April 15–17, 2014
Berlin, Germany

Association for
Computing Machinery

Advancing Computing as a Science & Profession

HSCC'14

Proceedings of the 17th International Conference on Hybrid Systems: Computation and Control (part of CPS Week)

Sponsored by:

ACM SIGBED

Supported by:

DENSO, MathWorks, and SFB-TR AVACS

Association for
Computing Machinery

Advancing Computing as a Science & Profession

The Association for Computing Machinery
2 Penn Plaza, Suite 701
New York, New York 10121-0701

ISBN: 978-1-4503-2732-9

Additional copies may be ordered prepaid from:

ACM Order Department
PO Box 30777
New York, NY 10087-0777, USA

Phone: 1-800-342-6626 (USA and Canada)
+1-212-626-0500 (Global)
Fax: +1-212-944-1318
E-mail: acmhelp@acm.org
Hours of Operation: 8:30 am – 4:30 pm ET

ACM Order Number: 100141

Printed in the USA

Program Chairs' Welcome

It is our great pleasure to welcome you to the 17th International Conference on Hybrid Systems: Computation and Control – HSCC'14. HSCC focuses on research that involves a blend of concepts, tools, and techniques from computer science, control theory, and applied mathematics for analysis and control of dynamical systems that exhibit combined continuous and discrete (hybrid) dynamics. By drawing on strategies from both computation and control, this field offers techniques applicable to both man-made, cyber-physical systems (ranging from mixed signal circuits and small robots to global infrastructure networks) and natural systems (ranging from biochemical networks to physiological models). HSCC has long been a leading, single-track conference for such rigorous, interdisciplinary approaches to dynamical systems with an emphasis on computational aspects, bringing together researchers from academia and industry with an interest in this exciting area. HSCC'14 was part of the 7th Cyber Physical Systems (CPS) Week, alongside the Real-Time and Embedded Technology and Applications Symposium (RTAS), the International Conference on Information Processing in Sensor Networks (IPSN), the Conference on High Confidence Networked Systems (HiCoNS), and the International Conference on Cyber-Physical Systems (ICCPS).

HSCC'14 attracted 69 submissions for regular papers, tool papers and case study papers from authors in 21 countries around the world: in Europe, Asia, North and South America and Australia. The program committee comprising 38 Associate Editors was able to secure 223 reviews for these papers, an average of 3.23 reviews per paper. The authors had the opportunity to comment on the reviews before a final decision was reached. In the end 29 regular papers, 2 tool papers and 1 case study paper were accepted for presentation, an overall acceptance rate of 46%. In a second round poster and demo submissions were solicited for a joint CPS Week Poster and Demo session. A total of 13 posters and demos were accepted by HSCC'14 for this joint session. The program was completed by an invited keynote presentation by Gregory Batt of the Institut National de Recherche en Informatique et Automatique (INRIA) on the topic of "Cells driven by computers: long-term model predictive control of gene expression in yeast" and by a panel discussion on "The Role of Robustness in Hybrid Systems", moderated by Martin Fränzle (Carl von Ossietzky Universität Oldenburg) and featuring Antoine Girard (Universite Joseph Fourier, Grenoble), Pieter Mosterman (MathWorks), Maria Prandini (Polytechnico di Milano), Stefan Ratschan (Academy of Sciences of the Czech Republic) and Thomas Stauner (BMW Group) as panelists .

We would like to thank the CPS Week organizing committee for giving us the opportunity to put together this exciting event and for their support throughout the process. We would also like to thank Calin Belta and Franjo Ivančic, the program chairs of HSCC'13, for their hints and guidance on the organization and Ian Mitchell for organizing the repeatability evaluation. We are especially grateful to Sriram Sankaranarayanan for taking care of the HSCC'14 publicity and of course to all the Program Committee members and the reviewers for the excellent job they did with the paper selection. We also express our gratitude to the HSCC steering committee, Rajeev Alur, Werner Damm, Bruce Krogh, Oded Maler, and Claire Tomlin, for their trust and guidance and to Lisa Tolles of Sheridan Communications for processing the proceedings in a timely manner. We thank our sponsor, ACM SIGBED, and our supporters, the DENSO Corporation, MathWorks and the SFB-TR AVACS.

Last, but not least, we would like to thank all the authors for entrusting us with their papers. Thanks to their contributions we were able to put together the high quality, exciting program, as you can witness in these proceedings.

Martin Fränzle
HSCC'14 Program co-Chair
Carl von Ossietzky Universität
Oldenburg, Germany

John Lygeros
HSCC'14 Program co-Chair
ETH Zürich, Switzerland

HSCC'14 Repeatability Evaluation

As its name implies, HSCC has a long and successful history of publishing papers featuring computation; for example, a brief scan through the proceedings of 2011–2013 shows that roughly two-thirds of the full papers contained significant computational elements. However, the details of these computational results are rarely documented to the same level as the proof of a theorem would be; consequently, it is often difficult or impossible to reproduce them at a later date. Furthermore, this reproducibility challenge is not just an affliction for our colleagues in other labs—all too often it strikes within the research group which produced the original paper, when newcomers (or even the same researchers) try to recreate and build on results a year or two later and struggle to find the right parameters, code, compilers, tool chains, environments, etc.

In order to help members of the HSCC community address this challenge, we have instituted an optional *repeatability evaluation* procedure for this year's conference. This procedure is independent of and occurred after the traditional program committee deliberations. All authors of accepted papers were invited to submit a *repeatability package* (RP) shortly after the submission deadline for the final version of their paper. The RPs were reviewed by a separate *repeatability evaluation committee* (REC) consisting of junior researchers, postdocs and senior graduate students from the HSCC community. The RPs are considered confidential and there is no requirement to make them publicly available; however, we will encourage authors to do so. RPs were judged according to a fixed set of criteria (available in advance), and those which were deemed sufficiently repeatable will be advertised as such at the conference.

Through this process we hope to provide authors:

- An incentive to improve the reproducibility of their computational results: If they are successful, they will receive additional acknowledgement at the conference.
- Guidance on how to do so: The criteria and submission process encourage authors to adopt standard practices known to improve reproducibility, such as use of version control, automating the generation of figures and tables, and documentation of at least the high level structure of the code.
- An opportunity to test whether they have achieved that goal: If a member of the REC can run their code, chances are that other members of their own lab will be able to do so.

Additional information can be found at the HSCC'14 repeatability evaluation website.

This process is based on similar efforts at other conferences, and we would particularly like to acknowledge Steve Blackburn and Mattias Hauswirth for their "Artifact Evaluation Artifact" describing the process at OOPSLA 2013 and Philippe Bonnet and colleagues for their description of the process at SIGMOD 2011. We would like to thank the steering committee and especially this year's program committee chairs for their support, the 2013 and 2014 program committee members for their nominations to the REC, and the members of the REC for volunteering their time. We look forward to reporting on the outcome of this experiment at the conference.

Ian M. Mitchell
Repeatability Evaluation Chair
University of British Columbia
Vancouver, Canada

Table of Contents

HSCC 2014 Conference Organization viii

HSCC 2014 Sponsors and Supporters xii

Session: Piecewise Affine and Switched Linear Systems

Session Chair: Pavithra Prabhakar *(IMDEA Software Institute)*

- **Computation of Piecewise Affine Terminal Cost Functions for Model Predictive Control** 1
  Florian D. Brunner *(University of Stuttgart)*, Mircea Lazar *(Eindhoven University of Technology)*, Frank Allgöwer *(University of Stuttgart)*
- **Stabilizing Discrete-Time Switched Linear Systems** 11
  Atreyee Kundu, Debasish Chatterjee *(Indian Institute of Technology Bombay)*
- **An LQ Sub-Optimal Stabilizing Feedback Law for Switched Linear Systems** 21
  Pierre Riedinger *(Université de Lorraine)*, Jean-Claude Vivalda *(Inria & Université de Lorraine)*
- **State-Feedback Stabilization of Discrete-Time Piecewise Affine Systems** 31
  Sihan Xiong, Ji-Woong Lee *(The Pennsylvania State University)*

Session: Stochastic Hybrid Systems

Session Chair: Benoît Caillaud *(IRISA)*

- **Bisimilar Symbolic Models for Stochastic Control Systems without State-Space Discretization** 41
  Majid Zamani, Ilya Tkachev *(Delft University of Technology)*, Alessandro Abate *(University of Oxford)*
- **Stochastic Reachability Based Motion Planning for Multiple Moving Obstacle Avoidance** 51
  Nick Malone, Kendra Lesser, Meeko Oishi, Lydia Tapia *(University of New Mexico)*
- **Timely Monitoring of Partially Observable Stochastic Systems** 61
  A. Prasad Sistla, Miloš Žefran, Yao Feng, Yue Ben *(University of Illinois at Chicago)*

Session: Hybrid System Modeling

Session Chair: Jens Oehlerking *(Robert Bosch GmbH)*

- **A Type-Based Analysis of Causality Loops in Hybrid Systems Modelers** 71
  Albert Benveniste *(INRIA)*, Timothy Bourke *(INRIA & ENS/DI)*, Benoît Caillaud *(INRIA)*, Bruno Pagano *(Esterel-Technologies)*, Marc Pouzet *(UPMC, ENS/DI & INRIA)*
- **A Hyperdense Semantic Domain for Hybrid Dynamic Systems to Model Different Classes of Discontinuities** 83
  Pieter J. Mosterman *(MathWorks)*, Gabor Simko *(Vanderbilt University)*, Justyna Zander *(HumanoidWay)*, Zhi Han *(MathWorks)*
- **Quasi-Dependent Variables in Hybrid Automata** 93
  Sergiy Bogomolov, Christian Herrera, Marco Muñiz, Bernd Westphal, Andreas Podelski *(Albert-Ludwigs-Universität Freiburg)*

Session: Stability and Control

Session Chair: Mircea Lazar *(Eindhoven University of Technology)*

- **Stability Analysis of Large-Scale Networked Control Systems with Local Networks: A Hybrid Small-Gain Approach** 103
  Dominicus P. Borgers, Maurice W.P.M.H. Heemels *(Eindhoven University of Technology)*
- **Model Reduction of Switched Affine Systems: A Method Based on Balanced Truncation and Randomized Optimization** 113
  Alessandro Vittorio Papadopoulos, Maria Prandini *(Politecnico di Milano)*

- **Control to Facet for Polynomial Systems** 123
  Christoffer Sloth, Rafael Wisniewski *(Aalborg University)*
- **Simulation-Guided Lyapunov Analysis for Hybrid Dynamical Systems** 133
  James Kapinski, Jyotirmoy V. Deshmukh *(Toyota Technical Center)*,
  Sriram Sankaranarayanan *(University of Colorado)*, Nikos Aréchiga *(Carnegie Mellon University)*

Session: Keynote Address

Session Chair: John Lygeros *(ETH Zürich)*

- **Cells Driven by Computers: Long-term Model Predictive Control of Gene Expression in Yeast** 143
  Gregory Batt *(INRIA Paris-Rocquencourt)*

Session: Tool and Case Study Presentations

Session Chair: Austin Jones *(Boston University)*

- **Component Based Design of Hybrid Systems: A Case Study on Concurrency and Coupling** 145
  Werner Damm, Eike Möhlmann, Astrid Rakow *(Carl von Ossietzky University of Oldenburg)*
- **JSR: A Toolbox to Compute the Joint Spectral Radius** 151
  Guillaume Vankeerberghen, Julien M. Hendrickx, Raphaël M. Jungers *(Université catholique de Louvain)*
- **A Bounded Model Checking Tool for Periodic Sample-Hold Systems** 157
  Gabor Simko *(Vanderbilt University)*, Ethan K. Jackson *(Microsoft Research)*

Session: Reachability

Session Chair: Goran Frehse *(Verimag)*

- **Inner Approximated Reachability Analysis** 163
  Eric Goubault, Olivier Mullier, Sylvie Putot *(CEA Saclay Nano-INNOV)*,
  Michel Kieffer *(Supélec-Université Paris-Sud)*
- **Sampling-Based Approximation of the Viability Kernel for High-Dimensional Linear Sampled-Data Systems** 173
  Jeremy H. Gillula, Shahab Kaynama, Claire J. Tomlin *(University of California, Berkeley)*
- **Proofs from Simulations and Modular Annotations** 183
  Zhenqi Huang, Sayan Mitra *(University of Illinois at Urbana-Champaign)*

Session: Approximation and Robustness

Session Chair: Jörg Raisch *(Technische Universität Berlin)*

- **On Approximation Metrics for Linear Temporal Model-Checking of Stochastic Systems** 193
  Ilya Tkachev *(Delft University of Technology)*, Alessandro Abate *(University of Oxford)*
- **Resilience to Intermittent Assumption Violations in Reactive Synthesis** 203
  Rüdiger Ehlers *(University of Bremen & University of Kassel)*, Ufuk Topcu *(University of Pennsylvania)*
- **Model Measuring for Hybrid Systems** 213
  Thomas A. Henzinger, Jan Otop *(Institute of Science & Technology Austria)*
- **Abstracting and Refining Robustness for Cyber-Physical Systems** 223
  Matthias Rungger, Paulo Tabuada *(University of California, Los Angeles)*

Session: Applications of Hybrid Systems

Session Chair: Pieter J. Mosterman *(The Mathworks, Inc.)*

- **Parameter Synthesis for Polynomial Biological Models** 233
  Tommaso Dreossi *(University of Udine, VERIMAG & University Joseph Fourier)*,
  Thao Dang *(VERIMAG & CNRS)*
- **Compositionality Results for Cardiac Cell Dynamics** 243
  Md. Ariful Islam, Abhishek Murthy *(Stony Brook University)*, Antoine Girard *(Université Joseph Fourier)*,
  Scott A. Smolka *(Stony Brook University)*, Radu Grosu *(Vienna University of Technology)*

- **Powertrain Control Verification Benchmark** 253
  Xiaoqing Jin, Jyotirmoy V. Deshmukh, James Kapinski, Koichi Ueda, Ken Butts *(Toyota Technical Center)*
- **Dynamic Multi-Domain Bipedal Walking with ATRIAS through SLIP based Human-Inspired Control** 263
  Ayonga Hereid, Shishir Kolathaya *(Texas A&M University)*,
  Mikhail S. Jones, Johnathan Van Why, Jonathan W. Hurst *(Oregon State University)*,
  Aaron D. Ames *(Texas A&M University)*

Session: Timed Systems and Temporal Specifications

Session Chair: Martin Fränzle *(Carl von Ossietzky Universität Oldenburg)*

- **Temporal Logic Inference for Classification and Prediction from Data** 273
  Zhaodan Kong, Austin Jones, Ana Medina Ayala, Ebru Aydin Gol, Calin Belta *(Boston University)*
- **Energy and Mean-Payoff Timed Games** 283
  Romain Brenguier *(Université Libre de Bruxelles)*,
  Franck Cassez *(NICTA)*, Jean-François Raskin *(Université Libre de Bruxelles)*
- **Abstraction, Discretization, and Robustness in Temporal Logic Control of Dynamical Systems** 293
  Jun Liu *(University of Sheffield)*, Necmiye Ozay *(University of Michigan)*
- **Edit Distance for Timed Automata** 303
  Krishnendu Chatterjee, Rasmus Ibsen-Jensen *(IST Austria)*, Rupak Majumdar *(MPI – SWS)*

HSCC'14 Posters 313

HSCC'14 Demonstrations 315

Author Index 316

HSCC 2014 Conference Organization

Program Chairs: Martin Fränzle, *Carl von Ossietziky Universität Oldenburg, Germany*
John Lygeros, *ETH Zurich, Switzerland*

Publicity Chair: Sriram Sankaranarayanan, *University of Colorado at Boulder, USA*

Repeatability Evaluation Chair: Ian Mitchell, *University of British Columbia, Canada*

Steering Committee: Rajeev Alur (Chair), *University of Pennsylvania, USA*
Bruce Krogh, *Carnegie-Mellon University, USA*
Oded Maler, *Verimag, France*
Claire Tomlin, *University of California Berkeley, USA*
Werner Damm, OFFIS, Germany

Program Committee: Alessandro Abate, *University of Oxford, UK*
Erika Abraham, *RWTH Aachen, Germany*
Matthias Althoff, *TU Ilmenau, Germany*
Calin Belta, *Boston University, USA*
Patricia Boyer, *CNRS, France*
Manfred Broy, *TU München, Germany*
Krishnendu Chaterjee, *IST Austria, Austria*
Patrick Cousot, *New York University, USA*
Stefano Di Cairano, *Mitsubishi, USA*
Alexandre Donze, *UC Berkeley, USA*
Georgios Fainekos, *Arizona State University, USA*
Goran Frehse, *Verimag, France*
Klaus Havelund, *NASA JPL, USA*
Ian Hiskens, *University of Michigan, USA*
Franjo Ivancic, *Google Inc., USA*
Xenofon Koutsoukos, *Vanderbilt University, USA*
Javad Lavaei, *Columbia University, USA*
Mircea Lazar, *TU Eindhoven, The Netherlands*
Rupak Majumdar, *MPI, Germany*
Pieter Mosterman, *Mathworks, USA*
Girish Nair, *University of Melbourne, Australia*
Jens Oehlerking, *Robert Bosch GmbH, Germany*
Andreas Podelski, *University of Freiburg, Germany*
Pavithra Prabhakar, *IMDEA, Spain*
Daniel Quevedo, *University of Newcastle, Australia*
Jörg Raisch, *TU Berlin, Germany*
Federico Ramponi, *University of Brescia, Italy*
Stefan Ratschan, *Academy of Sciences, Czech Republic*
Anders Ravn, *Aalborg University, Denmark*
Hendrik Sandberg, *KTH, Sweden*

Ricardo Sanfelice, *University Arizona, USA*
Sriram Sankaranarayanan, *University of Colorado at Boulder, USA*
Paulo Tabuada, *UCLA, USA*
Ufuk Topcu, *University of Pennsylvania, USA*
Ashutosh Trivedi, *IIT Bombay, India*
Verena Wolf, *Saarland Unversity, Germany*
Naijun Zhan, *Chinese Academy of Sciences, PR China*
Paolo Zuliani, *University of Newcastle, UK*

Repeatability Evaluation Committee:

Dieky Adzkiya, *Delft University of Technology, The Netherlands*
Ebru Aydin Gol, *Boston University, USA*
Ezio Bartocci, *TU Wien, Austria*
Sergiy Bogomolov, *Albert Ludwigs University of Freiburg, Germany*
Xin Chen, *RWTH Aachen University, Germany*
Liyun Dai, *Peking University, China*
Sadegh Esmaeil Zadeh Soudjani, *Delft University of Technology, The Netherlands*
Jie Fu, *University of Pennsylvania, USA*
Jeremy Gillula, *University of California at Berkeley, USA*
Ernst Moritz Hahn, *State Key Laboratory of Computer Science, Institute of Software, Chinese Academy of Sciences, China*
Pablo Ñañez, *Universidad de Los Andes, Colombia*
Akshay Rajhans, *The MathWorks, USA*
Christoffer Sloth, *Aalborg University, Denmark*

DENSO Corporation Best Student Paper Award Committee:

Franjo Ivancic, *Google Inc., USA*
Pieter Mosterman, *The Mathworks, USA*
Jörg Raisch, *TU Berlin, Germany*
Anders Ravn (Chair), *Aalborg University, Denmark*
Paulo Tabuada, *UCLA, USA*
Ashutosh Trivedi, *IIT Bombay, India*

Additional reviewers:

Houssam Abbas
S. Akshay
Eugene Asarin
James Aspnes
Nikolaos Athanasopoulos
Ana Medina Ayala
Amitabha Bagchi
Bart Besselink
Sergiy Bogomolov
Olivier Bouissou
Romain Brenguier

Thomas Brihaye
Alarico Campetelli
Debasish Chatterjee
Martin Chmelik
Samuel Coogan
David Copp
Yi Deng
Maria Domenica Di Benedetto
Jerry Ding
Alessandro D'Innocenzo
Peyman Mohajerin Esfahani
Emmanuel Filiot
Simone Garatti
Gilles Geeraerts
Khalil Ghorbal
Antoine Girard
Mario Gleirscher
Ebru Aydin Gol
Jessy Grizzle
Piyush Grover
Shibashis Guha
Vijay Gupta
Ernst Moritz Hahn
Arnd Hartmanns
Maurice Heemels
Peter Horvath
Richard Jensen
Barbara Jobstmann
Austin Jones
Maximilian Junker
Aditya Kanade
Sertac Karaman
Eric Kerrigan
Felix Klein
Yashar Kouhi
Gereon Kremer
Krishna S
Jan Kuratko
Colas Le Guernic
Thibaut Le Guilly
Jan Leike

Daniel Limon
Jun Liu
José Luis Mancilla-Aguilar
Nicolas Markey
Alexandru Mereacre
Linar Mikeev
Sayan Mitra
Eike Möhlmann
Behrang Nejad
Jan Otop
Thomas Pedersen
Giordano Pola
Vinayak Prabhu
Matteo Rubagotti
Matthias Rungger
Dorsa Sadigh
Anne-Kathrin Schmuck
Christian Schmuck
Thomas Schon
Wolfgang Schwitzer
Abhishek Sharma
Christoffer Sloth
Miriam Garcia Soto
Sadegh Esmaeil Zadeh Soudjani
Jiri Srba
Ilya Tkachev
Domagoj Toli
Guillaume Vankeerberghen
Eric Wolff
Tichackorn Wongpiromsarn
Bican Xia
Nan Xiao
Boyan Yordanov
Serdar Yuksel
Majid Zamani
Wei Zhang
Hengjun Zhao

HSCC 2014 Sponsor & Supporters

Sponsor: ACM SIGBED

Supporters: DENSO

MathWorks®

Institutional Supporter:

Carl von Ossietzky Universität Oldenburg

Albert-Ludwigs-Universität Freiburg

Universität des Saarlandes

SFB / TRR 14 AVACS
Automatic Verification and Analysis of Complex Systems

Computation of Piecewise Affine Terminal Cost Functions for Model Predictive Control

Florian D. Brunner
Institute for Systems Theory and Automatic Control
University of Stuttgart
Pfaffenwaldring 9
70569 Stuttgart
Germany
brunner@ist.uni-stuttgart.de

Mircea Lazar
Department of Electrical Engineering
Eindhoven University of Technology
P.O. Box 513
5600 MB Eindhoven
The Netherlands
m.lazar@tue.nl

Frank Allgöwer
Institute for Systems Theory and Automatic Control
University of Stuttgart
Pfaffenwaldring 9
70569 Stuttgart
Germany
allgower@ist.uni-stuttgart.de

ABSTRACT

This paper proposes a method for the construction of piecewise affine terminal cost functions for model predictive control (MPC). The terminal cost function is constructed on a predefined partition by solving a linear program for a given piecewise affine system, a stabilizing piecewise affine controller, an invariant set and a piecewise convex stage cost function. The constructed terminal cost function satisfies the sufficient conditions for asymptotic stability if it is used in an MPC scheme. In general, the constructed terminal cost function will be nonconvex. However, optional additional constraints in the linear program ensure that the cost function is convex, reducing the computational effort involved with solving the MPC optimization problem. Multiple examples illustrate the approach.

Categories and Subject Descriptors

I.2.8 [**Artificial Intelligence**]: Problem Solving, Control Methods, and Search—*Control theory*; G.1.6 [**Numerical Analysis**]: Optimization—*Linear Programming*

Keywords

hybrid systems; predictive control; terminal cost

1. INTRODUCTION

Model predictive control (MPC) is a well established control method based on solving finite horizon optimal control problems online at every sampling instant. The main appeal of MPC is the explicit consideration of constraints on the input and state of the plant. Furthermore, a performance criterion can be included in the optimization problem. For an overview of MPC refer to [18]. Stability of the origin of the closed loop system can a priori be guaranteed by including a terminal cost function in the optimization problem. Let the objective function of the MPC problem be given by

$$J(\mathbf{x}, \mathbf{u}) = \sum_{k=0}^{N-1} \ell(x_k, u_k) + V(x_N),$$

where $\mathbf{x} = (x_0, \ldots, x_N)$ is the predicted state trajectory, $\mathbf{u} = (u_0, \ldots, u_{N-1})$ is the predicted sequence of inputs, ℓ is a stage cost function, and V is a terminal cost function. Then stability of the origin of the closed loop system is guaranteed if there exists a terminal controller κ, such that the terminal cost V is a Lyapunov function for the closed loop system with the controller κ. More specifically, the terminal cost is required to satisfy

$$V(\Phi(x, \kappa(x)) - V(x) + \ell(x, \kappa(x)) \leq 0, \tag{1}$$

where Φ is the function mapping a state and an input onto the successor state [16]. Often, a terminal constraint $x_N \in \mathcal{X}_\mathrm{f}$ is added to the MPC problem, where $\mathcal{X}_\mathrm{f}$ is an invariant set for the closed-loop dynamics $x^+ = \Phi(x, \kappa(x))$. In this case, inequality (1) is only required to hold for all x in $\mathcal{X}_\mathrm{f}$, see also [16].

For linear dynamics and quadratic stage cost functions a quadratic terminal cost function can be obtained by solving a Lyapunov equation. However, depending on the application, more general types of stage cost functions might arise in the performance criterion. Furthermore, using nonquadratic cost functions might provide computational benefits. For example, optimization problems with piecewise affine cost functions such as functions based on infinity norms or one-norms might be solved by linear programming while quadratic cost functions require quadratic programming. Results for the computation of infinity norm Lyapunov functions can be found for example in [10] and in the references therein. Recently, terminal cost functions based on Minkowski gauge functions have been obtained in [17]. These functions may be asymmetric and therefore belong to a richer class of cost functions than infinity norms or one-norms.

In this paper, we consider the construction of *general* piecewise affine terminal cost functions. This class of functions includes as a special case Minkowski gauge functions based on polytopic sets and therefore also infinity norm and one-norm cost functions. However, piecewise affine functions

HSCC'14, April 15–17, 2014, Berlin, Germany.
Copyright 2014 ACM 978-1-4503-2732-9/14/04 ...$15.00.
http://dx.doi.org/10.1145/2562059.2562108.

need not be positively homogeneous. In fact, every piecewise continuous function can be approximated arbitrarily closely by a piecewise affine function. This allows the construction of nonconservative terminal cost functions for quite arbitrary stage cost functions. In [9, 5] piecewise quadratic Lyapunov functions were constructed for the stability analysis of hybrid systems. The main difference in this work is the inclusion of a stage cost function, allowing the approach to be used in the *synthesis* of controllers, that is, MPC algorithms. Specifically, an the inclusion of a terminal cost function satisfying (1) is sufficient for the stability of the origin of the closed loop system.

The algorithm proposed in this paper fits as follows into the MPC design flow. The stage cost function ℓ in the MPC objective is usually given by certain performance specifications. Ideally, on would choose the terminal cost equal to the infinite horizon optimal cost function associated with the optimal feedback law with respect to ℓ. This is, however, in general impossible even if the optimal feedback law is known, see also [16]. On the other hand, for many systems it is relatively easy to find a *locally stabilizing* controller which is linear or piecewise affine. For piecewise affine systems, a piecewise affine stabilizing controller can for example be obtained by multi-parametric programming, see [3]. In [14], stabilizing affine controllers are computed based on a piecewise affine control Lyapunov function. We assume in this paper that a stabilizing controller, and an associated invariant set, have already been constructed. The remaining step in the design of the MPC controller, and the step addressed in this paper, is then to find a terminal cost function satisfying (1) and being as close as possible to the infinite horizon cost function, that is, being as small as possible. Compare the approach in [4] where a quadratic cost function based on the LQR solution associated with the Jacobi-linearization at the origin of a nonlinear system is employed.

The inputs of the algorithm for the construction of the terminal cost function are a piecewise affine system, a stabilizing piecewise affine controller, a piecewise convex stage cost function, and an appropriate polyhedral partitioning of the state space. The algorithm returns a piecewise affine terminal cost function defined on this partitioning by solving a linear program. Optionally, a *convex* terminal cost function can be obtained by including additional constraints in the optimization problem. Convex cost functions offer considerable computational benefits over nonconvex functions. This is especially relevant in MPC, where optimization problems have to be solved online in real-time.

Summarizing, the proposed approach provides the following benefits. First, it is a novel way of constructing terminal cost functions for piecewise affine dynamics. These functions can not only be used in MPC schemes for the control of piecewise affine systems but also offer advantages in the control of linear systems if the chosen terminal controller is piecewise affine. Controllers of these type arise naturally if the inputs or the state of the system are subject to constraints. Second, the approach allows the construction of nonconservative terminal cost functions for a wide class of stage cost functions, especially piecewise affine functions. Hence, the method in this paper may be used to approximate an arbitrary objective function in an MPC scheme by piecewise affine functions while still guaranteeing stability. With the powerful solvers available for linear programming, this approach might provide computational benefits over solving the original problem by convex programming or even quadratic programming.

The remainder of the paper is structured in the following way. Section 2 contains the problem setup and some preliminary results. The main contribution of the paper is presented in Section 3 where the algorithm for the construction of the terminal cost functions is described. Section 4 contains some remarks on how the partitioning of the state space, one of the inputs for our algorithm, can be obtained. Examples illustrating the different aspects and applications of the approach are given in Section 5. Section 6 concludes the paper.

Notation: For natural numbers $a, b \in \mathbb{N}$, with $a \leq b$, the set $\{a, a+1, \dots, b\}$ is denoted by $\mathbb{N}_{[a,b]}$. The set of nonnegative real numbers is denoted by $\mathbb{R}_+$. For any matrix $H \in \mathbb{R}^{n \times m}$, $H \geq 0$ denotes the constraint that all entries of H are nonnegative. For sets $\mathcal{X}, \mathcal{Y} \subseteq \mathbb{R}^n$ define $\mathcal{X} \oplus \mathcal{Y} := \{z \in \mathbb{R}^n \mid z = x + y,\ x \in \mathcal{X},\ y \in \mathcal{Y}\}$. For vectors $v \in \mathbb{R}^n$ additionally define $\mathcal{X} \oplus v := \mathcal{X} \oplus \{v\}$. The closure of a set $\mathcal{X} \subseteq \mathbb{R}^n$ is denoted by $\mathrm{cl}(\mathcal{X})$, the interior by $\mathrm{int}(\mathcal{X})$. The convex hull is denoted by $\mathrm{convh}(\mathcal{X})$. Given a matrix $A \in \mathbb{R}^{m \times n}$ and sets $\mathcal{X} \subseteq \mathbb{R}^n$, and $\mathcal{Y} \subseteq \mathbb{R}^m$ define $A\mathcal{X} := \{y \in \mathbb{R}^m \mid \exists x \in \mathcal{X},\ y = Ax\}$ and $A^{-1}\mathcal{Y} := \{x \in \mathbb{R}^n | Ax \in \mathcal{Y}\}$. Note that $A^{-1}\mathcal{Y}$ is defined even if A^{-1} is not. A polyhedron is the intersection of open or closed halfspaces. A bounded polyhedron is called a polytope. For a polytope $\mathcal{P}$, define the set of extreme points by $\mathrm{extreme}(\mathcal{P})$. By convention, the set of extreme points of an empty set is empty. A compact and convex set containing the origin is called a C-set. We call a C set *proper* if it contains the origin in its nonempty interior. Given a proper C-set $\mathcal{X} \subseteq \mathbb{R}^n$, define for any $x \in \mathbb{R}^n$ the Minkowski gauge function $\psi(\mathcal{X}, x) = \inf\{c \in \mathbb{R} \mid c \geq 0,\ x \in c\mathcal{X}\}$.

2. PROBLEM SETUP AND PRELIMINARIES

We consider piecewise affine systems of the form

$$\begin{aligned} x^+ &= A_i x + B_i u + c_i \quad \text{if } x \in \mathcal{X}_i \\ &=: \Phi(x, u) \end{aligned} \tag{2}$$

where $x \in \mathbb{R}^n$ and $u \in \mathbb{R}^m$. We make the following assumptions on the partitioning of the state space.

Assumption 1. *It holds that for all $i \in \mathbb{N}_{[1,M]}$, $\mathcal{X}_i$ is a (not necessarily closed) polytope in $\mathbb{R}^n$ where $\mathrm{int}(\mathcal{X}_i) \neq \emptyset$. Furthermore, it holds that $\bigcup_{i=1}^{M} \mathcal{X}_i = \mathcal{X}$, where $\mathcal{X}$ is a closed and bounded set containing the origin in its (nonempty) interior. Finally, for any $i, j \in \mathbb{N}_{[1,M]}$ and $i \neq j$ it holds that $\mathcal{X}_i \cap \mathcal{X}_j = \emptyset$.*

We assume a piecewise affine controller $\kappa : \mathcal{X} \to \mathbb{R}^m$ to be given where

$$\kappa(x) = K_i x + d_i \quad \text{if } x \in \mathcal{X}_i. \tag{3}$$

The closed-loop system is defined by

$$\begin{aligned} x^+ &= \Phi(x, \kappa(x)) \\ &= A_i x + B_i(K_i x + d_i) + c_i \quad \text{if } x \in \mathcal{X}_i \end{aligned} \tag{4}$$

Assumption 2. *The origin of the closed-loop system (4) is asymptotically stable. Furthermore, the set $\mathcal{X}$ is positively invariant for the closed-loop system (4) and belongs to the region of attraction of the origin.*

Our goal is to define a piecewise affine, positive definite terminal cost function $V : \mathcal{X} \to \mathbb{R}_+$ with the property that for the closed-loop system (4) and all $x \in \mathcal{X}$ it holds that

$$V(\Phi(x, \kappa(x))) - V(x) + \ell(x, \kappa(x)) \leq 0 \tag{5}$$

where ℓ is a given positive definite function. We assume that

$$\ell(x, \kappa(x)) = \ell_i^\kappa(x) \quad \text{if } x \in \mathcal{X}_i \tag{6}$$

where for all $i \in \mathbb{N}_{[1,M]}$, $\ell_i^\kappa(x)$ is a convex function on $\mathcal{X}_i$. The function V is parameterized as

$$V(x) = V_i x + v_i \quad \text{if } x \in \mathcal{X}_i. \tag{7}$$

Hence, our goal is to find appropriate matrices $V_i \in \mathbb{R}^{1\times n}$ and scalars $v_i \in \mathbb{R}$ such that V is positive definite and (5) holds.

REMARK 1. *For simplicity of notation, the same partitioning is assumed for the open-loop system (2), the controller (3), the stage cost function ℓ, and the function V. However, as both the controller and the partitioning for the function V are assumed to be given in this paper, this assumption is not conservative. In fact, for any given different partitionings for the system, the controller, and the functions ℓ and V, the partitioning in this paper can be obtained by intersecting all the different partitionings. Further, the assumption that $\mathcal{X}$ is invariant can be satisfied by intersecting a given partitioning for the closed-loop system with a given invariant set.*

The following lemmas are used in this paper.

LEMMA 1. *Let a partition $\bigcup_{i=1}^M \mathcal{X}_i = \mathcal{X}$ satisfying Assumption 1 be given. Let further a function $g : \mathcal{X} \to \mathbb{R}$ be given, defined by*

$$g(x) = g_i(x) \quad \text{if } x \in \mathcal{X}_i \tag{8}$$

where all g_i are convex functions on $\mathcal{X}$. If and only if for all $x \in \mathcal{X}$ it holds that

$$\forall j \in \mathbb{N}_{[1,M]}: \; g_i(x) \geq g_j(x) \quad \text{if } x \in \mathcal{X}_i \tag{9}$$

it holds that

$$g(x) = \max_{j\in\mathbb{N}_{[1,M]}} g_j(x) \tag{10}$$

for all $x \in \mathcal{X}$. Furthermore, (9) implies that g is convex on $\mathcal{X}$.

PROOF. With g defined as in (8), the equivalence of (9) and (10) holds by definition. Furthermore, as (10) implies that g is the pointwise maximum of convex functions, it is convex, see for example Theorem 5.5 in [19]. This completes the proof. □

LEMMA 2 ([7]). *Given a nonempty polyhedron $\mathcal{P} := \{x \in \mathbb{R}^n \mid Gx \leq g\}$, the inequality $Fx \leq f$ is satisfied for all $x \in \mathcal{P}$ if and only if there exists a matrix $H \geq 0$ such that $HG = F$ and $Hg \leq f$.*

LEMMA 3 ([17]). *Let $\mathcal{X}$, $\mathcal{Y}$ and $\mathcal{Z}$ be any three proper C-sets in $\mathbb{R}^n$, $\mathbb{R}^m$, and $\mathbb{R}^n$ and let $K \in \mathbb{R}^{m\times n}$ be any matrix such that $\mathcal{Z} \subseteq \mathcal{X}$ and $K\mathcal{Z} \subseteq \mathcal{Y}$. Then, for all $a \in \mathbb{R}_+ \setminus \{0\}$ and all $x \in \mathbb{R}^n$, it holds that: (i) $\psi(a\mathcal{X}, x) = a^{-1}\psi(\mathcal{X}, x)$; (ii) $\psi(\mathcal{X}, x) \leq \psi(\mathcal{Z}, x)$; and (iii) $\psi(\mathcal{Y}, Kx) \leq \psi(\mathcal{Z}, x)$.*

LEMMA 4. *Let $\mathcal{X}$ be any proper C-set in $\mathbb{R}^n$ and let $x \in \mathbb{R}^n$ such that $x \notin \mathcal{X}$. Then it holds that $\psi(\mathcal{X}, x) > 1$.*

PROOF. The proof is by contradiction. As $\mathcal{X}$ is a proper C-set, it holds that $\psi(\mathcal{X}, x) > 0$. Hence, assume that $0 < \psi(\mathcal{X}, x) \leq 1$. By Lemma 3 (i) it follows that $1 = \psi(\mathcal{X}, x)^{-1}\psi(\mathcal{X}, x) = \psi(\psi(\mathcal{X}, x)\mathcal{X}, x)$ and, hence, $x \in \text{cl}(\psi(\mathcal{X}, x)\mathcal{X})$. However, with $\psi(\mathcal{X}, x) \leq 1$ and $\mathcal{X}$ being a proper C set it holds that $\psi(\mathcal{X}, x)\mathcal{X} \subseteq \mathcal{X}$, such that $x \in \mathcal{X}$, contradicting the assumption that $x \notin \mathcal{X}$. Hence it holds that $\psi(\mathcal{X}, x) > 1$, completing the proof. □

COROLLARY 1. *Let $\mathcal{X}$ and $\mathcal{Z}$ be any proper C-sets in $\mathbb{R}^n$ such that for any $y \in \mathbb{R}^n$ it holds that $\psi(\mathcal{X}, y) \leq \psi(\mathcal{Z}, y)$. Then it holds that $\mathcal{Z} \subseteq \mathcal{X}$.*

PROOF. The proof is by contradiction. Let an arbitrary $x \in \mathbb{R}^n$ be given such that $x \in \mathcal{Z}$ and $x \notin \mathcal{X}$. It holds that $\psi(\mathcal{Z}, x) \leq 1$, and, by Lemma 4, that $\psi(\mathcal{X}, x) > 1$, contradicting the assumption that $\psi(\mathcal{X}, x) \leq \psi(\mathcal{Z}, x)$. Hence it holds that $x \in \mathcal{X}$ and, as x was arbitrary, that $\mathcal{Z} \subseteq \mathcal{X}$, completing the proof. □

3. CONSTRUCTION OF THE PIECEWISE AFFINE TERMINAL COST FUNCTION

In this section, linear programs are defined that yield the parameters of the terminal cost function function V as a solution. The formulation of the optimization problems are different depending on whether the sets $\mathcal{X}_i$ are defined by their extreme points or by intersections of half-spaces.

In general, it is not necessary that the function V is convex. However, as a terminal cost function, V will be included in the objective function of an optimization problem. Therefore, convexity of V might be desirable from a computational point of view. As will be shown, depending on whether additional constraints are included in the optimization problem, convexity of V will be guaranteed.

REMARK 2. *In both formulations of the optimization problem, all constraints are enforced on $\text{cl}(\mathcal{X}_i)$ instead of $\mathcal{X}_i$. Hence, on the boundaries $\text{cl}(\mathcal{X}_i) \cap \text{cl}(\mathcal{X}_j)$ the constraints hold for both the realization of the closed-loop system (4) for $\mathcal{X}_i$ and $\mathcal{X}_j$. This approach has the advantage of being numerically more robust than enforcing the constraints only for $\mathcal{X}_i$, as this would require strict inequality constraints in the optimization problems. Further, it has been found that enforcing constraints on $\text{cl}(\mathcal{X}_i)$ instead of $\mathcal{X}_i$ also introduces robustness in terms of stability of the resulting closed-loop system, see [11].*

3.1 Vertex Representation

Define $P_i := \text{extreme}(\mathcal{X}_i)$ for all $i \in \mathbb{N}_{[1,M]}$, and $P_{ij}^\Phi := \text{extreme}(\mathcal{X}_i \cap (A_i + B_i K_i)^{-1}[\mathcal{X}_j \oplus (-B_i d_i - c_i)])$ for all $i, j \in \mathbb{N}_{[1,M]}$. Define the linear program

$$\underset{V_i, v_i}{\text{minimize}} \quad \sum_{i=1}^{M} \sum_{p\in\mathcal{P}_i} V_i p + v_i \tag{11a}$$

subject to

$$\forall i \text{ such that } 0 \in \text{cl}(\mathcal{X}_i): \quad v_i = 0 \tag{11b}$$

$$\forall i, j \in \mathbb{N}_{[1,M]}: \forall p \in P_{ij}^\Phi:$$
$$V_j(A_i p + B_i(K_i p + d_i) + c_i) + v_j - V_i p - v_i + \ell_i^\kappa(p) \leq 0 \tag{11c}$$

THEOREM 1. *Suppose Assumptions 1 and 2 hold and that the optimization problem in* (11) *admits a solution. Then for the closed-loop system and all* $x \in \mathcal{X}$ *inequality* (5) *holds.*

PROOF. By the piecewise definition of the dynamics and the cost functions, for all all $x \in \mathcal{X}$ it holds that

$$\begin{aligned} &V(\Phi(x, \kappa(x))) - V(x) + \ell(x, \kappa(x)) \\ &= V_j(A_i x + B_i K_i x + B_i d_i + c_i) + v_j - V_i x - v_i + \ell_i^\kappa(x) \\ &\quad \text{if } x \in \mathcal{X}_i \text{ and } A_i x + B_i K_i x + B_i d_i + c_i \in \mathcal{X}_j. \end{aligned} \quad (12)$$

The condition $x \in \mathcal{X}_i$ and $A_i x + B_i K_i x + B_i d_i + c_i \in \mathcal{X}_j$ is equivalent to $x \in \mathcal{X}_i \cap (A_i + B_i K_i)^{-1}[\mathcal{X}_j \oplus (-B_i d_i - c_i)]$. Therefore, considering that the left-hand side of (11c) is convex in p, the satisfaction of (11c) implies that (5) holds, completing the proof. □

LEMMA 5. *Suppose Assumptions 1 and 2 hold and that the optimization problem in* (11) *admits a solution. Then* V *is positive definite.*

PROOF. With k being an index denoting time, define the closed-loop system by

$$x_{k+1} = \Phi(x_k, \kappa(x_k)). \quad (13)$$

Let x_0 be any state in $\mathcal{X}$. As $\mathcal{X}$ was assumed to be belong to the region of attraction of the origin of the closed-loop system (13), it holds that $|x_N|$ converges to 0 for N approaching infinity. By (11b) it follows that $V(0) = 0$ and that V is piecewise linear in a neighborhood of the origin. Therefore, there exists an $\epsilon > 0$, a neighborhood $\mathcal{B}_\epsilon := \{x \in \mathbb{R}^n \mid |x| \leq \epsilon\}$ of the origin, and a constant $a \geq 0$, such that for all $x \in \mathcal{B}_\epsilon$ it holds that $|V(x)| \leq a|x|$. Hence, for the closed-loop system (13), $|V(x_N)|$ converges to zero. As ℓ was assumed to be positive definite, for any $x_0 \in \mathcal{X}$ there exists an $N \in \mathbb{N}$ such that $|V(x_N)| \leq \ell(x_0, \kappa(x_0))/2$. By Theorem 1, inequality (5) holds, such that for the closed-loop system (13) and any $N \in \mathbb{N}$ it follows that

$$\begin{aligned} V(x_0) &\geq \sum_{i=0}^{N-1} \ell(x_k, \kappa(x_k)) + V(x_N) \\ &\geq \ell(x_0, \kappa(x_0)) + V(x_N). \end{aligned} \quad (14)$$

Hence, for all $x_0 \in \mathcal{X}$ it holds that $V(x_0) \geq \ell(x_0, \kappa(x_0))/2$ such that V is positive definite. □

THEOREM 2. *Suppose Assumptions 1 and 2 hold and that the optimization problem in* (11) *admits a solution under the additional constraints*

$$\forall i, j \in \mathbb{N}_{[1,M]} : \forall p \in P_i : \quad V_i p + v_i \geq V_j p + v_j. \quad (15)$$

Then V *is a convex function on* $\mathcal{X}$.

PROOF. The constraints in (15) imply that for all $i, j \in \mathbb{N}_{[1,M]}$ and all x in $\mathcal{X}_i$ it holds that $V_i x + v_i \geq V_j x + v_j$. By Lemma 1 it follows that

$$V(x) = \max_i (V_i x + v_i), \quad (16)$$

implying that V is convex, completing the proof. □

3.2 Half-Space Representation

If the sets $\mathcal{X}_i$ are given as intersections of half-spaces, it might be more efficient to use this representation directly instead of first converting to a vertex representation, that is, computing extreme($\mathcal{X}_i$). However, if the half-space representation is used, it is necessary to bound the stage cost function by a piecewise affine function.

For $i \in \mathbb{N}_{[1,M]}$ let matrices $L_i \in \mathbb{R}^{1 \times n}$ and scalars $l_i \in \mathbb{R}$ be given.

ASSUMPTION 3. *For all* $i \in \mathbb{N}_{[1,M]}$ *and all* $x \in \mathcal{X}_i$ *it holds that*

$$\ell_i^\kappa(x) \leq L_i x + l_i. \quad (17)$$

REMARK 3. *As by assumption the sets* $\mathcal{X}_i$ *are bounded, there always exist* L_i *and* l_i *such that Assumption 3 is satisfied. It is of course desirable that for* $0 \in \mathcal{X}_i$ *it holds that* $\ell_i^\kappa(0) = 0 \Leftrightarrow L_i 0 + l_i = 0 \Leftrightarrow l_i = 0$. *As by assumption the functions* ℓ_i^κ *are convex, this is also always possible.*

Let $\mathrm{cl}(\mathcal{X}_i) = \{x \in \mathbb{R}^n \mid G_i x \leq g_i\}$ for all $\in \mathbb{N}_{[1,M]}$. Define the linear program

$$\underset{t_i, V_i, v_i, H_i^{\mathrm{t}}, H_{ij}^{\mathrm{d}}}{\text{minimize}} \quad \sum_{i=1}^{M} t_i \quad (18a)$$

subject to

$$\forall i, j \in \mathbb{N}_{[1,M]} : \quad H_i^{\mathrm{t}} \geq 0, \ H_{ij}^{\mathrm{d}} \geq 0 \quad (18b)$$

$$H_i^{\mathrm{t}} G_i = V_i, \ H_i^{\mathrm{t}} g_i \leq t_i - v_i \quad (18c)$$

$$\forall i \text{ such that } 0 \in \mathrm{cl}(\mathcal{X}_i) : \ v_i = 0 \quad (18d)$$

$\forall i, j \in \mathbb{N}_{[1,M]}$ such that

$\mathrm{cl}(\mathcal{X}_i) \cap (A_i + B_i K_i)^{-1}[\mathrm{cl}(\mathcal{X}_j) \oplus (-B_i d_i - c_i)] \neq \emptyset$:

$$H_{ij}^{\mathrm{d}} \begin{bmatrix} G_i \\ G_j(A_i + B_i K_i) \end{bmatrix} = V_j(A_i + B_i K_i) - V_i + L_i \quad (18e)$$

$$H_{ij}^{\mathrm{d}} \begin{bmatrix} g_i \\ g_j + G_j(-B_i d_i - c_i) \end{bmatrix} \leq -V_j(B_i d_i + c_i) - l_i + v_i - v_j. \quad (18f)$$

THEOREM 3. *Suppose Assumptions 1 and 2 hold and that the optimization problem in* (18) *admits a solution. Then for the closed-loop system and all* $x \in \mathcal{X}$ *inequality* (5) *holds.*

PROOF. The proof is similar to the proof of Theorem 1. The condition $x \in \mathcal{X}_i \cap (A_i + B_i K_i)^{-1}[\mathcal{X}_j \oplus (-B_i d_i - c_i)]$ is equivalent to

$$x \in \left\{ y \in \mathbb{R}^n \;\middle|\; \begin{bmatrix} G_i \\ G_j(A_i + B_i K_i) \end{bmatrix} y \leq \begin{bmatrix} g_i \\ g_j + G_j(-Bd_i - c_i) \end{bmatrix} \right\}. \quad (19)$$

Hence, considering Lemma 2 and Assumption 3, (18b), (18e), and (18f) imply that inequality (5) holds, completing the proof. □

LEMMA 6. *Suppose Assumptions 1 and 2 hold and that the optimization problem in* (18) *admits a solution. Then* V *is positive definite.*

PROOF. The proof is identical to the proof of Lemma 5. □

THEOREM 4. *Suppose Assumptions 1 and 2 hold and that the optimization problem in (18) with the additional variables H_{ij}^c admits a solution under the additional constraints*

$$H_{ij}^c \geq 0 \quad \text{(20a)}$$

$$\forall i,j \in \mathbb{N}_{[1,M]}: \ H_{ij}^c G_i = V_j - V_i, \ H_{ij}^c g_i \leq v_i - v_j. \quad \text{(20b)}$$

Then V is a convex function on $\mathcal{X}$.

PROOF. The proof is similar to the proof of Theorem 2. By Lemma 2, the constraints (20a) imply that for all $i, j \in \mathbb{N}_{[1,M]}$ and all x in $\mathcal{X}_i$ it holds that $V_i x + v_i \geq V_j x + v_j$. Hence it follows by Lemma 1, that

$$V(x) = \max_i (V_i x + v_i), \quad (21)$$

implying that V is convex, completing the proof. □

4. CONSTRUCTION OF THE PARTITION

Recalling Remark 1, the partition of the function V, and hence the sets $\mathcal{X}_i$ are design parameters. In this section we describe multiple ways of choosing this partition such that the optimization problems are guaranteed to be feasible. This also reveals useful applications of the proposed approach.

4.1 Linear Systems

Let the system be given by

$$x^+ = Ax + Bu, \quad (22)$$

the controller by $\kappa(x) = Kx$, and the closed-loop system by

$$x^+ = (A + BK)x. \quad (23)$$

We will construct a partition based on the approach in [17]. For this we require some results on Minkowski gauge functions.

LEMMA 7. *Let $\mathcal{Q}$ and $\mathcal{R}$ be proper polyhedral C-sets described by $\mathcal{Q} = \{x \in \mathbb{R}^n \mid \forall i \in \mathbb{N}_{[1,n_\mathcal{Q}]}: \ F_i^\mathcal{Q} x \leq 1\}$ and $\mathcal{R} = \{u \in \mathbb{R}^m \mid \forall i \in \mathbb{N}_{[1,n_\mathcal{R}]}: \ F_i^\mathcal{R} u \leq 1\}$, respectively. Then, for any matrix $K \in \mathbb{R}^{m \times n}$ it holds that*

$$\psi(\mathcal{Q}, x) + \psi(\mathcal{R}, Kx) = \psi(\mathcal{S}, x), \quad (24)$$

where

$$\mathcal{S} = \{x \in \mathbb{R}^n \mid \forall i \in \mathbb{N}_{[1,n_\mathcal{Q}]}, \forall j \in \mathbb{N}_{[1,n_\mathcal{R}]}: (F_i^\mathcal{Q} + F_j^\mathcal{R} K)x \leq 1\}. \quad (25)$$

PROOF. The result follows immediately from the fact that

$$\psi(\mathcal{Q}, x) + \psi(\mathcal{R}, Kx) = \max_{i \in \mathbb{N}_{[1,n_\mathcal{Q}]}} F_i^\mathcal{Q} x + \max_{j \in \mathbb{N}_{[1,n_\mathcal{R}]}} F_j^\mathcal{R} Kx. \quad (26)$$

□

Let now $\mathcal{P}$ be a proper polyhedral C-set defined by

$$\mathcal{P} = \{x \in \mathbb{R}^n \mid \forall j \in \mathbb{N}_{[1,n_\mathcal{P}]}: \ F_j^\mathcal{P} x \leq 1\}. \quad (27)$$

ASSUMPTION 4. *There exists a $\lambda \in [0, 1)$ such that $(A + BK)\mathcal{P} \subseteq \lambda \mathcal{P}$.*

REMARK 4. *For any stabilizable pair (A, B) and any stabilizing controller K there exists a set $\mathcal{P}$ such that Assumption 4 holds true.*

Define now for $i \in \mathbb{N}_{[1,n_\mathcal{P}]}$ the sets

$$\mathcal{P}_i := \{x \in \mathbb{R}^n \mid \forall j \in \mathbb{N}_{[1,n_\mathcal{P}]}: F_i^\mathcal{P} x \geq F_j^\mathcal{P} x\}, \quad (28)$$

such that for all $x \in \mathbb{R}^n$ it holds that

$$\psi(\mathcal{P}, x) = F_i^\mathcal{P} x \quad \text{if } x \in \mathcal{P}_i. \quad (29)$$

REMARK 5. *For any $x \in \mathbb{R}^n$ it holds that $x \in \mathcal{P}_i$ with $i = \arg\max_{j \in \mathbb{N}_{[1,n_\mathcal{P}]}} F_j^\mathcal{P} x$ and, hence, $\bigcup_{i \in \mathbb{N}_{[1,n_\mathcal{P}]}} \mathcal{P}_i = \mathbb{R}^n$.*

Let a stage cost function ℓ be given such that for all $x \in \mathcal{P}$ it holds that

$$\ell(x, u) \leq \psi(\mathcal{Q}, x) + \psi(\mathcal{R}, u), \quad (30)$$

for some proper polyhedral C-sets $\mathcal{Q}$ and $\mathcal{R}$. It follows that for all $x \in \mathcal{P}$

$$\ell(x, Kx) \leq \psi(\mathcal{S}, x) = \max_{j \in \mathbb{N}_{[1,n_\mathcal{S}]}} F_j^\mathcal{S} x, \quad (31)$$

where

$$\mathcal{S} = \{x \in \mathbb{R}^n \mid \forall j \in \mathbb{N}_{[1,n_\mathcal{S}]}: \ F_j^\mathcal{S} x \leq 1\} \quad (32)$$

for appropriate matrices $F_j^\mathcal{S}$, obtained with the help of Lemma 7. Define for $j \in \mathbb{N}_{[1,n_\mathcal{S}]}$ the sets

$$\mathcal{S}_i := \{x \in \mathbb{R}^n \mid \forall j \in \mathbb{N}_{[1,n_\mathcal{S}]}: F_i^\mathcal{S} x \geq F_j^\mathcal{S} x\}, \quad (33)$$

such that for all $x \in \mathcal{P}$ it holds that

$$\ell(x, Kx) \leq F_i^\mathcal{S} x \quad \text{if } x \in \mathcal{S}_i. \quad (34)$$

Define for all $i \in \mathbb{N}_{[1,n_\mathcal{P}]}, j \in \mathbb{N}_{[1,n_\mathcal{S}]}$ the sets

$$\mathcal{X}_{ij} := \mathcal{P} \cap \mathcal{P}_i \cap \mathcal{S}_j. \quad (35)$$

Define further

$$\mathcal{X} = \bigcup_{\substack{i \in \mathbb{N}_{[1,n_\mathcal{P}]} \\ j \in \mathbb{N}_{[1,n_\mathcal{S}]}}} \mathcal{X}_{ij}. \quad (36)$$

It holds that $\mathcal{X} = \mathcal{P}$ and, hence, $\mathcal{X}$ is invariant for the closed-loop system (23). Further, for all $x \in \mathcal{X}$ it holds that

$$\psi(\mathcal{P}, x) = F_i^\mathcal{P} x \quad \text{if } x \in \mathcal{X}_{ij}, \ \forall \ j \in \mathbb{N}_{[1,n_\mathcal{S}]} \quad \text{(37a)}$$

$$\ell(x, Kx) \leq L_{ij} x \quad \text{if } x \in \mathcal{X}_{ij}, \ \forall \ i \in \mathbb{N}_{[1,n_\mathcal{P}]} \quad \text{(37b)}$$

where $\forall i \in \mathbb{N}_{[1,n_\mathcal{P}]}: \ L_{ij} := F_j^\mathcal{S}$.

REMARK 6. *For simplicity, the fact that $\mathcal{X}_{ij} \cap \mathcal{X}_{kl} \neq \emptyset$ for some $(ij) \neq (kl)$, due to the fact that the sets are all compact is ignored here. It is of course possible to define the $\mathcal{X}_{ij}$ as general polytopes that may be neither closed nor open, such that Assumption 1 holds.*

Let $\alpha > 0$ be such that

$$\mathcal{P} \subseteq \alpha(1 - \lambda)\mathcal{S}. \quad (38)$$

By assumption, both $\mathcal{P}$ and $\mathcal{S}$ are bounded sets containing the origin in their nonempty interior. Hence, it is always possible to choose an $\alpha > 0$ satisfying (38). Let further $V(x)$ be parameterized as

$$V(x) = V_{ij} x + v_{ij} \quad \text{if } x \in \mathcal{X}_{ij}. \quad (39)$$

THEOREM 5. *Suppose Assumption 4 holds. Then the optimization problems (modulo double indices) in (11) and (18) are feasible with $V_{ij} = \alpha F_i^\mathcal{P}$ and $v_{ij} = 0$ for all $i \in \mathbb{N}_{[1,n_\mathcal{P}]}$ and $j \in \mathbb{N}_{[1,n_\mathcal{S}]}$.*

PROOF. In the following, let x be an arbitrary element of $\mathcal{X}$. Then it holds that $x \in \mathcal{X}_{ij}$ and $(A+BK)x \in \mathcal{X}_{kl}$ for appropriate $i,k \in \mathbb{N}_{[1,n_\mathcal{P}]}$ and $j,l \in \mathbb{N}_{[1,n_\mathcal{S}]}$. It follows from Assumption 4, that $F_k^\mathcal{P}(A+BK)x \leq \lambda F_i^\mathcal{P} x$. Further, with the choice of α in (38) it holds that $\alpha(1-\lambda)F_i^\mathcal{P} x \geq F_j^\mathcal{S} x$. Therefore, for any $x \in \mathcal{X}_{ij}$ it holds that

$$\begin{aligned} V_{kl}(A+BK)x - V_{ij}x + \ell(x,Kx) \\ \leq V_{kl}(A+BK)x - V_{ij}x + L_{ij}x \\ = \alpha F_k^\mathcal{P}(A+BK)x - \alpha F_i^\mathcal{P} x + F_j^\mathcal{S} x \\ \leq (\alpha\lambda - \alpha + \alpha(1-\lambda))F_i^\mathcal{P} x = 0, \end{aligned} \quad (40)$$

completing the proof. □

REMARK 7. *This choice of feasible V_{ij} leads to $V(x) = \alpha\psi(\mathcal{P},x)$ for all $x \in \mathcal{X}$. This is the same parameterization of the terminal cost function as in [17]. However, the value of α in [17] is required to satisfy $\mathcal{P} \subseteq 2^{-1}(1-\lambda)\alpha\mathcal{Q}$ and $K\mathcal{P} \subseteq 2^{-1}(1-\lambda)\alpha\mathcal{R}$. Considering that both $\mathcal{P}$ and $\mathcal{S}$ are proper C-sets, these constraints on α imply that for all $x \in \mathbb{R}^n$ it holds that*

$$\begin{aligned} \psi(\mathcal{S},x) &= \psi(\mathcal{Q},x) + \psi(\mathcal{R},Kx) \\ &\leq \psi\left(\frac{2\mathcal{P}}{\alpha(1-\lambda)},x\right) + \psi\left(\frac{2\mathcal{P}}{\alpha(1-\lambda)},x\right) \\ &= \psi\left(\frac{\mathcal{P}}{\alpha(1-\lambda)},x\right), \end{aligned} \quad (41)$$

where the second line follows from Lemma 3 (ii) and (iii) and the last line from Lemma 3 (i). Further, by Corollary 1 it follows that $\mathcal{P} \subseteq \alpha(1-\lambda)\mathcal{S}$, such that any α satisfying the requirements in [17] also satisfies the requirements in the present paper. Hence, the value of α obtained through the method in this paper will not be greater than when obtained through the method in [17].

The partitioning described above leads to a piecewise linear function V. A simple way of obtaining a more general piecewise affine function while still guaranteeing feasibility of the optimization problem is to intersect the partition above with any type of grid in $\mathbb{R}^n$. Alternatively, a refined partition can be obtained by intersecting with level-sets of the contractive set $\mathcal{P}$.

Summarizing, for linear systems the approach described in this paper allows the following applications. First, considering model predictive control, it is possible to define piecewise affine terminal cost functions on bounded terminal sets for arbitrary piecewise convex positive definite stage cost functions[1]. Second, it is straightforward to show that Theorem 5 holds for any piecewise linear closed loop dynamics defined on conic partitions, provided that the set $\mathcal{P}$ is contractive. Hence, the results in this section allow the construction of terminal cost functions on control contractive terminal sets, which are in general larger than invariant sets for linear controllers. Refer to Example 5.3 for an illustration.

4.2 Piecewise Affine Systems

For piecewise affine systems as given in (2), a piecewise affine stabilizing controller and an invariant set for the closed-loop system might be obtained by solving a finite horizon MPC problem parametrically, see for example [3]. The parametric solution also yields a Lyapunov function for the closed loop system. However, the MPC problem is usually defined based on an existing terminal cost function which is in general an overapproximation of the optimal infinite horizon cost function. Hence, for short horizons, the Lyapunov function returned by solving the MPC problem parametrically will in general be conservative. Longer horizons allow for a Lyapunov function that is closer to the optimal infinite horizon cost. On the other hand, solving MPC problems parametrically quickly becomes intractable for large horizon lengths. Furthermore, the approach in this paper allows the construction of *convex* functions V, which is an advantage if this function is to be used as a terminal cost function in a model predictive controller.

The following iterative procedure yields a suboptimal solution to the infinite horizon optimal control problem. After any iteration, the resulting Lyapunov function satisfies inequality (5), that is, it can be used as a terminal cost function.

Algorithm 1 Iterative Construction of the Terminal Controller and Cost

1: solve a short horizon MPC problem for a given terminal set and terminal cost function satisfying (5) parametrically
2: obtain the partition of the resulting stabilizing controller
3: solve optimization problem (11) or (18) on this partition
4: define the partition and the resulting Lyapunov function as the new terminal set and terminal cost function
5: go to 1

Note that the parametric solution of the MPC problem in step 1 of Algorithm 1 always satisfies inequality (5), such that, assuming the stage cost function is piecewise affine, the optimization problems in step 3 of Algorithm 1 will always be feasible.

5. NUMERICAL EXAMPLES

In this section we present multiple example illustrating the proposed approach. Terminal cost functions were computed for second and fifth order linear systems, for a linear system with a piecewise linear controller, and for two piecewise affine systems, where in the last example Algorithm 1 is demonstrated.

5.1 Linear System

Consider the linear system

$$x^+ = \begin{bmatrix} 1 & 1 \\ 0 & 1 \end{bmatrix} x + \begin{bmatrix} 0.5 \\ 1 \end{bmatrix} u \quad (42)$$

and the piecewise linear stage cost function

$$\ell(x,u) = \|Qx\|_\infty + \|Ru\|_\infty \quad (43)$$

with weighting matrices

$$Q = \begin{bmatrix} 1 & 0 \\ 0 & 1 \end{bmatrix} \quad \text{and} \quad R = 0.1. \quad (44)$$

A stabilizing controller $u = Kx$ is obtained by solving the LQR problem with the weighting matrices Q and R. A partition as described in Section 4.1 is obtained based on the maximal 0.81-contractive set under the constraint $x \in [-5,5] \times$

[1]It is assumed that the stage cost function is upper bounded by a convex piecewise affine positive definite function in a neighborhood of the origin.

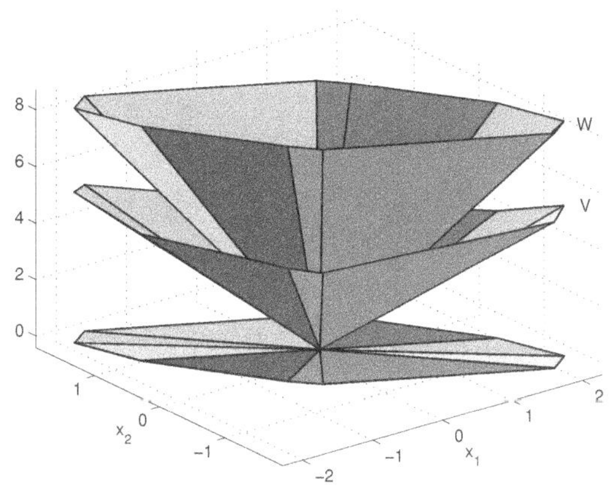

Figure 1: Cost function V computed by solving (11), cost function W calculated with the results from [17], and the associated partition for Example 5.1

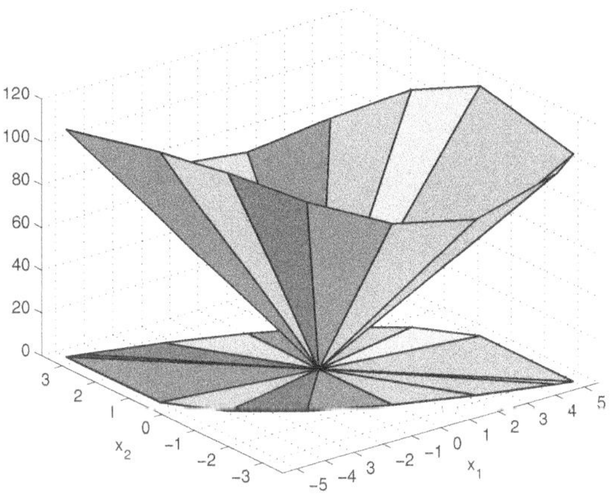

Figure 2: Terminal cost function and associated partition for Example 5.3.

$[-5, 5]$ and $u = Kx \in [-1, 1]$ with the help of the algorithm described in [6]. Figure 1 shows the partition, the piecewise linear function V obtained by solving the optimization problem (11), and the cost function W obtained with the algorithm in [17]. While the complexity of both functions is identical, the algorithm based on solving (11) yields a less conservative result.

5.2 Fifth-Order Linear System

Consider the linear system (quintuple integrator)

$$x^+ = \begin{bmatrix} 1 & 1 & \frac{1}{2} & \frac{1}{6} & \frac{1}{24} \\ 0 & 1 & 1 & \frac{1}{2} & \frac{1}{6} \\ 0 & 0 & 1 & 1 & \frac{1}{2} \\ 0 & 0 & 0 & 1 & 1 \\ 0 & 0 & 0 & 0 & 1 \end{bmatrix} x + \begin{bmatrix} \frac{1}{120} \\ \frac{1}{24} \\ \frac{1}{6} \\ \frac{1}{2} \\ 1 \end{bmatrix} u \tag{45}$$

and the piecewise convex stage cost function

$$\ell(x, u) = \|Qx\|_\infty^3 + (Ru^2)^{\frac{3}{4}} \tag{46}$$

with weighting matrices

$$Q = \begin{bmatrix} 1 & 0 & 0 & 0 & 0 \\ 0 & 1 & 0 & 0 & 0 \\ 0 & 0 & 1 & 0 & 0 \\ 0 & 0 & 0 & 1 & 0 \\ 0 & 0 & 0 & 0 & 1 \end{bmatrix} \quad \text{and} \quad R = 1. \tag{47}$$

A stabilizing controller $u = Kx$ was obtained by solving the LQR problem with the weighting matrices Q and R. A partition as described in Section 4.1 was obtained based on the maximal 0.64-contractive set under the constraints $\|x\|_\infty \leq 5$ and $\|u\|_\infty = \|Kx\|_\infty \leq 1$ with the help of the algorithm described in [6], resulting in 36 regions. A piecewise affine terminal cost function was then computed by solving (11) without the additional constraints for convexity included. The overall computation was completed in under 120 seconds on a standard laptop CPU. The largest part of the computation time was required for setting up the parameters of the optimization problem. The resulting linear program was solved in under 4 seconds.

5.3 Linear System with a Piecewise Linear Controller

It is well known that larger invariant sets can be achieved with nonlinear terminal controllers than with linear controllers. Consider the system from Example 5.1. An inner approximation of the maximal control-contractive set was computed for the constraints $x \in [-5, 5] \times [-5, 5]$ and $u \in [-1, 1]$ with a contraction constant of $\rho = 0.81$, using an algorithm in [2].

A piecewise linear controller was computed on this partition such that the overall set is contractive for the closed loop system. The optimization problem in (11) was solved with the quadratic stage cost function

$$\ell(x, u) = x^\top Q x + u^\top R u \tag{48}$$

with weighting matrices

$$Q = \begin{bmatrix} 1 & 0 \\ 0 & 1 \end{bmatrix} \quad \text{and} \quad R = 1. \tag{49}$$

The resulting terminal cost is shown in Figure 2. Refining the partition leads to a less conservative cost, as shown in Figure 3. In both cases the optimization problems were solved with the additional constraints for convexity included.

5.4 Piecewise Affine System

This example has been adapted from [12]. The system is given by

$$x^+ = A_i x + B_i u \quad \text{if } x \in \Omega_i \tag{50}$$

where

$$u = K_i x \quad \text{if } x \in \mathcal{X}_i \tag{51}$$

with the partition shown in Figure 4. The reader is referred to [12] for the numerical values of the system description. We chose the piecewise linear stage cost function

$$\ell(x, u) = \|Qx\|_\infty + \|Ru\|_\infty \tag{52}$$

with weighting matrices

$$Q = \begin{bmatrix} 1 & 0 \\ 0 & 1 \end{bmatrix} \quad \text{and} \quad R = 1. \tag{53}$$

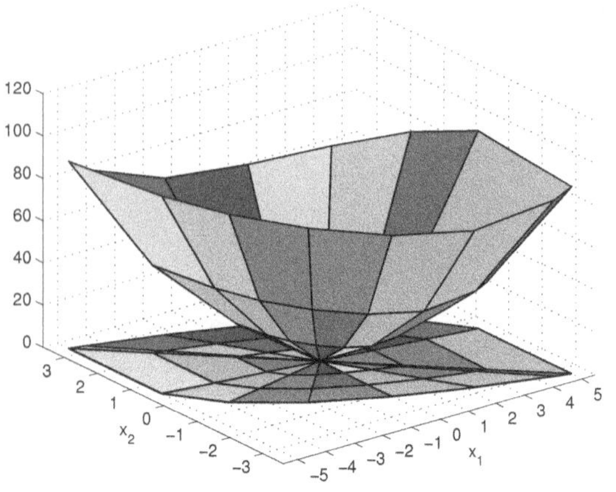

Figure 3: Terminal cost function on a refined partition for Example 5.3.

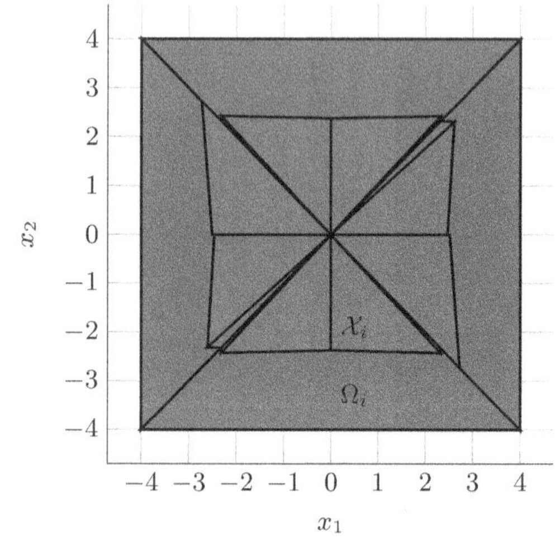

Figure 4: Partitioning of the state space for Example 5.4.

The optimization problem in (11) was solved on the partition defined by the sets $\mathcal{X}_i$ without and with the additional constraints for convexity. Figure 5 and Figure 6 show the resulting terminal cost functions.

5.5 Piecewise Affine System With a Partition Based on an Explicit MPC Solution

This example illustrates Algorithm 1. The setup has been adapted from [15]. Here, the system is given by

$$x^+ = A_i x + B_i u + c_i \quad \text{if } x \in \Omega_i \tag{54}$$

with

$$\begin{aligned}
\Omega_1 &= \{x \in \mathbb{R}^2 \mid [1\ 0]x \leq -1\},\\
\Omega_2 &= \{x \in \mathbb{R}^2 \mid -1 \leq [1\ 0]x \leq 1\},\\
\Omega_3 &= \{x \in \mathbb{R}^2 \mid 1 \leq [1\ 0]x\},\\
A_1 &= \begin{bmatrix} 0.5 & 0.2 \\ 0 & 1 \end{bmatrix},\ A_2 = \begin{bmatrix} 1 & 0.2 \\ 0 & 1 \end{bmatrix},\ A_3 = \begin{bmatrix} 0.5 & 0.2 \\ 0 & 1 \end{bmatrix}\\
B_1 &= B_2 = B_3 = \begin{bmatrix} 0 \\ 1 \end{bmatrix},\ c_1 = \begin{bmatrix} -0.5 \\ 0 \end{bmatrix},\ c_2 = \begin{bmatrix} 0 \\ 0 \end{bmatrix},\ c_2 = \begin{bmatrix} 0.5 \\ 0 \end{bmatrix}.
\end{aligned} \tag{55}$$

Note that the system in (54) is linear in a neighborhood of the origin. The stage cost function is defined by

$$\ell(x, u) = \|Qx\|_\infty + \|Ru\|_\infty \tag{56}$$

with weighting matrices

$$Q = \begin{bmatrix} 1 & 0 \\ 0 & 1 \end{bmatrix} \quad \text{and} \quad R = 0.1. \tag{57}$$

A terminal controller $u = Kx$ has been calculated as the solution of the LQR problem based on the linear system around the origin and the weighting matrices Q and R. The terminal set has been defined as the maximal constraint admissible set for the closed loop system $x^+ = (A_2 + B_2 K)x$ and the constraints $x \in [-1, 1] \times [-10, 10], u = Kx \in [-1, 1]$. Furthermore, the maximal 0.83-contractive set has been calculated for the same constraints. Similarly to Example 5.1, a convex, piecewise linear terminal cost function has been calculated based on this contractive set. One iteration of

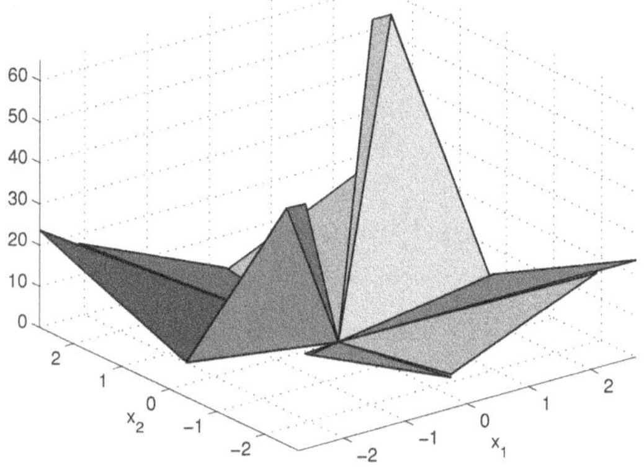

Figure 5: Nonconvex terminal cost function for Example 5.4.

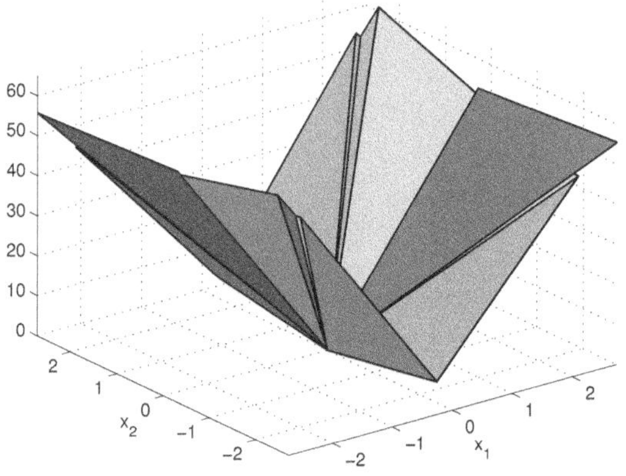

Figure 6: Convex terminal cost function for Example 5.4.

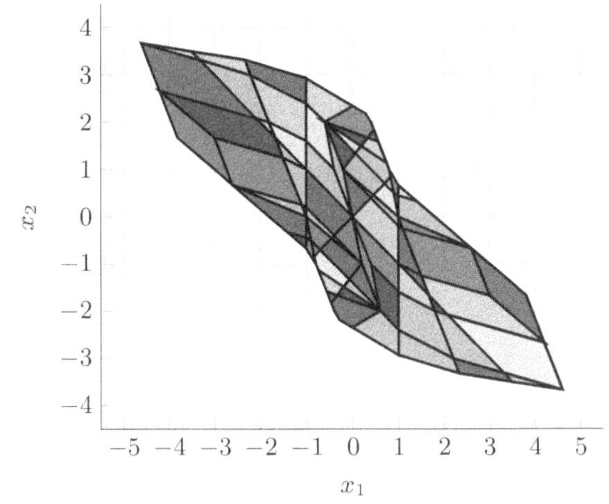

Figure 7: Partitioning of the state space for Example 5.5.

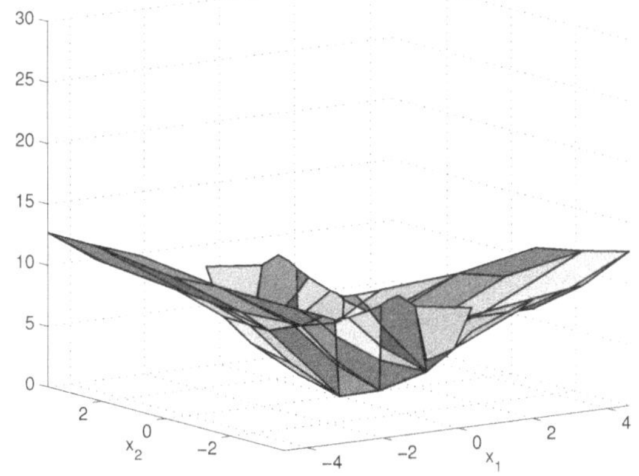

Figure 8: Nonconvex terminal cost function for Example 5.5.

Algorithm 1 was executed. With the terminal set and terminal cost function as defined above, the stage cost function in (56), and constraints $x \in [-5, 5] \times [-10, 10]$, $u \in [-1, 1]$, the explicit MPC solution has been obtained for a horizon length $N = 2$. The resulting partition of the state space is shown in Figure 7. Optimization problem (11) was solved without and with the additional constraints for convexity. The resulting piecewise affine functions are shown in Figure 8 and Figure 9, respectively. Not surprisingly, the Lyapunov function returned by (11) was almost identical to the solution of the explicit MPC problem in the nonconvex case. Hence, the iterative linear programming procedure proposed in this paper can result in a tractable method for computing approximate explicit MPC solutions for piecewise affine systems and large prediction horizons.

As demonstrated by this example, the approach in this paper may be used to obtain a convex piecewise affine terminal cost function from a given general piecewise affine terminal cost function. Note, however, that the feasibility of the optimization problem (11) is in general only guaranteed for the nonconvex case. In other words, the optimal value function

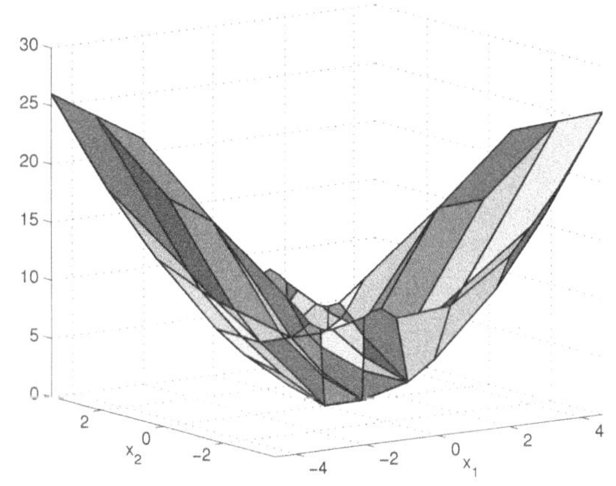

Figure 9: Convex terminal cost function for Example 5.5.

returned by the solution of the explicit MPC problem is a feasible solution for problem (11), but is in general nonconvex.

6. CONCLUSION AND OUTLOOK

In this paper we have presented an approach to constructing piecewise affine terminal cost functions for piecewise affine closed-loop dynamics. As shown in the examples, the approach improves on earlier results in terms of conservativeness of the terminal cost function. One particular strong point is the (optional) inclusion of constraints that lead to convex terminal cost functions, which are attractive from a computational point of view.

Future research will focus on general conditions on the partitioning of the state space such that the optimization problem in (11) is feasible. Another point is the approximation of general stage cost functions by piecewise affine stage cost functions, leading to MPC problems that can be solved by linear programming. Even in the case of quadratic stage cost functions, this might provide computational benefits, depending on the dimension of the state space and the level of approximation.

7. ACKNOWLEDGMENTS

The authors would like to thank the German Research Foundation (DFG) for financial support of the project within the Cluster of Excellence in Simulation Technology (EXC 310/1) at the University of Stuttgart. The authors would also like to thank the DFG for their financial support within the research grant in the frame of the collaborative research project "Optimization Based Control of Uncertain Systems".

The Multi-Parametric Toolbox [8], Yalmip [13], and Cplex-IBM [1] were used for the simulations.

8. REFERENCES

[1] IBM ILOG CPLEX Optimization Studio, 2013, `http://www-01.ibm.com/software/integration/optimization/cplex-optimization-studio/`.

[2] F. Blanchini and S. Miani. *Set-Theoretic Methods in Control*. Birkhäuser, Boston, Basel, Berlin, 2008.

[3] F. Borrelli, M. Baotic, A. Bemporad, and M. Morari. An efficient algorithm for computing the state feedback optimal control law for discrete time hybrid systems. In *Proc. American Control Conf. (ACC)*, pages 4717–4722, Denver, CO, USA, 2003.

[4] H. Chen and F. Allgöwer. A Quasi-Infinite Horizon Nonlinear Model Predictive Control Scheme with Guaranteed Stability. *Automatica*, 34(10):1205–1217, 1998.

[5] G. Feng. Stability Analysis of Piecewise Discrete-Time Linear Systems. *IEEE Trans. Automat. Control*, 47(7):1108–1112, 2002.

[6] E. Gilbert and K. Tan. Linear Systems with State and Control Constraints: The Theory and Application of Maximal Output Admissible Sets. *IEEE Trans. Automat. Control*, 36(9):1008–1020, 1991.

[7] J.-C. Hennet. Une extension du lemme de Farkas et son application au problème de ré egulation linéaire sous containtes. *Comptes-Rendus de l'Académie des Sciences, Série I*, 308:415–419, 1989.

[8] M. Herceg, M. Kvasnica, C. N. Jones, and M. Morari. Multi-Parametric Toolbox 3.0. In *European Control Conf. (ECC)*, pages 502–510, Zürich, Switzerland, 2013, `http://control.ee.ethz.ch/~mpt`.

[9] M. Johansson and A. Rantzer. Computation of piecewise quadratic Lyapunov functions for hybrid systems. *IEEE Trans. Automat. Control*, 43(4):555–559, 1998.

[10] M. Lazar. On infinity norms as Lyapunov functions: Alternative necessary and sufficient conditions. In *Proc. 49th IEEE Conf. Decision and Control (CDC)*, pages 5936–5942, Atlanta, GA, USA, 2010.

[11] M. Lazar, W. Heemels, and A. R. Teel. Lyapunov Functions , Stability and Input-to-State Stability Subtleties for Discrete-time Discontinuous Systems. *IEEE Trans. Automat. Control*, 54(10):2421–2425, 2009.

[12] M. Lazar and A. Jokić. On Infinity Norms as Lyapunov Functions for Piecewise Affine Systems. In *Proc. 13th Int. Conf. Hybrid Systems: Computation and Control (HSCC)*, pages 131–141, Stockholm, Sweden, 2010.

[13] J. Löfberg. YALMIP : A toolbox for modeling and optimization in MATLAB. In *Proc. CACSD Conference*, pages 284–289, Taipei, Taiwan, 2004, `http://users.isy.liu.se/johanl/yalmip`.

[14] L. Lu and W. P. M. H. Heemels and A. Bemporad. Synthesis of low-complexity stabilizing piecewise affine controllers: A control-Lyapunov function approach. In *Proc. IEEE Conf. Decision and Control (CDC), European Control Conf. (ECC)*, pages 1227–1232, Orlando, FL, USA, 2011.

[15] D. Q. Mayne and S. Raković. Model predictive control of constrained piecewise affine discrete-time systems. *Int. J. Robust and Nonlinear Control* , 13(3-4):261–279, 2003.

[16] D. Q. Mayne, J. B. Rawlings, C. V. Rao, and P. O. M. Scokaert. Constrained model predictive control : Stability and optimality. *Automatica*, 36(6):789–814, 2000.

[17] S. V. Raković and M. Lazar. Minkowski terminal cost functions for MPC. *Automatica*, 48(10):2721–2725, 2012.

[18] J. B. Rawlings and D. Q. Mayne. *Model Predictive Control: Theory and Design.* Nob Hill Publishing, Madison, WI, 2009.

[19] R. T. Rockafellar. *Convex Analysis.* Princeton University Press, Princeton, NJ, 1970.

Stabilizing Discrete-Time Switched Linear Systems

Atreyee Kundu
Systems & Control Engineering
Indian Institute of Technology Bombay
Mumbai 400076, India
atreyee@sc.iitb.ac.in

Debasish Chatterjee
Systems & Control Engineering
Indian Institute of Technology Bombay
Mumbai 400076, India
dchatter@iitb.ac.in

ABSTRACT

This article deals with stabilizing discrete-time switched linear systems. Our contributions are threefold: Firstly, given a family of linear systems possibly containing unstable dynamics, we propose a large class of switching signals that stabilize a switched system generated by the switching signal and the given family of systems. Secondly, given a switched system, a sufficient condition for the existence of the proposed switching signal is derived by expressing the switching signal as an infinite walk on a directed graph representing the switched system. Thirdly, given a family of linear systems, we propose an algorithmic technique to design a switching signal for stabilizing the corresponding switched system.

Categories and Subject Descriptors

J.2 [**Physical Sciences and Engineering**]: Engineering

Keywords

Discrete-time switched linear system; asymptotic stability; multiple Lyapunov-like functions; directed graphs.

1. INTRODUCTION

A *switched system* [10, §1.1.2] comprises of two components — a finite family of systems and a *switching signal* that selects an active subsystem from the family at every instant of time. Switched systems arise in a multitude of application areas such as networked systems, quantization, variable structure systems, etc; see e.g., [5, 3, 6, 16, 11] and the references therein.

Stability of switched systems has attracted considerable research attention over the past few decades, see [11, 5, 16] for detailed surveys. In this article we study stability of discrete-time switched linear systems under *constrained switching* [10, Chapter 3] as a continuation of our study of switched systems initiated in [9]. To wit, we are concerned with identifying classes of switching signals for which the switched system under consideration is globally asymptotically stable, as well as algorithmic synthesis of stabilizing switching signals.

Conditions for stability under constrained switching typically employ the idea of *slow switching* vis-a-vis *(average) dwell time* switching. Although these results were originally developed in the setting of continuous-time systems [10, Chapter 3], [7], they can be readily extended to the discrete-time setting, with the (average) dwell time expressed in terms of the number of time steps [11]. Most of these results apply to switched systems with all stable subsystems.

In the presence of unstable dynamics in the family, slow switching alone is not sufficient to guarantee stability of the switched system. Additional conditions are required to ensure that the switched system does not spend too much time on the unstable subsystems; see e.g., [11]. In [17] the authors discuss a class of switching signals for global exponential stability of a switched system in which not all subsystems are Schur stable (or even when no subsystem is Schur stable) but the unstable subsystems form a stable combination. The characterization of the stabilizing switching signal involves a modified definition of average dwell time and the method of activating the Schur stable subsystems (if any) arbitrarily but activating the unstable subsystems depending on a prespecified ratio. However, none of the above works ventured beyond switching signals with switching *frequencies* that are faster than a constant.

Keeping to the general tune of slow switching while extending its scope considerably, in this article we consider switched systems with unstable dynamics and design a class of stabilizing switching signals that transcends beyond the (average) dwell time regime. Moreover, given a switched system, we derive a sufficient condition for the existence of the proposed switching signal. This matter demands attention in the context of switched systems because given a switched system, a purely time-dependent stabilizing switching signal may be difficult to find. We also present an algorithmic approach to construct a switching signal that satisfies the proposed condition. More specifically, our contributions are:

- We propose a family of stabilizing switching signals such that:
  - ▷ The switching signals are more general than those having a certain average dwell time. In particular, switching rates that are faster than a constant are admissible.
  - ▷ We specify *only* certain asymptotic properties of the switching signal; there is, therefore plenty of flexibility insofar as the transient behaviour of the switching signals are concerned.

HSCC'14, April 15–17, 2014, Berlin, Germany.

http://dx.doi.org/10.1145/2562059.2562114.

▷ We allow unstable dynamics in the family of systems. Although this is not the first instance that stability of a discrete-time switched linear system containing unstable dynamics in the family has been considered, to the best of our knowledge, this is the first instance when a stabilizing switching signal for a discrete-time switched linear system containing unstable subsystems, is proposed *solely* in terms of asymptotic behaviour of the switching signal.

∘ We develop conditions for existence of switching signals having the properties that we propose. These conditions are algorithmic in nature, and can be readily tested for a given switched system.

∘ We provide an algorithmic procedure for synthesis of switching signals that ensure stability of discrete-time switched linear systems.

The analysis and the synthesis carried out in this article can be extended in a standard fashion to include the case of switched nonlinear systems; we do not strive for maximum generality in terms of applicability of the ideas presented here.

The remainder of this article is organized as follows: In §2 we formulate the problem under consideration and elaborate on the properties of the family of systems and the switching signal that we employ in our analysis. Our main results are stated in §3, and we illustrate our results with the aid of numerical examples in §4. We conclude in §5 with a brief summary of some of the natural future directions. The proofs of all facts and claims are presented in a consolidated fashion in §6.

Notation. $\mathbb{N} = \{1, 2, \cdots\}$ is the set of natural numbers, $\mathbb{N}_0 = \{0\} \cup \mathbb{N}$, and $\mathbb{R}$ is the set of real numbers. We denote by $k_1 : k_2$ the set $\{n \in \mathbb{N}_0 : k_1 \leqslant n \leqslant k_2\}$. We let $\mathbb{1}_A(\cdot)$ denote the indicator function of a set A, and $I_{d\times d}$ denote the d-dimensional identity matrix. Let $\|\cdot\|$ be the standard 2-norm and let $^\top$ denote the transpose operation.

2. PRELIMINARIES

We consider a discrete-time *switched linear system*

$$x(t+1) = A_{\sigma(t)}x(t),\ x(0) \text{ given},\ t \in \mathbb{N}_0, \tag{1}$$

generated by the following two components:

∘ a family of systems

$$x(t+1) = A_i x(t),\ x(0) \text{ given},\ i \in \mathcal{P},\ t \in \mathbb{N}_0, \tag{2}$$

where $x(t) \in \mathbb{R}^d$ is the vector of system states at time t, $\mathcal{P}$ is a finite index set, and $A_i \in \mathbb{R}^{d\times d}$ are known constant matrices.

∘ a *switching signal* $\sigma : \mathbb{N}_0 \to \mathcal{P}$ specifying at every time t, the index of the active subsystem from the family (2).

We assume that for each $i \in \mathcal{P}$ the matrix $A_i \in \mathbb{R}^{d\times d}$ has full rank. Consequently, $0 \in \mathbb{R}^d$ is the unique equilibrium point for each system in the family (2). Let $0 =: \tau_0 < \tau_1 < \cdots$ be the switching instants, i.e., those positive integers at which σ changes values. For $t > 0$ let N_t^σ denote the number of switches (before and including) t. The solution $(x(t))_{t\in\mathbb{N}_0}$ to the switched system (1) corresponding to a switching signal σ is given by

$$x(t) = A_{\sigma(\tau_{N_t^\sigma})}^{t-\tau_{N_t^\sigma}} A_{\sigma(\tau_{N_t^\sigma-1})}^{\tau_{N_t^\sigma}-\tau_{N_t^\sigma-1}} \cdots A_{\sigma(0)}^{\tau_1-\tau_0}x(0),\quad t \in \mathbb{N}_0, \tag{3}$$

where the dependence of $(x(t))_{t\in\mathbb{N}_0}$ on σ has been suppressed.

In this article we characterize a class of switching signals under which (1) is globally asymptotically stable (GAS). By definition,

Definition 1. The switched system (1) is *globally asymptotically stable* (GAS) for a given switching signal σ if (1) is

∘ Lyapunov stable, and

∘ globally asymptotically convergent, i.e., irrespective of the initial condition $x(0)$, $x(t) \to 0$ as $t \to +\infty$.

Prior to presenting our main result, we identify and derive key properties of the family of systems (2) and the switching signal σ, that will be used in our analysis.

2.1 Properties of the family (2)

Given the family of systems (2), the following fact captures the quantitative measure of (in)stability of each system.

Fact 1. For each $i \in \mathcal{P}$ there exists a pair (P_i, λ_i), where $P_i \in \mathbb{R}^{d\times d}$ is a symmetric and positive definite matrix, and

∘ if A_i is asymptotically stable, then $0 < \lambda_i < 1$;

∘ if A_i is marginally stable, then $\lambda_i = 1$; [1]

∘ if A_i is unstable, then $\lambda_i > 1$;

such that, with

$$\mathbb{R}^d \ni \xi \longmapsto V_i(\xi) := \langle P_i\xi, \xi\rangle \in [0, +\infty[, \tag{4}$$

we have

$$V_i(\gamma_i(t+1)) \leqslant \lambda_i V_i(\gamma_i(t)),\quad t \in \mathbb{N}_0, \tag{5}$$

and $\gamma_i(\cdot)$ solves the i-th recursion in (2), $i \in \mathcal{P}$.

The functions V_i, $i \in \mathcal{P}$, defined in (4) will be called Lyapunov-like functions in the sequel. Even though Fact 1 is a folklore result, in §6.1 we sketch a proof for completeness.

We observe that for all $i, j \in \mathcal{P}$ the respective Lyapunov-like functions are related as follows:

Fact 2. There exists $\mu_{ij} > 0$ such that

$$V_j(\xi) \leqslant \mu_{ij} V_i(\xi) \quad \text{for all} \quad \xi \in \mathbb{R}^d, \tag{6}$$

whenever the switching from system i to system j is admissible.

The assumption that there exists $\mu \geqslant 1$ such that $V_j(\xi) \leqslant \mu V_i(\xi)$ for all $i, j \in \mathcal{P}$ and $\xi \in \mathbb{R}^d$ is standard [17]. Clearly, the preceding inequality is a special case of (6). A *tight* estimate of the numbers μ_{ij} may be given as follows; we present a short proof of this estimate in §6.1.

Proposition 1. Let the Lyapunov-like functions be defined as in (4) with each P_i symmetric and positive definite, $i \in \mathcal{P}$. Then the smallest constant μ_{ij} in (6) is given by

$$\mu_{ij} = \lambda_{\max}(P_j P_i^{-1}),\quad i, j \in \mathcal{P}, \tag{7}$$

where for a matrix $M \in \mathbb{R}^{n\times n}$ having real spectrum, $\lambda_{\max}(M)$ denotes its maximal eigenvalue.

[1] Marginally stable systems are those systems in (2) that are Lyapunov stable but not asymptotically stable.

2.2 Properties of the switching signal

Recall that for a switching signal σ, $0 =: \tau_0 < \tau_1 < \cdots < \tau_{N_t^\sigma}$ are the switching instants before (and including) $t > 0$. We define the *i-th holding time* of a switching signal σ to be

$$S_{i+1} := \tau_{i+1} - \tau_i, \quad i = 0, 1, \cdots, \tag{8}$$

where τ_i and τ_{i+1} denote two consecutive switching instants. We let

$$\nu(t) := \frac{N_t^\sigma}{t}, \quad t > 0, \tag{9}$$

denote the *switching frequency* of σ at time t.

We associate a directed graph $G(\mathcal{P}, E(\mathcal{P}))$ with the given switched system (1) in the following fashion:[2] Let the finite index set $\mathcal{P}$ denote the set of vertices of the directed graph G, and let the set of edges $E(\mathcal{P})$ of G contain a directed edge from i to j, $i, j \in \mathcal{P}$, whenever a switching from system i to system j is admissible. If it is admissible to dwell on a system $i \in \mathcal{P}$ for at least two consecutive time steps, the vertex i has a self-loop.[3] For example:

Example 1. Given a family of systems with $\mathcal{P} = \{1, 2, 3\}$. Let a switching from system 1 to any other system and from system 2 to system 3 be admissible. Also, let it be admissible to dwell on systems 2 and 3 for at least two consecutive time steps. The corresponding directed graph representation is shown below:

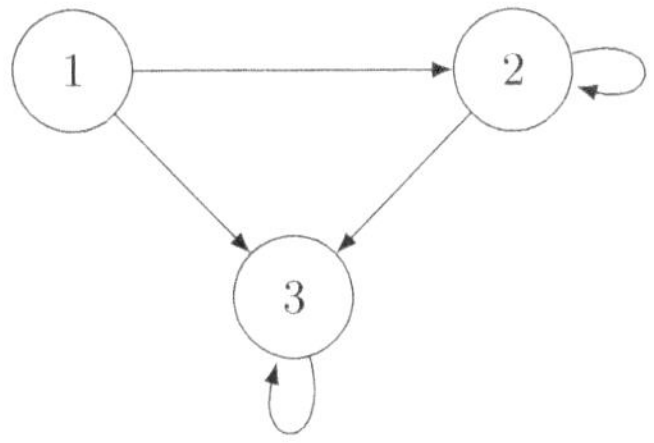

For the directed graph in figure

$$E(\mathcal{P}) = \{(1,2), (1,3), (2,2), (2,3), (3,3)\},$$

where the edges $(1,2), (1,3)$, and $(2,3)$ correspond to the admissible switches, and the self-loops $(2,2)$ and $(3,3)$ depict the fact that it is admissible to dwell on systems 2 and 3 for at least two consecutive time steps.

Recall [2, p.4] that a *walk* W on a directed graph $G(V, E)$ is an alternating sequence of vertices and edges, say $x_0, e_1, x_1, e_2, \cdots, e_\ell, x_\ell$, where $x_i \in V$, $e_i = (x_{i-1}, x_i) \in E$, $0 < i \leqslant \ell$. The length of a walk is its number of edges, counting repetitions, e.g., in the above case the length of the walk W is ℓ. In the sequel by the term *infinite walk* we mean a walk of infinite length, i.e., it has infinitely many edges.

Fact 3. The set of switching signals $\sigma : \mathbb{N}_0 \to \mathcal{P}$ and the set of infinite walks on $G(\mathcal{P}, E(\mathcal{P}))$ (defined as above) are in bijective correspondence.

A proof of Fact 3 is sketched in §6.1. Fix $t > 0$. For a switching signal σ and each pair $(k, \ell) \in E(\mathcal{P})$ we let

$$\rho_{k\ell}(t) := \#\{k \to \ell\}_t \tag{10}$$

denote the number of transitions from vertex (system) k to vertex (system) ℓ made by σ before (and including) t, and for each $j \in \mathcal{P}$ we define

$$\kappa_j(t) := \#\{j\}_t = \sum_{\substack{i:\sigma(\tau_i)=j \\ i=0,1,\cdots,N_t^\sigma}} S_{i+1} \tag{11}$$

to be the number of times the vertex (system) j is activated before (and including) t by σ. Here S_{i+1} is as defined in (8).

In the latter half of §3 we present some graph theoretic arguments, and there we use $\rho_{k\ell}(W)$ and $\kappa_j(W)$ in place of $\rho_{k\ell}(t)$ and $\kappa_j(t)$, where W is the walk (of length t) corresponding to $\sigma|_{0:t}$ à la Fact 3.

3. MAIN RESULTS

We are now in a position to present our first main result, a proof of which is presented in §6.2.

THEOREM 1. *Consider the family of systems (2). Let $\mathcal{P}_{AS}$ and $\mathcal{P}_U \subset \mathcal{P}$ denote the sets of indices of asymptotically stable and unstable systems in (2), respectively. For each $i, j \in \mathcal{P}$ let the constants λ_i and μ_{ij} be as in Fact 1 and (6), respectively. Then the switched system (1) is globally asymptotically stable for every switching signal σ satisfying*

$$\liminf_{t\to+\infty} \nu(t) > 0 \tag{12}$$

and

$$\limsup_{t\to+\infty} \frac{\sum_{(k,\ell)\in E(\mathcal{P})} (\ln \mu_{k\ell})\rho_{k\ell}(t) + \sum_{j\in\mathcal{P}_U} |\ln \lambda_j|\, \kappa_j(t)}{\sum_{j\in\mathcal{P}_{AS}} |\ln \lambda_j|\, \kappa_j(t)} < 1, \tag{13}$$

where $\nu(t)$, $\rho_{k\ell}(t)$, and $\kappa_j(t)$ are as defined in (9), (10), and (11), respectively.

Remark 1. The condition (12) is necessary to prevent the switched system from eventually "adhering to" an unstable system. This assumption is natural in our setting because we admit unstable systems in the family (2), and stipulates that switching continues to occur at a rate that is not asymptotically vanishingly small. However, (12) is not necessary when $\mathcal{P}_{AS} = \mathcal{P}$.

Remark 2. Condition (13) involves *only* the asymptotic behaviour of the switching signal. Indeed, (13) requires that the limit superior of the ratio

$$\frac{\sum_{(k,\ell)\in E(\mathcal{P})} (\ln \mu_{k\ell})\rho_{k\ell}(t) + \sum_{j\in\mathcal{P}_U} |\ln \lambda_j|\, \kappa_j(t)}{\sum_{j\in\mathcal{P}_{AS}} |\ln \lambda_j|\, \kappa_j(t)}$$

should be strictly less than 1. In the numerator of the above ratio, the term $\sum_{(k,\ell)\in E(\mathcal{P})} (\ln \mu_{k\ell})\rho_{k\ell}(t)$ captures the number of times each admissible transition $(k, \ell) \in E(\mathcal{P})$ occurs in σ till time t, weighted by $\ln \mu_{k\ell}$'s where $\mu_{k\ell}$ is as in Assumption 2. The terms $\sum_{j\in\mathcal{P}_{AS}} |\ln \lambda_j|\, \kappa_j(t)$ and $\sum_{j\in\mathcal{P}_U} |\ln \lambda_j|\, \kappa_j(t)$ capture the number of times a system $j \in \mathcal{P}_{AS}$ (resp. $\mathcal{P}_U$) is activated till time t by σ, weighted by the quantitative measure of (in)stability of the respective system.

[2] A directed graph is a set of nodes connected by edges, where each edge has a direction associated to it. Directed graphs have appeared before in the switched systems literature in [14, 8].

[3] A self-loop is an edge that connects a vertex to itself.

Remark 3. Recall [17, Theorem 3] the average dwell time condition for a given family of systems containing unstable subsystems: For any given $\lambda \in]\lambda_1, 1[$ there exists a finite constant τ_a^* such that the switched system under consideration is globally exponentially stable with stability degree λ if the switching signal σ satisfies $\inf_{k>0} \frac{K^-(k)}{K^+(k)} \geqslant \frac{\ln\lambda_2 - \ln\lambda^*}{\ln\lambda^* - \ln\lambda_1}$ for some scalar $\lambda^* \in]\lambda_1, \lambda[$, and the average dwell time is not smaller than τ_a^*. Here, $K^-(k)$ (resp. $K^+(k)$) denote the total activation time of Schur stable (resp. unstable) systems; $\lambda_1 < 1$ and $\lambda_2 \geqslant 1$ are as follows:

$$\left\|A_i^k\right\| \leqslant \begin{cases} h_i\lambda_1^k, & \text{if system } i \text{ is Schur stable} \\ h_i\lambda_2^k, & \text{if system } i \text{ is unstable} \end{cases}$$

for all $k \geqslant 1$ with $i = 0, \cdots, N$, and the number of switches $N_\sigma(0, k)$ on every time interval $0 : k-1$, $k \geqslant 1$, obeys $N_\sigma(0,k) \leqslant N_0 + \frac{k}{\tau_a}$ with chatter bound N_0, and average dwell time τ_a. Our condition (13) does not imply nor require any affine bound on the number of switches. Condition (13) also does not imply nor require a bound on the ratio of the activation time of Schur stable to unstable systems. Consequently, the number of switches N_t^σ on the interval $1 : t$ can grow faster than an affine function of t in our case; indeed, N_t^σ obeying $k_0 t - k_0'\sqrt{t} \leqslant N_t^\sigma \leqslant k_1 t + k_1' t + k_1''\sqrt{t}$ for positive constants $k_0, k_0', k_1, k_1', k_1''$, is perfectly admissible.

Remark 4. Theorem 1 does not assert any form of uniformity of global asymptotic stability of (1). Indeed, let σ and σ' be two switching signals satisfying the hypothesis of Theorem 1, and let $(x_\sigma(t))_{t\in\mathbb{N}_0}$ and $(x_{\sigma'}(t))_{t\in\mathbb{N}_0}$ be the corresponding solutions to (1), respectively. Theorem 1 asserts, in particular, that $x_\sigma(t)$ and $x_{\sigma'}(t) \to 0$ as $t \to +\infty$. However, Theorem 1 does *not* claim that the rates of convergence of the sequences $(x_\sigma(t))_{t\in\mathbb{N}_0}$ and $(x_{\sigma'}(t))_{t\in\mathbb{N}_0}$ are identical.

So far in this section we proposed a class of switching signals corresponding to a given switched system (1) such that global asymptotic stability of (1) is guaranteed. However, given a switched system (1) and a family of numbers μ_{ij} and λ_j, there may not exist a switching signal σ that satisfies condition (13). There is also a fair amount of latitude for selection of the Lyapunov functions for the constituent systems in (2), as is evident from Fact 2. Consequently, the sets of numbers $\{\mu_{ij} : (i,j) \in E(\mathcal{P})\}$ and $\{\lambda_j : j \in \mathcal{P}\}$ are not uniquely determined. These numbers enter the condition (13) in an essential way, and for a certain choice of Lyapunov functions, a.k.a the numbers $\{\mu_{ij}\}$ and $\{\lambda_j\}$, it may not be possible to verify(13) for any switching signal. For instance:

Example 2. Consider a family of systems with $\mathcal{P}_{AS} = \{1\}$ and $\mathcal{P}_U = \{2\}$. Let it be admissible to switch from system 1 to system 2 and vice-versa, and let it be not admissible to dwell on any of the systems for two consecutive time steps. Assume $\ln\mu_{12} = -1.5$, $\ln\mu_{21} = 1.8$, $\ln\lambda_1 = -0.2$, and $\ln\lambda_2 = 1.6$. In this case a switch occurs at every time t. The term $(\ln\mu_{12})\rho_{12}(t) + (\ln\mu_{21})\rho_{21}(t) + |\ln\lambda_2|\,\kappa_2(t)$ equals $-1.5\rho_{12}(t) + 1.8\rho_{21}(t) + 1.6\kappa_2(t)$. Consequently, condition (13) is not satisfied.

In view of Example 2, given a switched system (1), an important and natural problem concerns the existence of a switching signal σ that satisfies condition (13). We address this problem in the remainder of this section.

For a streamlined presentation of our second main result, we employ from §2.2 the directed graph $G(\mathcal{P}, E(\mathcal{P}))$ representation of the switched system (1). Given the family of systems (2), we get an estimate of the constants $\mu_{k\ell}$ for all $(k,\ell) \in E(\mathcal{P})$ and λ_j for all $j \in \mathcal{P}$, by applying Proposition 1 and Fact 1, respectively. The problem at hand, can now be rephrased in a purely graph theoretic language, as:

Problem 1. Given a directed graph $G(\mathcal{P}, E(\mathcal{P}))$ and two sets of real numbers $\{\mu_{k\ell} : (k,\ell) \in E(\mathcal{P})\}$, and $\{\lambda_j : j \in \mathcal{P}\}$, does there exist an infinite walk on $G(\mathcal{P}, E(\mathcal{P}))$ such that the corresponding switching signal *à* la Fact 3 satisfies condition (13)?

Remark 5. On the one hand, the issue of existence of a switching signal that satisfies condition (13) is trivial if the directed graph $G(\mathcal{P}, E(\mathcal{P}))$ has a self-loop for any vertex $j \in \mathcal{P}_{AS}$. Indeed, for a switching signal whose corresponding infinite walk (*à* la Fact 3) traverses this self-loop repeatedly, the denominator of the ratio on the left-hand side of (13) tends to $+\infty$ as t (a.k.a, the length of the walk) tends to $+\infty$. In the numerator of (13), $\ln\mu_{jj} = \ln(\lambda_{\max}(P_j P_j^{-1})) = 0$ by Proposition 1, and consequently, condition (13) holds. The design of an algorithm to detect such a walk is also simple: given $G(\mathcal{P}, E(\mathcal{P}))$, the algorithm needs to detect the vertex corresponding to an asymptotically stable subsystem with a self-loop. Beyond the preceding trivial case, on the other hand, given a weighted directed graph, the problem of algorithmically finding an *infinite* walk that satisfies some pre-specified conditions involving vertex and edge weights in the form of the numbers μ_{ij} and λ_j in Problem 1, is not a straightforward task.

Against the backdrop of Remark 5, we propose a partial solution to Problem 1 in the sequel: we provide a sufficient condition for the existence of a switching signal σ that satisfies condition (13), and an algorithm to design such a switching signal.

Recall [4, p.6] that a walk on a graph is called a *trail* if all its edges are distinct. A closed trail is called a *circuit*.

Let $A = [a_{ij}]$ be the (node arc) incidence matrix [15, §3.4] of $G(\mathcal{P}, E(\mathcal{P}))$, defined by

$$a_{ij} = \begin{cases} +1, & \text{if edge } (i,j) \text{ leaves node } i,\ i = 1, 2, \cdots, |\mathcal{P}|, \\ -1, & \text{if edge } (i,j) \text{ enters node } i,\ j = 1, 2, \cdots, |E(\mathcal{P})|, \\ 0, & \text{otherwise,} \end{cases} \tag{14}$$

where $|S|$ denotes the cardinality of a finite set S.

Remark 6. Incidence matrices are commonly defined for graphs without self-loops. Our purposes require us to define incidence matrices for directed graphs with self-loops, and we accommodate the latter in an incidence matrix A in the following way: Suppose that the given directed graph $G(\mathcal{P}, E(\mathcal{P}))$ has a self-loop on vertex $j \in \mathcal{P}$. We consider an auxiliary vertex j' corresponding to j and represent the self-loop as an edge from j to j'. Consequently, the number of rows of A becomes $|\mathcal{P}|+|$the set of vertices having self-loops$|$. Here is an illustration of this procedure:

Example 3. Consider the following directed graph:

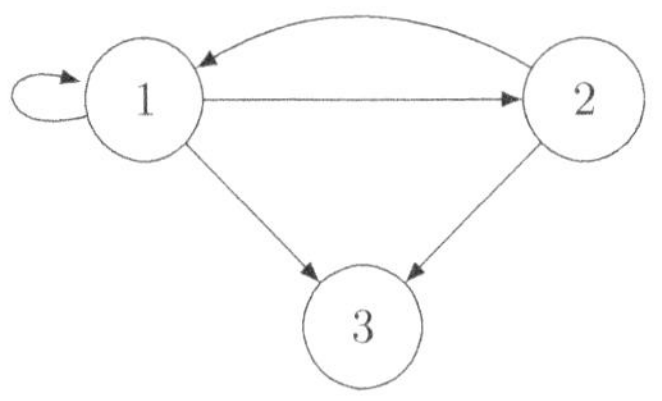

for which the incidence matrix is:

$$A = \begin{array}{c} \\ 1 \\ 1' \\ 2 \\ 3 \end{array} \begin{array}{c} \begin{array}{ccccc} (1,1') & (2,1) & (1,2) & (2,3) & (1,3) \end{array} \\ \left(\begin{array}{ccccc} +1 & -1 & +1 & 0 & +1 \\ -1 & 0 & 0 & 0 & 0 \\ 0 & +1 & -1 & +1 & 0 \\ 0 & 0 & 0 & -1 & -1 \end{array} \right) \end{array}.$$

Our second main result is as follows:

THEOREM 2. *Consider the switched system (2), and the directed graph $G(\mathcal{P}, E(\mathcal{P}))$ as in §2.2. Let the sets of real numbers $\{\mu_{k\ell} : (k,\ell) \in E(\mathcal{P})\}$ and $\{\lambda_j : j \in \mathcal{P}\}$ be calculated from Fact 1 and Proposition 1, respectively.*

(a) *If there exists a closed walk W on $G(\mathcal{P}, E(\mathcal{P}))$ that satisfies the inequality:*

$$\frac{\sum_{(k,\ell)\in E(\mathcal{P})} (\ln \mu_{k\ell})\rho_{k\ell}(W) + \sum_{j\in\mathcal{P}_U} |\ln \lambda_j|\, \kappa_j(W)}{\sum_{j\in\mathcal{P}_{AS}} |\ln \lambda_j|\, \kappa_j(W)} < 1, \tag{15}$$

then the switching signal corresponding to the infinite walk — obtained by repeating the closed walk W — satisfies (13).[4]

(b) *The existence of a circuit on $G(\mathcal{P}, E(\mathcal{P}))$ satisfying (15) is guaranteed by the existence of a solution to the following feasibility problem (linear program) in the variable $f \in \mathbb{R}^{|E(\mathcal{P})|}$:*

$$\text{minimize} \quad 1 \tag{16}$$

$$\text{subject to} \quad \begin{cases} Af = (0, 0, \cdots, 0)^\top, \\ \text{condition (15)}, \\ 0 \leqslant f_j \leqslant 1 \text{ for all } 1 \leqslant j \leqslant |E(\mathcal{P})|, \\ \sum_{j=1}^{|E(\mathcal{P})|} f_j \geqslant 1, \end{cases}$$

where the matrix A is as defined in (14), and $|E(P)|$ denotes the cardinality of the set $E(\mathcal{P})$.

(c) *If a solution to the feasibility problem (16) exists, then Hierholzer's algorithm can be used to obtain the circuit on $G(\mathcal{P}, E(\mathcal{P}))$ that satisfies (15).*

A detailed proof of Theorem 2 is provided in §6.2.

Remark 7. Theorem 2 gives a *sufficient condition* for the existence of an infinite walk on $G(\mathcal{P}, E(\mathcal{P}))$ corresponding to a switching signal σ that satisfies condition (13), thereby providing an answer to Problem 1. Given a directed graph representing the switched system (1), finding a *necessary condition* for the directed graph to admit an infinite walk such that condition (13) holds for the corresponding switching signal is a difficult problem. Armed with the sufficient condition proposed in Theorem 2, we need to algorithmically determine a closed walk on $G(\mathcal{P}, E(\mathcal{P}))$ that satisfies (15). We solve the last problem in two steps: Firstly, we employ the feasibility problem (16) to determine whether there exists a circuit on $G(\mathcal{P}, E(\mathcal{P}))$ that satisfies (15) by algorithmically calculating the vector f, each entry of which is either one or zero, corresponding to whether an edge is included in the circuit or not, respectively. If the feasibility problem (16) has a solution, we proceed to the second step with the calculated vector f, and apply Hierholzer's algorithm to find the circuit on $G(\mathcal{P}, E(\mathcal{P}))$ that satisfies (15). See also Remark 11 below.

[4]The correspondence refers to Fact 3.

Remark 8. We mentioned in Remark 7 that in a solution f to the feasibility problem (16), (if there is a solution,) each entry of the column vector f is either one or zero. This implies that the length of a circuit obtained as a solution to the feasibility problem (16) can at most be the total number of edges of the directed graph $G(\mathcal{P}, E(\mathcal{P}))$, i.e., the case when all entries of the vector f are one.

Remark 9. Condition (15) is included in the feasibility problem (16) in the following manner: We assume that the total number of times the closed walk W visits a vertex $j \in \mathcal{P}$ is the same as the total number of times W visits the outgoing edges of the vertex j. Consequently, for a vertex $j \in \mathcal{P}$, $\kappa_j(W)$ can be replaced by $\rho_{j\ell}(W)$, $(j,\ell) \in E(\mathcal{P})$. Since we are concerned with an infinite walk constructed by repeating the closed walk W satisfying (15), this assumption is no loss of generality.

Remark 10. The condition $Af = (0, 0, \cdots, 0)^\top$ in the feasibility problem (16) in Theorem 2 represents a closed walk. As such, the preceding equality always has a trivial solution where f is a vector with all entries equal to 0. The condition $\sum_j f_j \geqslant 1$ in (16) ensures that any solution f to (16) is not the zero vector.

Remark 11. Given an Eulerian graph G, Hierholzer's algorithm [4, p.57] finds an Eulerian circuit of G; see (c) of Theorem 2. The applicability of this algorithm in our context is explained in the proof of Theorem 2 in §6.2.

4. NUMERICAL EXAMPLES

Example 4. Consider a family of systems (2) with $\mathcal{P} = \{1, 2, 3, 4, 5\}$, and

$$A_1 = \begin{pmatrix} 0.4 & 0.8 \\ -0.7 & 0.6 \end{pmatrix}, \qquad A_2 = \begin{pmatrix} 0.3 & 0.6 \\ 0.1 & 0.4 \end{pmatrix},$$
$$A_3 = \begin{pmatrix} 1 & 0 \\ 0 & 0.5 \end{pmatrix}, \qquad A_4 = \begin{pmatrix} 1.2 & 0.7 \\ 1.6 & 0.1 \end{pmatrix},$$
$$A_5 = \begin{pmatrix} 1 & 0.1 \\ 0.1 & 1 \end{pmatrix}.$$

For this family $\mathcal{P}_{AS} = \{1, 2\}$ and $\mathcal{P}_U = \{4, 5\}$. Let all transitions among the systems in the given family be admissible. Let it also be permissible for switching signals to dwell on systems 3, 4, and 5 for at least two consecutive time steps.

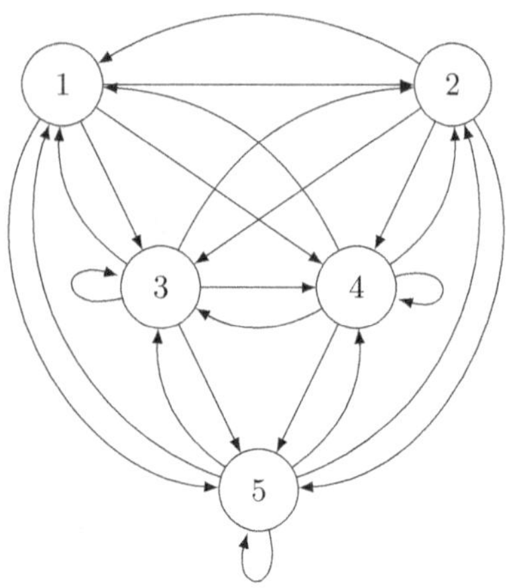

That is,

$$\begin{aligned}\mathcal{P} &= \{1,2,3,4,5\}, \quad \text{and}\\ E(\mathcal{P}) &= \{(1,2),(1,3),(1,4),(1,5),\\ &\quad (2,1),(2,3),(2,4),(2,5),\\ &\quad (3,1),(3,2),(3,3'),(3,4),(3,5),\\ &\quad (4,1),(4,2),(4,3),(4,4'),(4,5),\\ &\quad (5,1),(5,2),(5,3),(5,4),(5,5')\},\end{aligned}$$

where $3', 4'$ and $5'$ are as explained in Remark 6. We design the incidence matrix A from the above description of $E(\mathcal{P})$ and associate the elements of the column vector f with the entries of $E(\mathcal{P})$ as illustrated in Example 3. (We do not provide the rather large incidence matrix here for reasons of space.)

For the given family of systems (2), an estimate of the pairs (P_i, λ_i) as in Fact 1 are as follows:

$$(P_1,\lambda_1) = \left(\begin{pmatrix} 4.7545 & -0.5804\\ -0.5804 & 5.4464\end{pmatrix}, 0.8269\right),$$

$$(P_2,\lambda_2) = \left(\begin{pmatrix} 1.1421 & 0.3422\\ 0.3422 & 1.8755\end{pmatrix}, 0.5026\right),$$

$$(P_3,\lambda_3) = \left(\begin{pmatrix} 1 & 0\\ 0 & 1\end{pmatrix}, 1\right),$$

$$(P_4,\lambda_4) = \left(\begin{pmatrix} 1 & 0\\ 0 & 1\end{pmatrix}, 5.1306\right),$$

$$(P_5,\lambda_5) = \left(\begin{pmatrix} 1 & 0\\ 0 & 1\end{pmatrix}, 3.2000\right).$$

From Proposition 1, we obtain the following estimates for μ_{ij}:

$$\begin{array}{lll} \mu_{12} = 0.4185, & \mu_{13} = 0.2260, & \mu_{14} = 0.2260,\\ \mu_{15} = 0.2260, & \mu_{21} = 5.2823, & \mu_{23} = 0.9928,\\ \mu_{24} = 0.9928, & \mu_{25} = 0.9928, & \mu_{31} = 5.7761,\\ \mu_{32} = 2.0103, & \mu_{33} = 1, & \mu_{34} = 1,\\ \mu_{35} = 1, & \mu_{41} = 5.7761, & \mu_{42} = 2.0103,\\ \mu_{43} = 1, & \mu_{44} = 1, & \mu_{45} = 1,\\ \mu_{51} = 5.7761, & \mu_{52} = 2.0103, & \mu_{53} = 1,\\ \mu_{54} = 1, & \mu_{55} = 1. & \end{array}$$

Solving the feasibility problem (16) in the context of this example with the aid of MATLAB by employing the program YALMIP [12] and the solver SDPT3, we obtain the following solution:

$$f = (1,1,0,0,1,1,0,0,1,1,0,0,0,0,0,0,0,0,0,0,0,0,0)^\top,$$

with

$$\frac{\displaystyle\sum_{(k,\ell)\in E(\mathcal{P})} (\ln \mu_{k\ell})\rho_{k\ell}(W) + \sum_{j\in\mathcal{P}_U} |\ln\lambda_j|\,\kappa_j(W)}{\displaystyle\sum_{j\in\mathcal{P}_{AS}} |\ln\lambda_j|\,\kappa_j(W)} = 0.99 < 1.$$

Following is a circuit obtained from the vector f with the aid of Hierholzer's algorithm:

$$3,(3,1),1,(1,2),2,(2,1),1,(1,3),3,(3,2),2,(2,3),3,$$

which pictorially is as follows:

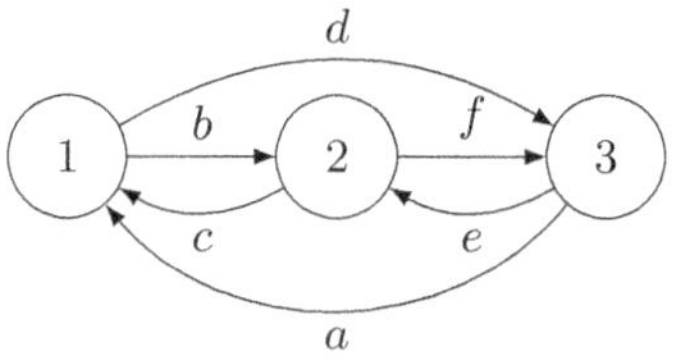

Here a, b, c, d and e denote the edges in consecutive order in which they appear in the above circuit.

We study the nature of $(x(t))_{t\in\mathbb{N}_0}$ for different initial conditions $x(0)$ and observe that in each case, $x(t) \to 0$ as $t \to +\infty$. In Figures 1 and 2 we present two representative solutions to (1) with $x(0) = (-1000, 1000)^\top$ and $x(0) = (1200, -500)^\top$, respectively.

Example 5. Consider a family of systems (2) with $\mathcal{P} = \{1,2,3,4\}$, and

$$A_1 = \begin{pmatrix} -0.5 & -0.7\\ 0.9 & -0.5\end{pmatrix}, \qquad A_2 = \begin{pmatrix} 1 & 0\\ 0 & 0.5\end{pmatrix},$$
$$A_3 = \begin{pmatrix} 0.2 & 0.1\\ 0.7 & 1\end{pmatrix}, \qquad A_4 = \begin{pmatrix} 1 & 0.1\\ 0.1 & 1\end{pmatrix}.$$

For this family $\mathcal{P}_{AS} = \{1\}$, $\mathcal{P}_{MS} = \{2\}$, and $\mathcal{P}_U = \{3,4\}$. Let all transitions among the systems in the given family be admissible. Let it also be permissible for switching signals to dwell on systems 2, 3, and 4 for at least two consecutive time steps.

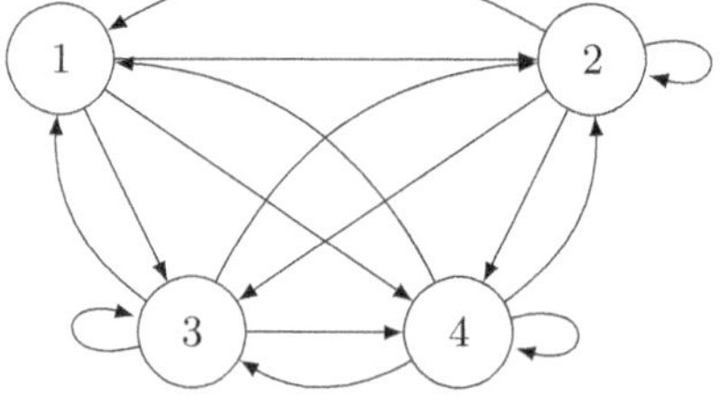

That is,

$$\begin{aligned}\mathcal{P} &= \{1,2,3,4\}, \quad \text{and}\\ E(\mathcal{P}) &= \{(1,2),(1,3),(1,4),\\ &\quad (2,1),(2,2'),(2,3),(2,4),\\ &\quad (3,1),(3,2),(3,3'),(3,4),\end{aligned}$$

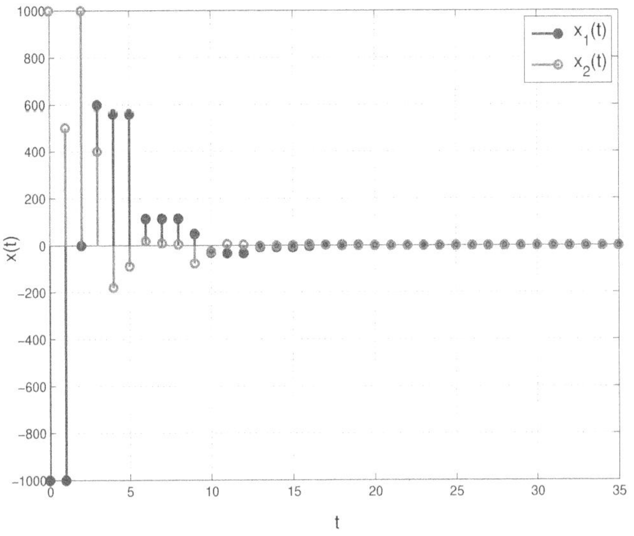

Figure 1: Solution to (1) with $x_1(0) = -1000, x_2(0) = 1000$.

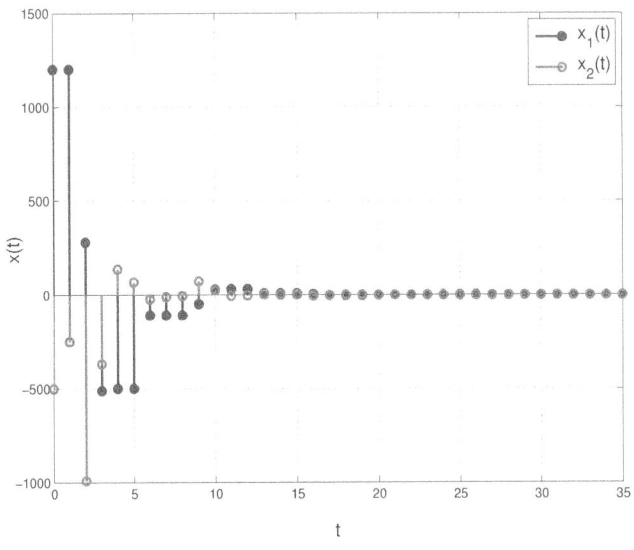

Figure 2: Solution to (1) with $x_1(0) = 1200, x_2(0) = -500$.

$$(4,1),(4,2),(4,3),(4,4')\},$$

where $2', 3'$ and $4'$ are as explained in Remark 6. We design the incidence matrix A and associate the elements of the column vector f as in the case of the previous example.

For the given family of systems (2), an estimate of the pairs (P_i, λ_i) as in Fact 1 are as follows:

$$(P_1,\lambda_1) = \left(\begin{pmatrix} 9.4460 & -0.0395 \\ -0.0395 & 7.4679 \end{pmatrix}, 0.8941\right),$$

$$(P_2,\lambda_2) = \left(\begin{pmatrix} 1 & 0 \\ 0 & 1 \end{pmatrix}, 1\right),$$

$$(P_3,\lambda_3) = \left(\begin{pmatrix} 1 & 0 \\ 0 & 1 \end{pmatrix}, 3.4730\right),$$

$$(P_4,\lambda_4) = \left(\begin{pmatrix} 1 & 0 \\ 0 & 1 \end{pmatrix}, 3.2000\right).$$

From Proposition 1, we obtain the following estimates for μ_{ij}:

$$\begin{array}{lll} \mu_{12} = 0.1339, & \mu_{13} = 0.1339, & \mu_{14} = 0.1339, \\ \mu_{21} = 9.4468, & \mu_{22} = 1, & \mu_{23} = 1, \\ \mu_{24} = 1 & \mu_{31} = 9.4468, & \mu_{32} = 1, \\ \mu_{33} = 1 & \mu_{34} = 1, & \mu_{41} = 9.4468, \\ \mu_{42} = 1, & \mu_{43} = 1, & \mu_{44} = 1. \end{array}$$

Solving the feasibility problem (16) in the context of this example in the same manner as in the previous example, we obtain that the solution for the same is infeasible.

5. CONCLUSION

In this article we proposed a class of switching signals under which global asymptotic stability of a discrete-time switched linear system is guaranteed. We considered unstable dynamics in the family and our characterization of the stabilizing switching signal involved only asymptotic behaviour of the switching signal. Moreover, given a switched system, we proposed a sufficient condition for the existence of a switching signal that satisfies our condition. We presented an algorithm to design such a switching signal.

Several open questions in this area remain. A necessary condition for the existence of the proposed switching signal is currently under investigation and will be reported elsewhere. A randomized algorithm for the synthesis of stabilizing switching signals for large-scale switched systems is also being developed.

6. PROOFS

6.1 Proofs of Fact 1, Proposition 1, and Fact 3

Proof of Fact 1. For asymptotically stable systems let $\mathbb{R}^d \ni z \longmapsto V_i(z) := z^\top P_i z$, where $P_i \in \mathbb{R}^{d\times d}$ is the symmetric and positive definite solution to the discrete-time Lyapunov equation

$$A_i^\top P_i A_i - P_i + Q_i = 0 \tag{17}$$

for some pre-selected symmetric and positive definite matrix $Q_i \in \mathbb{R}^{d\times d}$ [1, Proposition 11.10.5]. If A_i is marginally stable, it is known [1, Proposition 11.10.6] that there exists a symmetric and positive definite matrix $P_i \in \mathbb{R}^{d\times d}$ and a symmetric and non-negative definite matrix $Q_i \in \mathbb{R}^{d\times d}$ that solve the discrete-time Lyapunov equation (17); we put $\mathbb{R}^d \ni z \longmapsto V_i(z) := z^\top P_i z$ as the corresponding Lyapunov-like function. A straightforward calculation gives $V_i(z(t+1)) - V_i(z(t)) = -z(t)^\top Q_i z(t)$ in both the cases. An application of the standard inequality [1, Lemma 8.4.3] leads to $-z^\top Q_i z \leqslant -\frac{\lambda_{\min}(Q_i)}{\lambda_{\max}(P_i)} z^\top P_i z$. Defining $\bar{\lambda}_i = \frac{\lambda_{\min}(Q_i)}{\lambda_{\max}(P_i)}$, we arrive at

$$V_i(z(t+1)) \leqslant \lambda_i V_i(z(t)) \text{ with } \lambda_i = 1 - \bar{\lambda}_i,$$

which gives (5) with $0 < \lambda_i \leqslant 1$.

For unstable systems, let us consider the simplest case of a symmetric and positive definite matrix $P_i = I_{d\times d}$, and let $\mathbb{R}^d \ni z \longmapsto V_i(z) := \|z\|^2$. Then by the Cauchy-Schwarz inequality and sub-multiplicativity property of matrix norms,

$$|V_i(z(t+1)) - V_i(z(t))| \leqslant 2\|A_i\|\, V_i(z(t)).$$

To wit,

$$-2\|A_i\|\, V_i(z(t)) \leqslant V_i(z(t+1)) - V_i(z(t)) \leqslant 2\|A_i\|\, V_i(z(t))$$

for all $t \in \mathbb{N}_0$. Thus (5) holds for unstable systems with $\lambda_i = 1 + 2\|A_i\| > 1$. □

Proof of Proposition 1. Observe that $P_j P_i^{-1}$ is similar to $P_i^{-1/2}(P_j P_i^{-1})P_i^{1/2}$, and that the matrix $P_i^{-1/2}P_j P_i^{-1/2}$ is symmetric and positive definite. Since the spectrum of a matrix is invariant under similarity transformations, the eigenvalues of $P_j P_i^{-1}$ are the same as the eigenvalues of $P_i^{-1/2}P_j P_i^{-1/2}$; consequently, the eigenvalues of $P_j P_i^{-1}$ are real numbers. In addition,

$$\sup_{0\neq z\in\mathbb{R}^d} \frac{\langle P_j z, z\rangle}{\langle P_i z, z\rangle} = \sup_{0\neq z\in\mathbb{R}^d} \frac{\langle P_j z, z\rangle}{\langle P_i^{1/2} z, P_i^{1/2} z\rangle},$$

and, with $z := P_i^{-1/2} y$, the right-hand side above is

$$\begin{aligned}\sup_{0\neq y\in\mathbb{R}^d} \frac{\langle P_j(P_i^{-1/2}y), P_i^{-1/2}y\rangle}{\langle y, y\rangle} &= \sup_{0\neq y\in\mathbb{R}^d} \frac{\langle P_i^{-1/2}P_j P_i^{-1/2} y, y\rangle}{\langle y, y\rangle}\\ &= \lambda_{\max}(P_i^{-1/2}P_j P_i^{-1/2})\\ &= \lambda_{\max}(P_j P_i^{-1}).\end{aligned}$$

Since $V_j(z) \leqslant \mu_{ij} V_i(z)$ for all $z \in \mathbb{R}^d$, the smallest constant μ_{ij} satisfies (7). □

Proof of Fact 3. Let $\mathcal{P}^{\mathbb{N}_0}$ denote the set of all sequences $(x_n)_{n\in\mathbb{N}_0}$ with $x_n \in \mathcal{P}$. Define the map

$$\Phi : \mathcal{P}^{\mathbb{N}_0} \to \{W : W \text{ is an infinite walk on } G(\mathcal{P}, E(\mathcal{P}))\}$$

by $\sigma \longmapsto \Phi(\sigma) := (\sigma(0), (\sigma(0), \sigma(1)), \sigma(1), (\sigma(1), \sigma(2)), \sigma(2), \cdots)$, which is a unique infinite walk on $G(\mathcal{P}, E(\mathcal{P}))$. Indeed, for two different switching signals σ_1 and σ_2 the terms $\sigma_1(\ell), (\sigma_1(\ell), \sigma_1(\ell+1)), \sigma_1(\ell+1)$ and $\sigma_2(\ell), (\sigma_2(\ell), \sigma_2(\ell+1)), \sigma_2(\ell+1)$ are different at least for one $\ell \in \mathbb{N}_0$. Consequently, $\Phi(\sigma_1)$ and $\Phi(\sigma_2)$ are different, which ensures injectivity of Φ. Surjectivity is clear.

Conversely, for an infinite walk $W = (a_0, (a_0, a_1), a_1, (a_1, a_2), \cdots)$, we define $\sigma : \mathbb{N}_0 \to \mathcal{P}$ by $\sigma(i) = a_i$, (a_i, a_{i+1}) be the i-th transition of σ, i.e., $\sigma(i) = a_i, \sigma(i+1) = a_{i+1}, i = 0, 1, 2, \cdots$. Define the map

$$\Psi : \{W : W \text{ is an infinite walk on } G(\mathcal{P}, E(\mathcal{P}))\} \to \mathcal{P}^{\mathbb{N}_0}$$

by $W \longmapsto \Psi(W) := \sigma$, which is the switching signal corresponding to the infinite walk W constructed above. Standard arguments as above may be employed to assert bijectivity of Ψ. Finally, it is clear that Φ and Ψ are inverses of each other. □

6.2 Proofs of Theorems 1 and 2

Proof of Theorem 1. We will employ properties of the Lyapunov-like functions V_i for all $i \in \mathcal{P}$. Fix $t > 0$. Recall from §2 that $0 =: \tau_0 < \tau_1 < \cdots < \tau_{N_t^\sigma}$ are the switching instants before (and including) t. A straightforward iteration involving Fact 1 and Fact 2 leads to

$$V_{\sigma(t)}(x(t)) \leqslant V_{\sigma(0)}(x(0)) \times \left(\prod_{i=0}^{N_t^\sigma - 1} \mu_{\sigma(\tau_i)\sigma(\tau_{i+1})} \cdot \prod_{i=0}^{N_t^\sigma - 1} \lambda_{\sigma(\tau_i)}^{S_{i+1}} \cdot \lambda_{\sigma(N_t^\sigma)}^{t-\tau_{N_t^\sigma}}\right), \tag{18}$$

where S_{i+1} is as defined in (8). The second term on the right-hand side of the above inequality can be written as

$$\exp\Bigg(\ln\left(\prod_{i=0}^{N_t^\sigma - 1} \mu_{\sigma(\tau_i)\sigma(\tau_{i+1})}\right) + \ln\left(\prod_{i=0}^{N_t^\sigma - 1} \lambda_{\sigma(\tau_i)}^{S_{i+1}}\right) + \ln \lambda_{\sigma(\tau_{N_t^\sigma})}^{t-\tau_{N_t^\sigma}}\Bigg).$$

Now

$$\begin{aligned}\ln\left(\prod_{i=0}^{N_t^\sigma - 1} \mu_{\sigma(\tau_i)\sigma(\tau_{i+1})}\right) &= \sum_{i=0}^{N_t^\sigma - 1} \ln \mu_{\sigma(\tau_i)\sigma(\tau_{i+1})}\\ &= \sum_{k\in\mathcal{P}} \sum_{i=0}^{N_t^\sigma - 1} \sum_{\substack{k\to\ell:\\ \ell\in\mathcal{P},\\ k\neq\ell,\\ \sigma(\tau_i)=k,\\ \sigma(\tau_{i+1})=\ell}} \ln \mu_{k\ell}\\ &= \sum_{(k,\ell)\in E(\mathcal{P})} (\ln \mu_{k\ell})\rho_{k\ell}(t),\end{aligned} \tag{19}$$

where $\rho_{k\ell}(t)$ is as defined in (10), and

$$\begin{aligned}\ln\left(\prod_{i=0}^{N_t^\sigma - 1} \lambda_{\sigma(\tau_i)}^{S_{i+1}}\right) &= \sum_{i=0}^{N_t^\sigma - 1} S_{i+1} \ln \lambda_{\sigma(\tau_i)}\\ &= \sum_{i=0}^{N_t^\sigma - 1} \left(\sum_{j\in\mathcal{P}} \mathbb{1}_{\{j\}}(\sigma(\tau_i)) S_{i+1} \ln \lambda_j\right).\end{aligned}$$

Separating out the asymptotically stable, marginally stable, and unstable subsystems in the family (2) into the subsets $\mathcal{P}_{AS}$, $\mathcal{P}_{MS}$, and $\mathcal{P}_U \subset \mathcal{P}$, respectively, we see that the right-hand side of the above equation can be written as

$$\sum_{j\in\mathcal{P}_{AS}} \ln \lambda_j \sum_{\substack{i:\sigma(\tau_i)=j\\ i=0,1,\cdots,N_t^\sigma - 1}} S_{i+1} + \sum_{j\in\mathcal{P}_{MS}} \ln \lambda_j \sum_{\substack{i:\sigma(\tau_i)=j\\ i=0,1,\cdots,N_t^\sigma - 1}} S_{i+1} + \sum_{j\in\mathcal{P}_{U}} \ln \lambda_j \sum_{\substack{i:\sigma(\tau_i)=j\\ i=0,1,\cdots,N_t^\sigma - 1}} S_{i+1}.$$

Recall from Fact 1 that $0 < \lambda_j < 1$, $\lambda_j = 1$, and $\lambda_j > 1$ for the first, middle, and the last sums, respectively. Thus the last expression above equals

$$-\sum_{j\in\mathcal{P}_{AS}} |\ln\lambda_j|\,\kappa_j(t) + \sum_{j\in\mathcal{P}_U} |\ln\lambda_j|\,\kappa_j(t), \tag{20}$$

where $\kappa_j(t)$ is as defined in (11). We define two functions

$$\mathbb{N}\ni t\longmapsto g_1(t) := \sum_{j\in\mathcal{P}_{AS}} |\ln\lambda_j|\,\kappa_j(t), \tag{21}$$

and

$$\mathbb{N}\ni t\longmapsto g_2(t) := \sum_{(k,\ell)\in E(\mathcal{P})} (\ln\mu_{k\ell})\rho_{k\ell}(t) + \sum_{j\in\mathcal{P}_U} |\ln\lambda_j|\,\kappa_j(t) + (t-\tau_{N_t^\sigma})\ln\lambda_{\sigma(\tau_{N_t^\sigma})}. \tag{22}$$

Substituting (19) and (20) in (18) and applying the definitions of g_1 and g_2 from (21) and (22), respectively, we obtain

$$V_{\sigma(t)}(x(t)) \leqslant V_{\sigma(0)}(x(0))\exp\big(g_2(t)-g_1(t)\big). \tag{23}$$

To verify uniform global asymptotic convergence of the switched system (1), we need to find conditions such that

$$\lim_{t\to+\infty}\exp\big(g_2(t)-g_1(t)\big)=0, \tag{24}$$

and that

convergence is uniform for initial conditions $\tilde{x}(0)$ satisfying $\|\tilde{x}(0)\| \leqslant \|x(0)\|$. (25)

A sufficient condition for (24) is that

$$\liminf_{t\to+\infty}\big(g_1(t)-g_2(t)\big)=+\infty, \tag{26}$$

so our proof will be complete if we establish (26) and verify (25) separately. The following steps are geared towards establishing (26).

The hypothesis (12) guarantees that $t-\tau_{N_t^\sigma}$ in the definition of g_2 in (22) is $o(t)$ as $t\to+\infty$. Indeed, $t-\tau_{N_t^\sigma}\neq o(t)$ as $t\to+\infty$ implies that $\liminf_{t\to+\infty}\nu(t)=0$, which contradicts our assumption (12). Thus, we can omit this term in further analysis. Next, condition (26) is equivalent to

$$\liminf_{t\to+\infty}\left(g_1(t)\left(1-\frac{g_2(t)}{g_1(t)}\right)\right)=+\infty. \tag{27}$$

Note that the division by $g_1(t)$ on the left-hand side of the above expression is allowed for $t>0$ (large enough) because by the definition of $g_1(t)$, once an asymptotically stable subsystem is activated, $g_1(t)>0$. By the standard properties of lim inf, *à la* [13, §0.1],

$$\liminf_{t\to+\infty}\left(g_1(t)\left(1-\frac{g_2(t)}{g_1(t)}\right)\right) \geqslant \liminf_{t\to+\infty} g_1(t)\liminf_{t\to+\infty}\left(1-\frac{g_2(t)}{g_1(t)}\right), \tag{28}$$

because the right-hand side is not of the form $0\cdot\pm\infty$. Also, by definition of $g_1(t)$,

$$\liminf_{t\to+\infty} g_1(t)\in\,]0,+\infty].$$

Thus, to ensure that the right-hand side of (28) diverges, we need to find conditions such that

$$\liminf_{t\to+\infty}\left(1-\frac{g_2(t)}{g_1(t)}\right)>0,$$

which by standard properties of lim inf *à la* [13, §0.1], is equivalent to

$$\limsup_{t\to+\infty}\left(\frac{g_2(t)}{g_1(t)}-1\right)<0,$$

which is equivalent to

$$\limsup_{t\to+\infty}\frac{g_2(t)}{g_1(t)}<1. \tag{29}$$

Employing the definitions of $g_1(t)$ and $g_2(t)$ from (21) and (22), respectively, in (29), we see that (13) holds.

It remains to verify (25). To this end, we get back to (23). Since by (24), $\exp\big(g_2(t)-g_1(t)\big)$ is convergent, it is bounded. Let $[0,+\infty[\,\ni r\longmapsto\overline{\alpha}(r):=\lambda_{\max}\Big(\sum_{i\in\mathcal{P}}P_i\Big)r^2$ and $[0,+\infty[\,\ni r\longmapsto\underline{\alpha}(r):=\min_{i\in\mathcal{P}}\lambda_{\min}(P_i)r^2$, we see that

$$\underline{\alpha}(\|z\|)\leqslant V_i(z)\leqslant\overline{\alpha}(\|z\|)\text{ for all } i\in\mathcal{P}\text{ and } z\in\mathbb{R}^d.$$

In conjunction with (23), we get

$$\underline{\alpha}(\|z(t)\|)\leqslant V_{\sigma(t)}(x(t))\leqslant\overline{\alpha}(\|x(0)\|)\exp\big(g_2(t)-g_1(t)\big)\quad\text{for all } t\in\mathbb{N}_0,$$

which implies, for $c=\sqrt{\dfrac{\lambda_{\max}(\sum_{i\in\mathcal{P}}P_i)}{\min_{i\in\mathcal{P}}\lambda_{\min}(P_i)}}$,

$$\|x(t)\|\leqslant c\,\|x(0)\|\exp\big(g_2(t)-g_1(t)\big)\text{ for all } t\in\mathbb{N}_0. \tag{30}$$

Since on the right-hand side of (30), the initial condition $x(0)$ is decoupled from $g_2(t)-g_1(t)$ and $g_2(t)-g_1(t)$ depends on σ, if $\|x(t)\|<\varepsilon$ for all $t>T(\|x(0)\|,\varepsilon)$ for some pre-assigned $\varepsilon>0$, then the solution $(\tilde{x}(t))_{t\in\mathbb{N}_0}$ to (1) corresponding to an initial condition $\tilde{x}(0)$ such that $\|\tilde{x}(0)\|\leqslant\|x(0)\|$ satisfies $\|\tilde{x}(t)\|<\varepsilon$ for all $t>T(\|x(0)\|,\varepsilon)$.

We next verify Lyapunov stability of (1) under any switching signal σ that ensures uniform global asymptotic convergence of (1). We need to show that for all $\varepsilon>0$, there exists $\delta(\varepsilon)>0$ such that $\|x(0)\|<\delta(\varepsilon)$ implies $\|x(t)\|<\varepsilon$ for all $t>0$. To this end, fix $\varepsilon>0$. Let a switching signal σ be given such that σ ensures that (1) is uniformly globally asymptotically convergent. This implies that there exists $N_\sigma(\varepsilon)\in\mathbb{N}$ such that $\|x(t)\|<\varepsilon$ for all $t>N_\sigma(\varepsilon)$ whenever $\|x(0)\|<1$. Let $m:=\max_{i\in\mathcal{P}}\|A_i\|$. Let $(x(t))_{t\in\mathbb{N}_0}$ be the solution to (1) under any switching signal σ. From standard calculations, we have $\|x(N_\sigma(\varepsilon))\|\leqslant m^{N_\sigma(\varepsilon)}\|x_0\|$. Selecting $\delta'=\varepsilon m^{-N_\sigma(\varepsilon)}$, we see that $\|x(t)\|<\varepsilon$ for all $t\in 0:N_\sigma(\varepsilon)$ whenever $\|x(0)\|<\delta'$ and σ arbitrary. For σ that ensures uniform global asymptotic convergence of (1), we select $\delta=\min\{1,\delta'\}$ to guarantee Lyapunov stability of (1). The assertion of Theorem 1 follows at once. □

PROOF OF THEOREM 2. (a) Consider a closed walk W on $G(\mathcal{P},E(\mathcal{P}))$ of length τ that satisfies

$$\frac{N(W)}{D(W)}<1, \tag{31}$$

where

$$N(W):=\sum_{(k,\ell)\in E(\mathcal{P})}(\ln\mu_{k\ell})\rho_{k\ell}(W)+\sum_{j\in\mathcal{P}_U}|\ln\lambda_j|\,\kappa_j(W), \tag{32}$$

and

$$D(W) := \sum_{j \in \mathcal{P}_{AS}} |\ln \lambda_j| \, \kappa_j(W). \tag{33}$$

Fix $t \geqslant \tau$. Let a walk W' of length t be constructed by repeating the closed walk W of length τ. Therefore,

$$\frac{N(W')}{D(W')} = \frac{\lfloor \frac{t}{\tau} \rfloor N(W) + N(W'')}{\lfloor \frac{t}{\tau} \rfloor D(W) + D(W'')} \tag{34}$$

where W'' is a walk of length $t - \lfloor \frac{t}{\tau} \rfloor \tau$. As $t \to +\infty$, $N(W'')$ and $D(W'')$ are negligible compared to $N(W')$ and $D(W')$, respectively in the sense that $N(W'') = o(\lfloor \frac{t}{\tau} \rfloor)$ and $D(W'') = o(\lfloor \frac{t}{\tau} \rfloor)$ as $t \to +\infty$. Consequently,

$$\limsup_{t \to +\infty} \frac{N(W')}{D(W')} = \frac{\lfloor \frac{t}{\tau} \rfloor N(W)}{\lfloor \frac{t}{\tau} \rfloor D(W)} = \frac{N(W)}{D(W)} < 1 \quad \text{by (31)},$$

and the assertion in Theorem 2(a) follows.

(b) Step 1: We first show that every feasible solution to (16) is a trail. Recall from §3 the definition of (node arc) incidence matrix A of the directed graph $G(\mathcal{P}, E(\mathcal{P}))$. By the Corollary to Theorem 13.3 [15, p. 318], the feasibility problem (16) has only integer optimal solutions. By the constraint $0 \leqslant f_j \leqslant 1$ for all $1 \leqslant j \leqslant |E(\mathcal{P})|$, each element of the vector f is either zero or one. Consequently, the solution to (16) (if any) is a trail.

Step 2: It remains to verify that every feasible solution to (16) is a circuit. Suppose there exists a feasible solution which is a trail but not a circuit. By definition, the trail begins at a vertex $u \in \mathcal{P}$ and ends at a vertex $v \in \mathcal{P} \backslash \{u\}$. Then, $a_u f = +1$ and $a_v f = -1$, where a_u and a_v denote the rows of A corresponding to the distinct vertices u and v, respectively. Consequently, the vector Af has $+1$ and -1 values for the u-th and v-th row, respectively, and that contradicts our constraint that $Af = (0, \cdots, 0)^\top$ for every feasible f. It follows at once that every solution to (16) is a circuit.

(c) Let $G'(\mathcal{P}', E(\mathcal{P}'))$ denote a subgraph of the directed graph $G(\mathcal{P}, E(\mathcal{P}))$ such that the set of vertices $\mathcal{P}'$ and the set of edges $E(\mathcal{P}')$ contain the elements of $\mathcal{P}$ and $E(\mathcal{P})$ which are included in the circuit that satisfies condition (15), respectively. It is possible to construct $G'(\mathcal{P}', E(\mathcal{P}'))$ from the solution f to the feasibility problem (16) (if the solution exists). Since f represents a circuit (a closed walk with distinct edges), every vertex in $G'(\mathcal{P}', E(\mathcal{P}'))$ has even degree, i.e., $G'(\mathcal{P}', E(\mathcal{P}'))$ is Eulerian [4, p.56]. Given the Eulerian graph $G'(\mathcal{P}', E(\mathcal{P}'))$, we apply Hierholzer's algorithm [4, p.57] to obtain an Eulerian circuit on $G'(\mathcal{P}', E(\mathcal{P}'))$. □

Acknowledgement

We thank Ankur Kulkarni for discussions and a pointer to reference [15]. We also thank Niranjan Balachandran for several helpful discussions.

7. REFERENCES

[1] D. S. Bernstein, *Matrix mathematics*, Princeton University Press, Princeton, NJ, second ed., 2009. Theory, facts, and formulas.

[2] B. Bollobás, *Modern graph theory*, vol. 184 of Graduate Texts in Mathematics, Springer-Verlag, New York, 1998.

[3] M. C. F. Donkers, W. P. M. H. Heemels, N. van de Wouw, and L. Hetel, *Stability analysis of networked control systems using a switched linear systems approach*, IEEE Trans. Automat. Control, 56 (2011), pp. 2101–2115.

[4] J. M. Harris, J. L. Hirst, and M. J. Mossinghoff, *Combinatorics and graph theory*, Undergraduate Texts in Mathematics, Springer, New York, second ed., 2008.

[5] W. P. M. H. Heemels, B. De Schutter, J. Lunze, and M. Lazar, *Stability analysis and controller synthesis for hybrid dynamical systems*, Philos. Trans. R. Soc. Lond. Ser. A Math. Phys. Eng. Sci., 368 (2010), pp. 4937–4960.

[6] W. P. M. H. Heemels and N. van de Wouw, *Stability and stabilization of networked control systems*, vol. 406 of Lecture Notes in Control and Inform. Sci., Springer, Berlin, 2010.

[7] J. P. Hespanha and A. S. Morse, *Stability of switched systems with average dwell-time*, in Proc. of the 38th Conf. on Decision and Contr., Dec 1999, pp. 2655–2660.

[8] Ö. Karabacak, *Dwell time and average dwell time methods based on the cycle ratio of the switching graph*, Systems & Control Letters, 62 (2013), pp. 1032–1037.

[9] A. Kundu and D. Chatterjee, *Stabilizing switching signals for switched linear systems*. http://www.arxiv.org/abs/1303,1292.

[10] D. Liberzon, *Switching in systems and control*, Systems & Control: Foundations & Applications, Birkhäuser Boston Inc., Boston, MA, 2003.

[11] H. Lin and P. J. Antsaklis, *Stability and stabilizability of switched linear systems: a survey of recent results*, IEEE Trans. Automat. Control, 54 (2009), pp. 308–322.

[12] J. Löfberg, *YALMIP : a toolbox for modeling and optimization in matlab*, In Proceedings of IEEE International Symposium on Computer Aided Control Systems Design.

[13] S. Łojasiewicz, *An introduction to the theory of real functions*, A Wiley-Interscience Publication, John Wiley & Sons Ltd., Chichester, third ed., 1988. With contributions by M. Kosiek, W. Mlak and Z. Opial, Translated from the Polish by G. H. Lawden, Translation edited by A. V. Ferreira.

[14] J. L. Mancilla-Aguilar, R. García, E. Sontag, and Y. Wang, *Uniform stability properties of switched systems with switchings governed by digraphs*, Nonlinear Anal., 63 (2005), pp. 472–490.

[15] C. H. Papadimitriou and K. Steiglitz, *Combinatorial optimization: algorithms and complexity*, Dover Publications Inc., Mineola, NY, 1998. Corrected reprint of the 1982 original.

[16] R. Shorten, F. Wirth, O. Mason, K. Wulff, and C. King, *Stability criteria for switched and hybrid systems*, SIAM Rev., 49 (2007), pp. 545–592.

[17] G. Zhai, B. Hu, K. Yasuda, and A. Michel, *Qualitative analysis of discrete-time switched systems*, Proc. of the American Control Conference, (2002), pp. 1880–1885.

An LQ Sub-Optimal Stabilizing Feedback Law for Switched Linear Systems

Pierre Riedinger
Université de Lorraine, CRAN, UMR 7039,
2, avenue de la forêt de Haye,
Vandœuvre-lès-Nancy Cedex, 54516, France
CNRS, CRAN, UMR 7039, France
Pierre.Riedinger@univ-lorraine.fr

Jean-Claude Vivalda
Inria, CORIDA, Villers-lès-Nancy, F-54600, France
Université de Lorraine, IECL, UMR 7502, Vandœuvre-lès-Nancy, F-54506, France
CNRS, Institut Elie Cartan de Lorraine, UMR 7502, Vandœuvre-lès-Nancy, F-54506, France
Jean-Claude.Vivalda@inria.fr

ABSTRACT

The aim of this paper is the design of a stabilizing feedback law for continuous time linear switched system based on the optimization of a quadratic criterion. The main result provides a control Lyapunov function and a feedback switching law leading to sub-optimal solutions. As the Lyapunov function defines a tight upper bound on the value function of the optimization problem, the sub-optimality is guaranteed. Practically, the switching law is easy to apply and the design procedure is effective if there exists at least a controllable convex combination of the subsystems.

Keywords

Switched systems; optimization; stabilization

1. INTRODUCTION

Over the past decade, the design of stabilizing laws for switched systems (in continuous and discrete time) has been the focus of considerable research attention. Several approaches have been used to tackle this problem, one can cite for example [18, 26, 29, 30] for dynamic programming approaches, [1, 2, 27] for variational approaches, or [6, 8, 12] for Lyapunov based approaches. This problem is not easy, even numerically [24, 27] and the design of a stabilizing feedback law based on the optimization of a criterion is a challenging task.

LQ regulators are widely used for the control of linear systems because of their simple design and their robustness properties. These regulators can also been used for the design of stabilizing feedback laws for linear switched systems but, as yet, one cannot obtain the exact solution of a switched LQ problem. Moreover, the main drawback of this method is the difficulty to get a good numerical approximation of the solution of the optimal problem; this approximation is difficult to obtain even for small dimensional systems. Another possibility is to use open loop control law, which can be achieved through direct or indirect methods [27, 1], nevertheless, in this case singular solutions [22, 2] cause numerical complications [24].

In [12], the authors address two Lyapunov based strategies for stabilization of discrete time linear switched systems. The first one is of open loop nature while the second one is of closed-loop nature and is designed from the solution of the Lyapunov-Metzler inequalities. Their approach uses a family of quadratic Lyapunov functions and an upper bound on the cost is provided, but the distance from the optimality of the stabilizing feedback law is not estimated.

In this paper, we consider a linear and controlled switched linear system. Together with this system, we consider a quadratic cost function. Our aim is to design a stabilizing feedback law that approaches the solution of the optimal problem related to this cost function. To the best of our knowledge, the problem of finding a continuous stabilizing law which satisfies the optimal criterion has not yet been solved.

In Section 2, the problem statement is given as well as a relaxed version that takes into account all the convex combinations of the subsystems. We explain why this relaxation is useful to solve the problem. Then, the necessary condition of the Pontryagin Maximum Principle are recalled. We also discuss the numerical difficulties encountered when *singular controls* enter in the solution. To circumvent this, a numerical framework is proposed to solve properly the optimization problem.

In Section 3, we assume that there exists at least a globally asymptotically stable (GAS) convex combination of the subsystems. As the positive definite solution of an algebraic Riccati equation is a function continuous with respect to the constant matrices related to the equation, we are able to build a parametrized family of positive definite function whose parameters belong to a a compact set. A control Lyapunov function is then defined as the point-wise infimum of this familly.

We prove that the Lyapunov function is locally lipschitzian and homogenous of degree two. Then, we show that its directional Dini derivative is well defined along trajectories and we deduce a state feedback leading to a cost value less than the value of the Lyapunov function. In addition, we prove that this feedback makes the system globally exponentially stable. In section 4, we show that the sampled

HSCC'14, April 15–17, 2014, Berlin, Germany.
Copyright 2014 ACM 978-1-4503-2732-9/14/04 ...$15.00.
http://dx.doi.org/10.1145/2562059.2562121.

time version of the state feedback law is also globally exponentially stable. Finally, in Section 5, numerical examples are given which show actually that the optimal cost is finely approached.

2. PROBLEM STATEMENT AND NECESSARY CONDITIONS

We consider the class of continuous time linear switched systems:

$$\dot{x}(t) = A_{\sigma(t)}x(t) + B_{\sigma(t)}u_{\sigma(t)}(t) \quad x(0) = x_0 \tag{1}$$

where $\sigma : [0, +\infty) \to S = \{1, \cdots, s\}$ denotes the switching law that selects the active mode at time t by choosing among a finite collection of linear systems defined by the pairs $(A_i, B_i) \in \mathbf{R}^{n \times n} \times \mathbf{R}^{n \times m_i}$, $i \in S$. Each subsystem is also governed by a control $u_i(t) \in \mathbf{R}^{m_i}$, $0 \leq m_i \leq n$. Our aim is to design a state feedback switching law (i.e. $x \mapsto (\sigma(x), u_{\sigma(x)}(x))$) for system (1) that approaches the optimal solution of the following optimization problem:

Problem 1.

Minimize the switched quadratic criterion:

$$\min_{\sigma, u_\sigma} \frac{1}{2} \int_0^\infty x^{\mathrm{T}}(t)Q_{\sigma(t)}x(t) + u_{\sigma(t)}^{\mathrm{T}}(t)R_{\sigma(t)}u_{\sigma(t)}(t)\mathrm{d}t \tag{2}$$

where $Q_i = Q_i^{\mathrm{T}} \geq 0$, $R_i = R_i^{\mathrm{T}} > 0$, $i \in S$ subject to $\dot{x}(t) = A_{\sigma(t)}x(t) + B_{\sigma(t)}u_{\sigma(t)}(t)$, $x(0) = x_0$.

A usual framework [24, 2] to solve optimal control problems for switched systems ($\dot{x} = f_i(x)$, $i \in S$) is to solve its relaxed version, replacing the vector field set $\{ f_i(x) \mid i \in S \}$ by its convex hull ($\dot{x} = \mathrm{co}\{ f_i(x) \mid i \in S \}$). At least, three reasons justify the convexification of the problem: (i) the solutions are well defined [9]; (ii) the set of trajectories related to the switched system is dense into the set of trajectories of its relaxed version [13]; (iii) the existence of *singular* optimal solutions are taking into account [22, 2].

The relaxed version of Problem 1 is then given as a pure continuous time optimal control problem given by :

$$\dot{x}(t) = \sum_{i=1}^{s} \lambda_i(t)(A_i x(t) + B_i u_i(t)) \quad x(0) = x_0 \tag{3}$$

$$\lambda(t) \in \Lambda = \left\{ \lambda \in \mathbf{R}^s : \sum_{i=1}^{s} \lambda_i = 1 \quad \lambda_i \geq 0 \right\}. \tag{4}$$

and by the convexified cost:

$$\min_{\lambda(\cdot),\ u_i(\cdot)} \frac{1}{2} \int_0^\infty \sum_{i=1}^{s} \lambda_i(t)(x^T(t)Q_i x(t) + u_i^T(t)R_i u_i(t))dt \tag{5}$$

In the sequel we denote by u the s-tuple $u = (u_1, u_2, \cdots, u_s)$ and we use the following notation:

$$A(\lambda) = \sum_{i \in S} \lambda_i A_i, \quad B(\lambda) = [\lambda_1 B_1, \lambda_2 B_2, \cdots, \lambda_s B_s]$$

$$Q(\lambda) = \sum_{i \in S} \lambda_i Q_i, \quad R(\lambda) = \mathrm{diag}(\lambda_1 R_1, \lambda_2 R_2, \cdots, \lambda_s R_s).$$

Then the dynamics of the relaxed system can be redefined as:

$$\dot{x} = A(\lambda)x + B(\lambda)u$$

and the cost as

$$\min_{\lambda(\cdot), u(\cdot)} \frac{1}{2} \int_0^\infty x^T(t)Q(\lambda(t))x(t) + u^T(t)R(\lambda)u(t)dt.$$

To apply the Pontryagin Maximum Principle (PMP) for Problem 1 or its relaxed version, the Hamiltonian function is defined as follow:

$$\mathcal{H}(x, \lambda, u, p) = \sum_{i=1}^{s} \lambda_i \mathcal{H}_i(x, u_i, p) \tag{6}$$

with $\mathcal{H}_i(x, u_i, p) = p^T(A_i x + B_i u_i) + \frac{1}{2}(x^T Q_i x + u_i^T R_i u_i)$ and where p defines the co-state.

This leads to the following classical necessary conditions for optimality [23]:

THEOREM 1. *Suppose that (λ^*, u^*) is optimal with the corresponding state x^*. Then, there exists an absolutely continuous function p^*, called co-state, such that:*

1. $p^* \neq 0$,
2. $\dot{p}^* = \sum_{i=1}^{s} \lambda_i^*(t)(-A_i^T p^* - Q_i x^*)$ *for almost all* $t \in \mathbb{R}^+$,
3. $(\lambda^*(t), u^*(t)) \in \arg\min_{(\lambda \in \Lambda, u)} \mathcal{H}(x^*(t), \lambda, u, p^*(t))$,
4. $\mathcal{H}(x^*(t), \lambda^*(t), u^*, p^*(t)) = 0$.

Theorem 1 can be simplified thanks to the following lemma:

LEMMA 1. *The optimal value of the u_i's are given by $u_i^*(t) = -R_i^{-1}B_i^T p^*(t)$ and λ^* satisfies:*

$$\lambda^*(t) \in \arg\min_{\lambda \in \Lambda} \sum_{i=1}^{s} \lambda_i \mathcal{H}_i(x^*, -R_i^{-1}B_i^T p^*, p^*). \tag{7}$$

PROOF. From Equation 6, the minimum of $\mathcal{H}$ with respect to the u_i's is clearly independent of the value of λ and the result follows. □

From (7), it is clear that if there exists $i \in S$ at time t such that

$$\mathcal{H}_i(x^*(t), u_i^*, p^*(t)) < \mathcal{H}_j(x^*(t), u_j^*, p^*(t)), \quad \forall j \in S \setminus \{i\},$$

then the optimal control has to satisfy $\lambda_i^*(t) = 1$ and $\lambda_j^*(t) = 0$, $\forall j \in S \setminus \{i\}$.

A switching instant can occur at time t if there exists at least a pair $(i,j) \in S^2$ such that $\mathcal{H}_i = \mathcal{H}_j = 0$. At this time, the value of λ cannot be determined directly. Actually, if we suppose that $0 = \mathcal{H}_i = \mathcal{H}_j < \mathcal{H}_k$, $\forall k \in S \setminus \{i,j\}$ then the values that satisfy the relation, $\lambda_i + \lambda_j = 1$, are potential candidate for optimality. Moreover, a so called *singular control* λ can exist, for which $0 = \mathcal{H}_i = \mathcal{H}_j < \mathcal{H}_k$, $\forall k \in S \setminus \{i,j\}$ on a *non empty time interval* (a,b). This is a well known situation in the literature [25, 5, 4] and second order necessary conditions given by the generalized Legendre-Clebsh condition [28, 15] can be necessary to solve the optimal control problem.

Definition 1. We call *singular control*, a control $\lambda(.)$ such that there exist at least two indices i,j, for which $\mathcal{H}_i = \mathcal{H}_j = 0$ on a non zero measure time interval (a,b), and which satisfies $\lambda(t) \in \Lambda$, $\lambda_k(t) \neq 1$ $\forall k \in S$, $\forall t \in (a,b)$. The corresponding part of the trajectory is called a singular arc.

A singular control defines a Fillipov solution [7] for the original switched system (1). Hence, it allows to extend properly the notion of optimal solution for switched systems. Roughly speaking when an optimal solution of the relaxed problem possesses singular arcs, these arcs define sliding surfaces for the switched system (1) which lead to chattering if the surface is attractive. It is noteworthy that only suboptimal solutions can be achieved for the switched systems due to the limited switching frequency; see for example [2].

2.1 Numerical resolution

If one attempts to solve numerically an optimal control problem in which singular arcs appear, numerical difficulties will be encountered due to the insensitive of the Hamiltonian with respect to the control. On the one hand, standard indirect numerical methods such as multiple shooting methods are not appropriate to deal with singular arcs without a priori information on the structure of the trajectories (see [10], [20] and [3] to apply multiple shooting methods in this context). This information can be achieved using regularization techniques such as the continuation method used in [21], [14], [19]. On the other hand, when direct methods such as nonlinear programming (NLP) are used to solve (1)-(2), a very bad results are generally obtained on the optimal value for the control due to $\frac{\partial \mathcal{H}}{\partial u}=0$, $\forall u$ in an open subset of U. In [24], we have proposed to use a mix direct-indirect method.

The idea consists to take implicitly into account the singular arcs using the necessary condition of the PMP and the Hamiltonian systems and then to solve directly an augmented constraint optimization problem. As regard the LQ switched problem, this leads to the following constraint optimization problem (here $z=(x,p)$):

Problem 2.

Minimize (using NLP):

$$\min_{\lambda(\cdot)} \frac{1}{2}\int_0^{\infty}\sum_{i=1}^{s}\lambda_i(t)(x(t)^{\mathrm{T}}Q_i x(t)+p(t)^{\mathrm{T}}B_iR_i^{-1}B_i^T p(t))\mathrm{d}t \tag{8}$$

$$\text{subject to } \dot{z}(t)=\sum_{i=1}^{s}\lambda_i(t)\begin{pmatrix} A_i & -B_iR_i^{-1}B_i^T \\ -Q_i & -A_i^T\end{pmatrix} z(t) \tag{9}$$

$$0\le \lambda_i \perp \mathcal{H}_i(x,-R_i^{-1}B_i^T p,p)\ge 0,\quad i\in S \tag{10}$$

$$\lambda(t)\in\Lambda,\quad x(0)=x_0$$

where the sign $x\perp y$ means $xy=0$.

The complementarity constraints (10) allow λ to be multivalued function when the $\mathcal{H}_i$'s vanish for at least two subscripts. This is a key point since the necessary condition of PMP does not imply the unicity of solution of system (9) from an initial condition. When the admissible values for λ are multiple, this formulation by the minimization of the cost (8) yields the optimal value.

Practically, the complementarity constraints are taken into account with penalization terms $\rho\lambda_i\mathcal{H}_i$ in the cost with weight ρ. Hight order constraints can be also added to improve the result see [24] for more details.

3. LYAPUNOV BASED SWITCHING LAW

The aim of this part is to define a Lyapunov function as a tight upper bound on the value function. We means tight in the sense that the two functions may coincide at some points.

We denote by $B(\sqrt{\lambda})$ the matrix

$$B(\sqrt{\lambda})=\left[\sqrt{\lambda_1}B_1|\sqrt{\lambda_2}B_2|\dots|\sqrt{\lambda_s}B_s\right]$$

and we assume there exists a $\lambda^0\in\Lambda$ such that the pair $(A(\lambda^0),B(\sqrt{\lambda^0}))$ is controllable. Then, the Riccati equation:

$$A(\lambda)^T P_\lambda + P_\lambda A(\lambda) - P_\lambda B(\sqrt{\lambda})R^{-1}B(\sqrt{\lambda})^{\mathrm{T}}P_\lambda + Q(\lambda)=0. \tag{11}$$

(here $R=\operatorname{diag}([R_1,R_2,\cdots,R_s])$, admits a (unique) symmetric positive definite solution P_{λ^0} for $\lambda=\lambda^0$. Notice that the pack-writing term $P_\lambda B(\sqrt{\lambda})R^{-1}B(\sqrt{\lambda})^{\mathrm{T}}P_\lambda$ can be expanded as

$$P_\lambda B(\sqrt{\lambda})R^{-1}B(\sqrt{\lambda})^{\mathrm{T}}P_\lambda=\sum_{i\in S}\lambda_i(P_\lambda B_iR_i^{-1}B_i^{\mathrm{T}}P_\lambda).$$

In fact to ensure the existence of a positive definite solution to the Riccati equation (11), as the Q_i's are positive definite, it is enough to assume that the pair $(A(\lambda^0),B(\sqrt{\lambda^0}))$ is stabilizable (*cf.* Lemma 2). Now, the same is true if the pair $(A(\lambda^0),B(\sqrt{\lambda^0}))$ is controllable and if λ belongs to a sufficiently small neighborhood of λ^0; so the Riccati equation (11) admits a unique (positive definite) solution P_λ for every λ in some neighborhood of λ^0. Moreover, it is well known that the positive definite solution of a Riccati equation is a continuous function of $(A(\lambda),B(\sqrt{\lambda}),R,Q(\lambda))$ [17] and so P_λ is a continuous function of λ. Notice also that the condition for the existence of a symmetric nonnegative solution of the Riccati equation (11) can be weakened: in [16], V. Kučera proved that if the pair $(A(\lambda),B(\sqrt{\lambda}))$ is stabilizable and if the matrix

$$\mathcal{M}=\begin{pmatrix} A(\lambda) & -B(\sqrt{\lambda})R^{-1}B(\sqrt{\lambda})^{\mathrm{T}} \\ -Q(\lambda) & -A(\lambda)^{\mathrm{T}}\end{pmatrix}$$

has no purely imaginary eigenvalues, then there exists a symmetric nonnegative solution to equation (11). This result allow us to prove the following lemma about Eq. (11).

LEMMA 2. *If the pair $(A(\lambda),B(\sqrt{\lambda}))$ is stabilizable and $Q(\lambda)$ is positive definite, then there exists a positive definite solution to Eq.* (11).

PROOF. We denote by $S(\lambda)$ the matrix

$$S(\lambda):=B(\sqrt{\lambda})R^{-1}B(\sqrt{\lambda})^{\mathrm{T}},$$

and we take $x=(x_1^{\mathrm{T}},x_2^{\mathrm{T}})^{\mathrm{T}}$ a vector of $\mathbf{C}^{2n}$ such that $\mathcal{M}x=i\alpha x$ (with $\alpha\in\mathbf{R}$); we shall see that $x=0$. We have

$$A(\lambda)x_1-S(\lambda)x_2=i\alpha x_1 \tag{12}$$

$$-Q(\lambda)x_1-A(\lambda)^{\mathrm{T}}x_2=i\alpha x_2\,. \tag{13}$$

Multiplying on the left the members of equation (12) (resp. Eq. (13)) by $\bar{x}_2^{\mathrm{T}}$ (resp. by $\bar{x}_1^{\mathrm{T}}$, the bar denotes the conjugate), we get

$$\bar{x}_2^{\mathrm{T}}A(\lambda)x_1-\bar{x}_2^{\mathrm{T}}S(\lambda)x_2=i\alpha x_1 \tag{14}$$

$$-\bar{x}_1^{\mathrm{T}}Q(\lambda)x_1-\bar{x}_1^{\mathrm{T}}A(\lambda)^{\mathrm{T}}x_2=i\alpha x_2\,. \tag{15}$$

by adding the conjugate of the members of equation (14) to the members of equation (15), we get

$$-\bar{x}_1^{\mathrm{T}}Q(\lambda)x_1 - \bar{x}_2^{\mathrm{T}}S(\lambda)x_2 = 0.$$

If $x_1 \neq 0$, as $Q(\lambda)$ is positive definite, this last equality implies $\bar{x}_2^{\mathrm{T}}S(\lambda)x_2 < 0$, but this inequality cannot occur because $S(\lambda)$ is nonnegative, so we must have $x_1 = 0$ and reporting this equality in (12) and (13), we get $S(\lambda)x_2 = 0$ and $A(\lambda)^{\mathrm{T}}x_2 = -i\alpha\, x_2$, which in turn implies $A(\lambda)^{\mathrm{T}}x_2 = -i\alpha\, x_2$ and $B(\sqrt{\lambda})^{\mathrm{T}}x_2 = 0$. As the pair $(A(\lambda)^{\mathrm{T}}, B(\sqrt{\lambda})^{\mathrm{T}})$ is detectable, the Hautus lemma implies that $x_2 = 0$.

By applicantion of the above-mentionned result from Kučera, we deduce that there exists a symmetryc nonnegative solution P_λ to Eq. (11). Now this solution is necessarily definite, assume indeed that v is a vector such that $Pv = 0$, left-multiply both sides of (11) by $\bar{v}^{\mathrm{T}}$ and right-multiply by v, we get $\bar{v}^{\mathrm{T}}Qv = 0$ which implies $v = 0$ since Q is assumed to be positive definite. □

This lemma proves that for every $\lambda \in \Lambda$ such that the pair $(A(\lambda), B(\sqrt{\lambda}))$ is stabilizable, there exists a positive definite solution, denoted by P_λ, to the Riccati equation (11).

We denote by Λ^+ the set

$$\Lambda^+ = \{\, \lambda \in \Lambda \mid \text{the pair } (A(\lambda), B(\sqrt{\lambda})) \text{ is stabilizable and } \max \operatorname{spec}(P_\lambda) \leq \nu_{\max} \}$$

where $\operatorname{spec}(P_\lambda)$ denotes the spectrum of P_λ; this set Λ^+ satisfies the following property.

Lemma 3. *The matrices Q_i being positive definite, if one can find $\lambda^0 \in \Lambda$ such that $(A(\lambda^0), B(\sqrt{\lambda^0}))$ is controllable, then, for every $\nu_{\max}$ large enough, set Λ^+ is compact and its interior is not empty in Λ. Moreover, the two following real numbers, α_m and α_M, defined as*

$$\alpha_m = \min_{\lambda \in \Lambda^+} \min(\operatorname{spec}(P_\lambda)) \qquad \alpha_M = \max_{\lambda \in \Lambda^+} \max(\operatorname{spec}(P_\lambda))$$

are positive.

Proof. As noticed above, we can find a compact neighborhood $\mathscr{U}$ of λ^0 such that the Riccati equation (11) admits a positive definite solution P_λ for every $\lambda \in \mathscr{U}$. The mapping $\lambda \mapsto P_\lambda$ being continuous and $\mathscr{U}$ being compact, we have $\sup_{\lambda \in \mathscr{U}} \max \operatorname{spec}(P_\lambda) < \infty$; this implies that if $\nu_{\max}$ is chosen large enough, the interior of Λ^+ is non empty.

Now, set Λ^+ is included in Λ, therefore it is bounded; we shall show that it is also closed. Suppose that there exists a sequence $(\lambda^k)_{k \geq 1} \in \Lambda^+$ such that $\lim_{k\to\infty} \lambda^k = \bar{\lambda}$. As Λ is a compact set, $\bar{\lambda} \in \Lambda$. Moreover, the sequence $(P_{\lambda^k})_{k\geq 1}$ is bounded, so we can assume that it converges to a symmetric matrix P. As a limit of a sequence of positive definite matrices, this matrix is positive (semi) definite; moreover it is a solution of (11) with $\lambda = \bar{\lambda}$. We claim first that P is definite, assume indeed that v is a vector such that $Pv = 0$, left-multiply both sides of (11) by $\bar{v}^{\mathrm{T}}$ and right-multiply by v, we get $\bar{v}^{\mathrm{T}}Qv = 0$ which implies $v = 0$ since Q is assumed to be positive definite. Moreover the pair $(A(\lambda), B(\sqrt{\lambda})$ is stabilizable, to see this let μ be an eigenvalue of $A(\lambda)^{\mathrm{T}}$ such that $\Re(\mu) \geq 0$ ($\Re(\cdot)$ stands for the real part) and let $v \in \mathbf{R}^n$ be a vector such that $A(\lambda)^{\mathrm{T}}v = \mu\, v$ and $B^{\mathrm{T}}(\sqrt{\lambda})v = 0$, we shall see that $v = 0$ which implies that the rank of the matrix $(A(\lambda)^{\mathrm{T}} - \mu\,\mathrm{Id}, B^{\mathrm{T}}(\sqrt{\lambda}))^{\mathrm{T}}$ is equal to n for every μ in the closed right half plane and so the result will follow from the Hautus lemma. Matrix P being definite, there exists $x \in \mathbf{R}^n$ such that $Px = v$, left-multiply both sides of (11) by $\bar{x}^{\mathrm{T}}$ and right-multiply by x, we get

$$\mu\,\bar{x}^{\mathrm{T}}v + \bar{\mu}\,\bar{v}^{\mathrm{T}}x + \bar{x}^{\mathrm{T}}Q\,x = 0.$$

If $x \neq 0$, as matrix Q is positive definite , this equality implies that $\Re(\mu\,\bar{x}^{\mathrm{T}}v) < 0$ but $\bar{x}^{\mathrm{T}}v = \bar{x}^{\mathrm{T}}Px$ so $\bar{x}^{\mathrm{T}}v > 0$ since P is positive definite, therefore we must have $\Re(\mu) < 0$. This contradicts the fact that $\Re(\mu) \geq 0$, so, we must have $x = 0$, which implies that $v = 0$. Finally, the existence of α_m and α_M follows from the compactness of Λ^+ and the continuity of the mapping $\lambda \mapsto P_\lambda$. □

For the sake of readability, let us introduce the following notations. We denote by $M(\lambda)$ the matrix:

$$M(\lambda) := \sum_{i \in S} \lambda_i M_i(\lambda) \tag{16}$$

where

$$M_i(\lambda) := A_i - B_i K_i(\lambda) \tag{17}$$

$$K_i(\lambda) := R_i^{-1} B_i^T P_\lambda \tag{18}$$

and by $N(\lambda)$ the matrix:

$$N(\lambda) := \sum_{i \in S} \lambda_i N_i(\lambda) \tag{19}$$

where

$$N_i(\lambda) := Q_i + K_i(\lambda)^T R_i K_i(\lambda).$$

The Riccati equation (11) can then be rewritten as :

$$M(\lambda)^T P_\lambda + P_\lambda M(\lambda) + N(\lambda) = 0. \tag{20}$$

Lemma 4. *For every $(x, \lambda) \in (\mathbf{R}^n \smallsetminus \{0\}) \times \Lambda^+$, we have*

$$\min_{i \in S}\big(2x^{\mathrm{T}} M_i^{\mathrm{T}}(\lambda) P_\lambda x + x^{\mathrm{T}} N_i(\lambda) x\big) \leq 0.$$

Proof. Take $x \in \mathbf{R}^n \smallsetminus \{0\}$ and $\lambda \in \Lambda^+$, then equation (20) admits a solution and we can write

$$\sum_{i \in S} \lambda_i \big(2x^{\mathrm{T}} M_i^{\mathrm{T}}(\lambda) P_\lambda x + x^{\mathrm{T}} N_i(\lambda) x\big) = 0 \tag{21}$$

so we cannot have

$$2x^{\mathrm{T}} M_i^{\mathrm{T}}(\lambda) P_\lambda x + x^{\mathrm{T}} N_i(\lambda) x > 0 \tag{22}$$

for every $i \in S$ because in this case the left-hand member of equality (21) would be positive. Thus, for every pair (x, λ), there exists an index i which is such that the left-hand member in (22) is non positive. □

Let us now introduce the following Lyapunov function

$$V_m(x) := \inf_{\lambda \in \Lambda^+} x^{\mathrm{T}} P_\lambda x \tag{23}$$

where P_λ denotes the solution of equation (20). Clearly, as every P_λ is positive definite when λ belongs to Λ^+ and as the set $\{P_\lambda \mid \lambda \in \Lambda^+\}$ is compact, V_m is a positive definite function; notice also that V_m is homogeneous of degree 2 and locally Lipschitz.

Proposition 1. *The function defined by (23) is locally lipschitzian.*

PROOF. We have $z^T P_\lambda z \leq \alpha_M \|z\|^2$ for every $(z, \lambda) \in \mathbf{R}^n \times \Lambda^+$. So, if we take x and y in the ball $B(0, R)$, we obtain easily that, for every $\lambda \in \Lambda^+$,

$$|x^T P_\lambda x - y^T P_\lambda y| = |(x-y)^T P_\lambda (x+y)| \leq K\,\|x-y\|$$

where $K = 2\alpha_M R$. Thus, the family of functions indexed by $\lambda \in \Lambda^+$ and defined by $x \mapsto x^T P_\lambda x$ is uniformly locally Liptchitz with a Lipschitz constant equals to $K := 2\alpha_M R$ on the ball $B(0, R)$.

Now, as the function $\lambda \mapsto x^T P_\lambda x$ is continuous and set Λ^+ is compact, there exists a pair $(\lambda_1, \lambda_2) \in (\Lambda^+)^2$ such that:

$$V_m(x) = x^T P_{\lambda 1} x \qquad V_m(y) = y^T P_{\lambda 2} y.$$

From the definition of V_m, we deduce easily that

$$x^T P_{\lambda 1} x - x^T P_{\lambda 2} x \leq 0 \qquad y^T P_{\lambda 1} y - y^T P_{\lambda 2} y \geq 0$$

therefore, by continuity, there exists z on the line segment $[x\ y]$ such that $z^T P_{\lambda 1} z = z^T P_{\lambda 2} z$ and it follows:

$$\begin{aligned} |V_m(x) - V_m(y)| &\leq |x^T P_{\lambda_1} x - z^T P_{\lambda_1} z| \\ &\quad + |z^T P_{\lambda_2} z - y^T P_{\lambda_2} y| \\ &\leq K\|x-z\| + K\|z-y\| = K\|x-y\|. \end{aligned}$$

Finally function V_m is proper because it is continuous and $\alpha_m \|z\|^2 \leq V_m(z)$ for every $z \in \mathbf{R}^n$. □

Let f be a function defined on $\mathbf{R}^n$ and d be a vector of $\mathbf{R}^n$, as in [11] we shall denote by $f'(x; d)$ the following limit (if it exists)

$$f'(x; d) := \lim_{\substack{h \to 0 \\ h > 0}} \frac{f(x + h\,d) - f(x)}{h}. \tag{24}$$

For the sake of readability, we let $v_\lambda(x) := x^T P_\lambda x$. In order to compute $V'_m(x; d)$, we use Theorem 6.1 in [11] whose conditions of application are clearly met, thus we have

$$V'_m(x; d) = \inf_{\lambda \in \ell(x)} v'_\lambda(x; d). \tag{25}$$

Here $\ell(x)$ denotes the set of $\lambda \in \Lambda^+$ such that $V_m(x) = v_\lambda(x)$ (this set is clearly nonempty and compact because Λ^+ is compact and the function $\lambda \mapsto v_\lambda(x)$ is continuous). As the function $x \mapsto v_\lambda(x)$ is smooth, from (25), we infer that

$$V'_m(x; d) = 2 \inf_{\lambda \in \ell(x)} d^T P_\lambda x.$$

From this formula and from Lemma 4, we get the following properties.

LEMMA 5. *For every $(x, \lambda^0) \in \mathbf{R}^n \times \ell(x)$, there exist $i(x, \lambda^0)$ such that*

$$V'_m(x; M_{i(x,\lambda^0)}(\lambda^0) x) \leq -x^T N_{i(x,\lambda^0)}(\lambda^0) x \tag{26}$$

PROOF. For every $(x, \lambda^0) \in \mathbf{R}^n \times \ell(x)$, Lemma 4 implies that there exists $i(x, \lambda^0)$ such that

$$2x^T M^T_{i(x,\lambda^0)}(\lambda^0) P_{\lambda^0} x + x^T N_{i(x,\lambda^0)}(\lambda^0) x \leq 0$$

It follows directly that

$$\begin{aligned} V'_m(x; M_{i(x,\lambda^0)}(\lambda^0) x) &= \inf_{\lambda \in \ell(x)} 2x^T M^T_{i(x,\lambda^0)}(\lambda^0) P_\lambda x \\ &\leq 2x^T M^T_{i(x,\lambda^0)}(\lambda^0) P_{\lambda^0} x \\ &\leq -x^T N_{i(x,\lambda^0)}(\lambda^0) x. \quad \square \end{aligned}$$

In the following theorem, we shall consider mappings from $\mathbf{R}^n$ to $S \times \Lambda^+$ of the form $x \mapsto (i(x), \lambda(x))$ such that $\lambda(x) \in \ell(x)$. To such a mapping, we relate the following feedback law for system (1): the mode $\sigma(t)$ is equal to $i(x(t))$ for every $t \geq 0$ and $u_{\sigma(t)}$ is equal to $-K_{i(x)}(\lambda(x))\,x$.

THEOREM 2. *We assume that the matrices Q_i are positive definite and there exists at least a $\lambda \in \Lambda$ such that the pair $(A(\lambda), B(\sqrt{\lambda}))$ is controllable. For every $x \in \mathbf{R}^n$, we choose*

$$(i(x), \lambda(x)) \in \operatorname*{arg\,min}_{(i,\lambda) \in S \times \ell(x)} \left(2x^T M_i^T(\lambda) P_\lambda x + x^T N_i(\lambda) x\right).$$

Then the feedback related to $(i(x), \lambda(x))$ stabilizes system (1) with a cost smaller than $\frac{1}{2} V_m(x_0)$. Moreover the convergence is exponential with a rate $\beta = \frac{\eta_0}{\alpha_1}$ where η_0 and α_1 are given by:

$$\eta_0 = \min_{i \in S} \inf_{x \in S^{n-1}} \inf_{\lambda \in \ell(x)} x^T N_i(\lambda) x, \qquad \alpha_1 = \max_{x \in S^{n-1}} V_m(x)$$

Remark 1. From a practical point of view, Th. 2 remains still valid if the feedback switching law is simplified as follows: for a given x, choose $\lambda(x)$ in $\ell(x)$ and take $i(x)$ as

$$i(x) \in \operatorname*{arg\,min}_{(i) \in S} \left(2x^T M_i(\lambda) P_\lambda x + x^T N_i(\lambda) x\right).$$

PROOF PROOF OF TH. 2. We shall compute the derivative of V_m along the trajectories of system (1) in closed-loop with the feedback introduced in the theorem. Hereafter, for the sake of readability, we denote by $M_{i(x)}$ the matrix $M_{i(x)}(\lambda(x))$ and $\frac{\mathrm{d}}{\mathrm{d}t} V_m(x(t))$ denotes the Dini derivative (*cf.* (24)) of V_m.

$$\begin{aligned} \frac{\mathrm{d}}{\mathrm{d}t} V_m(x(t)) &= V'_m(x; M_{i(x)} x) \\ &= 2 \min_{\lambda \in \ell(x)} x^T M^T_{i(x)} P_\lambda x \\ &\leq 2x^T M^T_{i(x)} P_{\lambda(x)} x \\ &\leq -x^T N_{i(x)}(\lambda(x)) x \\ &\qquad \text{from the definition of } (i(x), \lambda(x)) \\ &\leq -\frac{\eta_0}{\alpha_1} V_m(x). \end{aligned}$$

This inequality implies that

$$V_m(x(t)) \leq e^{-\beta t} V_m(x_0)$$

with $\beta = \frac{\eta_0}{\alpha_1}$. As V_m is homogeneous of degree 2, this last inequality, implies the global exponential stability.

The upper bound on the cost $(1/2 V_m(x_0))$ comes from the fact that

$$\begin{aligned} x^T Q_{i(x)} x + x^T K^T_{i(x)} R_{i(x)} K_{i(x)} x &= x^T N_{i(x)} x \\ &\leq -\frac{\mathrm{d}}{\mathrm{d}t} V_m(x(t)). \quad \square \end{aligned}$$

Why do we claim that the Lyapunov function can be a tight upper bound on the value function? Observe first that in the case where all subsystems (related to the pairs (A_i, B_i)) are stabilizable, then the solution P_i of the Algebraic Riccati Equation exists for each mode i and the Lyapunov function satisfies always the following inequality:

$$\frac{1}{2} V_m(x) \leq \min_{i \in S} \frac{1}{2} x^T P_i x\,.$$

One can also observe that for a given state x_0, the value $\frac{1}{2}V_m(x_0)$ is the best cost related to every constant convex combination that stabilizes the relaxed system. The corresponding control is of the form : $\lambda(t) = \lambda(x_0), \forall t \geq 0$, $u_i(t) = -R_i^{-1}B_i^T P_\lambda x(t)$.

In the general case, when can we say that $\frac{1}{2}V_m(x_0)$ is optimal? The answer is: "Along the part of trajectories where the optimal control λ^* is constant to reach the origin". At least two cases can be mentioned: if the number of switchings is finite which means that a same mode is used after a time t or if the trajectory is steered to the origin by a constant singular control λ (*cf.* Definition 1) for which $P_\lambda > 0$. Note that singular control in dimension $n = 2$ can be algebraically determined [22] and are constant.

4. SAMPLED TIME SWITCHED CONTROL LAW

Practically, a sampled time version of the continuous time algorithm is applied. So, we shall show that the sampled time version of the above algorithm stabilizes the system for appropriate choice of sampled period.

Let τ be a given sampling period. The control is now piecewise constant and updated every times $t_k = k\tau$, $k \in \mathbb{N}$ following the state feedback provided by Theorem 2. To be more precise, at time $t_0 = 0$, we start with the initial condition x_0 and we choose the mode $i(x_0)$ and $\lambda(x_0)$ as in Theorem 2. Thus we have

$$2x_0^{\mathrm{T}} M_{i0(x_0)}^{\mathrm{T}} P_{\lambda(x_0)} x_0 \leq -x_0^{\mathrm{T}} N_{i(x_0)}(\lambda(x_0))x_0 \leq -\eta_0 \|x_0\|^2,$$

and, by the way, notice that $v_{\lambda(x_0)}(x_0) = V_m(x_0)$. We apply the feedback law related to $i(x_0), \lambda(x_0)$ to system (1), that is to say, we choose the mode $i(x_0)$ ($\sigma(t) = i(x_0)$) and $u_{\sigma(t)} = -K_{i(x_0)}(\lambda(x_0))$, we do so during a time $\tau > 0$. At time, $t_1 = t_0+\tau$, we arrive at a point x_1 and we choose a new index $i(x_1)$ and a new $\lambda(x_1)$ as in theorem 2. In this way, we build a sequence of points $(x_k)_{k\geq 0}$ together with a sequence of pairs $(i(x_k), \lambda(x_k))_{k\geq 0}$ chosen as in theorem 2. On each interval $[t_k, t_{k+1})$ ($t_k = t_0 + k\tau$), we choose the mode $i(x_k)$ and we apply the feedback $u = -K_{i(x_k)}(\lambda(x_k))$. The switched system (1) in closed loop with this feedback writes

$$\begin{cases} \dot{x} = (A_{i(x_k)} - B_{i(x_k)}K_{i(x_k)}(\lambda(x_k)))x, & t \in [t_k, t_{k+1}) \\ x_k = x(t_k) \end{cases} \tag{27}$$

We state the following theorem about this algorithm; notice that we still assume that the Q_i's are positive definite.

THEOREM 3. *If τ is chosen sufficiently small, the sampled time switching law described above stabilizes the switched system* (27) *globally exponentially*

For the proof of the theorem, we shall need the following lemma.

LEMMA 6. *Consider the solution $t \mapsto x(t)$ of* (27) *starting from x_0 at some time $t_0 = 0$ where the mode i is chosen such that*

$$x_0^{\mathrm{T}} P_{\lambda(x_0)} x_0 = V_m(x_0)$$
$$2x_0^{\mathrm{T}} M_i^{\mathrm{T}}(\lambda(x_0))P_{\lambda(x_0)}x_0 \leq -x_0^T N_i(\lambda(x_0))x_0 \leq -\eta_0\|x_0\|^2$$

where η_0 is defined in Theorem 2. We define the time T as

$$T = \inf\{\, t \geq 0 \mid 2x(t)^{\mathrm{T}} M_i^{\mathrm{T}}(\lambda(x_0))P_{\lambda(x_0)}x(t) \geq - \eta_0\gamma\,\|x(t)\|^2$$

where γ is a parameter chosen in the interval $(0,1)$. Then there exists $\tau_0 > 0$ independent from x_0 such that $T \geq \tau_0$.

PROOF. For the sake of readability, we shall denote by i and λ the terms $i(x_0)$ and $\lambda(x_0)$ respectively. We have

$$\begin{aligned} 2x(T)^{\mathrm{T}} M_i^{\mathrm{T}}(\lambda)P_\lambda x(T) - 2x_0^{\mathrm{T}} M_i^{\mathrm{T}}(\lambda)P_\lambda x_0 &= 2\int_0^T \frac{\mathrm{d}}{\mathrm{d}t} x(t)^{\mathrm{T}} M_i^{\mathrm{T}}(\lambda)P_\lambda x(t)\,\mathrm{d}t \\ &= 2\int_0^T \Big(x(t)^{\mathrm{T}}(M_i^{\mathrm{T}}(\lambda))^2 P_\lambda x(t) \\ &\quad + x(t)^{\mathrm{T}} M_i(\lambda)P_\lambda M_i(\lambda)x(t)\Big)\mathrm{d}t. \end{aligned} \tag{28}$$

Now, for every $t \in [0,T)$, we have $x(t) = e^{t\,M_i(\lambda)}x_0$ and so

$$\|x(t)\| \leq e^{t\,\|M_i(\lambda)\|}\,\|x_0\|.$$

Notice that the matrix $M_i(\lambda(x_0))$ is bounded because $\lambda(x_0)$ evolves on the compact set Λ^+ and the mapping $\lambda \mapsto M_{i_k}(\lambda)$ is continuous. So there exists $\mu > 0$ such that $\|M_i(\lambda)\| \leq \mu$ for every $(i,\lambda) \in S \times \Lambda^+$; also, from Lemma 3, we know that $\|P_\lambda\| \leq \alpha_M$ for every $\lambda \in \Lambda^+$. So, from equality (28), we deduce that

$$\begin{aligned} 2x(T)^{\mathrm{T}} M_i^{\mathrm{T}}(\lambda)P_\lambda x(T) - 2x_0^{\mathrm{T}} M_i^{\mathrm{T}}(\lambda)P_\lambda x_0 &\leq 4\mu^2\alpha_M\|x_0\|^2 \int_0^T e^{2t\,\mu}\mathrm{d}t \\ &= 2\mu\alpha_M(e^{2(T\,\mu} - 1)\|x_0\|^2. \end{aligned} \tag{29}$$

Now, since

$$2x_0^{\mathrm{T}} M_i^{\mathrm{T}}(\lambda)P_\lambda x_0 \leq -\eta_0\|x_0\|^2$$

and

$$2x(T)^{\mathrm{T}} M_i^{\mathrm{T}}(\lambda)P_\lambda x(T) = -\eta_0\gamma\,\|x(T)\|^2 \geq -\eta_0\gamma\, e^{2T\mu}\|x_0\|^2,$$

we have

$$2x(T)^{\mathrm{T}} M_i^{\mathrm{T}}(\lambda)P_\lambda x(T) - 2x_0^{\mathrm{T}} M_i^{\mathrm{T}}(\lambda)P_\lambda x_0 \geq \eta_0\|x_0\|^2(1 - \gamma\, e^{2T\mu}).$$

Substituting this inequality in (29), we get

$$2\mu\alpha_M(e^{2(T\,\mu} - 1)\|x_0\|^2 \geq \eta_0\|x_0\|^2(1 - \gamma\, e^{2T\mu})$$

and so

$$(2\mu\,\alpha_M + \eta_0\gamma)e^{2T\mu}) \geq 2\mu\,\alpha_M + \eta_0$$

which implies that

$$T \geq \tau_0 := \frac{1}{2\mu}\ln\left(\frac{2\mu\,\alpha_M + \eta_0}{2\mu\,\alpha_M + \eta_0\gamma}\right). \quad \square$$

PROOF OF THEOREM 3. We take a sampling time $\tau > 0$ no greater than τ_0, and we shall prove that system (27) is globally exponentially stable about the origin. Hereafter, for the sake of readability, we will denote by λ^k and i_k the terms $\lambda(x_k)$ and $i(x_k)$ respectively. Recall that, due to the choice of the pair (i_k, λ^k), we have $v_{\lambda^k}(x_k) = V_m(x_k)$ for every index k. Recall also that from Lemma 3, we have the inequality $x^{\mathrm{T}} P_\lambda x \geq \alpha_m\|x\|^2$ for every $\lambda \in \Lambda^+$ and every

$x \in \mathbf{R}^n$. The expression $2x(t)^{\mathrm{T}} M_{i_k}^{\mathrm{T}}(\lambda^k) P_{\lambda^k} x$ represents the derivative of v_{λ^k} along the trajectories of system (27) on the time interval $[t_k, t_{k+1})$. So, due to the choice of our feedback, this derivative is less or equal to $-\eta_0\gamma \|x(t)\|^2$ for every $t \in [t_k, t_{k+1})$, thus we have

$$\dot{v}_{\lambda^k}(x) \le -\eta_0\gamma \|x\|^2 \le -\frac{\eta_0\gamma}{\lambda_M(P_{\lambda^k})} v_{\lambda^k}(x)$$

where $\lambda_M(P_{\lambda^k})$ denotes the greatest eigenvalue of matrix P_{λ^k}. From Lemma 3, we have $\lambda_M(P_{\lambda^k}) \le \alpha_M$ and so we obtain

$$\dot{v}_{\lambda^k}(x) \le -\frac{\eta_0\gamma}{\alpha_M} v_{\lambda^k}(x)$$

which implies that

$$v_{\lambda^k}(x_{k+1}) \le v_{\lambda^k}(x_k) e^{-\frac{\eta_0\gamma}{\alpha_M}\tau} \tag{30}$$

for every index k. Now, we have $V_m(x_{k+1}) \le v_{\lambda^k}(x_{k+1})$ and $V_m(x_k) = v_{\lambda^k}(x_k)$, so from (30), we deduce

$$V_m(x_{k+1}) \le \theta\, V_m(x_k) \tag{31}$$

where $\theta = e^{-\frac{\eta_0\gamma}{\alpha_M}\tau} \in (0,1)$ and so

$$V_m(x_k) \le \theta^k\, V_m(x_0)$$

which implies , as $V_m(x) \ge \alpha_m \|x\|^2$,

$$\|x_k\|^2 \le \frac{1}{\alpha_m} \theta^k \|x_0\|^2. \tag{32}$$

Now, on the interval $[t_k, t_{k+1})$, we have $v_{\lambda^k}(x(t)) \le v_{\lambda^k}(x_k)$, this inequality together with (32), proves the result. □

5. ILLUSTRATIVE EXAMPLES

Before presenting some examples, it is important to mention that it is not necessary to ensure a stabilizing switched law to determine all the possible values of the set Λ^+. Only one value is sufficient to guarantee the stability. So, a reasonable finite number of values ensures performances. Practically, a finite number have been used using a discretization of the set Λ.

5.1 Example 1: a regular case

Consider a two mode switched system with the following design parameters:

$$A_1 = \begin{pmatrix} -2.7 & 3.9 \\ 4.4 & -12.6 \end{pmatrix}, \qquad A_2 = \begin{pmatrix} -9.5 & -5.1 \\ -7.5 & -3.3 \end{pmatrix},$$

$$B_1 = \begin{pmatrix} 0.1 \\ 0 \end{pmatrix}, \qquad B_2 = \begin{pmatrix} 4.6 \\ 0 \end{pmatrix},$$

$Q_1 = Q_2 = \mathrm{Id}$, $R_1 = 1$ and $R_2 = 2$.

For each subsystem, an LQ design can be be performed separately. Thus, in order to make some comparisons, Figure 1 shows the state space trajectories for the switching law given by (27) and the optimal one. The later is obtained by NL programming in a suitable formulation taking into account singular arcs [24]. If not, numerical difficulties in the control determination are often encountered. We can see that the two solutions match well together. In the example, it can be observed that two singular arcs (defined by two lines in the state space) occur in the solutions.

Figure 2 compares the optimal cost with the costs obtained by using the switching law, only mode 1 and only mode 2, respectively. This comparison is made for initial states taken on the unit ball, the x-axis represents the polar angle θ of these initial states. We have also added the guarantee on the cost provided by upper bound i.e. $\frac{1}{2}V_m(x)$. It can be observed that the cost associated to the switching law coincides with the cost of the optimal numerical solution. Of course, the essential difference is that the numerical solution is an open loop control while the switching law defines a closed loop control. It is also clear that the used of a single mode with no switching leads to lower performances.

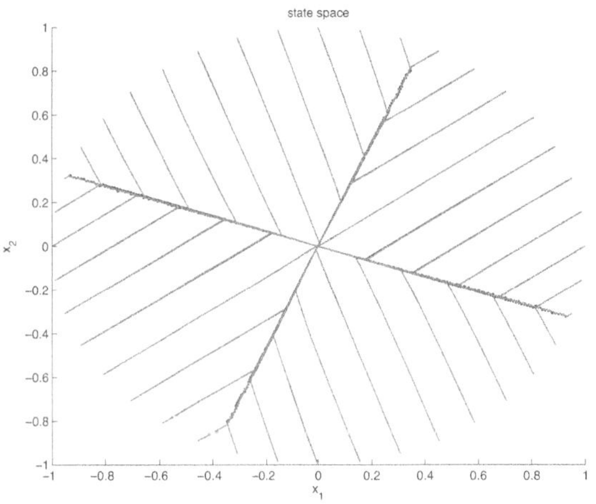

Figure 1: Ex. 1: State space trajectories: (red) optimal solution (NLP); (blue) switching law

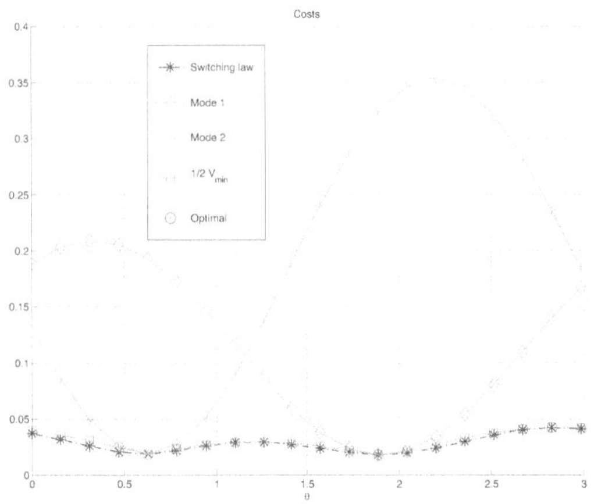

Figure 2: Ex. 1: Cost comparisons for different initial positions taken on the unit ball.

5.2 Example 2: non stabilizable subsystems

For this second example, we have chosen two non stabilizable subsystems:

$$A_1 = \begin{pmatrix} 1 & 0 \\ 1 & -1 \end{pmatrix}, \qquad A_2 = \begin{pmatrix} -2 & 1 \\ 0 & 1 \end{pmatrix},$$

$$B_1 = \begin{pmatrix} 0 \\ 1 \end{pmatrix}, \qquad B_2 = \begin{pmatrix} 1 \\ 0 \end{pmatrix}.$$

Therefore, there is no LQ design that can be defined separately for each subsystem. However, in a switched framework and taking $Q_1 = Q_2 = \mathrm{Id}$, $R_1 = 2$ and $R_2 = 1$, as the set Λ^+ is non empty, the switching law presented in this paper can be applied. Once again the optimal solution and the one provided by the switching law are very closed as showed by Figure 3. Figure 4 compares the optimal cost with the costs obtained by using the switching law. The upper bound V_m is also plotted.

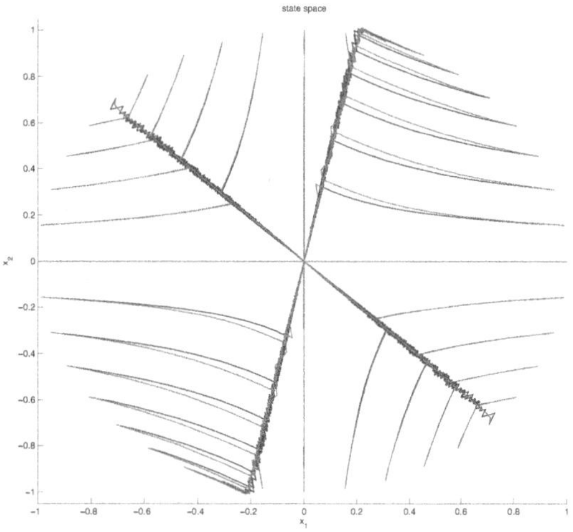

Figure 3: Ex. 2: State space trajectories: (red) optimal solution (NLP); (blue) switching law

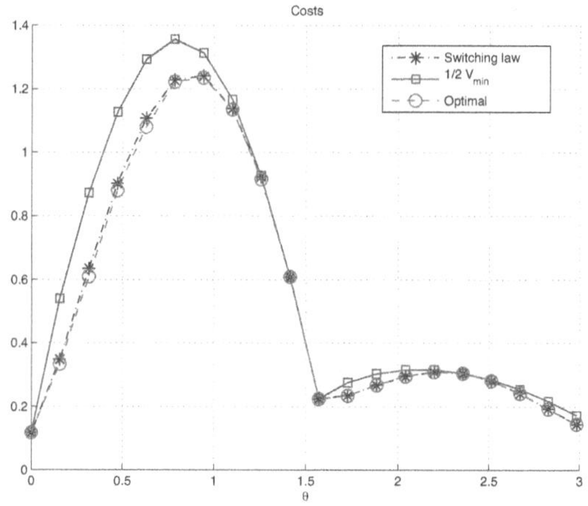

Figure 4: Ex. 2: Cost comparisons for different initial positions taken on the unit ball.

6. REFERENCES

[1] H. Axelsson, Y. Wardi, M. Egerstedt, and E. Verriest. Gradient descent approach to optimal mode scheduling in hybrid dynamical systems. *Journal of Optimization Theory and Applications*, 136(2):167–186, 2008.

[2] S. C. Bengea and R. A. DeCarlo. Optimal control of switching systems. *Automatica*, 41(1):11–27, 2005.

[3] F. Bonnans, P. Martinon, and E. Trélat. Singular arcs in the generalized Goddard's problem. *Journal of Optimization Theory and Applications*, 139(2):439–461, 2008.

[4] B. Bonnard and M. Chyba. *Singular Trajectories and Their Role in Control Theory*. Mathématiques et Applications. Springer, 2003.

[5] A. Bryson and Y. Ho. *Applied Optimal Control: Optimization, Estimation, and Control*. Halsted Press book'. Taylor & Francis, 1975.

[6] P. Colaneri, J. C. Geromel, and A. Astolfi. Stabilization of continuous-time switched nonlinear systems. *Systems & Control Letters*, 57(1):95–103, 2008.

[7] J. Cortes. Discontinuous dynamical systems. *Control Systems, IEEE*, 28(3):36–73, 2008.

[8] G. S. Deaecto, J. C. Geromel, and J. Daafouz. Switched state-feedback control for continuous time-varying polytopic systems. *International Journal of Control*, 84(9):1500–1508, 2011.

[9] A. Filippov and F. Arscott. *Differential Equations with Discontinuous Righthand Sides: Control Systems*. Mathematics and its Applications. Kluwer Academic Publishers, 1988.

[10] G. Fraser-Andrews. Finding candidate singular optimal controls: A state of the art survey. *Journal of Optimization Theory and Applications*, 60(2):173–190, 1989.

[11] N. Furukawa. Optimality conditions in nondifferentiable programming and their applications to best approximations. *Applied Mathematics and Optimization*, 9(1):337–371, 1982.

[12] J. C. Geromel and P. Colaneri. Stability and stabilization of discrete time switched systems. *International Journal of Control*, 79(7):719–728, 2006.

[13] B. Ingalls and E. D. Sontag. An infinite-time relaxation theorem for differential inclusions. In *Proc. Amer. Math. Soc*, pages 487–499, 2003.

[14] D. H. Jacobson, S. B. Gershwin, and M. M. Lele. Computation of optimal singular controls. *Automatic Control, IEEE Transactions on*, 15(1):67–73, 1970.

[15] A. J. Krener. The high order maximal principle and its application to singular extremals. *SIAM Journal on Control and Optimization*, 15(2):256–293, 1977.

[16] V. Kučera. A review of the matrix Riccati equation. *Kybernetika*, 9(1):42 61, 1973.

[17] P. Lancaster and L. Rodman. *Algebraic Riccati Equations*. Oxford science publications. Clarendon Press, 1995.

[18] B. Lincoln and A. Rantzer. Relaxing dynamic programming. *Automatic Control, IEEE Transactions on*, 51(8):1249–1260, 2006.

[19] P. Martinon. *Numerical resolution of optimal control problems by a simplicial method*. PhD thesis, Institut National Polytechnique de Toulouse, 2005.

[20] H. Maurer. Numerical solution of singular control problems using multiple shooting techniques. *Journal of Optimization Theory and Applications*, 18(2):235–257, 1976.

[21] P. Moylan and J. Moore. Generalizations of singular optimal control theory. *Automatica*, 7(5):591–598, 1971.

[22] D. Patino, P. Riedinger, and C. Iung. Practical optimal state feedback control law for continuous-time switched affine systems with cyclic steady state. *International Journal of Control*, 82(7):1357–1376, 2009.

[23] L. Pontryagin, V. Boltyanskii, R. Gamkrelidze, and E. Mishchenko. *The Mathematical Theory of Optimal Processes*. Pergamon, 1964.

[24] P. Riedinger and I.-C. Morărescu. A numerical framework for optimal control of switched input affine nonlinear systems subject to path constraint. *Mathematics and Computers in Simulation*, 95(0):63 – 77, 2014.

[25] H. M. Robbins. A generalized Legendre-Clebsch condition for the singular cases of optimal control. *IBM Journal of Research and Development*, 11(4):361–372, 1967.

[26] C. Seatzu, D. Corona, A. Giua, and A. Bemporad. Optimal control of continuous-time switched affine systems. *Automatic Control, IEEE Transactions on*, 51(5):726–741, 2006.

[27] M. Shahid Shaikh and P. E. Caines. On the hybrid optimal control problem: Theory and algorithms. *Automatic Control, IEEE Transactions on*, 52(9):1587–1603, 2007.

[28] M. Volker. Singular optimal control – the state of the art. Technical Report 169, Fachbereich Mathematik, 1996.

[29] X. Xu and P. J. Antsaklis. Optimal control of switched systems based on parameterization of the switching instants. *Automatic Control, IEEE Transactions on*, 49(1):2–16, 2004.

[30] W. Zhang, J. Hu, and A. Abate. On the value functions of the discrete-time switched LQR problem. *Automatic Control, IEEE Transactions on*, 54(11):2669–2674, 2009.

State-Feedback Stabilization of Discrete-Time Piecewise Affine Systems*

Sihan Xiong
Pennsylvania State University
Mechanical & Nuclear Engineering Dept.
University Park, PA 16802
sux101@psu.edu

Ji-Woong Lee
Pennsylvania State University
Mechanical & Nuclear Engineering Dept.
University Park, PA 16802
jiwoong@psu.edu

ABSTRACT

A symbolic abstraction method is used to synthesize stabilizing state-feedback controllers for piecewise affine plants. An increasing sequence of symbolic models of the piecewise affine plant and the corresponding sequence of convex synthesis conditions are obtained in the order of decreasing conservatism. Whenever one of these conditions is feasible, synthesis of a stabilizing piecewise affine controller is guaranteed. At least in principle, the synthesis conditions are capable of identifying the largest stabilizable region, and hence they do not suffer from inherent conservatism.

Categories and Subject Descriptors

J.2 [**Physical Sciences and Engineering**]: Engineering; I.1.4 [**Symbolic and Algebraic Manipulation**]: Applications

General Terms

Theory, design, verification

Keywords

Feedback control, hybrid systems, simulation, bisimulation

1. INTRODUCTION

A piecewise affine plant is a controlled nonlinear system defined by a collection of affine state-space models, and by a discrete logic that determines which of the affine models is active at each time instant based on the system state and input. That is, the product of state and input spaces is partitioned into a number of cells and an affine state-space model is assigned to each of these cells. In the context of nonlinear system modeling, the affine models are linearizations of a nonlinear system at different operating points [17]. Piecewise affine systems are equivalent to mixed-logic dynamical models [3], and are known to be capable of modeling a large class of hybrid dynamical systems [4].

In this paper, we focus on the discrete-time domain and develop a method for synthesizing piecewise affine state-feedback controllers that stabilize the piecewise affine plant. More specifically, we are concerned with the problem of finding a state-feedback controller for a given piecewise affine plant and a given set of initial states, so that, once the feedback loop is closed, all state trajectories starting from the given set of initial states converge to the origin with a uniform exponential decay rate.

Existing Lyapunov analysis–based synthesis methods for stabilization of piecewise affine systems typically require the existence of a common, or piecewise, quadratic Lyapunov function [5,6,13], or a polyhedral Lyapunov function [10,11], that decays along all trajectories of the closed-loop system. However, since the associated synthesis conditions do not explicitly involve the input variables, these methods cannot fully take into account the state-dependent switching structure or state-input constraints imposed by the underlying discrete logic. Moreover, these methods are inherently conservative because, if a specific type of Lyapunov functions does not exist, they do not suggest alternative Lyapunov function candidates. On the other hand, existing algorithmic approaches involving symbolic models are inherently discrete, and hence they either cannot be used for the purpose of stabilization [20] or require the existence of a finite-state symbolic model that is equivalent to the piecewise affine system [18].

We address the problem of stabilization by exploiting the link between the theory of maximal invariant sets [8] and a sequence of finite-state symbolic models of the piecewise affine plant. These symbolic models are said to be simulations of the piecewise affine plant because they describe the switching sequences that the underlying discrete logic can generate. Although simulations do not preserve stability in general [16], those in this approach suffice for stabilization under the assumption that a cell in the state-input partition contains the origin in its interior. This approach is scalable because, if a given symbolic model and the corresponding synthesis condition are deemed too conservative, one has the option to use the next, more refined symbolic model and obtain a less conservative synthesis condition by paying more computational cost. Furthermore, the approach does not suffer from inherent conservatism because the sequence of simulations converges to a finite-state or infinite-state bisimulation, which is an exact discrete-state representation of the piecewise affine system.

*This work was supported by the National Science Foundation under Grant Nos. ECCS-1201973 and CNS-1329422.

HSCC'14, April 15–17, 2014, Berlin, Germany.
Copyright 2014 ACM 978-1-4503-2732-9/14/04 ...$15.00.
http://dx.doi.org/10.1145/2562059.2562122.

While the features described above are common to the results presented in this paper and the stability analysis results in [15], a remarkable difference between feedback stabilization and stability analysis is that, while the symbolic models for system verification (e.g., those in [19]) can be used for stability analysis without alteration, those for controller synthesis are required to be adapted to the purpose of stabilization. In particular, the cell containing the origin of the state-input space must be such that its projection onto the state space is equal to its cross section along the state space. This is to ensure that an invariant set about the origin, which guarantees the exponential stability of the closed-loop system, is automatically obtained as a by-product of symbolic-model construction. Once a symbolic model leads to a feasible synthesis condition, a stabilizing state-feedback controller exists and can be taken to be piecewise affine.

This paper is organized as follows. Section 2 formulates our problem of stabilizability analysis and stabilizing controller synthesis. Section 3 then defines an increasing sequence of symbolic models and summarizes its properties. The main results on stabilizability analysis is presented in Section 4, and a guaranteed controller synthesis method, along with a numerical example, is provided in Section 5. Lastly, concluding remarks are given in Section 6.

Notation

The sets of real numbers, positive integers, and nonnegative integers are denoted by $\mathbb{R}$, $\mathbb{N}$, and $\mathbb{N}_0$, respectively. For vectors $\mathbf{x} \in \mathbb{R}^n$, denoted by $\|\mathbf{x}\|$ is the Euclidean norm of $\mathbf{x}$. The Euclidean norm induces the spectral norm $\|\mathbf{A}\|$ of matrices $\mathbf{A} \in \mathbb{R}^{m\times n}$. The n-by-n identity matrix is denoted by $\mathbf{I}_n$, and the m-by-n zero matrix by $\mathbf{0}_{m\times n}$; they are often written $\mathbf{I}$ and $\mathbf{0}$, respectively, with their dimensions understood. The interior and closure of sets $P \subset \mathbb{R}^n$ are denoted by $\mathrm{int}(P)$ and $\mathrm{cl}(P)$, respectively. If $\mathbf{A} \in \mathbb{R}^{m\times n}$ and $P \subset \mathbb{R}^n$, then $\mathbf{A}P$ denotes the set $\{\mathbf{Ax}\colon \mathbf{x} \in P\} \subset \mathbb{R}^m$.

2. PROBLEM DEFINITION

2.1 Piecewise Affine Plant

Let $\mathbf{A}_i \in \mathbb{R}^{n\times n}$, $\mathbf{B}_i \in \mathbb{R}^{n\times m}$, and $\mathbf{b}_i \in \mathbb{R}^n$ be given for each $i \in \mathbb{N}$. Let $D_1, D_2, \ldots \in \mathbb{R}^n \times \mathbb{R}^m$ be polyhedra that partition $\mathbb{R}^n \times \mathbb{R}^m$, so that $\bigcup_{i\in\mathbb{N}} D_i = \mathbb{R}^n \times \mathbb{R}^m$ and $D_i \cap D_j = \varnothing$ whenever $i \neq j$. Given the initial state $\mathbf{x}(0) \in \mathbb{R}^n$ and input sequence $\mathbf{u}(0)$, $\mathbf{u}(1)$, $\ldots \in \mathbb{R}^m$, the discrete-time piecewise affine plant generates the state sequence $\mathbf{x}(0)$, $\mathbf{x}(1)$, $\ldots \in \mathbb{R}^n$ and switching sequence $\theta(0)$, $\theta(1)$, $\ldots \in \mathbb{N}$ according to

$$\mathbf{x}(t+1) = \mathbf{A}_{\theta(t)}\mathbf{x}(t) + \mathbf{B}_{\theta(t)}\mathbf{u}(t) + \mathbf{b}_{\theta(t)}, \quad t \in \mathbb{N}_0; \tag{1a}$$

$$\theta(t) = i \quad \text{if } (\mathbf{x}(t), \mathbf{u}(t)) \in D_i, \quad i \in \mathbb{N},\ t \in \mathbb{N}_0. \tag{1b}$$

If $\theta = (\theta(0), \theta(1), \ldots)$ is a switching sequence generated by the piecewise affine plant (1) for some initial state $\mathbf{x}(0) \in \mathbb{R}^n$ and input sequence $\mathbf{u}(0)$, $\mathbf{u}(1)$, $\ldots \in \mathbb{R}^m$, then define

$$\mathbf{\Phi}_\theta(t, t_0) = \begin{cases} \mathbf{I}_n & \text{if } t = t_0; \\ \mathbf{A}_{\theta(t-1)} \cdots \mathbf{A}_{\theta(t_0)} & \text{if } t > t_0, \end{cases}$$

$$\mathbf{g}_\theta(t, t_0, \mathbf{u}) = \begin{cases} \mathbf{0}_{n\times 1} & \text{if } t = t_0; \\ \sum_{s=t_0}^{t-1} \mathbf{\Phi}_\theta(t, s+1)\mathbf{B}_{\theta(s)}\mathbf{u}(s) & \text{if } t > t_0, \end{cases}$$

$$\mathbf{f}_\theta(t, t_0) = \begin{cases} \mathbf{0}_{n\times 1} & \text{if } t = t_0; \\ \sum_{s=t_0}^{t-1} \mathbf{\Phi}_\theta(t, s+1)\mathbf{b}_{\theta(s)} & \text{if } t > t_0, \end{cases}$$

so that

$$\mathbf{x}(t) = \mathbf{\Phi}_\theta(t, t_0)\mathbf{x}(t_0) + \mathbf{g}_\theta(t, t_0, \mathbf{u}) + \mathbf{f}_\theta(t, t_0)$$

for all t, $t_0 \in \mathbb{N}_0$ with $t \geq t_0$.

2.2 Piecewise Affine Controller

Suppose $\mathbf{K}_i \in \mathbb{R}^{m\times n}$ and $\mathbf{l}_i \in \mathbb{R}^m$ for each $i \in \mathbb{N}$. Let X_1, $X_2, \ldots \in \mathbb{R}^n$ be polyhedra that partition the state space $\mathbb{R}^n$, so that $\bigcup_{i\in\mathbb{N}} X_i = \mathbb{R}^n$ and $X_i \cap X_j = \varnothing$ whenever $i \neq j$. Given the state $\mathbf{x}(t) \in \mathbb{R}^n$ of the piecewise affine plant at time $t \in \mathbb{N}_0$, the piecewise affine state-feedback controller generates the control input $\mathbf{u}(t) \in \mathbb{R}^m$ according to

$$\mathbf{u}(t) = \mathbf{K}_{\sigma(t)}\mathbf{x}(t) + \mathbf{l}_{\sigma(t)}, \quad t \in \mathbb{N}_0; \tag{2a}$$

$$\sigma(t) = j \quad \text{if } \mathbf{x}(t) \in X_j, \quad j \in \mathbb{N},\ t \in \mathbb{N}_0, \tag{2b}$$

where $\sigma(0)$, $\sigma(1)$, $\ldots$ is the controller switching sequence.

2.3 Closed-Loop Piecewise Affine System

The feedback interconnection of the plant (1) and controller (2) is described by

$$\begin{aligned}\mathbf{x}(t+1) = {}& \big(\mathbf{A}_{\theta(t)} + \mathbf{B}_{\theta(t)}\mathbf{K}_{\sigma(t)}\big)\mathbf{x}(t) \\ & + \mathbf{b}_{\theta(t)} + \mathbf{B}_{\theta(t)}\mathbf{l}_{\sigma(t)}, \quad t \in \mathbb{N}_0;\end{aligned} \tag{3a}$$

$$\begin{aligned}(\theta(t), \sigma(t)) = (i, j) \quad & \text{if } \mathbf{x}(t) \in P_{(i,j)}, \\ & i, j \in \mathbb{N},\ t \in \mathbb{N}_0,\end{aligned} \tag{3b}$$

where

$$P_{(i,j)} = \left\{\mathbf{x} \in X_j\colon \begin{bmatrix}\mathbf{I} \\ \mathbf{K}_j\end{bmatrix}\mathbf{x} + \begin{bmatrix}\mathbf{0} \\ \mathbf{l}_j\end{bmatrix} \in D_i\right\} \tag{3c}$$

for i, $j \in \mathbb{N}$. The closed-loop system (3) is a homogeneous piecewise affine system defined on the state-space partition formed by the polyhedra $P_{(i,j)}$, $(i, j) \in \mathbb{N}^2$.

If $\theta = (\theta(0), \theta(1), \ldots)$ and $\sigma = (\sigma(0), \sigma(1), \ldots)$ are the switching sequences generated by the closed-loop system for some initial state $\mathbf{x}(0) \in \mathbb{R}^n$, then define $\mathbf{\Phi}_{\theta,\sigma}(t_0, t_0) = \mathbf{I}_n$, $\mathbf{f}_{\theta,\sigma}(t_0, t_0) = \mathbf{0}_{n\times 1}$, and

$$\begin{aligned}\mathbf{\Phi}_{\theta,\sigma}(t, t_0) = {}& \big(\mathbf{A}_{\theta(t-1)} + \mathbf{B}_{\theta(t-1)}\mathbf{K}_{\sigma(t-1)}\big) \cdots \\ & \times \big(\mathbf{A}_{\theta(t_0)} + \mathbf{B}_{\theta(t_0)}\mathbf{K}_{\sigma(t_0)}\big),\end{aligned}$$

$$\mathbf{f}_{\theta,\sigma}(t, t_0) = \sum_{s=t_0}^{t-1} \mathbf{\Phi}_{\theta,\sigma}(t, s+1)\big(\mathbf{b}_{\theta(s)} + \mathbf{B}_{\theta(s)}\mathbf{l}_{\sigma(s)}\big)$$

for $t > t_0$, so that the closed-loop state sequence $\mathbf{x}(0)$, $\mathbf{x}(1)$, $\ldots$, satisfies

$$\mathbf{x}(t) = \mathbf{\Phi}_{\theta,\sigma}(t, t_0)\mathbf{x}(t_0) + \mathbf{f}_{\theta,\sigma}(t, t_0)$$

for all t, $t_0 \in \mathbb{N}_0$ with $t \geq t_0$.

2.4 Objectives

Without loss of generality, let $Q \subset \mathbb{R}^n \times \mathbb{R}^m$ be a given polytope (i.e., bounded polyhedron) such that

$$(\mathbf{0}, \mathbf{0}) \in \mathrm{int}(Q) \quad \text{and} \quad Q = \bigcup_{i=1}^{N} D_i$$

for some $N \in \mathbb{N}$. Correspondingly, let the pair $\Sigma = (\mathcal{S}, \mathcal{D})$ represent the piecewise affine plant restricted to Q, where

$$\mathcal{S} = \{(\mathbf{A}_1, \mathbf{B}_1, \mathbf{b}_1), \ldots, (\mathbf{A}_N, \mathbf{B}_N, \mathbf{b}_N)\},$$
$$\mathcal{D} = \{D_1, \ldots, D_N\}.$$

For $D \subset \mathbb{R}^n \times \mathbb{R}^m$, define the projection of D onto the state space as

$$\pi(D) = \{\mathbf{x} \in \mathbb{R}^n : (\mathbf{x}, \mathbf{u}) \in D,\ \mathbf{u} \in \mathbb{R}^m\}.$$

The set Q is our state-input constraint set. That is, we will require that the state-input pair $(\mathbf{x}(t), \mathbf{u}(t))$ be within the set Q for all $t \in \mathbb{N}_0$. This does not mean that Q is assumed invariant in some sense at the outset.

Definition 1. *A state-input pair $(\mathbf{x}, \mathbf{u}) \in \mathbb{R}^n \times \mathbb{R}^m$ is said to* satisfy constraint Q *for the piecewise affine system Σ if $(\mathbf{x}, \mathbf{u}) \in D_i \cap Q$ for some $i \in \{1, \dots, N\}$ and if $\mathbf{A}_i\mathbf{x} + \mathbf{B}_i\mathbf{u} + \mathbf{b}_i \in \pi(Q)$. A pair $(\mathbf{x}(0), u)$ of an initial state $\mathbf{x}(0)$ and an input sequence $u = (\mathbf{u}(0), \mathbf{u}(1), \dots)$ is said to satisfy constraint Q for Σ if $(\mathbf{x}(t), \mathbf{u}(t))$ satisfies constraint Q for Σ for every $t \in \mathbb{N}_0$.*

If $P \subset \pi(Q)$ is the set of initial states of our interest, then our first objective is to obtain a condition under which there exists an open-loop control scheme such that, for each initial state $\mathbf{x}(0) \in P$, an input sequence u forms a pair $(\mathbf{x}(0), u)$ that satisfies the state-input constraint Q, and such that the resulting state sequence converges to the origin with an exponential rate.

Definition 2. *The piecewise affine plant (1), or the pair $\Sigma = (\mathcal{S}, \mathcal{D})$, is said to be* (exponentially) stabilizable *on $P \subset \pi(Q)$ with constraint Q if there exist $c \geq 1$ and $\lambda \in (0, 1)$ such that, for each initial state $\mathbf{x}(0) \in P$, there exists an input sequence $\mathbf{u}(0), \mathbf{u}(1), \dots \in \mathbb{R}^m$ such that the corresponding switching sequence $\theta = (\theta(0), \theta(1), \dots)$ satisfies*

$$(\mathbf{\Phi}_\theta(t,0)\mathbf{x}(0) + \mathbf{g}_\theta(t,0,\mathbf{u}) + \mathbf{f}_\theta(t,0), \mathbf{u}(t)) \in Q, \tag{4a}$$

$$\|\mathbf{\Phi}_\theta(t,0)\mathbf{x}(0) + \mathbf{g}_\theta(t,0,\mathbf{u})\| \leq c\lambda^t \|\mathbf{x}(0)\| \tag{4b}$$

for all $t \in \mathbb{N}_0$, and

$$\|\mathbf{f}_\theta(t,0)\| \to 0 \tag{4c}$$

as $t \to \infty$.

Once the piecewise affine system is verified to be stabilizable, our second objective is to obtain a piecewise affine state-feedback realization of a stabilizing open-loop control scheme.

Definition 3. *The piecewise affine controller (2) is said to* (exponentially) stabilize *the plant (1), or the pair $\Sigma = (\mathcal{S}, \mathcal{D})$, on $P \subset \pi(Q)$ with constraint Q if there exist $c \geq 1$ and $\lambda \in (0, 1)$ such that, for each initial state $\mathbf{x}(0) \in P$, the closed-loop system (3) generates switching sequences $\theta = (\theta(0), \theta(1), \dots)$ and $\sigma = (\sigma(0), \sigma(1), \dots)$ that satisfy the following:*

$$(\mathbf{\Phi}_{\theta,\sigma}(t,0)\mathbf{x}(0) + \mathbf{f}_{\theta,\sigma}(t,0), \mathbf{u}(t)) \in Q, \tag{5a}$$

$$\|\mathbf{\Phi}_{\theta,\sigma}(t,0)\| \leq c\lambda^t \tag{5b}$$

for all $t \in \mathbb{N}_0$, and

$$\|\mathbf{f}_{\theta,\sigma}(t,0)\| \to 0 \tag{5c}$$

as $t \to \infty$.

2.5 Assumption on Central Cell

For the purpose of analyzing the stabilizability of piecewise affine plants, we will make the commonly made assumption that there exists a *central cell*, say D_1, in $\mathcal{D}$ that satisfies $(\mathbf{0}, \mathbf{0}) \in \mathrm{int}(D_1)$—see, e.g., [12]. This assumption is typically satisfied by piecewise affine approximations of nonlinear systems [17], and necessitates that the unique central cell be stabilizable in the following sense.

Definition 4. *Cell $D_1 \in \mathcal{D}$ is said to be* stabilizable *if the origin $(\mathbf{0}, \mathbf{0}) \in \mathrm{int}(D_1)$ (i.e., D_1 is a unique central cell in $\mathcal{D}$) and if there exist $\mathbf{K} \in \mathbb{R}^{m \times n}$ and $\mathbf{l} \in \mathbb{R}^m$ such that the spectral radius of $\mathbf{A}_1 + \mathbf{B}_1\mathbf{K}$ is less than one and such that $\mathbf{b}_1 + \mathbf{B}_1\mathbf{l} = \mathbf{0}$. In this case, the pair $(\mathbf{K}, \mathbf{l})$ is called a stabilizing pair for the triple $(\mathbf{A}_1, \mathbf{B}_1, \mathbf{b}_1)$.*

3. SYMBOLIC MODELS OF PLANT

3.1 Requirements for State-Input Partitions

Symbolic models constructed via successive partitioning and minimization procedures are well-suited for the purposes of system verification [1,19] and stability analysis [14, 15]. However, these stand-alone algorithmic procedures turn out to be inadequate for the purpose of stabilizability analysis. They need to be adapted to the physical constraints arising naturally from the objectives of stabilizability analysis and feedback controller synthesis.

Definition 5. *A partition $\mathcal{P}$ of Q is said to be* permissible *if the following hold:*

(a) If P_1, $P_2 \in \mathcal{P}$ are such that $\pi(P_1) \cap \pi(P_2) \neq \varnothing$, then $\pi(P_1) = \pi(P_2)$.

(b) If $P \in \mathcal{P}$ is such that $P \subset D_1$ and $(\mathbf{x}, \mathbf{0}) \in P$ for some $\mathbf{x} \in \mathbb{R}^n$, then $(\mathbf{x}, \mathbf{0}) \in P$ for all $\mathbf{x} \in \pi(P)$.

Condition (a) says that the state-space projections of two cells in a permissible state-input partition either coincide or are disjoint. This condition guarantees that there is no ambiguity in describing what part of the state space an input transfers a given state to. Condition (b) implies that, if a cell in a permissible state-input partition is a subset of the central cell, then its projection onto the state space is equal to its cross section along the state space. This condition ensures that the process of constructing the maximal invariant set detailed in [8] is a part of the procedure for successively partitioning the state-input space; see Section 4.2.

There is a close link between the process of constructing symbolic models of the piecewise affine plant and that of computing the maximal invariant set characterized in [8].the zero input suffices on a neighborhood of the origin of the state space as far as stabilization is concerned.

Any finite polyhedral partition of the state-input constraint Q can be further refined into a permissible partition as follows. Suppose $\mathcal{P} = \{P_1, \dots, P_r\}$ is a collection of polytopes that form a partition of Q. Compute all *minterms* of the collection $\{\pi(P_1), \dots, \pi(P_r)\}$—i.e., the nonempty sets of the form $\pi(P_1)' \cap \cdots \cap \pi(P_r)'$, where either $\pi(P_i)' = \pi(P_i)$ or $\pi(P_i)' = \pi(Q) \setminus \pi(P_i)$ for each i—based on [2, Theorem 3.3]. If any of these minterms is nonconvex, split it into a smallest number of disjoint convex polytopes using [7, Algorithm 1]. The resulting collection of disjoint subsets of minterms of $\{\pi(P_1), \dots, \pi(P_r)\}$ defines a convex polytopic partition $\mathcal{T}$

of $\pi(Q)$. If $\mathcal{C}$ is the collection of the cells in $\mathcal{P}$ that are subsets of the central cell D_1 (i.e., $\bigcup_{P\in\mathcal{C}} P = D_1$), then for each $(P,T) \in \mathcal{C}\times\mathcal{T}$ compute

$$U = \{\mathbf{x} \in \pi(Q) \colon (\mathbf{x},\mathbf{0}) \in P \cap (T \times \mathbb{R}^m)\},$$

and split T into U and $T \setminus U$ whenever both U and $T\setminus U$ are nonempty; if $T \setminus U$ is nonconvex, then split it further into disjoint convex polytopes using [7, Algorithm 1]. Now, the collection of all nonempty sets of the form $P\cap(T\times\mathbb{R}^m)$ over all $P \in \mathcal{P}$ and $T \in \mathcal{T}$, with a suitable redefinition of set boundaries, is a permissible partition of Q.

3.2 Construction of Symbolic Models

We assume, with little loss of generality, that the initial partition $\mathcal{D}$ of Q is permissible. Given $(\mathcal{S},\mathcal{D})$ as well as Q, a sequence of directed graphs G_0, G_1, ... is obtained by induction as follows.

Construction of G_0

Let

$$\mathcal{D}_0 = \mathcal{D},$$
$$V_0 = \{0,1,\dots,N\}.$$

For each $(i,j) \in (V_0\setminus\{0\})^2$, the set of all state-input pairs in cell D_i that lead to a next state that falls into the part of the state space on which cell D_j is projected is given by

$$D_{(i,j)} = \{(\mathbf{x},\mathbf{u}) \in D_i \colon \mathbf{A}_i\mathbf{x}+\mathbf{B}_i\mathbf{u}+\mathbf{b}_i \in \pi(D_j)\}.$$

Similarly, for $i \in V_0\setminus\{0\}$, the set of state-input pairs in D_i that lead to a next state outside $\pi(Q)$ is given by

$$D_{(i,0)} = \{(\mathbf{x},\mathbf{u}) \in D_i \colon \mathbf{A}_i\mathbf{x}+\mathbf{B}_i\mathbf{u}+\mathbf{b}_i \notin \pi(Q)\}.$$

Since $\mathcal{D}_0$ is permissible, we have either $\pi(D_i) = \pi(D_j)$ or $\pi(D_i)\cap\pi(D_j) = \varnothing$ for every $(i,j) \in (V_0\setminus\{0\})^2$. This guarantees that, after deleting repeated cells $D_{(i,j)}$, the collection

$$\widetilde{\mathcal{D}}_1 = \{D_{(i,j)} \neq \varnothing \colon i \in V_0\setminus\{0\},\ j\in V_0\}$$

defines a partition of Q that is finer than $\mathcal{D}_0$. Associated with this collection is

$$E_0 = \{(i,j)\colon D_{(i,j)} \neq \varnothing,\ i\in V_0\setminus\{0\},\ j\in V_0\}\cup\{(0,0)\},$$

which, together with V_0, defines the directed graph $G_0 = (V_0,E_0)$. The directed graph G_0 and the partition $\widetilde{\mathcal{D}}_1$ of Q form the basis for our induction.

Refinement of G_L, $L \in \mathbb{N}_0$

As an induction hypothesis, suppose $G_L = (V_L,E_L)$ and $\widetilde{\mathcal{D}}_{L+1}$ are given for some $L\in\mathbb{N}_0$. First of all, refine $\widetilde{\mathcal{D}}_{L+1}$ and obtain a permissible partition $\mathcal{D}_{L+1}$ of Q by following the procedure outlined in Section 3.1. Then, index the distinct cells in $\mathcal{D}_{L+1}$ by integers from $\max V_L + 1$ to $\max V_L + N_{L+1}$, where N_{L+1} denotes the number of distinct cells in $\mathcal{D}_{L+1}$. Let

$$V_{L+1} = \{0, \max V_L + 1, \dots, \max V_L + N_{L+1}\}.$$

For each $(i,j) \in (V_{L+1}\setminus\{0\})^2$, define

$$D_{(i,j)} = \{(\mathbf{x},\mathbf{u}) \in D_i \colon \mathbf{A}_{o(i)}\mathbf{x}+\mathbf{B}_{o(i)}\mathbf{u}+\mathbf{b}_{o(i)} \in \pi(D_j)\},$$

where $o(i) = j$ if and only if $D_i \subset D_j$ and $j\in\{1,\dots,N\}$. Similarly, define

$$D_{(i,0)} = \{(\mathbf{x},\mathbf{u}) \in D_i \colon \mathbf{A}_{o(i)}\mathbf{x}+\mathbf{B}_{o(i)}\mathbf{u}+\mathbf{b}_{o(i)} \notin \pi(Q)\}$$

for $i\in V_{L+1}\setminus\{0\}$. Then, we obtain a partition

$$\widetilde{\mathcal{D}}_{L+2} = \{D_{(i,j)} \neq\varnothing \colon i\in V_{L+1}\setminus\{0\},\ j\in V_{L+1}\}$$

of Q and the directed graph $G_{L+1} = (V_{L+1},E_{L+1})$, where

$$E_{L+1} = \{(i,j)\colon D_{(i,j)}\neq\varnothing,\ i\in V_{L+1}\setminus\{0\},\ j\in V_{L+1}\}\cup\{(0,0)\}.$$

This completes the induction step for constructing graphs G_0, G_1, ...

Symbolic Models

For each $L\in\mathbb{N}_0$, the pair $\Sigma_L = (G_L,\mathcal{D}_L)$ defines the L-th symbolic model of the piecewise affine plant $\Sigma = (\mathcal{S},\mathcal{D})$. There is a one-to-one correspondence between nodes $i \in V_L\setminus\{0\}$ in the graph G_L and cells $D_i\in\mathcal{D}_L$. More specifically, there is a directed edge from node $i\in V_L\setminus\{0\}$ to node $j\in V_L\setminus\{0\}$ in G_L if and only if there exists a state-input pair in $D_i\in\mathcal{D}_L$ that leads to a next state in $\pi(D_j)$. Also, there is a directed edge from node i to node 0 in G_L if either $i = 0$ or some state-input pair in D_i leads to a state outside $\pi(Q)$.

3.3 Plant Simulations and Bisimulations

The state-input partitions $\mathcal{D}_L$, $L\in\mathbb{N}_0$, are used for the controller synthesis purpose. The construction procedure for these partitions is similar to, and yet different from that used for stability analysis. While "coarsest" partitions of the "state space" are proved to be useful for stability analysis [14,15] and scalable system verification [19], the partitions of the state-input space must be adapted to the permissibility constraints (i.e., the conditions in Definition 5) that we impose for the purpose of stabilization. This is a major difference between the problem of stabilizing controller synthesis and the existing system analysis and verification problems.

Nevertheless, the symbolic models Σ_L, $L\in\mathbb{N}_0$, enjoy the same kind of properties of symbolic abstractions that are crucial for maintaining scalability in stability analysis [14,15]. That is, even if achieving a finite-state bisimulation is impossible or computationally infeasible, these models provide finite-state simulations of varying degrees of complexity and fidelity that can potentially be used for the purpose of stabilizability analysis and stabilizing controller synthesis. For nonempty $P\subset\pi(Q)$, let $\Theta(P)$ denote the set of all switching sequences $\theta = (\theta(0),\theta(1),\dots)$ that the piecewise affine plant (1) can generate from initial states in P while satisfying the state-input constraint Q. That is,

$$\Theta(P) = \{\theta\in\{1,\dots,N\}^\infty \colon \mathbf{x}(0)\in P,\ \mathbf{u}(t)\in\mathbb{R}^m \text{ and } (\mathbf{x}(t),\mathbf{u}(t))\in Q \text{ for all } t\in\mathbb{N}_0\}.$$

On the other hand, for nonempty $P\subset\pi(Q)$ and $L\in\mathbb{N}_0$, the set of all infinite paths in G_L that start from cells whose projections intersect P is

$$\widetilde{\Theta}_L(P) = \{(i_0,i_1,\dots)\in(V_L\setminus\{0\})^\infty \colon P\cap\pi(D_{i_0})\neq\varnothing,\ (i_t,i_{t+1})\in E_L \text{ for all } t\in\mathbb{N}_0\},$$

so the set of all switching sequences $\theta = (\theta(0),\theta(1),\dots)$ generated by the graph G_L starting from its nodes associated with initial states in P is

$$\Theta_L(P) = \{\theta \in \{1,\dots,N\}^\infty : \\ (i_0, i_1, \dots) \in \widetilde{\Theta}_L(P), \theta(t) = o(i_t) \text{ for all } t \in \mathbb{N}_0\}.$$

It can be shown as in [19] and [9, Theorem 1] that, in general, Σ_L defines a *simulation* of both Σ_{L+1} and Σ for $L \in \mathbb{N}_0$ in the sense that

$$\Theta(P) \subset \Theta_{L+1}(P) \subset \Theta_L(P), \quad P \in \pi(Q).$$

Given $L \in \mathbb{N}_0$, in the special case where each $D \in \mathcal{D}_L$ has a $\widetilde{D} \in \mathcal{D}_{L+1}$ such that $D = \widetilde{D}$, we shall say $\mathcal{D}_L$ is Σ-*invariant*. In this case, the state-input partition $\mathcal{D}_L$ is as fine as its refinement $\mathcal{D}_{L+1}$, and so no further partition of $\mathcal{D}_{L+1}$ is necessary. Moreover, if $\mathcal{D}_L$ is Σ-invariant, then the symbolic model $\mathcal{D}_L$ defines a *bisimulation* of the piecewise affine plant Σ in the sense that

$$\Theta(P) = \Theta_{L+1}(P) = \Theta_L(P), \quad P \in \pi(Q).$$

4. STABILIZABILITY ANALYSIS

4.1 Stabilizability of Central Cell

Suppose that the central cell $D_1 \in \mathcal{D}$ is stabilizable and that $F = (\mathbf{K}, \mathbf{l})$ is a stabilizing pair for $(\mathbf{A}_1, \mathbf{B}_1, \mathbf{b}_1)$. Then the state-input constraint Q and the piecewise affine plant $\Sigma = (\mathcal{S}, \mathcal{D})$ can be transformed to Q^F and $\Sigma^F = (\mathcal{S}^F, \mathcal{D}^F)$, respectively, where

$$\begin{aligned} Q^F &= \{(\mathbf{x},\mathbf{v}) \in \mathbb{R}^n \times \mathbb{R}^m : \mathbf{v} = \mathbf{u} - \mathbf{K}\mathbf{x} - \mathbf{l}, (\mathbf{x},\mathbf{u}) \in Q\}, \\ \mathcal{S}^F &= \{(\mathbf{A}_1^F, \mathbf{B}_1^F, \mathbf{b}_1^F), \dots, (\mathbf{A}_N^F, \mathbf{B}_N^F, \mathbf{b}_N^F)\}, \\ \mathcal{D}^F &= \{D_1^F, \dots, D_N^F\} \end{aligned}$$

with

$$\begin{aligned} \mathbf{A}_i^F &= \mathbf{A}_i + \mathbf{B}_i\mathbf{K}, \\ \mathbf{B}_i^F = \mathbf{B}_i, &\quad \mathbf{b}_i^F = \mathbf{b}_i + \mathbf{B}_i\mathbf{l}, \\ D_i^F &= \{(\mathbf{x},\mathbf{v}) \in Q^F : \mathbf{v} = \mathbf{u} - \mathbf{K}\mathbf{x} - \mathbf{l}, (\mathbf{x},\mathbf{u}) \in D_i\} \end{aligned}$$

for $i = 1, \dots, N$. Whenever an open-loop control scheme generates an input sequence $u = (\mathbf{u}(0), \mathbf{u}(1), \dots)$ for an initial state $\mathbf{x}(0) \in \pi(Q)$, the system equation (1) can be rewritten as

$$\begin{aligned} \mathbf{x}(t+1) &= \mathbf{A}_{\theta(t)}^F \mathbf{x}(t) + \mathbf{B}_{\theta(t)}^F \mathbf{v}(t) + \mathbf{b}_{\theta(t)}^F, \quad t \in \mathbb{N}_0; \\ \theta(t) &= i \quad \text{if } (\mathbf{x}(t), \mathbf{v}(t)) \in D_i^F, \quad i \in \mathbb{N}, \ t \in \mathbb{N}_0, \end{aligned}$$

where

$$\mathbf{v}(t) = \mathbf{u}(t) - \mathbf{K}\mathbf{x}(t) - \mathbf{B}_{\theta(t)}\mathbf{l}, \quad t \in \mathbb{N}_0.$$

This along with $\pi(Q) = \pi(Q^F)$ indicates that, for $P \subset \pi(Q)$, the plant $\Sigma = (\mathcal{S}, \mathcal{D})$ is stabilizable on P if and only if the transformed plant $\Sigma^F = (\mathcal{S}^F, \mathcal{D}^F)$ is stabilizable on P. Therefore, we assume, without loss of generality, that the central cell D_1 of the initial state-input partition $\mathcal{D}$ is in fact stable in the following sense.

DEFINITION 6. *Cell $D_1 \in \mathcal{D}$ is said to be* stable *if the origin $(\mathbf{0}, \mathbf{0}) \in \operatorname{int}(D_1)$, the spectral radius of $\mathbf{A}_1$ is less than one, and the affine term $\mathbf{b}_1 = \mathbf{0}$.*

4.2 Maximal Invariant Set

There is a close link between the process of constructing symbolic models of the piecewise affine plant and that of computing the maximal invariant set characterized in [8]. For $L \in \mathbb{N}_0$, define

$$O_L = \{\mathbf{x} \in \mathbb{R}^n : \mathbf{A}_1^t \mathbf{x} \in \pi(D_1) \text{ for all } t = 0, \dots, L\}.$$

Then, for $L \in \mathbb{N}_0$ and $\mathbf{x} \in \mathbb{R}^n$, we have $\mathbf{x} \in O_{L+1}$ if and only if $\mathbf{x} \in O_L$ and $\mathbf{A}_1\mathbf{x} \in O_L$. It is well-known that, if D_1 is stable, then the limit

$$O_\infty = \bigcap_{L=0}^{\infty} O_L$$

is well-defined and finitely determined. The set O_∞ is the maximal invariant set within $\pi(D_1)$ under zero inputs.

LEMMA 1. *If $D_1 \in \mathcal{D}$ is stable, then there exists $L \in \mathbb{N}_0$ such that $O_L = O_{L+1}$, $\mathbf{0} \in \operatorname{int}(O_L)$, and $\mathbf{A}_1\mathbf{x} \in O_L$ for all $\mathbf{x} \in O_L$.*

PROOF. The result follows from [8, Theorem 4.1]. □

Suppose the symbolic model $\Sigma_L = (\mathcal{G}_L, \mathcal{D}_L)$ is given for some $L \in \mathbb{N}_0$, where $G_L = (V_L, E_L)$ is a directed graph with node set V_L and edge set E_L. Because the state-input partition $\mathcal{D}_L$ is permissible, an equivalence class of $D \in \mathcal{D}_L$ is given by $[D] = \{\widetilde{D} : \pi(D) = \pi(\widetilde{D})\}$. Let the set of all equivalence classes in $\mathcal{D}_L$ be $\{[D_{i_1}], \dots, [D_{i_p}]\}$, where p is the number of distinct equivalence classes in $\mathcal{D}_L$. Then

$$\Pi_L = \{\pi(D_{i_1}), \dots, \pi(D_{i_p})\} \tag{6}$$

is a partition of $\pi(Q)$. For $i \in V_L \setminus \{0\}$, define $R_L(i)$ as the the state-space projection of the union of all cells in $\mathcal{D}_L$ reachable from cell $D_i \in \mathcal{D}_L$; that is,

$$R_L(i) = \bigcup \{\pi(D_j) : (i,j) \in E_L, \ j \in V_L \setminus \{0\}\}.$$

LEMMA 2. *Let $L \in \mathbb{N}_0$. If $i \in V_L \setminus \{0\}$ and $k \in V_{L+1} \setminus \{0\}$ are such that $R_L(i) \neq \varnothing$ and $D_k \subset D_i$, then*

$$R_{L+1}(k) \subset \pi(D_j) \subset R_L(i)$$

for some $j \in V_L \setminus \{0\}$ such that $(i,j) \in E_L$.

PROOF. Since $R_L(i) \neq \varnothing$, the inclusion $\pi(D_j) \subset R_L(i)$ is always valid for some $j \in V_L$ satisfying $(i,j) \in E_L$. If $R_{L+1}(k) = \varnothing$, then the desired result holds trivially. Suppose $R_{L+1}(k) \neq \varnothing$. Because $\mathcal{D}_{L+1}$ is finer than $\widetilde{\mathcal{D}}_{L+1}$, we have $D_k \subset D_{(i,j)} \subset D_i$ for some $j \in V_L$. By the definition of $D_{(i,j)}$, every state-input pair in $D_{(i,j)}$ leads to a state in $\pi(D_j)$. Therefore, it follows from $D_k \subset D_{(i,j)}$ that $R_{L+1}(k) \subset \pi(D_j)$. This proves the desired result. □

LEMMA 3. *Let $L \in \mathbb{N}_0$. Suppose that there are p equivalence classes in $\mathcal{D}_L$, and that they define a partition Π_L of $\pi(Q)$ as in (6). If $D_1 \in \mathcal{D}$ is stable, then there exists $\Lambda \subset \{1, \dots, p\}$ such that*

$$O_L = \bigcup_{k \in \Lambda} \pi(D_{i_k}). \tag{7}$$

PROOF. We will prove the desired result by induction on L. If $L = 0$, then $O_0 = \pi(D_1)$, so it is clear that $O_0 = \pi(D_{i_k})$ for some $k \in \{1, \dots, p\}$. This forms the basis for induction. As an induction hypothesis, suppose that there exists Λ such that (7) holds for some $L \in \mathbb{N}_0$. Let

$$\Pi_{L+1} = \{\pi(D_{j_1}), \dots, \pi(D_{j_q})\}$$

be a partition of $\pi(Q)$ defined by q equivalent classes in $\mathcal{D}_{L+1}$. Define

$$\Delta = \{k \in \{1,\ldots,q\}\colon \pi(D_{j_k}) = \pi(D_i) \subset O_L,\ \pi(D_{j_k}) \times \{\mathbf{0}\} \subset D_i \subset D_1,\ R_{L+1}(i) \subset O_L,\ i \in V_{L+1} \setminus \{0\}\}.$$

The induction step is completed by showing that $O_{L+1} = \bigcup_{k\in\Delta} \pi(D_{j_k})$.

Suppose $\mathbf{x} \in \bigcup_{k\in\Delta} \pi(D_{j_k})$. Then $\mathbf{x} \in \pi(D_{j_k})$ for some $k \in \Delta$, so $\mathbf{x} \in O_L$. Moreover, given this k, there exists $i \in V_{L+1}$ such that $(\mathbf{x},\mathbf{0}) \in \pi(D_{j_k}) \times \{\mathbf{0}\} \subset D_i$ and $R_{L+1}(i) \subset O_L$, and so the fact that $(\mathbf{x},\mathbf{0}) \in D_i$ and $\mathbf{b}_1 = \mathbf{0}$ gives $\mathbf{A}_1\mathbf{x} \in R_{L+1}(i) \subset O_L$. Thus, we have $\mathbf{x}$, $\mathbf{A}_1\mathbf{x} \in O_L$, which implies $\mathbf{x} \in O_{L+1}$. This establishes that $\bigcup_{k\in\Delta} \pi(D_{j_k}) \subset O_{L+1}$.

Conversely, suppose $\mathbf{x} \in O_{L+1}$, so that $\mathbf{x}$, $\mathbf{A}_1\mathbf{x} \in O_L$. Because $\mathbf{x} \in O_L$, there exists $k \in \{1,\ldots,p\}$ such that $\mathbf{x} \in \pi(D_{i_k}) \subset O_L \subset \pi(D_1)$ by the induction hypothesis. As Π_{L+1} is finer than Π_L, this implies there exists $l \in \{1,\ldots,q\}$ such that $\mathbf{x} \in \pi(D_{j_l}) \subset \pi(D_{i_k}) \subset O_L \subset \pi(D_1)$. On the other hand, since $\pi(D_{i_k}) \subset \pi(D_1)$, the permissibility of $\mathcal{D}_L$ (i.e., condition (a) in Definition 5) guarantees the existence of $i \in V_L$ such that $(\mathbf{x},\mathbf{0}) \in \pi(D_{i_k}) \times \{\mathbf{0}\} \subset D_i \subset D_1$. Thus, the permissibility of $\mathcal{D}_{L+1}$ yields the existence of $j \in V_{L+1}$ such that $D_j \subset D_i$ and such that

$$\mathbf{x} \in \pi(D_{j_l}) = \pi(D_j) \subset O_L, \tag{8}$$

$$(\mathbf{x},\mathbf{0}) \in \pi(D_{j_l}) \times \{\mathbf{0}\} \subset D_j \subset D_1. \tag{9}$$

As $(\mathbf{x},\mathbf{0}) \subset D_i$ and $\mathbf{A}_1\mathbf{x} \in O_L \subset \pi(D_1)$, we have $R_L(i) \neq \varnothing$. Since $R_L(i) \neq \varnothing$ and $D_j \subset D_i$, it is deduced from Lemma 2 that $R_{L+1}(j) \subset \pi(D_{i_{\tilde{k}}})$ for some $\tilde{k} \in \{1,\ldots,p\}$. By (9), we have $\mathbf{A}_1\mathbf{x} \in R_{L+1}(j)$. This, along with $\mathbf{A}_1\mathbf{x} \in O_L$ and the induction hypothesis, implies that $\tilde{k}$ can be taken to satisfy $\mathbf{A}_1\mathbf{x} \in \pi(D_{i_{\tilde{k}}}) \subset O_L$, which yields

$$R_{L+1}(j) \subset \pi(D_{i_{\tilde{k}}}) \subset O_L. \tag{10}$$

Therefore, we conclude from (8)–(10) that $\mathbf{x} \in \bigcup_{k\in\Delta} \pi(D_{j_k})$, which establishes $O_{L+1} \subset \bigcup_{k\in\Delta} \pi(D_{j_k})$. □

4.3 Stabilizability of Piecewise Affine Plants

Given $L \in \mathbb{N}_0$, suppose that there are p equivalence classes in $\mathcal{D}_L$, and that they define a partition Π_L of $\pi(Q)$ as in (6). For $\Lambda \subset \{1,\ldots,p\}$, define

$$S_0(\Lambda) = I_0(\Lambda) = \Lambda,$$

and

$$I_{t+1}(\Lambda) = \Big\{k \in \{1,\ldots,p\} \setminus S_t(\Lambda)\colon \pi(D_{i_k}) = \pi(D_i),\ R_L(i) \neq \varnothing,\ R_L(i) \subset \bigcup_{l\in S_t(\Lambda)} \pi(D_{i_l}),\ i \in V_L \setminus \{0\}\Big\},$$

$$S_{t+1}(\Lambda) = S_t(\Lambda) \cup I_{t+1}(\Lambda)$$

for $t \in \mathbb{N}_0$.

What we can deduce from the symbolic model Σ_L is that, if $k \in S_t(\Lambda)$, then every state in $\pi(D_{i_k})$ can be steered to a state in $\pi(D_{i_l})$ for some $l \in \Lambda$ within t steps. The following theorem is based on the simulation relation between Σ_L and Σ, and presents a sufficient condition for the stabilizability of the piecewise affine plant.

Theorem 1. *Let $L \in \mathbb{N}_0$ and $P \subset \pi(Q)$. Suppose that there are p equivalence classes in $\mathcal{D}_L$, and that they define a partition Π_L of $\pi(Q)$ as in (6). Suppose that $D_1 \in \mathcal{D}$ is stable. The piecewise affine plant (1) is exponentially stabilizable on P with constraint Q if the following hold:*

(a) There exists $\Lambda \subset \{1,\ldots,p\}$ such that

$$\mathbf{A}_1\Big(\bigcup_{k\in\Lambda} \pi(D_{i_k})\Big) \subset \bigcup_{k\in\Lambda} \pi(D_{i_k}) \subset \pi(D_1).$$

(b) There exists $t \in \mathbb{N}_0$ such that

$$P \subset \bigcup_{k\in S_t(\Lambda)} \pi(D_{i_k}).$$

Proof. It is readily seen that there exists a $t^* \in \mathbb{N}_0$ such that $S_{t^*}(\Lambda) = S_{t^*+1}(\Lambda) = \cdots$. Choose any $\mathbf{x}(0) \in \bigcup_{k\in S_{t^*}(\Lambda)} \pi(D_{i_k})$. Then we have $\mathbf{x}(0) \in \bigcup_{k\in I_{t_1}(\Lambda)} \pi(D_{i_k})$ for some $t_1 \in \mathbb{N}_0$ with $0 \le t_1 \le t^*$. If $t_1 = 0$, then $\mathbf{x}(0) \in \bigcup_{k\in\Lambda} \pi(D_{i_k})$. Otherwise, the definition of $I_{t_1}(\Lambda)$ guarantees the existence of $i \in V_L \setminus \{0\}$ and $\mathbf{u}(0) \in \mathbb{R}^m$ such that $(\mathbf{x}(0),\mathbf{u}(0)) \in D_i \subset Q$, which implies that $(\mathbf{x}(0),\mathbf{u}(0))$ satisfies constraint Q, and that $\mathbf{x}(1) \in \bigcup_{k\in S_{t_1-1}(\Lambda)} \pi(D_{i_k})$. This in turn implies that $\mathbf{x}(1) \in \bigcup_{k\in I_{t_2}(\Lambda)} \pi(D_{i_k})$ for some $t_2 \in \mathbb{N}_0$ with $0 \le t_2 \le t_1 - 1$. Proceeding in this manner, and noting condition (a) and the stability of D_1, we conclude that there exist $\tau \in \mathbb{N}_0$ and $\mathbf{u}(0)$, $\mathbf{u}(1)$, $\ldots \in \mathbb{R}^m$, with $\mathbf{u}(\tau) = \mathbf{u}(\tau+1) = \cdots = \mathbf{0}$, such that $(\mathbf{x}(0),\mathbf{u}(0))$, $(\mathbf{x}(1),\mathbf{u}(1))$, $\ldots \in Q$ and such that $\mathbf{x}(\tau)$, $\mathbf{x}(\tau+1)$, $\ldots \in \bigcup_{k\in\Lambda} \pi(D_{i_k})$. Since D_1 is stable, and since $\tau \le t^*$ for the arbitrarily chosen $\mathbf{x}(0)$, we conclude that the piecewise affine plant (1) is exponentially stabilizable on $\bigcup_{k\in S_{t^*}(\Lambda)} \pi(D_{i_k})$ with constraint Q. This, along with condition (b), yields the desired result. □

This theorem is intuitive; condition (a) requires the existence of an invariant subset of the state space that contains the origin in its interior, and condition (b) guarantees that all initial states of our interest are steered to this invariant set in a finite, bounded number of steps. These conditions are easy to check as the cells in $\mathcal{D}_L$ are convex polytopes.

The following theorem says that, when Σ_L is a bisimulation, conditions (a) and (b) become necessary, as well as sufficient, for stabilizability.

Theorem 2. *Let $L \in \mathbb{N}_0$ and $P \subset \pi(Q)$. Suppose that there are p equivalence classes in $\mathcal{D}_L$, and that they define a partition Π_L of $\pi(Q)$ as in (6). Suppose that $D_1 \in \mathcal{D}$ is stable, and that the state-input partition $\mathcal{D}_L$ is Σ-invariant. The piecewise affine plant (1) is exponentially stabilizable on P with constraint Q if and only if conditions (a) and (b) in Theorem 1 hold.*

Proof. Sufficiency is immediate from Theorem 1. To prove necessity, suppose the piecewise affine plant is exponentially stabilizable on P with constraint Q. By Lemmas 1 and 3, the Σ-invariance of $\mathcal{D}_L$ and the stability of D_1 imply the existence of $\Lambda \subset \{1,\ldots,p\}$ such that

$$\mathbf{0} \in \operatorname{int}(O_\infty) \quad \text{and} \quad O_\infty = \bigcup_{k\in\Lambda} \pi(D_{i_k}) \subset \pi(D_1).$$

Thus, condition (a) holds.

It remains to show condition (b) holds. Since $\mathbf{x}(t) \to \mathbf{0}$ exponentially for all $\mathbf{x}(0) \in P$, where P is bounded and $\mathbf{0} \in \operatorname{int}(O_\infty) \subset \pi(D_1)$, there exists $\tau \in \mathbb{N}$ such that $\mathbf{x}(\tau) \in O_\infty$

for all $\mathbf{x}(0) \in P$. Let t^* be such that $S_{t^*}(\Lambda) = S_{t^*+1}(\Lambda) = \cdots$. Suppose there exists $\mathbf{x}(0) \in P \setminus \bigcup_{k \in S_{t^*}(\Lambda)} \pi(D_{i_k})$. Then, for some input sequence $u = (\mathbf{u}(0), \mathbf{u}(1), \ldots)$, the pair $(\mathbf{x}(0), u)$ satisfies constraint Q as well as $\mathbf{x}(\tau) \in O_\infty$. In particular, since $(\mathbf{x}(\tau-1), \mathbf{u}(\tau-1))$ satisfies constraint Q, and since $\mathcal{D}_L$ is Σ-invariant, we have that $(\mathbf{x}(\tau-1), \mathbf{u}(\tau-1)) \in D_k = D_i$ for some $i \in V_L$ and $k \in V_{L+1}$, and that $R_L(i) \neq \varnothing$. Then, by Lemma 2, there exists $j \in V_L$ with $(i,j) \in E_L$ such that $R_{L+1}(k) \subset \pi(D_j)$. Now, because $\mathbf{x}(\tau) \in O_\infty \subset \bigcup_{l \in S_{t^*}(\Lambda)} \pi(D_{i_l})$, we obtain

$$\mathbf{x}(\tau) \in R_{L+1}(k) \subset \pi(D_j) \subset \bigcup_{l \in S_{t^*}(\Lambda)} \pi(D_{i_l}),$$

which implies $\mathbf{x}(\tau-1) \in \bigcup_{l \in S_{t^*}(\Lambda)} \pi(D_{i_l})$. Proceeding in this manner leads to $\mathbf{x}(0) \in \bigcup_{l \in S_{t^*}(\Lambda)} \pi(D_{i_l})$, which is a contradiction. Therefore, condition (b) follows. □

4.4 Largest Stabilizable Region

In this subsection, our analysis of stabilizability is shown to be nonconservative in the sense that, in principle, it is capable of identifying the largest region of the state space on which the piecewise affine plant is stabilizable. For each $L \in \mathbb{N}_0$, let Λ^* be the maximal Λ satisfying condition (a) in Theorem 1, and define

$$P_L = \lim_{t \to \infty} \bigcup_{k \in S_t(\Lambda^*)} \pi(D_{i_k}).$$

The set P_L indicates the part of the stabilizable region in $\pi(Q)$ that can be determined based on the symbolic model Σ_L.

LEMMA 4. *If $D_1 \in \mathcal{D}$ is stable, then $P_L \subset P_{L+1}$ for all $L \in \mathbb{N}_0$ and $\mathbf{0} \in \mathrm{int}(P_L)$ for some $L \in \mathbb{N}_0$.*

PROOF. By construction, we have $P_L \subset P_{L+1}$ for all $L \in \mathbb{N}_0$. By Lemma 1, there exists $L \in \mathbb{N}_0$ such that $O_L = O_\infty$. By Lemma 3, we have $O_L = \bigcup_{k \in \Lambda^*} \pi(D_{i_k}) \subset P_L$. Therefore, it follows from $\mathbf{0} \in \mathrm{int}(O_L)$ that $\mathbf{0} \in \mathrm{int}(P_L)$. □

The following theorem characterizes the largest stabilizable domain as the limit

$$P_\infty = \bigcup_{L=0}^{\infty} P_L,$$

which is a well-defined, nonempty subset of $\pi(Q)$ due to Lemma 4. That is, our stabilizability analysis does not suffer from inherent conservatism.

THEOREM 3. *Suppose $D_1 \in \mathcal{D}$ is stable. The piecewise affine plant (1) is exponentially stabilizable on P_L with constraint Q for each $L \in \mathbb{N}_0$, and is not exponentially stabilizable on any nonempty subset of $\pi(Q) \setminus P_\infty$ with constraint Q.*

PROOF. It is immediate from Theorem 1 that, for each $L \in \mathbb{N}_0$, the piecewise affine plant is stabilizable on P_L with constraint Q. Suppose there is $T \subset \pi(Q)$ with $T \cap P_\infty = \varnothing$ such that the plant is stabilizable on T with constraint Q. We will show that this leads to a contradiction.

Choose $\mathbf{x}(0) \in T$. By Lemma 4, there exists $L \in \mathbb{N}_0$ such that $\mathbf{0} \in \mathrm{int}(O_\infty) = \mathrm{int}(O_L) \subset \mathrm{int}(P_L)$, and so there exist $\tau \in \mathbb{N}$ and an input sequence $u = (\mathbf{u}(0), \mathbf{u}(1), \ldots)$ such that $\mathbf{x}(\tau) \in P_L$ and such that $(\mathbf{x}(0), u)$ satisfies constraint Q. Letting (6) be the partition of $\pi(Q)$ induced by the equivalence classes of $\mathcal{D}_L$, this implies that $\mathbf{x}(\tau) \in \pi(D_{i_k})$ for some $k \in S_t(\Lambda^*)$ and $t \in \mathbb{N}_0$, and that $(\mathbf{x}(\tau-1), \mathbf{u}(\tau-1)) \in D_k \subset D_i$ for some $i \in V_L$ and $k \in V_{L+1}$. These inclusions lead to $\mathbf{x}(\tau) \in R_L(i) \cap R_{L+1}(k)$, so Lemma 2 gives $\mathbf{x}(\tau) \in R_{L+1}(k) \subset \pi(D_j)$ for some j satisfying $(i,j) \in E_L$. It follows from $\mathbf{x}(\tau) \in P_L$ and from the permissibility of $\mathcal{D}_L$ that D_j can be taken to satisfy $\pi(D_j) = \pi(D_{i_l})$ for some $l \in S_{t^*}(\Lambda^*)$, where t^* is such that $S_{t^*}(\Lambda^*) = S_{t^*+1}(\Lambda^*) = \cdots$. Thus, by Lemma 4, we have $R_{L+1}(k) \subset \pi(D_j) \subset P_L \subset P_{L+1}$. On the other hand, the permissibility of $\mathcal{D}_{L+1}$, along with $(\mathbf{x}(\tau-1), \mathbf{u}(\tau-1)) \in D_k$, gives $\mathbf{x}(\tau-1) \in \pi(D_k)$. Now, it follows from $R_{L+1}(k) \subset P_{L+1}$ and $\mathbf{x}(\tau-1) \in \pi(D_k)$ that we must have $\mathbf{x}(\tau-1) \in P_{L+1}$. Proceeding in this manner, we conclude $\mathbf{x}(0) \in P_{L+\tau}$, which is a contradiction. □

4.5 Algorithm for Stabilizability Analysis

The analysis results presented so far lead to a scalable mathematical program for analyzing the stabilizability of a piecewise affine plant—see Algorithm 1. The algorithm assumes that the initial state-input partition $\mathcal{D}$ has a central cell D_1 which is stable. However, this assumption is not restrictive in the sense that the stabilizable domain P_∞ of the state space is independent of the feedback pair $(\mathbf{K}, \mathbf{l})$ that might have been used for the purpose of stabilizing the triple $(\mathbf{A}_1, \mathbf{B}_1, \mathbf{b}_1)$.

Algorithm 1 Analysis of Stabilizability

0. Set $L = 0$.
1. Construct the symbolic model Σ_L of the plant Σ.
2. Use Σ_L to obtain a subset P_L of the stabilizable domain.
3. [Case of bisimulation] If $\mathcal{D}_L$ is Σ-invariant, then stop.
4. [Case of simulation] If P_L is large enough or if the cost for computing P_{L+1} is prohibitive, then stop.
5. [Refinement of simulation] If P_L is too small and if there are sufficient computational resources, increment L to $L+1$ and go to Step 1.

PROPOSITION 1. *Suppose $D_1 \in \mathcal{D}$ is stabilizable. Let $F_1 = (\mathbf{K}_1, \mathbf{l}_1)$ and $F_2 = (\mathbf{K}_2, \mathbf{l}_2)$ be two stabilizing pairs for the triple $(\mathbf{A}_1, \mathbf{B}_1, \mathbf{b}_1)$. For $L \in \mathbb{N}_0$ and $i = 1, 2$, let $P_L^{F_i}$ be the stabilizable region that the symbolic model $\Sigma_L^{F_i}$ yields as in Step 1 of Algorithm 1. Then*

$$\bigcup_{L=0}^{\infty} P_L^{F_1} = \bigcup_{L=0}^{\infty} P_L^{F_2}.$$

PROOF. It suffices to show that, for each $L \in \mathbb{N}_0$, we have $P_L^{F_1} \subset \bigcup_{M=0}^{\infty} P_M^{F_2}$. Choose $L \in \mathbb{N}_0$ and $\mathbf{x}(0) \in P_L^{F_1}$. Then there exists an input sequence $v_1 = (\mathbf{v}_1(0), \mathbf{v}_1(1), \ldots)$ that stabilizes the transformed plant Σ^{F_1} on $\{\mathbf{x}(0)\}$ with constraint Q^{F_1}. This implies that the input sequence $\mathbf{u}(0) = \mathbf{v}_1(0) + \mathbf{K}_1\mathbf{x}(0) + \mathbf{l}_1$, $\mathbf{u}(1) = \mathbf{v}_1(1) + \mathbf{K}_1\mathbf{x}(0) + \mathbf{l}_1, \ldots$ stabilizes the plant Σ on $\{\mathbf{x}(0)\}$ with constraint Q. This in turn implies that the input sequence $v_2 = (\mathbf{v}_2(0), \mathbf{v}_2(1), \ldots)$, with $\mathbf{v}_2(0) = \mathbf{u}(0) - \mathbf{K}_2\mathbf{x}(0) - \mathbf{b}_2$, $\mathbf{v}_2(1) = \mathbf{u}(1) - \mathbf{K}_2\mathbf{x}(1) - \mathbf{b}_2$, ..., stabilizes the transformed plant Σ^{F_2} on $\{\mathbf{x}(0)\}$ with constraint Q^{F_2}. Therefore, Theorem 3 gives $\mathbf{x}(0) \in \bigcup_{M=0}^{\infty} P_M^{F_2}$, which establishes the desired result. □

5. STABILIZING CONTROLLERS

5.1 Algorithm for Controller Synthesis

Whenever the piecewise affine plant is stabilizable on a region with an input-output constraint, the plant admits a piecewise affine feedback controller that stabilizes the plant on the same region and satisfies the same constraint. To see this, suppose $D_1 \in \mathcal{D}$ is stable and fix $L \in \mathbb{N}_0$. Let $i \in V_L$ be such that $\pi(D_i) \subset P_L$, and let $j \in V_L$ be such that $(i, j) \in E_L$. Suppose $\pi(D_{(i,j)})$ has nonempty interior. If $\pi(D_{(i,j)})$ has vertices $\mathbf{v}_1, \ldots, \mathbf{v}_{m+1} \in \mathbb{R}^n$, then there exist $\mathbf{u}_1, \ldots, \mathbf{u}_{m+1} \in \mathbb{R}^m$ such that

$$(\mathbf{v}_k, \mathbf{u}_k) \in D_i, \quad \mathbf{A}_{o(i)}\mathbf{v}_k + \mathbf{B}_{o(i)}\mathbf{u}_k + \mathbf{b}_{o(i)} \in \pi(D_j) \quad (11)$$

for $k = 1, \ldots, m + 1$.

If $m \leq n$, then the linear independence of the vectors $\mathbf{v}_2 - \mathbf{v}_1, \mathbf{v}_3 - \mathbf{v}_1, \ldots, \mathbf{v}_{m+1} - \mathbf{v}_1$ implies that there exists a solution $(\mathbf{K}, \mathbf{l})$ to the equation

$$\begin{bmatrix} \mathbf{u}_1^{\mathrm{T}} \\ \vdots \\ \mathbf{u}_{m+1}^{\mathrm{T}} \end{bmatrix} = \begin{bmatrix} \mathbf{v}_1^{\mathrm{T}} & 1 \\ \vdots & \vdots \\ \mathbf{v}_{m+1}^{\mathrm{T}} & 1 \end{bmatrix} \begin{bmatrix} \mathbf{K}^{\mathrm{T}} \\ \mathbf{l}^{\mathrm{T}} \end{bmatrix}.$$

This means that an affine feedback law of the form

$$\mathbf{u}(t) = \mathbf{K}\mathbf{x}(t) + \mathbf{l}, \quad t \in \mathbb{N}_0,$$

steers all states $\mathbf{x}(t) \in \pi(D_{(i,j)})$ to $\mathbf{x}(t+1) \in \pi(D_j)$ in one step.

On the other hand, if $m > n$, then split $\pi(D_{(i,j)})$ into simplicies (i.e., n-dimensional polytopes with $n+1$ vertices) and form a simplicial partition $\mathcal{X} = \{X_1, \ldots, X_M\}$ of $\pi(D_{(i,j)})$. This way, we can associate each simplex $X \in \mathcal{X}$ with an affine feedback law that steers all states in X to $\pi(D_j)$ in one step. In other words, there exists a piecewise affine feedback law of the form

$$\mathbf{u}(t) = \mathbf{K}_{\sigma(t)}\mathbf{x}(t) + \mathbf{l}_{\sigma(t)}, \quad t \in \mathbb{N}_0,$$

where $\sigma(t) = j$ when $\mathbf{x}(t) \in X_j$ for $j = 1, \ldots, M$, that steers all $\mathbf{x}(t) \in \pi(D_{(i,j)})$ to $\mathbf{x}(t+1) \in \pi(D_j)$ in one step.

The above arguments suggest that stabilizability implies the following: (a) A stabilizing feedback controller exists; and (b) a guaranteed algorithm for synthesizing a stabilizing, piecewise affine feedback controller exists. Algorithm 2 is such an algorithm. It assumes D_1 is stable, and summarizes the synthesis steps discussed above for stabilizing the plant on P_L with constraint Q.

5.2 Numerical Example

This section is devoted to illustrating the main results by a simple numerical example. Let the state and input spaces be the real lines (i.e., $n = m = 1$). Let the state-input constraint be given by the box

$$Q = \{(x, u) \in \mathbb{R}^2 \colon -1 \leq x \leq 1, -1 \leq u \leq 1\},$$

which is partitioned into $N = 4$ cells $D_1, \ldots, D_4$ with

$$\mathrm{int}(D_1) = \{(x, u) \in \mathbb{R}^2 \colon -0.5 < x < 0.5, -1 < u < 1\},$$
$$\mathrm{int}(D_2) = \{(x, u) \in \mathbb{R}^2 \colon 0.5 < x < 1, (x-1)/3 < u < 1\},$$
$$\mathrm{int}(D_3) = \{(x, u) \in \mathbb{R}^2 \colon 0.5 < x < 1, -1 < u < (x-1)/3\},$$
$$\mathrm{int}(D_4) = \{(x, u) \in \mathbb{R}^2 \colon -1 < x < -0.5, -1 < u < 1\}.$$

Algorithm 2 Synthesis of Stabilizing Controller

0. For some $L \in \mathbb{N}_0$, obtain a nonempty
$$P_L = \bigcup_{t=0}^{t^*} \bigcup_{k \in I_t(\Lambda^*)} \pi(D_{i_k})$$
based on Σ_L. Put $t = 0$. Assign the zero control input to $\bigcup_{k \in I_0(\Lambda^*)} \pi(D_{i_k})$.

1. If $t = t^*$ or $I_{t+1}(\Lambda^*) = \varnothing$, then stop; otherwise, put
$$\Omega = \bigcup_{k \in I_t(\Lambda^*)} \pi(D_{i_k}).$$

2. For each $k \in I_{t+1}(\Lambda^*)$, obtain a simplicial refinement $\mathcal{X}$ of $\pi(D_{i_k})$, and assign a piecewise affine control to each $X \in \mathcal{X}$, so that the states in X are steered to Ω in one step.

3. Increment t to $t + 1$. Go to Step 1.

Let the piecewise affine plant Σ be defined as

$$x(t+1) = \begin{cases} -0.5x(t) + 0.5u(t), & (x(t), u(t)) \in D_1; \\ -x(t) + u(t), & (x(t), u(t)) \in D_2; \\ 2x(t) - 2u(t) + 3, & (x(t), u(t)) \in D_3; \\ -0.5x(t) + u(t), & (x(t), u(t)) \in D_4. \end{cases}$$

The first four partitions $\mathcal{D}_0, \mathcal{D}_1, \mathcal{D}_2, \mathcal{D}_3$ of Q, where $\mathcal{D}_0 = \mathcal{D} = \{D_1, D_2, D_3, D_4\}$, are shown in Figure 1, and the first three associated directed graphs G_0, G_1, G_2 are shown in Figure 2. It is readily seen that the maximal invariant set in $\pi(D_1)$ is equal to $\Omega_\infty = \pi(D_1)$. The graph G_0 indicates that none of the cells D_2, D_3, D_4 leads solely to $\pi(D_1)$ in one step, so the stabilizable region that can be obtained from the symbolic model $\Sigma_0 = (G_0, \mathcal{D}_0)$ is $P_0 = \pi(D_1)$.

Note that cells D_2 and D_4 in $\mathcal{D}_0$ can potentially be stabilizable because nodes 2 and 4 in G_0 have outgoing edges that are incident to node 1. This observation is verified when $L = 1$. The refined state-input partition $\mathcal{D}_1$ shows that cells D_2 and D_4 split into smaller cells, among which D_9 and D_{12} are identified as stabilizable. Since $\pi(D_1)$, $\pi(D_9)$, and $\pi(D_{12})$ cover the entire state space $\pi(Q) = [-1, 1]$ (i.e., $P_1 = \pi(Q)$), the symbolic model $\Sigma_1 = (G_1, \mathcal{D}_1)$, which merely simulates the plant Σ, suffices for the purpose of finding the maximal stabilizable region. As $\mathcal{D}_2$ and $\mathcal{D}_3$ define two identical partitions of Q, the partition $\mathcal{D}_2$ is Σ-invariant, and so Σ_2 is a bisimulation.

We have determined that the piecewise affine plant is stabilizable on $[-1, 1]$, which is partitioned into three regions $\pi(D_1) = [-0.5, 0.5]$, $\pi(D_9) = [0.5, 1]$, and $\pi(D_{12}) = [-1, -0.5]$. First, we assign the zero input to the first region. Next, observing that the vertices $v_1 = 0.5$ and $v_2 = 1$ of $\pi(D_9)$ can be transferred to $\pi(D_1)$ with inputs $u_1 = 0.5$ and $u_2 = 0.8$, respectively, we solve

$$\begin{bmatrix} 0.5 \\ 0.8 \end{bmatrix} = \begin{bmatrix} 0.5 & 1 \\ 1 & 1 \end{bmatrix} \begin{bmatrix} k \\ l \end{bmatrix}$$

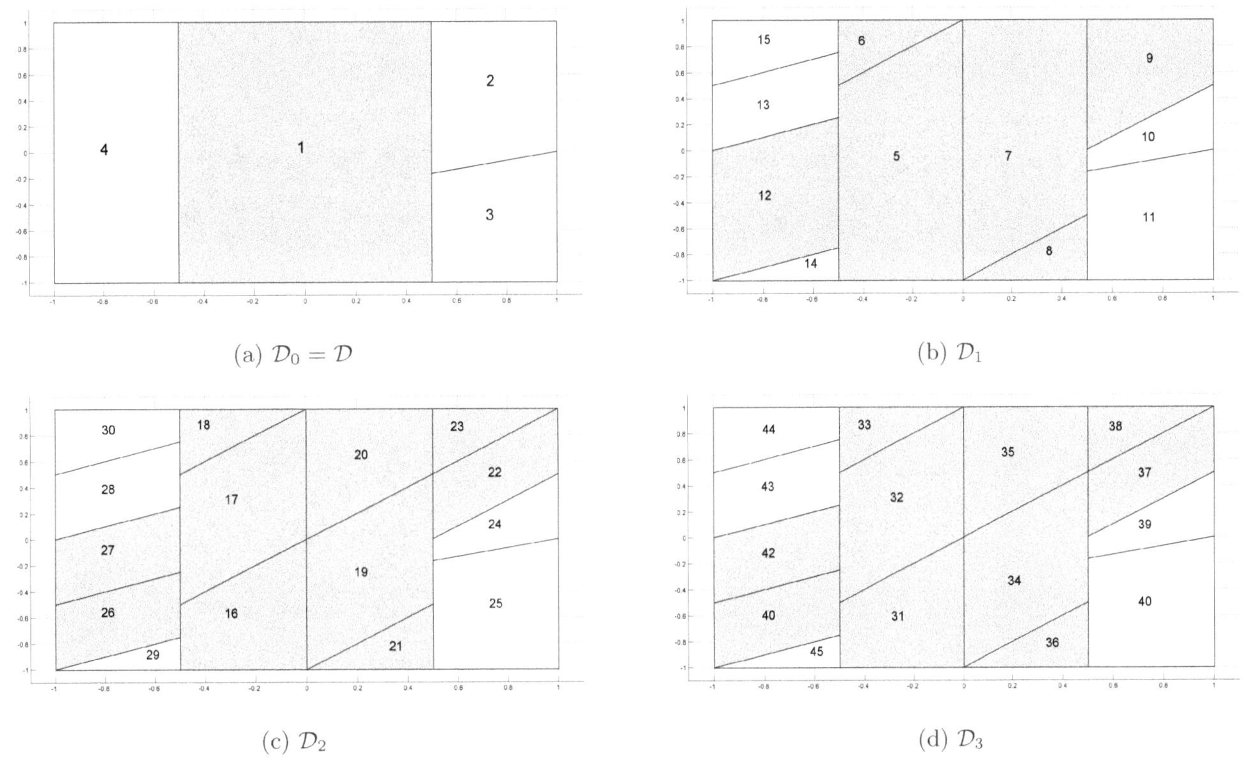

(a) $\mathcal{D}_0 = \mathcal{D}$

(b) $\mathcal{D}_1$

(c) $\mathcal{D}_2$

(d) $\mathcal{D}_3$

Figure 1: An increasing sequence of partitions $\mathcal{D}_0$, $\mathcal{D}_1$, $\mathcal{D}_2$, $\mathcal{D}_3$ of the state-input constraint set Q for the piecewise affine plant Σ in Section 5.2. The cells identified to be stabilizable by the corresponding symbolic models Σ_L are marked in gray. Partition $\mathcal{D}_2$ is Σ-invariant.

and obtain controller coefficients $k = 0.6$ and $l = 0.2$ for the region $\pi(D_9)$. Similarly, we solve

$$\begin{bmatrix} -0.4 \\ -0.4 \end{bmatrix} = \begin{bmatrix} -0.5 & 1 \\ -1 & 1 \end{bmatrix} \begin{bmatrix} k \\ l \end{bmatrix}$$

and obtain $k = 0$ and $l = -0.4$ for the region $\pi(D_{12})$. The resulting, stabilizing state-feedback controller is

$$u(t) = \begin{cases} -0.4 & x(t) \in [-1, -0.5), \\ 0 & x(t) \in [-0.5, 0.5], \\ 0.6x(t) + 0.2 & x(t) \in (0.5, 1]. \end{cases}$$

6. CONCLUSIONS

We analyzed the stabilizability of piecewise affine plants, and the feasibility of a state-input constraint, based on an increasing sequence of symbolic models that simulate the plant. A remarkable result was that this approach is, in principle, capable of identifying the largest region of the state space, on which the plant is stabilizable. We also showed that, whenever the piecewise affine plant is stabilizable on a region under a state-input constraint, a piecewise affine feedback controller stabilizes the system on the same region and satisfies the same constraint. A guaranteed method for synthesizing such a controller was shown.

A future research direction is to generalize the presented results to dynamic output feedback control and to performance optimization subject to stability. Another research direction is to relax the assumption that the state-input partition has a central cell that contains the origin in its interior; this will require discovery and creation of synergy between symbolic abstraction and Lyapunov analysis of piecewise affine systems.

7. ACKNOWLEDGMENTS

The authors thank the anonymous reviewers for their insightful comments and suggestions. The second author acknowledges discussions with Sanam Mirzazad-Barijough about some of the existing polyhedral algorithms, which are detailed in [2, 7] and form an integral part of this work.

8. REFERENCES

[1] R. Alur, T. Henzinger, G. Lafferriere, and G. Pappas. Discrete abstractions of hybrid systems. *Proceedings of the IEEE*, 88(7):971–984, 2000.

[2] D. Avis and K. Fukuda. Reverse search for enumeration. *Discrete Applied Mathematics*, 65(1–3):21–46, 1996.

[3] A. Bemporad, G. Ferrari-Trecate, and M. Morari. Observability and controllability of piecewise affine and hybrid systems. *IEEE Transactions on Automatic Control*, 45(10):1864–1876, 2000.

[4] A. Bemporad and M. Morari. Control of systems integrating logic, dynamics, and constraints. *Automatica*, 35(3):407–427, 1999.

[5] S. Boyd, L. El Ghaoui, E. Feron, and V. Balakrishnan. *Linear Matrix Inequalities in System and Control Theory*, volume 15 of *Studies in Applied Mathematics*. SIAM, Philadelphia, PA, 1994.

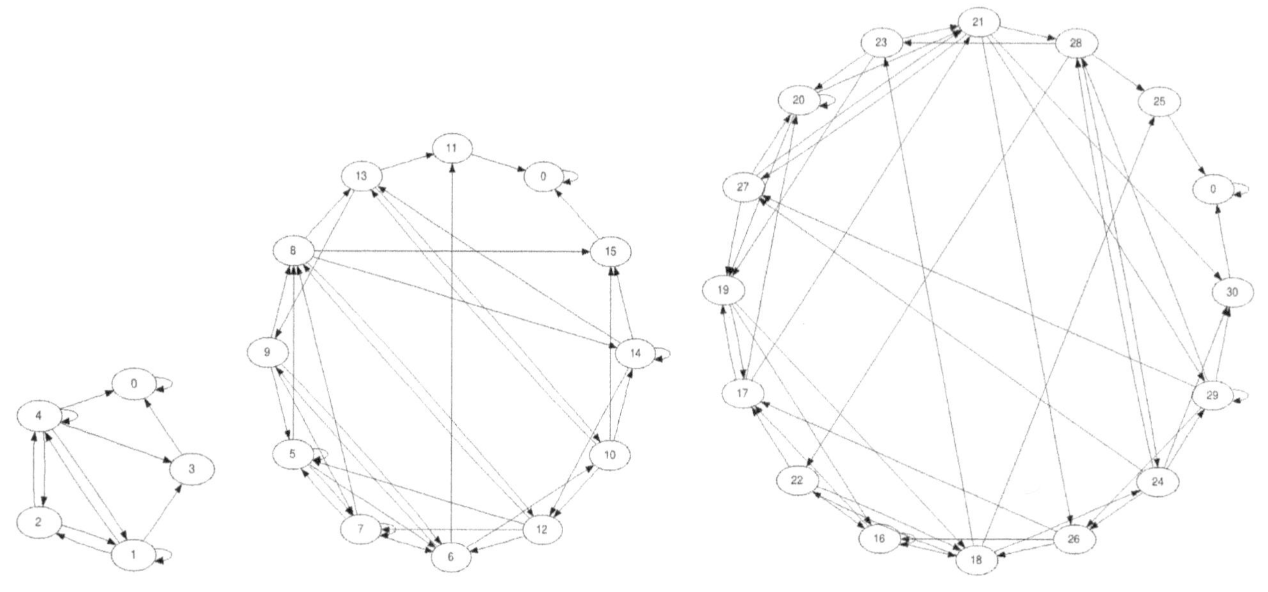

(a) G_0 (b) G_1 (c) G_2

Figure 2: The directed graphs G_0, G_1, G_2 associated with the state-input partitions $\mathcal{D}_L$ in Figure 1. While the symbolic model $\Sigma_2 = (G_2, \mathcal{D}_2)$ defines a bisimulation of the piecewise affine plant Σ in Section 5.2, the symbolic model $\Sigma_1 = (G_1, \mathcal{D}_1)$, which is a simulation of Σ, suffices for the purpose of stabilizing controller synthesis.

[6] F. A. Cuzzola and M. Morari. A generalized approach for analysis and control of discrete-time piecewise affine and hybrid systems. In M. D. Di Benedetto and A. Sangiovanni-Vincentelli, editors, *Hybrid Systems: Computation and Control*, volume 2034 of *Lecture Notes in Computer Science*, pages 189–203, London, UK, 2001. Springer-Verlag.

[7] T. Geyer, F. D. Torrisi, and M. Morari. Optimal complexity reduction of polyhedral piecewise affine systems. *Automatica*, 44(7):1728–1740, 2008.

[8] E. G. Gilbert and K. T. Tan. Linear systems with state and control constraints: The theory and application of maximal output admissible sets. *IEEE Transactions on Automatic Control*, 36(9):1008–1020, 1991.

[9] A. Girard and G. J. Pappas. Approximation metrics for discrete and continuous systems. *IEEE Transactions on Automatic Control*, 52(5):782–798, 2007.

[10] E. A. Gol, X. Ding, M. Lazar, and C. belta. Finite bisimulations for switched linear systems. In *Proceedings of the 51st IEEE Conference on Decision and Control*, pages 7632–7637, 2012.

[11] M. Lazar and A. Jokić. A generating function approach to the stability of discrete-time switched linear systems. In *Proceedings of the 13th ACM International Conference on Hybrid Systems: Computation and Control*, pages 131–140, 2010.

[12] D. Q. Mayne and S. Raković. Model predictive control of constrained piecewise affine discrete-time systems. *International Journal of Robust and Nonlinear Control*, 13(3–4):261–279, 2003.

[13] D. Mignone, G. Ferrari-Trecate, and M. Morari. Stability and stabilization of piecewise affine and hybrid systems: An LMI approach. In *Proceedings of the 39th IEEE Conference on Decision and Control*, volume 1, pages 504–509, 2000.

[14] S. Mirzazad-Barijough and J.-W. Lee. Robust stability and performance analysis of discrete-time piecewise affine systems with disturbances. In *Proceedings of the 51st IEEE Conference on Decision and Control*, pages 4229–4234, 2012.

[15] S. Mirzazad-Barijough and J.-W. Lee. Stability and transient performance of discrete-time piecewise affine systems. *IEEE Transactions on Automatic Control*, 57(4):936–949, 2012.

[16] P. Prabhakar, G. Dullerud, and M. Viswanathan. Pre-orders for reasoning about stability. In *Proceedings of the 15th ACM International Conference on Hybrid Systems: Computation and Control*, pages 197–206, 2012.

[17] E. D. Sontag. Nonlinear regulation: The piecewise linear approach. *IEEE Transactions on Automatic Control*, 26(2):346–358, 1981.

[18] P. Tabuada. Controller synthesis for bisimulation equivalence. *Systems & Control Letters*, 57(6):443–452, 2008.

[19] B. Yordanov and C. Belta. Formal analysis of discrete-time piecewise affine systems. *IEEE Transactions on Automatic Control*, 55(12):2834–2840, 2010.

[20] B. Yordanov, J. Tumova, I. Cerna, J. Barnat, and C. Belta. Temporal logic control of discrete-time piecewise affine systems. *IEEE Transactions on Automatic Control*, 57(6):1491–1504, 2012.

Bisimilar Symbolic Models for Stochastic Control Systems without State-Space Discretization *

Majid Zamani
Delft University of Technology
m.zamani@tudelft.nl

Ilya Tkachev
Delft University of Technology
i.tkachev@tudelft.nl

Alessandro Abate
University of Oxford
alessandro.abate@cs.ox.ac.uk

ABSTRACT

In the past few years different techniques have been developed for constructively deriving symbolic abstractions of (stochastic) control systems. The obtained symbolic models allow us to leverage the apparatus of finite-state reactive synthesis towards the problem of designing hybrid controllers enforcing rich logic specifications over the concrete models. Unfortunately, most of the existing techniques severely suffer from the curse of dimensionality due to the need to discretize state and input sets. In this paper we provide a symbolic abstraction technique for incrementally stable stochastic control systems, which only requires discretizing input sets. We show that for every incrementally stable stochastic control system, and for every given positive precision ε, the discretization of exclusively the input set allows constructing a symbolic model which is ε-approximate bisimilar (in moments) to the original stochastic control system. The details of the proposed technique are elucidated by synthesizing a control policy for a 6-dimensional linear stochastic control system satisfying some logic specifications, which would not be tractable using existing approaches based on state-space discretization.

1. INTRODUCTION

In the last decade several abstraction techniques have been developed, providing symbolic models for (stochastic) control systems obtained by replacing aggregates or collections of states of such systems by symbols. When a system with a finite number of states is obtained, one can use mature methodologies available in the literature [9] to leverage fixed-point computations in order to synthesize hybrid controllers enforcing rich complex specifications over the original system. Examples of such specifications include properties expressed as formulas in linear temporal logic (LTL) or as automata on infinite strings.

*This work is supported by the European Commission STREP project MoVeS 257005 and IAPP project AMBI 324432.

HSCC'14, April 15–17, 2014, Berlin, Germany.

http://dx.doi.org/10.1145/2562059.2562115.

The construction of symbolic models has been studied extensively for *continuous-time* non-probabilistic systems. This includes results on the construction of approximately bisimilar symbolic abstractions for incrementally stable control systems [8, 12], switched systems [4], and control systems with disturbances [13], as well as the construction of sound abstractions based on the convexity of reachable sets [14] and for unstable control systems [20]. Recently, there have been some results on the construction of symbolic models for *continuous-time* stochastic systems, including the construction of approximately bisimilar (in moments) symbolic models for incrementally stable stochastic control systems [18, 19] and for stochastic switched systems [16], as well as sound abstractions for unstable stochastic control systems [17]. The results in [6] propose abstraction notions for continuous-time stochastic hybrid systems, but with a different purpose: while we are interested in the construction of bisimilar abstractions that are finite, the work in [6] uses the notion of bisimulation to relate continuous (and thus infinite) stochastic hybrid systems. Note that all the abstraction techniques provided in [4, 8, 12, 13, 14, 16, 17, 18, 19, 20] are based on the discretization of state and input sets. Therefore, they suffer severely from *the curse of dimensionality* due to the need to grid both sets, which is especially tolling for models with high-dimensional state spaces.

In this paper, we construct approximately bisimilar symbolic models for incrementally stable continuous-time stochastic control systems, where only the input set requires to be discretized. This work is inspired by the recently proposed result in [2] for discrete-time non-probabilistic switched systems, in which mode sequences of a given length are considered as symbolic states. Since in the new approach we do not discretize the state space, this is potentially more efficient than the one proposed in [18, 19] when dealing with higher dimensional continuous-time stochastic systems. We provide a simple criterion that helps choosing the the most suitable among two approaches (in terms of the sizes of the symbolic models) for a given stochastic control system. Another advantage of the technique proposed here is that it allows us to construct symbolic models with probabilistic output values, resulting in less conservative symbolic abstractions than those proposed in [16, 17, 18, 19] that allow for non-probabilistic output values exclusively. We then explain how the proposed symbolic models with probabilistic output values can be used for synthesizing hybrid controllers enforcing logic specifications. The effectiveness of the proposed results is illustrated by synthesizing a control policy for a simple 6-dimensional linear stochastic control system against an LTL specification, which is not amenable to be dealt with the approaches proposed in [18, 19]. Due to space constraints, most of the proofs of the main results are omitted from this manuscript.

2. STOCHASTIC CONTROL SYSTEMS

2.1 Notation

The identity map on a set A is denoted by 1_A. The symbols $\mathbb{N}$, $\mathbb{N}_0$, $\mathbb{Z}$, $\mathbb{R}$, $\mathbb{R}^+$, and $\mathbb{R}_0^+$ denote the set of natural, nonnegative integer, integer, real, positive, and nonnegative real numbers, respectively. The symbols I_n, 0_n, and $0_{n\times m}$ denote the identity matrix, zero vector, and zero matrix in $\mathbb{R}^{n\times n}$, $\mathbb{R}^n$, and $\mathbb{R}^{n\times m}$, respectively. Given a vector $x\in\mathbb{R}^n$, we denote by x_i the i-th element of x, and by $\|x\|$ the infinity norm of x, namely, $\|x\|=\max\{|x_1|,|x_2|,...,|x_n|\}$, where $|x_i|$ denotes the absolute value of x_i. Given a matrix $P=\{p_{ij}\}\in\mathbb{R}^{n\times n}$, we denote by $\text{Tr}(P)=\sum_{i=1}^n p_{ii}$ the trace of P. We denote by $\lambda_{\min}(A)$ and $\lambda_{\max}(A)$ the minimum and maximum eigenvalues of symmetric matrix A, respectively. The diagonal set $\Delta\subset\mathbb{R}^n\times\mathbb{R}^n$ is defined as: $\Delta=\{(x,x)\mid x\in\mathbb{R}^n\}$.

The closed ball centered at $x\in\mathbb{R}^m$ with radius λ is defined by $\mathcal{B}_\lambda(x)=\{y\in\mathbb{R}^m\mid \|x-y\|\leq\lambda\}$. A set $B\subseteq\mathbb{R}^m$ is called a *box* if $B=\prod_{i=1}^m[c_i,d_i]$, where $c_i,d_i\in\mathbb{R}$ with $c_i<d_i$ for each $i\in\{1,\ldots,m\}$. The *span* of a box B is defined as $span(B)=\min\{|d_i-c_i|\mid i=1,\ldots,m\}$. For a box $B\subseteq\mathbb{R}^m$ and $\mu\leq span(B)$, define the μ-approximation $[B]_\mu=[\mathbb{R}^m]_\mu\cap B$, where $[\mathbb{R}^m]_\mu=\{a\in\mathbb{R}^m\mid a_i=k_i\mu, k_i\in\mathbb{Z}, i=1,\ldots,m\}$. Note that $[B]_\mu\neq\varnothing$ for any $\mu\leq span(B)$. Geometrically, for any $\mu\in\mathbb{R}^+$ with $\mu\leq span(B)$ and $\lambda\geq\mu$, the collection of sets $\{\mathcal{B}_\lambda(p)\}_{p\in[B]_\mu}$ is a finite covering of B, i.e. $B\subseteq\bigcup_{p\in[B]_\mu}\mathcal{B}_\lambda(p)$. We extend the notions of *span* and *approximation* to finite unions of boxes as follows. Let $A=\bigcup_{j=1}^M A_j$, where each A_j is a box. Define $span(A)=\min\{span(A_j)\mid j=1,\ldots,M\}$, and for any $\mu\leq span(A)$, define $[A]_\mu=\bigcup_{j=1}^M[A_j]_\mu$.

Given a measurable function $f:\mathbb{R}_0^+\rightarrow\mathbb{R}^n$, the (essential) supremum of f is denoted by $\|f\|_\infty:=\text{(ess)sup}\{\|f(t)\|, t\geq 0\}$. A continuous function $\gamma:\mathbb{R}_0^+\rightarrow\mathbb{R}_0^+$, is said to belong to class $\mathcal{K}$ if it is strictly increasing and $\gamma(0)=0$; γ is said to belong to class $\mathcal{K}_\infty$ if $\gamma\in\mathcal{K}$ and $\gamma(r)\rightarrow\infty$ as $r\rightarrow\infty$. A continuous function $\beta:\mathbb{R}_0^+\times\mathbb{R}_0^+\rightarrow\mathbb{R}_0^+$ is said to belong to class $\mathcal{KL}$ if, for each fixed s, the map $\beta(r,s)$ belongs to class $\mathcal{K}$ with respect to r and, for each fixed nonzero r, the map $\beta(r,s)$ is decreasing with respect to s and $\beta(r,s)\rightarrow 0$ as $s\rightarrow\infty$. We identify a relation $R\subseteq A\times B$ with the map $R:A\rightarrow 2^B$ defined by $b\in R(a)$ iff $(a,b)\in R$. Given a relation $R\subseteq A\times B$, R^{-1} denotes the inverse relation defined by $R^{-1}=\{(b,a)\in B\times A:(a,b)\in R\}$.

2.2 Stochastic control systems

Let $(\Omega,\mathcal{F},\mathbb{P})$ be a probability space endowed with a filtration $\mathbb{F}=(\mathcal{F}_s)_{s\geq0}$ satisfying the usual conditions of completeness and right continuity [7, p. 48]. Let $(W_s)_{s\geq0}$ be a p-dimensional $\mathbb{F}$-adapted Brownian motion.

Definition 2.1. *A stochastic control system is a tuple $\Sigma=(\mathbb{R}^n,\mathsf{U},\mathcal{U},f,\sigma)$, where*

- *$\mathbb{R}^n$ is the state space;*
- *$\mathsf{U}\subseteq\mathbb{R}^m$ is a compact input set;*
- *$\mathcal{U}$ is a subset of the set of all measurable functions of time from $\mathbb{R}_0^+$ to U;*
- *$f:\mathbb{R}^n\times\mathsf{U}\rightarrow\mathbb{R}^n$ satisfies the following Lipschitz assumption: there exist constants $L_x,L_u\in\mathbb{R}^+$ such that: $\|f(x,u)-f(x',u')\|\leq L_x\|x-x'\|+L_u\|u-u'\|$ for all $x,x'\in\mathbb{R}^n$ and all $u,u'\in\mathsf{U}$;*
- *$\sigma:\mathbb{R}^n\rightarrow\mathbb{R}^{n\times p}$ satisfies the following Lipschitz assumption: there exists a constant $Z\in\mathbb{R}^+$ such that: $\|\sigma(x)-\sigma(x')\|\leq Z\|x-x'\|$ for all $x,x'\in\mathbb{R}^n$.*

A continuous-time stochastic process $\xi:\Omega\times\mathbb{R}_0^+\rightarrow\mathbb{R}^n$ is said to be a *solution process* of Σ if there exists $\upsilon\in\mathcal{U}$ satisfying the following stochastic differential equation (SDE):

$$\mathrm{d}\xi=f(\xi,\upsilon)\,\mathrm{d}t+\sigma(\xi)\,\mathrm{d}W_t, \tag{2.1}$$

$\mathbb{P}$-almost surely ($\mathbb{P}$-a.s.), where f is known as the drift and σ as the diffusion. We also write $\xi_{a\upsilon}(t)$ to denote the value of the solution process at time $t\in\mathbb{R}_0^+$ under the input curve υ from initial condition $\xi_{a\upsilon}(0)=a$ $\mathbb{P}$-a.s., in which a is a random variable that is measurable in $\mathcal{F}_0$. Let us emphasize that the solution process is unambiguously determined, since the assumptions on f and σ ensure its existence and uniqueness [10, Theorem 5.2.1, p. 68].

3. INCREMENTAL STABILITY

We recall a stability notion for stochastic control systems, introduced in [19], on which the main results presented in this work rely.

Definition 3.1. *A stochastic control system Σ is incrementally input-to-state stable in the qth moment (δ-ISS-M$_q$), where $q\geq1$, if there exist a $\mathcal{KL}$ function β and a $\mathcal{K}_\infty$ function γ such that for any $t\in\mathbb{R}_0^+$, any $\mathbb{R}^n$-valued random variables a and a' that are measurable in $\mathcal{F}_0$, and any υ, $\upsilon'\in\mathcal{U}$, the following condition is satisfied:*

$$\mathbb{E}\left[\|\xi_{a\upsilon}(t)-\xi_{a'\upsilon'}(t)\|^q\right]\leq\beta\left(\mathbb{E}\left[\|a-a'\|^q\right],t\right)+\gamma\left(\|\upsilon-\upsilon'\|_\infty\right). \tag{3.1}$$

As showed in [19], one can describe δ-ISS-M$_q$ in terms of the existence of so-called *incremental Lyapunov functions*, as defined next.

Definition 3.2. *Consider a stochastic control system Σ and a continuous function $V:\mathbb{R}^n\times\mathbb{R}^n\rightarrow\mathbb{R}_0^+$ that is twice continuously differentiable on $\{\mathbb{R}^n\times\mathbb{R}^n\}\backslash\Delta$. The function V is called an incremental input-to-state stability in the qth moment (δ-ISS-M$_q$) Lyapunov function for Σ, where $q\geq1$, if there exist $\mathcal{K}_\infty$ functions $\underline{\alpha}$, $\overline{\alpha}$, ρ, and a constant $\kappa\in\mathbb{R}^+$, such that*

(i) $\underline{\alpha}$ (resp. $\overline{\alpha}$) is a convex (resp. concave) function;

(ii) for any $x,x'\in\mathbb{R}^n$, $\underline{\alpha}(\|x-x'\|^q)\leq V(x,x')\leq\overline{\alpha}(\|x-x'\|^q)$;

(iii) for any $x,x'\in\mathbb{R}^n$, $x\neq x'$, and for any $u,u'\in\mathsf{U}$,

$$\begin{aligned}\mathcal{L}^{u,u'}V(x,x'):=&\left[\partial_x V\ \ \partial_{x'}V\right]\begin{bmatrix}f(x,u)\\ f(x',u')\end{bmatrix}\\&+\frac{1}{2}Tr\left(\begin{bmatrix}\sigma(x)\\ \sigma(x')\end{bmatrix}\left[\sigma^T(x)\ \ \sigma^T(x')\right]\begin{bmatrix}\partial_{x,x}V & \partial_{x,x'}V\\ \partial_{x',x}V & \partial_{x',x'}V\end{bmatrix}\right)\\&\leq-\kappa V(x,x')+\rho(\|u-u'\|),\end{aligned}$$

where $\mathcal{L}^{u,u'}$ is the infinitesimal generator associated to the process $V(\xi, \xi')$ where ξ and ξ' are solution processes of the SDE (2.1) *[10, Section 7.3]. The symbols ∂_x and $\partial_{x,x'}$ denote first- and second-order partial derivatives with respect to x and (x, x'), respectively.*

Although condition *(ii)* in the above definition implies that the growth rate of functions $\overline{\alpha}$ and $\underline{\alpha}$ is linear, this condition does not restrict the behavior of $\overline{\alpha}$ and $\underline{\alpha}$ to only linear functions on a compact subset of $\mathbb{R}^n$. The following theorem, borrowed from [19], describes δ-ISS-M$_q$ in terms of the existence of δ-ISS-M$_q$ Lyapunov functions.

THEOREM 3.3. *A stochastic control system Σ is δ-ISS-M$_q$ if it admits a δ-ISS-M$_q$ Lyapunov function.*

One can resort to available software tools, such as SOSTOOLS [11], to search for appropriate δ-ISS-M$_q$ Lyapunov functions for polynomial type Σ. We refer the interested readers to the results in [19], providing special instances where these functions can be easily computed. For example, for linear stochastic control systems Σ (that is, for systems with linear drift and diffusion terms), one can search for appropriate δ-ISS-M$_q$ Lyapunov functions by solving a linear matrix inequality (LMI).

3.1 Noisy and noise-free trajectories

In order to introduce the symbolic models in Subsection 5.2 (Theorems 5.6 and 5.7) for a stochastic control system, we need the following technical result, borrowed from [19], which provides an upper bound on the distance (in the qth moment) between the solution process of Σ and the solution of the corresponding non-probabilistic control system obtained by disregarding the diffusion term σ. From now on, we use the notation $\overline{\xi}_{xv}$ to denote the solution of the ordinary differential equation (ODE) $\dot{\overline{\xi}}_{xv} = f\left(\overline{\xi}_{xv}, v\right)$ starting from the non-probabilistic initial condition x and under the input curve v.

LEMMA 3.4. *Consider a stochastic control system Σ such that $f(0_n, 0_m) = 0_n$ and $\sigma(0_n) = 0_{n\times p}$. Suppose that $q \geq 2$ and there exists a δ-ISS-M$_q$ Lyapunov function V for Σ such that its Hessian is a positive semidefinite matrix in $\mathbb{R}^{2n\times 2n}$ and $\partial_{x,x}V(x, x') \leq P$, for any $x, x' \in \mathbb{R}^n$, and some positive semidefinite matrix $P \in \mathbb{R}^{n\times n}$. Then for any $x \in \mathbb{R}^n$ and any $v \in \mathcal{U}$, we have*

$$\mathbb{E}\left[\left\|\xi_{xv}(t) - \overline{\xi}_{xv}(t)\right\|^q\right] \leq h_x(\sigma, t), \tag{3.2}$$

where

$$h_x(\sigma, t) = \underline{\alpha}^{-1}\left(\frac{1}{2}\left\|\sqrt{P}\right\|^2 n\min\{n,p\}Z^2\mathsf{e}^{-\kappa t} \cdot \int_0^t \left(\beta\left(\|x\|^q, s\right) + \gamma\left(\sup_{u\in\mathsf{U}}\{\|u\|\}\right)\right)^{\frac{2}{q}} \mathsf{d}s\right).$$

It can be readily seen that the nonnegative valued function h_x tends to zero as $t \to 0$, $t \to +\infty$, or as $Z \to 0$, where Z is the Lipschitz constant for the diffusion, introduced in Definition 2.1. The interested readers are referred to [19], which provides results in line with that of Lemma 3.4 for (linear) stochastic control systems Σ admitting a specific type of δ-ISS-M$_q$ Lyapunov functions.

4. SYSTEMS AND APPROXIMATE EQUIVALENCE RELATIONS

4.1 Systems

We employ the notion of system, introduced in [15], to describe both stochastic control systems as well as their symbolic models.

DEFINITION 4.1. *A system S is a tuple $S = (X, X_0, U, \longrightarrow, Y, H)$, where X is a set of states (possibly infinite), $X_0 \subseteq X$ is a set of initial states (possibly infinite), U is a set of inputs (possibly infinite), $\longrightarrow \subseteq X \times U \times X$ is a transition relation, Y is a set of outputs, and $H : X \to Y$ is an output map.*

A transition $(x, u, x') \in \longrightarrow$ is also denoted by $x \xrightarrow{u} x'$. For a transition $x \xrightarrow{u} x'$, state x' is called a u-successor, or simply a successor, of state x. We denote by $\mathbf{Post}_u(x)$ the set of all u-successors of a state x. For technical reasons, we assume that for any $x \in X$, there exists some u-successor of x, for some $u \in U$ — let us remark that this is always the case for the considered systems later in this paper.

System S is said to be

- *metric*, if the output set Y is equipped with a metric $\mathbf{d} : Y \times Y \to \mathbb{R}_0^+$;
- *finite* (or *symbolic*), if X and U are finite sets;
- *deterministic*, if for any state $x \in X$ and any input $u \in U$, $|\mathbf{Post}_u(x)| \leq 1$.

For a system $S = (X, X_0, U, \longrightarrow, Y, H)$ and given any initial state $x_0 \in X_0$, a finite state run generated from x_0 is a finite sequence of transitions:

$$x_0 \xrightarrow{u_0} x_1 \xrightarrow{u_1} \cdots \xrightarrow{u_{n-2}} x_{n-1} \xrightarrow{u_{n-1}} x_n, \tag{4.1}$$

such that $x_i \xrightarrow{u_i} x_{i+1}$ for all $0 \leq i < n$. A finite state run can be directly extended to an infinite state run as well. A finite output run is a sequence $\{y_0, y_1, \ldots, y_n\}$ such that there exists a finite state run of the form (4.1) with $y_i = H(x_i)$, for $i = 0, \ldots, n$. A finite output run can also be directly extended to an infinite output run as well.

4.2 Relations among systems

We recall the notion of approximate (bi)simulation relation, introduced in [3], which is useful when analyzing or synthesizing controllers for deterministic systems.

DEFINITION 4.2. *Let $S_a = (X_a, X_{a0}, U_a, \underset{a}{\longrightarrow}, Y_a, H_a)$ and $S_b = (X_b, X_{b0}, U_b, \underset{b}{\longrightarrow}, Y_b, H_b)$ be metric systems with the same output sets $Y_a = Y_b$ and metric $\mathbf{d}$. For $\varepsilon \in \mathbb{R}_0^+$, a relation $R \subseteq X_a \times X_b$ is said to be an ε-approximate simulation relation from S_a to S_b if, for all $(x_a, x_b) \in R$, the following two conditions are satisfied:*

(i) $\mathbf{d}(H_a(x_a), H_b(x_b)) \leq \varepsilon$;

(ii) $x_a \underset{a}{\xrightarrow{u_a}} x'_a$ *in S_a implies the existence of* $x_b \underset{b}{\xrightarrow{u_b}} x'_b$ *in S_b satisfying $(x'_a, x'_b) \in R$.*

A relation $R \subseteq X_a \times X_b$ is said to be an ε-approximate bisimulation relation between S_a and S_b if R is an ε-approximate simulation relation from S_a to S_b and R^{-1} is an ε-approximate simulation relation from S_b to S_a.

System S_a is ε-approximately simulated by S_b, or S_b ε-approximately simulates S_a, denoted by $S_a \preceq_S^\varepsilon S_b$, if there exists an ε-approximate simulation relation R from S_a to S_b such that:

- *for every $x_{a0} \in X_{a0}$, there exists $x_{b0} \in X_{b0}$ with $(x_{a0}, x_{b0}) \in R$.*

System S_a is ε-approximately bisimilar to S_b, denoted by $S_a \cong_S^\varepsilon S_b$, if there exists an ε-approximate bisimulation relation R between S_a and S_b such that:

- *for every $x_{a0} \in X_{a0}$, there exists $x_{b0} \in X_{b0}$ with $(x_{a0}, x_{b0}) \in R$;*
- *for every $x_{b0} \in X_{b0}$, there exists $x_{a0} \in X_{a0}$ with $(x_{a0}, x_{b0}) \in R$.*

5. SYMBOLIC MODELS FOR STOCHASTIC CONTROL SYSTEMS

5.1 Describing stochastic control systems as metric systems

In order to show the main results of the paper, we use the notion of system to abstractly represent a stochastic control system: given a stochastic control system Σ, we define an associated metric system $S(\Sigma) = (X, X_0, U, \longrightarrow, Y, H)$, where:

- X is the set of all $\mathbb{R}^n$-valued random variables defined on the probability space $(\Omega, \mathcal{F}, \mathbb{P})$;
- X_0 is a subset of the set of $\mathbb{R}^n$-valued random variables that are measurable over $\mathcal{F}_0$;
- $U = \mathcal{U}$;
- $x \xrightarrow{v} x'$ if x and x' are measurable in $\mathcal{F}_t$ and $\mathcal{F}_{t+\tau}$, respectively, for some $t \in \mathbb{R}_0^+$ and $\tau \in \mathbb{R}^+$, and there exists a solution process $\xi : \Omega \times \mathbb{R}_0^+ \to \mathbb{R}^n$ of Σ satisfying $\xi(t) = x$ and $\xi_{xv}(\tau) = x'$ $\mathbb{P}$-a.s.;
- $Y = X$;
- $H = 1_X$.

We assume that the output set Y is equipped with the metric $\mathbf{d}(y, y') = \left(\mathbb{E}\left[\|y - y'\|^q\right]\right)^{\frac{1}{q}}$, for any $y, y' \in Y$ and some $q \geq 1$. Let us remark that the set of states and inputs of $S(\Sigma)$ are uncountable and that $S(\Sigma)$ is a deterministic system in the sense of Definition 4.1, since (cf. Subsection 2.2) the solution process of Σ is uniquely determined.

As usual, since the concrete system $S(\Sigma)$ is infinite and does not allow for the direct control synthesis over itself, we are interested in finding a finite abstract system that is (bi)similar to the original concrete one. In order to talk about approximate (bi)simulation relations between two metric systems, such systems have to share the same output set (cf. Definition 4.2). The latter clearly determines the output behavior of the model that needs to be used to compare the concrete and the abstract models. Obviously, the system $S(\Sigma)$ inherits a classical trace-based semantics [15], and the only subtle point in our case is that the outputs of $S(\Sigma)$ (and those of any approximately (bi)similar one) are random variables. This fact is especially important due to the metric $\mathbf{d}$ with which the output set is endowed: for any non-probabilistic point one can always find a non-degenerate random variable which is as close as desired to the original point in the metric $\mathbf{d}$.

To elucidate the discussion in the previous paragraph, let us consider the following example. Let $A \subset \mathbb{R}^n$ be the set (of non-probabilistic points) whose safety we are interested in, so we formulate the problem as satisfying the LTL formula[1] $\Box A$. Suppose that over the abstract system we are able to synthesize a control strategy that makes an output run of the abstraction satisfy $\Box A$. Although the run would in general be consisting of random variables y, the fact that $y \in A$ means that y has a Dirac probability distribution centered at y, that is $y \in Y$ is a degenerate random variable that can be identified with a point in $A \subset \mathbb{R}^n \subset Y$: note that since any non-probabilistic point can be regarded as a random variable with a Dirac probability distribution centered at that point, $\mathbb{R}^n$ can be embedded in Y, which we denote as $\mathbb{R}^n \subset Y$ with a slight abuse of notation. As a result, satisfying $\Box A$ precisely means that the output run of the abstraction indeed stays in the set $A \subset \mathbb{R}^n$ forever. On the other hand, suppose that the original system is ε-approximate bisimilar to the abstraction. If we want to interpret the result $\Box A$ obtained over the abstraction, we can guarantee that the corresponding output run of the original system satisfies $\Box A_\varepsilon$, that is any output y of the run of the original system is within ε $\mathbf{d}$-distance from the set A: $\mathbf{d}(y, A) = \inf_{a \in A} \mathbf{d}(y, a) \leq \varepsilon$. Note that although the original set $A \subset Y$ is a subset of $\mathbb{R}^n \subset Y$, its ε-inflation $A_\varepsilon = \{y \in Y : \mathbf{d}(y, A) \leq \varepsilon\}$ is not a subset of $\mathbb{R}^n$ anymore and hence contains non-degenerate random variables. In particular, $A_\varepsilon \neq \{y \in \mathbb{R}^n : \inf_{a \in A} \|y - a\| \leq \varepsilon\}$ and is in fact bigger than the latter set of non-probabilistic points. As a result, although satisfying $\Box A_\varepsilon$ does not necessarily mean that a trajectory of Σ always stays within some non-probabilistic set, it means that the associated random variables always belong to A_ε and hence are close to the non-probabilistic set A with respect to the qth moment metric.

We are now able to provide two versions of finite abstractions: one whose outputs are always non-probabilistic points – that is degenerate random variables, elements of $\mathbb{R}^n \subset Y$, and one whose outputs can be non-degenerate random variables. Recall, however, that in both cases the output set is still the whole Y and the semantics is the same as for the original system $S(\Sigma)$.

5.2 Main results

This subsection contains the main contributions of the paper. We show that for any δ-ISS-M$_q$ stochastic control system Σ, and for any precision level $\varepsilon \in \mathbb{R}^+$, we can construct a finite system that is ε-approximate bisimilar to Σ. The results in this subsection rely on additional assumptions on the model Σ that are described next. We restrict our attention to stochastic control systems Σ with input sets U that are assumed to be finite unions of boxes (cf. Subsection 2.1). We further restrict our attention to sampled-data stochastic control systems, where input curves belong to set $\mathcal{U}_\tau$ which contains only curves that are constant over intervals of length $\tau \in \mathbb{R}^+$, i.e.

$$\mathcal{U}_\tau = \left\{v \in \mathcal{U} \mid v(t) = v((k-1)\tau), t \in [(k-1)\tau, k\tau[, k \in \mathbb{N}\right\}.$$

Let us denote by $S_\tau(\Sigma)$ a sub-system of $S(\Sigma)$ obtained by selecting those transitions of $S(\Sigma)$ corresponding to solution processes of duration τ and to control inputs in $\mathcal{U}_\tau$. This can be seen as the time discretization of Σ. More precisely,

[1]We refer the interested readers to [1] for the detailed definition of the safety property.

given a stochastic control system Σ, we define the associated metric system $S_\tau(\Sigma) = \left(X_\tau, X_{\tau 0}, U_\tau, \underset{\tau}{\longrightarrow}, Y_\tau, H_\tau\right)$, where $X_\tau = X$, $X_{\tau 0} = X_0$, $U_\tau = \mathcal{U}_\tau$, $Y_\tau = Y$, $H_\tau = H$, and

- $x_\tau \overset{\upsilon_\tau}{\underset{\tau}{\longrightarrow}} x'_\tau$ if x_τ and x'_τ are measurable, respectively, in $\mathcal{F}_{k\tau}$ and $\mathcal{F}_{(k+1)\tau}$ for some $k \in \mathbb{N}_0$, and there exists a solution process $\xi : \Omega \times \mathbb{R}_0^+ \to \mathbb{R}^n$ of Σ satisfying $\xi(k\tau) = x_\tau$ and $\xi_{x_\tau \upsilon_\tau}(\tau) = x'_\tau$ $\mathbb{P}$-a.s..

Notice that a finite state run $x_0 \overset{\upsilon_0}{\underset{\tau}{\longrightarrow}} x_1 \overset{\upsilon_1}{\underset{\tau}{\longrightarrow}} \cdots \overset{\upsilon_{N-1}}{\underset{\tau}{\longrightarrow}} x_N$ of $S_\tau(\Sigma)$, where $\upsilon_{i-1} \in \mathcal{U}_\tau$ and $x_i = \xi_{x_{i-1}\upsilon_{i-1}}(\tau)$ $\mathbb{P}$-a.s. for $i = 1, \ldots, N$, captures the solution process of Σ at times $t = 0, \tau, \ldots, N\tau$, started from the initial condition x_0 and resulting from a control input υ obtained by the concatenation of the input curves υ_{i-1} (i.e. $\upsilon(t) = \upsilon_{i-1}(t)$ for any $t \in [(i-1)\tau, i\tau[$), for $i = 1, \ldots, N$.

Let us proceed introducing two fully symbolic systems for the concrete model Σ. Consider a stochastic control system Σ and a tuple $\mathsf{q} = (\tau, \mu, N, x_s)$ of parameters, where τ is the sampling time, μ is the input set quantization, $N \in \mathbb{N}$ is a *temporal horizon*, and $x_s \in \mathbb{R}^n$ is a *source state*. Given Σ and q, consider the following systems:

$$S_\mathsf{q}(\Sigma) = (X_\mathsf{q}, X_{\mathsf{q}0}, U_\mathsf{q}, \underset{\mathsf{q}}{\longrightarrow}, Y_\mathsf{q}, H_\mathsf{q}),$$
$$\overline{S}_\mathsf{q}(\Sigma) = (X_\mathsf{q}, X_{\mathsf{q}0}, U_\mathsf{q}, \underset{\mathsf{q}}{\longrightarrow}, Y_\mathsf{q}, \overline{H}_\mathsf{q}),$$

consisting of:

- $X_\mathsf{q} = \{ (u_1, \ldots, u_N) \in \overbrace{[\mathsf{U}]_\mu \times \cdots \times [\mathsf{U}]_\mu}^{N \text{ times}} \}$;
- $X_{\mathsf{q}0} = X_\mathsf{q}$;
- $U_\mathsf{q} = [\mathsf{U}]_\mu$;
- $x_\mathsf{q} \overset{u_\mathsf{q}}{\underset{\mathsf{q}}{\longrightarrow}} x'_\mathsf{q}$, where $x_\mathsf{q} = (u_1, u_2, \ldots, u_N)$, if and only if $x'_\mathsf{q} = (u_2, \ldots, u_N, u_\mathsf{q})$;
- Y_q is the set of all $\mathbb{R}^n$-valued random variables defined on the probability space $(\Omega, \mathcal{F}, \mathbb{P})$;
- $H_\mathsf{q}(x_\mathsf{q}) = \xi_{x_s x_\mathsf{q}}(N\tau)$ $\left(\overline{H}_\mathsf{q}(x_\mathsf{q}) = \overline{\xi}_{x_s x_\mathsf{q}}(N\tau)\right)$.

Note that the transition relation in $S_\mathsf{q}(\Sigma)$ admits a very compact representation in the form of a shift operator. We have abused notation by identifying $u_\mathsf{q} \in [\mathsf{U}]_\mu$ with the constant input curve with domain $[0, \tau[$ and value u_q and identifying $x_\mathsf{q} \in [\mathsf{U}]_\mu^N$ with the concatenation of N control inputs $u_i \in [\mathsf{U}]_\mu$ (i.e. $x_\mathsf{q}(t) = u_i$ for any $t \in [(i-1)\tau, i\tau[$) for $i = 1, \ldots, N$. Notice that the proposed abstraction $S_\mathsf{q}(\Sigma)$ (resp. $\overline{S}_\mathsf{q}(\Sigma)$) is a deterministic system in the sense of Definition 4.1. Note that H_q and $\overline{H}_\mathsf{q}$ are mappings from a non-probabilistic point x_q to the random variable $\xi_{x_s x_\mathsf{q}}(N\tau)$ and to the one with a Dirac probability distribution centered at $\overline{\xi}_{x_s x_\mathsf{q}}(N\tau)$, respectively.

The control synthesis for $\overline{S}_\mathsf{q}(\Sigma)$ is simple as the outputs are non-probabilistic points. For $S_\mathsf{q}(\Sigma)$ it is perhaps less intuitive. Hence, we discuss it in more details later in Subsection 5.3.

An example of abstraction $S_\mathsf{q}(\Sigma)$ with $N = 2$ and $U_\mathsf{q} = \{0, 1\}$ is depicted in Figure 1, where the initial states are shown as targets of sourceless arrows. Note that $S_\mathsf{q}(\Sigma)$ only has four possible states: $X_\mathsf{q} = \{(0,0), (0,1), (1,0), (1,1)\}$.

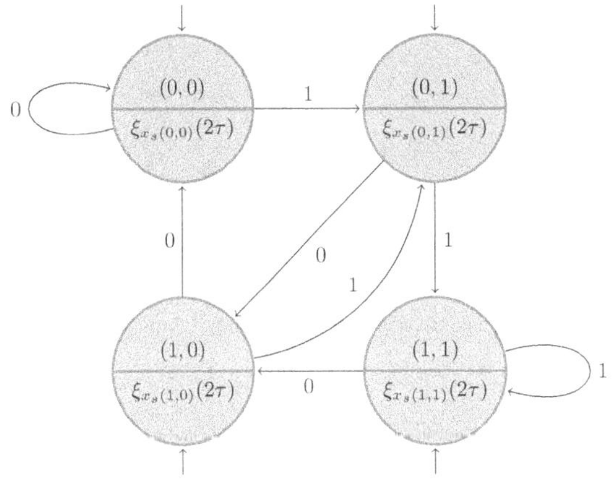

Figure 1: Example of abstraction $S_\mathsf{q}(\Sigma)$ with $N = 2$ and $U_\mathsf{q} = \{0, 1\}$. The lower part of the states are labeled with their output values.

If one chooses $N = 3$, then $S_\mathsf{q}(\Sigma)$ will have eight possible states.

In order to obtain some of the main results of this work, we raise an assumption on the δ-ISS-M$_q$ Lyapunov function V as follows:

$$|V(x, y) - V(x, z)| \leq \widehat{\gamma}(\|y - z\|), \tag{5.1}$$

for any $x, y, z \in \mathbb{R}^n$, and some $\mathcal{K}_\infty$ and concave function $\widehat{\gamma}$. As long as one is interested to work in a compact subset of $\mathbb{R}^n$, the function $\widehat{\gamma}$ in (5.1) can be readily computed. Indeed, for all $x, y, z \in \mathsf{D}$, where $\mathsf{D} \subset \mathbb{R}^n$ is compact, one can readily apply the mean value theorem to the function $y \to V(x, y)$ to get

$$|V(x, y) - V(x, z)| \leq \widehat{\gamma}\left(\|y - z\|\right),$$

$$\text{where } \widehat{\gamma}(r) = \left(\max_{x, y \in \mathsf{D} \setminus \Delta} \left\| \frac{\partial V(x, y)}{\partial y} \right\| \right) r.$$

In particular, for the δ-ISS-M$_1$ Lyapunov function $V(x, x') := \sqrt{(x - x')^T P (x - x')}$, for some positive definite matrix $P \in \mathbb{R}^{n \times n}$ and for all $x, x' \in \mathbb{R}^n$, one obtains $\widehat{\gamma}(r) = \frac{\lambda_{\max}(P)}{\sqrt{\lambda_{\min}(P)}} r$ [15, Proposition 10.5], which satisfies (5.1) globally on $\mathbb{R}^n$.

Before providing the main results of the paper, we need the following technical claims.

LEMMA 5.1. *Consider a stochastic control system Σ, admitting a δ-ISS-M$_q$ Lyapunov function V, and consider its corresponding symbolic model $\overline{S}_\mathsf{q}(\Sigma)$. We have:*

$$\eta \leq \left(\underline{\alpha}^{-1}\left(\mathsf{e}^{-\kappa N\tau} \max_{u_\mathsf{q} \in U_\mathsf{q}} V\left(\overline{\xi}_{x_s u_\mathsf{q}}(\tau), x_s\right)\right)\right)^{1/q}, \tag{5.2}$$

where

$$\eta := \max_{\substack{u_\mathsf{q} \in U_\mathsf{q}, x_\mathsf{q} \in X_\mathsf{q} \\ x'_\mathsf{q} \in \mathbf{Post}_{u_\mathsf{q}}(x_\mathsf{q})}} \left\| \xi_{\overline{H}_\mathsf{q}(x_\mathsf{q}) u_\mathsf{q}}(\tau) - \overline{H}_\mathsf{q}\left(x'_\mathsf{q}\right) \right\|. \tag{5.3}$$

The proof of Lemma 5.1 is provided in the Appendix. The next lemma provides similar result as the one in Lemma 5.1, but without explicitly using any Lyapunov function.

LEMMA 5.2. *Consider a δ-ISS-M_q stochastic control system Σ and its corresponding symbolic model $\overline{S}_{\mathsf{q}}(\Sigma)$. We have:*

$$\eta \leq \left(\beta\left(\max_{u_{\mathsf{q}}\in U_{\mathsf{q}}}\left\|\overline{\xi}_{x_s u_{\mathsf{q}}}(\tau)-x_s\right\|^q, N\tau\right)\right)^{1/q}, \quad (5.4)$$

where η is given in (5.3).

The proof of Lemma 5.2 is provided in the Appendix. The next two lemmas provide similar results as the ones of Lemmas 5.1 and 5.2, but by using the symbolic model $S_{\mathsf{q}}(\Sigma)$ rather than $\overline{S}_{\mathsf{q}}(\Sigma)$.

LEMMA 5.3. *Consider a stochastic control system Σ, admitting a δ-ISS-M_q Lyapunov function V, and consider its corresponding symbolic model $S_{\mathsf{q}}(\Sigma)$. One has:*

$$\widehat{\eta} \leq \left(\underline{\alpha}^{-1}\left(\mathsf{e}^{-\kappa N\tau}\max_{u_{\mathsf{q}}\in U_{\mathsf{q}}}\mathbb{E}\left[V\left(\xi_{x_s u_{\mathsf{q}}}(\tau), x_s\right)\right]\right)\right)^{1/q}, \quad (5.5)$$

where

$$\widehat{\eta} := \max_{\substack{u_{\mathsf{q}}\in U_{\mathsf{q}}, x_{\mathsf{q}}\in X_{\mathsf{q}}\\ x'_{\mathsf{q}}\in \mathbf{Post}_{u_{\mathsf{q}}}(x_{\mathsf{q}})}} \mathbb{E}\left[\left\|\xi_{H_{\mathsf{q}}(x_{\mathsf{q}})u_{\mathsf{q}}}(\tau) - H_{\mathsf{q}}\left(x'_{\mathsf{q}}\right)\right\|\right]. \quad (5.6)$$

PROOF. The proof is similar to the one of Lemma 5.1 and can be shown by using convexity of $\underline{\alpha}$ and Jensen inequality [10]. □

LEMMA 5.4. *Consider a δ-ISS-M_q stochastic control system Σ and its corresponding symbolic model $S_{\mathsf{q}}(\Sigma)$. We have:*

$$\widehat{\eta} \leq \left(\beta\left(\max_{u_{\mathsf{q}}\in U_{\mathsf{q}}}\mathbb{E}\left[\left\|\xi_{x_s u_{\mathsf{q}}}(\tau)-x_s\right\|^q\right], N\tau\right)\right)^{1/q}, \quad (5.7)$$

where $\widehat{\eta}$ is given in (5.6).

PROOF. The proof is similar to the one of Lemma 5.2 and can be shown by using Jensen inequality [10]. □

REMARK 5.5. *It can be readily verified that by choosing N sufficiently large, η and $\widehat{\eta}$ can be made arbitrarily small. One can even try to reduce the upper bound of η in* (5.2) *by choosing the source point x_s as the following:*

$$x_s = arg\min_{x\in\mathbb{R}^n}\max_{u_{\mathsf{q}}\in U_{\mathsf{q}}} V\left(\overline{\xi}_{xu_{\mathsf{q}}}(\tau), x\right). \quad (5.8)$$

We can now present the first main result of the paper, which relates the existence of a δ-ISS-M_q Lyapunov function to the construction of a symbolic model.

THEOREM 5.6. *Consider a stochastic control system Σ with $f(0_n, 0_m) = 0_n$ and $\sigma(0_n) = 0_{n\times p}$, admitting a δ-ISS-$M_q$ Lyapunov function V, of the form of the one explained in Lemma 3.4, such that* (5.1) *holds for some concave $\widehat{\gamma}\in\mathcal{K}_\infty$. Let η be given by* (5.3). *For any $\varepsilon\in\mathbb{R}^+$ and any tuple $\mathsf{q} = (\tau, \mu, N, x_s)$ of parameters satisfying $\mu \leq span(\mathsf{U})$ and*

$$\mathsf{e}^{-\kappa\tau}\underline{\alpha}(\varepsilon^q) + \frac{1}{\mathsf{e}\kappa}\rho(\mu) + \widehat{\gamma}\left((h_{x_s}(\sigma,(N+1)\tau))^{\frac{1}{q}} + \eta\right) \leq \underline{\alpha}(\varepsilon^q), \quad (5.9)$$

the relation

$$R = \left\{(x_\tau, x_{\mathsf{q}}) \in X_\tau \times X_{\mathsf{q}} \mid \mathbb{E}\left[V\left(x_\tau, \overline{H}_{\mathsf{q}}(x_{\mathsf{q}})\right)\right] \leq \underline{\alpha}(\varepsilon^q)\right\}$$

is an ε-approximate bisimulation relation between $\overline{S}_{\mathsf{q}}(\Sigma)$ and $S_\tau(\Sigma)$.

By choosing N sufficiently large, one can enforce $h_{x_s}(\sigma,(N+1)\tau)$ and η to be sufficiently small. Hence, it can be readily seen that for a given precision ε, there always exists a sufficiently small value of μ and a large value of N, such that the condition in (5.9) is satisfied.

In order to mitigate the conservativeness caused by using Lyapunov functions, the next theorem provides a result that is similar to the one of Theorem 5.6, which is however not obtained by explicit use of δ-ISS-M_q Lyapunov functions, but by using functions β and γ as in (3.1).

THEOREM 5.7. *Consider a δ-ISS-M_q stochastic control system Σ, satisfying the result of Lemma 3.4. Let η be given by* (5.3). *For any $\varepsilon\in\mathbb{R}^+$, and any tuple $\mathsf{q} = (\tau, \mu, N, x_s)$ of parameters satisfying $\mu \leq span(\mathsf{U})$ and*

$$(\beta(\varepsilon^q, \tau) + \gamma(\mu))^{\frac{1}{q}} + (h_{x_s}(\sigma,(N+1)\tau))^{\frac{1}{q}} + \eta \leq \varepsilon, \quad (5.10)$$

the relation

$$R = \left\{(x_\tau, x_{\mathsf{q}}) \in X_\tau \times X_{\mathsf{q}} \mid \left(\mathbb{E}\left[\left\|x_\tau - \overline{H}_{\mathsf{q}}(x_{\mathsf{q}})\right\|^q\right]\right)^{\frac{1}{q}} \leq \varepsilon\right\}$$

is an ε-approximate bisimulation relation between $\overline{S}_{\mathsf{q}}(\Sigma)$ and $S_\tau(\Sigma)$.

By choosing N sufficiently large, one can force $h_{x_s}(\sigma,(N+1)\tau)$ and η to be sufficiently small. Hence, it can be readily seen that for a given precision ε, there always exist a sufficiently large value of τ and N and small value of μ such that the condition in (5.10) is satisfied. However, unlike the result in Theorem 5.6, notice that here for a given fixed sampling time τ, one may not find any values of N and μ satisfying (5.10) because the quantity $(\beta(\varepsilon^q, \tau))^{\frac{1}{q}}$ may be larger than ε. The symbolic model $\overline{S}_{\mathsf{q}}(\Sigma)$, computed by using the parameter q provided in Theorem 5.7 whenever existing, is likely to have fewer states than the model computed by using the parameter q provided in Theorem 5.6. Similar observation has been verified in the first example in [19].

The next theorems provide results that are similar to those of Theorems 5.6 and 5.7, but by using the symbolic model $S_{\mathsf{q}}(\Sigma)$.

THEOREM 5.8. *Consider a stochastic control system Σ, admitting a δ-ISS-M_q Lyapunov function V such that* (5.1) *holds for some concave $\widehat{\gamma}\in\mathcal{K}_\infty$. Let $\widehat{\eta}$ be given by* (5.6). *For any $\varepsilon\in\mathbb{R}^+$ and any tuple $\mathsf{q} = (\tau, \mu, N, x_s)$ of parameters satisfying $\mu \leq span(\mathsf{U})$ and*

$$\mathsf{e}^{-\kappa\tau}\underline{\alpha}(\varepsilon^q) + \frac{1}{\mathsf{e}\kappa}\rho(\mu) + \widehat{\gamma}(\widehat{\eta}) \leq \underline{\alpha}(\varepsilon^q), \quad (5.11)$$

the relation

$$R = \{(x_\tau, x_{\mathsf{q}}) \in X_\tau \times X_{\mathsf{q}} \mid \mathbb{E}[V(x_\tau, H_{\mathsf{q}}(x_{\mathsf{q}}))] \leq \underline{\alpha}(\varepsilon^q)\}$$

is an ε-approximate bisimulation relation between $S_{\mathsf{q}}(\Sigma)$ and $S_\tau(\Sigma)$.

THEOREM 5.9. *Consider a δ-ISS-M_q stochastic control system Σ. Let $\widehat{\eta}$ be given by* (5.6). *For any $\varepsilon\in\mathbb{R}^+$, and any tuple $\mathsf{q} = (\tau, \mu, N, x_s)$ of parameters satisfying $\mu \leq span(\mathsf{U})$ and*

$$(\beta(\varepsilon^q, \tau) + \gamma(\mu))^{\frac{1}{q}} + \widehat{\eta} \leq \varepsilon, \quad (5.12)$$

the relation

$$R = \left\{(x_\tau, x_{\mathsf{q}}) \in X_\tau \times X_{\mathsf{q}} \mid \left(\mathbb{E}\left[\|x_\tau - H_{\mathsf{q}}(x_{\mathsf{q}})\|^q\right]\right)^{\frac{1}{q}} \leq \varepsilon\right\}$$

is an ε-approximate bisimulation relation between $S_{\mathsf{q}}(\Sigma)$ and $S_\tau(\Sigma)$.

REMARK 5.10. *The symbolic model $S_{\mathsf{q}}(\Sigma)$, computed using the parameter q provided in Theorem 5.8 (resp. Theorem 5.9), has fewer (or at most equal number of) states than the symbolic model $\overline{S}_{\mathsf{q}}(\Sigma)$, computed by using the parameter q provided in Theorem 5.6 (resp. Theorem 5.7) while having the same precision. However, the symbolic model $S_{\mathsf{q}}(\Sigma)$ has states with probabilistic output values, rather than non-probabilistic ones, which is likely to require more involved control synthesis procedures (cf. Subsection 5.3).*

REMARK 5.11. *Although we assume that the set U is infinite, Theorems 5.6, 5.7, 5.8, and 5.9 still hold when the set U is finite, with the following modifications. First, the system Σ is required to satisfy the property (3.1) for $\upsilon = \upsilon'$. Second, take $U_{\mathsf{q}} = \mathsf{U}$ in the definition of $\overline{S}_{\mathsf{q}}(\Sigma)$ (resp. $S_{\mathsf{q}}(\Sigma)$). Finally, in the conditions (5.9), (5.10),* (5.11), *and* (5.12) *set $\mu = 0$.*

Finally, we establish the results on the existence of symbolic model $\overline{S}_{\mathsf{q}}(\Sigma)$ (resp. $S_{\mathsf{q}}(\Sigma)$) such that $\overline{S}_{\mathsf{q}}(\Sigma) \cong^{\varepsilon}_{\mathcal{S}} S_\tau(\Sigma)$ (resp. $S_{\mathsf{q}}(\Sigma) \cong^{\varepsilon}_{\mathcal{S}} S_\tau(\Sigma)$).

THEOREM 5.12. *Consider the results in Theorem 5.6. If we select*

$$X_{\tau 0} = \left\{ x \in \mathbb{R}^n \middle| \left\| x - \overline{H}_{\mathsf{q}}(x_{\mathsf{q}0}) \right\| \leq \left(\overline{\alpha}^{-1}\left(\underline{\alpha}\left(\varepsilon^q\right)\right)\right)^{\frac{1}{q}}, \forall x_{\mathsf{q}0} \in X_{\mathsf{q}0} \right\},$$

then we have $\overline{S}_{\mathsf{q}}(\Sigma) \cong^{\varepsilon}_{\mathcal{S}} S_\tau(\Sigma)$.

PROOF. We start by proving that $S_\tau(\Sigma) \preceq^{\varepsilon}_{\mathcal{S}} \overline{S}_{\mathsf{q}}(\Sigma)$. For every $x_{\tau 0} \in X_{\tau 0}$ there always exists $x_{\mathsf{q}0} \in X_{\mathsf{q}0}$ such that $\|x_{\tau 0} - \overline{H}_{\mathsf{q}}(x_{\mathsf{q}0})\| \leq \left(\overline{\alpha}^{-1}\left(\underline{\alpha}\left(\varepsilon^q\right)\right)\right)^{\frac{1}{q}}$. Then,

$$\begin{aligned}\mathbb{E}\left[V\left(x_{\tau 0}, \overline{H}_{\mathsf{q}}(x_{\mathsf{q}0})\right)\right] &= V\left(x_{\tau 0}, \overline{H}_{\mathsf{q}}(x_{\mathsf{q}0})\right) \\ &\leq \overline{\alpha}(\|x_{\tau 0} - \overline{H}_{\mathsf{q}}(x_{\mathsf{q}0})\|^q) \leq \underline{\alpha}\left(\varepsilon^q\right),\end{aligned}$$

since $\overline{\alpha}$ is a $\mathcal{K}_\infty$ function. Hence, $(x_{\tau 0}, x_{\mathsf{q}0}) \in R$ implying that $S_\tau(\Sigma) \preceq^{\varepsilon}_{\mathcal{S}} \overline{S}_{\mathsf{q}}(\Sigma)$. In a similar way, we can show that $\overline{S}_{\mathsf{q}}(\Sigma) \preceq^{\varepsilon}_{\mathcal{S}} S_\tau(\Sigma)$ which completes the proof. □

The next theorem provides a similar result in line with the one of previous theorem, but by using a different relation.

THEOREM 5.13. *Consider the results in Theorem 5.7. If we select*

$$X_{\tau 0} = \left\{ x \in \mathbb{R}^n \mid \left\| x - \overline{H}_{\mathsf{q}}(x_{\mathsf{q}0}) \right\| \leq \varepsilon, \ \forall x_{\mathsf{q}0} \in X_{\mathsf{q}0} \right\},$$

then we have $\overline{S}_{\mathsf{q}}(\Sigma) \cong^{\varepsilon}_{\mathcal{S}} S_\tau(\Sigma)$.

PROOF. We start by proving that $S_\tau(\Sigma) \preceq^{\varepsilon}_{\mathcal{S}} \overline{S}_{\mathsf{q}}(\Sigma)$. For every $x_{\tau 0} \in X_{\tau 0}$ there always exists $x_{\mathsf{q}0} \in X_{\mathsf{q}0}$ such that $\|x_{\tau 0} - \overline{H}_{\mathsf{q}}(x_{\mathsf{q}0})\| \leq \varepsilon$ and $\left(\mathbb{E}\left[\left\|x_{\tau 0} - \overline{H}_{\mathsf{q}}(x_{\mathsf{q}0})\right\|^q\right]\right)^{\frac{1}{q}} \leq \varepsilon$. Hence, $(x_{\tau 0}, x_{\mathsf{q}0}) \in R$ implying that $S_\tau(\Sigma) \preceq^{\varepsilon}_{\mathcal{S}} \overline{S}_{\mathsf{q}}(\Sigma)$. In a similar way, we can show that $\overline{S}_{\mathsf{q}}(\Sigma) \preceq^{\varepsilon}_{\mathcal{S}} S_\tau(\Sigma)$ which completes the proof. □

The next two theorems provide similar results as the ones of Theorems 5.12 and 5.13, but by using the symbolic model $S_{\mathsf{q}}(\Sigma)$.

THEOREM 5.14. *Consider the results in Theorem 5.8. Let $\mathcal{A}$ denote the set of all $\mathbb{R}^n$-valued random variables, measurable over $\mathcal{F}_0$. If we select*

$$X_{\tau 0} = \left\{ a \in \mathcal{A} \middle| \left(\mathbb{E}\left[\|a - H_{\mathsf{q}}(x_{\mathsf{q}0})\|^q\right]\right)^{\frac{1}{q}} \leq \left(\overline{\alpha}^{-1}\left(\underline{\alpha}\left(\varepsilon^q\right)\right)\right)^{\frac{1}{q}}, \forall x_{\mathsf{q}0} \in X_{\mathsf{q}0} \right\},$$

then we have $S_{\mathsf{q}}(\Sigma) \cong^{\varepsilon}_{\mathcal{S}} S_\tau(\Sigma)$.

PROOF. The proof is similar to the one of Theorem 5.12. □

THEOREM 5.15. *Consider the results in Theorem 5.9. Let $\mathcal{A}$ denote the set of all $\mathbb{R}^n$-valued random variables, measurable over $\mathcal{F}_0$. If we select*

$$X_{\tau 0} = \left\{ a \in \mathcal{A} \mid \left(\mathbb{E}\left[\|a - H_{\mathsf{q}}(x_{\mathsf{q}0})\|^q\right]\right)^{\frac{1}{q}} \leq \varepsilon, \ \forall x_{\mathsf{q}0} \in X_{\mathsf{q}0} \right\},$$

then we have $S_{\mathsf{q}}(\Sigma) \cong^{\varepsilon}_{\mathcal{S}} S_\tau(\Sigma)$.

PROOF. The proof is similar to the one of Theorem 5.13. □

5.3 Control synthesis over $S_{\mathsf{q}}(\Sigma)$

Note that both $\overline{S}_{\mathsf{q}}(\Sigma)$ and $S_{\mathsf{q}}(\Sigma)$ are finite systems. The only difference is that the outputs of the former system are always non-probabilistic points, whereas those of the latter can be non-degenerate random variables. Let us describe the control synthesis for these systems over the safety formula $\Box A$, for $A \subset \mathbb{R}^n \subset Y$, which has already been used in Subsection 5.1. Clearly, since the original system $S_\tau(\Sigma)$ is stochastic in the sense that its outputs are non-degenerate random variables similarly to $S_{\mathsf{q}}(\Sigma)$, it would be too conservative to require that it satisfies the formula exactly. Thus, we are rather interested in an input policy that makes $S_\tau(\Sigma)$ satisfy $\Box A_\varepsilon$ with some $\varepsilon > 0$: recall from Subsection 5.1 that the latter LTL formula can be satisfied by non-degenerate random variables, in contrast to $\Box A$. Let us recap how to use abstractions for this task, and let us start with $\overline{S}_{\mathsf{q}}(\Sigma)$ belonging to a more familiar type of systems whose outputs are non-probabilistic.

We label a state x_{q} of $\overline{S}_{\mathsf{q}}(\Sigma)$ with A if $\overline{H}_{\mathsf{q}}(x_{\mathsf{q}}) \in A$ and, say, with B otherwise. As a result, we obtain a transition system with labels over the states and can synthesize a control strategy that makes an output run of $\overline{S}_{\mathsf{q}}(\Sigma)$ satisfy $\Box A$. After that, we can exploit ε-approximate bisimilarity to guarantee that the refined input policy makes the corresponding output run of the original system satisfy $\Box A_\varepsilon$.

The main subtlety in the case of $S_{\mathsf{q}}(\Sigma)$ is how to label its states. We cannot do this as for $\overline{S}_{\mathsf{q}}(\Sigma)$, since $H_{\mathsf{q}}(x_{\mathsf{q}})$ may never be an element of A for any $x_{\mathsf{q}} \in X_{\mathsf{q}}$: indeed, the latter is a set of non-probabilistic points, whereas all the outputs of $S_{\mathsf{q}}(\Sigma)$ can happen to be non-degenerate random variables. In order to cope with this issue, we propose to relax the original problem and at the same time to strengthen the quality of the abstraction. Namely, we can consider a relaxed problem $\Box A_\delta$ over the abstraction $S_{\mathsf{q}}(\Sigma)$, for some $\delta \in (0, \varepsilon)$, where the latter is now required to be $(\varepsilon - \delta)$-approximate (rather than just ε-approximate) bisimilar to the original system. Clearly $(A_\delta)_{\varepsilon-\delta} \subseteq A_\varepsilon$, so that whenever the control policy for $\Box A_\delta$ is synthesized over $S_{\mathsf{q}}(\Sigma)$, its refined version is guaranteed to force $\Box A_\varepsilon$ over the original system. Thanks to the fact that A_δ contains non-degenerate random variables, we eliminate the conservativeness presented before in the sense that it is likely that there are now points $x_{\mathsf{q}} \in X_{\mathsf{q}}$

in $S_q(\Sigma)$ such that $H_q(x_q) \in A_\delta$. The only remaining question is how to check whether $H_q(x_q) \in A_\delta$. To answer this question, we check that the distance

$$\mathbf{d}\left(H_q(x_q), A\right) = \inf_{a \in A} \left(\mathbb{E}\|\xi_{x_s x_q}(N\tau) - a\|^q\right)^{1/q} \qquad (5.13)$$

is smaller than δ, which involves both computing the expectation over the solution of the SDE, and optimizing the value of this expectation. Clearly, such a computation in general cannot be done analytically, and the evaluation of the expectation itself is a highly non-trivial task unless the SDE has a very special form.

We propose a Monte Carlo approach to compute an approximation of the quantity in (5.13) by means of empirical expectations. Using such an approach, we can estimate $\mathbf{d}\left(H_q(x_q), A\right)$ only up to some precision, say ϵ. If the estimated distance is less than $\delta - \epsilon$, we are safe to label x_q with A, whereas all other states are labeled by B. Furthermore, since this result is based on a Monte Carlo method, it holds true only with a certain confidence level $1 - \pi$ where $\pi \in [0, 1]$. The benefit of our approach is that it is not only valid asymptotically (as the number of samples tends to infinity), but we are also able to provide a number of simulations that is sufficient to estimate $\mathbf{d}\left(H_q(x_q), A\right)$ with any given precision ϵ and with any given confidence $1 - \pi$. This can be considered as an extension of the well-known Hoeffding's inequality [5] to the case when one has to deal with an optimization problem. Note that regardless of the specification of interest, the main task over $S_q(\Sigma)$ is always to compute some distance as in (5.13) for any set that appears in the specification, so the method below applies not only to the safety formula $\Box A$, but also to more general formulae, which are left as object of future research.

Due to space limitations, here we only consider the case $q = 1$. For $q \geq 2$, similar results can be derived. Suppose that A as in (5.13) is a compact subset of $\mathbb{R}^n$, and let A^r be the smallest subset of $[\mathbb{R}^n]_r$ such that $A \subseteq \bigcup_{p \in A^r} \mathcal{B}_{\frac{r}{2}}(p)$. Let M be the number of samples and let

$$\mathbf{d}_M^r := \min_{a \in A^r} \frac{1}{M} \sum_{i=1}^{M} \left\|\xi^i_{x_s x_q}(N\tau) - a\right\|,$$

where the superscript i denotes the number of samples. Now we have the following result.

THEOREM 5.16. *Consider a stochastic control system Σ and suppose that we are interested in its dynamics over a compact set D. It holds that $|\mathbf{d}\left(H_q(x_q), A\right) - \mathbf{d}_M^r| \leq \epsilon$ with confidence of at least $1 - \pi$ given that $r/2 < \epsilon$ and that*

$$M \geq \frac{D^2}{2\left(\epsilon - r/2\right)^2} \cdot \log \frac{2|A^r|}{\pi},$$

where $D = \sup\{\|x - y\| \mid x, y \in \mathsf{D}\}$.

Let us make some remarks regarding Theorem 5.16. First of all, no matter how many distances one has to evaluate, one can always use the same samples ξ^i and there is no need to generate new samples. Second, the number of samples is quadratic in the precision ϵ and is only logarithmic in the lack of confidence π, thus it is fairly fast and easy to satisfy the desired degree of accuracy with very high confidence.

5.4 Comparison with existing results in the literature

Note that given any precision ε and sampling time τ, one can always use the results in Theorem 5.12 to construct a symbolic model $\overline{S}_q(\Sigma)$ that is ε-approximate bisimilar to $S_\tau(\Sigma)$. However, the results in Theorem 5.1 in [19] cannot be applied for any sampling time τ if the precision ε is lower than the thresholds introduced in inequality (5.5) in [19]. Furthermore, while the results in [19] only provide symbolic models with non-probabilistic output values, the ones in this work provide symbolic models with probabilistic output values as well, which can result in less conservative symbolic models (cf. Remark 5.10 and the example section).

One can compare the results provided in Theorems 5.6 (corr. 5.12) and 5.7 (corr. 5.13) with the results provided in Theorems 5.1 and 5.3 in [19] in terms of the size of the generated symbolic models. One can readily verify that the precisions of the symbolic models proposed here and the ones proposed in [19] are approximately the same as long as both use the same input set quantization parameter μ and the state space quantization parameter, called ν, in [19] is equal to the parameter η in (5.3), i.e. $\nu \leq \left(\underline{\alpha}^{-1}\left(\mathsf{e}^{-\kappa N\tau}\eta_0\right)\right)^{1/q}$, where $\eta_0 = \max_{u_q \in U_q} V\left(\overline{\xi}_{x_s u_q}(\tau), x_s\right)$. The reason their precisions are approximately (rather than exactly) the same is because we use $h_{x_s}(\sigma, (N+1)\tau)$ in conditions (5.9) and (5.10) in this paper rather than $h(\sigma, \tau) = \sup_{x \in \mathsf{D}} h_x(\sigma, \tau)$ that is being used in conditions 5.4 and 5.14 in [19] for a compact set $\mathsf{D} \subset \mathbb{R}^n$. By assuming that $h_{x_s}(\sigma, (N+1)\tau)^{\frac{1}{q}}$ and $h(\sigma, \tau)^{\frac{1}{q}}$ are much smaller than η and ν, respectively, or $h_{x_s}(\sigma, (N+1)\tau) \approx h(\sigma, \tau)$, one should expect to obtain the same precisions for the symbolic models provided here and those provided in [19] under the aforementioned conditions.

The number of states of the proposed symbolic model in this paper is $\left|[\mathsf{U}]_\mu\right|^N$. Assume that we are interested in the dynamics of Σ on a compact set $\mathsf{D} \subset \mathbb{R}^n$. Since the set of states of the proposed symbolic model in [19] is $[\mathsf{D}]_\nu$, its size is $\left|[\mathsf{D}]_\nu\right| = \frac{K}{\nu^n}$, where K is a positive constant proportional to the volume of D. Hence, it is more convenient to use the proposed symbolic model here rather than the one proposed in [19] as long as:

$$\left|[\mathsf{U}]_\mu\right|^N \leq \frac{K}{\left(\underline{\alpha}^{-1}\left(\mathsf{e}^{-\kappa N\tau}\eta_0\right)\right)^{n/q}}.$$

Without loss of generality, one can assume that $\underline{\alpha}(r) = r$ for any $r \in \mathbb{R}_0^+$. Hence, for sufficiently large value of N, it is more convenient to use the proposed symbolic model here in comparison with the one proposed in [19] as long as:

$$\left|[\mathsf{U}]_\mu\right| \mathsf{e}^{\frac{-\kappa\tau n}{q}} \leq 1. \qquad (5.14)$$

Note that the methodology proposed in this paper allows us to construct less conservative symbolic models with probabilistic output values (see the example section) while the proposed one in [19] only provides conservative symbolic models with non-probabilistic output values.

6. EXAMPLE

We show the effectiveness of the results of the paper by constructing a bisimilar symbolic model for a simple 6-dimensional linear stochastic control system Σ, aiming mostly at elucidating the details. The model of Σ is described by:

$$\Sigma : \{\mathrm{d}\xi = (A\xi + Bv)\,\mathrm{d}t + 0.5\xi\,\mathrm{d}W_t, \qquad (6.1)$$

where

$$A = \begin{bmatrix} -20.73 & 0.45 & -0.77 & 0.92 & 0.68 & 1.28 \\ 0.95 & -22.41 & -1.73 & -0.14 & 0.47 & 0.77 \\ 0.57 & -0.74 & -23.57 & 0.37 & 0.58 & 0.57 \\ -0.71 & 0.07 & 1.04 & -21.41 & -1 & 0.14 \\ -0.95 & 0.47 & 0.96 & -1.34 & -23.96 & 0.11 \\ 1.72 & 0.37 & -0.21 & -0.43 & 0.89 & -22.91 \end{bmatrix}$$

$$B^T = [\,0 \;\; 0 \;\; 0 \;\; 0 \;\; 0 \;\; 100\,]^T.$$

We assume that $\mathsf{U} = [-1, 1]$ and that $\mathcal{U}_\tau$ contains curves taking values in $[\mathsf{U}]_1$. Hence, as explained in Remark 5.11, $\mu = 0$ is to be used in (5.9), (5.10), (5.11), and (5.12). One can readily verify that the function $V(x, x') = \sqrt{(x - x')^T I_6 (x - x')}$, for any $x, x' \in \mathbb{R}^6$, satisfies conditions (i)-(iii) in Definition 3.2 with $q = 1$, $\underline{\alpha}(r) = r$, $\overline{\alpha}(r) = \sqrt{6}r$, $\rho(r) = \sqrt{6}\|B\|r$, $\forall r \in \mathbb{R}_0^+$, and $\kappa = 19.5$. Hence, Σ is δ-ISS-M$_1$, equipped with the δ-ISS-M$_1$ Lyapunov function V. Using the results of Theorem 3.3, provided in [19], one gets that functions $\beta(r, s) = \sqrt{6}\mathsf{e}^{-\kappa s}r$ and $\gamma(r) = \frac{\sqrt{6}\|B\|r}{\mathsf{e}\kappa}$ satisfy property (3.1) for Σ. Given the Lyapunov function V, we solve the optimization problem in (5.8) using the function *fminimax* in Matlab and obtain $x_s \approx 0_6$.

For a given precision $\varepsilon = 1$ and fixed sampling time $\tau = 0.01$, the parameter N for $\overline{S}_\mathsf{q}(\Sigma)$, based on inequality (5.9) in Theorem 5.6, is obtained as 10. Therefore, the resulting cardinality of the set of states for $\overline{S}_\mathsf{q}(\Sigma)$ is $\left|[\mathsf{U}]_1\right|^{10} = 3^{10} = 59049$. Using the aforementioned parameters, one gets $\eta \leq 0.127$, where η is given in (5.3). Note that the results in Theorems 5.7 and 5.9 cannot be applied here because $(\beta(\varepsilon^q, \tau))^{\frac{1}{q}} > \varepsilon$. Using criterion (5.14), one has $\left|[\mathsf{U}]_\mu\right| \mathsf{e}^{\frac{-\kappa\tau n}{q}} = 0.93$, implying that the approach proposed in this paper is more appropriate in terms of the size of the abstraction than the one proposed in [19]. We elaborate more on this at the end of the section.

REMARK 6.1. *By considering the dynamics of Σ over the subset $\mathsf{D} = [-4, 4]^6$ of $\mathbb{R}^6$, at least $1 - 10^{-5}$ confidence level, and precision $\epsilon = 0.01$ and using Hoeffding's inequality [5], one can verify that the number of samples should be at least 3.9059×10^6 to empirically compute the upper bound of $\widehat{\eta}$ in (5.5). We compute $\widehat{\eta} \leq 0.1287$ when $N = 10$, $\tau = 0.01$, and $x_s \approx 0_6$. Using the results in Theorem 5.8 and the same parameters* q *as the ones in $\overline{S}_\mathsf{q}(\Sigma)$, one obtains $\varepsilon = 0.73$ in (5.11). Therefore, $S_\mathsf{q}(\Sigma)$, with confidence at least $1 - 10^{-5}$, provides less conservative precision than $\overline{S}_\mathsf{q}(\Sigma)$ while having the same size as $\overline{S}_\mathsf{q}(\Sigma)$.*

Now, consider that the objective is to design a control policy forcing the trajectories of Σ, starting from the initial condition $x_0 = 0_6$, to first sequentially visit (in the 1st moment metric) two regions of interest $W_1 = \{x \in \mathbb{R}^6 \mid x_6 = 0.3\}$ and $W_2 = \{x \in \mathbb{R}^6 \mid x_6 = -0.3\}$; then once the system has visited these regions, to reach the region $W_3 = \{x \in \mathbb{R}^6 \mid x_6 = 0.2\}$ in finite time and remain there forever (in the 1st moment metric). The LTL formula[2] representing this goal is $\Diamond\Box W_3 \wedge \Diamond(W_1 \wedge \Diamond W_2)$. Figure 2 displays a few realizations of the closed-loop solution process $\xi_{x_0 v}$ along the 6th dimension, as well as the corresponding evolution of the input signal v. In Figure 3, we show the average value (over 1000 experiments) of the distance in time of the solution process $\xi_{x_0 v}$ to the sets W_1, W_2, and W_3, namely $\|\xi_{x_0 v}(t)\|_{W_1}$, $\|\xi_{x_0 v}(t)\|_{W_2}$, and $\|\xi_{x_0 v}(t)\|_{W_3}$, where the point-to-set distance is defined as $\|x\|_W = \inf_{w \in W} \|x - w\|$.

[2]Note that the semantics of LTL are defined over the output behaviors of $S_\mathsf{q}(\Sigma)$.

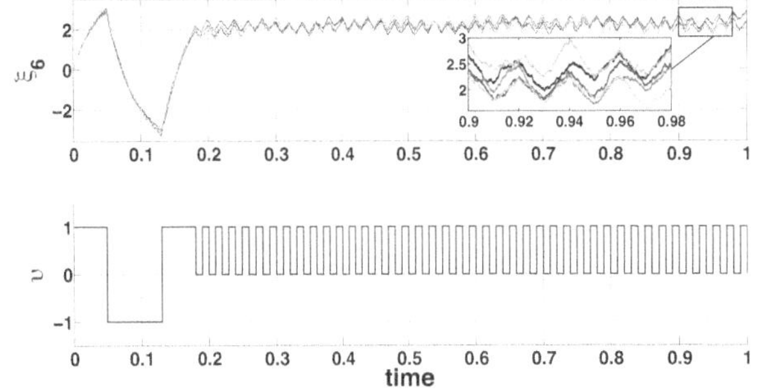

Figure 2: A few realizations of the closed-loop solution process $\xi_{x_0 v}$ along the 6th dimension (top panel) and the corresponding evolution of the obtained input signal v (bottom panel).

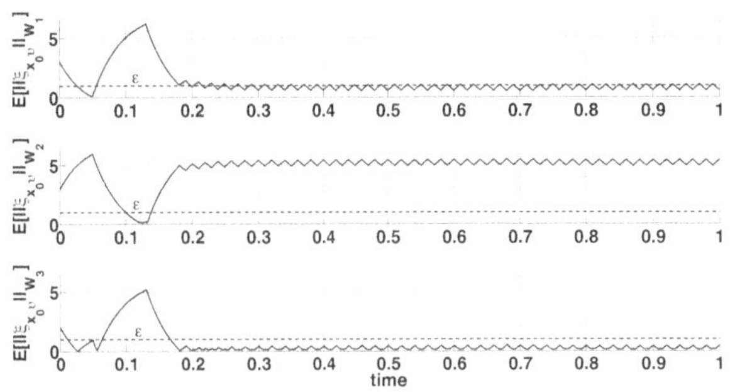

Figure 3: The average values (over 1000 experiments) of the distance of the solution process $\xi_{x_0 v}$ to the sets W_1 (top panel), W_2 (middle panel), and W_3 (bottom panel).

To compute exactly the size of the symbolic model, proposed in Theorem 5.1 in [19], we consider the dynamics of Σ over the subset $\mathsf{D} = [-4, 4]^6$ of $\mathbb{R}^6$. Note that Theorem 5.3 in [19] cannot be applied here because $(\beta(\varepsilon^q, \tau))^{\frac{1}{q}} > \varepsilon$. Using the same precision $\varepsilon = 1$ and sampling time $\tau = 0.01$ as the ones here, and the inequalities (5.3) and (5.4) in [19], we obtain the state space quantization parameter as $\nu \leq 0.01$. Therefore, if one uses $\nu = 0.01$, the cardinality of the state set of the symbolic model, provided by the results in Theorem 5.1 in [19], is equal to $\left(\frac{8}{0.01}\right)^6 = 2.62 \times 10^{17}$ which is much higher than the one proposed here, which amounts to 59049 points.

7. DISCUSSION

In this paper we have proposed a symbolic abstraction technique for incrementally stable stochastic control systems with only discretization of the input sets. The proposed approach is potentially more scalable than that proposed in [18, 19] for higher dimensional stochastic control systems.

Future work will concentrate on efficient implementations of the symbolic models proposed here, using Binary Decision Diagrams (BDD's) or Algebraic Decision Diagrams (ADD's) as well as efficient controller synthesis techniques.

8. REFERENCES

[1] C. Baier and J. P. Katoen. *Principles of model checking.* The MIT Press, April 2008.

[2] E. Le Corronc, A. Girard, and G. Goessler. Mode sequences as symbolic states in abstractions of incrementally stable switched systems. In *Proceedings of the 52nd IEEE Conference on Decision and Control*, pages 3225–3230, December 2013.

[3] A. Girard and G. J. Pappas. Approximation metrics for discrete and continuous systems. *IEEE Transactions on Automatic Control*, 25(5):782–798, May 2007.

[4] A. Girard, G. Pola, and P. Tabuada. Approximately bisimilar symbolic models for incrementally stable switched systems. *IEEE Transactions on Automatic Control*, 55(1):116–126, January 2009.

[5] W. Hoeffding. Probability inequalities for sums of bounded random variables. *Journal of the American Statistical Association*, 58(301):13–30, 1963.

[6] A. A. Julius and G. J. Pappas. Approximations of stochastic hybrid systems. *IEEE Transactions on Automatic Control*, 54(6):1193–1203, 2009.

[7] I. Karatzas and S. E. Shreve. *Brownian Motion and Stochastic Calculus*, volume 113 of *Graduate Texts in Mathematics*. Springer-Verlag, New York, 2nd edition, 1991.

[8] R. Majumdar and M. Zamani. Approximately bisimilar symbolic models for digital control systems. In M. Parthasarathy and S. A. Seshia, editors, *Computer Aided Verification (CAV)*, volume 7358 of *LNCS*, pages 362–377. Springer-Verlag, July 2012.

[9] O. Maler, A. Pnueli, and J. Sifakis. On the synthesis of discrete controllers for timed systems. In E. W. Mayr and C. Puech, editors, *Symposium on Theoretical Aspects of Computer Science*, volume 900 of *LNCS*, pages 229–242. Springer-Verlag, 1995.

[10] B. K. Oksendal. *Stochastic differential equations: An introduction with applications.* Springer, 5th edition, November 2002.

[11] A. Papachristodoulou, J. Anderson, G. Valmorbida, S. Prajna, P. Seiler, and P. A. Parrilo. SOSTOOLS version 3.00 - Sum of squares optimization toolbox for MATLAB. *arXiv: 1310.4716*, October 2013.

[12] G. Pola, A. Girard, and P. Tabuada. Approximately bisimilar symbolic models for nonlinear control systems. *Automatica*, 44(10):2508–2516, October 2008.

[13] G. Pola and P. Tabuada. Symbolic models for nonlinear control systems: Alternating approximate bisimulations. *SIAM Journal on Control and Optimization*, 48(2):719–733, February 2009.

[14] G. Reißig. Computing abstractions of nonlinear systems. *IEEE Transaction on Automatic Control*, 56(11):2583–2598, November 2011.

[15] P. Tabuada. *Verification and Control of Hybrid Systems, A symbolic approach.* Springer, 1st edition, June 2009.

[16] M. Zamani and A. Abate. Symbolic control of stochastic switched systems via finite abstractions. In K. Joshi, M. Siegle, M. Stoelinga, and P. R. D'Argenio, editors, *Quantitative Evaluation of Systems*, volume 8054 of *Lecture Notes in Computer Science*, pages 305–321. Springer Berlin Heidelberg, August 2013.

[17] M. Zamani, P. Mohajerin Esfahani, A. Abate, and J. Lygeros. Symbolic models for stochastic control systems without stability assumptions. *In Proceedings of European Control Conference (ECC)*, pages 4257–4262, July 2013.

[18] M. Zamani, P. Mohajerin Esfahani, R. Majumdar, A. Abate, and J. Lygeros. Bisimilar finite abstractions of stochastic control systems. *In Proceedings of the 52nd IEEE Conference on Decision and Control*, pages 3926–3931, December 2013.

[19] M. Zamani, P. Mohajerin Esfahani, R. Majumdar, A. Abate, and J. Lygeros. Symbolic control of stochastic systems via approximately bisimilar finite abstractions. *IEEE Transactions on Automatic Control, accepted, arXiv: 1302.3868*, 2014.

[20] M. Zamani, G. Pola, M. Mazo Jr., and P. Tabuada. Symbolic models for nonlinear control systems without stability assumptions. *IEEE Transactions on Automatic Control*, 57(7):1804–1809, July 2012.

Appendix

PROOF. of Lemma 5.1: Let $x_q \in X_q$, where $x_q = (u_1, u_2, \ldots, u_N)$, and $u_q \in U_q$. Using the definition of $\overline{S}_q(\Sigma)$, one obtains $x'_q = (u_2, \ldots, u_N, u_q) \in \mathbf{Post}_{u_q}(x_q)$. Since V is a δ-ISS-M$_q$ Lyapunov function for Σ, we have:

$$
\begin{aligned}
&\underline{\alpha}\left(\left\|\overline{\xi}_{\overline{H}_q(x_q)u_q}(\tau) - \overline{H}_q\left(x'_q\right)\right\|^q\right) \leq V\left(\overline{\xi}_{\overline{H}_q(x_q)u_q}(\tau), \overline{H}_q\left(x'_q\right)\right) \\
&= V\left(\overline{\xi}_{\overline{\xi}_{x_s x_q}(N\tau)u_q}(\tau), \overline{\xi}_{x_s x'_q}(N\tau)\right) \\
&= V\left(\overline{\xi}_{\overline{\xi}_{x_s u_1}(\tau)(u_2,\ldots,u_N,u_q)}(N\tau), \overline{\xi}_{x_s(u_2,\ldots,u_N,u_q)}(N\tau)\right) \\
&\leq \mathsf{e}^{-\kappa N\tau} V\left(\overline{\xi}_{x_s u_1}(\tau), x_s\right).
\end{aligned}
\tag{8.1}
$$

We refer the interested readers to the proof of Theorem 3.3 in [19] to see how we derived the inequality (8.1). Hence, one gets

$$
\left\|\overline{\xi}_{\overline{H}_q(x_q)u_q}(\tau) - \overline{H}_q\left(x'_q\right)\right\| \leq \left(\underline{\alpha}^{-1}\left(\mathsf{e}^{-\kappa N\tau} V\left(\overline{\xi}_{x_s u_1}(\tau), x_s\right)\right)\right)^{1/q},
\tag{8.2}
$$

because of $\underline{\alpha} \in \mathcal{K}_\infty$. Since the inequality (8.2) holds for all $x_q \in X_q$ and $u_q \in U_q$, and $\underline{\alpha} \in \mathcal{K}_\infty$, inequality (5.2) holds. □

PROOF. of Lemma 5.2: Let $x_q \in X_q$, where $x_q = (u_1, u_2, \ldots, u_N)$, and $u_q \in U_q$. Using the definition of $\overline{S}_q(\Sigma)$, one obtains $x'_q = (u_2, \ldots, u_N, u_q) \in \mathbf{Post}_{u_q}(x_q)$. Since Σ is δ-ISS-M$_q$ and using inequality (3.1), we have:

$$
\begin{aligned}
&\left\|\overline{\xi}_{\overline{H}_q(x_q)u_q}(\tau) - \overline{H}_q\left(x'_q\right)\right\|^q = \left\|\overline{\xi}_{\overline{\xi}_{x_s x_q}(N\tau)u_q}(\tau) - \overline{\xi}_{x_s x'_q}(N\tau)\right\|^q \\
&= \left\|\overline{\xi}_{\overline{\xi}_{x_s u_1}(\tau)(u_2,\ldots,u_N,u_q)}(N\tau) - \overline{\xi}_{x_s(u_2,\ldots,u_N,u_q)}(N\tau)\right\|^q \\
&\leq \beta\left(\left\|\overline{\xi}_{x_s u_1}(\tau) - x_s\right\|^q, N\tau\right).
\end{aligned}
$$

Hence, one gets

$$
\left\|\overline{\xi}_{\overline{H}_q(x_q)u_q}(\tau) - \overline{H}_q\left(x'_q\right)\right\| \leq \left(\beta\left(\left\|\overline{\xi}_{x_s u_1}(\tau) - x_s\right\|^q, N\tau\right)\right)^{1/q}.
\tag{8.3}
$$

Since the inequality (8.3) holds for all $x_q \in X_q$ and all $u_q \in U_q$, and β is a $\mathcal{K}_\infty$ function with respect to its first argument when the second one is fixed, inequality (5.4) holds. □

Stochastic Reachability Based Motion Planning for Multiple Moving Obstacle Avoidance

Nick Malone
Computer Science
University of New Mexico
Albuquerque, NM 87131, USA
nmalone@cs.unm.edu

Kendra Lesser
Electrical & Comp. Eng.
University of New Mexico
Albuquerque, NM 87131, USA
lesser@unm.edu

Meeko Oishi
Electrical & Comp. Eng.
University of New Mexico
Albuquerque, NM 87131, USA
oishi@unm.edu

Lydia Tapia
Computer Science
University of New Mexico
Albuquerque, NM 87131, USA
tapia@cs.unm.edu

ABSTRACT

One of the many challenges in designing autonomy for operation in uncertain and dynamic environments is the planning of collision-free paths. Roadmap-based motion planning is a popular technique for identifying collision-free paths, since it approximates the often infeasible space of all possible motions with a networked structure of valid configurations. We use stochastic reachable sets to identify regions of low collision probability, and to create roadmaps which incorporate likelihood of collision. We complete a small number of stochastic reachability calculations with individual obstacles a priori. This information is then associated with the weight, or preference for traversal, given to a transition in the roadmap structure. Our method is novel, and scales well with the number of obstacles, maintaining a relatively high probability of reaching the goal in a finite time horizon without collision, as compared to other methods. We demonstrate our method on systems with up to 50 dynamic obstacles.

Categories and Subject Descriptors

I.2.9 [**Artificial Intelligence**]: Robotics—*Autonomous Vehicles*; I.2.8 [**Artificial Intelligence**]: Problem Solving, Control Methods, and Search—*Control Theory, Dynamic Programming*; G.3 [**Mathematics of Computing**]: Probability and Statistics—*Stochastic Processes*

Keywords

Stochastic Reachability; Motion Planning; Probabilistic Roadmaps

HSCC'14, April 15–17, 2014, Berlin, Germany.
Copyright 2014 ACM 978-1-4503-2732-9/14/04 ...$15.00.
http://dx.doi.org/10.1145/2562059.2562127.

1. INTRODUCTION

One of the many challenges in designing autonomy for operation in uncertain and dynamic environments is the planning of collision-free paths. In applications such as search and rescue, coordinated sensing, collaborative monitoring, or automated manufacturing environments, a robot must traverse from a known start state to a goal state, in an environment that could contain many moving obstacles with stochastic dynamics. While theoretical solutions may be available via stochastic reachability, computational expense limits such an approach to a very small number of dynamic obstacles, depending on the model complexity of the robot and obstacle dynamics. Motion planning techniques provide a more computationally feasible alternative, depending on degrees of freedom of the robot, the nature of the environment, and the planning constraints. However, there is strong evidence that any complete planner will require exponential time in the number of DOFs of the robot [14], [11], [6].

In this paper, we present a novel, stochastic reachability based method to create probabilistic roadmaps that accommodate many moving obstacles that travel stochastically along straight line or arc trajectories. We use the likelihood of collision with a given object, computed a priori via stochastic reachability (SR), to inform the likelihood of collision along a given path. We demonstrate our method computationally on scenarios with up to 50 stochastic dynamic obstacles.

The robotic motion planning problem consists of finding a valid (collision-free) path for a robot from a start state to a goal state. One common solution to solving the planning problem is to use a roadmap, a network of valid configurations (nodes) and transitions between configurations (edges), that captures the topology of the collision-free space. Common approaches are cell-decomposition methods which place nodes at regular intervals [15], Probabilistic Roadmap Methods (PRMs) which place nodes probabilistically [14], and several variants which use heuristics to place nodes [2, 4]. However, planning in environments with dynamic obstacles remains a significant challenge.

Stochastic reachability analysis provides offline verification of dynamical systems, to assess whether the state of the system will, with a certain likelihood, remain within a desired subset of the state-space for some finite time, or avoid an undesired subset of the state-space [1]. To solve problems in collision avoidance, the region in the relative state-space which constitutes collision is defined as the set of states we wish the system to avoid [28, 13]. Unfortunately, the computation time for stochastic reachable sets (SR sets) is exponential in the dimension of the continuous state, making the assessment of collision probabilities with many simultaneously moving obstacles next to impossible (once the dynamics of each obstacle are incorporated into the state). However, while expensive, SR sets can be computed offline and the result queried online.

Our method combines multiple SR sets (computed pairwise between the robot and each dynamic obstacle), to generate appropriate weights associated with the edges in the roadmap. The SR sets are generated offline, computed individually for relative dynamics associated with each obstacle, and the results combined and queried at runtime by our algorithm. In an environment with multiple obstacles, the intersection of multiple SR sets clearly cannot provide a strict assurance of safety, since the reachable set is computed for one dynamic obstacle in isolation. However, such an approach can significantly improve the ability of the roadmap to reflect obstacle dynamics. Further, in simulation, we find that the SR - weighted roadmap is able to intelligently navigate in the presence of stochastic dynamic obstacles significantly more often than standard roadmap methods.

Our proposed combination of formal and ad-hoc methods has several advantages over existing moving obstacle solutions and over SR alone. First, at runtime, the method is fast since it does not have to make expensive collision detection calls and instead just queries the precomputed SR set. Second, it scales well with many obstacles. Furthermore, it provides a framework in which multiple SR sets can be combined to generate approximate collision avoidance probabilities with many moving obstacles, which would otherwise be impossible using a single SR set that accounts for all obstacles simultaneously. Finally, by using SR for the underlying collision probability calculation, the method provides an upper bound on the probability of collision avoidance, which can be used comparatively to select the best path.

Section 2 describes related literature in roadmaps with moving obstacles as well as in stochastic reachability for motion planning and collision avoidance. Section 3 presents the robot and obstacle dynamics, and known techniques for roadmap construction. Section 4 presents the computed stochastic reachable sets for collision avoidance with two types of stochastic dynamic obstacles, as well as our algorithm for roadmap construction that queries the stochastic reachable set. Section 5 describes our computational experiments, with two moving obstacles, and finally with 50 moving obstacles. Lastly, conclusions and directions for future work are offered in Section 6.

2. RELATED WORK

2.1 Roadmaps and moving obstacles

Several roadmap-based techniques including PRM variants have been developed to address planning in spaces with moving obstacles [23], [5], [30], [10], [24], [25]. Generally, these approaches adapt to moving obstacles using one of two approaches. The first category generates a roadmap with little obstacle information, and later filters paths at runtime with local obstacle information [23], [5]. These methods have low precomputation costs, but generally prove expensive during path selection. They start with an initial path that is collision free and incrementally modify the path to maintain a smooth, collision free path. These methods only rely on physical obstacle clearance by using protective bubbles to deform the path.

The second category approximates the environment and is cheap at runtime. These methods create an approximate roadmap and then use a heuristic approach to produce locally valid paths to avoid moving obstacles. These methods decrease runtime costs at the expense of path accuracy [24], [12]. In [24], a first stage constructs a dynamic roadmap that considers some obstacles and is shared across multiple moving robots. Then, in a second stage, a path is extracted by a single robot that is locally modified to account for neighboring robots (moving obstacles). Similarly, [30] repairs the existing roadmap when an obstacle makes an edge or group of edges invalid. The authors of [34] use a roadmap, but deform the edges around moving obstacles. The work in [2] trades off distance from the goal and the dynamic obstacles to path plan. Approaches in [32] and [22] utilize roadmap methods with heuristics to manage the moving obstacles, while [31] attempts to optimize the roadmap for moving obstacles under motion constraints.

2.2 Stochastic reachable sets

A Hamilton-Jacobi-Bellman (HJB) formulation [21] allows for both a control input and a disturbance input to model collision-avoidance scenarios [19], [9] for motion planning. The result of these reachability calculations is a maximal set of states within which collision between two objects is guaranteed (in the worst-case scenario), also known as the reachable set. The set which assures collision avoidance is simply the complement of the reachable set. In [29], reachable sets are calculated to assure a robot safely reaches a target while avoiding a single obstacle, whose motion is chosen to maximize collision, and the robot cannot modify its movements based on subsequent observations. In [8], a similar approach is taken, but with reachable sets computed iteratively so that the robot can modify its actions. In [17], multiple obstacles that each act as bounded, worst-case disturbances are avoided in an online fashion, based on precomputed invariant sets.

An alternative approach is to calculate an SR set that allows for obstacles whose dynamics include stochastic processes. Discrete-time SR generates probabilistic reachable sets [1], based on stochastic system dynamics. In [28], the desired target set is known, but the undesired sets that the robot should avoid are random and must be propagated over time. In [13] a two-player stochastic dynamical game is considered, and applied to a target tracking application in which the target acts in opposition to the tracker.

3. PRELIMINARIES

3.1 Obstacle Dynamics

We consider two representative types of dynamic obstacles, which have known trajectories but stochastic velocities. In particular, we consider straight-line and constant-arc trajectories, and presume that each obstacle is represented as a two-dimensional point mass. The obstacle dynamics are of the form $\dot{\overline{x}}^o = f(w,t)$, with obstacle state $\overline{x}^o = (x^o, y^o)$, and with w a discrete random variable that takes on values in $\mathcal{W}$ with probability distribution $p(w)$. We only consider a discrete random variable here for computational simplicity, although a continuous random variable could be introduced. The discretized obstacle dynamics (via an Euler approximation with time step Δ) are

$$\begin{aligned} x_{n+1}^o &= x_n^o + \Delta w_{n+1} \\ y_{n+1}^o &= \alpha x_{n+1}^o \end{aligned} \tag{1}$$

for straight-line movement, with speed $w \in \mathcal{W}$ and slope $\alpha \in \mathbb{R}$, and

$$\begin{aligned} x_{n+1}^o &= x_n^o + \Delta r\left(\cos(w_{n+1}(n+1)) - \cos(w_{n+1}n)\right) \\ y_{n+1}^o &= y_n^o + \Delta r\left(\sin(w_{n+1}(n+1)) - \sin(w_{n+1}n)\right) \end{aligned} \tag{2}$$

for constant-arc movement, with angular speed $w \in \mathcal{W}$.

3.2 Relative robot-obstacle dynamics

We presume a two-dimensional point-mass model for the robot with state $\overline{x}^r = (x^r, y^r)$ and dynamics in Cartesian coordinates

$$\begin{aligned} \dot{x}^r &= u_x \\ \dot{y}^r &= u_y \end{aligned} \tag{3}$$

with two-dimensional control input $u = (u_x, u_y)$ that is the velocity of the robot in both directions. While the obstacle is not trying to actively collide with the robot, its dynamics (1), (2) contain a stochastic component, which can be considered a disturbance that affects the robot's behavior. Discretizing the dynamics (3) using an Euler approximation with time step Δ results in

$$\overline{x}_{n+1}^r = \overline{x}_n^r + \Delta \cdot u. \tag{4}$$

A collision between the robot and the obstacle occurs when $|\overline{x}_n^r - \overline{x}_n^o| \leq \epsilon$ for some n and ϵ small. We construct a relative coordinate space that is fixed to the obstacle, with the relative state defined as $\tilde{x} = \overline{x}^r - \overline{x}^o$. Hence the dynamics of the robot *relative* to the obstacle are

$$\tilde{x}_{n+1} = \tilde{x}_n + \Delta u_n - \Delta f(w_n, t_n) \tag{5}$$

with $f(\cdot)$ as in (1) and (2), and a *collision* is defined as

$$|\tilde{x}_n| \leq \epsilon. \tag{6}$$

Using (5), we now have a dynamical system with state $\tilde{x} \in \mathcal{X}$, control input $u \in \mathcal{U}$ that is bounded, and stochastic disturbance w. Because $\tilde{x}_{n+1}$ is a function of a random variable, it is also a random variable. Its transitions are governed by a stochastic transition kernel, $\tau(\tilde{x}_{n+1} \mid \tilde{x}_n, u_n, n)$, that represents the probability distribution of $\tilde{x}_{n+1}$ conditioned on the known values $\tilde{x}_n$, u_n and time step n.

3.3 Roadmap Construction

Roadmap-based techniques attempt to approximate the topology of the collision-free C-space, the space of all possible robot configurations (where a configuration completely specifies the location of every point on the robot) [16]. They work by building a graph in collision-free C-space through sampling collision-free robot configurations (*node generation*), connecting neighboring nodes with weighted edges if a collision-free transition exists (*node connection*), and then querying the resulting roadmap by finding a path to a goal configuration (*roadmap query*). Node generation can be done via several different methods, e.g., using a cell decomposition of the space [15], a uniform random distribution

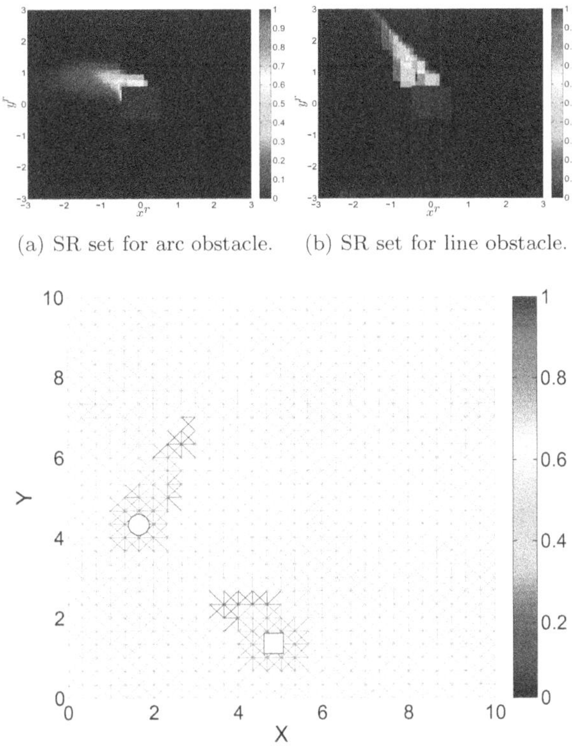

(a) SR set for arc obstacle. (b) SR set for line obstacle.

(c) Roadmap with edges weighted by SR sets

Figure 1: Two stochastic reachable sets for constant-arc and straight-line obstacles and their incorporation into a roadmap. (a) Stochastic reachable set that shows the likelihood of collision between the robot and an arc obstacle (in relative coordinates). (b) Stochastic reachable set for a straight-line obstacle with $\alpha = 1$. (c) Roadmap (Cartesian coordinates) with likelihood of collision indicated by edge color. The yellow circle (square) shows the line (arc) obstacle locations.

[14], obstacle boundaries [33], or visibility [26]. The utility of these various node generation methods varies with problem complexity. For example, cell decomposition methods are powerful, but their utility degrades with complex obstacle boundaries and in high-dimensional planning problems. On the other hand, uniform random placement, PRM, works well with high-dimensional problems, but has difficulty with obstacles that form tight narrow passages. Collision-free tests are often performed with static obstacles, and edge weights can be determined by several metrics of interest, e.g., distance [14], clearance from obstacles [18] [20], or other problem-specific measures [27].

4. METHODS

In this section, we present the novel methods for integrating SR sets with roadmap path extraction. First, we formulate the SR problem for collision avoidance with the straight-line and constant-arc dynamic obstacles. We then show how SR can be used to help build roadmaps that select a path that avoids multiple moving obstacles.

4.1 SR for Collision Avoidance

The SR problem can be formulated in the context of collision avoidance, where the probability of avoiding collisions within some finite time horizon is determined. The set $\overline{K}$ is defined as the set of states in which a collision is said to occur (6). To avoid collision with the obstacle, the robot should remain within K, the complement of $\overline{K}$. The probability that the robot will remain within K over N time steps, with initial relative position $\tilde{x}_0$, is given by

$$A_{\tilde{x}_0}^{\overline{u},N}(K) = \mathbb{P}\left[\tilde{x}_0, \ldots, \tilde{x}_N \in K \mid \tilde{x}_0, \overline{u}\right] \tag{7}$$

with $\mathbb{P}$ denoting probability and input sequence $\overline{u} = [u_0, u_1, \cdots, u_{N-1}]^T$.

Since $\mathbb{P}[x \in K] = \mathbb{E}[\mathbf{1}_K(x)]$, with $\mathbb{E}$ denoting expected value and $\mathbf{1}_K(x)$ denoting the indicator function defined as $\mathbf{1}_K(x) = 1$ for $x \in K$, and 0 otherwise, equation (7) can be rewritten as (see [1])

$$A_{\tilde{x}_0}^{\overline{u},N}(K) = \mathbb{E}\left[\prod_{n=0}^{N} \mathbf{1}_K(\tilde{x}_n) \mid \tilde{x}_0, \overline{u}\right], \tag{8}$$

since $\prod_{n=0}^{N} \mathbf{1}_K(\tilde{x}_n) = 1$ if $\tilde{x}_0, \ldots, \tilde{x}_N \in K$, and 0 otherwise.

Finally, instead of assuming a predetermined set of control inputs $\overline{u}$, we construct a state-feedback control input to maximize the likelihood of avoiding collision and to facilitate real-time control selection for motion planning. Equation (8) can then be reformulated as a stochastic optimal control problem.

$$A_{\tilde{x}_0}^{N}(K) = \max_{\pi \in \Pi} \mathbb{E}\left[\prod_{n=0}^{N} \mathbf{1}_K(\tilde{x}_n) \mid \tilde{x}_0\right] \tag{9}$$

Hence we define a policy $\pi = (\pi_0, \ldots, \pi_{N-1})$ with $\pi_n : \mathcal{X} \to \mathcal{U}$ and optimize (9) over all possible policies Π of this form. The resulting optimal policy π^* provides an upper bound on the probability of avoiding collision.

We implement a dynamic programming recursion [3], first introduced for the reachability problem in [1], to estimate the collision avoidance probability.

$$V_N(\tilde{x}) = \mathbf{1}_K(\tilde{x}) \tag{10}$$

$$V_n(\tilde{x}) = \mathbf{1}_K(\tilde{x}) \int_{\mathcal{X}} V_{n+1}(\tilde{x}')\tau(\tilde{x}' \mid \tilde{x}, u, n)\, d\tilde{x}' \tag{11}$$

Iterating (10), (11) backwards, the value function at time 0 provides the probability of avoiding collision,

$$V_0(\tilde{x}_0) = A_{\tilde{x}_0}^{N}(K). \tag{12}$$

The optimal control is determined by evaluating

$$V_n^*(\tilde{x}) = \sup_{u \in \mathcal{U}} \left\{ \mathbf{1}_K(\tilde{x}) \int_{\mathcal{X}} V_{n+1}^*(\tilde{x}')\tau(\tilde{x}' \mid \tilde{x}, u, n)\, d\tilde{x}' \right\} \tag{13}$$

which also returns the optimal policy π^*, with

$$\pi_n^*(\tilde{x}) = u_n = \arg\sup_{u \in \mathcal{U}} V_n^*(\tilde{x}). \tag{14}$$

Equation (13) can be simplified to

$$V_n^*(\tilde{x}) = \max_{u \in \mathcal{U}} \left\{ \mathbf{1}_K(\tilde{x}) \sum_{w \in \mathcal{W}} V_{n+1}^*\left(\tilde{x} + \Delta u - \Delta f(w, n)\right) p(w) \right\}. \tag{15}$$

Figure 1a shows the SR set for a constant-arc obstacle with radius $r = 5$, and probabilities $p(w) = \{0.2, 0.2, 0.3, 0.3\}$ associated with angular speeds $w \in \mathcal{W} = \left\{\frac{.4}{2\pi}, \frac{.6}{2\pi}, \frac{.9}{2\pi}, \frac{1.2}{2\pi}\right\}$. The slight curvature seen in the probability peaks corresponds to the obstacle trajectory. Similarly, Figure 1b shows the SR set for a straight-line obstacle with probabilities $p(w) = \{0.3, 0.4, 0.3\}$ associated with speeds $w \in \mathcal{W} = \{0.5, 0.7, 0.9\}$, and slope $\alpha = -1$. The peaks show higher probability of collision with the obstacle when the robot is in line with the obstacle trajectory. Intuitively, the closer the robot is to the obstacle, the higher the probability of collision.

On a single core of an Intel 3.40 GHz CORE i7-2600 CPU with 8 GB of RAM, Figure 1a took 1727.25 seconds to compute, over a horizon of $N = 30$ steps and a time step of length $\Delta = 1$. Figure 1b took 1751.87 seconds to compute, again with $N = 30$ and $\Delta = 1$. In both cases, we observed convergence in the stochastic reachable sets for $N > 5$ since the robot and obstacle traveled sufficiently far apart within this time frame.

With a single obstacle, $V_0^*(\tilde{x}_0)$ in (15) is the maximum probability of avoiding a collision, and hence a tight upper bound. For two obstacles with separately calculated avoidance probabilities $V_0^{*,1}(\tilde{x}_0^1)$, $V_0^{*,2}(\tilde{x}_0^2)$ (with relative position $\tilde{x}_0^i$ with respect to obstacle i), the probability of avoiding collision with *both* obstacles is

$$\begin{aligned} \mathbb{P}[B_1 \cap B_2] &= \mathbb{P}[B_1] + \mathbb{P}[B_2] - \mathbb{P}[B_1 \cup B_2] \\ &\leq \min\{\mathbb{P}[B_1], \mathbb{P}[B_2]\} \\ \mathbb{P}[B_1 \cap B_2] &\leq \min\{V_0^{*,1}(\tilde{x}_0^1), V_0^{*,2}(\tilde{x}_0^2)\} \end{aligned} \tag{16}$$

where B_i corresponds to the event that the robot avoids collision with obstacle i. We obtain an upper bound on the collision avoidance probability for two obstacles by taking the minimum of the individual avoidance probabilities. The same holds similarly for m obstacles. The minimum of the m individual avoidance probabilities provides an upper bound on the probability of avoiding collision with all m obstacles.

Lastly, we note that because we ultimately use the collision avoidance probabilities to determine routing choices on a roadmap, the true probabilities are of less interest than the relative probabilities at different locations. By generating an upper bound on the probability of avoiding collision with several moving obstacles, the robot can identify and travel along the path with the greatest upper bound. Further, if the obstacles are not so dense that avoiding the obstacle with the highest probability of collision implies a greater likelihood of avoiding all other obstacles as well, then this upper bound is fairly tight, and the robot can accurately identify the safest route through the roadmap.

4.2 SR Query

We now integrate SR sets (12) for straight-line and constant-arc obstacles into a pre-computed roadmap using techniques developed for static obstacles [15, 14]. Given a roadmap and an SR set for each moving obstacle, we identify paths that are likely to be free.

Algorithm 1 describes integration of the stochastic reachable sets into an existing roadmap via the roadmap query process. Although the SR calculation is performed offline, Algorithm 1 is intended to run in real time, using the information currently available to the robot (i.e. obstacle locations). Paths are extracted using Dijkstra's algorithm [7].

Algorithm 1 SR Query

Input: Obstacles O, $Roadmap$, Max time $T = N \cdot \Delta$
Output: boolean $Success$

1: $nextNode = start$
2: $previousNode = start$
3: **for** $t_n = 0$; $t_n < T$; $n = n + 1$ **do**
4:    **for** Obstacle $o \in O$ **do**
5:       $updateObstacle(o)$
6:    **end for**
7:    **if** $at(robot, nextNode)$ **then**
8:       **for** each edge $e \in Roadmap$ **do**
9:          $EdgeWeight = updateEdgeWeights(e, O)$
10:       **end for**
11:       $Path = Dijkstras(previousNode, GoalNode)$
12:       $nextNode = Path.next$
13:       $x^r_{n+1} = Path.next.getXVelocity()$
14:       $y^r_{n+1} = Path.next.getYVelocity()$
15:    **end if**
16:    $\overline{x}^r_{n+1} = interp(previousNode, nextNode, t_n)$
17: **end for**

However, to find paths of combined shortest distance and lowest probability of collision, the SR computation must be integrated into the roadmap edge weights. First, since the robot knows the location of each obstacle at the current time, the positions of the obstacles are updated to reflect their current locations. Second, we consider each node in the roadmap to be a waypoint. Updates of the roadmap weights are then performed at waypoints (see Algorithm 1, line 7). Updates consist of reweighting all edges (line 9), finding the path of lowest edge weight (line 11), querying the SR optimal control (14) to determine the robot's speed and resulting trajectory (lines 13 and 14), and traversing along that edge with the determined robot speed for the allotted time (line 15). If the robot is not at a waypoint, then it continues along the predetermined roadmap edge.

Two elements that are critical to the success of Algorithm 1 and atypical for probabilistic road maps are 1) updating of the obstacles, and 2) the subsequent effect on edge weights.

Regarding the first element, the likelihood of avoiding collision (12) and the optimal control (14) are evaluated over a discretized set of states, and are stored for use during run time for path planning. The algorithm propagates the location of the obstacles according to each obstacle's stochastic dynamics (1), (2). The stochastically determined obstacle speeds are chosen as per the randomization in Algorithm 2. The relative states are computed for every robot-obstacle pair in the environment.

Regarding the second element, edges define a transition between two configurations (see Section 3.3). These edges can be subdivided (often uniformly) into sets of discrete points defining the transition between configurations in the roadmap, and each point corresponds to a new intermediate configuration. The weight for a single edge is updated as in Algorithm 3. For each intermediate configuration associated with an edge, the relative distance to each obstacle is calculated and the probability of collision avoidance at the current relative distance is queried for each obstacle. The minimum of all avoidance probabilities is taken as the weight for

Algorithm 2 updateObstacle

Input: time $t_n = n \cdot \Delta$, obstacle o, velocities $w \in \mathcal{W} = \{w_1, w_2, ..., w_{n_W}\}$, probabilities $p(w)$

1: **if** $mod(t_n, 1) == 0$ **then**
2:    $s = rand(0, 1)$
3:    **for** $index = 0$; $index < n_W$; $index++$ **do**
4:       **if** $s \leq p(w)[index]$ **then**
5:          $o.w = w[index]$
6:          break
7:       **end if**
8:    **end for**
9: **end if**
10: $\overline{x}^o_{n+1} = \overline{x}^o_n + \Delta \cdot f(o.w, t_n)$

Algorithm 3 updateEdgeWeight

Input: Edge e, Obstacles O

1: $EdgeWeight = 0$
2: **for** Configuration $c \in e$ **do**
3:    $PROB = 1$
4:    **for** Obstacle $o \in O$ **do**
5:       $\tilde{x} = c - o$
6:       $PROB = \min\{PROB, o.V_0^*(\tilde{x})\}$
7:    **end for**
8:    **if** $PROB < EdgeWeight$ **then**
9:       $EdgeWeight = PROB$
10:    **end if**
11: **end for**
12: $e.Weight = \frac{1}{EdgeWeight}$

that configuration. This calculation is fast in comparison to standard collision detection methods whose computational complexity is defined by the number of polygons in the planning problem. The assigned edge weight is then the lowest probability of collision avoidance amongst all intermediate configurations for that edge, inverted for use in Dijkstra's algorithm (which finds minimum cost paths for graphs with nonnegative edge weights). Note that we presume the same time horizon N and time step Δ in Algorithm 1 as we do in the reachability calculations.

5. EXPERIMENTS

We evaluated our method on successful navigation in environments with several moving obstacles. Successful navigation is defined as the ability to find a path from a start state to goal state, without any collisions and within a specified time horizon. The stochastic reachable sets were computed in Matlab, and the SR Query was added to the Parasol Motion Planning Library (PMPL) from Texas A&M University. PMPL was also used to generate the initial roadmaps. Experiments were run on a single core of an Intel 3.40 GHz CORE i7-2600 CPU with 8 GB of RAM.

We compared our method (SR Query) to a Lazy-based method (Lazy) for moving obstacle avoidance [12]. The Lazy method updates the roadmap as obstacles move, by invalidating edges and nodes that are found to be in collision with the new position of the moving obstacles. This comparison

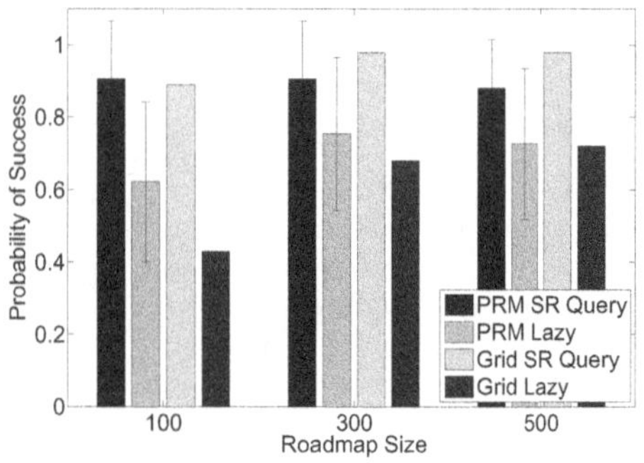

Figure 2: Comparison of SR Query and Lazy methods for the two dynamic obstacle experiment. Averaged likelihood of successfully traversing a collision-free path within the allotted time horizon for a given roadmap size, for Grid-based maps and PRM roadmaps. Note: Grid runs do not have error bars since there is only a single cell decomposition for a given roadmap size.

shows the accuracy gained by considering the probabilities of collision instead of just the obstacles' current locations.

Furthermore, we show the flexibility of the method by running experiments with node generation done with a uniform random distribution (PRM) [14] and with a regular cell decomposition (Grid) [15]. While cell decompositions can be ideal solutions, they are often infeasible for planning problems with several or complex static obstacles or of high dimensionality. In those cases, PRMs are often preferred. Since both types of roadmaps are treated the same way by the algorithm, we investigate how the topology of the roadmap can impact our method. In the Grid roadmaps, every node is connected with up to 8 adjacent neighbors. PRM roadmaps are constructed with uniform random sampling and each node is connected to its five closest neighbors.

5.1 Two Moving Obstacles

In this experiment, the robot navigates across a planning space while avoiding two dynamic obstacles that follow straight-line (1) and constant-arc (2) dynamics from initial conditions $\overline{x}_l^o(0)$, $\overline{x}_a^o(0)$. The robot's start state and goal state are at the opposite corners of a 20×20 planning space (Figure 3a). The obstacle trajectories are chosen to generate sufficient opportunities for conflict with the robot, and obstacles may exit the planning space.

In order to evaluate the performance of our algorithm, we constructed roadmaps of $|\mathcal{N}| = 100$, 300, and 500 nodes using the standard PRM method. For each map size, we used 10 random seeds to create 10 different PRM roadmaps. We also produced Grid roadmaps of size $\lfloor\sqrt{|\mathcal{N}|}\rfloor^2$ nodes, where $\mathcal{N}$ is the number of nodes in the corresponding PRM roadmap, to account for their square and unformly spaced node structure. We simulated 100 obstacle pair trajectories, resulting in $10 \times 100 = 1,000$ simulations for each map size. The success of the algorithm was measured by collision-free path completion (the robot reaching the target) within the given time horizon. To be conservative, we also declared instances in which the robot did not find a collision-free path within the allotted time horizon as unsuccessful. However, time horizons are only applicable for the SR Query method since the Lazy method is allowed to run until a path is found,

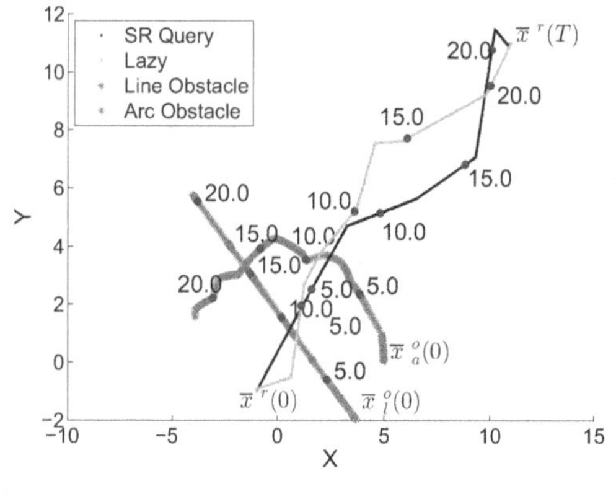

(a) Similar paths generated by SR Query and Lazy methods for two dynamic obstacle scenario.

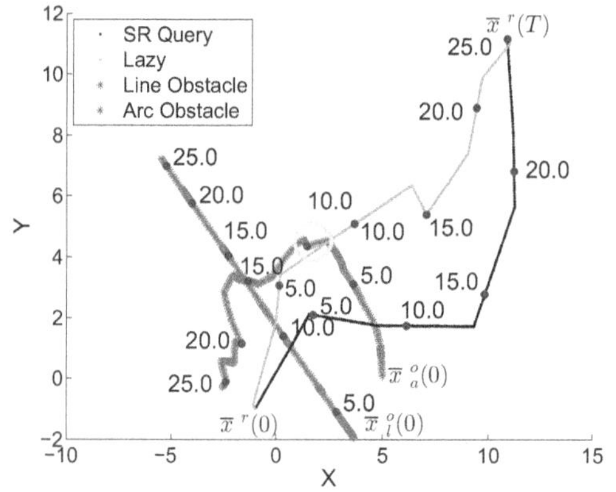

(b) Different paths generated by SR Query and Lazy methods for two dynamic obstacle scenario.

Figure 3: Sample trajectories found by SR Query (black line) and Lazy (blue line) methods on a PRM roadmap with two obstacles (red lines) over $T = N\Delta = 30$ seconds. (a) Both methods found qualitatively similar paths, due to little obstacle interference. (b) SR Query and Lazy found very different paths, likely due to a near miss with one of the dynamic obstacles (yellow circle).

no path exists, or a collision occurs. Each simulation was run for $T = 30$ seconds with a sampling interval of $\Delta = 1$ seconds ($N = 30$ time steps).

Figure 2 shows the effect of map size as well as the relative effectiveness of the two methods on PRM and Grid roadmaps in terms of the mean percentage of success. For the PRM roadmaps, SR Query was able to find successful paths 88% to 91% of the time, based on roadmap size. The error bars show how the randomized roadmap structures impact the success rate. In comparison, the Lazy method found successful paths 63% to 75% of the time. Unsuccessful runs of Lazy were due either to pruned nodes and edges that made traversal to the goal impossible, or direct collision with a moving obstacle. Error bars are not included for Grid due to the static map structure of a cell decomposition. In comparing Grid-based maps to PRM roadmaps, we find that the Grid-based maps produce better results for SR Query with larger map sizes, but poorer results for Lazy (for all map sizes). This is consistent with evidence that

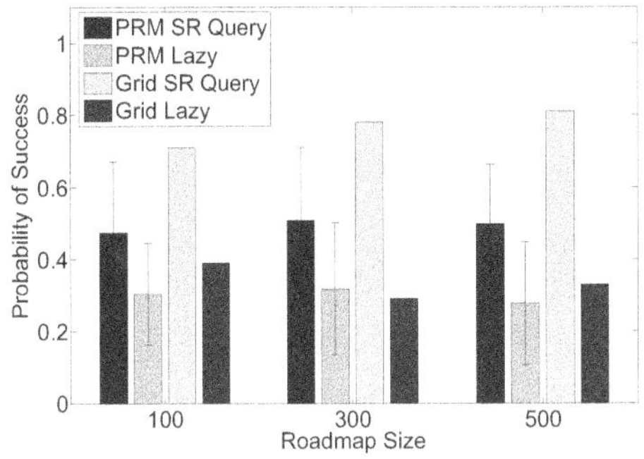

Figure 4: Comparison of SR Query and Lazy methods for the 50 dynamic obstacle experiment. Averaged likelihood of successfully traversing a collision-free path within the allotted time horizon for a given roadmap size, for Grid-based maps and PRM roadmaps. Note: Grid runs do not have error bars since there is only a single cell decomposition for a given roadmap size.

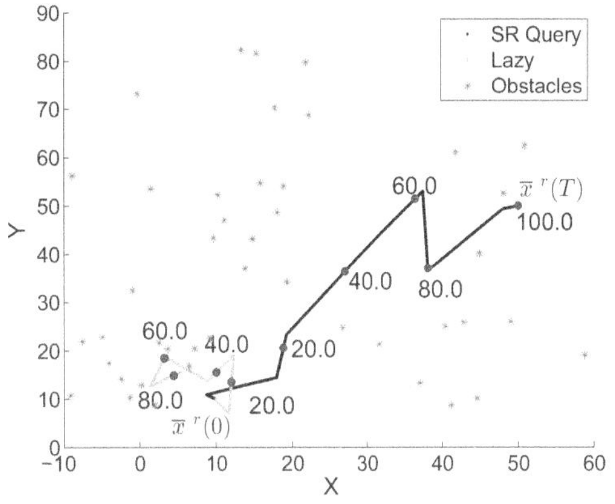

(a) Fifty dynamic obstacles scenario in which Lazy method results in collision, SR Query method does not.

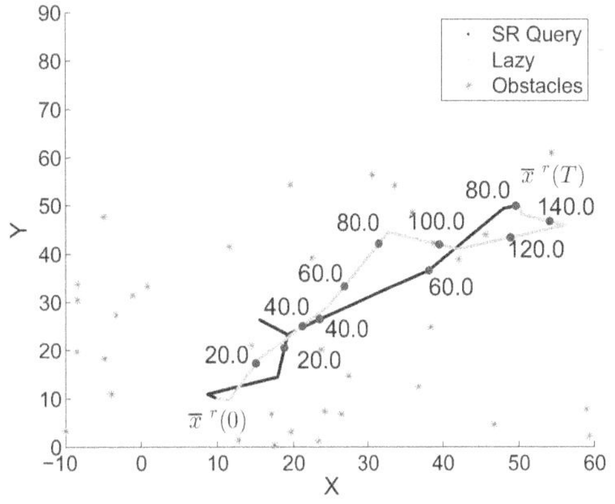

(b) Fifty dynamic obstacle scenario in which both methods successfully find collision-free paths.

Figure 5: Sample trajectories found by SR Query (black line) and Lazy (blue line) methods on a PRM roadmap with 50 obstacles shown at 80s into the simulation (red squares). Total simulation time $T = N\Delta = 100$s. (a) The Lazy method results in collision, but SR Query method successfully reaches the goal state without collision. (b) Sample trajectories (as in (a)), in which similar successful paths are found via both methods. *Movies of the 50 moving obstacle simulations are available at* `https://www.cs.unm.edu/amprg/Research/DO/`

Grids perform as well or better than randomized roadmaps in environments without static obstacles [15]. In all cases (Grid-based or PRM roadmaps), the SR Query method performs between 15% and 45% better than the Lazy method.

We further examine the paths selected by the two algorithms. In Figure 3a, the path generated via the SR Query method (black line) is fairly similar to the path generated via the Lazy method. The moving obstacles are shown in red, and time is indicated as labeled waypoints along each path. Both Lazy and SR Query methods follow the same path initially, but at around $t = 10$ seconds, the SR Query method identifies an incoming obstacle and moves the robot away from the obstacle. However, the Lazy method does not anticipate a possible collision, and so it does not change its path. In this case, the Lazy method allows the robot to barely pass in front of the obstacle. A similar near collision for the Lazy method is shown in Figure 3b. In this example, the paths for SR Query and Lazy are the same for the first 10 seconds. Again, SR Query anticipates an incoming obstacle and changes its path to avert a possible collision. The Lazy method generates a path for the robot that passes in front of the obstacle with very little clearance. This near miss is highlighted in Figure 3b inside the yellow circle.

5.2 Fifty Moving Obstacles

In this experiment, a robot navigates across a 60×60 planning space while avoiding 50 dynamic obstacles, O_i, $i \in \{1, \cdots, 50\}$. Twenty-five of the obstacles have straight-line dynamics (1), five each traveling along lines with $\alpha \in \{-1.5, -1, -0.5, +0.5, 1.0\}$, respectively. The other 25 dynamic obstacles have constant-arc dynamics (2), 10 each with radius $r = 50$, 10 with $r = 40$, and five with $r = 30$. The speeds and associated probabilities for each obstacle are as described in Section 4.1.

We constructed 10 each of the three roadmap sizes, as in Section 5.1. We again generated 100 obstacle trajectories, resulting in 1000 total simulations for each map size. Since obtaining a feasible path is more difficult with so many more obstacles, we increased the time horizon to $T = 100$ seconds.

Figure 4 shows the effect of map size as well as the average success rate of the two methods on PRM and Grid roadmaps. As this is a significantly harder problem, the percentages of success are lower as compared to the two obstacle scenario in Figure 2. However, in all cases the SR Query method is at least 20% better than the Lazy method. Interestingly, the Grid-based solution is significantly more successful than the PRM-based method. This is likely due to the regular spacing of the roadmap nodes, which prevents long edges and allows the algorithm to make quicker replanning decisions. However, this advantage would not likely exist in more complex environments. As in Section 5.1, the error bars in Figure 4 indicate the significant impact of randomization in the PRM roadmap.

The 50 obstacle test in Figure 4 has lower success rates than the two obstacle test in Figure 2 because of two factors. First, finding a collision-free path is significantly harder with

50 obstacles as opposed to merely two. Second, the roadmap density, defined as the number of nodes per area of the planning space, is lower with 50 obstacles than with two obstacles. Since the roadmap sizes are the same, but the area increases from 20×20 to 60×60, the 50 obstacle tests have *lower* roadmap density. Lower density roadmaps force the robot to travel greater distances before path replanning (which occurs in Algorithm 1 at roadmap nodes), and consequently should have more collisions. However, relatively high success rates are evident for the SR Query methods, especially via Grid methods, likely due to the even distribution of nodes that allow for consistent replanning.

Figures 5a and 5b show two sample trajectories, one in which the SR Query method significantly outperforms the Lazy method, and another in which the two methods behave comparably. Movies of the full 50 obstacle simulation are available at
`https://www.cs.unm.edu/amprg/Research/DO/`.

6. CONCLUSIONS

We have successfully incorporated stochastic reachability into motion planning roadmaps, in order to develop a novel planning algorithm that accounts for stochastically moving obstacles. We combined SR sets for individual obstacles into a single planning solution, generating an upper bound on the total avoidance probability with several obstacles. We demonstrated our method on an example with 50 obstacles and on two methods of roadmap construction. To date, SR has never been applied to such large systems. By combining roadmaps with stochastic reachability, our algorithm significantly outperforms another existing roadmap-based method for moving obstacles. Future work includes exploring better ways of integrating multiple SR sets to generate tighter upper bounds on total collision avoidance probabilities when incorporated into the roadmap. We also plan to investigate higher dimensional systems with more complex obstacle movement, by exploring approximate SR calculations. We believe the incorporation of SR into roadmaps is a promising technique for motion planning under uncertainty, as demonstrated by our simulations.

7. ACKNOWLEDGMENTS

Malone is supported in part by the UNM Manufacturing Engineering Program supported by Sandia National Laboratories PO# 1110220. Lesser and Oishi are supported in part by National Science Foundation (NSF) Career Award CMMI-1254990 and NSF Award CPS-1329878. Tapia is supported in part by the National Institutes of Health (NIH) Grant P20RR018754 to the Center for Evolutionary and Theoretical Immunology.

8. REFERENCES

[1] Abate, A., Prandini, M., Lygeros, J., and Sastry, S. Probabilistic reachability and safety for controlled discrete time stochastic hybrid systems. *Automatica* (2008), 2724–2734.

[2] Al-Hmouz, R., Gulrez, T., and Al-Jumaily, A. Probabilistic road maps with obstacle avoidance in cluttered dynamic environment. In *Intelligent Sensors, Sensor Networks and Information Processing Conf.* (2004), IEEE, pp. 241–245.

[3] Bertsekas, D. P. *Dynamic Programming and Optimal Control.* Athena Scientific, 2005.

[4] Bohlin, R., and Kavraki, L. E. Path planning using Lazy PRM. In *Proc. IEEE Int. Conf. Robot. Autom. (ICRA)* (2000), pp. 521–528.

[5] Brock, O., and Khatib, O. Elastic strips: Real-time path modification for mobile manipulation. *International Symposium of Robotics Research* (1997), 5–13.

[6] Choset, H., Lynch, K. M., Hutchinson, S., Kantor, G. A., Burgard, W., Kavraki, L. E., and Thrun, S. *Principles of Robot Motion: Theory, Algorithms, and Implementations.* MIT Press, 2005.

[7] Dijkstra, E. W. A note on two problems in connexion with graphs. *Numerische mathematik* (1959), 269–271.

[8] Ding, J., Li, E., Huang, H., and Tomlin, C. Reachability-based synthesis of feedback policies for motion planning under bounded disturbances. In *Proc. IEEE Int. Conf. Robot. Autom. (ICRA)* (2011), pp. 2160–2165.

[9] Gillula, J. H., Hoffmann, G. M., Haomiao, H., Vitus, M. P., and Tomlin, C. J. Applications of hybrid reachability analysis to robotic aerial vehicles. *The Int. Journal of Robotics Research* (2011), 335–354.

[10] Hsu, D., Kindel, R., Latombe, J. C., and Rock, S. Randomized kinodynamic motion planning with moving obstacles. In *Proc. Int. Workshop on Algorithmic Foundations of Robotics (WAFR)* (2000), pp. SA1–SA18.

[11] Hsu, D., Latombe, J.-C., and Kurniawati, H. Foundations of probabilistic roadmap planning. In *Proc. Int. Workshop on Algorithmic Foundations of Robotics (WAFR)* (2006).

[12] Jaillet, L., and Simeon, T. A PRM-based motion planner for dynamically changing environments. In *Proc. IEEE Int. Conf. Intel. Rob. Syst. (IROS)* (2004).

[13] Kamgarpour, M., Ding, J., Summers, S., Abate, A., Lygeros, J., and Tomlin, C. Discrete time stochastic hybrid dynamical games: Verification and controller synthesis. In *Conf. on Decision and Control* (2011), pp. 6122–6127.

[14] Kavraki, L. E., Švestka, P., Latombe, J. C., and Overmars, M. H. Probabilistic roadmaps for path planning in high-dimensional configuration spaces. *IEEE Trans. Robot. Automat.* (1996), 566–580.

[15] Lindemann, S. R., and LaValle, S. M. Current issues in sampling-based motion planning. In *Robotics Research.* Springer, 2005, pp. 36–54.

[16] Lozano-Pérez, T., and Wesley, M. A. An algorithm for planning collision-free paths among polyhedral obstacles. *Communications of the ACM* (1979), 560–570.

[17] Majumdar, A., and Tedrake, R. Robust online motion planning with regions of finite time invariance. In *Algorithmic Foundations of Robotics.* Springer, 2013, pp. 543–558.

[18] Malone, N., Manavi, K., Wood, J., and Tapia, L. Construction and use of roadmaps that incorporate workspace modeling errors. In *Proc. IEEE Int. Conf. Intel. Rob. Syst. (IROS)* (to appear, 2013).

[19] Margellos, K., and Lygeros, J. Hamilton-Jacobi formulation for reach-avoid problems with an application to air traffic management. *American Control Conf.* (2010), 3045–3050.

[20] Missiuro, P. E., and Roy, N. Adapting probabilistic roadmaps to handle uncertain maps. In *Proc. IEEE Int. Conf. Robot. Autom. (ICRA)* (2006), IEEE, pp. 1261–1267.

[21] Mitchell, I., Bayen, A., and Tomlin, C. A time-dependent Hamilton-Jacobi formulation of reachable sets for continuous dynamic games. *IEEE transactions on automatic control* (2005), 947–957.

[22] Nieuwenhuisen, D., van den Berg, J., and Overmars, M. Efficient path planning in changing environments. In *Proc. IEEE Int. Conf. Intel. Rob. Syst. (IROS)* (2007), IEEE, pp. 3295–3301.

[23] Quinlan, S., and Khatib, O. Elastic bands: Connecting path planning and control. In *Proc. IEEE Int. Conf. Robot. Autom. (ICRA)* (1993), pp. 802–807.

[24] Rodriguez, S., Lien, J.-M., and Amato, N. M. A framework for planning motion in environments with moving obstacles. In *Proc. IEEE Int. Conf. Intel. Rob. Syst. (IROS)* (2007), pp. 3309–3314.

[25] Shiller, Z., Large, F., and Sekhavat, S. Motion planning in dynamic environments: obstacles moving along arbitrary trajectories. In *Proc. IEEE Int. Conf. Robot. Autom. (ICRA)* (2001), vol. 4, pp. 3716–3721.

[26] Simeon, T., Laumond, J.-P., and Nissoux, C. Visibility-based probabilistic roadmaps for motion planning. *Advanced Robotics* (2000), 477–493.

[27] Song, G., Miller, S. L., and Amato, N. M. Customizing PRM roadmaps at query time. In *Proc. IEEE Int. Conf. Robot. Autom. (ICRA)* (2001), pp. 1500–1505.

[28] Summers, S., Kamgarpour, M., Lygeros, J., and Tomlin, C. A stochastic reach-avoid problem with random obstacles. In *Proc. Int. Conf. Hybrid Systems: Computation and Control (HSCC)* (2011), pp. 251–260.

[29] Takei, R., Huang, H., Ding, J., and Tomlin, C. Time-optimal multi-stage motion planning with guaranteed collision avoidance via an open-loop game formulation. In *Proc. IEEE Int. Conf. Robot. Autom. (ICRA)* (2012), pp. 323–329.

[30] Van Den Berg, J., Ferguson, D., and Kuffner, J. Anytime path planning and replanning in dynamic environments. In *Proc. IEEE Int. Conf. Robot. Autom. (ICRA)* (2006), IEEE, pp. 2366–2371.

[31] van den Berg, J. P., Nieuwenhuisen, D., Jaillet, L., and Overmars, M. H. Creating robust roadmaps for motion planning in changing environments. In *Proc. IEEE Int. Conf. Intel. Rob. Syst. (IROS)* (2005), IEEE, pp. 1053–1059.

[32] Van Den Berg, J. P., and Overmars, M. H. Roadmap-based motion planning in dynamic environments. *IEEE Transactions on Robotics* (2005), 885–897.

[33] Wu, Y. An obstacle-based probabilistic roadmap method for path planning. Master's thesis, Department of Computer Science, Texas A&M University, 1996.

[34] Yoshida, E., and Kanehiro, F. Reactive robot motion using path replanning and deformation. In *Proc. IEEE Int. Conf. Robot. Autom. (ICRA)* (2011), IEEE, pp. 5456–5462.

Timely Monitoring of Partially Observable Stochastic Systems

A. Prasad Sistla, Miloš Žefran, Yao Feng, and Yue Ben
University of Illinois at Chicago
{sistla,mzefran,yfeng9,yben2}@uic.edu

ABSTRACT

Ensuring the correct behavior of cyber physical systems at run time is of critical importance for their safe deployment. Any malfunctioning of such systems should be detected in a timely manner for further actions. This paper addresses the issue of how quickly a monitor raises an alarm after the occurrence of a failure in cyber physical systems. Towards this end, it introduces a class of systems called *exponentially converging* monitorable systems. The paper shows that failures in these systems can be detected fast by employing the traditional *threshold monitors*. It shows that the expected failure detection time for exponentially converging monitorable systems has logarithmic relationship with the inverse of the chosen threshold value. The paper identifies well defined natural classes of these systems. Experimental results are presented that confirm the theoretical results on the relationship between the failure detection time and the chosen threshold values.

1. INTRODUCTION

The modern cyber physical systems are becoming increasingly complex and require novel approaches to guarantee their correct functioning. This is especially so for safety critical systems such as medical devices and transportation systems where a failure can have catastrophic consequences.

Monitoring the behavior of a system at run time is an effective way of detecting failures. The monitor observes the inputs and outputs of the system and checks whether the behavior of the system is consistent with the expected behavior. Monitors can be especially useful if a fail-safe shutdown procedures can be developed, which is true for a broad class of systems. The fundamental advantage of monitors is that they are in principle easy to implement, and they are independent of the design procedures used to develop a component. While wrong assumptions might lead to a faulty design, the monitor is independent of design decisions and can therefore easily detect that the component is failing to perform its function. This paper, for the first time, addresses the time complexity of monitors and presents a number of important results.

Many cyber physical systems involve control systems where it is commonly assumed that system behavior is stochastic and its state is not directly observable. Furthermore, in digital control systems the state is typically quantized. We thus consider Hidden Markov Chains (HMC) to model such discrete state systems. In our earlier work [24, 25], we addressed the problem of monitoring a system, modeled as a HMC H, when the correctness specification is given by a deterministic Streett automaton $\mathcal{A}$ on the computations of the system. There we considered accuracy measures of a monitor that capture its rates of false alarms and missed alarms. There we also introduced two notions of monitorability, called *monitorability* and *strong monitorability*, of a HMC H with respect to a property specified by an automaton $\mathcal{A}$, and presented necessary and sufficient conditions for them. Monitoring algorithms for achieving arbitrary high values of accuracies were presented when the system is monitorable with respect to the property. These monitoring algorithms observe the outputs of the system, and in real-time, estimate the *acceptance probability*, which is the probability that the output sequence is generated by a correct computation of the system. They raise an alarm if this estimated probability goes below a given threshold, called *acceptance threshold*.

In this paper, we address the time taken for a monitor to raise an alarm after the occurrence of a system failure. We define a new notion of monitorability, called *exponentially converging* monitorability which takes time into consideration. Intuitively, a system H is exponentially converging monitorable with respect to a correctness specification $\mathcal{A}$, if after a failure the *acceptance probability* of an output sequence goes to zero exponentially with time with increasingly high probability, that also converges to 1 exponentially. For a threshold based monitoring algorithm, the time taken for it to raise an alarm, called *monitoring time*, is a random variable. We show that, if the system is exponentially converging monitorable with respect to the correctness specification, then the expected value, as well as the standard deviation, of the monitoring time for a threshold based monitor, is $O(\log(\frac{1}{atr}))$ where atr is the acceptance threshold used.

We show that the class of strongly monitorable systems introduced in [24] are exponentially converging monitorable. We also show that a subclass of well defined monitorable systems, called *bounded uniform* systems, are also exponentially converging monitorable. For these systems, our results show

HSCC'14, April 15–17, 2014, Berlin, Germany.

http://dx.doi.org/10.1145/2562059.2562136.

that the expected time for raising an alarm after a failure is $O(c \cdot \log(\frac{1}{atr}))$ where atr is as the acceptance threshold used and c is the inverse of the well known $KL\_divergence$ (also known as relative entropy) between the distributions of outputs on bad computations and good computations, respectively. We employ Quantized Probabilistic Hybrid Automata (QPHA) to model realistic systems and give their semantics as HMCs. We present experimental results, for examples described using QPHAs, that corroborate our theoretical analysis.

In summary the main contributions of the paper are as follows: (1) introduction of exponentially converging monitorable systems and results on the logarithmic bounds on expected monitoring time for threshold monitors; (2) results showing that strongly monitorable finite state systems, and bounded uniform monitorable systems are both exponentially converging monitorable; (3) experimental results corroborating the above results.

The paper is organized as follows. Section 2 contains related work. Section 3 presents the model, the definitions and review of relevant earlier work. Section 4 introduces exponentially converging monitorability. It also presents results showing that strongly monitorable finite state systems, and uniform bounded monitorable systems are exponentially converging monitorable. Finally, in Section 5 we demonstrate the validity of the theoretical predictions with an example motivated by a car braking system. Due to the space limitations, most proofs have been omitted in the current version. For complete details we refer the reader to [26].

2. RELATED WORK

In our earlier works [8], we considered *external monitoring*, where the correctness property to be monitored is specified on the outputs of the system. In these cases, it is easy to see that every safety property is strongly monitorable (i.e., there exists a monitor with zero false alarm rate and zero missed alarm rate) and [8] shows that, for finite state systems, all properties including liveness properties are monitorable. The work [27] also considers external monitoring where the outputs have gaps, i.e., periods where the outputs are not recorded. This work employs interesting techniques for handling gaps through state estimation and evaluated them on realistic examples. However, it does not consider time complexity of the monitoring algorithms. As opposed to these, our earlier works [24,25] and the current work, consider *internal* monitoring where the correctness property is specified on the computations of the system which are not directly observable.

Several authors consider monitoring temporal properties of deterministic systems capable of measuring system state [2,5,7,18,31]. Some of them define monitorability, but only with respect to a property. In contrast, we consider partially observable stochastic systems (i.e., HMCs). In this case, the monitoring problem is significantly more difficult and both the system and the property need to be considered when defining monitorability.

A problem that has been extensively studied is monitoring and diagnosis of a hybrid automaton modeling a system [1, 3,12,15,30], where the aim is to detect when the automaton enters a fail state. The techniques employed in most of these works assume and depend on the specific possible modes of failure that take the automaton to the fail state. None of these works address the general problem of monitoring a system against properties specified in an expressive formal system such as automata. Furthermore, they do not address the problem of monitoring liveness properties.

Control synthesis for stochastic discrete-event systems has been studied in [13,16]. In contrast to our work, the authors only consider finite-state systems with directly observable state. Similarly, the literature on diagnosability of partially-observable discrete-event systems (e.g. [33]) only considers deterministic finite-state systems.

A method for monitoring and checking quantitative and probabilistic properties of real-time systems has been given in [22], [19] considers monitoring interfaces for faults using game-theoretical framework, and *conservative* run time monitors were proposed in [14, 23]; none of these works is intended for monitoring of hybrid systems.

The area of sequential analysis in statistics, pioneered by Wald (see [32]), deals with the problem of hypothesis testing using repeated and unbounded sampling. Similarly, the work on "Quickest Detection" pioneered by Vincent Poor [20] deals with detecting change in the distribution of signals generated by a source. They consider false alarm and missed alarm rates and the time for detection of change. However, they do not consider monitoring correctness properties specified by automata on infinite strings as we do here. Furthermore, in our scheme, both correct and incorrect executions are generated by a single Hidden Markov Chain.To the best of our knowledge, the notion of exponentially converging monitorability for such systems, has not been defined and studied in these works.

3. DEFINITIONS AND NOTATION

Sequences. Let S be a set. We let S^*, S^ω denote the set of finite sequences and the set of infinite sequences over S. For a finite sequence α over S, let $|\alpha|$ denote the length of α. For any $\alpha \in S^*$ and $b \in S$, we let $nbr(\alpha, b)$ denote the number of occurrences of b in α. Let $\sigma = s_0, s_1, \ldots$ be a possibly infinite sequence over S. For any $i \geq 0$, $\sigma[0,i]$ denotes the prefix of σ up to s_i. If α_1 is a finite sequence and α_2 is either a finite or an ω-sequence then $\alpha_1\alpha_2$ denotes the concatenation of the two sequences in that order. If $C \subseteq S^\omega$ and $\alpha \in S^*$ then αC denotes the set $\{\alpha\beta : \beta \in C\}$.

Safety Properties. For any $\sigma \in S^\omega$, let prefixes(σ) denote the set of prefixes of σ and for any $C \subseteq S^\omega$, let prefixes(C) $= \cup_{\sigma \in C}$(prefixes(σ)). We say that $C \subseteq S^\omega$ is a *safety* property if the following condition holds: for any $\sigma \in S^\omega$, if prefixes(σ) $\subseteq$ prefixes(C) then $\sigma \in C$.

Automata. A deterministic Streett automaton $\mathcal{A}$ is a tuple $(Q, \Sigma, \delta, q_0, F)$ where Q is it set of states, Σ is its input alphabet, $\delta : Q \times \Sigma \to Q$ is the next state function, q_0 is the starting state and F is a collection of pairs of subsets of states. A run $r = (r_0, ...r_i, ...)$ of the automaton on an infinite input sequence $\sigma = (\sigma_0, ...)$ is the unique infinite sequence of states such that $r_0 = q_0$ and $\forall i \geq 0$, $r_{i+1} = \delta(r_i, \sigma_i)$. A run $(r_0, ...)$ is said to be *accepting* if for every pair $(C, D) \in F$ the following holds: if there exist infinite values of i such that $r_i \in C$ then there are infinite values of j such that $r_j \in D$. An input string is accepted if there is an accepting run of the automaton on the input starting from the initial state. We let $L(\mathcal{A})$ denote the set of strings accepted by $\mathcal{A}$. An automaton $\mathcal{A}$, as given above, is called a *safety automaton* if F has a single pair $(\{q_{error}\}, \emptyset)$ where q_{error} is an absorbing state, i.e., all transitions from it go back to itself. The state q_{error} is called the error state and it is easy to see that an infinite input sequence is accepted iff the error state is never reached on this input.

Markov Chains. We assume that the reader is familiar with basic probability theory, random variables and Markov chains. We consider stochastic systems given as Markov Chains [17] and monitor their computations for satisfaction of a given property specified by an automaton or a temporal formula. A Markov chain $G = (S, R, \phi)$ is a triple satisfying the following: S is a set of countable states; $R \subseteq S \times S$ is a total binary relation (i.e., for every $s \in S$, there exists some $t \in S$ such that $(s,t) \in R$); and $\phi : R \rightarrow (0,1]$ is a probability function such that for each $s \in S$, $\sum_{(s,t)\in R} \phi((s,t)) = 1$. Note that, for every $(s,t) \in R$, $\phi((s,t))$ is non-zero. Intuitively, if at any time the system is in a state $s \in S$, then in one step, it goes to some state t such that $(s,t) \in R$ with probability $\phi((s,t))$. A finite path p of G is a sequence $s_0, s_1, \ldots, s_n$ of states such that $(s_i, s_{i+1}) \in R$ for $0 \leq i < n$. For any such p, if $n > 0$, then let $\phi(p) = \prod_{0\leq i<n} \phi((s_i, s_{i+1}))$; if $n = 0$ then let $\phi(p) = 1$. An infinite path of G is an infinite sequence of states $s_0, s_1, \ldots$ such that $\forall i \geq 0$, $(s_i, s_{i+1}) \in R$.

For any Markov chain G, as given above, we define a class $\mathcal{E}_G$ of measurable sets of infinite sequences over S. $\mathcal{E}_G$ is the σ-algebra [17] generated by sets of sequences of the form pS^ω where $p \in S^*$. Now, for any system state $r \in S$, we define a probability function $\mathcal{F}_{G,r}$ defined on $\mathcal{E}_G$ as follows. Intuitively, for any $C \in \mathcal{E}_G$, $\mathcal{F}_{G,r}(C)$ denotes the probability that a sequence of states generated from the system state r, is in C. $\mathcal{F}_{G,r}$ is the unique probability measure satisfying all the probability axioms [17], such that for every $p \in S^*$ and $C = pS^\omega$, if p is the empty sequence then $\mathcal{F}_{G,r}(C) = 1$, if p is a finite path starting from state r then $\mathcal{F}_{G,r}(C) = \phi(p)$, otherwise $\mathcal{F}_{G,r}(C) = 0$. Note that, by this definitions, any $C \subset S^\omega$ whose elements are not paths in G, has zero probability measure.

For any $D \in \mathcal{E}_G$ such that $\mathcal{F}_{G,r}(D) > 0$, we let $\mathcal{F}_{G,r|D}$ denote the conditional probability function given D; formally, for any $C, D \in \mathcal{E}_G$, $\mathcal{F}_{G,r|D}(C) = \frac{\mathcal{F}_{G,r}(C\cap D)}{\mathcal{F}_{G,r}(D)}$. For any $\alpha \in S^*$ and $C = \alpha S^\omega$, we let $\mathcal{F}_{G,r}(\alpha)$ denote the probability $\mathcal{F}_{G,r}(C)$ and $\mathcal{F}_{G,r|\alpha}$ denote the conditional probability function $\mathcal{F}_{G,r|C}$. For a set $C \subseteq S^*$, we let $\mathcal{F}_{G,r}(C)$ denote $\mathcal{F}_{G,r}(CS^\omega)$.

We will use automata to specify properties over sequences of states of a Markov chain G. The input symbols to the automata are states of G, i.e., members of S. It has been shown that, for any automaton $\mathcal{A}$, $L(\mathcal{A})$ is measurable [29]. We will be interested in monitoring sequences of states of a system modeled by G, i.e., computations generated by G, to ensure that it satisfies the property given by an automaton $\mathcal{A}$. However, the monitor can not observe the actual states of the system.

Classification and decomposition of states. We take the following definitions from [17]. For any two states $s, t \in S$ and any integer $n \geq 0$, let $f^n_{s,t}$ denote the probability of reaching state t starting from state s exactly after n steps for the first time, i.e., $f^n_{s,t} = \sum_p \phi(p)$ where the sum is taken over all paths, of length n, starting from s and ending in t and not containing t in between. Let $f_{s,t} = \sum_{n>0} f^n_{s,t}$. Intuitively, $f_{s,t}$ denotes the probability of eventually reaching t from s in one or more steps. We say that state s is *persistent* if $f_{s,s} = 1$, i.e., the probability of eventually returning to s, when started in s, is one. A state that is not persistent is called a *transient* state. A *terminal strongly connected component* (tscc) of G is a maximal subset X of S such that for every pair of states $s, t \in X$, there is a path from s to t and no state outside X is reachable from any state in X. For every tscc, either all of its nodes are persistent or all of them are transient. A *persistent tscc* (ptscc) is a tscc all of whose states are persistent. It is established [17] that the set S of states can be decomposed into disjoint sets $T, C_1, C_2, \ldots$ such that T is the set of transient states, and $\mathcal{C} = \{C_1, C_2, \ldots\}$ is the set of all persistent tscc's , i.e., ptscc's. Note that $\mathcal{C}$ can be infinite when G is infinite.

Hidden Markov Chains. A Hidden Markov Chain (HMC) [4] $H = (G, \Sigma, O, r_0)$ is a quadruple where $G = (S, R, \phi)$ is a Markov chain, Σ is a set of symbols called *output* symbols, $O : S \rightarrow \Sigma$ is the output function and $r_0 \in S$ is the initial state. Intuitively, for any $s \in S$, $O(s)$ is the output generated in state s and this output is generated when ever a transition entering state s is taken. The generated symbols become inputs to the monitor. H is called Hidden Markov chain because one only observes the outputs generated in each state but not the actual state. We extend the output function O to paths of G as follows. For any finite or infinite path $p = s_0, s_1, \ldots, s_i, \ldots$ in G, $O(p) = O(s_0), O(s_1), \ldots, O(s_i), \ldots$. For any finite or infinite sequence α in $\Sigma^* \cup \Sigma^\omega$, we let $O^{-1}(\alpha)$ denote the set of $p \in S^* \cup S^\omega$ such that $O(p) = \alpha$. For any $C' \subseteq \Sigma^* \cup \Sigma^\omega$, we let $O^{-1}(C') = \cup_{\alpha\in C'}(O^{-1}(\alpha))$.

For any HMC H as given above, we define a class $\mathcal{E}_H$ of sets of infinite sequences over Σ and for any $r \in S$, we define a probability measure $\mathcal{F}_{H,r}$ on $\mathcal{E}_H$ as follows. $\mathcal{E}_H$ is the σ-algebra generated by the sets $\alpha\Sigma^\omega$ for $\alpha \in \Sigma^*$, and for any $C \in \mathcal{E}_H$, $\mathcal{F}_{H,r}(C) = \mathcal{F}_{G,r}(O^{-1}(C))$. It can easily be shown that $\mathcal{F}_{H,r}$ is the unique probability measure such that for any $\alpha \in \Sigma^*$, $\mathcal{F}_{H,r}(\alpha\Sigma^\omega) = \mathcal{F}_{G,r}(O^{-1}(\alpha)S^\omega)$. Intuitively, $\mathcal{F}_{H,r}(C')$ denotes the probability that an output sequence generated from the system state r, is in C'. For any measurable sets $C, C' \in \mathcal{E}_H$ such that $\mathcal{F}_{H,r}(C) > 0$, we define the conditional probability

$$\mathcal{F}_{H,r|C}(C') = \mathcal{F}_{G,r|O^{-1}(C)}(O^{-1}(C')).$$

Monitors. A monitor $M : \Sigma^* \rightarrow \{0,1\}$ is a function with the property that, for any $\alpha \in \Sigma^*$, if $M(\alpha) = 0$ then $M(\alpha\beta) = 0$ for every $\beta \in \Sigma^*$. For an $\alpha \in \Sigma^*$, we say that M rejects α, if $M(\alpha) = 0$, otherwise we say M accepts α. Thus if M rejects α then it rejects all its extensions. For an infinite sequence $\sigma \in \Sigma^\omega$, we say that M rejects σ iff there exists a prefix α of σ that is rejected by M; we say M accepts σ if it does not reject it. Let $L(M)$ denote the set of infinite sequences accepted by M. It is not difficult to see that $L(M)$ is a safety property and $O^{-1}(L(M))$ is measurable (it is in $\mathcal{E}_G$).

Accuracy Measures. Let $\mathcal{A}$ be an automaton on states of H. The *acceptance accuracy* of M for $\mathcal{A}$ with respect to the HMC H, denoted by $AA(M, H, \mathcal{A})$, is the probability $\mathcal{F}_{G,r_0|L(\mathcal{A})}(O^{-1}(L(M)))$ where r_0 is the initial state of H. Intuitively, it is the conditional probability that a sequence generated by the system is accepted by M, given that it is in $L(\mathcal{A})$. The *rejection accuracy* of M for $\mathcal{A}$ with respect to H, denoted by $RA(M, H, \mathcal{A})$, is the probability that a sequence generated by the system is rejected by M, given that it is not in $L(\mathcal{A})$; formally, it is the probability $\mathcal{F}_{G,r_0|C}(D)$, where C, D are the complements of $L(\mathcal{A})$ and $O^{-1}(L(M))$ respectively.

Monitorability. We say that a system H is *strongly monitorable* with respect to an automaton $\mathcal{A}$ if there exists a monitor M such that $AA(M, H, \mathcal{A}) = 1$ and $RA(M, H, \mathcal{A}) = 1$. We say that a system H is *monitorable* with respect to an automaton $\mathcal{A}$ if for every $x \in [0, 1)$ there exists a monitor M such that $AA(M, H, \mathcal{A}) \geq x$ and $RA(M, H, \mathcal{A}) \geq x$.

Previous Results. Here we briefly review the results proved in [24]. These results provide necessary and sufficient conditions for monitorability. Let $H = (G, \Sigma, O, r_0)$ be a HMC where $G = (S, R, \phi)$ is the associated Markov chain. Let $\mathcal{A}$ be an automaton with input alphabet S.

Consider any $\alpha \in \Sigma^*$. Note that $\mathcal{F}_{H,r}(\alpha)$ is the probability that an output sequence of length n, generated by H from state r, is α. Let $\alpha \in \Sigma^*$ be such that $\mathcal{F}_{H,r}(\alpha) > 0$. Now, we define a probability measure $AccProb(\alpha)$ which is the conditional probability that an execution of the system H that initially generated the output sequence α is accepted by $\mathcal{A}$. Formally, $AccProb(\alpha) = \mathcal{F}_{H,r_0|C}(L(\mathcal{A}))$ where $C = O^{-1}(\alpha)S^\omega$. We call $AccProb(\alpha)$, $1 - AccProb(\alpha)$ as the acceptance and rejection probabilities of α, respectively.

Recall that for any $\beta \in \Sigma^\omega$ and integer $i \geq 0$, $\beta[0, i]$ denotes the prefix of β of length $i + 1$. Let $OneSeq(H, \mathcal{A})$ be the set of $\beta \in \Sigma^\omega$ such that $\lim_{i \to \infty} AccProb(\beta[0, i])$ exists and its value is 1. Similarly, let $ZeroSeq(H, \mathcal{A})$ be the set of all $\beta \in \Sigma^\omega$ such that the above limit exists and is equal to 0. We refer to elements of $ZeroSeq(H, \mathcal{A})$ and $OneSeq(H, \mathcal{A})$ as zero and one sequences, respectively. The sets $OneSeq(H, \mathcal{A})$ and $ZeroSeq(H, \mathcal{A})$ are measurable. Let $ZeroOneSeq(H, \mathcal{A}) = OneSeq(H, \mathcal{A}) \cup ZeroSeq(H, \mathcal{A})$. It has been shown in the earlier work [24] that for any HMC H and deterministic Streett H is monitorable with respect to $\mathcal{A}$ iff

$$\mathcal{F}_{H,r_0}(ZeroOneSeq(H, \mathcal{A})) = 1.$$

Comparison of Probability Distributions. For a probability distribution $\psi : \Delta \to [0, 1]$ over the set Δ, the *support* of ψ is defined to be the set $\{a \in \Delta : \psi(a) > 0\}$. Let ψ_1, ψ_2 be probability distributions on Δ having the same support. The divergence $KL\_div(\psi_1, \psi_2)$ between the two distributions (called Kullback-Leibler Divergence), is given by

$$KL\_div(\psi_1, \psi_2) = \sum_{a \in \Delta} \psi_1(a) \cdot f(a)$$

where $f(a) = \log(\frac{\psi_1(a)}{\psi_2(a)})$ when $\psi_1(a) > 0$, and $f(a) = 0$ otherwise, i.e., when $\psi_1(a) = \psi_2(a) = 0$. $KL\_div(\psi_1, \psi_2)$ is also known as the relative entropy and is commonly used in information theory. It is a well known that $KL\_div(\psi_1, \psi_2) > 0$ when $\psi_1 \neq \psi_2$. Obviously, this value is zero when $\psi_1 = \psi_2$.

4. TIMELY DETECTION OF FAILURES

In monitoring systems for detecting failures, in addition to accurately detecting failures, the time taken for detection of failures is also of paramount importance. Essentially, the time for failure detection is defined to be the time that elapses from the point a failure occurs to the time when the monitor raises an alarm. The time instance when a failure occurs is only well defined when the correctness property is a safety property.

Let $H = (G, \Sigma, O, r_0)$ be a HMC where $G = (S, R, \phi)$ is the associated finite Markov chain and $O : S \to \Sigma$ assigns output symbols from Σ to each state in S. We do not require S to be finite. Without loss of generality, we assume that every state in S is reachable from r_0. Let $\mathcal{A} = (Q, S, \delta, q_0, F)$ be a safety automaton with input alphabet S. $\mathcal{A}$ specifies the correctness property to be monitored. Recall that Q has a single error state q_{error} which is an absorbing state and F has the single pair $(\{q_{error}\}, \emptyset)$ and an input sequence is rejected if $\mathcal{A}$ ever reaches the q_{error}. We assume that Q is a finite set having cardinality m. Note that the number of transitions of $\mathcal{A}$ can be infinite since its input alphabet is S which can be countably infinite.

Safety Properties and Bad prefixes. Consider an incorrect, i.e. bad, computation σ of H, i.e., a computation that is rejected by $\mathcal{A}$. Any prefix of σ that is rejected by $\mathcal{A}$ (i.e., on which $\mathcal{A}$ goes to the error state) is called a *bad prefix* of σ. We consider the instance of failure of σ to be the first occurrence of a bad prefix, i.e., the smallest bad prefix of σ.

We consider *conservative monitors*. These monitors eventually reject every bad computation with probability 1. More specifically, we consider threshold based monitors. These monitors observe the outputs of the system in real-time. After each output, they compute $AccProb(\alpha)$ where α is the output sequence thus far, and they reject if this value is less than a given threshold atr.

As before, let σ be an infinite bad computation of the system, i.e., a computation that is rejected by $\mathcal{A}$. Let $\sigma[0:t]$ be the smallest bad prefix of σ, and let t' be the instance when the monitor raised an alarm. The difference $t' - t$ is the elapsed time before the monitor raises an alarm. We study this elapsed time under the condition that the system failed, i.e., generated a bad computation. Then, this elapsed time is a random variable and we let $MTIME(atr)$ denote this random variable when the monitor uses the threshold of atr for $AccProb()$. We let $E[MTIME(atr)]$ denote the expected value of this random variable. Recall that, for $C \subseteq \Sigma^\omega$, $\mathcal{F}_{H,r_0|ZeroSeq(H,\mathcal{A})}(C)$ denotes the conditional probability that an output sequence in C is generated given that the output sequences are from $ZeroSeq(H, \mathcal{A})$. For notational simplicity, we let $\mathcal{F}'(C)$ represent this value.

Observe that the monitor makes a decision solely based on the outputs generated by σ since this is all the information it has. Let $\alpha \in ZeroSeq(H, \mathcal{A})$. Most of the computations in $O^{-1}(ZeroSeq(H, \mathcal{A}))$ are bad computations, i.e., those rejected by $\mathcal{A}$. For any $\alpha \in ZeroSeq(H, \mathcal{A})$, let $f(\alpha)$ be the length of the smallest bad prefix in the set $prefixes(O^{-1}(\alpha))$. Furthermore, for any real constants $c, c' > 0$ and integer $t > 0$, let $ExConverge(c, c', t) = \{\alpha \in ZeroSeq(H, \mathcal{A}) : AccProb(\alpha[0 : f(\alpha) + t]) \leq c \cdot 2^{-c' \cdot t}\}$. Intuitively, this is the set of $\alpha \in ZeroSeq(H, \mathcal{A})$, for which the $AccProb()$ is $\leq c \cdot 2^{-c' \cdot t}$ after t time units from the earliest failure point. We say that H is *exponentially converging* monitorable with respect to $\mathcal{A}$, if there exist real numbers $c, c', d, d' > 0$ such that for all integers $t \geq 0$, $\mathcal{F}'(ExConverge(c, c', t)) \geq (1 - d \cdot 2^{-d' \cdot t})$. Intuitively, this means $AccProb()$ converges to zero exponentially from the earliest failure point with high probability, which goes to 1 exponentially as $t \to \infty$. In the above case, we call H to be exponentially converging monitorable with constants c, c', d, d'. The constant c' denotes the rate of convergence of the acceptance probability for outputs in $ZeroSeq(H, \mathcal{A})$.

The following theorem shows that if H is exponentially converging monitorable with respect to $\mathcal{A}$ and the monitor uses a threshold atr, then $E[MTIME(atr)] = O(\log(\frac{1}{atr}))$. Note that to get high accuracy, we need to make atr close to zero. This logarithmic dependence on $\frac{1}{atr}$ is a nice characteristic of exponentially converging monitorable systems.

THEOREM 1. *If H is exponentially converging monitorable, with respect to $\mathcal{A}$, with constants c, c', d, d', then*

$$E[MTIME(atr)] \leq \frac{1}{c'} \cdot \lceil \log(\frac{c}{atr}) \rceil + d \cdot \frac{1}{1 - 2^{-d'}} \quad (1)$$

PROOF. Assume that H is exponentially converging monitorable with constants c, c', d, d'. Now, consider any $\alpha \in ZeroSeq(H, \mathcal{A})$ and let t' be the smallest integer $\geq f(\alpha)$ such that $AccProb(\alpha[0 : t']) \leq atr$. The monitor will reject (raise an alarm) at time t'. Now consider the random variable $t' - f(\alpha)$ defined over the probability space $ZeroSeq(H, \mathcal{A})$ and call it $AMTIME(atr)$. Observe that multiple bad computations may generate the same α. According to our definition, the earliest failure time among all these bad computations is $f(\alpha)$. Hence the random variable $MTIME(atr)$, which we defined earlier, is less than or equal to $AMTIME(atr)$. Hence $E[MTIME(atr)] \leq E[AMTIME(atr)]$. We prove the theorem by showing that $E[AMTIME(atr)]$ satisfies the inequality (1).

According to [17],

$$E[AMTIME(atr)] = \sum_{n \geq 0} Prob\{AMTIME(atr) > n\}.$$

Let $C_n = \{\alpha \in ZeroSeq(H, \mathcal{A}) : AccProb(\alpha[0 : f(\alpha)+n]) > atr\}$. Now we have, $Prob\{AMTIME(atr) > n\} = \mathcal{F}'(C_n)$.

Let n_0 be the smallest integer t such that $c \cdot 2^{-c' \cdot t} \leq atr$, i.e., $n_0 = \lceil (\frac{1}{c'} \cdot \log(\frac{c}{atr})) \rceil$. Now, for all $n < n_0$, we use value 1 as the upper bound of $\mathcal{F}'(C_n)$, and for all $n \geq n_0$, we use $d \cdot 2^{-d' \cdot n}$ as its upper bound. Notice that the later upper bound is valid, since, for all $n \geq n_0$, $C_n \subseteq D_n = \{\alpha \in ZeroSeq(H, \mathcal{A}) : AccProb(\alpha[0 : f(\alpha)+n]) > c \cdot 2^{-c' \cdot n}\}$ and $\mathcal{F}'(D_n) \leq d \cdot 2^{-d' \cdot n}$. From this we see that,

$$E[AMTIME(atr)] \leq n_0 + \sum_{t \geq n_0} d \cdot 2^{-d' \cdot t},$$

which is $\leq n_0 + d \cdot (atr)^{\frac{d'}{c'}} \cdot \frac{1}{1-2^{-d'}}$. Using an upper bound of 1 for $atr^{\frac{d'}{c'}}$, we get the upper bound given by the inequality (1). □

Using the same proof technique, we can extend Theorem 1 showing that the variance of $MTIME(atr)$ is bounded by $n_0^2 + e$ and hence its standard deviation is bounded by $n_0 + e$ where $n_0 = \lceil (\frac{1}{c'} \cdot \log(\frac{c}{atr})) \rceil$ and $e = d \cdot \frac{1}{1-2^{-d'}}$. In fact, we can bound the higher order moments similarly, i.e., it can be shown that the expected value of $(MTIME(atr))^k$ is bounded by $n_0^k + e$ for all $k \geq 2$.

Examples. Consider the example HMC given in Figure 1 with s as the start state and a, b being the output symbols. Let the good computations, i.e., those accepted by the correctness automaton, be exactly all the computations that start with the transition from s to v. Observe that outputs are generated with different distributions in the good and bad computations. From theorem 3, given later, it follows that this HMC is exponentially converging monitorable with respect to the correctness property that requires that state v be the second state in the computation.

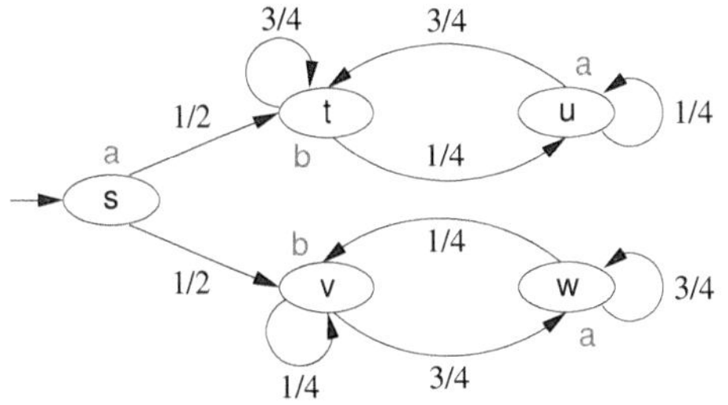

Figure 1: A HMC that is exponentially converging monitorable

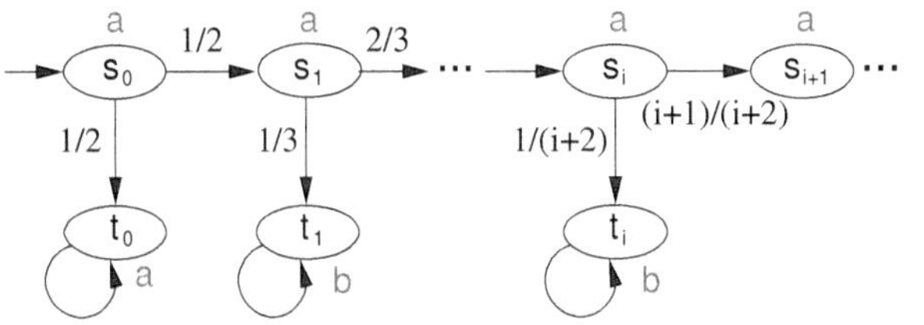

Figure 2: An example of a system that is not exponentially converging monitorable.

Now, we give an example HMC, given in Figure 2, which is monitorable but is not exponentially converging monitorable. The HMC has infinite number of states. The set of states is given by $\{s_i, t_i : i \geq 0\}$. All the states in the set $\{s_i : i \geq 0\}$ and the state t_0 generate the output symbol a. All the states in the set $\{t_i : i > 0\}$ generate the output b. The state s_0 is the initial state and has transitions to t_0, s_1 with probabilities $\frac{1}{2}$. Each state t_i, for $i \geq 0$, is an absorbing state. For each $i > 0$, there are transitions from s_i to t_i and to s_{i+1} with probabilities $\frac{1}{i+2}$ and $\frac{i+1}{i+2}$, respectively. This system has only one bad computation which is the computation from s_0 to t_0. All other computations are good computations. It is not difficult to see that this system is monitorable with respect to the above correctness property. This system has only one zero sequence which is the infinite sequence a^ω. It is easily seen that $AccProb(a^n) = \frac{1}{n+1}$ for $n \geq 2$. Thus it is not exponentially converging monitorable.

The following theorem is proved using the property that, in finite state Markov chains the probability that the system stays in transient states t steps goes to 0 exponentially, i.e., $\exists\, c, c' > 0$ such that the probability that the system is in a transient state after t steps is $\leq c \cdot 2^{-c' \cdot t}$.

THEOREM 2. *If $H, \mathcal{A}$ are finite state systems and H is strongly monitorable with respect to $\mathcal{A}$ then H is exponentially converging monitorable with respect to $\mathcal{A}$.*

Now, we consider the product of the Markov chain $G = (S, R, \phi)$ and the automaton $\mathcal{A} = (Q, S, \delta, q_0, F)$. We denote this as $Prod(G, \mathcal{A})$. Formally $Prod(G, \mathcal{A})$ is given by the Markov chain (PS, R', ϕ') where PS be the smallest subset of $S \times Q$ such that $(r_0, q_0) \in PS$ and for every $(s, q) \in PS$ and every $(s, t) \in R$ the pair $(t, \delta(q, s))$ is also in PS. $R' = \{((s, q), (s', q')) : (s, q) \in PS, (s, s') \in R, \delta(q, s) = \{q'\}\}$ and $\phi'((s, q), (s', q')) = \phi(s, s')$. The members of $S \times Q$ are called *product* states. We also define the product HMC, $Prod(H, \mathcal{A}) = (Prod(G, \mathcal{A}), \Sigma, O', (r_0, q_0))$ where for every $(s, q) \in S \times Q$, $O'(s, q) = O(s)$.

We let M, H' denote $Prod(G, \mathcal{A})$ and $Prod(H, \mathcal{A})$, respectively. Let T be the set of transient states and $\mathcal{C}$ be the collection of ptscc's of G. Let T' be the set of transient states and $\mathcal{D}$ be the collection of ptscc's of $Prod(G, \mathcal{A})$, respectively. For any $D \in \mathcal{D}$, let $Proj(D) = \{s : (s, q) \in D\}$. It is easy to see that $Proj(D)$ is a ptscc of G, i.e., is a member of $\mathcal{C}$. Thus, each ptscc of $Prod(G, \mathcal{A})$ corresponds to a unique ptscc of G, but a ptscc of G may correspond to more than one ptscc in $\mathcal{D}$. Since $\mathcal{A}$ has m number of states, it is easily seen that each ptscc in $\mathcal{C}$ corresponds to at most m ptscc's in $\mathcal{D}$.

We say that H is absorbing if the Markov chain G, when started in state r_0, eventually gets absorbed in a ptscc with probability one. Observe that if H is absorbing then H' is also absorbing. Note that all finite state HMCs are absorbing.

For any $s \in S$, let $out\_distr(s)$ be the unique distribution on the output alphabet Σ defined as follows: $out\_distr(s)(a)$ is the sum of $\phi(s, t)$ for all $(s, t) \in R$ such that $O(t) = a$; that is, $out\_distr(s)$ gives the probability of generating different outputs in the next step. We say that H is *uniform* if for every ptscc C of G, $out\_distr(s)$ is the same for all $s \in C$; that is once the system is in a state in C, future outputs are generated with the same distribution. In this case, for any ptscc C of H, we refer to $out\_distr(s)$, for any $s \in C$, as the output distribution of C and denote it by $out\_distr(C)$. It is easy to see that the HMC given in Figure 1 is an absorbing uniform HMC.

It is not difficult to see that if H is uniform then also $Prod(H, \mathcal{A})$ is uniform. Furthermore, if the ptscc D of $Prod(G, \mathcal{A})$ corresponds to the ptscc C of G then the output distributions of D and C are same, i.e., $out\_distr(D) = out\_distr(C)$. We say that a ptscc D of $Prod(G, \mathcal{A})$ is *rejecting* if it contains a product state of the form (s, q_{error}). (Observe that if D contains a product state of the form (s, q_{error}) then all product states in it are of the same form, i.e., the automaton component of the state is the error state.) A ptscc that is not rejecting is called *accepting*.

We say that ptsccs D_1 and D_2 in $\mathcal{D}$ conflict if one of them is an accepting ptscc and the other is a rejecting ptscc and there exist finite paths p_1, p_2 in $Prod(G, \mathcal{A})$ starting from (r_0, q_0) and ending in some product states in D_1, D_2, respectively, such that $O'(p_1) = O'(p_2)$. If D_1, D_2 conflict and they correspond to the ptsccs C_1, C_2 in $\mathcal{C}$, respectively, then we say that C_1 and C_2 also conflict. Intuitively, if C_1 conflicts with C_2 then there may be paths of G ending in C_1, that are rejected by $\mathcal{A}$, and that generate the same output sequences of some paths that end in C_2 and that are accepted by $\mathcal{A}$.

The following lemma is proved using the strong law of large numbers.

LEMMA 1. *An absorbing uniform HMC H is monitorable with respect to an automaton $\mathcal{A}$ iff for every pair D_1, D_2 of conflicting ptscc's in $Prod(G, \mathcal{A})$ we have $out\_distr(D_1) \neq out\_distr(D_2)$.*

Recall that we defined the notion of conflicting ptsccs in the HMC H with respect to $\mathcal{A}$ using this notion for $Prod(G, \mathcal{A})$. From this, it should be straightforward to see that a uniform absorbing HMC H is monitorable with respect to a correctness automaton $\mathcal{A}$ iff for every pair of conflicting ptsccs C_1, C_2 in H with respect to $\mathcal{A}$ we have $OutDistr(C_1) \neq OutDistr(C_2)$.

Let $Min\_KL\_div(H, \mathcal{A})$ denote the greatest lower bound of the set of all values $KL\_div(\psi_1, \psi_2)$ where ψ_1, ψ_2, respectively, are the output distributions of some pair of rejecting,accepting ptsccs of M. For an integer $k > 0$, we say that the HMC $H = (G, \Sigma, O, r_0)$ is *k-bounded* with respect to $\mathcal{A}$ if the following conditions are satisfied: (i) every path in G starting from r_0 and containing only transient states is of length at most k; (ii) every path in G starting from r_0 which is a bad computation, i.e., is rejected by $\mathcal{A}$, has bad prefix of length $\leq k$; that is, if a failure occurs it occurs in the first k states; (iii) $Min\_KL\_div(H, \mathcal{A}) > 0$. We say that H is *bounded* if it is $k-$bounded for some $k > 0$.

Let H be the HMC given in the Figure 1 with start state s. Let $\mathcal{A}$ be the safety correctness automaton having two states q_0, q_{error}. In state q_0, the automaton goes to the error state on the input symbol t, but stays in q_0 on any other input symbol. Now, it should be easy to see that the two ptsccs $\{v, w\}$ and $\{t, u\}$ of H are conflicting and have different output distributions. Hence this H is monitorable with respect to the $\mathcal{A}$ given above. Furthermore, it should be easy to see that H is 3-bounded.

THEOREM 3. *If H is a bounded uniform HMC that is monitorable with respect to a safety automaton $\mathcal{A}$, then H is exponentially converging monitorable with respect to $\mathcal{A}$.*

For H satisfying the given condition, the proof of the theorem actually shows that H is exponentially converging monitorable with parameters c, c', d, d' where $c' = (CF-t) \cdot \log(e)$, $d' = \frac{2 \cdot t^2}{DF} \cdot \log(e)$, e is the Euler's constant, t is any value such that $0 < t < CF$ and $CF = Min\_KL\_div(H, \mathcal{A})$.

Recall that c' gives the rate of convergence. From theorem 1, we see that the expected time for a monitor to raise an alarm after failure is $O(\frac{1}{c'} \cdot \log(\frac{c}{atr}))$ where atr is the threshold used by the monitor. Using $t = \frac{CF}{2}$, we see that the expected time for the monitor to raise an alarm is $O(\frac{1}{CF} \cdot \log(\frac{1}{atr}))$. This shows that if the output distributions of two conflicting ptsccs are close, i.e., $Min\_KL\_div(H, \mathcal{A})$ is small, then the time for raising the alarm is high.

The HMC given in the Figure 1 is 3-bounded with respect to the correctness automaton that rejects all computations that contain the state t. By the theorem, it is exponentially converging monitorable. Also, the discussion above implies that the rate of convergence is determined by the $KL\_div(out\_distr(C_1), out\_distr(C_2))$. where C_1, C_2 are the two ptsccs in the HMC.

The theorem is proved by considering all pairs of conflicting ptsccs in M and using Hoeffding's inequality [9] . The proof is left out due to lack of space.

5. EXPERIMENTAL EVALUATION

In this section, we present experimental results validating the theoretical results given in the previous section. For this, we consider a realistic example specified as Quantized Probabilistic Hybrid Automata (QPHA). First, we define QPHAs and define their

5.1 Quantized Probabilistic Hybrid Automata (QPHA)

Quantized probabilistic hybrid automata (QPHA) are probabilistic hybrid automata [10] in which the noise distributions are quantized. Their semantics is given by a HMC,

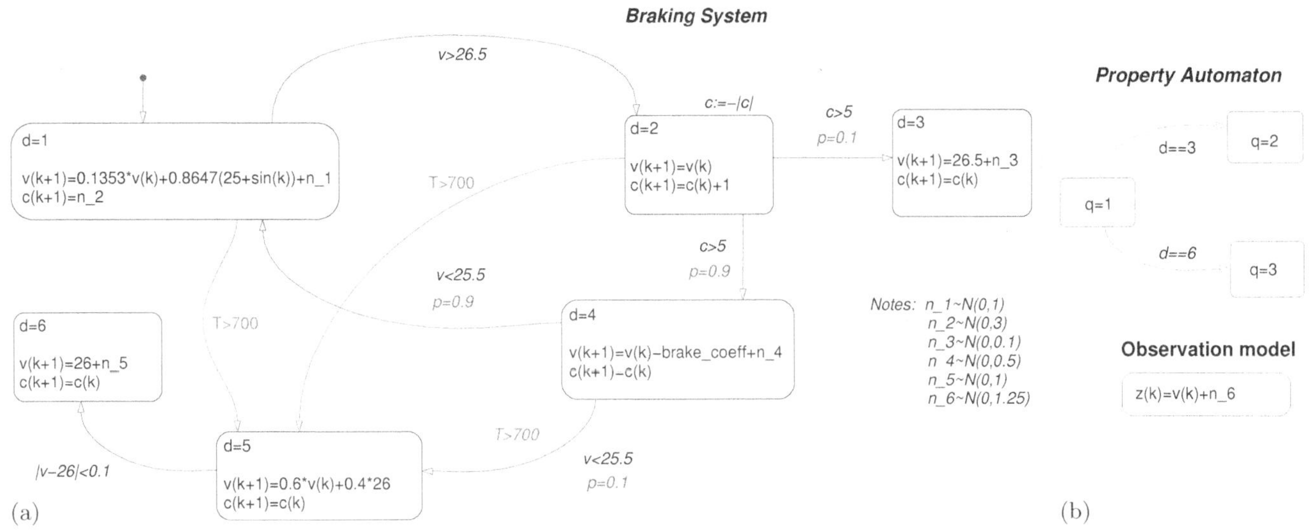

Figure 3: (a) Model of a car braking system. (b) Property automaton and output model.

but they provide a convenient formalism for specifying systems. A quantized probabilistic hybrid automaton $\mathcal{H}$ is a tuple $(Q, V, Y, \mathcal{E}, \mathcal{T}, c_0)$ defined as follows.

- Q is a finite set of *discrete* states, called *modes*.
- $V = \{x_1, ..., x_n\}$ is a finite set of real-valued variables, called *state* variables, that define the continuous state of the automaton.
- $Y = \{y_1, ..., y_m\}$ is another finite set of real-valued variables called *output* variables.
- $\mathcal{E}$ is a function that with each $q \in Q$ associates a set $\mathcal{E}(q)$ of difference equations describing the evolution of the continuous state and the outputs over time. For each $q \in Q$ and $z \in V \cup Y$, $\mathcal{E}(q)$ contains exactly one difference equation of the form $z = f(x_1, ..., x_n) + h$ where f is a function of the state variables $x_1, .., x_n$ and h is a random noise with known distribution; if $z \in V$, then this equation gives the value of the state variable z at the next time instance; if $z \in Y$, then this equation gives the value of the output variable z at the current time as a function of the values of the state variables at the same time.
- $\mathcal{T}$ is a function that assigns to each $q \in Q$ a set of transitions (ϕ, U) where ϕ is a condition (called *guard*) on the state variables and U is a set of $(n+2)$-tuples of the form $(p, r, f_1(x_1, ..., x_n), ..., f_n(x_1, ..., x_n))$ where $p \in [0, 1]$ is a probability value, $r \in Q$ and each $f_i(x_1, ..., x_n)$ is a function called *reset* function. We require that the guards in the transitions in $\mathcal{T}(q)$ be mutually exclusive and exhaustive (i.e., in each continuous state, exactly one guard is true) and for each transition $(\phi, U) \in \mathcal{T}(q)$ the following conditions hold: the sum of all values of p such that $(p, r, f_1(), ..., f_n()) \in U$ equals 1 and no two tuples in U have the same second component, i.e., same value for r.
- c_0 denotes the initial discrete and continuous states of the automaton.

We give the semantics of the QPHA $\mathcal{H} = (Q, V, Y, \mathcal{E}, \mathcal{T}, c_0)$ as a HMC as follows. The difficulty arises due to the fact that the state space of a HMC is discrete (i.e., countable), while the noise terms in the state equations, associated with each discrete state in Q, are defined by continuous probability distributions. We overcome this difficulty by converting these continuous distributions into discrete distributions by quantizing the real line using a quantization constant δ. The value of δ is taken to be sufficiently small and may be determined by the required precision. In the reminder of this section, we chose and fix such a value for δ. We use the following notation. Let $Z, \mathbf{R}$ denote the set of all integers and real numbers, respectively. For a probability distribution function N on the real line and an interval I on the real line, let $prob(N, I)$ be the probability that the value of N is in the interval I. The semantics of $\mathcal{H}$ is given by the HMC $H = (G, \Sigma, O, r_0)$ where $G = (S, R, \Phi)$ defined as follows.

The set S is defined inductively using a fixed point definition. From our definition, it automatically follows that S, Σ are countable sets. Recall that c_0 is a single $(n+1)-$*tuple* giving the initial discrete and continuous state; we let $(q_0, c_1', ..., c_n')$ be this tuple where $c_1', c_2', ..., c_n'$ are arbitrary real numbers defining the continuous state. $S = \{r_0\} \cup S'$ where r_0 is an arbitrary dummy initial state and S' consists of $n+m+1$ tuples of the form $(q, d_1, ..., d_{n+m})$ where $q \in Q$ and $d_1, ..., d_{n+m} \in \mathbf{R}$. Each such tuple specifies the discrete state, the values of the state variables and those of the output variables in that order. The output function O is defined so that for each $(q, d_1, ..., d_{m+n}) \in S'$, $O(q, d_1, ..., d_{n+m}) = (d_{n+1}, ..., d_{n+m})$, i.e., the last m components of a state define the output generated in that state, and $O(r_0)$ is taken as simply the m-tuple $(0, ..., 0)$. The correctness property to be monitored will be modified to refer to the computation starting from the second state.

Let $t = (q, c_1, ..., c_n) \in Q \times \mathbf{R}^n$. Each such t represents a state of $\mathcal{H}$ consisting of the discrete state q and continuous state $(c_1, ..., c_n)$. With respect to t, we define two functions g_t' and h_t', both with domain Z^m, which are used to define the outputs that are generated in t by discretizing the noise distributions. For each $(k_1, ..., k_m) \in Z^m$, $g_t'(k_1, ..., k_m)$ specifies an output and $h_t'(k_1, ..., k_m)$ specifies the probability of generating the output. For $j = 1, ..., m$, let the equation in $\mathcal{E}(q)$ defining the value of the output variable y_j, be $y_j = f_{n+j}(x_1, ..., x_n) + N_{n+j}$ where $x_1, ..., x_n$ are the continuous state variables and N_{n+j} is the noise term. Now, $g'_t(k_1, ..., k_m) = (e_1, ..., e_m)$ where $e_j = f_{n+j}(c_1, ..., c_n)+k_j \cdot \delta$ for $j = 1, ..., m$ and $h'_t(k_1, ..., k_m) = \prod_{1 \leq j \leq m} Prob(N_{n+j}, I_j)$ where I_j is the real interval $[k_j\, \delta,\, (k_j + 1)\, \delta)$.

To define the set S', we fist define an initial set S_0 from which other states will be defined. Let $c_0 = (q_0, c'_1, ..., c'_n)$ be the initial state of $\mathcal{H}$. For each $(k_1, ..., k_m) \in Z^m$, S_0 has the state $(q_0, c'_1, ..., c'_n, e_1, ..., e_m)$ as a member where $(e_1, ..., e_m) = g'_{c_0}(k_1, ..., k_m)$ and there is a transition in R from the initial state r_0 to this state and the probability of this transition is $h'_{c_0}(k_1, ..., k_m)$. These are the only states in S_0. Observe that S_0 is countable. Now the set S is the smallest set containing $\{r_0\} \cup S_0$ and satisfying the following closure properties.

Consider a state $s = (q, c_1, ..., c_n, o_1, ..., o_m) \in S$ and define its successor states (i.e., the transitions in R) and their associated transition probabilities as follows. First, we define two functions g_s, h_s with domain Z^n. For each $i = 1, ..., n$, let $x_i = f_i(x_1, ..., x_n)+N_i$ be the unique equation in $\mathcal{T}(q)$. Let $d_i = f_i(c_1, ..., c_n)$. For each $(k_1, ..., k_n) \in Z^n$, $g_s(k_1, ..., k_n)$ is the tuple $((d_1 + k_1 \cdot \delta), ..., (d_i + k_i \cdot \delta), ...)$ and $h_s(k_1, ..., k_n)$ is the probability $\prod_{1 \leq j \leq n} prob(N_j, I_{k_j})$, where I_{k_j} is the interval $[k_j \cdot \delta,\, (k_j + 1) \cdot \delta))$. Intuitively, the continuous state will evolve to an intermediate state $g_s(k_1, ..., k_n)$ with probability $h_s(k_1, ..., k_n)$ at the next time instance. However, exactly one of the transitions in $\mathcal{T}(q)$ is going to be triggered in the intermediate state which may further cause a change in the discrete state as well as the continuous state. Define another function W_s with domain Z^n such that for each $(k_1, ..., k_n) \in Z^n$, $W_s(k_1, ..., k_n)$ is a finite set of pairs of the form (p, t) where p is a probability value and $t \in Q \times \mathbf{R}^n$; here t denotes the next possible discrete and continuous states, and p the associated probability. Fix $(k_1, ..., k_n) \in Z^n$ and let (ϕ, U) be the unique transition in $\mathcal{T}(q)$ such that guard ϕ is satisfied in the continuous state $g_s(k_1, ..., k_n)$. Let $\{\tau_1, ..., \tau_u\}$ be the set of all $n + 2$ tuples in U. For each $\ell = 1, .., u$, let $\tau_\ell = (p_\ell, r_\ell, f_{\ell,1}(), ..., f_{\ell,u}()))$. Observe that each τ_ℓ is taken with probability p_ℓ. As a result, the discrete part of the state changes to r_ℓ and the continuous variables are reset using the reset functions applied to the intermediate continuous state. Then let $W_s(k_1, ..., k_n) = \{ ((h_s(k_1, ..., k_n) \cdot p_\ell), (r_\ell, f_{\ell,1}(g_s(k_1, ..., k_n)), ..., f_{\ell,n}(g_s(k_1, ..., k_n)))) : 1 \leq \ell \leq u\}$.

Let V_s be the set of all $t \in Q \times \mathbf{R}^n$ such that for some $(k_1, ..., k_n) \in Z^n$ and some p', $(p', t) \in W_s(k_1, ..., k_n)$. For each $t \in V_s$, let p''_t be the sum of all p' such that $(p', t) \in W_s(k_1, ..., k_n)$ for some $(k_1, ..., k_n) \in Z^n$. We then extend each $t = (r, e_1, ..., e_n) \in V_s$ with output values which are computed by using the functions g'_t and h'_t defined earlier. For each $(k_1, ..., k_m) \in Z^m$, the $n + m + 1$ tuple $s' = (r, e_1, ..., e_n, ...e_{n+m})$ is in S and $(s, s') \in R$ and $\Phi(s, s') = p''_t \cdot h'_t(k_1, ..., k_m)$ where $(e_{n+1}, ..., e_{n+m}) = g'_t(k_1, ..., k_m)$.

It is not difficult to see that the smallest set of states S satisfying the above closure conditions and containing the set $\{r_0\} \cup S_0$ as a subset is a countable set.

5.2 Example

In order to verify the theory we consider the example of a car braking system during the burn-in phase. Many systems exhibit a burn-in period as they are manufactured, during which the manufacturing defects typically manifest.

The hybrid automaton representing the evolution of the car velocity is shown in Figure 3.a. The car starts in the discrete state $d = 1$. In state $d = 1$ the car accelerates to velocity $v = 25$ and oscillates around that value with the magnitude 0.86. The car velocity is also affected by a Gaussian noise n_1. If the velocity exceeds a threshold $v = 26.5$ due to noise, it switches to the discrete state $d = 2$. The system remains in that state until the timer c_1 (that increases with each time step) reaches $c = 5$ (modeling delays in actuation and computational delays). Note that the initial value of the timer c_1 as the system enters the state $d = 2$ is not deterministic, so the duration of time the system remains in $d = 2$ is a random variable. After the timer reaches $c = 5$, the car brake can fail with a probability $p = 0.1$ (transition probabilities are marked in green in the figure) and permanently switch to the (bad) state $d = 3$. With the probability $p = 0.9$ it switches to $d = 4$, where the brake engages, decelerating the car. As the velocity falls below $v = 25.5$, the brake disengages. At that instant the system can either return to the state $d = 1$ with probability $p = 0.9$, or exit the burn-in period with probability $p = 0.1$, entering the state $d = 5$. In the state $d = 5$ the car adjusts the velocity to $v = 26$ and enters the terminal state $d = 6$.

We assume that the burn-in period lasts for at most 700 time units. After that time, unless the brake failed, the system thus switches to the state $d = 5$, from which it quickly (since the velocity in that state exponentially converges to $v = 26$) switches to the terminal (good) state $d = 6$. These transitions are marked with red on the figure. It can be also observed that the output distributions in the accepting and rejecting terminal state are constant, corresponding to the Gaussians n_5 and n_3, respectively. In our model the noise terms n_1, n_2, n_4 are truncated Gaussian distributions, truncated at $10 \cdot \sigma$ where σ is the standard deviation. From this, we see that the velocity v is bounded when the mode $d = 5$ and the system stays in this mode for a bounded amount of time. As a consequence we see that the HMC that defines the system stays in the transient states for at most k time steps for some $k > 700$ and that it is absorbing.

The property automaton, as well as the output model for the system, are shown in Figure 3.b. The state of the property automaton is indicated by the value q and $q = 2$ is the error state, i.e., q_{error}, as per our earlier notation. The property automaton simply states that $d = 3$ is the bad mode. From our previous discussion, it is not difficult to see that the HMC that captures the semantics of the Hybrid automaton, is k-bounded for some $k > 700$, with respect to the above correctness property.

State estimation. Let $\mathcal{S}$ be the system automaton and $\mathcal{P}$ the property automaton given in Figure 3. Note that $\mathcal{P}$ has a single error/bad state $q = 2$. We construct the product of $\mathcal{S}$ and $\mathcal{P}$ to obtain the product automaton $\mathcal{S} \times \mathcal{P}$. Using this product automaton, we compute the acceptance and rejection probabilities of the observed output sequence α. We do so by estimating, at each step, the probability distribution over the discrete states of the product automaton $\mathcal{S} \times \mathcal{P}$. This can be achieved by propagating the belief (probability distribution over the states of the product automaton) from the current state to the next state, given the new observation [21]. We employed Particle filters for estimation and these were developed as a computationally efficient ap-

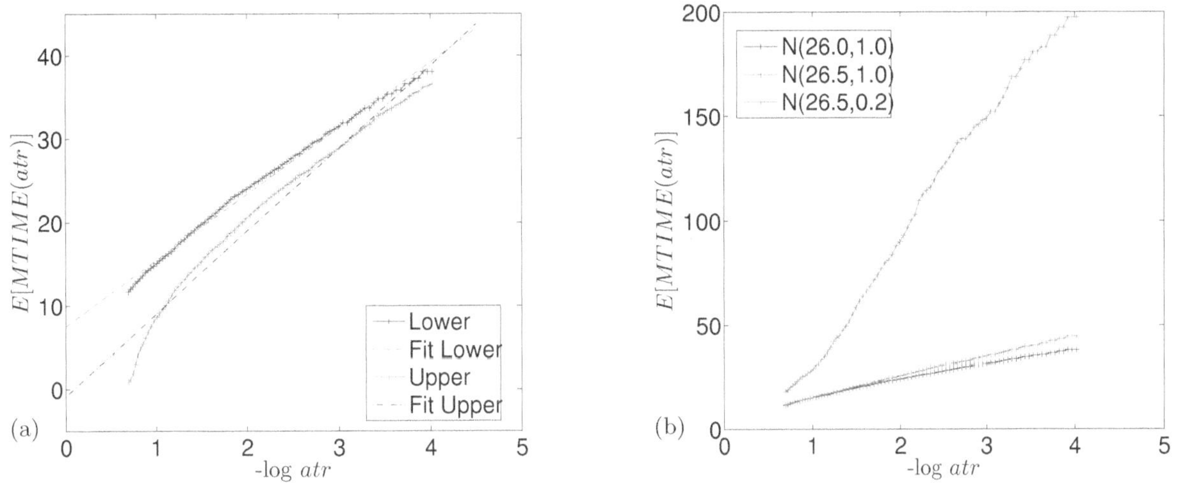

Figure 4: (a) Plot of $E[MTIME(atr)]$ vs. $\log atr$. (b) Dependence of $E[MTIME(atr)]$ on the KL divergence between n_3 and n_5.

proximation of the belief propagation [6, 11, 28]. They have been successfully applied in the hybrid system community for state estimation [3, 12, 15, 30].

Even if the probability distribution over the discrete states of the product automaton is known, estimating the acceptance probability is non-trivial because of the transitions at $T = 700$. However, we can obtain upper and lower bounds on the acceptance probability. First, observe that the lower bound on the rejection probability is simply the probability that the state d equals 3, $P[d = 3]$. Thus, the upper bound on the acceptance probability is $AccProb^U(\alpha) = 1 - P[d = 3]$. To obtain the lower bound, observe that the acceptance probability increases due to the transitions at $T = 700$ compared to the system where those transitions were not there. Thus, the lower bound on the acceptance probability can be obtained by computing the acceptance probability of the system without those transitions. It can be easily seen that the corresponding expression is $AccProb^L(\alpha) = 1 - P[d = 3] - (P[d = 1] + P[d = 2] + 0.9P[d = 4])\frac{0.1}{1-0.9^2}$.

Experimental results. In order to verify the theoretical results in the paper we ran the system for 800 steps. At each time step, we estimate the acceptance and rejection probabilities, using the particle filter to estimate the probabilities of the discrete states of the product automaton $\mathcal{S} \times \mathcal{P}$. We can then verify the validity of Theorem 1. To obtain an estimate of $E[MTIME(atr)]$, the system was run 400 times. A set of thresholds atr was chosen and then the average of $MTIME(atr)$ over the 400 runs was computed for each threshold atr. The results are shown in Figure 4(a).

As can been seen in the figure, the experimental data can be fit well with a straight line, confirming the result in Theorem 1. We only used the first term of the inequality (1), of Theorem 1, to fit the data as the second term is a constant independent of atr. For lower values of $-\log atr$ the linear fit is not that good. This may be due to the inaccuracies in state estimation. The lower curves correspond to the upper estimate of the acceptance probability while the upper curves to the lower estimate. The real curve lies between these two and it would clearly also be well approximated by a line.

Figure 4(b) shows how the curves change as the KL divergence between the Gaussians n_3 and n_5 changes. For the plot, the Gaussians n_3 was $N(26.5, 0.1)$ while n_5 was $N(26, 1)$, $N(26.5, 1)$, and $N(26.5, 0.2)$, respectively. As expected, as the KL divergence decreases, $E[MTIME(atr)]$ increases.

It is worth pointing out that we also performed experiments with a system that was bounded but not uniform. The results in that case were similar to those reported here. This indicates that while uniformity is sufficient for exponential convergence they are not necessary. Necessary conditions for exponential convergence are a subject of future work.

6. CONCLUSIONS

In this paper, we introduced a new class of monitorable systems, called exponentially converging monitorable systems. For these systems, we presented results giving upper bounds on the expected value of the monitoring time for threshold monitors. We also showed that finite state strongly monitoring systems and bounded uniform monitorable systems are both exponentially converging monitorable. Experimental results corroborating our theoretical results are presented.

7. ACKNOWLEDGMENTS

This research was supported in part by NSF grants IIS-0905593, CNS-0910988, CNS-1035914, CCF-0916438, CCF-1319754 and CNS-13-14485.

8. REFERENCES

[1] A. Balluchi, L. Benvenuti, M. Di Benedetto, and A. Sangiovanni-Vincentelli. Design of observers for hybrid systems. In *Hybrid Systems: Computation and Control*, volume 2289 of *Lecture Notes in Computer Science*, pages 59–80. Springer, 2002.

[2] A. Bauer, M. Leucker, and C. Schallhart. Runtime verification for LTL and TLTL. *ACM Transactions on Software Engineering and Methodology*, 2011.

[3] H. Blom and E. Bloem. Particle filtering for stochastic hybrid systems. In *IEEE Conference on Decision and Control*, pages 3221–3226, 2004.

[4] O. Cappe, E. Moulines, and T. Riden. *Inferencing in Hidden Markov Models*. Springer, 2005.

[5] M. d'Amorim and G. Roşu. Efficient monitoring of ω-languages. In *Computer Aided Verification*, volume 3576 of *Lecture Notes in Computer Science*, pages 311–318. Springer, 2005.

[6] A. Doucet, N. de Freitas, K. Murphy, and S. Russell. Rao-Blackwellised particle filtering for dynamic Bayesian networks. In *Uncertainty in AI (UAI)*, pages 176–183, 2000.

[7] Y. Falcone, J. C. Fernandez, and L. Mounier. Run-time verification of safety-progress properties. In *RV*, volume 5779 of *Lecture Notes in Computer Science*, pages 40–59. Springer, 2009.

[8] K. Gondi, Y. Patel, and A. Sistla. Monitoring the full range of ω-regular properties of stochastic systems. In *Verification, Model Checking, and Abstract Interpretation*, volume 5403 of *Lecture Notes in Computer Science*, pages 105–119. Springer, 2009.

[9] W. Hoeffding. Probability inequalities for sums of bounded random varoables. *Journal of the American Statistical Association*, 58(301):13–30, 1963.

[10] M. Hofbaur and B. Williams. Mode estimation of probabilistic hybrid systems. In *Hybrid Systems: Computation and Control*, volume 2289 of *Lecture Notes in Computer Science*, pages 81–91. Springer, 2002.

[11] M. Isard and A. Blake. Condensation–conditional density propagation for visual tracking. *International journal of computer vision*, 29(1):5–28, 1998.

[12] X. Koutsoukos, J. Kurien, and F. Zhao. Estimation of distributed hybrid systems using particle filtering methods. In *Hybrid Systems: Computation and Control*, volume 2623 of *Lecture Notes in Computer Science*, pages 298–313. Springer, 2003.

[13] R. Kumar and V. Garg. Control of stochastic discrete event systems modeled by probabilistic languages. *IEEE Transactions on Automatic Control*, 46(4):593–606, 2001.

[14] T. Margaria, A. Sistla, B. Steffen, and L. Zuck. Taming interface specifications. In *CONCUR 2005 – Concurrency Theory*, volume 3653 of *Lecture Notes in Computer Science*, pages 548–561. Springer, 2005.

[15] S. McIlraith, G. Biswas, D. Clancy, and V. Gupta. Hybrid systems diagnosis. In *Hybrid Systems: Computation and Control*, volume 1790 of *Lecture Notes in Computer Science*, pages 282–295. Springer, 2000.

[16] V. Pantelic, S. Postma, and M. Lawford. Probabilistic Supervisory Control of Probabilistic Discrete Event Systems. *IEEE Transactions on Automatic Control*, 54(8):2013–2018, 2009.

[17] A. Papoulis and S. U. Pillai. *Probability, Random Variables and Stochastic Processes*. McGrawHill, NewYork, 2002.

[18] A. Pnueli and A. Zaks. PSL model checking and run-time verification via testers. In *FM*, volume 4085 of *Lecture Notes in Computer Science*, pages 573–586. Springer, 2006.

[19] A. Pnueli, A. Zaks, and L. D. Zuck. Monitoring interfaces for faults. In *Runtime Verification (RV'05)*, 2005.

[20] H. V. Poor and O. Hadjiliadis. *Quickest Detection*. Cambridge University Press, Boston, MA, 2008.

[21] S. J. Russell and P. Norvig. *Artificial Intelligence: A Modern Approach*. Prentice Hall, second edition, December 2002.

[22] U. Sammapun, I. Lee, and O. Sokolsky. Rt-mac:runtime monitoring and checking of quantitative and probabilistic properties. In *Proc. of 11th IEEE International Conference on Embedded and Real-time Computing Systems and Applications (RTCSA 2005)*, pages 147–153, 2005.

[23] A. Sistla, M. Zhou, and L. Zuck. Monitoring off-the-shelf components. In *Verification, Model Checking, and Abstract Interpretation*, volume 3855 of *Lecture Notes in Computer Science*, pages 222–236. Springer, 2006.

[24] A. P. Sistla, M. Žefran, and Y. Feng. Monitorability in stochastic dynamic systems. In *Computer Aided Verification (CAV 2011)*, 2011.

[25] A. P. Sistla, M. Žefran, and Y. Feng. Runtime monitoring of stochastic cyber physical systems with hybrid states. In *2nd International Conference on Runtime Verification (RV2011)*, 2011.

[26] A. P. Sistla, M. Žefran, Y. Feng, and Y. Ben. Timely monitoring of partially observable stochastic systems. Technical report, University of Illinois at Chicago, 2013.

[27] S. Stoller, E. Bartocci, J. Seyster, R. Grosu, K. Havelund, S. Smolka, and E. Zado. Runtime verification with state estimation. In *Run Time Verification (RV2011)*, 2011.

[28] S. Thrun, D. Fox, W. Burgard, and F. Dellaert. Robust Monte Carlo localization for mobile robots. *Artificial Intelligence*, 128(1-2):99–141, 2001.

[29] M. Vardi. Automatic verification of probabilistic concurrent systems. In *26th annual Symposium on Foundations of Computer Science*, pages 327–338. IEEE Computer Society Press, 1985.

[30] V. Verma, G. Gordon, R. Simmons, and S. Thrun. Real-time fault diagnosis. *IEEE Robotics & Automation Magazine*, 11(2):56–66, 2004.

[31] M. Viswanathan and M. Kim. Foundations for runtime monitoring of reactive systems - fundamentals of the mac language. In *ICTAC*, volume 3407 of *Lecture Notes in Computer Science*, pages 543–556. Springer, 2004.

[32] B. Wetherill and K. Glazenbrook. *Sequential Methods in Statistics*. Chapman and Hall, 1986.

[33] T. Yoo and S. Lafortune. Polynomial-time verification of diagnosability of partially observed discrete-event systems. *IEEE Transactions on Automatic Control*, 47(9):1491–1495, 2002.

A Type-based Analysis of Causality Loops in Hybrid Systems Modelers*

Albert Benveniste
INRIA, Rennes

Timothy Bourke
INRIA and ENS/DI, Paris

Benoit Caillaud
INRIA, Rennes

Bruno Pagano
Esterel-Technologies, Toulouse

Marc Pouzet
UPMC, ENS/DI and INRIA, Paris

ABSTRACT

Explicit hybrid systems modelers like *Simulink/Stateflow* allow for programming both discrete- and continuous-time behaviors with complex interactions between them. A key issue in their compilation is the static detection of algebraic or *causality* loops. Such loops can cause simulations to deadlock and prevent the generation of statically scheduled code.

This paper addresses this issue for a hybrid modeling language that combines synchronous data-flow equations with Ordinary Differential Equations (ODEs). We introduce the operator `last`(x) for the left-limit of a signal x. This operator is used to break causality loops and permits a uniform treatment of discrete and continuous state variables. The semantics relies on non-standard analysis, defining an execution as a sequence of infinitesimally small steps. A signal is deemed *causally correct* when it can be computed sequentially and only changes infinitesimally outside of announced discrete events like zero-crossings. The causality analysis takes the form of a type system that expresses dependences between signals. In well-typed programs, signals are provably continuous during integration provided that imported external functions are also continuous.

The effectiveness of this system is illustrated with several examples written in ZÉLUS, a LUSTRE-like synchronous language extended with hierarchical automata and ODEs.

Categories and Subject Descriptors

I.6.2 [**Simulation and Modeling**]: Simulation Languages

Keywords

Hybrid systems; Synchronous programming languages; Type systems; Block diagrams; Static analysis.

*The full version of this paper with proofs and examples can be found at: `http://zelus.di.ens.fr/hscc2014/`. This work has been partially funded by the Sys2Soft, *Briques Génériques du Logiciel Embarqué, Investissements d'Avenir* French national project.

HSCC'14, April 15–17, 2014, Berlin, Germany

ACM 978-1-4503-2732-9/14/04 ...$15.00.
http://dx.doi.org/10.1145/2562059.2562125.

1. CAUSALITY AND SCHEDULING

Tools for modeling hybrid systems [7] such as MODELICA,[1] LABVIEW,[2] and SIMULINK/STATEFLOW,[3] are now rightly understood and studied as programming languages. Indeed, models are used not only for simulation, but also for test-case generation, formal verification and translation to embedded code. This explains the need for formal operational semantics for specifying their implementations and proving them correct [15, 9].

The underlying mathematical model is the synchronous parallel composition of stream equations, Ordinary Differential Equations (ODEs), hierarchical automata, and imperative features. While each of these features taken separately is precisely understood, real languages allow them to be combined in sophisticated ways. One major difficulty in such languages is the treatment of causality loops.

Causality or *algebraic* loops [20, 2-34] pose problems of well-definedness and compilation. They can lead to mathematically unsound models. They can prevent simulators from statically ensuring the existence of a fixed point, and compilers from generating statically scheduled code. The static detection of such loops, termed *causality analysis*, has been studied and implemented since the mid-1980s in synchronous data-flow language compilers [12, 13, 1]. The classical and simplest solution is to reject cycles (feed-back loops) which do not cross a unit delay. For instance, the LUSTRE-like equations:[4]

```
x = 0 -> pre y     and     y = if c then x + 1 else x
```

define the two sequences $(x_n)_{n\in\mathbb{N}}$ and $(y_n)_{n\in\mathbb{N}}$ such that:

$$x(0) = 0 \qquad y(n) = \texttt{if}\, c(n)\, \texttt{then}\, x(n) + 1\, \texttt{else}\, x(n)$$
$$x(n) = y(n-1)$$

They are causally correct since the feedback loop for `x` contains a unit delay `pre y` ('previous'). Replacing `pre y` with `y` gives two non-causal equations. Causally correct equations can be statically scheduled to produce a sequential, loop-free *step* function. Below is an excerpt of the C code generated by the HEPTAGON compiler [11] of LUSTRE:

```
if (self->v_1) {x = 0;} else {x = self->v_2;};
if (c) {y = x+1;} else {y = x;};
self->v_2 = y; self->v_1 = false;
```

[1] `http://www.modelica.org`
[2] `http://www.ni.com/labview`
[3] `http://www.mathworks.com/products/simulink`
[4] The unit delay $0 \texttt{->} \texttt{pre}(\cdot)$, initialized to 0, is sometimes written as $0\,\texttt{fby}\cdot$ ('0 followed by'), or in SIMULINK: $\frac{1}{z}$.

It computes current values of x and y from that of c. The internal memory of function *step* is in self, with self->v_1 initialized to true and set to false (to encode the LUSTRE operator ->) and self->v_2 storing the value of pre y.

ODEs with resets: Consider now the situation of a program defining continuous-time signals only, made of ODEs and equations. For example:

```
der y = z init 4.0 and z = 10.0 - 0.1 * y and k = y + 1.0
```

defines signals y, z and k, where for all $t \in \mathbb{R}^+$, $\frac{dy}{dt}(t) = z(t)$, $y(0) = 4$, $z(t) = 10 - 0.1 \cdot y(t)$, and $k(t) = y(t) + 1$.[5] This program is causal simply because it is possible to generate a sequential function $derivative(y) = \texttt{let}\, z = 10 - 0.1 * y\, \texttt{in}\, z$ returning the current derivative of y and initial value 4 for y so that a numeric solver [8] can compute a sequence of approximations $y(t_n)$ for increasing values of time $t_n \in \mathbb{R}^+$ and $n \in \mathbb{N}$. Thus, for continuous-time signals, integrators break algebraic loops just as delays do for discrete-time signals.

Can we reuse the simple justification we used for data-flow equations to justify that the above program is causal? Consider the value that y would have if computed by an ideal solver taking an infinitesimal step of duration ∂ [4]. Writing ${}^\star y(n)$, ${}^\star z(n)$ and ${}^\star k(n)$ for the values of y, z and k at instant $n\partial$, with $n \in {}^\star\mathbb{N}$ a non-standard integer, we have:

$$ {}^\star y(0) = 4 \qquad {}^\star z(n) = 10 - 0.1 \cdot {}^\star y(n) $$
$$ {}^\star y(n+1) = {}^\star y(n) + {}^\star z(n) \cdot \partial \qquad {}^\star k(n) = {}^\star y(n) + 1 $$

where ${}^\star y(n)$ is defined sequentially from past values and ${}^\star y(n)$ and ${}^\star y(n+1)$ are infinitesimally close, for all $n \in {}^\star\mathbb{N}$, yielding a unique solution for y, z and k. The equations are thus causally correct.

Troubles arise when ODEs interact with discrete-time constructs, for example when a reset occurs at every occurrence of an event. E.g., the sawtooth signal $y : \mathbb{R}^+ \mapsto \mathbb{R}^+$ such that $\frac{dy}{dt}(t) = 1$ and $y(t) = 0$ if $t \in \mathbb{N}$ can be defined by an ODE with reset,

```
der y = 1.0 init 0.0 reset up(y - 1.0) -> 0.0
```

where y is initialized with 0.0, has derivative 1.0, and is reset to 0.0 every time the zero-crossing up(y - 1.0) is true, that is, whenever y - 1.0 crosses 0.0 from negative to positive. Is this program causal? Again, consider the value y would have were it calculated by an ideal solver taking infinitesimal steps of length ∂. The value of ${}^\star y(n)$ at instant $n\partial$, for all $n \in {}^\star\mathbb{N}$ would be:

$$ {}^\star y(0) = 0 \qquad {}^\star y(n) = \texttt{if}\ {}^\star z(n)\ \texttt{then}\ 0.0\ \texttt{else}\ {}^\star ly(n) $$
$$ {}^\star ly(n) = {}^\star y(n-1) + \partial \qquad {}^\star c(n) = ({}^\star y(n) - 1) \geq 0 $$
$$ {}^\star z(0) = \texttt{false} \qquad {}^\star z(n) = {}^\star c(n) \wedge \neg {}^\star c(n-1) $$

This set of equations is clearly not causal: the value of ${}^\star y(n)$ depends instantaneously on ${}^\star z(n)$ which itself depends on ${}^\star y(n)$. There are two ways to break this cycle: (*a*) consider that the effect of the zero-crossing is delayed by one cycle, that is, the test is made on ${}^\star z(n-1)$ instead of on $z(n)$, or, (*b*) distinguish the current value of ${}^\star y(n)$ from the value it would have had were there no reset, namely ${}^\star ly(n)$. Testing a zero-crossing of ly (instead of y),

$$ {}^\star c(n) = ({}^\star ly(n) - 1) \geq 0, $$

gives a program that is causal since ${}^\star y(n)$ no longer depends instantaneously on itself. We propose writing this ♣[6]:

```
der y = 1.0 init 0.0 reset up(last y - 1.0) -> 0.0
```

where $\texttt{last}(y)$ stands for ly, that is, the *left-limit* of y. In non-standard semantics [4], it is infinitely close to the previous value of y, and written $ly(n) \approx y(n-1)$. When y is defined by its derivative, $\texttt{last}(y)$ corresponds to the so-called 'state port' of the integrator block $\frac{1}{s}$ of SIMULINK, which is introduced expressly to break causality loops like the one above ♣.[7] According to the documentation [19, 2-685]:

> "The output of the state port is the same as the output of the block's standard output port except for the following case. If the block is reset in the current time step, the output of the state port is the value that would have appeared at the block's standard output if the block had not been reset."

SIMULINK restricts the use of the state port. It is only defined for the integrator block and cannot be returned as a block output: it may only be referred to in the same context as its integrator block and used to break algebraic loops. The use of the state port reveals subtle bugs in the SIMULINK compiler. Consider the SIMULINK model shown in Figure 1a with the simulation results given by the tool for x and y in Figure 1b. The model contains two integrators. The one at left, named 'Integrator0' and producing x, integrates the constant 1. The one at right, named 'Integrator1' and producing y, integrates x; its state port is fed back through a bias block to reset both integrators, and through a gain of -3 to provide a new value for Integrator0. The new value for Integrator1 comes from the state port of Integrator0 multiplied by a gain of -4. In our syntax ♣:

```
    der x = 1.0 init 0.0 reset z -> -3.0 * last y
and der y = x init 0.0 reset z -> -4.0 * last x
and z = up(last x - 2.0)
```

In the non-standard interpretation of signals, the equations above are perfectly causal: the current values of ${}^\star x(n)$ and ${}^\star y(n)$ only depend on previous values, that is:

$$ {}^\star x(n) = \texttt{if}\ {}^\star z(n)\ \texttt{then}\ {-3} \cdot {}^\star y(n-1)\ \texttt{else}\ {}^\star x(n-1) + \partial $$
$$ {}^\star y(n) = \texttt{if}\ {}^\star z(n)\ \texttt{then}\ {-4} \cdot {}^\star x(n-1)\ \texttt{else}\ {}^\star y(n-1) + \partial \cdot {}^\star x(n-1) $$

$$ {}^\star x(0) = 0 \qquad {}^\star y(0) = 0 $$
$$ {}^\star c(n) = ({}^\star x(n-1) - 2) \geq 0 \qquad {}^\star z(n) = {}^\star c(n) \wedge \neg {}^\star c(n-1) $$

Yet, can you guess the behavior of the model and explain why the trajectories computed by SIMULINK are wrong?

Initially, both x and y are 0. At time $t = 2$, the state port of Integrator1 becomes equal to 2 triggering resets at each integrator as the output of block $u - 2.0$ crosses zero. The results show that Integrator0 is reset to -6 $(= 2 \cdot -3)$

[5] $\texttt{der}\, y = e\ \texttt{init}\ v_0$ stands for $y = \frac{1}{s}(e)$ inititialized to v_0 in SIMULINK.

[6] The ♣'s link to http://zelus.di.ens.fr/hscc2014/.

[7] The SIMULINK integrator block outputs both an integrated signal and a state port. We write $(x, lx) = \frac{1}{s}(x_0, \texttt{up}(z), x')$ for the integral of x', reset with value x_0 every time z crosses zero from negative to positive, with output x and state port lx. The example would thus be written: $(y, ly) = \frac{1}{s}(0.0, \texttt{up}(ly - 1.0), 1.0)$.

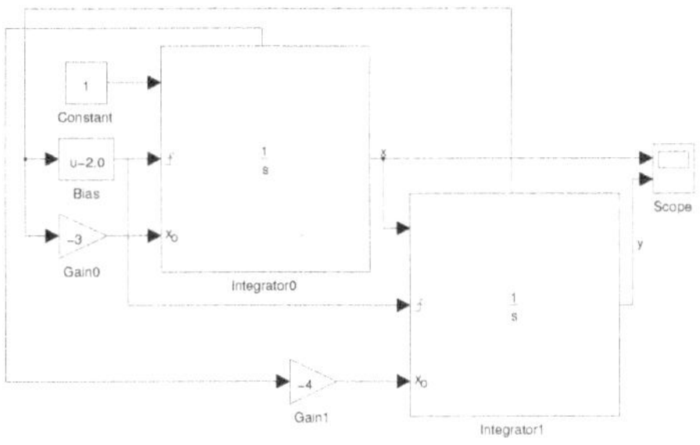

(a) Simulink model

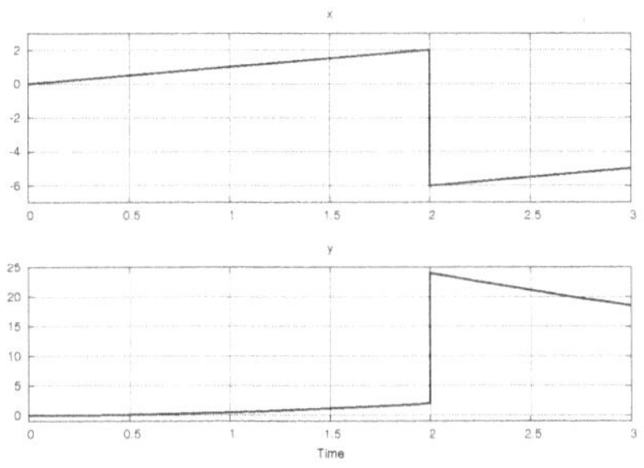

(b) Simulation results

Figure 1: A miscompiled Simulink model (R2009b) ♣

```
// P_0 = -2.0 P_1 = -3.0 P_2 = -4.0 P_3 = 1.0

static void mdlOutputs(SimStruct * S, int_T tid)
{ _rtX = (ssGetContStates(S));
  ...
  _rtB = (_ssGetBlockIO(S));

  _rtB->B_0_0_0 = _rtX->Integrator1_CSTATE + _rtP->P_0;
  _rtB->B_0_1_0 = _rtP->P_1 * _rtX->Integrator1_CSTATE;

  if (ssIsMajorTimeStep (S))
   { ...
     if (zcEvent || ...)
      { (ssGetContStates (S))->Integrator0_CSTATE =
            _ssGetBlockIO (S)->B_0_1_0;
      }
     ... }

  (_ssGetBlockIO (S))->B_0_2_0 =
    (ssGetContStates (S))->Integrator0_CSTATE;
    _rtB->B_0_3_0 = _rtP->P_2 * _rtX->Integrator0_CSTATE;

    if (ssIsMajorTimeStep (S))
    { ...
      if (zcEvent || ...)
       { (ssGetContStates (S))-> Integrator1_CSTATE =
             (ssGetBlockIO (S))->B_0_3_0;
       }
      ...
    }
    ... }
```

Figure 2: Excerpt of C code produced by RTW (R2009b)

and that Integrator1 is reset to 24 ($= -6 \cdot -4$). The latter result is surprising since, at this instant, the state port of Integrator0 should also be equal to 2, and we would thus expect Integrator1 to be reset to -8 ($= 2 \cdot -4$)!

The SIMULINK implementation does not satisfy its documented behavior [19, 2-685]. Inspecting the C function which computes the current outputs, `mdlOutput` in Figure 2, the code of the two integrators appears in an incorrectly scheduled sequence.[8] At the instant of the zero-crossing (conditions `ssIsMajorTimeStep(S)` and `zcEvent` are true), the state port of Integrator0 (stored in `sGetContStates(S) -> Integrator0_CSTATE`) is reset using the state port value of Integrator1. Thus, Integrator1 does not read the value of Integrator0's state port (that is ${}^\star x(n-1)$) but rather the current value (${}^\star x(n)$) leading to an incorrect output. The SIMULINK model is not correctly compiled—it needs another variable to store the value of ${}^\star x(n-1)$, just as a third variable is normally needed to swap the values of two others. We argue that such a program should either be scheduled correctly or give rise to a warning or error message. Providing a means to statically detect and explain causality issues in a hybrid model is a key motivation of this paper.

Any loop in SIMULINK, whether of discrete- or continuous-time signals, can be broken by inserting the so-called memory block [19, 2-831].[9] If x is a signal, $\texttt{mem}(x)$ is a piecewise constant signal which refers to the value of x at the previous integration step (or *major* step). If those steps are taken at increasing instants $t_i \in \mathbb{R}$, $\texttt{mem}(x)(t_0) = x_0$ where $t_0 = 0$ and x_0 is an explicitly defined initial value, $\texttt{mem}(x)(t_i) = x(t_{i-1})$ for $i > 0$ and $\texttt{mem}(x)(t_i + \delta) = x(t_{i-1})$ for $0 \leq \delta < t_{i+1} - t_i$. As integration is performed globally, $\texttt{mem}(y)$ may cause strange behaviors as the previous value of a continuously changing signal x depends precisely on when the solver decides to stop! ♣ Writing $\texttt{mem}(y)$ is thus unsafe in general [3].[10] There is nonetheless a situation where the use of the memory block is mandatory and still safe: *The program only refers to the previous integration step during a discrete step.* This situation is very common: it is typically that of a system with continuous modes M_1 and M_2 producing a signal x, with each of them being started with the value computed previously by the solver, and $\texttt{mem}(x)$ being used to pass a value from one mode to the other ♣. Instead of using the unsafe operator $\texttt{mem}(x)$, we could better refer to the *left limit* of x, and write it again $\texttt{last}(x)$. Yet, the unrestricted use of this operation may cause a new kind of causality loop which has to be statically rejected. Consider the following equation activated on a continuous time base:

```
y = -1.0 * (last y) and init y = 1.0
```

which defines, for all $n \in {}^\star\mathbb{N}$, the sequence ${}^\star y(n)$ such that:

$$ {}^\star y(n) = -{}^\star y(n-1) \quad {}^\star y(0) = 1 $$

Indeed, this differs little from the equation `y = -1.0 * y`. Even though ${}^\star y(n)$ can be computed sequentially, its value does not increase infinitesimally at each step, that is, y is not left continuous even though no zero-crossing occurs. For any time $t \in \mathbb{R}$, the set $\{n\partial \mid n \in {}^\star\mathbb{N} \wedge n\partial \approx t \wedge {}^\star y(n) \not\approx {}^\star y(n+1)\}$ is infinite. Thus, the value of $y(t)$ at any standard instant $t \in \mathbb{R}$ is undefined.

Contribution and organization of the paper: This paper presents the causality problem for a core language

[8]The same issue exists in release R2014a.

[9]In contrast, the application of a unit delay $\frac{1}{z}$ to a continuous-time signal is statically detected and results in a warning.

[10]Quoting the SIMULINK manual (**http://www.mathworks.com/help/simulink/slref/memory.html**), "Avoid using the Memory block when both these conditions are true: - Your model uses the variable-step solver ode15s or ode113. - The input to the block changes during simulation."

that combines LUSTRE-like stream equations, ODEs with reset and a basic control structure. The operator $\texttt{last}(x)$ stands for the previous value of x in non-standard semantics and coincides with its left-limit when x is left-continuous. This operation plays the role of a delay but is safer than the memory block $\texttt{mem}(x)$ as its semantics does not depend on when a particular solver decides to stop. When x is a continuous-state variable, it coincides with the so-called SIMULINK *state port*. We develop a non-standard semantics following [4] and a compile-time *causality analysis* in order to detect possible instantaneous loops. The static analysis takes the form of a type system, reminiscent of the simple Hindley-Milner type system for core ML [21]. A type signature for a function expresses the instantaneous dependencies between its inputs and outputs. We prove that well typed programs only progress by infinitely small steps outside of zero-crossing events, that is, signals are continuous during integration provided imported operations applied point-wise are continuous. We are not aware of such a correctness theorem based on a static typing discipline for hybrid modelers.

The presented material is implemented in ZÉLUS [6], a synchronous LUSTRE-like language extended with ODEs. Moreover, all examples in the paper are written in ZÉLUS.

The paper is organized as follows. Section 2 introduces a core synchronous language with ODEs. Section 3 presents its semantics based on non-standard analysis. Section 4 presents a type system for causality and Section 5 a major property: any well-typed program is proved not to have any discontinuities during integration. Section 6 discusses related work and we conclude in Section 7.

2. A SYNCHRONOUS LANGUAGE + ODES

We now introduce a kernel language. It is not intended to be a full language but a minimal one for the purpose of the present paper. It includes data-flow equations, ordinary differential equations and control structures. Its syntax is:

$$d ::= \texttt{let}\, x = e \mid \texttt{let}\, k\, f(p) = e\, \texttt{where}\, E \mid d; d$$

$$e ::= x \mid v \mid op(e) \mid e\, \texttt{fby}\, e \mid \texttt{last}(x) \mid f(e) \mid (e, e) \mid \texttt{up}(e)$$

$$p ::= (p, p) \mid x$$

$$\begin{aligned} E ::= &\ () \mid x = e \mid \texttt{init}\ x = e \mid \texttt{next}\ x = e \mid \texttt{der}\, x = e \\ &\mid E\ \texttt{and}\ E \mid \texttt{local}\ x\ \texttt{in}\ E \mid \texttt{if}\, e\, \texttt{then}\, E\, \texttt{else}\, E \\ &\mid \texttt{present}\ e\ \texttt{then}\ E\ \texttt{else}\ E \end{aligned}$$

$$k ::= \texttt{D} \mid \texttt{C} \mid \texttt{A}$$

A program is a sequence of definitions (d), that either bind the value of expression e to x ($\texttt{let}\, x = e$) or define a function ($\texttt{let}\, k\, f(p) = e\, \texttt{where}\, E$). In a function definition, k is the kind of the function f, p denotes formal parameters, and the result is the value of an expression e which may contain variables defined in the auxiliary equations E. There are three kinds of function: $k = \texttt{A}$ means that f is a *combinational* function (typically a function imported from the host language, e.g., addition); $k = \texttt{D}$ means that f is a *sequential* function that must be activated at discrete instants (typically a LUSTRE function with an internal discrete state); $k = \texttt{C}$ denotes a hybrid function that may contain ODEs and which must be activated continuously.

An expression e can be a variable (x), an immediate value (v), e.g., a boolean, integer or floating point value, the point-wise application of an imported function ($op(e)$) such as $+$, $*$ or $\texttt{not}(\cdot)$, an initialized unit delay ($e_1\, \texttt{fby}\, e_2$), the left-limit of a signal ($\texttt{last}(x)$), a function application ($f(e)$), a pair (e, e) or a rising zero-crossing detection ($\texttt{up}(e)$), which, in this language kernel, is the only basic construct to produce an event from a continuous-time signal (e). A pattern p is a tree structure of identifiers (x). A set of equations E is either an empty equation ($()$); an equality stating that a pattern equals the value of an expression at every instant ($x = e$); the initialization of a state variable x with a value e ($\texttt{init}\ x = e$); the value of a state variable x at the next instant ($\texttt{next}\ x = e$); or, the current value of the derivative of x ($\texttt{der}\, x = e$). An equation can also be the conjunction of two sets of equations ($E_1\ \texttt{and}\ E_2$); the declaration that a variable x is defined within, and local to, a set of equations ($\texttt{local}\ x\ \texttt{in}\ E$); a conditional that activates a branch according to the value of a boolean expression ($\texttt{if}\, e\, \texttt{then}\, E_1\, \texttt{else}\, E_2$), and a variant that operates on an event expression ($\texttt{present}\ e\ \texttt{then}\ E_1\ \texttt{else}\ E_2$).

Notational abbreviations:

(*a*) $\texttt{if}\ e\ \texttt{then}\ E \stackrel{def}{=} \texttt{if}\, e\, \texttt{then}\, E\, \texttt{else}\, ()$.

(*b*) $\texttt{present}\ e\ \texttt{then}\ E \stackrel{def}{=} \texttt{present}\ e\ \texttt{then}\ E\ \texttt{else}\ ()$.

(*c*) $\texttt{der}\, x = e\ \texttt{init}\ e_0 \stackrel{def}{=} \texttt{init}\ x = e_0\ \texttt{and}\ \texttt{der}\, x = e$

(*d*) $\texttt{der}\, x = e\ \texttt{init}\ e_0\ \texttt{reset}\ z \rightarrow e_1 \stackrel{def}{=}$
$\texttt{init}\ x = e_0\ \texttt{and}\ \texttt{present}\ z\ \texttt{then}\ x = e_1\ \texttt{else}\ \texttt{der}\, x = e$

Equations (E) must be in Static Single Assignment (SSA) form: every variable has a unique definition at every instant.

3. NON-STANDARD SEMANTICS

3.1 Semantics

Let $^*\mathbb{R}$ and $^*\mathbb{N}$ be the non-standard extensions of $\mathbb{R}$ and $\mathbb{N}$. $^*\mathbb{N}$ is totally ordered and every set bounded from above (resp. below) has a unique maximal (resp. minimal) element. Let $\partial \in {}^*\mathbb{R}$ be an infinitesimal, i.e., $\partial > 0$, $\partial \approx 0$. Let the global time base or *base clock* be the infinite set of instants:

$$\mathbb{T}_\partial = \{t_n = n\partial \mid n \in {}^*\mathbb{N}\}$$

$\mathbb{T}_\partial$ inherits a total order from $^*\mathbb{N}$; in addition, for each element of $\mathbb{R}_+$ there exists an infinitesimally close element of $\mathbb{T}_\partial$. Whenever possible we leave ∂ implicit and write $\mathbb{T}$ instead of $\mathbb{T}_\partial$. Let $T = \{t'_n \mid n \in {}^*\mathbb{N}\} \subseteq \mathbb{T}$. $T(i)$ stands for t'_i, the i-th element of T. In the sequel, we only consider subsets of the time base $\mathbb{T}$ obtained by sampling a time base on a boolean condition or a zero-crossing event. Any element of a time base will thus be of the form $k\partial$ where $k \in {}^*\mathbb{N}$. If $T \subseteq \mathbb{T}$, we write $^\bullet T(t)$ for the immediate predecessor of t in T and $T^\bullet(t)$ for the immediate successor of t in T. For an instant t, we write its immediate predecessor and successor as, respectively, $^\bullet t$ and $t^\bullet$, rather than as $^\bullet\mathbb{T}(t)$ and $\mathbb{T}^\bullet(t)$. For $t \in T \subseteq \mathbb{T}$, neither $^\bullet t$ nor $t^\bullet$ necessarily belong to T. $min(T)$ is the minimal element of T and $t \leq_T t'$ means that t is a predecessor of t' in T.

DEFINITION 1 (SIGNALS). *Let $V_\perp = V + \{\perp\}$ where V is a set. $S(V) = \mathbb{T} \mapsto V_\perp$ is the set of signals. A signal $x : T \mapsto V_\perp$ is a total function from a time base $T \subseteq \mathbb{T}$ to $V_\perp$. Moreover, for all $t \notin T, x(t) = \perp$. If T is a time base, $x(T(n))$ and $x(t_n)$ are the value of x at instant t_n where*

$n \in {}^\star\mathbb{N}$ *is the n-th element of T. The clock of a signal x is* $clock(x) = \{t \in \mathbb{T} \mid x(t) \neq \bot\}$.

Sampling: Let $\texttt{bool} = \{\texttt{false}, \texttt{true}\}$ and $x : T \mapsto \texttt{bool}_\bot$. The *sampling of T according to x*, written $T \texttt{ on } x$, is the subset of instants defined by:

$$T \texttt{ on } x = \{t \mid (t \in T) \wedge x(t) = \texttt{true}\}$$

Note that as $T \texttt{ on } x \subseteq T$, it is also totally ordered. The zero-crossing of $x : T \mapsto {}^\star\mathbb{R}_\bot$ is $up(x) : T \mapsto \texttt{bool}_\bot$. To emphasize that $up(x)$ is defined only for $t \in T$, we write its value at time t as $up(x)(T)(t)$. For $t \notin T$, $up(x)(T)(t) = \bot$. In the definition below $<$ is the total order on ${}^\star\mathbb{R}$.

$$\begin{array}{rcl} up(x)(T)(t_0) & = & \texttt{false} \text{ where } t_0 = min(T) \\ up(x)(T)(t) & = & \exists n \in {}^\star\mathbb{N}, n \geq 1. \; \wedge (x(t-n\partial) < 0) \\ & & \wedge (x(t-(n-1)\partial) = 0) \\ & & \wedge \ldots \\ & & \wedge (x(t-\partial) = 0) \\ & & \wedge (x(t) > 0) \\ & & \text{where } t \in T \end{array} \quad (1)$$

The above definition means that a zero-crossing on x occurs when x goes from a strictly negative to a strictly positive value, possibly with intermediate values equal to 0.

Let V be a set of values closed under product and sum. ${}^\star V$ is its non-standard extension such that ${}^\star(V_1 \times V_2) = {}^\star V_1 \times {}^\star V_2$, ${}^\star V = V$ for any finite set V. ${}^\star V_\bot = {}^\star V + \{\bot\}$ with $\bot$ as the minimum element. Let $L = \{x_1, ..., x_n, ...\}$ be a set of local variables and $L_g = \{f_1, ..., f_n, ...\}$ a set of global variables. An environment associates names to values. A local environment ρ and a global environment G map names to signals and signal functions:

$$\rho : L \mapsto S({}^\star V) \qquad G : L_g \mapsto (S({}^\star V) \mapsto S({}^\star V))$$

Operations on environments: Consider ρ_1 and ρ_2.

- $(\rho_1 + \rho_2)(x)(t)$ is $\rho_1(x)(t)$ if $\rho_2(x)(t) = \bot$, $\rho_2(x)(t)$ if $\rho_1(x)(t) = \bot$, and $\bot$ otherwise.
- $\rho = merge\,(T)\,(s)\,(\rho_1)\,(\rho_2)$ is the merge of two environments according to a signal $s \in S(\texttt{bool})$. The value of a signal x at instant $t \in T$ is the one given by ρ_1 if $s(t)$ is true and that of ρ_2 otherwise. Nonetheless, in case x is not defined in ρ_1 (respectively ρ_2), it implicitly keeps its previous value, that is $\rho_1({}^\bullet clock(x)(t))$. This corresponds to adding an equation $x = \texttt{last}(x)$ when no equation is given in one branch of a conditional.

  For all x and $t \in T$, $\rho(x)(t) = \rho_1(x)(t)$ if $s(t) = \texttt{true}$ and $x \in Dom(\rho_1)$; $\rho(x)(t) = \rho(x)({}^\bullet clock(x)(t))$ if $s(t) = \texttt{true}$ and $x \notin Dom(\rho_1)$. $\rho(x)(t) = \rho_2(x)(t)$ if $s(t) = \texttt{false}$ and $x \in Dom(\rho_2)$; finally, $\rho(x)(t) = \rho(x)({}^\bullet clock(x)(t))$ otherwise.

Expressions: Expressions are interpreted as signals and node definitions as functions from signals to signals. For expressions, we define ${}^\star[\![e]\!]^\rho_G(T)(t)$ to give at every instant $t \in T$ both the value of e and a Boolean value true if e raises a zero-crossing event. The definition is given in Figure 3.

Let us explain the definition. The value of expression e is considered undefined outside of T. The current value of an immediate constant v is v and no zero-crossing event is raised. The current value of x is the one stored in the environment $\rho(x)$ and no event is raised. The semantics of

$$\begin{array}{rcl}
{}^\star[\![e]\!]^\rho_G(T)(t) & = & \bot, \bot \text{ if } t \notin T \\
{}^\star[\![v]\!]^\rho_G(T)(t) & = & v, \texttt{false} \\
{}^\star[\![x]\!]^\rho_G(T)(t) & = & \rho(x)(t), \texttt{false} \\
{}^\star[\![op(e)]\!]^\rho_G(T)(t) & = & \texttt{let } v, z = {}^\star[\![e]\!]^\rho_G(T)(t) \texttt{ in} \\
& & op(v), z \\
{}^\star[\![(e_1, e_2)]\!]^\rho_G(T)(t) & = & \texttt{let } v_1, z_1 = {}^\star[\![e_1]\!]^\rho_G(T)(t) \texttt{ in} \\
& & \texttt{let } v_2, z_2 = {}^\star[\![e_2]\!]^\rho_G(T)(t) \texttt{ in} \\
& & (v_1, v_2), (z_1 \vee z_2) \\
{}^\star[\![e_1 \texttt{ fby } e_2]\!]^\rho_G(T)(t_0) & = & {}^\star[\![e_1]\!]^\rho_G(T)(t_0) \text{ if } t_0 = min(T) \\
{}^\star[\![e_1 \texttt{ fby } e_2]\!]^\rho_G(T)(t) & = & {}^\star[\![e_2]\!]^\rho_G(T)({}^\bullet T(t)) \text{ otherwise} \\
{}^\star[\![\texttt{last}(x)]\!]^\rho_G(T)(t) & = & \rho(x)({}^\bullet clock(x)(t)), \texttt{false} \\
{}^\star[\![f(e)]\!]^\rho_G(T)(t) & = & \texttt{let } s(t'), z(t') = {}^\star[\![e]\!]^\rho_G(T)(t') \texttt{ in} \\
& & \texttt{let } v', z' = G(f)(s)(t) \texttt{ in} \\
& & v', z(t) \vee z' \\
{}^\star[\![\texttt{up}(e)]\!]^\rho_G(T)(t) & = & \texttt{let } s(t'), z(t') = {}^\star[\![e]\!]^\rho_G(T)(t') \texttt{ in} \\
& & \texttt{let } v' = up(s)(T)(t) \texttt{ in} \\
& & v', z(t) \vee v'
\end{array}$$

Figure 3: The non-standard semantics of expressions

$op(e)$ is obtained by applying the operation op to e at every instant, an event is raised only if e raises one. An expression (e_1, e_2) returns a pair at every instant and raises an event if either of e_1 or e_2 does. The initial value of a delay $e_1 \texttt{ fby } e_2$ is that of e_1. Afterward, it is the previous value of e_2 according to clock T. E.g., the value of $0 \texttt{ fby } x$ on clock T is the value x had at the previous instant that T was active. This is not necessarily the previous value of x. On the contrary, $\texttt{last}(x)$ is the previous value of x the last time x was defined. The semantics of $f(e)$ is the application of the function f to the signal value of e, which raises an event when either e or the body of f does. Finally, the semantics of $\texttt{up}(e)$ is given by operator $up(.)$, which raises a zero-crossing event when either e does or $up(s)(T)(t)$ is true.

Equations: If E is an equation, G is a global environment, ρ is a local environment and T is a time base, ${}^\star[\![E]\!]^\rho_G(T) = \rho', z$ means that the evaluation of E on the time base T returns a local environment ρ' and a zero-crossing signal z. As for expressions, the value of E is undefined outside of T, that is, for all $t \notin T$, $\rho'(x)(t) = \bot$ and $z(t) = \bot$. For all $t \in T$, $z(t) = \texttt{true}$ signals that a zero-crossing occurs at instant t and $z(t) = \texttt{false}$ means that no zero-crossing occurred at that instant. The semantics of equations is given in Figure 4, where the following notation is used: if $z_1 : T \mapsto \texttt{bool}_\bot$ and $z_2 : T \mapsto \texttt{bool}_\bot$ then $z_1 \; or \; z_2 : T \mapsto \texttt{bool}_\bot$ and $\forall t \in T.(z_1 \; or \; z_2)(t) = z_1(t) \vee z_2(t)$ if $z_1(t) \neq \bot$ and $z_2(t) \neq \bot$, and otherwise, $(z_1 \; or \; z_2)(t) = \bot$.

Function definitions: Function definition is our final concern: we must show the existence of fixed points in the sense of Kahn process network semantics based on Scott domains.

The prefix order on signals $S(V)$ indexed by $\mathbb{T}$ is defined as: signal x is a *prefix* of signal y, written $x \leq_{S(V)} y$, if

$$\star[\![x = e]\!]^{\rho}_{G}(T) = [s/x], z \quad \textit{where} \quad \forall t \in T.s(t), z(t) = \star[\![e]\!]^{\rho}_{G}(T)(t)$$

$$\star[\![E_1 \,\texttt{and}\, E_2]\!]^{\rho}_{G}(T) = \rho_1 + \rho_2, z_1 \textit{ or } z_2 \quad \textit{where} \quad \rho_1, z_1 = \star[\![E_1]\!]^{\rho}_{G}(T) \wedge \rho_2, z_2 = \star[\![E_2]\!]^{\rho}_{G}(T)$$

$$\begin{aligned}\star[\![\texttt{present}\ e\ \texttt{then}\ E_1\ \texttt{else}\ E_2]\!]^{\rho}_{G}(T) = \rho', z \textit{ or } z_1 \textit{ or } z_2 \quad & \textit{where} \quad \forall t \in T.s(t), z(t) = \star[\![e]\!]^{\rho}_{G}(T)(t) \\ & \textit{and} \quad \rho_1, z_1 = \star[\![E_1]\!]^{\rho}_{G}(T\ \texttt{on}\ s) \\ & \textit{and} \quad \rho_2, z_2 = \star[\![E_2]\!]^{\rho}_{G}(T\ \texttt{on}\ not(s)) \\ & \textit{and} \quad \rho' = merge\,(T)\,(s)\,(\rho_1)\,(\rho_2)\end{aligned}$$

$$\star[\![\texttt{if}\ e\ \texttt{then}\ E_1\ \texttt{else}\ E_2]\!]^{\rho}_{G}(T) = \rho', z \textit{ or } z_1 \textit{ or } z_2 \quad \text{as for } \texttt{present} \text{ (see extended version)}$$

$$\begin{aligned}\star[\![\texttt{init}\ x = e]\!]^{\rho}_{G}(T) = [s/x], z \quad & \textit{where} \quad s(t_0), z(t_0) = \star[\![e]\!]^{\rho}_{G}(T)(t_0) \\ & \textit{and} \quad t_0 = min(T) \\ & \textit{and} \quad \forall t \neq t_0.s(t) = \rho(x)(t) \wedge z(t) = \texttt{false}\end{aligned}$$

$$\star[\![\texttt{next}\ x = e]\!]^{\rho}_{G}(T) = [s/x], z \quad \textit{where} \quad \forall t \in T.\ (v, z = \star[\![e]\!]^{\rho}_{G}(T)(t)) \wedge (s(t^{\bullet}) = v)$$

$$\star[\![\texttt{der}\ x = e]\!]^{\rho}_{G}(T) = [s/x], z \quad \textit{where} \quad \forall t \in T.\ (v, z = \star[\![e]\!]^{\rho}_{G}(T)(t)) \wedge (s(t^{\bullet}) = s(t) + \partial \times v)$$

Figure 4: The non-standard semantics of equations

$x(t) \neq y(t)$ implies $x(t') = \bot$ for all t' such that $t \leq t'$. The minimum element is the undefined signal $\bot_{S(V)}$ for which $\forall t \in \mathbb{T}, \bot_{S(V)}(t) = \bot$. When possible, we write $\bot$ for $\bot_{S(V)}$ and $x \leq y$ for $x \leq_{S(V)} y$. The symbol $\bigvee$ denotes a supremum in the prefix order. A function $f : S(^\star V) \mapsto S(^\star V)$ is continuous if $\bigvee_i f(x_i) = f(\bigvee_i x_i)$ for every increasing chain of signals, where increasing refers to the prefix order. If f is continuous, then equation $x = f(x)$ has a least solution denoted by $\mathit{fix}(f)$, and equal to $\bigvee_i f^i(\bot)$. We name such continuity on the prefix order *Kahn continuity* [14].

The prefix order is lifted to environments so that $\rho \leq \rho'$ iff for all $x \in \mathit{Dom}(\rho) \cup \mathit{Dom}(\rho')$, $\rho(x) \leq \rho'(x)$. It is lifted to pairs such that $(x, y) \leq (x', y')$ iff $x \leq x'$ and $y \leq y'$.

PROPERTY 1 (KAHN CONTINUITY). *Let $[s/p]$ be an environment, G a global environment of Kahn-continuous functions and T a clock. The function:*

$$F : (L \mapsto S(^\star V)) \times S(\texttt{bool}) \mapsto (L \mapsto S(^\star V)) \times S(\texttt{bool})$$

such that:

$$F(\rho, z) = \texttt{let}\ \rho', z' = \star[\![E]\!]^{\rho+[s/p]}_{G}(T)\ \texttt{in}\ \rho', z \textit{ or } z'$$

is Kahn continuous, that is, for any sequence $(\rho_i, z_i)_{i \geq 0}$:

$$F(\textstyle\bigvee_{i \in I}(\rho_i, z_i)) = \bigvee_{i \in I}(F(\rho_i, z_i))$$

As a consequence, an equation $(\rho, z) = F(\rho, z)$ admits a least fixed point $\mathit{fix}(F) = \bigvee_i(F^i(\bot, \bot))$.

The declaration of $\star[\![\texttt{let}\ k\ f(p) = e\ \texttt{where}\ E]\!]_G(T)$ defines a Kahn-continuous function $^\star f$ such that

$$\star[\![\texttt{let}\ k\ f(p) = e\ \texttt{where}\ E]\!]_G(T)(s)(t) = {}^\star f(T)(s)(t)$$

where

$$\begin{aligned}{}^\star f(T)(s)(t) = \texttt{let}\ & s'(t'), z(t') = \star[\![e]\!]^{\rho'+[s/p]}_{G}(T)(t')\ \texttt{in} \\ & s'(t), z(t) \vee z'(t)\end{aligned}$$

and with

$$(\rho', z') = \mathit{fix}((\rho, z) \mapsto \star[\![E]\!]^{\rho+[s/p]}_{G}(T))$$

Yet, Kahn-continuity of $^\star f$ does not mean that the function computes anything interesting. In particular, the semantics gives a meaning to functions that become 'stuck', like[11]

```
let hybrid f(x) = y where rec y = y + x
```

The semantics of `f` is $^\star f(x) = \bot$ since the minimal solution of equation $y = y + x$ is $\bot$. The purpose of the causality analysis is to statically reject this kind of program.

3.2 Standardization

We now relate the non-standard semantics to the usual super-dense semantics of hybrid systems. Following [18], the execution of a hybrid system alternates between integration steps and discrete steps. Signals are now interpreted as total functions from the time index $\mathbb{S} = \mathbb{R} \times \mathbb{N}$ to $V_\bot$. This time index is called *super-dense time* [18, 15] and is ordered lexically, $(t, n) <_{\mathbb{S}} (t', n')$ iff $t <_{\mathbb{R}} t'$, or $t = t'$ and $n <_{\mathbb{N}} n'$. Moreover, for any (t, n) and (t, n') where $n \leq_{\mathbb{N}} n'$, if $x(t, n') \neq \bot$ then $x(t, n) \neq \bot$.

A *timeline* for a signal x is a function $N_x : \mathbb{R}_+ \mapsto \mathbb{N}_\bot$. $N_x(t)$ is the number of instants of x that occur at a real date t and such timelines thus specify a subset of super-dense time $\mathbb{S}_{N_x} = \{(t, n) \in \mathbb{S} \mid n \leq_{\mathbb{N}} N_x(t)\}$. In particular, if N_x is always 0, then $\mathbb{S}_{N_x}$ is isomorphic to $\mathbb{R}_+$. For $t \in \mathbb{R}$ and $T \subseteq \mathbb{T}$, define:

$$set(T)(t) \stackrel{def}{=} \{t' \in T \mid t' \approx t \wedge t \in \mathbb{R}\} \subseteq \mathbb{T}$$

that is, the set of all instants infinitely close to t. T is totally ordered and hence so is $set(T)(t)$. Let $x : T \mapsto {}^\star V_\bot$.

We now proceed to the definition of the *timeline* N_x of x and the *standardization* of x, written

$$st(x) : \mathbb{R} \times \mathbb{N} \mapsto V_\bot,$$

such that $st(x)(t, n) = \bot$ for $n > N_x(t)$.

Let $T' \stackrel{def}{=} set(T)(t)$ and consider

$$st(x(T')) \stackrel{def}{=} \{st(x(t')) \mid t' \in T'\}.$$

[11]The keyword `hybrid` stands for $k = \texttt{C}$ and `node` for $k = \texttt{D}$.

(a) If $st(x(T')) = \{v\}$ then, at instant t, x's timeline is $N_x(t) = 0$ and its standardization is $st(x)(t, 0) = v$.

(b) If $st(x(T'))$ is not a singleton set, then let

$$Z \stackrel{def}{=} \{t' \mid t' \in T' \wedge x(t') \not\approx x(T'^{\bullet}(t'))\}$$

i.e., Z collects the instants at which x experiences a non-infinitesimal change. Z is either finite or infinite:

(i) If $Z = \{t_{z_0}, \ldots, t_{z_m}\}$ is finite, timeline $N_x(t) = m$ and the standard value of signal x at time t is:

$$\forall n \in \{0, \ldots, m\}.st(x)(t, n) = st(x(t_{z_n}))$$

(ii) If Z is infinite (it may even lack a minimum element), let

$$N_x(t) = \perp \text{ and } \forall n.st(x)(t, n) = \perp$$

which corresponds to a Zeno behavior.

Our approach differs slightly from [15], where the value of a signal is frozen for $n > N(t)$. We decide instead to set it to the value $\perp$. Each approach has its merits. For ours, parts of signals that do not experience jumps are simply indexed by $(t, 0)$ which we identify with t. In turn, we squander the undefined value $\perp$ which is usually devoted to Scott-Kahn semantics and causality issues.

3.3 Key properties

We now define two main properties that reasonable programs should satisfy. The first one states that discontinuities do not occur outside of zero-crossing events, that is, signals are continuous during integration. The second one states that the semantics should not depend on the choice of the infinitesimal. These two invariants are sufficient conditions to ensure that a standardization exists.

INVARIANT 1 (ZERO-CROSSINGS). *An expression e evaluated under G, ρ and a base time T has no discontinuity outside of zero-crossing events. Formally, define $s(t), z(t) = {}^\star[\![e]\!]_G^\rho(T)(t)$, then $\forall t, t' \in T$ such that $t \leq t'$:*

$$t \approx t' \Rightarrow (\exists t'' \in T, t \leq t'' \leq t' \wedge z(t'')) \vee s(t) \approx s(t')$$

This invariant states that all discontinuities are aligned on zero-crossings, that is, signals must evolve continuously during integration. Discrete changes must be announced to the solver using the construct `up(.)`. Not all programs satisfy the invariant, e.g.,

```
let hybrid f()= y where rec y = last y + 1 and init y = 0
```

`f` takes a single argument `()` of type `unit` and returns a value `y`. Writing ${}^\star y(n)$ for the value of y at instant $n\partial$ with $n \in {}^\star\mathbb{N}$, we get ${}^\star y(0) = 0$ and ${}^\star y(n) = {}^\star y(n-1) + 1$. Yet, ${}^\star y(n) \not\approx {}^\star y(n-1)$ while no zero-crossing is registered for any instant $n \in {}^\star\mathbb{N}$. This program will be statically rejected by using the type system developed in the next section.

INVARIANT 2 (INDEPENDENCE FROM ∂). *The semantics of e evaluated under G, ρ and a base time T is independent of the infinitesimal time step. Formally, define $s(t) = fst({}^\star[\![e]\!]_G^\rho(T_\partial)(t))$ and $s'(t) = fst({}^\star[\![e]\!]_G^\rho(T_{\partial'})(t))$, then:*

$$\forall t \in \mathbb{R},\ n \in \mathbb{N},\ st(s)(t, n) = st(s')(t, n)$$

When satisfied, this invariant ensures that properties and values on non-standard time carry over to standard time and values.

4. A LUSTRE-LIKE CAUSALITY

Programs are statically typed. We adopt, for our language, the type system presented in [3]. Well-typed programs may still exhibit causality issues, that is, the definition of a signal at instant t may instantaneously depend on itself. A classical causality analysis is to reject loops which do not cross a delay. This ensures that outputs can be computed sequentially from current inputs and an internal state. This simple solution is used in the academic LUSTRE compiler [12], LUCID SYNCHRONE [22] and SCADE 6.[12] We propose generalizing it to a language mixing stream equations, ODEs and their synchronous composition. The causality analysis essentially amounts to checking that every loop is broken either by a unit delay or an integrator.

The analysis gives sufficient conditions for invariants 1 and 2. We adopt the convention quoted below [3, 4]. A signal is termed *discrete* if it only changes on a *discrete clock*:

> A clock is termed *discrete* if it has been declared so or if it is the result of a zero-crossing or a sub-sampling of a discrete clock. Otherwise, it is termed *continuous*.

A discrete change on x at instant $t \in \mathbb{T}$ means that $x({}^\bullet t) \not\approx x(t)$ or $x(t) \not\approx x(t^\bullet)$. Said differently, all discontinuities have to be announced using the programming construct `up(.)`.

Two classes of approaches exist to formalize causality analyses. In the first, causality is defined as an abstract preorder relation on signal names. The causality preorder evolves dynamically at each reaction. A program is causally correct if its associated causality preorder is provably a partial order at every reaction. In the second class, causality is defined as the tagging of each event by a 'stamp' taken from some preordered set. The considered program is causally correct if its set of stamps can be partially ordered—similarly to Lamport vector clocks. Previous works [1, 4] belong to the first class whereas this paper belongs to the second.

Our analysis associates a type to every expression and function via two predicates: (TYP-EXP) states that, under constraints C, global environment G, local environment H, and kind $k \in \{\mathtt{A}, \mathtt{D}, \mathtt{C}\}$, an expression e has type ct; (TYP-ENV) states that under constraints C, global environment G, local environment H, and kind k, the equation E produces the type environment H'.

(TYP-EXP) $\quad C \mid G, H \vdash_k e : ct$ $\qquad$ (TYP-ENV) $\quad C \mid G, H \vdash_k E : H'$

The type language is

$$\begin{array}{rcl} \sigma & ::= & \forall \alpha_1, ..., \alpha_n : C.\ ct \xrightarrow{k} ct \\ ct & ::= & ct \times ct \mid \alpha \\ k & ::= & \mathtt{D} \mid \mathtt{C} \mid \mathtt{A} \end{array}$$

where σ defines type schemes, $\alpha_1, ..., \alpha_n$ are type variables and C is a set of constraints. A type is either a pair $(ct \times ct)$ or a type variable (α). The typing rules for causality are defined with respect to an environment of causality types. G is a global environment mapping each function name to a type scheme (σ). H is a local environment mapping each variable x to its type ct:

$$G ::= [\sigma_1/f_1, ..., \sigma_k/f_k] \qquad H ::= [ct_1/x_1, ..., ct_n/x_n]$$

[12] `http://www.esterel-technologies.com/scade`

(TAUT)
$$C + \alpha_1 < \alpha_2 \vdash \alpha_1 < \alpha_2$$

(TRANS)
$$\frac{C \vdash ct_1 < ct' \qquad C \vdash ct' < ct_2}{C \vdash ct_1 < ct_2}$$

(PAIR)
$$\frac{C \vdash ct_1 < ct_1' \qquad C \vdash ct_2 < ct_2'}{C \vdash ct_1 \times ct_2 < ct_1' \times ct_2'}$$

(ENV)
$$\frac{\forall i \in \{1,..,n\}, C \vdash ct_i < ct_i'}{C \vdash [x_1 : ct_1; ...; x_n : ct_n] < [x_1 : ct_1'; ...; x_n : ct_n']}$$

Figure 5: Constraints between types

If H_1 and H_2 are environments, $H_1 + H_2$ is their disjoint union. H_1, H_2 is their concatenation; and $H_1 * H_2$ is a new environment such that $(H_1 + [x : ct]) * (H_2 + [x : ct]) = (H_1 * H_2) + [x : ct]$ where $+$ and $*$ are associative and commutative.

Precedence relation: C is a precedence relation between variables with the following intuition. If $C \mid G, H \vdash_k e : \alpha_1$ holds and $\alpha_1 < \alpha_2$, the current value of e is ready at α_1 and also later, within the execution of the same reaction, at α_2. $<$ must be a strict partial order: it must not be possible to deduce both $\alpha_1 < \alpha_2$ and $\alpha_2 < \alpha_1$ from the transitive closure of C.

$$C ::= \{\alpha_1 < \alpha_1', ..., \alpha_n < \alpha_n'\}$$

The predicate $C \vdash ct_1 < ct_2$, defined in Figure 5, means that ct_1 precedes ct_2 according to C. All rules are simple distribution rules.

The initial environment G_0 gives type signatures to imported operators, synchronous primitives and the zero-crossing function.

$$\begin{array}{lll} (+), (-), (*), (/) & : & \forall \alpha.\ \alpha \times \alpha \xrightarrow{\mathtt{A}} \alpha \\ \mathtt{pre}(\cdot) & : & \forall \alpha_1, \alpha_2 : \{\alpha_2 < \alpha_1\}.\alpha_1 \xrightarrow{\mathtt{D}} \alpha_2 \\ \cdot\,\mathtt{fby}\,\cdot & : & \forall \alpha_1, \alpha_2 : \{\alpha_2 < \alpha_1\}.\alpha_1 \times \alpha_2 \xrightarrow{\mathtt{D}} \alpha_1 \end{array}$$

For example, the operation $x + y$ depends on both x and y, that is, it must be computed after x and y have been computed. Indeed, if $C \mid G, H \vdash x : \alpha_1$ and $C \mid G, H \vdash y : \alpha_2$, $C \vdash \alpha_1 < \alpha$ and $C \vdash \alpha_2 < \alpha$, then $C \mid G, H \vdash x : \alpha$, $C \mid G, H \vdash y : \alpha$. Thus $C \mid G, H \vdash x + y : \alpha$. $\mathtt{pre}(x)$ does not depend on x. For $\mathtt{up}(x)$, two policies can be considered:

$$\mathtt{up}(\cdot) : \forall \alpha_1, \alpha_2 : \{\alpha_2 < \alpha_1\}.\alpha_1 \xrightarrow{\mathtt{C}} \alpha_2 \quad \mathtt{up}(\cdot) : \forall \alpha_1 : \alpha_1 \xrightarrow{\mathtt{C}} \alpha_1$$

With the first one, the effect of a zero-crossing is delayed by one cycle. Hence, $\mathtt{up}(x)$ does not depend instantaneously on x. With the second, the effect is instantaneous.

Instantiation/Generalization The types of global definitions are generalized to types schemes (σ) by quantifying over free variables.

$$Gen(C)(ct_1 \xrightarrow{k} ct_2) = \forall \alpha_1, ..., \alpha_n : C.ct_1 \xrightarrow{k} ct_2$$

where $\{\alpha_1, ..., \alpha_n\} = Vars(C) \cup Vars(ct_1) \cup Vars(ct_2)$. The variables in a type scheme σ can be instantiated. $ct \in Inst(\sigma)$ means that ct is an instance of σ. For $\vec{\alpha'}$ and $k \leq k'$:

$$C[\vec{\alpha'}/\vec{\alpha}], ct_1[\vec{\alpha'}/\vec{\alpha}] \xrightarrow{k'} ct_2[\vec{\alpha'}/\vec{\alpha}] \in Inst(\forall \vec{\alpha} : C.ty_1 \xrightarrow{k} ty_2)$$

The typing relation is defined in Figure 6:

Rule (VAR). A variable x inherits the declared type ct.

Rule (CONST). A constant v has any causality type.

Rule (APP). An application $f(e)$ has type ct_2 if f has function type $ct_1 \xrightarrow{k} ct_2$ from the instantiation of a type scheme giving a new set of constraints C, and e has type ct_1.

Rule (LAST). $\mathtt{last}(x)$ is the previous value of x. In this system, we only allow $\mathtt{last}(x)$ to appear during a discrete step (of kind $\mathtt{D}$).

Rule (EQ). An equation $x = e$ defines an environment $[ct/x]$ if x and e are of type ct.

Rule (SUB). If e is of type ct and $ct < ct'$ then e can also be given the type ct'.

Rule (DER). An integrator has a similar role as a unit delay: it breaks dependencies during integration. If $e : ct_1$ then any use of x does not depend instantaneously on the computation of e and can thus be given a type ct_2.

Rules (PRESENT) and (IF). The present statement returns an environment $H_1 * H_2$. The first handler is activated during discrete steps and the second one has kind $\mathtt{C}$. The rule for conditionals is the same except that the handlers and condition must all be of kind k.

Rule (LOCAL). The declaration of a local variable x is valid if E gives an equation for x which is itself causal.

Rule (DEF). For a function f with parameter p and result e, the body E is first typed under an environment H and constraints C. The resulting environment H' must be strictly less than H. This forbids any direct use of variables in H when typing E.

We can now illustrate the system on several examples.

Example: The following program is a classic synchronous (thus discrete-time) program written in the concrete syntax of ZÉLUS. Calling the forward Euler integrator `integr` below, the function `heat` is valid since `temp` does not depend instantaneously on `gain - temp`. `step` is a global constant.

```
let node integr(xi, x') = x where
  rec x = xi fby (x + x' * step)

let node heat(temp0, gain) = temp where
  rec temp = integr(temp0, gain - temp))
```

The causality signatures are:

```
val integr : {'a < 'b}.'a * 'b -C-> 'a
val heat   : {'a < 'b}.'a * 'b -C-> 'a
```

The signature for `integr` states that the output depends instantaneously on its first argument but not the second one. The following program is statically rejected:

```
let cycle() = (x, y) where rec y = x + 1 and x = y + 2
```

Indeed, taken $x : \alpha_x$ and $y : \alpha_y$, the first equation is correct if both $C \vdash \alpha_x < \alpha_y$ and $C \vdash \alpha_y < \alpha_x$. This means that C must contain $\{\alpha_x < \alpha_y, \alpha_y < \alpha_x\}$ which is cyclic. This following two are correct, `der` playing the role of a delay:

$$\frac{}{C \mid G, H + x : ct \vdash_k x : ct}\ (\text{VAR}) \qquad \frac{}{C \mid G, H \vdash_k v : ct}\ (\text{CONST}) \qquad \frac{C, ct_1 \xrightarrow{k} ct_2 \in \mathit{Inst}(G(f)) \quad C \mid G, H \vdash_k e : ct_1}{C \mid G, H \vdash_k f(e) : ct_2}\ (\text{APP})$$

$$\frac{C \vdash ct_2 < ct_1}{C \mid G, H + x : ct_1 \vdash_{\mathtt{D}} \mathtt{last}(x) : ct_2}\ (\text{LAST}) \qquad \frac{C \mid G, H \vdash_k x : ct \quad C \mid G, H \vdash_k e : ct}{C \mid G, H \vdash_k x = e : [ct/x]}\ (\text{EQ}) \qquad \frac{C \mid G, H \vdash_{\mathtt{C}} e : ct_1 \quad C \vdash ct_2 < ct_1}{C \mid G, H \vdash_{\mathtt{C}} \mathtt{der}\, x = e : [ct_2/x]}\ (\text{DER})$$

$$\frac{C \mid G, H \vdash_{\mathtt{C}} e : ct}{C \mid G, H \vdash_{\mathtt{C}} \mathtt{init}\, x = e : [ct/x]}\ (\text{INIT}) \qquad \frac{C \mid G, H \vdash_{\mathtt{D}} e : ct_1 \quad C \vdash ct_2 < ct_1}{C \mid G, H \vdash_{\mathtt{D}} \mathtt{next}\, x = e : [ct_2/x]}\ (\text{NEXT}) \qquad \frac{C \mid G, H \vdash_k e : ct \quad C \vdash ct < ct'}{C \mid G, H \vdash_k e : ct'}\ (\text{SUB})$$

$$\frac{C \mid G, H \vdash_{\mathtt{C}} e : ct \quad C \mid G, H \vdash_{\mathtt{D}} E_1 : H_1 \quad C \mid G, H \vdash_{\mathtt{C}} E_2 : H_2}{C \mid G, H \vdash_{\mathtt{C}} \mathtt{present}\ e\ \mathtt{then}\ E_1\ \mathtt{else}\ E_2 : H_1 * H_2}\ (\text{PRESENT}) \qquad \frac{C \mid G, H \vdash_k e : ct \quad \forall i \in \{1,2\} : C \mid G, H \vdash_k E_i : H_i}{C \mid G, H \vdash_k \mathtt{if}\ e\ \mathtt{then}\ E_1\ \mathtt{else}\ E_2 : H_1 * H_2}\ (\text{IF})$$

$$\frac{C \mid G, H \vdash_k E_1 : H_1 \quad C \mid G, H \vdash_k E_2 : H_2}{C \mid G, H \vdash_k E_1\ \mathtt{and}\ E_2 : H_1 * H_2}\ (\text{AND}) \qquad \frac{C \mid G, H + [x : ct_1] \vdash_k E : H' + [x : ct_2] \quad C \vdash ct_2 < ct_1}{C \mid G, H \vdash_k \mathtt{local}\ x\ \mathtt{in}\ E : H'}\ (\text{LOCAL})$$

$$\frac{\forall i \in \{1,2\} : C \mid G, H \vdash_k e_i : ct_i}{C \mid G, H \vdash_k (e_1, e_2) : ct_1 \times ct_2}\ (\text{PAIR}) \qquad \frac{C \mid G, H \vdash_k E : H' \quad C \vdash H' < H \quad C \mid G, H \vdash_k p : ct_1 \quad C \mid G, H \vdash_k e : ct_2}{\vdash \mathtt{let}\ k\ f(p) = e\ \mathtt{where}\ E : [\mathit{Gen}(C)(ct_1 \xrightarrow{k} ct_2)/f]}\ (\text{DEF})$$

Figure 6: A Lustre-like Causality Analysis

```
let hybrid f(x) = o where
  rec der y = 1.0 - x init 0.0 and o = y + 1.0

let hybrid loop(x) = y where rec y = f(y) + x

val f    : {'b < 'a }.'a -C-> 'b
val loop : 'a -C-> 'a
```

In the present system, $\mathtt{last}(x)$ is restricted to only appear in a discrete context. Hence, the following program is rejected.

```
let hybrid g(x) = o where
  rec der y = 1.0 init 0.0
  and x = last x + y and init x = 0.0
```

If $\mathtt{up}(.)$ is considered to instantaneously depend on its input, `loop` is rejected:

```
let hybrid f(z) = y where
  der y = 1.0 init -1.0 reset up(z) -> -1.0

let hybrid loop() = y where rec y = f(y)
```

Indeed, `f` has signature $\forall \alpha.\alpha \rightarrow \alpha$. For `loop` to be well-typed, we would need to be able to state an equation $\alpha_y < \alpha_y$ where $y : \alpha_y$.

Type simplification: The ZÉLUS compiler implements a simplification algorithm to eliminate useless constraints. It follows the algorithm [23] to partition type variables according to *Input-Output* (IO) relations. Moreover, as causality analysis is performed after typing, some relations can be removed. E.g., the actual signature of the unit delay is simply:

$$\mathtt{pre}(\cdot) \quad : \quad \forall \alpha_1, \alpha_2 : \alpha_1 \xrightarrow{\mathtt{D}} \alpha_2$$

The State Port: The present causality analysis restricts the use of $\mathtt{last}(x)$ to appear only under a discrete context. An extension is to allow $\mathtt{last}(x)$ to appear in a continuous context provided x is a continuous state variable, i.e., it is defined by an equation $\mathtt{der}\, x = e$. Indeed, during integration $\mathtt{last}(x)$ and x are infinitely close to each other (${}^\star x(n-1) \approx {}^\star x(n)$). The ZÉLUS compiler implements this minor extension.

5. THE MAIN THEOREM

We can now state the main result of this paper: The semantics of well-typed programs satisfies Invariants 1 and 2. This theorem requires assumptions on primitive operators and imported functions, as the following example shows.

A Nonsmooth Model ♣: It comprises several modules (written in ZÉLUS syntax). The first two are an integrator and a time base with a parameterized initial value t_0:

```
let hybrid integrator(y0, x) = y where
  rec init y = y0 and der y = x

let hybrid time(t0) = integrator(t0, 1.0)
```

Then a function producing a quasi-Dirac (Dirac with a width strictly greater than 0). It yields a function $\mathrm{dirac}(d, t)$ such that $\int_{-\infty}^{+\infty} \mathrm{dirac}(d, t)dt = 1$ for every constant $d > 0$.

```
let dirac(d, t) = 1.0 / pi * d / (d * d + t * t)
```

Our goal is to produce, using a hybrid program, an infinitesimal value for d, so that $\mathrm{dirac}(d, t)$ standardizes as a Dirac measure centered on $t = 0$. This can be achieved by integrating a pulse of magnitude 1, but of infinitesimal width. Such a pulse can be produced using a variable that is reset twice by the successive occurrences, separated by a ∂, of two zero-crossings:

```
let hybrid doublecrossing(t) = (x + 1.0) / 2.0 where
  rec init x = -1.0
  and present up(t) then do next x = 1.0 done else
      present up(x) then do next x = -1.0 done
                    else do der x = 0.0 done

let hybrid infinitesimal(t1,t) =
  integrator(0.0, doublecrossing(t1))
```

The first zero-crossing in **doublecrossing** occurs when t crosses zero and causes an immediate reset of x from -1 to $+1$, this in turn triggers an immediate zero-crossing on x and a reset of x back to -1. The input of the integrator is thus one for one ∂-step; the output of the integrator, initially 0, becomes ∂ at time $t_1 + \partial$.

The main program is the following, where $t_0 < t_1 < t_2$:

```
let hybrid nonsmooth(t0, t1, t2) = x where
  rec t = time(t0) and d = infinitesimal(t - t1)
  and x = integrator(0.0, dirac(d,(t - t2)))
```

What is the point of this example? It is causally correct and yet its standardization has a discontinuity at t_2 though no zero-crossing occurs. This is because dirac standardizes to a Dirac mass.

Discussion: In the previous example, the problem arises with the function dirac, that is not defined when $t = 0$ and $d = 0$. However, it is defined everywhere when $d \neq 0$. In particular, it is defined for $d = \partial$. The solution seems clear: *if a standard function $f(x)$ of a real variable x is such that $f(x_0) = \perp$, then the semantics must enforce $f(x) = \perp$ for any $x \approx x_0$.* Applying this to the function $d \mapsto \frac{d}{d^2+t^2}$ where $t = 0$ is fixed gives $\frac{\partial}{\partial^2+t^2} = \perp$. This is formalized through the assumptions on operators and functions given below.

Given $x, y \in {}^\star\mathbb{R}$, relation $x \approx y$ holds iff $st(x - y) = 0$. Recall that function $f : {}^\star\mathbb{R} \mapsto {}^\star\mathbb{R}$ is *microcontinuous* iff for all $x, y \in {}^\star\mathbb{R}$, $x \approx y$ implies $f(x) \approx f(y)$. Recall that the microcontinuity of f implies the uniform continuity of $st(f){:}\mathbb{R}{\mapsto}\mathbb{R}$ [17]. Denote $[t_0, t_1]_{\mathbb{T}} = \{t \in \mathbb{T} \mid t_0 \leq t \leq t_1\}$, with $t_0, t_1 \in \mathbb{T}$ finite.

ASSUMPTION 1. *Operators $op(\cdot)$ of kind* C *are standard and satisfy the following definedness, finiteness and continuity properties:*

$$\left\{\begin{array}{l} op(\perp) = \perp \\ \forall v, op(v) \neq \perp \textit{ implies } op(v) \textit{ finite} \\ \forall u, v, u \approx v \textit{ and } op(u) \not\approx op(v) \textit{ implies } op(u) = \perp \end{array}\right.$$

ASSUMPTION 2. *Environment G is assumed to satisfy the following assumption, for all external functions f of kind* C*: for any bounded interval $K = [t_1, t_2]_{\mathbb{T}}$, for any input u that is defined, finite and microcontinuous on K, if function $G(f)(u)$ is defined and produces no zero-crossing in K, then it is assumed to be finite and microcontinuous on K:*

$$\left[\forall t \in K, \left\{\begin{array}{rl} fst(G(f)(u)(t)) & \neq \perp \text{ and} \\ snd(G(f)(u)(t)) & = \texttt{false} \end{array}\right.\right]$$
$$\Downarrow$$
$$\left[\begin{array}{l} \forall t \in K, fst(G(f)(u)(t)) \textit{ finite, and} \\ \forall t, t' \in K, t \approx t' \textit{ implies} \\ fst(G(f)(u)(t)) \approx fst(G(f)(u)(t')) \end{array}\right]$$

Assumption 1 has several implications on the definitions of the usual operators. For the square root function: $\sqrt{\epsilon} = \sqrt{-\epsilon} = \sqrt{0}$, for all $\epsilon \approx 0$, which yields two meaningful solutions: $\sqrt{\epsilon} = \perp$ or $\sqrt{\epsilon} = 0$ For the inverse: $1/\epsilon = \perp$ for any infinitesimal ϵ is the only solution.

THEOREM 1. *Under Assumptions 1 and 2, the semantics of every causally correct equation E (wrt. typing rules of Section 4) satisfies Invariants 1 and 2 and is standardizable.*

This is a direct consequence of the following lemmas.

LEMMA 1. *Assume that Assumptions 1 and 2 hold. For any activation clock $T \subseteq \mathbb{T}$, for any bounded interval $K = [t_1, t_2]_{\mathbb{T}}$, for any environment ρ that is defined, finite and microcontinuous on K, if expression e, of kind* A *or* C*, is defined and produces no zero-crossing on K, then it is finite and microcontinuous on K:*

$$\left[\forall t \in K, \left\{\begin{array}{rl} fst({}^\star[\![e]\!]^\rho_G(T)(t)) & \neq \perp \text{ and} \\ snd({}^\star[\![e]\!]^\rho_G(T)(t)) & = \texttt{false} \end{array}\right.\right]$$
$$\Downarrow$$
$$\left[\begin{array}{l} \forall t \in K, fst({}^\star[\![e]\!]^\rho_G(T)(t)) \textit{ finite, and} \\ \forall t, t' \in K, t \approx t' \textit{ implies} \\ fst({}^\star[\![e]\!]^\rho_G(T)(t)) \approx fst({}^\star[\![e]\!]^\rho_G(T)(t')) \end{array}\right]$$

Given a bounded interval $T = [t_0, t_1]_{\mathbb{T}}$, define the following nonstandard dynamical system on T:

$$\left\{\begin{array}{rcl} x(t_0) & = & x_0 \text{ finite} \\ \forall t \in T \setminus \{t_1\}, x(t + \partial) & = & x(t) + \partial \times f(t, x(t)) \end{array}\right.$$

LEMMA 2. *If the solution $x : T \mapsto {}^\star\mathbb{R}$ of the dynamical system defined above is infinite or discontinuous at t, then there exists $t' < t$ such that $f(t', x(t'))$ is infinite.*

The corollary of this lemma, is that under Assumptions 1 and 2, the semantics of $\texttt{der}\, x = e$ is smooth provided that expression e is defined and triggers no zero-crossing:

COROLLARY 1. *Assume that Assumptions 1 and 2 hold, and that e is a causally correct expression of kind* A *or* C*. For any activation clock $T \subseteq \mathbb{T}$, for any bounded interval $K = [t_1, t_2]_{\mathbb{T}}$, for any environment ρ that is defined, finite and microcontinuous on K, if the least fixed point of the operator $\rho', z' \mapsto {}^\star[\![\texttt{der}\, x = e]\!]^{\rho'+\rho}_G(T)$ is defined and raises no zero-crossing on K, then ρ' is microcontinuous on K.*

LEMMA 3. *Assume that Assumptions 1 and 2 hold. For any activation clock $T \subseteq \mathbb{T}$, for any bounded interval $K = [t_1, t_2]_{\mathbb{T}}$, for any environment ρ that is defined, finite and microcontinuous on K, if the semantics of E, a causally correct equation of kind* C*, is defined and produces no zero-crossing on K, then it is finite and microcontinuous on K:*

$$\left[\forall x, \forall t \in K, \left\{\begin{array}{rl} fst({}^\star[\![E]\!]^\rho_G(T))(x)(t) & \neq \perp \text{ and} \\ snd({}^\star[\![E]\!]^\rho_G(T))(t) & = \texttt{false} \end{array}\right.\right]$$
$$\Downarrow$$
$$\left[\begin{array}{l} \forall x, (\forall t \in K, fst({}^\star[\![E]\!]^\rho_G(T))(x)(t) \textit{ finite, and} \\ \forall t, t' \in K, t \approx t' \textit{ implies} \\ fst({}^\star[\![E]\!]^\rho_G(T))(x)(t) \approx fst({}^\star[\![E]\!]^\rho_G(T))(x)(t')) \end{array}\right]$$

6. DISCUSSION AND RELATED WORK

The present work continues that of Benveniste et al. [4], by exploiting non-standard semantics to define causality in a hybrid program. The proposed analysis gives a sufficient condition for the program to be statically scheduled.

The present work is related to Ptolemy [10] and the use of synchronous language concepts to define the semantics of hybrid modelers [16]. We follow the same path, replacing super-dense semantics by non-standard semantics that we found more helpful to explain causality constraints and generalize solutions adopted in synchronous compilers. The presented material is implemented in ZÉLUS, a synchronous language extended with ODEs [6]. It is more single-minded than Ptolemy but ZÉLUS programs are turned into sequential code whereas Ptolemy only provides an interpreter.

Causality has been extensively studied for the synchronous languages SIGNAL [1] and ESTEREL [5]. Instead of imposing that every feedback loop crosses a delay, *constructive causality* checks that the corresponding circuit is constructive. A circuit is constructive if its outputs stabilize in bounded time when inputs are fed with a constant input. In the present work, we adapted the simpler causality of LUSTRE and LUCID SYNCHRONE based on a precedence relation in order to focus on specific issues raised when mixing discrete and continuous-time signals. Schneider et al. [2] have considered the causality problem for a hybrid extension of Quartz, a variant of ESTEREL, with ODEs. But, they did not address issues due to the interaction of discrete and continuous behaviors.

Regarding tools like SIMULINK, we think that the synchronous interpretation of signals where time advances by infinitesimal steps can be helpful to define causality constraints and safe interactions between mixed signals.

7. CONCLUSION

Causality in system modelers is a sufficient condition for ensuring that a hybrid system can be implemented: general fix-point equations may have solutions or not, but the subset of causally correct systems can definitely be computed sequentially using off-the-shelf solvers. The notion of causality we propose is that of a synchronous language where instantaneous feedback loops are statically rejected. An integrator plays the role of a unit delay for continuous signals as the previous value is infinitesimally close to the current value.

We introduced the construction `last`(x) which stands for the previous value of a signal and coincides with the *left limit* when the signal is left continuous. Then, we introduced a causality analysis to check for the absence of instantaneous algebraic loops. Finally, we established the main result: causally correct programs have no discontinuous changes during integration.

8. REFERENCES

[1] T. Amagbegnon, L. Besnard, and P. Le Guernic. Implementation of the data-flow synchronous language Signal. In *Programming Languages Design and Implementation (PLDI)*, pages 163–173. ACM, 1995.

[2] K. Bauer and K. Schneider. From synchronous programs to symbolic representations of hybrid systems. In *HSCC*, pages 41–50, 2010.

[3] A. Benveniste, T. Bourke, B. Caillaud, and M. Pouzet. Divide and recycle: types and compilation for a hybrid synchronous language. In *LCTES*, Chicago, USA, Apr. 2011. ACM.

[4] A. Benveniste, T. Bourke, B. Caillaud, and M. Pouzet. Non-Standard Semantics of Hybrid Systems Modelers. *Journal of Computer and System Sciences (JCSS)*, 78(3):877–910, May 2012.

[5] G. Berry. The constructive semantics of pure Esterel. 1999.

[6] T. Bourke and M. Pouzet. Zélus, a Synchronous Language with ODEs. In *HSCC*, Philadelphia, USA, April 8–11 2013. ACM.

[7] L. Carloni, R. Passerone, A. Pinto, and A. Sangiovanni-Vincentelli. Languages and tools for hybrid systems design. *Foundations & Trends in Electronic Design Automation*, vol. 1, 2006.

[8] G. Dahlquist and Å. Björck. *Numerical Methods in Scientific Computing: Volume 1.* SIAM, 2008.

[9] B. Denckla and P. Mosterman. Stream- and state-based semantics of hierarchy in block diagrams. In *17th IFAC World Congress*, pages 7955–7960, South Korea, 2008.

[10] J. Eker, J. W. Janneck, E. A. Lee, J. Liu, X. Liu, J. Ludvig, S. Neuendorffer, S. Sachs, and Y. Xiong. Taming heterogeneity—the Ptolemy approach. *Proc. IEEE*, 91(1):127–144, Jan. 2003.

[11] L. Gérard, A. Guatto, C. Pasteur, and M. Pouzet. A Modular Memory Optimization for Synchronous Data-Flow Languages. Application to Arrays in a Lustre Compiler. In *LCTES*, Beijing, June 12-13 2012.

[12] N. Halbwachs, P. Caspi, P. Raymond, and D. Pilaud. The synchronous dataflow programming language LUSTRE. *Proceedings of the IEEE*, 79(9):1305–1320, September 1991.

[13] N. Halbwachs, P. Raymond, and C. Ratel. Generating efficient code from data-flow programs. In *PLILP*, LNCS, Passau (Germany), August 1991.

[14] G. Kahn. The semantics of a simple language for parallel programming. In *IFIP 74 Congress*. North Holland, Amsterdam, 1974.

[15] E. A. Lee and H. Zheng. Operational semantics of hybrid systems. In *HSCC*, Zurich, Switzerland, Mar. 2005.

[16] E. A. Lee and H. Zheng. Leveraging synchronous language principles for heterogeneous modeling and design of embedded systems. In *EMSOFT*, 2007.

[17] T. Lindstrom. An invitation to non standard analysis. In N. Cutland, editor, *Nonstandard analysis and its applications*. Cambridge Univ. Press, 1988.

[18] O. Maler, Z. Manna, and A. Pnueli. From Timed to Hybrid Systems. In *Real-Time: Theory in Practice*, volume 600 of *LNCS*, pages 447–484. Springer, 1992.

[19] The Mathworks, Natick, MA, U.S.A. *Simulink 7—Reference*, 7.6 edition, Sept. 2010.

[20] The Mathworks, Natick, MA, U.S.A. *Simulink 7—User's Guide*, 7.5 edition, Mar. 2010.

[21] B. C. Pierce. *Types and Programming Languages.* MIT Press, 2002.

[22] M. Pouzet. *Lucid Synchrone, version 3. Tutorial and reference manual.* Université Paris-Sud, LRI, Apr. 2006.

[23] M. Pouzet and P. Raymond. Modular Static Scheduling of Synchronous Data-flow Networks: An efficient symbolic representation. In *EMSOFT*, Grenoble, France, Oct. 2009. ACM.

A Hyperdense Semantic Domain for Hybrid Dynamic Systems to Model Different Classes of Discontinuities

Pieter J. Mosterman
MathWorks
Natick, MA, USA
pmosterm@mathworks.com

Gabor Simko
Vanderbilt University
Nashville, TN, USA
tsg@isis.vanderbilt.edu

Justyna Zander
HumanoidWay
Natick, MA, USA
justyna.zander@gmail.com

Zhi Han
MathWorks
Natick, MA, USA
zhan@mathworks.com

ABSTRACT

The physics of technical systems, such as embedded and cyber-physical systems, is frequently modeled using the notion of continuous time. The underlying continuous phenomena may, however, occur at a time scale much faster than the system behavior of interest. In such situations, it is desirable to approximate the detailed continuous-time behavior by discontinuous change. Two classes of discontinuous change can be identified: pinnacles and mythical modes. This work shows how pinnacles are well modeled using a hyperreal notion of time while a superdense notion of time applies well to mythical modes. Thus, the combination, called *hyperdense* time, is proposed to allow for the expression of the semantics of both pinnacles and mythical modes. Further, the hyperdense semantic domain is translated into a computational representation as a three-dimensional model of time. In particular, continuous-time behavior is mapped onto floating point numbers, while the mythical mode and pinnacle event iterations each map onto an integer dimension. A modified Newton's cradle is used as a case study and to illustrate the computational implementation.

1. INTRODUCTION

With the advent of ubiquitous embedded computation, the complexity of engineered systems has grown by leaps and bounds. Where much of the increase in complexity has been driven by the availability of higher level programming languages combined with powerful compilers, more recently engineers have been turning to yet a higher level of abstraction. This higher level of abstraction is often somewhat colloquially referred to as 'models', making the implicit assumption that the computer code is the system under study rather than the actual implementation for which requirements are formulated.

HSCC'14, April 15–17, 2014, Berlin, Germany.

ACM 978-1-4503-2732-9/14/04.
http://dx.doi.org/10.1145/2562059.2562135 .

Recently attention has been gained by the notion of *Cyber-Physical Systems* (CPS). These systems tightly integrate the physical world, the computation, and the information space in a technological sense. Model-Based Design [14, 30] is a prime exponent to develop such systems [40]. Given the open nature of CPS and the necessity to include abstract representations in their development process, the availability of quality models for system-level studies is fundamental to a successful design effort.

In other work [29], the use of models has indeed been explored as an approach to mitigate system integration issues. Because of the delicate interaction between the various component and subsystem behaviors in their implementation, the use of models in addressing system integration challenges is not straightforward, however. In particular, it becomes essential to create 'good' models of the physics, that is, models that embody correctly the pertinent physical effects while not giving rise to behaviors that have no physical manifestation.

A critical characteristic of physics models for system-level studies is the manner in which their dynamics are captured. Generally, physical systems are well described by continuous-time behavior, for example, based on the foundations of thermodynamics [6, 13]. However, the dynamics of some of the continuous behavior is much faster than the time scale of interest, and, therefore, it may be efficient to model the resulting effect by discontinuous changes instead. The corresponding models then combine continuous behavior with discontinuous effects, which can be represented as a mathematical system with hybrid dynamics.

Complications arise because, as recognized by previous work [10, 27], certain laws of physics do not hold when discontinuities are introduced in the model behavior. For example, *continuity of power* is violated much like *conservation of energy* because of *instantaneous dissipation*. Other laws, however, do hold across discontinuities (e.g., *conservation of charge*, *conservation of momentum*, etc.) and these laws help determine consistent transfer across discontinuities of the dynamic state in a physics model. It is the objective of the work presented here to further develop these domain-specific constraints while formalizing their behavior so as to support multiparadigm modeling [32] across the fields of signal processing, control engineering, computer science, and thermodynamics.

Because of a natural bias toward computational implementations, a first approach to formalizing discontinuities in models of physical systems is to employ a semantic domain that is continuous but interspersed with discontinuous changes. In such a computational implementation, it is tempting to model sequences of discontinuous changes as occurring at a single point in time, which naturally leads to an orthogonal integer dimension so as to attribute an order to consecutive discontinuous changes. However, the resulting *superdense time* [21], $\mathbb{R}\times\mathbb{N}$ is insufficient to precisely describe the intricate behavior of discontinuities in physical system models [31]. In particular, an ontology of hybrid dynamics in physical system models that was developed in previous work [34] includes a class of behaviors referred to as *mythical modes* [35] that can be well formalized in superdense time. The ontology also includes a class of behaviors called *pinnacles*, though, which requires a time advance during discontinuous change, and, therefore, cannot be formalized by the integer dimensions of superdense time.

As an alternative, related work [17] proposed another approach to formalizing discontinuities based on the *hyperreals* of nonstandard analysis [19]. More recently, this approach has been further developed in an effort to define the semantics of hybrid dynamic systems [2, 3]. Because hyperreals allow an infinitesimal time advance, they present a semantic domain onto which pinnacles map well. With mythical modes being well presented by an orthogonal integer dimension, this paper proposes a semantic domain that combines the two in order to be able to span the range of discontinuous behaviors that have been identified in previous work [23, 32].

The resulting *hyperdense* semantic domain enables modeling of physics from first principles based on the theory of thermodynamics. A formalization of the intricate behavior on a hyperdense domain is then mapped onto a computational implementation. The corresponding executable models generate consistent and physically meaningful behavior even in the face of complicated interactions between classes of discontinuities. The conceptual modeling from first principles reduces the conceptual investment that is generally required when introducing discontinuities in physics models [7], an investment that is significantly (if not prohibitively) exacerbated in the case of interacting discontinuities.

Section 2 discusses the notion of discontinuity in physical modeling. In particular, hybrid bond graphs are introduced as a means to represent the nuances of physical phenomena. Examples of models are provided to explain the discontinuities, such as pinnacles and mythical mode. Section 3 relates the discontinuous changes to the notion of time. Superdense and hyperreal time semantic domains are discussed to provide a basis for a combination thereof. The resulting hyperdense time notion is then related to mythical mode and pinnacle behavior. In Section 4, a computational representation for hyperdense time is provided. A case study of a variant of Newton's cradle illustrates the value of the approach and its computational implementation is discussed. Section 5 discusses related work on the topic. Section 6 completes the treatise.

2. DISCONTINUITIES IN PHYSICS MODELS

The Heaviside principle [15] forms the foundation of a continuity assumption that is well developed in the theory of thermodynamics (e.g., [9]). In previous work [18, 36], *bond graphs* have been developed as a formalism to model continuous-time behavior of physical systems. After a brief introduction to thermodynamics and bond graphs, this section reviews how the bond graph formalism may be extended with an ideal switching element to form *hybrid bond graphs* [25]. Note that the principles apply to physics modeling languages in general such as Modelica [12] and MathWorks® Simscape™ [22].

2.1 Bond graphs for physical modeling

Modeling physics for system-level studies is often based on the concept of *reticulation* [5]. This is the foundation of the *lumped parameter assumption*, that is, physical phenomena can be isolated and represented by well-defined parameter values. For example, a spring may exert a varying force along its longitudinal dimension but is often represented by a spring constant that captures the force between two points of attachment given a displacement between these two points.

Across physics domains (e.g., electrical, hydraulic, thermal, chemical, etc.) thermodynamics identifies two types of variables that are subject to dynamic behavior. These variables represent either: (i) *extensive* quantities or (ii) *intensive* quantities. The extensive quantities depend on the extent of a lumped phenomenon whereas the intensive quantities do not. For example, momentum is an extensive quantity because halving the mass that stores it also halves the momentum. In contrast, velocity is an intensive quantity as halving a mass with a given velocity does not change the velocity of the two halves.

The dynamics of extensities and intensities are related by *conduction*, that is, when there is a difference in intensities, a change in extensity follows. For example, a difference in velocities between two bodies results in a force acting between them that causes a change in momentum ($F = m\frac{dv}{dt} = \frac{dp}{dt}$). Because of the generality across physical domains of this phenomena, it is useful to define a generalized measure based on a notion of intensity difference, *effort*, and a notion of corresponding change in extensity *flow*. If this measure is taken to be the product, it corresponds to the well-known notion of *power* (change of energy). For example, $v \cdot F$ equates power much like in the electrical domain the product of the intensity difference (voltage, v) and change of extensity (current i) equates power.

The relations in thermodynamics models can then be summarized as illustrated in Fig. 1 as a 'triangle of state' (after Henry Paynter's 'tetrahedron of state'). A component represents a lumped parameter. This component may store a quantity as its extensity. Based on the constituent behavior of the component, this extensity relates to an intensity. Given the connection structure that the component is part of, the intensity results in a change of extensity, a flow. The flow adds to the stored extensity (by means of integration over time). Generally, the relation between intensity and extensity is one of a storage element whereas the relation between the intensity and flow is one of dissipation. Note that the role of a quantity depends on the physical domain

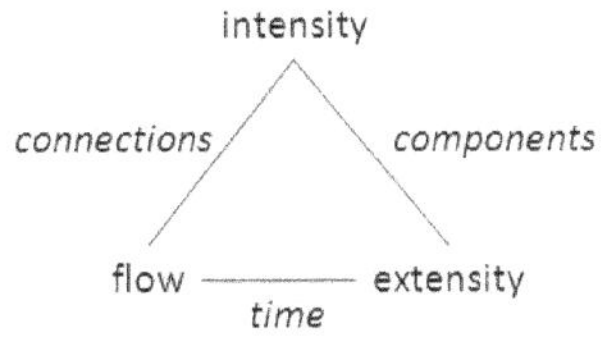

Figure 1: Triangle of state

(e.g., whereas a voltage is an intensity in the electrical domain, it is a flow in the magnetic domain).

In an energy-based representation, any change in dynamic variable values then is the result of two variables acting: an effort, e, and a flow, f. Moreover, in a model there are two basic energy-based phenomena: (i) storage of either effort (C) or flow (I) and (ii) dissipation (R) while the context of the model is defined by ideal sources of either effort (Se) or flow (Sf).

With the various idealized physical phenomena identified as I, C, R, Se, and Sf, the final step is to establish how they can be connected. Turning to reticulation again it is desirable to identify ideal connection behavior. Given the energy-based approach, this connection behavior should center around flow of energy, power, between physical phenomena. Moreover, the connection behavior should be ideal in that it neither dissipates nor stores energy (the latter condition implying continuity of power).

Given these conditions, a connection element between a number of physical phenomena relates the efforts and the flows of all of these interacting phenomena in such a way that the sum of their product equates 0 (otherwise, there would be either dissipation or storage), $\sum_i e_i \cdot f_i = 0$. The two orthogonal implementations of this are that either all efforts are the same while the flows sum to zero, or the other way around. In the electrical domain, this corresponds to either Kirchhoff's current law or Kirchhoff's voltage law. In bond graph terminology these connections are represented by *junctions*, the former by a 0 junction ($\forall_{i \neq j} e_i = e_j$ and $\sum_i f_i = 0$) and the latter by a 1 junction ($\forall_{i \neq j} f_i = f_j$ and $\sum_i e_i = 0$).

To introduce discontinuities into the bond graph modeling formalism again the principle of reticulation is followed. This requires an idealized form of discontinuous change in dynamic behavior, which is well represented by a change in the junction structure because this structure is ideal, void of dissipation and storage. Implementing discontinuities then becomes a matter of dynamically modifying the junction structure in an idealized manner. This idealized reconfiguration amounts to a junction between phenomena being active or not [41]. In other words, a 0 junction can be active ($\forall_{i \neq j} e_i = e_j$ and $\sum_i f_i = 0$) or not ($\forall_i Se_i = 0$) and a 1 junction exhibits the dual behavior when active ($\forall_{i \neq j} f_i = f_j$ and $\sum_i e_i = 0$) or not ($\forall_i Sf_i = 0$). Note that when a junction is not active, indeed no power flows across it. These junctions that can change their mode from active (*on*) to inactive (*off*) are called *controlled junctions*.

2.2 Discontinuities in physics models

With the ability for a junction to switch its mode it becomes necessary to specify when a mode switch should occur. Given the popularity of finite state machines (FSM) to capture discrete event logic, a controlled junction is equipped with a FSM that determines the *on* or *off* mode of the junction. This determination requires two aspects of the state logic to be captured: (i) how the state of the FSM maps onto the *on* and *off* mode of the junction and (ii) how the physical quantities map onto transition conditions of the FSM. Continuity of power leads to the notion that discontinuities in physical quantities result from a lack of detail in modeled phenomena, which come in two classes: (i) storage and (ii) dissipation. The discontinuous behavior that emerges in turn for each of these is discussed next.

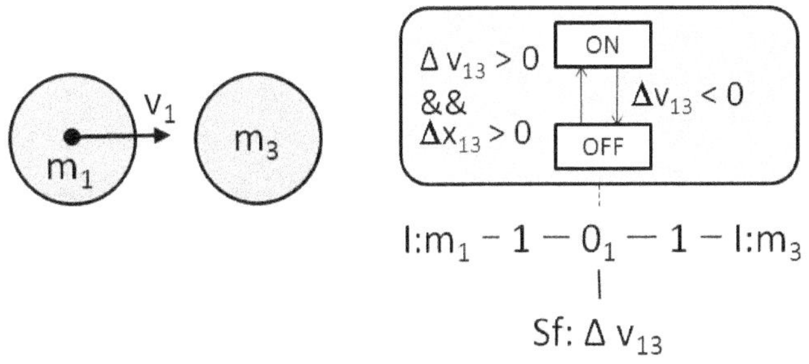

Figure 2: Ideally plastic collision

2.2.1 *Pinnacles*

Discontinuities in physics models are often studied based on multibody collisions, albeit with impact models that generally are subject to a large set of assumptions (e.g., perfectly simultaneous collisions, that are ideally plastic, along the normal direction, with only a translational component, and between bodies of equal mass). In a hybrid bond graph model, the impact of such a collision between two bodies, m_1 and m_3, can be modeled as depicted in Fig. 2. The two bodies are modeled as inertias, I, connected to a common velocity, 1, junction. These junctions represent the respective velocities, v_1 and v_3, which are connected via a common force, 0, junction. This 0 junction is controlled and when *off* it exerts force 0 on both bodies. Upon collision, the 0 junction turns *on* and it now enforces a velocity balance such that $v_1 - v_3 + \Delta v = 0$, where Δv_{13} is computed by an ideal flow source, Sf, as $\Delta v_{13} = v_1^- - v_3^-$, with the '-' superscript referring to signals immediately preceding the collision.

The FSM controlling the *on/off* mode of the 0 junction models the impact by switching from *off* to *on* when the bodies make contact ($\Delta x > 0$) and when they are moving toward one another ($\Delta v > 0$). Here the $\Delta v > 0$ is essential to model that there is impact because of a collision as opposed to the bodies only being in contact. As soon as the bodies move away from one another ($\Delta v < 0$), the 0 junction switches to *off*, irrespective of whether the bodies are touching.

During behavior generation, when $\Delta x > 0$ && $\Delta v > 0$ holds, a collision occurs and the flow source enforcing the velocity difference Δv^- because of impact becomes active. Based on this velocity difference and conservation of momentum ($\sum_i m_i v_i^- = \sum_i m_i v_i$), the velocities upon collision can be computed. The state of the velocity of the bodies is then reinitialized and this leads to the condition $\Delta v < 0$ being satisfied. Thus, a consecutive mode change occurs where the FSM moves to the *off* mode again. In the *off* mode the bodies behave as independent masses, and, therefore, no further changes in the physical state occur. Since the discrete mode

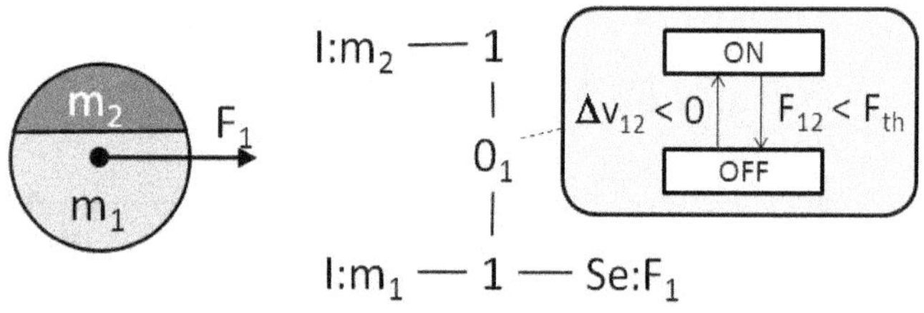

Figure 3: Two bodies with a breakaway force

changes have thus converged, the system proceeds to evolve in continuous time.

The end result is that the bodies m_1 and m_2 evolve according to a mode of continuous evolution. With a point in time at which two mode changes occur: (i) first, a collision mode occurs to model the impact that necessitates a reinitialization (discontinuous change) and (ii) second, the system changes back to a mode of continuous evolution. The collision mode that is active only to effect a reinitialization of physical state is referred to as a *pinnacle* [27]. Note that in more detail this collision mode would comprise a *storage* effect that captures the compression and expansion of the bodies.

2.2.2 *Mythical mode changes*

A different interaction effect between two bodies takes place based on friction effects. For example, consider two bodies m_1 and m_2 with m_2 at rest on top of m_1. When at a point in time a large enough external force is exerted on m_1, m_1 will start moving with a corresponding velocity. However, if the force is sufficiently large that the breakaway friction force $F_{breakaway}$ between m_1 and m_2 is exceeded, m_2 may remain at rest.

A hybrid bond graph model of such a system is depicted in Fig. 3. In this model, an ideal source of effort exerts an external force F_{in}. This force is applied to m_1 because it is connected to the common velocity 1 junction that represents the velocity of m_1. When *on*, a controlled 0 junction connects the 1 junction that represents the velocity of m_2, which forces m_1 and m_2 to move with the same velocity. The FSM for the controlled 0 junctions shows that the junction changes to its *off* mode when the force between m_1 and m_2 exceeds the breakaway force, $F > F_{breakaway}$. In the *off* mode, the 0 junction exerts 0 force on both m_1 and m_2, and so they move independently. The FSM also shows that if the velocity difference between m_1 and m_2 falls below a threshold velocity ($\Delta V < v_{th}$) the two bodies 'stick' to each other again. Note that this model does not account for viscous friction when the two bodies move relative to one another as the focus of this paper is on the discontinuous behavior.

During behavior generation, initially the 0 junction is in its *on* mode because the bodies are at rest on top of one another and the system evolves in continuous time. When the point in time occurs at which F_{in} changes discontinuously, new velocities for both m_1 and m_2 are computed. These velocities, however, may require a force to be exerted on m_2 that causes the condition $F > F_{breakaway}$ to be satisfied and the 0 junction changes to its *off* mode. Once in the *off* mode, if the velocity difference is sufficiently large, no further mode changes occur. Since the discrete mode changes have thus converged, the system proceeds to evolve in continuous time.

The end result is that the two bodies m_1 and m_2 evolve according to a mode of continuous evolution until a point in time at which a force is exerted. At this point in time, the corresponding velocities and forces are computed and based on the newly computed values the connection between the two bodies changes mode such that they are dynamically independent. In the mode of independence the system evolves in continuous time again. Since there is no effect of the external force on the velocity of m_2, in order to arrive at the proper values for reinitialization of v_1 and v_2, the mode where the external force becomes active while m_1 and m_2 are still connected is considered to have no effect on the physical state, which is referred to as a *mythical mode* [27]. Note that in more detail the mythical mode would comprise a very small nonlinear *dissipation* effect that captures the quick buildup of force before disconnecting.

3. MODELS OF TIME

In the following subsections, background information on superdense and hyperreal time models is provided. These time semantics are required to arrive at a combination in the form of a hyperdense time that allows for representing pinnacles and mythical modes in concert. It is shown how previous results can now be mapped onto a hyperdense semantic domain.

3.1 Introduction to superdense time

Time-event sequence is a semantic domain for describing event-based models. Intuitively, time-event sequences are instantaneous events separated by non-negative real numbers that describe time durations between the events. Events separated by zero duration are simultaneous, but have a well-defined causal ordering.

Superdense time was introduced to represent time-event sequences as functions of time [21]. Superdense time is a totally ordered subset of $\mathbb{R}_+ \times \mathbb{N}$, where the non-negative real number represents the real time and the natural number represents the causal ordering. Simultaneous events at time t are mapped to $(t, 0), (t, 1), \ldots$ superdense time instants such that the ordering of the events is preserved.

The (total) ordering of superdense time is given by the following definitions: $(t, n) = (t', n') \Leftrightarrow t = t' \wedge n = n'$, and $(t, n) < (t', n') \Leftrightarrow t < t' \vee (t = t' \wedge n < n')$. Therefore, superdense time is a time model that can be used to describe simultaneous events as functions of time, while retaining the causality of events.

Mythical modes emerge as an artifact of logical inference to determine a new mode in which physical state can change. As such, mythical modes do not affect the dynamic state of a physical system. Moreover, different logic formulations may traverse different mythical modes yet still arrive at the same resulting mode where physical state changes can occur. Consequently, the logical evaluation has no corresponding manifestation in the dynamic state of a physical system and occurs at a single point in time along a logical inferencing dimension. This behavior corresponds to the superdense semantic domain.

3.2 Introduction to hyperreal time

The system of hyperreals extends the theories with real numbers to a larger number system that includes infinitesimal and infinite numbers. An infinitesimal ϵ is any nonzero number, such that $|\epsilon| < \frac{1}{n}$ for any $n \in \mathbb{N}$. Intuitively, the idea behind hyperreals is to extend the dense field of $\mathbb{R}$ with infinitely many points around each real number such that any real sentence that holds for one or more real functions also holds for the hyperreal natural extensions of these functions [19] (transfer principle).

In the ultrapower construction [16], hyperreals are represented as infinite sequences of real numbers $\langle u_1, u_2, \ldots \rangle \in \mathbb{R}^{\mathbb{N}}$ with real numbers embedded as constant sequences (i.e., a real number r is the sequence of $\langle r, r, \ldots \rangle \in \mathbb{R}^{\mathbb{N}}$). These sequences, together with elementwise addition and multiplication operations, form a commutative ring but not a field (since the multiplication of two non-zero numbers could result in zero: $\langle 0, 1, 0, \ldots \rangle \times \langle 1, 0, 1, \ldots \rangle = \langle 0, 0, \ldots \rangle$). This issue is remedied by considering equivalence classes of $\mathbb{R}^{\mathbb{N}}$ defined by a free ultrafilter U of $\mathbb{N}$.

Let J be a nonempty set. An ultrafilter on J is a nonempty collection U of subsets of J having the following properties: $\emptyset \notin U$; $A \in U$ and $B \in U$ implies $A \cap B \in U$; $A \in U$ and $A \subseteq B \subseteq J$ implies $B \in U$; for all $A \subseteq J$, either $A \in U$ or $J \setminus A \in U$. The ultrafilter U is free if the intersection of all its members is the empty set: $\bigcap_{A \in U} A = \emptyset$.

Given a free ultrafilter U of $\mathbb{N}$, an equivalence relation $=_U$ can be defined over $\mathbb{R}^{\mathbb{N}}$: $u =_U v$ holds for sequences $u = \langle u_1, u_2, \ldots \rangle$ and $v = \langle v_1, v_2, \ldots \rangle$ iff $\{i \mid u_i = v_i\} \in U$. The hyperreals are then defined as the quotient of $\mathbb{R}^{\mathbb{N}}$ by U, ${}^*\mathbb{R} = \mathbb{R}^{\mathbb{N}}/U$.

As a semantic domain, hyperreals have the advantage that around any real time instant there are hyperreal time instants that are closer to it than any other real time instant. Such extension of time greatly simplifies the semantic specification of discontinuities, in particular, the description of pinnacles that represent fast physical behaviors where the dynamic state changes discontinuously. As a result, a pinnacle corresponds to a distinct state of physical behavior. In physics, such a distinct state corresponds to a distinct point in time. Because the continuous behavior represented by a pinnacle is considered to occur infinitely fast, time is considered to advance by an infinitesimal amount for a pinnacle to implement the physical state change. This behavior corresponds to the hyperreal domain.

3.3 Hyperdense time

The models of time provide the ingredients for a semantic domain that is sufficiently rich to formalize the behavior at discontinuities in physical system models including mythical mode behavior and pinnacle behavior, as well as combinations of both. It is a straightforward extension to introduce a hyperdense time model as a "combination" of the superdense and hyperreal time models. We define the hyperdense time ${}^*\mathbb{R}_+ \times \mathbb{N}$ as the product of the non-negative hyperreals and natural numbers. Such a time model can be used for representing both infinitesimal time advancements as different hyperreals, as well as establishing a causal ordering among superdense time instances with the same hyperreal. The particular value of such a precise semantic description lies in the ability to develop consistent computational behavior generation algorithms.

As discussed before, mythical mode changes correspond to immediate (zero-time) changes during which the state variables are not updated, i.e., 0/0. Pinnacles, on the other hand, are found at $\epsilon/\mathbb{R}$ since they correspond to real jumps in an infinitesimally small time interval.

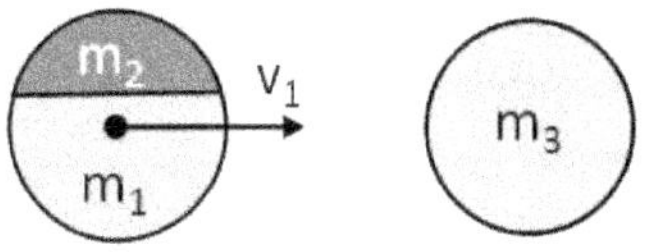

Figure 4: A variant of Newton's cradle

4. COMPUTATIONAL REPRESENTATION OF HYPERDENSE SEMANTICS

Because of the discreteness of computational values and limited precision of a computational implementation, the semantic domain of computational models cannot represent superdense nor hyperreal domains. Therefore, (i) a modeling formalism must include a means for the modeler to distinguish between pinnacles and mythical modes and (ii) the behavior generation algorithms must include sophistication that addresses the differences between superdense and hyperreal semantic domains. The resulting semantic domain for the computational implementation maps continuous time behavior onto floating point numbers, $\mathbb{F}$, while the mythical mode and pinnacle event iteration each map onto an integer domain. The first principle hyperdense semantic domain ${}^*\mathbb{R}_+ \times \mathbb{N}$ then maps onto a three-dimensional model of time $\mathbb{F} \times \mathbb{N}^{-1} \times \mathbb{N}$ in a computational implementation, where the pinnacle domain comprises the natural numbers extended with -1 in order to capture the physical state immediately preceding the point in time at which discontinuities occur. This section first presents a paradigmatic example followed by a computational implementation. This implementation can now be formalized based on mapping the first principles hyperdense semantic domain onto a computational three-dimensional time semantic domain.

4.1 A paradigmatic example

In Fig. 4, a variant of Newton's cradle is shown. One of the bodies, m_1, has another body, m_2, positioned on top of it. Stiction effects between m_1 and m_2 cause them to behave as one body with combined mass as long as the breakaway force between them, $F_{breakaway}$, is not exceeded. The body m_1 may collide with another body, m_3, according to a perfectly elastic collision, $\Delta v_{32} = -\Delta v_{32}^-$, where Δv is the difference in velocities ($v_3 - v_2$) after the collision and Δv_{32}^- is the difference in velocities before the collision.

The bond graph model in Fig. 5 shows the three masses as inertias, I, each of them connected to a common velocity junction, 1, which have as velocity on all connected ports the velocity of the directly connected mass. The 1 junctions are connected by common force junctions, 0. The 0 junctions are *controlled junctions* in that a finite state machine determines whether their *on* or *off* state is active. The plastic collision is modeled as ideally plastic (i.e., a coefficient of restitution $\epsilon = 1$) by a modulated flow source *MSf*. If the controlled junction 0_1 is in its *on* state, this flow source enforces a difference in velocities of m_1 and m_3, possibly accounting for the rigidly connected mass m_2. If the controlled junction 0_1 is in its *off* state, a 0 force is exerted on both m_1 and m_3 (possibly accounting for m_2). The controlled junction 0_2 exerts a 0 force in its *off* state as well, which is when the force at the contact point between m_1 and m_2 exceeds the breakaway force. Note that for clarity no viscous friction in case m_1 and m_2 move independently in continuous time

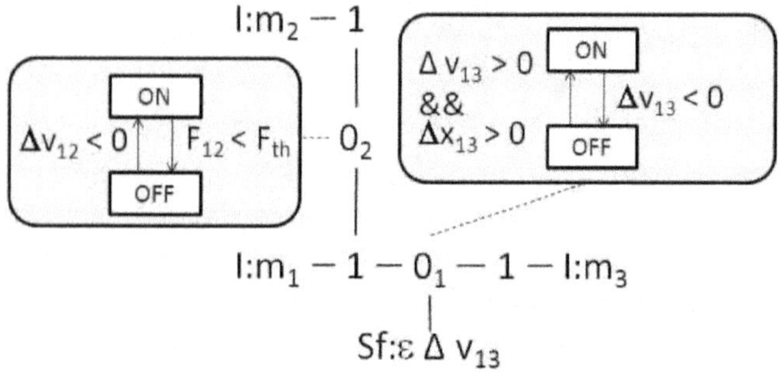

Figure 5: Model of the variant of Newton's cradle

is modeled. If the difference in velocities between m_1 and m_2 falls below a threshold level, the stiction effect becomes active, which is modeled by 0_2 changing to its *on* state. In the *on* state, a difference in velocities of m_2 and m_3 of 0 is enforced.

Upon collision of m_1 and m_3, if the difference in velocities v_1 and v_2, Δv_{12}, is less than the threshold velocity v_{th}, stiction is active and m_1 and m_2 behave as one body with mass $m_1 + m_2$. In case $m_1 + m_2 < m_3$, this would result in a return velocity of m_1 (i.e., m_1 would start moving in the opposite direction compared to the velocity before the collision). However, the momentum of m_1 may be such that an impulsive force [8] arises between m_1 and m_2 that triggers the $F_{breakaway}$ transition, causing the two bodies to move independently. In this case, if $m_1 = m_3$ and $\epsilon = 1$, there is no return velocity for m_1 but instead it acts as in the case of Newton's cradle where m_3 assumes all of the momentum of m_1 while m_1 comes to rest. In this case the velocity of m_2 is not affected by the collision.

The importance of a semantic domain that combines both superdense as well as hyperreals is prominently displayed by this example. While the condition for 0_2 to switch from *on* to *off* occurs in 0 time, the condition for 0_1 to switch from *on* to *off* occurs in infinitesimal, ϵ, time. A critical consequence of this phenomenon is that, although in reasoning about the system, 0_1 first changes its state to *on*, after which the change of state in 0_2 to *off* is determined, the change of state in 0_1 back to *off* is not effected until *after* the change of state in 0_2 to *off*.

4.2 A computational implementation

To generate behaviors for the system in Fig. 4, a computational model is designed based on the hybrid bond graph model in Fig. 5 by using the hybrid bond graph modeling and simulation tool HyBrSim [28]. Figure 6 shows the hybrid bond graph in Fig. 5 modeled in HyBrSim with the finite state machines of the controlled junctions shown in Fig. 7.

The HyBrSim model shows the power bonds in the hybrid bond graph as harpoons (i.e., one-sided arrow heads). The bond graph elements are shown as black rectangles with their type on the right-hand side of each rectangle. The left-hand side of each rectangle displays the name of the element as well as its parameter. Mapping the bond graph elements (0, 1, I, and Sf) onto the model in Fig. 5 is straightforward, where the HyBrSim models shows that the masses all are

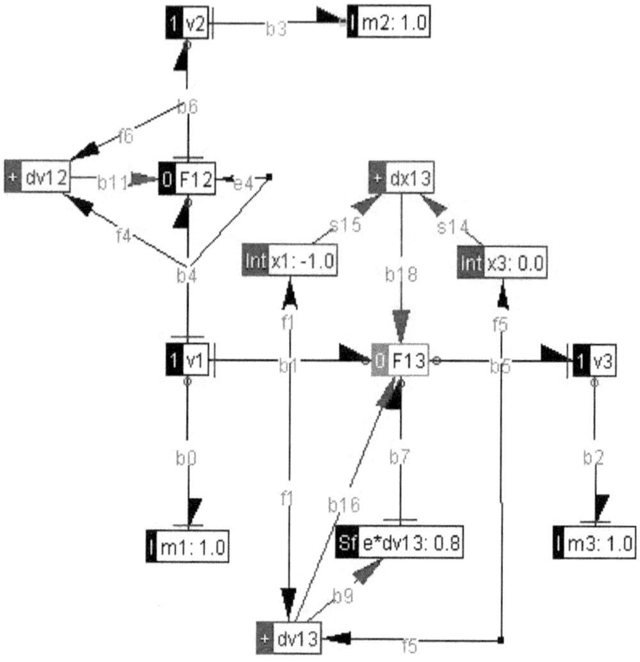

Figure 6: Hybrid bond graph of the modified Newton's cradle

chosen as 1.0 and the coefficient of restitution, ϵ, is chosen to be 0.8.

In addition to the bond graph elements, Fig. 6 shows signal elements of type + and *Int*. The latter integrate their input with respect to time, which in Fig. 6 is either $f1$ (the flow variable of bond $b1$ that represents the velocity of m_1) or $f5$ (the flow variable of bond $b5$ that represents the velocity of m_3). The result of the integration is the position of m_1 and m_3, respectively.

The type + elements add their input (with possible negative sign, which is a property of each particular element) and so the *dx13* element subtracts the position of m_3, represented by signal *s14*, from the position of m_1, represented by signal *s15*. The resulting output of *dx13* is input to the controlled 0-junction *F13* and so become a source in the state transition diagram in Fig. 7(b) that controls the mode of *F13*. Similarly, the + element *dv13* subtracts the velocity of m_3, represented by *f5* from the velocity of m_1 represented by *f1*. The resulting output is input to the controlled 0-junction *F13* as well and so also becomes a source (with two incarnations) in the state transition diagram Fig. 7(b).

Finally, the + element *dv12* subtracts the velocity of m_2, represented by the flow *f6* on bond *b6* from the velocity of m_1 represented by the flow *f4* on bond *b4*. The resulting output is input to the controlled 0-junction *F12* and so becomes a source (with two incarnations) in the state transition diagram Fig. 7(a). In addition, the state transition diagram shows a source *e4*, which is shown in the HyBrSim model to be the effort on bond *b4* and this corresponds to the force exerted across the 0 junction *F12*.

4.3 Behavior generation

A key aspect of the computational model in HyBrSim is the language elements that allow a modeler to map the conceptual differences in discontinuities on a hyperdense seman-

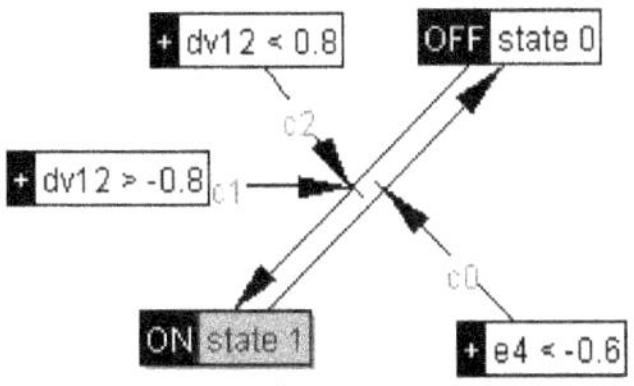

(a) F12

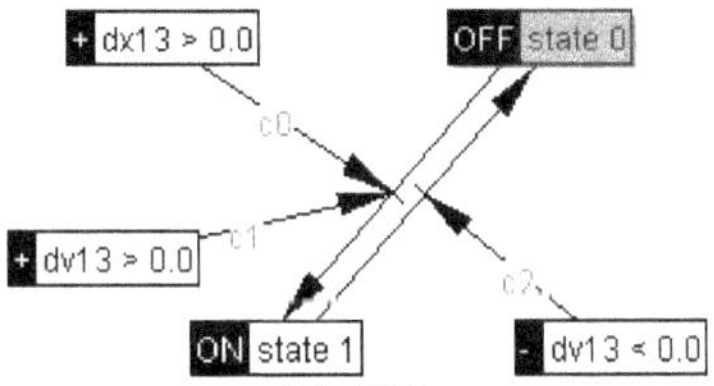

(b) F13

Figure 7: Finite state machines for controlled junctions

tic domain onto a computational three-dimensional model of time. In HyBrSim this is facilitated by allowing the modeler to state whether a guard in the state transition diagrams is evaluated based on *a priori* or *a posteriori* variable values in the model. This is illustrated in the state transition diagrams of Fig. 7 by the guard elements being annotated on the left-hand side by either a '-' sign (e.g., $dv13 < 0.0$) or a '+' sign (e.g., $dv13 > 0.0$), respectively.

In the case of an *a priori* guard, the variable values that are employed are those of the most recent hyperreal advance. In other words, while the model iterates across mythical modes, the truth value of the *a priori* guard does not change. In contrast, in the case of an *a posteriori* guard, the most recent variable values (either of a pinnacle or a mythical mode) are employed to compute its truth value. In addition to the language elements for expressing the different types of discontinuous behaviors, the behavior generation of HyBrSim is based on the *mythical mode algorithm* [26] to enable evaluating *a posteriori* truth values in between hyperreal advances (corresponding to 'accepted' and *physically meaningful* states). Finally, it should be noted that HyBrSim implements conservation of physical extensities (charge, mass, flux, etc.) to hold across structural changes in a hybrid bond graph [28], which completes the necessary computational machinery for behavior generation.

Parameter studies can now be conducted to analyze three qualitatively different behaviors: (i) a partially plastic collision between the combined $m_1 + m_2$ mass and m_3 may occur without further discontinuous effects; (ii) the collision may cause the breakaway force F_{th} to be exceeded so that m_1 and m_2 behave as independent masses, after which continuous behavior resumes; and (iii) before continuous behavior resumes, the difference in velocities of m_1 and m_2 is such that it falls below the threshold velocity and m_1 and m_2 act as a single mass again. The studies are presented based on computational behavior generation with the progression of behavior on both the hyperdense (as a 2 tuple $\langle time, mythical\ mode\rangle$ with time as hyperreals that progress by infinitesimals, ϵ, to represent pinnacles) and the three-dimensional (as a corresponding 3 tuple $\langle time, pinnacle, mythical\ mode\rangle$) semantic domains. This

time	0_{F12}	0_{F13}	p_{m1}	p_{m2}	p_{m3}
$\langle t_{collide} - \epsilon, 0\rangle$ $\langle t_{collide}, -1, 0\rangle$	*on*	*off*	0.95	0.95	0
$\langle t_{collide}, 0\rangle$ $\langle t_{collide}, 0, 0\rangle$	*on*	*on*	0.38	0.38	1.14
$\langle t_{collide} + \epsilon, 0\rangle$ $\langle t_{collide}, 1, 0\rangle$	*on*	*off*	0.38	0.38	1.14

Table 1: Sequence of mode changes in infinitesimal steps for $v_{th} = 0.8$ and $F_{th} = -0.6$

notation is used in the following tables while referring to the column labeled time.

Behavior generation for the first case is shown in Fig. 8(a) with the numerical values of the detailed discontinuous behavior upon collision shown in Table 1. With the chosen parameters ($m_1 = m_2 = m_3 = 1.0$ and $\epsilon = 0.8$) and initial conditions for the velocities and momenta ($v_{1,0} = p_{1,0} = v_{2,0} = p_{2,0} = 0.95$, $v_{3,0} = 0$), the table shows how upon collision, the mode of controlled 0 junction F_{13} changes from *off* to *on*. The resulting collision causes a change in momentum across all three bodies involved and time advances by an infinitesimal amount. Upon the advance the collision mode of F_{13} turns *off* and the bodies proceed to move in a continous fashion with the changed momentum.

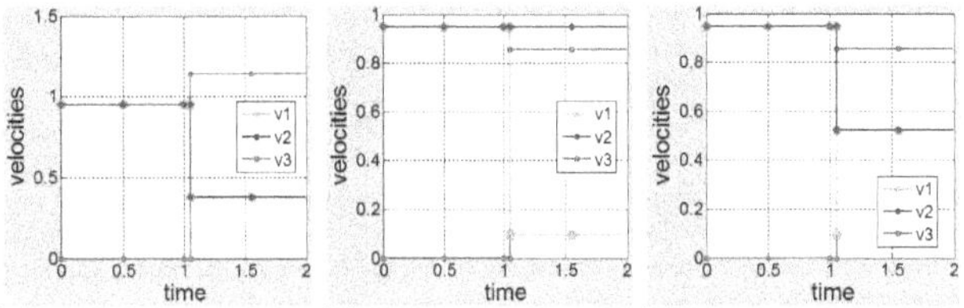

(a) $F_{th} = -0.6$ and $v_{th} = 0.8$ (b) $F_{th} = -0.5$ and $v_{th} = 0.8$ (c) $F_{th} = -0.5$ and $v_{th} = 0.875$

Figure 8: Simulation results of the computational algorithm ($m_1 = m_2 = m_3 = 1.0$, $v_{1,0} = v_{2,0} = 0.95$, $v_{3,0} = 0$, $\epsilon = 0.8$)

Behavior generation for the second case is shown in Fig. 8(b) with the numerical values of the detailed discontinuous behavior upon collision shown in Table 2. With the $F_{th} = -0.5$ parameter, the change in momenta upon collision ($t = \langle t_{collide}, 0\rangle$) exceeds the breakaway force and before an infinitesimal advance, a consecutive mode change occurs at $t = \langle t_{collide}, 1\rangle$ that causes the controlled 0 junction between m_1 and m_2 to turn *off*. This new set of modes of the controlled junctions effects a further change in momenta after which no further instantaneous mode changes occur. Therefore, time advances by an infinitesimal step ($t = \langle t_{collide} + \epsilon, 0\rangle$), after which the system proceeds to evolve continuously.

Behavior generation for the third case is shown in Fig. 8(c) with the numerical values of the detailed discontinuous behavior upon collision shown in Table 3. Here, the previous scenario is followed up till $t = \langle t_{collide} + \epsilon, 0\rangle$. However, after the controlled 0 junction that models the collision effect changes its mode to *off*, the difference in velocities of m_1 and m_2 falls below the threshold velocity and the masses become rigidly connected again by the 0 junction F_{12} switching back *on* instantaneously (i.e., at $t = \langle t_{collide} + \epsilon, 1\rangle$). Once in this mode, no further mode changes occur and the system proceeds to evolve continuously.

time	0_{F12}	0_{F13}	p_{m1}	p_{m2}	p_{m3}
$\langle t_{collide} - \epsilon, 0\rangle$ $\langle t_{collide}, -1, 0\rangle$	*on*	*off*	0.95	0.95	0
$\langle t_{collide}, 0\rangle$ $\langle t_{collide}, 0, 0\rangle$	*on*	*on*	0.38	0.38	1.14
$\langle t_{collide}, 1\rangle$ $\langle t_{collide}, 0, 1\rangle$	*off*	*on*	0.095	0.95	0.855
$\langle t_{collide} + \epsilon, 0\rangle$ $\langle t_{collide}, 1, 0\rangle$	*off*	*off*	0.095	0.95	0.855

Table 2: Sequence of mode changes in 0 and infinitesimal steps for $v_{th} = 0.8$ and $F_{th} = -0.5$

time (t)	0_{F12}	0_{F13}	p_{m1}	p_{m2}	p_{m3}
$\langle t_{collide} - \epsilon, 0\rangle$ $\langle t_{collide}, -1, 0\rangle$	*on*	*off*	0.95	0.95	0
$\langle t_{collide}, 0\rangle$ $\langle t_{collide}, 0, 0\rangle$	*on*	*on*	0.38	0.38	1.14
$\langle t_{collide}, 1\rangle$ $\langle t_{collide}, 0, 1\rangle$	*off*	*on*	0.095	0.95	0.855
$\langle t_{collide} + \epsilon, 0\rangle$ $\langle t_{collide}, 1, 0\rangle$	*off*	*off*	0.095	0.95	0.855
$\langle t_{collide} + \epsilon, 1\rangle$ $\langle t_{collide}, 1, 1\rangle$	*on*	*off*	0.5225	0.5225	0.855
$\langle t_{collide} + 2\epsilon, 0\rangle$ $\langle t_{collide}, 2, 0\rangle$	*on*	*off*	0.5225	0.5225	0.855

Table 3: Sequence of mode changes in 0 and infinitesimal steps for $v_{th} = 0.875$ and $F_{th} = -0.5$

The sequences of mode changes is depicted in Table 3, which clearly shows the difference in effects as the model evolves in the computational representation of superdense and hyperreal time. The ability to differentiate between $t = \langle t_{collide}, 1\rangle$ and $t = \langle t_{collide} + \epsilon, 0\rangle$ enables making the distinction between the pinnacle effect of 0 junction F_{13} and the mythical mode effect of 0 junction F_{12}. Otherwise, 0 junction F_{13} would have switched back *off* simultaneously with 0 junction F_{12} switching *off*. This would either: (i) not allow modeling of inferencing (mythical) modes or (ii) have the collision effect (incorrectly) computed for m_1 and m_2 comprising a combined mass of $m_1 + m_2$.

Note that in evaluating the truth value of the guard with F_{th} as a variable requires the ability to evaluate impulses. Because of the discontinuous changes in velocities, the accelerations become impulsive, and, therefore, the forces that are compared against F_{th} become impulsive as well. Because of the infinite magnitude of an impulse, F_{th} would always be exceeded and the guard would always evaluate to true. Instead, HyBrSim allows the use of either a numerical approximation of the impulse (based on a small numerical delta in time) or the use of the impulsive area in the comparison to evaluate the truth value of the guard [24]. For example, in the case of the model in Fig. 6, the area of the impulse corresponds to the discontinuous change in momentum of m_1.

5. RELATED WORK

A number of research activities are presently being explored in the hybrid dynamic system community. Based on the superdense time notion of Maler, Manna, and Pnueli [21], Lee and Zheng have developed an operational semantics of hybrid systems [20]. Because of the focus on tool development, their work concentrates on computational models, in which case the notion of hyperreals can be reduced to an integer dimension. In contrast with the three-dimensional model of time developed for computational models in this paper, support for mythical mode iterations is not considered in their work. Moreover, employing superdense time for impact modeling requires a direct mapping of physics onto a computational representation that differs in the first principles semantic domain. In turn, this requires a high conceptual investment and relies on additional validation to compensate for the omission of a modeling stage based on a theory of physics (e.g., [38]).

In a different exploration, Bliudze and Krob [3] and Benveniste, Bourke, and Pouzet have pursued nonstandard analysis [2, 3] to formalize the semantics of hybrid automata models. Though the intent is less about developing a first principles modeling approach, by developing a mathematical representation that helps in formulating a computational implementation, the work provides an unbiased foundation that does relate well to an underlying physics theory. Still, compared to the work presented in this paper, their work currently does not support a semantics for mythical mode behavior. Generally, the choice of hybrid automata as a modeling formalism requires explicit formulation of much of the behavior of a system that is being modeled and so in the context of the work presented here it would require a conceptual investment to explicitly determine the mythical mode overall end effects.

Other work on formalizing hybrid automata [1] relies on a superdense semantic domain and so comparisons with a hyperdense semantic domain apply. Similar to hybrid automata, related work on dynamic logic [37] requires an explicit formulation of discontinuities with the corresponding conceptual investment that it necessitates.

Somewhat further removed but still related in the underlying intent are efforts by Bourke and Pouzet [4] to formalize the semantics of hybrid system modeling languages. In particular, formalizing the combination of synchronous behavior and continuous-time behavior generated by a variable-step numerical solver requires a precise understanding of discrete event behavior and its bearing on continuous evolution. Focus in their work is an eventual computational implementation and as such other work by Mosterman, Zander, Hamon, and Deckla [33] has taken a perspective in which continuous-time differential equations behavior is defined by a numerical solver that is applied in the computational approximation. In addition to the lack of support for mythical mode iteration, this work also does not specifically focus on a first principles theory for modeling physics.

While the challenges of mythical mode iteration are acknowledged in related work by Söderman and Strömberg [39], the classification of *transient*, *semi-transient*, and *nontransient* modes in the implementation by Edström, Strömberg, Söderman, and Top [11] does not provide support for mythical modes. In their work, a mode transition system (MTS) is derived from a declarative formulation of a *switched bond graph*. Depending on the execution semantics of the operational MTS, a parallel execution may handle mythical modes by compiling a static transition structure that accounts for these modes. Furthermore, though the use of bond graphs bases the work by Edström , Strömberg, Söderman, and Top [11] on a solid theory of physics, the MTS concentrates on a computational implementation (i.e., interpreted as integer semantics), and, therefore, the use of hyperreals to represent pinnacles (*semi-transient* modes in MTS) is not part of their work [10].

Previous work by Mosterman and Biswas [27] provided a theory of physics to support mythical mode iteration but did not elaborate to the same extent on pinnacle iteration. The lack of a hyperreals in the semantic domain lead to modeling a sequence of collisions as a sequence of isolated points on the reals. The resulting gaps in time between these points challenged the understanding of physics from a thermodynamics perspective, because it includes continuity principles. Hyperreals allow formulating such collision sequences with infinitesimal advances between the collisions and thus, the semantic pitfall of gaps in time are avoided.

6. CONCLUSION

A critical characteristic of physical system models is the manner in which the system dynamics are captured and abstracted. Generally, physical systems are well described by continuous-time behavior. However, if the dynamics of some of the continuous behavior is much faster than the time scale of interest it is sometimes more efficient to model the resulting effect by discontinuous change. The corresponding models then combine continuous behavior with discontinuous change and the system comprises hybrid dynamics.

In this paper, the discontinuous change is represented by pinnacles and mythical modes. These two classes of modes, in turn, are represented by different temporal semantics. Pinnacles require physical time to advance during discontinuous change. This change is modeled using a notion of time as hyperreals. Mythical modes do not allow changes in the physical state and so occur without time increment. As such, these modes are represented by a notion of superdense time.

Consequently, a combined notion of time that allows for the expression of both semantics is required in order to analyze pinnacles and mythical modes in concert. Moreover, so as to support behavior generation, a computational representation is necessary that captures the interaction between these two classes of discontinuities in a consistent and executable manner.

In the presented work, a *hyperdense* notion of time is introduced as a combination of superdense and hyperreal domains. The particular value of using such a precise semantic description lies in the ability to develop consistent computational behavior generation algorithms. To this end, the hyperdense notion of time is mapped onto a three-dimensional computational model of time. In particular, continuous-time behavior is mapped onto floating point numbers, while the mythical mode and pinnacle event iteration each map onto an integer domain. A modified Newton's cradle is used as a case study and to illustrate the implementation.

The benefits of having a hyperdense semantics include support for combining the expertise of physics modeling with computer science and control engineering. Such combined expertise becomes increasingly valuable as cyber-physical systems are rising to prominence in the realm of modern technical systems. Moreover, providing a computational semantics based on the hyperdense semantic domain allows for designing better interdisciplinary behavioral models derived from first principle foundations. Impact scenarios, for example, in multibody systems can be studied with a sound theoretical foundation about the physical interactions and nuances that are taking place before, during, and after the collision moment.

Moreover, the work provides support for implicit modeling that is ubiquitous in industry as well as a foundation for relating implicit models to explicit models that are often used in academia. For example, nonterminating behavior in the superdense sense (causing time to halt) can now be strictly separated from nonterminating behavior in the hyperreal sense (causing time to advance by infinitesimals).

7. REFERENCES

[1] R. Alur, C. Courcoubetis, T. A. Henzinger, and P.-H. Ho. Hybrid automata: An algorithmic approach to the specification and verification of hybrid systems. In R. Grossman, A. Nerode, A. Ravn, and H. Rischel, editors, *Lecture Notes in Computer Science*, volume 736, pages 209–229. Springer-Verlag, 1993.

[2] A. Benveniste, T. Bourke, B. Caillaud, and M. Pouzet. Non-standard semantics of hybrid systems modelers. *Journal of Computer and System Sciences*, 78(3):877–910, May 2012.

[3] S. Bliudze and D. Krob. Modelling of complex systems: Systems as dataflow machines. *Fundamenta Informaticae*, 91:1–24, 2009.

[4] T. Bourke and M. Pouzet. Zélus, a Synchronous Language with ODEs. In *International Conference on Hybrid Systems: Computation and Control (HSCC 2013)*, Philadelphia, USA, April 8–11 2013. ACM.

[5] P. Breedveld. Multibond graph elements in physical systems theory. *Journal of the Franklin Institute*, 319(1/2):1–36, January/February 1985.

[6] P. C. Breedveld. *Physical Systems Theory in Terms of Bond Graphs*. PhD dissertation, University of Twente, Enschede, Netherlands, 1984.

[7] P. C. Breedveld. The context-dependent trade-off between conceptual and computational complexity illustrated by the modeling and simulation of colliding objects. In *CESA '96 IMACS Multiconference*, Lille, France, July 1996. Ecole Centrale de Lille.

[8] B. Brogliato. *Nonsmooth Mechanics*. Springer-Verlag, London, 1999. ISBN 1-85233-143-7.

[9] H. Callen. *Thermodynamics*. John Wiley & Sons, Inc., New York/London, 1960.

[10] K. Edström. *Switched Bond Graphs: Simulation and Analysis*. PhD dissertation, Linköping University, Sweden, 1999.

[11] K. Edström, J.-E. Strömberg, U. Söderman, and J. Top. Modelling and simulation of a switched power converter. In F. E. Cellier and J. J. Granda, editors, *1997 International Conference on Bond Graph Modeling and Simulation (ICBGM '97)*, pages 195–200, Phoenix, AZ, Jan. 1997. Society for Computer Simulation.

[12] H. Elmqvist, B. Bachmann, F. Boudaud, J. Broenink, D. Brück, T. Ernst, R. Franke, P. Fritzson, A. Jeandel, P. Grozman, K. Juslin, D. Kågedahl, M. Klose, N. Loubere, S. E. Mattsson, P. Mosterman, H. Nilsson, M. Otter, P. Sahlin, A. Schneider, H. Tummescheit, and H. Vangheluwe. Modelica^{tm}–a unified object-oriented langauge for physical systems modeling: Language specification, Dec. 1999. version 1.3, http://www.modelica.org/.

[13] G. Falk and W. Ruppel. *Energie und Entropie: Eine Einführung in die Thermodynamik*. Springer-Verlag, Berlin, Heidelberg, New York, 1976. ISBN 3-540-07814-2.

[14] J. Friedman and J. Ghidella. Using model-based design for automotive systems engineering – requirements analysis of the power window example.

In *Proceedings of the SAE 2006 World Congress & Exhibition*, pages CD–ROM: 2006–01–1217, Detroit, MI, Apr. 2006.

[15] O. Heaviside. On the forces, stresses, and fluxes of energy in the electromagnetic field. *Proceedings of the Royal Society of London*, 50:126–129, 1891.

[16] A. Hurd and P. Loeb. *An Introduction to Nonstandard Real Analysis*. Pure and Applied Mathematics. Elsevier Science, 1985.

[17] Y. Iwasaki, A. Farquhar, V. Saraswat, D. Bobrow, and V. Gupta. Modeling time in hybrid systems: How fast is "instantaneous"? In *1995 International Conference on Qualitative Reasoning*, pages 94–103, Amsterdam, May 1995. University of Amsterdam.

[18] D. Karnopp, D. Margolis, and R. Rosenberg. *Systems Dynamics: A Unified Approach*. John Wiley and Sons, New York, 2 edition, 1990.

[19] H. J. Keisler. *Elementary Calculus: An Infinitesimal Approach*. Prindle, Weber and Schmidt, Dover, 3 edition, 2012.

[20] E. Lee and H. Zheng. Operational semantics of hybrid systems. In *International Conference on Hybrid Systems: Computation and Control (HSCC 2005)*, pages 25–53, Zürich, Switzerland, Mar. 2005.

[21] O. Maler, Z. Manna, and A. Pnueli. From timed to hybrid systems. In *Real-Time: Theory in Practice*, Lecture Notes in Computer Science, pages 447–484. Springer, 1992.

[22] MathWorks®. *MATLAB® and Simulink® product families*, Sept. 2012.

[23] P. J. Mosterman. *Hybrid Dynamic Systems: A hybrid bond graph modeling paradigm and its application in diagnosis*. PhD dissertation, Vanderbilt University, 1997.

[24] P. J. Mosterman. HyBrSim—a modeling and simulation environment for hybrid bond graphs. *Journal of Systems and Control Engineering*, 216(1):35–46, 2002.

[25] P. J. Mosterman and G. Biswas. Behavior generation using model switching a hybrid bond graph modeling technique. In F. E. Cellier and J. J. Granda, editors, *1995 International Conference on Bond Graph Modeling and Simulation (ICBGM '95)*, number 1 in Simulation, pages 177–182, Las Vegas, Jan. 1995. Society for Computer Simulation, Simulation Councils, Inc. Volume 27.

[26] P. J. Mosterman and G. Biswas. Modeling discontinuous behavior with hybrid bond graphs. In *1995 International Workshop on Qualitative Reasoning*, pages 139–147, Amsterdam, May 1995. University of Amsterdam.

[27] P. J. Mosterman and G. Biswas. A theory of discontinuities in dynamic physical systems. *Journal of the Franklin Institute*, 335B(3):401–439, Jan. 1998.

[28] P. J. Mosterman and G. Biswas. A java implementation of an environment for hybrid modeling and simulation of physical systems. In *Proceedings of the International Conference on Bond Graph Modeling*, pages 750–755, Mexico City, Mexico, Sept. 1999.

[29] P. J. Mosterman, J. Ghidella, and J. Friedman. Model-based design for system integration. In *Proceedings of The Second CDEN International Conference on Design Education, Innovation, and Practice*, pages CD–ROM: TB–3–1 through TB–3–10, Kananaskis, Alberta, Canada, July 2005.

[30] P. J. Mosterman, S. Prabhu, and T. Erkkinen. An industrial embedded control system design process. In *Proceedings of The Inaugural CDEN Design Conference (CDEN'04)*, Montreal, Canada, July 2004. CD-ROM: 02B6.

[31] P. J. Mosterman, G. Simko, and J. Zander. A hyperdense semantic domain for discontinuous behavior in physical system models. In *Proceedings of the 7th International Workshop on Multi-Paradigm Modeling at the ACM/IEEE 16th International Conference on Model Driven Engineering Languages and Systems (MoDELS) conference*, Miami, FL, Sept. 2013.

[32] P. J. Mosterman and H. Vangheluwe. Computer automated multi-paradigm modeling in control system design. In *Proceedings of the IEEE International Symposium on Computer-Aided Control System Design*, pages 65–70, Anchorage, Alaska, Sept. 2000.

[33] P. J. Mosterman, J. Zander, G. Hamon, and B. Denckla. A computational model of time for stiff hybrid systems applied to control synthesis. *Control Engineering Practice*, 20(1):2–13, 2012.

[34] P. J. Mosterman, F. Zhao, and G. Biswas. An ontology for transitions in physical dynamic systems. In *AAAI98*, pages 219–224, July 1998.

[35] T. Nishida and S. Doshita. Reasoning about discontinuous change. In *Proceedings AAAI-87*, pages 643–648, Seattle, Washington, 1987.

[36] H. M. Paynter. *Analysis and Design of Engineering Systems*. The M.I.T. Press, Cambridge, Massachusetts, 1961.

[37] A. Platzer. Differential dynamic logic for hybrid systems. *Journal of Automated Reasoning*, 41(2):143–189, 2008.

[38] D. E. Post and L. G. Votta. Computational science demands a new paradigm. *Physics Today*, 58(8):35–41, Jan. 2005.

[39] U. Söderman and J.-E. Strömberg. Switched bond graphs: Multiport switches, mathematical characterization and systematic composition of computational models. Technical Report LiTH-IDA-R-95-7, Department of Computer and Information Science, Linköping University, Linköping, Sweden, 1995.

[40] Steering Committee for Foundations in Innovation for Cyber-Physical Systems. Foundations for Innovation: Strategic Opportunities for the 21st Century Cyber-Physical Systems—Connecting computer and information systems with the physical world. Technical report, National Institute of Standards and Technology (NIST), Mar. 2013.

[41] J.-E. Strömberg, J. Top, and U. Söderman. Variable causality in bond graphs caused by discrete effects. In *Proceedings of the International Conference on Bond Graph Modeling*, pages 115–119, San Diego, California, 1993.

Quasi-Dependent Variables in Hybrid Automata*

Sergiy Bogomolov
Albert-Ludwigs-Universität Freiburg

Christian Herrera
Albert-Ludwigs-Universität Freiburg

Marco Muñiz
Albert-Ludwigs-Universität Freiburg

Bernd Westphal
Albert-Ludwigs-Universität Freiburg

Andreas Podelski
Albert-Ludwigs-Universität Freiburg

ABSTRACT

The concept of hybrid automata provides a powerful framework to model and analyze real-world systems. Due to the structural complexity of hybrid systems it is important to ensure the *scalability* of analysis algorithms. We approach this problem by providing an effective generalisation of the recently introduced notion of *quasi-equal* clocks to hybrid systems. For this purpose, we introduce the concept of *quasi-dependent* variables. Our contribution is two-fold: we demonstrate how such variables can be automatically *detected*, and we present a *transformation* leading to an abstraction with a smaller state space which, however, still retains the same properties as the original system. We demonstrate the practical applicability of our methods on a range of industrial benchmarks.

Categories and Subject Descriptors

G.1.7 [**Numerical Analysis**]: Ordinary Differential Equations; I.6.4 [**Simulation and Modeling**]: Model Validation and Analysis

Keywords

Hybrid systems, quasi-dependent variables, model transformation, abstraction, reachability analysis

1. INTRODUCTION

Real-time systems often employ distributed architectures where every component uses an independent clock for internal purposes. The classes of TDMA- [2] and EPL-based [3] protocols are prominent examples of this particular class of systems. In such settings, the information exchange among the components proceeds periodically; components are assigned to certain time ranges for communication. In the end of every period, the components reset their clocks to ensure correct system behavior. This leads to an exponential blow-up of the set of states to be considered due to the interleaving semantics of distributed resets in timed automata.

We have attacked this problem in our previous work [4–6] by proposing the notion of *quasi-equal* clocks for timed automata to efficiently reduce the system complexity. Intuitively, two clocks are *quasi-equal* if they always agree on their values except possibly when those clocks are reset.

Hybrid automata provide an expressive framework to model and analyze real-world systems exhibiting complex continuous behavior described by differential equations. Therefore, the handling of continuous dynamics takes an essential part of the analysis run-time. Due to this reason, the reduction of the number of variables in the system and of interleaving resets might lead to crucial performance improvements. To this end, we propose to move from an *equality* relation between quasi-equal clocks to a general *dependency* relation and thus *quasi-dependent* variables. The notion of quasi-equality is a special case of quasi-dependency of variables.

We present an approach consisting of two parts. First, we detect quasi-dependent variables. Here, in some sense, we transfer the idea of variable relations already explored in program verification [7, 8] into the context of hybrid automata. Second, based on this knowledge, we reduce the original system. This line of research is particularly motivated by industrial time-based protocols where the timers of the individual components advance at *different* rates.

The crux behind our detection algorithm is the application of abstraction techniques while analyzing the relations between variables. Both continuous and discrete evolution can break the quasi-dependency between variables. However, interestingly, we only need to be precise while considering discrete jumps whereas in case of continuous evolution we can just check which quasi-dependencies still hold in the considered location. The intuition is that we can abstract away constraints other than the ones reflecting the quasi-dependencies because if a quasi-dependency holds before computing continuous successors (which is checked without precision loss in the preceding discrete step) then the continuous evolution obeys the quasi-dependency. The quasi-dependent variables can also be detected by a hybrid model checker, however, it would explore the state space of the system in a great detail, whereas our detection algorithm conducts a coarse analysis with the focus on the state space parts relevant for establishing quasi-dependencies. These ideas lead to an abstraction that is rather imprecise, yet

*Partly supported by the German Research Council (DFG) as part of the Transregional Collaborative Research Center SFB/TR 14 AVACS (`http://www.avacs.org`), and by CONACYT (Mexico) and DAAD (Germany).

HSCC'14, April 15–17, 2014, Berlin, Germany.
Copyright 2014 ACM 978-1-4503-2732-9/14/04 ...$15.00.
http://dx.doi.org/10.1145/2562059.2562142.

results in a dramatic performance improvement of quasi-dependent variables detection.

Our transformation replaces quasi-dependent variables by one representative variable and updates the system structure appropriately. Properties of the original system are reflected, that is, a forbidden configuration is reachable in the transformed system if and only if it is reachable in the original system. System complexity is reduced in two ways. First, we reduce the number of variables in the system. This step alone leads to a more efficient system handling as the underlying data structures become more compact. Furthermore, in many cases we can achieve an even larger performance boost by completely avoiding interleavings of resets of quasi-dependent variables.

The paper is organized as follows. Section 2 introduces necessary preliminaries. Section 3 describes and discusses the concept of quasi-dependency. The detection algorithm is discussed and evaluated in Section 4, the transformation in Section 5. We conclude the paper with Section 6.

Related Work.

The state space reduction for different classes of systems by deriving dependencies between their variables has been an active research topic since the inception of the area of verification. In particular, deriving (affine) relationships between variables of a program is classical since [7, 8]. This idea has also been successfully applied to the domain of timed automata. Daws et al. [9] suggest an approach to reduce the number of clocks in a single automaton based on the notion of active and equal clocks. This work was extended by Daws et al. [10] to handle networks of automata. Active clocks were used by Étienne [11] to analyze parametric timed automata. The work [12] proposes an abstraction method for a restricted class of systems with multiple clocks being activated in a sequential manner for some bounded time. Clearly, with our approach we can handle timed automata as a subclass of hybrid automata, however, we impose weaker structural requirements compared to the above mentioned works.

In the scope of hybrid automata, dependency detection and appropriate reduction becomes especially complicated. The main efforts in this area were concentrated towards reducing hybrid automata by finding appropriate (bi-)simulation relations. In particular, Pappas [13] and van der Schaft [14] presented a theoretical framework of bisimulation for linear systems. The idea of simulation was extended to its approximate version by Girard et al. [15] where the distance between the observed behavior of the reduced and original should be bounded. Finally, the notion of approximate simulations was lifted to hybrid automata by Girard et al. [16].

In this paper, we pose weaker requirements on the structure of the reduced system. Departing from strong bisimulation towards *weak* bisimulation between the reduced and original systems allows us to completely eliminate some configurations which are induced by interleavings. In order to ensure the preservation of the property to be checked, we rewrite the property itself. In this way, we access the information which is no longer explicitly encoded in the reduced system.

2. PRELIMINARIES

In the following, we recall the definitions of hybrid automata [17], (non-Zeno) run, and observable behaviour for self-containedness. In addition, we introduce the notions of update point and instantaneous valuations. The latter denotes the non-empty, possibly non-singleton set of valuations observable at a given point in time.

Given a set of real-valued variables Var, we use V to denote the set $(Var \to \mathbb{R})$ of *valuations* of Var. A *hybrid automaton* is a tuple $\mathcal{H} = (Loc, Var, Lab, Edge, Act, Inv, Init)$ where Loc is a finite set of *locations*, Var is a finite set of real-valued variables, Lab is a set of *synchronisation labels* including the *stutter label* $\tau \in Lab$, $Edge \subseteq Loc \times Lab \times 2^{V^2} \times Loc$ is a finite set of directed *edges* including a *stutter edge* (ℓ, τ, id, ℓ) for each location $\ell \in Loc$. An edge (ℓ, a, μ, ℓ') from location ℓ to ℓ' is labelled with a label $a \in Lab$ and a *conditional update* μ. $Act : Loc \to 2^{\mathbb{R}_0^+ \to V}$ is a function which assigns a set of *activities* $f : \mathbb{R}_0^+ \to V$ to each location. The activity sets are time-invariant, i.e., for each $t' \in \mathbb{R}_0^+$, $f \in Act(\ell)$ implies $(f + t) \in Act(\ell)$, where $(f + t)(t') = f(t + t')$. $Inv : Loc \to 2^V$ is a function which assigns an *invariant* $Inv(\ell) \subseteq V$ to each location ℓ, and $Init : Loc \to 2^V$ is a function which assigns an *initial value invariant* $Init(\ell) \subseteq V$ to each location ℓ. Locations ℓ with $Init(\ell) \neq \emptyset$ are called *initial locations.*

A *network* $\mathcal{N} = \{\mathcal{H}_1, \ldots, \mathcal{H}_n\}$ is a finite set of hybrid automata each with variables Var and with pairwise disjoint sets of locations. We write $\mathcal{H} \in \mathcal{N}$ if and only if $\mathcal{H} \in \{\mathcal{H}_1, \ldots, \mathcal{H}_n\}$. We use $Lab(\mathcal{H}), Edge(\mathcal{H})$, etc. to denote the set of labels, edges, etc. of automaton $\mathcal{H}$.

The *operational semantics* of a network $\mathcal{N}$ is defined by the (labelled) transition system

$$\mathcal{T}(\mathcal{N}) = (Conf(\mathcal{N}), \Lambda, \{\xrightarrow{\lambda} \mid \lambda \in \Lambda\}, C_{ini})$$

where $Conf(\mathcal{N}) = Loc \times V$, and $\Lambda := (\mathbb{R}_0^+ \times Act(\mathcal{N})) \cup \bigcup_{1 \le i \le n} Lab_i$ is the set of transition labels. The set of configurations $Conf(\mathcal{N})$ consists of pairs of *location vectors* $\vec{\ell} = \langle \ell_1, \ldots, \ell_N \rangle \in \times_{i=1}^n Loc(\mathcal{H}_i)$ and valuations. We write $\ell_{s,i}$, $1 \le i \le N$, to denote the location that automaton $\mathcal{H}_i$ assumes in a configuration $s = \langle \vec{\ell}_s, \nu_s \rangle$ and ν_s to denote $\nu_s|_{Var}$. The set of initial configurations is $C_{ini} = \{\langle \vec{\ell}, \nu \rangle \in Conf(\mathcal{N}) \mid \nu \in \cap_{1 \le i \le n} Init_i(\ell_i)\}$. There is a *discrete transition* $s \xrightarrow{a} s'$ from configuration $s = \langle (\ell_1, \ldots, \ell_n), \nu \rangle$ to configuration $s' = \langle (\ell'_1, \ldots, \ell'_n), \nu' \rangle$ if and only if there are edges $(\ell_i, a_i, \mu_i, \ell'_i) \in Edge_i$, $1 \le i \le n$, such that for each i, either $a_i = a$, or $a_i = \tau$ and $a \notin Lab_i$, and the edges are enabled by valuation ν and ν' is an effect of the updates applied to ν, i.e. $(\nu, \nu') \in \bigcap_{1 \le i \le n} \mu_i$, $\nu' \in \bigcap_{1 \le i \le n} Inv(\ell'_i)$. There is a *time transition* $s \xrightarrow{d,f} s'$ with delay $d \in \mathbb{R}_0^+$ from configuration s to configuration s' if and only if action f is in $\bigcap_{1 \le i \le n} Act(\ell_{s,i})$ and $f(0) = \nu_s$, $f(d) = \nu_{s'}$, $\forall 0 \le t \le d \bullet f(t) \in \bigcap_{1 \le i \le n} Inv(\ell_{s,i})$.

Note that multiple automata in a network can take labelled edges simultaneously; asynchronous labelled edges are only possible for local labels, i.e., labels that only occur in the set of labels of a single hybrid automaton $\mathcal{H} \in \mathcal{N}$.

Figure 1 shows an example of a network $\mathcal{N}$ consisting of the hybrid automata $\mathcal{H}_1$ and $\mathcal{H}_2$ with variables x and y. Variables x and y with respective initial values 0 and -3 are set to 3 at the point in time 5. In the strict interleaving

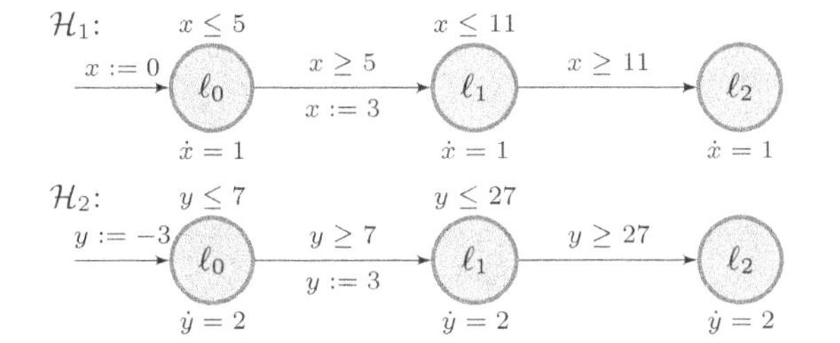

Figure 1: Example of a network $\mathcal{N}$ of hybrid automata.

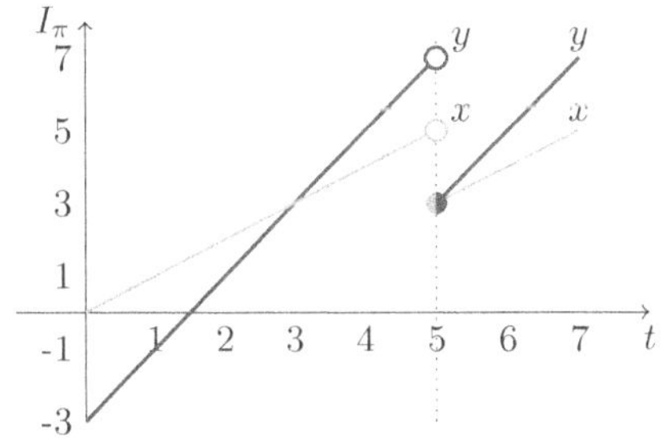

Figure 2: Observable behavior of variables x and y from $\mathcal{N}$.

semantics of networks of hybrid automata, these updates occur one after the other.

A sequence $\pi = \langle \ell_0, \nu_0 \rangle, t_0 \xrightarrow{\lambda_1} \langle \ell_1, \nu_1 \rangle, t_1 \xrightarrow{\lambda_2} \cdots$ of time-stamped configurations is called *run* of $\mathcal{H}$ if and only if $\langle \ell_0, \nu_0 \rangle \in C_{ini}$, $t_0 = 0$, and for all $i \in \mathbb{N}_0$, we have $\lambda_{i+1} \in Lab$ and $t_i = t_{i+1}$ or $\lambda_{i+1} \in \{t_{i+1} - t_i\} \times Act$, and the transition relation $\langle \ell_i, \nu_i \rangle \xrightarrow{\lambda_{i+1}} \langle \ell_{i+1}, \nu_{i+1} \rangle$. We use $\Pi(\mathcal{H})$ to denote the set of all runs of $\mathcal{H}$; a hybrid automaton need not have a run.

One run of network $\mathcal{N}$ in Figure 1 is $\pi = \langle (\ell_0, \ell_0), (0, -3) \rangle$, $0 \xrightarrow{5,f} \langle (\ell_0, \ell_0), (5, 7) \rangle, 5 \xrightarrow{\tau} \langle (\ell_1, \ell_0), (3, 7) \rangle, 5 \xrightarrow{\tau} \langle (\ell_1, \ell_1), (3, 3) \rangle, 5 \xrightarrow{2,f} \langle (\ell_1, \ell_1), (5, 7) \rangle, 7 \cdots$

In the following, we assume infinite runs without Zeno behaviour, i.e. where the sequence of time stamps diverges. A configuration s is called *reachable* in $\mathcal{H}$ if and only if there is a run $\pi \in \Pi(\mathcal{H})$ such that s occurs in π.

Update Points and Instantaneous Valuations.

The *observable behaviour* of run π is a function $\mathcal{I}^\pi : \mathbb{R}_0^+ \to V$ which assigns to each point in time the valuation defined by an action during a non-zero delay in π, i.e. $\mathcal{I}^\pi(t) := f_{i+1}(t - t_i)$ where $i \in \mathbb{N}_0$ is the (unique) index such that $t_i \le t < t_{i+1}$ and $\lambda_{i+1} = (d_{i+1}, f_{i+1})$. Figure 2 shows the observable behaviour of the network in Figure 1 corresponding to the example run π above.

A point in time $t \in \mathbb{R}_0^+$ is called *update point* of π if and only if a discrete transition occurs in π at t, i.e. if

$$\exists i \in \mathbb{N}_0 \bullet \langle \ell_i, \nu_i \rangle, t_i \xrightarrow{a_{i+1}} \langle \ell_{i+1}, \nu_{i+1} \rangle, t_{i+1} \land t = t_{i+1}.$$

We use $\mathcal{U}^\pi$ to denote the set of update points of π, the index may be omitted if clear from context. The *instantaneous valuations* of π is a function $\mathcal{V}^\pi : \mathbb{R}_0^+ \to 2^V \setminus \{\emptyset\}$ which assigns to each point in time the (non-empty) set of valuations that occur at that point in time, i.e.

$$\mathcal{V}^\pi(t) := \{\mathcal{I}^\pi(t)\} \cup \{\nu_i \mid t_i = t\}.$$

We use $\mathcal{I}_x^\pi : \mathbb{R}_0^+ \to \mathbb{R}$ and $\mathcal{V}_x^\pi : \mathbb{R}_0^+ \to 2^{\mathbb{R}} \setminus \{\emptyset\}$ to denote the functions which are point-wise defined as $\mathcal{I}_x^\pi(t) := \mathcal{I}^\pi(t)(x)$ and $\mathcal{V}_x^\pi(t) := \{\nu(x) \mid \nu \in \mathcal{V}^\pi(t)\}$ for $t \in \mathbb{R}_0^+$, respectively. We may omit the superscript if it is clear from the context.

In the following we assume that a set of *forbidden configurations* for network $\mathcal{N}$ is given in form of a *configuration formula CF*. *CF* is any logical connection of *basic formulae* over $\mathcal{N}$ which are given by the grammar $\beta ::= \ell \mid \neg\ell \mid \varphi$ where $\ell \in L_i$, $1 \le i \le n$, and where φ is any arithmetical constraint over the variables in *Var*. A basic formula β is *satisfied* by a configuration $s \in Conf(\mathcal{N})$, denoted by $s \models \beta$, if and only if $\ell_{s,i} = \ell$, $\ell_{s,i} \ne \ell$, and $\nu_s \models \varphi$, respectively. We say *CF* is *reachable* in $\mathcal{N}$ if only if there is a configuration s reachable in $\mathcal{T}(\mathcal{N})$ which satisfies *CF*.

3. QUASI-DEPENDENT VARIABLES

In the following, we define quasi-dependency between variables in terms of the *observable behaviour* of a hybrid automaton. We discuss two alternative characterisations of quasi-dependency and show how quasi-dependency induces an equivalence relation.

Definition 1. (Quasi-f-Dependent Variables) Let $x, y \in Var$ be two variables of the hybrid automaton $\mathcal{H}$. We say x *quasi-depends on* y via function f, denoted by $x \simeq_f y$, if and only if for each run of $\mathcal{H}$ and for each point in time, the value of x in the observable behaviour is the value of f applied to the value of y in the observable behaviour, i.e. if

$$\forall \pi \in \Pi(\mathcal{H})\ \forall t \in \mathbb{R}_0^+ \bullet \mathcal{I}_x^\pi(t) = f(\mathcal{I}_y^\pi(t)).$$

f is called *dependency function* for x wrt. y. ◇

In the example of the network $\mathcal{N}$ from Figure 1, the variable x quasi-depends on y via dependency function $f(z) = 2z - 3$. At time 5, there are configurations where their values don't satisfy $f(y) = 2x - 3$, but these configurations do not contribute to the observable behaviour as there is no delay possible afterwards (cf. Figure 2).

Note that dependency functions are in general not unique. For example, if only value a occurs in the observable behaviour of variable x and only value b for variable y, then x and y are quasi-dependent via any function f with $f(a) = b$.

We can alternatively state quasi-dependency using instantaneous valuations and update points. The instantaneous values of quasi-dependent variables are related by the dependency function f everywhere except for update points. At update points, the values given by the observable behaviour have to adhere to f.

Lemma 3.1. *Let $x, y \in Var$ be two variables of the hybrid automaton $\mathcal{H}$ such that $x \simeq_f y$ with dependency function f. Then $x \simeq_f y$ if and only if $\forall \pi \in \Pi(\mathcal{H}) \bullet$*

$$\mathcal{V}_x^\pi|_{\mathbb{R}_0^+ \setminus \mathcal{U}} = (f \circ \mathcal{V}_y^\pi)|_{\mathbb{R}_0^+ \setminus \mathcal{U}} \land \forall t \in \mathcal{U} \bullet \mathcal{I}_x^\pi(t) = f(\mathcal{I}_y^\pi(t))$$

where $f \circ \mathcal{V}_y^\pi$ is the set-valued function which yields the set of values obtained by applying f to all values in $\mathcal{V}_y$. ◇

The following lemma states a third approach to quasi-dependency: two variables are quasi-dependent if the accumulated duration where their values are not related by the dependency function is 0.

Lemma 3.2. *Let $x, y \in Var$ be two variables of the hybrid automaton $\mathcal{H}$. Let $\pi \in \Pi(\mathcal{H})$ be a run of $\mathcal{H}$. Let $\Delta : \mathbb{R}_0^+ \to \{0, 1\}$ be the characteristic function of the points* *in time where the value of x is* not *obtained by applying the dependency function f to the value of y, i.e.*

$$\Delta(t) = \begin{cases} 1, & \text{if there exist } v \in \mathcal{V}_x^\pi(t), w \in \mathcal{V}_y^\pi(t) \text{ s.t. } v \neq f(w) \\ 0, & \text{otherwise.} \end{cases}$$

Then $x \simeq_f y$ *implies* $\int_0^\infty \Delta(t)dt = 0.$ ◇

Note that Lemma 3.2 is only an implication. The opposite direction does not hold, e.g., with actions that non-continuously change their value at isolated points during a time transition. The integral is blind for such changes, in the observable behaviour (and thus for Definition 1) they are present.

Definition 2. (Quasi-Dependent Variables) Let $x, y \in Var$ be variables of hybrid automaton $\mathcal{H}$. We say x *quasi-depends on* y, denoted by $x \equiv y$, if and only if there exist dependency functions f and g such that $x \simeq_f y$ and $y \simeq_g x$. ◇

Quasi-dependency induces an equivalence relation as follows.

LEMMA 3.3 (EQUIVALENCE RELATION). *Let $\mathcal{H}$ be a hybrid automaton. Quasi-dependency $\equiv$ is an equivalence relation on the variables Var of $\mathcal{H}$.* ◇

In the following, we use $\mathcal{QD}_\mathcal{N}$ to denote the set $\{Y \in Var/\equiv \mid 1 < |Y|\}$ of equivalence classes of quasi-dependent variables of $\mathcal{N}$ with at least two elements. For each $Y \in \mathcal{QD}_\mathcal{N}$, we assume a designated representative variable denoted by $rep(Y)$. For each $x \in Y$, we use $rep(x)$ to denote $rep(Y)$.

LEMMA 3.4. *Let $x, y \in Var$ be variables of hybrid automaton $\mathcal{H}$ such that $x \simeq_f y$ and $y \simeq_g x$. Then f is the inverse of g, i.e.*

$$\forall \pi \in \Pi(\mathcal{H})\ \forall t \in \mathbb{R}_0^+ \bullet g(f(\mathcal{I}_y^\pi(t))) = \mathcal{I}_y^\pi(t).$$ ◇

Note that the notion of quasi-dependency of variables substantially generalizes the existing notion of quasi-equal clocks from [4]. Firstly, timed automata are a subclass of hybrid automata where all continuous variables increase with rate 1 and can only be assigned to 0. Two clocks in a timed automaton are quasi-equal if and only if they are quasi-dependent via the identity function.

4. QUASI-DEPENDENCY DETECTION

For our detection of quasi-dependent variables in hybrid automata, we consider the well-known symbolic semantics of hybrid automata where sets of valuations are represented by so called *regions*. For the rest of this section, let $\mathcal{H}$ denote the hybrid automaton $(Loc, Var, Lab, Edge, Act, Inv, Init)$.

Definition 3. (Symbolic Semantics) The *symbolic semantics* of a hybrid automaton $\mathcal{H}$ is defined by the region transition system $\mathcal{T}(\mathcal{H}) = (Conf'(\mathcal{H}), \Longrightarrow, C_{ini})$ where

- $Conf'(\mathcal{H}) = Loc \times (2^V \setminus \{\emptyset\})$ is the set of configurations, consisting of pairs of a location and a set of valuations,
- $C_{ini} = \{\langle \ell, Z\rangle \in Conf'(\mathcal{H}) \mid Z \subseteq Init(\ell)\}$ is the set of initial configurations, and
- $\Longrightarrow$ is the transition relation where
  - there is a *discrete transition* $\langle \ell, Z\rangle \Longrightarrow \langle \ell', Z'\rangle$ induced by edge $(\ell, a, \mu, \ell') \in Edge$ if $Z' = \{\nu' \mid \exists \nu \in Z \bullet (\nu, \nu') \in \mu$ and $\nu' \in Inv(\ell')\}$, and
  - there is a *time transition* $\langle \ell, Z\rangle \Longrightarrow \langle \ell, Z'\rangle$ if $Z' = \{\nu' \mid \exists f \in Act(\ell), \nu \in Z, t \in \mathbb{R}_0^+ \bullet f(0) = \nu \wedge f(t) = \nu' \wedge \forall 0 \leq t' \leq t \bullet f(t') \in Inv(\ell)\}$. ◇

We call configurations where no flow of positive duration is possible, i.e. the only possible flow has duration zero, zero time configurations.

Definition 4. (Zero time configuration) A configuration $\langle \ell, Z\rangle$ is called *zero time*, if and only if the invariant of ℓ does not allow time to elapse from any valuation in Z, i.e. if

$$\forall f \in Act(\ell), \nu \in Z, t \in \mathbb{R}_0^+ \bullet f(0) = \nu \wedge f(t) \in Inv(\ell)$$
$$\wedge \forall 0 \leq t' \leq t \bullet f(t') \in Inv(\ell) \implies t = 0.$$

We write $\mathsf{zt}(\ell, Z)$ if and only if $\langle \ell, Z\rangle$ is zero time. ◇

Note that the values of quasi-dependent variables are *not* related by the dependency function at most in zero time configurations, and that they may assume any value in zero-time configurations without violating quasi-dependency. Stated the other way around, quasi-dependecy is violated in each non-zero time configuration where the values of the variables are not related by the given dependency function. Thus our analysis tries to establish that for each transition sequence involving only zero-time configurations, whenever two variables are related by the quasi-dependency function when entering a zero-time configuration, they will be related by the quasi-dependency function again when entering a non zero-time configuration.

To this end, our analysis uses precise values for variables only during zero-time configurations. For non zero-time configurations, the *relax operator* only preserves the information which variables are related by which dependency function.

Definition 5. (Relax operator) The *relax operator* rlx applied to the configuration $\langle \ell, Z\rangle$ of $\mathcal{H}$ over-approximates the region Z by a conjunction of the quasi-dependent functions it entails. Formally, $\mathsf{rlx}(\ell, Z) := \langle \ell, Z'\rangle$ where

$$Z' = \bigwedge \{y = f(x) \mid x, y \in Var \text{ and } \forall g \in Act(\ell), \nu \in Z \bullet$$
$$g(0)(x) = \nu(x) \wedge g(0)(y) = \nu(y)$$
$$\implies \forall t \in \mathbb{R}_+^0 \bullet g(t)(y) = f(g(t)(x))\}.$$

Our abstraction function (see below) depends on whether the given configuration is zero time. If it is zero time, then the abstraction goes as precise as possible by preserving all information in the given region. If the configuration is not zero time, then the abstraction will preserve only quasi-dependency relations. In practice, the number of zero time configurations is often small compared to the number of non-zero time configurations. Since for every non-zero time configuration the abstraction function maps given regions to much bigger ones, the size of the resulting abstract system is then much smaller than the corresponding concrete one.

Definition 6. (Zero time abstraction function) The abstraction function α_{zt} applied to a configuration $\langle \ell, Z\rangle$ leaves

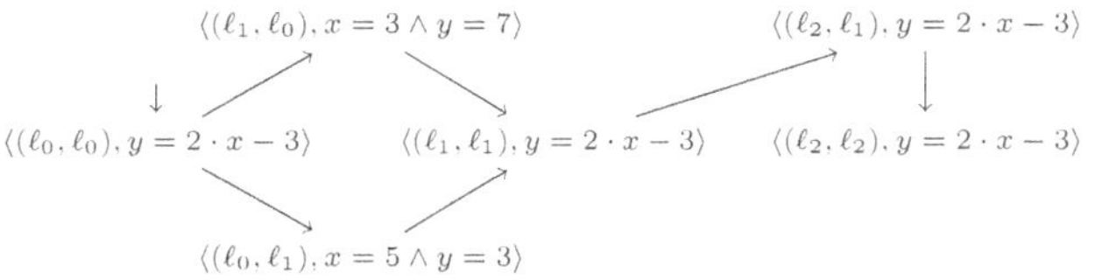

Figure 3: Abstract region graph of network $\mathcal{N}$ from Figure 1.

the configuration unaffected if the configuration is zero time and it abstracts it using the relax operator otherwise, i.e.

$$\alpha_{\mathsf{zt}}(\langle \ell, Z\rangle) := \begin{cases} \langle \ell, Z\rangle & \text{if } \mathsf{zt}(\ell, Z) \\ \mathsf{rlx}(\ell, Z) & \text{otherwise.} \end{cases}$$

The following lemma ensures that the abstraction function applied to a configuration produces a configuration with a bigger or equal region.

LEMMA 4.1. *The abstraction function is increasing and idempotent, i.e., let $\langle \ell, Z\rangle \in Conf'(\mathcal{H})$ be a configuration.*

1. $Z \subseteq Z'$ *if* $\langle \ell, Z'\rangle = \alpha_{\mathsf{zt}}(\langle \ell, Z\rangle)$, *and*
2. $\alpha_{\mathsf{zt}}(\alpha_{\mathsf{zt}}(\langle \ell, Z\rangle)) = \alpha_{\mathsf{zt}}(\langle \ell, Z\rangle)$. $\diamondsuit$

Our technique generates an abstract region graph, where quasi-dependent variables can be soundly detected by traversing the graph. The following definition is constructive in the sense that it tells how to construct the abstract region graph: compute the initial configurations firstly and then for each configuration, compute its successors using the abstraction function α_{zt}. It is important to note that there are only discrete transitions in the abstract region graph. This is because, by definition of the abstraction function there are two possibilities: either a configuration is zero time, meaning it does not have time successors, or the configuration is non-zero time. In the latter case the relax operator is applied, and yields a region which includes all time successors.

Definition 7. (Abstract region graph) $\mathcal{H}$ induces the abstract region graph $\mathcal{T}^{\#}(\mathcal{H}) = (Conf'(\mathcal{H}), \Longrightarrow^{\#}, C_0^{\#})$ where

- $\Longrightarrow^{\#} \subseteq Conf'(\mathcal{H}) \times Conf'(\mathcal{H})$ is the transition relation. There is a transition $\langle \ell, Z\rangle \Longrightarrow^{\#} \alpha_{\mathsf{zt}}(\langle \ell', Z'\rangle)$ if there is an edge $(\ell, a, \mu, \ell') \in E$ such that $Z' = \{\nu' \mid \exists \nu \in Z \bullet (\nu, \nu') \in \mu$ and $\nu' \in Inv(\ell')\}$ is not empty, and
- $C_0^{\#} = \{\alpha_{\mathsf{zt}}(\langle \ell, Z\rangle) \mid \langle \ell, Z\rangle \in Conf'(\mathcal{H}) \wedge Z = Init(\ell)\}$ is the set of initial configurations. $\diamondsuit$

Figure 3 shows the abstract region graph for the running example. The abstract region graph simulates the region transition system thus quasi-dependency detection on the abstract region graph is sound.

Definition 8. (Simulation relation) A simulation relation $\preceq$ for two region transition systems $\mathcal{T}_i = (Conf'(\mathcal{H}), \Longrightarrow_i, C_{ini_i})$, $i \in \{1,2\}$, is a binary relation on $Conf'(\mathcal{H})$ satisfying the following properties:

1. for all $c_{ini_1} \in C_{ini_1}$ there exists c_{ini_2} with $c_{ini_1} \preceq c_{ini_2}$,
2. $\langle \ell_1, Z_1\rangle \preceq \langle \ell_2, Z_2\rangle$ implies $\ell_1 = \ell_2$, $Z_1 \subseteq Z_2$, and
3. $\langle \ell_1, Z_1\rangle \preceq \langle \ell_2, Z_2\rangle$ and $\langle \ell_1, Z_1\rangle \Longrightarrow_1 \langle \ell_1', Z_1'\rangle$ implies that there exists a configuration $\langle \ell_2', Z_2'\rangle$ such that $\langle \ell_2, Z_2\rangle \Longrightarrow_2 \langle \ell_2', Z_2'\rangle$ and $\langle \ell_1', Z_1'\rangle \preceq \langle \ell_2', Z_2'\rangle$.

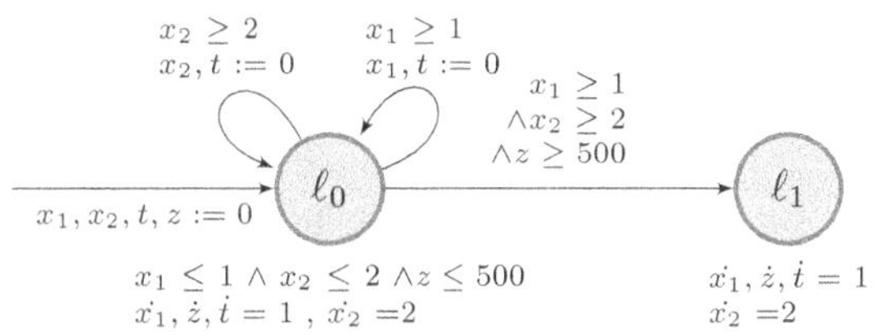

Figure 4: Class B benchmark: $x_1 \simeq_f x_2$ via $f(x) = 0.5 \cdot x$.

We say that $\mathcal{T}_2$ *simulates* $\mathcal{T}_1$ if and only if there exists a simulation relation for $\mathcal{T}_1, \mathcal{T}_2$. $\diamondsuit$

THEOREM 4.2. $\mathcal{T}^{\#}(\mathcal{H})$ *simulates* $\mathcal{T}(\mathcal{H})$. $\diamondsuit$

Quasi-dependency of two variables x and y via depedency function f is checked on the abstract region graph $\mathcal{T}^{\#}(\mathcal{H})$ by checking, for each non-zero time configuration $\langle \ell, Z\rangle$ of $\mathcal{T}^{\#}(\mathcal{H})$ whether Z entails $x = f(y)$. If there is a (possibly spurious) counter-example for the quasi-dependency, the corresponding application of the relax operator removes this dependency from the region.

Note that Definition 5 needs a given dependency function candidate f. For *linear* hybrid automata, also known as *multi-rate* automata, dependency function candidates can easily be constructed from the locations' actions (rates) and initial values of variables. Further note that two variables x, y having the same rate in each location does not imply quasi-dependency between x and y; similarly, having different rates for x and y in some (even reachable) location does not imply that there is no quasi-dependency between them.

4.1 Experimental Results

We have implemented our approach in our tool sAsEt. We have implemented regions as predicates over reals and use the SMT solver Z3 [18] to compute the result of the relax operator, whether a configuration is zero time, and whether guards are satisfied. As Z3 is restricted to linear arithmetics, the scope of our implementation is restricted to *linear* hybrid automata. sAsEt is based on the Jahob system [19]. It takes as input a network of hybrid automata in the SpaceEx [20] format and computes successors on the fly.

Table 1 compares the run-time of sAsEt with SpaceEx on two artificial benchmarks which represent two typical cases for quasi-dependent variables in hybrid models. As SpaceEx does not support the detection of quasi-dependency directly, we introduced an auxiliary continuous variable t with rate $\dot{t} = 1$ in all locations which is set to 0 on all edges. Then checking for quasi-equality, e.g., for the running example amounts to checking $(y < 2x + 3 \vee y > 2x + 3) \wedge t > 0$.

In the Class A benchmark, there exists an ordering on the assignments of quasi-dependent variables. This yields a linear increase of the number of zero time configurations. Both sAsEt and SpaceEx scale, but the non quasi-dependent variables are early abstracted away by our approach yielding a very small abstract region graph in comparison with the one obtained by SpaceEx. In the Class B benchmark (cf. Figure 4), there is non-determinism between the assignments of quasi-dependent variables which yields an exponential growth of the number of zero time configurations in

[1]AMD Opteron 6174, 2.2GHz, 16GB, Linux 2.6.32-5-amd64; SpaceEx 0.9.7c (32bit); t(s) gives user+system time.

Cl.	n	sAsEt SMT-calls	states	t (s)	SpaceEx iterat.	t (s)
A	1	4	3	0.34	1003	2.35
	2	5	4	0.64	1503	4.21
	3	6	5	1.00	2003	6.79
	4	7	6	1.48	2503	10.23
B	1	17	4	0.91	1502	7.52
	2	71	8	5.12	3502	49.14
	3	278	16	25.72	7502	283.70
	4	1255	35	142.20	-	-

Table 1: $x_0 \simeq_{f_i} x_i$ via $f_i(x) = x/i + 1$. Timeout 1200 sec.[1]

the interleaving semantics. Hence the number of SMT calls grows exponentially. Yet in addition of being faster, the abstraction is more space efficient than SpaceEx. Note that the use of SMT calls amounts to 80% of the computation time.

5. TRANSFORMATION

In this section we present our transformation for networks of hybrid automata which reduces a given set of quasi-dependent variables and reflects reachability of forbidden configurations. For simplicity, we impose a set of syntactical criteria called well-formedness rules on networks.

Firstly, we introduce some notions which we need to state our rules. Let $W \subseteq V$ be a set of valuations. We use $vars(W) \subseteq Var$ to denote the set of variables that are constrained by W, i.e. $vars(W) = \{x \in Var \mid \{\nu(x) \mid \nu \in W\} \neq \mathbb{R}\}$. Analogously, for update $\mu \subseteq V \times V$ and action f, we use $vars(\mu)$ and $vars(f)$, to denote the set of variables that are constrained by μ and f, respectively. We use $\mathcal{V}(\mathcal{H})$ to denote the set of variables that are constrained by some initial condition, location invariant, update, or action in $\mathcal{H}$.

We use $\mathcal{SE}_Y(\mathcal{H})$ to denote the set of *simple resetting edges* of hybrid automaton $\mathcal{H}$ where only quasi-dependent variables from $Y \in \mathcal{QD}_\mathcal{N}$ are constrained by the conditional update and which have action τ, i.e., $\mathcal{SE}_Y(\mathcal{H}) = \{(\ell, \tau, \mu, \ell') \in Edge(\mathcal{H}) \mid vars(\mu) \subseteq Y\}$. We use $\mathcal{CE}_Y(\mathcal{H})$ to denote the set of *complex resetting edges* of $\mathcal{H}$ where quasi-dependent and non-quasi-dependent variables occur in the conditional update, or which have a label different from τ, i.e., $\mathcal{CE}_Y(\mathcal{H}) = \{(\ell, a, \mu, \ell') \in Edge(\mathcal{H}) \mid vars(\mu) \cap Y \neq \emptyset \wedge (vars(\mu) \setminus Y \neq \emptyset \vee a \neq \tau)\}$. We use $\mathcal{E}_Y(\mathcal{H}) = \mathcal{SE}_Y(\mathcal{H}) \cup \mathcal{CE}_Y(\mathcal{H})$ to denote the set of resetting edges of $\mathcal{H}$ wrt. Y, and $\mathcal{RES}_Y(\mathcal{N})$ to denote the set of automata in $\mathcal{N}$ which have a Y-resetting edge, i.e., $\mathcal{RES}_Y(\mathcal{N}) = \{\mathcal{H} \in \mathcal{N} \mid \mathcal{E}_Y(\mathcal{H}) \neq \emptyset\}$.

We use $\mathcal{SL}_Y(\mathcal{H})$ and $\mathcal{CL}_Y(\mathcal{H})$ to respectively denote the set of source and destination locations of simple and complex resetting edges of $\mathcal{H}$. A location ℓ (ℓ') is called *reset (successor) location* wrt. Y in $\mathcal{N}$ if and only if there is a resetting edge in $\mathcal{E}_Y(\mathcal{H})$ from (to) ℓ (ℓ'). We use $\mathcal{RL}_Y^-$ ($\mathcal{RL}_Y^+$) to denote the set of reset (successor) locations wrt. Y in $\mathcal{N}$. We define $\mathcal{RL}_\mathcal{N}^- := \bigcup_{Y \in \mathcal{QD}_\mathcal{N}} \mathcal{RL}_Y^-$ and similarly $\mathcal{RL}_\mathcal{N}^+$.

Definition 9. (Well-formed Network) A network $\mathcal{N}$ is called *well-formed* if and only if it satisfies the following restrictions for each set of quasi-dependent variables $Y \in \mathcal{QD}_\mathcal{N}$:

(R1) All resetting edges update at most one variable $x \in Y$, and, given $x \simeq_f y$, the guard of the edge and the invariant of its source location and the assignment, resp., determine unique values $C_Y, O_Y \in \mathbb{R}$, i.e.

$$\exists C_Y, O_Y \in \mathbb{R}\ \forall (\ell, a, \mu, \ell') \in \mathcal{E}_Y(\mathcal{N})\ \exists x \in Y \bullet$$
$$\forall (\nu, \nu') \in \mu \bullet \nu|_{\mathcal{V}\setminus\{x\}} = \nu'|_{\mathcal{V}\setminus\{x\}}$$
$$\wedge \forall \nu \in (\mu \downarrow_1) \cap Inv(\ell) \bullet \nu(x) = C_Y$$
$$\wedge \forall \nu \in (\mu \downarrow_2) \bullet \nu(x) = O_Y,$$

where $\mu \downarrow_i$ denotes projection onto the i-th component.

(R2) There are no two resetting edges from one location, i.e.

$$\forall e_1 = (\ell_1, a_1, \mu_1, \ell_1'), e_2 = (\ell_2, a_2, \mu_2, \ell_2') \in \mathcal{E}_Y(\mathcal{N}) \bullet$$
$$e_1 \neq e_2 \implies \ell_1 \neq \ell_2.$$

(R3) All edges that synchronise on some label either all reset a clock from Y or none does, i.e.,

$$\forall a \in Lab \bullet (\exists e = (\ell, a, \mu, \ell') \in Edge(\mathcal{N}) \bullet e \in \mathcal{E}_Y(\mathcal{N}))$$
$$\implies (\forall e = (\ell, a, \mu, \ell') \in Edge(\mathcal{N}) \bullet e \in \mathcal{E}_Y(\mathcal{N})).$$

(R4) No guard relates two or more variables from Y, i.e.

$$\forall e = (\ell, a, \mu, \ell') \in Edge(\mathcal{N})\ \forall x \in Y \bullet (\mu \downarrow_1)|_{\{x\}} \subsetneq \mathbb{R}$$
$$\implies \forall y \in Y \setminus \{x\} \bullet (\mu \downarrow_1)|_{\{y\}} = \mathbb{R}.$$

Note that network $\mathcal{N}$ from Figure 1 is well-formed.

In the following we describe our transformation procedure $\mathcal{K}$. It works with two given inputs, a well-formed network $\mathcal{N} = \{\mathcal{H}_1, \dots, \mathcal{H}_n\}$ and a set of equivalence classes $\mathcal{QD}_\mathcal{N}$ of quasi-dependent variables. The output is the transformed network $\mathcal{N}' = \{\mathcal{H}_1', \dots, \mathcal{H}_n'\} \cup \{\mathcal{R}_Y \mid Y \in \mathcal{QD}_\mathcal{N}\}$ which consists of hybrid automata $\mathcal{H}_i' = (Loc'(\mathcal{H}_i), Var', Lab'(\mathcal{H}_i), Edge'(\mathcal{H}_i), Act'(\mathcal{H}_i), Inv'(\mathcal{H}_i), Init'(\mathcal{H}_i))$ which are obtained as modifications of the $\mathcal{H}_i$, and one *resetter* automaton for each equivalence class $Y \in \mathcal{QD}_\mathcal{N}$.

The common set of variables Var' consists of the non-quasi-dependent variables in $\mathcal{N}$, one representative $rep(Y)$ for each equivalence class, and bookkeeping variables $rst_Y^{I_\mathcal{H}}$ and $rst_Y^{O_\mathcal{H}}$, $\mathcal{H} \in \mathcal{N}$. For each equivalence class $Y \in \mathcal{QD}_\mathcal{N}$, the set of labels of $\mathcal{H}$ is extended by the fresh label $reset_Y$ if $\mathcal{H} \in \mathcal{RES}_Y(\mathcal{N})$.

For each automaton $\mathcal{H} \in \mathcal{N}$, and for each complex edge $e \in \mathcal{CE}_Y(\mathcal{H})$, the set of locations is extended by one fresh location $\ell_{\xi_{Y,e}}$ and the set of edges is extended by one edge with label $reset_Y$ and no guard and no assignment from the source of e to $\ell_{\xi_{Y,e}}$. The source location of e is changed to be $\ell_{\xi_{Y,e}}$, any guard on and any assignment of quasi-dependent variables is removed from its μ. For each simple edge, its label τ is replaced by $reset_Y$ and any guard on and assignment of quasi-dependent variables is removed from its μ.

In order to keep track of whether a hybrid automaton is ready to reset a quasi-dependent variable or has just reset its variable, the assignments of all edges with a reset location as destination are changed such that $rst_Y^{I_\mathcal{H}}$ is assigned 1, the assignments of all non-resetting edges with a reset location as source are changed such that $rst_Y^{I_\mathcal{H}}$ is assigned 0, and the assignments of all resetting edges (including those redirected to have source $\ell_{\xi_{Y,e}}$) is changed such that $rst_Y^{O_\mathcal{H}}$ is assigned 0. Note that $rst_Y^{I_\mathcal{H}}$ may also be assigned 1 on resetting edges in case of loops.

For each location, any action $f \in Act(\mathcal{H})$ is restricted to Var' and modified such that $rst_Y^{I_\mathcal{H}}$ and $rst_Y^{O_\mathcal{H}}$ keep their value over time, and such that the evolution of the representative variables is unconstrained. Their evolution is

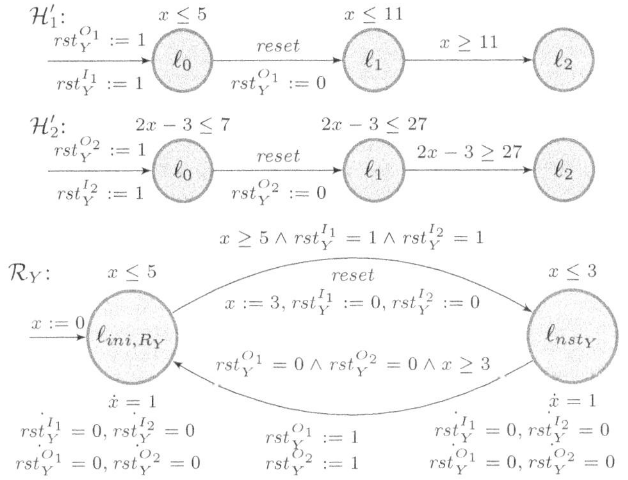

Figure 5: Network $\mathcal{N}'$ after applying the transformation.

determined by the resetter automata. The actions of the locations $\ell_{\xi_{Y,e}}$ keep all values constant. For each location, the valuations in the invariant and the initial valuations set are modified such that they express the original guard in terms of the representative variable and the dependency function.

For example, applying $\mathcal{K}$ to network $\mathcal{N}$ from Figure 1 with the set of quasi-dependent variables $Y = \{x, y\}$ yields the automata $\mathcal{H}_1'$ and $\mathcal{H}_2'$ as shown in Figure 5. Note that only the representative variable of Y remains, namely variable x.

The *resetter* for equivalence class Y is the hybrid automaton $\mathcal{R}_Y$ with two locations $\ell_{ini,\mathcal{R}_Y}$ and $\ell_{nst,Y}$ and two edges $(\ell_{ini,\mathcal{R}_Y}, reset_Y, \mu_1, \ell_{nst,Y})$ and $(\ell_{nst,Y}, \tau, \mu_2, \ell_{ini,\mathcal{R}_Y})$. The first edge obtains a guard μ_1 which checks whether the representative variable of equivalence class Y equals C_Y and whether the $rst_Y^{I_\mathcal{H}}$ evaluate to 1. μ_1 assigns all $rst_Y^{I_\mathcal{H}}$ to 0 and the representative variable to O_Y. The second edge obtains a guard μ_2 which checks whether $rst_Y^{O_\mathcal{H}}$ evaluates to 0, and assigns 1 to $rst_Y^{O_\mathcal{H}}$.

Both locations of $\mathcal{R}_Y$ inherit the actions for the representative variable x from the automaton constraining x. Additionally, from the same automaton, location $\ell_{ini,\mathcal{R}_Y}$ inherits the invariant of the reset location with an outgoing edge updating x. Location $\ell_{ini,\mathcal{R}_Y}$ is set as the initial location and in $\ell_{nst,Y}$ we require that the value of the representative is O_Y. The variables $rst_Y^{I_\mathcal{H}}$ and $rst_Y^{O_\mathcal{H}}$ keep their value over time. $rst_Y^{I_\mathcal{H}}$ is initialised to 1 on initial locations which are reset locations and to 0 otherwise; $rst_Y^{O_\mathcal{H}}$ is initialised to 1.

See Figure 5 for an example resetter. Note that the guard and the update operation are delegated to the resetter. Further note that well-formedness together with the counter variables $rst_Y^{I_\mathcal{H}}$ enforces blocking multicast synchronisation, i.e., always all automata from $\mathcal{RES}_Y(\mathcal{N})$ participate in the reset.

To support all possible queries, we use the location $\ell_{nst,Y}$ to summarise information from configurations that are induced by interleaving updates of quasi-dependent variables. The variables $rst_Y^{O_\mathcal{H}}$ are introduced to indicate how many automata still need to take their reset edges. The following function Ω (cf. Table 2) syntactically transforms properties over a well-formed network $\mathcal{N}$ into equivalent properties over $\mathcal{N}'$ (cf. Theorem 5.2).

Function Ω treats queries for source or destination locations of resetting edges special, by referring these queries to the summary location $\ell_{nst,Y}$. For instance, for a simple resetting edge $e \in \mathcal{SE}_Y(\mathcal{H})$ of some $\mathcal{H} \in \mathcal{N}$, the source location ℓ of e can be assumed in $\mathcal{N}$ in different configurations: either the reset time is not yet reached, or the reset time is reached but $\mathcal{H}$ did not reset yet, while other automata in $\mathcal{RES}_Y(\mathcal{N})$ may have reset their quasi-dependent variables already. In $\mathcal{N}'$, all edges resulting from simple edges fire at once on the synchronisation on $reset_Y$, so all source locations are left together. With this synchronisation, the resetter moves to $\ell_{nst,Y}$, which represents all configurations of $\mathcal{N}$ where all simple edges are in their source or destination location and the variables updated on these edges have value C_Y or O_Y. Thus the location ℓ is reachable in $\mathcal{N}$ if and only if, for $\mathcal{N}'$, (i) $\ell_{nst,Y}$ is reachable, or (ii) ℓ is reached while being stable, i.e., not being in $\ell_{nst,Y}$.

Note that $\Omega(CF)$ consists of two parts: a transformation of CF by Ω_0 which uses fresh existentially quantified variables and a feasibility condition for these fresh variables. Thereby we represent that, although involving two choices of location and variable value each, there are actually only two cases (not four) summarised by $\ell_{nst,Y}$. Namely, assuming the source location of a simple resetting edge implies that the representative has value C_Y, and assuming the destination location implies the value O_Y. Furthermore, we can only assume either the source or the destination location of the simple resetting edge. By *R1*, we only need to consider, e.g., O_Y and C_Y as values of $\tilde{x}$, thus the existential quantification can be rewritten into a big disjunction, and hence is a proper configuration formula.

In the following, we observe that our transformation yields a network whose stable configurations (see below) directly relate to the stable configurations of $\mathcal{N}$ (one-to-one). For unstable configurations from both networks the relation between them is more involved (one-to-many), i.e., this relation depends on information from simple and complex resetting edges, as well as on values from *rst*-variables.

Definition 10. (Stable and Unstable Configurations) Let $\mathcal{N}$ be a network and let $Y \in \mathcal{QD}_\mathcal{N}$ be a set of quasi-dependent variables. A configuration $s \in Conf(\mathcal{N})$ is called *stable wrt.* $Y \in \mathcal{QD}_\mathcal{N}$ if and only if $\forall x \in Y, x \simeq_f rep(x) \bullet \nu_s(x) = f(\nu_s(rep(x)))$. We use $\mathcal{SC}_\mathcal{N}^Y$ to denote the set of all configurations that are stable wrt. Y and $\mathcal{SC}_\mathcal{N}$ to denote the set $\bigcap_{Y \in \mathcal{QD}_\mathcal{N}} \mathcal{SC}_\mathcal{N}^Y$ of *globally stable* configurations of $\mathcal{N}$. Configurations not in $\mathcal{SC}_\mathcal{N}$ are called *unstable*.

A configuration $r \in Conf(\mathcal{N}')$ of $\mathcal{N}' = \mathcal{K}(\mathcal{N}, \mathcal{QD}_\mathcal{N})$ is called *stable wrt.* Y if and only if the initial location $\ell_{ini,\mathcal{R}_Y}$ of resetter $\mathcal{R}_Y \in \mathcal{N}'$ occurs in r, i.e., if $\ell_r = \ell_{ini,\mathcal{R}_Y}$. ◇

The following definition allows us to define a weak bisimulation relation between $\mathcal{N}$ and $\mathcal{N}'$.

Definition 11. (Delayed Edge) An edge e of a hybrid automaton $\mathcal{H}$ in network $\mathcal{N}$ is called *delayed* if and only if time must pass before e can be taken, i.e., if

$$\forall s_0 \xrightarrow{\lambda_1}_{E_1} \dots s_{n-1} \xrightarrow{\lambda_n}_{E_n} s_n \in \Pi(\mathcal{H}) \bullet e \in E_n \implies \exists 0 \le j < n \bullet \lambda_j \in \mathbb{R}_0^+ \setminus \{0\} \wedge \forall j \le i < n \bullet Edge(\mathcal{H}) \cap E_i = \emptyset.$$

Here, we write $s_i \xrightarrow{\lambda_i}_{E_i} s_{i+1}$, $i \in \mathbb{N}^+$, to denote that the transition $s_i \xrightarrow{\lambda_i} s_{i+1}$ is justified by the set of edges E_i; E_i is empty for time transitions, i.e., if $\lambda_i \in \mathbb{R}_0^+ \times Lab$.

We say *$\mathcal{QD}_\mathcal{N}$-reset edges are pre/post delayed in well-formed network $\mathcal{N}$* if and only if all edges originating in

$$\Omega_0(\beta) = \begin{cases} (\ell \wedge \neg \ell_{nst,Y}) \vee (\ell_{nst,Y} \wedge \tilde{\ell}) & \text{, if } \beta = \ell, \ell \in \mathcal{SL}_Y(\mathcal{N}) \cup (\mathcal{CL}_Y(\mathcal{N}) \cap \mathcal{RL}_Y^-), Y \in \mathcal{QD}_\mathcal{N}. \\ (\neg\ell \wedge \neg \ell_{nst,Y}) \vee (\ell_{nst,Y} \wedge \neg\tilde{\ell}) & \text{, if } \beta = \neg\ell, \ell \in \mathcal{SL}_Y(\mathcal{N}) \cup (\mathcal{CL}_Y(\mathcal{N}) \cap \mathcal{RL}_Y^-), Y \in \mathcal{QD}_\mathcal{N}. \\ \big(\varphi[x/rep(x) \mid x \in Var] \wedge \neg \ell_{nst,Y}\big) \vee \big(\ell_{nst,Y} \wedge \tilde{\varphi}\big) & \text{, if } \beta = \varphi, \tilde{\varphi} = \varphi[x/\tilde{x} \mid x \in Var], Y \in \mathcal{QD}_\mathcal{N}. \\ \beta & \text{, otherwise} \end{cases}$$

$$\Omega(CF) = \exists\, \tilde{x}_1, \ldots, \tilde{x}_k \; \exists\, \tilde{\ell}_1, \ldots, \tilde{\ell}_m \bullet$$

$$\Omega_0(CF) \wedge \bigwedge_{\substack{1 \le i \le k, 1 \le j \le m, \\ x_j \in \mathcal{X}_p \cap Y, 1 \le p \le n, \\ \ell_i \in L_p \cap (\mathcal{RL}_Y^- \setminus \mathcal{RL}_Y^+)}} (\tilde{\ell}_i \implies \tilde{x}_j = C_Y) \wedge \bigwedge_{\substack{1 \le i \le k, 1 \le j \le m, \\ x_j \in \mathcal{X}_p \cap Y, 1 \le p \le n, \\ \ell_i \in L_p \cap (\mathcal{RL}_Y^+ \setminus \mathcal{RL}_Y^-)}} (\tilde{\ell}_i \implies \tilde{x}_j = O_Y) \wedge \bigwedge_{\substack{(\ell, a, \mu, \ell') \\ \in \mathcal{SE}_Y(\mathcal{H}), \\ \ell_i \in \{\ell, \ell'\}}} (\tilde{\ell}_i \implies \ell') \wedge \bigwedge_{\substack{(\ell, a, \mu, \ell') \\ \in \mathcal{CE}_Y(\mathcal{H}), \\ \ell_i = \ell}} (\tilde{\ell}_i \implies \ell_{\xi_{Y,e}}) \wedge \bigwedge_{\substack{1 \le i \ne j \le m, \\ 1 \le p \le n \\ \ell_i, \ell_j \in L_p,}} \neg(\tilde{\ell}_i \wedge \tilde{\ell}_j)$$

Table 2: Formula transformation function Ω. $\Omega_0(CF)$ denotes applying Ω_0 to each basic formula in CF.

reset (successor) locations are delayed, i.e., if for all $e = (\ell, a, \mu, \ell') \in Edge(\mathcal{N})$, $\ell \in \mathcal{RL}_\mathcal{N}^- \cup \mathcal{RL}_\mathcal{N}^+$ implies that e is delayed. ◇

There are *sufficient* syntactic criteria for an edge $e = (\ell_1, a_1, \mu_1, \ell_2)$ being delayed. For instance, if $(\ell_0, a_0, \mu_0, \ell_1)$ is the only incoming edge to ℓ_1 and if the condition of μ_0 is $(x \ge C \wedge x \le C)$ and the condition of μ_1 is $(x \ge D \wedge x \le D)$ and $C < D$, then e is delayed. It is also delayed if $(\ell_0, a_0, \mu_0, \ell_1)$ is the only incoming edge to ℓ_1, μ_0 updates x, and the condition of μ_1 is $(x > 0)$.

Both patterns occur, e.g., in the FSN case-study (cf. Section 5.1). There, the reset location is entered via an edge following the former pattern, and the edges originating at the reset successor location follow the latter pattern. Thus $\mathcal{QD}_\mathcal{N}$-reset edges are pre/post delayed in FSN.

LEMMA 5.1. *(Weak Bisimulation) Any well-formed network $\mathcal{N}$ where $\mathcal{QD}_\mathcal{N}$-reset edges are pre/post delayed, is* weakly bisimilar *to $\mathcal{N}' = \mathcal{K}(\mathcal{N}, \mathcal{QD}_\mathcal{N})$, i.e., there is a* weak bisimulation relation *$\mathcal{S} \subseteq Conf(\mathcal{N}) \times Conf(\mathcal{N}')$ such that*

1. *$\forall\, s \in Conf(\mathcal{N})\; \exists\, r \bullet (s, r) \in \mathcal{S}$ and $\forall\, r \in Conf(\mathcal{N})\; \exists\, s \bullet (s, r) \in \mathcal{S}$.*

2. *For all configuration formulae CF over $\mathcal{N}$, $\forall\, (s, r) \in \mathcal{S} \bullet s \models CF \implies r \models \Omega(CF)$ and $\forall\, r \in CONS_{\mathcal{QD}_\mathcal{N}} \bullet r \models \Omega(CF) \implies \exists\, s \in Conf(\mathcal{N}) \bullet (s, r) \in \mathcal{S} \wedge s \models CF$. Where $r \in CONS_{\mathcal{QD}_\mathcal{N}}$ iff*

$$\forall\, Y \in \mathcal{QD}_\mathcal{N} \bullet \nu_r(rst_Y^{I_\mathcal{H}}) = |\{\ell_{r,1}, \ldots, \ell_{r,n}\} \cap \mathcal{RL}_Y^-| \wedge \ell_{r,\mathcal{R}_Y} = \ell_{ini,\mathcal{R}_Y} \implies \nu_r(rst_Y^{O_\mathcal{H}}) = |Y| \wedge \ell_{r,\mathcal{R}_Y} = \ell_{nst,\mathcal{R}_Y} \implies \nu_r(rst_Y^{O_\mathcal{H}}) = |\{\ell_{r,1}, \ldots, \ell_{r,n}\} \cap \Xi_Y|.$$

3. *For all $(s, r) \in \mathcal{S}$, if $s \xrightarrow{\lambda} s'$ with*

   (a) *$s, s' \notin \mathcal{SC}_\mathcal{N}^Y$, where $Y \in \mathcal{QD}_\mathcal{N}$, and justified by a simple resetting edge, or $s \notin \mathcal{SC}_\mathcal{N}^Y$, $s' \in \mathcal{SC}_\mathcal{N}^Y$, where $Y \in \mathcal{QD}_\mathcal{N}$, and justified by a simple resetting edge, then $r \xrightarrow{0} r$ and $(s', r) \in \mathcal{S}$.*

   (b) *$s \in \mathcal{SC}_\mathcal{N}^Y$, $s' \notin \mathcal{SC}_\mathcal{N}^Y$, where $Y \in \mathcal{QD}_\mathcal{N}$, and justified by the set $CE_Y^1 \subseteq \mathcal{CE}_Y(\mathcal{N})$ of complex resetting edges wrt. Y, or $s, s' \in \mathcal{SC}_\mathcal{N}^Y$, where $Y \in \mathcal{QD}_\mathcal{N}$, and justified by $CE_Y \subseteq \mathcal{CE}_Y(\mathcal{N})$, or $s, s' \in \mathcal{SC}_\mathcal{N}^Y$, $\ell_r = \ell_{nst,\mathcal{R}_Y}$ for some $Y \in \mathcal{QD}_\mathcal{N}$, and $\lambda = d > 0$, then there exist r', r'' such that $r \xrightarrow{\tau} r' \xrightarrow{\lambda} r''$ and $(s, r'), (s', r'') \in \mathcal{S}$.*

   (c) *Otherwise there is r' s.t. $r \xrightarrow{\lambda} r'$ and $(s', r') \in \mathcal{S}$.*

and if $r \xrightarrow{\lambda} r'$ with

   (a) *$r \in \mathcal{SC}_{\mathcal{N}'}^Y, r' \notin \mathcal{SC}_{\mathcal{N}'}^Y$, where $Y \in \mathcal{QD}_\mathcal{N}$, $\nu_{r'}(rst_Y^{O_\mathcal{H}}) < N$, where $N = \nu_r(rst_Y^{O_\mathcal{H}})$, there exist $s_1, \ldots, s_n$ where $n = N - \nu_{r'}(rst_Y^{O_\mathcal{H}})$, such that $s \xrightarrow{\tau} s_1 \xrightarrow{\tau} \ldots \xrightarrow{\tau} s_n$ and $(s_i, r') \in \mathcal{S}$, $1 \le i \le n$.*

   (b) *$r \in \mathcal{SC}_{\mathcal{N}'}^Y, r' \notin \mathcal{SC}_{\mathcal{N}'}^Y$, $\nu_{r'}(rst_Y^{O_\mathcal{H}}) = \nu_r(rst_Y^{O_\mathcal{H}})$, where $Y \in \mathcal{QD}_\mathcal{N}$, or $\ell_r = \ell_{nst,\mathcal{R}_Y}$, $\ell_{r'} \ne \ell_{nst,\mathcal{R}_Y}$, $Y \in \mathcal{QD}_\mathcal{N}$, then $s \xrightarrow{0} s$ and $(s, r') \in \mathcal{S}$.*

   (c) *Otherwise there is s' s.t. $s \xrightarrow{\lambda} s'$ and $(s', r') \in \mathcal{S}$.*

THEOREM 5.2. *Let CF be a configuration formula over well-formed network $\mathcal{N}$ with pre/post delayed $\mathcal{QD}_\mathcal{N}$-resets. CF is reachable in $\mathcal{N}$ iff $\Omega(CF)$ is reachable in $\mathcal{K}(\mathcal{N}, \mathcal{QD}_\mathcal{N})$.*

5.1 Experimental Results

For our experimental evaluation[1] we have chosen two industrial time-based protocols for wireless sensor networks where the timers of the individual sensors advance at different rates (each rate being constant). In our case studies we have verified queries which were proposed by the respective authors. Our first benchmark, the FSN fire alarm protocol from [21] belongs to the class of TDMA protocols. It consists of one controller and, in our setting, from 10 to 130 sensors. Each sensor has only one (simple) resetting edge. We verified that the communication between controller and sensors is successful, i.e., each message received by the controller is replied to and reaches the transmitting sensor. The results are reported in Table 3; we have used the same machine as in Section 4.1. We compare the number of iterations and analysis runtime needed by SpaceEx for the original and the transformed systems (the latter denoted in the table by the suffix K). Furthermore, we report time spent in the detection phase. It is important to note that the detection can be done in a compositional manner by considering only *pairs* of sensors and their variables. These detections can run in parallel; the final set of quasi-dependent variables can be derived using transitivity. Therefore, in column "Detect" of Table 3, we show the results of pair-wise detection. Overall, our approach shows better performance starting from the smallest instances. Furthermore, our combined approach

[1] Tools and benchmarks are available for download [1].

	Detect		Check		
	pairs	Σ t(s)	iter.	t(s)	Σ
10			2086	47.18	47.18
10_K	9	27.68	41	0.14	27.82
11			4138	134.53	134.53
11_K	10	30.74	45	0.17	30.91
12			-	-	-
12_K	11	33.78	49	0.19	33.97
110_K	109	334.28	441	46.35	380.63
120_K	119	364.93	481	59.72	424.65
130_K	129	395.48	521	75.55	471.03

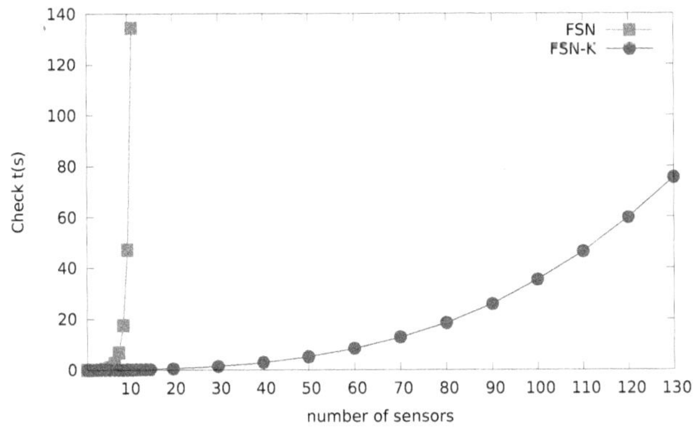

Table 3: Benchmark FSN: For each pair of quasi-dependent variables, detect needs 41 SMT calls, 14 states.[1]

	Detect		Check		
	pairs	Σ t(s)	iter.	t(s)	Σ
7			396	5.45	5.45
7_K	5	48.53	408	2.05	50.58
8			781	15.51	15.51
8_K	6	58.21	794	5.28	63.49
9			1550	43.75	43.75
9_K	7	68.25	1564	14.27	82.52
10			-	-	-
10_K	8	77.85	3102	41.89	119.74
11_K	9	87.49	6176	139.91	227.40

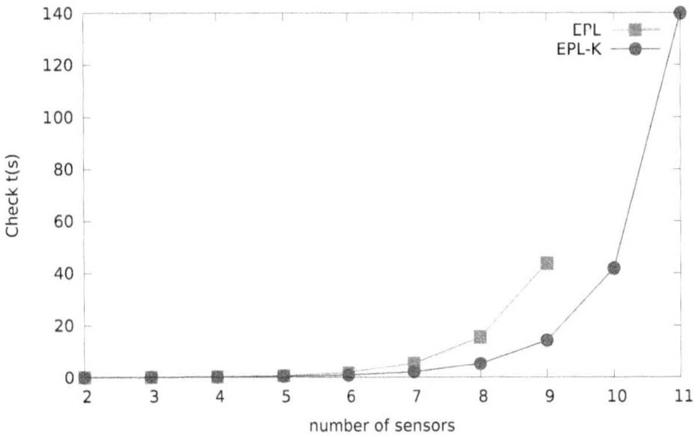

Table 4: Benchmark EPL: For each pair of quasi-dependent variables, detect needs 120 SMT calls, 34 states.[1]

uses much less memory thus we can treat larger system instances. Our approach scales up to 130 sensors whereas the analysis of the original system runs out of memory already for the instance with 12 sensors.

Our second case study [3] belongs to the class of EPL protocols. Once again there is one controller with multiple sensors, each sensor has a single (complex) resetting edge where quasi-dependent and non-quasi-dependent variables are updated. We verified that all sensors receive and acknowledge each message sent by the controller. The results for our settings range from 7 to 11 sensors and are presented in Table 4. Although it always takes SpaceEx less time to analyse the transformed system than to analyse the original system, we observe that the speed-up is smaller than for the FSN benchmark. This can be explained by the fact that we are able to completely remove the interleaving "diamond" in case of FSN because of only simple resetting edges, whereas for EPL we only reduce the number of variables while still having to analyze the interleavings induced by the update of non-quasi-dependent variables in complex resetting edges. Those interleavings also have an impact on the detection phase performance as we need to consider more paths in the abstract region graph. Still, we can observe that the analysis of the original system runs out of memory for 10 sensors, our approach can analyze larger instances.

As SpaceEx supports only continuous variables, we have, for the sake of efficiency, represented values of the discrete counter variables $rst_Y^{I_\mathcal{H}}$ and $rst_Y^{O_\mathcal{H}}$ by corresponding locations in the resetter automata.

6. CONCLUSION

In this paper, we have presented techniques to efficiently exploit the dependencies between continuous variables in hybrid automata.

The technical contribution comprises two methods: an automatic detection of quasi-dependent variables and a method to automatically transform and reduce the original system. The current prototypical implementation of our detection algorithm is backed by a linear SMT solver. Although using a rather straight-forward, constraint-based representation of regions in the abstract region graph, we have been able to achieve a significant performance speed-up. Thus, we can expect to achieve even better performance when using elaborated data structures to represent regions. Our transformation technique shrinks the set of states emerging during discrete updates of quasi-dependent variables due to the interleaving semantics. This leads to an abstracted hybrid automaton with a much smaller state space, which, however, reflects all properties of the original system.

Overall, a combination of our methods, i.e. the detection part and consequent transformation, shows very promising results compared to the application of the hybrid model checker SpaceEx to original models. Although we have only evaluated our approach on linear hybrid automata motivated by industrial, time-based protocols where the timers of the individual sensors advance at measurably different rates, our theory is generic as it uses the SMT solver (for the detecting part) and SpaceEx (for the analysis of a reduced hybrid automaton) as black-boxes. In particular, our detection algorithm leverages the power of the underlying SMT-solver, thus using dReal [22] or HySAT [23], which can handle non-linear constraints, would immediately support detection for systems with non-linear behaviour. The transformation does not depend on the class of continuous dynamics at all.

Acknowledgments.
We thank Goran Frehse for his assistance with SpaceEx during the preparation of our benchmark suite.

7. REFERENCES

[1] `http://swt.informatik.uni-freiburg.de/projects/CaseStudyRepository/hybridqdv`.

[2] T.S. Rappaport. *Wireless communications*, volume 2. Prentice Hall, 2002.

[3] G. Cena et al. Performance analysis of ethernet powerlink networks for distributed control and automation systems. *CSI*, 31(3):566–572, 2009.

[4] C. Herrera, B. Westphal, S. Feo-Arenis, M. Muñiz, and A. Podelski. Reducing quasi-equal clocks in networks of timed automata. In *FORMATS*, pages 155–170. Springer, 2012.

[5] C. Herrera, Westphal, and A. Podelski. Quasi-equal clock reduction: More networks, more queries. In *TACAS*. Springer, 2014.

[6] M. Muñiz, B. Westphal, and A. Podelski. Detecting quasi-equal clocks in timed automata. In *FORMATS*, pages 198–212. Springer, 2013.

[7] M. Karr. Affine relationships among variables of a program. *Acta Informatica*, 6(2):133–151, 1976.

[8] P. Cousot and R. Cousot. Abstract interpretation: a unified lattice model for static analysis of programs by construction or approximation of fixpoints. In *POPL*, pages 238–252. ACM, 1977.

[9] C. Daws and S. Yovine. Reducing the number of clock variables of timed automata. In *RTSS*, pages 73–81. IEEE, 1996.

[10] C. Daws and S. Tripakis. Model checking of real-time reachability properties using abstractions. In *TACAS*, pages 313–329. Springer, 1998.

[11] A. Étienne. Dynamic clock elimination in parametric timed automata. In *FSFMA*, volume 31, pages 18–31. Schloss Dagstuhl, 2013.

[12] R. Ben Salah et al. Compositional timing analysis. In *EMSOFT*, pages 39–48. ACM, 2009.

[13] G. J. Pappas. Bisimilar linear systems. *Automatica*, 39(12):2035–2047, 2003.

[14] A. J. Van der Schaft. Equivalence of dynamical systems by bisimulation. *IEEE Trans. Automatic Control*, 49(12):2160–2172, 2004.

[15] A. Girarda and G. J. Pappas. Approximate bisimulation relations for constrained linear systems. *Automatica*, 43:1307–1317, 2007.

[16] A. Girard, A. A. Julius, and G. J. Pappas. Approximate simulation relations for hybrid systems. *Discrete Event Dynamic Systems*, 18(2):163–179, 2008.

[17] R. Alur, C. Courcoubetis, et al. The algorithmic analysis of hybrid systems. *TCS*, 138(3):34, 1995.

[18] L. De Moura and N. Bjørner. Z3: An efficient smt solver. *TACAS*, pages 337–340, 2008.

[19] K. Zee, V. Kuncak, and M. Rinard. Full functional verification of linked data structures. In *PLDI*, pages 349–361. ACM, 2008.

[20] G. Frehse et al. SpaceEx: Scalable verification of hybrid systems. In *CAV*, LNCS. Springer, 2011.

[21] D. Dietsch, S. Feo Arenis, B. Westphal, and A. Podelski. Disambiguation of industrial standards through formalization and graphical languages. In *RE*, pages 265–270. IEEE, 2011.

[22] S. Gao, S. Kong, and E. M. Clarke. dReal: An SMT solver for nonlinear theories over the reals. In *CADE*, pages 208–214. Springer, 2013.

[23] M. Fränzle, C. Herde, et al. Efficient solving of large non-linear arithmetic constraint systems with complex boolean structure. *JSAT*, 1(3-4):209–236, 2007.

Stability Analysis of Large-scale Networked Control Systems with Local Networks: A Hybrid Small-gain Approach

Dominicus P. Borgers
d.p.borgers@tue.nl

W.P. Maurice H. Heemels
m.heemels@tue.nl

Control Systems Technology Group, Department of Mechanical Engineering
Eindhoven University of Technology
Eindhoven, The Netherlands

ABSTRACT

In this paper we consider large-scale networked control systems (NCSs) with multiple communication networks connecting sensors, controllers and actuators. Using a recently developed small-gain theorem for general interconnections of hybrid systems, we are able to find to find a maximum allowable transmission interval (MATI) and a maximum allowable delay (MAD) for each individual network, such that input-to-state stability of the complete NCS is guaranteed.

Categories and Subject Descriptors

G.0 [**Mathematics of Computing**]: General; J.2 [**Physical Sciences and Engineering**]: Engineering

Keywords

Networked control systems; Hybrid systems; Small-gain theorem; Input-to-state stability; Protocols

1. INTRODUCTION

Networked control systems (NCSs) are control systems in which sensor and actuation data is transmitted via a shared (wired or wireless) communication network. This offers several advantages over conventional control systems, in which sensor and actuation data is transmitted using dedicated point-to-point wired links. These advantages include reduced installation costs, better maintainability and greater flexibility. However, next to these advantages, NCSs are adversely affected by several network effects, including varying transmission intervals and delays, quantization errors and packet losses. In addition, since the network is usually shared by multiple sensor, controller and actuator nodes, there is a need for a network protocol that governs the access of the nodes to the network in order to prevent packet losses. As a result, one needs to design the network and controller in such a way that the NCS is robust to these network-induced phenomena.

In most of the available literature on NCSs it is assumed that all sensor and actuation data is transmitted over *one* single communication network, see, e.g., [14–16, 24], and the required network performance ("quality-of-service", expressed in terms of, e.g., maximum allowable transmission interval (MATI), maximum allowable delay (MAD), required network reliability, etc.) to guarantee certain stability requirements is formulated globally.

However, it is not always reasonable to assume that there is one global communication network. For example, in the control of large-scale systems it is often more convenient and cost-efficient to use a local controller for each subsystem than one global controller for the whole system. Analogously, it is much more reasonable to close the local control loops over several local communication networks, instead of one global communication network. This leads to large-scale NCSs with local communication networks operating independently and asynchronously. Clearly, the required network parameters are to be formulated locally for each individual network.

Only very few papers consider NCSs in which sensors, controllers and actuators transmit via asynchronous communication links. Included in this small collection are [10] and [8].

In [10], we derive MATIs for each local network using a small-gain approach in order to guarantee closed-loop stability. In this paper we tackle a similar problem, but we take a different approach and make use of a small-gain theorem for general networks of interconnected (hybrid) systems which are input-to-state stable (ISS), developed in [3,4], to derive network parameters for each local network, which guarantee ISS of the complete system. Since the stability analysis is based on the ISS gains of the interconnected systems, the analysis is based mostly on local information. This leads to a very systematic and modular setup, since when changing one subsystem, one only needs to find the ISS gains related to the changed subsystem in order to redo the stability analysis. Another advantage of the new approach is that it is much more general than the approach of [10], which makes it much easier to extend the results to more general control setups, to include other network-induced phenomena (e.g., quantization, transmission delays, packet losses, etc.), and even to include different types of communication networks,

HSCC'14, April 15–17, 2014, Berlin, Germany.

http://dx.doi.org/10.1145/2562059.2562129 .

such as perhaps event-triggered networks. Already in this paper we consider a more general networked control setup than in [10], and, next to varying transmission intervals, we also consider varying transmission delays. Furthermore, the current analysis leads to a tradeoff between networks in terms of their required quality-of-service, and for each local network leads to a tradeoff between its network parameters. In this way, one can design an NCS on two levels. First, on a high level, one can tradeoff the quality-of-service requirements between networks that guarantee ISS of the complete NCS. Second, for each local communication network, one can tradeoff the various network parameters to arrive at the required network quality-of-service.

The recent paper [8] also bases its result on the general small-gain theorem of [3, 4] in order to guarantee stability of the complete system. However, the paper remains at a rather abstract mathematical level without connecting local quality-of-service parameters such as MATI and MAD to input-to-state stability (ISS) gains of the communication links in order to apply the small-gain theorems of [3,4]. In this paper we derive these connections explicitly, which enables the use of these results in engineering practise. Besides, in [8] it is argued that extensions of the hybrid small-gain theorems of [3,4] are needed, as data channels are assumed to be pre-globally stable (pre-GS). Here we show that for an important class of network protocols, and in the presence of varying delays and varying transmission intervals, such an extension is not needed and one can rely on more "classical" small-gain theorems as in [3,4].

The paper is organized as follows. In Section 2 we present necessary preliminaries, and in Section 3 we describe the class of large-scale NCS considered in the paper and derive the resulting hybrid system models. We present the stability analysis in Section 4. How to find the important ISS gains is described explicitly in Section 5, and in Section 6 we demonstrate the usefulness and modularity of our results via a numerical example. Finally, possible extensions and future work are discussed in Section 7, and we end with our conclusions in Section 8.

1.1 Notation

For a vector $x \in \mathbb{R}^{n_x}$, we denote by $|x| := \sqrt{x^\top x}$ its 2-norm. For a symmetric matrix $A \in \mathbb{R}^{n\times n}$, we denote by $\lambda_M(A)$ and $\lambda_m(A)$ its maximum and minimum eigenvalue, respectively. For a matrix $A \in \mathbb{R}^{n\times m}$, we denote by $|A| := \sqrt{\lambda_M(A^\top A)}$ its induced 2-norm. By I we denote the identity matrix of appropriate size. By $\mathbb{N}$ we denote the set of natural numbers excluding zero, i.e., $\mathbb{N} := \{1, 2, \dots\}$. For $N \in \mathbb{N}$ we define the set $\bar{N} := \{1, 2, \cdots, N\}$. With $\mathcal{L}_\infty^n$ we denote the space of all essentially bounded functions of dimension n, and for a signal $w : \mathbb{R}_{\geqslant 0} \to \mathbb{R}^{n_w}$, $w \in \mathcal{L}_\infty^{n_w}$, we denote by $\|w\| = \operatorname{ess\,sup}_{t\in\mathbb{R}_{\geqslant 0}} \|w(t)\|$ its $\mathcal{L}_\infty$-norm. A function $\gamma : \mathbb{R}_{\geqslant 0} \to \mathbb{R}_{\geqslant 0}$ is a $\mathcal{K}$-function if it is continuous, strictly increasing and $\gamma(0) = 0$, and a $\mathcal{K}_\infty$-function if it is a $\mathcal{K}$-function and, in addition, $\gamma(s) \to \infty$ as $s \to \infty$. A function $\beta : \mathbb{R}_{\geqslant 0} \times \mathbb{R}_{\geqslant 0} \to \mathbb{R}_{\geqslant 0}$ is a $\mathcal{KL}$-function if for each fixed $t \geqslant 0$ the function $\beta(\cdot, t)$ is a $\mathcal{K}$-function and for each fixed $s \geqslant 0$, $\beta(s, t)$ is decreasing in t and $\beta(s, t) \to 0$ as $t \to \infty$. For a square matrix Z we write $Z \succ 0$ if Z is positive definite, and $Z \prec 0$ if Z is negative definite. For vectors $x_i \in \mathbb{R}^{n_i}$, $i \in \bar{N}$, we denote by $(x_1, \cdots, x_N)$ the vector $\begin{bmatrix} x_1^\top \cdots x_N^\top \end{bmatrix}^\top$. With $\bar{e}_i$ we denote the compound vector of all $e_j, j \in \bar{N} \setminus \{i\}$, i.e., $\bar{e}_i = (e_1, \dots, e_{i-1}, e_{i+1}, \dots, e_N)$.

For vectors $x, y \in \mathbb{R}^n$ we write $x \ngeq y$ if $x_i < y_i$ for at least one $i \in \bar{n}$. For a function $f : \mathbb{R}_{\geqslant 0} \to \mathbb{R}^n$, we use $f(t^+)$ to denote the limit $f(t^+) = \lim_{t\leftarrow s} f(s)$.

2. PRELIMINARIES

Consider a collection of N interconnected subsystems described by

$$\dot{x}_i = f_i(x, u),\ i \in \bar{N}, \tag{1}$$

where $x = (x_1, \cdots, x_N)$ is the state of the complete system, and u is an input. Note that the complete system of interconnected subsystems can be described by

$$\dot{x} = f(x, u), \tag{2}$$

where $f(x, u) = (f_1(x, u), f_2(x, u), \cdots, f_N(x, u))$.

Definition 2.1 ([18]). *The i-th subsystem of (1) is input-to-state stable (ISS) with respect to x_j, $j \in \bar{N}\setminus\{i\}$ and u, if there exist $\beta_i \in \mathcal{KL}$ and $\gamma_{ij}, \gamma_i^u \in \mathcal{K}\cup\{0\}$, with $\gamma_{ii} = 0$, such that for all $x_j \in \mathcal{L}_\infty^{n_{x_j}}$ and all $u \in \mathcal{L}_\infty^{n_u}$ the corresponding solution $x_i(t)$ starting in $x_i(0)$ satisfies*

$$|x_i(t)| \leqslant \beta_i(|x_i(0)|, t) + \sum_{j=1}^{N} \gamma_{ij}(\|x_j\|) + \gamma_i^u(\|u\|) \tag{3}$$

for all $x_i(0) \in \mathbb{R}^{n_{x_i}}$ and all $t \in \mathbb{R}_{\geqslant 0}$.

The functions γ_{ij}, γ_i^u are called (nonlinear) gains. Following [3], we can collect all γ_{ij} in a *gain matrix* $\Gamma = (\gamma_{ij})_{i,j=1}^N$, which defines the map $\Gamma : \mathbb{R}_{\geqslant 0}^N \to \mathbb{R}_{\geqslant 0}^N$ by

$$\Gamma(s) := \begin{bmatrix} \gamma_{11}(s_1) + \cdots + \gamma_{1N}(s_N) \\ \vdots \\ \gamma_{N1}(s_1) + \cdots + \gamma_{NN}(s_N) \end{bmatrix} \tag{4}$$

For functions $\alpha_i \in \mathcal{K}_\infty$, $i \in \bar{N}$, we define the diagonal operator $D : \mathbb{R}_{\geqslant 0}^N \to \mathbb{R}_{\geqslant 0}^N$ by

$$D(s) = \begin{bmatrix} (Id + \alpha_1)(s_1) \\ \vdots \\ (Id + \alpha_N)(s_N) \end{bmatrix}. \tag{5}$$

Definition 2.2 ([3]). *A gain matrix Γ satisfies the* strong small gain condition *if there exists an operator D as in (5), such that for all $s \in \mathbb{R}_{\geqslant 0}^N, s \neq 0$ we have*

$$D \circ \Gamma(s) := D(\Gamma(s)) \ngeq s. \tag{6}$$

Lemma 2.1 ([3, Theorem 4.4]). *Consider the system (1) and suppose that each subsystem is ISS with respect to x_j, $j \in \bar{N}\setminus\{i\}$ and u, i.e., (3) holds for all $i \in \bar{N}$. If Γ given by (4) satisfies the strong small gain condition (6), then the system (2) is ISS with respect to u.*

Lemma 2.2 ([3, Corollary 4.9]). *Let $\Gamma \in (\mathcal{K}\cup\{0\})^{N\times N}$ be a gain matrix. If Γ is linear, i.e., $\Gamma(s) = Gs$, then Γ satisfies the strong small gain condition (6) if and only if the spectral radius of G is less than one.*

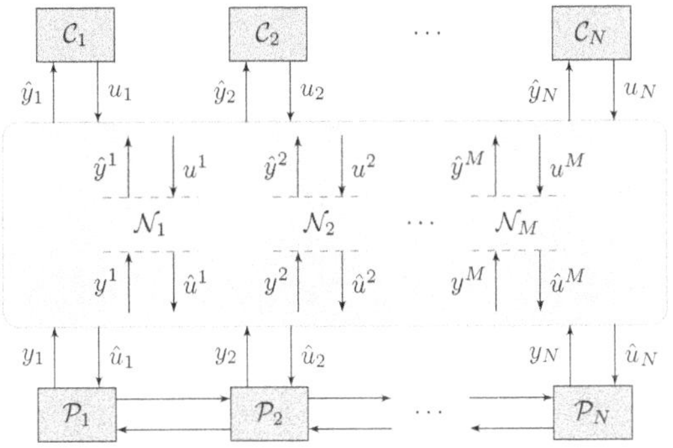

Figure 1: Networked control setup.

3. NETWORKED CONTROL SETUP

We consider the networked control setup shown in Figure 1, consisting of N physically coupled nonlinear continuous-time plants $\mathcal{P}_i$, $i \in \bar{N}$, controlled by N local controllers $\mathcal{C}_i$, $i \in \bar{N}$. The dynamics of the plants $\mathcal{P}_i$ are given by

$$\mathcal{P}_i : \begin{cases} \dot{x}_i^p &= f_i^p(x^p, \hat{u}_i, w), \\ y_i &= g_i^p(x_i^p, w), \end{cases} \tag{7}$$

where x_i^p is the state of plant $\mathcal{P}_i$, $x^p = (x_1^p, x_2^p, \cdots, x_N^p)$, y_i is the output of plant $\mathcal{P}_i$, $\hat{u}_i$ is the latest control input received by plant $\mathcal{P}_i$ and w is a disturbance signal. The dependence of f_i^p on the complete vector x^p describes the physical coupling of the plants. The controllers $\mathcal{C}_i$ are given by

$$\mathcal{C}_i : \begin{cases} \dot{x}_i^c &= f_i^c(x_i^c, \hat{y}_i, w), \\ u_i &= g_i^c(x_i^c, w), \end{cases} \tag{8}$$

where x_i^c is the state of controller $\mathcal{C}_i$, u_i its generated control input, and $\hat{y}_i$ is the latest output information received by controller $\mathcal{C}_i$, $i \in \bar{N}$.

The plant outputs y_i and control inputs u_i, $i \in \bar{N}$, are transmitted via M communication networks $\mathcal{N}_k$, $k \in \bar{M}$, which are operating independently from each other. We allow that multiple control loops are closed over one single network, or that a single control loop is closed over several different networks. This means that the output vector y_i might be transmitted via several networks. Each component in y_i and u_i, $i \in \bar{N}$, is transmitted via *exactly one* communication network, so redundant transmissions over multiple communication networks are not allowed.

We denote by y_i^k the part of y_i which is transmitted over network $\mathcal{N}_k$. Similarly, by u_i^k we denote the part of u_i which is transmitted over network $\mathcal{N}_k$. Thus, network $\mathcal{N}_k$, $k \in \bar{M}$, transmits the vector (y^k, u^k), where $y^k = (y_1^k, y_2^k, \cdots, y_N^k)$ and $u^k = (u_1^k, u_2^k, \cdots, u_N^k)$. We introduce the network-induced errors $e_k^y = \hat{y}^k - y^k$ and $e_k^u = \hat{u}^k - u^k$, which we group per network in $e_k = (e_k^y, e_k^u)$, $k \in \bar{M}$, and also into one vector $e = (e_1, e_2, \cdots, e_M)$. As a result, we can write

$$\hat{y}_i = y_i + Y_i e, \ i \in \bar{N}, \tag{9}$$

$$\hat{u}_i = u_i + U_i e, \ i \in \bar{N}, \tag{10}$$

where the matrices $Y_i \in \mathbb{R}^{n_{y_i} \times n_e}$ and $U_i \in \mathbb{R}^{n_{u_i} \times n_e}$ contain only ones and zeros. The interconnection of plants $\mathcal{P}_i$, $i \in \bar{N}$, and controllers $\mathcal{C}_i$, $i \in \bar{N}$, over the networks $\mathcal{N}_k$, $k \in \bar{M}$, leads to N controlled subsystems $\mathcal{G}_i$, given by the ordinary nonlinear dynamical systems

$$\mathcal{G}_i : \dot{x}_i = f_i(x, e, w), \ i \in \bar{N}, \tag{11}$$

where $x_i = (x_i^p, x_i^c)$, $x = (x_1, x_2, \cdots, x_N)$ and f_i is given by

$$f_i(x, e, w) = \begin{bmatrix} f_i^p(x^p, g_i^c(x_i^c, w) + U_i e, w) \\ f_i^c(x_i^c, g_i^p(x_i^p, w) + Y_i e, w) \end{bmatrix}. \tag{12}$$

We assume that the controller $\mathcal{C}_i$ is designed such that the *isolated* subsystem $\mathcal{G}_i$ is stable in the absence of disturbances and network-induced errors, i.e., the system $\dot{x}_i = f_i(x_i, 0, 0)$ is stable in an appropriate sense.

Each network $\mathcal{N}_k$, $k \in \bar{M}$, consists of several nodes, with each node corresponding to one or more elements in (y^k, u^k). At transmission times $t_{\kappa_k}^k$, the network protocol grants one of the nodes access to the network, where $\kappa_k \in \mathbb{N}$ is a counter keeping track of the transmission number of network $\mathcal{N}_k$, $k \in \bar{M}$. The node that is granted access collects the values of its corresponding entries in $(y^k(t_{\kappa_k}^k), u^k(t_{\kappa_k}^k))$, which will be transmitted over the network. This information arrives after a delay of $\tau_{\kappa_k}^k$ time units at its destination, and results in an update of the corresponding values in $(\hat{y}^k(t_{\kappa_k}^k + \tau_{\kappa_k}^k), \hat{u}^k(t_{\kappa_k}^k + \tau_{\kappa_k}^k))$, i.e., the updates of $\hat{y}^k$ and $\hat{u}^k$ satisfy

$$\hat{y}^k\left(\left(t_{\kappa_k}^k + \tau_{\kappa_k}^k\right)^+\right) = y^k\left(t_{\kappa_k}^k\right) + h_k^y\left(\kappa_k, e_k^y\left(t_{\kappa_k}^k\right)\right), \tag{13a}$$

$$\hat{u}^k\left(\left(t_{\kappa_k}^k + \tau_{\kappa_k}^k\right)^+\right) = u^k\left(t_{\kappa_k}^k\right) + h_k^u\left(\kappa_k, e_k^u\left(t_{\kappa_k}^k\right)\right). \tag{13b}$$

We will refer to $h_k = (h_k^y, h_k^u)$ as the network protocol corresponding to network $\mathcal{N}_k$, $k \in \bar{M}$.

REMARK 3.1. *The communication networks $\mathcal{N}_k$, $k \in \bar{M}$, might be of a different nature, in the sense that they might employ different network protocols, or even different communication media. For example, some networks might be wired (using e.g., CAN or HART), while others might be wireless (using e.g., Zigbee, WirelessHART or WIFI).*

For each network $\mathcal{N}_k$, $k \in \bar{M}$, we assume that the time between two subsequent transmissions is upper bounded by a maximum allowable transmission interval (MATI) τ_{mati}^k, and that the delays are upper bounded by a maximum allowable delay (MAD) τ_{mad}^k.

ASSUMPTION 3.1. *The transmission times $t_{\kappa_k}^k$ satisfy*

$$0 \leqslant t_1^k \leqslant \tau_{mati}^k, \tag{14}$$

and

$$\delta_k \leqslant t_{\kappa_k+1}^k - t_{\kappa_k}^k \leqslant \tau_{mati}^k, \tag{15}$$

for all $\kappa_k \in \mathbb{N}$, where $\delta_k \in (0, \tau_{mati}^k]$, $k \in \bar{M}$, is arbitrary. Furthermore, the communication delays $\tau_{\kappa_k}^k$ satisfy

$$0 \leqslant \tau_{\kappa_k}^k \leqslant \max\{\tau_{mad}^k, t_{\kappa_k+1}^k - t_{\kappa_k}^k\}, \tag{16}$$

for all $\kappa_k \in \mathbb{N}$.

Furthermore, we assume that $\hat{y}^k$ and $\hat{u}^k$ are held constant in between updates, i.e., the networks operate in a zero-order hold (ZOH) fashion.

To model the network-induced error dynamics in a hybrid system formulation [9], we make use of the ideas in [14] and introduce the auxiliary variables $s_k \in \mathbb{R}^{n_{e_k}}$, $\kappa_k \in \mathbb{N}$, $\tau_k \in \mathbb{R}_{\geqslant 0}$ and $l_k \in \{0,1\}$, $k \in \bar{M}$. For each network $\mathcal{N}_k$, $k \in \bar{M}$, the variable s_k is used to store information, κ_k is a counter keeping track of the transmission number, τ_k is a timer to constrain both the transmission interval and the delay, and l_k is a Boolean variable keeping track of whether the next event is a transmission or an update. To be precise, when $l_k = 0$ the next event will be a transmission and when $l_k = 1$ the next event will be an update.

Further details on this modelling approach can be found in [14]. Because of space reasons we omit these details here and just state the resulting model.

By defining $\xi_k = (e_k, s_k, \tau_k, \kappa_k, l_k)$, the network-induced error dynamics for $\mathcal{N}_k$, $k \in \bar{M}$, is given by the hybrid model [9] consisting of the flow dynamics (17a) and the jump dynamics (17b),

$$\mathcal{E}_k : \begin{cases} \left.\begin{array}{l} \dot{e}_k = g_k(x, e, w) \\ \dot{s}_k = 0 \\ \dot{\tau}_k = 1 \\ \dot{\kappa}_k = 0 \\ \dot{l}_k = 0 \end{array}\right\} & \xi_k \in \mathcal{F}_k, \quad (17a) \\ \xi_k^+ = G_k(\xi_k), & \xi_k \in \mathcal{J}_k. \quad (17b) \end{cases}$$

In (17a) the flow set $\mathcal{F}_k$ is given by

$$\mathcal{F}_k := \Big\{ \xi_k \in \mathbb{R}^{2n_{e_k}+1} \times \mathbb{N} \times \{0,1\} \Big| \\ (l_k = 0 \wedge \tau_k \in [0, \tau_{mati}^k]) \vee (l_k = 1 \wedge \tau_k \in [0, \tau_{mad}^k]) \Big\}, \quad (18)$$

and the jump set $\mathcal{J}_k$ in (17b) is given by

$$\mathcal{J}_k : \Big\{ \xi_k \in \mathbb{R}^{2n_{e_k}+1} \times \mathbb{N} \times \{0,1\} \Big| \\ (l_k = 0 \wedge \tau_k \in [\delta_k, \tau_{mati}^k]) \vee (l_k = 1 \wedge \tau_k \in [\delta_k, \tau_{mad}^k]) \Big\}. \quad (19)$$

The reset equations in (17b) are given by the transmission resets (i.e., when $l_k = 0$)

$$G_k(e_k, s_k, \tau_k, \kappa_k, 0) = (e_k, h_k(\kappa_k, e_k) - e_k, 0, \kappa_k + 1, 1) \quad (20)$$

and the update resets (i.e., when $l_k = 1$)

$$G_k(e_k, s_k, \tau_k, \kappa_k, 1) = (s_k + e_k, -s_k - e_k, \tau_k, \kappa_k, 0). \quad (21)$$

Finally, $\delta_k \in (0, \tau_{mati}^k]$, $k \in \bar{M}$, is an arbitrary parameter used to prevent Zeno behavior. See [14] for more details on this modelling approach, including the definition of the function g_k.

The networked control setup of Figure 1 can thus be viewed as an interconnection of N controlled subsystems $\mathcal{G}_i$, $i \in \bar{N}$, given by the nonlinear model (11), and M network-induced error systems $\mathcal{E}_k$, $k \in \bar{M}$, given by the hybrid model (17), leading to the control setup shown in Figure 2.

Remark 3.2. *In this paper we could allow even more general networked control setups, but for the sake of clarity and readability we will not do so. Note that the presented control setup is still very general and contains as special cases the class of systems which employ only one global communication network, and the class of systems described in [10].*

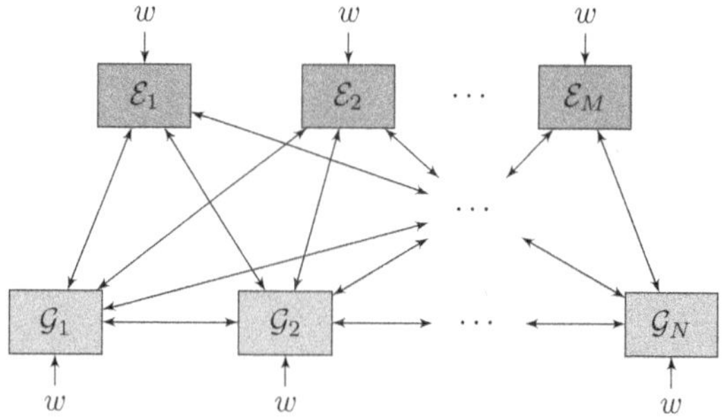

Figure 2: The networked control setup of Figure 1, viewed as an interconnection of N controlled subsystems $\mathcal{G}_i$, $i \in \bar{N}$, and M network-induced error systems $\mathcal{E}_k$, $k \in \bar{M}$.

Finally, to guarantee the existence of solutions of (11) and (17), we assume that for all $i \in \bar{N}$ and all $k \in \bar{M}$ it holds that f_i and g_k are continuous and h_k is locally bounded.

4. STABILITY ANALYSIS

By assuming ISS of all (closed-loop) subsystems (11) and all network-induced error systems (17), we can determine the stability of the complete system using the general small-gain theorem formulated in [3]. More specifically, we assume that each closed-loop subsystem (11) is ISS with respect to w, x_j, $j \in \bar{N} \setminus \{i\}$ and e_h, $h \in \bar{M}$, i.e., for each subsystem (11) the following condition holds.

Condition 4.1. *For all $x_j \in \mathcal{L}_\infty^{n_{x_j}}$, $j \in \bar{N} \setminus \{i\}$ all $e_h \in \mathcal{L}_\infty^{n_{e_h}}$, $h \in \bar{M}$, and all $w \in \mathcal{L}_\infty^{n_w}$, any corresponding solution to* (11) *satisfies*

$$|x_i(t)| \leqslant \beta_i(|x_i(0)|, t) + \sum_{j=1}^{N} \gamma_{ij}(\|x_j\|) \\ + \sum_{h=1}^{M} \gamma_{ih}^e(\|e_h\|) + \gamma_i^w(\|w\|), \quad (22)$$

where $\beta_i \in \mathcal{KL}$ and $\gamma_{ij}, \gamma_{ih}^e, \gamma_i^w \in \mathcal{K} \cup \{0\}$, and $\gamma_{ii} \equiv 0$.

Additionally, we assume that each network-induced error system (17) is ISS with respect to w, x_j, $j \in \bar{N}$, and e_h, $h \in \bar{M} \setminus \{k\}$, and the corresponding gains can be scaled by a scalar ϕ_k, where ϕ_k is a function of the network parameters, i.e., for each network-induced error system (17) the following condition holds[1].

Condition 4.2. *Under Assumption 3.1 and for all $x_j \in \mathcal{L}_\infty^{n_{x_j}}$, $j \in \bar{N}$, all $e_h \in \mathcal{L}_\infty^{n_{e_h}}$, $h \in \bar{M} \setminus \{k\}$, and all $w \in \mathcal{L}_\infty^{n_w}$,*

[1]Strictly speaking, Condition 4.2 does not imply ISS of the error system (17), but rather (a strong version of) input-to-output stability. However, since we guarantee ISS bounds as in [3] for the state variables x and e, even though the auxiliary state variables $s_k, \tau_k, \kappa_k, l_k$, $k \in \bar{M}$, do not behave in an ISS manner, we still use the term ISS here with some abuse of terminology.

any corresponding solution to (17) *satisfies*

$$|e_k(t)| \leqslant \bar{\beta}_k(|e_k(0)|, t) + \phi_k \left[\sum_{j=1}^{N} \bar{\gamma}_{kj}(\|x_j\|) + \sum_{h=1}^{M} \bar{\gamma}_{kh}^{e}(\|e_h\|) + \bar{\gamma}_k^{w}(\|w\|) \right], \quad (23)$$

where ϕ_k *is a function of the network parameters* τ_{mati}^k *and* τ_{mad}^k, $\bar{\beta}_k \in \mathcal{KL}$, $\bar{\gamma}_{kj}, \bar{\gamma}_{kh}^e, \bar{\gamma}_k^w \in \mathcal{K} \cup \{0\}$ *and* $\bar{\gamma}_{kk}^e \equiv 0$.

The scaling functions ϕ_k, $k \in \bar{M}$, depend only on the network parameters τ_{mati}^k and τ_{mad}^k, and can therefore be regarded as a measure for the network performance (quality-of-service). How to find ϕ_k, $\bar{\beta}_k$, $\bar{\gamma}_{kj}$, $\bar{\gamma}_{kh}^e$ and $\bar{\gamma}_k^w$ will be discussed in detail in Section 5.2 for uniformly globally exponentially stable (UGES) protocols [15].

If Conditions 4.1 and 4.2 and Assumption 3.1 are satisfied, then given ϕ_k, $k \in \bar{M}$, we can verify the input-to-state stability of the complete system using the following lemma, which obviously follows from Lemma 2.1.

LEMMA 4.1. *If Condition 4.1 holds for all* $i \in \bar{N}$, *Condition 4.2 holds for all* $k \in \bar{M}$, *and the gain matrix* Γ, *given by*

$$\Gamma = \begin{bmatrix} \gamma_{11} & \cdots & \gamma_{1N} & \gamma_{11}^e & \cdots & \gamma_{1M}^e \\ \vdots & & \vdots & \vdots & & \vdots \\ \gamma_{N1} & \cdots & \gamma_{NN} & \gamma_{N1}^e & \cdots & \gamma_{NM}^e \\ \phi_1\bar{\gamma}_{11} & \cdots & \phi_1\bar{\gamma}_{1N} & \phi_1\bar{\gamma}_{11}^e & \cdots & \phi_1\bar{\gamma}_{1M}^e \\ \vdots & & \vdots & \vdots & & \vdots \\ \phi_M\bar{\gamma}_{M1} & \cdots & \phi_M\bar{\gamma}_{MN} & \phi_M\bar{\gamma}_{M1}^e & \cdots & \phi_M\bar{\gamma}_{MM}^e \end{bmatrix}$$

satisfies the strong small gain condition (6), *then the complete system* (11), (17) *is ISS with respect to* w.

Concluding, once we have all the ISS gains and scaling functions, we can check the input-to-state stability of the complete NCS. For linear systems Lemma 4.1 can be easily checked using Lemma 2.2. Using these tools, we can maximize the values of ϕ_k, $k \in \bar{M}$, in Pareto optimal sense, for which the condition $D \circ \Gamma(s) \ngeq s$ holds, see also [8]. Based on the values of ϕ_k, we can derive corresponding values for τ_{mati}^k and τ_{mad}^k using the results of Section 5, where the link between ϕ_k and τ_{mati}^k and τ_{mad}^k will be made explicit.

In short, one can find network parameters for each local network that guarantee ISS of the complete NCS by using the following procedure.

PROCEDURE 4.1.

1. *Find ISS gains as in Condition 4.1 for each controlled subsystem* $\mathcal{G}_i$, $i \in \bar{N}$, *given by* (11).
2. *Determine the protocol for each network* $\mathcal{N}_k$, $k \in \bar{M}$.
3. *Find ISS gains as in Condition 4.2 for each network-induced error system* $\mathcal{E}_k$, $k \in \bar{M}$, *given by* (17).
4. *Using Lemma 4.1, find appropriate scaling functions* ϕ_k, $k \in \bar{M}$, *such that the complete NCS is ISS.*
5. *For each network* $\mathcal{N}_k$, $k \in \bar{M}$, *find appropriate network parameters (MATI and MAD), which lead to the required scaling* ϕ_k, *by using the results of Section 5.2.*

5. ISS GAINS

In this section we first show that Condition 4.1 holds for linear systems that are asymptotically stable in the absence of disturbances. Next, we derive the ISS gains and scaling factors of the network-induced error systems (17) for networks which employ UGES protocols.

5.1 Linear subsystems

Here we show that Condition 4.1 is a reasonable restriction for linear subsystems which are asymptotically stable in the absence of inputs x_j, $j \in \bar{N} \setminus \{i\}$, e_h, $h \in \bar{M}$ and w. To show this, consider the following linear subsystem $\mathcal{G}_i$

$$\dot{x}_i = A_i x_i + \sum_{\substack{j=1 \\ j \neq i}}^{N} \Delta_{ij} x_j + \sum_{h=1}^{M} B_{ih} e_h + E_i w \quad (24)$$

with A_i Hurwitz. Hence, we can find $P_i \succ 0$, $Q_i \succ 0$ such that $A_i^\top P_i + P_i A_i = -Q_i$ and $V_i(x_i) = x_i^\top P_i x_i$ satisfies

$$\underline{a}_i |x_i|^2 \leqslant V_i(x_i) \leqslant \bar{a}_i |x_i|^2$$

with $\underline{a}_i = \lambda_m(P_i)$ and $\bar{a}_i = \lambda_M(P_i)$. Moreover,

$$\dot{V}_i(x_i) \leqslant -c_i|x_i|^2 + 2|x_i| \left(\sum_{\substack{j=1 \\ j \neq i}}^{N} |P_i \Delta_{ij}||x_j| + \sum_{h=1}^{M} |P_i B_{ih}||e_h| + |P_i E_i||w| \right)$$

with $c_i = \lambda_{min}(Q_i)$. So, $\dot{V}_i(x_i) \leqslant -\varepsilon c_i |x_i|^2$, $0 < \varepsilon < 1$, if

$$|x_i| \geqslant \left(\frac{2}{c_i(1-\varepsilon)} \right) \left(\sum_{\substack{j=1 \\ j \neq i}}^{N} |P_i \Delta_{ij}||x_j| + \sum_{h=1}^{M} |P_i B_{ih}||e_h| + |P_i E_i||w| \right),$$

from which we derive that

$$|x_i(t)| \leqslant \beta_i(|x_i(0)|, t) + \sum_{j=1}^{N} \gamma_{ij}(\|x_j\|) + \sum_{h=1}^{M} \gamma_{ih}^e(\|e_h\|) + \gamma_i^w(\|w\|),$$

where

$$\beta(s,t) = \sqrt{\frac{\bar{a}_i}{\underline{a}_i}} e^{-\frac{\varepsilon c_i}{2\bar{a}_i} t} s,$$

$$\gamma_{ih}^e(s) = \left(\frac{2}{c_i(1-\varepsilon)} \right) |P_i B_{ih}| s,$$

$$\gamma_{ij}(s) = \left(\frac{2}{c_i(1-\varepsilon)} \right) |P_i \Delta_{ij}| s, \; j \neq i,$$

$$\gamma_i^w(s) = \left(\frac{2}{c_i(1-\varepsilon)} \right) |P_i E_i| s.$$

Thus, Assumption 4.1 is satisfied with linear gain functions $\gamma_{ij}, \gamma_{ih}^e, \gamma_i^w$.

5.2 Network-induced error systems with UGES protocols

In this section we derive the ISS gains and scaling factors in (23) of the network-induced error systems (17) under appropriate assumptions. We consider communication networks that suffer only from varying transmission intervals and varying delays, and which employ a uniformly globally exponentially stable (UGES) protocol [15]. This class of protocols includes the well-known Try-Once-Discard (TOD) and Round Robin (RR) protocols.

We need the following assumptions.

ASSUMPTION 5.1. *For each network-induced error system* (17)*, the protocol given by h_k is UGES, meaning that there exists a function $W_k : \mathbb{N} \times \mathbb{R}^{n_{e_k}} \to \mathbb{R}_{\geqslant 0}$ that is locally Lipschitz in its second argument such that for all $\kappa_k \in \mathbb{N}$ and all $e_k \in \mathbb{R}^{n_{e_k}}$*

$$\underline{a}_k^W |e_k| < W_k(\kappa_k, e_k) \leqslant \bar{a}_k^W |e_k| \tag{25}$$

$$W_k(\kappa_k + 1, h_k(\kappa_k, e_k)) \leqslant \lambda_k W_k(\kappa_k, e_k) \tag{26}$$

for constants $0 \leqslant \underline{a}_k^W \leqslant \bar{a}_k^W$ and $0 < \lambda_k < 1$.

ASSUMPTION 5.2. *For each network-induced error system* (17)*, the function W_k satisfies for all $\kappa_k \in \mathbb{N}$ and all $e_k \in \mathbb{R}^{n_{e_k}}$*

$$W_k(\kappa_k + 1, e_k) \leqslant \lambda_k^W W_k(\kappa_k, e_k) \tag{27}$$

for some constant $\lambda_k^W \geqslant 1$, and satisfies for almost all $e_k \in \mathbb{R}^{n_{e_k}}$ and all $\kappa_k \in \mathbb{N}$

$$\left| \frac{\partial W_k}{\partial e_k}(\kappa_k, e_k) \right| \leqslant M_k^W \tag{28}$$

for some $M_k^W > 0$. Additionally, for all $x_j \in \mathbb{R}^{n_{x_j}}$, $j \in \bar{N}$ and all $e_h \in \mathbb{R}^{n_{e_h}}$, $h \in \bar{M} \setminus \{k\}$, the growth of e_k is bounded during flow by

$$|g_k(x, e, w)| \leqslant M_k^e |e_k| + \sum_{j=1}^{N} \hat{\gamma}_{kj}(|x_j|) + \sum_{\substack{h=1 \\ h \neq k}}^{M} \hat{\gamma}_{kh}^e(|e_h|) + \hat{\gamma}_k^w(|w|), \tag{29}$$

where $M_k^e \geqslant 0$, and $\hat{\gamma}_{kj}, \hat{\gamma}_{kh}^e, \hat{\gamma}_k^w \in \mathcal{K} \cup \{0\}$ for all $j \in \bar{N}$ and all $h \in \bar{M} \setminus \{k\}$.

Note that for $x_j \in \mathcal{L}_\infty^{n_{x_j}}$, $j \in \bar{N}$, and $e_h \in \mathcal{L}_\infty^{n_{e_h}}$, $h \in \bar{M}$, the right-hand side of (29) is upper bounded by $M_k^e |e_k| + m_k(x, \bar{e}_k, w)$ with $m_k : \mathbb{R}_{\geqslant 0}^{N+M} \to \mathbb{R}_{\geqslant 0}$ given by

$$m_k(x, \bar{e}_k, w) := \sum_{j=1}^{N} \hat{\gamma}_{kj}(\|x_j\|) + \sum_{\substack{h=1 \\ h \neq k}}^{M} \hat{\gamma}_{kh}^e(\|e_h\|) + \hat{\gamma}_k^w(\|w\|). \tag{30}$$

From Assumptions 5.1 and 5.2 it follows that for almost all e_k and all κ_k

$$\left\langle \frac{\partial W_k(\kappa_k, e_k)}{\partial e_k}, g_k(x, e, w) \right\rangle \leqslant L_k W_k(\kappa_k, e_k) + M_k^W m_k(x, \bar{e}_k, w), \tag{31}$$

where

$$L_k = \frac{M_k^W M_k^e}{\underline{a}_k^W} \tag{32}$$

and $\langle \cdot, \cdot \rangle$ denotes the inner product. We are now ready to derive the scaling factors and ISS gains, which we will first do for the case without delays in Section 5.2.1, and then for the case with delays in Section 5.2.2.

5.2.1 Varying transmission intervals

First we state our results for communication networks without delays, i.e., $\tau_{\kappa_k}^k = 0$ for all $\kappa_k \in \mathbb{N}$. Since there are no delays, we do not need the variables s_k and l_k to fully describe the network-induced error dynamics, and (17) reduces to

$$\mathcal{E}_k : \begin{cases} \left.\begin{array}{l} \dot{e}_k = g_k(x, e, w) \\ \dot{\tau}_k = 1 \\ \dot{\kappa}_k = 0 \end{array}\right\}, & \tau_k \in [0, \tau_{mati}^k], \\ \left.\begin{array}{l} e_k^+ = h_k(\kappa_k, e_k) \\ \tau_k^+ = 0 \\ \kappa_k^+ = \kappa_k + 1 \end{array}\right\}, & \tau_k \in [\delta_k, \tau_{mati}^k]. \end{cases} \tag{33}$$

THEOREM 5.1. *If*

- *Assumptions 3.1, 5.1 and 5.2,*
- $\lambda_k e^{L_k \tau_{mati}^k} < 1$,
- $\tau_{\kappa_k}^k = 0$ *for all* $\kappa_k \in \mathbb{N}$,

hold, then e_k satisfying (33) *is ISS with respect to w, x_j, $j \in \bar{N}$, and e_h, $h \in \bar{M} \setminus \{k\}$, and Condition 4.2 holds with*

$$\phi_k(\tau_{mati}^k) = \frac{e^{L_k \tau_{mati}^k} - 1}{L_k(1 - \lambda_k e^{L_k \tau_{mati}^k})}, \tag{34}$$

and

$$\bar{\gamma}_k^w = \frac{M_k^W}{\underline{a}_k^W} \hat{\gamma}_k^w, \tag{35a}$$

$$\bar{\gamma}_{kj} = \frac{M_k^W}{\underline{a}_k^W} \hat{\gamma}_{kj}, \text{ for all } j \in \bar{N}, \tag{35b}$$

$$\bar{\gamma}_{kh}^e = \frac{M_k^W}{\underline{a}_k^W} \hat{\gamma}_{kh}^e, \text{ for all } h \in \bar{M} \setminus \{k\}. \tag{35c}$$

The proof can be obtained following similar arguments as in [15, 20] and can be found in [2].

5.2.2 Varying transmission intervals and delays

Next we also allow nonzero communication delays bounded by τ_{mad}^k and $t_{\kappa_k+1}^k - t_{\kappa_k}^k$ as in Assumption 3.1, next to time-varying transmission intervals. Thus the obtained network-induced error is described by (17). In order to guarantee ISS of the network-induced errors, we make the following assumption.

ASSUMPTION 5.3. *For each network-induced error system* (17) *there exist a function $\tilde{W}_k : \mathbb{N} \times \{0, 1\} \times \mathbb{R}^{n_{e_k}} \times \mathbb{R}^{n_{e_k}} \to \mathbb{R}_{\geqslant 0}$ with $\tilde{W}_k(\kappa_k, l_k, \cdot, \cdot)$ locally Lipschitz for all $\kappa_k \in \mathbb{N}$ and $l_k \in \{0, 1\}$, continuous functions $H_{l_k}^k : \mathbb{R}^{n_x} \times \mathbb{R}^{n_w} \times \mathbb{R}^{n_e - n_{e_k}} \to \mathbb{R}_{\geqslant 0}$, functions $\underline{b}_k^W, \bar{b}_k^W \in \mathcal{K}_\infty$ and constants $0 \leqslant \lambda_k < 1$, $L_{l_k}^k \geqslant 0$ such that:*

- *for all $\kappa_k \in \mathbb{N}$ and all $s_k, e_k \in \mathbb{R}^{n_{e_k}}$ it holds that*

$$\tilde{W}_k(\kappa_k + 1, 1, e_k, h_k(\kappa_k, e_k) - e_k) \leqslant \lambda_k \tilde{W}_k(\kappa_k, 0, e_k, s_k) \tag{36}$$

$$\tilde{W}_k(\kappa_k, 0, s_k + e_k, -s_k - e_k) \leqslant \tilde{W}_k(\kappa_k, 1, e_k, s_k); \tag{37}$$

- *for all $\kappa_k \in \mathbb{N}$, $l_k \in \{0,1\}$ and all $s_k, e_k \in \mathbb{R}^{n_{e_k}}$ it holds that*

$$\underline{b}_k^W(|(e_k, s_k)|) \leqslant \tilde{W}_k(\kappa_k, l_k, e_k, s_k) \leqslant \bar{b}_k^W(|(e_k, s_k)|); \tag{38}$$

- *for all $\kappa_k \in \mathbb{N}$, $l_k \in \{0,1\}$, $s_k \in \mathbb{R}^{n_{e_k}}$, $x \in \mathbb{R}^{n_x}$ and almost all $e \in \mathbb{R}^{n_e}$ it holds that*

$$\left\langle \frac{\partial \tilde{W}_k(\kappa_k, l_k, e_k, s_k)}{\partial e_k}, g_k(x, e, w) \right\rangle \leqslant L_{l_k}^k \tilde{W}_k(\kappa_k, l_k, e_k, s_k) + H_{l_k}^k(x, w, \bar{e}_k). \tag{39}$$

THEOREM 5.2. *If Assumptions 3.1, 5.1 and 5.2 hold, then the function $\tilde{W}_k$ given by*

$$\tilde{W}_k(\kappa_k, l_k, e_k, s_k) := \begin{cases} \max\left\{W_k(\kappa_k, e_k), W_k(\kappa_k, e_k + s_k)\right\}, & l_k = 0, \\ \max\left\{\frac{\lambda_k}{\lambda_k^W} W_k(\kappa_k, e_k), W_k(\kappa_k, e_k + s_k)\right\}, & l_k = 1, \end{cases} \tag{40}$$

satisfies Assumption 5.3 with

$$H_0^k(x, \bar{e}_k, w) = H_1^k(x, \bar{e}_k, w) = M_W^k m^k(x, \bar{e}_k, w), \tag{41}$$

$$L_0^k = \frac{M_k^W M_k^e}{\underline{a}_k^W} \text{ and } L_1^k = \frac{\lambda_k^W M_k^W M_k^e}{\lambda_k \underline{a}_k^W}, \tag{42}$$

$\underline{b}_k^W(r) = \underline{b}_k^W r$ and $\bar{b}_k^W(r) = \bar{b}_k^W r$, where $\underline{b}_k^W$ and $\bar{b}_k^W$ are some positive constants.

If, in addition, τ_{mati}^k and τ_{mad}^k are such that

$$\lambda_k e^{L_0^k(\tau_{mati}^k - \tau_{mad}^k)} e^{L_1^k \tau_{mad}^k} < 1, \tag{43}$$

then Condition 4.2 holds with

$$\bar{\gamma}_k^w = \frac{\lambda_k^W}{\lambda_k} \frac{M_k^W}{\underline{a}_k^W} \hat{\gamma}_k^w, \tag{44a}$$

$$\bar{\gamma}_{kj} = \frac{\lambda_k^W}{\lambda_k} \frac{M_k^W}{\underline{a}_k^W} \hat{\gamma}_{kj}, \text{ for all } j \in \bar{N}, \tag{44b}$$

$$\bar{\gamma}_{kh}^e = \frac{\lambda_k^W}{\lambda_k} \frac{M_k^W}{\underline{a}_k^W} \hat{\gamma}_{kh}^e, \text{ for all } h \in \bar{M} \setminus \{k\}, \tag{44c}$$

and

$$\phi_k(\tau_{mati}^k, \tau_{mad}^k) = \frac{L_0^k F_0^k F_1^k + (L_1^k - L_0^k) F_0^k - L_1^k}{L_0^k L_1^k \left(1 - \lambda_k F_0^k F_1^k\right)}, \tag{45}$$

where

$$F_0^k = e^{L_0^k(\tau_{mati}^k - \tau_{mad}^k)} \tag{46}$$

and

$$F_1^k = e^{L_1^k \tau_{mad}^k}. \tag{47}$$

The proof can be found in [2].

REMARK 5.3. *Note that $\phi_k(\tau_{mati}^k, 0)$ in (45) is larger than $\phi_k(\tau_{mati}^k)$ in (34), and that the gains $\gamma_{kj}, \gamma_{kh}^e$ of (44) are larger than the gains $\gamma_{kj}, \gamma_{kh}^e$ of (35). In other words, by introducing transmission delays in the analysis, the estimates of the scaling factors and ISS gains of the network-induced errors immediately become more conservative.*

To show how $\phi_k(\tau_{mati}^k, \tau_{mad}^k)$ depends on τ_{mati}^k and τ_{mad}^k, we show in Figure 3 which combinations of τ_{mati}^k and τ_{mad}^k lead to a certain value of ϕ_k, for a communication network with $\lambda_k^W = 1$, $\lambda_k = \sqrt{1/2}$, $L_0^k = 50$ and $L_1^k = \lambda_k^W L_0^k / \lambda_k$. From this figure it is apparent that there is a tradeoff of MATI versus MAD, and that the size of the tradeoff depends on the value of ϕ_k.

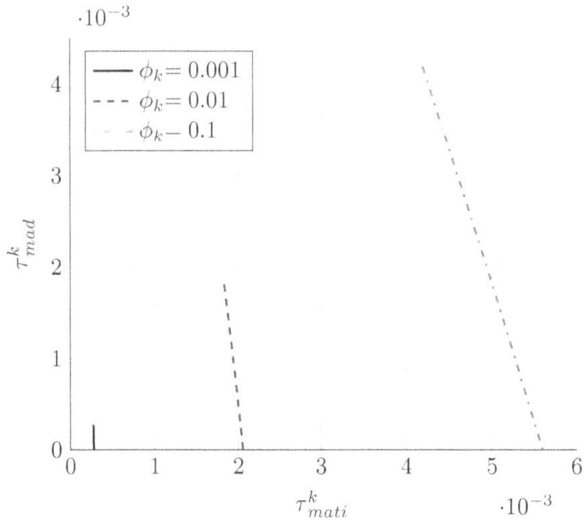

Figure 3: Tradeoff of MATI versus MAD for a network with $\lambda_k^W = 1$, $\lambda_k = \sqrt{1/2}$, $L_0^k = 50$, $L_1^k = \lambda_k^W L_0^k / \lambda_k$.

6. NUMERICAL EXAMPLE

To illustrate the findings of the paper, we consider the problem of stabilizing two coupled cart-pendulum systems $\mathcal{P}_i$, $i = 1, 2$, with the pendula in their (unstable) upright equilibrium, see Figure 4. This is the same example as in [10]. Each subsystem consists of a moving support (cart) with mass M_i, a rigid massless beam of length l_i, and a point mass m_i attached to the end of the beam, $i = 1, 2$. The pendula are coupled via a linear spring with stiffness k. The system is actuated via input forces $\hat{u}_i$, $i = 1, 2$.

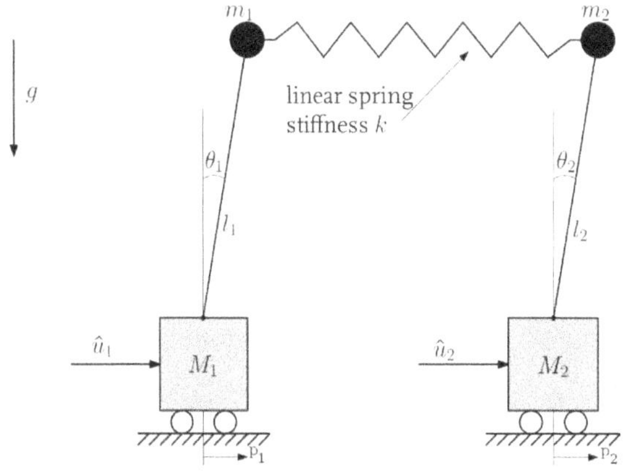

Figure 4: Schematic of the two coupled cart-pendulum systems.

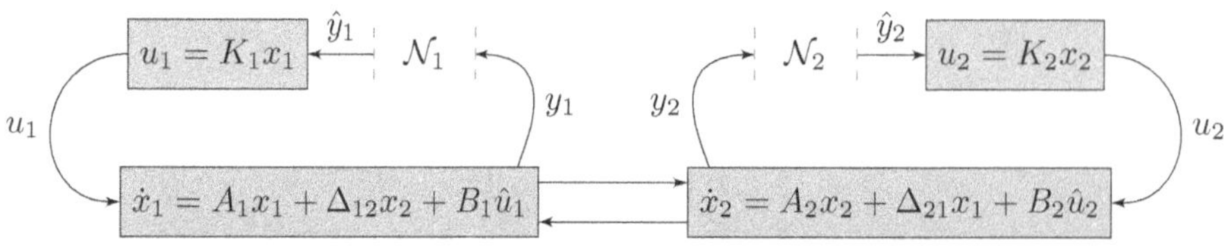

Figure 5: Networked control setup of the two coupled cart-pendulum systems.

Linearizing the pendula around their unstable upright equilibria, we find,

$$\dot{x}_1 = A_1 x_1 + \Delta_{12} x_2 + B_1 \hat{u}_1, \tag{48}$$
$$\dot{x}_2 = A_2 x_2 + \Delta_{21} x_1 + B_2 \hat{u}_2, \tag{49}$$

where $x_i = (p_i, \dot{p}_i, \theta_i, \dot{\theta}_i)$ is the state variable of subsystem $\mathcal{P}_i$, $i = 1, 2$. The numerical values of all parameters and matrices that are used in this example can be found in [10].

Each subsystem has its own decentralized controller collocated with the actuator (and thus $\hat{u}_i = u_i$, $i = 1, 2$), given by $u_i = K_i \hat{x}_i$, where K_i are such that the eigenvalues of $A_1 + B_1 K_1$ are $\{-1, -2, -3, -4\}$, and the eigenvalues of $A_2 + B_2 K_2$ are $\{-2, -3, -4, -5\}$.

Furthermore, each subsystem employs its own local network as in Figure 5, over which the state values $y_i = x_i$ are transmitted to the controller. The flow dynamics of the closed-loop hybrid model can then be written in the form

$$\dot{x}_1 = (A_1 + B_1 K_1) x_1 + \Delta_{12} x_2 + B_1 K_1 e_1, \tag{50a}$$
$$\dot{x}_2 = (A_2 + B_2 K_2) x_2 + \Delta_{21} x_1 + B_2 K_2 e_2, \tag{50b}$$
$$\dot{e}_1 = -\dot{x}_1, \tag{50c}$$
$$\dot{e}_2 = -\dot{x}_2 \tag{50d}$$

in which $e_k = \hat{x}_k - x_k$, $k = 1, 2$ are the network-induced (state) errors.

For subsystems (50a) and (50b) we derive ISS gains γ_{12}, γ_{11}^e, γ_{21} and γ_{22}^e satisfying Condition 4.1 by using the procedure described in Section 5.1 and local Lyapunov functions $V_i(x_i) = x_i^\top P_i x_i$ satisfying

$$(A_i + B_i K_i)^\top P_i + P_i (A_i + B_i K_i) = -3I. \tag{51}$$

We assume that the networks suffer from varying transmission intervals and varying delays, satisfying Assumption 3.1, but not from other network effects, such as packet dropouts and quantization. Furthermore, we assume that both networks employ the TOD protocol, which satisfies Assumption 5.1 with $W_k(\kappa_k, e_k) = |e_k|$, $\underline{a}_k^W = \bar{a}_k^W = 1$, and $\lambda_k = \sqrt{(n_k - 1)/n_k}$, where n_k is the number of nodes in network $\mathcal{N}_k$ [15]. Then, using (50), we find that Assumption 5.2 is satisfied with

$$\lambda_k^W = 1, \tag{52a}$$
$$M_k^W = 1, \tag{52b}$$
$$M_k^e = |B_k K_k|, \tag{52c}$$
$$\hat{\gamma}_{kk}(|x_k|) = |A_k + B_k K_k||x_k|, \tag{52d}$$
$$\hat{\gamma}_{kj}(|x_j|) = |\Delta_{kj}||x_j|, \; j \neq k, \tag{52e}$$
$$\hat{\gamma}_{kh}^e(|e_h|) = 0, \; h \neq k. \tag{52f}$$

The gain matrix now becomes

$$\Gamma = \begin{bmatrix} 0 & \gamma_{12} & \gamma_{11}^e & 0 \\ \gamma_{21} & 0 & 0 & \gamma_{22}^e \\ \phi_1 \bar{\gamma}_{11} & \phi_1 \bar{\gamma}_{12} & 0 & 0 \\ \phi_2 \bar{\gamma}_{21} & \phi_2 \bar{\gamma}_{22} & 0 & 0 \end{bmatrix}. \tag{53}$$

We can now use Procedure 4.1 and the results of Section 5.2 to find suitable values for $\tau_{mati}^k, \tau_{mad}^k$, $k = 1, 2$. Since in this case $\Gamma(s)$ is linear we use Lemma 2.2 to maximize ϕ_2 for each given scalar ϕ_1 thus finding Pareto optimal values for ϕ_1 and ϕ_2 such that $\Gamma(s)$ satisfies the strong small gain condition,

First we consider the delay-free case. Using Theorem 5.1, we find a tradeoff of τ_{mati}^1 versus τ_{mati}^2, shown in Figure 6. From Figure 6 we can see that by decreasing τ_{mati}^1 we can allow a larger τ_{mati}^2, and vice versa. This is a very useful result, since it implies that we can decrease the required performance of one network by improving the other. The figure also shows the MATIs found in [10], and we can see that the approach of Section 5.2.1 is, at least for this example, no more conservative than the approach of [10], while we gain the freedom of trading MATIs.

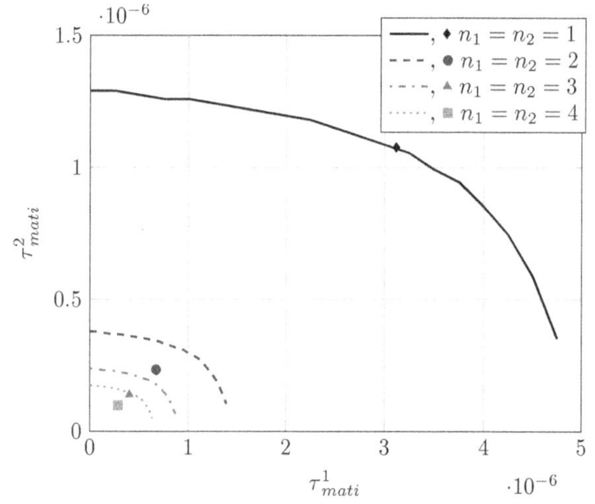

Figure 6: Tradeoff of τ_{mati}^1 versus τ_{mati}^2 for the delay-free case, for varying number of nodes per network n_i. The MATIs found in [10] are shown with marks for comparison.

Next we also allow delays, so we have to use the results of Section 5.2.2 for finding $\tau_{mati}^k, \tau_{mad}^k$, $i = 1, 2$. Again maximizing ϕ_2 for each ϕ_1, we find a tradeoff curve of ϕ_1 versus ϕ_2, shown in Figure 7(a) for $n_1 = n_2 = 2$. For each network we can now trade τ_{mati}^i versus τ_{mad}^i to arrive at a given value of ϕ_k, $k = 1, 2$. For network $\mathcal{N}_1$ this tradeoff is shown in Figure 7(b), again for $n_1 = 2$. From this figure we can

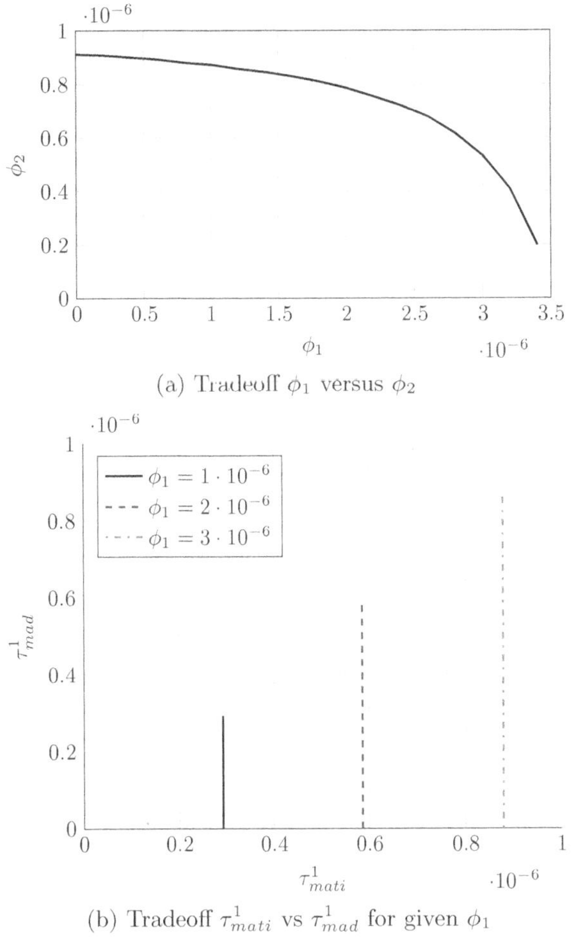

(a) Tradeoff ϕ_1 versus ϕ_2

(b) Tradeoff τ^1_{mati} vs τ^1_{mad} for given ϕ_1

Figure 7: The tradeoff curve of ϕ_1 versus ϕ_2, and the tradeoff of τ^i_{mati} versus τ^i_{mad} for network $\mathcal{N}_1$, for the case with delays and with $n_1 = n_2 = 2$.

see that for this example, the dependence of ϕ_1 on τ^1_{mad} is negligible, and that we can allow any delay bounded by the transmission interval, without any significant change in τ^1_{mati}.

7. POSSIBLE EXTENSIONS AND FUTURE WORK

The presented stability analysis is of course not limited to the communication networks described in this paper. An important observation from [8] is that ISS of the communication networks is sufficient, but not necessary to guarantee ISS of the plant and controller states of the interconnected system. For this, it is sufficient that the network-induced errors are globally stable (GS). Certainly, non-UGES protocols can be allowed, as long the resulting network-induced error systems are GS, see, e.g., [15].

Furthermore, instead of only considering time-triggered networks (characterized by MATIs), also event-triggered networks can be allowed. In an event-triggered network, the transmission times are not determined (or restricted) based on time, but based on the actual information content of the involved signals, see, e.g., [12] for a recent overview. This guarantees that transmissions only occur when necessary, reducing the load on the network. For such networks it is trivial to find the ISS gains of the network-induced error system, since these gains can be directly enforced by the choice of event-triggering mechanism (ETM), see, e.g., [21]. Interesting and useful results in this direction have already been published in [6], where decentralized ETMs are derived using the general small-gain theorem of [4]. Furthermore, in [17] event-triggered control is studied in the setting of networks using UGES protocols. The key problem in event-triggered control is preventing Zeno behavior, i.e., it is necessary that a nonzero minimum transmission interval is guaranteed, and that this minimum transmission interval is robust to disturbances [1]. Most works in the literature guaranteeing this property only consider setups in which events are generated based on the full state of the system, however, when only using output information it is in general an open question how to prevent Zeno behavior. Possible solutions would be to resort to periodic event-triggered control (PETC) systems [11], in which the event-triggering mechanism is not evaluated continuously, but rather periodically, or to evaluate the ETM only after a predetermined lower time threshold has elapsed [5, 13, 22, 23]. These approaches automatically guarantee a positive minimum transmission interval. Such event-triggered communication networks can then directly be incorporated in the above stability analysis, without any significant changes. Another option would be to add an absolute threshold to the triggering condition as in [7], for which a semi-global lower bound on the inter-event times can be guaranteed. This would lead to input-to-state practically stable (ISpS) systems, which also fit into the framework proposed in this paper.

Furthermore, we aim to extend the current results to packet losses (with [19] being an interesting starting point), delays greater than the transmission interval and quantization effects. Finally, we hope to reduce the conservatism of the current results, to get larger MATIs and MADs guaranteeing stability of the complete system.

8. CONCLUSIONS

We used a recently introduced small-gain theorem for general networks to analyze the stability of a large class of large-scale networked control systems with multiple communication networks.

The class of NCSs we considered can be modelled as an interconnection of ordinary nonlinear systems (the controlled subsystems) and hybrid systems (the communication networks). We assumed that all controlled subsystems are ISS, and we showed that networks that employ UGES protocols give rise to ISS error systems with ISS gains that can be scaled by a function ϕ, which is a function of the network parameters (MATI and MAD). Then, by using the general small-gain theorem, we can optimize the scaling functions ϕ_k corresponding to networks $\mathcal{N}_k$, $k \in \bar{M}$ in a Pareto optimal sense. This leads to a tradeoff between the scaling functions. Once the scaling function of a network is determined, one can tradeoff its MATI versus its MAD to meet the required value of ϕ.

Based on this analysis we find that by increasing the performance of one network (where the performance of a network is characterized by its scaling function ϕ), we can decrease the required performance of other networks. Furthermore, by decreasing the MATI of a network, we can allow a larger MAD, while not decreasing the network performance.

Since the stability analysis is only based on the ISS gains of the subsystems and the network-induced error systems, it is very easy to use different types of communication networks in one NCS. For example, it is possible to mix both time-triggered and event-triggered networks, and also to mix different UGES or even non-UGES protocols, as discussed in Section 7. Furthermore, when changing, removing or adding a communication network, one only needs to find the ISS gains related to the changed or added network in order to redo the stability analysis.

9. ACKNOWLEDGEMENTS

This work is supported by the Innovational Research Incentives Scheme under the VICI grant "Wireless control systems: A new frontier in automation" (No. 11382) awarded by NWO (The Netherlands Organization for Scientific Research) and STW (Dutch Science Foundation), and the European 7th Framework Network of Excellence "Highly-complex and networked control systems" (HYCON2) (grant agreement no. 257462).

10. REFERENCES

[1] D.P. Borgers and W.P.M.H. Heemels, *On minimum inter-event times in event-triggered control*, Decision and Control (CDC), 2013 52nd IEEE Conference on, 2013, to appear.

[2] ———, *Stability analysis of large-scale networked control systems with local networks: A hybrid small-gain approach*, Tech. report, Eindhoven University of Technology, 2014, Technical report, available online at http://www.heemels.tue.nl/content/papers/BorHee_TUE14a.pdf.

[3] S.N. Dashkovskiy, B.S. Rüffer, and F.R. Wirth, *An ISS small gain theorem for general networks*, Mathematics of Control, Signals, and Systems **19** (2007), no. 2, 93–122.

[4] ———, *Small gain theorems for large scale systems and construction of ISS lyapunov functions*, SIAM Journal on Control and Optimization **48** (2010), no. 6, 4089–4118.

[5] C. De Persis, R. Sailer, and F. Wirth, *On inter-sampling times for event-triggered large-scale linear systems*, Decision and Control (CDC), 2013 52nd IEEE Conference on, 2013, to appear.

[6] C. De Persis, R. Sailer, and H. Wirth, *Parsimonious event-triggered distributed control: A zeno free approach*, Automatica **49** (2013), no. 7, 2116–2124.

[7] M.C.F. Donkers and W.P.M.H. Heemels, *Output-based event-triggered control with guaranteed $\mathcal{L}_\infty$-gain and improved and decentralized event-triggering*, Automatic Control, IEEE Transactions on **57** (2012), no. 6, 1362–1376.

[8] R. Geiselhart and F.R. Wirth, *On maximal gains guaranteeing a small-gain condition*, Submitted for publication.

[9] R. Goebel, R.G. Sanfelice, and A.R. Teel, *Hybrid dynamical systems: Modeling, stability, and robustness*, Princeton University Press, 2012.

[10] W.P.M.H. Heemels, D.P. Borgers, N. Van de Wouw, D. Nešić, and A.R. Teel, *Stability analysis of nonlinear networked control systems with asynchronous communication: A small-gain approach*, Decision and Control (CDC), 2013 52nd IEEE Conference on, 2013, to appear, available online at http://www.dct.tue.nl/New/Heemels/Conferences/HeeBor_CDC_13.pdf.

[11] W.P.M.H. Heemels, M.C.F. Donkers, and A.R. Teel, *Periodic event-triggered control for linear systems*, Automatic Control, IEEE Transactions on **58** (2013), no. 4, 847–861.

[12] W.P.M.H. Heemels, K.H. Johansson, and P. Tabuada, *An introduction to event-triggered and self-triggered control*, Decision and Control (CDC), 2012 IEEE 51st Annual Conference on, 2012, pp. 3270–3285.

[13] W.P.M.H. Heemels, J.H. Sandee, and P.P.J. Van Den Bosch, *Analysis of event-driven controllers for linear systems*, International journal of control **81** (2008), no. 4, 571–590.

[14] W.P.M.H. Heemels, A.R. Teel, N. Van de Wouw, and D. Nešić, *Networked control systems with communication constraints: Tradeoffs between transmission intervals, delays and performance*, Automatic Control, IEEE Transactions on **55** (2010), no. 8, 1781–1796.

[15] D. Nešić and A.R. Teel, *Input-output stability properties of networked control systems*, Automatic Control, IEEE Transactions on **49** (2004), no. 10, 1650–1667.

[16] ———, *Input-to-state stability of networked control systems*, Automatica **40** (2004), no. 12, 2121–2128.

[17] R. Postoyan, P. Tabuada, D. Nešić, and A. Anta, *Event-triggered and self-triggered stabilization of distributed networked control systems*, Decision and Control and European Control Conference (CDC-ECC), 2011 50th IEEE Conference on, 2011, pp. 2565–2570.

[18] E. D. Sontag and Y. Wang, *On characterizations of the input-to-state stability property*, Systems and Control Letters **24** (1995), no. 5, 351–359.

[19] M. Tabbara and D. Nešić, *Input-output stability of networked control systems with stochastic protocols and channels*, Automatic Control, IEEE Transactions on **53** (2008), no. 5, 1160–1175.

[20] ———, *Input-output stability with input-to-state stable protocols for quantized and networked control systems*, Decision and Control (CDC), 2008 47th IEEE Conference on, 2008, pp. 2680–2685.

[21] P. Tabuada, *Event-triggered real-time scheduling of stabilizing control tasks*, Automatic Control, IEEE Transactions on **52** (2007), no. 9, 1680–1685.

[22] P. Tallapragada and N. Chopra, *Event-triggered decentralized dynamic output feedback control for LTI systems*, IFAC Workshop on Distributed Estimation and Control in Networked Systems, 2012, pp. 31–36.

[23] ———, *Event-triggered dynamic output feedback control for LTI systems*, Decision and Control (CDC), 2012 IEEE 51st Annual Conference on, 2012, pp. 6597–6602.

[24] G.C. Walsh, O. Beldiman, and L.G. Bushnell, *Asymptotic behavior of nonlinear networked control systems*, Automatic Control, IEEE Transactions on **46** (2001), no. 7, 1093–1097.

Model Reduction of Switched Affine Systems: a Method Based on Balanced Truncation and Randomized Optimization

Alessandro Vittorio Papadopoulos
Politecnico di Milano, Dipartimento di Elettronica, Informazione e Bioingegneria
Milano, Italy
papadopoulos@elet.polimi.it

Maria Prandini
Politecnico di Milano, Dipartimento di Elettronica, Informazione e Bioingegneria
Milano, Italy
prandini@elet.polimi.it

ABSTRACT

This paper proposes an approach to build a reduced order model for a Switched Affine (SA) system. The main idea is to transform the SA system into an equivalent Switched Linear (SL) system with state reset, and then apply balanced truncation to each mode and redefine the reset maps so as to best reproduce the free evolution of the system output. A randomized method is proposed for order selection in the case when the input is stochastic and one is interested in reproducing the output of the original SA system over a finite time-horizon. The performance of the approach is shown on a benchmark example.

Categories and Subject Descriptors

G.1.2 [**Mathematics of Computing**]: Approximation;
G.1.6 [**Mathematics of Computing**]: Optimization—*Stochastic programming*

Keywords

Model reduction; Switched systems; Randomized algorithms

1. INTRODUCTION

This paper deals with the problem of approximating a hybrid system by means of some simpler model, see e.g. [12,13,15,19,22,26] to cite a few. Hybrid systems are characterized by intertwined continuous and discrete dynamics, and are suitable for modeling complex, large scale systems, as shown in [18] where an overview on the application of hybrid models to various domains is presented. The study of hybrid systems is more challenging than that for other classes of systems, and many problems still lack an effective solution. In particular, this is the case for the design of reduced order models.

In this paper, we focus on the design of an approximate model for a switched affine system. More specifically, our goal is to obtain a simpler model of the system which can be effectively used for system verification over some finite horizon T.

HSCC'14, April 15–17, 2014, Berlin, Germany.
Copyright 2014 ACM 978-1-4503-2732-9/14/04 ...$15.00.
http://dx.doi.org/10.1145/2562059.2562131.

Verification of properties related to the hybrid system evolution, like, e.g., safety and reach/avoid properties, are typically addressed through numerical methods that scale badly with the state-space dimension, [1,2,9,11,16,20,24,27]. The aim of the approximation is then to build a model that mimics the behavior of the original system and that can be used in place of the system to scale-up numerical methods for the verification of the property of interest. When the hybrid system input is stochastic, the notion of approximate simulation introduced in [15] can be used to quantify the model performance.

The approach proposed in this paper is inspired by [19], where a balanced truncation is adopted for reducing the order of the linear dynamics governing the evolution of the continuous component of an hybrid system. The main advances with respect to [19] are

- the extension to the class of switched affine systems;
- the introduction of a novel method for defining the state reset map that provides better performance than the one adopted in [19]; and
- the introduction of a procedure to select the order of the reduced model based on a randomized approach, when the input is stochastic.

Note that, differently from most of the works on switched affine (or linear) system reduction, [23, 26], the transitions between discrete modes in the considered switched affine system class are determined by an endogenous signal that depends on the continuous state evolution, which makes the approximation problem more challenging.

The rest of the paper is organized as follows. We start with a brief review of balanced truncation for linear systems in Section 2. We then describe the considered switched affine system class (Section 3) and the proposed model reduction method (Section 4). The randomized approach to model order selection is illustrated in Section 5, whilst a numerical example showing the performance of the approach is presented in Section 6. Finally, some concluding remarks are drawn in Section 7.

2. BALANCED TRUNCATION FOR LINEAR SYSTEMS: A BRIEF REVIEW

There is a vast literature on model order reduction for linear systems (see e.g. [4, 14, 21]). In particular, balanced truncation is one of the more popular techniques, and the one adopted here for reducing the order of the continuous dynamics within each mode. The balanced truncation method rests on the representation of the system in the balanced realization form, which is recalled next for the purpose of self-containedness.

Let $\mathscr{S}$ be a continuous-time linear time-invariant dynamic system described in state-space form through a 4-tuple of matrices $(\mathscr{A},\mathscr{B},\mathscr{C},\mathscr{D})$:

$$\mathscr{S}:\begin{pmatrix}\mathscr{A} & \mathscr{B}\\ \mathscr{C} & \mathscr{D}\end{pmatrix}.$$

Suppose that $\mathscr{S}$ is controllable, observable and asymptotically stable.

DEFINITION 1 (BALANCED SYSTEM). *System $\mathscr{S}$ is* balanced *if $\mathscr{W}_c=\mathscr{W}_o$, where*

$$\mathscr{W}_c=\int_0^\infty e^{\mathscr{A}\tau}\mathscr{B}\mathscr{B}^T e^{\mathscr{A}^T\tau}\,\mathrm{d}\tau$$
$$\mathscr{W}_o=\int_0^\infty e^{\mathscr{A}^T\tau}\mathscr{C}^T\mathscr{C}e^{\mathscr{A}\tau}\,\mathrm{d}\tau$$

are, respectively, the infinite controllability *and* observability Gramians *of $\mathscr{S}$. Furthermore, $\mathscr{S}$ is* principal-axis balanced *if $\mathscr{W}_c=\mathscr{W}_o=\Sigma$, with*

$$\Sigma=\mathrm{diag}\{\sigma_1,\sigma_2,\ldots,\sigma_n\},$$

where σ_i are the Hankel singular values of $\mathscr{S}$, listed in decreasing order.

The problem of finding the balanced realization of a system is equivalent to that of determining a balancing transformation matrix T such that

$$\begin{cases}W_c=T\mathscr{W}_cT^*\\ W_o=T^{-*}\mathscr{W}_oT^{-1}\end{cases}\Rightarrow W_cW_o=T\left(\mathscr{W}_c\mathscr{W}_o\right)T^{-1}=\Sigma^2,$$

where T^* denotes the Hermitian adjoint of T, which, in turn, reduces to solving the following minimization problem [4]

$$\min_T \mathrm{tr}\left[T\mathscr{W}_cT^*+T^{-*}\mathscr{W}_oT^{-1}\right]=2\,\mathrm{tr}\{\Sigma\}. \tag{1}$$

The system in the balanced state-space form is then obtained by applying the transformation matrix T, i.e.,

$$S:\begin{pmatrix}A & B\\ C & D\end{pmatrix}=\begin{pmatrix}T\mathscr{A}T^{-1} & T\mathscr{B}\\ \mathscr{C}T^{-1} & \mathscr{D}\end{pmatrix}.$$

The idea of the balanced truncation method is that in the balanced realization the state variables are ordered by decreasing importance as for their contribution to the input/output map, so that one can decompose the state vector (and the system) into two parts and neglect that with lowest importance. Formally, vector x is separated into two components

$$x=\begin{bmatrix}x_1\\ x_2\end{bmatrix},\quad S:\begin{pmatrix}A_{11} & A_{12} & B_1\\ A_{21} & A_{22} & B_2\\ C_1 & C_2 & D\end{pmatrix}.$$

with $x_1\in\mathbb{R}^{n_r}$ and $x_2\in\mathbb{R}^{n-n_r}$. Correspondingly,

$$\Sigma=\begin{bmatrix}\Sigma_1 & 0\\ 0 & \Sigma_2\end{bmatrix},$$

and if Σ_1 and Σ_2 do not contain any common element, then, the matrices A_{ii} $(i=1,2)$ are asymptotically stable [17].

A reduced order model S_r of the system can then be obtained by setting $x_2=0$ and eliminating its contribution, thus getting:

$$S_r:\begin{pmatrix}A_r & B_r\\ C_r & D_r\end{pmatrix}=\begin{pmatrix}A_{11} & B_1\\ C_1 & D\end{pmatrix}.$$

Alternatively, one can set $\dot{x}_2=0$, thus obtaining

$$S_r:\begin{pmatrix}A_r & B_r\\ C_r & D_r\end{pmatrix}=\begin{pmatrix}A_{11}-A_{12}A_{22}^{-1}A_{21} & B_1-A_{12}A_{22}^{-1}B_2\\ C_1-C_2A_{22}^{-1}A_{21} & D-C_2A_{22}^{-1}B_2\end{pmatrix}. \tag{2}$$

An estimate of the neglected state x_2 is then given by

$$\widehat{x}_2=-A_{22}^{-1}A_{21}x_1-A_{22}^{-1}B_2u, \tag{3}$$

which corresponds to the condition $\dot{x}_2=0$. If Σ_1 and Σ_2 do not contain any common element, then, S_r is asymptotically stable, controllable and observable [17]. Moreover, the static gain of S_r is equal to that of the original system S.

In order to select the order of the reduced model, one can choose $\gamma\in[0,1]$ and set

$$n_r=\min\{i\in\{1,2,\ldots,n\}:\psi(i)<\gamma\},$$

where $\psi:\{1,2,\ldots n\}\to[0,1)$ is defined based on the Hankel singular values $\sigma_1\geq\sigma_2\geq\cdots\geq\sigma_n$ of system S as follows:

$$\psi(i)=1-\frac{\sum_{j=1}^{i}\sigma_j}{\sum_{j=1}^{n}\sigma_j}. \tag{4}$$

The bound γ can be used as a knob to control the tradeoff between the dimension of the reduced state and the quality of the approximation.

Approximation by balanced truncation preserves stability and the difference between system S and its reduced model S_r has its $\mathscr{H}_\infty$-norm bounded by the sum of the neglected Hankel singular values as follows:

$$\|S-S_r\|_{\mathscr{H}_\infty}\leq 2\,\mathrm{tr}\{\Sigma_2\}.$$

3. MODELING FRAMEWORK

We consider the class of Switched Affine (SA) systems, whose evolution is characterized through a discrete state component q_a taking values in $Q=\{1,2,\ldots,m\}$ and a continuous component $\xi_a\in\Xi_a=\mathbb{R}^n$ evolving according to an affine dynamics that depends on the operating mode q_a. Correspondingly, the output $y_a\in Y_a=\mathbb{R}^p$ is an affine function of the state and the input $u\in U=\mathbb{R}^m$ that depends on q_a as well. In formulas:

$$\begin{cases}\dot{\xi}_a(t)=\mathscr{A}_{q_a}\xi_a(t)+\mathscr{B}_{q_a}u(t)+f_{q_a}\\ y_a(t)=\mathscr{C}_{q_a}\xi_a(t)+g_{q_a}.\end{cases} \tag{5}$$

A collection of polyhedra $\{Dom_{a,i}\subseteq Y_a\times U, i\in Q\}$ is given, which covers the whole set $Y_a\times U$[1]. Each polyhedron $Dom_{a,i}$ is defined through a system of r_i linear inequalities:

$$Dom_{a,i}=\{(y_a,u)\in Y_a\times U: G_i^{y_a}y_a+G_i^u u\leq G_i\},$$

with $G_i^{y_a}\in\mathbb{R}^{r_i\times p}$, $G_i^u\in\mathbb{R}^{r_i\times m}$ and $G_i\in\mathbb{R}^{r_i}$.
The system evolves according to the dynamics associated with mode i as long as (ξ_a,u) is such that (y_a,u) keeps evolving within $Dom_{a,i}$ and commute to the dynamics associated with $j\in Q$ as soon as (y_a,u) exits $Dom_{a,i}$ and enters into $Dom_{a,j}$.

REMARK 1. *$Dom_{a,i}$ appears to be a function of both y_a and u. However, if $G_i^u=0$, then, the dependence on u is not present. Furthermore, those cases when the transition condition depends on the whole state ξ_a can be reframed in our setting by including ξ_a in the output variables.*

[1] $\cup_{i\in Q}Dom_{a,i}=Y_a\times U$

REMARK 2. *Note that if $\{Dom_{a,i}, i \in Q\}$ is a polyhedral subdivision of $Y_a \times U$ (i.e., a finite collection of polyhedra on $Y_a \times U$ such that $\cup_{i\in Q} Dom_{a,i} = Y_a \times U$, each polyhedron $Dom_{a,i}$ is of dimension $p+m$, and the intersection $Dom_{a,i} \cap Dom_{a,j}$, $i \neq j$, is either empty or a common proper face of both polyhedra), then, the SA system reduces to a piecewise affine system.*

4. SYSTEM REDUCTION

In this section, we introduce a procedure for designing a reduced order model of the SA system (5) that tries to best reproduce its output y_a. The proposed procedure rests on Assumption 1 below, and is based on the following key steps:

- reformulation of the SA system as a Switched Linear (SL) system with state reset;
- model reduction of the SL system through balanced truncation of the continuous dynamics and definition of appropriate state reset maps when a mode transition occurs;
- reconstruction of the output of the SA system based on the reduced SL system.

ASSUMPTION 1. *For any $i \in Q$, matrix $\mathscr{A}_i$ is Hurwitz, $(\mathscr{A}_i, \mathscr{B}_i)$ is controllable, and $(\mathscr{A}_i, \mathscr{C}_i)$ is observable.*

4.1 Reformulation of the SA system as a SL system with state reset

We next build a SL system with state reset that is equivalent to the original SA system, in that (ξ_a, q_a) and y_a can be recovered exactly from the state and output variables of such a system.

Let $\xi \in \Xi = \Xi_a$ evolve according to a linear dynamics that depends on the operating mode $q \in Q$ as follows:

$$\begin{cases} \dot{\xi}(t) = \mathscr{A}_q \xi(t) + \mathscr{B}_q u(t) \\ y(t) = \mathscr{C}_q \xi(t) \end{cases} \tag{6}$$

where $y \in Y = Y_a$.

Set $\bar{y}_{a,q} = \mathscr{C}_q \bar{\xi}_{a,q} + g_q$, where $\bar{\xi}_{a,q} = -\mathscr{A}_q^{-1} f_q$, with $\mathscr{A}_q$ invertible by Assumption 1. A transition from mode $i \in Q$ to mode $j \in Q$ occurs as soon as $(y + \bar{y}_{a,i}, u)$ exits Dom_i and enters Dom_j, where $Dom_q = Dom_{a,q}$, $q \in Q$.

When a discrete transition from mode $i \in Q$ to mode $j \in Q$ occurs at time t^-, then, ξ is reset as follows

$$\xi(t) = \xi(t^-) + \bar{\xi}_{a,i} - \bar{\xi}_{a,j}. \tag{7}$$

PROPOSITION 4.1. *Suppose that the SA and SL systems are initialized with $\xi_a(0) = \xi_{a,0}$, $q_a(0) = q_{a,0}$, and $\xi(0) = \xi_{a,0} - \bar{\xi}_{a,q_{a,0}}$, $q(0) = q_{a,0}$, respectively, and are both fed by the same input $u(t)$, $t \in [0,T]$. Then, the execution of ξ_a, q_a and y_a over $[0,T]$ can be recovered from those of ξ, q and y as follows:*

$$\begin{aligned} q_a(t) &= q(t) \\ \xi_a(t) &= \xi(t) + \bar{\xi}_{a,q(t)} \\ y_a(t) &= y(t) + \bar{y}_{a,q(t)}. \end{aligned} \tag{8}$$

PROOF. The result immediately follows by observing that $\bar{\xi}_{a,q}$ and $\bar{y}_{a,q}$ are the state and output equilibria of system (5) associated with $u = 0$. □

REMARK 3. *Note that the reset condition in (7) is such that variable ξ_a reconstructed from ξ according to (8) is continuous. Continuity of ξ_a is generally not guaranteed if ξ is approximated through a reduced order model of the SL system.*

4.2 Reduction of the SL system

A reduced order model of the SL system with reset defined before can be obtained by applying balanced truncation (2) to each single linear dynamics in (6). This is is in order to best reproduce the evolution of the output y within a fixed mode, and also the discrete transitions between modes, since they are defined through a condition involving y.
We associate to each mode $q_r \in Q$ a reduced model of order $n_{r,q} \leq n$:

$$\begin{cases} \dot{x}_{r,q_r}(t) = A_{r,q_r} x_{r,q_r}(t) + B_{r,q_r} u(t) \\ \hat{y}(t) = C_{r,q_r} x_{r,q_r}(t) + D_{r,q_r} u(t) \end{cases} \tag{9}$$

and define transitions between modes, say from mode i to mode j, by evaluating when $(\hat{y} + \bar{y}_{a,i}, u)$ exits from domain Dom_i and enters into Dom_j. As for the state reset map (7) associated with a transition from mode $i \in Q$ to mode $j \in Q$, we shall reformulate it in the following form

$$x_{r,j}(t) = L_{ji} x_{r,i}(t^-) + M_{ji} u(t^-) + N_{ji}. \tag{10}$$

where $x_{r,i}(t^-) \in \mathbb{R}^{n_{r,i}}$, $x_{r,j}(t) \in \mathbb{R}^{n_{r,j}}$, and L_{ji}, M_{ji}, N_{ji} are matrices of appropriate dimensions.

We shall present next two methods to define matrices L_{ji}, M_{ji}, N_{ji}. In both of them we shall refer to the following variables:

1. the estimate $\hat{x}_i$ of the state of the SL system dynamics associated with mode $i \in Q$ in balanced form. $\hat{x}_i$ is reconstructed from the reduced state $x_{r,i}$ according to:

$$\begin{aligned} \hat{x}_i &= \begin{bmatrix} x_{r,i} \\ -A_{i,22}^{-1} A_{i,21} x_{r,i} - A_{i,22}^{-1} B_{i,2} u \end{bmatrix} \\ &= \begin{bmatrix} I_{n_{r,i} \times n_{r,i}} \\ -A_{i,22}^{-1} A_{i,21} \end{bmatrix} x_{r,i} + \begin{bmatrix} \mathbf{0}_{n_{r,i} \times 1} \\ -A_{i,22}^{-1} B_{i,2} \end{bmatrix} u \end{aligned} \tag{11}$$

   Expression (11) can be rewritten in compact form as

$$\hat{x}_i = H_i x_{r,i} + K_i u, \tag{12}$$

   with

$$H_i = \begin{bmatrix} I_{n_{r,i} \times n_{r,i}} \\ -A_{i,22}^{-1} A_{i,21} \end{bmatrix} \qquad K_i = \begin{bmatrix} \mathbf{0}_{n_{r,i} \times 1} \\ -A_{i,22}^{-1} B_{i,2} \end{bmatrix}$$

   where $I_{n_{r,i} \times n_{r,i}}$ is an identity matrix of dimension $n_{r,i} \times n_{r,i}$, and $\mathbf{0}_{n_{r,i} \times 1}$ is a zero vector of $n_{r,i}$ elements;

2. the estimate $\hat{\xi}_i$ of the state of the SL system associated with mode $i \in Q$:

$$\hat{\xi}_i = T_i^{-1} \hat{x}_i, \tag{13}$$

   obtained from $\hat{x}_i$ through the balanced transformation matrix T_i.

We are now in a position to defined the reduced state reset maps for a transition from $i \in Q$ at time t^- to $j \in Q$ at time t.

a) reset map proposed in [19]:

We start setting

$$x_{r,j}(t) = E_{n_{r,j}} \hat{x}_j(t)$$

where $E_{n_{r,j}}$ is a matrix that extracts the first $n_{r,j}$ rows from $\hat{x}_j(t)$, being $n_{r,j}$ the dimension of $x_{r,j}$ in mode j. Now,

$$\begin{aligned} \hat{x}_j(t) &= T_j \hat{\xi}_j(t) = T_j \left(\hat{\xi}_i(t^-) + \bar{\xi}_{a,i} - \bar{\xi}_{a,j} \right) \\ &= T_j \left(T_i^{-1} \hat{x}_i(t^-) + \bar{\xi}_{a,i} - \bar{\xi}_{a,j} \right) \\ &= T_j \left(T_i^{-1} H_i x_{r,i}(t^-) + T_i^{-1} K_i u(t^-) + \bar{\xi}_{a,i} - \bar{\xi}_{a,j} \right), \end{aligned}$$

so that

$$x_{r,j}(t) = E_{n_{r,j}} T_j \left(T_i^{-1} H_i x_{r,i}(t^-) + T_i^{-1} K_i u(t^-) + \bar{\xi}_{a,i} - \bar{\xi}_{a,j} \right). \tag{14}$$

By direct comparison of this expression with (10), we get the reset matrices:

$$L_{ji} = E_{n_{r,j}} T_j T_i^{-1} H_i$$
$$M_{ji} = E_{n_{r,j}} T_j T_i^{-1} K_i$$
$$N_{ji} = E_{n_{r,j}} T_j \left(\bar{\xi}_{a,i} - \bar{\xi}_{a,j} \right).$$

According to a similar reasoning, the system is initialized as follows

$$q_r(0) = q_a(0) = q_0$$
$$x_{r,q_0}(0) = E_{n_{r,q_0}} T_{q_0} \left(\xi_a(0) - \bar{\xi}_{a,q_0} \right),$$

with the understanding that $(y_a(0), u(0))$ is an interior point of Dom_{a,q_0} for any admissible $u(0)$.

b) reset map best reproducing the output free evolution:

Model reduction techniques for asymptotically stable linear systems aim at finding a model that best reproduce the forced response of the system, while neglecting the free evolution. This motivates the introduction of an alternative reset map that minimizes the norm-2 error when reproducing the free evolution of the output y. More precisely, we set

$$x_{r,j} = \Psi_j \hat{\xi}_j$$

and choose Ψ_j so as to minimize

$$J = \int_0^{+\infty} \| y_{fr,j}(t) - \hat{y}_{fr,j}(t) \|^2 \, dt, \tag{15}$$

where $y_{fr,j}$ and $\hat{y}_{fr,j}$ respectively denote the free evolution of the original linear dynamics (6) initialized with $\hat{\xi}_j$ and that of the reduced order dynamics (9) initialized with $x_{r,j} = \Psi_j \hat{\xi}_j$. The solution to this optimization problem can be found analytically as shown in Proposition 4.2.

PROPOSITION 4.2. *Matrix Ψ_j minimizing (15) for any $\hat{\xi}_j$ is given by*

$$\Psi_j = \mathscr{W}_{r,o,j}^{-1} \mathscr{W}_{\times,j}.$$

where

$$\mathscr{W}_{r,o,j} = \int_0^{+\infty} (e^{A_{r,j}t})^T C_{r,j}^T C_{r,j} e^{A_{r,j}t} \, dt \tag{16}$$

$$\mathscr{W}_{\times,j} = \int_0^{+\infty} (e^{A_j t})^T C_j^T C_{r,j} e^{A_{r,j}t} \, dt \tag{17}$$

and invertibility of the infinite observability Gramian $\mathscr{W}_{r,o,j}$ is guaranteed by the observability of the reduced order model (9) with $q = j$.

PROOF. The cost function J can be written as

$$J = \int_0^{+\infty} (C_j e^{A_j t} \hat{\xi}_j - C_{r,j} e^{A_{r,j}t} x_{r,j})^T (C_j e^{A_j t} \hat{\xi}_j - C_{r,j} e^{A_{r,j}t} x_{r,j}) \, dt$$
$$= x_{r,j}^T \mathscr{W}_{r,o,j} x_{r,j} - 2 x_{r,j} \mathscr{W}_{\times,j} \hat{\xi}_j + \hat{\xi}_j^T \mathscr{W}_{o,j} \hat{\xi},$$

where we set

$$\mathscr{W}_{o,j} = \int_0^{+\infty} (e^{A_j t})^T C_j^T C_j e^{A_j t} \, dt.$$

Then, the minimum of J as a function of $x_{r,j}$ satisfies

$$\frac{\partial J}{\partial x_{r,j}} = 2 \mathscr{W}_{r,o,j} x_{r,j} - 2 \mathscr{W}_{\times,q'} \hat{\xi}_j = 0$$

yielding the reset map

$$x_{r,j} = \mathscr{W}_{r,o,j}^{-1} \mathscr{W}_{\times,j} \hat{\xi}_j.$$

□

Note that the quantity (16) is the solution of the Lyapunov equation

$$A_{r,j} \mathscr{W}_{r,o,j} + \mathscr{W}_{r,o,j} A_{r,j}^T + C_{r,j}^T C_{r,j} = 0,$$

while quantity (17) is the solution of the Sylvester equation

$$A_{r,j}^T \mathscr{W}_{\times,j} + \mathscr{W}_{\times,j} A_j + C_{r,j}^T C_j = 0.$$

Given Ψ_j, the following derivations

$$x_{r,j}(t) = \Psi_j \hat{\xi}_j(t) = \Psi_j \left(\hat{\xi}_i(t^-) + \bar{\xi}_{a,i} - \bar{\xi}_{a,j} \right) =$$
$$= \Psi_j \left(T_i^{-1} \hat{x}_i(t^-) + \bar{\xi}_{a,i} - \bar{\xi}_{a,j} \right)$$
$$= \Psi_j \left(T_i^{-1} H_i x_{r,i}(t^-) + T_i^{-1} K_i u(t^-) + \bar{\xi}_{a,i} - \bar{\xi}_{a,j} \right) \tag{18}$$

using the reset map (7) and equations (13) and (12) lead to the following definition of the matrices in the reset map (10):

$$L_{ji} = \Psi_j T_i^{-1} H_i,$$
$$M_{ji} = \Psi_j T_i^{-1} K_i,$$
$$N_{ji} = \Psi_j \left(\bar{\xi}_{a,i} - \bar{\xi}_{a,j} \right).$$

As for the system initialization, we set

$$q_r(0) = q_a(0) = q_0$$
$$x_{r,q_0}(0) = \Psi_j \left(\xi_a(0) - \bar{\xi}_{a,q_0} \right).$$

A different reset map that accounts for the switching nature of the system can be obtained by considering a finite horizon $[0, \tau]$ for the minimization of the free evolution error:

$$J = \int_0^{\tau} \| y_{fr,j}(t) - \hat{y}_{fr,j}(t) \|^2 \, dt.$$

The resulting optimal $\Psi_j^{(\tau)}$ can be computed through the following expression

$$\Psi_j^{(\tau)} = \mathscr{W}_{r,o,j}^{-1}(\tau) \mathscr{W}_{\times,j}(\tau),$$

with

$$\mathscr{W}_{r,o,j}(\tau) = \int_0^{\tau} (e^{A_{r,j}t})^T C_{r,j}^T C_{r,j} e^{A_{r,j}t} \, dt$$
$$\mathscr{W}_{\times,j}(\tau) = \int_0^{\tau} (e^{A_j t})^T C_j^T C_{r,j} e^{A_{r,j}t} \, dt,$$

the proof being analogous to that in the infinite horizon case. The above finite horizon quantities can be computed as

$$\mathscr{W}_{r,o,j}(\tau) = \mathscr{W}_{r,o,j} - \int_{\tau}^{+\infty} (e^{A_{r,j}t})^T C_{r,j}^T C_{r,j} e^{A_{r,j}t} \, dt = \mathscr{W}_{r,o,j} - \mathscr{W}_{r,o,j}^{(\tau,\infty)},$$
$$\mathscr{W}_{\times,j}(\tau) = \mathscr{W}_{\times,j} - \int_{\tau}^{\infty} (e^{A_j t})^T C_j^T C_{r,j} e^{A_{r,j}t} \, dt = \mathscr{W}_{\times,j} - W_{\times,j}^{(\tau,\infty)},$$

where the quantities $\mathscr{W}_{r,o,j}^{(\tau,\infty)}$ and $\mathscr{W}_{\times,j}^{(\tau,\infty)}$ can be obtained respectively as the solution of the Lyapunov and Sylvester equations

$$A_{r,j} \mathscr{W}_{r,o,j}^{(\tau,\infty)} + \mathscr{W}_{r,o,j}^{(\tau,\infty)} A_{r,j}^T + \left(e^{A_{r,j}\tau} \right)^T C_{r,j}^T C_{r,j} e^{A_{r,j}\tau} = 0,$$
$$A_{r,j}^T \mathscr{W}_{\times,j}^{(\tau,\infty)} + \mathscr{W}_{\times,j}^{(\tau,\infty)} A_j + \left(e^{A_{r,j}\tau} \right)^T C_{r,j}^T C_j e^{A_j\tau} = 0,$$

which are identical to the previous ones except for the fact that C_j and $C_{r.j}$ are replaced by $C_j e^{A_j \tau}$ and $C_{r.j} e^{A_{r.j} \tau}$, respectively. Note that well-posedness of the above equations is guaranteed by the fact that A_j and $A_{r.j}$ are Hurwitz.

The matrices in the reset map (10) and the system initialization are given by:

$$L_{ji} = \Psi_j^{(\tau)} T_i^{-1} H_i,$$
$$M_{ji} = \Psi_j^{(\tau)} T_i^{-1} K_i,$$
$$N_{ji} = \Psi_j^{(\tau)} \left(\bar{\xi}_{a.i} - \bar{\xi}_{a.j}\right)$$

and

$$q_r(0) = q_a(0) = q_0$$
$$x_{r.q_0}(0) = \Psi_j^{(\tau)} \left(\xi_a(0) - \bar{\xi}_{a.q_0}\right).$$

The choice for τ depends on the settling times of the different mode dynamics. A sensible choice is suggested in the numerical example of Section 6.

4.3 Reconstruction of the SA system output

The output of the SA system is reconstructed based on (8) using the output $\hat{y}$ of the SL reduced system as an estimate of the output y of the SL system:

$$\hat{y}_a(t) = \hat{y}(t) + \bar{y}_{a.q_r(t)}.$$

5. A RANDOMIZED METHOD FOR MODEL ORDER SELECTION

In this section, a randomized method is described for selecting the order of the reduced order model of the SA system when the input u is stochastic and the goal is verifying a finite horizon property that depends on the behavior of the SA system output y_a along the time horizon T.

The proposed method involves feeding the reduced model and the system with some realizations of the stochastic input. This in practice means that either the distribution of the input is known, or some of its realizations are available as historical time series.

As discussed in Section 2, a sensible way of choosing the order of the reduced model for a linear system is setting a threshold value for the ψ function in (4) and then define the order accordingly. By following the same logic as in [19], a function $\psi_q : \{1,2,\dots n\} \to [0,1)$ can then be considered for each mode $q \in Q$

$$\psi_q(i) = 1 - \frac{\sum_{j=1}^{i} \sigma_{j.q}}{\sum_{j=1}^{n} \sigma_{j.q}},$$

where $\sigma_{1.q} \geq \sigma_{2.q} \geq \cdots \geq \sigma_{n.q}$ are the Hankel singular values of the SL system dynamics (6) in mode q, and the order of the model (9) defining the reduced SL system can be set according to

$$n_{r.q} = \min\{i \in \{1,2,\dots,n\} : \psi_q(i) < \gamma\},$$

for each $q \in Q$.

Our goal is now to introduce a method for choosing an appropriate value for γ.

To this purpose, we denote by $\hat{y}_a^{\gamma}$ the estimate of y_a obtained through the reduced SL system with parameter γ, and by Γ the (finite) set of threshold values for γ, those that result in a different choice for $\{n_{r.q},\ q \in Q\}$.

In order to choose an appropriate order for the reduced dynamics associated to each mode, we quantify the approximation error through some function $d_T(\cdot,\cdot)$ that maps each pair of trajectories $y_a(t), t \in T$, and $\hat{y}_a^{\gamma}(t), t \in T$, into a positive real number $d_T(y_a, \hat{y}_a^{\gamma})$ that represents the extent to which the output y_a of the SA system differs from its estimate $\hat{y}_a^{\gamma}$ along the time horizon T. Obviously, if we set $\gamma = 0$, then, no reduction is performed and $d_T(y_a, \hat{y}_a^{\gamma}) = 0$ since $\hat{y}_a^{\gamma}(t) = y_a(t), t \in T$.

Note that $d_T(y_a, \hat{y}_a^{\gamma})$ is a random quantity since it depends on the realization of the stochastic input $u(t)$ and the (possibly) stochastic initialization $\xi_a(0)$ of the SA system.

According to the notion of approximate simulation in [3, 10, 15], we assess the approximation quality of the reduced order model with parameter γ through the maximal value $\rho_\gamma^\star$ taken by $d_T(y_a, \hat{y}_a^{\gamma})$ over all realizations of the stochastic input and initial state except for a set of probability at most $\varepsilon \in (0,1)$. An 'optimal' value for γ can then be chosen by inspecting the values of $\rho_\gamma^\star$ as a function of γ and selecting the appropriate compromise between quality of the approximation and tractability of the resulting reduced order model.

For each $\gamma \in \Gamma \subset [0,1]$, the approximation quality $\rho_\gamma^\star$ of the reduced order model with parameter γ is the solution to the following chance-constrained optimization problem:

$$CCP_\gamma : \min_\rho \rho \quad (19)$$
$$\text{subject to: } \mathbb{P}\{d_T(y_a, \hat{y}_a^{\gamma}) \leq \rho\} \geq 1 - \varepsilon.$$

REMARK 4 (CHOICE OF $d_T(y_a, \hat{y}_a^{\gamma})$). *As argued in [3], the directional Hausdorff distance*

$$d_T(y_a, \hat{y}_a^{\gamma}) = \sup_{t \in T} \inf_{\tau \in T} \|y_a(t) - \hat{y}_a^{\gamma}(\tau)\| \quad (20)$$

is a sensible choice for $d_T(y_a, \hat{y}_a^{\gamma})$ when performing probabilistic verification such as, e.g., estimating of the probability that y_a will enter some set within the time horizon T. For the verification of more complex reachability properties, such as that of reaching some set only after passing through some region within a given finite time interval, however, this choice for $d_T(y_a, \hat{y}_a^{\gamma})$ is not adequate since the timing information is lost, and one can opt for

$$d_T(y_a, \hat{y}_a^{\gamma}) = \sup_{t \in T} \|y_a(t) - \hat{y}_a^{\gamma}(t)\|.$$

Irrespectively of the choice for $d_T(y_a, \hat{y}_a^{\gamma})$, solving the chance-constrained problem (19) is known to be difficult, [25], since it involves determining, among all sets of realizations of the stochastic input and initial state that have a probability $1 - \varepsilon$, the one that provides the best (lowest) value for $d_T(y_a, \hat{y}_a^{\gamma})$. We then head for an approximate solution where instead of considering all the possible realizations for the stochastic uncertainty, we consider only a finite number N of them called "scenarios", extracted at random according to their probability distribution, and treat them as if they were the only admissible uncertainty instances. This leads to the formulation of Algorithm 1, where the chance-constrained solution is determined using some empirical violation parameter $\eta \in (0, \varepsilon)$.

Notably, if the number N of extractions is appropriately chosen, the obtained estimate of $\rho_\gamma^\star$ is chance-constrained feasible, uniformly with respect to $\gamma \in \Gamma$, with a-priori specified (high) probability. This result is based on the "scenario theory", [7], which was first introduced for solving uncertain convex programs via randomization [5] and then extended to chance-constrained optimization problems in [6].

PROPOSITION 5.1. *Select a confidence parameter $\beta \in (0,1)$ and an empirical violation parameter $\eta \in (0, \varepsilon)$. If N is such that*

$$\sum_{i=0}^{\lfloor \eta N \rfloor} \binom{N}{i} \varepsilon^i (1-\varepsilon)^{N-i} \leq \frac{\beta}{|\Gamma|}, \quad (21)$$

Algorithm 1 Randomized solution

1: extract N realizations of the stochastic input $u^{(i)}(t)$, $t \in T$, $i = 1, 2, \ldots, N$, and N samples of the initial condition $\xi_a(0)^{(i)}$, $i = 1, 2, \ldots, N$, and let $k = \lfloor \eta N \rfloor$;

2: for all $\gamma \in \Gamma$ do

2.1: determine the N realizations of the output signals $y_a^{(i)}(t)$ and $\hat{y}_a^{\gamma,(i)}(t)$, $t \in T$, $i = 1, 2, \ldots, N$, when the SL system and the reduced order model with parameter γ are fed by the extracted uncertainty instances;

2.2: compute

$$\hat{\rho}^{(i)} := d_T(y_a^{(i)}, \hat{y}_a^{\gamma,(i)}), \; i = 1, 2, \ldots, N;$$

and determine the indices $\{h_1, h_2, \ldots h_k\} \subset \{1, 2, \ldots, N\}$ of the k largest values of $\{\hat{\rho}^{(i)}, i = 1, 2, \ldots, N\}$

2.3: set

$$\hat{\rho}_\gamma^\star = \max_{i \in \{1,2,\ldots,N\} \setminus \{h_1, h_2, \ldots, h_k\}} \hat{\rho}^{(i)}.$$

then, the solution $\hat{\rho}_\gamma^\star$, $\gamma \in \Gamma$, to Algorithm 1 satisfies

$$\mathbb{P}\{d_T(y_a, \hat{y}_a^\gamma) \le \hat{\rho}_\gamma^\star\} \ge 1 - \varepsilon, \; \forall \gamma \in \Gamma, \tag{22}$$

with probability at least $1 - \beta$. □

If we discard the confidence parameter β for a moment, this proposition states that for any $\gamma \in \Gamma$, the randomized solution $\hat{\rho}_\gamma^\star$ obtained through Algorithm 1 is feasible for the chance-constrained problem (19). As η tends to ε, $\hat{\rho}_\gamma^\star$ approaches the desired optimal chance constrained solution $\rho_\gamma^\star$. In turn, the computational effort grows unbounded since N scales as $\frac{1}{\varepsilon - \eta}$, [6], therefore, the value for η depends in practice from the available computational resources.

As for the confidence parameter β, one should note that $\hat{\rho}_\gamma^\star$ is a random quantity that depends on the randomly extracted input realizations and initial conditions. It may happen that the extracted samples are not representative enough, in which case the size of the violation set will be larger than ε. Parameter β controls the probability that this happens and the final result holds with probability $1 - \beta$. N satisfying (21) depend logarithmically on $|\Gamma|/\beta$, [6], so that β can be chosen as small as 10^{-10} (and, hence, $1 - \beta \simeq 1$) without growing significantly N.

PROOF (PROPOSITION 5.1). Note that the chance-constrained problem (19) needs to be solved for a finite number $|\Gamma|$ of values for γ. The application of Theorem 2.1 in [6] to the randomized solution obtained with Algorithm 1 for each given $\bar{\gamma} \in \Gamma$, provides the following guarantees on the solution $\hat{\rho}_{\bar{\gamma}}^\star$:

$$\mathbb{P}\{d_T(y_a, \hat{y}_a^{\bar{\gamma}}) \le \hat{\rho}_{\bar{\gamma}}^\star\} \ge 1 - \varepsilon, \text{ with probability at least } 1 - \frac{\beta}{|\Gamma|}.$$

As a result, guarantee (22) involving all $\gamma \in \Gamma$ holds except for a set whose probability can be upper bounded by $\sum_{i=1}^{|\Gamma|} \frac{\beta}{|\Gamma|} = \beta$, thus proving the thesis. □

Notice that the guarantees provided by Proposition 5.1 are valid irrespectively of the underlying probability distribution of the input, which may even not be known explicitly, e.g., when feeding Algorithm 1 with historical time series as realizations of the stochastic input u.

6. A NUMERICAL EXAMPLE

In this section we present a numerical example to show the performance of the proposed approach for model reduction. The example is inspired by a benchmark for hybrid system verification presented in [8].

6.1 Model description

The example deals with the heating of a number of rooms in a house. Each room has one single heater, but there is some constraint on the number of "active" heaters that can possibly be on at the same time. The temperature in each room depends on the temperature of the adjacent rooms, on the outside temperature, and on whether a heater is on in the room or not. The heater is controlled by a typical thermostat, i.e., it is switched on if the temperature is below a certain threshold, and off if it is beyond another (higher) threshold. Differently from the original benchmark in [8], we model also the dynamic of the heaters.

When the temperature in a room, say room i, falls below a certain level, its heater may become active (and eventually be switched on) if a heater was active in one of the adjacent rooms, say room j, provided that the temperature in room j is significantly higher than that in room i. In this case, we shall say for brevity that the heater is "moved" from room i to room j. The underlying *rationale* of the control policy is that, even if all the rooms have their own heater, the number of heaters that can be on at the same time must be limited, so as to exploit also the heat exchange among the rooms in order to maintain some minimum temperature in all rooms.

Let T_i be the temperature in room i, T_{ext} the outside temperature, and h_i a boolean variable that is 1 when the heater is on in room i, and 0 otherwise.

The heat transfer coefficient between room i and room j is k_{ij}, and the one between room i and the external environment is $k_{e,i}$. We assume that the heat exchange is symmetric, i.e., $k_{ij} = k_{ji}$. We say that rooms i and j are adjacent if $k_{ij} > 0$. The volume of the room is V_i, and the wall surface between room i and room j is $S_{r,ij}$, while that between room i and the environment is $S_{e,i}$. Air density and heat capacity are $\rho_a = 1.225\,\text{kg/m}^3$ and $c = 1005\,\text{J/(kg K)}$, respectively. Letting $\phi_i = \rho_a c V_i$, we can formulate the following dynamic model for room i and its heater:

$$\begin{aligned} \phi_i \dot{T}_i &= \sum_{j \neq i} S_{r,ij} k_{ij} (T_j - T_i) + S_{e_i} k_{e,i} (T_{\text{ext}} - T_i) + \kappa_i \theta_i \\ \tau_{h,i} \dot{\theta}_i &= -\theta_i + h_i \cdot p_i - \chi_i T_{\text{ext}} \end{aligned} \tag{23}$$

which is an affine system, with T_i representing the temperature in the i-th room, κ_i representing the maximum heat flow rate that the heater can provide, while $p_i \in \{0, 1\}$ is a binary variable indicating if the heater is active in room i. The heater dynamics is represented by a first-order system with a time constant $\tau_{h,i}$. If we neglect the term $-\chi_i T_{\text{ext}}$ in the heater dynamics and set $h_i = p_i = 1$, the heater state variable θ_i will tend to 1 so that the heater will provide its maximum heat flow rate κ_i to the room when it is active and on. The term $-\chi_i T_{\text{ext}}$ is introduced to account for the influence of the external temperature on the effectiveness of the heating system.

6.2 The switching control policy

There is a *room policy*, which decides whether or not to switch on the heater of a single room, and a *building policy* which decides how to "move" the heaters that can be switched on.

As for the room policy, each room has a thermostat that switches the heater on if the measured temperature is below a certain threshold, and off when the temperature reaches a higher temperature. For each room we define thresholds on_i and off_i: the heater in room i is on if $T_i \leq on_i$ and off if $T_i \geq off_i$.

On the other hand, the building policy can be defined as follows. A heater is moved from room j to an adjacent room i if the following holds

- room i has no active heater;
- room j has an active heater;
- temperature $T_i \leq get_i$;
- the difference $T_j - T_i \geq dif_i$.

Notice that the control policy may have non-deterministic behaviors, since a room j may have more than one room, e.g., rooms i_1 and i_2, that is adjacent, and it may happen that conditions for the building policy to move the heater to room i_1 and to room i_2 are satisfied at the same time. To avoid non-deterministic choices in the policy, each room is identified by some integer index, and, in the previously mentioned situation, the heater is always moved to the room with higher index.

Apparently enough, the switching nature of the system originates from the control policy. The complexity of the considered system significantly increases with the number of rooms, thus making the problem particularly suitable for reduction when dealing with realistic cases.

6.3 The considered system

In the following we consider four adjacent rooms as represented in Figure 1, having each its own heater, but with the constraint that only three heaters can be active at the same time, i.e., $\sum_{i=1}^{4} p_i = 3$.

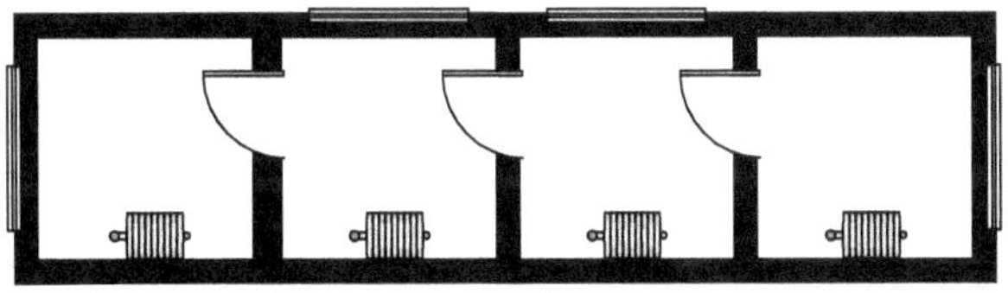

Figure 1: Scheme of the four rooms.

The rooms have different heat transfer coefficients among them, but identical geometric characteristics. The considered parameters are reported in Table 1.

Parameters			
k_{12}	2 W/(m^{2}K)	$S_{r,ij}$	12 m^2
k_{23}	5 W/(m^{2}K)	$S_{e,i}$	24 m^2
k_{34}	2 W/(m^{2}K)	V_i	48 m^3
$k_{e,i}$	1 W/(m^{2}K)	χ_i	10^{-5}

Table 1: Four rooms parameters.

The outside temperature is modeled as a sinusoidal source of period 24 hours with an offset of 4°C, affected by a band-limited Gaussian noise with zero mean and variance 4.

We assume that the initial conditions are deterministic and given by

$$T(0) = \begin{bmatrix} 20 \\ 20 \\ 20 \\ 20 \end{bmatrix}, \quad \theta(0) = \begin{bmatrix} 0 \\ 0 \\ 0 \\ 0 \end{bmatrix}, \quad h(0) = p(0) = \begin{bmatrix} 0 \\ 1 \\ 1 \\ 1 \end{bmatrix},$$

where T is the vector of the 4 rooms temperatures, θ is the vector of the heaters states, h and p are the vectors denoting, respectively, the on/off status and the active/inactive status of the heaters. Obviously, $p(0)$ satisfies the condition that only 3 over the 4 heaters are active. As for the (switching) control policy parameters, we use

$$off = \begin{bmatrix} 21 \\ 21 \\ 21 \\ 21 \end{bmatrix}, \quad on = \begin{bmatrix} 20 \\ 20 \\ 20 \\ 20 \end{bmatrix}, \quad get = \begin{bmatrix} 19 \\ 19 \\ 19 \\ 19 \end{bmatrix}, \quad dif = \begin{bmatrix} 1 \\ 1 \\ 1 \\ 1 \end{bmatrix}. \tag{24}$$

According to the described policy, model (23) can be represented as a SA system with continuous state $\xi_a = \begin{bmatrix} T' & \theta' \end{bmatrix}'$, input $u = T_{\text{ext}}$, and output $y_a = T$:

$$\begin{aligned} \dot{\xi}_a &= \mathscr{A}\,\xi_a + \mathscr{B}\,u + f_{q_a} \\ y_a &= \mathscr{C}\,\xi_a. \end{aligned} \tag{25}$$

As for the mode q_a, it is identified by the value of h and p, which determine the affine term entering the dynamics of ξ_a. The polyhedral sets Dom_{a,q_a} are determined by the building and room control policies through the threshold values (24) as described in Section 6.2.

Notice that in this example only the affine term f_{q_a} depends on the discrete mode $q_a \in Q$, while the state-space matrices $(\mathscr{A}, \mathscr{B}, \mathscr{C})$ are constant.

As for the choice of the order of the reduced model, the standard approach used in balanced truncation techniques [19] and resting on classical Hankel Singular Values (HSV) analysis can be applied so as to identify to what extent reducing the system dynamics in each single mode. This analysis is independent of the discrete mode. More importantly, it does not consider the impact of the choice of the order on the switched system approximation, which involves also mode transitions.

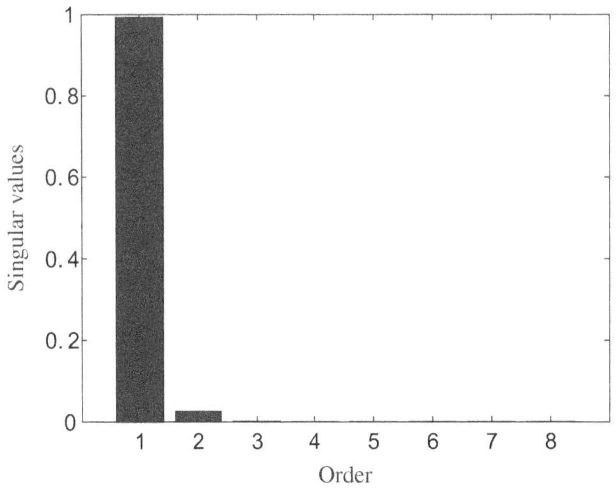

Figure 2: Hankel Singular Values sorted by decreasing magnitude.

Figure 2 shows the HSV of system (25) sorted by decreasing magnitude. On the basis of the HSV, it seems that most of the dynamics can be caught by reducing the continuous dynamics of the SA system to a first-order one. Indeed, computing the distance (4) used in [19] results in $\psi(1) \cdot 100 = 2.64\%$.

As anticipated, this evaluation of the quality of the reduced model does not account for the impact of mode transitions, thus care has to be taken when applying it to the context of SA systems. In fact, classical balanced truncation techniques are typically based on the assumption that the free evolution of the system can be neglected since it asymptotically vanishes in an asymptotically stable linear system, fact that notoriously does not hold true when dealing with hybrid behaviors.

6.4 Proposed model reduction method

We apply now the proposed model reduction method to the considered system, including the randomized method for order selection based on the directional Hausdorff distance (20). In particular, referring to the chance constrained optimization problem (19), we choose $\varepsilon = 0.1$, $\beta = 10^{-6}$. Thus, setting $\eta = 0.05$, and solving the implicit formula (21), the number of experiments to be performed for each possible threshold value for γ is $N = 778$, corresponding to a number $\lfloor \eta N \rfloor = 38$ of realizations to be removed, as described in Algorithm 1.

The randomized order selection is performed with the reset maps (14) proposed in [19], map (18) proposed here for the first time, both in its finite and infinite horizon versions. As for the choice of the finite horizon, the time constant τ_h of the heater is chosen.

Figure 3 shows a realization of the temperatures obtained with the original model and with the reduced models of order 5 implementing the three reset maps.

Notice that there is a discrete map $m_\gamma : \Gamma \to \{1, 2, \ldots, n\}$ between the threshold values of γ and the corresponding order n_r of the reduced order model. In formulas

$$n_r = \underset{i=\{1,2,\ldots,n\}}{\arg\min} \left\{ d_T(y_a, \hat{y}_a^\gamma) \leq \hat{\rho}_\gamma^\star \right\}.$$

For the sake of clarity, it is more convenient to express the estimate of $\rho_\gamma^\star$ as a function of the reduced order n_r. The values for $\hat{\rho}_\gamma^\star$ obtained with the different reset methods are presented in Figure 4 as a function of n_r.

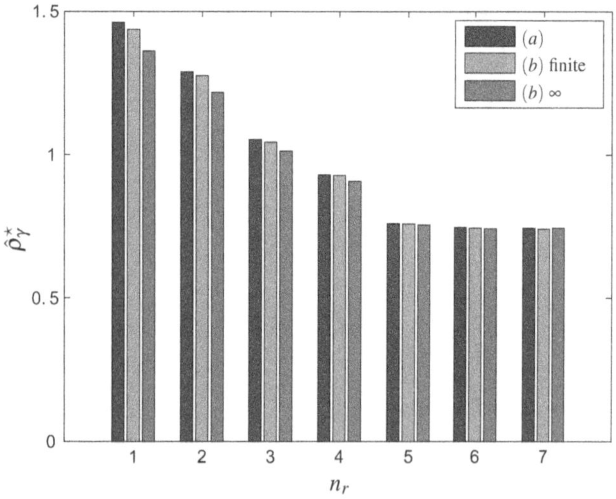

Figure 4: Performance of different reduced models as a function of the order n_r and of the adopted reset map.

6.5 Discussion

Two facts can be noticed by analyzing the results presented in Figure 4. First of all, the reset map affects the value of the directional Hausdorff distance, and the novel reset maps exhibit a better performance for any order n_r chosen for the reduction.

Furthermore, the outcome of our analysis through the randomized approach is quite different from that based on the HSV only (see Figure 2). In fact, reducing the system to a first-order approximation results in quite bad performance when the goal of the approximation is the analysis of reachability properties for which the directional Hausdorff distance is a suitable accuracy measure. In addition, such a drastic reduction yields discontinuities in the state reset that may possibly produce chattering behaviors. On the other hand, from the randomized based analysis it appears that one can push the reduction up to a fifth order without degrading significantly the accuracy of the model.

7. CONCLUSIONS

In this work, we presented a novel approach to model reduction of switched affine systems using balanced truncation for reducing the continuous affine dynamics. The main novel ingredients of the approach are:

- the introduction of suitable state reset maps that serve the purpose of making the reduced model best reproduce the free evolution of the original system; and
- the integration in the reduced order model design of a randomized procedure for model order selection.

The considered class of switched systems is characterized by an endogenous switching signal, in that the transitions between modes are determined by the evolution of the continuous state component. The method can be applied also to the case when transitions are determined by some exogenous switching signal, possibly probabilistic as in the case of Markov jump linear systems, [28]. In the case when the switching signal is subject to some dwell time τ_D and the approximated dynamics has a settling time smaller than τ_D, then, the approximation error introduced by the state reset will be negligible.

8. REFERENCES

[1] A. Abate, S. Amin, M. Prandini, J. Lygeros, and S. Sastry. Computational approaches to reachability analysis of stochastic hybrid systems. In A. Bemporad, A. Bicchi, and G. Buttazzo, editors, *Hybrid Systems: Computation and Control*, volume 4416 of *Lecture Notes in Computer Science*, pages 4–17. Springer Berlin Heidelberg, apr 2007.

[2] A. Abate, J.-P. Katoen, J. Lygeros, and M. Prandini. Approximate model checking of stochastic hybrid systems. *European Journal of Control, special issue on Stochastic hybrid systems*, 16(6):624–641, Dec. 2010.

[3] A. Abate and M. Prandini. Approximate abstractions of stochastic systems: a randomized method. In *50th IEEE Conference on Decision and Control and European Control Conference (CDC-ECC)*, pages 4861–4866. IEEE, Dec 2011.

[4] A. Antoulas. *Approximation of large-scale dynamical systems*, volume 6. Society for Industrial Mathematics, 2005.

[5] G. Calafiore and M. Campi. Uncertain convex programs: randomized solutions and confidence levels. *Mathematical Programming*, 102(1):25–46, 2005.

[6] M. Campi and S. Garatti. A sampling-and-discarding approach to chance-constrained optimization: Feasibility and

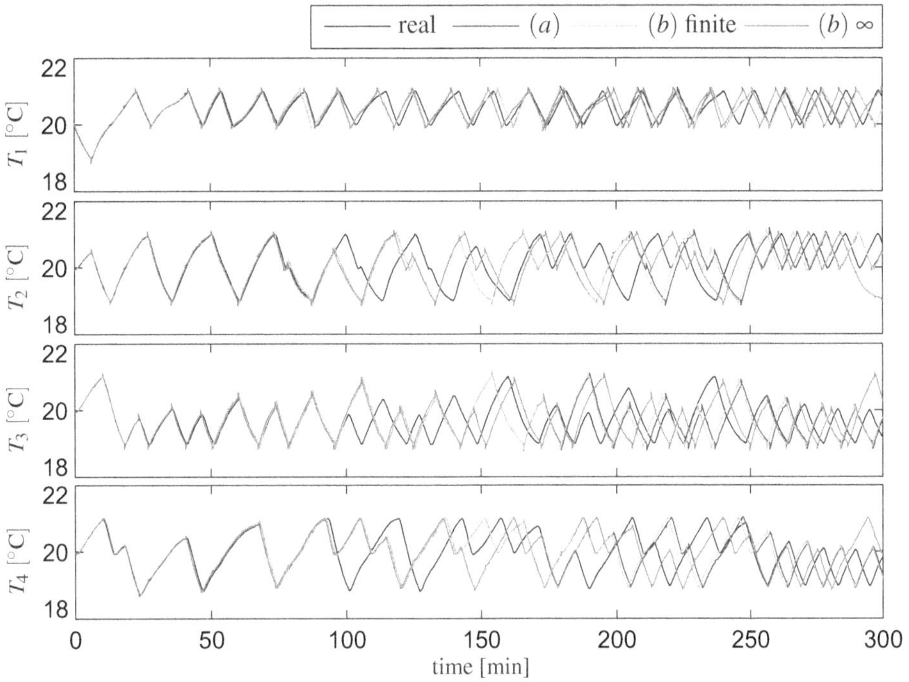

Figure 3: Comparison of the temperatures evolution obtained with the original model and with the reduced ones implementing the considered reset maps.

optimality. *Journal of Optimization Theory and Applications*, 148(2):257–280, 2011.

[7] M. C. Campi, S. Garatti, and M. Prandini. The scenario approach for systems and control design. *Annual Reviews in Control*, 33(2):149–157, 2009.

[8] A. Fehnker and F. Ivancic. Benchmarks for hybrid systems verification. In *In Hybrid Systems: Computation and Control (HSCC 2004)*, pages 326–341. Springer, 2004.

[9] G. Frehse. Phaver: Algorithmic verification of hybrid systems past hytech. In *Hybrid Systems: Computation and Control*, pages 258–273. Springer, 2005.

[10] S. Garatti and M. Prandini. A simulation-based approach to the approximation of stochastic hybrid systems. In *Analysis and Design of Hybrid Systems*, pages 406–411, 2012.

[11] A. Girard and C. Guernic. Zonotope/hyperplane intersection for hybrid systems reachability analysis. In *Proceedings of the 11th international workshop on Hybrid Systems: Computation and Control*, HSCC '08, pages 215–228, Berlin, Heidelberg, 2008. Springer-Verlag.

[12] A. Girard and G. Pappas. Approximation metrics for discrete and continuous systems. *IEEE Trans. on Automatic Control*, 52(5):782–798, 2007.

[13] A. Girard, G. Pola, and P. Tabuada. Approximately bisimilar symbolic models for incrementally stable switched systems. *IEEE Transactions on Automatic Control*, 55(1):116–126, Jan 2010.

[14] S. Gugercin and A. C. Antoulas. A survey of model reduction by balanced truncation and some new results. *International Journal of Control*, 77(8):748–766, 2004.

[15] A. Julius and G. Pappas. Approximations of stochastic hybrid systems. *IEEE Transactions on Automatic Control*, 54(6):1193–1203, 2009.

[16] A. B. Kurzhanski and P. Varaiya. Ellipsoidal techniques for hybrid dynamics: the reachability problem. In *in New Directions and Applications in Control Theory*, pages 193–205. Springer, 2005.

[17] Y. Liu and B. D. Anderson. Singular perturbation approximation of balanced systems. *International Journal of Control*, 50(4):1379–1405, 1989.

[18] J. Lunze and F. Lamnabhi-Lagarrigue, editors. *Handbook of Hybrid Systems Control – Theory, Tools, Applications*. Cambridge University Press, Cambridge, UK, 2009.

[19] E. Mazzi, A. Sangiovanni Vincentelli, A. Balluchi, and A. Bicchi. Hybrid system reduction. In *47th IEEE Conference on Decision and Control*, pages 227–232. IEEE, Dec 2008.

[20] I. Mitchell. *Application of Level Set Methods to Control and Reachability Problems in Continuous and Hybrid Systems*. PhD thesis, Ph.D. Dissertation. Dept. Scientific Computing and Computational Mathematics, Stanford Univ., CA, 2002.

[21] B. Moore. Principal component analysis in linear systems: Controllability, observability, and model reduction. *IEEE Transactions on Automatic Control*, 26(1):17–32, Feb 1981.

[22] M. Petreczky and R. Vidal. Metrics and topology for nonlinear and hybrid systems. In *Proceedings of the 10th International Conference on Hybrid Systems: Computation and Control*, volume 4416 of *Lecture Notes in Computer Sciences*, pages 459–472, 2007.

[23] M. Petreczky, R. Wisniewski, and J. Leth. Theoretical analysis of balanced truncation for linear switched systems. In *Analysis and Design of Hybrid Systems*, pages 240–247, 2012.

[24] M. Prandini and J. Hu. Stochastic reachability: Theoretical foundations and numerical approximation. In *Stochastic*

hybrid systems, volume 24 of *Control Engineering Series*, pages 107–138. Taylor & Francis Group/CRC Press, 2006.

[25] A. Prèkopa. Probabilistic programming. In A. Ruszczyǹski and A. Shapiro, editors, *Stochastic Programming*, volume 10 of *handbooks in operations research and management science*, London, UK, 2003. Elsevier.

[26] H. R. Shaker and R. Wisniewski. Model reduction of switched systems based on switching generalized gramians. *International Journal of Innovative Computing, Information and Control*, 8(7(B)):5025–5044, 2012.

[27] C. Tomlin, I. Mitchell, A. Bayen, and M. Oishi. Computational techniques for the verification of hybrid systems. *Proceedings of the IEEE*, 91(7):986–1001, 2003.

[28] L. Zhang, B. Huang, and J. Lam. H_∞ model reduction of Markovian jump linear systems. *Systems & Control Letters*, 50(2):103–118, 2003.

Control to Facet for Polynomial Systems

Christoffer Sloth
Section of Automation & Control, Aalborg University
9220 Aalborg East, Denmark
ces@es.aau.dk

Rafael Wisniewski
Section of Automation & Control, Aalborg University
9220 Aalborg East, Denmark
raf@es.aau.dk

ABSTRACT

This paper presents a solution to the control to facet problem for arbitrary polynomial vector fields defined on simplices. The novelty of the work is to use Bernstein coefficients of polynomials for determining certificates of positivity. Specifically, the constraints that are set up for the controller design are solved by searching for polynomials in Bernstein form. This allows the controller design problem to be formulated as a linear programming problem. Examples are provided that demonstrate the efficiency of the method for designing controls for polynomial systems.

Categories and Subject Descriptors

G.1 [**Mathematics of Computing**]: Numerical Analysis

General Terms

Theory, Algorithms

Keywords

Bernstein polynomials, Certificates of positivity, Polynomial systems, Control to facet

1. INTRODUCTION

The control to facet problem originates from [8], and has been studied for more than a decade by various researchers. Control to facet is concerned with two control problems: 1) forcing all trajectories to exit a subset of the state space through a specific subset of its boundary, 2) ensuring that a subset of the state space is positively invariant. The considered subsets are usually simplices or rectangles. By partitioning the state space into simplices, a global control problem can be decomposed into several local control problems. This eases the controller design.

Control to facet can for instance be used to design controls that comply with temporal logic specifications, where the predicates of the logic are defined over subsets of the state space [12]. This makes it possible to take safety constraints into consideration [10, 20].

Control to facet has been considered for different classes of systems: affine systems [8], multi-affine systems [3], and polynomial systems [21]. Additionally, a tool for designing controls that obey temporal logic specifications using the control to facet technique was presented in [12]. Previous works exploit the affine nature of the problem, which allows the synthesis of a control to be reduced to solving linear constraints defined on the vertices of a polyhedral set. To extend the above idea to polynomial vector fields, [21] proposes to transform polynomials into higher dimensional multi-affine functions using blossoming [23].

In this work, we generalize previous results on control to facet. To this end, we exploit a certificate of positivity for polynomials in Bernstein form. In a nutshell, a certificate of positivity is an algorithmically checkable condition that determines if a function is positive. As an example, linear matrix inequalities (LMIs) are used extensively in control to certify the positivity of quadratic forms. LMI-based methods exploit that a quadratic form is positive at every point except of the origin if its defining matrix is positive definite. In other words, the positive definiteness of the matrix defining the form is a certificate of positivity.

Certificates of positivity for polynomials have been identified in the field of real algebraic geometry [17, 22, 5]. Our results lean upon the well-known certificate of positivity given by Bernstein's Theorem, where the positivity of a polynomial is certified by checking its coordinates in Bernstein basis of a degree d, and if necessary raising its degree [6].

THEOREM 1 (BERNSTEIN'S THEOREM). *If a nonzero polynomial P of degree p is positive on a simplex, then there exists $d \geq p$ such that all coefficients of P given in the Bernstein basis of degree d are positive.*

Bernstein theorem can be used to certify the positivity of any positive polynomial on a simplicial complex. It is worth mentioning that this is not possible with the sum of squares method, which is currently used to certify the positivity of polynomials in control [11].

Recently, [14] established bounds for the degree d in Bernstein's Theorem. This result makes the certificates of positivity based on Bernstein's Theorem very attractive for solving the control to facet problem. Remark that the positivity of a linear function can be certified with Bernstein's Theorem without raising the degree [7].

The contributions of this paper are:

HSCC'14, April 15–17, 2014, Berlin, Germany.

http://dx.doi.org/10.1145/2562059.2562132.

- Provide a necessary and sufficient condition for a simplex to be positive invariant for a Lipschitz continuous vector field.
- Provide a necessary and sufficient condition for a polynomial state feedback to impose positive invariance of a simplex.
- Derive an algorithm for synthesizing a polynomial state feedback that imposes positive invariance of a simplex.
- Provide a necessary and sufficient condition for all solutions of a Lipschitz continuous vector field to exit a simplex in finite time.
- Derive a method for synthesizing a state feedback that ensures that all solutions of a polynomial system exit a simplex in finite time through an admissible exit facet.
- Combined, we have derived results that give a solution to the control to facet problem for polynomial vector fields.

The paper starts by introducing the notation of simplex and face maps in Section 2, and properties of polynomials in Bernstein form are provided in Section 3. Section 4 formulates the two control problems that are addressed in Section 5. Finally, Section 6 demonstrates the method on several classical examples, and Section 7 comprises conclusions.

2. SIMPLICES

The control laws designed in this work are defined over simplicial domains, which are introduced in this section. We introduce a novel notation for concise description of complex combinatorial operations, inspired by Chapter 1 in [16] and Section 7.5 in [13].

NOTATION 1. *We denote by* $\mathbb{R}[X_1,\dots,X_n]$ *the ring of polynomials over* $\mathbb{R}$, *and by* $\mathbb{R}^m[X_1,\dots,X_n]$ *the set of maps* $f:\mathbb{R}^n\to\mathbb{R}^m$ *with polynomial coordinate functions* f_i *for* $i=1,\dots,m$. *Similarly, the set of rational functions is denoted by* $\mathbb{R}(X_1,\dots,X_n)$. *We let* $\mathbb{N}_0$ *denote* $\mathbb{N}\cup\{0\}$, *and let* $e_i = [\underbrace{0\dots0}_{i\ 0s}1 0\dots0]$ *be the* i^{th} *canonical unit vector on* $\mathbb{N}_0^{n+1}$.

Consider the following definition of ordinal numbers. Let 0 denote the empty set, and inductively n is defined by

$$n=\{0,1,\cdots,n-1\}.$$

The objects of the simplicial category $\triangle$ are ordinal numbers, arrows, and $f:m\to n$ all order preserving functions, i.e., for $i,j\in m$ with $i\le j$ $(i\subseteq j)$ then $f(i)\le f(j)$. In the sequel, we write $f_i\equiv f(i)$.

We consider the family of maps $\delta_k^n : n\to n+1$ defined by

$$\delta_k^n:\{0,\dots,n-1\}\mapsto\{0,\dots,\hat{k},\dots,n\}, \tag{1}$$

where $\hat{k}$ is omitted. In particular, $\delta_k^n(k-1)=k-1$, and $\delta_k^n(k)=k+1$.

We utilize Bernstein polynomials defined over simplices via barycentric coordinates. Bernstein polynomials can alternatively be defined over boxes [4], resulting in a similar construction.

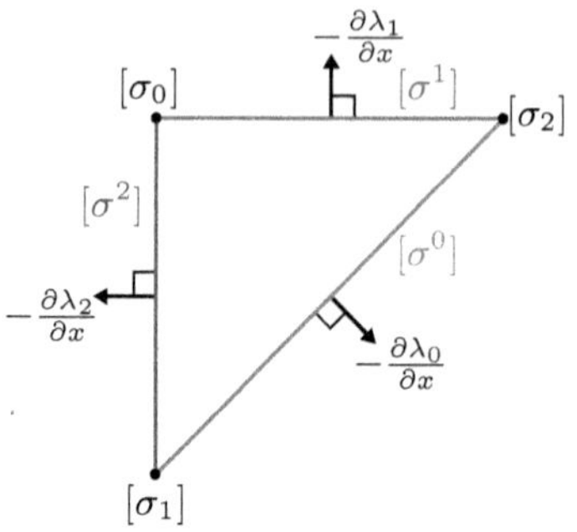

Figure 1: Simplex σ with vertices $[\sigma_i]$ and facets $[\sigma^i]$.

DEFINITION 1 (BARYCENTRIC COORDINATES). *Let* $\lambda_0,\dots,\lambda_n\in\mathbb{R}[X_1,\dots,X_n]$ *be affine polynomials and let* $v_0,\dots,v_n\in\mathbb{R}^n$ *be affinely independent. If*

$$\sum_{i=0}^{n}\lambda_i=1 \quad \textit{and}$$
$$x=\lambda_0(x)v_0+\cdots+\lambda_n(x)v_n \quad \forall x\in\mathbb{R}^n$$

then $\lambda_0,\dots,\lambda_n$ *are said to be barycentric coordinates associated to* $v_0,\dots,v_n$.

Let $\lambda_0,\dots,\lambda_n$ be barycentric coordinates associated to the points $(v_0,\dots,v_n)\equiv(0,e_0,\dots,e_{n-1})$. The standard n-simplex is

$$\triangle_n\equiv\{x=\sum_{i=0}^{n}\lambda_i v_i|\ \lambda_i(x)\ge0, i=0,\dots,n\}\subset\mathbb{R}^n.$$

We define a simplex as a map $\sigma:n+1\to\mathbb{R}^n$; hence, a simplex is an $(n+1)$-tuple $(\sigma_0,\dots,\sigma_n)$.

An affine simplex $[\sigma]\equiv[\sigma_0,\dots,\sigma_n]$ is the affine map

$$[\sigma]:\ \triangle_n\to\mathbb{R}^n,\ \sum_{i=0}^{n}\lambda_i v_i\mapsto\sum_{i=0}^{n}\lambda_i\sigma_i.$$

In the sequel, we identify the map $[\sigma]$ with its image $[\sigma](\triangle_n)$. Finally, we define the kth face of simplex σ by

$$\sigma^k=\sigma\circ\delta_k^n : n\to\mathbb{R}^n.$$

This finalizes the exposition of simplices. We have defined a simplex $[\sigma]$, its facets $[\sigma^k]$, and vertices $[\sigma_k]$. Figure 1 illustrates a simplex and its relation to vertices and facets. Throughout the paper, we assume that all simplices are nondegenerate, i.e., the vertices are affinely independent.

3. POLYNOMIALS IN BERNSTEIN FORM

This section introduces classical results on polynomials in Bernstein form. The exposition leans on [14, 7].

First, we define the main component of this paper - a Bernstein polynomial.

DEFINITION 2 (BERNSTEIN POLYNOMIAL). *Let* $d\in\mathbb{N}_0$, $n\in\mathbb{N}$, $\alpha:n+1\to\mathbb{N}_0$, *and let* $\lambda_0,\dots,\lambda_n\in\mathbb{R}[X_1,\dots,X_n]$ *be barycentric coordinates associated to a simplex* σ. *The Bernstein polynomials of degree* d *on the simplex* σ *are*

$$\mathcal{B}_\alpha^d=\binom{d}{\alpha}\lambda^\alpha \tag{2}$$

for

$$|\alpha| \equiv \sum_{i=0}^{n} \alpha_i = d$$

where

$$\binom{d}{\alpha} = \frac{d!}{\alpha_0!\alpha_1!\cdots\alpha_n!} \quad \text{and} \quad \lambda^\alpha \equiv \prod_{i=0}^{n} \lambda_i^{\alpha_i}.$$

Figure 2 shows the graphs of the 2-dimensional Bernstein polynomials of degree 3, with respect to the standard simplex $\triangle_n$.

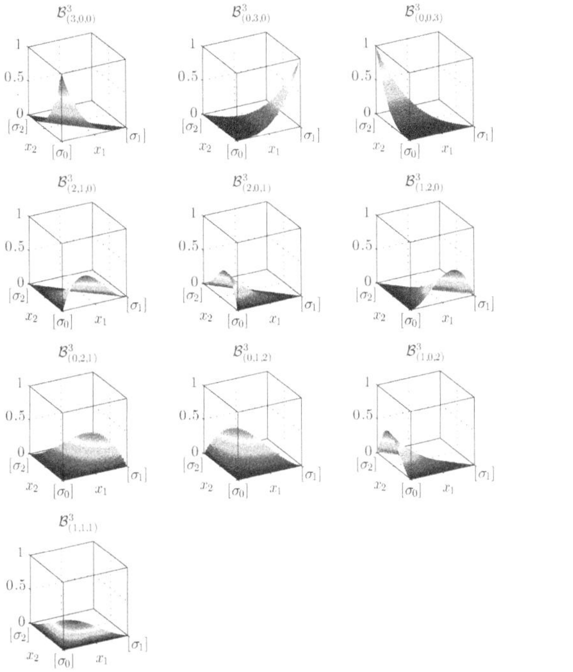

Figure 2: Graphs of Bernstein polynomials with $|\alpha| = d = 3$ and $n = 2$.

Bernstein polynomials have numerous desirable properties [7]. We explain a few of the properties in the remainder of the section.

Any polynomial can be expressed in terms of Bernstein polynomials, as they form a basis of the vector space of polynomials [14].

PROPOSITION 1. *The Bernstein polynomials of degree $d \in \mathbb{N}_0$ on the simplex σ form a basis of the vector space of polynomials of degree at most d.*

Proposition 1 says that every polynomial $f \in \mathbb{R}[X_1, \ldots, X_n]$ of degree no greater than d can be written uniquely as

$$f = \sum_{|\alpha|=d} b_\alpha(f, d, \sigma)\mathcal{B}^d_\alpha = \sum_{|\alpha|=d} b^d_\alpha \mathcal{B}^d_\alpha = b^d \mathcal{B}^d, \qquad (3)$$

where $b_\alpha(f, d, \sigma) \in \mathbb{R}$ is a Bernstein coefficient of f of degree d with respect to σ. We say that (3) is a *polynomial in Bernstein form*. When f and σ are clear from the context, we denote a Bernstein coefficient by b^d_α, the row vector of Bernstein coefficient by b^d, and the column vector with Bernstein polynomials by $\mathcal{B}^d$.

This paper is concerned with the positivity of a polynomial on a simplex as well as on its facets. The following proposition provides the key to this study.

PROPOSITION 2. *Let $d \in \mathbb{N}_0$, $n \in \mathbb{N}$, $\alpha : n+1 \to \mathbb{N}_0$, and let σ be a simplex with associated Bernstein basis $\mathcal{B}^d_\alpha$. Then*

$$\mathcal{B}^d_\alpha(x) \begin{cases} = 0 & \text{for } x \in \bigcup_{i\in\alpha^{-1}(\mathbb{N})}[\sigma^i] \\ > 0 & \text{for } x \in [\sigma]\setminus\bigcup_{i\in\alpha^{-1}(\mathbb{N})}[\sigma^i]. \end{cases}$$

PROOF. From Definition 1, it is seen that

$$\lambda_i(x) \begin{cases} = 0 & \text{for } x \in [\sigma^i] \\ > 0 & \text{for } x \in [\sigma]\setminus[\sigma^i] \end{cases}$$

since any point in the simplex σ is a convex combination of its vertices. A Bernstein polynomial $\mathcal{B}^d_\alpha$ is zero at any point where a zero valued barycentric coordinate is raised to a nonzero power. The indices of $\alpha_i \neq 0$ are given by the set $\alpha^{-1}(\mathbb{N})$. Proposition 2 follows directly from these observations. □

From Proposition 2, it is seen that all Bernstein polynomials except $\mathcal{B}^d_{de_i}([\sigma_i])$ are zero at the vertex $[\sigma_i]$; hence, $\mathcal{B}^d_{de_i}([\sigma_i]) = 1$. As an example, consider the Bernstein polynomial $\mathcal{B}^3_{(1,1,1)}$. For this polynomial $\alpha = (1,1,1)$; thus, $\{0,1,2\} = \alpha^{-1}(\mathbb{N})$. This implies that the value of $\mathcal{B}^3_{(1,1,1)}$ is zero at all facets of σ. This is also seen in Figure 2, where the graph of $\mathcal{B}^3_{(1,1,1)}$ is illustrated in the bottom left subplot.

We study the positivity of polynomials, which can be determined by the following condition on the Bernstein coefficients given in [14]. For a vector $a \in \mathbb{R}^n$, we say that $a \geq 0$ ($a > 0$) if and only if $a_i \geq 0$ ($a_i > 0$) for $i = 1, \ldots, n$.

The next proposition reveals why the study of polynomials in Bernstein form is particularly interesting for defining certificates of positivity. In short, it shows that checking positivity of the Bernstein coefficients determines positivity of the polynomial.

PROPOSITION 3 (POSITIVENESS [14]). *Let $d \in \mathbb{N}_0$, $n \in \mathbb{N}$, and let σ be a simplex with associated Bernstein basis $\mathcal{B}^d_\alpha$. Let*

$$f = b^d \mathcal{B}^d$$

be a polynomial in Bernstein form. If

$$b^d \geq 0 \quad \text{and} \quad b^d_{de_i} > 0 \quad \forall i \in \{0, \ldots, n\} \qquad (4)$$

then

$$f(x) > 0 \quad \forall x \in [\sigma].$$

It is seen from Proposition 3 that when a polynomial in Bernstein form has positive coefficients, then the value of the polynomial is positive in the simplex over which it is defined. The conditions for positiveness of the Bernstein coefficients in (4) can easily be checked. Thus, we will exploit this certificate of positivity in the remainder of the paper.

To certify the positivity of a polynomial, we rely on the following theorem [14].

THEOREM 2 (MULTIVARIATE BERNSTEIN THEOREM). *If a nonzero polynomial $P \in \mathbb{R}[X_1, \ldots, X_n]$ of degree $p \in \mathbb{N}_0$ is positive on a simplex σ, then there exists $d \geq p$ such that all entries of b^d are positive.*

From Theorem 2, it is seen that it is always possible to find a certificate of positivity of a positive polynomial, by a polynomial in Bernstein form of sufficiently high degree. Bounds on the degree d in Theorem 2 are given in [14]. To find a certificate of positive, it may be necessary to raise the degree of the polynomial. This procedure is explained in [14] and will not be detailed in this paper. In short, for any $r \in \mathbb{N}$ a given polynomial

$$f = b^d \mathcal{B}^d$$

can be expressed in the Bernstein basis of degree $n + r$ as

$$f = b^{d+r} \mathcal{B}^{d+r}.$$

4. PROBLEM FORMULATION

Control to facet methods are concerned with two separate problems: 1) ensure that all solutions stay in a simplex, and 2) ensure that all solution trajectories exit a simplex in finite time through an admissible exit facet.

We shall extend the results of [9], by solving the control to facet problem for polynomial vector fields. The solutions are given in the Section 5.

The first problem is to ensure that a simplex σ is positively invariant.

PROBLEM 1. *Let $f \in \mathbb{R}^n[X_1, \ldots, X_n]$ be a vector field and $g \in \mathbb{R}^{n \times m}[X_1, \ldots, X_n]$ be a polynomial input matrix. Consider the polynomial system*

$$\dot{x} = f(x) + g(x)u$$

on simplex σ, with input $u \in U$. Find a map $k : \mathbb{R}^n \to \mathbb{R}^m$ such that the feedback control law $u = k(x)$ is admissible, and all solutions of the corresponding closed-loop system

$$\dot{x} = f(x) + g(x)k(x), \quad x(0) = z$$

for all $z \in [\sigma]$ and all $t \geq 0$ satisfy

$$x(t, z) \in [\sigma].$$

PROBLEM 2. *Let $f \in \mathbb{R}^n[X_1, \ldots, X_n]$ be a vector field and $g \in \mathbb{R}^{n \times m}[X_1, \ldots, X_n]$ be a polynomial input matrix. Consider the polynomial system*

$$\dot{x} = f(x) + g(x)u$$

on simplex σ, with input $u \in U$. Let $\mathcal{I} \subseteq \{0, \ldots, n\}$ be a nonempty set. Find a map $k : \mathbb{R}^n \to \mathbb{R}^m$ such that the state feedback control law $u = k(x)$ is admissible, i.e., $k(x) \in U$ for all $x \in [\sigma]$, and all solutions of the corresponding closed-loop system

$$\dot{x} = f(x) + g(x)k(x), \quad x(0) = z \tag{5}$$

have the following property: for every $z \in [\sigma]$ there exist $T \geq 0$ and $\epsilon > 0$ such that the solution $x(t, z)$ of (5) satisfies

1. *$x(t, z) \in [\sigma]$ for all $t \in [0, T]$,*
2. *$x(t, z) \notin [\sigma]$ for all $t \in (T, T + \epsilon)$,*
3. *$\exists k \in \mathcal{I}$ such that $x(T, z) \in [\sigma^k]$.*

A solution to Problem 2 ensures that all trajectories initialized in simplex σ exit an admissible exit facet given by $\{\sigma^k | k \in \mathcal{I}\}$ in finite time.

5. CONTROL TO FACET

Solutions to the two control problems are provided in this section. In the controller design, we consider only one simplex, since the control on each simplex can be designed independently. The framework provided in [12] can be exploited to design a control that fulfills a temporal logic specification defined a set partitioned by simplices.

5.1 Positively Invariant Simplex

This subsection provides a controller design method for making a simplex positively invariant, i.e., it solves Problem 1. Initially, we provide a necessary and sufficient condition for a simplex to be positively invariant. This condition is used to form a necessary and sufficient condition for the solution of Problem 1. Finally, an algorithm is proposed for computing the control. The algorithm is based on certificates of positivity in the Bernstein basis.

A simplex is positively invariant under the following condition.

PROPOSITION 4 (POSITIVELY INVARIANT SIMPLEX). *Let σ be a simplex, where n_i is an outwards pointing normal vector for facet σ^i, and let $V \subseteq \mathbb{R}^n$ be an open neighborhood of $[\sigma]$. Suppose that $f : V \to \mathbb{R}^n$ is a Lipschitz continuous vector field. The simplex σ is positively invariant for*

$$\dot{x} = f(x) \tag{6}$$

if and only if for all $i \in \{0, \ldots, n\}$

$$n_i^T f(x) \leq 0 \quad \forall x \in [\sigma^i].$$

PROOF. The contingent cone $T_{[\sigma]}(x)$ at $x \in [\sigma]$ is $\mathbb{R}^n$ if x is an interior point of $[\sigma]$, and

$$T_{[\sigma]}(x) = \bigcap_{k \in \{i \in \{0,\ldots,n\} | \; x \in [\sigma^i]\}} \{v \in \mathbb{R}^n | \; v^{\mathrm{T}} n_k \leq 0\}$$

if $x \in \partial[\sigma]$.

By Nagumo Theorem (Theorem 1.2.1 in [2]), $[\sigma]$ is locally viable if and only if for all $x \in [\sigma]$, $f(x) \in T_{[\sigma]}(x)$. By compactness of $[\sigma]$, the solution $x(t, z)$ is defined for all $t \in [0, \infty]$, from which the proposition follows. □

The next theorem gives conditions for solving Problem 1 in terms of a polynomial state feedback control. We defined the set of admissible controls U as

$$U = \{u \in \mathbb{R}^m | g_U(u) \geq 0\}, \tag{7}$$

where $g_U : \mathbb{R}^m \to \mathbb{R}^l$.

THEOREM 3. *Let σ be a simplex, where n_i is an outwards pointing normal vector for facet σ^i, let $f \in \mathbb{R}^n[X_1, \ldots, X_n]$ be a vector field, $g \in \mathbb{R}^{n \times m}[X_1, \ldots, X_n]$ be a polynomial input matrix, and let U be defined as shown in (7). Consider the system*

$$\dot{x} = f(x) + g(x)u \tag{8}$$

with $u \in U$. Let $k \in \mathbb{R}^m[X_1, \ldots, X_n]$. Then $u = k(x)$ is an admissible state feedback that solves Problem 1 if and only if

1. *$g_U \circ k(x) \geq 0$ for all $x \in [\sigma]$,*
2. *For all $i \in \{0, \ldots, n\}$*

$$n_i^T (f(x) + g(x)k(x)) \leq 0 \quad \forall x \in [\sigma^i].$$

PROOF. Condition 1 is necessary and sufficient for $k(x)$ to be an admissible state feedback by the definition of U in (7). Condition 2 is a necessity and sufficiency condition for σ to be positively invariant by Proposition 4. Thus, the theorem gives a necessary and sufficient condition for solving Problem 1 with a polynomial state feedback. □

It is not possible to directly check the conditions given in Theorem 3, as it requires the evaluation of the conditions at every point in the simplex. Therefore, they are rewritten in terms of Bernstein coefficients. This requires a relation between normal vectors to facets, and the value of a polynomial restricted to a facet.

As indicated in Figure 1, the partial derivatives of barycentric coordinates are normal to facets.

LEMMA 1. *Let $\lambda_0, \dots, \lambda_n \in \mathbb{R}[X_1, \dots, X_n]$ be barycentric coordinates associated to the simplex σ. Then*

$$-\frac{\partial \lambda_k}{\partial x}$$

is a normal vector to the facet σ^k, pointing out of σ.

PROOF. Recall that for $x \in \mathbb{R}^n$, if $f^{-1}(0)$ is a plane in $\mathbb{R}^n$. Then $\partial f/\partial x = \begin{bmatrix} \frac{\partial f}{\partial x_1} & \cdots & \frac{\partial f}{\partial x_n} \end{bmatrix}$ is normal to the plane $f^{-1}(0)$.

It is seen that $[\sigma^k] \subset \lambda_k^{-1}(0)$; hence, $\partial\lambda_k/\partial x$ is normal to $[\sigma^k]$. Since λ_k is affine in x its partial derivatives are constant on the facet $[\sigma^k]$. The vector $\partial\lambda_k/\partial x$ is pointing into the simplex σ, as λ_k per definition is positive in the interior of $[\sigma]$; thus, by changing its sign it is an outwards pointing normal vector. □

To get the value of a polynomial restricted to a facet of a simplex, we define the following

$$\alpha^k = \alpha \circ \delta_k^n : n \to \mathbb{N}_0.$$

This is similar to the face map σ^k. The next corollary shows that the value of a polynomial at $[\sigma^k]$ is given by the index α^k.

COROLLARY 1. *Let*

$$f = \sum_{|\alpha|=d} F_\alpha^d \mathcal{B}_\alpha^d$$

be a polynomial in Bernstein form on simplex σ. Then

$$f|_{[\sigma^k]} = \sum_{|\alpha^k|=d} F_\alpha^d \mathcal{B}_\alpha^d|_{[\sigma^k]}.$$

PROOF. Recall from Proposition 2 that

$$\mathcal{B}_\alpha^d(x) = 0 \quad \forall x \in \bigcup_{k \in \alpha^{-1}(\mathbb{N})} [\sigma^k].$$

Thus, if $\alpha_k \neq 0$ then

$$\mathcal{B}_\alpha^d(x) = 0 \quad \forall x \in [\sigma^k].$$

If $|\alpha^k| = d$ then $\alpha_k = 0$, and we conclude that

$$f(x) = \sum_{|\alpha^k|=d} F_\alpha^d \mathcal{B}_\alpha^d(x) \quad \forall x \in [\sigma^k].$$

□

We consider a vector field $f : \mathbb{R}^n \to \mathbb{R}^n$ and assume that it is polynomial. The vector field $f \in \mathbb{R}^n[X_1, \dots, X_n]$ can be represented in Bernstein form similar to (3)

$$f = \sum_{|\alpha|=d_f} F_\alpha^{d_f} \mathcal{B}_\alpha^{d_f} = F^{d_f} \mathcal{B}^{d_f}$$

where $F_\alpha^{d_f} \in \mathbb{R}^n$ is a vector of Bernstein coefficients, and F^{d_f} is a matrix of Bernstein coefficients. The system equations

$$\dot{x} = f(x) + g(x)k(x) = f(x) + \sum_{i=1}^{m} g_i(x)k_i(x)$$

can be written as

$$\dot{x} = F^{d_f}\mathcal{B}^{d_f}(x) + \sum_{i=1}^{m} G_i^{d_g}\mathcal{B}^{d_g}(x)K_i^{d_k}\mathcal{B}^{d_k}(x) \tag{9}$$

where

$$g_i = G_i^{d_g}\mathcal{B}^{d_g},\ k_i = K_i^{d_k}\mathcal{B}^{d_k},\ \text{and } k = K^{d_k}\mathcal{B}^{d_k}.$$

It should be noted that (9) is linear in the coefficients of the control K^{d_k}.

Let $d = \max(d_f, d_g + d_k)$. It is possible to represent the two summands of (9) in the same degree d, and write the closed-loop system as

$$\dot{x} = B^d(K^{d_k})\mathcal{B}^d(x). \tag{10}$$

We write $B^d(K^{d_k})$ to indicate that the coefficients B^d are affine functions of the entries of K^{d_k}. This notation is utilized in the remainder of the paper. Let $u \in \mathbb{R}^m$ be a control input. To obtain a linear problem for the controller design, we restrict the set U to be given by affine functions, i.e., $g_U(u) = Au + b$.

PROPOSITION 5. *Let σ be a simplex, $f \in \mathbb{R}^n[X_1, \dots, X_n]$ be a vector field, $g \in \mathbb{R}^{n\times m}[X_1, \dots, X_n]$ be an input matrix, and $k \in \mathbb{R}^m[X_1, \dots, X_n]$ be the control. Consider the system*

$$\dot{x} = f_{cl}(x) = f(x) + g(x)k(x) = B^d(K^{d_k})\mathcal{B}^d(x). \tag{11}$$

Define the polynomial

$$g_U \circ k = Q^{d_q}(K^{d_k})\mathcal{B}^{d_q}. \tag{12}$$

Then $u = k(x)$ is an admissible state feedback that solves Problem 1 if

$$Q^{d_q}(K^{d_k}) \geq 0, \tag{13a}$$

$$\frac{\partial \lambda_i}{\partial x} B_\alpha^d(K^{d_k}) \geq 0 \quad \forall i \in \{0, \dots, n\} \tag{13b}$$

where $|\alpha^i| = d$.

PROOF. By Proposition 3, (13a) is equivalent to $g_U \circ k(x) \geq 0$ for all $x \in [\sigma]$. Recall from Lemma 1 that $\frac{\partial \lambda_i}{\partial x}$ is normal to facet σ^i and from Corollary 1 that

$$\sum_{|\alpha^i|=d} b_\alpha^d \mathcal{B}_\alpha^d(x) = \sum_{|\alpha|=d} b_\alpha^d \mathcal{B}_\alpha^d(x) \quad \forall x \in [\sigma^i].$$

Thus, by Proposition 3 and (11), (13b) is equivalent to $n_i^T f_{cl}(x) \leq 0$ for all $x \in [\sigma^i]$. This proves the proposition. □

It is seen that the coefficients of the closed-loop system $B^d(K^{d_k})$ as well as the input constraints $Q^{d_g}(K^{d_k})$ are affine in the coefficients of the control K^{d_k}. This implies that the constraints in (13) are linear in the unknown control coefficients K^{d_k}. Thus, we can find K^{d_k} with a linear program. Notice that Proposition 5 provides only a sufficient condition, but via Bernstein theorem, one can raise the degree of the polynomials and find a solution. A control solving Problem 1 can be found using the following algorithm.

ALGORITHM 1.
Input: *Vector field* $f \in \mathbb{R}^n[X_1, \ldots, X_n]$, *input matrix* $g \in \mathbb{R}^{n \times m}[X_1, \ldots, X_n]$, *input constraints* g_U, *simplex* σ, *degree of the control* $d_k \in \mathbb{N}_0$, *and maximum iterations* $j_{max} \in \mathbb{N}_0$.
Output: *Feedback control law of degree* d_k.
Procedure:

0. *Initialization: Declare the coefficients* $Q^{d_q}(K^{d_k})$ *and* $B^d_\alpha(K^{d_k})$ $(d = \max(d_f, d_g + d_k))$ *from* (11) *and* (12), *and calculate the matrix* $\frac{\partial \lambda}{\partial x}$. *Set* $j = 0$.
1. *Search for coefficients of* K^{d_k} *satisfying* (13).
2. *If step 1 has failed and* $j < j_{max}$, *then raise the degree of* $Q^{d_q}(K^{d_k})$ *and* $B^d(K^{d_k})$ *by one, set* $j \equiv j + 1$, *and go to step 1.*
3. *Output* K^{d_k}.

5.2 Leaving a Simplex

To solve Problem 2, a control must be designed which ensures that all trajectories initialized in a simplex exit it in finite time through an admissible exit facet. Initially, we provide a necessary and sufficient condition for all solutions to exit a simplex in finite time. This condition is used to form a necessary and sufficient condition for the solution of Problem 2. Finally, the conditions are derived that makes it possible to compute the control. The proposed algorithm is based on certificates of positivity in the Bernstein basis.

PROPOSITION 6. *Let* σ *be a simplex and* $V \subset \mathbb{R}^n$ *be an open neighborhood of* $[\sigma]$. *Suppose* $f : V \to \mathbb{R}^n$ *is a Lipschitz continuous vector field. Consider the autonomous system*

$$\dot{x} = f(x), \quad x(0) = z, \tag{14}$$

and let $x(t, z)$ *denote the solution trajectory of* (14) *with initial state* z. *Then the trajectory* $x(t, z)$ *leaves* σ *in finite time for all* $z \in [\sigma]$ *if and only if there exist an open neighborhood* $W \subset V$ *of* $[\sigma]$, *and an upper semicontinuous function* $p : W \to \mathbb{R}$ *such that*

$$\frac{\mathrm{d}}{\mathrm{d}t}|_{t=0} p(x(t, z)) < 0 \quad \forall z \in [\sigma]. \tag{15}$$

If p *is smooth, then* (15) *is equivalent to*

$$\frac{\partial p}{\partial x}(x) f(x) < 0 \quad \forall x \in [\sigma].$$

PROOF. First, we show by contradiction that (15) is a necessary condition.

Fix $z \in [\sigma]$, and suppose that $x(t, z) \in [\sigma]$ for all $t \geq 0$. Since $[\sigma]$ is a closed positive invariant set, $[\sigma]$ contains ω-limit sets for every point in it.

Let $y \in \omega(z) \subseteq [\sigma]$. In other words, there is a sequence $\{t_n\}$ with $t_n \to \infty$ and $\lim_{n\to\infty} x(t_n, z) = y$. As a consequence, also $x(t, y) \in \omega(z)$ for all $t \geq 0$. Fix any $t \geq 0$, then there is a sequence $\{\tau_n\}$ with $\tau_n \to \infty$ and $\lim_{n\to\infty} x(\tau_n, z) = x(t, y)$.

By Bolzano-Weierstrass property [1], there are points α and β such that $\lim_{n\to\infty} p \circ x(t_n, z) = \alpha$ and $\lim_{n\to\infty} p \circ x(\tau_n, z) = \beta$. The function $p \circ x(\cdot, z)$ is decreasing, thus $\alpha = \beta$ (can be shown by the contradiction argument). This implies ($p \circ x(\cdot, z)$ is continuous by the premise) that $p(x(t, y)) = p(y)$, which contradicts (15).

Next, we show that the condition is sufficient. To this end, let W be a bounded open set with $[\sigma] \subset W \subset V$, and such that if the trajectory leaves $[\sigma]$ then it may enter $[\sigma]$ only after leaving $\mathrm{cl}(W)$. Such a neighbourhood exists because the flow map $x(\cdot, \cdot)$ is continuous and the boundary $\partial[\sigma]$ of $[\sigma]$ is compact.

By the premise, for any z, there is a finite time $t \equiv t(z)$ such that $x(t, z) \in \mathbb{R}^n \setminus [\sigma]$. Since $\mathrm{cl}(W)$ is compact, there are times T_1 and T_2 such that $T_1 < t(z) < T_2$ for all $z \in [\sigma]$.

For a union I of disjoint intervals $I_1, \ldots, I_n$ in $\mathbb{R}$ ($n \in \mathbb{N}_0 \cup \{\infty\}$) , $I = I_1 \cup \ldots \cup I_n$, we define a set-valued map $\mathrm{Min} : 2^{\mathbb{R}} \to 2^{\mathbb{R}}$ by

$$\mathrm{Min} : I_1 \cup \ldots \cup I_n \mapsto I_k,$$

where k is the (unique) index of the interval with the property: $t, \tau \in I$ and $t > \tau$ implies $t, \tau \in I_k$ (k is the set with smallest elements).

Equipped with the set valued map Min, we define a function $R : \mathrm{cl}(W) \to [T_1, T_2]$ by

$$R : z \mapsto \mathrm{Min}\{t \in \mathbb{R} |\ \partial[\sigma] \cap x(t, z) \neq \emptyset\}.$$

The map R is well defines, since there is finite time such that the solution trajectory $x(\cdot, z)$ leaves $[\sigma]$. Furthermore, both the domain and the range are compact.

We show that R is upper semicontinuous. To this end, we consider a sequence $\{(t_n, z_n)\}$ on the graph of R converging to (t, z). In particular $x(t_n, z_n) \in \partial[\sigma]$. Since $\partial[\sigma]$ is closed and the flow map $x(\cdot, \cdot)$ is continuous, $x(t, z) \in \partial[\sigma]$. Thus, the graph of R is closed. As a consequence, R is upper semicontinuous. By Theorem 1, Sec. 2.1.6 in [2], the maximal selection $p : x \mapsto \max R(x)$ is upper semicontinuous. To complete the proof, we compute the derivative of p in the direction of the vector field f

$$\frac{\mathrm{d}}{\mathrm{d}t} p \circ x(t, z) = \frac{\mathrm{d}}{\mathrm{d}t}(p(z) - t) = -1.$$

□

An autonomous system that solves Problem 2 satisfies the following conditions.

PROPOSITION 7. *Let* σ *be a simplex, where* n_i *is an outwards pointing normal vector of facet* σ^i, *let* $V \subseteq \mathbb{R}^n$ *be an open neighborhood of* $[\sigma]$, *and let* $\mathcal{I} \subseteq \{0, \ldots, n\}$ *be nonempty. Suppose* $f : V \to \mathbb{R}^n$ *is a Lipschitz continuous vector field. Consider the autonomous system*

$$\dot{x} = f(x), \quad x(0) = z, \tag{16}$$

and let $x(t, z)$ *denote the solution trajectory of* (16) *with initial state* z. *Then for all* $z \in [\sigma]$, *the solution trajectory* $x(t, z)$ *leaves* σ *in finite time through an admissible exit facet* $\{\sigma^i |\ i \in \mathcal{I}\}$ *if and only if*

1. *There exists an upper semicontinuous function* $p : V \to \mathbb{R}$ *such that* $\frac{\mathrm{d}}{\mathrm{d}t}|_{t=0} p(x(t, z)) < 0$ *for all* $z \in [\sigma]$. *(If* p *is smooth, then* $\frac{\partial p}{\partial x}(x) f(x) < 0$ *for all* $x \in [\sigma]$.*)*

2. *For all $i \in \{0, \dots, n\} \backslash \mathcal{I}$*

$$n_i^T f(x) \leq 0 \quad \forall x \in [\sigma^i].$$

PROOF. By Proposition 6, Condition 1 is equivalent to the property that the solution trajectory $x(t, z)$ leaves $[\sigma]$ in finite time.

For $i \in \{0, \dots, n\}$, let H_i be the supporting hyperplane of the polyhedral set $[\sigma]$ such that $[\sigma^i] = [\sigma] \cap H_i$; furthermore, let H_i^+ be a half space with supporting hyperplane H_i and $[\sigma] \subset H_i^+$. Define a polyhedral set

$$P = \bigcap_{i \in \{0, \dots, n\} \backslash \mathcal{I}} H_i^+.$$

Since $[\sigma^i]$ is compact there exists $\epsilon > 0$ such that the solution $x(t, z)$ is defined for any $-\epsilon < t < \epsilon$ and $z \in [\sigma^i]$. By Nagumo Theorem, Condition 2 is equivalent to positive local invariance of the set

$$P \cap x((-\epsilon, \epsilon), [\sigma^i]).$$

As a conclusion, Conditions 1 and 2 are equivalent to the statement that the solution trajectory $x(\cdot, z)$, for any $z \in [\sigma]$, leaves $[\sigma]$ and passes through one of the facets $[\sigma^i]$ with $i \in \mathcal{I}$. □

To design a closed-loop system that satisfies the previous condition, it is necessary to rewrite the condition such that the inequalities are linear in the unknown polynomials. The problem to be solved is: Find p and k such that

$$\frac{\partial p}{\partial x}(x)(f(x) + g(x)k(x)) < 0 \quad \forall x \in [\sigma]$$

$$n_i^T (f(x) + g(x)k(x)) \geq 0 \quad \forall x \in [\sigma^i].$$

The difficulty of this problem is to simultaneously find p and k, when their coefficients are multiplied together. A similar problem is solved in [19] where a Lyapunov measure is used, and in [18] where the problem is solved using sums of squares with restrictions imposed on the structure of the Lyapunov function. We solve the problem by restricting the structure of p. We denote the input matrix by $g = [g_1 \ \dots \ g_m]$ and define

$$\bar{g}^T = [g_1^T \ \dots \ g_m^T]$$

and let f_{n_i} be the projection of f onto n_i, and accordingly let $g_{j_{n_i}}$ be the projection of g_j onto n_i; hence,

$$\bar{g}_{n_i}^T = \left[g_{1_{n_i}}^T(x) \ \dots \ g_{m_{n_i}}^T(x) \right].$$

THEOREM 4. *Let σ be a simplex, $f \in \mathbb{R}^n[X_1, \dots, X_n]$ be a vector field, $g = [g_1 \ \dots \ g_m]$ with $g_i \in \mathbb{R}^n[X_1, \dots, X_n]$ be an input matrix, and let $\mathcal{I} \subseteq \{0, \dots, n\}$ be nonempty. Assume that each vector $g_i(x)$ is nonzero for all $x \in [\sigma]$. If there exist a map $y \in \mathbb{R}^{mn}[X_1, \dots, X_n]$ and a function $p \in \mathbb{R}[X_1, \dots, X_n]$ satisfying*

$$\frac{\partial p}{\partial x} = \sum_{i=1}^{m} g_i^T H^i, \tag{17a}$$

where $H^i \in \mathbb{R}^{n \times n}[X_1, \dots, X_n]$ such that

$$\frac{\partial p}{\partial x}(x)f(x) + \bar{g}^T y(x) < 0 \quad \forall x \in [\sigma], \tag{18}$$

$$\sum_{i=1}^{m} g_i^T(x) H^i(x) g_i(x) < 0 \quad \forall x \in [\sigma], \tag{19}$$

$$g_i^T H^i g_j = 0 \quad \forall i \neq j, \tag{20}$$

and for all $i \in \{0, \dots, n\} \backslash \mathcal{I}$

$$\frac{\partial p}{\partial x}(x) f_{n_i}(x) + \bar{g}_{n_i}^T(x) y(x) \leq 0 \quad \forall x \in [\sigma^i], \tag{21}$$

$$\frac{\partial p}{\partial x}(x) n_i \geq 0 \quad \forall x \in [\sigma^i], \tag{22}$$

there exists $k \in \mathbb{R}^m(X_1, ..., X_n)$ that solves

$$\bar{g}^T y(x) = \frac{\partial p}{\partial x}(x) g(x) k(x). \tag{23}$$

Furthermore for all $z \in [\sigma]$, trajectory $x(t, z)$ of system

$$\dot{x} = f(x) + g(x)k(x)$$

with state feedback control $k \in \mathbb{R}^m(X_1, \dots, X_n)$ given by (23) leaves σ in finite time through an admissible exit facet given by $\{\sigma^i | \ i \in \mathcal{I}\}$.

PROOF. First, we show that the existence of a function $p \in \mathbb{R}[X_1, \dots, X_n]$ and a map $y \in \mathbb{R}^{mn}[X_1, \dots, X_n]$ such that

$$\frac{\partial p}{\partial x}(x) f(x) + \bar{g}^T(x) y(x) < 0 \quad \forall x \in [\sigma]$$

implies that with the same $p \in \mathbb{R}[X_1, \dots, X_n]$ there exists a map $k \in \mathbb{R}^m(X_1, \dots, X_n)$ such that

$$\frac{\partial p}{\partial x}(x)(f(x) + g(x)k(x)) < 0 \quad \forall x \in [\sigma]. \tag{24}$$

By (19) and (20), for any $x \in [\sigma]$ there exists $i \in \{1, \dots, m\}$ such that

$$\frac{\partial p}{\partial x}(x) g_i(x) \neq 0.$$

Thereby there exists a rational map $k(x) \in \mathbb{R}^m(X_1, \dots, X_n)$ such that

$$\bar{g}^T(x) y(x) = \frac{\partial p}{\partial x}(x) g(x) k(x) \quad \forall x \in [\sigma].$$

Next, we show that

$$\frac{\partial p}{\partial x}(x) f_{n_i}(x) + \bar{g}_{n_i}^T(x) y(x) \leq 0 \quad \forall x \in [\sigma^i], \tag{25a}$$

$$\frac{\partial p}{\partial x}(x) n_i > 0 \quad \forall x \in [\sigma^i] \tag{25b}$$

implies that

$$n_i^T(f(x) + g(x)k(x)) \leq 0 \quad \forall x \in [\sigma^i]. \tag{26}$$

By (25b), the vector $\frac{\partial p}{\partial x}(x)$ points out of σ for all $x \in [\sigma^i]$. Therefore, the closed-loop vector field projected onto n_i must point in the opposite direction of $\frac{\partial p}{\partial x}(x)$ for all $x \in [\sigma^i]$, i.e.,

$$\frac{\partial p}{\partial x}(x)(f_{n_i}(x) + g_{n_i}(x)k(x)) \leq 0 \quad \forall x \in [\sigma^i]. \tag{27}$$

This is ensured by (21) and (23), as

$$\bar{g}_{n_i}^T y(x) = \frac{\partial p}{\partial x}(x) g_{n_i}(x) k(x). \tag{28}$$

□

The theorem can be solved by rephrasing the inequalities to certificates of positivity in the Bernstein basis. It is seen that the constraints are linear in unknown coefficients.

In the algorithm, we search directly for $\partial p / \partial x$; thus, we must ensure that there exists a function $p \in \mathbb{R}[X_1, \dots, X_n]$

with a partial derivative given as shown in (17a). Since $[\sigma]$ is contractible, there exists p such that $dp = h$ if and only if $dh = 0$ [15]. Thus, there exists p with partial derivative given by (17a) if and only if

$$\sum_{i=1}^{m} \frac{\partial g_i}{\partial x_k} H_j^i - \frac{\partial g_i}{\partial x_j} H_k^i + g_i^T \left(\frac{\partial H_j^i}{\partial x_k} - \frac{\partial H_k^i}{\partial x_j} \right) = 0 \quad (29)$$

for any pair $(j,k) \in \{1,\ldots,n\}^2$ with $i > k$, where H_j^i denotes the jth column of H^i.

For the subsequent work, it is important to note that the Bernstein coefficients of $\partial f/\partial x$ are linear combinations of the Bernstein coefficients of f, as expected.

COROLLARY 2. *Let σ be a simplex, $f \in \mathbb{R}^n[X_1,\ldots,X_n]$ be a vector field, $g \in \mathbb{R}^{n\times m}[X_1,\ldots,X_n]$ be an input matrix, and let $\mathcal{I} \subseteq \{0,\ldots,n\}$ be nonempty. Consider the system*

$$\dot{x} = f(x) + g(x)k(x). \quad (30)$$

Fix polynomials $\partial p/\partial x$, y, and define the polynomials

$$y(x) = Y^{d_y}\mathcal{B}^{d_y}(x)$$
$$\frac{\partial p}{\partial x}(x) = P^{d_p}\mathcal{B}^{d_p}(x)$$
$$\frac{\partial p}{\partial x}(x)f(x) + \bar{g}^T y(x) = F^{d_f}(P^{d_p}, Y^{d_y})\mathcal{B}^{d_f}(x),$$
$$g_i^T(x)H^i(x)g_j(x) = \bar{H}^{i,j,d_h}(P^{d_p})\mathcal{B}^{d_h}(x)$$
$$\frac{\partial p}{\partial x}(x)f_{n_i}(x) + \bar{g}_{n_i}^T(x)y(x) = F^{i,d_f}(P^{d_p}, Y^{d_y})\mathcal{B}^{d_f}(x)$$
$$\frac{\partial p}{\partial x}(x)n_i = N^{i,d_n}(P^{d_p})\mathcal{B}^{d_n}(x)$$

and impose the structure from (29) on $\partial p/\partial x$. Then the control $u = k(x)$ given by

$$\bar{g}^T y(x) = \frac{\partial p}{\partial x}(x)g(x)k(x) \quad (31)$$

is an admissible state feedback that solves Problem 2 if the coefficients F^{d_f}, $\bar{H}^{i,j,d_h}$, and N^{i,d_n} satisfy

$$F_\alpha^{d_f}(P^{d_p}, Y^{d_y}) \le 0 \quad \text{for } |\alpha| = d \quad (32a)$$
$$F_{e_i}^{d_f}(P^{d_p}, Y^{d_y}) < 0 \quad \text{for } i \in \{0,\ldots,n\} \quad (32b)$$
$$\sum_{j=1}^{m} \bar{H}_\alpha^{j,j,d_h}(P^{d_p}) \le 0 \quad \text{for } |\alpha| = d \quad (32c)$$
$$\sum_{j=1}^{m} \bar{H}_{e_i}^{j,j,d_h}(P^{d_p}) < 0 \quad \text{for } i \in \{0,\ldots,n\} \quad (32d)$$
$$\bar{H}_\alpha^{i,j,d_h}(P^{d_p}) = 0 \quad \text{for } |\alpha| = d \text{ and } j \ne i \quad (32e)$$

and for $i \in \{0,\ldots,n\} \setminus \mathcal{I}$

$$F^{i,d_f}(P^{d_p}, Y^{d_y}) \ge 0 \quad \text{for } |\alpha^i| = d \quad (32f)$$
$$N^{i,d_n}(P^{d_p}) \ge 0 \quad \text{for } |\alpha^i| = d. \quad (32g)$$

6. EXAMPLES

To validate the proposed algorithms, we will apply them to examples from [10] and [21] comprising affine and polynomial systems.

6.1 Affine System

Example 5.7 in [10] presents a controller design for affine vector fields defined on the standard simplex. We recalculate the example using the proposed algorithm. Notice that we are sure to find linear controls without raising the degree of our expression, due to the linear precision of Bernstein forms [7].

We consider the control system

$$\dot{x} = \begin{bmatrix} -x_1 + u \\ x_1 - x_2 + u \end{bmatrix}$$

and design a state feedback control $k \in \mathbb{R}[X_1, X_2]$ such that $u \in [-1 \;\; 1]$, and all solutions exit the simplex σ through the admissible exit facet $[\sigma^2]$, where the vertices are $[\sigma_0] = (1,0) \in \mathbb{R}^2$, $[\sigma_1] = (0,1) \in \mathbb{R}^2$, and $[\sigma_2] = (0,0) \in \mathbb{R}^2$. Thus, we solve Problem 2 with an iterative method.

The control is realized from p and y found to be

$$p(x) = 0.1352x_1 - 0.999x_2 + 0.999$$
$$y(x) = \begin{bmatrix} 0.5255 - 0.5255x_1 \\ -0.8639x_1 - 1.9981x_2 \\ 0.7623 - 0.4995x_2 - 1.2618x_1 \end{bmatrix}.$$

The resulting feedback control is

$$k(x) = 1.1564x_2 - 1.3129x_1 + 1.1564.$$

A phase plot of the closed-loop system is illustrated in Figure 3. It is seen that the vector field only points out of facet $[\sigma^2]$; hence, the problem is solved and all solutions trajectories exit the simplex through $[\sigma^2]$.

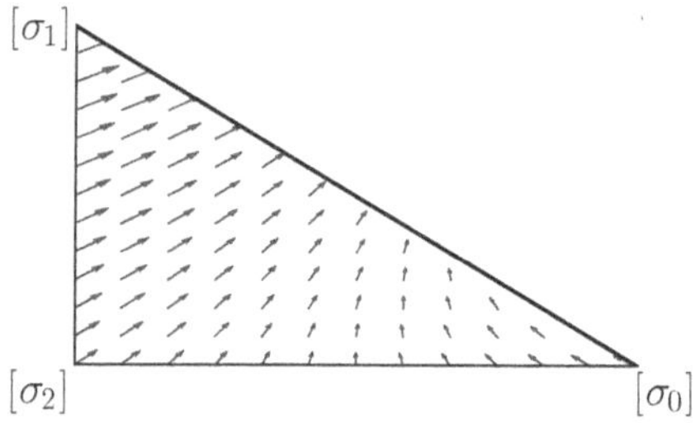

Figure 3: Phase plot of a vector field solving Problem 2, with admissible exit facet $[\sigma^2]$.

We consider the control system

$$\dot{x} = \begin{bmatrix} 1 - x_1 + 2u \\ x_1 - x_2 + u \end{bmatrix}$$

and design a state feedback control $k \in \mathbb{R}[X_1, X_2]$ such that $u \in [-1 \;\; 1]$ and the simplex σ is positively invariant, where $[\sigma_0] = (1,0)$, $[\sigma_1] = (0,1)$, and $[\sigma_2] = (0,0)$. Thus, we solve Problem 1 using Algorithm 1.

The resulting feedback control is found to be

$$k(x) = 0.3459 - 0.5485x_2 - 0.8547x_1.$$

A phase plot of the closed-loop system is illustrated in Figure 4. It is seen that the vector field points into the simplex at all facets; thus, the problem is solved.

6.2 Polynomial System

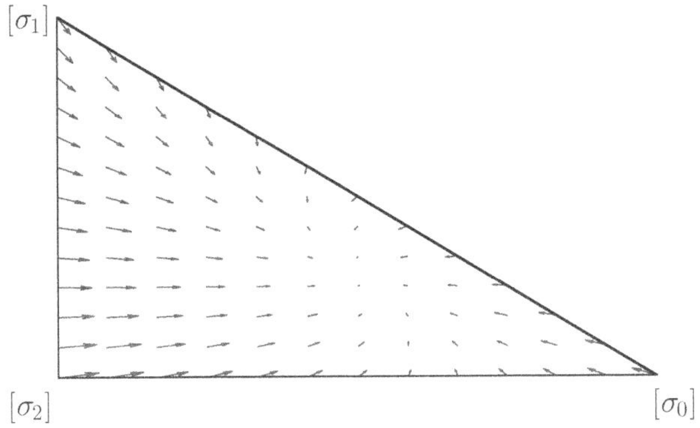

Figure 4: Phase plot of a vector field solving Problem 1.

We solve the control problems for a polynomial system presented in [21]. In contrast to [21], we consider a simplicial subset of the state space for the design.

We consider the control system

$$\dot{x} = \begin{bmatrix} -x_2 - 1.5x_1 - 0.5x_1^3 + u_1 \\ x_1 + u_2 \end{bmatrix} \tag{33}$$

and design a state feedback control $k \in \mathbb{R}^2[X_1, X_2]$ such that $u \in [-10 \quad 10]$ and all solutions exit the simplex σ through the admissible exit facet $[\sigma^2]$. The simplex is defined by the vertices $[\sigma_0] = (2, -1.5)$, $[\sigma_1] = (-2, 3)$, and $[\sigma_2] = (-2, -1.5)$. We solve Problem 2 with an iterative method.

Choosing the degree of the controller to 2, the feedback control is found to be

$$k(x) = \begin{bmatrix} 0.0055x_1^2 - 0.3107x_1x_2 - 0.1798x_1 \\ 0.0726x_1^2 + 0.3072x_1x_2 - 0.9436x_1 \end{bmatrix.$$
$$\begin{matrix} +0.0561x_2^2 - 0.8656x_2 + 6.1825 \\ +0.2626x_2^2 - 0.8722x_2 - 1.1669 \end{bmatrix} .$$

A phase plot of the closed-loop system is illustrated in Figure 5. It is seen that the vector field only points out of facet $[\sigma^2]$ as required.

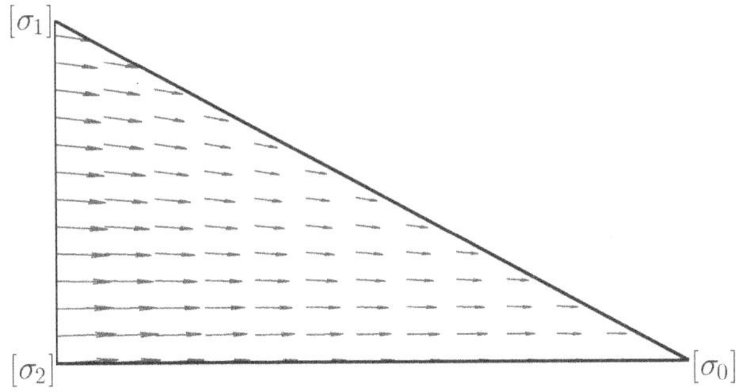

Figure 5: Phase plot of a vector field solving Problem 2, with admissible exit facet $[\sigma^2]$.

Next, we again consider the control system in (33) and design a state feedback control $k \in \mathbb{R}^2[X_1, X_2]$ such that $u \in [-10 \quad 10]$ and the simplex σ is positively invariant.

The resulting feedback control is found to be

$$k(x) = \begin{bmatrix} -3.1212 - 1.0696x_2 - 2.9672x_1 \\ 0.0295 - 3.1893x_2 - 1.2078x_1 \end{bmatrix} .$$

A phase plot of the closed-loop system is illustrated in Figure 6. It is seen that the simplex is positively invariant, as the vector field points into the simplex at every facet.

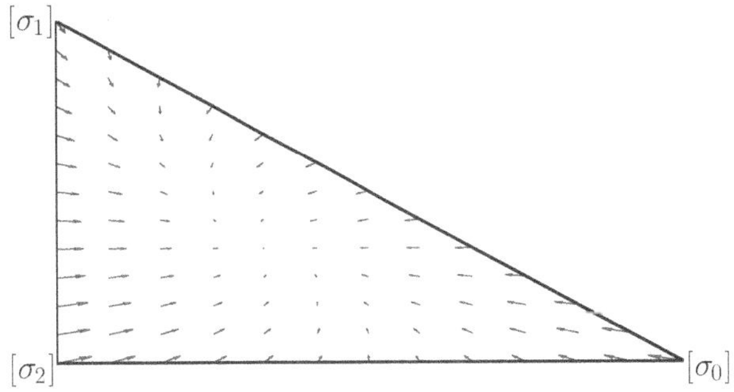

Figure 6: Phase plot of a vector field solving Problem 1.

7. CONCLUSIONS

In this paper, the control to facet problem for polynomial vector fields was considered. The main contribution was to show that polynomial inequalities can be accommodated by the use of Bernstein coefficients. Thus, it is possible to design polynomial control laws for polynomial systems via linear programming.

In contrast to the certificate of positivity sum of squares, the positivity of any polynomial can be certified by the presented certificate of positivity. This opens the opportunity to synthesize controls for general polynomial systems.

8. REFERENCES

[1] T. M. Apostol. *Mathematical Analysis.* Addison-Wesley Publishing Company, 2nd edition, 1974.

[2] J.-P. Aubin. *Viability Theory.* Birkhäuser, 1991.

[3] C. Belta and L. C. Habets. Controlling a class of nonlinear systems on rectangles. *IEEE Transactions on Automatic Control*, 51(11):1749–1759, November 2006.

[4] J. Berchtold and A. Bowyer. Robust arithmetic for multivariate Bernstein-form polynomials. *Computer-Aided Design*, 32(11):681 – 689, 2000.

[5] J. Bochnak, M. Coste, and M.-F. Roy. *Real Algebraic Geometry.* Springer, 1998.

[6] F. Boudaoud, F. Caruso, and M.-F. Roy. Certificates of positivity in the Bernstein basis. *Discrete & Computational Geometry*, 39:639–655, 2008.

[7] R. T. Farouki. The Bernstein polynomial basis: A centennial retrospective. *Computer Aided Geometric Design*, 29(6):379 – 419, 2012.

[8] L. Habets and J. Schuppen. Control of piecewise-linear hybrid systems on simplices and rectangles. In M. Benedetto and A. Sangiovanni-Vincentelli, editors, *Hybrid Systems: Computation and Control*, volume 2034 of *Lecture Notes in Computer Science*, pages 261–274. Springer Berlin Heidelberg, 2001.

[9] L. Habets and J. van Schuppen. Control to facet problems for affine systems on simplices and polytopes - with applications to control of hybrid systems. In

44th IEEE Conference on Decision and Control and 2005 European Control Conference, pages 4175–4180, December 2005.

[10] L. C. G. J. M. Habets, P. J. Collins, and J. H. van Schuppen. Reachability and control synthesis for piecewise-affine hybrid systems on simplices. *IEEE Transactions on Automatic Control*, 51(6):938–948, June 2006.

[11] D. Henrion and A. Garulli, editors. *Positive Polynomials in Control*, volume 312 of *Lecture Notes in Control and Information Science*. Springer Berlin Heidelberg, 2005.

[12] M. Kloetzer and C. Belta. A fully automated framework for control of linear systems from temporal logic specifications. *IEEE Transactions on Automatic Control*, 53(1):287–297, February 2008.

[13] S. M. Lane. *Categories for the Working Mathematician*, volume 5 of *Graduate Texts in Mathematics*. Springer New York, 2nd edition, 1978.

[14] R. Leroy. Certificates of positivity in the simplicial Bernstein basis. 2009.

[15] I. H. Madsen and J. Tornehave. *From Calculus to Cohomology: De Rham Cohomology and Characteristic Classes*. Cambridge University Press, 1997.

[16] J. P. May. *Simplicial Objects in Algebraic Topology*. Chicago Lectures in Mathematics. University of Chicago Press, 1967.

[17] V. Powers. Positive polynomials and sums of squares: Theory and practice. *Real Algebraic Geometry*, 2011.

[18] S. Prajna, A. Papachristodoulou, and F. Wu. Nonlinear control synthesis by sum of squares optimization: A lyapunov-based approach.

[19] A. Rantzer. A dual to Lyapunov's stability theorem. *Systems & Control Letters*, 42:161–168, 2001.

[20] B. Roszak and M. E. Broucke. Necessary and sufficient conditions for reachability on a simplex. In *Proceedings of the 44th IEEE Conference on Decision and Control, and the European Control Conference*, pages 4706–4711, 2005.

[21] M. A. B. Sassi and A. Girard. Control polynomial dynamical systems on rectangles. In *Proceedings of the 12th European Control Conference*, 2013.

[22] C. Scheiderer. Positivity and sums of squares: a guide to recent results. In *Emerging applications of algebraic geometry*, pages 271–324. Springer, 2009.

[23] H. P. Seidel. An introduction to polar forms. *IEEE Computer Graphics and Applications*, 13(1):38–46, 1993.

Simulation-guided Lyapunov Analysis for Hybrid Dynamical Systems

James Kapinski*
Toyota Technical Center

Jyotirmoy V. Deshmukh
Toyota Technical Center

Sriram Sankaranarayanan
Univ. of Colorado

Nikos Aréchiga
Carnegie Mellon University

ABSTRACT

Lyapunov functions are used to prove stability and to obtain performance bounds on system behaviors for nonlinear and hybrid dynamical systems, but discovering Lyapunov functions is a difficult task in general. We present a technique for discovering Lyapunov functions and barrier certificates for nonlinear and hybrid dynamical systems using a search-based approach. Our approach uses concrete executions, such as those obtained through simulation, to formulate a series of linear programming (LP) optimization problems; the solution to each LP creates a candidate Lyapunov function. Intermediate candidates are iteratively improved using a global optimizer guided by the Lie derivative of the candidate Lyapunov function. The analysis is refined using counterexamples from a Satisfiability Modulo Theories (SMT) solver. When no counterexamples are found, the soundness of the analysis is verified using an arithmetic solver. The technique can be applied to a broad class of nonlinear dynamical systems, including hybrid systems and systems with polynomial and even transcendental dynamics. We present several examples illustrating the efficacy of the technique, including two automotive powertrain control examples.

Categories and Subject Descriptors

I.2.8 [**Artificial Intelligence**]: Problem Solving, Control Methods, and Search—*Control theory*; I.6 [**Simulation and Modeling**]: Simulation Output Analysis; G.1.6 [**Numerical Analysis**]: Optimization—*Global optimization*

*The authors can be contacted at the following email addresses, respectively: `jim.kapinski@tema.toyota.com`, `jyotirmoy.deshmukh@tema.toyota.com`, `srirams@colorado.edu`, and `narechig@ece.cmu.edu`.

HSCC'14, April 15–17, 2014, Berlin, Germany.

http://dx.doi.org/10.1145/2562059.2562139.

Keywords

Lyapunov functions, Stability, Invariant Sets, Barrier certificates, Simulation

1. INTRODUCTION

Analysis techniques for hybrid systems range from formal techniques that can provide mathematical proofs of correctness to testing-based techniques that rely on a large number of simulations to gain confidence in system correctness. Formal techniques provide better guarantees but are often intractable for large, complex system designs. On the other hand, simulation-based methods work well for systems of arbitrary complexity but cannot be used for verification. In this paper, we describe our effort to bridge this gap by formally addressing prominent analysis problems for hybrid systems while leveraging data obtained from simulations. In particular, we address the problems of proving stability of a system, characterizing performance bounds by computing forward invariant sets, and proving system safety by automatically synthesizing barrier certificates.

It is well-known that each of these problems can be effectively addressed if the designer is able to supply a function v that satisfies the following *Lyapunov conditions* in a given region of interest: (1) v is positive definite, and (2) the Lie derivative of v along the system dynamics is negative (semi-)definite. While the search for a Lyapunov function is widely recognized as a hard problem, sum-of-squares (SoS) optimization-based techniques have been used successfully to obtain Lyapunov functions for systems with polynomial [17, 21] , nonpolynomial [16], and hybrid [18] dynamics. While these techniques have mature tool support [20, 14], they often involve solving problems that are numerically sensitive. For instance, a function computed by such a technique may not strictly satisfy the Lyapunov conditions for all points in the region of interest.

Our key contribution is a novel technique to exploit the results obtained by simulating a system to obtain a *provably correct* and *numerically robust* certificate of stability or safety for the system. The decision to use simulation data and test results is natural in the context of complex dynamical systems, such as those in industrial control systems. In such systems, simulations are often used to validate system designs and increase confidence in system performance. Powerful tools for performing simulation are readily available and are commonly used in, for example, the automotive industry to perform model-based design (e.g., Simulink from the MathWorks [1]).

We now give a brief overview of our technique. We assume that the desired Lyapunov function has a certain parameterized template form: an SoS polynomial of fixed degree. We derive a set of linear constraints on the parameters in the Lyapunov function from concrete execution traces. Given a set of such constraints, the search for a Lyapunov function then reduces to solving a linear program (LP) to obtain a *candidate Lyapunov function*. A key step is then to use a stochastic global optimizer to search the region of interest for states that violate the Lyapunov conditions for the given candidate. The search is guided by a cost function that is based on the Lie derivative of the candidate Lyapunov function; if the minimum cost is less than zero, then the minimizing argument provides a witness (which we call a *counterexample*) that the candidate Lyapunov function is invalid. After the global optimizer obtains counterexamples, the associated linear constraints are included in the LP problem and the candidate Lyapunov function is updated. The process terminates when the global optimizer is unable to identify counterexamples.

As global optimization is not exhaustive, it is imperative to validate any analysis based on the candidate Lyapunov function obtained by the counterexample-guided iterative technique described above. To do so, we use an ensemble of solvers: SMT solvers with nonlinear capabilities such as z3 [6] and dReal [8] and symbolic tools such as quantifier elimination as implemented by the `Reduce` command in Mathematica [24].

Using the candidate Lyapunov function and a suitable solver, we can perform various types of analysis: showing Lyapunov stability or producing a forward invariant set or a barrier certificate. To show Lyapunov stability, we employ one of the solvers to verify the soundness of the candidate Lyapunov function. To produce a forward invariant set, we generate a *sublevelset* of the candidate Lyapunov function S_ℓ of v (i.e., the set $\{\mathbf{x} \mid v(\mathbf{x}) \leq \ell\}$) and then validate that S_ℓ is an invariant using one of the solvers mentioned above.This can be formulated as a single convex optimization problem. Given an initial set of states X_0, and a set of unsafe states U, we can also use it to obtain a *barrier certificate* that includes the initial states while excluding the unsafe set. In this instance, we formulate the barrier certificate as a suitable *levelset* of v that separates X_0 from U.

To demonstrate the efficacy of our techniques, we present examples of dynamical systems, ranging from simple nonlinear systems and systems with transcendental, time-varying dynamics, to switched and nonpolynomial dynamical systems. Our examples include two systems inspired by the automotive engine control domain. The first automotive example is an Air-to-Fuel ratio (A/F) control system with nonlinear, nonpolynomial dynamics, and we construct a forward invariant, which provides performance bounds for the system. The second automotive example is a closed-loop model-predictive control system, modeled as a switched-mode system with piecewise affine dynamics in each of its 69 modes. For this system, we are able to obtain a Lyapunov function for the region of interest (27 modes), thus providing a proof of stability as well as a means to compute performance bounds.

The use of simulations to obtain Lyapunov functions and estimate the maximal region of attraction has been investigated in the past by Topcu et al. [21]. Their approach uses simulation traces to estimate the region of attraction (ROA) for a dynamical system: converting a set of bilinear matrix inequalities (which are computationally expensive to solve) into linear matrix inequalities, which are computationally less expensive. We provide the following extensions to that work: a.) We provide a procedure that uses a guided approach to iteratively improve the quality of the candidate Lyapunov functions, and b.) Our technique is not restricted to the class of systems with polynomial dynamics.

Related work was proposed by Gupta et al. [9] for program analysis. Their approach uses traces of discrete programs to compute termination proofs in the form of ranking functions and linear invariants.

The layout of the paper is as follows: We review the theoretical background in Sec. 2. In Sec. 3, we present our technique for generating candidate Lyapunov functions and for iteratively improving the candidates. In Sec. 4, we explain how SMT solvers can be used to verify the soundness of the candidates and we also explain how counterexamples can be used to further improve the candidate Lyapunov functions. We demonstrate our technique on interesting nonlinear and hybrid examples in Sec. 5, and finally conclude with a discussion of future work in Sec. 6.

2. PRELIMINARIES

Continuous-time switched-mode systems (CSMS). A CSMS is a dynamical system described by a set of ODEs:

$$\dot{\mathbf{x}}(t) \;=\; f_i(\mathbf{x}(t)),\ \forall \mathbf{x}(t) \in X_i, \qquad (1)$$

where $\mathbf{x}(t) \in \mathbb{R}^n$ is the state of the system at time t, and X_i, $i = 1, \ldots, I$ is a partition of the state space $\mathcal{X} \subseteq \mathbb{R}^n$. Each f_i is a nonlinear vector field that is Lipschitz-continuous. We abuse notation and take $\mathbf{x} \in \mathbb{R}^n$ to be a singleton and $\mathbf{x}(\cdot)$ to be a differentiable function $\mathbf{x} : \mathbb{R} \to \mathbb{R}^n$.

Given an initial condition $\mathbf{x}_0 \in \mathbb{R}^n$, a *trace* of a CSMS is a function $\mathbf{x}(t) : \mathbb{R}_{\geq 0} \to \mathbb{R}^n$, where $\mathbf{x}(0) = \mathbf{x}_0$ and (1) holds for all $t \in \mathbb{R}_{\geq 0}$.

We assume that the system has no Zeno behavior, that is, we assume that there are finite switches in finite time. Given an initial condition $\mathbf{x}(0)$, a unique solution $\mathbf{x}(t)$ to (1) exists.

We define $\phi(t)$ as a discrete-time *trace* of system (1). That is, $\phi(t)$ is a function $\phi : T \to \mathbb{R}^n$, where $T = \{t_1, \ldots, t_N\} \subset \mathbb{R}$, where $N \in \mathbb{Z}_{>0}$, and there exists an $\mathbf{x}(t)$, such that for each $1 \leq j < N$, $\phi(t_j) = \mathbf{x}(t_j)$ and (1) holds for all $t \in [t_j, t_{j+1}]$.

DEFINITION 2.1 (EQUILIBRIUM POINT). *A state $\mathbf{x}^*$ is called an* equilibrium point *of a* CSMS *if a trace of the system with $\mathbf{x}(0) = \mathbf{x}^*$ is given by $\mathbf{x}(t) = \mathbf{x}^*$ for all time t.*

In standard fashion, we use $\|\mathbf{x}\|$ to denote the Euclidean norm $\sqrt{\mathbf{x}^T\mathbf{x}}$, i.e. the distance of a point in $\mathbb{R}^n$ from the origin. A^T denotes the transpose of the matrix A.

DEFINITION 2.2 (FORWARD INVARIANT SET). *A set of states $I \subseteq \mathbb{R}^n$ of a* CSMS *is called a* forward invariant set *if for all $\mathbf{x}(0) \in I$ and for all $t \geq 0$, $\mathbf{x}(t) \in I$.*

The goal of Lyapunov's direct method is to show stability of a system by identifying a *Lyapunov function*.

Definition 2.3 (Lyapunov function). *Given a* CSMS, *a function* $v : \mathcal{X} \to \mathbb{R}_{\geq 0}$ *is called a Lyapunov function if the following holds for all* i *[13]:*

$$\forall \mathbf{x} \in X_i \backslash \mathbf{0} : v(\mathbf{x}) \ > 0,\ v(\mathbf{0}) = 0 \tag{2}$$
$$\forall \mathbf{x} \in X_i : \nabla v(\mathbf{x}(t))^T \cdot f_i(\mathbf{x}(t)) \ \leq 0. \tag{3}$$

The existence of a Lyapunov function, as specified above, guarantees non-asymptotic stability. For switched systems, such a Lyapunov function can take the form of a single, continuous and differentiable *common Lyapunov function*. When a common Lyapunov function cannot be found, it is sometimes possible to define a *piecewise Lyapunov function*, where a unique Lyapunov-like function is defined for each mode, with additional conditions on the behavior of the Lyapunov-like functions at the switching instances [4].

For certain classes of systems, such as stable linear time-invariant systems, techniques exist to identify Lyapunov functions and invariant sets. For continuous systems with dynamics given by polynomial equations, relaxations based on SoS techniques exist that allow Lyapunov functions and invariant sets to be identified for certain cases. For general nonlinear systems, however, no such techniques exist. For hybrid systems with linear continuous dynamics, several techniques exist for identifying Lyapunov functions, such as LMI solutions for simultaneous Lyapunov functions and piecewise quadratic Lyapunov functions, but these techniques are not complete (i.e., they can fail to identify a Lyapunov function even when one exists).

The *sublevelset* of a Lyapunov function $v(\mathbf{x})$ is the set $\{\mathbf{x} \mid v(\mathbf{x}) \leq \ell\}$. It is well known that sublevelsets of Lyapunov functions are forward invariant sets. While forward invariant sets can be used to characterize performance bounds of a given CSMS, the closely related notion of a *barrier certificate* can be used to verify safety of a given system.

Definition 2.4 (Barrier Certificate). *Given a* CSMS, *an initial set* $X_0 \subset \mathcal{X}$, *and an unsafe set* $U \subset \mathcal{X}$ *such that* $U \cap X_0$ *is empty, a function* $B : \mathcal{X} \to \mathbb{R}$ *is called a barrier certificate if it satisfies the following conditions for all* i*:*

$$B(\mathbf{x}) \leq 0 \qquad \forall \mathbf{x} \in X_0 \tag{4}$$
$$B(\mathbf{x}) > 0 \qquad \forall \mathbf{x} \in U \tag{5}$$
$$\nabla B(\mathbf{x})^T \cdot f_i(\mathbf{x}) < 0 \quad \forall \mathbf{x} \in X_i \ s.t.\ B(\mathbf{x}) = 0. \tag{6}$$

Note that a Lyapunov function can be used to construct a barrier certificate as follows. Given an $l \in \mathbb{R}_{>0}$, if we select $B(\mathbf{x}) = v(\mathbf{x}) - l$ and define $S_\ell = \{\mathbf{x} \mid B(\mathbf{x}) = 0\}$, then $B(\mathbf{x})$ satisfies (6) if $S_\ell \subseteq \mathcal{X}$. As long as (4) and (5) hold, then $B(\mathbf{x})$ is a barrier certificate.

Discrete-time Switched-Mode Systems (DSMS). We also consider discrete-time switched-mode systems (DSMS), where $\mathbf{x}[k+1] = f_i(\mathbf{x}[k])$. When discussing a discrete-time context, we use $\hat{\mathbf{x}} = f_i(\mathbf{x})$. The notions defined above for CSMS carry over for DSMS. For example, an invariant set for a DSMS is defined as a set I such that for all $\mathbf{x}[0] \in I$, and for all $k \in \mathbb{Z}_{>0}$, $\mathbf{x}[k] \in I$. Similarly, the Lyapunov conditions for a DSMS are:

$$\forall \mathbf{x} \in X_i \backslash \mathbf{0} : v(\mathbf{x}) \ > 0,\ v(\mathbf{0}) = 0 \tag{7}$$
$$\forall \mathbf{x} \in X_i : v(\mathbf{x}) - v(\hat{\mathbf{x}}) \ > 0. \tag{8}$$

3. ITERATIVELY IMPROVED LYAPUNOV CANDIDATES

We present a technique to compute candidate Lyapunov functions for switched-mode systems using simulation traces. The technique relies on a *falsification* tool to produce a series of successively improved candidate functions. The falsification tool is a global optimizer that is guided by direction information provided by the intermediate Lyapunov candidates. The falsifier adds constraints to a series of LPs by selecting initial conditions for simulation traces. We go on to describe how to use the resulting candidates and automated reasoning tools to: a.) show that the candidates are Lyapunov functions, or b.) produce invariant sets and barrier certificates.

Topcu et al. [21] employ simulation traces to formulate a convex optimization problem to compute candidate Lyapunov functions and invariant sets. The goal for their work is to characterize a region of attraction of a given continuous-time dynamical system. In this paper, we go further and provide a technique to iteratively improve the candidates using a stochastic global optimization-based approach that is guided by a cost function based on the Lie derivative of the candidate Lyapunov function.

3.1 Constructing Candidates

In the following, we assume the system has a stable equilibrium point, which is, without loss of generality, at the origin. Let Φ_i be a collection of p traces within mode i. We assume we can obtain discrete-time traces, $\phi_i(t)$.

We obtain candidates for functions v that satisfy conditions (2) and (3) by using the following alternate conditions:

1. We restrict each v to the class of polynomials of some fixed degree;
2. We require that a necessary condition for constraints (2) and (3) hold for every trace in Φ_i.

We impose condition (1) by requiring $v(\mathbf{x}) = \mathbf{z}^T \mathbf{P} \mathbf{z}$, where $\mathbf{z}$ is some vector of m monomials in $\mathbf{x}$ and $\mathbf{P} \in \mathbb{R}^{m \times m}$ is symmetric. We impose condition (2) by requiring the following:

$$v(\phi(t_j)) \ > \ 0 \tag{9}$$
$$v(\phi(t_j)) - v(\phi(t_{i+j})) - \gamma \|\phi(t_j)\|^2 \ > \ 0 \tag{10}$$
$$\gamma \ > \ \epsilon, \tag{11}$$

for all $\phi_i \in \Phi$, $j \in \{1, \ldots, N-1\}$. The parameter $\epsilon \in \mathbb{R}_{\geq 0}$ is a fixed positive value. Note that (9) is a series of necessary conditions for constraint (2) to hold. For (3) to hold, it must be that $v(\phi(t_j)) - v(\phi(t_{i+j})) > 0$; constraint (10) is stronger in that it bounds $v(\phi(t_j)) - v(\phi(t_{i+j}))$ away from zero. We call any v that satisfies (9) through (11) a *Lyapunov candidate*. To distinguish between a Lyapunov function and a Lyapunov candidate, we use the term *proper Lyapunov function* to refer to a Lyapunov function.

Remark 3.1. *We reiterate that constraints (9) and (10) impose necessary* but not sufficient *conditions for (2) and (3) to hold. Therefore, to enforce (2) and (3), we have to perform a formal validation of our final Lyapunov candidate, as discussed in Section 4.1. In practice, we find that adding more simulation traces, and thus more constraints (9) and (10) improves the likelihood that a Lyapunov candidate also satisfies (2) and (3).*

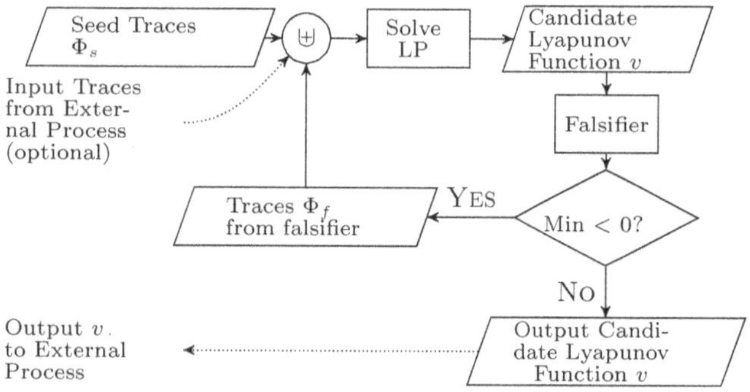

Figure 1: Procedure to iteratively improve candidate Lyapunov functions for system (1).

Note that (9) and (10) are linear constraints since they are linear in the matrix variable $\mathbf{P}$. Conditions (9) through (11) represent a set of linear constraints for which a feasible solution can be found using a standard LP solver.

Note that (2) could be imposed directly by replacing the constraint (9) with the alternative linear matrix inequality (LMI) constraint $\mathbf{P} \succ 0$, but this would require solving a potentially large scale semidefinite programming (SDP) problem (if, for example, there are a large number of simulation traces). Our experience indicates that SDP solvers are not as mature as LP solvers and are more prone to numerical difficulties. Thus, we elect to use the linear constraint (9).

REMARK 3.2. *Given a Lyapunov template $v(\mathbf{x}) = \mathbf{z}^T\mathbf{P}\mathbf{z}$, the set of feasible solutions that satisfy (2) and (3) is convex in the decision variable $\mathbf{P}$. Adding constraints (9) to (11) bounds the feasible set with linear constraints. Thus the feasible set lies on the interior of the linear constraints. If an interior point algorithm is used to provide a feasible solution to the LP, the solution returned is the* analytic center *of the LP problem [23]. We rely on this, since our intuition is that for many problems, the analytic center of the LP problem coincides with the interior of the feasible set for (2) and (3).*

3.2 Iterative Candidate Improvement

We present procedures to automatically select execution traces for system (1) to iteratively improve the quality of a series of Lyapunov candidates. We equate the quality of a Lyapunov candidate with the amount of time it takes a search procedure to identify a point that violates constraint (10). We rely on a falsification tool to automatically identify points within some domain $\mathcal{D} \subseteq \mathcal{X}$ that violate (10). Our falsification tool is a global optimizer that minimizes the LHS of (10) to find examples of points that violate the constraint.

The inputs to the procedures are:

- A parameter $\beta \in \mathbb{R}_{\geq 0}$ representing the size of an open ball centered around the origin, $B_\beta = \{\mathbf{x} \mid \|\mathbf{x}\| < \beta\}$, that will *not* be included in the analysis;
- A domain of interest, $\mathcal{D}$;
- A time step $T \in \mathbb{R}_{>0}$;
- A bound on the degree of the Lyapunov candidate function;
- A description of system (1) and a mechanism for generating concrete execution traces, such as simulations.

Also, we provide an initial collection of traces, Φ_s, to seed the procedure. The step-by-step process of the algorithm to construct candidate Lyapunov functions is shown in Figure 1. We elaborate on important steps in the procedure below.

Solve LP. In this stage, we obtain a Lyapunov candidate by solving the feasibility problem given by (9) through (11), based on the the set of all simulation traces explored by a.) the manually selected set of seed traces and b.) the falsification tool. If the LP is successfully solved, then we move to the Falsification Stage. If the LP is deemed infeasible, then we halt and report that the technique failed to find a Lyapunov candidate; this could occur due to a.) no Lyapunov function of the given template form exists or b.) numerical problems.

Falsifier. In this step we use a non-convex, global optimizer, which we call a *falsifier*, to search for a simulation trace that violates the Lyapunov conditions for the candidate Lyapunov function. The optimization problem is given by:

$$J^* = \min_{\phi(t_0)\in\mathcal{D}} \left(\min_{\substack{i\in\\ \{1,\ldots,N-1\}}} v(\phi(t_i)) - v(\phi(t_{i+1})) - \gamma\|\phi(t_i)\|^2 \right). \tag{12}$$

If $J^* < 0$, then the minimizing trace, ϕ_f, demonstrates that the Lyapunov candidate, v, does not satisfy condition (10). We call such a trace a *counterexample.* Note that the cost function in (12) is based on an estimate of the Lie derivative (i.e., $v(\phi(t_i)) - v(\phi(t_{i+1}))$ is proportional to the Lie derivative). If counterexamples Φ_f are found, then we add the linear constraints corresponding to the counterexamples in Φ_f to the set of LP constraints and return to the Solve LP stage. If no counterexample is found, we halt and return the candidate Lyapunov function.

A prototype of the technique has been implemented in the MATLAB programming environment, using the freely available SeDuMi and YALMIP optimization packages [15, 20, 14]. Our implementation of the falsification tool uses a Nelder-Mead algorithm for the global optimizer.

REMARK 3.3. *Note that our search for a Lyapunov function can also be used for black-box systems, where we have no analytic representation of system dynamics because the system is either proprietary or is modeled in a graphical language with obscure semantics, such as Simulink [1]. In such a scenario, the Lyapunov candidate we obtain cannot be formally vetted, but can be used to give semi-formal guarantees. For some gray-box systems, where we have only limited knowledge of the system dynamics, such as the Lipschitz constant for the dynamics and the maximum absolute value of the vector field within the region of interest, we can give formal guarantees by using a dense sampling of the region of interest as the set of initial states and a small enough simulation time-step. We omit these results for brevity.*

4. VERIFICATION WITH SOLVERS

In this section, we describe how we use a variety of solvers to formally validate the results of the simulation-guided Lyapunov analysis techniques.

4.1 Formal validation

Verifying Lyapunov conditions. Let the predicate $R(\mathbf{x}) < 0$ be true when $\mathbf{x}$ is in the region of interest X. We formulate the query for checking positive definiteness conditions (2,7) within a given region of interest for a CSMS or DSMS as follows:

$$\exists \mathbf{x} : (\mathbf{x} \neq \mathbf{0}) \wedge (R(\mathbf{x}) < 0) \wedge (v(\mathbf{x}) \leq 0). \tag{13}$$

If the above query is unsatisfiable, it proves positive definiteness of v. For checking if the Lie derivative $\dot{v}$ is negative definite (in the region of interest), we formulate the following queries for CSMS (14) and DSMS (15) respectively:

$$\exists \mathbf{x} : (\mathbf{x} \neq \mathbf{0}) \wedge (R(\mathbf{x}) < 0) \wedge (\nabla v^T \cdot f_q(\mathbf{x}) > 0) \tag{14}$$

$$\exists \mathbf{x} : (\mathbf{x} \neq \mathbf{0}) \wedge (R(\mathbf{x}) < 0) \wedge (v(\mathbf{x}) - v(f_q(\mathbf{x})) < 0). \tag{15}$$

If such a query is unsatisfiable, then it proves that for all points within the region of interest, the Lie derivative is nonincreasing.

Verifying Barrier certificate conditions. Recall that we use a barrier function B of the form $v(\mathbf{x}) - \ell$. Let the predicate $I(\mathbf{x}) < 0$ be true when $\mathbf{x} \in X_0$ (the set of initial states). Similarly, let the predicate $U(\mathbf{x}) < 0$ be true when $\mathbf{x} \in U$ (the set of unsafe states). We use ϵ to denote a small positive real constant (e.g., 0.00001). The unsatisfiability of each of the first three queries below respectively establishes the barrier conditions (4-6):

$$\exists \mathbf{x} : (I(\mathbf{x}) < 0) \wedge (v(\mathbf{x}) - \ell > 0) \tag{16}$$

$$\exists \mathbf{x} : (U(\mathbf{x}) < 0) \wedge (v(\mathbf{x}) - \ell < 0) \tag{17}$$

$$\exists \mathbf{x} : (v(\mathbf{x}) - \ell = 0) \wedge (\nabla v^T \cdot f_q(\mathbf{x}) > -\epsilon). \tag{18}$$

While the above treatment may seem like an obvious translation of the Lyapunov conditions or the barrier certificate conditions, we wish to point out that each of these queries is essentially a satisfiability query formulated in a suitable theory. If the candidate Lyapunov function that we obtain is a polynomial (or SoS) expression, and if the system dynamics are also polynomial, then each of these queries is a sentence in the decidable theory of real closed fields. If the system dynamics are nonpolynomial, then the query may belong to an undecidable theory. Nevertheless, advanced nonlinear solver technologies can often provide answers for these cases. We now briefly discuss the solvers that we use and their underlying technical principle.

4.2 Solver Engines

Symbolic solvers. The most popular algorithm for deciding sentences over algebraic expressions uses Partial Cylindrical Algebraic Decomposition (PCAD) [5]. A number of tools either directly implement PCAD or CAD based algorithms, or use them for specific sub-tasks. Examples include Mathematica [24], the Conflict-driven Clause Learning style search used by z3 [6], and QEPCAD. While algebra-based solvers seem to perform well with a single polynomial inequality, in our experience these solvers do not scale when faced with a conjunction of polynomial inequalities (they either exceed a generous time-out that we specify, or run out of memory). Another interesting solver in this space is MetiTarksi [2]. This is a resolution-based theorem prover modified to call a decision procedure for the theory of real closed fields. Nonpolynomial functions are approximated by upper and lower bounds that are rational functions derived from Taylor expansion representations.

Solvers based on optimization and numeric techniques. SoS techniques have been employed to synthesize and to check the validity of Lyapunov functions for dynamical systems with polynomial dynamics. Basically, an SoS problem is formulated to show that the negative of the Lie derivative is in the set of SoS polynomials (thus, guaranteeing that the Lie derivative is always decreasing). This can be accomplished for polynomial systems, as the Lie derivative is polynomial in the state variables [17, 21]. Further, for some dynamical systems with nonpolynomial dynamics, variable transformations can be performed, which allow the test of the Lie derivative to again be posed as an SoS problem [16]. For some hybrid systems, the test of the validity of a candidate Lyapunov function may be performed, as in [18].

SoS techniques address an important class of dynamical systems, but it should be noted that even if the Lie derivative is negative definite, an SoS certificate is not guaranteed to exist. Further, even if an SoS certificate for the Lie derivative exists, an SDP solver will sometimes fail to generate the desired result. This is due to the lack of maturity in SDP solvers, which can often fail due to numerical problems.

Solvers based on interval methods. Interval constraint propagation (ICP) is a technique for contracting interval domains associated with a set of variables without removing any value that is consistent with a set of constraints. When combined with a branch and bound algorithm, ICP can be used to obtain quick but approximate results for satisfiability of nonlinear constraints. For example, dReal [8] and iSat [7] are such solvers, and we focus on using dReal for our validation problems. dReal supports various nonlinear elementary functions in the framework of δ-complete decision procedures, and returns "unsat" or "δ-sat" for a given query, where δ is a precision value specified by the user. When the answer is "unsat", dReal produces a proof of unsatisfiability; when it returns "δ-sat", it gives an interval of size δ, which contains points that may possibly satisfy the query. We remark that when using dReal, for some queries, it often helps if we add additional constraints bounding the free variables in the queries to intervals. This often produces less conservative results.

4.3 Solver-guided Improvement and Validation

We use the above-mentioned solvers in a procedure to verify the soundness of results that are based on the Lyapunov candidates produced by the procedure in Figure 1. The procedure utilizes counterexamples from the solver to iteratively improve the quality of the Lyapunov candidate functions. The result is a proof of soundness for either a.) a Lyapunov function b.) a forward invariant set or c.) a barrier certificate.

Figure 2 illustrates a process that incorporates the formal validation techniques discussed in Sec. 4.2 with the iterative Lyapunov candidate improvement procedure shown in Figure 1. The following describes the important aspects of the procedure.

Formulate Solver Query. This operation creates one of the queries described in Section 4.1 to validate the result of the Lyapunov candidate analysis produced by the proce-

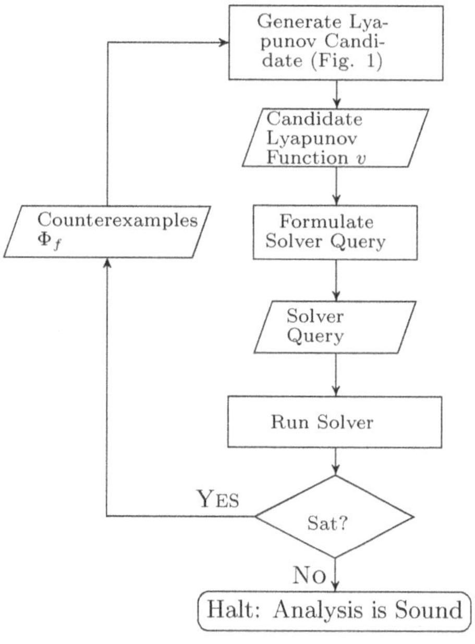

Figure 2: Incorporating solver technologies to verify soundness of the Lyapunov anlyses.

dure described in Section 3. When the desired output is a proper Lyapunov function, the Lyapunov candidate v may be tested directly using the procedure described in Section 4.1. When the desired output is a forward invariant set or a barrier certificate, a candidate certificate must first be generated. This is done by selecting a levelset size of the Lyapunov candidate v (i.e., a size l such that the sublevelset is given by $\{\mathbf{x}|v(\mathbf{x}) \leq l\}$). An appropriate levelset size may be computed by maximizing the levelset size such that the levelset remains within $\mathcal{D}$. This can be formulated as a convex optimization problem that can be solved efficiently using an SDP solver. The result is a candidate barrier certificate, which can be validated using the technique described in Section 4.1.

Run Solver. This operation applies one of the technologies described in Section 4.2 to the generated query. If the result is that the query is unsatisfiable, then the Lyapunov analysis (based on the candidate Lyapunov function and the construction produced by the Formulate Solver Query operation) is sound, and the procedure may halt. If the result is that the query is satisfiable, then a counterexample may be used to refine the Lyapunov candidate on which the query was based. Note that all of the technologies described in Section 4.2 produce some form of counterexamples except for the SoS-based techniques; for this case, some other method of refinement must be selected (e.g., selecting a different Lyapunov function template or adding several new simulation traces randomly).

5. EXAMPLE CASE STUDIES

We present several examples involving nonlinear and hybrid dynamical systems. In some cases, the analysis task is to produce a Lyapunov function within some designated domain; in other examples, the analysis task is to produce a forward invariant set. Our examples include systems with ODEs that are polynomial, transcendental, and switched. For systems with ODEs, traces are produced by the `ode45` numerical integration algorithm provided in MATLAB®.

A summary of the results for the examples is given in Table 2. For each example, the table lists the following: the example name, the number of continuous state variables, the computation time taken for the procedure in Figure 1 to produce a candidate Lyapunov function, the number of simulation points explored by the falsification tool, the computation time required by the arithmetic solver, and the arithmetic solver used to verify the result.

5.1 Example 1: Normalized Pendulum

Consider a standard pendulum system with normalized parameters:

$$\begin{bmatrix} \dot{x}_1 \\ \dot{x}_2 \end{bmatrix} = \begin{bmatrix} x_2 \\ -\sin(x_1) - x_2 \end{bmatrix}.$$

Here, x_1 represents angular position and x_2 angular velocity. The system has only one mode of operation. The continuous dynamics contain a transcendental function, which we note is difficult for most other techniques to handle. This system is guaranteed to be stable, as it is a representation of a passive physical system with damping (i.e., the system will tend to a zero-energy state over time).

The task for this example is to identify a Lyapunov function for the system that is valid within the domain $\mathcal{D} = \{\mathbf{x}|\mathbf{x}^T\mathbf{x} \leq 1\}$ and also to identify a forward invariant set. We select $\mathbf{z} = \mathbf{x}$, that is, the Lyapunov candidates are quadratic.

The procedure from Figure 1 produces the candidate Lyapunov function $v(\mathbf{x}) = \mathbf{x}^T\mathbf{P}\mathbf{x}$, where, after rounding:

$$\mathbf{P} = \begin{bmatrix} 100.0 & 24.0 \\ 24.0 & 92.0 \end{bmatrix}.$$

The procedure takes 74.22 seconds. A total of 300 simulation traces were explored by the falsification tool, each with 10 time steps of 0.1 seconds each.

A query of the form given by (13) and (14) was posed to the Mathematica arithmetic solver and was able to prove that the query is unsatisfiable in 7.72 seconds, thus proving that the above candidate Lyapunov function is a proper Lyapunov function.

A convex optimization provides the size of the largest levelset of the Lyapunov function that is contained within the domain. The resulting levelset size was $l = 71.51$, where the invariant set is given by $\{\mathbf{x}|v(\mathbf{x}) \leq l\}$. The SDP solver returns this result in 1.36 seconds. Figure 3 illustrates the results. Simulation traces explored by the falsification tool appear as dotted lines, with the associated initial conditions marked with an asterisk. The dashed line indicates the domain for the example (the unit ball). The dash-dotted line represents the invariant set.

5.2 Example 2: Constrained Pendulum

Consider the following constrained pendulum example [22]:

$$\begin{aligned} \dot{x}_1 &= \begin{cases} \frac{1}{2}x_2 & x_1 \geq -\frac{\pi}{18} \\ x_2 & \text{otherwise} \end{cases} \\ \dot{x}_2 &= -g\sin(x_1) - x_2, \end{aligned}$$

where x_1 is the angular position, x_2 is the angular velocity, and $g = 9.8$ is the acceleration due to gravity. The behavior is similar to the previous example, except a pin constrains

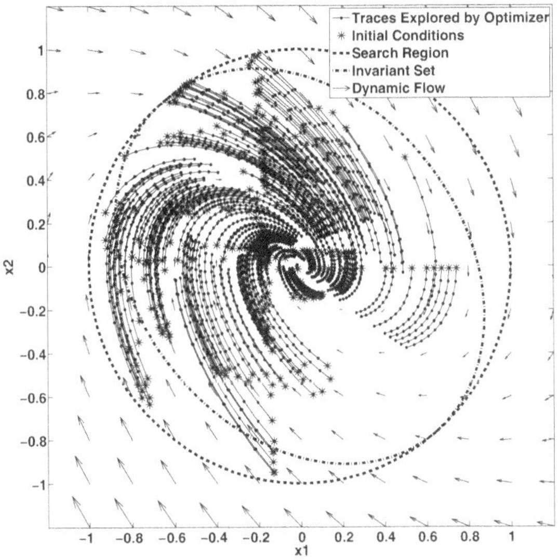

Figure 3: Optimization results of analysis for the Normalized Pendulum example.

the swing of the pendulum. Thus, the system has two modes of operation. If $x_1 \geq \frac{\pi}{18}$, the pendulum is unconstrained by the pin, and the effective length of the pendulum is 2.0 m. When $x_1 < \frac{\pi}{18}$, the pin constrains the pendulum swing, and effective length of the pendulum is 1.0 m.

As in the previous example, the system is guaranteed to be stable as it is a physical system with damping. For this example, we consider the task of constructing a forward invariant set for the system. To highlight the feature that we can supply different templates during the search for candidate Lyapunov functions, in this example, we specify a piecewise Lyapunov function template. In [12], Chapter 4.4, the author proposes a way to frame a piecewise Lyapunov function for piecewise linear systems that is continuous across the switching boundary. We can extend this idea to general switched systems; here, we show how it can be applied to this example. Consider a CSMS with two modes. The basic idea is to search for a Lyapunov function that has the following form:

$$v(\mathbf{x}) = \mathbf{z}_1^T Q \mathbf{z}_1 + \mathbf{z}_2^T P_i \mathbf{z}_2 \cdot (h(\mathbf{x}))^2, \qquad (19)$$

where $i \in \{1, 2\}$. Here, $\mathbf{z}_1$ and $\mathbf{z}_2$ are monomial vectors, where the degree of $\mathbf{z}_1$ is higher than the degree of $\mathbf{z}_2$ [1].

The expression $h(\mathbf{x})$ is a function such that $h(\mathbf{x}) = 0$ specifies the switching surface separating the two modes. For this example, $h(\mathbf{x}) = x_1 + \frac{\pi}{18}$. Observe that on the switching surface the right summand evaluates to 0, and hence the Lyapunov function becomes continuous at the switching boundary.

The search procedure returns a candidate Lyapunov candidate after 2,308.54 seconds. The resulting Q and P_i matrices are omitted for brevity. After the candidate Lyapunov function is returned, a search returns a levelset size, which is used to define a candidate forward invariant set. dReal returns a verification result for the forward invariant set in 0.084 seconds.

[1]This constraint is necessary to prevent the terms in h from making the Lyapunov candidate trivially positive.

5.3 Example 3: Damped Mathieu System

Consider the damped Mathieu system (page 315 in [10]):

$$\begin{bmatrix} \dot{x}_1 \\ \dot{x}_2 \end{bmatrix} = \begin{bmatrix} x_2 \\ -x_2 - (2 + \sin(t))x_1 \end{bmatrix}.$$

The task for this example is to identify a Lyapunov function within the domain given by the unit ball centered at the origin. Note that the Mathieu dynamics are time varying. That is, $\dot{\mathbf{x}} = f(t, \mathbf{x})$. To construct Lyapunov candidates for this system, we use a variation on Lyapunov's direct method. We invoke Barbalat's Lemma, as in [19] (page 125). This requires that a.) $\dot{v} < 0$ for all $t \geq 0$ and b.) the second derivative of v be uniformly continuous in time. We apply condition (10) over simulations of duration 6 seconds (the intuition being that 6 seconds is representative of the dynamics for all $t > 0$). Also, it can be shown that the second derivative of v is continuous.

Again, we select a quadratic form for the candidate Lyapunov function. The procedure from Figure 1 produces the candidate Lyapunov function $v(\mathbf{x}) = \mathbf{x}^T \mathbf{P} \mathbf{x}$, where, after rounding:

$$\mathbf{P} = \begin{bmatrix} 98.0 & 24.0 \\ 24.0 & 55.0 \end{bmatrix}.$$

The above result was returned after 216.61 seconds and a total of 200 simulation traces were explored by the falsification tool, each with 60 time steps of 0.1 seconds each.

A query of the form given by (13) and (14) was posed to the dReal SMT solver and was able to prove that the query is unsatisfiable in 0.044 seconds, thus proving that the above candidate Lyapunov function is a proper Lyapunov function.

5.4 Example 4: Switched-Mode System

Consider the following CSMS system, which is a modified version of an example from Johansson[12]:

$$\dot{\mathbf{x}} = \begin{cases} \begin{bmatrix} -0.1 & 1.0 \\ -10 & -0.1 \end{bmatrix} \mathbf{x} & \begin{matrix} (x_1 \geq 0 \land x_2 \geq g(x_1)) \lor \\ (x_1 \leq 0 \land x_2 \leq g(x_1)) \end{matrix} \\ \begin{bmatrix} -0.1 & 10 \\ -1 & -0.1 \end{bmatrix} \mathbf{x} & \begin{matrix} (x_1 < 0 \land x_2 > g(x_1)) \lor \\ (x_1 > 0 \land x_2 < g(x_1)) \end{matrix} \end{cases}, \qquad (20)$$

where $g(x_1) = 0.1e^{x_1} - 0.1$. The task for this example is to identify an invariant set within the unit ball.

Invariant sets can be obtained from Lyapunov functions for switched-mode systems, and there are techniques that attempt to obtain a common Lyapunov function by solving the convex optimization feasibility problem $\mathbf{P} \succ 0$, $A_i^T \mathbf{P} + \mathbf{P} A_i \prec 0$ for every mode i. Note, however, that no solution (i.e., a common Lyapunov function) for the continuous dynamics in this system exists, as shown in [12]. While techniques such as LMI solutions based on the so called *S-procedure* [3] could succeed for the original example in [12], these techniques fail to capture the transcendental switching surface in this example. As we show, our technique can compute an invariant set for this system, indicating that our technique offers a viable alternative when other techniques fail.

The falsification tool uses traces of the system with a step size of 0.02 seconds, out to 1.0 seconds. We select a quadratic Lyapunov function template. The falsification tool produces

$$\mathbf{P} = \begin{bmatrix} 11.0 & 1.0 \\ 1.0 & 100.0 \end{bmatrix}$$

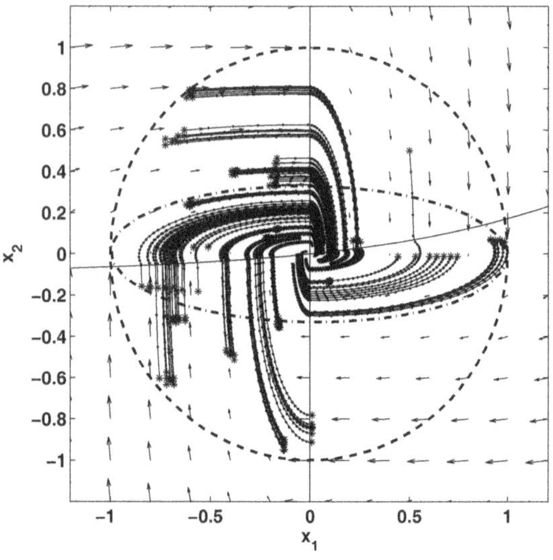

Figure 4: Optimization results of analysis for the Switched-Mode example.

in 170.75 seconds. A total of 196 simulation traces were explored by the falsification tool. The SDP solver returned a levelset size of $l = 10.8$ in 0.79 seconds. Mathematica is able to verify the candidate invariant set in 1.476 seconds.

Figure 4 illustrates the results. The arrows indicate the direction of the vector field. The dashed surface represents the domain of interest (the unit ball). The solid traces are the simulations that were used to compute a Lyapunov candidate function. The vertical axis and the curved surface passing through the origin define the switching boundaries.

5.5 Example 5: Powertrain Control System

We consider a fuel controller for an automotive application, and evaluate its ability to maintain the air-fuel (A/F) ratio within a given range of an optimal value. Environmental concerns and government legislation require that the rate of emissions (e.g., hydrocarbons, carbon monoxide, and nitrogen oxides) be minimized; control of automobile engine A/F ratio is crucial to minimize emissions. Ideal A/F levels are given by the *stoichiometric* value; we present an A/F control system model whose purpose is to maintain the A/F ratio to within 10% of the stoichiometric value when running under normal operating conditions.

The experiment that we model involves an engine connected to a dynamometer, which is a device that can control the speed of the engine and measure the output torque. For our experiment, the dynamometer maintains the engine at a constant rotational velocity, as the engine is tested.

The dynamical system we consider is a CSMS representing the parallel composition of a plant subsystem with a controller subsystem. This system has four state variables: two associated with the plant and two associated the controller. The two states associated with the plant represent the manifold pressure p and the normalized A/F ratio r (this is the ratio of the actual air-fuel ratio to the stoichiometric value 14.7). The controller implements a feedforward open-loop estimator to observe the state p of the plant; the output of the estimator is the state p_{est}. It also implements a feedback

Table 1: Model Parameters for the PTC Example.

Parameter	Value
c_1	0.41328
c_2	200.0
c_3	−0.366
c_4	0.08979
c_5	−0.0337
c_6	0.0001
c_7	2.821
c_8	−0.05231
c_9	0.10299
c_{10}	−0.00063
c_{11}	1.0
c_{12}	14.7
c_{13}	0.9
c_{14}	0.4
c_{15}	0.4
c_{16}	1.0
$\hat{u_1}$	23.0829

PI control law, and the state i represents the internal state of the integrator. We present the system dynamics in Fig. 5 and then tabulate the model parameters in Table 1.

We translate the system so that the origin coincides with the equilibrium point $p \approx 0.8987$, $r = 1.0$, $p_{est} \approx 1.077$, $i \approx 0.0$ and call the translated variables $\hat{p}$, $\hat{r}$, $\hat{p}_{est}$, and, $\hat{i}$, respectively. Using $\mathbf{x} = [\hat{p}\ \hat{r}\ \hat{p}_{est}\ \hat{i}]^T$, we define the following unsafe set:

$$U = \{\mathbf{x} |\ \|\hat{r}\| > 0.1\},$$

which corresponds to unacceptable A/F ratio values. The requirement is that the system should never enter U, given an initial condition in X_0, where

$$X_0 = \{\mathbf{x} |\ \|\mathbf{x}\| \leq 0.02\}.$$

We apply our technique to identify a barrier certificate for this system to verify that this system satisfies the requirement. We select a domain of $\mathcal{D} = \{\mathbf{x} |\ \|\mathbf{x}\| \leq 0.1\}$, which we note does not intersect with U. We use a candidate Lyapunov function of the form $v(\mathbf{x}) = \mathbf{z}^T\mathbf{P}\mathbf{z}$, where $\mathbf{z}$ is a vector of all monomials of degree ≤ 2 of the state variables $\hat{p}$, $\hat{r}$, $\hat{p}_{est}$ and $\hat{i}$. Note that $\mathbf{z}$ thus contains 14 monomials, and the $\mathbf{P}$ that we wish to find is a 14x14 matrix. The procedure from Figure 1 produces a candidate Lyapunov function of the desired form. We omit the resulting $\mathbf{P}$ matrix for brevity but note that the minimum and maximum eigenvalues are approximately 7.6 and 489.0, respectively.

The computation takes $1,413.73$ seconds. An appropriate levelset size of the Lyapunov candidate was found to be 0.07. The candidate barrier certificate is thus $B(\mathbf{x}) = \mathbf{z}^T\mathbf{P}\mathbf{z} - l$, where $l = 0.07$. The dReal solver is used to prove that B is a barrier certificate using a query similar to (16) through (18). dReal is able to prove that the query is unsatisfiable in $1,157.42$ seconds.

5.6 Example 6: MPC for Engine Control System

Lastly, we consider a representation of a model predictive control (MPC) system for a turbocharged diesel engine application. This system has been the subject of recent experimental work in the automotive industry and has appeared

$$
\begin{aligned}
\dot{p} &= c_1\left(2\hat{u}_1\sqrt{\frac{p}{c_{11}}-\left(\frac{p}{c_{11}}\right)^2}-\left(c_3+c_4c_2p+c_5c_2p^2+c_6c_2^2p\right)\right)\\
\dot{r} &= 4\left(\frac{c_3+c_4c_2p+c_5c_2p^2+c_6c_2^2p}{c_{13}(c_3+c_4c_2p_{est}^2+c_5c_2p_{est}^2+c_6c_2^2p_{est})(1+i+c_{14}(r-c_{16}))}-r\right)\\
\dot{p}_{est} &= c_1\left(2\hat{u}_1\sqrt{\tfrac{p}{c_{11}}-\left(\tfrac{p}{c_{11}}\right)^2}-c_{13}\left(c_3+c_4c_2p_{est}+c_5c_2p_{est}^2+c_6c_2^2p_{est}\right)\right)\\
\dot{i} &= c_{15}(r-c_{16})
\end{aligned}
\tag{21}
$$

Figure 5: System dynamics for the Powertrain Control System.

recently in the literature [11]. There has been interest in adopting MPC in the automotive industry, but several hurdles remain, such as the ability to prove safety properties of the closed-loop system. A technique that provides a means to, for example, prove stability or to provide guarantees on performance bounds would help to ease the way for this new technology to find application in industry. Below, we apply our technique to prove this system is stable by discovering a discrete-time Lyapunov function that is valid over a given domain.

The purpose of the MPC system for this application is to regulate the manifold pressure (MAP) and exhaust gas recirculation (EGR) rate. The MAP affects the amount of air injected into the cylinder for the combustion phase of the engine; accurately controlling the MAP directly affects the power output of the engine as well as the efficiency. The EGR subsystem allows some portion of the exhaust gas to be reinjected into the cylinder, with the ultimate effect of increasing efficiency and decreasing the rate of emissions.

The actuators are the variable geometry turbine (VGT) and the EGR valve. The VGT controls how much air is forced into the manifold due to pressure from the exhaust gases. The EGR valve regulates the rate at which exhaust gases are recirculated into the intake manifold.

The model we consider is a DSMS. The continuous-valued dynamics are given by affine difference equations. The plant is highly nonlinear with at least eight state variables. The version of the plant that we consider is first linearized, producing a linear time-invariant model with eight state variables. Then the number of state variables is reduced by applying a model-order reduction technique. The controller has 69 modes of operation (27 modes within the domain of interest); in each mode a unique linear feedback law is applied. The resulting closed-loop model of the system has three continuous-valued state variables and 27 modes.

The control space is divided into so called *controller regions*, $X_i \subset \mathbb{R}^3$ for $i \in \{1,\ldots,27\}$, where each region is associated with a unique mode of the controller. The collection of regions partitions the domain of interest; the boundaries of each region are polyhedral sets. The dynamics are given by:

$$
\mathbf{x}[k+1] = \mathbf{A}_i\mathbf{x}[k]+\mathbf{b}_i,\ \forall \mathbf{x}[k]\in X_i,
$$

where $\mathbf{A}_i \in \mathbb{R}^{n\times n}$ and $\mathbf{b}_i \in \mathbb{R}^n$.

Note that existing LMI techniques failed to identify a Lyapunov function for this example, but as we describe below, our search-based technique is able to discover a solution.

We use a quadratic Lyapunov template and define the domain as the ball of radius 20.0 centered at the origin. The search procedure produces the following Lyapunov candidate in 107.29 seconds:

$$
\mathbf{P} = \begin{bmatrix} 1.625 & -0.309 & 0.740\\ -0.309 & 0.886 & 0.208\\ 0.740 & 0.208 & 1.688 \end{bmatrix}.
$$

A query to dReal takes 133 seconds to prove that the resulting candidate Lyapunov function is a proper Lyapunov function over the domain. This provides a proof of stability as well as a mechanism to produce forward invariant sets for the MPC system.

6. CONCLUSIONS

We presented a Lyapunov-based technique for the analysis of systems based on simulation data. The technique leverages numerical optimization and automated reasoning technologies such as SMT solvers and can be used to demonstrate stability and to provide performance bounds and safety guarantees for nonlinear and hybrid dynamical systems. This technique directly targets industrial applications, where simulation data is easily obtainable but application of traditional formal methods is not yet feasible.

The foundation of our analysis is a technique to automatically generate and iteratively improve upon candidate Lyapunov functions. The candidates are generated based on linear constraints provided by simulation traces; the feasible solution to an LP problem provides the Lyapunov candidates. We iteratively improve upon a series of candidates by using a tool that we call a falsifier, which is a global optimizer guided by a cost function that is based on the Lie derivative of the candidate Lyapunov function. An SMT solver is then used to validate the soundness of the resulting analysis, which can be a stability proof, a forward invariant set, or a barrier certificate. If necessary, we refine the candidate Lyapunov functions using counterexamples from the SMT solver.

We provided several examples, including two examples from the automotive engine control domain. No guarantees exist that our procedure will terminate with a sound analysis result, but our examples show that the technique can be applied to challenging industrial problems.

[1]For a Intel Xeon E5606 2.13GHz Dual Processor machine, with 24 GB RAM, running Windows 7, SP1

[2]For a 4x Intel Core i7 at 2.7 GHz with 8 GB RAM, running Ubuntu 13.04

Table 2: Results from Lyapunov analysis for various examples.

Model	Name	Degree	Candidate Time (sec.)[1]	No. Sim. Points	Verif. Time (sec.)[2]	Solver
1	Pendulum	2	74.22	3,000	7.72	Mathematica
2	Constrained Pendulum	2	2,308.54	57,240	0.084	dReal
3	Mathieu	2	216.61	12,000	0.044	Mathematica
4	Switched-Mode	2	170.75	9,800	1.476	Mathematica
5	PTC	3	1,413.73	258,078	1,157.42	dReal
6	MPC	3	107.29	4,480	133	dReal

Future work will consider non-autonomous systems and will explore alternative search strategies based on, for example, machine learning.

Acknowledgements

The authors would like to thank Ken Butts from the Toyota Technical Center and Mike Huang from the University of Michigan for their help with the automotive control models, Ufuk Topcu from the University of Pennsylvania for insightful discussions on numerical techniques for obtaining Lyapunov functions, and the anonymous reviewers for their constructive comments.

7. REFERENCES

[1] *Using Simulink.* The MathWorks, 2007.

[2] B. Akbarpour and L. C. Paulson. Metitarski: An automatic theorem prover for real-valued special functions. *Journal of Automated Reasoning*, 44(3):175–205, 2010.

[3] S. Boyd, L. E. Ghaoui, E. Feron, and V. Balakrishnan. *Linear Matrix Inequalities in System and Control Theory*, volume 15 of *SIAM Studies in Applied Mathematics.* SIAM, 1994.

[4] M. Branicky. Multiple lyapunov functions and other analysis tools for switched and hybrid systems. *IEEE Transactions on Automatic Control*, 43(4):475–482, April 1998.

[5] G. E. Collins and H. Hong. Partial cylindrical algebraic decomposition for quantifier elimination. *Journal of Symbolic Computation*, 12(3):299–328, 1991.

[6] L. De Moura and N. Bjørner. Z3: An efficient smt solver. In *Proc. of Tools and Algorithms for the Construction and Analysis of Systems*, pages 337–340, 2008.

[7] M. Fränzle, C. Herde, T. Teige, S. Ratschan, and T. Schubert. Efficient solving of large non-linear arithmetic constraint systems with complex boolean structure. *JSAT*, 1(3-4):209–236, 2007.

[8] S. Gao, J. Avigad, and E. M. Clarke. δ-complete decision procedures for satisfiability over the reals. In *Automated Reasoning*, pages 286–300. Springer, 2012.

[9] A. Gupta, R. Majumdar, and A. Rybalchenko. From tests to proofs. In *Proc. of Tools and Algorithms for Construction and Analysis of Systems*, pages 262–276, 2009.

[10] W. Haddad and V. Chellaboina. *Nonlinear Dynamical Systems and Control: A Lyapunov-Based Approach.* Princeton University Press, 2011.

[11] M. Huang, H. Nakada, S. Polavarapu, R. Choroszucha, K. Butts, and I. Kolmanovsky. Towards combining nonlinear and predictive control of diesel engines. In *American Control Conference, 2013. Proceedings of the 2004*, pages 2852–2859. IEEE, 2013.

[12] M. Johansson. *Piecewise Linear Control Systems*, volume 284 of *Lecture Notes in Control and Information Sciences.* Springer, 2003.

[13] D. Liberzon. Basic problems in stability and design of switched systems. *IEEE Control Systems*, 19(5):59–70, Oct. 1999.

[14] J. Löfberg. Yalmip : A toolbox for modeling and optimization in MATLAB. In *Proc. of Computatational Aspects of Control System Design*, Taipei, Taiwan, 2004.

[15] MATLAB. *version 7.12.0 (R2011a).* The MathWorks Inc., Natick, Massachusetts, 2011.

[16] A. Papachristodoulou and S. Prajna. Analysis of Non-polynomial Systems Using the Sum of Squares Decomposition. In D. Henrion and A. Garulli, editors, *Positive Polynomials in Control*, volume 312 of *Lecture Notes in Control and Information Sciences*, pages 23–43. Springer Berlin / Heidelberg, 2005.

[17] P. A. Parrilo. *Structured Semidefinite Programs and Semialgebraic Geometry Methods in Robustness and Optimization.* PhD thesis, California Institute of Technology, 2000.

[18] S. Prajna. *Optimization-based methods for nonlinear and hybrid systems verification.* PhD thesis, California Institute of Technology, Caltech, Pasadena, CA, USA, 2005.

[19] J. Slotine and W. Li. *Applied nonlinear control.* Prentice Hall, 1991.

[20] J. F. Sturm. Using SeDuMi 1.02, A MATLAB Toolbox for Optimization over Symmetric Cones. *Optimization Methods and Software*, 11/12(1-4):625–653, 1999.

[21] U. Topcu, P. Seiler, and A. Packard. Local stability analysis using simulations and sum-of-squares programming. *Automatica*, 44:2669–2675, 2008.

[22] A. van der Schaft and J. Schumacher. *An Introduction to Hybrid Dynamical Systems.* Lecture Notes in Control and Information Sciences. Springer, 2000.

[23] L. Vandenberghe and S. Boyd. Semidefinite Programming. *SIAM Review*, 38(1):49–95, March 1996.

[24] S. Wolfram. *The Mathematica® Book, Version 4.* Cambridge University Press, 1999.

Cells Driven by Computers: Long-term Model Predictive Control of Gene Expression in Yeast

Gregory Batt
INRIA Paris-Rocquencourt, 78153 Le Chesnay, France
gregory.batt@inria.fr

ABSTRACT

Real-time control has been recently applied to drive actual intracellular processes with unprecedented accuracy. Here we introduce the motivations for the development of these approaches and then present a platform for the real-time control of gene expression in yeast cells. We conclude by surveying related works and discussing possible future directions.

Categories and Subject Descriptors

J.3 [**Computer Applications**]: Life and Medical Sciences

Keywords

Computational Biology, Gene Expression, Systems Biology, Synthetic Biology, Yeast

1. MOTIVATION

The application of control theory to systems biology is not novel. However, until recently, control theory has been mostly employed to understand general principles of the functioning of biological systems at the molecular and cellular level [8, 7]. Quite surprisingly, only a handful of research groups have investigated the problem of controlling actual biological processes at the cellular levels so far. This problem is of importance not only for the systems biology community but also for the synthetic biology community.

In the first case, to understand the functioning of biomolecular processes one typically applies perturbations to the system and observes the system response, following a grey-box modeling strategy. Using current methods it is very difficult to perturb intracellular factors, like protein concentrations, with good precision and in a time-varying manner. This severely limits the range of perturbations that can be applied and consequently the informativeness of the experiments. Having means to control the level of proteins in a precise and temporally-controlled manner offers significant perspectives to better understand cellular processes.

HSCC'14, April 15–17, 2014, Berlin, Germany.
ACM 978-1-4503-2732-9/14/04.
http://dx.doi.org/10.1145/2562059.2562144.

In the second case, the objective is to engineer biological systems to perform useful tasks. Cells are often seen as biochemical plants whose capabilities can be extended via genetic engineering. Although this approach has been highly successful in a few cases, obtaining efficient solutions necessitates that the new demand is properly integrated with the rest of the cell metabolism. Obtaining a proper (re-)orchestration of the metabolic efforts is a major bottleneck. This is generally implemented at the molecular level by using genetic regulatory systems to tune protein levels. This control task is delicate and necessitates a global view on the process. Therefore externalizing the control and using computers to drive metabolic pathways could be highly beneficial for the optimization of the process.

Regardless of whether the motivation originates from systems biology (understanding) or synthetic biology (engineering), the first step towards demonstrating the biological relevance of these approaches is to develop a platform for controlling the intracellular level of a protein of interest with good accuracy and over extended durations.

2. A CONTROL PLATFORM FOR REAL-TIME CONTROL OF GENE EXPRESSION IN YEAST

Here we present an approach described in detail in [6] (Fig. 1). We use yeast cells engineered such that hyperosmotic stresses trigger pSTL1 gene expression and the subsequent synthesis of a fluorescent protein, YFP, whose concentration can be measured. Yeast cells grow as a monolayer in a microfluidic device that is used to rapidly change the cells' osmotic environment and image their response. After cell segmentation and cell tracking the measured fluorescence is sent to a state estimator connected to an MPC controller. A model of the pSTL1 gene induction is used to find the best possible series of osmotic pulses to apply in the future so that the predicted YFP level follows a target profile. At the present time point, the system state is estimated, and the MPC searches for the best input (pulse duration and number of pulses) which minimizes the distance of the MPC predictions to the target profile for the next 2 h. Here, the osmotic series of pulses that corresponds to the blue curve (Fig. 1, #4) is selected and sent to the microfluidic command. This control loop is iterated every 6 min. Using this platform, we were able to control gene expression at the cell population level but also at the single cell level during many cell generations (Fig. 2). Such performances can not be obtained using more conventional (open-loop) induction strategies.

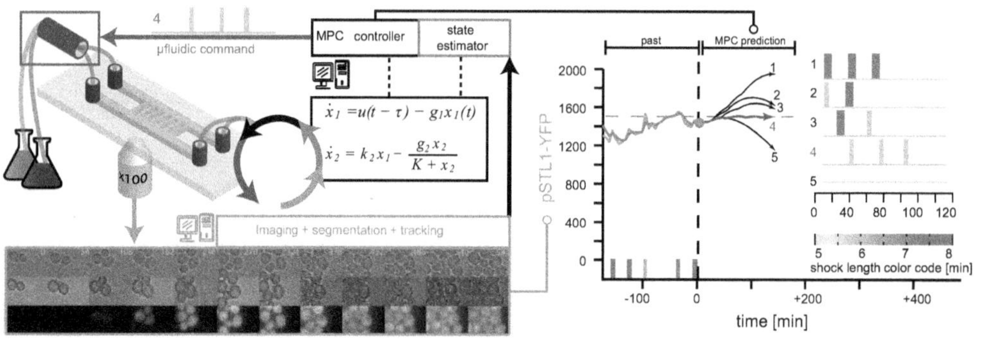

Figure 1: A platform for real-time control of gene expression in yeast.

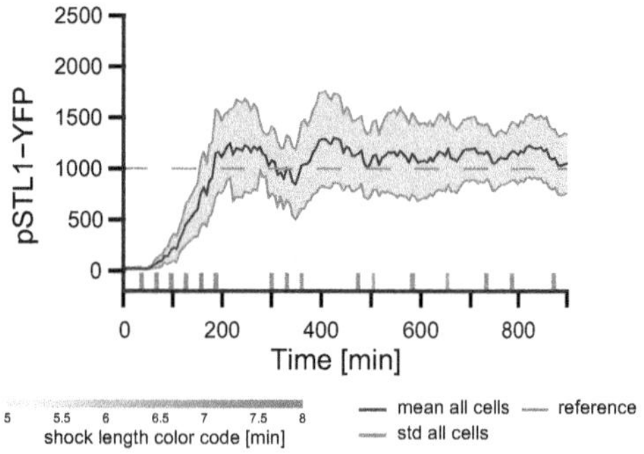

Figure 2: A typical set-point control experiment.

3. RELATED WORKS

As mentioned earlier, the actual use of in silico feedback loops to control intracellular processes has been proposed only recently. In 2011, we showed that the signaling activity in live yeast cells can be controlled by an *in silico* feedback loop [5]. Using a proportional-integral controller we controlled the output of a signal transduction pathway by modulating the osmotic environment of cells in real time. A similar framework has been proposed by Menolascina et al. to control a large synthetic gene network [2]. Toettcher et al. used elaborate microscopy techniques and optogenetics to control in real time and at the single cell level the localization and activity of a signal transduction protein in eukaryotic cells [4]. They were able to buffer external stimuli by clamping a cell messenger for short time scales. With this approach, the authors were able to reduce cell-to-cell variability of the cells output by applying different inputs to each cell. The most closely-related work is that of Milias-Argeitis et al. [3]. Using optogenetic techniques, they managed to control the expression of a yeast gene to a constant target value over several hours in a chemostat culture. In particular they are able to control the system to a fixed setpoint after they have sent a random series of pulses. These works have been reviewed in more depth by Chen et al. [1].

4. PERSPECTIVES

Connecting living cells to computers is a promising field of research both for applied and fundamental research. By maintaining a system around specific operating points or by driving it out of its standard operating regions, real-time control approaches offer unprecedented opportunities to investigate how gene networks process dynamical information at the cell level. We also anticipate that such platforms will be used to help the development of synthetic biology via the creation of hybrid systems resulting from the interconnection of *in vivo* and *in silico* computing devices.

From a control point of view, solving model-based control problems at the cell level raises novel issues. Indeed, a cell microcolony is a (growing) collection of different individuals, each behaving in a stochastic manner and slowly changing in time. Finding suitable frameworks for modeling and identification, and then state estimation and stochastic control, is a topic of high importance both in control and in biology.

5. ACKNOWLEDGMENTS

I would like to thank Alessandro Abate, Kirill Batmanov, Eugenio Cinquemani, Giancarlo Ferrari-Trecate, Andres Gonzalez, Pascal Hersen, Artemis Llamosi, Jean-Baptiste Lugagne, Valentina Peschetola, Ilya Tkachev, and Cristian Versari for stimulating interactions on this problem.

6. REFERENCES

[1] S. Chen *et al.* Building robust functionality in synthetic circuits using engineered feedback regulation. *Current Opinion in Biotechnology*, 24(4):790–6, 2013.

[2] F. Menolascina, M. di Bernardo, and D. di Bernardo. Analysis, design and implementation of a novel scheme for in-vivo control of synthetic gene regulatory networks. *Automatica*, 47(6):1265–70, 2011.

[3] A. Milias-Argeitis *et al.* In silico feedback for in vivo regulation of a gene expression circuit. *Nature Biotechnology*, 29:1114–6, 2011.

[4] J. E. Toettcher *et al.* Light-based feedback for controlling intracellular signaling dynamics. *Nature Methods*, 8:837–9, 2011.

[5] J. Uhlendorf *et al.* Towards real-time control of gene expression: controlling the hog signaling cascade. In *PSB'11*, pages 338–49, 2011.

[6] J. Uhlendorf *et al.* Long-term model predictive control of gene expression at the population and single-cell levels. *PNAS*, 109(35):14271–6, 2012.

[7] D. Del Vecchio, A. Ninfa, and E. Sontag. Modular cell biology: retroactivity and insulation. *Molecular Systems Biology*, 4:161, 2008.

[8] T. M. Yi *et al.* Robust perfect adaptation in bacterial chemotaxis through integral feedback control. *PNAS*, 97(9):4649–53, 2000.

Component Based Design of Hybrid Systems: A Case Study on Concurrency and Coupling*

Werner Damm and Eike Möhlmann and Astrid Rakow
Carl von Ossietzky University of Oldenburg
Department of Computer Science
D-26111 Oldenburg, Germany
{damm,eike.moehlmann,astrid.rakow}@informatik.uni-oldenburg.de

ABSTRACT

In the search of design principles that allow compositional reasoning about safety and stability properties of hybrid controllers we examine a case study on a simplified driver assistance system for lane keeping and velocity control. We thereby target loosely coupled systems: the composed system has to accomplish a task that may depend on several of its subcomponents while little coordination between them is necessary. Our assistance system has to accomplish a comfortable centrifugal force, lane keeping and velocity control. This leads to an architecture composed of a velocity controller and a steering controller, where each controller has its local objectives and together they maintain a global objective. The steering controller makes time bounded promises about its steering, which the velocity controller uses for optimization. For this system, we deductively prove from the components' properties that the objectives of the composed system are accomplished.

Categories and Subject Descriptors

D.2.4 [**Software Engineering**]: Software/Program Verification

General Terms

Design, Verification

Keywords

Hybrid Systems; Automatic Verification; Stability; Safety; Composition; Interfaces; Specifications; Assume-Guarantee; Computer-Aided Design

1. INTRODUCTION

In [2] Damm et al. proposed a library based design methodology for constructing hybrid controllers from a component library. The suggested framework preserves safety and stability properties. Verification conditions were identified to alleviate the support by automatic verification tools.

While in [2], control components are sequentially active, our research aims to extend this approach by allowing sequential as well as concurrent control components. A first step towards this goal is this case study on an advanced driver assistance system (ADAS) as a loosely coupled concurrent control application. In the following presentation of our case study we highlight what we identified as fundamental characteristics of the application domain and resulting key insights for the extension of [2].

Basically, a component can be thought of as an encapsulation of an implementation that interacts with its environment via a its interface and that can be (re-)used in certain deployment contexts, where it guarantees to provide its services. The importance of contract-based compositional design has long been recognized as an instrument to reduce the number of late integration errors [11] and to boost reuse of components [6]. Contract-based specifications have been integrated into the Core meta Model underlying the CESAR reference technology platform for critical system design, which is recognized by the Artemis Industrial Association as the unifying platform for building a suite of interopable methods and tools covering the complete system life cycle for critical systems [1]. Projects like Speeds[1] have provided formal contract based component interface specifications for real-time and safety requirements (as in [4, 5]).

Determining an appropriate system decomposition into subcomponents is a challenging task though. There certainly is an area of conflict arising from the benefits of re-using components and the cost payed for decoupling the component from its environment in order to make it reusable. We therefore focus on *loosely coupled systems*, where one component needs to know little about its concurrent environment.

We examine a simplified ADAS in the setting of single lane country roads with no additional traffic. The ADAS has to **(o1)** maintain a centrifugal force comfortable for a driver, **(o2)** bring and then keep the car on the center of its lane, **(o3)** control the speed also considering driver requests for a certain speed value. Our ADAS consists of two concurrent controllers, a velocity controller, VC, and a steering controller, SC. The velocity controller is responsible for its *local objective* of controlling the speed, the steering controller is responsible for lane keeping and together they have to accomplish the *global objective* of guaranteeing a comfortable centrifugal force. The global objective implies a loose coupling between VC and SC, because maintaining a comfortable centrifugal force means that a car cannot be arbitrarily

*This work has been partly supported by the German Research Foundation (DFG) as part of the Transregional Collaborative Research Center "Automatic Verification and Analysis of Complex Systems" (SFB/TR 14 AVACS).

HSCC'14, April 15–17, 2014, Berlin, Germany.

http://dx.doi.org/10.1145/2562059.2562120.

[1]IST Project 03347, see www.speeds.eu.com

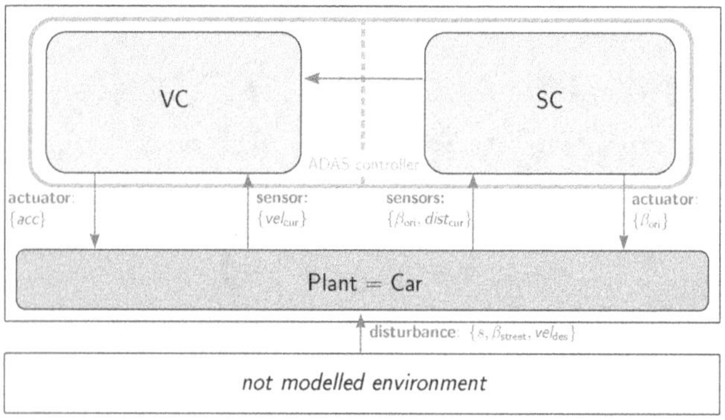

Figure 1: Overall architecture

fast in a narrow turn and a fast car may not decide to change its steering angle too abruptly. But as steering angles usually are small, the coupling is quite loose.
In the sequel, we will develop hybrid interfaces for the two controllers and suggest a way of coordination between them. In particular, we suggest (a) to use an assume-guarantee approach and annotate assumptions and guarantees as part of the interface. A component's guarantee describes its services. The assumption specifies a component's deployment context. Any deployment context has to refine the assumption. We further suggest (b) the use of events encoding time bounded promises for communication between concurrent controllers. By this means, SC can tell VC that it will do a good turn, so that the VC can increase the velocity. Finally we will deductively prove that our ADAS accomplishes its objectives, (o2) to (o3), using automatic verification tools.

2. SPECIFYING THE ADAS

Our driver assistance system has to perform concurrently steering and velocity control for a car on a road. With other words, we study a system of a plant, which is the controlled car, and a composite ADAS controller with its two subcomponents, velocity controller VC and steering controller SC. The ADAS controller perceives the plant via sensors and controls the plant via actuators. We specify all components of our system as hybrid automata with inputs and outputs. The modelled system has as inputs disturbances, that is variable values whose evolution is not captured by our model: a disturbance s on the actuator acc, the user's desired speed vel_{des} and the course of the road (cf. Fig. 1). The desired speed vel_{des} may only take integer values within the considered velocity range of $[5\frac{m}{s}, 50\frac{m}{s}]$. Actuators of the ADAS are the acceleration acc and steering, β_{steer}. The ADAS reads via sensors plant variables: the car's orientation β_{ori}, its position relative to the mid of the lane $dist_{cur}$ (cf. Fig. 2), and the current velocity vel_{cur}. The plant defines the continuous evolution of plant variables and builds an open system with actuators (and possibly disturbances) as inputs. Our plant model is illustrated in Fig. 3 To rule out write conflicts, each actuator belongs to one concurrent controller only. SC controls β_{steer} and VC actuator acc. Consequently SC is in charge of lane keeping (o2), and VC of speed control (o3).

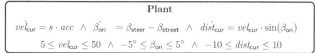

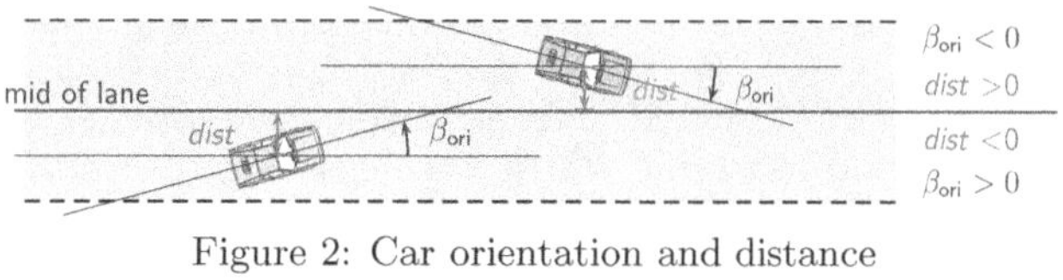

Figure 2: Car orientation and distance

Plant

$$\dot{vel}_{cur} = s \cdot acc \;\wedge\; \dot{\beta}_{ori} = \beta_{steer} - \beta_{street} \;\wedge\; \dot{dist}_{cur} = vel_{cur} \cdot \sin(\beta_{ori})$$
$$5 \le vel_{cur} \le 50 \;\wedge\; -5^\circ \le \beta_{ori} \le 5^\circ \;\wedge\; -10 \le dist_{cur} \le 10$$

Figure 3: Hybrid automaton of the plant.

These objectives canonically imply, that SC reads via sensors β_{ori}, $dist_{cur}$ and VC reads vel_{cur}. SC and VC together have to establish the global objective (o1), guaranteeing a comfortable centrifugal force.
In the remainder of this section we will discuss design decisions on the coordination between VC and SC.

2.1 Coordination

To summarize, we want to design a composite ADAS controller that accomplishes objectives (o1) to (o3). Lane keeping (o2) is a local objective of subcomponent SC and speed control (o3) is local to VC. Both subcomponents influence the (hence global) objective of guaranteeing comfortable centrifugal forces (o1).
We aim to extend the framework of [2], which targets to bridge the gap between specification and implementation models. Following [2] we aim to support distributed component based design of control systems taking realistic assumptions about reaction times into account. Thus we target a setting where instantaneous reactions are considered as inadequate, because of time penalties for task switching and delays in sensing and actuating and where coordination messages may get lost between controllers on different ECUs.

Events. As we aim to support the design of safety critical systems, critical objectives always have to be guaranteed, even if all messages are lost. Hence we suggest to use coordination messages, so called *events*, that are optional for the receiving component. By sending an event, the sender promises a certain future behaviour. Promises are tagged with a time stamp and a validity duration. While being aware of signal latencies, the receiving component can make use of this information for optimisation, but has to be able to fulfill its guarantees even without any events.

Assumptions. To specify a component's deployment context, the assumptions φ^{assm} of the component are specified as part of its interface. A component with assumption φ^{assm} has to be able to deal with any behaviour that satisfies φ^{assm}.

Control Hierarchies. For coordination between coupled components, we derive a hierarchy on the controller's subcomponents from the priorities of controller's objectives. We give top priority to the driver's well-being, that is maintaining a comfortable centrifugal force F_{cntrif}. As $F_{cntrif} = mass \cdot \omega^2 \cdot r$ [2], both VC and SC influence whether F_{cntrif} is comfortable. Hence the two controllers are coupled: VC may not choose an arbitrary speed, when SC is currently on a narrow curve and vice versa. VC becomes subordinate to SC, as lane keeping is considered as more important than reaching the user desired speed. This means that VC has to be able to deal with what ever steering the SC chooses, whereas SC assumes a cooperative VC, that never jeopardises a comfortable F_{cntrif}. As VC cannot simultaneously be ready to deal with arbitrary steering and reach the user requested speed, we have to adopt the objective (o3): vel_{des} has to be reached if compatible with steering.

[2] ω is the angular rate, r is the radius of the curve the car is on, and $mass$ is the mass of the passenger

2.2 Interface Ingredients

In this section we briefly elaborate on the main ingredients for interfaces of concurrent control components in our framework.

Assumptions and Guarantees. Assumptions express constraints on the component's environment. Our components specify *base assumptions* and *event assumptions*. A base assumption φ^{assm} has to hold unless the component is bound to fulfill an event promise. When it is bound to a promise, it may be able to relax its assumptions, hence it declares at its interface event assumptions. Assumptions may refer to inputs of the composite of plant and controller, Var_A. A control component specifies *guarantees* φ^{guara}, which may refer to Var_G, the outputs of the composite of plant and controller. Basically, as long as its base assumption holds, the component has to accomplish its guarantees. To cope with sensing delays, the component has to even accomplish its guarantees for a limited future of $\Delta_{\mathsf{lat}}^{time}$ after the base assumption expires. At the moment we think of φ^{assm} and φ^{guara} as simple predicates of the form $\Box \bigwedge_{v \in Var_A \cup \dot{Var_A}} (v \in I_a(v))$ and $\Box \bigwedge_{v \in Var_G \cup \dot{Var_G}} (v \in I_g(v))$ with intervals I_a, I_g, but plan to extend their expressiveness.

Events. An event $\mathcal{E}$ is defined as $(f^{prom}, dueTime, duration)$ with f^{prom} a predicate over a set of variables the event refers to, $dueTime$ a due time, and $duration$ a validity duration. At its interface a component declares the set of outgoing events EvP^{out}. Similar to guarantees, f^{prom} encodes intervals for variables, i.e. f^{prom} has the form $\bigwedge_{v \in Var_G}(v \in I_o(v))$. But unlike guarantees, promises are time-limited: The sending component has to guarantee that variable values are within I_o after the due time elapses and at least for the promised validity duration. A component is bound to fulfill its promises, so if there are several promises for the same point in time, the most restrictive promise has to be realized. A component may not send contradictory promises. As there also is a latency for sending events between distributed components, we further demand a separation of at least $\Delta_{\mathsf{sep}}^{time}$.

An interface specifies for each outgoing event $\mathcal{E} \in EvP^{out}$ an event assumption $\varphi_{\mathcal{E}}^{assm}$, which may relax the base assumption φ^{assm}. Analogously an interface specifies for each incoming event $\mathcal{E} \in EvP^{in}$ an event guarantee, which may relax the base guarantee φ^{guara}. That way communication allows more behavior: when controller C_A sends an event signaling that it is ready to tolerate more behavior, another controller C_G within C_A's environment receiving that event might exhibit compatible extra behavior.

Incoming events EvP^{in} at the interface, declare what kinds of events the component can use for optimization. Note, that in our framework events are only used to optimize a controller's behavior. The controller guarantees have to accomplished given its assumptions hold, with or without events.

Signal Latencies and Sending Events. We assume that there is a global maximal latency $\Delta_{\mathsf{mlat}}^{time}$ between sending an event and receiving the event. In order to take this latency conservatively into account, the event's time gets adjusted: The time-limited promise of event $\mathcal{E} = (f^{prom}, dueTime, duration)$ sent at time t, implies that the receiving component can rely on the promise encoded by $\mathcal{E}' = (f^{prom}, dueTime, \max(0, duration - \Delta_{\mathsf{mlat}}^{time}))$ received at time t' with $t < t' \leq t + \Delta_{\mathsf{mlat}}^{time}$. Event $\mathcal{E}'$ has the same due time as $\mathcal{E}$, as the event may be received with (nearly) no latency. The validity duration in $\mathcal{E}'$ is shortened by the maximal latency, because the event may be received after $\Delta_{\mathsf{mlat}}^{time}$ the latest.

3. SYSTEM MODEL SPECIFICATION

In this section we describe the ADAS system model, for which we compositionally derive in Sect. 4 that objectives (o1) to (o3) hold.

3.1 Plant

In Fig. 3 of Sect. 2 we have already presented the hybrid automaton modelling the plant. For now we consider only straight lanes, that is the mid of lane is fixed and we set the disturbance s to 1. Whereas the latter restriction can be easily dropped, the first is conceptual:

In the following we will use that controllers stabilize to their certain equilibrium point. Having a dynamic road course, implies that there is no fixed equilibrium point. In control theory this is called reference tracking and a clever embedding in our framework needs further investigation.

3.2 Velocity Controller

The VC is composed of two subcomponents: one component regulates the velocity, the other handles received events. In the sequel we refer to the regulating component as VC_PI (PI velocity controller) and the other component is called VC_ER (event receiver VC).

In Sect. 2.1, we explained why we chose VC to be subordinate to SC. VC being subordinate implies, that it sacrifices its objective (o3), if necessary. So, VC aims for the user desired velocity vel_{des}, but if this is too fast, it targets for a comfortable velocity.

For a given centrifugal force F_{comf} that a passenger still experiences as comfortable, we can derive the according velocity vel_{comf} at the current steering $\dot{\beta}_{\mathsf{ori}}$ via $vel_{\mathsf{comf}} = \frac{F_{\mathsf{comf}}}{mass \cdot \dot{\beta}_{\mathsf{ori}}}$ (Eq. 1) from $F_{\mathsf{cntrif}} = mass \cdot \omega^2 \cdot r$, $\omega = \dot{\beta}_{\mathsf{ori}}$ and $vel_{\mathsf{cur}} = \omega \cdot r$.

Within VC, VC_ER will use the events send by SC to determine the setpoint vel_{goal} for VC_PI. VC_ER derives a maximal, comfortable velocity and sets vel_{goal} to $\min(vel_{\mathsf{des}}, vel_{\mathsf{comf}})$.

A PI Velocity Controller. The VC_PI (cf. Fig. 4) has three modes: **Norm**, **Accl**, **Decl**. In mode **Norm** the controller uses a PI rule to fine tune the velocity control. In modes **Accl** and **Decl**, the, respectively, maximal tolerated acceleration and deceleration are applied.

Event Receiver. The event receiver, VC_ER, runs in parallel to VC_PI (cf. Fig. 5). It receives events and sets the velocity setpoint vel_{goal} for VC_PI appropriately. VC is prepared to use events that promise $\dot{\beta}_{\mathsf{ori}} \in [-0.3, 0.3]$. So VC_ER receives events $\mathcal{E} = ([min, max], dueTime, duration)$ with $-0.3 \leq \mathcal{E}.min \leq \mathcal{E}.max \leq 0.3$.

Exploiting An Event. If no events are received, the VC has to guarantee that its velocity is comfortable at all as-

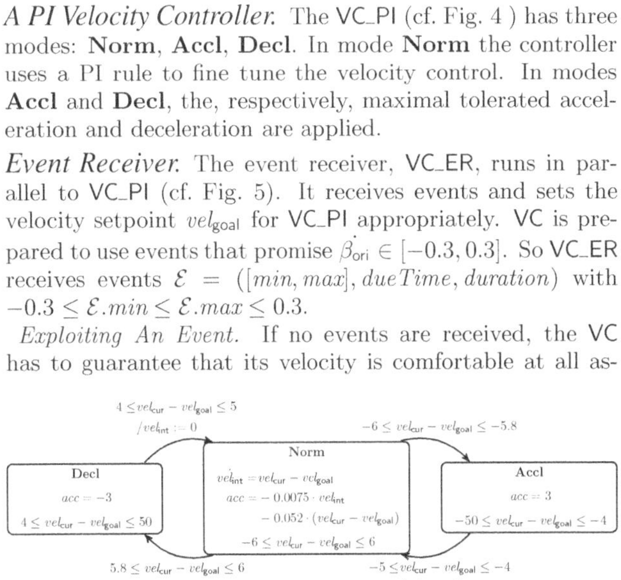

Figure 4: Hybrid Automaton Visualizing the VC_PI.

$\mathcal{E}.f^{prom} \subseteq [-0.05, 0.05]$	$vel_{\mathsf{comf}} = vel_{\mathsf{crit}} = 50$
$\mathcal{E}.f^{prom} \subseteq [-\frac{1}{15}, \frac{1}{15}]$	$vel_{\mathsf{comf}} = 45$
$\mathcal{E}.f^{prom} \subseteq [-0.12, 0.12]$	$vel_{\mathsf{comf}} = 25$
$\mathcal{E}.f^{prom} \subseteq [-0.2, 0.2]$	$vel_{\mathsf{comf}} = 15$
$\mathcal{E}.f^{prom} \subseteq [-0.3, 0.3]$	$vel_{\mathsf{comf}} = vel_{\mathsf{safe}} = 10$

Table 1: Look up table for the comfortable velocity vel_{comf}.

$\lvert vel_{\mathsf{cur}} - vel_{\mathsf{comf}} \rvert \geq 3$	$peakOvershoot = 3$
$\lvert vel_{\mathsf{cur}} - vel_{\mathsf{comf}} \rvert \in [2, 3[$	$peakOvershoot = 2$
$\lvert vel_{\mathsf{cur}} - vel_{\mathsf{comf}} \rvert \in [0, 2[$	$peakOvershoot = 1$

Table 2: Look up table for the peak overshoot *peakOvershoot*.

sumed steering. It therefore makes the car drive at most with velocity vel_{safe}, which guarantees comfortable centrifugal forces at all assumed steering activities. To guarantee, that VC is ready again for arbitrary steering when a promise $\mathcal{E}$ ends, vel_{goal} gets increased for a duration of $\mathcal{E}.duration - maxConvTime(vel_{\mathsf{cur}}, vel_{\mathsf{safe}})$ where the time $maxConvTime(vel_{\mathsf{cur}}, vel_{\mathsf{safe}})$ is sufficient for VC_PI to reach vel_{safe}. Likewise, VC_ER ignores events that have a duration less than $maxConvTime(vel_{\mathsf{cur}}, vel_{\mathsf{safe}})$.

For event $\mathcal{E}$, VC_ER sets vel_{goal} according to Eq. (1) to the maximal velocity that is comfortable for all announced steering actions, $\dot{\beta}_{\mathsf{ori}} \in \mathcal{E}.f^{prom}$ and additionally takes into account that VC_PI may overshoot the new vel_{goal} on its way to stabilizing on it. We refer to the maximal overshoot as the peak overshoot. The following equation summarizes how VC_ER determines the maximal velocity according to a given event $\mathcal{E}$: $velFor(\mathcal{E}) = \max(\frac{|F_{\mathsf{comf}}|}{|mass| \cdot \max(|\mathcal{E}.f^{prom}|)} - peakOvershoot, vel_{\mathsf{goal}}^{\mathsf{min}})$ (Eq. 2), where $\max(|\mathcal{E}.f^{prom}|)$ is the maximum change of orientation according to $\mathcal{E}$ and $vel_{\mathsf{goal}}^{\mathsf{min}}$ is the least allowed velocity setpoint due to overshoots. Based on *velFor*, $velFor(\mathcal{E}, vel_{\mathsf{des}}) = \min\{velFor(\mathcal{E}), vel_{\mathsf{des}}\}$ is defined to take into account the user's wishes vel_{des}.

For the composition (cf. 4.3) we have implemented VC_ER (i.e. the *velFor*-function) using the lookup tables (cf. Table 1, Table 2).

Managing Events. Within a current validity duration new events can be received that may trigger themselves new setpoints and new validity durations. Such events are only exploited if their due time ends before the current promise ends, so that contiguously promises can be exploited and the new promise is better than or equals the current promise. To simplify VC_ER, we assume that VC_ER has a mailbox subcomponent, VC_MB, that preprocesses events. VC_MB sorts, stores and manages events and notifies VC_ER in time by providing optimized events.

3.3 Steering Controller

The steering controller SC also consists of two subcomponents: a component for setting the actuator and a component for event generation.

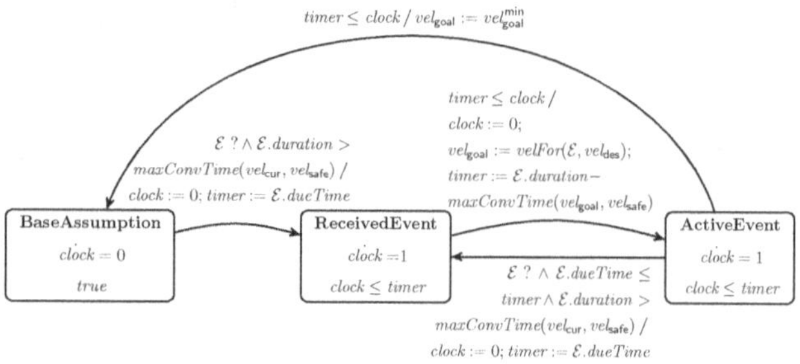

Figure 5: VC_ER adjusts the setpoint of the VC_PI.

Steering Control. In the plant the change of the distance to the mid of the street evolves according to $\dot{dist} = vel_{\mathsf{cur}} \cdot \sin(\beta_{\mathsf{ori}})$. SC's area of operation is partitioned into three regions, which correspond to mode names: **Keep**, **Left**, **Right** (cf. Fig. 6). In **Keep** the orientation is controlled in a PI-like manner exploiting the distance as an integrator. Both, **Left** and **Right**, split up into three modes that represent distance categories (**Close**, **Mid**, **Far**). In each such mode SC aims for an orientation which is proportional to the distance.

Event Generation. SC has to conservatively overapproximate its future steering in order to send valid events to the VC. As an event communicates guaranteed improvements for the announced window of time, its due time may be greater or equals the actual start time of the guaranteeable steering improvement, its duration may be smaller, but its end time has to be before the improvement ends.

The steering angle will converge to the equilibrium, which exists as we assume the road is straight. For curved roads, the SC could overapproximate its future steering based on sensor data of the road course.

We did not formally specify an event generator for SC, but assume that this component only sends events that can be mapped using Table 1 and that the sending of events is separated by at least $\Delta_{\mathsf{sep}}^{time}$.

4. PROVING ADAS'S OBJECTIVES

In Sections 4.1 and 4.2 we will obtain local properties of VC and SC by examining them isolated within their respective assumed environment. We consider a centrifugal force of maximal $\frac{F_{\mathsf{comf}}}{mass} = \frac{240}{80} = 3$ as comfortable. We globally assume that the disturbance s is 1 (GLB.A3). We can easily drop this restriction, by replacing the differential equation for vel_{cur} with a differential inclusion. In the sequel, we will describe which assumptions are used to obtain which properties. Due to space limitation we sketch some proof only. A detailed version can be found in [3].

4.1 Properties of the SC

For obtaining properties of SC we used that the velocity will stay slow i.e. $vel_{\mathsf{cur}} \in [5, 10]$ until the SC allows VC to increase its setpoint. Particularly, we derive from base as-

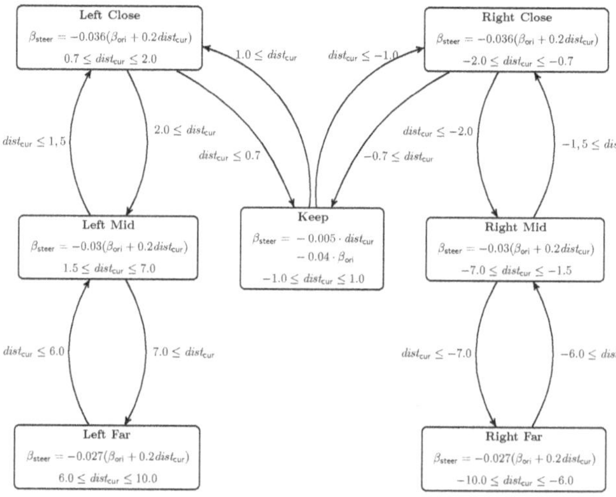

Figure 6: Hybrid automaton of SC.

sumptions and event assumptions of SC that $vel_{cur} \leq vel_{comf}$ always holds.

SC's assumptions (SC.A1, SC.A2, and SC.A3) and SC's guarantees (SC.G1, SC.G2, SC.G3, and SC.G4) are summarized in Table 3 and specify SC's achievements in an environment satisfying its assumptions.

To derive guarantees we replaced vel_{cur} in the composite of SC and the **Plant** by the whole domain and thereby the differential equation for $dist_{cur}$ becomes a differential inclusion. Further we approximated the sinus in two different ways: 1. by further exploiting differential inclusions as the convex combination $convex(\{x/57.59, x/57.25\})$, or 2. by differential equations with bounded inputs and manual state space partioning along β_{ori}.

A proof for SC.G1 can be obtained using the first approximation and the Stabhyli tool[9]. Stabhyli is a tool that proves non-linear hybrid systems to be stable based on Lyapunov functions. Stability, i.e. convergence to an equilibrium, is guaranteed, when a Lyapunov function is found, since the function value decreases along every trajectory of the system and function has its minimum at the equilibrium. To proof SC.G2 we transformed the invariant property SC.G2 to a time-bounded property. We used the Lyapunov functions to compute a barrier certificate[3] delimiting a sink set, such that trajectories after entering the sink will never reach states violating SC.G2. We also derived from the Lyapunov function an upper time bound for reaching this sink set. We then showed that SC eventually reaches states in mode **Keep** that were also in its init set, or SC reaches the sink box, where all trajectories satisfy SC.G2. For these proofs we used iSAT's bounded model checking interface for hybrid systems [7] and the symbolic forward model checker SoapBox [8] in combination on models with the second approximation.

4.2 Properties of the VC

To analyze the VC, we use that VC has finitely many possible setpoints. The number of setpoints is the product of the number of receivable events of VC (cf. Table 1), the possible values of *peakOvershoot* (cf. Table 2) and the number of possible values for vel_{des}. For each of VC's setpoints, i.e. for each value of vel_{goal}, we obtain an instance $\mathsf{VC}(vel_{goal_i})$. Appropriate discrete switching between these instances, leads to an automaton chaining the $\mathsf{VC}(vel_{goal_i})$. We instead analyze an equivalent but more compact version, that adopts the mode invariants in the original VC and resets vel_{goal}.

From the declaration of receivable events in VC's interface and the implementation of VC_ER we derive that $vel_{comf} \in [10, 50]$. This and the other guarantees (VC.G1 to VC.G6) as well as VC's assumptions (VC.A1 to VC.A5) are summarized in Table 3.

To proof VC.G1 we shifted VC i.e. by setting $vel'_{cur} = vel_{cur} - vel_{goal}$ and adjusted the invariants such that a single VC subsumes all individual $\mathsf{VC}(vel_{goal_i})$. We used Stabhyli to determine Lyapunov functions that certify convergence towards $vel'_{cur} = 0$ for the resulting system model. Note, how close vel_{cur} will approach vel_{goal} depends on how long vel_{goal} remains constant.

[3] Roughly speaking, a barrier certificate can be used to establish a border between two state sets such that one set cannot be reached though any trajectory starting in the other set. Each level set of a Lyapunov function can be used as barrier certificate [10].

Name	Property	Proof
VC.A1	$vel_{cur} \in [5, 10]$	directly by GLB.A2
VC.A2	G ($vel_{comf} \in [10, 50]$)	directly by SC.G3 and GLB.A6
VC.A3	G ($s = 1$)	directly by GLB.A3
VC.A4	G ($vel_{des} \in [10, 45]$)	directly by GLB.A4
VC.A5	There is a lower time bound greater 0 on event separation	directly by GLB.A5
VC.G1	vel_{cur} converges to vel_{goal}	complex, tool-supported
*VC.G2**	If vel_{goal} is (re)set so that $vel_{goal} \leq vel_{comf} - peakOvershoot$ holds, then $vel_{cur} \leq vel_{comf}$ always holds	complex, tool-supported
*VC.G3**	For every $vel'_{cur} \in [-50, 50]$ a time $maxConvTime$ after which a trajectory finally reaches a 1-region around any vel_{goal} exists. Further a time $maxTimeToSafeVel$ after which any trajectory finally reaches a 1-region around a $vel_{goal} = vel_{goal}^{min}$ exists.	directly by VC.G1
VC.G4	G ($vel_{cur} \leq vel_{comf}$)	complex, tool-supported
VC.G5	G ($vel_{cur} \in [5, 50]$)	complex, tool-supported
VC.G6	VC is lock free	complex, by-hand
SC.A1	init conf. restricting β_{ori} depending on $dist$	directly by GLB.A1
SC.A2	G ($vel_{cur} \in [5, 50]$)	directly by **Plant** invariant
SC.A3	G ($vel_{cur} \leq vel_{comf}$)	directly by VC.G4
SC.G1	converg. to $(\beta_{ori}, dist_{cur})=(0,0)$	complex, tool-supported
SC.G2	G ($dist_{cur} \in [-10, 10]$) and $\beta_{ori} \in [-5^\circ, 5^\circ]$	complex, tool-supported
SC.G3	G ($\beta_{steer} \in [-0.3, 0.3]$)	complex, tool-supported
SC.G4	SC is lock free	complex, by-hand
GLB.A1	init conf. restricting β_{ori} depending on $dist$	assumption of ADAS
GLB.A2	$vel_{cur} \in [5, 10]$	assumption of ADAS
GLB.A3	G ($s = 1$)	assumption of ADAS
GLB.A4	G ($vel_{des} \in [10, 45]$)	assumption of ADAS
GLB.A5	The events sent by SC are separated at least by Δ_{sep}^{time}	by-construction
GLB.A6	Event promises of SC are truthful and events have to conform with Table 1	by-construction of event generator
GLB.G1	The ADAS converges to the middle of the lane	directly by SC.G1
GLB.G2	The ADAS converges to the user's desired velocity	directly by VC.G1
GLB.G3	The comfortable centrifugal force is never exceeded	directly by VC.G4 and GLB.A6
GLB.G4	The ADAS is lock free	directly by SC.G4 and VC.G6

Table 3: Summary of Assumptions and Guarantees. * marks intermediate proof steps, G abreviates globally

To show that the *peakOvershoot* is sufficiently large (VC.G2), we again combined Lyapunov functions with bounded model checking by first using Lyapunov functions to calculate a barrier certificate delimiting a sink state set that implies that any trajectory reaching it will then satisfy $vel_{cur} \leq vel_{comf}$ and an upper time bound on reaching this set. Then we used SoapBox to prove that VC.G2 globally holds until either the upper time bound or that set is reached.

To obtain upper time bounds for convergence as required for VC.G3 we use the Lyapunov functions to calculate an upper bound on the time spent outside a particular region. Such an upper bound is usually a very rough overapproximation and better bounds can be found by again combining sink sets with bounded model checking like we did for VC.G2.

To proof VC.G4 one first has to see that the value of vel_{goal} is always set according to Eq. (2). Using VC.G2 it remains to show that vel_{goal} is set on time. VC will always reach a safe velocity, i.e. a velocity that is sufficiently low to be comfortable for the future steering, before the end of an event promise is reached, as $t = maxTimeToSafeVel$ is sufficiently large (VC.G3) and the automaton in Fig. 5 will set vel_{goal} to vel_{goal}^{min} at least t time units before the promise ends.

To show VC.G5 it is sufficient to see vel_{goal}^{min} is the least value for vel_{goal} and that vel_{goal}^{min} is chosen such that even with overshooting peaks the lower velocity bound of 5 is respected. Likewise, the maximal velocity setpoint is chosen such that even with overshooting peaks the upper velocity bound is respected. This can again be proven just like VC.G2.

The guarantee VC.G6 holds, since the union of all invariants covers the component's state space i.e. $[-50 + vel_{goal}, 50 + vel_{goal}] \supseteq [5, 50]$, and there is at least one enabled transition at the mode boundaries. VC does not stall time by firing discrete transitions, since for a given constant vel_{des} it converges towards vel_{goal}. By VC.A5, it follows that there is no discrete divergence.

4.3 Deducing properties of the composed system

We now use the properties proven for the isolated SC and VC to derive properties for the composed ADAS controller. Within our framework we have developed a calculus for deriving properties of the composed system. Due to the lack of space, we only sketch the grounds of reasoning here. Basically the composed component makes assumptions, that imply the assumptions of its subcomponents. Thus the subcomponents are bound to deliver their guarantees. Assumptions of the composed component take into account though, that its subcomponents contribute to satisfying assumptions of other subcomponents.

Table 3 summarizes the remaining assumptions and the guarantees of the composed ADAS. The assumptions GLB.A1, GLB.A2, GLB.A3, and GLB.A4 specify a valid deployment context for the ADAS and GLB.A5 and GLB.A6 are remaining assumptions for the event generator for SC. The guarantees GLB.G1, GLB.G2, GLB.G3, and GLB.G4 are what the ADAS will be able to achieve in a valid deployment context and imply our initial objectives (o1), (o2), and (o3).

5. CONCLUSION

We have presented a design methodology based on an exemplary composition of a steering controller (SC) and a velocity controller (VC) together implementing a simple ADAS. We gave an overview on the system's architecture, specified the controllers as hybrid automata and explained their event-based communication. We have explained how to show that each controller fulfills its local objective i.e. VC controls the velocity to be safe but stabilizes to a user chosen velocity if this is safe and SC brings and then keeps the car to the middle of its lane. Further, in the composite ADAS, they still achieve their objectives and together they also maintain the global objective, *the centrifugal force a passenger is experiencing does not exceed a certain threshold.*

In the future, we plan to extend our case study towards curved lanes, for which we have to consider reference tracking. However, our main target is to develop a formalized design methodology which allows library-based design of controllers, so that the properties of a composed controller can be compositionally derived –without examining the global system– from properties annotated in the components' interface.

Acknowledgement We would like to thank Andreas Eggers for support with iSAT and Willem Hagemann for support and access to his tool SoapBox.

6. REFERENCES

[1] L. J. Alun Foster, Iris Hamelink, editor. *ARTEMIS Book of Successes*. ARTEMIS, 2013.

[2] W. Damm, H. Dierks, J. Oehlerking, and A. Pnueli. Towards component based design of hybrid systems: Safety and stability. In Z. Manna and D. Peled, editors, *Essays in Memory of Amir Pnueli*, volume 6200 of *LNCS*. Springer, 2010.

[3] W. Damm, W. Hagemann, E. Möhlmann, and A. Rakow. Component based design of hybrid systems: A case study on concurrency and coupling. Reports of SFB/TR 14 AVACS 95, 2014.

[4] W. Damm, A. Mikschl, J. Oehlerking, E.-R. Olderog, J. Pang, A. Platzer, M. Segelken, and B. Wirtz. Automating Verification of Cooperation, Control, and Design in Traffic Applications. In *Formal Methods and Hybrid Real-Time Systems, Essays in Honor of Dines Bjørner and Chaochen Zhou on the Occasion of Their 70th Birthdays*, 2007.

[5] W. Damm, T. Peikenkamp, and B. Josko. Contract Based ISO CD 26262 Safety Analysis. In *SAE World Congress – Session on Safety-Critical Systems*, 2009.

[6] W. Damm, A. Votintseva, A. Metzner, B. Josko, and E. Peikenkamp, Thomas; Böde. Boosting re–use of embedded automotive applications through rich components. In *Proceedings of FIT 2005*, 08 2005.

[7] A. Eggers, N. Ramdani, N. S. Nedialkov, and M. Fränzle. Improving the SAT modulo ODE approach to hybrid systems analysis by combining different enclosure methods. *Software & Systems Modeling*, 2012.

[8] W. Hagemann. Reachability analysis of hybrid systems using symbolic orthogonal projections. *CAV*, 2014. submitted.

[9] E. Möhlmann and O. E. Theel. Stabhyli: a Tool for Automatic Stability Verification of Non-Linear Hybrid Systems. In C. Belta and F. Ivancic, editors, *HSCC*. ACM, 2013.

[10] S. Prajna and A. Jadbabaie. Safety verification of hybrid systems using barrier certificates. In R. Alur and G. J. Pappas, editors, *HSCC*, volume 2993 of *LNCS*. Springer, 2004.

[11] A. L. Sangiovanni-Vincentelli, W. Damm, and R. Passerone. Taming Dr. Frankenstein: Contract-based design for cyber-physical systems. *Eur. J. Control*, 18(3), 2012.

JSR: A Toolbox to Compute the Joint Spectral Radius

Guillaume Vankeerberghen [*]
ICTEAM, Université catholique de Louvain
4, Av. G. Lemaître
1348 Louvain-la-Neuve, Belgium
guillaume.vankeerberghen@uclouvain.be

Julien M. Hendrickx
ICTEAM, Université catholique de Louvain
4, Av. G. Lemaître
1348 Louvain-la-Neuve, Belgium
julien.hendrickx@uclouvain.be

Raphaël M. Jungers [†]
ICTEAM, Université catholique de Louvain
4, Av. G. Lemaître
1348 Louvain-la-Neuve, Belgium
raphael.jungers@uclouvain.be

ABSTRACT

We present a toolbox for computing the Joint Spectral Radius of a set of matrices, i.e., the maximal asymptotic growth rate of products of matrices taken in that set. The Joint Spectral Radius has a wide range of applications, including switched and hybrid systems, combinatorial words theory, or the study of wavelets. However, it is notoriously difficult to compute or approximate; it is actually uncomputable, and its approximation is NP-hard. The toolbox compiles several recent computation and approximation methods, and also contains an automatic blackbox method for inexperienced users, selecting the most appropriate methods based on an automatic study of the matrix set provided. The tool is implemented in Matlab and is freely downloadable (with documentation and demos) from Matlab Central[1].

Categories and Subject Descriptors

G.1.0.f [**Mathematics of Computing**]: Numerical Analysis—*General - Numerical algorithms*; G.4.a [**Mathematics of Computing**]: Mathematical Software—*Algorithm design and analysis*; F.2.1 [**Theory of Computation**]: Analysis of Algorithms and Problem Complexity—*Numerical algorithms and problems*

Keywords

Matlab; Joint Spectral Radius; Switched Systems; Stability

[*]G. V. is a F.R.I.A. Fellow

[†]R. M. J. is a F.R.S.-FNRS Research Associate

[1]`http://www.mathworks.com/matlabcentral/fileexchange/33202-the-jsr-toolbox`. Some of the methods also require SeDuMi, `http://coral.ie.lehigh.edu/~newsedumi/` [31].

HSCC'14, April 15–17, 2014, Berlin, Germany.

ACM 978-1-4503-2732-9/14/04 ...$15.00.
http://dx.doi.org/10.1145/2562059.2562124 .

1. INTRODUCTION

The Joint Spectral Radius (JSR) of a finite set of matrices $\mathcal{M}$ is defined by

$$\rho(\mathcal{M}) = \lim_{k\to\infty} \max\{\|A_{d_1}\cdots A_{d_k}\|^{1/k} : A_{d_i} \in \mathcal{M}\}. \quad (1)$$

It thus represents the largest asymptotic growth rate of all possible products of matrices in $\mathcal{M}$. Note that it can more generally be defined for compact (or even larger) sets $\mathcal{M}$, but we will restrict our attention to finite sets here. See [18] for a recent monograph on the topic. The JSR was introduced by Rota and Strang in 1960 [30], and has since then been the object of extensive research, partly due to its surprisingly diverse spectrum of applications.

Maybe the most natural application concerns the stability of *switched linear dynamical systems*. In these systems, the state $x(t)$ evolves as $x(t+1) = A_t x(t)$, where A_t can be any matrix in a given set $\mathcal{M}$. Such systems can be unstable for certain sequences of matrices even when every individual matrix in $\mathcal{M}$ is stable.

The evolution of the state depends of course on the particular sequence of matrices selected, but it can be easily seen that all possible trajectories converge to 0 if $\rho(\mathcal{M}) < 1$. On the other hand, one can prove that if $\rho(\mathcal{M}) \geq 1$, then there exists a sequence of matrices $A_0, A_1, A_2, \ldots$ and an initial condition $x(0)$ for which $x(t)$ does not converge to 0. Similarly, if $\rho(\mathcal{M}) > 1$ there exists a sequence of matrices and an initial condition such that $||x(t)||$ diverges [18, Corollary 1.1].

Switched systems are present in an increasing number of contexts, including systems relying on complex communication networks subject to failures and unreliabilities, which can temporarily modify the system behavior [12, 19]. They can also be used to derive bounds for more general hybrid systems. In various natural contexts, the behaviour of the system can be modeled in the following way $x(t+1) = A_{\sigma(\mathbf{x};t)} x(t)$; where $\sigma(.;.)$ takes its values in a set indexing some set of matrices $\mathcal{M}$, and may depend on x, the history of x, and on time. This is for example typically the case when analyzing multi-agent systems where the ability of agents to communicate depends on their position (see for example [5, 33] and references therein). Analyzing the behavior of these systems is often extremely challenging due to their nonlinear and sometimes discontinuous behavior. However, the JSR $\rho(\mathcal{M})$ provides an upper bound on their convergence or divergence rate.

The JSR also has very different applications in engineering and computer science. For instance, it characterizes the smoothness properties of certain wavelet functions, among which the celebrated Daubechies' finitely supported wavelets [11]. Recently, the value of the JSR also proved useful in combinatorics on words. Overlap-free words are words on a finite alphabet satifsying certain combinatorial properties, and an important question in their study is to characterize the rate at which the number of words of length n grows with n. It has been shown that this number could be obtained by taking the largest of all possible products (of a certain length related to n) of two matrices. By computing bounds on the JSR of these two matrices, a new approximation of the growth rate of the number of overlap-free words was obtained, outperforming previous bounds that were obtained by ad hoc methods [21]. Similar results were obtained for α-power-free words [4]. The JSR also plays a key role in the trackability of malicious agents in sensor networks [10], or the computation of the capacity of codes subject to particular constraints [24].

Unfortunately, the JSR of a set of matrices is very hard to compute or even to approximate. More specifically, the question of determining whether $\rho(\mathcal{M}) \leq 1$ is undecidable, even if $\mathcal{M}$ only consists of two matrices [9]. In addition, it is also NP-hard to approximate, even if $\mathcal{M}$ consists of two matrices whose nonzero entries are all equal to one [32]. Meaning that there is no single algorithm that will work well on all cases.

Nevertheless, several approximation methods have been proposed over the years (see Section 2), and it appears that the JSR can be computed to a satisfactory level of accuracy at an acceptable cost in many applications.

However, even if more than a dozen approximation methods are available in the literature, very little work has been done on comparing their accuracy and efficacy on given classes of problems. We also found that several of these methods were hard to obtain, so that the interested users essentially needed to re-implement them.

More importantly, implementing and using these methods, and selecting the appropriate one for a given problem, is far from trivial, and often requires some experience in the domain. As a result, it is rather difficult for researchers of other fields to test the application of the JSR to their problems. The application of the JSR to certain combinatorial word problems was for example only made possible by the collaboration between experts in the two fields [4], and many other possible applicatons of the JSR may have been left unexplored due to the lack of such collaborations.

These two issues motivated the development of the toolbox presented here, which contains two main features.
a) A compilation of fourteen recent methods for approximating the JSR in a unified interface. The goal of this part is to allow experienced users to use and test different techniques on their problems, to compare the efficiency of different methods (tuning some methods' parameters when relevant), or to help them comparing new methods that they have developed with the existing ones. Note that the toolbox will be open and that the addition of any new method by an interested contributor is welcome. Our goal is also to propose a benchmark of matrices that would be available to test new methods.
b) A ready-to-use `jsr` function with which the user can compute the JSR of a set of matrices in blackbox and that requires no understanding of the methods used. This function analyzes the set of matrices provided by the user, pre-treats them when relevant, and then selects the methods that appear the most appropriate. Our goal here is to provide researchers from other fields with a simple way of computing the JSR and to test if the results can help them in their research field.

2. DESCRIPTION OF THE METHODS

We describe here the theoretical ideas behind the methods implemented in the toolbox. The precise way to use each method in Matlab is extensively described in the `help` and the toolbox itself contains demos. A list of all implementations can be obtained in Matlab with the command `help JSR_louvain` if the toolbox's folder is named `JSR_louvain`.

Most methods to approach the JSR rely on the following inequalities, bounding it from above and from below.

$$\max\{\rho(A) : A \in \mathcal{M}^k\} \leq \rho(\mathcal{M})^k \leq \max\{||A|| : A \in \mathcal{M}^k\} \quad (2)$$

where $\mathcal{M}^k = \left\{A_{d_1}\cdots A_{d_k} \;\middle|\; A_{d_j} \in \mathcal{M},\ j = 1,\ldots,k\right\}$.

After preprocessing steps, which we review in Section 2.1, there are essentially two families of methods. A first one consists in computing the spectral radius and/or the norm of products of k matrices of $\mathcal{M}$, and using the results to bound $\rho(\mathcal{M})$ from below and/or above using the general bounds (2). We review some of these methods in Section 2.2.

The second class of methods uses the fact that the upper bound in (2) is valid for any submultiplicative norm. They consist in building specific norms for which this upper bound is as small as possible. Some methods achieve this by an iterative procedure using the matrices of $\mathcal{M}$. Others directly build the norm using optimization techniques. We review the former in Section 2.3 and the latter in Section 2.4.

2.1 Preprocessing

2.1.1 *Joint triangularizability (`jointTriangul`)*

If the set of matrices is jointly triangularizable (i.e., if the matrices share a common nontrivial invariant subspace), then the matrices can be split into blocks so that the JSR is equal to the maximum of the JSR of the different diagonal blocks (see [18, Proposition 1.5]). To the best of our knowledge, no efficient algorithm is known to decide whether a set of matrices has a nontrivial invariant subspace. The toolbox uses a heuristic search that allows in some cases to find such a subspace if it exists.

2.1.2 *Joint triangularizability under permutation (`permTriangul`)*

Contrary to the above general triangularizability case, it is possible to decide in polynomial time whether a set of matrices is triangularizable *under a common permutation of the entries of the matrix* (that is, to decide whether a coordinate hyperplane is invariant). See [18, Lemma 3.1].

2.1.3 *The products lifting (`itMeth`)*

From Equation (2), for any natural number k, one can first compute all the products of length k of the matrices in $\mathcal{M}$, and then apply any method to compute the JSR of the new set in order to compute the JSR of the initial set. Note that for instance, computing the maximal spectral radius (or the maximal norm, for an arbitrary norm) of the set for increasing k already gives a method that asymptotically converges towards the JSR (this is straightforward from Equations (1) and (2)). This method is described in Section 2.2.1.

2.1.4 *The semidefinite lifting (`jsr_lift_semidefinite`)*

The semidefinite lifting introduced in [7] is another way of constructing a new set of matrices in the same spirit as in the previous subsection. That is, for any natural k, it builds a new set of matrices $\mathcal{M}^{[k]}$ such that

$$\rho(\mathcal{M}^{[k]}) = \rho(\mathcal{M})^{2k}.$$

Even though any method could be applied on the set $\mathcal{M}^{[k]}$, the main motivation of this lifting is that it allows for the use of a very fast method to obtain converging upper and lower bounds on the JSR, by summing all the matrices in $\mathcal{M}^{[k]}$, and computing the spectral radius of the obtained matrix [7, Theorem 5]. Since it is the principal motivation of performing the semidefinite lifting, we directly implemented it within the function `jsr_lift_semidefinite`. See also [18, Section 2.3.6].

2.1.5 *The Kronecker lifting (*`itMeth`*)*

The Kronecker lifting also consists in building a new set of matrices formed by taking the Kronecker product of each matrix with itself. This lifting has the same effect as taking all products of a certain length [7]. The method `itMeth` can apply the Kronecker lifting and call user-specified methods on the new set of matrices.

2.2 Enumeration based methods

2.2.1 *Brute force (*`jsr_prod_bruteForce`*)*

This method iteratively computes the products sets $\mathcal{M}^k$ and returns the simple upper and lower bounds provided by (2) with the euclidean norm.

2.2.2 *Pruning method for nonnegative matrices (*`jsr_prod_pruningAlgorithm`*)*

Thanks to the partial order implied by the positive orthant, if the matrices have nonnegative entries, it is possible to modify the brute force method described above by pruning the set of products at every step in order to save both time and space during the computations. This technique can prove extremely fast in some cases. See [6, 18, Section 2.3.3] for more explanations.

2.2.3 *Gripenberg's algorithm (*`jsr_prod_Gripenberg`*)*

This method, introduced in [14], is an adaptation of the brute force technique described above, which carefully prunes some of the products with the guarantee that the lower and upper bounds are still valid, up to a certain prespecified arbitrary maximal error. If this maximal error is not taken too small, this method is quite efficient, and is usually used as a first way of getting quick bounds on the JSR. Since it works by generating the products, it has the additional advantage that it provides a guess for the optimal product.

2.3 Iterative norm methods

In this section and the next one we describe methods that work on the upper bound part of Equation (2). They consist in finding a good norm so that the upper bound is as small as possible, hence providing an approximation of the JSR *even without having to compute products of matrices.* They rely on the following fundamental theorem:

THEOREM 1. *If a set of matrices $\mathcal{M}$ is irreducible (i.e. it does not have a common nontrivial invariant subspace), then there exists a norm $||\cdot||$ such that*

$$\rho(\mathcal{M}) = \max\{||A_i|| : A_i \in \mathcal{M}\}.$$

The idea of the iterative methods is to start with a candidate optimal product, an optimal product being a product $A \in \mathcal{M}^k$ for which the left-hand side inequality in (2) is tight. If the product is really optimal, then $\mathcal{M}/(\rho(A)^{1/k})$ has JSR equal to one. One can show that one can converge to a norm as in Theorem 1 by iteratively applying the matrices of $\mathcal{M}$ to the unit ball of a particular initial norm. If the candidate product was not optimal, then $\mathcal{M}/(\rho(A)^{1/k})$ has JSR larger than one, and one can detect that when iteratively applying the matrices. See for instance [16, 17] for proofs and developments.

A significant advantage of these methods is that they can end in finite time, if the upper bound provided by the norm obtained at some step is equal to the lower bound provided by the candidate optimal product A. This actually happens rather frequently, provided that one starts with a particular initial norm, which is constructed with the leading eigenvectors of the candidate optimal product. See [18, 27] for more explanation on this phenomena, and for other similar methods not implemented in this toolbox.

2.3.1 *Balanced Real Polytope method (*`jsr_norm_balancedRealPolytope`*)*

This method, described in [17], can be used if the leading eigenvectors of the candidate product are real. Fig. 1 illustrates a Balanced Real Polytope, i.e., a polytope with nonempty interior and symmetric around the origin, (plain polytope) such that its image by any of the matrices in $\mathcal{M}$ (dashed polytopes) is contained in the polytope. This proves that $\rho(\mathcal{M}) \leq 1$ (we do not present here the set $\mathcal{M}$ because of length constraints).

Figure 1: A Balanced real Polytope (plain lines) and its images by two matrices in $\mathbb{R}^{2\times 2}$ (dashed lines). This provides a guarantee that the JSR is smaller than or equal to one.

2.3.2 *Balanced Complex Polytope (BCP) method (*`jsr_norm_balancedComplexPolytope`*)*

This method, described in [15, 16] can be used in the general case where the leading eigenvectors of the candidate product have complex values.

2.3.3 *Lifted Polytope method (*`jsr_norm_conitope`*)*

This method, recently introduced in [20], mixes the spirit of the iterative methods with algebraic properties of liftings like the ones described above. The authors of [20] introduce new types of norms, which allow to prune vertices of the norm constructed at every step, hence allowing to save computational time and space. They also sometimes allow to deliver shorter certificates of optimality.

2.3.4 *Kozyakin's numerical algorithms (*`jsr_norm_linearRelaxation2D`, `jsr_norm_maxRelaxation2D`, `jsr_norm_maxRelaxation`*)*

These methods implement the numerical algorithms described in [22, 23]. In these papers, the author proposes numerical ways to approximate the norm provided by Theorem 1 and proves that they asymptotically converge towards the true value.

2.4 Optimization-based norm methods

The methods described here also try to compute a norm in order to provide a small upper bound in Equation (2). However, contrary to Section 2.3, they do not rely on iterative application of the matrices in $\mathcal{M}$. Instead, they make use of optimization methods in order to minimize this upper bound, by creating a norm *ab initio*. A significant advantage of these methods is that they come with a guarantee of accuracy: for each of them, one can compute an $\varepsilon(n)$, depending only on the dimension of the matrices, such that the upper bound ρ^* obtained with this method satisfies

$$(1-\varepsilon)\rho^* \leq \rho \leq \rho^*.$$

2.4.1 *The linear norms for nonnegative matrices* (`jsr_conic_linear`)

If the matrices have nonnegative entries, norms yielding a bound ρ^* arbitrarily close to ρ can be obtained as the solution of linear optimization problems. See [29] for more details and an expression of $\varepsilon(n)$.

2.4.2 *The ellipsoid method* (`jsr_conic_ellipsoid`)

Thanks to Semidefinite Programming techniques, one can optimize on the set of ellipsoidal norms in order to minimize the upper bound ρ^*. Fig. 2 illustrates this for 2 matrices in $\mathbb{R}^{2\times 2}$. In Fig. 2, the plain ellipse corresponds to the unit ball of an ellipsoidal norm such that its image by any of the two matrices is contained in the unit ball. This provides a guarantee that the JSR is smaller than or equal to one. Upper-bounds other than one can be found by scaling the matrices. See [2,8] for more details and an expression of $\varepsilon(n)$.

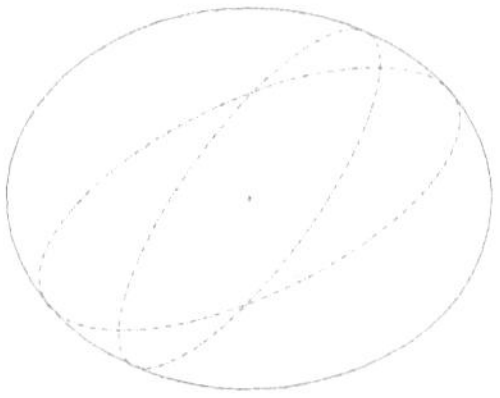

Figure 2: The ellipse corresponding to the unit ball of a norm (plain line) and its images by two matrices in $\mathbb{R}^{2\times 2}$ (dashed lines). This provides a guarantee that the JSR is smaller than or equal to one.

2.4.3 *Sum-Of-Squares* (`jsr_opti_sos`)

It has been shown in [26] that the idea of the ellipsoidal norm can be pushed further, by replacing ellipsoidal norms (represented by Sum-of-squares of degree 2) with higher degree Sum-Of-Squares functions in order to improve the accuracy of the bound. See [18, 26, Section 2.3.7] for more details and an expression of $\varepsilon(n)$.

3. BLACKBOX METHOD: `JSR`

In the previous section we introduced and briefly described the different algorithms implemented in the JSR Toolbox. As explained in the introduction however, selecting the best method to use for a given problem is not necessarily easy and may require some experience in the domain. As a result, a user unfamiliar with these methods might find them difficult to use. Therefore, we have included in the toolbox an easily callable function that automatically checks conditions on the set of matrices and then sequentially runs appropriate methods with the goal of providing as good as possible bounds in a reasonable time. This function is named `jsr`. Our goal is to allow anyone to check the approximate value of the JSR of a set of matrices, without requiring her or him to know anything about the computation methods used. The implementation is assorted with explanatory outputs that are understandable by non-experts. See Fig. 3 for a flow-chart of the algorithm.

The algorithm first checks if the matrices are real and nonnegative. Indeed, many applications lead to nonnegative matrices [4, 10,21,24], and it turns out that specific and more efficient methods can be applied in that case. Then, `jsr` checks if the matrices can be jointly block-triangularized. The method first checks for block-triangularization by permutation with `permTriangul` and if it did not work it tries with the heuristic `jointTriangul`. If none is found, it will assume that there is no joint block-triangularization. In this case it can be proved that the methods called by `jsr` will still converge to the true value, even if the matrices are in fact block-triangularizable [20]. Depending on the results of this test, it selects one of the three options described below.

Joint block-triangularizable matrices

As mentioned in Section 2.1.1, when matrices can be block-triangularized, the JSR of the set is equal to the maximum of the joint spectral radii of the sets of diagonal blocks [18]. Hence in this case, the computation of the JSR can be done by computing the JSR of each set of blocks and taking the largest one, which can usually be done at a smaller cost. Because the JSR of the set is the largest JSR of the sets of blocks, it is not always necessary to compute precisely the JSR of every block: we can ignore all those for which we know that their JSR will not be the largest one. Hence, when a block-triangularization could be found, `jsr` computes quick bounds with the pruning method in the nonnegative real case and with brute force method in the case with complex or negative and positive entries. It then checks if the upper bound on some set is lower than the lower bound on some other set so as to stop the analysis on the former. After this quick pruning attempt, `jsr` calls itself on each remaining set of blocks. As these blocks have a smaller size than the original matrices these recursive calls always stop. When the recursive `jsr` calls have provided bounds on each set of blocks, `jsr` tries to prune sets of blocks in the same way as described above. If only one set of blocks remains it outputs the bounds on this set which also bound the JSR of the original set of matrices. If more than one set of blocks remain, `jsr` prints a message explaining the situation and outputs the different blocks and the best bounds found on each of them to allow the user to pursue the analysis.

Nonnegative matrices with no joint block-triangularization

For real nonnegative matrices that cannot be block-triangularized, `jsr` first launches the pruning method. Then the bounds obtained are successively refined by the linear norm and the ellipsoid methods. Finally, the iterative lifted polytope method is launched with the product attaining the pruning method's lower bound as candidate optimal product. The rationale for applying these methods is as follows. First, the pruning method on nonnegative matrices iteratively generates long products by keeping only the interesting ones, so it has a chance of finding an optimal product. Then, the linear and ellipsoid norm methods might refine the upper-bound found. Finally, lifted polytope might provide very tight bounds if the candidate optimal product is good and if it has enough time remaining.

General matrices with no joint block-triangularization found

For matrices with entries that are complex or of both signs and that could not be block-triangularized, `jsr` starts by using Gripenberg's method. This method is good to generate products of long length by keeping only the interesting ones. Then, `jsr` launches the ellipsoid method to try refining the upper-bound from Gripenberg. Finally, `jsr` launches the lifted polytope method with as input candidate optimal product the candidate optimal product output by Gripenberg. This method has the potential to find tight bounds when it is initialized with a good candidate optimal product and is given enough time.

Additional options of `jsr`

There are three options that can be specified to `jsr`:
Computation time: One can specify an approximate time-limit on the execution. In the implementation of `jsr`, the desired time-

limit is divided in smaller time-limits that are given, to the various methods used. Note that the time cannot be checked after each operation and it is hard to predict the time a future iteration will take. Therefore, the desired time-limit is not always strictly respected. By default this time-limit is set to 120 seconds.
Tolerance: The tolerance fed as option to the methods called. Its precise implication depends on the particular methods called. We refer the reader to the `help` of these methods. By default it is set to 10^{-6}.
Block-triangularization (boolean): This boolean variable allows disabling the tests for block-triangularization. There are indeed situations where it is preferable not to launch the `jointTriangul` heuristic which could take too much time, such as for instance, when dealing with many big matrices with positive and negative entries. By default, `jsr` will try to block-triangularize as described in Fig. 3.

4. EXAMPLES

4.1 Random matrices

As a first example, we use the toolbox to compare two methods on a set of 3 random matrices in $[0,1]^{10\times 10}$. The two methods are `jsr_prod_pruningAlgorithm` and `jsr_norm_conitope`. The bounds found at each depth, or product length, by these methods is represented on Fig. 4. We see that for a comparable length of products the conitope algorithm gives substantially tighter bounds. However, this comes at the expense of time as the pruning algorithm took around 3 seconds whereas the conitope one took around 2 minutes on our personal computer. The candidate product with highest growth-rate output by these two methods is the same and is A_2A_3.

The matrices, the plot of Fig. 4, and more outputs can be generated by the script `demo2_JSR.m` in the toolbox.

4.2 Wavelet

The function `waveletMat` in the toolbox generates the set of two matrices corresponding to the Nth Daubechies wavelet, for N up to 19. We launched `jsr` on the two matrices in $\mathbb{R}^{7\times 7}$ corresponding to the wavelets of index $N = 15$. The method computes upper and lower bounds in less than 2 minutes, the lower bound found is the actual value of the JSR, 0.14754035... [14], and the upper bound is $2.171 \cdot 10^{-5}$ more.

5. CONCLUSION

The JSR toolbox has been implemented and released in beta version in 2011 with two goals: to provide the practitioner with quick and efficient tools to approximate the JSR of a set of matrices, a task that can be cumbersome and sometimes necessitates to delve into quite an intricate theory; and to provide researchers with benchmarks and solid implementations of most available methods in the literature in order to compare them, adapt them to particular cases, or create new methods. We are confident that the currently available version is sufficiently solid to achieve these goals.

In the future, we plan to implement newly proposed methods that appear to outperform previous ones in some particular cases, like the so-called path-dependent Lyapunov functions recently proposed in [1]. Another development would be to broaden the scope of the toolbox towards more general tools to analyze switched systems, like the top Lyapunov exponent of matrices (see [13,28]), the joint spectral subradius [3,29], the p-radius [25], etc.

Figure 3: Flow chart of the jsr algorithm.

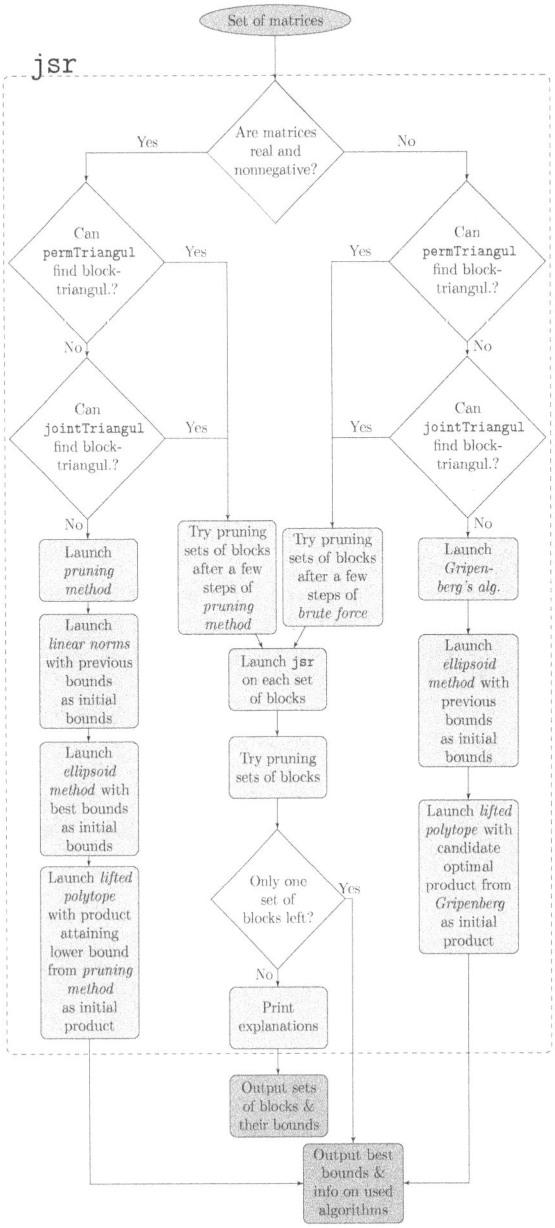

6. ACKNOWLEDGMENTS

We are grateful to Chia-Tche Chang and Vincent Blondel for providing their own codes for certain methods, which served as a basis for the implementation of some of the algorithms contained in the Toolbox. The research was funded by the Belgian Network DYSCO initiated by the Belgian State and by an ARC of the French Community of Belgium.

7. REFERENCES

[1] A. A. Ahmadi, R. M. Jungers, P. A. Parrilo, and M. Roozbehani. Analysis of the joint spectral radius via lyapunov functions on path-complete graphs. In *Proceedings of HSCC '11*, pages 13–22, 2011.

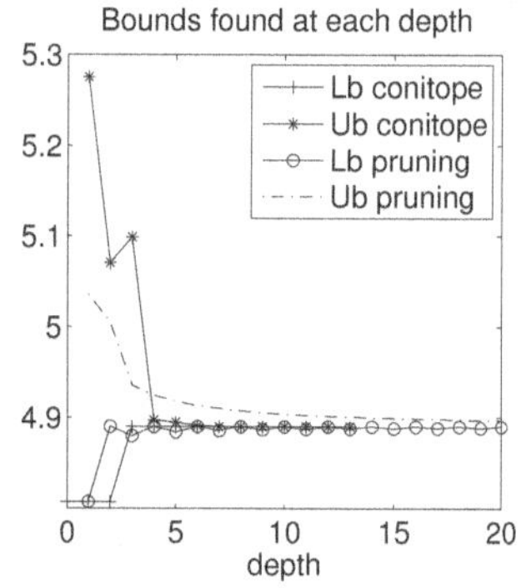

Figure 4: Bounds on the JSR found at each depth (i.e., product length) by `jsr_prod_pruningAlgorithm` and `jsr_norm_conitope`.

[2] T. Ando and M.-H. Shih. Simultaneous contractibility. *SIAM Journal on Matrix Analysis and Applications*, 19(2):487–498, 1998.

[3] F. Blanchini, P. Colaneri, and M.E. Valcher. Co-positive lyapunov functions for the stabilization of positive switched systems. *Automatic Control, IEEE Transactions on*, 57(12):3038–3050, 2012.

[4] V. D. Blondel, J. Cassaigne, and R. M. Jungers. On the number of α-power-free words for $2 < \alpha < 7/3$. *Theoretical Computer Science*, 410(38-40):2823–2833, 2009.

[5] V. D. Blondel, J. M. Hendrickx, and J. N. Tsitsiklis. On Krause's multi-agent consensus model with state-dependent connectivity. *Automatic Control, IEEE Transactions on*, 54(11):2586–2597, 2009.

[6] V. D. Blondel, R. M. Jungers, and V. Y. Protasov. On the complexity of computing the capacity of codes that avoid forbidden difference patterns. *Information Theory, IEEE Transactions on*, 52(11):5122–5127, 2006.

[7] V. D. Blondel and Y. Nesterov. Computationally efficient approximations of the joint spectral radius. *SIAM Journal on Matrix Analysis and Applications*, 27(1):256–272, 2005.

[8] V. D. Blondel, Y. Nesterov, and J. Theys. Approximations of the Rate of Growth of Switched Linear Systems. In *Proceedings of HSCC '04*, pages 173–186, 2004.

[9] V. D. Blondel and J. N. Tsitsiklis. The boundedness of all products of a pair of matrices is undecidable. *Systems & Control Letters*, 41(2):135–140, 2000.

[10] V. Crespi, G. Cybenko, and G. Jiang. The theory of trackability with applications to sensor networks. *ACM Transactions on Sensor Networks*, 4(3):1–42, 2008.

[11] I. Daubechies and J. C. Lagarias. Two-scale difference equations. ii. local regularity, infinite products of matrices and fractals. *SIAM Journal of Mathematical Analysis*, 23:1031–1079, 1992.

[12] P. Frasca and J. M. Hendrickx. On the mean square error of randomized averaging algorithms. *to appear in Automatica*, 2013.

[13] R. Gharavi and V. Anantharam. An upper bound for the largest lyapunov exponent of a markovian product of nonnegative matrices. *Theoretical Computer Science*, 332:543–557, 2005.

[14] G. Gripenberg. Computing the joint spectral radius. *Linear Algebra and its Applications*, 234:43–60, 1996.

[15] N. Guglielmi and V. Y. Protasov. Exact computation of joint spectral characteristics of linear operators. *Foundations of Computational Mathematics*, 13(1):37–97, 2013.

[16] N. Guglielmi, F. Wirth, and M. Zennaro. Complex polytope extremality results for families of matrices. *SIAM Journal on Matrix Analysis and Applications*, 27(3):721–743, 2005.

[17] N. Guglielmi and M. Zennaro. Finding extremal complex polytope norms for families of real matrices. *SIAM Journal on Matrix Analysis and Applications*, 31(2):602–620, 2009.

[18] R. M. Jungers. The joint spectral radius, Theory and applications. In *Lecture Notes in Control and Information Sciences*, volume 385. Springer-Verlag, Berlin, 2009.

[19] R. M. Jungers, A. D'Innocenzo, and M. D. Di Benedetto. Feedback stabilization of dynamical systems with switched delays. *Proceedings of the IEEE CDC2012*, 2012.

[20] R. M. Jungers, N. Guglielmi, and A. Cicone. Lifted polytope methods for computing the joint spectral radius. *SIAM Journal on Matrix Analysis and Applications*, 2014.

[21] R. M. Jungers, V. Y. Protasov, and V. D. Blondel. Overlap-free words and spectra of matrices. *Theoretical Computer Science*, 410:3670–3684, 2009.

[22] V. Kozyakin. Iterative building of barabanov norms and computation of the joint spectral radius for matrix. *Discrete and Continuous Dynamical Systems-series B*, 14(1):143–158, 2010.

[23] V. Kozyakin. A relaxation scheme for computation of the joint spectral radius of matrix sets. *Journal of Difference Equations and Applications*, 17(2):185–201, 2011.

[24] B. E. Moision, A. Orlitsky, and P. H. Siegel. On codes that avoid specified differences. *Information Theory, IEEE Transactions on*, 47:433–442, 2001.

[25] M. Ogura and C. F. Martin. Stability of switching systems and generalized joint spectral radius. *Proceedings of the IEEE ECC 2013*, 2013.

[26] P. A. Parrilo and A. Jadbabaie. Approximation of the joint spectral radius using Sum Of Squares. *Linear Algebra and its Applications*, 428(10):2385–2402, 2008.

[27] V. Y. Protasov. The geometric approach for computing the joint spectral radius. In *Proceedings of the 44th IEEE CDC-ECC*, pages 3001–3006, 2005.

[28] V. Y. Protasov and R. M. Jungers. Lower and Upper Bounds for the Largest Lyapunov Exponent of matrices. *To appear in: Linear Algebra and its Applications*, 2013.

[29] V. Y. Protasov, R. M. Jungers, and V. D. Blondel. Joint spectral characteristics of matrices: a conic programming approach. *SIAM Journal on Matrix Analysis and Applications*, 31(4):2146–2162, 2010.

[30] G. C. Rota and W. G. Strang. A note on the joint spectral radius. *Indag. Math.*, 22:379–381, 1960.

[31] J.F. Sturm. Using SeDuMi 1.02, a MATLAB toolbox for optimization over symmetric cones. *Optimization Methods and Software*, 11–12:625–653, 1999.

[32] J. N. Tsitsiklis and V. D. Blondel. The Lyapunov exponent and joint spectral radius of pairs of matrices are hard - when not impossible - to compute and to approximate. *Mathematics of Control, Signals, and Systems*, 10:31–40, 1997.

[33] T. Vicsek, A. Czirók, E. Ben-Jacob, I. Cohen, and O. Shochet. Novel type of phase transition in a system of self-driven particles. *Physical Review Letters*, 75(6):1226, 1995.

A Bounded Model Checking Tool for Periodic Sample-hold Systems

Gabor Simko
Vanderbilt University
Nashville, TN, USA
gabor.simko@isis.vanderbilt.edu

Ethan K. Jackson
Microsoft Research
Redmond, WA, USA
ejackson@microsoft.com

ABSTRACT

Safety verification of a plant together with its controller is an important part of controller design. If the controller is implemented in software, then a formal model such as *hybrid automata* is needed to model the composite system. However, classic hybrid automata scale poorly for complex software controllers due to their eager representation of discrete states. In this paper we present safety verification for software controllers without constructing hybrid automata. Our approach targets a common class of software controllers, where the plant is periodically sampled and actuated by the controller. The resulting systems exhibit a regular alternation of discrete steps and fixed length continuous-time evolution. We show that these systems can be verified by a combination of *SMT solving* and *Taylor models*. SMT formulas accurately capture control software in a compact form, and Taylor models accurately capture continuous trajectories up to guaranteed error bounds.

Categories and Subject Descriptors

D.2.2 [**Software Engineering**]: Design Tools and Techniques

1. INTRODUCTION

Safety verification of a plant together with its controller is an important part of controller design. Proving safety is notoriously hard for discrete controllers (e.g. software controllers) operating on continuous-time (CT) plants (e.g. mechanical plants). A standard approach is to represent the composite system with *hybrid automata* (HA), which can capture both the discrete and continuous aspects. Given an HA model, possible trajectories (i.e. *flowpipes*) can be computed and checked for safety [5, 4, 10]. However, representing software controllers with classic HA is often impractical, because all possible states of a software controller must be enumerated in its HA model. In other words, there is an explosion of discrete states in the HA representation. Introduction of discrete state variables as syntactic sugar also does not solve the problem.

HSCC'14, April 15–17, 2014, Berlin, Germany.
Copyright 2014 ACM 978-1-4503-2732-9/14/04 ...$15.00.
http://dx.doi.org/10.1145/2562059.2562134.

In this paper we present safety verification that does not rely on HA models. Our approach works for controllers that periodically sample and actuate their CT plants. These systems exhibit a regular alternation of discrete steps and fixed length CT evolution. Because of this property, the discrete evolution can be represented accurately and compactly using *satisfiability modulo theories* (SMT) formulas [6]. CT evolution of continuous state variables can be represented with *Taylor models* [2] providing guaranteed error bounds. Finally, the two representations can be composed by sampling and discretizing a Taylor model (continuous-to-discrete), and then holding predicted discrete control outputs for a fixed amount of time (discrete-to-continuous).

The benefits of our approch are:

- *Accuracy* - The controller implementation is modeled accurately, e.g. rounding, discretization, and saturation effects are modeled.
- *Convenience* - Periodic sample-hold systems are common. We directly account for their semantics.
- *Scalability* - Our approach avoids eager expansion of discrete states. Due to sampling assumptions, there is no need for costly evaluation of guard intersections and state reinitializations.

Concretely, users specify software controllers as discrete dataflow systems in a style similar to *Simulink*. The dataflow system periodically samples the plant's state variables, computes the next control response, and holds this control response for an entire sample period. We assume computation of the control response to be instantaneous and the ith response is presented to the plant at the t_{i+1} sample time. (These assumptions can be found in many formalisms ([13, 12].) The plant is modeled as a set of non-linear ODEs with initial conditions constrained to be within some intervals.

This paper is organized as follows. Section 2 presents related work. Section 3 describes our approach in detail. Section 4 presents our implementation and Section 5 describes case studies. We conclude in Section 6.

2. RELATED WORK

Taylor models are now commonly employed in safety verification of hybrid systems. Ramdani et al. [14] use Taylor models to perform validated integration and *interval constraint propagation* (ICP) to find the flowpipe guard intersections. Chen et al. [4] propose the usage of Taylor mod-

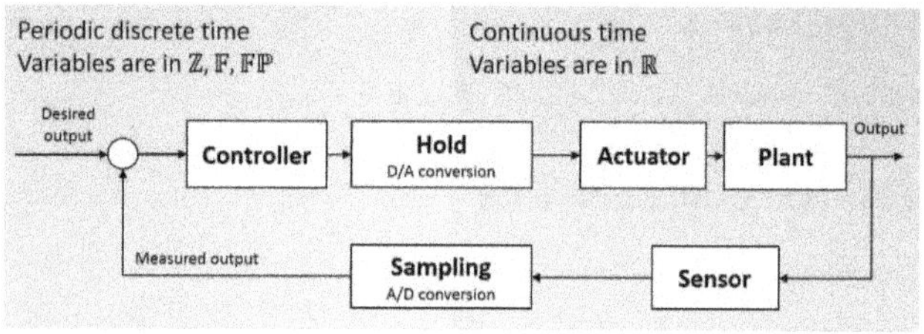

Figure 1: A periodic sample-hold system

els as well, but instead of ICP they performed the flow-pipe intersection using domain contraction and range over-approximation. A different line of research is based on SAT solvers for finding reachability. Gao et al. [11] introduce delta-reachability based on *DReal*, a delta-complete SAT solver. Similarly, *HySAT/iSAT* [9] are SAT-based bounded model checkers for hybrid systems based on interval constraints.

Boiussou et al. [3] describe a static analyser ANSI C programs within a continuous environment described using a set of ODEs, which also accounts for numerical issues regarding floating-point inaccuracies. They use a guaranteed integrator for over-approximating the continuous trajectories, and their *Fluctuat* tool for performing the analysis of the floating-point computations.

More generally, the hazards of translating mathematical arithmetic into computer arithmetic are well-known and are the sources of many bugs in software systems. The problem is well-studied in the program verification community and tools based on *abstract interpretation* [7] and SMT solving [16] are state-of-the-art.

Sampled data hybrid systems are hybrid systems driven by clocks – similar to the systems presented in this work. Silva and Krogh [15] discuss the modeling and verification of sampled data hybrid systems using their *CheckMate* verification tool. Relational abstractions have also been applied [17].

3. PERIODIC SAMPLE-HOLD SYSTEMS

Figure 1 illustrates a prototypical sample-hold system. Here, the plant variables are periodically sampled on the tick of a clock, and the discrete output of the controller is held at constant values with a zero-order hold. The controller has input, output and memory variables with a wide range of possible values (typically 2^8 to 2^{16}), and exhibits implementation-specific behaviors related to number representation and data/time discretization. For instance, controllers may misbehave due to numerical overflows and underflows.

Formally, a sample-hold system is a structure

$$H = \langle X, I, Q, J, f, g, \tau \rangle$$

where:

- X is a vector of m continuous-time variables,
- $I \in (\mathbb{R} \times \mathbb{R})^m$ is an m-vector of intervals initial conditions for X,
- Q is a vector of n discrete variables with domain $\mathbb{D}$,
- $J \in (\mathbb{D} \times \mathbb{D})^n$ is an n-vector of intervals of Q initial conditions,

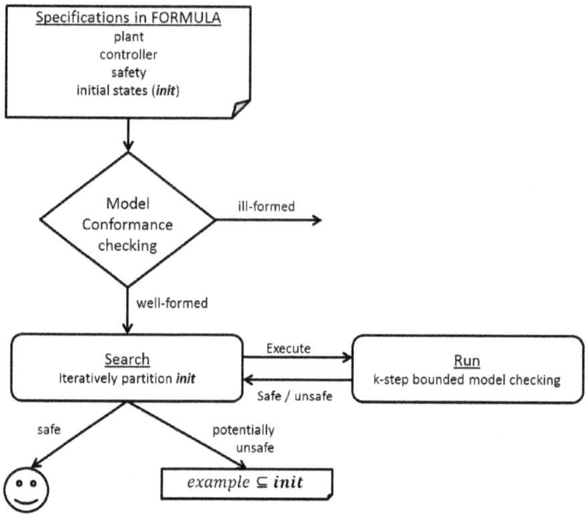

Figure 2: Control flow of the tool

- $f\colon \mathbb{R}^m \times \mathbb{D}^n \to \mathbb{R}^m$ is a flow function,
- $g\colon \mathbb{R}^m \times \mathbb{D}^n \to \mathbb{D}^n$ is a discrete update function,
- τ is the sample period.

We write $X(t)$ to denote the values of continuous-time variables at time t, and $Q(i)$ to denote the values of discrete variables at step i. A sample-hold system initially satisfies:

$$X(0) \in I. \quad Q(0) \in J.$$

The continuous variables evolve through a series of trajectories satisfying:

$$\forall i \in \mathbb{N}.\ t \in [\tau \times i, \tau \times (i+1)) \Rightarrow \dot{X} = f(X, Q(i)).$$

In other words, the continuous systems evolves as if the ith control response was held constant for τ time. The discrete variables evolve by sampling the continuous variables and computing the next control response:

$$\forall i \in \mathbb{N}.\ Q(i+1) = g(X(\tau \times i), Q(i)).$$

The run of a periodic sample-hold system is an alternating sequence of continuous-time and discrete steps where each continuous-time step describes the continuous-time evolution of the system for exactly τ time, and between each continuous-time step there is exactly one discrete step, which is executed synchronously (i.e. in zero time).

4. THE TOOL

Our tool is the integration of two efforts: We use Taylor models for over-approximating the CT steps, and SMT solvers for over-approximating the discrete steps. Figure 2 shows the control flow of the tool. We use the *FORMULA* specification language [1] to define a domain-specific language for representing periodic sample-hold systems. This allows us to give a formal grammar for our class of sample-hold systems, and to notify the user if the input model violates basic consistency constraints.

If the model is well-formed, we load it and initialize a *search* with the specified initial intervals. The search initiates *runs*, where each run performs a k-step bounded model checking by over-approximating the reachable states from

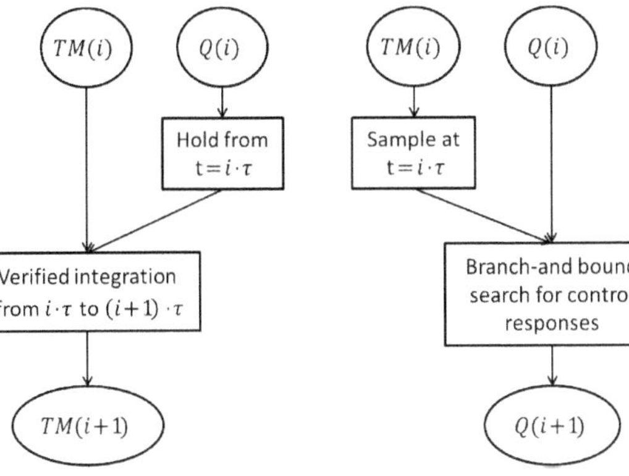

Figure 3: One step during a run

the given initial states, and returns whether the system is safe or (potentionally) unsafe during the run. If the system is unsafe, the search performs an iterative partitioning of the initial states. The premise is that by starting from a smaller set of initial states, the runs become more precise. The search procedure finishes if either all the runs are safe, or the states are potentially unsafe within an error bound.

The result of a search is conservative. If a search returns the *safe* result, the system is guaranteed to be safe for k-step long operations. Otherwise, the system might be unsafe, but is not necessarily so. In this case, we can obtain the refined set of initial states *example* which led to the unsafe state.

A run consists of k steps, and Figure 3 shows the anatomy of a step. Taylor Models are denoted TM and they are the symbolic encoding of a set of continuous states. A Taylor Model is a polynomial (in the initial values of the variables) and a remainder bound, such that the sum of the polynomial and the remainder bound is a superset of the reachable continuous states. Discrete states (and response) are denoted with Q and they are represented as integer hyper-rectangles (boxes).

On the left side of Figure 3, the next continuous state $TM(i+1)$ is calculated by performing a rigorous integration from the last state $TM(i)$ of the continuous-time system, and the previous discrete control response $Q(i)$. The right side shows the evaluation of the discrete controller. Based on the last continuous state $TM(i)$ and discrete state $Q(i)$, we use a branch-and-bound search to find an over-approximation for the possible control states and responses at $Q(i+1)$, which is the hyper-rectangle used in the computation of the next Taylor model.

4.1 Implementation

Our *SAHVY* (Sample And Hold Verification) tool is available under a source-license and can be downloaded as part of the FORMULA tool-suite [1]. For performing rigorous integration, we used the Taylor model implementation developed for *Flow** [4]. The branch-and-bound search is performed using Microsoft *Z3* [6], a state of the art SMT solver, in which we created a theory for the fixed-point numbers by extending the theory of bitvectors.

These two steps are the most time-consuming processes for the tool. Fortunately, since they are independent at every step, they can be executed in parallel. In our implementation, during each computation of a step, the next continuous and discrete states are computed concurrently and the results are joined at the end of the transition.

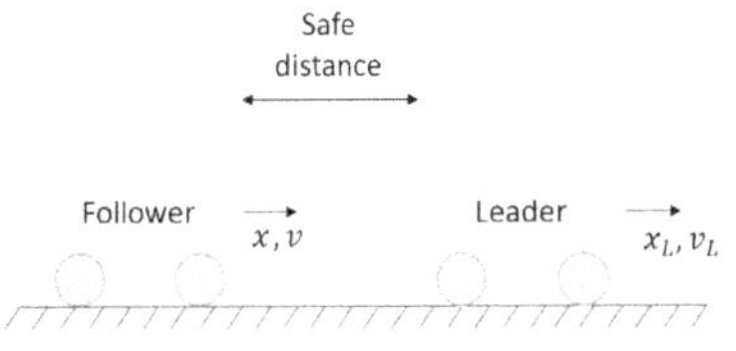

(a) Adaptive cruise control setup

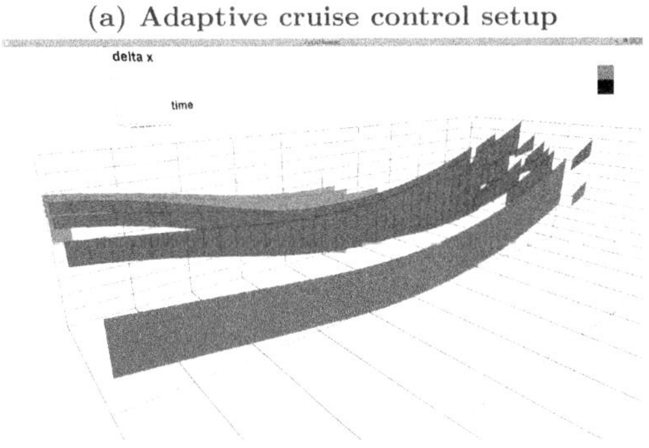

(b) Real-time visualization

Figure 4: Adaptive cruise control. The generated flowpipes are displayed on-the-fly with our real-time visualizator. The y axis is the distance between the cars, the x axis is time from 0 to 4 seconds, and the z axis (depth) represents the *runs*. Red means unsafe run, green means safe run, and the blue color is used for the current flowpipe under verification.

5. CASE STUDIES

In this section, we present some case studies demonstrating typical sample-hold controllers, and some case studies that are sample-hold implementations of well-known hybrid automata models exhibiting only a few modes. We performed all the tests on a desktop computer with 8GB of RAM and a 3.4Ghz Intel Core i7-2600 CPU.

Adaptive Cruise Control.

Our first case study shows an adaptive cruise control (Figure 4). The continuous-time dynamics for the system is the following:

$$\frac{\Delta x}{dt} = v_L - v, \quad \frac{v}{dt} = a, \quad \frac{v_L}{dt} = a_L$$

where Δx is the distance between the two cars, v is the speed of the follower car, v_L is the speed of the leader car, and a and a_L are the acceleration of the follower and leader car, respectively. Furthermore, we specify the following initial conditions:

```
InitialRangeC(v, 30, 30).
InitialRangeC(delta_x, 30, 81).
InitialRangeC(vL, 20, 21).
```

Meaning that the initial velocity of the follower car is $v \in [30, 30]$, the initial velocity of the leader car is $v_L \in [20, 21]$, and the initial distance between the two cars is $\Delta x \in [30, 81]$.

We assume that the leader decelerates with $a_L = -20$ until the leader car has not stopped. Currently, the tool does not support saturation functions for the continuous-time dynamics, thus we model this deceleration with a controller for the leader car. The controller measures v_L and if it is above

0, it keeps decelerating. Otherwise, the car has come to a complete stop and the acceleration a_L is set to 0.

The more interesting controller is the one implemented by the follower car. It runs with a frequency of 10 Hz, and uses 10 bit fixed point numbers without any decimals, i.e., the discrete variables store integers ranging from −512 to 511. Equivalently, in the FORMULA specification we have the following declarations for the controller variables:

```
ctrl is C.Var("control", 10, 0).
meas_v is C.Var("measured␣v", 10, 0).
meas_dx is C.Var("measured␣delta␣x", 10, 0).
meas_dv is C.Var("measured␣delta␣v", 10, 0).
```

And the relations between the controller and physical variables are the following:

```
Sample(delta_x, meas_dx).
Sample(O.Sub(vL,v), meas_dv).
Sample(v, meas_v).
Hold(ctrl, a).
```

In words, control variable *meas_dx* is measured (sampled) from Δx, control variable *meas_dv* is sampled from $v_L - v$ (i.e., the speed difference between the cars), control variable *meas_v* is sampled from v, and the acceleration a of the follower car is produced by zero-order holding the control variable *ctrl*.

The controller code is the following:

```
zero    is C.RConst( 0, 10, 0).
maxDec is C.RConst(-20, 10, 0).
maxAcc is C.RConst( 10, 10, 0).
K2      is C.RConst( -2, 10, 0).
desiredDist is C.RConst( 70, 10, 0).
value   is C.Mul(K2,Sub(desiredDist,meas_dx)).
prevValue is C.Pre(value).
avgValue  is C.Div(Add(prevValue,value),Two).
Assign(control,
    C.Max(Min(avgValue,maxAcc),maxDec)).
```

In the first lines, we define constants $zero = 0$, $maxDec = -20$, $maxAcc = 10$, $K2 = -2$ and $desiredDistance = 70$ as 10 bit fixed point numbers with 0 bits reserved for the decimals. In this case, the constants are represented without loss of precision and without any need for scaling, but if the number of decimals would be greater than zero, the tool would automatically perform the necessary conversions. Then, the behavior of the controller is described as:

$$\begin{aligned} value[i] &:= K_2(desiredDist - meas\_dx[i]) \\ prevValue[i] &:= value[i-1] \\ avgValue[i] &:= \frac{value[i] + prevValue[i]}{2} \\ ctrl[i] &:= \min(\max(value, maxDec), maxAcc) \end{aligned}$$

Note that here the control inputs and control output have the same index i, but as discussed before the inputs represent the state of the physical system at an earlier time.

Since the first step of the simulation is the execution of a continuous-time step, we need initial values for the output variables (*ctrl*), as well as for the initial content of the memory variable *prevValue*):

```
InitialRangeD(ctrl, 0, 0).
InitialRangeD(prevValue, 0, 0).
```

In this case, they are initialized to the integer interval $[0, 0]$, i.e., they are strictly zero. Finally, the safety property is:

```
Safe(GE(delta_x, 3)).
```

Meaning that the cars will never get closer to each other than 3 units.

We performed the verification of this model for 40 steps, which is equivalent to 4 seconds of simulation time. Note that the leader car comes to a complete stop after approximately 1 second, so if the controller is incorrectly implemented it is reasonable to expect a safety violation within in the first 4 seconds. The verification took several *search* iterations as shown in Figure 4. The red flowpipes show that the initial states had to be partitioned, otherwise the over-approximation could not reject the violation of the safety property. The complete verification took 27 seconds and successfully verified that the controller is safe.

Diabetic control.

In diabetic control, a physical model is used for modeling the dynamics of glucose and insulin levels, and the goal of the controller is to stabilize the glucose level by controlling the injection of insulin. In the Bergman minimal model, we have the following differential equations for the physical system:

$$\begin{aligned} \frac{dG}{dt} &= -p_1 G - X(G + G_b) + g(t) \\ \frac{dX}{dt} &= -p_2 X + p_3 I \\ \frac{dI}{dt} &= -n(I + I_b) + \frac{i(t)}{V_I} \end{aligned}$$

Here G is a plasma glucose concentration above the basal value G_b, X is the insulin concentration in the interstitial chamber, I is the insulin concentration above I_b, $g(t)$ expresses the glucose consumption and $i(t)$ is the insulin injection. The parameters are $p_1 = 0.01$, $p_2 = 0.025$, $p_3 = 0.000013$, $V_I = 12$, $n = 0.093$, $G_b = 4.5$ and $I_b = 15$.

A diabetic controller was introduced by Fisher [8] for this model. We modeled the system by taking measurements of the glucose level every second (1 Hz). The measurement is stored in a signed 16-bit fixed-point variable $G_d[i] = sample(G(t))$ (with 10 bits reserved for the integer part and 6 bits for decimals). The control output value is then:

$$i_d[i] := \begin{cases} 1 + \frac{2}{9} G_d[i] & \text{if } G_d[i] < 6 \\ 16.66 & \text{else} \end{cases}$$

Note that the tool will automatically convert the constants to match the number representation of the discrete system. In this case, there are 6 bits used for the decimals, so the constants are multiplied by 2^6 and the integer part is taken (therefore 16.66 is stored as 1066, which actually represents 16.65625. This is a prime example how the actual implementation differs from the idealized model). Finally, the value of $i(t) = hold(i_d[i])$ is a piecewise constant function, updated once per second.

We model the glucose input of the system with another discrete controller:

$$g_d[i] := \begin{cases} 0 & \text{if } T_d[i] \geq 120 \\ \frac{T_d[i]}{60} & \text{if } T_d[i] \leq 30 \\ \frac{120 - T_d[i]}{180} & \text{else} \end{cases}$$

where $T_d[i] := sample(T(t))$ is the local time (i.e., the local time of the hardware platform), and the glucose input $g(t) = hold(g_d[i])$ is a piecewise constant.

Chen et al. [4] performed the verification of this system based on a hybrid automata model using the Flow* tool. In order to make the comparison of the results possible, we used

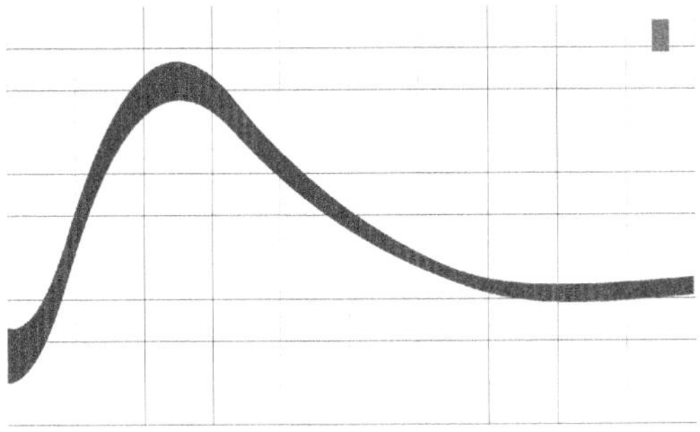

Figure 5: The behavior of a diabetic control system.

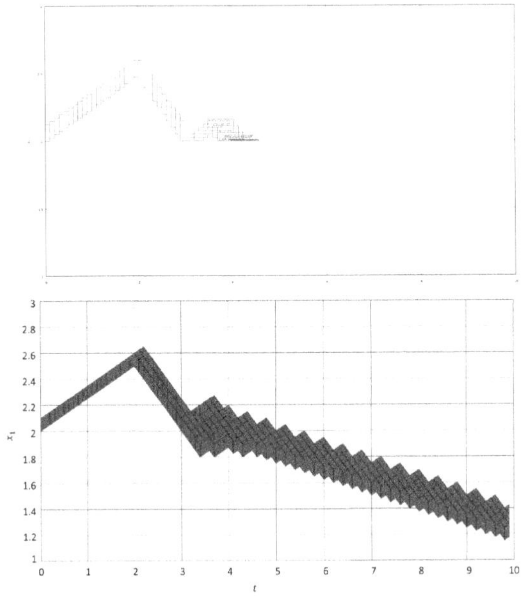

Figure 6: Behavior of the two tanks system. Zeno execution for hybrid automata based approach using Flow* (top) and our sample-hold based approach (bottom)

the same initial values for the state variables: $G(0) \in [-2, 2]$, $I(0) \in [-0.1, 0.1]$, $X(0) = 0$ and $T(0) = 0$.

Figure 5 shows the results of our approach, which is qualitatively very similar to Figure 4 in [4], and the calculations took 35 seconds (which is 1.5 times faster than *Flow** on our system, but note that this is not conclusive because we compiled and ran the Linux native application under Windows). The results show that our approach results in a coarser over-approximation compared to the very tight over-approximation obtained with Flow* due to the low frequency of our control system.

Two watertanks.

In the next case study, we evaluate the classic two watertank system exhibiting Zeno behavior. The continuous-time dynamics of the system is:

$$\frac{dx_1}{dt} = i(t) \cdot w - v_1$$
$$\frac{dx_2}{dt} = (0.0625 - i(t)) \cdot w - v2$$

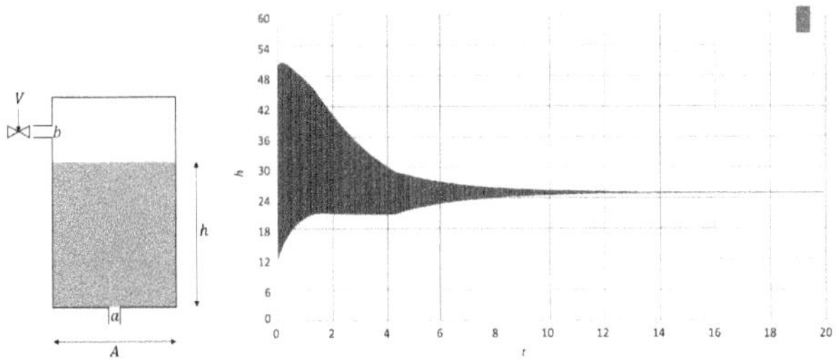

(a) Tank (b) Controller running on 10 Hz.

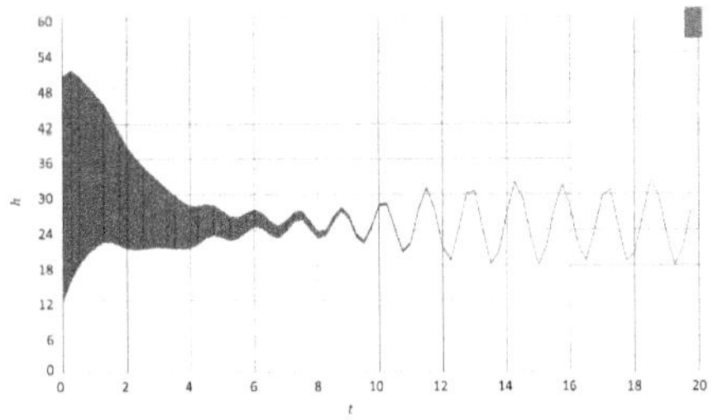

(c) Controller running on 4 Hz.

Figure 7: The behavior of the watertank controller system implementing the same control algorithms but running on different frequencies.

where $i(t)$ controls the in-flow of the watertanks. If $i(t) = 0.0625$, all water flows in the first tank, if $i(t) = 0$, all water flows in the second tank.

The controller operates with a frequency of 10 Hz and the discrete variables are 8-bit fixed point numbers with 4 bits reserved for the decimals. It has two input measurements x_{1d} and x_{2d} that reflect the water levels in the tank. Furthermore, it has an output variable i_d, and a state variable *prev* that stores the last output of the system. The control code is then:

$$i_d[i] := \begin{cases} 0 & \text{if } prev[i] = 1 \text{ and } x_{1d}[k] \leq 2 \\ 0 & \text{if } prev[i] = 0 \text{ and } x_{2d}[k] > 2 \\ 1 & \text{else} \end{cases}$$
$$prev[i] := i_d[i-1]$$

Remember that the constants are automatically converted between fixed-point numbers and mathematical reals, so the output of $i_d[i] = 1$ really corresponds to $i(t) = 0.0625$.

As shown in Figure 6, a periodic sample-hold system moves past the point in time where Zeno behavior would be observed in the corresponding hybrid automata model. The verification took 14 seconds with our tool, and required many backtracking steps during search. While in the case of hybrid automata it is possible to "zoom in" to the point where the guards are satisfied, in the software-implemented sample-hold controller the finite arithmetic leads to interesting corner cases. For instance, one might expect the controller to mode switch at $t = 2s$, but due to numeric errors it may actually change its mode a period later at $t = 2.1s$. Since the initial set of states allow for both behaviors, our flowpipes exhibit both possible branches.

A single watertank controller.

Our final case study is another water tank system shown in Figure 7a, which has an outflow based on the height of the water and an inlet through which a controller can let more water in the tank.

The plant dynamics is given by the following flow:

$$\frac{dh}{dt} = 5 \cdot V - 5 \cdot \sqrt{h},$$

and initially the water level h is between 12 and 50. The safety condition expresses that the water level always stays within 5 and 55 units.

We performed two experiments, one with a controller running at 10 Hz, and another with the controller running at 4 Hz. In both cases, we used 16 bit fixed point numbers with 6 bits reserved for the decimals. The controller output *cout* is calculated from the sampled water height *cin*[*i*] as follows:

```
Sample(h, cin).
Hold(cout, Vin).
desiredH is C.RConst(30, 16, 6).
minC is C.RConst(0, 16, 6).
maxC is C.RConst(10, 16, 6).
Assign(cout,Max(Min(Sub(desiredH,cin),maxC),
                minC)).
```

Implementing the following control law:

$$cout[i] := \max(\min(30 - cin[i]), 10, 0)$$

Verifying the system for up to 125 steps took 4 seconds in both cases, and the results are shown in Figure 7. While it is easy to show that the system is safe assuming an ideal controller (without time and data discretization), verifying the real plant-control system is clearly challenging. In particular, in the case of low frequencies the system behavior may become erratic compared to the ideal case.

6. CONCLUSION

In this paper we introduced a hybrid verification tool that is capable of verifying periodic sample-hold systems accounting for non-linear plant dynamics and implementation-specific behaviors of the controller code.

The presented use cases demonstrate its applicability to hybrid systems and some practical use-cases. In its current form, we see it as a complementary tool to other verification tools. It solves verification problems that are challenging for other tools. One disadvantage of our method is that it works for periodic sample-hold systems only, and this has important consequences: The physical system model cannot have discontinuities, and our approach works best for controllers that operate at a relatively low frequency.

Future work is plentiful. An important next step is the integration of our approach with other hybrid automata based tools, in particular incorporating the SMT-based controller verification tool into the hybrid automata workflow. Another important feature is to add support for floating-point numbers. As future work, we also plan to examine more realistic models for quantization in fixed-point hardware.

Acknowledgement

We are grateful to Xin Chen for the useful discussions about Taylor models and for providing us with the latest implementations of *Flow**. Also, we are thankful for the anonymous reviewers for their useful comments.

7. REFERENCES

[1] *FORMULA*. `http://formula.codeplex.com`.

[2] M. Berz and K. Makino. Verified integration of odes and flows using differential algebraic methods on high-order taylor models. *Reliable Computing*, 4(4):361–369, 1998.

[3] O. Bouissou, E. Goubault, S. Putot, K. Tekkal, and F. Vedrine. Hybridfluctuat: A static analyzer of numerical programs within a continuous environment. In *Computer Aided Verification*, pages 620–626. Springer, 2009.

[4] X. Chen, E. Abrahám, and S. Sankaranarayanan. Taylor model flowpipe construction for non-linear hybrid systems. In *Real-Time Systems Symposium*, pages 183–192, 2012.

[5] A. Chutinan and B. H. Krogh. Verification of polyhedral-invariant hybrid automata using polygonal flow pipe approximations. In *Hybrid Systems: Computation and Control*, pages 76–90. 1999.

[6] L. De Moura and N. Bjørner. Z3: An efficient smt solver. In *Tools and Algorithms for the Construction and Analysis of Systems*, pages 337–340. 2008.

[7] M. Fähndrich and F. Logozzo. Checking compatibility of bit sizes in floating point comparison operations. *Electr. Notes Theor. Comput. Sci.*, 288:15–23, 2012.

[8] M. E. Fisher. A semiclosed-loop algorithm for the control of blood glucose levels in diabetics. *IEEE Trans. on Biomedical Engineering*, 38(1):57–61, 1991.

[9] M. Fränzle and C. Herde. Hysat: An efficient proof engine for bounded model checking of hybrid systems. *Formal Methods in System Design*, 30(3):179–198, 2007.

[10] G. Frehse, C. Le Guernic, A. Donzé, S. Cotton, R. Ray, O. Lebeltel, R. Ripado, A. Girard, T. Dang, and O. Maler. Spaceex: Scalable verification of hybrid systems. In *Computer Aided Verification*, pages 379–395, 2011.

[11] S. Gao, S. Kong, and E. Clarke. dreach: Reachability analysis for nonlinear hybrid systems (tool paper). In *Hybrid Systems: Computation and Control*, 2013.

[12] N. Halbwachs, P. Caspi, P. Raymond, and D. Pilaud. The synchronous data flow programming language lustre. *Proc. of the IEEE*, 79(9):1305–1320, 1991.

[13] T. A. Henzinger, B. Horowitz, and C. M. Kirsch. Giotto: A time-triggered language for embedded programming. *Proc. of the IEEE*, 91(1):84–99, 2003.

[14] N. Ramdani and N. S. Nedialkov. Computing reachable sets for uncertain nonlinear hybrid systems using interval constraint-propagation techniques. *Nonlinear Analysis: Hybrid Systems*, 5(2):149–162, 2011.

[15] B. I. Silva and B. H. Krogh. Modeling and verification of sampled-data hybrid systems. In *Proc. 4th Int. Conf. on Automation of Mixed Processes: Hybrid Dynamic Systems*, pages 237–242, 2000.

[16] D. Vanoverberghe, N. Bjørner, J. de Halleux, W. Schulte, and N. Tillmann. Using dynamic symbolic execution to improve deductive verification. In *SPIN*, pages 9–25, 2008.

[17] A. Zutshi, S. Sankaranarayanan, and A. Tiwari. Timed relational abstractions for sampled data control systems. In *CAV*, pages 343–361, 2012.

Inner Approximated Reachability Analysis

Eric Goubault, Olivier Mullier, Sylvie Putot
CEA LIST, CEA Saclay Nano-INNOV
91 191 Gif-sur-Yvette, France
firstname.lastname@cea.fr

Michel Kieffer
L2S - CNRS - Supélec - Univ Paris-Sud
91192 Gif-sur-Yvette
kieffer@lss.supelec.fr

ABSTRACT

Computing a tight inner approximation of the range of a function over some set is notoriously difficult, way beyond obtaining outer approximations. We propose here a new method to compute a tight inner approximation of the set of reachable states of non-linear dynamical systems on a bounded time interval. This approach involves affine forms and Kaucher arithmetic, plus a number of extra ingredients from set-based methods. An implementation of the method is discussed, and illustrated on representative numerical schemes, discrete-time and continuous-time dynamical systems.

Categories and Subject Descriptors

F.3.1 [**Logics and Meanings of Programs**]: Specifying and Verifying and Reasoning about Programs—*invariants,mechanical verification*; G.1.0 [**Numerical Analysis**]: General—*Interval arithmetic,Numerical algorithms*; G.4 [**Mathematical Software**]: Reliability and robustness

General Terms

Theory, Verification

Keywords

Inner approximation; modal intervals; affine arithmetic

1. INTRODUCTION

Analyzing the reachability of dynamical systems is essential to many areas of computer science, numerical analysis, and control theory. For the validation of computer programs for instance, determining an outer approximation of the set of states that can be reached by a program, can help to prove that it cannot reach erroneous states. On the other hand, inner approximations are useful to prove the reachability of some desired states. Combined, outer and inner approximations provide an indication of the precision of the estimates of the exact reachability region, as shown in [17].

HSCC'14, April 15–17, 2014, Berlin, Germany.
Copyright 2014 ACM 978-1-4503-2732-9/14/04 ...$15.00.
http://dx.doi.org/10.1145/2562059.2562113.

In numerical analysis and control theory, reachability problems using outer and inner approximations are also of primary importance for similar reasons, both for discrete-time and continuous-time dynamical systems [26]. Inner approximations can also be useful for viability problems [2], to prove that there exists a controller for which the system under study behaves in a satisfying way. In the linear case, inner approximations are useful for the design of controllers [13].

In this paper, we propose a method to produce a tractable inner approximation of the set of reachable states of a non-linear dynamical system, at each (discrete or continuous) time step, over a bounded time interval. The main contributions are the following :

- We introduce a generalization of zonotopic abstractions (by vectors of affine forms, as will be recalled in the preliminaries), that produces implicit representations of inner (and outer) approximations (Section 3). The method introduced in [17] can be seen as a special zeroth-order case of the approximation presented here.
- We show how we can extract from these generalized affine vectors, either inner approximations of each component of the vector-valued dynamical system (Section 4.1), using ideas from modal or Kaucher arithmetic, or, if necessary, a joint inner range (Section 4.3). Note that this joint range is more costly but does not have to be computed at each time step.
- Section 5 presents results obtained with our implementation, first for the convergence study of numerical algorithms, where no joint range is necessary, then for discrete and finally continuous-time dynamical systems. The inner approximation for a small hybrid system, requiring the extra ingredient of the interpretation of guard conditions, is finally quickly exemplified.

Related work.

Many methods have been proposed to evaluate outer approximations of reachability sets of linear discrete or continuous-time dynamical systems. They are generally based on interval methods, zonotopes [12], support functions [20], ellipsoids [26], etc. Evaluation of inner approximations has been considered in the linear case in [1], by inner approximating the exponential of a matrix, or using ellipsoidal techniques [26]. Outer approximations of reachability sets have also been obtained for non-linear systems, albeit more recently, e.g., for polynomials systems [7, 29]. Nevertheless, methods to evaluate inner approximations of such sets are far less developed, since most methods in the non-linear case rely on conservative linearizations, which necessarily produce outer approximations. Under-approximate bounded vertex representation of polyhedra have been proposed for the analysis of Simulink/Stateflow models [24], but they are restricted to linear systems. Hybrid system falsification [28] relies on simulation-based local inner approximations. There exist few methods to compute global inner approximations of the image of non-linear vector-valued functions, mostly based on bisections of the input domain, see for instance [15], later extended by the authors in [16], or inner approximating sets of (semi-algebraic) constraints [21]. But these bisections are very costly if an accurate approximation is needed, and they are not directly applicable to the problem of inner reachability of dynamical systems. For the case of discrete-time dynamical systems for instance, this would require to apply these methods separately to each iterate, with a very costly symbolic representation. To the best of our knowledge, the abstraction described here, generalizing and improving over [17], is the only one to propose such kind of direct inner approximation in a general setting.

2. PRELIMINARIES

Let us first introduce the ingredients that will be instrumental in the computation of inner approximations. In Section 2.1, we formulate the problem of computing an inner or an outer approximation of the image of a function in terms of quantified expressions, for which partial solutions can be given using generalized intervals and Kaucher arithmetic. Section 2.2 introduces affine vectors (also called affine sets in some references [11,19]) which extend (classical) interval arithmetic to improve the accuracy of outer approximation computations. The rest of the paper mixes these two notions to obtain tight inner approximations in a general setting.

2.1 Generalized intervals for outer and inner approximations

The results and notations quickly introduced in this section are mostly based on the work of Goldsztejn *et al.* on modal intervals [14].

Interval extensions, outer and inner approximations.

Classical intervals are used in many situations to rigorously compute with interval domains instead of reals, usually leading to outer approximations of function ranges over boxes. The set of classical intervals is denoted by $\mathbb{IR} = \{[a, b],\ a \in \mathbb{R}, b \in \mathbb{R}, a \leqslant b\}$. In what follows, intervals are in bold. An outer approximating extension of a function $f : \mathbb{R}^n \to \mathbb{R}$ is a function $\boldsymbol{f} : \mathbb{IR}^n \to \mathbb{IR}$ such that $\forall \boldsymbol{x} \in \mathbb{IR}^n, \text{range}(f, \boldsymbol{x}) = \{f(x), x \in \boldsymbol{x}\} \subseteq \boldsymbol{f}(\boldsymbol{x})$. The natural interval extension consists in replacing real operations by their interval counterparts in the expression of the function. A generally more accurate extension relies on the mean-value theorem, linearizing the function to compute.

Classical interval computations can be interpreted as quantified propositions. Consider for example $f(x) = x^2 - x$. Its natural interval extension, evaluated on $[2,3]$, is $\boldsymbol{f}([2,3]) = [2,3]^2 - [2,3] = [1,7]$, which can be interpreted as the proposition

$$(\forall x \in [2,3])\,(\exists z \in [1,7])\,(f(x) = z).$$

The mean-value extension gives $f(2.5) + \boldsymbol{f}'([2,3]) \times ([2,3] - 2.5) = [1.25, 6.25]$, and can be interpreted similarly.

The drawback of these extensions is that the ranges they yield can be pessimistic, i.e., largely over-estimate the actual range. Inner approximations can be used to evaluate this pessimism, by determining a set of values proved to belong to the range of the function over some input box. The fact that some $\boldsymbol{z} \in \mathbb{IR}$ satisfies $\boldsymbol{z} \subseteq \text{range}(f, \boldsymbol{x})$, i.e., is an inner approximation of the range of f over $\boldsymbol{x}$, can again be written using quantifiers :

$$(\forall z \in \boldsymbol{z})\,(\exists x \in \boldsymbol{x})\,(f(x) = z).$$

Modal intervals and generalized intervals.

A modal interval [9] is an interval supplemented by a quantifier. Extensions of modal intervals were proposed in the framework of generalized intervals, and called AE extensions because universal quantifiers (All) always precede existential ones (Exist) in the interpretations. They give rise to a generalized interval arithmetic which coincides with Kaucher arithmetic [25].

Let us first introduce generalized intervals, i.e., intervals whose bounds are not ordered. The set of generalized intervals is denoted by $\mathbb{IK} = \{[a, b],\ a \in \mathbb{R}, b \in \mathbb{R}\}$. Considering a set of real numbers $\{x \in \mathbb{R},\ a \leqslant x \leqslant b\}$, one can define two generalized intervals, $[a, b]$, which is called *proper*, and $[b, a]$, which is called *improper*. We define the operations dual $[a, b] = [b, a]$ and pro $[a, b] = [\min(a, b), \max(a, b)]$. The generalized intervals are partially ordered by inclusion which extends inclusion of classical intervals. Given two generalized intervals $\boldsymbol{x} = [\underline{x}, \overline{x}]$ and $\boldsymbol{y} = [\underline{y}, \overline{y}]$, the inclusion is defined by $\boldsymbol{x} \sqsubseteq \boldsymbol{y} \Leftrightarrow \underline{y} \leqslant \underline{x} \wedge \overline{x} \leqslant \overline{y}$. The inclusion is then related to the dual interval by $\boldsymbol{x} \sqsubseteq \boldsymbol{y} \Leftrightarrow$ dual $\boldsymbol{x} \sqsupseteq$ dual $\boldsymbol{y}$.

Definition 1. *Let $f : \mathbb{R}^n \to \mathbb{R}$ be a continuous function and $\boldsymbol{x} \in \mathbb{IK}^n$, which we can decompose in $\boldsymbol{x}_{\mathcal{A}} \in \mathbb{IR}^p$ and $\boldsymbol{x}_{\mathcal{E}} \in (\text{dual}\,\mathbb{IR})^q$ with $p + q = n$. A generalized interval $\boldsymbol{z} \in \mathbb{IK}$ is $(f, \boldsymbol{x})$-interpretable if*

$$(\forall x_{\mathcal{A}} \in \boldsymbol{x}_{\mathcal{A}})\,(Q_z z \in \textit{pro}\ \boldsymbol{z})\,(\exists x_{\mathcal{E}} \in \textit{pro}\ \boldsymbol{x}_{\mathcal{E}}), (f(x) = z) \quad (1)$$

where $Q_z = \exists$ if $\boldsymbol{z}$ is proper, and $Q_z = \forall$ otherwise.

We will later be interested in a generalization of this definition to vector functions $f : \mathbb{R}^n \to \mathbb{R}^p$. In the present context of intervals, we can only consider each component of f independently.

When all intervals in (1) are proper, we retrieve the interpretation of classical interval computation, which gives an outer approximation of range$(f, \boldsymbol{x})$

$$(\forall x \in \boldsymbol{x})\,(\exists z \in \boldsymbol{z})\,(f(x) = z).$$

When all intervals are improper, (1) becomes an inner approximation of range$(f, \boldsymbol{x})$

$$(\forall z \in \text{pro}\ \boldsymbol{z})\,(\exists x \in \text{pro}\ \boldsymbol{x})\,(f(x) = z).$$

Kaucher arithmetic and the generalized interval natural extension.

Kaucher arithmetic [25] returns intervals that are interpretable as inner approximations in some simple cases. Kaucher addition extends addition on classical intervals by $\boldsymbol{x} + \boldsymbol{y} = [\underline{x} + \underline{y}, \overline{x} + \overline{y}]$ and $\boldsymbol{x} - \boldsymbol{y} = [\underline{x} - \overline{y}, \overline{x} - \underline{y}]$. We now decompose $\mathbb{IK}$ in $\mathcal{P} = \{\boldsymbol{x} = [\underline{x}, \overline{x}],\ \underline{x} \geqslant 0 \wedge \overline{x} \geqslant 0\}$, $-\mathcal{P} = \{\boldsymbol{x} =$

$\boldsymbol{x} \times \boldsymbol{y}$	$\boldsymbol{y} \in \mathcal{P}$	$\mathcal{Z}$	$-\mathcal{P}$	dual$\mathcal{Z}$
$\boldsymbol{x} \in \mathcal{P}$	$[\underline{x}\underline{y}, \overline{x}\overline{y}]$	$[\overline{x}\underline{y}, \overline{x}\overline{y}]$	$[\overline{x}\underline{y}, \underline{x}\overline{y}]$	$[\underline{x}\underline{y}, \underline{x}\overline{y}]$
$\mathcal{Z}$	$[\underline{x}\overline{y}, \overline{x}\overline{y}]$	$[\min(\underline{x}\overline{y}, \overline{x}\underline{y}), \max(\underline{x}\underline{y}, \overline{x}\overline{y})]$	$[\overline{x}\underline{y}, \underline{x}\underline{y}]$	0
$-\mathcal{P}$	$[\underline{x}\overline{y}, \overline{x}\underline{y}]$	$[\underline{x}\overline{y}, \underline{x}\underline{y}]$	$[\overline{x}\overline{y}, \underline{x}\underline{y}]$	$[\overline{x}\overline{y}, \overline{x}\underline{y}]$
dual$\mathcal{Z}$	$[\underline{x}\underline{y}, \overline{x}\underline{y}]$	0	$[\overline{x}\overline{y}, \underline{x}\overline{y}]$	$[\max(\underline{x}\underline{y}, \overline{x}\overline{y}), \min(\underline{x}\overline{y}, \overline{x}\underline{y})]$

Table 1: Kaucher multiplication

$[\underline{x}, \overline{x}],\ \underline{x} \leqslant 0 \wedge \overline{x} \leqslant 0\}$, $\mathcal{Z} = \{\boldsymbol{x} = [\underline{x}, \overline{x}],\ \underline{x} \leqslant 0 \leqslant \overline{x}\}$, and dual $\mathcal{Z} = \{\boldsymbol{x} = [\underline{x}, \overline{x}],\ \underline{x} \geqslant 0 \geqslant \overline{x}\}$. Kaucher multiplication $\boldsymbol{x} \times \boldsymbol{y}$ is described in Table 1. In Sections 3 and 4, we will have $\boldsymbol{y} = [1, -1]$, belonging to dual $\mathcal{Z}$.

Let us interpret the result of the multiplication $\boldsymbol{z} = \boldsymbol{x} \times \boldsymbol{y}$ in one of the cases encountered when $\boldsymbol{y} \in$ dual $\mathcal{Z}$, for instance for $\boldsymbol{x} \in \mathcal{Z}$. Proposition 1 will express the fact that the result can be interpreted as in Definition 1. Interval $\boldsymbol{z}$ can a priori either be proper or improper, let us consider the improper case. We obtain an inner approximation of the range of the multiplication: according to the quantifiers in Definition 1, computing $\boldsymbol{z} = \boldsymbol{x} \times \boldsymbol{y}$ consists in finding $\boldsymbol{z}$ such that for all $x \in \boldsymbol{x}$, for all $z \in$ pro $\boldsymbol{z}$, there exists $y \in$ pro $\boldsymbol{y}$ such that $z = x \times y$. If $\boldsymbol{x}$ contains zero, which is the case when $\boldsymbol{x} \in \mathcal{Z}$, then $\boldsymbol{z}$ is necessarily 0, the result given in Table 1. Indeed, a property that holds for all $x \in \boldsymbol{x}$, holds in particular for $x = 0$, from which we deduce that for all $z \in$ pro $\boldsymbol{z}$, (there exists $y \in$ pro $\boldsymbol{y}$) $z = 0$.

Kaucher division is defined for all $\boldsymbol{y}$ such that $0 \notin$ pro $\boldsymbol{y}$ by $\boldsymbol{x}/\boldsymbol{y} = \boldsymbol{x} \times [1/\overline{y}, 1/\underline{y}]$.

When restricted to proper intervals, these operations coincide with the classical interval operations. Kaucher arithmetic defines a generalized interval natural extension [14] :

PROPOSITION 1. *Let $f : \mathbb{R}^n \to \mathbb{R}$ be a function, given by an arithmetic expression with only single occurrences of variables. Then for $\boldsymbol{x} \in \mathbb{IK}^n$, $f(\boldsymbol{x})$, computed using Kaucher arithmetic, is $(f, \boldsymbol{x})$-interpretable.*

Kaucher arithmetic can thus be used in some cases to compute an inner approximation of range$(f, \boldsymbol{x})$. But the restriction to functions f with single occurrences of variables, that is with no dependency, prevents its direct use. A mean-value extension allows us to by-pass this limitation.

Generalized interval mean-value extension.

In the general case of a differentiable function f, the mean-value theorem can be extended to define a generalized interval mean-value extension (see [14]) :

THEOREM 1. *Let $f : \mathbb{R}^n \to \mathbb{R}$ be differentiable, $\boldsymbol{x} \in \mathbb{IK}^n$ and suppose that for each $i \in \{1, \dots, n\}$, we can compute $\boldsymbol{\Delta}_i \in \mathbb{IR}$ such that*

$$\left\{ \frac{\partial f}{\partial x_i}(x),\ x \in \textit{pro}\ \boldsymbol{x} \right\} \sqsubseteq \boldsymbol{\Delta}_i. \tag{2}$$

Then, for all $\tilde{x} \in$ pro $\boldsymbol{x}$, the following interval is $(f, \boldsymbol{x})$-interpretable :

$$\tilde{f}(\boldsymbol{x}) = f(\tilde{x}) + \sum_{i=1}^{n} \boldsymbol{\Delta}_i(\boldsymbol{x}_i - \tilde{x}_i). \tag{3}$$

EXAMPLE 1. *Let f be defined by $f(x) = x^2 - x$, for which we want to compute an inner approximation of the range over $\boldsymbol{x} = [2, 3]$. Due to the two occurrences of x, $f(\boldsymbol{x})$, computed with Kaucher arithmetic, is not $(f, \boldsymbol{x})$-interpretable. The interval $\tilde{f}(\boldsymbol{x}) = f(2.5) + \boldsymbol{f}'([2, 3])(\boldsymbol{x} - 2.5) = 3.75 + [3, 5](\boldsymbol{x} - 2.5)$ given by its mean-value extension, computed with Kaucher arithmetic, is $(f, \boldsymbol{x})$-interpretable. For $\boldsymbol{x} = [3, 2]$, using the multiplication rule for $\mathcal{P} \times$ dual $\mathcal{Z}$, we get $\tilde{f}(\boldsymbol{x}) = 3.75 + [3, 5]([3, 2] - 2.5) = 3.75 + [3, 5][0.5, -0.5] = 3.75 + [1.5, -1.5] = [5.25, 2.25]$, that can be interpreted as: $\forall z \in [2.25, 5.25]$, $\exists x \in [2, 3]$, $z = f(x)$. Thus, $[2.25, 5.25]$ is an inner approximation of* range$(f, [2, 3])$.

2.2 Affine vectors for outer approximations

Affine arithmetic.

Affine arithmetic [6] is an extension of (classical) interval arithmetic, that takes into account affine correlations between variables. Affine operations are exact in affine arithmetic, so that affine forms are good candidates to define inner approximations, as we will see.

An affine form is a sum over a set of noise symbols ε_i

$$\hat{x} = x_0 + \sum_{i=1}^{n} x_i \varepsilon_i, \tag{4}$$

with $x_i \in \mathbb{R}$ for all i. Each noise symbol ε_i stands for an independent component of the total uncertainty on $\hat{x}$, its value is unknown but bounded in $[-1, 1]$. The same noise symbol can be shared by several variables, expressing correlations between these variables. The set of values represented by an affine form $\hat{x}$ is the box $\left[x_0 - \sum_{i=1}^{n} |x_i|, x_0 + \sum_{i=1}^{n} |x_i|\right]$. Conversely, the assignment of a variable x whose value is given in a range $[a, b]$, is defined as a centered form using a fresh noise symbol $\varepsilon_{n+1} \in [-1, 1]$, which indicates unknown dependency with other variables: $\hat{x} = \frac{(a+b)}{2} + \frac{(b-a)}{2} \varepsilon_{n+1}$.

The result of linear operations on affine forms is an affine form, and is thus interpreted exactly. For two affine forms $\hat{x}$ and $\hat{y}$, and a real number λ, we have $\lambda \hat{x} + \hat{y} = (\lambda x_0 + y_0) + \sum_{i=1}^{n} (\lambda x_i + y_i) \varepsilon_i$.

Affine vectors for outer approximations.

In (classical) affine arithmetic, non-affine operations are linearized, and new noise symbols are introduced to handle the approximation term. In our use, we distinguish, as detailed in [18, 19], these new noise symbols denoted by η_j noise symbols,from the ε_i. The ε_i noise symbols model uncertainty in data or parameters, while the η_j noise symbols model uncertainty coming from the analysis. For instance, a possible (simple) abstraction of the multiplication of two affine forms, defined, for simplicity, on ε_i only, writes

$$\hat{x}\hat{y} = x_0 y_0 + \sum_{i=1}^{n} (x_i y_0 + y_i x_0) \varepsilon_i + \frac{1}{2} \sum_{1 \leqslant i, j \leqslant n} |\, x_i y_j + x_j y_i \,| \, \eta_1.$$

More generally, non-affine operations are abstracted by an approximate affine form obtained for instance by a first-order Taylor expansion, plus an approximation term attached to a new noise symbol. Affine operations have linear complexity in the number of noise symbols, whereas non-affine operations can be evaluated with quadratic cost.

EXAMPLE 2. *Consider the arithmetic expressions $x = a * b; y = x + b$, starting from $a \in [-2, 0]$ and $b \in [1, 3]$. The assignments of a and b create two new noise symbols ε_1, ε_2: $\hat{a} = -1 + \varepsilon_1$, $\hat{b} = 2 + \varepsilon_2$. The multiplication produces a new*

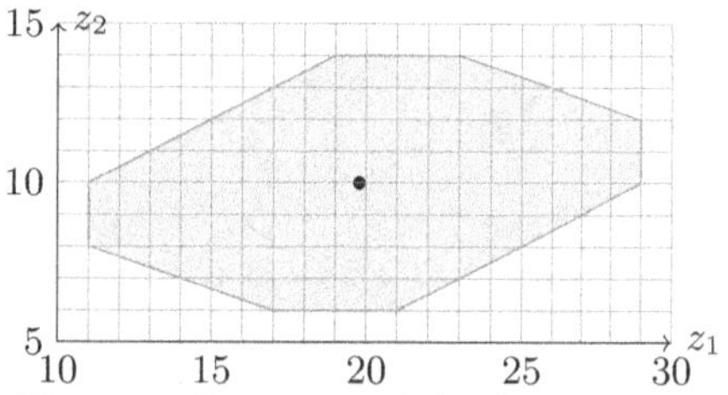

Figure 1: Zonotope $\gamma(Z)$ of Example 3.

η_1 symbol, we get $\hat{x} = -2 + 2\varepsilon_1 - \varepsilon_2 + \eta_1$. Affine expressions are handled exactly, we get $\hat{y} = 2\varepsilon_1 + \eta_1$. The range of y given by $\hat{y}$ is $[-3, 3]$, which is also the exact range, while the range obtained with the natural interval extension is $[-5, 3]$.

In what follows, we use matrix notations to handle affine vectors, that is vectors of affine forms. We denote $\mathcal{M}(n,p)$ the space of matrices with n lines and p columns of real coefficients, and ${}^tX$ the transpose of a matrix X.

DEFINITION 2. *An affine vector is a vector of p affine forms over n noise symbols ε_i, $1 \leqslant i \leqslant n$ and m noise symbols η_j, $1 \leqslant j \leqslant m$. It is represented by a matrix $Z \in \mathcal{M}(n+m+1, p)$ decomposed in sub-matrices $Z_0 = (z_{0,k})_{1 \leqslant k \leqslant p}$, $Z_\varepsilon = (z_{i,k})_{\substack{1 \leqslant k \leqslant p \\ 1 \leqslant i \leqslant n}}$ and $Z_\eta = (z_{j,k})_{\substack{1 \leqslant k \leqslant p \\ n+1 \leqslant j \leqslant n+m}}$. The set of values it represents is the zonotope*

$$\gamma(Z) = \left\{ {}^tZ_0 + {}^tZ_\varepsilon \varepsilon + {}^tZ_\eta \eta \mid (\varepsilon, \eta) \in [-1,1]^{n+m} \right\}. \quad (5)$$

In Definition 2, the k-th component of the vector is given by the affine form $\hat{z}_k = z_{0,k} + \sum_{i=1}^{n} z_{i,k}\varepsilon_i + \sum_{j=n+1}^{n+m} z_{j,k}\eta_j$.

EXAMPLE 3. *For $n = 4$ and $p = 2$, the set of values represented by the affine vector $(\hat{z}_1, \hat{z}_2)$ with $\hat{z}_1 = 20 - 4\varepsilon_1 + 2\varepsilon_3 + 3\varepsilon_4$, and $\hat{z}_2 = 10 - 2\varepsilon_1 + \varepsilon_2 - \varepsilon_4$, is the gray zonotope of Figure 1. Of course, the range of each variable considered independently can also be computed: $\gamma(\hat{z}_1) = [20-4-2-3, 20+4+2+3] = [11, 29]$ and $\gamma(\hat{z}_2) = [6, 14]$.*

The affine vector introduced in Definition 2 can also be seen as a linear function of the n inputs or noise symbols to the p variables it represents, plus an uncertain part given as a linear transform of a box (the zonotope ${}^tZ_\eta\eta$). It represents a set of functions from $\mathbb{R}^n$ to $\mathbb{R}^p$:

$$\gamma_{\text{func}}(Z) = \left\{ g_Z : \mathbb{R}^n \to \mathbb{R}^p \mid \begin{array}{l} \forall \varepsilon \in [-1,1]^n, \exists \eta \in [-1,1]^m, \\ g_Z(\varepsilon) = {}^tZ_0 + {}^tZ_\varepsilon \varepsilon + {}^tZ_\eta \eta \end{array} \right\}$$

This will be instrumental in the definition of outer and inner approximations, by allowing to state Properties 1 and 2. Property 1 states that affine vectors are interpretable as over-approximations.

PROPERTY 1. *Let $f : \mathbb{R}^n \to \mathbb{R}^p$ be a function, $\boldsymbol{x} \in \mathbb{IR}^n$, and $Z \in \mathcal{M}(n+m+1, p)$ the abstraction in affine vectors of the p components of $f(x), x \in \boldsymbol{x}$. Then Z is $(f, \boldsymbol{x})$-interpretable :*

$$(\forall x \in \boldsymbol{x})\,(\exists z \in \gamma(Z)),\ (f(x) = z).$$

Equivalently, using the interpretation of affine vectors as sets of functions, Z is $(f, \boldsymbol{\varepsilon})$-interpretable :

$$(\forall \varepsilon \in \boldsymbol{\varepsilon})\,(\exists \eta \in \boldsymbol{\eta}),\ (f(x(\varepsilon)) = {}^tZ_0 + {}^tZ_\varepsilon \varepsilon + {}^tZ_\eta \eta).$$

In Definition 1, an *interval* is considered (f, x)-interpretable. In Property 1, Definition 1 is implicitly extended to zonotopic sets of values z, for vector-valued functions f. However, we will not be able to obtain sets that are (f, x)-interpretable in the same way for inner approximation.

Constrained affine vectors.
As described in [11], we can interpret conditions in these affine vectors by adding some constraints on the noise symbols ε_i. Instead of letting them vary freely into $[-1, 1]$, we restrain ourselves to inputs that satisfy these constraints. This idea allows us to interpret conditions in programs, or guard conditions for hybrid systems, for outer approximations as well as inner approximations: we do not detail this in this paper, but quickly illustrate this on a simple example in Section 5.5.

3. GENERALIZED AFFINE VECTORS

We consider again the problem of finding an $(f, \boldsymbol{x})$ interpretable set as in Definition 1, but with the affine arithmetic point-of-view.

To each component $\boldsymbol{x}_i$, $i = 1, \ldots, n$ of the input box $\boldsymbol{x} \in \mathbb{IK}^n$, we associate a noise symbol ε_i, by writing $\hat{x}_i(\varepsilon_i) = \frac{\underline{x}_i + \overline{x}_i}{2} + \frac{\overline{x}_i - \underline{x}_i}{2}\varepsilon_i$, where $\boldsymbol{x}_i = [\underline{x}_i, \overline{x}_i]$. Then any function $f : \mathbb{R}^n \to \mathbb{R}$, for some input $\boldsymbol{x} \in \mathbb{IK}^n$, can be seen as a function f^ε of the vector $\varepsilon = (\varepsilon_1, \ldots, \varepsilon_n)$. f^ε is said to be the function induced on $\varepsilon = (\varepsilon_1, \ldots, \varepsilon_n)$ by the substitution of $\hat{x}_i(\varepsilon_i)$, $i = 1, \ldots, n$ in f.

As already mentionned in [17], we can now restate the generalized mean-value extension of Theorem 1 on f^ε.

THEOREM 2. *Let $f : \mathbb{R}^n \to \mathbb{R}$ be a differentiable function, $\boldsymbol{x} \in \mathbb{IK}^n$, and $f^\varepsilon : \mathbb{R}^n \to \mathbb{R}$ the function induced on $\varepsilon = (\varepsilon_1, \ldots, \varepsilon_n)$. Suppose that $\boldsymbol{\Delta}_i$ is an outer approximation of the partial derivative $\frac{\partial f^\varepsilon}{\partial \varepsilon_i}$:*

$$\left\{ \frac{\partial f^\varepsilon}{\partial \varepsilon_i}(\varepsilon),\ \varepsilon \in [-1,1]^n \right\} \sqsubseteq \boldsymbol{\Delta}_i. \quad (6)$$

Then, $\forall (t_1, \ldots, t_n) \in \text{pro}\ \boldsymbol{\varepsilon} = [-1, 1]^n$,

$$\tilde{f}^\varepsilon(\boldsymbol{\varepsilon}_1, \ldots, \boldsymbol{\varepsilon}_n) = f^\varepsilon(t_1, \ldots, t_n) + \sum_{i=1}^{n} \boldsymbol{\Delta}_i(\boldsymbol{\varepsilon}_i - t_i), \quad (7)$$

is $(f, \boldsymbol{x})$-interpretable. In particular,

- *if $\tilde{f}^\varepsilon([1, -1]^n)$, computed with Kaucher arithmetic, is improper, then pro $\tilde{f}^\varepsilon([1, -1]^n)$ is an inner approximation of $\{f^\varepsilon(\varepsilon),\ \varepsilon \in [-1,1]^n\} = \{f(x),\ x \in \boldsymbol{x}\}$.*
- *if $\tilde{f}^\varepsilon([-1, 1]^n)$ is a proper interval, then it is an outer approximation of $\{f(x),\ x \in \boldsymbol{x}\}$.*

Theorem 2 [17] allows us to compute outer and inner approximating intervals of the ranges of expressions. But we also have more than just ranges, as we define generalized affine forms over the noise symbols ε_i, generalized in the sense that multiplicative coefficients of the noise symbols are no longer just real numbers but represent sets of values. We will characterize the joint inner approximation defined by these forms in Section 4.

Affine vectors with interval coefficients, which we refer to as zeroth-order generalized affine vectors, are obtained by bounding the partial derivatives in intervals $\boldsymbol{\Delta}_i$. This is what was proposed in [17], and will not be detailed here. Operations on these zeroth-order sets involve interval computations, and thus suffer from the drawbacks of interval arithmetic.

Affine vectors with affine vector coefficients are obtained when an outer approximation of the Jacobian matrix of the function is computed using affine vectors. They are called first-order generalized affine vectors, and are introduced in the next section. We will compare results of the zeroth and first-order sets in Section 5.

3.1 First-order generalized affine vectors

In this section, we start by defining the first-order generalized affine vectors and the property we expect them to satisfy (Property 2) to be able to use them for inner approximation. We then explicit the construction of such sets.

DEFINITION 3. *A first-order generalized affine vector from $\mathbb{R}^n$ to $\mathbb{R}^p$ is a triple (Z, c, J) consisting of an affine vector $Z \in \mathcal{M}(n+m+1, p)$, a vector $c \in \mathbb{R}^p$, and a vector of affine vectors $J \in (\mathcal{M}(n,p))^n$.*

In order to use Theorem 2 to derive an inner approximation of range$(f, \boldsymbol{x})$ from these first-order generalized affine vectors, we want them to satisfy the following property.

PROPERTY 2. *A first-order generalized affine vector (Z, c, J) abstracts the function $f : \mathbb{R}^n \to \mathbb{R}^p$, if $c = f^\varepsilon(0)$ and*

$$(\forall \varepsilon \in \boldsymbol{\varepsilon})\,(\exists \eta \in \boldsymbol{\eta}),\ \begin{cases} f^\varepsilon(\varepsilon) = {}^tZ_0 + {}^tZ_\varepsilon \varepsilon + {}^tZ_\eta \eta \\ \frac{\partial f^\varepsilon}{\partial \varepsilon_i}(\varepsilon) = {}^tJ_{i,0} + {}^tJ_{i,\varepsilon}\varepsilon + {}^tJ_{i,\eta}\eta, \\ \forall i = 1, \ldots, n \end{cases} \quad (8)$$

Equation 8 expresses that for a given $\varepsilon \in [-1,1]^n$, (Z, c, J) defines an outer approximation of $f^\varepsilon(\varepsilon)$ and of $(\frac{\partial f^\varepsilon}{\partial \varepsilon_i})_i(\varepsilon)$ relying on the same parametrization in the η noise symbols.

We thus now define arithmetic operations that preserve Property 2, starting from a generalized affine vector defined as in Definition 3, where to each component $\boldsymbol{x}_i$ of the input box $\boldsymbol{x}$, corresponds a noise symbol ε_i, $i = 1, \ldots, n$. Note that the k-th component of the vector represented by the affine vector Z, is given by the affine form $\hat{z}^k = z_{0,k} + \sum_{i=1}^{n} z_{i,k}\varepsilon_i + \sum_{j=n+1}^{n+m} z_{j,k}\eta_j$. Similarly, the k-th component of the affine vector J_i, noted $\hat{j}_{ik}$, is a vector that represents an affine form that outer approximates the component $\frac{\partial f_k^\varepsilon}{\partial \varepsilon_i}$. In the following, for a more compact definition of operations, we will see the affine vector matrix Z as its equivalent vector of affine forms $\hat{z}_k$, $1 \leqslant k \leqslant p$, and the vector of affine vectors J as its equivalent matrix of affine forms $\hat{j}_{i,k}$, $1 \leqslant i \leqslant n, 1 \leqslant k \leqslant p$.

The following example will illustrate the arithmetic operations on first-order generalized affine vectors.

EXAMPLE 4. *Let $x = (x_1, x_2) \in [2,3] \times [3,4]$ and*

$$f(x) = \begin{pmatrix} x_1^3 - 2x_1x_2 \\ x_2^3 - 2x_1x_2 \end{pmatrix}$$

Assignment.

The generalized affine vector $(Z', c', J') \in \mathcal{M}(n+m+1, p+1) \times \mathbb{R}^{p+1} \times (\mathcal{M}(n, p+1))^n$ for $f' : \mathbb{R}^n \to \mathbb{R}^{p+1}$ where $f_{p+1} := [a, b]$, with $a < b$ and corresponding noise symbol ε_i, is defined by :

$$\begin{cases} Z' &= \begin{pmatrix} Z & \frac{a+b}{2} + \frac{b-a}{2}\varepsilon_i \end{pmatrix} \\ c' &= \begin{pmatrix} c & \frac{a+b}{2} \end{pmatrix} \\ J' &= \begin{pmatrix} & 0 \\ J & \frac{b-a}{2} \\ & 0 \end{pmatrix} \leftarrow i\text{-th line} \end{cases}$$

EXAMPLE 5. *In Example 4, let us interpret the assignments $x_1 := [2,3]$ and $x_2 := [3,4]$. The affine forms for x_1 and x_2 are $\hat{x}_1 = \frac{5}{2} + \frac{1}{2}\varepsilon_1$ and $\hat{x}_2 = \frac{7}{2} + \frac{1}{2}\varepsilon_2$. The centers are $c_1 = \frac{5}{2}$ and $c_2 = \frac{7}{2}$. Finally, the Jacobian of the function which associates (x_1, x_2) to $(\varepsilon_1, \varepsilon_2)$ is $J = \begin{pmatrix} \frac{1}{2} & 0 \\ 0 & \frac{1}{2} \end{pmatrix}$.*

Affine operations.

Affine operations are handled exactly; we will examplify them later on the function of Example 4, at the same time as multiplication. For $(\lambda_1, \lambda_2) \in \mathbb{R}^2$, the generalized affine vector $(Z', c', J') \in \mathcal{M}(n+m+1, p+1) \times \mathbb{R}^{p+1} \times (\mathcal{M}(n, p+1))^n$ for $f' : \mathbb{R}^n \to \mathbb{R}^{p+1}$ where $f_{p+1} = \lambda_1 f_i + \lambda_2 f_j$, is defined by :

$$\begin{cases} Z' &= \begin{pmatrix} Z & \lambda_1\hat{z}_i + \lambda_2\hat{z}_j \end{pmatrix} \\ c' &= \begin{pmatrix} c & \lambda_1 c_i + \lambda_2 c_j \end{pmatrix} \\ J' &= \begin{pmatrix} & \lambda_1\hat{j}_{1,i} + \lambda_2\hat{j}_{1,j} \\ J & \vdots \\ & \lambda_1\hat{j}_{n,i} + \lambda_2\hat{j}_{n,j} \end{pmatrix} \end{cases}$$

Multiplication.

The generalized affine vector $(Z', c', J') \in \mathcal{M}(n+m+2, p+1) \times \mathbb{R}^{p+1} \times (\mathcal{M}(n, p+1))^n$ for $f' : \mathbb{R}^n \to \mathbb{R}^{p+1}$ where $f_{p+1} = f_i \times f_j$, is defined by :

$$\begin{cases} Z' &= \begin{pmatrix} Z & \hat{z}_i\hat{z}_j \end{pmatrix} \\ c' &= \begin{pmatrix} c & c_i c_j \end{pmatrix} \\ J' &= \begin{pmatrix} & \hat{z}_j\hat{j}_{1,i} + \hat{z}_i\hat{j}_{1,j} \\ J & \vdots \\ & \hat{z}_j\hat{j}_{n,i} + \hat{z}_i\hat{j}_{n,j} \end{pmatrix} \end{cases}$$

EXAMPLE 6. *In Example 4, one needs to compute $\hat{x}_1\hat{x}_2$, $\hat{x}_1^3$ and $\hat{x}_2^3$. First, we get, using rules from Section 2.2, $\hat{x}_1\hat{x}_2 = \frac{35}{4} + \frac{7}{4}\varepsilon_1 + \frac{5}{4}\varepsilon_2 + \frac{1}{4}\eta_1$. This adds a (third) column to Z and a new center, $c_3 = \frac{35}{4}$. Moreover,*

$$\begin{aligned} \frac{\partial(\hat{x}_1\hat{x}_2)}{\partial\varepsilon_1} &= \frac{\partial\hat{x}_1}{\partial\varepsilon_1}\hat{x}_2 + \hat{x}_1\frac{\partial\hat{x}_2}{\partial\varepsilon_1} \\ &= \frac{7}{4} + \frac{1}{4}\varepsilon_2 \end{aligned}$$

Similarly, $\frac{\partial(\hat{x}_1\hat{x}_2)}{\partial\varepsilon_2} = \frac{5}{4} + \frac{1}{4}\varepsilon_1$. This adds a (third) column to J: ${}^t\begin{pmatrix} \frac{7}{4} + \frac{1}{4}\varepsilon_2 & \frac{5}{4} + \frac{1}{4}\varepsilon_1 \end{pmatrix}$.
Then we compute successively $\hat{x}_1\hat{x}_1$, $\hat{x}_1(\hat{x}_1\hat{x}_1)$, $\hat{x}_2\hat{x}_2$, $\hat{x}_2(\hat{x}_2\hat{x}_2)$ adding each time a new column to Z, a new center and a new column to J (computing the outer approximations of the partial derivatives of these expressions along the ε_j). One gets

$$\begin{aligned} \hat{x}_1^3 - 2\hat{x}_1\hat{x}_2 &= -\frac{25}{16} + \frac{95}{16}\varepsilon_1 + \frac{17}{8}\eta_3 \\ \hat{x}_2^3 - 2\hat{x}_1\hat{x}_2 &= \frac{427}{16} - \frac{7}{4}\varepsilon_1 + \frac{255}{16}\varepsilon_2 + \frac{15}{8}\eta_5 \end{aligned}$$

with the centers $c_1 = -\frac{15}{8}$ *and* $c_2 = \frac{203}{8}$*, and the following last two columns of the Jacobian* J

$$\begin{pmatrix} \frac{97}{16}+\frac{15}{4}\varepsilon_1-\frac{1}{2}\varepsilon_2+\frac{15}{8}\eta_6 & -\frac{5}{2}-\frac{1}{2}\varepsilon_1 \\ -\frac{7}{2}-\frac{1}{2}\varepsilon_2 & \frac{257}{16}-\frac{1}{2}\varepsilon_1+\frac{21}{4}\varepsilon_2+\frac{15}{8}\eta_7 \end{pmatrix}$$

The fact that the arithmetic operations defined above preserve Property 2 results from the property that operations on (classical) affine vectors outer approximate the concrete operations [18], combined with the rules of derivation of sum and product of functions.

4. INTERVAL AND JOINT INNER RANGE OF GENERALIZED AFFINE VECTORS

This section describes the information we can derive from the generalized affine vectors on the inner range of vector-valued functions, first component-by-component, then considering components jointly.

4.1 Interval inner approximation of the range

From a first-order generalized affine vector (Z, c, J) abstracting a function $f : \mathbb{R}^n \to \mathbb{R}^p$, a zeroth-order generalized affine vector is easily obtained as

$$\tilde{x}_k = c_k + \sum_{i=1}^{n} [a_{ik}, b_{ik}]\varepsilon_i, \ \forall k = 1, \ldots, p,$$

where $[a_{ik}, b_{ik}]$ is the interval concretization of the affine form $\hat{j}_{ik}$.

We can then define the following (inner) interval concretization for each variable x_k, $k = 1, \ldots, p$:

$$\underline{\gamma}(\tilde{x}_k) \;=\; \text{pro}\ (c_k + \textstyle\sum_{i=1}^{n} [a_{ik}, b_{ik}] \times [1, -1])$$

computed using Kaucher arithmetic, see Section 2.1. As noted in [17], the improper interval $[1, -1]$ being in dual $\mathcal{Z}$, the types of (proper) intervals $[a_{ik}, b_{ik}]$ that do not lead to a multiplication equal to zero can be deduced from Table 1. It must be in $\mathcal{P}$ or in $-\mathcal{P}$, that is the interval bounding the Jacobian coefficient should not contain zero.

By Theorem 2, as the intervals $[a_{ik}, b_{ik}]$ outer approximate the partial derivative of the kth component of f^{ε} with respect to ε_i, $\underline{\gamma}(\tilde{x}_k)$ is guaranteed to be inside the set of reachable values for x_k, i.e., of the k-th projection of the image of f.

EXAMPLE 7. *With the first-order inner approximating set of Example 6, we get the following concretization in terms of inner approximating forms of order zero :*

$$\begin{aligned} \tilde{x}_1 &= -1.875 + [-0.0625, 12.1875]\varepsilon_1 + [-3, -2]\varepsilon_2 \\ \tilde{x}_2 &= 25.375 + [-4, -3]\varepsilon_1 + [8.4375, 23.6875]\varepsilon_2 \end{aligned}$$

and the interval concretizations using Kaucher arithmetic: $\underline{\gamma}(\tilde{x}_1) = \textit{pro}\ (-1.875 + [-0.0625, 12.1875] \times [1, -1] + [-3, -2] \times [1, -1]) = \textit{pro}\ (-1.875 + [2, -2]) = [-3.875, 0.125]$ *and* $\underline{\gamma}(\tilde{x}_2) = \textit{pro}\ (25.375 + [3, -3] + [8.437, -8.437]) = [13.937, 36.812]$.

On this example, we get better interval concretizations with the direct computation of zeroth-order forms of [17],

$$\begin{aligned} \tilde{x}'_1 &= -1.875 + [2, 10.5]\varepsilon_1 + [-3, -2]\varepsilon_2 \\ \tilde{x}'_2 &= 25.375 + [-4, -3]\varepsilon_1 + [10.5, 22]\varepsilon_2 \end{aligned}$$

that give $\underline{\gamma}(\tilde{x}'_1) = [-5.875, 2.125]$ *and* $\underline{\gamma}(\tilde{x}'_2) = [11.875, 38.875]$. *There is no general rule about the relative precision of the interval concretizations of zeroth-order and first-order generalized affine forms. Nevertheless, the joint range will be better with first-order forms. This result is similar to that obtained when comparing interval arithmetic to affine arithmetic. When the considered function* f *is more involved, see e.g., Section 5, interval concretizations of first-order generalized affine forms are usually much more precise than the ones obtained with zeroth-order generalized affine forms.*

The next section describes a tool for the inner approximation of vector-valued functions, which will allow us in Section 4.3 to characterize an inner approximation of the joint inner range of first-order generalized affine forms.

4.2 Inner range of vector-valued functions

This section recalls the main result of [15] to evaluate an inner approximation of the range of a function with domain and co-domain of the same dimension. We refer the reader to [16] for the extension of this method to functions from $\mathbb{R}^n$ to $\mathbb{R}^p$ with p not necessarily equal to n.

THEOREM 3. *(Corollary 3.1 of [15]) Let* $\mathbf{x} \in \mathbb{IR}^n$ *and* $f : \mathbf{x} \to \mathbb{R}^n$ *be a continuous function, continuously differentiable in the interior of* $\mathbf{x}$*,* $\text{int}(\mathbf{x})$*. Consider* $\mathbf{y} \in \mathbb{IR}^n$ *and* $\tilde{x} \in \mathbf{x}$ *such that* $f(\tilde{x}) \in \mathbf{y}$*. Consider also an interval matrix* $\mathbf{J} \in \mathbb{IR}^{n\times n}$ *such that* $f'(x) \in \mathbf{J}$ *for all* $x \in \mathbf{x}$*. Assume that* $0 \notin \mathbf{J}_{ii}$ *for all* $i \in [1, \ldots, n]$*. Calling* $\text{Diag}\,\mathbf{J}$ *the diagonal part of* $\mathbf{J}$ *and* $\text{OffDiag}\,\mathbf{J}$ *its off diagonal part, consider*

$$H(\mathbf{J}, \tilde{x}, \mathbf{x}, \mathbf{y}) = \tilde{x} + (\text{Diag}^{-1}\,\mathbf{J})\Big(\mathbf{y} - f(\tilde{x}) - (\text{OffDiag}\,\mathbf{J})(\mathbf{x} - \tilde{x})\Big). \tag{9}$$

If $H(\mathbf{J}, \tilde{x}, \mathbf{x}, \mathbf{y}) \sqsubseteq \text{int}(\mathbf{x})$ *then* $\mathbf{y} \sqsubseteq \text{range}(f, \mathbf{x})$.

This theorem provides an efficient test for a box $\mathbf{y}$ to be a subset of the range of a vector-valued function, see Figure 2 for an illustration. The restriction on f having the same dimension of domain and co-domain comes from the matrix inversion of $\text{Diag}\,\mathbf{J}$ in (9).

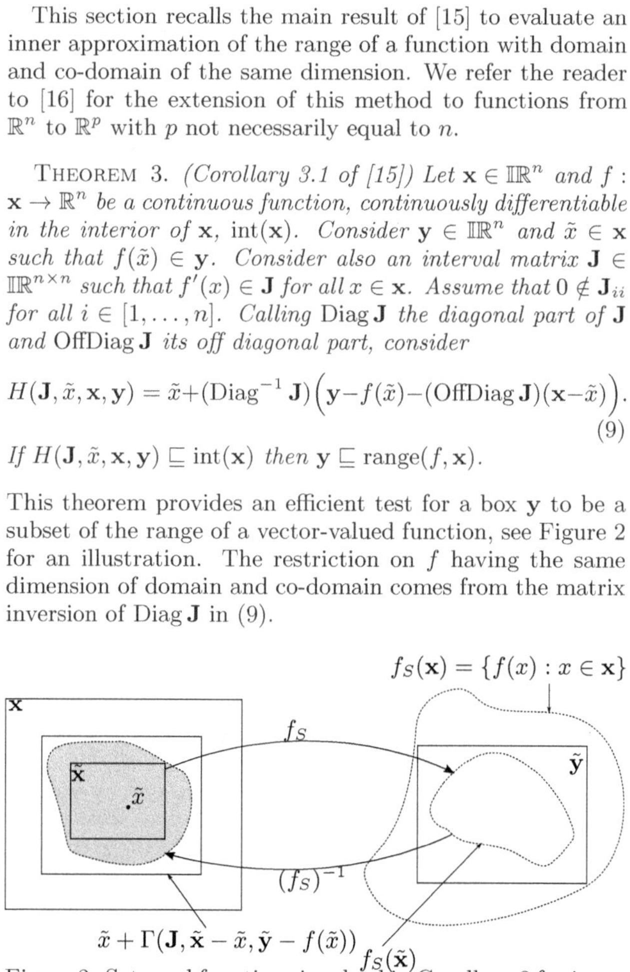

Figure 2: Sets and functions involved in Corollary 3 for inner approximation.

The algorithm relying on Corollary 3 to obtain an inner approximation of $\text{range}(f, \boldsymbol{x})$ is as follows. The algorithm starts with a function f, a box $\mathbf{x} \in \mathbb{IR}^n$ on which an inner approximation of the range of f must be evaluated, and a parameter ϵ, which will determine the precision for the inner approximation of $\text{range}(f, \boldsymbol{x})$. We start by using an outer approximation of the image of f on $\mathbf{x}$, called $\mathbf{y}$ (using interval analysis, and the mean-value theorem as in Section 2.1). If condition (9) on $\mathbf{x}$ and $\mathbf{y}$ is satisfied, then $\mathbf{y}$ is in the image of f. Otherwise, we bisect $\mathbf{y}$ and carry on testing condition (9) on each of the generated sub-boxes, until they are proven to be in $\text{range}(f, \boldsymbol{x})$, or their width is less than ϵ, so as to ensure termination of the algorithm.

Hence this method gives a paving of boxes proven to be inside the image of f on $\mathbf{x}$. We illustrate this on the particular case of a vector-valued function given by a generalized affine vector in the next section.

4.3 Inner range of generalized affine vectors

Corollary 3 gives a criterion to prove that boxes belong to range$(f, \boldsymbol{x})$, by only evaluating an outer approximation of the Jacobian of f on sub-boxes of $\mathbf{x}$. Both zeroth-order and first-order generalized affine vectors compute an outer approximation of this Jacobian. A joint concretization Γ is thus calculated using the algorithm presented in Section 4.2, using the center $c_1, \ldots, c_p$ for $f(\tilde{x})$ and J in place of the exact Jacobian of f.

EXAMPLE 8. *The joint concretization of the first-order generalized affine vector for Example 4 is represented in Figure 3 and compared to the exact range. The joint concretization for the zeroth-order generalized affine vector only contains the point* $(-1.875, 25.375)$ *here, because it does not track dependencies between the coefficients of the Jacobian.*

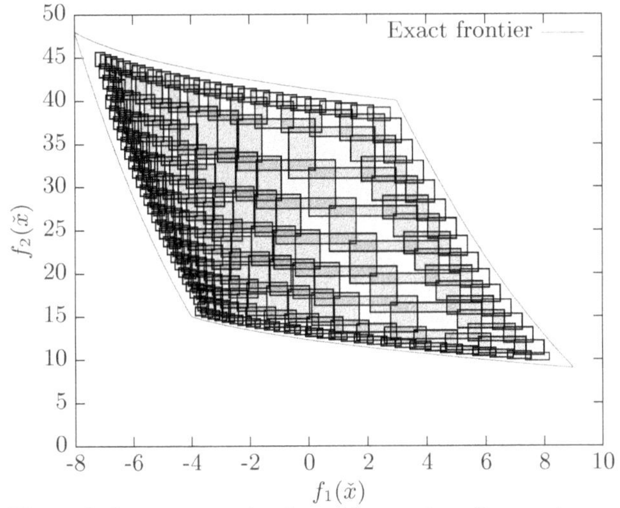

Figure 3: Inner concretization of first-order affine vector and exact function border for Example 8: 269 proved inner boxes in 0.03s with ϵ=0.1.

5. EXPERIMENTS

5.1 Implementation

A C library[1] has been written, that implements both zeroth-order and first-order generalized affine vectors; these abstractions are interfaced to the Apron [23] library of abstract domains, and rely on the Taylor1+ [10] implementation for the outer approximating affine vectors.

In the previous sections, we relied on real numbers to compute the generalized affine vectors. In the implementation, one important point is to ensure guaranteed results while using finite-precision numbers. We use the multi-precision floating-point library MPFR [8] which allows us to increase precision if necessary. To get a sound and tractable implementation, we make sure the outer approximation of the variables and the Jacobian of the function by affine vectors or intervals is sound with respect to finite-precision. For intervals, this is obvious using outward rounding (rounding towards $-\infty$ for the first bound and towards $+\infty$ for the second bound). For affine vectors, this can also be achieved quite easily, see [10] for instance. Then, the center c_k of the generalized affine form for a variable x_k, can be soundly computed by a small interval with outward rounding, $[\underline{c_k}, \overline{c_k}]$. Finally, we want a sound interval inner approximation using Kaucher arithmetic

$$\underline{\gamma}(\check{x}_k) = \text{pro}\left([\underline{c_k}, \overline{c_k}] + \sum_{j=1}^{n} [a_{ik}, b_{ik}] \times [1, -1]\right),$$

$[\underline{c_k}, \overline{c_k}]$ is a proper interval while each $[a_{ik}, b_{ik}] \times [1, -1]$ is an improper interval. We get an inner approximation of the range of x_k if the addition of these generalized intervals is an improper interval $\boldsymbol{r}$: computing this addition again with outward rounding ensures correctness: indeed if the finite precision approximation $\boldsymbol{r}_p$ of $\boldsymbol{r}$, is such that $\boldsymbol{r} \sqsubseteq \boldsymbol{r}_p$, then dual $(\boldsymbol{r}_p) \sqsubseteq$ dual $(\boldsymbol{r})$, that is we obtain a smaller (thus correct) inner approximation than the one that would be computed with real numbers.

Note that, in the extreme case, if too much precision is lost in the computation due to the use of finite precision compared to the width of the inner approximation given by $[a_{ik}, b_{ik}] \times [1, -1]$, then $[\underline{c_k}, \overline{c_k}] + \sum_{j=1}^{n} [a_{ik}, b_{ik}] \times [1, -1]$ may become proper, so that we no longer get any inner approximation.

5.2 Convergence of numerical schemes

Inner approximations are useful to state properties of numerical algorithms, as shown below.

5.2.1 A Newton iteration

We consider the (non-linear) iteration of the Newton algorithm $x(k+1) = 2x(k) - ax(k)^2$, for $a \in [1.95, 2.]$. If we take $x(0)$ not too far away from the inverse of a, this iteration converges to $1/a$. We start here from $x(0) = 0.6$.

Figure 4 represents 10 iterates of this Newton algorithm, computed with the outer approximating affine vectors (Taylor1+ [10] Apron implementation), and the zeroth-order and first-order inner approximating affine vectors, all with double precision. While the zeroth-order inner approximation quickly tends to a unique point, the first-order inner aproximation remains very close to the outer approximation (actually so close we do not see the difference on the figure). Let us now show how we can usefully combine the information from the inner and outer approximation on this simple scheme. If we ask to iterate this scheme until $|x(k+1) - x(k)| < 5.10^{-4}$, we can prove, thanks to the outer approximation, that the stopping criterion of the loop is always satisfied after 4 iterations (we have $|x(4) - x(3)| \subseteq [-2.6\,10^{-4}, 2.6\,10^{-4}]$). While the inner approximation of $x(k+1) - x(k)$ proves that there exist some inputs for which the criterion is not satisfied for the first 3 iterations (for instance, $[-7.7\,10^{-4}, -4.1\,10^{-4}] \subseteq x(3) - x(2)$). The inner and outer approximation can be used to prove that when the criterion is satisfied, $[.4999244, .5127338] \subseteq x(4) \subseteq [0.499831, 0.512906]$, which is actually quite tight.

[1]available at `http://www.lix.polytechnique.fr/Labo/Sylvie.Putot/hscc14.html`

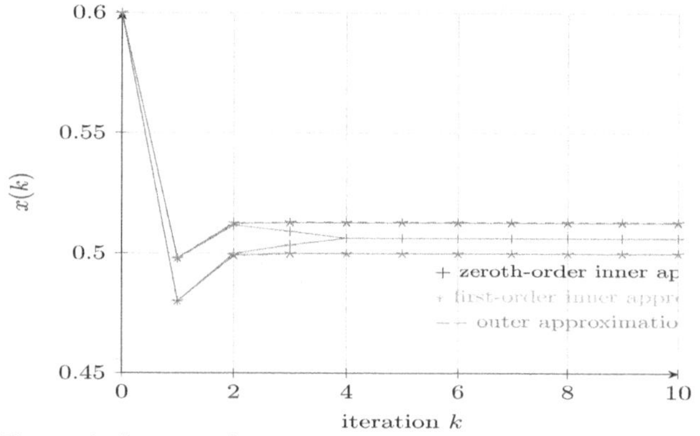

Figure 4: Inner and outer approximations for the Newton iterates

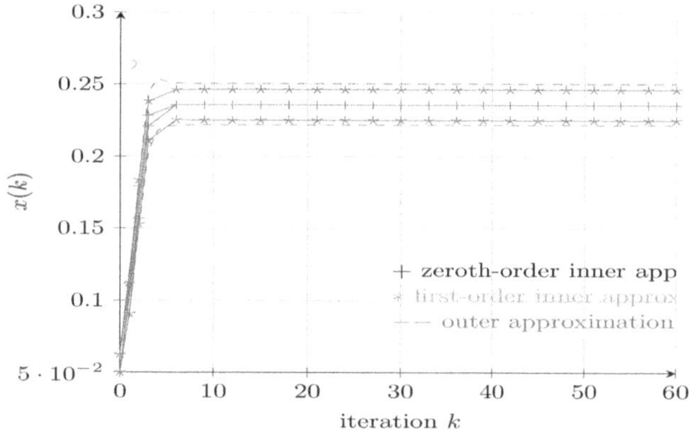

Figure 5: Inner and outer approximations for the Householder iterates

5.2.2 *A Householder iteration*

Consider the following Householder scheme

$$x(k+1) = x(k) + x(k)\left(\frac{1}{2}h(k) + \frac{3}{8}h(k)^2\right)$$

with $h(k) = 1 - ax(k)^2$ and $a \in [16, 20]$, starting from $x(0) = [\frac{1}{20}, \frac{1}{16}]$. The results by inner and outer approximation are presented Figure 5. It is even clearer here than on the Newton example that the zeroth-order inner approximation is not accurate enough for such a non-linear scheme, while the first-order inner approximation manages to remain stable along iterations and not far from the outer approximation.

We represent in Figure 6 the execution times for the three methods: not surprisingly, the outer approximation is the fastest, as an inner approximation needs the evaluation of an outer approximation. The cost of the zeroth-order inner approximation remains close to that of the outer approximation. The first-order inner approximation is naturally more costly, as it involves outer approximation of every component of the Jacobian matrix of the function composed of every elementary sub-expressions involved in the scheme (the inner approximation is built inductively on the arithmetic expressions, in order to be automatically computed on any program). As expected, the cost remains almost linear compared to the cost of the outer approximation. Note that a study of the cost and behaviour of this outer approximation

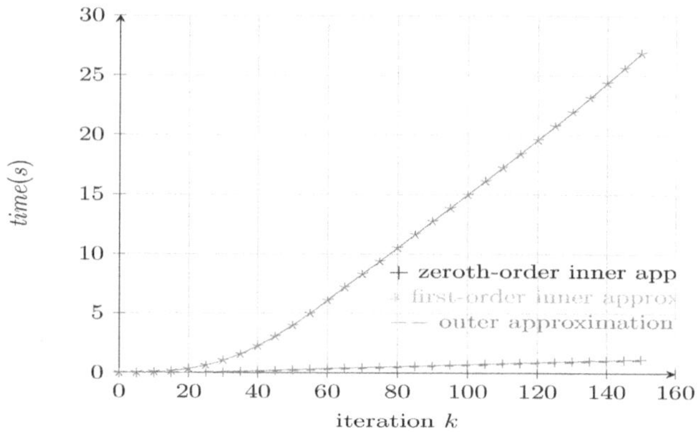

Figure 6: Comparison of execution times for the Householder scheme

was reported in [10], where its good tradeoff between cost and accuracy was demonstrated.

5.3 Reachability of discrete dynamical systems: FitzHugh-Nagumo neuron model

This polynomial discrete-time dynamical system is derived from a continuous-time dynamical system modeling the electrical activity of a neuron, using an Euler time-discretization scheme, see [29]:

$$\begin{cases} x_1(k+1) = x_1(k) + h\left(x_1(k) - \frac{x_1(k)^3}{3} - x_2(k) + I\right) \\ x_2(k+1) = x_2(k) + h\left(0.08(x_1(k) + 0.7 - 0.8x_2(k))\right) \end{cases}$$

where $h = 0.2$, $I = \frac{7}{8}$, and the initial set is the bounding box $[1, 1.25] \times [2.25, 2.5]$

Using first-order affine vectors, we obtain for instance, at iteration 100 (in 11.54 seconds), the inner and outer ranges : $[-.737783, -.716137] \subseteq x_1 \subseteq [-.857537, -.595651]$, and $[.450016, .506109] \subseteq x_2 \subseteq [.429873, .542796]$. Figure 7 represents both approximations, for the 100 iterations: note that we do not present the joint range defined in Section 4.3, but only the interval ranges in both coordinates: at each iteration, each interval corresponding to the two coordinates for the inner approximating boxes (in plain lines) is guaranteed to be in the reachability set for each of the two variables x_1 and x_2. The boxes themselves are not guaranteed to be within the reachability set. Of course, the outer approximating boxes (in dotted lines), that enclose the zonotopes that were actually computed, are guaranteed to be an outer approximation of the reachable values. We see that, even for 100 iterations of a non-trivial non-linear dynamical system, we get outer and inner approximations which are quite close to each other, demonstrating the quality of the analysis performed - the reader may also compare these results with the very similar corresponding figure in [29].

5.4 Reachability of ODEs: Brusselator

Our inner approximation basically relies on a calculation of an outer approximation of a Jacobian (plus a center). For ODEs, it is simple to derive an ODE that gives the evolution over time of each entry of the Jacobian of the solution with respect to the initial conditions. We can then use any method (here, Taylor models) to outer approximate solutions of this derived system of ODEs, and use the result as a starting point for our inner approximation.

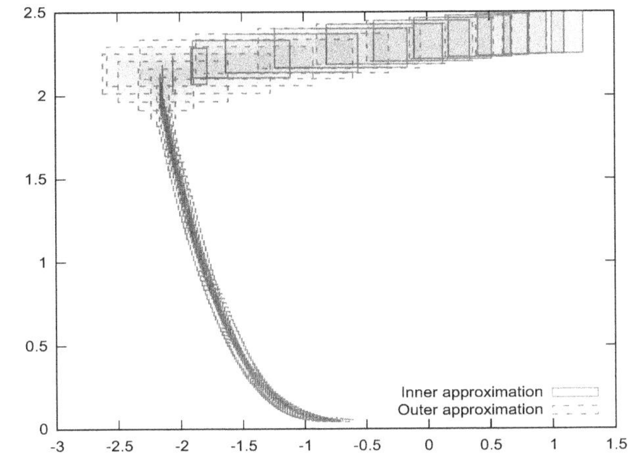

Figure 7: Outer and inner approximations of reachable sets for 100 iterations of the FitzHugh-Nagumo model

This is now detailed on the generic system

$$\dot{x}_i = f_i(x_1, \ldots, x_n) \text{ for } i = 1, \ldots, n \tag{10}$$

with initial condition $x(0) = (x_1(0), \ldots, x_n(0)) \in \mathbf{x_0} \sqsubseteq \mathbb{R}^n$. Under some regularity conditions on the functions f_i, $i = 1, \ldots, n$, the Cauchy-Lipschitz theorem asserts the existence of a unique solution $g : \mathbb{R}^{n+1} \to \mathbb{R}^n$ to (10) on a time interval $[0, \tau]$, for some positive τ. We could derive from set-integration methods (see, e.g., Lohner's method [27]), a method that would directly use our inner approximating arithmetic, in the style of what has been done in [3] using zonotopes. This needs too many developments for an inclusion in this paper, we choose instead to use a Taylor model of the dynamics [4] and of the dynamics of its Jacobian with respect to initial conditions.

When the functions f_i in (10) are at least continuously differentiable in all their arguments, we can write down a new "derived" system of ordinary differential equations describing the evolution in time of a solution g of (10), and its Jacobian $J_g = \left(g_{i,j} = \frac{\partial g_i}{\partial x_j(0)} \right)$. The functions $g_{i,j}$ and g_l satisfy the following systems of ordinary differential equations:

$$\left\{ \begin{array}{rcl} \dot{y}_{i,j} & = & \sum_{k=1}^{n} \frac{\partial f_i}{\partial x_k} y_{k,j} \\ \dot{x}_l & = & f_l(x_1, \ldots, x_n) \end{array} \right.$$

for $i = 1, \ldots, n$, $j = 1, \ldots, n$ and $\ell = 1, \ldots, n$, with $y_{i,i}(0) = 1$ and $y_{i,j}(0) = 0$ for $i \neq j$. Using Taylor models, the derived ODE is now modeled by polynomials P_k in $x_1(0), \ldots, x_n(0)$ and in t (the current time), and a box remainder $\mathbf{I}_k$ for a time interval $[t_k, t_{k+1}]$, $k = 0, \ldots, l$, $t_0 = 0$. These polynomials and interval remainders are such that $P_k([t_k, t_{k+1}]) + \mathbf{I}_k$ are guaranteed to contain the solutions to the derived ODE (hence the Jacobian of the solutions of the initial ODE) for all initial conditions within $\mathbf{x_0}$. We can now use our outer approximation methods using affine arithmetic to get an inner approximation in terms of first-order generalized affine forms.

EXAMPLE 9. *Consider the Brusselator studied e.g. in [3], [4]:*

$$\left\{ \begin{array}{rcl} \dot{x}_1 & = & 1 + x_1^2 x_2 - 2.5 x_1 \\ \dot{x}_2 & = & 1.5 x_1 - x_1^2 x_2 \end{array} \right.$$

with $x_1(0) \in [0.9, 1]$ and $x_2(0) \in [0, 0.1]$.

We use the tool Flow [5] to derive the Taylor models of order 5, up to time $t = 4$, with fixed steps equal to 0.1 (hence we get 40 Taylor models) and remainder estimation parameter equal to 0.1 (we will get a rather coarse estimate of the flowpipe, given that we allow for quite large box remainders) for the derived system of ODEs.*

We now look at the inner approximation derived from the zonotopic outer approximations of the Taylor model $(P_{39}, \mathbf{I}_{39})$, i.e., describing the solutions for the Brusselator in the time interval $[3.9s, 4s]$. As an indication, the Taylor model derived by Flow for x_1, within the latter time interval is a fifth-order polynomial in the initial conditions of the ODE and in time t, composed of 56 monomials. We find $(x_1, x_2) \in [0.700684, 0.763468] \times [1.851165, 1.894451]$ with centers $c_1 = 0.732$ and $c_2 = 1.873$, and the Jacobian is outer approximated by forms which are within the interval matrix:*

$$\frac{1}{20} \left(\begin{array}{cc} [0.1347, 0.1624] & [0.2427, 0.2963] \\ [-0.0049, 0.1091] & [0.03129, 0.2039] \end{array} \right)$$

Hence an inner approximation of the range of x_1 and x_2 are respectively pro $(0.732 + \frac{1}{20}[0.1347, 0.1624] \times [1, -1] + \frac{1}{20}[0.2427, 0.2963] \times [1, -1]) = [0.7132, 0.751]$ and pro $(1.873 + \frac{1}{20}[-0.0049, 0.1091] \times [1, -1] + \frac{1}{20}[0.03129, 0.2039] \times [1, -1]) = [1.87124, 1.87437]$. We see that for x_1, we get a tight inner approximation with respect to the outer approximation.

5.5 Guard conditions in hybrid automata

We briefly illustrate in this section how to interpret in our framework guard conditions in dynamical systems, such as the ones defining mode changes in hybrid automata. We concentrate here on a particular case, exemplified below. The general case is out of the scope of this paper.

We consider a simple 1D mass-spring system, where the mass decreases linearly over time, until some minimum mass is reached. As a hybrid automaton, this can be modeled by two modes m_1 and m_2 with transition from m_1 to m_2 if $k > k_m$ and from m_2 to m_1 if $k \leqslant k_m$. Each of the modes is normally governed by an ODE, but to keep things simple, we discretize them using a simple Euler scheme, with time constant $h = 0.04$. In all modes $x(n+1) = x(n) - hk(n)(x(n) - x_c)$, but in m_1, $k(n+1) = k(n) - hg_k$ $(k(n+1) > k_m)$, and in m_2, $k(n+1) = k(n)$ $(k(n+1) \leqslant k_m)$. The initial values for k and x are $k(0) \in [2, 2.5]$ (i.e. $k(0) = 2.25 + 0.25\varepsilon_1$), $x(0) \in [10, 11]$ (i.e. $x(0) = 10.5 + 0.5\varepsilon_2$), and constants $g_k = 2$, $k_m = 1$, $x_c = 8$.

The system starts in mode m_1, and some states can change mode only from iterate 13 on, as a simple analysis by our inner and outer approximations show. At iterate 13, the first-order generalized affine form (which coincides here with the outer approximation) of $k(13)$ is $1.21 + 0.25\varepsilon_1$. Therefore the states that will stay in mode m_1 at iterate 13 are exactly those for which $1.21 + 0.25\varepsilon_1 > 1$, i.e. $\varepsilon_1 > -0.84$, that is for initial state $k(0) \in [2.04, 2.5]$. At iterate 13, the Jacobian of $x(13)$ is outer approximated by: $J = (-0.006650 - 0.0009165\varepsilon_1 - 0.002021\varepsilon_2 + 0.0729218\eta_1 \;\; 0.3863 - 0.05388\varepsilon_2 + 0.001809\eta_4)$. The outer approximation of $x(13)$ is $7.7003 - 0.005278\varepsilon_1 - 0.4234\varepsilon_2 + 1.3824\eta_3$. It proves that $x(13) \in [5.8891, 9.5114]$ if we ignore the mode change, and if not, that is if we take into account $\varepsilon_1 > -0.84$, we get a slightly tighter value: $x(13) \in [5.8891, 9.5106]$. From the first-order generalized affine form, we also deduce that the inner interval range for $x(13)$ is in all cases $[7.369694594, 8.030894409]$:

this is still a fairly wide inner approximation even in the case of the mode change.

In this example, we have been able to handle the guard condition exactly as a restriction of the values that ε_1 can take: $1 \geq \varepsilon_1 > -0.84$ instead of $1 \geq \varepsilon_1 > -1$. In the general case, the guard condition will be expressed as a set of inequalities involving several noise symbols, for which we will have to compute inner boxes, or joint interval inner approximations, for instance using the work of Isshii *et al.* [22] on an interval-based projection method for under-constrained systems, that relies on similar ideas as described in Section 4.2 for the computation of boxes guaranteed to be in the image of a vector-valued function.

6. CONCLUSION

The method we developed for inner approximating reachable sets of dynamical systems can still be improved in several directions. First, we can directly integrate the first-order generalized affine forms arithmetic in the Picard operator approach to solving continuous-time ODEs. This would relieve us from the preliminary step of obtaining a Taylor model of the ODE. Second, we can use more general set-based methods for representing the Jacobian we need at each step of our method, in particular, we would like to investigate the use of higher Taylor methods.

7. ACKNOWLEDGEMENTS

This work was partly supported by the Digiteo SANSCRIT and ANR-12-INSE-0007-02 CAFEIN projects.

Michel Kieffer is partly supported by the Institut Universitaire de France, 75005 Paris.

8. REFERENCES

[1] M. Althoff, O. Stursberg, and M. Buss. Reachability analysis of linear systems with uncertain parameters and inputs. In *IEEE CDC*, 2007.

[2] J. Aubin and H. Frankowska. *Set-Valued Analysis*. Birkhäuser, Boston, 1990.

[3] O. Bouissou, A. Chapoutot, and A. Djoudi. Enclosing temporal evolution of dynamical systems using numerical methods. In *NASA Formal Methods*, 2013.

[4] X. Chen, E. Ábrahám, and S. Sankaranarayanan. Taylor model flowpipe construction for non-linear hybrid systems. In *RTSS*, pages 183–192, 2012.

[5] X. Chen, E. Ábrahám, and S. Sankaranarayanan. Flow*: An analyzer for non-linear hybrid systems. In *CAV*, pages 258–263, 2013.

[6] J. L. D. Comba and J. Stolfi. Affine arithmetic and its applications to computer graphics. *SIBGRAPI*, 1993.

[7] T. Dang and R. Testylier. Hybridization domain construction using curvature estimation. In *HSCC*, pages 123–132, 2011.

[8] L. Fousse, G. Hanrot, V. Lefèvre, P. Pélissier, and P. Zimmermann. Mpfr: A multiple-precision binary floating-point library with correct rounding. *ACM Trans. Math. Softw*, 33(2):13, 2007.

[9] E. Gardeñes, M. Sainz, L. Jorba, R. Calm, R. Estela, H. Mielgo, and A. Trepat. Model intervals. *Reliable Computing*, 7(2):77–111, 2001.

[10] K. Ghorbal, E. Goubault, and S. Putot. The zonotope abstract domain taylor1+. In *CAV'09*, volume 5643 of *LNCS*, pages 627–633. Springer, 2009.

[11] K. Ghorbal, E. Goubault, and S. Putot. A logical product approach to zonotope intersection. In *CAV'10*, volume 6174 of *LNCS*, 2010.

[12] A. Girard. Reachability of uncertain linear systems using zonotopes. In *HSCC'05*. Springer, 2005.

[13] A. Girard, C. Le Guernic, and O. Maler. Efficient computation of reachable sets of linear time-invariant systems with inputs. In *HSCC 2006*, volume 3927 of *LNCS*, pages 257–271. Springer, 2006.

[14] A. Goldsztejn, D. Daney, M. Rueher, and P. Taillibert. Modal intervals revisited: a mean-value extension to generalized intervals. In *QCP'05*, 2005.

[15] A. Goldsztejn, L. Jaulin, et al. Inner approximation of the range of vector-valued functions. *Reliable Computing*, 14:1–23, 2010.

[16] E. Goubault, M. Kieffer, O. Mullier, and S. Putot. General inner approximation of vector-valued functions. *Reliable Computing*, 18:117–143, 2013.

[17] E. Goubault and S. Putot. Under-approximations of computations in real numbers based on generalized affine arithmetic. In *SAS*, pages 137–152, 2007.

[18] E. Goubault and S. Putot. A zonotopic framework for functional abstractions. *CoRR*, abs/0910.1763, 2009.

[19] E. Goubault, S. Putot, and F. Vedrine. Modular static analysis with zonotopes. In *SAS'12*, volume 7460 of *LNCS*, pages 24–40. Springer, 2012.

[20] C. L. Guernic and A. Girard. Reachability analysis of hybrid systems using support functions. In *CAV*, 2009.

[21] D. Henrion and C. Louembet. Convex inner approximations of nonconvex semialgebraic sets applied to fixed-order controller design. *International Journal of Control*, 85(8):1083–1092, 2012.

[22] D. Ishii, A. Goldsztejn, and C. Jermann. Interval-based projection method for under-constrained numerical systems. *Constraints*, 17(4):432–460, 2012.

[23] B. Jeannet and A. Miné. Apron: A library of numerical abstract domains for static analysis. In *CAV'09*, pages 661–667. Springer, 2009.

[24] A. Kanade, R. Alur, F. Ivančić, S. Ramesh, S. Sankaranarayanan, and K. C. Shashidhar. Generating and analyzing symbolic traces of simulink/stateflow models. In *CAV'09*. Springer, 2009.

[25] E. Kaucher. Interval analysis in the extended interval space IR. *Comput. (Supplementum) 2*, 1980.

[26] A. B. Kurzhanski and P. Varaiya. Ellipsoidal techniques for reachability analysis. In *HSCC '00*, pages 202–214. Springer, 2000.

[27] R. J. Lohner. Enclosing the solutions of ordinary initial and boundary value problems. In *Computer Arithmetic: Scientific Computation and Programming Languages*, pages 255–286. Wiley-Teubner, 1987.

[28] T. Nghiem, S. Sankaranarayanan, G. Fainekos, F. Ivancić, A. Gupta, and G. J. Pappas. Monte-carlo techniques for falsification of temporal properties of non-linear hybrid systems. In *HSCC'10*. ACM, 2010.

[29] M. A. B. Sassi, R. Testylier, T. Dang, and A. Girard. Reachability analysis of polynomial systems using linear programming relaxations. In *ATVA*, 2012.

Sampling-Based Approximation of the Viability Kernel for High-Dimensional Linear Sampled-Data Systems

Jeremy H. Gillula
Electrical Engineering and Computer Sciences Dept.
UC Berkeley
301 Cory Hall
Berkeley, CA 94720
jgillula@eecs.berkeley.edu

Shahab Kaynama
Electrical Engineering and Computer Sciences Dept.
UC Berkeley
307 Cory Hall
Berkeley, CA 94720
kaynama@berkeley.edu

Claire J. Tomlin
Electrical Engineering and Computer Sciences Dept.
UC Berkeley
721 Sutardja Dai Hall
Berkeley, CA 94720
tomlin@eecs.berkeley.edu

ABSTRACT

Proving that systems satisfy hard input and state constraints is frequently desirable when designing cyber-physical systems. One method for doing so is to compute the viability kernel, the subset of the state space for which a control signal exists that is guaranteed to keep the system within the constraints over some time horizon. In this paper we present a novel method for approximating the viability kernel for linear sampled-data systems using a sampling-based algorithm, which by its construction offers a direct trade-off between scalability and accuracy. We also prove that the algorithm is correct, that its convergence properties are optimal, and demonstrate it on a simple example. We conclude by briefly describing additional results which are omitted due to space constraints.

Categories and Subject Descriptors

I.2.8 [**Artificial Intelligence**]: Problem Solving, Control Methods, and Search—*control theory*

Keywords

constrained sampled-data systems; viability kernel approximations; sampling-based algorithms

1. INTRODUCTION

As we enter the twenty-first century, cyber-physical systems are increasingly being used in "workspaces" which are shared with the general public and thus for which safety is critical. In order to guarantee the safety of these robots as well as the humans working with them it is vitally important that we be able to prove that these systems satisfy hard input and state constraints.

One method for doing so is to compute the *viability kernel* [2], the subset of the state space for which a control signal exists which is guaranteed to keep the system state within some hard constraints over some finite time horizon. (In the infinite horizon case this set is also known as the maximal controlled-invariant set [4].) In this paper we present a novel method for approximating the viability kernel for sampled-data systems using a sampling-based algorithm which offers a direct trade-off between scalability and accuracy. In addition to presenting the algorithm we will prove its correctness, analyze its convergence properties (and prove that they are optimal), and demonstrate the algorithm on a simple example.

1.1 Related Work

A great deal of prior work has been done on methods for computing the viability kernel, e.g. [25, 29]. Since these particular techniques represent the viability kernel using a grid over the state space, however, they have historically been limited to use on low-dimensional systems (usually 5D or less). Efforts to overcome this limitation, although still grid-based, include imposing and/or taking advantage of the structure of the dynamics [16, 24], or using approximate dynamic programming techniques [6].

An alternative to computing the viability kernel on a grid is to follow the flow of the system while using compact set representations (similar in spirit to Lagrangian techniques for maximal reachability [10, 11, 13]). For example [15] utilizes a recursive method to under-approximate the viability kernel for continuous-time systems, and proposes a scalable piecewise ellipsoidal algorithm (based on ellipsoidal techniques for maximal reachability [17]) for linear time-invariant (LTI) dynamics.

The model-predictive control (MPC) community has also developed algorithms that enable the computation of the viability kernel for discrete-time LTI systems with polytopic constraints [4]. Due to the high computational cost of the operations involved (Minkowski sums, intersections, and vertex-to-facet enumerations of polytopes) these algorithms can only be applied to low-dimensional systems. Alternatively, [21] proposed an efficient and scalable algorithm based on support vector representations for discrete-time LTI systems.

Approximating the viability kernel can also be viewed as a search for an appropriate control Lyapunov function, subject to additional input and state constraints. In this spirit, sums-of-squares (SOS) optimization-based techniques have been proposed [22, 28, 32–35] for polynomial systems with semi-algebraic constraints, which either directly calculate an approximation of the viability kernel or can be modified to do so. Such techniques strike a tradeoff between conservatism and complexity (as determined, e.g., by the chosen degree of the SOS multipliers). A related SOS-based technique is the method of occupation measures [14, 23] that, while convex and thus scalable, can only compute an over-approximation of the desired set (which is not sufficient for safety).

Despite this rich body of literature, all of the above work has focused on either continuous- or discrete-time systems, and very little work has been done on computing the viability kernel for *sampled-data* systems, i.e. systems with continuous dynamics in which the

HSCC'14, April 15–17, 2014, Berlin, Germany.
ACM 978-1-4503-2732-9/14/04.
http://dx.doi.org/10.1145/2562059.2562117 .

state of the system is measured at every time instant $t_k := k\delta$ for $k \in \mathbb{Z}_+$ and fixed sampling interval $\delta \in \mathbb{R}_+$, and for which the input is applied at the beginning of each sampling interval and kept constant until the next sampling instant. We believe that this class of systems more accurately represents modern cyber-physical systems in that most controllers are implemented on digital platforms while the system itself is analog and evolves continuously [12]. [1] Unfortunately continuous-time analysis on a system cannot provide guarantees about the behavior of the sampled-data system where the input is restricted to draw from the class of piecewise constant signals [26] and the state can only be measured at a fixed frequency. Similarly, simply discretizing the dynamics and designing control policies in discrete time would not account for the behavior of the underlying analog system between sampling instants, and could result in loss of safety. These complications make the work described above difficult to adapt to sampled-data systems. Instead our proposed algorithm handles sampled-data systems directly.

To the authors' knowledge the only other scalable work on computing the viability kernel for sampled-data systems is presented in [26], and applies to LTI systems and represents the constraints in a piecewise-ellipsoidal manner. Unfortunately due to the operations involved the results of that algorithm are extremely conservative. By contrast our approach (which is also scalable) yields a tight approximation of the viability kernel in the sense that the resulting set touches the boundary of the true viability kernel with arbitrary precision.

1.2 Definitions and Problem Formulation

In order to more formally state the problem our algorithm solves, we must first present some additional definitions and notation.

The $\|\cdot\|_p$-distance of a point $\mathbf{x} \in \mathcal{X}$ from a nonempty set $\mathcal{A} \subset \mathcal{X}$ is defined as $\mathrm{dist}_p(\mathbf{x}, \mathcal{A}) := \inf_{\mathbf{a}\in\mathcal{A}} \|\mathbf{x} - \mathbf{a}\|_p$.

We say that the vector field f is bounded on $\mathcal{A}$ if a norm $\|\cdot\|_p$ and a real number $M > 0$ exist for some norm $\|\cdot\|_p$ such that $\|f(\mathbf{x}, \mathbf{u})\|_p \leq M \ \forall (\mathbf{x}, \mathbf{u}) \in \mathcal{A} \times \mathcal{U}$. If $\mathcal{A}$ is compact, every continuous vector field f is bounded on $\mathcal{A}$.

The *Minkowski sum* of any two nonempty subsets $\mathcal{A}$ and $\mathcal{C}$ is $\mathcal{A} \oplus \mathcal{C} := \{\mathbf{a} + \mathbf{c} \mid \mathbf{a} \in \mathcal{A},\ \mathbf{c} \in \mathcal{C}\}$; their *Pontryagin difference* (or, the *erosion* of $\mathcal{A}$ by $\mathcal{C}$) is $\mathcal{A} \ominus \mathcal{C} := \{\mathbf{a} \mid \mathbf{a} \oplus \mathcal{C} \subseteq \mathcal{A}\}$.

We denote by $\partial\mathcal{C}$ the boundary of $\mathcal{C}$, and by $\mathcal{C}^c$ its complement. $\mathcal{B}_p^n(\mathbf{x}, \alpha)$ denotes a closed p-norm ball of radius $\alpha \in \mathbb{R}_+$ about a point $\mathbf{x}$ in $\mathbb{R}^n$, and $\mathcal{S}_p^{n-1}$ the codimension one boundary $\partial\mathcal{B}_p^n(0, 1)$ of the unit ball centered at the origin.

A *ray* in $\mathbb{R}^n$ is the set of points $\vec{r} = \{\mathbf{r}_0 + s\mathbf{r}_d \mid s \in \mathbb{R}_+\}$, where $\mathbf{r}_0 \in \mathbb{R}^n$ is the *origin* of the ray, and $\mathbf{r}_d \in \mathbb{R}^n$ is a unit vector giving the *direction* of the ray.

We denote by $\mathrm{conv}(\{\mathbf{v}_0, \ldots, \mathbf{v}_N\})$ the convex hull of the points $\mathbf{v}_0, \ldots, \mathbf{v}_N$, and by $\mathrm{vol}(\mathcal{C})$ the volume of a set $\mathcal{C}$.

Finally, consider the LTI system of the form:

$$\dot{\mathbf{x}}(t) = f(\mathbf{x}(t), \mathbf{u}(t)) = A\mathbf{x}(t) + B\mathbf{u}(t), \quad \mathbf{x}(0) = \mathbf{x}_0 \qquad (1)$$

with a finite-dimensional normed vector state space $\mathcal{X} := \mathbb{R}^n$, state vector $\mathbf{x}(t) \in \mathcal{X}$, and control input $\mathbf{u}(t) \in \mathcal{U}$, where $\mathcal{U}$ is a compact convex subset of $\mathbb{R}^m$. A and B are constant matrices of appropriate dimensions. We are concerned with the evolution of the system over the interval $\mathbb{T} := [0, \tau]$ with arbitrary, finite time horizon $\tau \in \mathbb{R}_+$. We denote by $N_\delta := \tau/\delta \in \mathbb{Z}_+$ the number of sampling intervals in $\mathbb{T}$. Since we are concerned with sampled-data systems, the input signal draws from the set of piecewise constant functions

$$\begin{aligned} \mathscr{U}_{\mathbb{T}}^{\mathrm{pw}} := \{\mathbf{u} \colon \mathbb{T} \to \mathbb{R}^m \text{ piecewise const., } \mathbf{u}(t_k) \in \mathcal{U}\ \forall k, \\ \mathbf{u}(t) = \mathbf{u}(t_k)\ \forall t \in [t_k, t_{k+1})\}. \end{aligned} \qquad (2)$$

For every $\mathbf{x}_0 \in \mathcal{X}$ and $\mathbf{u}(\cdot) \in \mathscr{U}_{\mathbb{T}}^{\mathrm{pw}}$, we denote the (unique) trajectory of (1) by $\mathbf{x}_{\mathbf{x}_0}^{\mathbf{u}} : \mathbb{T} \to \mathcal{X}$ with initial condition $\mathbf{x}_{\mathbf{x}_0}^{\mathbf{u}}(0) = \mathbf{x}_0$. When clear from the context, we shall drop the subscript and superscript from the trajectory notation.

For a nonempty compact convex state constraint set $\mathcal{A} \subset \mathcal{X}$ (deemed *safe*), we examine the following backward construct:

Definition 1 (Sampled-Data Viability Kernel). *The finite-horizon sampled-data viability kernel of $\mathcal{A}$ is the set of all initial states in $\mathcal{A}$ for which there exists a control law such that the trajectories emanating from those states remain in $\mathcal{A}$ over the horizon $\mathbb{T}$:*

$$\begin{aligned} \mathrm{Viab}_{\mathbb{T}}^{\mathrm{sd}}(\mathcal{A}) := \{\mathbf{x}_0 \in \mathcal{A} \mid \exists \mathbf{u}(\cdot) \in \mathscr{U}_{\mathbb{T}}^{\mathrm{pw}}, \\ \text{s.t. } \mathbf{x}_{\mathbf{x}_0}^{\mathbf{u}}(t) \in \mathcal{A}\ \forall t \in \mathbb{T}\}. \end{aligned} \qquad (3)$$

We note that any approximation to the viability kernel must be in the form of an under-approximation in order to guarantee safety; thus the goal of our algorithm will be to find an efficient and scalable technique that under-approximates the viability kernel.

2. THE SAMPLING-BASED REACHABILITY ALGORITHM

At a high level the algorithm we propose works by sampling from points in $\mathcal{A}$. We then verify whether each sampled point is within the viability kernel by formulating a convex program which attempts to find a piecewise constant control input that keeps the system trajectory, starting from the sampled point, inside the safe set $\mathcal{A}$ over the period $\mathbb{T}$. If such a control signal can be found, then the sampled point is inside the viability kernel. Finally, since we are working with linear systems, we use the fact that the sets $\mathcal{U}$ and $\mathcal{A}$ are convex to construct an under-approximation to the viability kernel from the convex hull of the sampled points.

2.1 Checking Point Feasibility

An important aspect of our algorithm is that it constructs an approximation to the viability kernel by iteratively adding to a list of points known to be just inside its boundary. To do this we need a way of checking whether or not a sampled point $\mathbf{x}_0$ is in $\mathrm{Viab}_{\mathbb{T}}^{\mathrm{sd}}(\mathcal{A})$. We will call a point *feasible* if it is inside the viability kernel, and *infeasible* otherwise.

2.1.1 From Continuous to Pointwise Feasibility

By definition if we can find a piecewise constant control signal $\mathbf{u}(\cdot)$ such that $\mathbf{x}_{\mathbf{x}_0}^{\mathbf{u}}(t) \in \mathcal{A}\ \forall t \in \mathbb{T}$, then $\mathbf{x}_0 \in \mathrm{Viab}_{\mathbb{T}}^{\mathrm{sd}}(\mathcal{A})$. Of course without an analytical representation for the trajectory $\mathbf{x}_{\mathbf{x}_0}^{\mathbf{u}}(t)$, checking that all points along the trajectory are within $\mathcal{A}$ is impossible. Thus instead of verifying that the entire trajectory is inside the safe set, we will instead verify that discrete points $\mathbf{x}_k := \mathbf{x}_{\mathbf{x}_0}^{\mathbf{u}}(t_k)$ are within $\mathcal{A}$. However, since the trajectories in between two sampling instants could escape safety even when the end points are within $\mathcal{A}$ (Figure 1(a)), we will instead verify that the points are within an appropriately constructed subset of $\mathcal{A}$ such that the entire trajectory is guaranteed to maintain safety. The following lemma describes how to construct such a subset, called $\mathcal{A}_\downarrow$.

Lemma 1 ([15]). *Suppose that f is uniformly bounded on $\mathcal{A}$ in some norm $\|\cdot\|_{p_1}$ by M. With a sampling interval $\delta > 0$,*

[1] Note that even though some systems can be treated continuously because the controllers run at a much higher frequency than the time scales of the system dynamics, there are still many systems for which this is not the case, such as the automated anesthesia system described in [21].

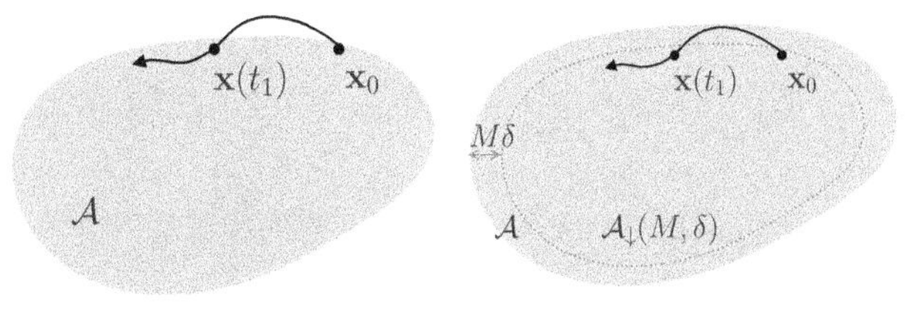

(a) (b)

Figure 1: (a) Even though the sampled points x_0 and $x(t_1)$ are contained in $\mathcal{A}$, the continuous trajectory may not be. (b) Erosion of the set $\mathcal{A}$ ensures that the curvature of the continuous trajectory in between two sampling time instants does not escape safety.

define a set

$$\begin{aligned}\mathcal{A}_{\downarrow}(M,\delta) &:= \{\mathbf{x} \in \mathcal{A} \mid \mathrm{dist}_{p1}(\mathbf{x}, \mathcal{A}^c) \geq M\delta\} \\ &= \mathcal{A} \ominus \mathcal{B}^n_{p1}(0, M\delta).\end{aligned} \tag{4}$$

For a given initial condition $\mathbf{x}_0$*, if there exists a piecewise constant control signal* $\mathbf{u}(\cdot) \in \mathscr{U}^{\mathrm{pw}}_{\mathbb{T}}$ *such that* $\mathbf{x}(t_k) \in \mathcal{A}_{\downarrow}(M,\delta)$ $\forall k \in \{0,\dots,N_\delta\}$*, then* $\mathbf{x}_0 \in \mathrm{Viab}^{\mathrm{sd}}_{\mathbb{T}}(\mathcal{A})$.

PROOF. Over any sampling interval $[t_k, t_{k+1}]$ the trajectory can travel a distance of at most

$$\|\mathbf{x}(t_{k+1}) - \mathbf{x}(t_k)\|_{p_1} \leq \int_{t_k}^{t_k+\delta} \|\dot{\mathbf{x}}(\lambda)\|_{p_1} d\lambda \leq M\delta. \tag{5}$$

Thus for any $s \in [t_k, t_{k+1})$ we have that

$$\|\mathbf{x}(s) - \mathbf{x}(t_k)\|_{p_1} \leq M(s - t_k) < M\delta. \tag{6}$$

Since $\mathbf{x}(t_k) \in \mathcal{A}_{\downarrow}(M,\delta)$, we know that $\mathrm{dist}_{p_1}(\mathbf{x}(t_k), \mathcal{A}^c) \geq M\delta$. Therefore,

$$\begin{aligned}\mathrm{dist}_{p_1}(\mathbf{x}(s), \mathcal{A}^c) &\geq \mathrm{dist}_{p_1}(\mathbf{x}(t_k), \mathcal{A}^c) - \|\mathbf{x}(s) - \mathbf{x}(t_k)\|_{p_1} \\ &> M\delta - M\delta = 0.\end{aligned} \tag{7}$$

Thus $\mathbf{x}(t) \in \mathcal{A}$ over any closed sub-interval $[t_k, t_{k+1}]$ and therefore $\mathbf{x}(t) \in \mathcal{A}\ \forall t \in \mathbb{T}$. Hence, $\mathbf{x}_0 \in \mathrm{Viab}^{\mathrm{sd}}_{\mathbb{T}}(\mathcal{A})$. □

We have thus reduced a continuous feasibility problem (checking if an entire trajectory is in $\mathcal{A}$) to a pointwise feasibility problem (checking if the points $\mathbf{x}_k$ are in $\mathcal{A}_{\downarrow}$, see Figure 1(b)).

2.1.2 Discretization Error

To solve this pointwise feasibility problem we will use forward simulation to determine whether a piecewise constant control signal exists that satisfies $\mathbf{x}(t_k) \in \mathcal{A}_{\downarrow}\ \forall k \in \{0,\dots,N_\delta\}$ when applied to the true sampled-data system. To do this we will use a finite-difference approximation of the dynamics, and thus need to take into account the effect of the discretization error introduced by the truncation of the Taylor series expansion of the dynamics [1].

Recall that the solution $\mathbf{x}_{k+1} = \mathbf{x}(t_{k+1})$ of the sampled-data system (1) at time t_{k+1} for any sampling interval $[t_k, t_k+\delta]$ starting from $\mathbf{x}_k = \mathbf{x}(t_k)$ using a constant input $\mathbf{u}_k$ is given by

$$\mathbf{x}_{k+1} = e^{A\delta}\mathbf{x}_k + \int_0^\delta e^{A(\delta-r)}B\mathbf{u}_k dr \tag{8}$$

$$= e^{A\delta}\mathbf{x}_k + \left(\int_0^\delta e^{A\lambda} d\lambda \cdot B\right)\mathbf{u}_k. \tag{9}$$

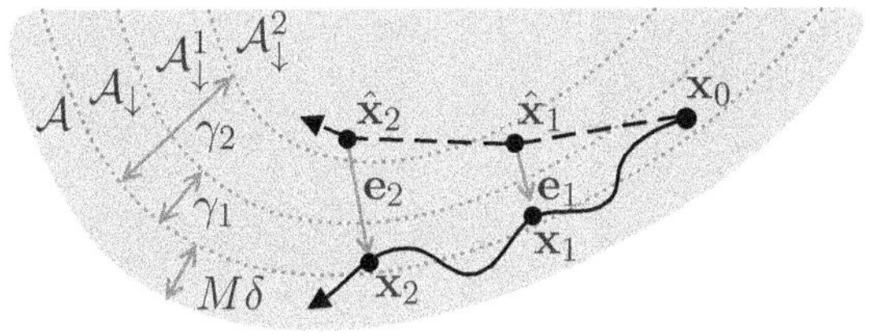

Figure 2: The discretization error $\mathbf{e}_k$ due to the mismatch between the true sampled-data state $\mathbf{x}_k = \mathbf{x}(t_k)$ at sampling time t_k and the nominal state $\hat{\mathbf{x}}_k$ of the discretized system propagates in time. If not accounted for in forward simulations, this mismatch could jeopardize the safety of the sampled-data system. By ensuring that $\hat{\mathbf{x}}_k \in \mathcal{A}^k_{\downarrow}$, we can guarantee $\mathbf{x}_k \in \mathcal{A}_{\downarrow}$ and thus guarantee safety.

Consider the Taylor series expansion of the matrix exponential

$$e^{As} = \sum_{i=0}^{\infty} \frac{(As)^i}{i!}. \tag{10}$$

We approximate the above infinite sum by a ζ-th order finite sum

$$A_s := \sum_{i=0}^{\zeta} \frac{(As)^i}{i!} \approx e^{As}, \quad \zeta < \infty \tag{11}$$

with *truncation error*

$$E_s := e^{As} - A_s = \sum_{i=\zeta+1}^{\infty} \frac{(As)^i}{i!}. \tag{12}$$

The trajectory of the resulting finite-difference equation is

$$\hat{\mathbf{x}}_{k+1} = A_\delta \hat{\mathbf{x}}_k + \left(\int_0^\delta A_\lambda d\lambda \cdot B\right)\mathbf{u}_k. \tag{13}$$

We denote $\hat{\mathbf{x}}$ as the *nominal* state of the system.

Truncating the tail of the Taylor series expansion introduces a *discretization error* $\mathbf{e}_k$ that results in a mismatch between the true values of the system trajectory $\mathbf{x}_k = \mathbf{x}(t_k)$ at discrete time instants and the values generated by the finite-difference model, i.e. $\hat{\mathbf{x}}_k = \mathbf{x}_k - \mathbf{e}_k$. Thus to guarantee an under-approximation of the viability kernel using a pointwise feasibility check, we must take into account this error and its forward propagation in time (Figure 2).

LEMMA 2. *Suppose that there exist constants* $\gamma_k \geq 0$ *and a norm* $\|\cdot\|_{p_2}$ *such that* $\|\mathbf{e}_k\|_{p_2} \leq \gamma_k\ \forall k$*. Let*

$$\mathcal{A}^k_{\downarrow}(M,\delta,\gamma_k) := \mathcal{A}_{\downarrow}(M,\delta) \ominus \mathcal{B}^n_{p_2}(0,\gamma_k) \neq \emptyset. \tag{14}$$

Then we have that

$$\hat{\mathbf{x}}_k \in \mathcal{A}^k_{\downarrow}(M,\delta,\gamma_k) \Rightarrow \mathbf{x}_k \in \mathcal{A}_{\downarrow}(M,\delta). \tag{15}$$

PROOF. Since $\mathbf{e}_k \in \mathcal{B}^n_{p_2}(0,\gamma_k)$, regardless of the perturbation caused by the error, we have $\mathbf{x}_k \in \hat{\mathbf{x}}_k \oplus \mathcal{B}^n_{p_2}(0,\gamma_k)$. By enforcing $\hat{\mathbf{x}}_k \in \mathcal{A}^k_{\downarrow}(M,\delta,\gamma_k)$ we guarantee that

$$\mathbf{x}_k \in \left(\mathcal{A}_{\downarrow}(M,\delta) \ominus \mathcal{B}^n_{p_2}(0,\gamma_k)\right) \oplus \mathcal{B}^n_{p_2}(0,\gamma_k) \subseteq \mathcal{A}_{\downarrow}(M,\delta), \tag{16}$$

since for every two sets $\mathcal{X}$ and $\mathcal{Y}$ we have $(\mathcal{X} \ominus \mathcal{Y}) \oplus \mathcal{Y} \subseteq \mathcal{X}$ (Figure 2). □

For any initial condition $\mathbf{x}_0$ we trivially have that $e_0 = 0$ and thus $\mathcal{A}^0_{\downarrow}(M,\delta,\gamma_0) = \mathcal{A}_{\downarrow}(M,\delta)$. We now describe a procedure to compute error bounds γ_k for $k \in \{1,\dots,N_\delta\}$ which will be used for *a priori* (offline) construction of the sets $\mathcal{A}^k_{\downarrow}(M,\delta,\gamma_k)$.

Using the identity $e^{As} = A_s + E_s$ in equation (9) yields

$$\mathbf{x}_k = (A_\delta + E_\delta)\mathbf{x}_{k-1} + \left(\int_0^\delta (A_\lambda + E_\lambda) d\lambda \cdot B\right) \mathbf{u}_{k-1}$$
$$= \underbrace{A_\delta \mathbf{x}_{k-1} + \left(\int_0^\delta A_\lambda d\lambda \cdot B\right) \mathbf{u}_{k-1}}_{\hat{\mathbf{x}}_k} +$$
$$\underbrace{E_\delta \mathbf{x}_{k-1} + \left(\int_0^\delta E_\lambda d\lambda \cdot B\right) \mathbf{u}_{k-1}}_{\mathbf{e}_k}. \quad (17)$$

Recall that for any discrete-time LTI system $\mathbf{x}_k = \Phi \mathbf{x}_{k-1} + \Psi \mathbf{u}_{k-1}$ we can rewrite the solution $\mathbf{x}_k$ in terms of the initial condition $\mathbf{x}_0$ and the past inputs as

$$\mathbf{x}_k = \Phi^k \mathbf{x}_0 + \sum_{i=0}^{k-1} \Phi^i \Psi \mathbf{u}_{k-1-i}. \quad (18)$$

Back-substituting the solutions $\mathbf{x}_{k-1}$ into $\mathbf{x}_k$, and $\hat{\mathbf{x}}_{k-1}$ into $\hat{\mathbf{x}}_k$ for every $k = 1, \ldots, N_\delta$ we can rewrite $\mathbf{e}_k = \mathbf{x}_k - \hat{\mathbf{x}}_k$ as

$$\mathbf{e}_k = \left((A_\delta + E_\delta)^k - A_\delta^k\right) \mathbf{x}_0 +$$
$$\sum_{i=0}^{k-1} \Big[\left((A_\delta + E_\delta)^i - A_\delta^i\right) \int_0^\delta A_\lambda d\lambda +$$
$$(A_\delta + E_\delta)^i \int_0^\delta E_\lambda d\lambda\Big] B \mathbf{u}_{k-1-i}. \quad (19)$$

To compute the upper-bound γ_k on (19), invoke

i) the inequality $\|A^k\| \leq \|A\|^k$ which holds for any matrix A and positive constant k,
ii) the multiplicative and triangular inequalities, and
iii) the binomial expansion for $(A_\delta + E_\delta)^k$ (which is valid since $A_s E_s = E_s A_s$ [31]).

We obtain

$$\|\mathbf{e}_k\| \leq \left\|(A_\delta + E_\delta)^k - A_\delta^k\right\| \|\mathbf{x}_0\|$$
$$+ \sum_{i=0}^{k-1} \Big[\left\|\left((A_\delta + E_\delta)^i - A_\delta^i\right) \int_0^\delta A_\lambda d\lambda\right\|$$
$$+ \left\|(A_\delta + E_\delta)^i \int_0^\delta E_\lambda d\lambda\right\|\Big] \sup_{u \in \mathcal{U}} \|B\mathbf{u}\| \quad (20)$$
$$\leq \left\|\sum_{l=0}^{k} \binom{k}{l} A_\delta^l E_\delta^{k-l} - A_\delta^k\right\| \|\mathbf{x}_0\|$$
$$+ \sum_{i=0}^{k-1} \Big[\left\|\sum_{l=0}^{i} \binom{i}{l} A_\delta^l E_\delta^{i-l} - A_\delta^i\right\| \left\|\int_0^\delta A_\lambda d\lambda\right\|$$
$$+ \|A_\delta + E_\delta\|^i \left\|\int_0^\delta E_\lambda d\lambda\right\|\Big] \sup_{u \in \mathcal{U}} \|B\mathbf{u}\|. \quad (21)$$

For $k > 1$ we find

$$\|\mathbf{e}_k\| \leq \sum_{l=0}^{k-1} \binom{k}{l} \left\|A_\delta^l\right\| \|E_\delta\|^{k-l} \|\mathbf{x}_0\|$$
$$+ \sum_{i=1}^{k-1} \Big[\sum_{l=0}^{i-1} \binom{i}{l} \left\|A_\delta^l\right\| \|E_\delta\|^{i-l} \left\|\int_0^\delta A_\lambda d\lambda\right\|$$
$$+ (\|A_\delta\| + \|E_\delta\|)^i \left\|\int_0^\delta E_\lambda d\lambda\right\|\Big] \sup_{u \in \mathcal{U}} \|B\mathbf{u}\|, \quad (22)$$

and for $k = 1$ this inequality is

$$\|\mathbf{e}_1\| \leq \|E_\delta\| \|\mathbf{x}_0\| + \left\|\int_0^\delta E_\lambda d\lambda\right\| \sup_{u \in \mathcal{U}} \|B\mathbf{u}\|. \quad (23)$$

The term $\int_0^\delta A_\lambda d\lambda$ is a definite integral of a finite sum. Therefore, it can be easily computed:

$$\int_0^\delta A_\lambda d\lambda = \int_0^\delta \sum_{i=0}^{\zeta} \frac{(A\lambda)^i}{i!} d\lambda = \sum_{i=0}^{\zeta} \frac{A^i \delta^{i+1}}{(i+1)!}. \quad (24)$$

Evaluating $\int_0^\delta E_\lambda d\lambda$ and $\|E_\delta\|$ is trickier. We can, however, formulate upper-bounds on their infinity norm. To do so, we use the following property [19]:

$$\|E_\delta\|_\infty \leq \sum_{i=\zeta+1}^{\infty} \frac{(\|A\|_\infty \delta)^i}{i!} \quad (25)$$
$$\leq \frac{(\|A\|_\infty \delta)^{\zeta+1}}{(\zeta+1)!} \cdot (1 + \varepsilon + \varepsilon^2 + \cdots) \quad (26)$$
$$\leq \frac{(\|A\|_\infty \delta)^{\zeta+1}}{(\zeta+1)!} \cdot \frac{1}{1-\varepsilon}, \quad \varepsilon := \frac{\|A\|_\infty \delta}{\zeta+2}, \quad (27)$$

where the order of approximation ζ is chosen such that $\varepsilon < 1$. Denote (27) as

$$\psi_\delta := \frac{(\|A\|_\infty \delta)^{\zeta+1}}{(\zeta+1)!} \cdot \frac{1}{1-\varepsilon}. \quad (28)$$

Similarly we have that

$$\left\|\int_0^\delta E_\lambda d\lambda\right\|_\infty \leq \int_0^\delta \|E_\lambda\|_\infty d\lambda \leq \int_0^\delta \sum_{i=\zeta+1}^{\infty} \frac{\|A\|_\infty^i \lambda^i}{i!} d\lambda$$
$$= \sum_{i=\zeta+1}^{\infty} \int_0^\delta \frac{\|A\|_\infty^i \lambda^i}{i!} d\lambda = \sum_{i=\zeta+1}^{\infty} \frac{\|A\|_\infty^i \delta^{i+1}}{(i+1)!}$$
$$\leq \frac{\|A\|_\infty^{\zeta+1} \delta^{\zeta+2}}{(\zeta+2)!} \cdot (1 + \eta + \eta^2 + \cdots) \quad (29)$$
$$\leq \frac{\|A\|_\infty^{\zeta+1} \delta^{\zeta+2}}{(\zeta+2)!} \cdot \frac{1}{1-\eta}, \quad \eta := \frac{\|A\|_\infty \delta}{\zeta+3} \quad (30)$$

(and note that since $\eta < \varepsilon$, $\varepsilon < 1 \Rightarrow \eta < 1$). Denote (30) as

$$\phi_\delta := \frac{\|A\|_\infty^{\zeta+1} \delta^{\zeta+2}}{(\zeta+2)!} \cdot \frac{1}{1-\eta}. \quad (31)$$

Substituting (24), (27), and (30) in (23) and (22) for the infinity norm we obtain a conservative upper-bound on the error:

$$\|\mathbf{e}_1\|_\infty \leq \psi_\delta \|\mathbf{x}_0\|_\infty + \phi_\delta \sup_{u \in \mathcal{U}} \|B\mathbf{u}\|_\infty =: \tilde{\gamma}_1 \quad (32)$$

and, for $k > 1$,

$$\|\mathbf{e}_k\|_\infty \leq \sum_{l=0}^{k-1} \binom{k}{l} \left\|A_\delta^l\right\|_\infty \psi_\delta^{k-l} \|\mathbf{x}_0\|_\infty$$
$$+ \sum_{i=1}^{k-1} \Big[\sum_{l=0}^{i-1} \binom{i}{l} \left\|A_\delta^l\right\|_\infty \psi_\delta^{i-l} \left\|\sum_{j=0}^{\zeta} \frac{A^j \delta^{j+1}}{(j+1)!}\right\|_\infty$$
$$+ \left(\|A_\delta\|_\infty + \psi_\delta\right)^i \phi_\delta\Big] \sup_{u \in \mathcal{U}} \|B\mathbf{u}\|_\infty$$
$$=: \tilde{\gamma}_k. \quad (33)$$

Using $\tilde{\gamma}_k$ in (32)–(33) in Lemma 2 will allow us to check for feasibility of a given point $\mathbf{x}_0$ via only the nominal (finite-difference approximation) system, while ensuring that safety will not be violated due to discretization error.

REMARK 1. *The bound $\tilde{\gamma}_k$ is asymptotically tight in the sense that for any k, $\lim_{\zeta\to\infty} \tilde{\gamma}_k = 0$.*

In practice, the chosen order of approximation ζ must be large enough such that it ensures convergence of the power series in (26) (and thus (29)) as well as non-emptiness of the eroded sets $\mathcal{A}_{\downarrow}^{k}(M,\delta,\tilde{\gamma}_k)$ in Lemma 2.

2.1.3 Verifying Feasibility via Forward Simulation

We can now use the discretized model

$$\hat{\mathbf{x}}_{k+1} = A_\delta \hat{\mathbf{x}}_k + \underbrace{\left(\int_0^\delta A_\lambda d\lambda \cdot B\right)}_{B_\delta} \mathbf{u}_k \tag{34}$$

to determine feasibility of a given initial condition $\mathbf{x}_0$ without worrying about the impact on safety of the discretization error or the behavior of the continuous trajectory of (1) in between sampling times. If there exists a sequence of controls $\{\mathbf{u}_k\}$ so that the nominal states $\hat{\mathbf{x}}_k$ of the closed-loop system belong to the precomputed sets $\mathcal{A}_{\downarrow}^{k}(M,\delta,\tilde{\gamma}_k)$ described above, then via Lemmas 2 and 1 the trajectories of the original sampled-data system will never exit $\mathcal{A}$.

We can construct the prediction equation as

$$\begin{bmatrix} \hat{\mathbf{x}}_0 \\ \hat{\mathbf{x}}_1 \\ \hat{\mathbf{x}}_2 \\ \vdots \\ \hat{\mathbf{x}}_{N_\delta} \end{bmatrix} = \underbrace{\begin{bmatrix} I \\ A_\delta \\ A_\delta^2 \\ \vdots \\ A_\delta^{N_\delta} \end{bmatrix}}_{G} \mathbf{x}_0 + \underbrace{\begin{bmatrix} 0 & 0 & \dots & 0 \\ B_\delta & 0 & \dots & 0 \\ A_\delta B_\delta & B_\delta & \dots & 0 \\ \vdots & \vdots & \ddots & \vdots \\ A_\delta^{N_\delta-1} B_\delta & A_\delta^{N_\delta-2} B_\delta & \dots & B_\delta \end{bmatrix}}_{H} \underbrace{\begin{bmatrix} \mathbf{u}_0 \\ \mathbf{u}_1 \\ \vdots \\ \mathbf{u}_{N_\delta-1} \end{bmatrix}}_{U}, \tag{35}$$

and formulate the finite horizon feasibility program

$$\begin{aligned} \min_{U}.\quad & 0 && (36a) \\ \text{s.t.}\quad & U \in \mathcal{U}^{N_\delta} && (36b) \\ & \hat{\mathbf{x}}_k \in \mathcal{A}_{\downarrow}^{k}(M,\delta,\tilde{\gamma}_k), \quad k = 0,\dots,N_\delta && (36c) \\ & \begin{bmatrix} \hat{\mathbf{x}}_0 & \cdots & \hat{\mathbf{x}}_{N_\delta} \end{bmatrix}^T = G\mathbf{x}_0 + HU. && (36d) \end{aligned}$$

THEOREM 1. *If $\exists U^*$ satisfying (36), then $\mathbf{x}_0 \in \mathrm{Viab}_{\mathbb{T}}^{\mathrm{sd}}(\mathcal{A})$.*

PROOF. The proof follows directly from Lemmas 1 and 2. For a fixed input sequence U the prediction equation (35) generates a forward simulation of the trajectory of the finite-difference system (34) over the horizon $[0, N_\delta]$ corresponding to the continuous time horizon $[0, N_\delta \delta] = \mathbb{T}$. Constraint (36b) ensures that this input sequence is point-wise admissible, while constraint (36c) restricts $\hat{\mathbf{x}}_k$ so that the trajectory of the sampled-data system (1) evaluated at t_k belongs to $\mathcal{A}_{\downarrow}(M,\delta)$ since via Lemma 2, $\hat{\mathbf{x}}_k \in \mathcal{A}_{\downarrow}^{k}(M,\delta,\tilde{\gamma}_k) \Rightarrow \mathbf{x}_k = \mathbf{x}(t_k) \in \mathcal{A}_{\downarrow}(M,\delta)$. Lemma 1 then automatically guarantees $\mathbf{x}(t) \in \mathcal{A}\ \forall t \in [0,\tau]$ which implies $\mathbf{x}_0 \in \mathrm{Viab}_{\mathbb{T}}^{\mathrm{sd}}(\mathcal{A})$. □

In terms of practical implementation, if $\mathcal{U} = \{\mathbf{u} \in \mathbb{R}^m \mid \mathbf{u}_{\min} \le \mathbf{u} \le \mathbf{u}_{\max}\}$ for some limits $\mathbf{u}_{\min}$ and $\mathbf{u}_{\max}$, and the sets $\mathcal{A}_{\downarrow}^{k}(M,\delta,\tilde{\gamma}_k)$ are represented by polytopes $\{\mathbf{x} \mid P_k\mathbf{x} \le \mathbf{p}_k\}$, then to determine if a given point $\mathbf{x}_0$ is feasible we can simply check for feasibility of the linear convex program

$$\begin{aligned} \min_{U}.\quad & 0 && (37a) \\ \text{s.t.}\quad & \mathbf{1}_{N_\delta} \otimes \mathbf{u}_{\min} \le I_{N_\delta m} U \le \mathbf{1}_{N_\delta} \otimes \mathbf{u}_{\max} && (37b) \\ & P_k \hat{\mathbf{x}}_k \le \mathbf{p}_k, \quad k = 0,\dots,N_\delta && (37c) \\ & \begin{bmatrix} \hat{\mathbf{x}}_0 & \cdots & \hat{\mathbf{x}}_{N_\delta} \end{bmatrix}^T = G\mathbf{x}_0 + HU, && (37d) \end{aligned}$$

where $\otimes$ denotes the Kronecker product.[2]

In the algorithm below we will encapsulate Theorem 1 to determine the feasibility of a given sample point $\mathbf{x}_0$ in the subroutine FEASIBLE. Its computational complexity is proportional to the complexity of the program (36), which in turn depends only on the shape of the sets $\mathcal{U}$ and $\mathcal{A}$.

2.2 Additional Subroutines

In addition to the feasibility-checking subroutine FEASIBLE described above, our algorithm will also make use of the following subroutines which we describe in less detail due to their more straightforward nature.

- FIND-INTERSECTION-ON-BOUNDARY$(\mathcal{C}, \vec{r})$ – Input: A convex compact set $\mathcal{C} \subset \mathcal{X}$, and a ray $\vec{r}$ with origin $\mathbf{r}_0 \in \mathcal{C}$. Returns a point $\mathbf{x}$ along the ray $\vec{r}$ on ∂C. We note that since $\mathcal{C}$ is convex and compact, and since $\mathbf{r}_0 \in \mathcal{C}$, there is exactly one such point $\mathbf{x}$. Runs in time proportional to the number of faces of $\mathcal{C}$ if $\mathcal{C}$ is a polytope, and constant time if $\mathcal{C}$ is an ellipsoid.
- SAMPLE-RAY$(\mathbf{x})$ – Input: A point $\mathbf{x} \in \mathbb{R}^n$. First samples a point $\mathbf{r}_d \in \mathcal{S}_2^{n-1}$ at random[3] from the Euclidean unit ball in $\mathbb{R}^n$, then returns the ray $\vec{r} = \{\mathbf{x} + s\mathbf{r}_d\}$, i.e. a ray with random direction and origin $\mathbf{x}$. Runs in time linear in n.

We will also use BISECTION-FEASIBILITY-SEARCH$(\mathbf{a}, \mathbf{b}, \mathcal{A})$ as defined in Algorithm 1, which searches along the line segment between $\mathbf{a}$ and $\mathbf{b}$ to find a point $\mathbf{c}$ such that $\mathrm{dist}_p(\mathbf{c}, \partial\,\mathrm{Viab}_{\mathbb{T}}^{\mathrm{sd}}(\mathcal{A})) < \epsilon$.

Algorithm 1 Determines an ϵ-accurate intersection of $\partial\,\mathrm{Viab}_{\mathbb{T}}^{\mathrm{sd}}(\mathcal{A})$ on the line segment between $\mathbf{a}$ and $\mathbf{b}$.

```
function BISECTION-FEASIBILITY-SEARCH(a, b, A)
    c ← a + (b − a)/2
    if FEASIBLE(c, A) then
        if dist_p(b, c) < ε then
            return c
        else
            return BISECTION-FEASIBILITY-SEARCH(c, b, A)
        end if
    else
        return BISECTION-FEASIBILITY-SEARCH(a, c, A)
    end if
end function
```

[2] A similar quadratically-constrained program can be formulated if the state or input constraints are instead represented by ellipsoids. Additionally, if the system being analyzed is a switched system then the LP (37) becomes a Mixed-Integer LP. Both extensions are straightforward, and are omitted due to space constraints.

[3] Any probability distribution may be used; for our implementation in the examples that follow we used the uniform distribution.

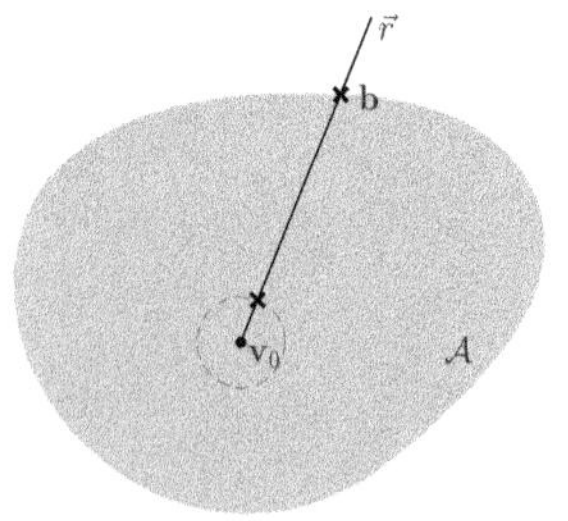

(a) Sample a ray $\vec{r}$ at random, and find $\mathbf{b}$, its intersection with $\mathcal{A}$ (lines 4 and 5).

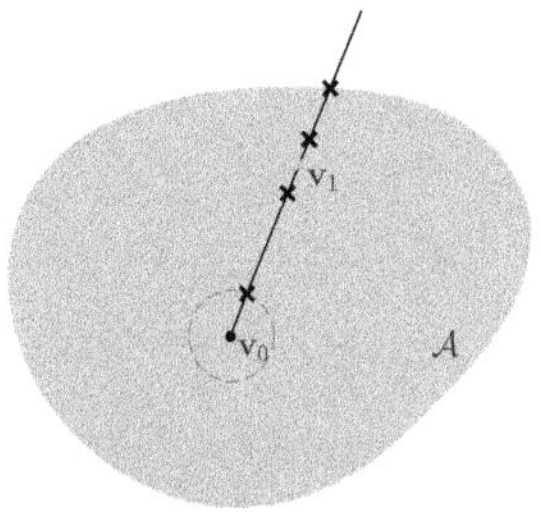

(b) Perform a bisection search along $\vec{r}$ between $\mathbf{v}_0$ and $\mathbf{b}$ to find $\mathbf{v}_1 \in \mathrm{Viab}_{\mathbb{T}}^{\mathrm{sd}}(\mathcal{A})$, where $\mathrm{dist}_p(\mathbf{v}_1, \partial\,\mathrm{Viab}_{\mathbb{T}}^{\mathrm{sd}}(\mathcal{A})) < \epsilon$ (line 6).

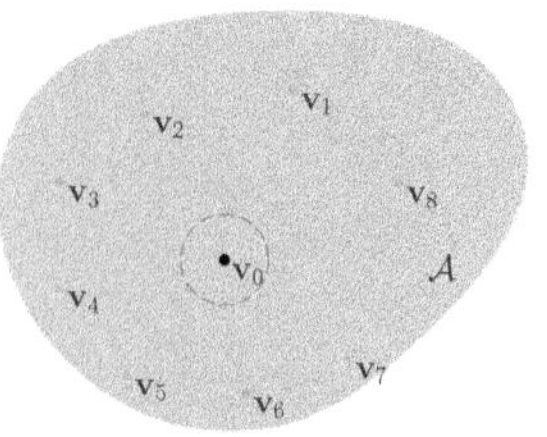

(c) Repeat this procedure for N samples.

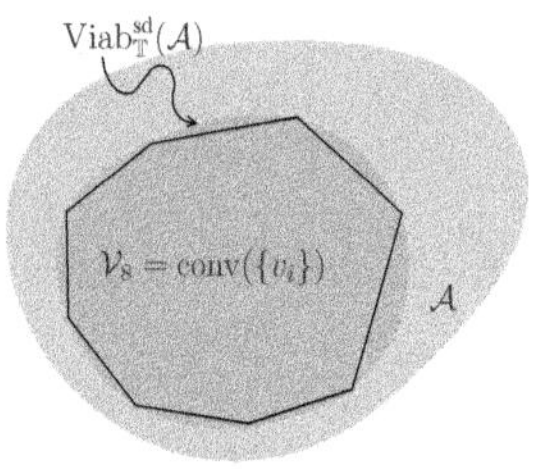

(d) Return the polytope $\mathcal{V}_N := \mathrm{conv}(\{\mathbf{v}_0, \ldots, \mathbf{v}_N\})$.

Figure 3: Illustration of Algorithm 2.

2.3 The Algorithm

Given the subroutines described above, our algorithm for computing a polytopic under-approximation of the viability kernel for an LTI sampled-data system is given by Algorithm 2. It proceeds as follows (see Figure 3). We assume as input a description of the safe constraint set $\mathcal{A}$, as well as some initial point $\mathbf{v}_0 \in \mathrm{Viab}_{\mathbb{T}}^{\mathrm{sd}}(\mathcal{A})$.[4] We then construct a polytopic approximation of $\mathrm{Viab}_{\mathbb{T}}^{\mathrm{sd}}(\mathcal{A})$ by iteratively sampling a direction $\vec{r}$ (line 4); finding the point $\mathbf{b} \in \mathbb{R}^n$ where the ray with that direction (centered at $\mathbf{v}_0$) intersects the boundary of the safe set $\mathcal{A}$ (line 5); and then performing a bisection search between $\mathbf{v}_0$ and $\mathbf{b}$ until we find a point $\mathbf{v}_i$ such that $\mathbf{v}_i \in \mathrm{Viab}_{\mathbb{T}}^{\mathrm{sd}}(\mathcal{A})$ and $\mathrm{dist}_p(\mathbf{v}_i, \partial\,\mathrm{Viab}_{\mathbb{T}}^{\mathrm{sd}}(\mathcal{A})) < \epsilon$ in some desired norm $\|\cdot\|_p$ (see Algorithm 1). By taking the convex hull of these points $\{\mathbf{v}_0, \ldots, \mathbf{v}_N\}$ we arrive at a polytope $\mathcal{V}_N \subseteq \mathrm{Viab}_{\mathbb{T}}^{\mathrm{sd}}(\mathcal{A})$ which converges to $\mathrm{Viab}_{\mathbb{T}}^{\mathrm{sd}}(\mathcal{A})$ (in a manner we will formalize after we have proved the algorithm's correctness).

3. ALGORITHM PROPERTIES

3.1 Correctness

THEOREM 2. *Given convex sets $\mathcal{A}$ and $\mathcal{U}$ and an initial point $\mathbf{v}_0 \in \mathrm{Viab}_{\mathbb{T}}^{\mathrm{sd}}(\mathcal{A})$, and let $\mathcal{V}_N =$* POLYTOPIC-APPROX$(\mathcal{A}, \mathbf{v}_0, N)$, *then $\mathcal{V}_N \subseteq \mathrm{Viab}_{\mathbb{T}}^{\mathrm{sd}}(\mathcal{A})$.*

PROOF. We use proof by induction. First, it is obvious that for $N = 0$, $\mathcal{V}_0 =$ POLYTOPIC-APPROX$(\mathcal{A}, \mathbf{v}_0, 0) = \mathrm{conv}(\{\mathbf{v}_0\}) \subseteq \mathrm{Viab}_{\mathbb{T}}^{\mathrm{sd}}(\mathcal{A})$, since we are given that $\mathbf{v}_0 \in \mathrm{Viab}_{\mathbb{T}}^{\mathrm{sd}}(\mathcal{A})$.

[4]For linear systems we have that if $0 \in \mathcal{A}$ and $0 \in \mathcal{U}$, then $0 \in \mathrm{Viab}_{\mathbb{T}}^{\mathrm{sd}}(\mathcal{A})$, and thus we can use $\mathbf{v}_0 = 0$. However, if the origin is not inside the constraint set, then we assume we can sample points $\mathbf{x}$ at random over the interior of $\mathcal{A}$ and check if they are inside $\mathrm{Viab}_{\mathbb{T}}^{\mathrm{sd}}(\mathcal{A})$ using the subroutine FEASIBLE$(\mathbf{x}, \mathcal{A})$.

Algorithm 2 Computes a polytopic under-approximation of $\mathrm{Viab}_{\mathbb{T}}^{\mathrm{sd}}(\mathcal{A})$ with at most $N+1$ vertices

```
1: procedure POLYTOPIC-APPROX(A, v_0, N)
2:     V_0 ← {v_0}
3:     for i = 1 to N do                                  ▷ N samples
4:         r ← SAMPLE-RAY(v_0)
5:         b ← FIND-INTERSECTION-ON-BOUNDARY(A, r)
6:         v_i ← BISECTION-FEASIBILITY-SEARCH(v_0, b, A)
7:         V_i ← conv(V_{i-1} ∪ {v_i})
8:     end for
9:     return V_N
10: end procedure
```

Next assume that $\mathcal{V}_N = \mathrm{conv}(\{\mathbf{v}_0, \ldots, \mathbf{v}_N\}) \subseteq \mathrm{Viab}_{\mathbb{T}}^{\mathrm{sd}}(\mathcal{A})$, and that we have $\mathbf{v}_{N+1} =$ BISECTION-FEASIBILITY-SEARCH$(\mathbf{v}_0, \mathbf{b}, \mathcal{A})$ for some point $\mathbf{b} \in \partial\mathcal{A}$ (as returned by FIND-INTERSECTION-ON-BOUNDARY). Then since BISECTION-FEASIBILITY-SEARCH only returns points which are inside $\mathrm{Viab}_{\mathbb{T}}^{\mathrm{sd}}(\mathcal{A})$, we have $\mathbf{v}_{N+1} \in \mathrm{Viab}_{\mathbb{T}}^{\mathrm{sd}}(\mathcal{A})$. Let $\mathcal{V}_{N+1} = \mathrm{conv}(\mathcal{V}_N \cup \{\mathbf{v}_{N+1}\})$. Now since $\mathcal{V}_{N+1}$ is convex, $\forall \mathbf{x}_0 \in \mathcal{V}_{N+1}$, $\exists \mathbf{x}_0' \in \mathcal{V}_N$ and $\exists \theta \in [0,1]$ such that $\mathbf{x}_0 = \theta\mathbf{x}_0' + (1-\theta)\mathbf{v}_{N+1}$. For $\mathbf{x}_0'$ we know (by the induction hypothesis) that $\exists \mathbf{u}_{x_0'}(\cdot) \in \mathscr{U}_{\mathbb{T}}^{\mathrm{pw}}$ such that

$$\mathbf{x}_{\mathbf{x}_0'}^{\mathbf{u}_{\mathbf{x}_0'}}(t) = e^{At}\mathbf{x}_0' + \int_0^t e^{A(t-r)} B\mathbf{u}_{\mathbf{x}_0'}(r)dr \in \mathcal{A} \quad \forall t \in \mathbb{T}. \tag{38}$$

For $\mathbf{v}_{N+1}$ we also know $\exists \mathbf{u}_{\mathbf{v}_{N+1}}(\cdot) \in \mathscr{U}_{\mathbb{T}}^{\mathrm{pw}}$ such that

$$\begin{aligned} \mathbf{x}_{\mathbf{v}_{N+1}}^{\mathbf{u}_{\mathbf{v}_{N+1}}}(t) =& e^{At}\mathbf{v}_{N+1} + \\ & \int_0^t e^{A(t-r)} B\mathbf{u}_{\mathbf{v}_{N+1}}(r)dr \in \mathcal{A} \ \forall t \in \mathbb{T}. \end{aligned} \tag{39}$$

Let $\mathbf{u}_{\mathbf{x}_0}(\cdot) = \theta\mathbf{u}_{\mathbf{x}_0'}(\cdot) + (1-\theta)\mathbf{u}_{\mathbf{v}_{N+1}}(\cdot) \in \mathscr{U}_{\mathbb{T}}^{\mathrm{pw}}$, then

$$\begin{aligned} \mathbf{x}_{\mathbf{x}_0}^{\mathbf{u}_{\mathbf{x}_0}}(t) :=& e^{At}\mathbf{x}_0 + \int_0^t e^{A(t-r)} B\mathbf{u}_{\mathbf{x}_0}(r)dr \\ =& e^{At}\left(\theta\mathbf{x}_0' + (1-\theta)\mathbf{v}_{N+1}\right) + \\ & \int_0^t e^{A(t-r)} B\left(\theta\mathbf{u}_{\mathbf{x}_0'}(r) + (1-\theta)\mathbf{u}_{\mathbf{v}_{N+1}}(r)\right) dr \\ =& \theta\mathbf{x}_{\mathbf{x}_0'}^{\mathbf{u}_{\mathbf{x}_0'}}(t) + (1-\theta)\mathbf{x}_{\mathbf{v}_{N+1}}^{\mathbf{u}_{\mathbf{v}_{N+1}}}(t) \in \mathcal{A} \quad \forall t \in \mathbb{T} \end{aligned} \tag{40}$$

since $\mathcal{A}$ and $\mathcal{U}$ are convex and compact. Thus $\mathbf{u}_{\mathbf{x}_0}(\cdot)$ is safety-preserving and $\mathbf{x}_0 \in \mathrm{Viab}_{\mathbb{T}}^{\mathrm{sd}}(\mathcal{A})$. Because $\mathbf{x}_0$ was chosen arbitrarily in $\mathcal{V}_{N+1}$, we conclude that $\mathcal{V}_{N+1} \subseteq \mathrm{Viab}_{\mathbb{T}}^{\mathrm{sd}}(\mathcal{A})$. □

3.2 Convergence

One of the striking features of our algorithm is that it is random; additional points on the boundary of the polytopic approximation of $\mathrm{Viab}_{\mathbb{T}}^{\mathrm{sd}}(\mathcal{A})$ are generated based on random sampling. This is necessary because $\partial\,\mathrm{Viab}_{\mathbb{T}}^{\mathrm{sd}}(\mathcal{A})$ is unknown *a priori* so it is impossible to know deterministically what points to sample in order to construct a polytope that converges to $\mathrm{Viab}_{\mathbb{T}}^{\mathrm{sd}}(\mathcal{A})$ as quickly as possible. In fact any algorithm which deterministically chooses such points could be presented with a safe set $\mathcal{A}$ and system dynamics for which the algorithm would converge arbitrarily poorly. This result comes from the literature of estimating the volume of convex bodies using a *separation oracle*, which is a function that accepts as input a convex set and a point, and returns whether or not that point is inside the convex set.[5] More specifically it can be shown

[5]Such an oracle is primarily used when the representation of the body is too complicated to be tractable for analytical volume cal-

that for any algorithm that deterministically queries a separation oracle a polynomial number of times in order to build a polytopic approximation, the error (the difference in volume between the approximation and the true set) could be exponential in the number of dimensions [3]. Random algorithms, on the other hand, can perform provably better [7], and we use a proof from the literature [30] to prove our algorithm's asymptotic convergence. First, however, we must introduce several new definitions.

First, let $\widehat{\text{Viab}}^{\text{sd}}_{\mathbb{T}}(\mathcal{A})$ be the subset of the viability kernel our algorithm actually approximates, i.e.

$$\widehat{\text{Viab}}^{\text{sd}}_{\mathbb{T}}(\mathcal{A}) := \{\mathbf{x}_0 \in \mathcal{A}_{\downarrow}(M,\delta) \mid \exists \mathbf{u}(\cdot) \in \mathscr{U}^{\text{pw}}_{\mathbb{T}}, \\ \forall k \in \{0,\dots,N_\delta\}, \mathbf{x}(t_k) \in \mathcal{A}_{\downarrow}(M,\delta)\}. \tag{41}$$

While the true viability kernel $\text{Viab}^{\text{sd}}_{\mathbb{T}}(\mathcal{A})$ encompasses all initial conditions for which a piecewise constant control keeps $\mathbf{x}(t) \in \mathcal{A}$, the set $\widehat{\text{Viab}}^{\text{sd}}_{\mathbb{T}}(\mathcal{A})$ only encompasses initial conditions for which $\mathbf{x}(t_k) \in \mathcal{A}_{\downarrow}(M,\delta)$ (which is a sufficient — but not necessary — condition to imply $\mathbf{x}(t) \in \mathcal{A}$; cf. Lemma 1). Thus, $\widehat{\text{Viab}}^{\text{sd}}_{\mathbb{T}}(\mathcal{A}) \subseteq \text{Viab}^{\text{sd}}_{\mathbb{T}}(\mathcal{A})$. Define the volumetric error between these two sets as

$$e_{M\delta} := \text{vol}(\text{Viab}^{\text{sd}}_{\mathbb{T}}(\mathcal{A})) - \text{vol}(\widehat{\text{Viab}}^{\text{sd}}_{\mathbb{T}}(\mathcal{A})). \tag{42}$$

and note that it depends only on the term $M\delta$, due to the definition of $\mathcal{A}_{\downarrow}(M,\delta)$ in (4).

Of course for a given choice of ζ for the discretization (Section 2.1.2) and ϵ in the bisection search (Algorithm 1), the points our algorithm samples will not be precisely on the boundary $\partial\widehat{\text{Viab}}^{\text{sd}}_{\mathbb{T}}(\mathcal{A})$, so it will also be useful to define $\widehat{\text{Viab}}^{\text{sd}}_{\mathbb{T}}(\mathcal{A},\zeta,\epsilon)$ as the subset of $\widehat{\text{Viab}}^{\text{sd}}_{\mathbb{T}}(\mathcal{A})$ which our algorithm approximates as $N \to \infty$. Thus using the extended notation $\mathcal{V}^{\zeta,\epsilon}_N$ = POLYTOPIC-APPROX$(\mathcal{A},\mathbf{v}_0,N)$ for a given choice of ζ and ϵ:[6]

$$\widehat{\text{Viab}}^{\text{sd}}_{\mathbb{T}}(\mathcal{A},\zeta,\epsilon) := \lim_{N\to\infty} \mathcal{V}^{\zeta,\epsilon}_N \tag{43}$$

$$\lim_{\substack{\zeta\to\infty\\ \epsilon\to 0}} \widehat{\text{Viab}}^{\text{sd}}_{\mathbb{T}}(\mathcal{A},\zeta,\epsilon) = \widehat{\text{Viab}}^{\text{sd}}_{\mathbb{T}}(\mathcal{A}). \tag{44}$$

Finally we will need the key lemma which describes the *convergence rate* of random algorithms for estimating the boundary of a convex body, which we restate from [30], omitting some of the details that are unnecessary for our purposes:

LEMMA 3 ([30]). *Let $\mathcal{C}$ be a convex body in $\mathbb{R}^n$ with $\partial\mathcal{C}$ C^2, let $h : \partial\mathcal{C} \to \mathbb{R}_+$ be a probability density function defined on $\partial\mathcal{C}$, let $\mathbb{P}_h$ be the probability measure defined by h, and let $\mathbb{E}(h,N)$ be the expected volume of the convex hull of N points chosen randomly on $\partial\mathcal{C}$ with respect to $\mathbb{P}_h$. Then*

$$\lim_{N\to\infty} (\text{vol}(\mathcal{C}) - \mathbb{E}(h,N))\, N^{\frac{2}{n-1}} = c_n(\mathcal{C}), \tag{45}$$

where $c_n(\mathcal{C})$ is a constant which depends only on the dimension n, the distribution of h, and the shape of $\mathcal{C}$ (more specifically its Gauss-Kronecker curvature).

The key point of this lemma is that any algorithm which builds a polytopic approximation to a convex body by randomly sampling points on its boundary will converge with a rate that is proportional to $1/N^{\frac{2}{n-1}}$. Additionally, [30] also shows that this convergence rate is optimal (up to a numerical constant) with respect to all algorithms which build polytopic approximations via boundary sampling.

With this lemma and these definitions in hand, we can state the convergence of our algorithm.

PROPOSITION 1 (RATE OF CONVERGENCE). *Let $e_{\text{vol}}(N,\zeta,\epsilon)$ represent the volumetric error between the viability kernel and the result of our algorithm, minus the error $e_{M\delta}$ between the true viability kernel and $\widehat{\text{Viab}}^{\text{sd}}_{\mathbb{T}}(\mathcal{A})$, i.e.*

$$e_{\text{vol}}(N,\zeta,\epsilon) := \text{vol}(\text{Viab}^{\text{sd}}_{\mathbb{T}}(\mathcal{A})) - \text{vol}(\mathcal{V}^{\zeta,\epsilon}_N) - e_{M\delta}. \tag{46}$$

Then our algorithm converges as

$$\lim_{\substack{N\to\infty\\ \zeta\to\infty\\ \epsilon\to 0}} e_{\text{vol}}(N,\zeta,\epsilon) N^{\frac{2}{n-1}} = c_n(\text{Viab}^{\text{sd}}_{\mathbb{T}}(\mathcal{A}), M\delta), \tag{47}$$

where $c_n(\text{Viab}^{\text{sd}}_{\mathbb{T}}(\mathcal{A}), M\delta)$ is a constant dependent on the dimension n, the shape of the viability kernel, and the value $M\delta$.

Proposition 1 asserts that the volumetric error between the outcome of our algorithm and the true viability kernel asymptotically converges at the exponential rate of $c_n(\text{Viab}^{\text{sd}}_{\mathbb{T}}(\mathcal{A}))/N^{\frac{2}{n-1}}$ to a numerical constant (due to the sampled-data nature of the system).

To prove this proposition we first need to introduce the following lemma, which introduces a fictitious source of error ϵ_{smooth} between the result of our algorithm and the viability kernel:

LEMMA 4 ([8,9]). *For every compact convex set $\mathcal{C}$, there exists a compact convex set $\tilde{\mathcal{C}} \subseteq \mathcal{C}$ whose boundary $\partial\tilde{\mathcal{C}}$ is C^2, and $\text{vol}(\mathcal{C}) - \text{vol}(\tilde{\mathcal{C}}) = e_{\text{smooth}}$ for some arbitrarily small positive scalar constant e_{smooth}.*

We use Lemma 4 to define a convex body $\widetilde{\text{Viab}}^{\text{sd}}_{\mathbb{T}}(\mathcal{A},\zeta,\epsilon)$ that is a C^2 approximation of $\widehat{\text{Viab}}^{\text{sd}}_{\mathbb{T}}(\mathcal{A},\zeta,\epsilon)$ such that

$$\text{vol}(\widehat{\text{Viab}}^{\text{sd}}_{\mathbb{T}}(\mathcal{A},\zeta,\epsilon)) - \text{vol}(\widetilde{\text{Viab}}^{\text{sd}}_{\mathbb{T}}(\mathcal{A},\zeta,\epsilon)) = e_{\text{smooth}}. \tag{48}$$

We will also require the following lemma (which we state without proof):

LEMMA 5. *Any compact convex set $\mathcal{C}$ with $\mathbf{v}_0 \in \mathcal{C}$ is homeomorphic to $\mathcal{B}^n_2(\mathbf{v}_0,1)$ [5], and in particular taking $\mathcal{C} = \widehat{\text{Viab}}^{\text{sd}}_{\mathbb{T}}(\mathcal{A},\zeta,\epsilon)$, we can define the invertible mapping $\mathbf{m} : S^{n-1}_2(\mathbf{v}_0) \to \partial\widehat{\text{Viab}}^{\text{sd}}_{\mathbb{T}}(\mathcal{A},\zeta,\epsilon)$ as $\mathbf{m}(\mathbf{r}_d) \equiv$ BISECTION-FEASIBILITY-SEARCH$(\mathbf{v}_0$, FIND-INTERSECTION-ON-BOUNDARY$(\mathcal{C},\vec{r}),\mathcal{C})$, where $\vec{r}$ has origin $\mathbf{v}_0 \in \mathcal{C}$ and direction $\mathbf{r}_d$.*

We are now ready to prove Proposition 1.

PROOF OF PROPOSITION 1. By Lemma 3, if we have a probability density function $\tilde{g}$ that samples from $\partial\widetilde{\text{Viab}}^{\text{sd}}_{\mathbb{T}}(\mathcal{A},\zeta,\epsilon)$, then we have

$$\lim_{N\to\infty} \left(\text{vol}(\widetilde{\text{Viab}}^{\text{sd}}_{\mathbb{T}}(\mathcal{A},\zeta,\epsilon)) - \mathbb{E}(\tilde{g},N)\right) N^{\frac{2}{n-1}} = \\ \tilde{c}_n(\widetilde{\text{Viab}}^{\text{sd}}_{\mathbb{T}}(\mathcal{A},\zeta,\epsilon))) \tag{49}$$

for some constant $\tilde{c}_n(\widetilde{\text{Viab}}^{\text{sd}}_{\mathbb{T}}(\mathcal{A},\zeta,\epsilon))$ which depends only on the dimension n, the distribution $\tilde{g}$, and the shape of $\widetilde{\text{Viab}}^{\text{sd}}_{\mathbb{T}}(\mathcal{A},\zeta,\epsilon)$.

culations, or as in our case (where FEASIBLE$(\mathbf{x},\mathcal{A})$ plays the role of the separation oracle) when the representation of the body is not actually known in form besides the oracle.

[6]Note that Theorem 2, restated in terms of the extended notation, asserts that $\mathcal{V}^{\zeta,\epsilon}_N \subseteq \text{Viab}^{\text{sd}}_{\mathbb{T}}(\mathcal{A}), \forall\zeta,\epsilon,N$.

Now let $h(\mathbf{x})$ be the probability distribution used by SAMPLE-RAY($\mathbf{v}_0$) to generate samples on the unit sphere. Then since the mapping $\mathbf{m}(\mathbf{r}_d)$ from Lemma 5 returns points on $\widehat{\text{Viab}_{\mathbb{T}}^{\text{sd}}}(\mathcal{A}, \zeta, \epsilon)$, we can use $\mathbf{m}$ to perform a change of variables to define a new probability density function $g(\mathbf{m}(\mathbf{r}_d))$ on $\partial\widehat{\text{Viab}_{\mathbb{T}}^{\text{sd}}}(\mathcal{A}, \zeta, \epsilon)$ [27]. Then by Lemma 4, we can take $e_{\text{smooth}} \to 0$, and thus $\widetilde{\text{Viab}_{\mathbb{T}}^{\text{sd}}}(\mathcal{A}, \zeta, \epsilon) \to \widehat{\text{Viab}_{\mathbb{T}}^{\text{sd}}}(\mathcal{A}, \zeta, \epsilon)$ and $\tilde{g} \to g$. Thus we can write (49) as:

$$\lim_{N\to\infty} \left(\text{vol}(\widehat{\text{Viab}_{\mathbb{T}}^{\text{sd}}}(\mathcal{A}, \zeta, \epsilon)) - \mathbb{E}(g, N)\right) N^{\frac{2}{n-1}} = \tilde{c}_n(\widehat{\text{Viab}_{\mathbb{T}}^{\text{sd}}}(\mathcal{A}, \zeta, \epsilon))), \quad (50)$$

which, since $\mathbb{E}(g, N) = \text{vol}(\mathcal{V}_N^{\zeta,\epsilon})$, becomes

$$\lim_{N\to\infty} \left(\text{vol}(\widehat{\text{Viab}_{\mathbb{T}}^{\text{sd}}}(\mathcal{A}, \zeta, \epsilon)) - \text{vol}(\mathcal{V}_N^{\zeta,\epsilon})\right) N^{\frac{2}{n-1}} = \tilde{c}_n(\widehat{\text{Viab}_{\mathbb{T}}^{\text{sd}}}(\mathcal{A}, \zeta, \epsilon))). \quad (51)$$

Then by (44), taking the limit as $\zeta \to \infty$ and $\epsilon \to 0$ on both sides of (51) gives:

$$\lim_{\substack{N\to\infty \\ \zeta\to\infty \\ \epsilon\to 0}} \left(\text{vol}(\widehat{\text{Viab}_{\mathbb{T}}^{\text{sd}}}(\mathcal{A})) - \text{vol}(\mathcal{V}_N^{\zeta,\epsilon})\right) N^{\frac{2}{n-1}} = \tilde{c}_n(\widehat{\text{Viab}_{\mathbb{T}}^{\text{sd}}}(\mathcal{A})). \quad (52)$$

Now, by (42), we can replace $\text{vol}(\widehat{\text{Viab}_{\mathbb{T}}^{\text{sd}}}(\mathcal{A}))$ to get

$$\lim_{\substack{N\to\infty \\ \zeta\to\infty \\ \epsilon\to 0}} \left(\text{vol}(\text{Viab}_{\mathbb{T}}^{\text{sd}}(\mathcal{A})) - e_{M\delta} - \text{vol}(\mathcal{V}_N^{\zeta,\epsilon})\right) N^{\frac{2}{n-1}} = \tilde{c}_n(\widehat{\text{Viab}_{\mathbb{T}}^{\text{sd}}}(\mathcal{A})). \quad (53)$$

Since the shape of $\widehat{\text{Viab}_{\mathbb{T}}^{\text{sd}}}(\mathcal{A})$ depends only on the shape of $\text{Viab}_{\mathbb{T}}^{\text{sd}}(\mathcal{A})$ and the value of $M\delta$, we can write $\tilde{c}_n(\widehat{\text{Viab}_{\mathbb{T}}^{\text{sd}}}(\mathcal{A})) := c_n(\text{Viab}_{\mathbb{T}}^{\text{sd}}(\mathcal{A}), M\delta)$ for some appropriate function c_n, and we arrive at

$$\lim_{\substack{N\to\infty \\ \zeta\to\infty \\ \epsilon\to 0}} e_{\text{vol}}(N, \zeta, \epsilon) N^{\frac{2}{n-1}} = c_n(\text{Viab}_{\mathbb{T}}^{\text{sd}}(\mathcal{A}), M\delta). \quad (54)$$

□

It is worth emphasizing once again that due to the results in [30], this convergence rate is optimal (up to a multiplicative constant depending on the probability density function used for sampling); no other algorithm which approximates the viability kernel by sampling from its boundary will be able to converge at a faster rate.

3.3 Computational Complexity & Scalability

The run time complexity of our algorithm (for a fixed number of time sampling intervals N_δ) is $O(N \log(d)\Phi(n))$, where

- N is the number of samples/vertices,
- d is the "diameter" of the set $\mathcal{A}$, and
- Φ is the complexity of the feasibility program (36) as a function of the state dimension n.

That is, the algorithm runs in time linear in the number of samples N, logarithmic in the diameter d of $\mathcal{A}$ due to the bisection search, and proportional to Φ in the complexity of the appropriate feasibility program (36). For instance with polytopic constraints the feasibility problem is an LP and thus the run time complexity of the proposed algorithm is super-quadratic but sub-cubic in n. This is a direct improvement over existing techniques for approximating the sampled-data viability kernel.

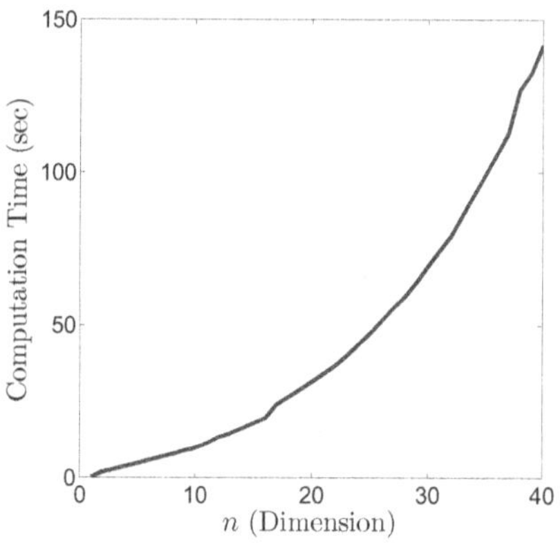

Figure 4: Run time of the proposed algorithm for a chain of n-integrators.

We note that the spatial complexity of the algorithm is still exponential in the number of samples N as the dimension n increases: The convergence rate (47) says that to keep the same approximation accuracy as $n \to kn$, we would need an increase of $N \to N^{\frac{kn-1}{n-1}}$ in the number of samples. However, the fact that we only store samples on the boundary of the viability kernel to describe that set (as opposed to storing a grid of the entire set $\mathcal{A}$ and possibly beyond) requires significantly less memory than conventional approaches such as the level-set method presented in [26]. Additionally, the computed approximation is far more accurate (and possibly more scalable) than the piecewise ellipsoidal technique also presented in [26]. In essence our algorithm strikes a balance between accuracy and scalability that to the best of our knowledge no other algorithm has yet achieved for sampled-data systems.

To examine the scalability of our algorithm empirically, consider the chain of n-integrators $\partial^n x/\partial t^n = u$ with input and state constraints $\mathcal{U} = [-0.15, 0.15]$ and $\mathcal{A} = \{\mathbf{x} \mid \|\mathbf{x}\|_\infty \leq 0.5\}$. The trajectory $\mathbf{x}(\cdot)$ is measured every $\delta = 0.05$ s and safety is to be maintained over $\mathbb{T} = [0, 1]$. We use a discretization order of $\zeta = 4$, bisection accuracy of $\epsilon = 0.01$ and employ YALMIP [20] to implement (36) and MPT [18] for simple operations with polytopes. All of these parameters are kept constant as we increase the dimension n and the number of samples $N = 2n$ to examine the scalability of our algorithm. The results are shown in Figure 4. The algorithm was implemented in MATLAB version 7.13 (R2011b) and tested on an Intel Core i7 at 2.9 GHz with 16 GB RAM running 64-bit Windows 7 Professional (without optimizing the code for speed). As would be expected given that the feasibility problem is a linear program for this example, the resulting runtime is a super-quadratic but sub-cubic function in n.

4. NUMERICAL EXAMPLE

To further examine the performance of the algorithm, we will examine how it performs on a trivial system, the double-integrator:

$$\dot{\mathbf{x}} = \begin{bmatrix} 0 & 1 \\ 0 & 0 \end{bmatrix} \mathbf{x} + \begin{bmatrix} 0 \\ 1 \end{bmatrix} u. \quad (55)$$

Consider a similar setting as before, where $\mathcal{U} = [-0.15, 0.15]$, $\mathcal{A} = \{\mathbf{x} \mid \|\mathbf{x}\|_\infty \leq 0.5\}$, the sampling interval is $\delta = 0.05$ s, and safety is to be maintained over $\mathbb{T} = [0, 1]$. The bound M on the vector field is simply calculated as 0.5 in the infinity norm. Using $\zeta = $ 4th order discretization and $\epsilon = 0.01$-accurate bisection

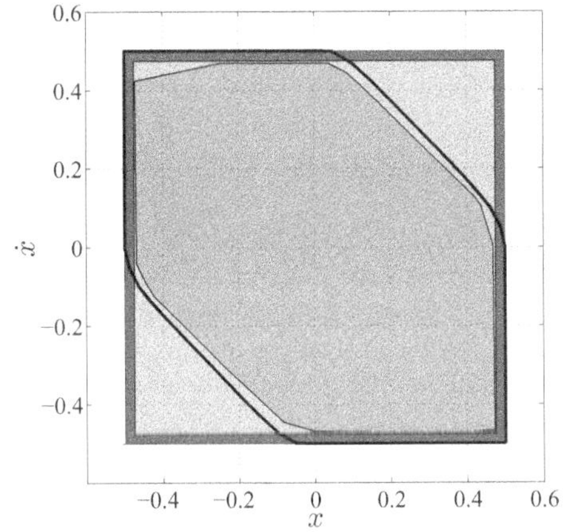

Figure 5: Polytopic under-approximation $\mathcal{V}_N$ (the inner-most set in light blue color) of $\text{Viab}_{\mathbb{T}}^{\text{sd}}(\mathcal{A})$ for the double-integrator using $N = 44$ samples via Algorithm 2. The outer-most set (dark green) is $\mathcal{A}$, separated from the eroded set $\mathcal{A}_{\downarrow}(M, \delta)$ (light green) by a margin determined by $M\delta$. The sampled-data level-set approximation [26] is also shown (outlined by thick black lines), though this approximation is not conservative; cf. [26, Section 5.4.4]).

search we approximate $\text{Viab}_{\mathbb{T}}^{\text{sd}}(\mathcal{A})$ by the set $\mathcal{V}_N$ via $N = 44$ randomly generated samples in approximately 28 seconds (Figure 5).

A quantitative upper-bound on the total volumetric error between $\mathcal{V}_N$ and the true viability kernel can be formulated using the following procedure.[7] Let L be the number of faces in $\mathcal{V}_N$. Consider the facet representation of $\mathcal{V}_N$, i.e. $\mathcal{V}_N = \{\mathbf{x} \mid F_{\mathcal{V}_N}\mathbf{x} \leq \mathbf{f}_{\mathcal{V}_N}\}$ with

$$F_{\mathcal{V}_N} = \begin{bmatrix} F_{\mathcal{V}_N 1} \\ F_{\mathcal{V}_N 2} \\ \vdots \\ F_{\mathcal{V}_N L} \end{bmatrix} \in \mathbb{R}^{L \times n}, \quad \mathbf{f}_{\mathcal{V}_N} = \begin{bmatrix} f_{\mathcal{V}_N 1} \\ f_{\mathcal{V}_N 2} \\ \vdots \\ f_{\mathcal{V}_N L} \end{bmatrix} \in \mathbb{R}^{L}. \tag{56}$$

Let $F_{\mathcal{V}_N \setminus i} \in \mathbb{R}^{(L-1)\times n}$ and $\mathbf{f}_{\mathcal{V}_N \setminus i} \in \mathbb{R}^{L-1}$ denote $F_{\mathcal{V}_N}$ and $\mathbf{f}_{\mathcal{V}_N}$ with their i-th rows removed:

$$F_{\mathcal{V}_N \setminus i} := \begin{bmatrix} F_{\mathcal{V}_N 1} \\ \vdots \\ F_{\mathcal{V}_N i-1} \\ F_{\mathcal{V}_N i+1} \\ \vdots \\ F_{\mathcal{V}_N L} \end{bmatrix}, \quad \mathbf{f}_{\mathcal{V}_N \setminus i} := \begin{bmatrix} f_{\mathcal{V}_N 1} \\ \vdots \\ f_{\mathcal{V}_N i-1} \\ f_{\mathcal{V}_N i+1} \\ \vdots \\ f_{\mathcal{V}_N L} \end{bmatrix}. \tag{57}$$

Suppose we also rewrite $\mathcal{A}$ using its facet representation as $\mathcal{A} = \{\mathbf{x} \mid F_{\mathcal{A}}\mathbf{x} \leq \mathbf{f}_{\mathcal{A}}\}$. Then an overestimate of the error can defined as

$$\text{err} = \sum_{i=1}^{L} \left(\text{vol}\left(\left\{ x \mid \begin{bmatrix} F_{\mathcal{V}_N \setminus i} \\ F_{\mathcal{A}} \end{bmatrix} x \leq \begin{bmatrix} \mathbf{f}_{\mathcal{V}_N \setminus i} \\ \mathbf{f}_{\mathcal{A}} \end{bmatrix} \right\} \right) - \text{vol}(\mathcal{V}_N) \right), \tag{58}$$

i.e. for every possible face, we compute what the difference in volume would be if we removed it (while still restricting the approximation to be inside $\mathcal{A}$), and then sum up these differences. This gives a (very) conservative estimate of what the maximum possible error could be, in that it computes an over-estimate of the maximum possible volume of a convex body with the points $\{\mathbf{v}_i\}$ on its

[7] Although this procedure is in general not scalable, it will work for this simple example.

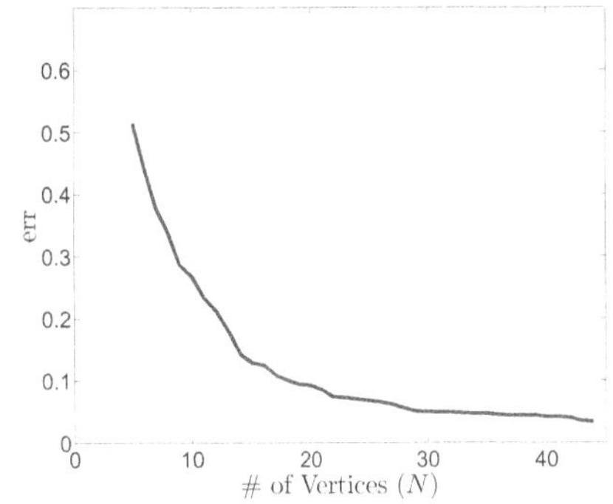

Figure 6: The upper-bound on the total volumetric error (58) between $\mathcal{V}_N$ and $\text{Viab}_{\mathbb{T}}^{\text{sd}}(\mathcal{A})$ for the double-integrator as a function of the number of samples N (averaged over 10 runs).

boundary. Note that this error is not guaranteed to decrease monotonically as the number of vertices increases, though we expect it to converge in the limit as $N \to \infty$. Figure 6 plots this upper-bound for the double-integrator example (averaged over 10 runs).

5. CONCLUSIONS, ONGOING, & FUTURE WORK

We have presented a new algorithm for computing the viability kernel for LTI sampled-data systems. This algorithm, which takes a novel sampling-based approach to calculating the viability kernel, allows the user to explicitly balance computation resources with desired accuracy. In addition to proving the algorithm's correctness, convergence properties, and complexity, we also demonstrated its use on a simple example.

One important area we are actively investigating is the extension to systems with bounded disturbances (i.e. calculating the *discriminating kernel*). One possible approach would involve further erosion of the safe sets used to check feasibility during forward simulation in the same way as the error due to discretization of the continuous system. This sort of robustification of our algorithm would also enable our system to handle nonlinear dynamics by bounding the error between the nonlinear system and its linear approximation, and treating this error as another disturbance.

There are also several areas of ongoing work for which we have results, but cannot present here due to space constraints. We have recently developed a more scalable way of over-approximating the viability kernel, again in a tight manner, by making use of support functions. By taking the difference in volume between this over-approximation and our under-approximation of the viability kernel, we have been able to construct a better approximation of the error in our results. By approximating the gradient of this error we are able to better guide the random sampling we use to generate new directions along which to constrain the under-approximation, which may result in faster convergence to the true viability kernel while making use of fewer samples. Using these improvements we have been able to apply our algorithm to a practical high-dimensional system (a 12D quadrotor model) with promising results.

We have also developed control synthesis methods based on the results of our under-approximation which construct control signals (either open-loop or feedback-based). Finally, we have also developed a sufficient condition which we can use to determine if the under-approximation of the viability kernel generated by our algorithm is control-invariant (and thus can be used as the terminal constraint in an MPC framework).

6. ACKNOWLEDGMENTS

This research was funded in part by the US National Science Foundation under CPS:ActionWebs (CNS-931843), by the US Office of Naval Research under the HUNT (N0014-08-0696) and SMARTS (N00014-09-1-1051) MURIs and by grant N00014-12-1-0609, and by the US Air Force Office of Scientific Research under the CHASE MURI (FA9550-10-1-0567).

7. REFERENCES

[1] M. Althoff, O. Stursberg, and M. Buss. Reachability analysis of linear systems with uncertain parameters and inputs. In *Proc. IEEE Conf. Decis. Contr.*, pages 726–732, 2007.

[2] J.-P. Aubin. *Viability Theory*. Systems and Control: Foundations and Applications. Birkhäuser, Boston, 1991.

[3] I. Bárány and Z. Füredi. Computing the volume is difficult. *Discrete Comput. Geom.*, 2(1):319–326, 1987.

[4] F. Blanchini and S. Miani. *Set-Theoretic Methods in Control*. Springer, 2008.

[5] G. E. Bredon. *Topology and Geometry*, volume 139. Springer, 1993.

[6] P.-A. Coquelin, S. Martin, and R. Munos. A dynamic programming approach to viability problems. In *Proc. IEEE Symp. Adapt. Dyn. Program. Reinf. Learn.*, pages 178–184, 2007.

[7] M. Dyer. Computing the volume of convex bodies: a case where randomness provably helps. *Probabilistic combinatorics and its applications*, 44:123–170, 1991.

[8] M. Ghomi. The problem of optimal smoothing for convex functions. *Proc. Am. Math. Soc.*, 130(8):2255–2260, 2002.

[9] M. Ghomi. Optimal Smoothing for Convex Polytopes. *Bull. London Math. Soc.*, 36(4):483–492, July 2004.

[10] A. Girard and C. Le Guernic. Efficient reachability analysis for linear systems using support functions. In *Proc. IFAC World Congr.*, Seoul, Korea, July 2008.

[11] A. Girard, C. Le Guernic, and O. Maler. Efficient computation of reachable sets of linear time-invariant systems with inputs. In J. Hespanha and A. Tiwari, editors, *Proc. Hybrid Syst.: Comput. Contr.*, pages 257–271. Springer-Verlag, 2006.

[12] G. Goodwin, J. Aguero, M. Cea Garridos, M. Salgado, and J. Yuz. Sampling and sampled-data models: The interface between the continuous world and digital algorithms. *IEEE Contr. Syst. Mag.*, 33(5):34–53, 2013.

[13] Z. Han and B. H. Krogh. Reachability analysis of nonlinear systems using trajectory piecewise linearized models. In *Proc. Am. Contr. Conf.*, pages 1505–1510, Minneapolis, MN, 2006.

[14] D. Henrion and M. Korda. Convex computation of the region of attraction of polynomial control systems. *preprint arXiv:1208.1751*, 2012.

[15] S. Kaynama, J. Maidens, M. Oishi, I. M. Mitchell, and G. A. Dumont. Computing the viability kernel using maximal reachable sets. In *Proc. Hybrid Syst.: Comput. Contr.*, pages 55–63, Beijing, 2012.

[16] S. Kaynama and M. Oishi. A modified Riccati transformation for decentralized computation of the viability kernel under LTI dynamics. *IEEE Trans. Autom. Contr.*, 58(11):2878–2892, 2013.

[17] A. B. Kurzhanski and P. Varaiya. Ellipsoidal techniques for reachability analysis: internal approximation. *Syst. Contr. Lett.*, 41:201–211, 2000.

[18] M. Kvasnica, P. Grieder, M. Baotić, and M. Morari. Multi-Parametric Toolbox (MPT). In R. Alur and G. J. Pappas, editors, *Proc. Hybrid Syst.: Comput. Contr., LNCS 2993*, pages 448–462, Berlin, Germany, 2004. Springer.

[19] M. Liou. A novel method of evaluating transient response. *Proceedings of the IEEE*, 54(1):20–23, 1966.

[20] J. Löfberg. YALMIP: a toolbox for modeling and optimization in MATLAB. In *Proc. Comput. Aided Contr. Syst. Des.*, pages 284–289, 2004.

[21] J. Maidens, S. Kaynama, I. M. Mitchell, M. Oishi, and G. A. Dumont. Lagrangian methods for approximating the viability kernel in high-dimensional systems. *Automatica*, 49(7):2017–2029, 2013.

[22] A. Majumdar and R. Tedrake. Robust online motion planning with regions of finite time invariance. In E. Frazzoli, T. Lozano-Perez, N. Roy, and D. Rus, editors, *Algorithmic Found. Robot. X*, pages 543–558. Springer Berlin Heidelberg, 2013.

[23] A. Majumdar, R. Vasudevan, M. M. Tobenkin, and R. Tedrake. Technical report: Convex optimization of nonlinear feedback controllers via occupation measures. *preprint arXiv:1305.7484*, 2013.

[24] I. M. Mitchell. Scalable calculation of reach sets and tubes for nonlinear systems with terminal integrators: a mixed implicit explicit formulation. In *Proc. Hybrid Syst.: Comput. Contr.*, pages 103–112, Chicago, IL, 2011. ACM.

[25] I. M. Mitchell, A. M. Bayen, and C. J. Tomlin. A time-dependent Hamilton-Jacobi formulation of reachable sets for continuous dynamic games. *IEEE Trans. Autom. Contr.*, 50(7):947–957, July 2005.

[26] I. M. Mitchell, S. Kaynama, M. Chen, and M. Oishi. Safety preserving control synthesis for sampled data systems. *Nonlinear Anal.: Hybrid Syst.*, 10:63–82, 2013.

[27] J. Pitman. *Probability*. Springer-Verlag, New York, 1993.

[28] S. Prajna and A. Jadbabaie. Safety verification of hybrid systems using barrier certificates. In *Proc. Hybrid Syst.: Comput. Contr.*, pages 477–492, 2004.

[29] P. Saint-Pierre. Approximation of the viability kernel. *Appl. Math. Optim.*, 29(2):187–209, Mar 1994.

[30] C. Schütt and E. Werner. Polytopes with Vertices Chosen Randomly from the Boundary of a Convex Body. In V. Milman and G. Schechtman, editors, *Geom. Aspects Funct. Anal.*, volume 1807 of *Lect. Notes Math.*, pages 241–422. Springer Berlin, 2003.

[31] C. Standish. Truncated Taylor series approximation to the state transition matrix of a continuous parameter finite Markov chain. *Linear Algebra Appl.*, 12(2):179–183, 1975.

[32] W. Tan and A. Packard. Searching for control lyapunov functions using sums of squares programming. In *Annual Allerton Conf.*, pages 210–219, 2004.

[33] R. Tedrake, I. R. Manchester, M. Tobenkin, and J. W. Roberts. LQR-trees: Feedback motion planning via sums-of-squares verification. *Int. J. Robot. Res.*, 29(8):1038–1052, 2010.

[34] M. Tobenkin, I. Manchester, and R. Tedrake. Invariant funnels around trajectories using sum-of-squares programming. In *Proc. IFAC World Congr.*, volume 18, pages 9218–9223, Milano, Italy, 2011.

[35] U. Topcu, A. Packard, and P. Seiler. Local stability analysis using simulations and sum-of-squares programming. *Automatica*, 44(10):2669–2675, 2008.

Proofs from Simulations and Modular Annotations *

Zhenqi Huang Sayan Mitra

{zhuang25, mitras}@illinois.edu
Coordinate Science Laboratory
University of Illinois at Urbana Champaign
Urbana, IL 61801

ABSTRACT

We present a modular technique for simulation-based bounded verification for nonlinear dynamical systems. We introduce the notion of input-to-state discrepancy of each subsystem A_i in a larger nonlinear dynamical system A which bounds the distance between two (possibly diverging) trajectories of A_i in terms of their initial states and inputs. Using the IS discrepancy functions, we construct a low dimensional deterministic dynamical system $M(\delta)$. For any two trajectories of A starting δ distance apart, we show that one of them bloated by a factor determined by the trajectory of M contains the other. Further, by choosing appropriately small δ's the overapproximations computed by the above method can be made arbitrarily precise. Using the above results we develop a sound and relatively complete algorithm for bounded safety verification of nonlinear ODEs. Our preliminary experiments with a prototype implementation of the algorithm show that the approach can be effective for verification of nonlinear models.

Keywords

Compositional Verification, Dynamical Systems, Simulation-based Verification, Input-to-state Stability

1. INTRODUCTION

For nonlinear dynamical systems that do not admit analytic solutions, one has to exclusively rely on numerical simulations. Though simulations give sufficient confidence for design, testing, and performance analysis in many application scenarios, for mathematical guarantees or verification, they are of limited use. Particularly resistant to simulation-based verification are nonlinear models with large sets of initial conditions, inputs, and unknown parameters.

Several recent papers [1–4] present techniques for proving or disproving properties of such models. The details vary to some extent, but the common strategy relies on the following simulate-and-bloat step: For a particular initial state $\mathbf{x}$ and a time bound T, compute a (possibly inaccurate) simulation of the system $\xi_{\mathbf{x}}$ starting from $\mathbf{x}$ upto time T. Then, the simulated trajectory $\xi_{\mathbf{x}}$ is bloated by some factor, to get a *tube* $\mathbf{B}(\xi_{\mathbf{x}})$ that contains all the trajectories starting from a neighborhood $B(\mathbf{x})$ of initial states around $\mathbf{x}$ upto T. The simulate-and-bloat step is repeated for finitely many initial states and their union is guaranteed to over-approximate the reach set of the system from all the initial states up to time T. The technique works as well for dynamical systems with bounded number of unknown parameters, by encoding all the nondeterministic choices in the initial state and it is embarrassingly parallel as the each simulate-and-bloat can be computed independently.

The bloating factor is crucial for performance of verification with the above strategy. From basic continuity of the trajectories, we know that neighboring initial states have trajectories that remain close over time. With more information about the sensitivity of the trajectories to the initial state we get bounds on the distance between neighboring trajectories [5]. For example, Lipschitz continuity of the dynamic function gives a bound on the distance between the neighboring trajectories that grows exponentially with time. Stronger notions like sensitivity, incremental Lyapunov functions, and contraction metrics for dynamical system are used in [6] to obtain more practically useful bounds.

In [3] we defined *discrepancy functions* that generalizes several of these properties and bounds the boating factor as a function of the size of the initial neighborhoods; we used these discrepancy functions for bounded time verification of nonlinear and switched models. But there are no general techniques for computing discrepancy functions (or for that matter sensitivity, contraction metrics and incremental Lyapunov functions) from the syntactic description of a dynamical system. One typically assumes a template polynomial for the candidate function and then solves an optimization problem to find the coefficients or assumes that this information is provided by the system designer as an annotation to the model. Obviously, the problem of finding these annotations becomes harder for larger models in which many components interact [7]. In [7, 8], stability and safety of a composed system can be checked by solving a subsystem-level optimization problems. However, this approach does not guarantee completeness.

*Zhenqi Huang is supported by an NSA SoS grant (Contract No W911NSF-13-0086). Sayan Mitra is supported by an NSF CAREER grant (Contract No NSF CNS 10-54247).

HSCC'14, April 15–17, 2014, Berlin, Germany.

ACM 978-1-4503-2732-9/14/04 ...$15.00.
http://dx.doi.org/10.1145/2562059.2562126 .

In this paper, present a new technique for simulation and approximation-based verification for large dynamical systems which only uses *input-to-state discrepancy* for the smaller constituent subsystems. Consider a large dynamical system A consisting of several interacting subsystems $A_1, \ldots, A_N$, that is, the input signals of a subsystem A_i are driven by the outputs (or states) of some other components A_j. Lets say that each A_i is n-dimensional which makes A nN-dimensional. Our main idea in this paper is to use a new type of input-to-state discrepancy function (IS discrepancy) for each subsystem A_i to construct a (small) $N+1$-dimensional dynamical system M that bounds the needed bloating factor for A. An IS discrepancy for A_i (together with its witnesses) gives a bound on the distance between two trajectories as a function of (a) their initial states and (b) the inputs they experience.

Input-to-state stability (ISS), its variants and their characterization in terms of necessary and sufficient conditions have been one of the major advances of nonlinear control theory in the last two decades [9–11]. Incremental ISS has been used to construct discrete symbolic models that approximately bisimulate continuous systems [12, 13]. Under additional assumptions about the stability of the overall system, it has been shown that a large system can be reduced to a smaller system with similar behaviors [14]. Our work is the first to connect these ideas to simulation-based safety verification of composed systems. Moreover, our technique does not rely on any stability assumptions of the composed system. Though our results do not give new techniques for computing IS discrepancy functions, but they do reassure that if such techniques are developed for smaller or special types of nonlinear models, then larger compositions of such subsystems can be automatically verified.

Contributions. (i) We introduce a method for constructing an approximation of a composed dynamical system using the IS discrepancy functions of the components (Definition 4). Specifically, we use the collection of IS discrepancy functions for the subsystems to define a family of dynamical systems $M(\delta)$, where the parameter δ defines the initial state of M.

(ii) We show that $M(\delta)$ has a unique trajectory μ, and that any trajectory $\xi_{\mathbf{x}}$ of A point-wise bloated by the value of $\mu(t)$ contains the reach set of all the trajectories of A starting from a δ-ball around $\mathbf{x}$ (Theorem 5.4). Thus, by simulating A and (the smaller) M we can compute bounded-time reach set overapproximations of A.

(iii) We also show that by choosing appropriately small δ's the overapproximations computed by the above method can be made arbitrarily precise; modulo the precision of the numerical simulations (Theorem 5.7).

(iv) Using the above results we develop an algorithm for bounded safety verification of nonlinear dynamical systems that iteratively refines initial set partitions (Algorithm 1). We show that the algorithm is sound and is guaranteed to terminate whenever the model is robustly safe or unsafe with respect to a given unsafe set. Our preliminary experimental results with a prototype implementation of the algorithm validates the approach and underscore its promise.

2. PRELIMINARIES

We will use the notations from the hybrid I/O automaton (HIOA) framework for modeling compositions of dynamical systems [15, 16]. For a natural number $n \in \mathbb{N}$, $[n]$ is the set $\{1, 2, \ldots, n\}$. For a sequence A of objects of any type with n elements, we refer to the ith element, $i \leq n$ by A_i. Let V be a finite set of real-valued variables. Variables are names for state and input components. A *valuation* $\mathbf{v}$ *for* V is a function mapping each variable name to its value in $\mathbb{R}$. The set of valuations for V is denoted by $Val(V)$.

For any function $f : A \rightarrow B$ and a set $S \subseteq A$, $f \lceil S$ is the restriction of f to S. That is, $(f \lceil S)(s) = f(s)$ for each $s \in S$. So, for a variable $v \in V$ and a valuation $\mathbf{v} \in Val(V)$, $\mathbf{v} \lceil v$ is the function mapping $\{v\}$ to the value $\mathbf{v}(v)$.

Trajectories model the continuous evolution of variable valuations over time. A *trajectory* for V is a differentiable function $\tau : \mathbb{R}_{\geq 0} \rightarrow Val(V)$. The set of all possible trajectories for V is denoted by $Traj(V)$. For any function $f : C \rightarrow [A \rightarrow B]$ and a set $S \subseteq A$, $f \downarrow S$ is the restriction of $f(c)$ to S. That is, $(f \downarrow S)(c) = f(c) \lceil S$ for each $c \in C$. In particular, for a variable $v \in V$ and a trajectory $\tau \in Traj(V)$, $\tau \downarrow v$ is the trajectory of v defined by τ.

Valuations can be viewed as vectors in $\mathbb{R}^{|V|}$ dimensional space by fixing some arbitrary ordering on variables. For a valuation $\mathbf{v}$, $|\mathbf{v}|$ is ℓ^2-norm of the vector of variable values. $B_\delta(\mathbf{v}) \subseteq Val(V)$ is the closed ball of valuations with radius δ centered at $\mathbf{v}$. The notions of continuity, differentiability, and integration are lifted to functions defined over sets of valuations in the usual way.

A function $f : A \rightarrow \mathbb{R}$ is *Lipschitz* if there exists a constant $L \geq 0$—called the *Lipschitz constant*—such that for all $a_1, a_2 \in A$ $|f(a_1) - f(a_2)| \leq L|a_1 - a_2|$. A continuous function $\alpha : \mathbb{R}_{\geq 0} \rightarrow \mathbb{R}_{\geq 0}$ is in the *class of $\mathcal{K}$ functions* if $\alpha(0) = 0$ and it is strictly increasing. Class $\mathcal{K}$ functions are closed under composition and inversion. A class $\mathcal{K}$ function α is a *class $\mathcal{K}_\infty$* function if $\alpha(x) \rightarrow \infty$ as $x \rightarrow \infty$. A continuous function $\beta : \mathbb{R}_{\geq 0} \times \mathbb{R}_{\geq 0} \rightarrow \mathbb{R}_{\geq 0}$ is called a *class $\mathcal{KL}$ function* if for any t, $\beta(x, t)$ is a class $\mathcal{K}$ function in x and for any x, $\beta(x, t) \rightarrow 0$ as $t \rightarrow \infty$.

3. MODELS AND COMPOSITION

3.1 Dynamical System Modules

A dynamical system is specified by a collection of ordinary differential equations (ODEs), possibly with inputs, and a set of initial states. For reducing notational complexity, we identify output variables with state variables in this paper but our results can be extended to systems where outputs are distinct in a straightforward manner. The following definition introduces this class of dynamical systems.

Definition 1. *A dynamical system A is a tuple $\langle X, U, \Theta, f \rangle$ where*

(i) X is a set of variables called the state variables*; valuations of X are called* state*;*

(ii) U is a set of variables called the input variables *that are distinct from the state variables;*

(iii) $\Theta \subseteq Val(X)$ is a compact set of initial states*;*

(iv) $f : Val(X) \times Val(U) \rightarrow Val(X)$ is called the dynamic mapping*. In addition, f is Lipschitz continuous with respect to both arguments.*

An *input signal* of A is a trajectory of input variables $\eta \in Traj(U)$. For a given input signal $\eta \in Traj(U)$ and an initial state $\mathbf{x} \in \Theta$, the *solution* (or trajectory) of A is a state trajectory $\xi \in Traj(X)$ satisfying: (a) $\xi(0) = \mathbf{x}$,

(b) for any $t \in \mathbb{R}_{\geq 0}$, the time derivative of ξ at t satisfies the differential equation:

$$\dot{\xi}(t) = f(\xi(t), \eta(t)). \quad (1)$$

Under the Lipschitz assumption of the dynamic mapping (iv) and the differentiability of η, the differential equation (1) admits a unique solution. This solution ξ is uniquely defined by the initial state $\mathbf{x} \in Val(X)$ and the input signal $\eta \in Traj(U)$. A dynamical system without inputs ($U = \varnothing$) is said to be *closed*; otherwise, it is *open*. For closed system, for any $\mathbf{x} \in Val(X)$, $Traj(A, \mathbf{x})$ is a singleton.

Notations. The set of all trajectories of A with respect to a set of initial states $\Theta' \subseteq Val(X)$ and a set of input signals $H \subseteq Traj(U)$ is denoted by $Traj(A, \Theta', H)$. We will drop the argument H for closed dynamical systems. The components of dynamical system A and A_i are denoted by X_A, U_A, Θ_A, f_A and X_i, U_i, Θ_i, f_i, respectively. We will drop the subscripts when they are clear from context.

Next, for a closed dynamical system A we define reachable states and safety. A state $\mathbf{x} \in Val(X)$ is *T-reachable* if there exists a trajectory $\xi \in Traj(A, \Theta, \varnothing)$ and a time $t \leq T$ such that the trajectory $\xi(t) = \mathbf{x}$. The set of T-reachable states is denoted by $\mathsf{Reach}_A(\Theta, T)$ and the set of all reachable states is denoted by $\mathsf{Reach}_A(\Theta)$.

Definition 2. *For $\epsilon \geq 0$ and time $T \geq 0$, and an open unsafe set $\mathbb{U} \subseteq Val(X)$, A is ϵ-*robustly safe up to T with respect to $\mathbb{U}$ *if $B_\epsilon(\mathsf{Reach}_A(\Theta, T)) \cap \mathbb{U} = \varnothing$. If there exists some $\epsilon > 0$ for which this condition holds, then A is* robustly safe up to T with respect to $\mathbb{U}$.

There are a rich body of studies where static analysis is used to compute reachable sets (see for example [?, ?, ?]). In this paper, we present an approach uses modular annotations for dynamic analysis.

3.2 Composition of Modules

Large and complex dynamical system models are created by *composing* smaller modules or subsystems. Formally, the composition operation takes a pair of compatible subsystems and defines a new dynamical system by plugging-in or identifying the input variables of one subsystem with state variables of another. Several subsystems can be composed inductively. The resulting system may still have input variables that are not identified with any of the state variables. A pair of dynamical subsystems A_1 and A_2 are *compatible* if they do not share any of the state variables $X_1 \cap X_2 = \varnothing$.

Definition 3. *For a pair of compatible dynamical systems $A_1 = \langle X_1, U_1 \Theta_1, f_1 \rangle$ and $A_2 = X_2, U_2, \Theta_2, f_2 \rangle$, their composition $A = A_1 \| A_2$ is the tuple $\langle X, U, \Theta, f \rangle$, where*

(i) $X = X_1 \cup X_2$,

(ii) $U = U_1 \cup U_2 \setminus (X_1 \cup X_2)$,

(iii) $\Theta = \{\mathbf{x} \in Val(X) \mid (\mathbf{x} \lceil X_i) \in \Theta_i, i \in \{1, 2\}\}$, *and*

(iv) $f : Val(X) \times Val(U) \to Val(X)$ *is defined as: For each* $\mathbf{x} \in Val(X), \mathbf{u} \in Val(U)$, $i \in \{1, 2\}$,
$f(\mathbf{x}, \mathbf{u}) \lceil X_i = f_i(\mathbf{x} \lceil X_i, \mathbf{w})$, *where for each* $u \in U_i$*:*

$$\mathbf{w}(u) = \begin{cases} \mathbf{x}(u) & \text{if } u \in X \backslash X_i, \\ \mathbf{u}(u) & \text{otherwise.} \end{cases}$$

The definition of $\mathbf{w}$ creates a valuation for U_1 by combining valuations of X_2 and U, (creates a valuation for U_2 by combining valuations of X_1 and U). The definition for f ensures that the inputs to A_1 that come from A_2 are mapped correctly and those that are left unmapped remain as inputs variables in A. It can be checked that f is Lipschitz since f_1 and f_2 are. Therefore $\mathcal{A}$ is indeed a dynamical system and has well-defined trajectories for differentiable input signals.

Example 1. *Consider a dynamical synchronization problem where multiple subsystems start from different initial states and communicate to agree on a trajectory [17]. The interaction is shown by the graph in Figure 1. Each A_i, $i \in \{1, 2, 3\}$, is a dynamical system with the following components: (i) $X_i = \{x_{i1}, x_{i2}, x_{i3}, x_{i4}\}$, (ii) Θ_i is a compact subset of $Val(X_i)$, (iii) $U_1 = X_2, U_2 = X_1 \cup X_3$ and $U_3 = X_1$,* [1] *and (iv) for all $\mathbf{x}_1 \in Val(X_1), \mathbf{u}_1 \in Val(U_1)$, $f_1(\mathbf{x}_1, \mathbf{u}_1) = D\mathbf{x}_1 + \mathbf{u}_1$. Similarly, $f_2(\mathbf{x}_2, \mathbf{u}_2) = D\mathbf{x}_2 + \frac{1}{2}[I, I]\mathbf{u}_2$ and $f_3(\mathbf{x}_3, \mathbf{u}_3) = D\mathbf{x}_3 + \mathbf{u}_3$, where D is a 4×4 matrix, I is the identity matrix.*

According to Definition 3, the overall system $A = A_1 \| A_2 \| A_3$ with (i) $U_A = \varnothing$, and (ii) for any $\mathbf{x} \in Val(X_A)$,

$$f_{\mathcal{A}}(\mathbf{x}) = \begin{bmatrix} D & I & 0 \\ 0.5I & D & 0.5I \\ I & 0 & D \end{bmatrix} \mathbf{x}.$$

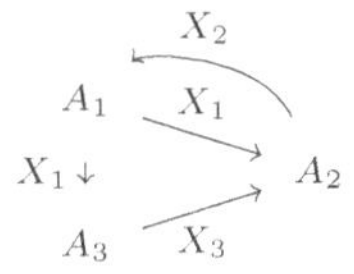

Figure 1: Illustration of Example 1.

For a closed composed system $A = A_1 \| \ldots \| A_N$, a subsystem A_i's input variables are in the set of state variables of A: $U_i \subseteq X_A$. For any state $\mathbf{x}$ of A, let $\xi = Traj(A, \mathbf{x})$ be the trajectory of A. It can be shown that for any subsystem A_i, the restriction of ξ onto A_i's state variables is a trajectory of A_i under the input signal η_i, where η_i is defined as ξ restricted to A_i's input variables. That is $\xi \downarrow X_i = Traj(A_i, \mathbf{x}(X_i), \xi \downarrow U_i)$.

4. INPUT-TO-STATE ANNOTATIONS

For bounded time safety verification of complex dynamical systems, we propose to use annotations for the individual modules. We rely on designers to provide these annotations, perhaps based on their insights about module's designed behavior or through additional computations performed explicitly for finding annotations. In Section 4.2 we relate these annotations to several existing concepts that are used in the control theory literature for stability analysis.

4.1 IS Discrepancy

Roughly, the annotation of a module A bounds the distance between two trajectories of A with different initial states and inputs. We call such an annotation an *input-to-state discrepancy function* or simply an IS discrepancy function.

Definition 4. *For a dynamical system A, a continuous functions $V : Val(X)^2 \to \mathbb{R}_{\geq 0}$ is an* input-to-state discrepancy function *if*

[1]Here we assume that $Val(U_1)$ and $Val(X_2)$ has the same variables ordering, etc.

(i) $\exists$ *class-*$\mathcal{K}$ *functions* $\underline{\alpha}, \overline{\alpha}$ *such that for any* $\mathbf{x}, \mathbf{x}' \in Val(X)$, $\underline{\alpha}(|\mathbf{x}-\mathbf{x}'|) \leq V(\mathbf{x}, \mathbf{x}') \leq \overline{\alpha}(|\mathbf{x}-\mathbf{x}'|)$, *and*

(ii) $\exists \beta : \mathbb{R}_{\geq 0} \times \mathbb{R}_{\geq 0} \to \mathbb{R}_{\geq 0}$ *of class-*$\mathcal{K}$ *in the first argument and* $\gamma \in \mathcal{K}$ *such that for any* $\theta, \theta' \in \Theta$, *input trajectories* $\eta, \eta' \in Traj(U)$, *and* $t \in \mathbb{R}_{\geq 0}$,

$$V(\xi(t), \xi'(t)) \leq \beta(|\theta-\theta'|, t) + \int_0^t \gamma(|\eta(s) - \eta'(s)|)ds, \tag{2}$$

where $\xi = Traj(A, \theta, \eta)$ *and* $\xi' = Traj(A, \theta', \eta')$.

$(\underline{\alpha}, \overline{\alpha}, \beta, \gamma)$ *are the* witnesses *of the discrepancy function.*

The discrepancy function (and it's witnesses) bounds the maximum distance between two trajectories in terms of the ℓ^2 distance between their input signals and their initial states. In the rest of the paper, we further assume that $\underline{\alpha}^{-1}$ and γ are Lipschitz, and $\beta(\cdot, \cdot)$ has a Lipschitz continuous derivative in the second argument. In general the IS discrepancy annotations have to be provided with the system model. However for some classes of models, annotations may be computed automatically or obtained from other certificates used for stability proofs.

4.2 Finding IS discrepancy

We note 3 different ways of obtaining IS discrepancy functions.

Lipschitz Dynamics. If the dynamic mapping f of system A is Lipschitz, then for any bounded time $T > 0$, we can find a IS discrepancy function of A that holds for all $t \in [0, T]$. This version of IS discrepancy will be enough for bounded safety proofs. The Lipschitz constants can be computed for linear, polynomial and some several other types of functions [18].

Proposition 4.1. *Suppose the dynamic mapping* f *of system* A *is Lipschitz in both arguments. For any time bound* $T > 0$, $V(\mathbf{x}, \mathbf{x}') = |\mathbf{x}-\mathbf{x}'|$ *is a discrepancy function with witnesses* $(\underline{\alpha}, \overline{\alpha}, \beta, \gamma)$ *where* $\underline{\alpha}(|\mathbf{x}-\mathbf{x}'|) = \overline{\alpha}(|\mathbf{x}-\mathbf{x}'|) = |\mathbf{x}-\mathbf{x}'|$, $\beta(|\theta-\theta'|, t) = e^{Lt}|\theta-\theta'|$ *and* $\gamma(|\mathbf{u}-\mathbf{u}'|) = Le^{LT}|\mathbf{u}-\mathbf{u}'|$.

IS discrepancy functions obtain in this way will have witnesses β and γ exponentially growing in time.

Stable Linear Systems. Suppose A' dynamic mapping $f(\mathbf{x}, \mathbf{u}) = C\mathbf{x} + D\mathbf{u}$, where C is a $n \times n$ matrix and D is a $n \times m$ matrix. If C is asymptotically stable, then its trajectories converge exponentially. And we can get an IS dependency function with exponentially convergent witnesses.

Proposition 4.2. *For linear system* A *with dynamic mapping* $f(\mathbf{x}, \mathbf{u}) = C\mathbf{x} + D\mathbf{u}$ *with* C *stable, there exists* $\lambda > 0$, $V(\mathbf{x}, \mathbf{x}') = |\mathbf{x}-\mathbf{x}'|$ *is a discrepancy function with witnesses* $(\underline{\alpha}, \overline{\alpha}, \beta, \gamma)$ *where* $\underline{\alpha}(|\mathbf{x}-\mathbf{x}'|) = \overline{\alpha}(|\mathbf{x}-\mathbf{x}'|) = |\mathbf{x}-\mathbf{x}'|$, $\beta(|\theta-\theta'|, t) = e^{-\lambda t}|\theta-\theta'|$ *and* $\gamma(|\mathbf{u}-\mathbf{u}'|) = |D||\mathbf{u}-\mathbf{u}'|$.

The positive constant λ can be found algorithmically through solving Lyapunov equation [19].

Incremental Integral ISS. The notion of incremental integral input-to-state stability (incremental integral ISS) of dynamical systems [11] is a generalization of the standard notions of input-to-state stability [9, 10, 20]. A Lyapunov like theorem of proving incremental integral ISS as well as a converse Lyapunov theorem are presented in [11]. Given a proof of an incremental integral ISS property of a model, we get its IS discrepancy function (with witnesses) for free.

Definition 5. *A dynamical system* A *is called incremental integral input-to-state stable (ISS) if there exists a class-*$\mathcal{K}_\infty$ *function* α, *a class-*$\mathcal{KL}$ *function* β *and a class-*$\mathcal{K}$ *function* γ *such that, for any initial states* $\theta, \theta' \in \Theta_A$, *for any input signal* $\eta, \eta' \in U_A$ *and any* $t > 0$,

$$|\alpha(|\xi(t)-\xi'(t)|)| \leq \beta(|\theta-\theta'|, t) + \int_0^t \gamma(|\eta(s)-\eta'(s)|)ds. \tag{3}$$

where $\xi = Traj(A, \theta, \eta)$ *and* $\xi' = Traj(A, \theta', \eta')$.

Proposition 4.3. *Given an incremental integral ISS system* A *with* (α, β, γ) *as in Definition 5, then* $V(\mathbf{x}, \mathbf{x}') = \alpha(|\mathbf{x}-\mathbf{x}'|)$ *is a discrepancy function with witnesses* $(\underline{\alpha}, \overline{\alpha}, \beta, \gamma)$ *where* $\underline{\alpha}(|\mathbf{x}-\mathbf{x}'|) = \overline{\alpha}(|\mathbf{x}-\mathbf{x}'|) = \alpha(|\mathbf{x}-\mathbf{x}'|)$, *and* β, γ *given above.*

5. SMALL APPROXIMANTS FROM IS DISCREPANCY

In this section we define an one-dimensional approximation for dynamical subsystems (Definition 6) that use input-to-state discrepancy functions. For the sake of a cleaner presentation, we develop the results for a dynamical system consisting of two modules with a two-dimensional approximation. The general results follow by straightforward extension and are stated in Section 5.4.

5.1 IS Approximation of $A_1 \| A_2$

Consider the closed dynamical system $A = A_1 \| A_2$, with $X_1 = U_2$ and $X_2 = U_1$ as shown in Figure 2. Let V_i be

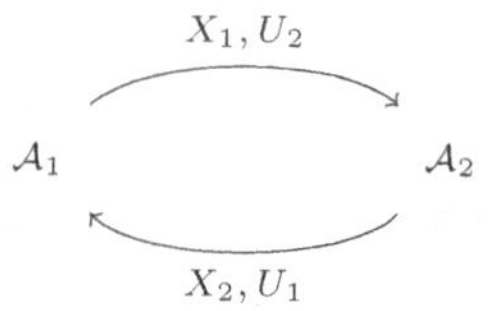

Figure 2: A dynamical system with two modules.

the IS discrepancy function for $A_i, i \in \{1, 2\}$ with witness $(\underline{\alpha}_i, \overline{\alpha}_i, \beta_i, \gamma_i)$. For any pair of initial states θ, θ' in Θ_A, let $\xi = Traj(A, \theta)$ and $\xi' = Traj(A, \theta')$ be the unique trajectories starting from them. We define $\xi_i = \xi \downarrow X_i$ and $\xi_i' = \xi' \downarrow X_i$. From Section 3.2, the restriction of ξ_i and ξ_i' to X_i are trajectories of A_i from $\theta \lceil X_i$ and $\theta' \lceil X_i$. From Definition 4, for every $t \in [0, T]$ the following holds:

$$V_1(\xi_1(t), \xi_1'(t)) \leq \beta_1(|\theta_1 - \theta_1'|, t) + \int_0^t \gamma_1(|\xi_2(s) - \xi_2'(s)|)ds,$$
$$V_2(\xi_2(t), \xi_2'(t)) \leq \beta_2(|\theta_2 - \theta_2'|, t) + \int_0^t \gamma_2(|\xi_1(s) - \xi_1'(s)|)ds. \tag{4}$$

Next, we introduce the key notion of a family of IS approximations for A. Each approximation is parameterized by nonnegative reals δ_1 and δ_2 and is a closed dynamical system M with two main variables m_1 and m_2. As we shall see in Theorem 5.4, at any time t, m_1 gives an upper-bound on the distance between two state trajectories of A_1 that start from neighboring states at most δ_1 apart. Similarly, m_2 gives an upper-bound on neighboring trajectories of A_2.

Of course, the distance between two neighboring state trajectories of A_1 depends on (a) their initial states and (b) on the inputs they experience. These inputs in turn, depend on the corresponding state trajectories of A_2. So, the dynamics of m_1 (and m_2) takes into account the impact of both of these factors using the witnesses of the IS discrepancy functions. Since the β witness bounds the impact of initial states on the discrepancy as a function of time, the dynamics of m_1 (and m_2) is time varying. For convenience, we have therefore introduced a third clock variable (clk) in M.

Definition 6. *For any pair of nonnegative constants (δ_1, δ_2), the (δ_1, δ_2)-IS* approximation *of A is a closed dynamical system $M = \langle X_M, \Theta_M, U_M, f_M\rangle$ where*

(i) $X_M = \{m_1, m_2, clk\}$,

(ii) $\Theta_M = \{\theta\}$ *where θ defined by $\theta(m_i) = \beta_i(\delta_i, 0)$, for $i \in \{1,2\}$, and $\theta(clk) = 0$,*

(iii) $U_M = \varnothing$, *and*

(iv) for any valuation $\mathbf{x} \in Val(X_M)$,

$$f_M(\mathbf{x}) = \begin{bmatrix} \dot\beta_1(\delta_1, \mathbf{x}(clk)) + \gamma_1 \circ \underline{\alpha}_2^{-1}(\mathbf{x}(m_2)) \\ \dot\beta_2(\delta_2, \mathbf{x}(clk)) + \gamma_2 \circ \underline{\alpha}_1^{-1}(\mathbf{x}(m_1)) \\ 1 \end{bmatrix}^{2}. \quad (5)$$

The last component of f_M is the constant 1 and in the initial state $clk = 0$; it follows that along any trajectory μ of M, clk tracks the real time: $\mu(t) \lceil clk = t$. The witness functions $\underline{\alpha}_1^{-1}, \gamma_1$, etc., are Lipschitz and Lipschitz functions are closed under composition, and therefore, f_M is Lipschitz with respect to m_1 and m_2. $\beta_i(\cdot,\cdot)$ has Lipschitz derivatives in the second argument which implies that f_M is also Lipschitz with respect to clk. Thus, M is indeed a closed, deterministic dynamical system with a single initial state and a unique trajectory. Note that both the initial state and the dynamics of M depend on the choice of the parameters δ_1 and δ_2. In Theorem 5.4 we relate m_1 and m_2 with the divergence between trajectories of A_1 and A_2. Specifically, if μ is the trajectory of a (δ_1, δ_2)-IS approximation then $\mu_i = \mu \downarrow m_i(t)$ gives an upperbound on the distance between the trajectories of A_i starting from initial states that are at most δ_i apart.

5.2 Overapproximation with IS Discrepancy

Before diving into technical details, we introduce a couple of notations. For any pair of non-negative reals $\delta = (\delta_1, \delta_2)$ and any state $\mathbf{x} \in Val(X_A)$, we define

$$B_\delta(\mathbf{x}) = B_{\delta_1} \lceil \mathbf{x}(X_1) \times B_{\delta_2}(\mathbf{x} \lceil X_2)$$

as the product of the δ_i-balls around $\mathbf{x} \lceil X_i$. Given a pair of discrepancy functions $V = (V_1, V_2)$ for A_1 and A_2, a state $\mathbf{m} \in Val(X_M)$ of M naturally defines a sublevel set in $Val(X_A) \times Val(X_A)$. In what follows, we denote by $L_V(\mathbf{m}) \subseteq Val(X_A) \times Val(X_A)$ the set

$$\{(\mathbf{x}, \mathbf{x}') \mid \forall i \in \{1,2\},\ V_i(\mathbf{x} \lceil X_i), \mathbf{x}' \lceil X_i) \leq \mathbf{m} \lceil m_i\}.$$

This set is the intersection of the ($\mathbf{m} \lceil m_i$)-*sublevel sets* of V_i. For a state $\mathbf{x} \in Val(X_A)$ of A and a state $\mathbf{m} \in Val(X_M)$ we define

$$B^V_{\mathbf{m}}(\mathbf{x}) = \{\mathbf{x}' \in Val(X_A) \mid (\mathbf{x}, \mathbf{x}') \in L_V(\mathbf{m})\}$$

as the subset of states of A for which $(\mathbf{x}, \mathbf{x}')$ lies in the sublevel set defined by $\mathbf{m}$.

We ultimately show that the trajectory of M always upper bounds the right-hand side of Equation (4), that is,

$$\begin{aligned} \mu_1(t) &\geq \beta_1(|\theta_1 - \theta_1'|, t) + \int_0^t \gamma_1(|\xi_2(s) - \xi_2'(s)|)ds, \\ \mu_2(t) &\geq \beta_2(|\theta_2 - \theta_2'|, t) + \int_0^t \gamma_2(|\xi_1(s) - \xi_1'(s)|)ds. \end{aligned} \quad (6)$$

From the construction of M, we observe that at time $t = 0$, the above inequalities hold. Moreover, the first derivatives of the left-hand sides upper bound those of the right-hand sides at time $t = 0$. However, this property at $t = 0$ cannot immediately be generalized to all $t > 0$. In our proof, we first construct a strict upper bound of the right-hand sides of (6) that holds for all t, and then show that this bound converges to $\mu(\cdot)$.

First, for any positive $\epsilon > 0$, we construct a pair of ϵ-factor trajectories $(\mu_{1\epsilon}, \mu_{2\epsilon})$ with derivatives ϵ-close to the first two components of f_M and show that these trajectories strictly upper-bound the discrepancy functions of V_1 and V_2.

For any $\delta_1, \delta_2 \geq 0$ and any $\epsilon > 0$, a pair of trajectories $\mu_{1\epsilon}, \mu_{2\epsilon} : \mathbb{R}_{\geq 0} \to \mathbb{R}_{\geq 0}$ are defined as solutions to the differential equations:

$$\dot\mu_{1\epsilon} = \dot\beta_1(\delta_1, t) + \gamma_1 \circ \underline{\alpha}_2^{-1}(\mu_{2\epsilon}) + \epsilon, \text{ and} \quad (7)$$

$$\dot\mu_{2\epsilon} = \dot\beta_2(\delta_2, t) + \gamma_2 \circ \underline{\alpha}_1^{-1}(\mu_{1\epsilon}) + \epsilon, \quad (8)$$

with $\mu_{1\epsilon}(0) = \beta_1(\delta_1, 0) + \epsilon$ and $\mu_{2\epsilon}(0) = \beta_2(\delta_2, 0) + \epsilon$. The right-hand side of Equation (7) is Lipschitz, and therefore, $\mu_{1\epsilon}$ and $\mu_{2\epsilon}$ are well-defined. For any two initial states of A θ, θ', we define two differentiable functions $g_1, g_2 : \mathbb{R}_{\geq 0} \to \mathbb{R}$:

$$\begin{aligned} g_1(t) &= \mu_{1\epsilon}(t) - \beta_1(\delta_1, t) - \textstyle\int_0^t \gamma_1(|\xi_2(s) - \xi_2'(s)|)ds, \\ g_2(t) &= \mu_{2\epsilon}(t) - \beta_2(\delta_2, t) - \textstyle\int_0^t \gamma_2(|\xi_1(s) - \xi_1'(s)|)ds. \end{aligned} \quad (9)$$

Recall that $\xi = Traj(A, \theta)$ and $\xi' = Traj(A, \theta')$ are the trajectories of A starting from θ and θ'.

Proposition 5.1. *Consider any non-negative pair $\delta = (\delta_1, \delta_2)$ and initial states $\theta, \theta' \in \Theta_A$ such that $\theta' \in B_\delta(\theta)$. Let $\xi = Traj(A, \theta)$ and $\xi' = Traj(A, \theta')$. Then, for any $\epsilon > 0, t \geq 0$, if $g_1(t), g_2(t) > 0$, then*

$$V_1(\xi_1(t), \xi_1'(t)) < \mu_{1\epsilon}(t), \text{ and } V_2(\xi_2(t), \xi_2'(t)) < \mu_{2\epsilon}(t).$$

PROOF. Here we prove the bound for V_1; the bound for V_2 follows by symmetry. For any $t \geq 0$, since $g_1(t) > 0$,

$$\mu_{1\epsilon}(t) > \beta_1(\delta_1, t) + \int_0^t \gamma_1(|\xi_2(s) - \xi_2'(s)|)ds. \quad (10)$$

From $\theta' \in B_\delta(\theta)$, we have $|\theta_1 - \theta_1'| \leq \delta_1$. Since $\beta_1(\cdot, t)$ is a class-$\mathcal{K}$ function, it follows that

$$\beta_1(\delta_1, t) \geq \beta_1(|\theta_1 - \theta_1'|, t).$$

Thus, Equation (10) becomes

$$\mu_{1\epsilon}(t) > \beta_1(|\theta_1 - \theta_1'|, t) + \int_0^t \gamma_1(|\xi_2(s) - \xi_2'(s)|)ds.$$

[2] $\dot\beta_i(\delta_i, \mathbf{x}(clk))$ is a short hand for $\frac{\partial \beta_i}{\partial t}(\delta_i, \mathbf{x}(clk))$.

By applying Equation (4), it follows that

$$\begin{aligned}\mu_{1\epsilon}(t) &> \beta_1(|\theta_1-\theta_1'|,t)+\textstyle\int_0^t \gamma_1(|\xi_2(s)-\xi_2'(s)|)ds\\ &\geq V_1(\xi_1(t),\xi_1'(t)).\end{aligned}$$

The next lemma, establishes that we can drop the assumption about the positivity of g_1 and g_2 and still arrive at the conclusion of Proposition 5.1.

Lemma 5.2. *Consider any non-negative pair $\delta=(\delta_1,\delta_2)$, and initial states $\theta,\theta'\in\Theta_A$ such that $\theta'\in B_\delta(\theta)$. Let $\xi = Traj(A,\theta)$ and $\xi'=Traj(A,\theta')$. Thus, for any $\epsilon>0, t\geq 0$,*

$$V_1(\xi_1(t),\xi_1'(t))<\mu_{1\epsilon}(t) \text{ and } V_2(\xi_2(t),\xi_2'(t))<\mu_{2\epsilon}(t).$$

PROOF. By Proposition 5.1, it suffices to prove that for all $t\geq 0$, $g_1(t),g_2(t)>0$. At $t=0$,

$$g_1(0)=\beta_1(\delta_1,0)+\epsilon-\beta_1(\delta_1,0)=\epsilon>0.$$

Similarly, $g_2(0)>0$. Suppose for the sake of contradiction that $t_a>0$ is the first time when $g_1(t),g_2(t)>0$ is violated. From the continuity of g_1,g_2, we have that the both following conditions hold:

(i) $g_1(t),g_2(t)>0$ for all $t\in[0,t_a)$, and

(ii) $g_1(t_a)=0$ or $g_2(t_a)=0$.

Without loss of generality, we assume $g_1(t_a)=0$. From mean value theorem, there exists some time $t_b\in(0,t_a)$ such that

$$\dot{g}_1(t_b)=\frac{g_1(0)-g_1(t_a)}{0-t_a}\leq-\frac{\epsilon}{t_a}<0. \tag{11}$$

We can bound the derivative $\dot{g}_1(t_b)$ as:

$$\dot{g}_1(t_b)=\dot{\mu}_{1\epsilon}(t_b)-\frac{d}{dt}\left(\beta_1(\delta_1,t_b)+\int_0^{t_b}\gamma_1(|\xi_2(s)-\xi_2'(s)|)ds\right).$$

Plugging the right-hand side of Equation (7) into the above equation, it follows:

$$\begin{aligned}\dot{g}_1(t_b) &= \dot{\beta}_1(\delta_1,t_b)+\gamma_1\circ\underline{\alpha}_2^{-1}(\mu_{2\epsilon}(t_b))+\epsilon\\ &\quad -\dot{\beta}_1(\delta_1,t_b)-\gamma_1(|\xi_2(t_b)-\xi_2'(t_b)|)\\ &= \epsilon+\left(\gamma_1\circ\underline{\alpha}_2^{-1}(\mu_{2\epsilon}(t_b))-\gamma_1(|x_2(t_b)-x_2'(t_b)|)\right).\end{aligned} \tag{12}$$

From condition (i), we know $g_2(t_b)>0$. It follows from Proposition 5.1 that

$$\mu_{2\epsilon}(t_b)>V_2(\xi_2(t_b),\xi_2'(t_b)). \tag{13}$$

From Definition 4, we have $V_2(\xi_2(t_b),\xi_2'(t_b))\geq\underline{\alpha}_2(|\xi_2(t_b)-\xi_2'(t_b)|)$. Equation (13) yields $\mu_{2\epsilon}(t_b)>\underline{\alpha}_2(|\xi_2(t_b)-\xi_2'(t_b)|)$. Because $\gamma\circ\underline{\alpha}_2^{-1}$ is a class-$\mathcal{K}$ function, it follows that

$$\gamma_1\circ\underline{\alpha}_2^{-1}(\mu_{2\epsilon}(t_b))\geq\gamma_1(|\xi_2(t_b)-\xi_2'(t_b)|).$$

Combining the above equation with Equation (12), we have that $\dot{g}_1(t_b)\geq\epsilon>0$, which contradicts to Equation (11).

Lemma 5.2 shows that for any $\epsilon>0$, the ϵ-factor trajectories $\mu_{1\epsilon}$ and $\mu_{2\epsilon}$ give strict upper bounds on the distance between corresponding trajectories of A_1 and A_2. In the following lemma, we show that as $\epsilon\to 0$, $\mu_{i\epsilon}$ converges to the trajectory $\mu\downarrow m_i$; recall that μ is the trajectory of the IS approximation M. It follows that the trajectory μ indeed bounds the divergence of any trajectories of A.

Lemma 5.3. *Consider any non-negative pair $\delta=(\delta_1,\delta_2)$ and initial states $\theta,\theta'\in\Theta_A$ such that $\theta'\in B_\delta(\theta)$. Let $\xi = Traj((A,\theta))$, $\xi'=Traj((A,\theta'))$, and μ be the trajectory of A's (δ_1,δ_2)-IS approximation M. Then for all $t\geq 0$,*

$$(\xi(t),\xi'(t))\in L_V(\mu(t)).$$

PROOF. For brevity we write $\mu\downarrow m_i$ as μ_i and $\mu\downarrow clk$ as clk. Recall, we have $clk(t)=t$. Rewiriting the condition that the solution μ of M satisfies the differential equation defined by f_M, we have

$$\begin{aligned}\dot{\mu}_1(t) &= \dot{\beta}_1(\delta_1,t)+\gamma_1\circ\underline{\alpha}_2^{-1}(\mu_2(s))ds,\\ \dot{\mu}_2(t) &= \dot{\beta}_2(\delta_2,t)+\gamma_2\circ\underline{\alpha}_1^{-1}(\mu_1(s))ds,\\ \dot{clk}(t) &= 1.\end{aligned} \tag{14}$$

By integrating both sides with initial condition $\mu_1(0)=\beta_1(\delta_1,0)$ and $\mu_2(0)=\beta_2(\delta_2,0)$, we have,

$$\begin{aligned}\mu_1(t) &= \beta_1(\delta_1,t)+\textstyle\int_0^t\gamma_1\circ\underline{\alpha}_2^{-1}(\mu_2(s))ds,\\ \mu_2(t) &= \beta_2(\delta_2,t)+\textstyle\int_0^t\gamma_2\circ\underline{\alpha}_1^{-1}(\mu_1(s))ds,\\ clk(t) &= t.\end{aligned} \tag{15}$$

Similarly, by integrating Equation (7), we have

$$\begin{aligned}\mu_{1\epsilon}(t) &= \beta_1(\delta_1,t)+\textstyle\int_0^t\gamma_1\circ\underline{\alpha}_2^{-1}(\mu_{2\epsilon}(s))ds+\epsilon(1+t)\\ \mu_{2\epsilon}(t) &= \beta_2(\delta_1,t)+\textstyle\int_0^t\gamma_2\circ\underline{\alpha}_1^{-1}(\mu_{1\epsilon}(s))ds+\epsilon(1+t).\end{aligned} \tag{16}$$

Define $h(t)\triangleq|\mu_1(t)-\mu_{1\epsilon}(t)|+|\mu_2(t)-\mu_{2\epsilon}(t)|$. Plugging in Equation (15) and (16) into the definition of $h(t)$, we have:

$$\begin{aligned}h(t) &\leq 2\epsilon(t+1)+\int_0^t|\gamma_1\circ\underline{\alpha}_2^{-1}(\mu_{1\epsilon}(s))-\gamma_1\circ\underline{\alpha}_2^{-1}(\mu_1(s))|ds\\ &\quad+\int_0^t|\gamma_2\circ\underline{\alpha}_1^{-1}(\mu_{2\epsilon}(t))-\gamma_2\circ\underline{\alpha}_1^{-1}(\mu_2(t))|ds.\end{aligned}$$

From the Lipschitz property of $\gamma_1\circ\underline{\alpha}_2^{-1}$ and $\gamma_2\circ\underline{\alpha}_1^{-1}$, we can find a constant $L>0$ such that $|\gamma_1\circ\underline{\alpha}_2^{-1}(\mu_{1\epsilon}(s))-\gamma_1\circ\underline{\alpha}_2^{-1}(\mu_1(s))|\leq L|\mu_1(t)-\mu_{1\epsilon}(t)|$ and $|\gamma_2\circ\underline{\alpha}_1^{-1}(\mu_{2\epsilon}(s))-\gamma_2\circ\underline{\alpha}_1^{-1}(\mu_2(s))|\leq L|\mu_2(t)-\mu_{2\epsilon}(t)|$. It follows that

$$h(t)\leq 2\epsilon(t+1)+\int_0^t Lh(s)ds.$$

By Gronwall-Bellman inequality [21], it follows that

$$h(t)\leq 2\epsilon(t+1)+2\epsilon L\int_0^t(s+1)e^{L(t-s)}ds. \tag{17}$$

It follows that for any $t\in\mathbb{R}_{\geq 0}$, the integral $\int_0^t(s+1)e^{L(t-s)}ds$ is bounded. Thus $h(t)\to 0$ as $\epsilon\to 0$, which implies both $|\mu_1(t)-\mu_{1\epsilon}(t)|$ and $|\mu_2(t)-\mu_{2\epsilon}(t)|$ converge to 0. Using Lemma 5.2, and taking the limit of $\epsilon\to 0$, it follows that

$$V_1(\xi_1(t),\xi_1'(t))\leq\mu_1(t) \text{ and } V_2(\xi_2(t),\xi_2'(t))\leq\mu_2(t).$$

That is, for any $t\geq 0$, $(\xi(t),\xi'(t))\in L_V(\mu(t))$.

Theorem 5.4 states that the reach set of any (large) dynamical system $A=A_1\|A_2$ from a set of states can be overapproximated by bloating an individual execution ξ of A by a factor that is entirely determined by (a) IS discrepancy functions V_1 and V_2 of its (smaller) subsystems, and (b) the trajectory μ of a (small, 2-dimensional) dynamical system M that is its IS approximation.

Theorem 5.4. *Consider a closed dynamical system $A = A_1 \| A_2$ with IS discrepancy functions $V = (V_1, V_2)$. Let $\xi = Traj(A, \theta)$ for some initial state $\theta \in \Theta_A$. For any nonnegative pair $\delta = (\delta_1, \delta_2)$ suppose μ is the trajectory of the (δ_1, δ_2)-IS approximation M. Then, for any $T \geq 0$*

$$\mathsf{Reach}_A(B_\delta(\theta), T) \subseteq \bigcup_{t \in [0,T]} B^V_{\mu(t)}(\xi(t)).$$

PROOF. For any $\mathbf{x} \in \mathsf{Reach}_\mathcal{A}(B_\delta(\theta), T)$, there exists an initial state $\theta' \in B_\delta(\theta)$, a trajectory $\xi' = Traj(A, \theta')$ and a time $t \in [0, T]$ such that $\xi'(t) = \mathbf{x}$. It follows Lemma 5.3 that $(\xi(t), \xi'(t)) \in L_V(\mu(t))$, and therefore, $\mathbf{x} \in B^V_{\mu(t)}(\xi(t))$.

Theorem 5.4 establishes an overapproximation of set of reachable states from a δ-ball $B_\delta(\theta)$. To compute the set of reachable state from a compact initial set Θ_A, we can first compute a δ-cover of Θ_A, and then compute the union of reach set of the covers.

Remark 1. Theorem 5.4 does not require A to be stable or any global property to hold for the IS discrepancy functions.

Remark 2. To use Theorem 5.4 we need to (a) find IS discrepancy functions for the subsystems, and (b) compute individual executions ξ of A and μ of M. Fortunately, for large classes of nonlinear dynamical systems there exist scalable numerical techniques for (b). This is one of the motivations of this work. For linear and some special classes of nonlinear systems (a) can be solved automatically (see Section 4.2).

5.3 Precision of IS Approximation

The precision of this overapproximation is determined by $|\mu(t)|$. In the following, we show that the precision can be made arbitrarily high with sufficiently small but positive δ_1, δ_2.

Lemma 5.5. *Consider any $T > 0$, $t \in [0, T]$, and a sequence of pairs of positive reals $\delta^k = (\delta^k_1, \delta^k_2)$ converging to $(0, 0)$. For the trajectory (μ^k) of the corresponding (δ^k_1, δ^k_2)-IS approximation M^k, $|(\mu^k \downarrow m_i(t)| \to 0$ for $i \in \{1, 2\}$.*

PROOF. Fix a $T > 0$ and $\delta^k = (\delta^k_1, \delta^k_2)$. This defines the (δ^k_1, δ^k_2)-IS approximation M^k and its trajectory μ^k. We will prove that for all $t \in [0, T]$,

$$|(\mu^k \downarrow m_1)(t)| + |(\mu^k \downarrow m_2)(t)| \to 0,$$

as $\delta^k \to 0$. Here on we drop the superscript k and use the notations setup earlier: $\mu_i = \mu \downarrow m_i$, etc.

From the first row in Equation (15), we have that

$$|\mu_1(t)| \leq \beta_1(\delta_1, t) + \int_0^t |\gamma_1 \circ \underline{\alpha}_2^{-1}(\mu_2(s))| ds \tag{18}$$

From the Lipschitz property of $\gamma_1 \circ \underline{\alpha}_2^{-1}$, there exists some $L_1 > 0$, such that $|\gamma_1 \circ \underline{\alpha}_2^{-1}(\mu_2(s)) - \gamma_1 \circ \underline{\alpha}_2^{-1}(0)| \leq L|\mu_2(s) - 0|$. Since $\gamma_1 \circ \underline{\alpha}_2^{-1}$ is of class-$\mathcal{K}$, it follows that

$$|\gamma_1 \circ \underline{\alpha}_2^{-1}(\mu_2(s))| \leq L|\mu_2(s)|.$$

From Equation (15), we observe that $i \in \{1, 2\}$ $\mu_i(t)$ are nonnegative scalers. We drop the absolute value symbols $|\cdot|$. Then Equation (18) reduces to

$$|\mu_1(t)| \leq \beta_1(\delta_1, t) + \int_0^t L|\mu_2(s)| ds. \tag{19}$$

Since $\beta_1(\delta_1, t)$ is bounded in compact intervals, define

$$B^T_1(\delta_1) = \sup_{t \in [0,T]} \beta_1(\delta_1, t), \tag{20}$$

as the upper bound of the function $\beta_1(\cdot, t)$ in interval $t \in [0, T]$. It follows from Equation (19) that

$$|\mu_1(t)| \leq B^T_1(\delta_1) + \int_0^t L|\mu_2(s)| ds. \tag{21}$$

Starting from the second row of Equation (15), by following similar steps from Equation (18)-(21), we have:

$$|\mu_2(t)| \leq B^T_2(\delta_2) + \int_0^t L|\mu_1(s)| ds. \tag{22}$$

Summing up Equation (21) and (22), by applying Gronwall-Bellman inequality, we have

$$|\mu_1(t)| + |\mu_2(t)| \leq (B^T_1(\delta_1) + B^T_2(\delta_2)) e^{Lt}.$$

For $i \in \{1, 2\}$, since $\beta_i(\cdot, \cdot)$ is a class-$\mathcal{K}$ function in the first argument, it follows from Equation (20) that $B_i(\delta^k_i) \to 0$ as $\delta^k_i \to 0$. It follows that, $|\mu^k_1(t)| + |\mu^k_2(t)| \to 0$ as $\delta^k \to 0$.

Proposition 5.6 follows from the fact that for $i \in \{1, 2\}$, for any $\mathbf{x}, \mathbf{x}' \in X_i$, $\underline{\alpha}_i(\mathbf{x} - \mathbf{x}') \leq V_i(\mathbf{x}, \mathbf{x}')$ (Definition 4).

Proposition 5.6. *For dynamical system A with discrepancy function V_1, V_2, fix any $\mathbf{x} \in X_A$. For any $\epsilon > 0$, there exist $r > 0$, such that $B^V_r(\mathbf{x}) \subseteq B_\epsilon(\mathbf{x})$.*

With Lemma 5.5 and Proposition 5.6, the following theorem is straightforward.

Theorem 5.7. *Consider a closed dynamical system $A = A_1 || A_2$ with IS discrepancy $V = \{V_1, V_2\}$. Let $\xi = Traj(A, \theta)$ for some initial state $\theta \in \Theta_A$. For any $\epsilon > 0$, there exists a positive pair $\delta_1, \delta_2 > 0$ such that , for A's (δ_1, δ_2)-IS approximation M, for any $T \geq 0$*

$$\bigcup_{t \in [0,T]} B^V_{\mu(t)}(\xi(t)) \subseteq B_\epsilon(\mathsf{Reach}_\mathcal{A}(B_\delta(\theta), T)),$$

where μ is the unique trajectory of M.

Remark 3. If the overapproximation obtained from Theorem 5.4 is not precise enough to prove safety, then, we can refine the parameters δ_1 and δ_2. Then we can compute $B^V_{\mu(t)}(\xi(t))$ for each of the smaller partitions with higher precision. This is the approach used for developing Algorithm 1.

5.4 Approximations for $A_1 \| A_2 \| \ldots A_N$

The approximation and its analysis presented in the previous section can be extended to a closed systems with N components: $A = A_1 \| A_2 \ldots \| A_N$. For any trajectories $\xi, \xi' \in Traj(A, \Theta)$, like the notations we used in Section 5.1, for each $i \in [N]$, we denfine $\xi_i = \xi \downarrow X_i$ and $\xi'_i = \xi \downarrow X_i$.

The natural generalization of Definition 4 to a set of discrepancy functions according to the composition topology for A is given below:

Definition 7. *A set of input-to-state discrepancy functions of $\mathcal{A}$ is a set of continuous functions $V = \{V_i\}_{i \in [N]}$ with class-$\mathcal{K}$ witnesses $\{(\underline{\alpha}_i, \overline{\alpha}_i, \beta_i)\}_{i \in [N]}$ and $\{\gamma_{ji}\}_{(j,i): X_j \cap U_i \neq \varnothing}$, where for any $\theta, \theta' \in \Theta_A$, , for each $t \geq 0$ each $i \in [N]$*

$$V_i(\xi_i(t), \xi'_i(t)) \leq \beta_i(|\xi_i(0) - \xi'_i(0)|, t) + \int_0^t \sum_{j: X_j \cap U_i \neq \varnothing} \gamma_{ji}(|\xi_j(s) - \xi'_j(s)|) ds,$$

where $\xi = Traj(A, \theta)$ and $\xi' = Traj(A, \theta')$.

The set $\{A_j | X_j \cap U_i \neq \varnothing\}$ is the set of modules that provide inputs to module A_i. Similar to Definition 4, Definition 7 requires that each module A_i, is associated with functions V_i and witnesses $(\underline{\alpha}_i, \overline{\alpha}_i, \beta_i)$. Furthermore, each pair (A_j, A_i), where part of A_i's input comes from A_j's state, is associated with a witness function γ_{ji}. Generalizing Definition 6, the IS approximation of A is a $(N+1)$-dimensional closed deterministic dynamical system M.

Definition 8. *For any $\delta = (\delta_1, \ldots, \delta_N) \in {\mathbb{R}_{\geq 0}}^N$, the δ-IS approximation of A is a closed dynamical system $M = \langle X_M, \Theta_M, U_M, f_M \rangle$, where*

(i) $X_M = \{m_1, m_2, \ldots, m_N, clk\}$,

(ii) $\Theta_M = \{\theta\}$, *where θ is defined by $\theta(m_i) = \beta_i(\delta_i, 0)$, for $i \in [N]$, and $\theta(clk) = 0$,*

(iii) $\mathcal{U}_B = \varnothing$,

(iv) For any valuation $\mathbf{x} \in Val(X_M)$ and each $i \in [N]$:

$$f_M \downarrow m_i(\mathbf{x}) = \dot{\beta}_i(\delta_i, \mathbf{x}(clk)) + \sum_{j: X_j \cap U_i \neq \varnothing} \gamma_{ji} \circ \underline{\alpha}_j^{-1}(\mathbf{x}(m_j)),$$

$$f_M \downarrow clk(\mathbf{x}) = 1.$$

For any state $\mathbf{m} \in Val(X_M)$, the intersection of all sublevel sets of $\{V_i\}_{i \in [N]}$ is denoted as $L_V(\mathbf{m})$ as a generalization of the $A_1 || A_2$ case.

Remark 4. The IS approximation M is $N+1$-dimensional. Construction of M only uses (a) information of individual modules (IS discrepancy functions etc.) and (b) the topology of the composition. No additional information about the behavior of the composed system A is needed.

It follows that for a closed composed system $A = A_1 || \ldots A_N$ and its IS approximation M, the conclusions of Theorem 5.4 and 5.7 hold with the obvious changes.

6. FROM SIMULATIONS TO PROOFS

In Section 5, from a closed dynamical system A composed of N subsystems and a set of IS discrepancy functions for the subsystems, we constructed an $(N+1)$-dimensional IS approximation M. With Theorem 5.4, by computing trajectories $\xi = Traj(A, \theta)$ of A and a trajectories μ of M, we can compute overapproximations $\mathsf{Reach}_A(B_\delta(\theta), T)$. Computing precise overapproximations of $\mathsf{Reach}_A(\Theta_A, T)$ then reduce to computing finitely many trajectories of A and Ms which can be accomplished using numerical ODE solvers. In this section, we present a safety verification algorithm using this idea.

6.1 Simulations of Dynamical Systems

Given a closed dynamical system A, an initial state θ, let $\xi = \{A, \theta\}$. For a step size $\tau > 0$, validated ODE solvers (such as [22–24]) compute a sequence of boxes $R_1, R_2, \ldots, R_l \subseteq Val(X_A)$, such that for each $k \in [l]$, $t \in [(k-1)\tau, k\tau]$, $\xi(t) \in R_k$. For a desired error bound $\epsilon > 0$, by reducing the step size τ, the diameter of R_k can be made smaller then ϵ. We capture such simulation trace in the definition below.

Definition 9. *Given a dynamical system A, an initial state θ, a time bound T, an error bound $\epsilon > 0$, and time step $\tau > 0$, for $\xi = Traj(A, \theta)$, a $(\theta, T, \epsilon, \tau)$-simulation trace is a finite sequence $\phi = (R_0, t_0), (R_1, t_1), \ldots, (R_l, t_l)$ where*

(i) $t_0 = 0$, $t_l = T$, and $\forall\ k \in [l]$, $t_i - t_{i-1} \leq \tau$,

(ii) $\forall k \in [l]$ and $\forall t \in [t_{k-1}, t_k]$, $\xi(t) \in R_k$, and

(iii) $\forall k \in [l]$, $dia(R_k) \leq \epsilon$.

In Algorithm 1 presented in Section 6.2, the subroutine $Simulate(A, \theta, T, \epsilon, \tau)$ (line 5,7) computes a $(\theta, T, \epsilon, \tau)$-simulation as defines in Definition 9. For the completeness of the algorithm, we require that for any precision parameters $\epsilon, \tau > 0$, a simulation trace fulfill such precision can be computed.

6.2 Verification Algorithm

Algorithm 1: Verifying interconnecting systems

input: $A, \mathbb{U}, \epsilon_0, \delta_0, T, \{V_i, \underline{\alpha}_i, \overline{\alpha}_i, \beta_i, \gamma_{ij}\}$

1 $\delta \leftarrow \delta_0$; $\epsilon \leftarrow \epsilon_0$; $\mathcal{R} \leftarrow \varnothing$;
2 $\mathcal{C} \leftarrow Partition(\Theta_{\mathcal{A}}, \delta, \epsilon)$;
3 **while** $\mathcal{C} \neq \varnothing$ **do**
4   **for** $(\theta, \delta, \epsilon) \in \mathcal{X}$ **do**
5     $\psi \leftarrow Simulate(A, \theta, T, \epsilon, \tau)$;
6     $M \leftarrow ISApprox(\delta, \{V_i, \underline{\alpha}_i, \overline{\alpha}_i, \beta_i, \gamma_{ij}\})$;
7     $\phi \leftarrow Simulate(M, \theta_M, T, \epsilon, \tau)$;
8     $\rho \leftarrow SupByTime(\phi)$;
9     $S \leftarrow B_\rho^V(\psi)$;
10   **if** $S \cap \mathbb{U} = \varnothing$ **then**
11       $\mathcal{C} \leftarrow \mathcal{C} \backslash \{(\theta, \delta, \epsilon)\}$; $\mathcal{R} \leftarrow \mathcal{R} \cup S$;
12   **else if** $\exists k, R_k \subseteq \mathbb{U}$ **then**
13   **return** (UNSAFE, $\mathcal{R}$)
14   **else**
15       $\mathcal{C} \leftarrow \mathcal{C} \backslash \{(\theta, \delta, \epsilon)\}$;
16       $\mathcal{C} \leftarrow \mathcal{C} \cup Partition(\Theta \cap B_\delta(\theta), (\frac{\delta_1}{2}, \ldots, \frac{\delta_N}{2}), \frac{\epsilon}{2})$;
17 **return** (SAFE, $\mathcal{R}$);

We introduce Algorithm 1 to verify a closed composed system $A = A_1 || \ldots || A_N$. Let each subsystem A_i be equipped with discrepancy functions V_i with witnesses $(\underline{\alpha}_i, \overline{\alpha}_i, \beta_i, \{\gamma_{ji}\})$. The set $\mathcal{C}$ computed in line 2 is a finite set of triples $\{(\theta_c, \delta, \epsilon)\}_{c \in |\mathcal{C}|}$, such that $\{\theta_c\}_{c \in |\mathcal{C}|}$ is a δ-cover of the initial set Θ_A. Each θ_c is associated with precession parameter $\epsilon > 0$ and positive real-valued vector δ. For each triple $(\theta, \delta, \epsilon)$ in the cover set $\mathcal{C}$, an δ-IS approximation M (line 6) is constructed following Definition 8.

The $Simulate()$ (line 5, 7) function is used in two ways:

(i) in computing a simulation trace $\psi = \langle R_0, t_0 \rangle, \ldots, \langle R_p, t_p \rangle$ containing the trajectory $\xi = Traj(A, \theta)$ of the (large) dynamical system A, and

(ii) in computing a simulation trace $\phi = \langle Q_0, t_0 \rangle, \ldots, \langle Q_p, t_p \rangle$ of the trajectory $\mu = Traj(M, \theta_M)$, of the (smaller) IS approximation M.

Here we assume the time stamps of the sequence ψ matches up with that of ϕ. This can be achieved by using a fixed step solver or through resimulating using smaller step sizes. The sequence ρ computed in line 8 is a sequence of the pair $\langle r_0, t_0 \rangle, \ldots, \langle r_p, t_p \rangle$, where for each $k \in [p]$, r_k is a nonnegative real defined as $r_k = \sup_{\mathbf{m} \in Q_k} |\mathbf{m}|$. In line 9, the sequence of sets $\{R_k\}$ is bloated by the sequence of factors $\{r_k\}$ element-wise to construct a tube S. We claim that the tube S contains the set of reachable state of $\mathcal{A}$ from the set of initial state $B_\delta(\theta)$. Then the algorithm checks whether this tube is safe or not, or further refinement is needed.

6.3 Analysis of the Algorithm

We establish the soundness and relative completeness of the algorithm in Theorems 6.3 and 6.4.

Proposition 6.1. *For any* $(\theta, \delta, \epsilon) \in \mathcal{C}$, $\xi \in Traj(A, B_\delta(\theta))$ *and* $t \in [t_{k-1}, t_k]$: $\xi(t) \in B^V_{r_k}(R_k)$.

This follows directly from Theorem 5.4. It also straightforward to check the following invariant of Algorithm 1.

Proposition 6.2. *For compact initial set* Θ_A*, during a run of Algorithm 1,* $\mathcal{C}$ *is finite. And,* $\bigcup_{(\theta,\delta,\epsilon)\in\mathcal{C}} B_\delta(\theta) \supseteq \Theta_A$.

Theorem 6.3. *Algorithm 1 is sound. That is, if it returns* SAFE *then A is safe up to T, and if it returns* UNSAFE *then A is unsafe.*

PROOF. Suppose the algorithm returns SAFE. For any cover $(\theta, \delta, \epsilon) \in \mathcal{C}$, S computed in line 9 is the union of a sequence of regions $\{B^V_{r_k}(R_k)\}$. It follows from Proposition 6.1 that $\mathsf{Reach}_A(B_\delta(\theta), T) \subseteq S$. Thus if $S \cap \mathbb{U} = \varnothing$, then $\mathsf{Reach}_A(B_\delta(\theta)) \cap \mathbb{U} = \varnothing$. The algorithm returns SAFE, if all such covers are checked safe. From Proposition 6.2, we conclude $\mathsf{Reach}_A(\Theta_A, T) \cap \mathbb{U} = \varnothing$.

Otherwise if the algorithm returns UNSAFE, there exists at least one set R_k contained in the unsafe set $\mathbb{U}$. It follows from Proposition 6.1 that for the trajectory $\xi = Traj(A, \theta)$ and some $t \in [t_{k-1}, t_k]$, $\xi(t) \in \mathbb{U}$.

Theorem 6.4. *Algorithm 1 is relatively complete. That is, if A is robustly safe then Algorithm 1 terminates and returns* SAFE *and if A is unsafe then it terminates and returns* UNSAFE.

PROOF. Suppose that for some $\epsilon' > 0$, A is ϵ'-robustly safe up to time T. It follows from Definition 2 that

$$B_{\epsilon'}(\mathsf{Reach}_A(\Theta_A, T)) \cap \mathbb{U} = \varnothing.$$

It follows that line 11 is never executed. For any $\theta \in \Theta$, we will show that for small enough refinement parameters $\delta, \epsilon > 0$, for any k, $dia(B^V_{r_k}(R_k)) < \epsilon'$. From Proposition 5.6, we can show that exists $e > 0$ such that for $r_k < e$,

$$B^V_{r_k}(R_k) \subseteq B_{\epsilon'/3}(R_k). \tag{23}$$

From Lemma 5.5, there exists a $\delta > 0$, for all $t \in [0, T]$, $\forall i \in [N]$, $|\mu(t)| \leq e/2$. For a simulation trace $\phi = \langle M_0, t_0\rangle, \ldots, \langle M_q, t_q\rangle$ (line 7), for $\epsilon \leq e/2$, it follows from Definition 9 that for all $k \in [q]$, the diameter $dia(M_k) \leq e/2$. Thus for any $k \in [q]$, $r_k = \sup_{\mathbf{m}\in M_k} |\mathbf{m}| \leq \epsilon + \sup_{t\in[t'_{l-1}, t'_l]} |\mu(t)| \leq e/2 + e/2 = e$. It follows from Equation (23) that by choosing $\delta \leq d$ and $\epsilon \leq e/2$, we have $B^V_{r_k}(R_k) \subseteq B_{\epsilon'/3}(R_k)$. Notice that the diameter of R_k is bounded by the refinement parameter ϵ. By choosing $\epsilon = \min\{\epsilon'/3, e\}$, it follows that

$$dia(B_{\epsilon'/3}(R_k)) \leq \epsilon'/3 + dia(R_k) \leq \epsilon'/3 + \epsilon'/3 < \epsilon'.$$

Thus, after a number of $\max\{\log(\frac{\epsilon_0}{\min\{\epsilon'/3, e\}}), \log\frac{\delta_0}{d}\}$ refinements, the parameters δ, ϵ are small enough to guarantee that $S \cap \mathbb{U} = \varnothing$. Thus the algorithm returns SAFE.

On the other hand, suppose A is unsafe with respect to an open unsafe set $\mathbb{U}$. There exists an initial state θ, a time $t \geq 0$ and a $\epsilon' > 0$ such that $B_{\epsilon'}\xi(\theta, t) \subseteq \mathbb{U}$. For the same number of refinement as the robustly safe case, it can be shown that there exists an $B^V_{r_k}(R_k) \subseteq B_{\epsilon'}\xi(\theta, t)$. It follows that the algorithm returns UNSAFE.

7. EXPERIMENTAL VALIDATION

We have created a prototype implementation of Algorithm 1 in Matlab using the built-in ODE solvers. Currently, we assume that the error bounds of the computation in line 5-7 are indeed met by the Matlab's ODE solver. To make this step rigorous, in the future, we will use a validated ODE solver like [22–24].

We verify the safety of several linear and nonlinear models. Each module in the linear synchronization examples (Example 1, see [17] for detail) is a 4-dimensional linear dynamical system and the overall system is composed of several modules in different topologies.

The nonlinear water tank network example is a modified version of the one presented in [25]. In this example, each module captures the fluid levels in a group of tanks, which depends on the flows from other groups of tanks.

The closed loop robotic arm system consists of two modules: a 4-dimensional model of the robotic arm (see [10]), and a 2-dimensional adaptive controller.

We perform several experiments for time bound $T = 20s$ on a Intel i5-3470 CPU. The columns in Table 1 present (i) the system being verified, (ii) the number of total state variables, (iii) the number of modules, (iv) the number of covers for the initial set, (v) the total number of simulation boxes generated, and (vi) the running time of the algorithm. Our experimental results show that the running time roughly scales linearly with the total number of simulation boxes generated for both the original system A and its IS approximation M. The number of simulation boxes generated is proportional to the product of the total number of covers and the time bound. Fixed a compact initial set, the number of covers generated depends on the level of precision needed to prove (or disprove) safety, which depends on the distance between the unsafe set to the reachable states. We also observe that the dimension and non-linearity of the system does not explicitly influence the running time.

System	# V	# N	# C	# sim	RT (s)
Lin. Sync I	12	3	128	42112	115.7
Lin. Sync II	16	4	128	45440	129.2
Lin. Sync III	24	6	128	45649	135.1
Nonli. WT I	10	2	128	45184	127.4
Nonli. WT II	15	3	128	47232	134.9
Nonli. WT III	30	6	128	47232	140.0
Nonli. Rob. I	6	2	64	22592	49.3
Nonli. Rob. II	6	2	216	76248	166.8

Table 1: Experimental results. The columns represent: (1) the system being verified, (2) # state variables, (3) # modules, (4) # covers of initial set, (5) # total simulation boxes, (6) run time.

8. CONCLUSIONS

The technique we present for proving bounded time safety properties of (possibly unstable) nonlinear dynamical systems uses numerical simulations and IS discrepancy functions for the subsystems. IS discrepancy of a subsystem A_i, bounds the distance between two (possibly diverging) trajectories of A_i in terms of their initial states and input signals. It is closely related to the notion of input-to-state stability that is well studied in control theory, but importantly, does not require the subsystems or the overall system to be stable. Consequently, our construction of the low dimensional dynamical system $M(\delta)$ that gives a bound on the divergence of trajectories of A, does not rely on any global properties like small-gain of the interconnection nor stability of A, but instead only uses the individual discrepancy functions and the numerical simulations of A and $M(\delta)$. Further, we also show that by choosing appropriately small δ's the overapproximations can be made arbitrarily precise; and therefore our verification algorithm is sound and relatively complete.

To make this technique practical, we have to develop systematic methods for finding these discrepancy functions for nonlinear models. While there are existing approaches based on static analysis, one alternative direction would be to used simulations themselves to bootstrap the search for discrepancy function [3,26]. A orthogonal direction is to extend the results to switched or hybrid systems.

9. REFERENCES

[1] A. Donzé, "Breach, a toolbox for verification and parameter synthesis of hybrid systems," in *Computer Aided Verification*. Springer, 2010, pp. 167–170.

[2] Y. Annpureddy, C. Liu, G. Fainekos, and S. Sankaranarayanan, *S-taliro: A tool for temporal logic falsification for hybrid systems*. Springer, 2011.

[3] P. Duggirala, S. Mitra, and M. Viswanathan, "Verification of annotated models from executions," in *International Conference on Embedded Software*, 2013.

[4] Z. Huang, "On simulation based verification of nonlinear nondeterministic hybrid systems," 2013.

[5] Z. Han and P. J. Mosterman, "Towards sensitivity analysis of hybrid systems using simulink," in *Proceedings of the 16th international conference on Hybrid systems: computation and control*. ACM, 2013, pp. 95–100.

[6] E. M. Aylward, P. A. Parrilo, and J.-J. E. Slotine, "Stability and robustness analysis of nonlinear systems via contraction metrics and sos programming," *Automatica*, vol. 44, no. 8, pp. 2163–2170, 2008.

[7] U. Topcu, A. Packard, and R. Murray, "Compositional stability analysis based on dual decomposition," in *Decision and Control, 2009 held jointly with the 2009 28th Chinese Control Conference. CDC/CCC 2009. Proceedings of the 48th IEEE Conference on*, Dec 2009, pp. 1175–1180.

[8] C. Sloth, R. Wisniewski, and G. Pappas, "On the existence of compositional barrier certificates," in *Decision and Control (CDC), 2012 IEEE 51st Annual Conference on*, Dec 2012, pp. 4580–4585.

[9] E. D. Sontag, "Comments on integral variants of iss," *Systems & Control Letters*, vol. 34, no. 1-2, pp. 93 – 100, 1998. [Online]. Available: http://www.sciencedirect.com/science/article/pii/S0167691198000036

[10] D. Angeli, E. D. Sontag, and Y. Wang, "A characterization of integral input-to-state stability," *Automatic Control, IEEE Transactions on*, vol. 45, no. 6, pp. 1082–1097, 2000.

[11] D. Angeli, "Further results on incremental input-to-state stability," *Automatic Control, IEEE Transactions on*, vol. 54, no. 6, pp. 1386–1391, 2009.

[12] A. Girard, G. Pola, and P. Tabuada, "Approximately bisimilar symbolic models for incrementally stable switched systems," *Automatic Control, IEEE Transactions on*, vol. 55, no. 1, pp. 116–126, 2010.

[13] G. Pola, A. Girard, and P. Tabuada, "Approximately bisimilar symbolic models for nonlinear control systems," *Automatica*, vol. 44, no. 10, pp. 2508–2516, 2008.

[14] P. Tabuada, A. D. Ames, A. Julius, and G. J. Pappas, "Approximate reduction of dynamic systems," *Systems & Control Letters*, vol. 57, no. 7, pp. 538–545, 2008.

[15] S. Mitra and N. A. Lynch, *A verification framework for hybrid systems*, 2007, vol. 68, no. 12.

[16] D. K. Kaynar, N. Lynch, R. Segala, and F. Vaandrager, *The Theory of Timed I/O Automata*. Morgan Claypool, November 2005, also available as Technical Report MIT-LCS-TR-917.

[17] L. Scardovi and R. Sepulchre, "Synchronization in networks of identical linear systems," *Automatica*, vol. 45, no. 11, pp. 2557–2562, 2009.

[18] G. Wood and B. Zhang, "Estimation of the lipschitz constant of a function," *Journal of Global Optimization*, vol. 8, no. 1, pp. 91–103, 1996.

[19] P. Benner, J.-R. Li, and T. Penzl, "Numerical solution of large-scale lyapunov equations, riccati equations, and linear-quadratic optimal control problems," *Numerical Linear Algebra with Applications*, vol. 15, no. 9, pp. 755–777, 2008.

[20] D. Angeli, "A lyapunov approach to incremental stability properties," *Automatic Control, IEEE Transactions on*, vol. 47, no. 3, pp. 410–421, 2002.

[21] H. K. Khalil, *Nonlinear Systems*, 3rd ed. Prentice Hall, 1992.

[22] CAPD, "Computer assisted proofs in dynamics," 2002. [Online]. Available: http://www.capd.ii.uj.edu.pl/

[23] N. S. Nedialkov, K. R. Jackson, and G. F. Corliss, "Validated solutions of initial value problems for ordinary differential equations," *Applied Mathematics and Computation*, vol. 105, no. 1, pp. 21–68, 1999.

[24] O. Bouissou and M. Martel, "Grklib: a guaranteed runge kutta library," in *Scientific Computing, Computer Arithmetic and Validated Numerics, 2006. SCAN 2006. 12th GAMM-IMACS International Symposium on*. IEEE, 2006, pp. 8–8.

[25] X. Chen, E. Abrahám, and S. Sankaranarayanan, "Taylor model flowpipe construction for non-linear hybrid systems," in *Real-Time Systems Symposium (RTSS), 2012 IEEE 33rd*. IEEE, 2012, pp. 183–192.

[26] Z. Huang and S. Mitra, "Computing bounded reach sets from sampled simulation traces," in *The 15th International Conference on Hybrid Systems: Computation and Control (HSCC 2012), Beijing, China.*, 2012.

On Approximation Metrics for Linear Temporal Model-checking of Stochastic Systems*

Ilya Tkachev
Delft University of Technology
i.tkachev@tudelft.nl

Alessandro Abate
University of Oxford
aabate@cs.ox.ac.uk

ABSTRACT

This paper proposes criteria for metrics between stochastic systems with a focus on the task of linear temporal model-checking. It explicitly puts forward two metrics which partially satisfy those criteria, and discusses their connection with other metrics studied in the literature. In particular, the notion of coupling between stochastic processes is shown to be crucial: omitting the explicit choice of coupling may lead to conservative results. The theoretical claims in the paper are supported by numerical examples.

1. INTRODUCTION

Stochastic systems have found broad applications in diverse areas where uncertainty can be quantified (cf. references in [31]). One particularly interesting class of problems concerns linear temporal (LT) model-checking of stochastic systems [8], which seeks to find the expectation of a path-dependent reward (or cost) functional, e.g. the probability that a realization of a system satisfies a given specification. Among the specifications of interest are reachability, safety, reach-avoid, and richer properties over a trajectory. If the system allows for a control input, one may further be interested in optimizing such an expectation or probability over all the admissible control policies [32]. Clearly, the simpler the system the easier the resulting model-checking procedure. In particular, if the state space of the process is finite, then model-checking can be performed algorithmically, by means of a specialized software [18, 21]. It is thus of interest to develop metrics[1] between stochastic systems that allow quantifying an error over LT properties when substituting a complex, concrete system with a simpler, abstract one.

*A. Abate is also affiliated with the Delft University of Technology. This work is supported by the European Commission STREP project MoVeS 257005, by the European Commission Marie Curie grant MANTRAS 249295, by the European Commission IAPP project AMBI 324432, by the European Commission NoE Hycon2 257462, and by the NWO VENI grant 016.103.020.

[1] In this paper we mostly deal with pseudo-metrics, which are allowed to be equal to zero for two different elements that are equivalent, in a certain sense. Since the difference between a metric and a pseudo-metric is not of importance to us, we refer to both objects simply as metrics.

HSCC'14, April 15–17, 2014, Berlin, Germany.

ACM 978-1-4503-2732-9/14/04 ...$15.00.
http://dx.doi.org/10.1145/2562059.2562118 .

A recent survey on stochastic metrics can be found in [3]. Here we briefly recapitulate two main approaches to defining and using such metrics. The first one has been taken in the Computer Science community, whereas the second has been proposed in the Systems & Control area.

The work in [11] has been the first to emphasize the necessity for metrics between stochastic systems, justifying their relevance by the conservative nature and lack of robustness of the notion of exact probabilistic bisimulation relation [22]. According to the notion in [22], an infinite system is bisimilar to a finite one only if the former has a certain "lumpable" structure relating the two models, and any small perturbation of the models can violate such a structure, thus resulting in systems that originally were precisely related and that become now completely unrelated. In contrast, the metric introduced in [11] both admits the bisimulation as its zero level set, and varies continuously with respect to perturbations of the system dynamics. A few other metrics have been developed along the same lines (see e.g. [35] and references therein), however in all these cases the applicability to LT model-checking has not been discussed.

Similar ideas have been later applied to non-stochastic systems [16]. The approach there is different from the one in [11, 35], as it starts from trace-like metrics over the global dynamics (paths), and then relates the former metrics on path spaces to a bisimulation-like metric over the local dynamics (transitions), the latter being more conservative but easier to compute. The developed metrics were designed to quantify errors over LT properties. The extension of this technique to stochastic systems has been proposed in [19], however the obtained results appear to be rather conservative, possibly due to the fact that the work with stochastic systems has been done at the level of random elements (rather than distributions), and as their coupling procedure is not addressed explicitly (cfr. Sections 2.1 and 3.2).

In summary, there are two main approaches to metrics between stochastic systems that are currently available. The first, taken in the Computer Science community [35, 11], does not provide an explicit way of using metrics for LT model-checking. The second, originated in the area of Systems & Control [19], although applicable to the aforementioned task, leads to conservative results. These reasons suggest to look into alternative approaches to define metrics between stochastic systems. We propose the following criteria for such metrics:

i. a metric between two systems quantifies the difference between LT specifications computed over such systems;

ii. given any two systems the metric between them is computable, either analytically or at least by means of Monte Carlo simulations;

iii. there is a class of "nice" infinite systems that allow for finite abstractions that are arbitrarily close in a given metric.

With focus on the criteria above, in this work we provide two new metrics. Unlike [19], we do not assume any form of stability over the systems under study, hence most of the results in this work hold true over a finite time horizon n, the dependence on which we then explicitly mention in the notation for the metrics. The first metric d_{TV^n} is based on the total variation distance between measures, whereas the second metric d_{W^n} is inspired by the Wasserstein distance.[2] Similar to [16, 19], we start with trace-like metrics to assure that the first criterion is satisfied. We also provide Monte Carlo methods to quantify both metrics in order to meet the requirements of the second criterion. Finally, we provide precise (rather than simulation-based) bounds on d_{TV^n} in terms of a bisimulation-like analogue, here called d_{B}: this allows us to characterize a class of systems that satisfy the last criterion with respect to d_{TV^n}, which in turn aligns with results on formula-free abstractions proposed in [31]. Unfortunately, such analytic results are much harder to obtain for the metric d_{W^n}.

The rest of the work is structured as follows. The majority of our ideas and methods rely upon the notion of random elements, their distributions, and their couplings. We briefly go over this theory in Section 2, which also introduces labelled discrete-time Markov processes (ldt-MP), the class of systems we focus on in this paper. The metrics d_{TV^n} and d_{W^n}, and relations between them, are discussed in Section 3. Theoretical and computational examples are further provided in Section 4, and the paper is concluded in Section 5. The notation can be found in Section 7.

2. PRELIMINARIES

2.1 Coupling

The notion of coupling [23] is crucial when considering an interplay between two stochastic processes, particularly in case one wants to quantify the difference between them. To introduce this notion, we need to elaborate on the definition of stochastic processes and on their representations. Recall that a stochastic process is a special case of a random element – this concept is often used to model probabilistic phenomena.

DEFINITION 1. *A* random element *on a measurable space $(E,\mathscr{E})$ is a tuple $(\Omega,\mathscr{F},\mathsf{P},f)$, where $(\Omega,\mathscr{F},\mathsf{P})$ is a probability space and $f:\Omega\to E$ is a measurable map. We say that $(\Omega,\mathscr{F},\mathsf{P})$ is the* sample space *of the random element, and that $(E,\mathscr{E})$ is its* range. *The* distribution *of the random element $(\Omega,\mathscr{F},\mathsf{P},f)$ is the probability measure $f_*\mathsf{P}\in\mathscr{P}(E,\mathscr{E})$ on its range.*

We will shortly discuss that distributions can be induced by different random elements, thus one can think of the latter as particular *representations* of distributions. More precisely, we say that a random element $(\Omega,\mathscr{F},\mathsf{P},f)$ is the representation of a probability measure Q whenever it holds that $f_*\mathsf{P}=\mathsf{Q}$. Note that, for any distribution $\mathsf{Q}\in\mathscr{P}(E,\mathscr{E})$, there always exists at least one representation over its range, given by $(E,\mathscr{E},\mathsf{Q},\mathrm{id}_E)$ since $(\mathrm{id}_E)_*\mathsf{Q}=\mathsf{Q}$. This is also known as the *canonical representation* of the distribution Q[3]. Let us provide some examples to further clarify the concept of representation. The first example shows that for any distribution a representation is never unique.

[2] The Wasserstein metric is also known as Kantorovich or Hutchinson metric [35],[14, footnote in Section 2.2].

[3] The existence of a canonical representation in particular means that in order to represent any given distribution its range suffices and there is no necessity in coming up with a "bigger" sample space $(\Omega,\mathscr{F})$.

EXAMPLE 1. *Consider a distribution Q and let $(\Omega,\mathscr{F},\mathsf{P},f)$ be its arbitrary representation. For any probability space $(\Omega',\mathscr{F}',\mathsf{P}')$ it holds that $(\Omega\times\Omega',\mathscr{F}\otimes\mathscr{F}',\mathsf{P}\otimes\mathsf{P}',f\circ\pi)$ is another representation of Q, where $\pi:\Omega\times\Omega'\to\Omega$ denotes the projection map.*

In the previous example it is crucial that the sample space is modified. The next example emphasizes this fact by showing that if the sample space is fixed, then there may exist distributions that admit a unique representation over this sample space.

EXAMPLE 2. *Let $E:=\{-1,1\}$, $\mathscr{E}:=2^E$, and let $\mathsf{Q}(\{1\})=\frac{1}{3}$. Note that there exist four distinct maps $f:E\to E$, that is id_E, $-\mathrm{id}_E$, and the constant maps -1 and 1. Clearly, $\mathsf{Q}=(\mathrm{id}_E)_*\mathsf{Q}$ but $\mathsf{Q}\neq f_*\mathsf{Q}$ if $f\neq\mathrm{id}_E$, so that Q can be represented in the unique (canonical) way if the sample space is $(E,\mathscr{E})$. On the other hand, a symmetrical distribution Q' given by $\mathsf{Q}'(\{1\})=\frac{1}{2}$ can be represented in two ways since $\mathsf{Q}'=(-\mathrm{id}_E)_*\mathsf{Q}'$. More generally, if a distribution admits distinct representations over its range, they can be considered as symmetries of this distribution.*

According to [24, Section 2.1], a stochastic process on a measurable space $(X,\mathscr{X})$ is a parameterized collection of X-valued random elements $(\mathbf{x}_t)_{t\in T}$, all defined over the same probability space $(\Omega,\mathscr{F},\mathsf{P})$. Clearly, one can equivalently consider a stochastic process as a single random element $(\Omega,\mathscr{F},\mathsf{P},f)$ where the map $f:\Omega\to X^T$ is uniquely determined by $f\circ\pi_t=\mathbf{x}_t$ for any t, $\pi_t:X^T\to X$ being obvious projection maps. Recall that here X^T is the product measurable space consisting of all maps from T to X. As a consequence, all the results on random elements above now apply to stochastic processes. In particular, it is important for us that any stochastic process can be understood also in a "weak" form – as a distribution over X^T, rather than only in a perhaps more intuitive "strong" form – as a random element inducing such a distribution. This approach is important in the context of this work, since only distributions matter for LT model checking, rather than particular representations of a stochastic process. A representation, especially if it is not canonical, is sometimes provided to show a constructive definition of a distribution, as in the following example.

EXAMPLE 3. *A one-dimensional Itô diffusion [24, Chapter 7]*

$$\mathrm{d}\mathbf{x}_t=a(\mathbf{x}_t)\mathrm{d}t+b(\mathbf{x}_t)\mathrm{d}B_t,\quad \mathbf{x}_0=x\in\mathbb{R},\tag{1}$$

is a stochastic process with trajectories in $E=\mathscr{C}([0,\infty))$. Since the diffusion (1) is Markovian, it can be considered from two perspectives: either as a solution of the stochastic differential equation (SDE) (1), or as a Markov process on $X=\mathbb{R}$.

In order to treat a diffusion as a solution of an SDE, we consider a probability space $(\Omega,\mathscr{B}(\Omega),\mathsf{P})$, where $\Omega=\mathscr{C}_0([0,\infty))$ is a set of all $\omega\in E$ satisfying $\omega(0)=0$ and where P is the Wiener measure (the distribution of the Brownian motion $(B_t)_{t\in[0,\infty)}$). In this setting a diffusion is constructed as a random element $(\Omega,\mathscr{F},\mathsf{P},f)$, where f is the strong solution *of an SDE [24, Section 5.3] with the initial condition x. Let us denote the induced distribution by $\mathsf{Q}:=f_*\mathsf{P}$.*

Alternatively, one can treat the diffusion in (1) as a Markov process, and construct a distribution Q directly on E using the transition function associated with the diffusion [13, Section 4.1]. The stochastic process for the diffusion (in a strong sense) would be a canonical representation of Q. In this Markovian setting there is no need to define an auxiliary probability space $(\Omega,\mathscr{F},\mathsf{P})$ for the

Brownian motion, so the current Markovian approach is more direct. On the other hand, such a construction is perhaps less intuitive as it does not emphasize the connection between the diffusion and the Brownian motion it is driven by.

Note that both methods lead to the same stochastic process in a weak sense (at the level of distributions), but to different stochastic processes in a strong sense (at the level of random elements). At the same time, if one needs to compute the probability that a trajectory of (1) *reaches a target set, it does not matter which representation of a diffusion is used, since such a probability is uniquely determined by the distribution of the diffusion.*

The motivation behind approximate abstractions of stochastic systems is to use the information obtained over a simpler abstract system to deduce properties of a more complicated concrete system. Assume that the range $(E, \mathscr{E})$ is endowed with a metric d_E. Given a concrete random element $(\Omega, \mathscr{F}, \mathsf{P}, f)$ and its approximation $(\tilde{\Omega}, \tilde{\mathscr{F}}, \tilde{\mathsf{P}}, \tilde{f})$ one wants to obtain an inequality

$$\mathbb{P}\big(d_E(f, \tilde{f}) > \delta\big) \leq \varepsilon \tag{2}$$

to be able to interpret over f the results obtained for $\tilde{f}$. As an example [6], if we know the probability $p = \tilde{\mathsf{P}}(\tilde{f} \in A)$ for some set $A \in \tilde{\mathscr{F}}$, we can use (2) to provide bounds on $\mathsf{P}(f \in A_\delta)$, where $A_\delta = \{x \in E : d_E(x, A) \leq \delta\}$ is the δ-inflation of the set A:

$$\begin{aligned}\mathsf{P}(f \in A_\delta) = \mathbb{P}(f \in A_\delta) &\geq \mathbb{P}\big(\{\tilde{f} \in A\} \cap \{d_E(f, \tilde{f}) \leq \delta\}\big) \\ &\geq \mathbb{P}(\tilde{f} \in A) - \mathbb{P}(d_E(f, \tilde{f}) > \delta) \geq p - \varepsilon.\end{aligned}$$

Whenever f and $\tilde{f}$ are stochastic processes and A is a reachability specification, the result allows using the probabilistic reachability analysis over $\tilde{f}$ to study that over f. Recall that the abstraction is a random element on its own, and that the analysis over the abstraction can be carried out regardless of its relation to the concrete system: such a relation only matters when extrapolating results of this analysis from the abstraction back to the concrete system. For this purpose one has to define a *common* sample space for both systems in order to specify the probability measure in (2). The procedure of building a common sample space for *a priori* unrelated distributions or random elements is called coupling.

DEFINITION 2. *A* coupling *of* $\mathsf{Q}, \tilde{\mathsf{Q}} \in \mathscr{P}(E, \mathscr{E})$ *is a probability measure* $\mathbb{Q} \in \mathscr{P}(E^2, \mathscr{E}^2)$ *satisfying the following equalities:*

$$\pi_* \mathbb{Q} = \mathsf{Q}, \qquad \tilde{\pi}_* \mathbb{Q} = \tilde{\mathsf{Q}}, \tag{3}$$

where $\pi(x, \tilde{x}) = x$ *and* $\tilde{\pi}(x, \tilde{x}) = \tilde{x}$ *for all* $(x, \tilde{x}) \in E^2$ *are obvious projection maps. A coupling of two random elements* $(\Omega, \mathscr{F}, \mathsf{P}, f)$ *and* $(\tilde{\Omega}, \tilde{\mathscr{F}}, \tilde{\mathsf{P}}, \tilde{f})$ *is any random element* $(\Xi, \mathscr{G}, \mathbb{P}, (g, \tilde{g}))$ *such that* $(g, \tilde{g})_* \mathbb{P}$ *is a coupling of* $f_* \mathsf{P}$ *and* $\tilde{f}_* \tilde{\mathsf{P}}$*, and* $(\Xi, \mathscr{G})$ *is an arbitrary measurable space.*

Whenever (3) holds true, we say that Q and $\tilde{\mathsf{Q}}$ are *marginals* of $\mathbb{Q}$. It shall be clear that given any two marginal distributions, there always exists at least one coupling of them, called the *independence coupling*, which is given by $\mathbb{Q} := \mathsf{Q} \otimes \tilde{\mathsf{Q}}$. The most important point about the coupling is that it is only unique when one of the marginals Q or $\tilde{\mathsf{Q}}$ is the Dirac measure, or equivalently when one of the random elements is deterministic. In particular, since the concrete system and the abstraction are almost never coupled a priori (neither at the level of random elements, nor at the level of distributions), one can e.g. optimize over all admissible couplings to choose the best for inequality (2). This idea constitutes to the core of our method. Before going into the details of it, let us provide examples of couplings.

EXAMPLE 4. *Consider the diffusion* $\mathbf{x}$ *as per* (1)*, and let*

$$\mathrm{d}\tilde{\mathbf{x}}_t = \tilde{a}(\tilde{\mathbf{x}}_t)\mathrm{d}t + \tilde{b}(\tilde{\mathbf{x}}_t)\mathrm{d}\tilde{B}_t, \quad \tilde{\mathbf{x}}_0 = \tilde{x} \in \mathbb{R}, \tag{4}$$

be another diffusion. Let us represent both of them as solutions of SDEs, that is as random elements on the sample spaces $(\Omega, \mathscr{F}, \mathsf{P})$ *and* $(\tilde{\Omega}, \tilde{\mathscr{F}}, \tilde{\mathsf{P}})$*, where the former is defined in Example 3, and the latter is defined for* (4) *analogously. We provide three versions of couplings obtained via the Brownian motions driving these diffusions:*

a. $\Xi = \Omega$, $\mathscr{G} = \mathscr{F}$, $\mathbb{P} = \mathsf{P}$ *and* $(g, \tilde{g}) = (f, \tilde{f})$*. This coupling corresponds to the case* $B_t = \tilde{B}_t$ *when diffusions are "sharing" the same noise [19].*

b. $\Xi = \Omega \times \tilde{\Omega}$, $\mathscr{G} = \mathscr{F} \otimes \tilde{\mathscr{F}}$, $\mathbb{P} = \mathsf{P} \otimes \tilde{\mathsf{P}}$ *and* $(g, \tilde{g}) = (f \circ \pi, \tilde{f} \circ \tilde{\pi})$ *where the projection maps* $\pi : \Xi \to \Omega$ *and* $\tilde{\pi} : \Xi \to \tilde{\Omega}$ *are as in Definition 2. This clearly corresponds to the case of the independence coupling, that is* $B_t \perp \tilde{B}_t$ *[2].*

c. $\Xi = \Omega$, $\mathscr{G} = \mathscr{F}$, $\mathbb{P} = \mathsf{P}$ *and* $(g, \tilde{g}) = (f, \tilde{f} \circ n)$ *where* $n(\omega) = -\omega$ *for any* $\omega \in \Omega$*. In this case* $B_t = -\tilde{B}_t$*: noises driving diffusions are "reflected". Such a construction is possible thanks to the fact that* n *is a symmetry of* P *(i.e.* $n_* \mathsf{P} = \mathsf{P}$*), or in other words* $-\tilde{B}_t$ *is a Brownian motion whenever* $\tilde{B}_t$ *is.*

Finally, let us mention that as much as any distribution of a single random element admits a representation over its range, the distribution of any coupling of two random elements admits a representation over the product of the ranges: this follows directly from Definition 2. In particular, if $(\Omega, \mathscr{F}, \mathsf{P}, f)$ and $(\tilde{\Omega}, \tilde{\mathscr{F}}, \tilde{\mathsf{P}}, \tilde{f})$ are any random elements with a range $(E, \mathscr{E})$ endowed with a metric d, and $(\Xi, \mathscr{G}, \mathbb{P}, (g, \tilde{g}))$ is one of their couplings with a distribution $\mathbb{Q} = (g, \tilde{g})_* \mathbb{P}$, then the probability in (2) can be expressed as

$$\mathbb{P}(d(g, \tilde{g}) > \delta) = \mathbb{Q}(E^2 \setminus \Delta_E^\delta),$$

where $\Delta_E^\delta := \{(x, \tilde{x}) : d(x, \tilde{x}) \leq \varepsilon\}$ is a diagonal ε-strip in E^2. The benefit of dealing with stochastic systems (and their couplings) at the level of distributions lies the easy introduction of the distance between the concrete and the abstract systems. To support this point, let us mention that in probability theory distances are classically introduced between distributions, rather than between random elements [15, 25].

2.2 Behaviors of ldt-MP

Although most of the concepts and methods we have introduced apply to arbitrary stochastic processes, a focus on discrete-time Markov processes (dt-MP) allows us to provide a more detailed analysis. A dt-MP is a pair (X, P), where X is a Borel space referred to as the state space, and $P : X \to \mathscr{P}(X)$ is a stochastic kernel on X. It follows from [26, Theorem 2.8] that given any initial state $x \in X$ there exists a unique probability measure P_x on the state-path space X^ω satisfying

$$\mathsf{P}_x\left(\prod_{k=0}^{\infty} \mathrm{d}x_k\right) = 1_{\{x\}}(x) \cdot \prod_{k=0}^{\infty} P(x_k, \mathrm{d}x_k). \tag{5}$$

We say that (X, P) is finite whenever X is a finite set.

REMARK 1. *Similar to Example 3, for a given dt-MP and a fixed initial state,* (5) *provides a weak stochastic process. The corresponding canonical strong stochastic process can be introduced by defining the coordinate maps* $\mathbf{x}_k : X^\omega \to X$ *as obvious projections. As an alternative, it follows from [20, Proposition 7.6] that any dt-MP can be expressed as a stochastic difference equation*

$\mathbf{x}_{k+1} = F(\mathbf{x}_k, w_k)$, *where* w_k *is a sequence of iid uniform random variables on* $[0,1]$. *With focus on Section 2.1, this means that any dt-MP with a fixed initial state* $x \in X$ *admits the following non-canonical representation:* $([0,1]^\omega, \mathscr{B}([0,1]^\omega), \lambda^\omega, f)$, *where* λ *is the Lebesgue measure on* $[0,1]$ *and the map* f *is obtained by iterating* F *starting from* x.

For a non-stochastic system on a state space X, its internal behavior is any element of X^ω where each transition $\mathbf{x}_k \to \mathbf{x}_{k+1}$ is allowed in the system [29, Section 1.2]. For stochastic systems such a definition is not suitable since formally all transitions are allowed, so that any single element of X^ω is a possible internal behavior of a dt-MP, albeit possibly of zero probability. Due to this reason, it is more appropriate to talk about *behavioral distributions*, that is P_x shall be understood as a distribution of internal behaviors that indicates which behaviors are more likely appear as trajectories of a dt-MP.

Often one is not interested in each single behavior, but rather in collections thereof that can be characterised by means of observations (or labels). A labeled dt-MP (ldt-MP for short) is a tuple (X, P, Y, L) where (X, P) is a dt-MP, Y is a Borel space and $\mathsf{L} : X \to Y$ is a measurable map [31]. In an ldt-MP, to any internal behavior $(x_0, x_1, \dots)$ there corresponds an *external behavior*, or a *trace*, given by an output of the trace map:

$$\mathsf{L}_\omega(x_0, x_1, \dots) := (\mathsf{L}(x_0), \mathsf{L}(x_1), \dots).$$

For non-stochastic system a collection of its all admissible external behaviors is also called a *language* of a system [17]. Similar to the case of internal behaviors, in our setting it is more appropriate to talk about distributions of external behaviors as all of them are allowed in the ldt-MP. We refer to such distributions as *trace distributions* [27]: let us emphasize again that trace distributions are analogues of languages for non-stochastic systems. Since the map $\mathsf{L}_\omega : X^\omega \to Y^\omega$ is measurable [31, Theorem 1], for any ldt-MP its trace distribution can be expressed as $(\mathsf{L}_\omega)_* \mathsf{P}_x$. We can formulate the LT model-checking problem for ldt-MP as follows:

PROBLEM 1. *Given an ldt-MP* (X, P, Y, L) *and the observation-path dependent functional* $f \in \mathscr{B}(Y^\omega)$, *compute the expectation* $((L_\omega)_* \mathsf{P}_x) f$ *for any initial state* $x \in X$.

An important case of a functional f in Problem 1 is the indicator function $f = 1_A$ of some event of interest $A \in \mathscr{B}(Y^\omega)$: in such a case the expectation to be computed turns out to be the probability $((L_\omega)_* \mathsf{P}_x)(A) = \mathsf{P}_x(L_\omega(\mathbf{x}) \in A)$. A common example of an observation space is given by finite sets Y, also called *alphabets*. Over alphabets the event A can be for instance an ω-regular language[4] expressed as an automaton, or an LTL formula - for a detailed exposition see e.g. [8, Chapters 4, 5].

Dealing with stochastic systems at the level of observations allows one to compare systems possibly endowed with different state spaces. This feature is extremely important since a complex ldt-MP can be approximated by a simpler one over a smaller state space - for example, by a finite ldt-MP: for the latter LT model-checking allows for analytical solutions, and numerical procedures can be computationally efficient. In order to be able to quantitatively argue about the original ldt-MP using results obtained over its abstract approximation, it is useful to endow the trace space with some metrics [16]. The choice of the latter depends on how one wants to interpret over the original system the results obtained over the abstraction. Along the lines of the discussion in Section 2.1, for ldt-MP we define these metrics to measure the difference (or similarity) between trace distributions, regardless of the way the latter are represented. The trace equivalence for any two ldt-MP can be defined by requiring them to have the same trace distributions, however there may be several choices of metrics whose zero level sets coincide with such trace equivalence. The next section proposes two such metrics for the trace distributions over the ldt-MP with the same observation spaces based on the *total variation* distance TV and on the *Wasserstein* distance W.

[4] Indeed, ω-regular languages over a finite Y are always elements of $\mathscr{B}(Y^\omega)$, for the proof see e.g. [36, Proposition 2.3].

3. METRICS FOR LDT-MP

3.1 Total variation distance

Perhaps the most direct way to define a distance between two probability measures that fits the purposes of Problem 1 is to maximize over all functionals (or events) the difference between the corresponding expectations. Interestingly, such seemingly naïve approach yields a useful metric called the total variation distance (see Section 7.2).

Let us consider two ldt-MP $\mathscr{D} = (X, P, Y, \mathsf{L})$ and $\tilde{\mathscr{D}} = (\tilde{X}, \tilde{P}, Y, \tilde{\mathsf{L}})$ over the same observation space Y. Given initial states $x \in X$ and $\tilde{x} \in \tilde{X}$, we denote the trace distributions of $\mathscr{D}$ and $\tilde{\mathscr{D}}$ by Q_x and $\tilde{\mathsf{Q}}_{\tilde{x}}$, respectively. Suppose for example that $\tilde{\mathscr{D}}$ is finite, Y is a finite alphabet and Φ is some LTL formula over Y. If we know the value of $\mathsf{TV}(\mathsf{Q}_x, \tilde{\mathsf{Q}}_{\tilde{x}})$, we can compute $\tilde{\mathsf{Q}}_{\tilde{x}}(\Phi)$ and use it to estimate $\mathsf{Q}_x(\Phi)$, since by definition of TV (12)

$$|\mathsf{Q}_x(\Phi) - \tilde{\mathsf{Q}}_{\tilde{x}}(\Phi)| \le \frac{1}{2} \mathsf{TV}(\mathsf{Q}_x, \tilde{\mathsf{Q}}_{\tilde{x}}).$$

From the definition of TV (for details see Section 7.2), it follows that similar bounds in terms of $\mathsf{TV}(\mathsf{Q}_x, \tilde{\mathsf{Q}}_{\tilde{x}})$ can be also obtained on the difference of expectations for more general cost functionals, rather than just indicator functions of LTL formulae. As a result, the TV satisfies the first criterion from Section 1 and can thus represent a good candidate for a metric. However, notice that $\mathsf{TV}(\mathsf{Q}_x, \tilde{\mathsf{Q}}_{\tilde{x}})$ quantifies the distance between probabilities on the infinite time horizon: this may be a too conservative requirement, as mentioned in [33, Section 3.1] and as the following example shows.

EXAMPLE 5. *Let us consider two simple ldt-MP with only two states:* $\tilde{X} = X = \{0, 1\}$, $Y = X$, $\mathsf{L} = \tilde{\mathsf{L}} = \mathrm{id}_X$, *and suppose that transition matrices* $P \neq \tilde{P}$ *have only positive entries. It follows that these ldt-MP are ergodic; we denote their unique invariant distributions by* μ *and* $\tilde{\mu}$, *respectively. For any* $h : X^2 \to \mathbb{R}$ *define*

$$A_h := \left\{ \lim_{n\to\infty} \frac{1}{n} \sum_{k=0}^{n-1} h(\mathbf{x}_k, \mathbf{x}_{k+1}) = \int_{X^2} h(x, y) P(x, \mathrm{d}y) \mu(\mathrm{d}y) \right\}.$$

It holds that $\mathsf{P}_x(A_h) = 1$ *for any initial state* x. *A similar fact can be obtained for* $\tilde{\mathsf{P}}_x$. *Clearly, we can always find an* h *such that*

$$\int_{X^2} h(x, y) P(x, \mathrm{d}y) \mu(\mathrm{d}y) \neq \int_{X^2} h(x, y) \tilde{P}(x, \mathrm{d}y) \tilde{\mu}(\mathrm{d}y).$$

Since $\mathsf{Q}_x = \mathsf{P}_x$ *and* $\tilde{\mathsf{Q}}_x = \tilde{\mathsf{P}}_x$ *we get* $\mathsf{TV}(\mathsf{Q}_x, \tilde{\mathsf{Q}}_x) = 2$ *by putting* A_h *in (12), no matter how small the difference between* P *and* $\tilde{P}$ *is.*

Due to the reasons discussed above, we focus our attention to finite-horizon behaviors of ldt-MP, characterized by restrictions of the trace distribution Q_x and $\tilde{\mathsf{Q}}_{\tilde{x}}$ to the set Y^{n+1}: we denote them by Q^n_x and $\tilde{\mathsf{Q}}^n_{\tilde{x}}$, respectively. Since given an initial state over the concrete ldt-MP one has the freedom of choosing that over the abstraction, let us define the TV-like distance between ldt-MPs with the same observation spaces by

$$d_{\mathsf{TV}^n}(\mathscr{D},\tilde{\mathscr{D}}) := \sup_{x\in X}\inf_{\tilde{x}\in\tilde{X}} \mathsf{TV}(\mathsf{Q}^n_x,\tilde{\mathsf{Q}}^n_{\tilde{x}}). \tag{6}$$

DEFINITION 3. *We say that two ldt-MP* $\mathscr{D}$ *and* $\tilde{\mathscr{D}}$ *are* ε-trace equivalent in the d_{TV^n} *metrics if* $d_{\mathsf{TV}^n}(\mathscr{D},\tilde{\mathscr{D}}) \le \varepsilon$.

Although the approximate trace equivalence of ldt-MP in d_{TV^n} for $n<\infty$ is not in general useful in infinite-horizon LT model-checking, it is sufficient to argue about finite-horizon properties, for example those expressed as BLTL formulae [31, Section 2.4]. Until the end of Section 3.1 we focus exclusively on the case when Y is a finite alphabet. A finite alphabet on a finite time horizon contains only a finite number of elements, which justifies the use of the following formula for the total variation [9]:

$$\mathsf{TV}(\mathsf{Q}^n_x,\tilde{\mathsf{Q}}^n_{\tilde{x}}) = \sum_{y\in Y^{n+1}} |\mathsf{Q}_x(\{y\}) - \tilde{\mathsf{Q}}_{\tilde{x}}(\{y\})|. \tag{7}$$

Though the expression above is still challenging to compute precisely even over finite-state ldt-MPs, it can be computed by means of Monte Carlo simulations, which shows that d_{TV^n} satisfies the second criterion mentioned in Section 1.

Let us fix the time horizon n, and let us sample independently N copies of the observations of $\mathscr{D}$ and $\tilde{\mathscr{D}}$ over the given time horizon, which we further denote by $(\mathbf{y}^i)_{i=1}^N$ and $(\tilde{\mathbf{y}}^i)_{i=1}^N$ respectively.[5] The index i refers to different runs: each of them can be obtained e.g. by sampling the state-path of $\mathscr{D}$, say $\mathbf{x}^i$, on the time horizon n, and then by mapping $\mathbf{x}^i$ into $\mathbf{y}^i$ by means of map L. Define

$$\mathsf{Q}^{n,N}_x(\cdot) := \frac{1}{N}\sum_{i=1}^N 1\{\mathbf{y}^i\in\cdot\}, \qquad \tilde{\mathsf{Q}}^{n,N}_{\tilde{x}}(\cdot) := \frac{1}{N}\sum_{i=1}^N 1\{\tilde{\mathbf{y}}^i\in\cdot\} \tag{8}$$

to be empirical distributions. It is fairly simple to compute the approximate distance $\hat{v}_N := \mathsf{TV}(\mathsf{Q}^{n,N}_x,\tilde{\mathsf{Q}}^{n,N}_{\tilde{x}})$ using (7), which leads to assess how good such an approximation of the original distance $v := \mathsf{TV}(\mathsf{Q}^n_x,\tilde{\mathsf{Q}}^n_{\tilde{x}})$ is. Let us denote by Π the joint probability distribution of the two iid sequences $(\mathbf{y}^i)_{i=1}^N$ and $(\tilde{\mathbf{y}}^i)_{i=1}^N$.

THEOREM 1. *For any* $\delta>0$ *it holds that*

$$\Pi(|v-\hat{v}_N|\le 2\delta) \ge \left(1-(N+1)^{|Y^{n+1}|}\mathrm{e}^{-N\delta^2}\right)^2, \tag{9}$$

provided that $(N+1)^{|Y^{n+1}|}\mathrm{e}^{-N\delta^2}\le 1$.

PROOF. The idea of the proof is to start with $\mathsf{TV}(\mathsf{Q}^n_x,\mathsf{Q}^{n,N}_x)$:

$$\Pi\left(\mathsf{TV}(\mathsf{Q}^n_x,\mathsf{Q}^{n,N}_x)\ge\delta\right) = \sum_{v\in L^\delta_N}\Pi\left(\mathsf{Q}^{n,N}_x = v\right) \le \sum_{v\in L^\delta_N}\mathrm{e}^{-N\cdot\mathsf{KL}(v,\mathsf{Q}^n_x)},$$

where by KL we denote the Kullback-Leibler divergence between probability measures [15], L^δ_N is the set of all empirical measures v satisfying $\mathsf{TV}(\mathsf{Q}^n_x,v)\ge\delta$, and the last inequality immediately follows from [9, Lemma 2.1.9]. Since for all $v\in L^\delta_N$ it holds that $\mathsf{KL}(v,\mathsf{Q}^n_x)\ge(\mathsf{TV}(v,\mathsf{Q}^n_x))^2$, and [9, Lemma 2.1.2(a)] implies that $|L^\delta_N|\le(N+1)^{|Y^{n+1}|}$, we obtain:

$$\Pi\left(\mathsf{TV}(\mathsf{Q}^n_x,\mathsf{Q}^{n,N}_x)\ge\delta\right)\le(N+1)^{|Y^{n+1}|}\mathrm{e}^{-N\delta^2}. \tag{10}$$

A similar estimate obviously can be derived for $\mathsf{TV}(\tilde{\mathsf{Q}}^n_{\tilde{x}},\tilde{\mathsf{Q}}^{n,N}_{\tilde{x}})$. By triangular inequality we further get

$$|v-\hat{v}_N|\le\mathsf{TV}(\mathsf{Q}^n_x,\mathsf{Q}^{n,N}_x)+\mathsf{TV}(\tilde{\mathsf{Q}}^n_{\tilde{x}},\tilde{\mathsf{Q}}^{n,N}_{\tilde{x}}),$$

which together with (10) yields (9) as desired. □

Clearly, (9) implies that the estimator $\hat{v}_N$ converges in Π to the true distance v, and further provides an explicit bound on the confidence level. Note also that for fixed sizes of the alphabet and of the time horizon, the bound in (9) depends quadratically on the precision δ, and logarithmically on the confidence level. Unfortunately, such a dependence is only asymptotical, and for N not sufficiently large the polynomial term $(N+1)^{|Y^{n+1}|}$ dominates the exponential term $\mathrm{e}^{-N\delta^2}$. Moreover, such polynomial term grows very fast with respect to the size of the alphabet, and even faster with respect to the time horizon. For example, even if $|Y|=2$, $n=9$ and $\delta=0.1$, one needs approximately an order of $N=1.5\times10^6$ samples to obtain good confidence levels, whereas for $n=10$ around $N=3.5\times10^6$ samples are required. In addition, the precision of the estimator $\hat{v}_N$ can be only guaranteed with some confidence as its computation relies on randomized methods. Finally, Theorem 1 only gives a way to estimate $\mathsf{TV}(\mathsf{Q}^n_x,\tilde{\mathsf{Q}}^n_{\tilde{x}})$ for given initial states, whereas (6) requires solving an optimization problem. All of this motivates looking into alternative methods for computing the d_{TV^n} metric.

We start with the case when both ldt-MPs $\mathscr{D}$ and $\tilde{\mathscr{D}}$ have the same state space, say X; let P and $\tilde{P}$ be the corresponding stochastic kernels. Recall that each of them acts as a linear operator on the Banach space $\mathrm{b}\mathscr{B}(X)$, e.g. $Pf(x)=\int_X f(y)P(x,\mathrm{d}y)$. Since $\mathrm{b}\mathscr{B}(X)$ is endowed with a sup-norm, one can define an induced norm on operators, as follows:

$$\|P-\tilde{P}\| := \sup_{f\in\mathrm{b}\mathscr{B}(X),\|f\|\le1}\|(P-\tilde{P})f\|.$$

We obtain that $\|P-\tilde{P}\| = \sup_{x\in X}\mathsf{TV}(P(x,\cdot),\tilde{P}(x,\cdot))$ and as a result $\|P-\tilde{P}\|\ge\mathsf{TV}^1(\mathsf{Q}_x,\tilde{\mathsf{Q}}_x)$. We define a new metric as

$$d_{\mathsf{B}}(\mathscr{D},\tilde{\mathscr{D}}) := \|P-\tilde{P}\|.$$

The next theorem shows how the latter metric can be used in order to derive upper bounds on d_{TV^n}.

THEOREM 2. *For any* $n\in\mathbb{N}_0$ *it holds that*

$$d_{\mathsf{TV}^n}(\mathscr{D},\tilde{\mathscr{D}})\le 2-2\left(1-\frac{1}{2}d_{\mathsf{B}}(\mathscr{D},\tilde{\mathscr{D}})\right)^n. \tag{11}$$

PROOF. From [7, Theorem 2] it follows that

$$\mathsf{TV}(\mathsf{P}^n_x,\tilde{\mathsf{P}}^n_x)\le 2-2\left(1-\frac{1}{2}d_{\mathsf{B}}(\mathscr{D},\tilde{\mathscr{D}})\right)^n,$$

for any initial state $x\in X$. Since Q^n_x and $\tilde{\mathsf{Q}}^n_x$ are image measures generated by P^n_x and $\tilde{\mathsf{P}}^n_x$ respectively, it holds that $\mathsf{TV}(\mathsf{Q}^n_x,\tilde{\mathsf{Q}}^n_x)\le\mathsf{TV}(\mathsf{P}^n_x,\tilde{\mathsf{P}}^n_x)$. Finally, it clearly holds that

$$d_{\mathsf{TV}^n}(\mathscr{D},\tilde{\mathscr{D}})\le\sup_{x\in X}\mathsf{TV}(\mathsf{Q}^n_x,\tilde{\mathsf{Q}}^n_x),$$

which further leads to (11). □

Before we elaborate on Theorem 2, let us first show an example of how it can be applied to construct finite abstractions with any given precision: that would assure that d_{TV^n} satisfies the third criterion in Section 1. Suppose that we are given an ldt-MP $\mathscr{D}=(X,Y,P,\mathsf{L})$, where Y is a finite alphabet and P is an integral kernel, that is $P(x,\mathrm{d}y)=p(x,y)\mu(\mathrm{d}y)$. Here p is a jointly measurable function and μ is a σ-additive measure on X. We say that p is a density of P with respect to the measure μ: for example if $X=\mathbb{R}^m$ and μ is the Lebesgue measure, p is a common density function. Assume further that the state space

[5] Note that for any $i\in[1;N]$, we have that $\mathbf{y}^i$ is a vector of elements of Y of length $n+1$: that is a vector of observations of $\mathscr{D}$ over the time horizon n.

X is endowed with some metric d_X compatible with its topology, and is bounded with respect to this metric. Let $(X_i)_{i=1}^m$ be a finite partition of X such that L is constant when restricted to any X_i, and denote by δ_i the diameter of X_i in the metric d_X. Let $x_i \in X_i$ be arbitrary points, and define the finite ldt-MP $\tilde{\mathscr{D}} = (\tilde{X}, \tilde{P}, Y, \tilde{\mathsf{L}})$ as follows: $\tilde{X} = [1;m]$, $\tilde{P}(i,\{j\}) := P(x_i, X_j)$ and $\tilde{\mathsf{L}}(i) = \mathsf{L}(x_i)$. Notice that we cannot compare $\mathscr{D}$ and $\tilde{\mathscr{D}}$ directly using the metric d_{B}: the latter is only defined for ldt-MP that share the same state space. Due to this reason, below we construct an auxiliary ldt-MP $\hat{\mathscr{D}}$ which has an infinite state space X so that $d_{\mathsf{B}}(\mathscr{D},\hat{\mathscr{D}})$ is well-defined, but whose structure makes it trace-equivalent to the finite ldt-MP $\tilde{\mathscr{D}}$. We require the following Lipschitz-like condition.

ASSUMPTION 1. *There exist measurable non-negative functions* $\kappa_i : X \to [0,\infty)$, *such that* $K_i := \int_X \kappa_i(y)\mu(dy) < \infty$ *for all* $i \in [1;m]$, *and such that*

$$|p(x',y)-p(x'',y)| \le \kappa_i(y) d_X(x',x'') \quad \forall x',x'' \in X_i, \quad \forall y \in X.$$

THEOREM 3. *Under Assumption 1 for any* $n \in \mathbb{N}_0$ *it holds that*

$$d_{\mathsf{TV}^n}(\mathscr{D},\tilde{\mathscr{D}}) \le 2 - 2\left(1 - \max_{i\in[1;m]} K_i\delta_i\right)^n.$$

PROOF. We construct an auxiliary ldt-MP $\hat{D} = (X, \hat{P}, Y, \mathsf{L})$ with a lumpable structure to assure that $d_{\mathsf{TV}^n}(\hat{\mathscr{D}},\tilde{\mathscr{D}}) = 0$, and to compare $d_{\mathsf{TV}^n}(\mathscr{D},\hat{\mathscr{D}})$ using Theorem 2. For this purpose we let $\hat{P}(x,dy) = \hat{p}(x,y)\mu(dy)$ to be an integral kernel where the density $\hat{p}$ is defined as $\hat{p}(x,y) = p(x_i,y)$ for all points $x \in X_i$ and $y \in X$. For any $f \in \mathrm{b}\mathscr{B}(X)$, $\|f\| \le 1$ and $x \in X_i$ it holds that

$$|(P-\hat{P})f(x)| = \left|\int_X f(y)(p(x,y)-p(x_i,y))\mu(dy)\right| \le \int_X |f(y)|\delta_i\kappa_i(y)\mu(dy) \le K_i\delta_i,$$

and hence $\|P-\hat{P}\| \le \max_{i\in[1;m]} K_i\delta_i$, so that

$$d_{\mathsf{TV}^n}(\mathscr{D},\hat{\mathscr{D}}) \le 2 - 2\left(1 - \max_{i\in[1;m]} K_i\delta_i\right)^n$$

by Theorem 2. Let $\iota : X \to \tilde{X}$ be the map defined by $\iota(x) = i$ iff $x \in X_i$. For any initial state $x \in X$ it holds that $\mathsf{Q}^n_x = \tilde{\mathsf{Q}}^n_{\iota_* x}$: indeed, these measures coincide on each element of the finite set Y^{n+1} by construction. As a result, $d_{\mathsf{TV}^n}(\hat{\mathscr{D}},\tilde{\mathscr{D}}) = 0$, which completes the proof of the theorem. □

This theorem shows that in case an original ldt-MP satisfies Assumption 1, for any $\varepsilon > 0$ it is possible to construct a finite ldt-MP that is ε-trace equivalent to the original one in the d_{TV^n} metric. As a result, the metric d_{TV^n} satisfies all the criteria in Section 1. Note also that to estimate the metric d_{TV^n}, which quantifies the difference between path measures, namely the *global* (in time) dynamics, we have used the metric d_{B}, which compares the stochastic kernels, hence measuring the difference between transitions of ldt-MP – their *local* dynamics. The difference in local dynamics is often easier to assess, which in turn provides a method to argue about similarity of the global dynamics – see also the discussion in [16, Section II.B]. To formally speak about the similarity of the local dynamics for the processes with different state spaces, we would need to introduce notions of approximate bisimulations. For example, in such a case we could compare $\mathscr{D}$ and $\tilde{\mathscr{D}}$ in the proof of Theorem 3 directly, without the need to introduce the auxiliary ldt-MP $\hat{\mathscr{D}}$. However the discussion on approximate bisimulation goes beyond the scope of this contribution.

Theorems 2 and 3 further improve the formula-free abstraction procedure for ldt-MP introduced in [31]: the bounds on the path measures there increase linearly in the time horizon, whereas (11) provides bounds which never exceed 2 – the maximal meaningful value of the total variation distance. Moreover, such bounds are tight, that is in some special cases the equality in (11) holds.

3.2 Wasserstein distance

Above we have shown the usefulness of the metric d_{TV^n} for LT model-checking. Although this metric is based on the total variation distance, which has an important characterization through coupling (13), we have not used extensively the notion of coupling in the discussion on d_{TV^n} (though it is important in the proof [7, Theorem 2] used in Theorem 2).

The notion of coupling appears to be much more important for another metric that we consider next. Suppose that we are given two ldt-MP $\mathscr{D} = (X, Y, P, \mathsf{L})$ and $\tilde{\mathscr{D}} = (\tilde{X}, \tilde{P}, Y, \tilde{\mathsf{L}})$ expressed as

$$\begin{cases} \mathbf{x}_{k+1} &= F(\mathbf{x}_k, w_k), \\ \mathbf{y}_k &= \mathsf{L}(\mathbf{x}_k) \end{cases} \qquad \begin{cases} \tilde{\mathbf{x}}_{k+1} &= \tilde{F}(\tilde{\mathbf{x}}_k, \tilde{w}_k), \\ \tilde{\mathbf{y}}_k &= \tilde{\mathsf{L}}(\tilde{\mathbf{x}}_k) \end{cases}$$

where each of the $(w_k)_{k\in\mathbb{N}_0}, (\tilde{w}_k)_{k\in\mathbb{N}_0}$ is a sequence of iid random variables. Suppose further that we are interested in approximating $\mathscr{D}$ with $\tilde{\mathscr{D}}$. If the observation space Y is endowed with some metric d_Y, we can endow Y^{n+1} with the product metric

$$d_{Y^{n+1}}((y_0,\dots,y_n),(\tilde{y}_0,\dots,\tilde{y}_n)) := \max_{k\in[0;n]} d_Y(y_k,\tilde{y}_k).$$

If we are able to assure that $d_{Y^{n+1}}(\mathbf{y},\tilde{\mathbf{y}}) \le \delta$ with a high probability, the fact that $\tilde{\mathbf{y}}$ satisfies some property $\Phi \in \mathrm{b}\mathscr{B}(Y^{n+1})$ would imply that $\mathbf{y}$ satisfies the modified (inflated) property

$$\Phi_\delta = \{y \in Y^{n+1} : d_{Y^{n+1}}(y,\Phi) \le \delta\}.$$

See [19, Theorem 7] for the case when Φ is a reachability specification. However, in order to talk about the probability of the value of $d_{Y^{n+1}}(\mathbf{y},\tilde{\mathbf{y}})$ being less than δ, we need to consider a coupling between $\mathbf{y}$ and $\tilde{\mathbf{y}}$. The work in [19] has considered the case of linear jump-diffusions, and implicitly suggested to use a coupling that matches the noises, that is $\tilde{w}_k = w_k$. In the follow-up paper [2] the coupling was considered to be the independent one (cf. Example 4). However, one has a complete freedom in choosing the coupling, so we can define a metric as follows:

$$d_{\mathsf{W}^n}(\mathscr{D},\tilde{\mathscr{D}}) := \sup_{x\in X}\inf_{\tilde{x}\in\tilde{X}} \mathsf{W}(\mathsf{Q}^n_x, \tilde{\mathsf{Q}}^n_{\tilde{x}}),$$

thanks to the coupling characterization of the Wasserstein distance in (14). In case we know $d_{\mathsf{W}^n}(\mathscr{D},\tilde{\mathscr{D}})$, for any initial state $x \in X$ we can find a corresponding $\tilde{x} \in \tilde{X}$ such that

$$\mathbb{Q}(d_{Y^{n+1}}(\mathbf{y},\tilde{\mathbf{y}}) \ge \delta) \le \frac{d_{\mathsf{W}^n}(\mathscr{D},\tilde{\mathscr{D}})}{\delta},$$

thanks to Markov's inequality, where $\mathbb{Q} \in \Gamma(\mathsf{Q}^n_x, \tilde{\mathsf{Q}}^n_{\tilde{x}})$ is any among the optimal couplings in (14). As a result, the metric d_{W^n} as well satisfies the first criterion in Section 1. Randomized methods to compute this metric can be found in [14, Sections 2.2, 2.3] and [28], thus assuring that d_{W^n} satisfies the second criterion we have raised. These methods are based on the representation of W as an integral metric (see Section 7.2), for example the one in [28] suggests solving a linear programming problem to evaluate $\mathsf{W}(\mathsf{Q}^{n,N}_x, \tilde{\mathsf{Q}}^{n,N}_{\tilde{x}})$ over empirical distributions (8).

Both TV and W are integral metrics, and for bounded metric spaces TV is always bigger than W, multiplied by a constant.

Hence, one may expect that d_{W^n} provides less conservative estimates than d_{TV^n}. Unfortunately, although one can try defining an analogue of the transition-based metric d_B for d_{W^n}, obtaining estimates similar to Theorem 2 is not an easy task. Thus we are not able to claim that d_{W^n} satisfies the third criterion.

Let us also mention that the Wasserstein metric has also been applied for purposes of abstractions of controlled ldt-MP in [14] with focus on discounted additive cost functionals. Furthermore, [30] has employed the Wasserstein metric to compare outputs of stochastic processes. However, the results in both papers are not suitable for Problem 1.

4. COMPARISON WITH THE LITERATURE

4.1 Total Variation distance

Recent literature on approximate probabilistic bisimulations has led to several metrics for discrete-time stochastic systems that are related to the metrics d_B and d_{TV^n} considered here. Before we elaborate on their similarity, let us first recall a few of these metrics.

One of the first metrics for stochastic systems is introduced in [11] and [12] for finite and infinite systems, respectively. As we discussed in Section 1, the notion of exact probabilistic bisimulation, introduced for finite systems in [22] and extended to infinite systems in [10], appears to be too restrictive and to lack robustness: this motivates looking for more flexible relations between systems. The notion of exact probabilistic bisimulation is characterized via a binary logic $\mathscr{L}$, so that two states are bisimilar if and only if they satisfy the same formulae in $\mathscr{L}$. The extension of $\mathscr{L}$ to some *real-valued* logic $\mathscr{L}_r$ leads to the definition of a distance between two states x and $\tilde{x}$ as the maximal difference between all formulae of $\mathscr{L}_r$ computed over such states: $d_{\mathscr{L}_r}(x,\tilde{x}) := \sup_{f\in\mathscr{L}_r}|f(x)-f(\tilde{x})|$. The fact that $\mathscr{L}_r$ is an extension of $\mathscr{L}$ requires that $d_{\mathscr{L}_r}$ is equal to zero over bisimilar states. The value of the metric between two stochastic systems is defined (over the disjoint union of the two systems) as the $d_{\mathscr{L}_r}$ distance between their initial conditions.

A different approach is taken in [35], where stochastic systems are represented as co-algebras, namely pairs (X,P), where X is a state space and $P : X \to \mathscr{P}(X)$ (note the similarity with dt-MP models considered in this work). The state spaces are assumed to be endowed with a metric, and the functor $\mathscr{P}$ is assumed to push the original metric of X into a Kantorovich metric over $\mathscr{P}(X)$.[6] It is further shown that a final co-algebra exists for such a functor, and since the final co-algebra is often thought of as a collection of behaviors, [35] introduces a metric between two states $x,\tilde{x}\in X$ as $d_{co}(x,\tilde{x}) = d_{fin}(!(x),!(\tilde{x}))$, where ! is the unique map from X to the final co-algebra.

Although $d_{\mathscr{L}_r}$ and d_{co} are introduced in completely different ways, it is shown in [35] that under certain conditions $d_{co} = d_{\mathscr{L}_r}$. This could be considered as evidence that any of these two (equal) metrics is the natural metric for the intended applications. However, it is of interest whether either of the two approaches is *the* natural one. Indeed, the definition of $d_{\mathscr{L}_r}$ depends on the choice of the real-valued logic $\mathscr{L}_r$, which in [12] is chosen to be just one of many possible extensions of the binary logic $\mathscr{L}$. Similarly, given a metric on the Borel space X, there are many ways to introduce a related metric on $\mathscr{P}(X)$: besides the Kantorovich metric proposed in [35] one could employ a Prokhorov metric [15] which would lead to a different value for d_{co}. As convergence in Prokhorov metric is equivalent to weak convergence of measures, and hence to the topology of $\mathscr{P}(X)$, arguably the latter may be a more natural choice for a metric on $\mathscr{P}(X)$ than the Kantorovich one. In conclusion, we contend that it is in general not possible to assert how good or natural the choice of a particular metric is, based on the way this metric is defined: the usefulness of a metric is rather determined by the applications it is meant to be used for. From this more practical perspective, it is unfortunately not clear which applications the models studied in [12, 35] are suitable for, besides their use in testing [34]: in fact, their semantics has not been defined explicitly and constructively. Besides, up to the best of the authors knowledge, in the case of testing there exist no precise bounds on the difference between testing probabilities over two system given their d_{co} or $d_{\mathscr{L}_r}$ distances.

From the perspective of the preceding discussion, we aim next to elaborate on the similarity between $d_{\mathscr{L}_r}$ and d_{TV^n}. Let us in particular show how $d_{\mathscr{L}_r}$ can be applied on BLTL model-checking over ldt-MP (which are the models we have defined d_{TV^n} over). Since $d_{\mathscr{L}_r}$ has been introduced over Labelled Markov Processes (LMP) [10], we need to provide a way of transform an ldt-MP into a corresponding LMP[7]. Consider a ldt-MP $\mathscr{D} = (X,Y,P,\mathsf{L})$ with a finite observation space Y; we define a corresponding LMP $(X,Y,\{\tau_y\}_{y\in Y})$, endowed with a state space X, a labels set Y, and the transition kernel

$$\tau_y(x,\mathrm{d}x') := 1_{\mathsf{L}^{-1}(y)}(x)\cdot P(x,\mathrm{d}x'),$$

that is, we enable the label y in the LMP exactly in those states x that are labeled with y in $\mathscr{D}$. Suppose we would like to compute over $\mathscr{D}$ a probability of some basic BLTL formula, that is a finite word $y_0\dots y_n \in Y^{n+1}$: i.e. we are to find $\mathsf{Q}^n_x(y_0\dots y_n)$, where Q^n_x is the trace distribution $\mathscr{D}$ induces on Y^{n+1}. As LMP do not have explicitly-defined trace semantics, we can interpret $\mathsf{Q}^n_x(y_0\dots y_n)$ as a value of the $\mathscr{L}_r$ formula $\langle y_0\rangle\dots\langle y_n\rangle 1(x)$.[8] The latter interpretation tells us that the LMP can be applied to compute probabilities of basic BLTL formulae over a corresponding ldt-MP, and hence it can be applied to any BLTL formula [31, Section 2.4]. Note however, that probabilities of more general BLTL formulae over ldt-MP are not necessarily elements of $\mathscr{L}_r$ for the corresponding LMP: the disjunction and conjunction in BLTL are not related to max and min in $\mathscr{L}_r$ at all. As a result, although any BLTL formula over an ldt-MP can be computed via functions in $\mathscr{L}_r$ over the corresponding LMP, such computations may require summation of $\mathscr{L}_r$ functions. Hence, if any function in $\mathscr{L}_r$ is known only with some error, this operation will require accumulating errors – this issue was already discussed in [31, Section 3] concerning the possible extensions of safety-focused results in [4] to the whole BLTL. Thus, although [12, Proposition 7.5] concerning $d_{\mathscr{L}_r}$ provides an analysis similar to Theorem 2, the bounds from the former result when interpreted over ldt-MP only apply to basic BLTL formulae, whereas the latter result provides bounds for any BLTL formula.

Let us also mention that Theorems 2 and 3 concerning the d_{TV^n} metric improve formula-free guarantees for ldt-MP introduced in [31] by providing tighter bounds on the difference between trace distributions: indeed, [31, Lemma 1, Theorem 3] derives similar bounds as Theorem 2, but provide more conservative results. An alternative approach [5] suggests expressing an LT property as an automaton, and solving a safety problem over the product

[6] Note however, that despite a strong connection between Kantorovich and Wasserstein metrics (see e.g. [14, Section 2.4.6]), this approach differs from the one we apply here in Section 3.2.

[7] Up to our knowledge, this paper is the first to explicitly elaborate on such a transformation.

[8] We assume here a version of $\mathscr{L}_r$ without discounting.

system. Unfortunately, the overall error associated to the abstraction needed for the solution of the safety problem depends on the size of the automaton, which is particularly crucial in case of BLTL formulae for which automata can be large [31, Section 3.4]. The formula-free guarantees do not depend on a particular BLTL formula (as the name suggests), and provide arguably less conservative bounds than safety-based approximate model-checking of complex LT properties (cf. [31, Section 5]).

4.2 Wasserstein distance

As we have mentioned in Section 3.2, the definition of the d_{W^n} metric is inspired by the work [19], which introduces an analogous metric restricted to a fixed coupling structure. We contend that this feature substantially increases the conservatism of the results, since in general one has the freedom to optimize over the coupling. The notions in [19] hinge upon similar ones developed over non-stochastic systems [16], where the coupling is necessarily unique so that its choice does not play a role. The choice of coupling for stochastic processes is especially important when it is not meaningful to claim that both processes are driven by the same noise. For instance, if it is clear how to compare noises that drive two diffusions (cf. Example 4), it is much less clear how to couple a diffusion with a finite-space continuous-time Markov Chain serving as its approximation [2]: in the latter case the only natural coupling seems to be the independent one, and it is rather unlikely that this coupling is the optimal one.

The work in [19] suggests how to compute a metric over a fixed coupling under rather strong assumptions on the stability of the models (over a fixed coupling). In particular, these technique require Lyapunov-like functions to synthesize a metric, and provide practically relevant sufficient conditions for these functions only in the linear case. In contrast, [6] introduces randomized methods to compute fixed coupling metrics without any stability assumptions – as in our case the results are valid over a finite time horizon. It is of interest to compare those results with ours, to see whether the choice of the coupling leads to a reduced conservatism, as expected.

Let us consider an example drawn form [1] and also studied in [32]. We consider a regional power network consisting of two local subnetworks: each of them has its own energy storage capacity. There are two sources of the energy: a coal plant shared by both networks, and two separate wind farms producing renewable energy. [32] studied the approximate abstraction of this model, with the objective of coal plant energy production and distribution optimizing some desired property over the whole network. On the other hand, here we are interested in studying the effect of the correlation over the energy produced by the two wind farms – it practically makes sense to consider this correlation when the two local subnetworks are close geographically. We assume that the coal plant energy is evenly distributed between both networks, which leads to the following (autonomous) dt-MP model of the network:

$$\begin{cases} \mathbf{x}^1_{k+1} = \beta\left(\mathbf{x}^1_k + \tfrac{1}{2}p_k + r^1_k - d^1_k\right) \vee 0 \wedge M, \\ \mathbf{x}^2_{k+1} = \beta\left(\mathbf{x}^2_k + \tfrac{1}{2}p_k + r^2_k - d^2_k\right) \vee 0 \wedge M, \end{cases}$$

where $\mathbf{x}^i$ it the amount of the stored energy in the i-th subnetwork, $\beta = 0.8$ is the loss rate of the stored energy, p_k is the energy produced by the coal plant, r^i_k is a renewable energy produced by the i-th wind farm, d^i_k is the energy demand in the i-th network, and $M = 30$ is the max storage capacity. We assume that $p_k \sim U([3,5])$ and $d^i_k \sim U([1,2])$ are distributed uniformly. The distribution of the renewable energy instead consists of two components: $r^i_k = (1-\rho)e^i_k + \rho r_k$, where $e^i_k, r_k \in \mathcal{E}(1)$ are distributed exponentially and $\rho \in [0,1]$ measures the correlation level of the distributions r^1_k and r^2_k. The initial conditions $\mathbf{x}^i_0 \sim U([5,10])$ are distributed uniformly.

We study two copies of the model distinguished by the choice of parameter $\rho = 0.2$ and $\rho = 0$ respectively. Recall that we only know the distribution of the stochastic process associated to each of the two models, but not their joint distribution: this allows to choose the coupling. We then consider three possible choices: coupling via the same noise, independence coupling, and reflected coupling. In the former case we use the same samples of $\tilde{d}^i_k = d^i_k$, $\tilde{p}_k = p_k$ and $\tilde{\mathbf{x}}^i_0 = \mathbf{x}^i_0$ for both systems, whereas in the latter case we use the symmetry of the uniform distribution to define $\tilde{d}^i_k$, $\tilde{p}_k$ and $\tilde{\mathbf{x}}^i_0$ as d^i_k, p_k and $\mathbf{x}^i_0$ reflect with respect to their mean values. Finally, in case of the independence coupling all samples are assumed to be independent, that is $\tilde{d}^i_k \perp d^i_k$, $\tilde{p}_k \perp p_k$ and $\tilde{\mathbf{x}}^i_0 \perp \mathbf{x}^i_0$. We assume that the observation space corresponds to the state space endowed with the Euclidean metric, thus the observation map is the identity function.

The results are presented in Figure 1. The computations are run over a time horizon $n = 100$ for $N \in [2; 1000]$ samples. From the figure it can be seen that over the number of samples considered, for each estimator the convergence does hold. One can also observe that although the coupling via the same noise performs better than the independence coupling, or than that via reflected noise, their associated distance is greater than the distance $d_{\mathsf{W}^{100}}$ obtained by optimizing over all the possible couplings. This optimization is performed using the method in [28], by means of solving a linear programming problem: the latter clearly represents the computational bottleneck of the method, as it requires $2N$ variables and $N(N-1)$ constraints. The complexity then depends on the number of samples, and although there is no explicit connection between the complexity of the linear programming problem and the dimension of original systems (or the time horizon), the latter factor may affect the number of samples needed for convergence to the true solution. Unfortunately, up to our knowledge there are no explicit results on the convergence for the W metric, similar to Theorem 1 for the TV metric. Methods mentioned in [14, Sections 2.2, 2.3] can be explored as possible computationally efficient alternatives. Let us finally mention that we do not provide here a comparison over the d_{TV^n} metric as it would not enlighten the importance of coupling as significantly as the d_{W^n} metric does.

5. CONCLUSIONS

This paper has discussed the formulation of two new metrics for stochastic transition systems, with focus on their applications for linear-time model-checking. Such metrics are shown to be useful according to three criteria defined in the article, and are claimed to perform better compared to other metrics proposed in the literature. Table 1 further shows which of those criteria the metrics introduced in this paper satisfy, and according to which result. A promising direction of future research concerns the connections of the metrics proposed in this work with notions of approximate probabilistic simulation and bisimulation.

Criterion	TV^n	W^n
[i.]	YES. By definition.	YES. By definition.
[ii.]	YES. By Theorem 1.	YES. See e.g. [28].
[iii.]	YES. By Theorems 2, 3.	???

Table 1: Satisfaction of criteria by metrics TV^n and W^n.

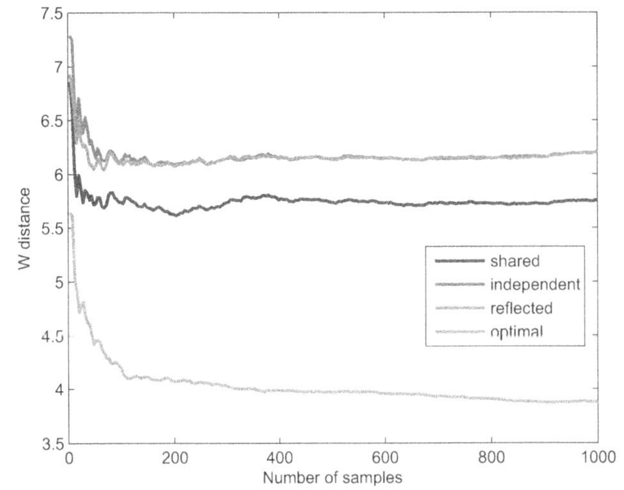

Figure 1: Evaluation of expected distances between x and x̃ depending on the number of samples, over different couplings: shared (blue line in the middle), independent and reflected noises (resp. red and gray lines on the top), optimal coupling (green line at the bottom).

6. REFERENCES

[1] MoVeS website. http://www.movesproject.eu.

[2] A. Abate. A contractivity approach for probabilistic bisimulations of diffusion processes. In *Proceedings of the 48th IEEE Conference on Decision and Control and 28th Chinese Control Conference*, pages 2230–2235, 2009.

[3] A. Abate. Approximation metrics based on probabilistic bisimulations for general state-space markov processes: a survey. *Electronic Notes in Theoretical Computer Sciences*, 2013. In Print.

[4] A. Abate, J.-P. Katoen, J. Lygeros, and M. Prandini. Approximate model checking of stochastic hybrid systems. *European Journal of Control*, 16:624–641, 2010.

[5] A. Abate, J.-P. Katoen, and A. Mereacre. Quantitative automata model checking of autonomous stochastic hybrid systems. In *Proceedings of the 14th international conference on Hybrid Systems: Computation and Control*, HSCC '11, pages 83–92, New York, NY, USA, 2011. ACM.

[6] A. Abate and M. Prandini. Approximate abstractions of stochastic systems: A randomized method. In *Proceedings of the 50th IEEE Conference on Decision and Control and European Control Conference*, pages 4861–4866, 2011.

[7] A. Abate, F. Redig, and I. Tkachev. On the effect of perturbation of conditional probabilities in total variation. *Statistics & Probability Letters*, 2014. In Press.

[8] C. Baier and J.-P. Katoen. *Principles of model checking*. The MIT Press, 2008.

[9] A. Dembo and O. Zeitouni. *Large deviations techniques and applications*. Springer-Verlag, Berlin, 2010.

[10] J. Desharnais, A. Edalat, and P. Panangaden. Bisimulation for Labelled Markov Processes. *Information and Computation*, 179(2):163 – 193, 2002.

[11] J. Desharnais, V. Gupta, R. Jagadeesan, and P. Panangaden. Metrics for Labeled Markov Systems. In *Proceedings of the 10th International Conference on Concurrency Theory*, CONCUR '99, pages 258–273, London, UK, 1999. Springer-Verlag.

[12] J. Desharnais, V. Gupta, R. Jagadeesan, and P. Panangaden. Metrics for labelled Markov processes. *Theoretical Computer Science*, 318(3):323–354, 2004.

[13] S. N. Ethier and T. G. Kurtz. *Markov processes: characterization and convergence*. Wiley Series in Probability and Mathematical Statistics: Probability and Mathematical Statistics. John Wiley & Sons Inc., New York, 1986.

[14] N. Ferns, P. Panangaden, and D. Precup. Bisimulation metrics for continuous Markov decision processes. *SIAM Journal on Computing*, 40(6):1662–1714, 2011.

[15] A. L. Gibbs and F. E. Su. On choosing and bounding probability metrics. *International Statistical Review*, 70(3):419–435, 2002.

[16] A. Girard and G. J. Pappas. Approximation metrics for discrete and continuous systems. *IEEE Transactions on Automatic Control*, 52(5):782 –798, 2007.

[17] A. Girard and G. J. Pappas. Approximate bisimulation: A bridge between computer science and control theory. *European Journal of Control*, 17(5-6):568–578, 2011.

[18] A. Hinton, M. Kwiatkowska, G. Norman, and D. Parker. PRISM: A tool for automatic verification of probabilistic systems. In H. Hermanns and J. Palsberg, editors, *Tools and Algorithms for the Construction and Analysis of Systems*, volume 3920 of *Lecture Notes in Computer Science*, pages 441–444. Springer Verlag, 2006.

[19] A.A. Julius and G.J. Pappas. Approximations of stochastic hybrid systems. *IEEE Transactions on Automatic Control*, 54(6):1193–1203, 2009.

[20] O. Kallenberg. *Foundations of modern probability*. Probability and its Applications. Springer-Verlag, New York, 1997.

[21] J.-P. Katoen, M. Khattri, and I. S. Zapreev. A Markov reward model checker. In *Proceedings of the Second International Conference on the Quantitative Evaluation of Systems*, QEST '05, pages 243–244, Washington, DC, USA, 2005. IEEE Computer Society.

[22] K. G. Larsen and A. Skou. Bisimulation through probabilistic testing. *Information and Computation*, 94(1):1–28, 1991.

[23] T. Lindvall. *Lectures on the coupling method*. Wiley Series in Probability and Mathematical Statistics: Probability and Mathematical Statistics. John Wiley & Sons Inc., New York, 1992.

[24] B. Øksendal. *Stochastic differential equations: an introduction with applications*. Universitext. Springer-Verlag, Berlin, sixth edition, 2003.

[25] K. R. Parthasarathy. *Probability measures on metric spaces*. Probability and Mathematical Statistics, No. 3. Academic Press Inc., New York, 1967.

[26] D. Revuz. *Markov chains*. North-Holland Publishing, Amsterdam, second edition, 1984.

[27] R. Segala. A compositional trace-based semantics for probabilistic automata. In I. Lee and S. A. Smolka, editors, *CONCUR '95: Concurrency Theory*, volume 962 of *Lecture Notes in Computer Science*, pages 234–248. Springer Berlin Heidelberg, 1995.

[28] B. K. Sriperumbudur, K. Fukumizu, A. Gretton, B. Schölkopf, and G. Lanckriet. On the empirical estimation of integral probability metrics. *Electronic Journal of Statistics*, 6:1550–1599, 2012.

[29] P. Tabuada. *Verification and control of hybrid systems: A symbolic approach*. Springer Verlag, New York, 2009.

[30] D. Thorsley and E. Klavins. Approximating stochastic biochemical processes with Wasserstein pseudometrics. *Systems Biology, IET*, 4(3):193 -211, May 2010.

[31] I. Tkachev and A. Abate. Formula-free finite abstractions for linear temporal verification of stochastic hybrid systems. In *Proceedings of the 16th international conference on Hybrid Systems: Computation and Control*, HSCC '13, pages 283–292, New York, NY, USA, 2013. ACM.

[32] I. Tkachev, A. Mereacre, J.-P. Katoen, and A. Abate. Quantitative automata-based controller synthesis for non-autonomous stochastic hybrid systems. In *Proceedings of the 16th international conference on Hybrid Systems: Computation and Control*, HSCC '13, pages 293–302, New York, NY, USA, 2013. ACM.

[33] Ilya Tkachev and Alessandro Abate. Characterization and computation of infinite-horizon specifications over markov processes. *Theoretical Computer Science*, 515(0):1 – 18, 2014.

[34] F. van Breugel, S. Shalit, and J. Worrell. Testing labelled Markov processes. In *Proceedings of the 29th International Colloquium on Automata, Languages and Programming*, ICALP '02, pages 537–548, London, UK, 2002. Springer-Verlag.

[35] F. van Breugel and J. Worrell. Towards quantitative verification of probabilistic transition systems. In *Proceedings of the 28th International Colloquium on Automata, Languages and Programming*, ICALP '01, pages 421–432, London, UK, 2001. Springer-Verlag.

[36] M.Y. Vardi. Automatic verification of probabilistic concurrent finite state programs. In *26th Annual Symposium on Foundations of Computer Science*, pages 327–338, 1985.

7. APPENDIX

7.1 General notation

We use extensively standard notions from measure and probability theory, for precise definitions see e.g. [20]. A measurable space is a pair $(E,\mathscr{E})$ where E is an arbitrary set and $\mathscr{E}$ is a σ-algebra on E. The space of all probability measures on $(E,\mathscr{E})$ is denoted by $\mathscr{P}(E,\mathscr{E})$; it is assumed to be endowed with the smallest σ-algebra that makes any evaluation map $\theta_A : \mathscr{P}(E,\mathscr{E}) \to \mathbb{R}$, defined by $\theta_A(p) = p(A)$ for all $p \in \mathscr{P}(E,\mathscr{E})$ and $A \in \mathscr{E}$, measurable. A stochastic kernel on $(E,\mathscr{E})$ is a measurable map $K : E \to \mathscr{P}(E,\mathscr{E})$. A probability space is a triple $(E,\mathscr{E},p)$, where $(E,\mathscr{E})$ is a measurable space and $p \in \mathscr{P}(E,\mathscr{E})$. If $(\Omega,\mathscr{F},\mathsf{P})$ is a probability space and $f : (\Omega,\mathscr{F}) \to (E,\mathscr{E})$ is a measurable map then

$$(f_*\mathsf{P})(A) := \mathsf{P}\left(f^{-1}(A)\right), \quad \forall A \in \mathscr{E}$$

defines the probability measure in $\mathscr{P}(E,\mathscr{E})$. We say that f induces the measure $f_*\mathsf{P}$. We further denote by id_Ω the identity map on Ω; clearly, it holds that $(\mathrm{id}_\Omega)_*\mathsf{P} = \mathsf{P}$ for any $\mathsf{P} \in \mathscr{P}(\Omega,\mathscr{F})$. By $\otimes$ we denote the product of measures or σ-algebras. The set of real numbers is denote by $\mathbb{R}$, the set of natural numbers by $\mathbb{N}$ and we write $\mathbb{N}_0 := \mathbb{N} \cup \{0\}$. We write E^ω in place of $E^{\mathbb{N}_0}$.

Any topological space X is assumed to be endowed with its Borel σ-algebra $\mathscr{B}(X)$ generated by all open subsets of X. For topological spaces we simply write $\mathscr{P}(X)$ in place of $\mathscr{P}(X,\mathscr{B}(X))$. We refer to elements of $\mathscr{B}(X)$ as Borel subsets of X. A (standard) Borel space is a topological space that is homeomorphic to a Borel subset of complete separable metric space. By $\mathscr{C}(X)$ we denote the linear space of all continuous real-valued functions on X.

Given a measurable space $(E,\mathscr{E})$, we denote by $\mathrm{b}\mathscr{E}$ the linear space of all bounded functions $f : E \to \mathbb{R}$. It is a Banach space endowed with a sup-norm $\|f\| := \sup_{x\in E}|f(x)|$.

7.2 Distances between probability measures

For a brief overview on distance between probability measures see [15]; a detailed exposition can be found in [25]. In this paper we focus on two metrics: the total variation distance TV that applies to measures over any measurable spaces, and the Wasserstein distance W that requires the underlying space to be a metric space. Both metrics fall into the class of integral probability metrics: let $(E,\mathscr{E})$ be an some measurable space and let $\mathscr{G}$ be any collection real-valued measurable functions on E. The corresponding metric on $\mathscr{P}(E,\mathscr{E})$ is defined as

$$I_{\mathscr{G}}(\mu,\tilde{\mu}) := \sup_{g\in\mathscr{G}}\left|\int_E g\,\mathrm{d}(\mu-\tilde{\mu})\right|.$$

The total variation metric is given by $\mathsf{TV} = I_{\mathrm{b}\mathscr{E}_1}$ where $g \in \mathrm{b}\mathscr{E}_1$ iff $g \in \mathrm{b}\mathscr{E}$ and $\|g\| \le 1$. Alternatively, the metric TV can be introduced via the difference of μ and $\tilde{\mu}$ over sets as follows:

$$\mathsf{TV}(\mu,\tilde{\mu}) = 2\cdot\sup_{A\in\mathscr{E}}|\mu(A)-\tilde{\mu}(A)|. \qquad (12)$$

Unlike the total variation distance that depends exclusively on the measurability structure of the set E, the Wasserstein distance requires E to be a metric space. Let E be endowed with the metric d_E such that $\mathscr{E} = \mathscr{B}(E)$. For any $g \in \mathrm{b}\mathscr{E}$ let

$$\mathrm{Lip}(g) := \sup_{x\neq x'}\frac{|g(x)-g(x')|}{d_E(x,x')}$$

denote the Lipschitz constant of g. The Wasserstein distance is defined as $\mathsf{W} = I_{\mathscr{C}_1}$, where $g \in \mathscr{C}_1$ iff $\mathrm{Lip}(g) \le 1$. Provided that $\mathrm{diam}(E) := \sup_{x,x'\in E} d_E(x,x') < \infty$, the following inequality relates the two metrics: $\mathsf{TV} \ge \frac{1}{\mathrm{diam}(E)}\mathsf{W}$ [15], so that the convergence in TV implies the convergence in W in case the latter is defined using a metric in which E is bounded.

Another relation between TV and W can be derived via recalling that each of the metric can be characterized by a coupling, optimal in a certain sense. For $\mu,\tilde{\mu} \in \mathscr{P}(E,\mathscr{E})$ let us denote by $\Gamma(\mu,\tilde{\mu}) \subset \mathscr{P}(E^2,\mathscr{E}^2)$ the collection of all coupling measures for μ and $\tilde{\mu}$. Provided that E is a Borel space and $\mathscr{E} = \mathscr{B}(E)$:

$$\mathsf{TV}(\mu,\tilde{\mu}) = 2\cdot\sup_{M\in\Gamma(\mu,\tilde{\mu})} M(\Delta_E) \qquad (13)$$

and if (E,d_E) is a bounded complete separable metric space:

$$\mathsf{W}(\mu,\tilde{\mu}) = \inf_{M\in\Gamma(\mu,\tilde{\mu})}\int_{E\times E} d_E(x,\tilde{x})M(\mathrm{d}x\times\mathrm{d}\tilde{x}). \qquad (14)$$

If we consider any two random elements f and $\tilde{f}$ that represent distributions μ and $\tilde{\mu}$, then the total variation distance can be obtained via the coupling that maximizes the probability that $f = \tilde{f}$, whereas the Wasserstein distance is exactly the minimal expected value of $d_E(f,\tilde{f})$ over all possible couplings.

Resilience to Intermittent Assumption Violations in Reactive Synthesis

Rüdiger Ehlers
University of Bremen, Bremen, Germany
University of Kassel, Kassel, Germany

Ufuk Topcu
University of Pennsylvania
Philadelphia, Pennsylvania, United States

ABSTRACT

We consider the synthesis of reactive systems that are robust against intermittent violations of their environment assumptions. Such assumptions are needed to allow many systems that work in a larger context to fulfill their tasks. Yet, due to glitches in hardware or exceptional operating conditions, these assumptions do not always hold in the field. Manually constructed systems often exhibit *error-resilience* and can continue to work correctly in such cases. With the development cycles of reactive systems becoming shorter, and thus reactive synthesis becoming an increasingly suitable alternative to the manual design of such systems, automatically synthesized systems are also expected to feature such resilience.

The framework for achieving this goal that we present in this paper builds on generalized reactivity(1) synthesis, a synthesis approach that is well-known to be scalable enough for many practical applications. We show how, starting from a specification that is supported by this synthesis approach, we can modify it in order to use a standard generalized reactivity(1) synthesis procedure to find error-resilient systems. As an added benefit, this approach allows exploring the possible trade-offs in error resilience that a system designer has to make, and to give the designer a list of all Pareto-optimal implementations.

1. INTRODUCTION

Automatically synthesizing reactive systems from their specifications is an attractive alternative to constructing these by hand. Even when a complete specification is not available, formal synthesis is a useful approach to analyze the specifications for the parts of the system to be constructed and allows to explore the design alternatives in a structured way.

To fully benefit from synthesis technology, measures have to be taken to ensure that the implementations computed in the process are of good quality [1, 7, 11]. Example quality criteria include energy consumption, size of the implementation, and the resilience of the implementation against changes in the conditions under which the system operates. Intuitively, the latter criterion means that a system should work as well as possible in scenarios in which the assumptions about its environment are violated. In other words, the system shall degrade gracefully, and all safety-relevant properties of the system should be fulfilled "whenever" possible.

While it would obviously be best if a synthesized system does not rely on any environment assumptions being satisfied, this is typically not possible. For example, if we require a robot to go from one point in a workspace to another point and there is an obstacle in between, then the assumption that the position of the robot is updated according to its actions (move left, move right, etc.) needs to be made. Manually constructed reactive system controllers typically only rely on these environment assumptions being satisfied in situations in which they are crucially needed. A reactive synthesis procedure on the other hand will typically compute a controller that lets it come very close to the obstacle, and thus the resulting controller cannot even tolerate a single "glitch" in the environment assumptions. The reason for this is by default, reactive synthesis procedures do not optimize towards controller behavior that allows for error-resilience (such as staying away from an obstacle as far as possible). Even worse, once an assumption is violated, the system is free to behave in an arbitrary manner and in particular, possibly fail to fulfill its requirements. The violation of assumptions in the field does also not necessarily mean that they have been modeled incorrectly, as typically not all eventualities can be modeled correctly and precisely, like components of the robot breaking at runtime or dirt on sensors leading to imperfect measurements.

In this paper, we solve the problem of synthesizing error-resilient systems from specifications in temporal logic. We concentrate on the generalized reactivity(1) fragment of linear-time temporal logic (LTL), for which an efficient and symbolic synthesis algorithm is known [4]. We show how to add the requirement of being k-resilient [10] to such a specification. That is the system has to tolerate arbitrarily many violations of safety assumptions ("*glitches*"), as long as in between every k such glitches, there is a long enough period in which no glitch occurs so that the system can recover from the earlier k glitches. By not exceeding the class of generalized reactivity(1) specification in this process, we ensure that also the synthesis problem for the resulting specification can be solved efficiently.

HSCC'14, April 15–17, 2014, Berlin, Germany.

ACM 978-1-4503-2732-9/14/04 ...$15.00.
http://dx.doi.org/10.1145/2562059.2562128.

Automatically synthesizing error-resilient systems enables to effectively perform *design space exploration*: we compute (1) which assumptions need to be seen as strict, i.e., need to be satisfied all of the time, (2) for which assumptions arbitrarily many glitches can be tolerated, and (3) for which assumption some glitches can be tolerated, and whose violations should count towards the value of k. We present an exploration algorithm that searches for all Pareto-optimal assignments of the assumptions to these categories that represent implementable error-resilience guarantees. Searching for these optimal solutions gives the system designer the insight of what the specifications imply with respect to the system's resilience and thus to select the most reasonable solution for the practical application in mind, without the need to formalize the preferences in advance. Additionally, it allows the system designer to state the assumptions in a very conservative manner whenever a precise model of the assumptions cannot be given. In the robot example, we might for instance know that dislocations of the robot do not happen "very often," but a more precise characterization of the environment cannot be given. By assuming that these never happen, and applying error-resilient synthesis, we can explore the possible error-resilience levels with our synthesis approach and by picking the most suitable one save the effort to analyze the possible environment behavior more closely in order to obtain a most suitable controller.

The rest of the paper is structured as follows: In the next section, we recall some preliminaries. Then, we formally describe the error-resilient system synthesis problem in Section 3, and explain how a generalized reactivity(1) specification can be modified in order to add error-resilience as a requirement in Section 4. We state how to search for all Pareto-optimal solutions in Section 5 and show the usefulness of our new techniques experimentally in Section 6. Afterwards, we discuss related work in Section 7 and conclude with a summary in Section 8.

2. PRELIMINARIES

A *controller* is a reactive system with an *interface* $\mathcal{I} = (\mathsf{AP}_I, \mathsf{AP}_O)$, where AP_I is the set of *input signals* and AP_O is the set of *output signals*. Given an interface $\mathcal{I}$, we describe a controller as a finite-state machine $\mathcal{M} = (S, \mathsf{AP}_I, \mathsf{AP}_O, s_0, \delta)$ for which S is a finite set of states, $s_0 \in S$ is the initial state, and $\delta : S \times 2^{\mathsf{AP}_I} \to S \times 2^{\mathsf{AP}_O}$ is the transition function. We say that some word $w = (w_0^I, w_0^O)(w_1^I, w_1^O)(w_2^I, w_2^O)\ldots \in (2^{\mathsf{AP}_I} \times 2^{\mathsf{AP}_O})^\omega$ is a *trace* of $\mathcal{M}$ if there exists a *run* $\pi = \pi_0\pi_1\ldots \in S^\omega$ such that $\pi_0 = s_0$ and for every $i \in \mathbb{N}$, we have $(\pi_{i+1}, w_i^O) = \delta(\pi_i, w_i^I)$. We call a sequence of states $s_1 s_2 \ldots s_n \in S$ a *loop* in $\mathcal{M}$ if $s_1 = s_n$ and for all $i \in \{1, \ldots, n-1\}$, there exist $x \subseteq \mathsf{AP}_I$ and $y \subseteq \mathsf{AP}_O$ such that $(s_{i+1}, y) = \delta(s_i, x)$.

In *reactive synthesis*, we compute a finite-state machine for which all of its traces satisfy some specification, which we describe in *temporal logic*. We consider a subset of *linear-time temporal logic (LTL)* [13] in this paper. Formulas in LTL are evaluated at positions i in a word $w = w_0 w_1 \ldots \in (2^{\mathsf{AP}})^\omega$ over a set of atomic propositions AP. In addition to the standard Boolean operators, we have the temporal operators G, F, and X that connect the truth values at some position in a word to those at future positions. Formally, we have (1) $w, i \models \mathsf{X}\phi$ iff $w, (i+1) \models \phi$, (2) $w, i \models \mathsf{G}\phi$ iff $\forall j \geq i : w, j \models \phi$, and (3) $w, i \models \mathsf{F}\phi$ iff $\exists j \geq i : w, j \models \phi$ (for every trace w, index i and sub-formula ϕ). The *until* operator of LTL is not used in this paper and not defined here. We say that a finite-state machine $\mathcal{M} = (S, \mathsf{AP}_I, \mathsf{AP}_O, s_0, \delta)$ satisfies some LTL specification ψ if and only if all of its traces (over $\mathsf{AP} = \mathsf{AP}_I \cup \mathsf{AP}_O$) satisfy the LTL formula at position $i = 0$. Given an interface $\mathcal{I} = (\mathsf{AP}_I, \mathsf{AP}_O)$ and an LTL specification ψ over the set of atomic propositions $\mathsf{AP}_I \cup \mathsf{AP}_O$, the *synthesis problem* is to decide whether there exists a finite-state machine $\mathcal{M} = (S, \mathsf{AP}_I, \mathsf{AP}_O, s_0, \delta)$ that satisfies ψ, and to compute such a finite-state machine in case of a positive answer.

A particularly interesting sub-class of LTL for the purpose of synthesis is the class of *generalized reactivity(1)* specifications [4], which is abbreviated as *GR(1)* in the following. Such specifications are of the form

$$\psi = (\psi_i^a \wedge \psi_s^a \wedge \psi_l^a) \to (\psi_i^g \wedge \psi_s^g \wedge \psi_l^g),$$

where the parts left of the implication operator are the *assumptions* and the parts right of the implication operator are the *guarantees*. In both of these property groups, we have *initialization properties* (ψ_i^a and ψ_i^g), which are free of temporal operators, *safety properties* (ψ_s^a and ψ_s^g), which are of the form $\mathsf{G}\phi$ for some LTL sub-formula ϕ in which the only temporal operator allowed is X, and *liveness properties* (ψ_l^a and ψ_l^g), which are of the form $\mathsf{GF}\phi$ for some LTL sub-formula ϕ in which the only temporal operator allowed is X. In all of these properties, the X operator is not allowed to be nested. In ψ_s^a and ψ_l^a, variables from AP_O may not occur within the scope of an X operator. Synthesizing from GR(1) specifications can be performed in time exponential in $|\mathsf{AP}_I| + |\mathsf{AP}_O|$, and tools that circumvent this worst-case computation time for many practical cases have been developed [12, 6]. It must be noted however that these typically implement a *strict semantics* of GR(1), where in order for a system to be considered to satisfy ψ, we have that ψ_s^g may only be violated after ψ_s^a has already been violated. This choice has no conceptual reasons – a specification for the classical Boolean implication semantics between the assumptions and guarantees can be encoded into one for the strict semantics with a minor blow-up of adding only one atomic proposition. For more details, the reader is referred to Bloem et al. [4]. In contrast to older GR(1) synthesis literature, we also allow the next-time operator in liveness assumptions and guarantees, which has been shown to only require a minor change to the standard GR(1) synthesis procedure [14].

3. DEFINING ERROR-RESILIENCE

In this section, we introduce a series of notions of resilience and state the main problems solved in the subsequent sections. Let AP be the set of signals of a reactive system and $\psi = \psi^a \to \psi^g = (\psi_i^a \wedge \psi_s^a \wedge \psi_l^a) \to (\psi_i^a \wedge \psi_s^a \wedge \psi_l^a)$ be its specification. Recall that ψ_s^a is a conjunction of basic safety properties, i.e., we have $\psi_s^a = \psi_{s,1}^a \wedge \ldots \wedge \psi_{s,n}^a$ with $\psi_{s,j}^a = \mathsf{G}\phi_{s,j}^a$ for all $j \in \{1, \ldots, n\}$.

3.1 Uniform Error-Resilience

Let $w = w_0 w_1 w_2 \ldots \in (2^{\mathsf{AP}})^\omega$ be a trace of a reactive system. We say that we have an *intermittent assumption violation at some position* $i \in \mathbb{N}$ for property $\psi_{s,j}^a = \mathsf{G}\phi_{s,j}^a$ in the trace if $w_{i-1} w_i w' \not\models \phi_{s_j}^a$ for every $w' \in (2^{\mathsf{AP}})^\omega$. For simplicity, let us also call intermittent assumption violations *glitches*. We say that $l \in \mathbb{N}$ glitches occur at some position

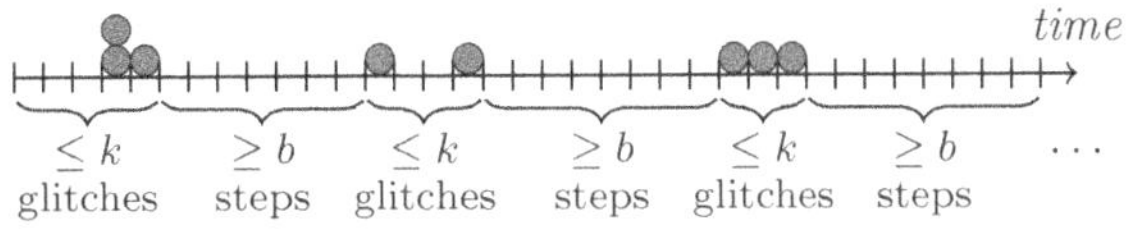

Figure 1: Graphical description of a (k,b)-sane input stream for some system and $(k,b) = (3,6)$; glitches along the system's execution are marked by circles.

$i \in \mathbb{N}$ in w if the maximal subset $P \subseteq \{\psi^a_{s,1}, \ldots, \psi^a_{s,n}\}$ such that for every $\psi' \in P$, we have a glitch for ψ' at position i, has cardinality l.

Definition 1. *Let $(\psi^a_i \wedge \psi^a_s \wedge \psi^a_l) \rightarrow \psi^g$ be a specification for some interface $\mathcal{I} = (\mathsf{AP}_I, \mathsf{AP}_O)$ and $k, b \in \mathbb{N}$. We say that some trace w is* (k,b)-sane *if in w,*

1. *there are infinitely many sequences of at least b consecutive steps in which no glitch occurs,*
2. *in between every of these glitch-free sequences, there are at most k glitches, and*
3. *there are only finitely many glitches in total.*

We say that a reactive system $\mathcal{M}$ with the interface $\mathcal{I}$ is (k,b)-resilient *if every of its traces satisfies ψ^g if it is (k,b)-sane and satisfies ψ^a_i and ψ^a_l.*

Figure 1 explains the concept graphically. Note that our definition of glitches is concerned with both the input and output part of a trace, which may be a bit unintuitive at first. It allows us to define the allowed *next* input signal valuations in the safety assumptions based on the system's previous output, however.

Intuitively, if a system is (k,b)-resilient, then it can from time to time tolerate a sequence of up to k intermittent assumption violations (not necessarily consecutive), provided that there are at least b steps to recover from the glitches afterwards. The restriction to finitely many glitches ensures that in cases in which the environment of a reactive system uses the glitches to prevent the system from fulfilling its liveness objectives, the system does not need to satisfy its guarantees. Since the system may have to wait for progress with respect to the environment satisfying its liveness assumptions before it can make progress towards satisfying the liveness guarantees, a recovery period of b steps may be insufficient for any value of b in the case of infinitely many glitches. The restriction to finitely many glitches does not affect the idea of error resilience, however, as a system can never know when a glitch has been the last one. Thus, it always has to return to normal operation mode after some finite number of steps and has to work towards satisfying its liveness guarantees even in the case of infinitely many glitches.

Note that we excluded the initialization assumptions and the liveness assumptions from being considered in the definition of error-resilience. The reason is simply that we want to make the system under design robust against *intermittent* violations of the assumptions. Liveness and initialization assumptions cannot be violated temporarily. If we are able to synthesize a reactive system even for the case that one such assumption is violated, then it is not needed. It can be assumed that in a formal development process of a reactive system, in which a specification is built step-by-step, such an assumption would never be added, so not considering this case does not restrict the practical impact of our error-resilient synthesis techniques to follow.

We are now ready to define the error-resilient synthesis problems.

Definition 2. *Given a specification $\psi = \psi^a \rightarrow \psi^g$, an interface $\mathcal{I} = (\mathsf{AP}_I, \mathsf{AP}_O)$, and values $k, b \in \mathbb{N}$, we define the reactive (k,b)-resilient synthesis problem for ψ and $\mathcal{I}$ to check if there exists a (k,b)-resilient system for $\mathcal{I}$ that satisfies ψ, and to compute such a system whenever it exists. In the reactive k-resilient synthesis problem [10] for $\mathcal{I}$ and ψ, we want to find a system for $\mathcal{I}$ whose traces satisfy ψ and that is (k,b)-resilient for some $b \in \mathbb{N}$, if it exists.*

3.2 Mixed Error-Resilience

The k-resilience definition introduced above treats all (safety) assumptions alike. In practical specifications, they however often differ in how likely they are to be violated at runtime. For example, for a robot, the assumption that the sensed position does not jump from one end of the workspace to another one is less likely to be violated compared to the assumption that the robot position is always updated precisely according to the actuators involved, as people can bump into the robot and thus cause small dislocations. As we cannot expect the robot to work correctly if people bump into it too often, this assumption is nevertheless justified and typically also needed. To account for these different likelihoods of intermittent assumption violations, we now refine the idea of k-resilience accordingly.

Definition 3. *Let $\psi^a_s = \psi^a_{s,1} \wedge \ldots \wedge \psi^a_{s,n}$ be the set of safety assumptions of a given specification. We define a* resilience signature *for ψ^a_s to be a function $s : \{1, \ldots, n\} \rightarrow \{any, some, none\}$.*

The idea of a resilience signature is that it augments a reactive system specification with information about the relative significance of the violations in its safety assumptions with respect to its resilience. More specifically, it classifies the assumptions as those for which (1) any number of glitches shall be tolerated, (2) a particular pre-specified number of glitches shall be tolerated, or (3) no glitches are guaranteed to be tolerated. Only case (2) shall count toward the value of k that we define resilience over.

Definition 4. *Let $(\psi^a_i \wedge \psi^a_s \wedge \psi^a_l) \rightarrow \psi^g$ be a specification for some interface $\mathcal{I} = (\mathsf{AP}_I, \mathsf{AP}_O)$, s be a resilience signature for ψ^a_s, and $k, b \in \mathbb{N}$. We say that some trace w is (s,k,b)-sane if in w,*

1. *there are infinitely many sequences of at least b consecutive steps in which no glitch occurs,*
2. *no glitches occur at all for all safety assumptions $\psi^a_{s,j}$ with $s(\psi^a_{s,j}) = none$,*
3. *in between every of these glitch-free sequences, there are at most k glitches of safety assumptions $\psi^a_{s,j}$ with $s(\psi^a_{s,j}) = some$, and*
4. *there are only finitely many glitches in total.*

We say that a reactive system $\mathcal{M}$ is (s,k,b)-resilient *if every trace of the system satisfies ψ^g if the trace is (s,k,b)-sane and satisfies ψ^a_i and ψ^a_l.*

The resilient synthesis problem can now be modified accordingly as follows.

Definition 5. *Given a specification $\psi = \psi^a \rightarrow \psi^g$, an interface $\mathcal{I} = (\mathsf{AP}_I, \mathsf{AP}_O)$, values $b, k \in \mathbb{N}$, and some resilience signature s, we define the reactive (s,k,b)-resilient synthesis problem for ψ and $\mathcal{I}$ to check if there exists a (s,k,b)-resilient system for $\mathcal{I}$ that satisfies ψ, and to compute such a system whenever it exists. The (s,k)-resilient synthesis problem for ψ and $\mathcal{I}$ is to decide whether for some $b \in \mathbb{N}$, a (s,k,b)-resilient system exists and to find such a system.*

For the brevity of presentation, we only consider the (s,k)-resilient synthesis problem in the following. This choice is motivated by the fact that in practice, glitches often come in bursts, so optimizing towards the maximum possible length of such bursts should have the highest priority.

To simplify the presentation of examples in the following, we will also just list the values that s maps to whenever the assumption list is fixed. For instance, we will write $(\mathit{some}, \mathit{none}, 2)$ instead of $(\{1 \mapsto \mathit{some}, 2 \mapsto \mathit{none}\}, 2)$. For some fixed specification and a fixed interface, we will also call a resilience signature (s,k) *realizable* if there exists a (s,k)-resilient implementation for the specification with the defined interface.

4. SYNTHESIZING ERROR-RESILIENT SYSTEMS

We now show how given a specification $\psi = \psi^a \rightarrow \psi^g$, an interface $\mathcal{I} = (\mathsf{AP}_I, \mathsf{AP}_O)$, a resilience signature s for ψ and a value $k \in \mathbb{N}$, we can perform (s,k)-resilient synthesis. While ψ and $\mathcal{I}$ are necessarily given in any reactive synthesis problem, the latter two describe how error-resilient we want our implementation to be. We show in the next section how to optimize over these, i.e., find the strongest possible values for s and k that are implementable. For the scope of this section, we assume them to be given.

The following construction shows how to modify a GR(1) specification in order to enforce (s,k)-resilience of the implementation along with satisfying the specification. As a consequence, for synthesizing an (s,k)-resilient implementation, we can modify the specification (automatically) and use a standard GR(1) synthesis tool.

For $k \in \mathbb{N}$, we define AP_k to represent a set of signals $\{x_0, \ldots, x_m\}$ such that $m = \lceil \log_2(k+1) \rceil$, and we denote the binary encoding of a number $0 \leq j \leq k$ into AP_k as $(\!|j|\!)$. We also call AP_k the *counter signals.*

Definition 6 (Modified Specification). *Given ψ with the set of safety assumptions $\{\psi^a_{s,1}, \ldots, \psi^a_{s,n}\}$, $\mathcal{I}$, s and k, we define the modified interface $\mathcal{I}'$ and the modified specification ψ' as follows:*

$$\begin{aligned} \mathcal{I}' &= (\mathsf{AP}_I, \mathsf{AP}_O \cup \mathsf{AP}_k) \text{ and} \\ \psi' &= (\psi^a_i \wedge \psi'^a_s \wedge \psi'^a_l) \rightarrow (\psi'^g_i \wedge \psi'^g_s \wedge \psi'^g_l) \end{aligned}$$

with

$$\begin{aligned} \psi'^a_s &= \bigwedge_{j \in \{1,\ldots,n\}, s(j)=\mathit{none}} \mathsf{G}\,\phi^a_{s,j} \\ &\quad \wedge \bigwedge_{\substack{h \in \{0,\ldots,k\}, \\ D \subseteq \{1,\ldots,n\}, \\ |D| = h+1, \\ \forall j \in D: s(j)=\mathit{some}}} \mathsf{G}\left((\!|h|\!) \rightarrow \bigvee_{j \in D} \phi^a_{s,j} \right), \\ \psi'^a_l &= \bigwedge_{j \in \{1,\ldots,n'\}} \mathsf{GF}(\neg(\!|k|\!) \vee \phi^a_{l,j}) \end{aligned}$$

for $\psi^a_l = \mathsf{GF}\phi^a_{l,1} \wedge \ldots \wedge \mathsf{GF}\phi^a_{l,n'}$,

$$\begin{aligned} \psi'^g_i &= \psi^g_i \wedge (\!|k|\!), \\ \psi'^g_s &= \psi^g_s \wedge \bigwedge_{\substack{h \in \{0,\ldots,k\}, \\ D \subseteq \{1,\ldots,n\}, \\ |D| \leq h, \\ \forall j \in D: s(j)=\mathit{some}}} \mathsf{G}\left((\!|h|\!) \wedge \bigwedge_{j \notin D} \phi^a_{s,j} \rightarrow \mathsf{X} \bigvee_{h' \geq h - |D|} (\!|h'|\!) \right), \\ \psi'^g_l &= \mathsf{GF}\left((\!|k|\!) \vee \bigvee_{j \in \{1,\ldots,n\}} \neg\phi^a_{s,j} \right) \\ &\quad \wedge \bigwedge_{j' \in \{1,\ldots,n'\}} \mathsf{GF}\left(\phi^s_{l,j'} \vee \bigvee_{j \in \{1,\ldots,n\}} \neg\phi^a_{s,j} \right) \end{aligned}$$

for $\psi^g_l = \mathsf{GF}\phi^g_{l,1} \wedge \ldots \wedge \mathsf{GF}\phi^g_{l,n'}$.

Intuitively, when constructing a modified specification, we add a set of output signals that the system can use to declare how often assumption violations can be tolerated in the near future. The modified formula ψ'^g_i describes that the system should start with a value of k. The progress of the values of AP_k is constrained in ψ'^g_s, which describes that in every step of the system's execution, it can only decrease the value of the counter by the number of assumptions violated. However, the counter value can always be increased. We modify the safety assumptions such that those assumptions that s maps to *some* must only be satisfied if otherwise the counter would drop below 0. As the system can only decrease the counter values with assumption violations, this witnesses that recently k glitches with respect to the *some*-properties have occurred.

The modified liveness guarantees only require the system to satisfy its original liveness guarantees when finitely many assumption violations occur. Also, in that case, the counter must infinitely often have a value of k. While, intuitively, this does not require the existence of a bound $b \in \mathbb{N}$ such that the system is (s,k,b)-resilient, applying a synthesis tool to a specification that we modified according to Definition 6 yields only implementations that have such a bound b. This is because GR(1) synthesis procedures only produce finite-state solutions, for which b is bounded from above by the number of states in the system.

Let us now prove that using the modified specification, we can synthesize (s,k)-resilient systems.

Theorem 1. *Let $\mathcal{I}$ be an interface, ψ be a generalized reactivity(1) specification, s be a resilience signature, $k \in \mathbb{N}$, and $\mathcal{I}'$ and ψ' be the modified interface and specification constructed from $\mathcal{I}$, ψ, s, and k using Definition 6. We have:*

- *If there exists an (s,k)-resilient system with interface $\mathcal{I}$ for ψ, then there exists a system that satisfies ψ' for the interface $\mathcal{I}'$.*
- *If a system satisfies ψ' for the interface $\mathcal{I}'$, then it is (s,k)-resilient and satisfies ψ.*

Proof. *Part 1:* Assume that we are given some (s,k)-resilient finite-state machine $\mathcal{M}$. We can augment every state in $\mathcal{M}$ by some counter value that represents the maximum number (in $\mathbb{N} \cup \{\infty\}$) of violations of *some*-assumptions that it is guaranteed to tolerate from the state (along any path). Note that along any transition, the counter can only decrease by as much as the number of assumption glitches witnessed by the transition, as otherwise the counter value of the predecessor state of a transition would be incorrect. This fact also holds if we cap every number to k. Consider that we augment the output of the system by the additional signals AP_k that it uses to output the current counter value. The set of states and the transitions between the states of the system's finite-state machine are not altered by adding these signals as the counter value only depends on the current state. The modified assumptions $\psi_s^{\prime a}$ are engineered to hold along all (s,k)-sane traces then. These are the traces that the system can cope with by the assumption that it is (s,k)-resilient, so it must satisfy ψ_s^g on them. As $\psi_s^{\prime g}$ consists of two conjuncts, namely ψ_s^g and the requirement that the counter is updated correctly, it also satisfies $\psi_s^{\prime g}$ for (s,k)-sane input streams. Fulfillment of the initialization constraints is trivial.

Since $\mathcal{M}$ is (s,k)-resilient, we must be able to label every state that lies at a loop of states that can be taken infinitely often without violating a safety assumption with k. Otherwise, some input could delay the recovery of the system to a stage at which it can tolerate k more glitches of *some*-properties arbitrarily, so the system would not be (s,k,b)-resilient for any value of b. At the same time, along all loops in the system that can be taken without glitches and while satisfying the liveness assumptions of the system when being taken infinitely often (a "*good*" loop), it must satisfy ψ_l^g when taken infinitely often. Thus, if ψ_l^a is fulfilled and the trace is (s,k)-sane, then $\psi_l^{\prime g}$ is fulfilled as then eventually the counter is k and ψ_l^g is fulfilled.

Part 2: Let a finite-state machine with interface $\mathcal{I}'$ be given that satisfies ψ'. We show that this system is (s,k)-resilient for ψ. That is ψ is satisfied for all traces that are (s,k,b)-sane for some $b \in \mathbb{N}$. We set b to be the number of states in the finite-state machine. Note that the counter represented by the AP_k signals can only be decreased by glitches for *some*-assumptions. Furthermore, in between every b steps of the machine's execution without a glitch, the counter has to be reset to k, as otherwise we have found a loop in the execution that can eventually be taken forever and that violates the first conjunct of $\psi_l^{\prime g}$. Since continuously having a counter value of less than k also satisfies the liveness assumptions, such a loop would witness the non-satisfaction of ψ' by the system. Since, after at most b steps, we have always found a loop, the claim follows. As the counter value can only be decreased with glitches (by the definition of $\psi_s^{\prime g}$), the value always represents an over-approximation of how many glitches still need to be tolerated for a (s,k,b)-sane trace before a b-length recovery phase. The only way to violate ψ_a' is to violate a *none*-assumption or to violate more assumptions than allowed by the counter value in a step. Both cases witness that the trace is not (s,k,b)-sane. Thus, the safety assumptions of ψ' only excluded cases that do not need to be considered for establishing the (s,k)-resilience of a system. On the other hand, if at some point glitches stop occurring, then the system has to satisfy ψ_l^g. Also, ψ_s^g and ψ_i^g are included in the guarantees of ψ'. Therefore, all (s,k,b)-sane traces of the finite-state machine satisfy ψ^g. □

Note that we can just ignore the additional output signals that a system has for a modified specification, so an implementation for a modified specification can also be used for the original specification. Also observe that starting from a GR(1) specification, a modified specification is still in GR(1) form. Thus, we can solve the (s,k)-resilient synthesis problem for a GR(1) specification using a classical GR(1) synthesis procedure by just modifying the specification with the construction of Definition 6.

When applying Definition 6, the number of signals in the specification grows only logarithmically in k, and the number of liveness assumptions and guarantees grows only by 1. Thus, the complexity of a GR(1) synthesis process (which is polynomial in the number of liveness assumptions and guarantees and exponential in the number of signals) grows only polynomially in k. This fact does not contradict the exponential growth of the formula length, as complexity-wise, it is subsumed in the increase of the number of signals.

In Definition 6, we assumed the strict semantics of the implication that connects the assumptions and guarantees in a GR(1) specification. For specifications for the non-strict semantics, one can use the construction from [4] to translate it to an equivalent specification for the strict semantics, and then apply Definition 6. The resulting specification is suitable for one of the many GR(1) synthesis tools with strict implication semantics.

5. FINDING ALL PARETO-OPTIMAL ERROR-RESILIENCE CONFIGURATIONS

In the previous section, we explained how to synthesize (s,k)-resilient systems for given values of s and k. In a formal system development process, we want to automate the task of searching for the best values of s and k in order to ensure that we obtain an as-good-as-possible system. In particular, we want to find all Pareto-optimal solutions. A value pair (s,k) is Pareto-optimal for a specification ψ if there exists no other realizable value pair $(s',k') \neq (s,k)$ that *dominates* (s,k), i.e., such that for all $i \in \{1,\ldots,n\}$, we have $s'(i) \geq s(i)$ (for the total order $none < some < any$) and $k' \geq k$, with the restriction that we treat all values of k as equal if s does not map any assumption to *some* (as then the value of k does not matter). We also call such value pairs (s,k) *resilience configurations* in the following.

As the set of possible resilience configurations (s,k) is infinite, we cannot just enumerate all configurations and check for each of them if an (s,k)-resilient system can be found. Even if we could, such an approach would be inefficient, as we can make use of *monotonicity* – if for some (s,k), we find an implementation, then we can surely find one for a configuration (s',k') that represents weaker resilience requirements to the system.

We propose the following two-step process. We first search for the Pareto-optimal implementable resilience configurations (s,k) for $s:\{1,\ldots,n\} \rightarrow \{none, any\}$. Observe that here, the value of k does not matter, so without loss of generality, we can set $k=0$. In the second step, starting from the realizable resilience configurations found in the first step, we check if we can upgrade some *none*-assumptions to *some*-assumptions and raise the value of k as much as possible. The maximally permissible values of k are always bounded, as otherwise this would witness that we could make all *some*-assumptions to *any*-assumptions, which contradicts the fact that we started from a Pareto-optimal solution for $s:\{1,\ldots,n\} \rightarrow \{none, any\}$.

We formalize both steps as a search problem for all maximal elements in a lattice $(P,\leq)$ that are mapped to **true** by some antitone function $f: P \rightarrow \mathbb{B}$. In the first step,

Algorithm 1 Pareto-optima finding algorithm

```
procedure SEARCH((P, ≤),x,succ,f,found,missed,done)
    if x ∈ done then return ;
    if ∃p ∈ missed : p ≤ x then return ;
    if (∃p ∈ found : p ≥ x) ∨ f(x) then
        for x' ∈ succ(x) do
            SEARCH(x',succ,f,found,missed,done);
        if ∄p ∈ found : x ≤ p then
            found ← found ∪ {x};
    else
        missed ← missed ∪ {x};
    done ← done ∪ {x};
end procedure
```

Algorithm 2 Lattice successor computation function and antitone function definition for step 1 of the Pareto-optimal solution finding procedure

```
function f1(x)
    return REALIZABLE({i ↦ any | i ∈ {1,...,n}, i ∈ x} ∪ {i ↦ none | i ∈ {1,...,n}, i ∉ x}, 0, ψ);
end function

function succ1(A)
    return {A ∪ {x} | x ∈ {1,...,n}} \ {A};
end function
```

P is simply $2^{\{1,\ldots,n\}}$ and $\leq$ is set inclusion. An element of P then contains all assumption indices i that are mapped to *any*. To search for all Pareto-optimal solutions in this context, we can apply algorithms from the field of computational learning, in particular for learning a monotone Boolean function from an oracle. However, such algorithms are typically geared towards minimizing the number of evaluations of f in the context of Boolean functions (see [8] for an overview of classical algorithms), and are not applicable to the second step of our construction, in which a non-Boolean lattice is considered. For simplicity, we use the search algorithm given in Algorithm 1 for both cases, which is suitable for all lattices with a least element. It is based on a solution idea by Gainanov [9] to traverse the lattice from the least element until a Pareto-optimal element is found, but uses a caching scheme to reduce the number of evaluations of f. The first step in our two-step process can be executed through the call

SEARCH($(P_1, \leq_1)$, $\emptyset$, succ_1, f_1, $found_1$, $missed_1$, $done_1$)

where the parameters are set as

$found_1 \leftarrow \emptyset$;
$missed_1 \leftarrow \emptyset$;
$done_1 \leftarrow \emptyset$;
$(P_1, \leq_1) \leftarrow (2^{\{1,\ldots,m\}}, \subseteq)$.

For reasons of readability, the functions f_1 and $succ_1$ are given in Algorithm 2. The function REALIZABLE(s, k, ψ) denotes checking (s, k)-resilient realizability of the specification ψ using Definition 6 and a GR(1) synthesis procedure. The parameters to SEARCH are passed by reference, so that the contents of $found_1$, $missed_1$, and $done_1$ are retained during the recursive evaluation of SEARCH and can be used for caching the results already computed.

After we have identified the realizable resilience configurations that are restricted to *none* and *any* entries, we turn towards the second step of the construction, in which we search for the remaining ones. We apply the SEARCH procedure

SEARCH($(P_2, \leq_2)$, $(\{\{1,\ldots,n\} \mapsto none\}, 1)$, succ_2, REALIZABLE, $found_2$, $missed_2$, $done_2$)

with the following parameters:

$found_2 \leftarrow \text{conv}(found_1)$;
$missed_2 \leftarrow \text{conv}(missed_1)$;
$done_2 \leftarrow \emptyset$;
$(P_2, \leq_2) \leftarrow ((\{1,\ldots,n\} \rightarrow \{any, some, none\}) \times \mathbb{N}_{\geq 1} \setminus (\{1,\ldots,n\} \rightarrow \{any, none\}) \times \mathbb{N}_{\geq 2}, \text{cmp}_2)$.

Here, the function *conv* translates a resilience signature of the shape used in step 1 to a resilience configuration for step 2, i.e., for every $x \subseteq \{1,\ldots,n\}$, we have

$$\text{conv}(x) = \{(\{i \mapsto \tau(x(i)) \mid i \in \{1,\ldots,n\}\}, 1) \mid x \in found_1\}$$

for $\tau(x) = any$ if $x = \textbf{true}$ and $\tau(x) = none$ if $x = \textbf{false}$.

The comparison operator cmp_2 and the function succ_2 for computing the direct successors of an element in the lattice $(P_2, \leq_2)$ are given in Algorithm 3. Note that the succ_2 function computes *any* direct successors of a resilience configuration, but we have a slightly more complicated definition of the lattice in step two than in step one. It excludes all resilience configurations (s, k) that are dominated by the ones found to be realizable in step 1 (i.e., are contained in $found_1$) and for which $k > 1$. As we know that in such cases, for any value of k, our specification is (s, k)-resiliently realizable, we prevent to needlessly search for larger values of k in this way. Note that any resilience configuration in the lattice is still reachable by succ_2 steps from the least element $(\{\{1,\ldots,n\} \mapsto none\}, 1)$, so we do not miss any solutions in this way. However, it is ensured that our search only needs finite time due to this modification since only finitely many reachable resilience configurations are mapped to **true** by REALIZABLE. The reason is that for cases (s, k) not covered by the ones from step one, there is a maximum number for k such that the specification is (s, k)-realizable, but not $(s, k+1)$-realizable. To see this, assume that there exists a value of s such that the specification is (s, k)-resiliently realizable for any value of k. Then it is also realizable for $(s', 0)$ for which s' results from setting all $i \in \{1,\ldots,n\}$ to *any* if they are set to *some* or *any* in s. Such configurations would have been found in step 1 however, and as a consequence, $succ_2$ would have never computed (s, k) as a possible successor of any resilience configuration for $k > 1$.

To speed up the computation in step 2, $found_2$ and $missed_2$ are initialized with information stored into $found_1$ and $missed_1$ after the first step. Setting $k = 1$ for entries added to $found_2$ is motivated by the fact that in $(P_2, \leq_2)$, a value of $k = 1$ can only be exceeded for resilience configurations (s, k) for which s is not dominated by some resilience configuration that is found to be realizable during the first step of the overall search procedure, which would not be covered by a case stored in $found_1$ anyway. Note that some of the configurations by which we initialize $found_2$ may be Pareto-optimal, whereas others might not. Thus, after the call to SEARCH, the set $found_2$ can contain non-Pareto-optimal configurations. Whenever this is a concern, we can post-process the set $found_2$ after the call to SEARCH by simply removing resilience configurations that are dominated by other configurations in $found_2$.

Algorithm 3 Lattice navigation functions for step 2 of the Pareto-optimal solution finding procedure

> **function** $\text{cmp}_2((s,k),(s',k'))$
>   **return** $(\forall i \in \{1,\ldots,n\} : s(k) \leq s'(k)) \wedge (k \leq k')$;
> **end function**
>
> **function** $\text{succ}_2(s,k)$
> $X \leftarrow \{(s',k) \mid s' \neq s, \exists i \in \{1,\ldots,n\} : \forall j \in \{1,\ldots,n\} \setminus \{i\} : s'(j) = s(j), (s(i) = \mathit{none} \wedge s'(i) = \mathit{some}) \vee (s(i) = \mathit{some} \wedge s'(i) = \mathit{any})\}$;
>   **if** $\exists i \in \{1,\ldots,n\} : f(i) = \mathit{some} \wedge \forall f \in \mathit{found}_1, \exists i \in \{1,\ldots,n\} : \neg f(i) \wedge (s(i) \neq \mathit{none})$ **then**
> $X \leftarrow X \cup \{(s,k+1)\}$;
>   **return** X
> **end function**

To illustrate the search algorithm, Figure 2 depicts the call graph of the SEARCH function for a specification with two assumptions for the set of Pareto optima $\{(\mathit{any},\mathit{none},1),(\mathit{none},\mathit{any},1),(\mathit{some},\mathit{some},2)\}$. Step one yields $\{(\mathbf{true},\mathbf{false}),(\mathbf{false},\mathbf{true})\}$ in this case, so that found_2 is initialized with $\{(\mathit{any},\mathit{none},1),(\mathit{none},\mathit{any},1)\}$.

The graph represents the candidate resilience configurations during the recursive evaluation of the SEARCH procedure. Every configuration is labeled by whether it is realizable ($^+$) or not ($^-$). The return edges are dotted, whereas calls that cause the SEARCH function to return in the first two lines due to caching in the sets missed_2 and done_2 are dashed. All other edges represent that the third line of Algorithm 1 is reached and thus the function f given to the algorithm is evaluated or a resilience configuration is covered by one of found_2 already. The latter is the case for the edges 1, 2, 21, and 24 in the figure. Thus, the GR(1) synthesis procedure needs to be called six times in this example.

It can be seen that the SEARCH algorithm mitigates the problem that a lattice element can be reached from multiple successors by caching whether an element has already been considered in done. This happens at the edges 7, 22, and 25. For edge 12, the unrealizability of the configuration $(\mathit{any},\mathit{some},2)$ is deduced from the fact that before return edge 4, $(\mathit{any},\mathit{some},1)$ is stored in missed_2.

In terms of complexity, the number of calls to the REALIZABLE function in both steps of the algorithm is bounded from above by $2(n+1)\cdot\#\mathit{Sig}$, where $\#\mathit{Sig}$ is the number of realizable resilience configurations (s,k) in P_2 for which k is not needlessly ≥ 1, i.e., for which there is no realizable resilience configuration $(s',1)$ that dominates (s,k).

6. EXAMPLES AND EXPERIMENTS

We implemented the constructions from Section 4 and Section 5 in a Python script that interfaces the GR(1) Synthesis tool `slugs` [6], using strict implication semantics. We consider three benchmarks to evaluate the practical applicability of our resilient synthesis approach, which we describe in the following. All computation times are given for an Intel Xeon 2.40GHz computer running Linux, with a 4 GB memory limit, which was never exceeded. All computations are performed single-threaded. During the computation of the realizable resilience configurations, only realizability is checked, but no implementation is computed. All implementation sizes are given in states for explicit-state implementations that were computed in additional runs of `slugs`.

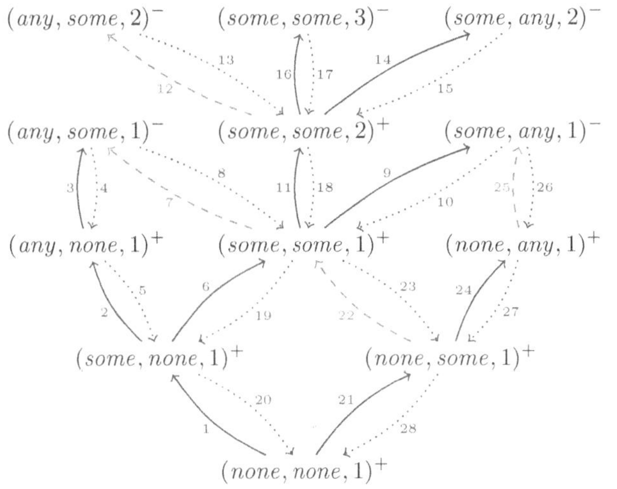

Figure 2: Graphical representation of the call structure during step 2 of the search algorithm for some specification with two assumptions.

6.1 Water Reservoir Level

As a simple introductory example, we consider a water reservoir controller. The reservoir is required to always hold between 10 and 99 gallons of water. There are two in-flows that are uncontrollable for the system. Each of them either delivers no water at all or two gallons of water at every time step. The controller can decide to release three gallons of water in a time step. We start with a reservoir level of 10 gallons.

By default, this setting is unrealizable as the controller cannot avoid the reservoir to overflow. This can be seen from the fact that in every step, four gallons of water can be added, but only three gallons can be released. With the two assumptions for each of the in-flows that they can only release water in every second time step, the setting becomes realizable.

Applying the constructions from the previous sections yields $\{(\mathit{any},\mathit{some},87),(\mathit{some},\mathit{any},87),(\mathit{some},\mathit{some},175)\}$ as the set of Pareto-optimal realizable resilience configurations. Obtaining this set takes 4 minutes and 52 seconds of computation time (including 270 calls to the `slugs` synthesis tool). For comparison, synthesizing a non-error-resilient controller for the water reservoir controller takes 0.35 seconds. Checking the realizability of a modified specification takes 1.07 seconds in the mean, and the number of (reachable) states of the computed implementations increases from 2043 for the non-resilient implementation to 2383 for the Pareto optima with $k = 87$, and 2489 for the other optimum.

The structure of the set of Pareto-optimal solutions can be explained from the fact that we need glitches for both of the in-flows in order to reach a situation in which the 3 gallons/time unit of the out-flow are insufficient to cope with the in-flows. Due to the difference of one gallon per time unit between the maximum in-flow and the maximum out-flow one would expect $(\mathit{any},\mathit{some},89)$ to be a realizable resilience configuration, but in fact it is not. The reason is that the environment can initially trigger only a single in-flow, which yields a reservoir level of 12 gallons, which the controller cannot reduce without violating its specification. Starting

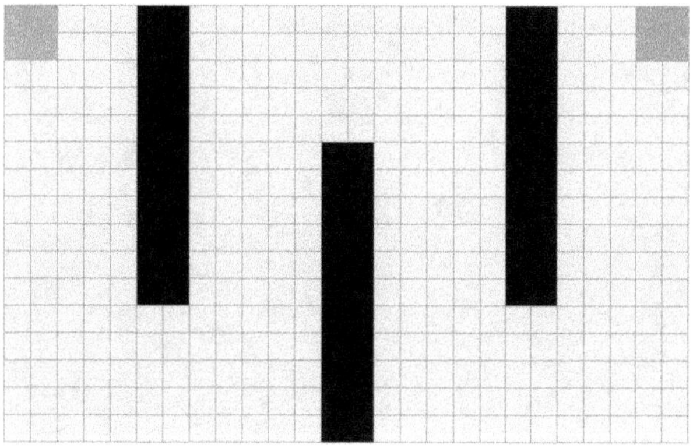

Figure 3: Workspace of the robot for the scenario of Section 6.2.

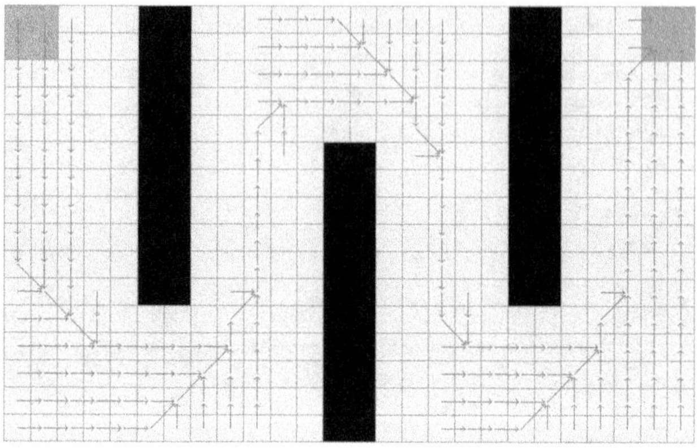

Figure 4: Robot behavior in the absence of glitches.

from 12 gallons, 87 cycles with two glitches in every cycle are then needed for the environment to enforce exceeding the 99 maximally allowed gallons in the reservoir. If one of the assumptions is an *any*-assumption, only one of the glitches counts towards k, leading to a maximum value for k of 87. If both glitches count, we get a maximally possible value of $k = 175$. The difference of one is explained by the fact that a computation cycle with a single glitch is never a problem for the system, as this means that our in-flow is at most 3 gallons, which can be handled. Thus, one additional glitch is permitted.

6.2 Robot Motion Planning

As a second example, we consider a problem in which a robot is required to deliver a package from the top left corner of a workspace (shown in Figure 3) to the top right corner of a workspace whenever it is triggered by some input signal. The workspace features some obstacles that the robot must not collide with. Running into the boundaries of the workspace is allowed. The robot has a sensor for its current position and can trigger motion into eight directions (north west, north, north east, etc.). Let us call the directions along the width and height as x and y direction, respectively.

We have three safety assumptions in this setting: (1) the robot position cannot change by more than one cell (horizontally, vertically, or diagonally) per execution step, (2) the x-position of the robot is updated according to whether it moves westwards or eastwards, and (3) the y-position of the robot is updated according to whether it moves northwards or southwards.

Finding all Pareto-optimal resilience configurations $\{(any, none, none, 1), (some, some, some, 1), (none, some, any, 1), (none, some, some, 2)\}$ takes 16.8 seconds (including the 22 calls to **slugs**). As assumptions (2) and (3) together imply assumption (1), the first two of these configurations are not interesting. The third configuration allows arbitrarily many glitches in the y-direction, but only a single one in the x-direction. The asymmetry between the x and y directions is due to that there are a columns along the y direction in the workspace without obstacles. Whenever we get a sequence of glitches for assumption (3), the robot can move to these columns to avoid bumping into obstacles, and later return to fulfilling its delivery task. The last of the resilience configurations is the one in which the robot maximizes its resilience against small dislocations. Since the resulting implementation has more reachable workspace cells, its size increases from 164 states of the non-resilient implementation to 7136 states. Figure 4 shows the paths taken by the robot for getting the package to the top right corner in case that no glitch occurred so far for the synthesized implementation with resilience configuration $(none, some, some, 2)$. In this figure, the arrows show the transitions that the robot shall take if it ends up in a cell from which an arrow originates. The robot does not reach the cells without outgoing arrows under the corresponding strategy. It can be seen that the robot keeps a good distance to the obstacles. In case of dislocations of the robot, it performs different actions. Figure 5 shows the actions of the robot for the case that recently two glitches have been observed, but no delivery is to be made, i.e., the only task of the robot at the respective point in time is to avoid obstacles.

6.3 Robot Motion Planning with Moving Obstacles

We now consider a variant of the motion planning problem of Section 6.2 with a moving obstacle introduced to the workspace shown in Figure 6. The robot to be controlled starts in the upper left corner and has the assumptions and guarantees described in Section 6.2. The controller also obtains as input the position of the moving obstacle that has a width of two cells and an equal height. In addition to the three assumptions about the robot position updates, we have two additional ones: (4) that the obstacle can only move in every second execution step, and (5) that the obstacle can only move to adjacent cells in every step while never touching the fixed obstacles (black) and the gray boundary cells, which can only be crossed by the robot to be controlled. Assumption (4) is necessary to prevent the obstacle from moving into the path of the robot all of the time, while (5) ensures that the obstacle cannot jump onto the robot and can also not block the pickup and delivery regions, which are colored in Figure 6 in the same way as in Figure 3.

Analyzing the scenario takes 361 minutes (with 75 calls to **slugs** for modified specifications and an average computation time of 288.5 seconds per call). The set of Pareto optima is $A = \{(any, none, none, some, none, 47)\}$, and synthesis without error-resilience for the original specification takes 9 minutes and 23 seconds. The number of states in the implementation increases from 133819 to 1587114 for the resilience signature in A. As again the satisfaction of

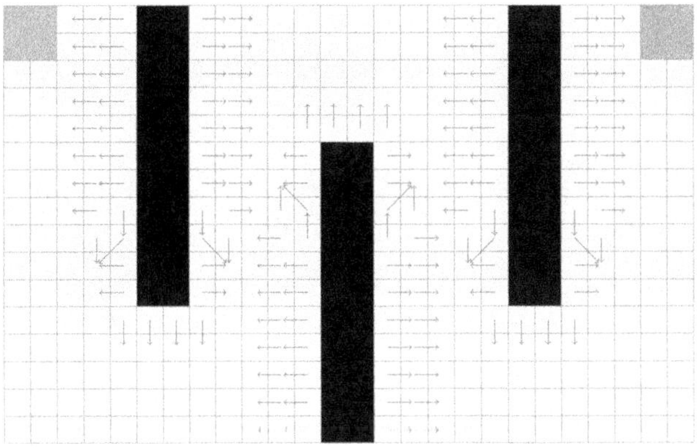

Figure 5: Robot backup behavior after two glitches.

assumptions (2) and (3) together imply the satisfaction of assumption (1), the singular set of Pareto optima shows that the only assumption for which we can tolerate glitches is the one that disallows the obstacle to move at the same speed as the robot (i.e., one cell per cycle for both x and y directions). However, we can tolerate bursts of glitches of length 47 for this assumption. Intuitively, the space available for the robot to pass by the obstacle is not sufficient to tolerate a glitch in its motion, but the obstacle being too fast a few times can be compensated.

We also considered a moving obstacle in a 16×16 grid without fixed obstacles in which the only task for the robot is to avoid colliding with the moving obstacle. The assumptions are the same as in the previous case. After 4 minutes and 29 seconds (90 calls to `slugs`), we obtain the following Pareto-optimal resilience configurations:

1. $(any, none, none, some, none, 20)$
2. $(some, some, some, some, none, 1)$
3. $(none, some, some, some, none, 2)$
4. $(none, some, none, some, none, 3)$
5. $(none, none, some, some, none, 3)$
6. $(none, some, none, none, none, 5)$
7. $(none, none, some, none, none, 5)$

Due to the smaller workspace, only 20 glitches of the assumption that the obstacle must not move too quickly can be tolerated (if all other assumptions are strict). Again, due to the implication between assumptions (2), (3), and (1), the second resilience configuration can be ignored. This time, robot motion glitches and speed glitches for the moving obstacle can be tolerated in combination, namely 2 glitches in total if the direction of the robot motion glitch is not fixed, and 3 glitches otherwise. If only robot motion glitches in x or y direction need to be tolerated, then 5 glitches are admissible. If both of them can occur, then only 2 glitches can be tolerated (which is a special case of resilience configuration number 3).

7. RELATED WORK

Reasoning about the changes (or preservations) of system's properties under uncertainties and disturbances has been considered not only in the control theory literature but also in synthesis of discrete reactive controllers. Numerous notions of robustness (and sensitivity) have been defined for different applications. For example, Tabuada et al. [15] consider the problem of synthesizing a program whose behavior in case of disturbances stays close to the nominal-case behavior and at the same time the effect of disturbances vanishes over time. It can be seen that this robustness criterion is motivated by similar notions in controls [18, 16] and heavily depends on the existence of a distance notion between different input/output streams, in contrast to the error-resilience criterion that we use in this paper. Additional work includes [3] which focuses on safety properties and uses the ratio of the distances between allowed and observed system behavior to that of the environment behavior as a measure of sensitivity. Reference [17] on the other hand synthesizes reactive controllers that are robust to uncertainties in the underlying open finite transition systems (e.g., due to unmodeled transitions).

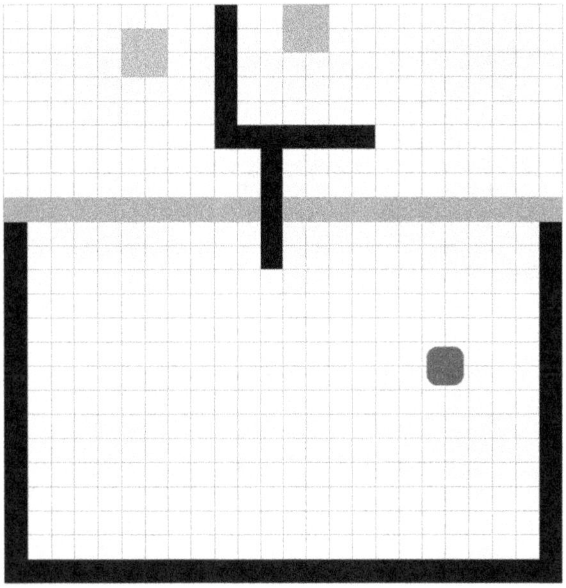

Figure 6: Robot workspace with a moving obstacle.

Ehlers [5] discusses the synthesis of systems that are robust in the sense that after safety assumption violations, the system must return to an operation mode in which the safety guarantees are satisfied again after only finitely many violations of these. Thus, such systems have a backup strategy for anomalous operating conditions without the need for the system engineer to specify one. Bloem et al. [2] consider a strengthened version of the approach in which a robust system is required to satisfy its liveness guarantees even in the presence of infinitely many safety assumption violations. In the approaches of [5] and [2], the robustness criteria are purely qualitative. In contrast to these works, in our new approach, all of the guarantees should always be satisfied without deviation. We systematically extend the set of environment behaviors that can be dealt with by the system synthesized. Our error-resilience definition is thus closer to the classical notions of robustness in control, in which the admissible environment conditions of the computed controllers are to be loosened as much as possible.

8. CONCLUSION & DISCUSSION

In this paper, we considered the problem of synthesizing systems that are resilient against environment assumption violations. The key contribution is a construction to change a generalized reactivity(1) specification to one of the same type, but that encodes the search for an implementation that exhibits the desired error-resilience level. This encoding allows to use off-the-shelf generalized reactivity(1) synthesis tools for obtaining error-resilient systems. Our construction distinguishes between two types of error-resilience for every assumption: resilience against arbitrarily long sequence of glitches, and resilience against at most k glitches (for some k). To find all Pareto-optimal assignments of the assumptions to these types and to maximize the value of k, we described an algorithm to search for these Pareto optima and thus provided a fully-automated method to explore how resilient an implementation for a specification can be made.

Our contribution not only allows to synthesize error-resilient implementations, but also helps a system engineer with the manual construction of error-resilient systems. Starting with a specification for the system to be constructed and a corresponding implementation, we can analyze whether the implementation is already optimal with respect to error-resilience by comparing the error-resilience level of the implementation against the Pareto optima found in the synthesis process.

The definition of the synthesis problem for error-resilient systems that we considered in this paper has many conceivable variants that we did not discuss in detail. For example, we could require that the length of a recovery period (referred to as the value of the variable b in Section 3) shall be minimized. We can approximate this behavior by changing the definition of $\psi_l'^g$ in our specification modification construction (by replacing all liveness guarantees $\mathsf{GF}\phi$ in $\psi_l'^g$ by $\mathsf{GF}((\llparenthesis k \rrparenthesis \wedge \phi) \vee \bigvee_{i=0}^{k-1} \llparenthesis i \rrparenthesis \wedge \neg \mathsf{X} \llparenthesis i \rrparenthesis)$ in order to count changing the counter value as progress whenever it is not yet k). However, a slight modification of the GR(1) synthesis tool is advisable in order to let the implementation favor transitions that make progress towards the unmodified liveness guarantees whenever possible while working towards increasing the counter value.

Another variant of practical relevance is strengthening the definition of error-resilience to require the satisfaction of a specification's liveness guarantees also in the case of infinitely many safety assumption violations. Note that this variant only makes sense if the resilience signature does not map some assumptions to *any*, as otherwise the implementability of a system for this error-resilience definition would witness that the *any*-assumptions are actually not needed. Synthesis for such a variant of the error-resilience definition is best performed by using a modified synthesis algorithm, in which we use the unmodified liveness assumptions and guarantees, but at the same time force the system to always eventually set the counter to a value closer to k or k itself, regardless of the satisfaction of the liveness assumptions.

These two variants of the methods proposed in this paper retain the same complexity of the synthesis process.

Acknowledgements

The first author was partially supported by the ERC under grant agreement no. 259267 and NSF ExCAPE CCF-1139025/1139138. The second author was partially supported by the AFOSR (FA9550-12-1-0302) and ONR (N00014-13-1-0778).

9. REFERENCES

[1] S. Almagor, U. Boker, and O. Kupferman. Formalizing and reasoning about quality. In *ICALP (2)*, pages 15–27, 2013.

[2] R. Bloem, H.-J. Gamauf, G. Hofferek, B. Könighofer, and R. Könighofer. Synthesizing robust systems with RATSY. In *SYNT*, volume 84 of *EPTCS*, pages 47–53, 2012.

[3] R. Bloem, K. Greimel, T. A. Henzinger, and B. Jobstmann. Synthesizing robust systems. In *FMCAD*, pages 85–92, 2009.

[4] R. Bloem, B. Jobstmann, N. Piterman, A. Pnueli, and Y. Sa'ar. Synthesis of reactive(1) designs. *Journal of Computer and System Sciences*, 78(3):911–938, 2012.

[5] R. Ehlers. Generalized Rabin(1) synthesis with applications to robust system synthesis. In *NASA Formal Methods*, pages 101–115, 2011.

[6] R. Ehlers, C. Finucane, and V. Raman. Slugs GR(1) synthesizer. `http://github.com/ltlmop/slugs`, 2013.

[7] R. Ehlers, R. Könighofer, and G. Hofferek. Symbolically synthesizing small circuits. In G. Cabodi and S. Singh, editors, *FMCAD*, pages 91–100. IEEE, 2012.

[8] T. Eiter, K. Makino, and G. Gottlob. Computational aspects of monotone dualization: A brief survey. *Discrete Applied Mathematics*, 156(11):2035–2049, 2008.

[9] D. Gainanov. On one criterion of the optimality of an algorithm for evaluating monotonic boolean functions. *USSR Computational Mathematics and Mathematical Physics*, 24(4):176–181, 1984.

[10] C.-H. Huang, D. Peled, S. Schewe, and F. Wang. Rapid recovery for systems with scarce faults. In M. Faella and A. Murano, editors, *GandALF*, volume 96 of *EPTCS*, pages 15–28, 2012.

[11] G. Jing, R. Ehlers, and H. Kress-Gazit. Shortcut through an evil door: Optimality of correct-by-construction controllers in adversarial environments. In *IROS*, pages 4796–4802. IEEE, 2013.

[12] S. C. Livingston. gr1c GR(1) synthesizer. `http://github.com/slivingston/gr1c`, 2013.

[13] A. Pnueli. The temporal logic of programs. In *FOCS*, pages 46–57. IEEE Computer Society, 1977.

[14] V. Raman, N. Piterman, and H. Kress-Gazit. Provably correct continuous control for high-level robot behaviors with actions of arbitrary execution durations. In *ICRA*. IEEE, 2013.

[15] P. Tabuada, A. Balkan, S. Y. Caliskan, Y. Shoukry, and R. Majumdar. Input-output robustness for discrete systems. In *EMSOFT*, pages 217–226, 2012.

[16] D. C. Tarraf, A. Megretski, and M. A. Dahleh. A framework for robust stability of systems over finite alphabets. *IEEE Transactions on Automatic Control*, 53(5):1133–1146, 2008.

[17] U. Topcu, N. Ozay, J. Liu, and R. M. Murray. On synthesizing robust discrete controllers under modeling uncertainty. In *Hybrid System: Computation and Control*, pages 85–94, 2012.

[18] J. C. Willems. Dissipative dynamical systems part i: General theory. *Archive for rational mechanics and analysis*, 45(5):321–351, 1972.

Model Measuring for Hybrid Systems

Thomas A. Henzinger
tah@ist.ac.at

Jan Otop*
jotop@ist.ac.at

Institute of Science and Technology Austria (IST Austria)

ABSTRACT

As hybrid systems involve continuous behaviors, they should be evaluated by quantitative methods, rather than qualitative methods. In this paper we adapt a quantitative framework, called model measuring, to the hybrid systems domain. The model-measuring problem asks, given a model M and a specification, what is the maximal distance such that all models within that distance from M satisfy (or violate) the specification. A distance function on models is given as part of the input of the problem. Distances, especially related to continuous behaviors are more natural in the hybrid case than the discrete case. We are interested in distances represented by monotonic hybrid automata, a hybrid counterpart of (discrete) weighted automata, whose recognized timed languages are monotone (w.r.t. inclusion) in the values of parameters.

The contributions of this paper are twofold. First, we give sufficient conditions under which the model-measuring problem can be solved. Second, we discuss the modeling of distances and applications of the model-measuring problem.

Categories and Subject Descriptors

D.2.4 [**Software/Program Verification**]: Model checking

Keywords

Quantitative model checking, parametric hybrid automata, model measuring

1. INTRODUCTION

Hybrid systems combine discrete control and continuous dynamics. Hybrid automata, which are used to model hybrid systems, specify discrete control and continuous behaviors by, respectively, finite automata and continuous functions parametrized by time. These two aspects of hybrid automata influence each other. The current state of the discrete control determines a system of differential inequalities that specify the evolution of continuous functions. The transitions of the discrete control are labeled by linear inequalities, called guards. A transition is enabled only if its guards are satisfied by the current values of continuous functions.

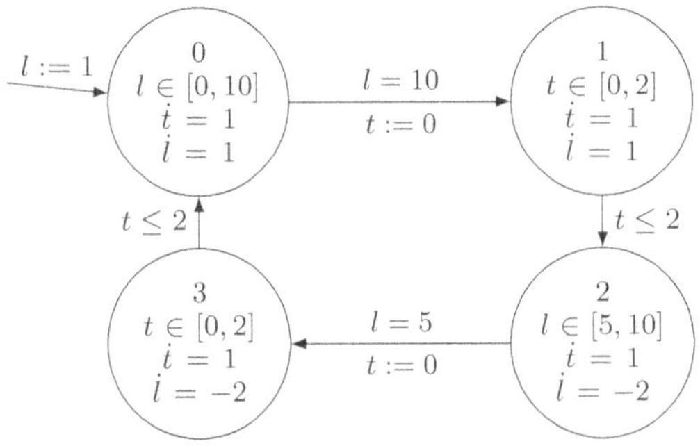

Figure 1: The water-level monitor from [1].

Hybrid automata allow for the precise modeling of physical features. Consider a model of a water-level monitor depicted in Figure 1. The system monitors the level of water in a tank by switching the pump on and off to keep the water level between 0 and 13 units; it works as follows. If the pump is on, the water level rises constantly at pace 1 units per time unit. When the pump is off, the water level drops constantly at pace 2. Finally, there is a latency of (at most) 2 time units between the decision of the monitor to shut down (turn on) the pump and the effect. The functions t, l represent a clock and the water level.

However, while modeling of the system's physical part, the designer has to come up with numerical bounds occurring in guards, like the aforementioned latency of the pump. Those values are often estimated by the designer. In consequence, guards are often too restrictive. In the water-level monitor example, the latency of the pump can be safely increased from 2 to 2.5. That issue can be avoided by employing automatic parameter synthesis, which can be expressed as an instance of the model-measuring problem.

The *model-measuring problem* asks, given a model M and specification P, what is the maximal distance ρ such that all models M' within that distance from M satisfy (or violate) P. That distance ρ is called the *stability radius*.

To determine the stability radius, it suffices to have a unary function that, for a given transition system M', specifies its distance from M. Such a function, called a *similarity measure*, is an input to the model-measuring problem. As

*The second author is on the leave from University of Wrocław.

HSCC'14, April 15–17, 2014, Berlin, Germany.

ACM 978-1-4503-2732-9/14/04 ...$15.00.
http://dx.doi.org/10.1145/2562059.2562130 .

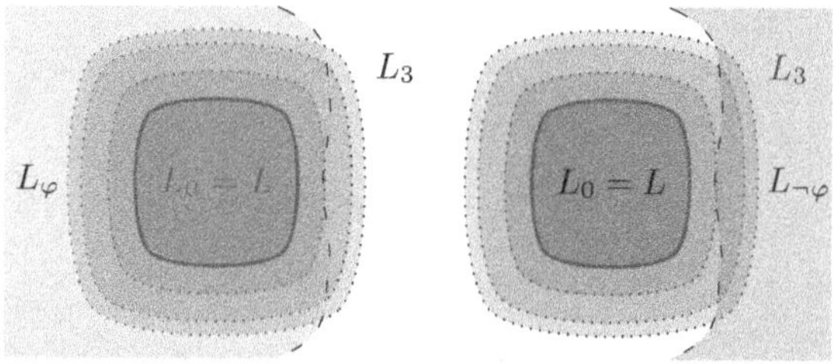

(a) Containment (b) Disjointness

Figure 2: A similarity measure and sets of traces satisfying (a) and violating (b) the specification. The model checking problem reduces to containment (a) and disjointness (b).

inputs are required to be finitely represented, we are interested in *automatic* similarity measures that are represented by parametrized hybrid automata in the following way.

Consider a parametrized hybrid automaton $\mathcal{A}[p]$ with a single parameter p, which occurs in its guards. E.g. a parameter p in $x < p$. Assume that with p instantiated to 0, $\mathcal{A}$ recognizes precisely the set of traces of M and the timed languages recognized by $\mathcal{A}$ are monotonic (w.r.t. inclusion) in the values of the parameter p. Such a hybrid automaton defines a monotonic function from $[0, \infty]$ to the set of timed languages (ordered by inclusion), $x \mapsto \{L_x\}$, where L_x is the language of $\mathcal{A}$ with p instantiated to x (cf. Figure 2). Then, $\mathcal{A}$ defines a similarity measure in the following way, the distance of M' from M is the minimal value x such that L_x contains all traces of M'. This definition of a similarity measure allows for effective computation of the stability-radius.

The model satisfies the specification if its set of traces is contained in the language of all admissible traces. In consequence, the stability radius in the model-measuring problem is the supremum of the values x of the parameter p such that L_x is contained in the language of the specification (Figure 2.a). Indeed, the set of traces of each model whose distance from M is less then x is contained in L_x. On the other hand, maximality of x implies that x is the maximal distance.

However, if the specification L_P is given as the complement of the set of all valid traces, the model checking problem reduces to disjointness. Similarly, the model-measuring problem reduces to finding the supremum of the values of x of the parameter p such that L_x and L_P are disjoint (Figure 2.b). Finding that supremum, in turn, reduces to finding the infimum of values of the parameter p such that a given parametrized hybrid automaton with the parameter instantiated to this value recognizes a nonempty language. That problem for discrete weighted automata is referred to as the quantitative emptiness problem or the optimal-weight problem.

We discuss the optimal-weight problem for parametrized hybrid automata in Section 3. We give sufficient conditions, which guarantee that a class of parametrized hybrid automata admits an effective procedure for approximating the infimum of the values of parameters, such that the hybrid automaton with parameters instantiated to these values recognizes a nonempty language.

Having an algorithmic foundation for the model-measuring problem, we can focus on its applications. Returning to the water-level monitor, the guard $t \in [0, 2]$ in the transitions from 1 to 2 and from 3 to 0, and the invariants in 1, 3, can be substituted by a parametrized guard $t \in [0, 2 + p]$, which states that the latency of the pump is bounded by $2 + p$. Such a parametrized hybrid automaton defines a similarity measure and the model-measuring problem answers the question: what is the maximal latency of the pump tolerated by the system?

However, the model-measuring problem is far more general than parameter synthesis. It can be used to measure the resilience of the model under perturbations. For instance, one can model a pipeline failure scenario, which manifests itself as either water shortage or water absence. In case of water shortage the pump is able to pump only 0.5 water units per second and in water absence 0 units per second. The question "what is the maximal overall time of water shortage tolerated by the water-level monitor" can be expressed as an instance of the model-measuring problem.

Contributions. We continue the line of research set in [11]. We introduce basic notions and notation in Section 2. The remaining part of the paper contains the following contributions:

1. We develop the theory of monotonic parametric hybrid automata, that can be thought of as "weighted" counterparts of hybrid automata (Section 3).
2. We adapt the model-measuring framework [11] to the hybrid automata case (Section 4).
3. We discuss constructions of similarity measures defined by hybrid automata (Section 5).
4. We study which distances on timed words can be expressed by hybrid automata (Section 6).

Related work. Parameter synthesis for hybrid automata, which is a special case of model measuring for hybrid automata, has been extensively studied [7, 8]. However, parameter synthesis is usually considered for arbitrary parameterizations (in particular in [8]), whereas, we are interested only in monotonic parameterizations. The (non-monotonic) parameter synthesis problem becomes quickly undecidable; it is already undecidable for timed automata. Therefore, the methods for (non-monotonic) parameter synthesis are necessarily incomplete or nonterminating.

Monotonic parameterizations of timed automata have been studied in [12]. Our approach is more general. First, it is defined on affine hybrid automata. Second, it allows constraints of the form $t \in [-p, p]$, which are disallowed in [12]. Third, parameter synthesis is a special case of our model-measuring framework.

Evaluation of hybrid systems based on distances has been discussed in [6], where the Skorohod distance has been suggested as the right distance between continuous behaviors. It can be expressed by a hybrid automaton, but it is not known whether that automaton belongs to a class enjoying decidability of the emptiness problem.

2. PRELIMINARIES

A *labeled transition system* is a quadruple (S, Σ, E, s_0), where S is a (finite or infinite) set of states, Σ is an alphabet, E is a relation on $S \times \Sigma \times S$ and s_0 is an initial state. All models considered in this paper are (finite or infinite) transition systems. A word $w = a_1a_2\ldots$ is a *trace* of a (labeled) transition system M if there is a path $s_0s_1\ldots$ in M such that for every $i \in [1, |w|]$, $(s_{i-1}, a_i, s_i) \in E$. Such a path is said to be *associated* with w.

2.1 Hybrid automata

We briefly present basic notions regarding hybrid automata and its special case, timed automata. Timed-automata and related topics are discussed in a comprehensive survey [2]. Hybrid automata in general and their connections to timed automata are discussed in [3,9]. In the following, we consider only automata over finite timed words.

Let X be a set of real-valued variables. An *affine constraint* is a conjunction of terms of the form $s(X) \sim c$, where $c \in \mathbb{Q}$, $\sim \in \{<, \leq, =, \geq, >\}$ and $s(X)$ is a linear combination of the variables from X with rational coefficients. Denote by $\mathrm{AFF}(X)$ the set of affine constraints over X. A *valuation* ν is a mapping $\nu : X \mapsto \mathbb{R}$ (written also as $\nu \in \mathbb{R}^X$). A valuation ν satisfies $g \in \mathrm{AFF}(X)$, denoted by $\nu \models g$, if the formula $\nu(g)$, obtained from g by instantiating variables from X by their values in ν, is true.

An (affine) *hybrid automaton* $\mathcal{A}$ is a tuple $(\Sigma, L, X, \langle l_0, \nu_0\rangle, Inv, Flow, \delta, F)$, where (1) Σ is the alphabet of $\mathcal{A}$ (called labels in [9]), (2) L, X are sets of locations and variables, (3) l_0, ν_0 are the initial location and valuation, (4) $Inv : L \mapsto \mathrm{AFF}(X)$ defines location invariants, (5) $Flow : L \mapsto \mathrm{AFF}(\dot{X})$ defines dynamics of each variable at a given location, where $\dot{x}$ is the derivative of x (also called its *rate*), and $\dot{X} = \{\dot{x} : x \in X\}$ (6) $\delta \subseteq L \times \mathrm{AFF}(X \cup X^+) \times (\Sigma \cup \{\epsilon\}) \times L$ is the switch relation, where x^+ denotes the value of x after taking the switch and $X^+ = \{x^+ : x \in X\}$. A switch (l, s, a, l') resets a value of x, if s is consistent with $x \neq x^+$, (7) F is a finite set of acceptance conditions of the form $\langle l, s\rangle$, where $l \in L$ and $s \in \mathrm{AFF}(X)$ is a constraint on variables.

Notice that $Flow(l)$ consists of only derivatives and constants, i.e., $\dot{x} \in [0, 2]$ is allowed and $x = \dot{x}$ is not.

We assume that each hybrid automaton has the *time variable* $t \in X$, whose rate is 1 at every location.

We settled for the class of affine hybrid automata, therefore we omit the word "affine".

We define the size of the automaton $\mathcal{A}$, denoted by $|\mathcal{A}|$, as the length of its binary representation, where the constants are represented in binary notation.

An *event* over Σ and X is a pair $\langle a, \nu\rangle$ of a discrete action from $\Sigma \cup \{\epsilon\}$ and a valuation $\nu : X \mapsto \mathbb{R}$. A *timed word* over Σ and X is a finite sequence of events $\langle a_0, \nu_0\rangle \ldots \langle a_k, \nu_k\rangle$ such that the time variable $\nu_0(t), \nu_1(t), \ldots$ is a weakly increasing sequence. For a timed word w, we define $untime(w)$ as the projection of w on Σ^*. A *state* $q = \langle l, \nu\rangle$ of $\mathcal{A}$ is a pair of a location $l \in L$ and a valuation ν.

There are two kinds of transitions between states of $\mathcal{A}$: *(i) elapse of time*: $\langle l, \nu\rangle \xrightarrow{\tau} \langle l, \nu'\rangle$ iff there is a differentiable function $f : [0, \tau] \mapsto \mathbb{R}^X$, such that $f(0) = \nu$, $f(\tau) = \nu'$ and for all $\lambda \in [0, \tau]$, the valuation $\mu_\lambda : X \cup \dot{X} \mapsto \mathbb{R}$, defined for all $x \in X$ as $\mu_\lambda(x) = f(\lambda)[x]$, $\mu_\lambda(\dot{x}) = (\frac{\partial}{\partial t} f(\lambda))[x]$, satisfies $Flow(l)$, *(ii) location switch*: $\langle l, \nu\rangle \underset{a}{\rightarrow} \langle l', \nu'\rangle$ iff there is a switch of $\mathcal{A}$, (l, s, a, l'), such that the valuation $\tau : X \cup X^+ \mapsto \mathbb{R}$, defined for all $x \in X$ as $\tau(x) = \nu(x)$ and $\tau(x^+) = \nu'(x)$, satisfies s. An elapse of time is usually followed by a location switch, thus we define the composition $\xrightarrow{\tau} \circ \underset{a}{\rightarrow}$, denoted by $\underset{a}{\xrightarrow{\tau}}$.

We associate with $\mathcal{A}$ a transition system $\mathrm{Pre}_{\mathcal{A}} = (L \times \mathbb{R}^X, (\Sigma \cup \{\epsilon\}) \times \mathbb{R}^X, E, \langle l_0, \nu_0\rangle)$ such that $\langle l_0, \nu_0\rangle$ is the initial state of $\mathcal{A}$ and $(\langle l, \nu\rangle, \alpha, \langle l', \nu'\rangle) \in E$ if $\alpha \in \Sigma \cup \{\epsilon\}$ and there is $\tau > 0$ such that $\mathcal{A}$ has a transition $\langle l, \nu\rangle \underset{\alpha}{\xrightarrow{\tau}} \langle l', \nu'\rangle$. Paths in $\mathrm{Pre}_{\mathcal{A}}$ are called *runs* of $\mathcal{A}$.

A state $\langle l, \nu\rangle$ of $\mathrm{Pre}_{\mathcal{A}}$ is *accepting* iff there is a constraint $(l', s) \in F$ from $\mathcal{A}$ such that $l = l'$ and ν satisfies s.

For a hybrid automaton $\mathcal{A}$, we define $[\mathcal{A}]$ as the set of traces from $[\mathrm{Pre}_{\mathcal{A}}]$ whose last state is accepting. A timed word w is accepted by $\mathcal{A}$ iff there is a trace $v \in [\mathcal{A}]$ whose projection to $\Sigma \times \mathbb{R}^X$ is w. We will write $\mathcal{A}_M$ to indicate that $\mathcal{A}_M$ generates a transition system M such that $[M] = [\mathcal{A}_M]$.

The *emptiness problem* for hybrid automata asks, given hybrid automaton $\mathcal{A}$, is $[\mathcal{A}]$ nonempty? That problem is also referred to as the *reachability* problem as it is equivalent to reachability of an accepting state in $\mathrm{Pre}_{\mathcal{A}}$.

2.2 Product of hybrid automata

Let $\mathcal{A}_i = (\Sigma, L_i, X_i, \langle l_{0,i}, \nu_{0,i}\rangle, Inv_i, Flow_i, \delta_i, F_i)$, for $i \in \{1, 2\}$, be hybrid automata over Σ. We define *the product* of $\mathcal{A}_1$ and $\mathcal{A}_2$, denoted by $\mathcal{A}_1 \times \mathcal{A}_2$, as the hybrid automaton $\mathcal{A}_1 \times \mathcal{A}_2 = (\Sigma, L, X, \langle l_0, \nu_0\rangle, Inv, Flow, \delta, F)$ such that:

(i) $L = L_1 \times L_2$ and $X = X_1 \cup X_2$,

(ii) $l_0 = \langle l_{0,1}, l_{0,2}\rangle$, $\nu_0 = \nu_{0,1} \cup \nu_{0,2}$, and

for all $l_1 \in L_1, l_2 \in L_2$:

(iv) $Inv(\langle l_1, l_2\rangle) \equiv Inv_1(l_1) \wedge Inv_2(l_2)$

(v) $Flow(\langle l_1, l_2\rangle) \equiv Flow_1(l_1) \wedge Flow_2(l_2)$

(vi) $\delta = \{(\langle l_1, l_2\rangle, s_1 \wedge s_2, a, \langle l_1', l_2'\rangle) : (l_1, s_1, a, l_1') \in \delta_1, (l_2, s_2, a, l_2') \in \delta_2\}$

(vii) $F = \{(\langle l_1, l_2\rangle, s_1 \wedge s_2) : (l_1, s_1) \in F_1, (l_2, s_2) \in F_2\}$

The automaton $\mathcal{A}_1 \times \mathcal{A}_2$ recognizes the intersection of languages recognized by $\mathcal{A}_1$ and $\mathcal{A}_2$. (This holds only for affine hybrid automata, as they have piecewise-linear trajectories.)

2.3 Rectangular hybrid automata

An affine constraint is *rectangular* iff it is a finite conjunction of expressions $x \sim c$, where $c \in \mathbb{Q}$ and $\sim \in \{<, \leq, =, \geq, >\}$. A hybrid automaton is *rectangular* iff all constraints, are rectangular or of the form $x = x^+$ (which occur only in switches).

A rectangular hybrid automaton is *initialized* iff for each switch (l_1, s, a, l_2) and every $x \in X$, if the flow of x changes, i.e, $Flow(l_1) \restriction_x \neq Flow(l_2) \restriction_x$, then x is reset at that switch. E.g. every timed automaton is an initialized rectangular automaton [10].

THEOREM 1 ([10]). *The emptiness problem for initialized rectangular automata is PSPACE-complete.*

A subset of $\mathbb{R}^n$ is *compact* iff it is bounded and closed. A constraint is *compact* iff it defines a compact subset of $\mathbb{R}^n$. Finally, a hybrid automaton is *compact* iff all constraints defining its invariants, flows, the transition relation and the acceptance conditions are compact.

2.4 Parametric hybrid automata

A variable x is a *parameter* in a hybrid automaton if its rate at each location is 0 and in every switch we have the constraint $x = x^+$. A *parametric hybrid automaton* $\mathcal{A}$ is a hybrid automaton with distinguished subsets of variables that are parameters. We write $\mathcal{A}[\vec{p}]$ to indicate that $\mathcal{A}$ has parameters $\vec{p}$. Since parameters values do not change during a run, they can be instantiated to (rational) constants.

We say that a parametric hybrid automaton belongs to a class $\mathcal{C}$ iff for every instantiation of parameters, the resulting automaton belongs to $\mathcal{C}$. E.g. even though a parametric hybrid automaton $\mathcal{A}$ has a non-rectangular constraint $x \leq p$, each instantiation of p makes $x \leq p$ rectangular and we consider such an automaton to be rectangular.

The emptiness problem has its parametric counterpart. *The parametric emptiness problem* asks, given a parametric hybrid automaton, is there an instantiation of its parameters (by rational numbers) such that the resulting automaton recognizes a nonempty language.

Observe that parameters in a hybrid automaton are instantiated in ν_0, whereas in the parametric emptiness problem they can be arbitrarily instantiated. It follows that the emptiness problem implies the parametric emptiness problem, but not vice versa.

2.5 Weighted timed automata

A *weighted timed automaton* is a timed automaton augmented by weights associated with its locations and switches, $C : L \cup \delta \mapsto \mathbb{N}$. The value of a run $\langle l_0, \nu_0 \rangle \overset{\tau_1}{\underset{a_1}{\to}} \langle l_1, \nu_1 \rangle \overset{\tau_2}{\underset{a_2}{\to}} \ldots \overset{\tau_k}{\underset{a_k}{\to}} \langle l_k, \nu_k \rangle$ is given by $\sum_{i=0}^{k-1} C(l_i)\tau_{i+1} + \sum_{i=0}^{k-1} C(e_i)$, where e_i is the switch taken in the transition $\langle l_i, \nu_i \rangle \overset{\tau_{i+1}}{\underset{a_{i+1}}{\to}} \langle l_{i+1}, \nu_{i+1} \rangle$. The value of a timed word w assigned by a weighted timed automaton $\mathcal{A}$, denoted by $L_{\mathcal{A}}(w)$, is the infimum of the set of values of all accepting runs of $\mathcal{A}$ on w. Timed words that are rejected by $\mathcal{A}$ have infinite value.

The emptiness question for non-weighted automata has the following weighted counterpart:

DEFINITION 2. *The* optimal-value question *asks, given a weighted timed automaton $\mathcal{A}$, to compute the infimum of $L_{\mathcal{A}}(w)$ over all timed words.*

It has been shown in [4] that:

THEOREM 3. *The optimal-value question for timed automata can be computed in polynomial space.*

Weighted timed automata defined as above are referred to in the literature as *linearly-priced timed automata*. Observe that weighted timed automata are a special kind of parametric affine hybrid automata. Indeed, a timed part of a timed automaton is translated directly to an affine hybrid automaton and the value is represented by a *value variable* val. For a switch e, val is updated according to $\text{val}^+ = \text{val} + C(e)$. In a location l, the rate of val is equal $C(l)$. The value of val does not appear in any constraints except for acceptance conditions, where val is compared with a threshold parameter tr, where val $\leq$ tr states that we are interested in runs whose values are bounded by tr.

3. PARAMETRIC HYBRID AUTOMATA

In this section we develop a unified theory of "weighted" hybrid automata over finite timed words, which is applied in Section 4. Richness of hybrid automata allows encoding value directly as a continuous variable and avoiding auxiliary components as in discrete weighted automata. However, that richness raises decidability issues.

However, the emptiness problem for the whole class of (affine) hybrid automata is undecidable. Thus, we shall restrict ourselves to subclasses of hybrid automata that have the emptiness and parametric emptiness problems decidable (weighted timed automata, initialized rectangular automata). The following definitions help us to address decidability issues.

DEFINITION 4. *A class of hybrid automata $\mathfrak{C}$ is: (1)* weakly decidable *iff the membership (of an automaton to $\mathfrak{C}$) and the emptiness problems are decidable over $\mathfrak{C}$ (2)* strongly decidable *iff the membership, the emptiness and parametric emptiness problems are decidable over $\mathfrak{C}$.*

The class of parametric timed automata is weakly decidable but not strongly decidable. This implies that even if there is a (rational) instantiation of parameters such that the resulting automaton recognizes a nonempty language, there is no bound on the length of binary representation rational parameters. If there was a bound, there would be finitely many instances of the automaton preserving the bound, and one could just test for emptiness all of those instances. Thus, instead of computing exact values of parameters, we have to settle for approximation.

We define the class of admissible parameters for $\mathcal{A}$, denoted by $\mathfrak{Par}(\mathcal{A})$, as $\{\vec{p} : [\mathcal{A}[\vec{p}]] \neq \emptyset\}$. We are interested in approximation of "minimal" elements of $\mathfrak{Par}(\mathcal{A})$ (which is called the *quantitative emptiness problem* or the *optimal-value problem* in the weighted automata case.) Approximation and minimality are defined by a vector norm $|\cdot|$. For a given norm and $\epsilon > 0$, we say that $\vec{q}$ is an ϵ-approximation of $\vec{p}$ iff $|\vec{q} - \vec{p}| \leq \epsilon$. A vector $\vec{p}$ is minimal in a set A if $\vec{p} \in A$, and for every $\vec{q} \in \mathcal{A}$, $|\vec{p}| \leq |\vec{q}|$. As $\mathfrak{Par}(\mathcal{A})$ may not have minimal elements, we consider its closure in $\mathbb{R}^n$, $cl(\mathfrak{Par}(\mathcal{A}))$. Each coordinate of $\mathfrak{Par}(\mathcal{A})$ is positive, hence $cl(\mathfrak{Par}(\mathcal{A}))$ contains minimal elements.

DEFINITION 5. *A class of hybrid automata $\mathfrak{C}$ admits* parameter approximation *iff there is a procedure that for a given $n > 0$ and $\mathcal{A} \in \mathfrak{C}$, returns a 2^{-n}-approximation of a minimal element of $cl(\mathfrak{Par}(\mathcal{A}))$ if $\mathfrak{Par}(\mathcal{A})$ is nonempty and $\emptyset$ otherwise.*

In the rest of this section we give sufficient conditions for a class $\mathfrak{C}$ to admit effective parameter approximation. The complexity of parameter approximation is given separately w.r.t. the size of an automaton $|\mathcal{A}|$ and a precision n.

Assume that a class of hybrid automata $\mathfrak{C}$ is weakly decidable, but not strongly decidable. There are two possible reasons for the undecidability: density and unboundedness of the domain of possible parameters, the rational numbers, which corresponds to infinite domain of denominators (density) and numerators (unboundedness). The undecidability of the parametric emptiness problem for timed automata is caused by the density. Indeed, even a restricted problem, are there parameters from the interval $[1, 2]$ such that $[\mathcal{A}[\vec{p}]]$ is nonempty, is undecidable [13]. Density, as a source of undecidability, can be eliminated by restricting parameterizations to be monotonic:

DEFINITION 6. *We say that a parametric hybrid automaton $\mathcal{A}$ is* monotonic *iff for all $\vec{p}, \vec{q} \in \mathbb{Q}^k$, $\vec{p} \leq \vec{q}$ ($\vec{q}$ is greater than $\vec{q}$ component-wise) implies $[\mathcal{A}[\vec{p}]] \subseteq [\mathcal{A}[\vec{q}]]$*

There are simple sufficient conditions that guarantee monotonicity of a given hybrid automaton. E.g. an automaton with constraints $x - p \leq 0$ or $x + p \geq 0$ is monotonic w.r.t. p

as higher values of p lead to weakening the constraints and admittance of more runs. Still, given a hybrid automaton, even a timed automaton, it is not possible to decide whether it is monotonic.

PROPOSITION 7. *Monotonicity of parametric timed automata is undecidable.*

All monotonic timed automata are strongly decidable, but in the rich class of hybrid automata, monotonicity alone does not make a weakly decidable class strongly decidable. The unboundedness of the domain of parameters may cause undecidability of the parametric emptiness problem even with monotonic parametrizations. Indeed, consider the class stopwatch automata over bounded time, i.e., parametric stopwatch automata that have a single parameter bounding the duration of each run. Such automata are monotonic and their class is weakly decidable [5]. However, that class is not strongly decidable as its strong decidability is equivalent to weak decidability of the class of stopwatch automata.

In order to eliminate unboundedness as a source of undecidability, we define a small parameter property called f-*boundedness*.

DEFINITION 8. *Let f be a computable function. A class of hybrid automata $\mathfrak{C}$ is* f-bounded *iff for every $\mathcal{A} \in \mathfrak{C}$, if there is a tuple $\vec{p}$ such that $[\mathcal{A}[\vec{p}]] \neq \emptyset$, then there a tuple $\vec{q}$ whose components are from $[0, f(|\mathcal{A}|)]$ such that $[\mathcal{A}[\vec{q}]] \neq \emptyset$.*

An f-bounded class of parametric hybrid automata that are monotonic admits effective parameter approximation procedure. Basically, for a given $\mathcal{A} \in \mathfrak{C}$ and $\epsilon = 2^{-n}$, one can do binary search for parameters with the minimal norm, where each parameter is from the set $\{\frac{i}{j} : j \in \{1, \ldots, 2^n\}, i \in \{0, \ldots, j \cdot f(|\mathcal{A}|)\}\}$. Observe that the length of instantiated parameters in the fixed-point representation is bounded by $log(f(|\mathcal{A}|)) + n$. It follows that each automaton that results from such an instantiation of $\mathcal{A}$ has the size bounded by $\mathcal{A} + PM(\mathcal{A})(log(f(|\mathcal{A}|)) + n)$, where $PM(\mathcal{A})$ is the number of instances of parameters in $\mathcal{A}$.

PROPOSITION 9. *Every weakly decidable and f-bounded class of monotonic hybrid automata $\mathfrak{C}$ admits parameter approximation in time $O((f(|\mathcal{A}|) + n) \cdot T(|\mathcal{A}| + PM(\mathcal{A}) \cdot (log(f(|\mathcal{A}|))+n)))$, where $T(\cdot)$ is the complexity of the emptiness problem for $\mathfrak{C}$.*

f-boundedness of a class of weakly decidable hybrid automata, which are monotonic, is equivalent to strong decidability in the following sense.

PROPOSITION 10. *Let $\mathfrak{C}$ be a weakly decidable class of monotonic hybrid automata. The class $\mathfrak{C}$ is strongly decidable iff there is a computable function f such that $\mathfrak{C}$ is f-bounded.*

The classes of monotonic weighted timed automata and compact initialized rectangular automata are exponentially bounded classes. Parameters in (affine) hybrid automata occur only in affine terms. Thus, to show that a class $\mathfrak{C}$ is exponentially bounded, it is sufficient to show that if an automaton from $\mathfrak{C}$ has an accepting run, it has an accepting run in which all variables are exponentially bounded.

A straightforward analysis of the region graph of a timed automaton yields that if a timed automaton has an accepting run, then there is a timed word $(a_0, t_0) \ldots (a_k, t_k)$ accepted by this timed automaton with k and $t_k - t_0$ exponentially bounded in the size of the automaton. It follows that each timed automaton that recognizes a nonempty language has a run in which values of all clocks and the value are exponentially bounded.

PROPOSITION 11. *The class of monotonic weighted timed automata (over finite words) is exponentially bounded.*

Compact initialized rectangular automata have bounded rates of their variables and they recognize precisely timed languages recognized by timed automata [10]. Thus, if a compact initialized rectangular automaton has an accepting run, it accepts a timed word $(a_0, t_0) \ldots (a_k, t_k)$ such that k, $t_k - t_0$ are exponentially bounded in the size of the automaton. It follows, that it has an accepting run in which the values of all variables are exponentially bounded. Hence, we have:

PROPOSITION 12. *The class of monotonic compact initialized rectangular automata (over finite words) is exponentially bounded.*

In consequence, we have:

COROLLARY 13. *Let $|\cdot|$ be a vector norm computable in linear time. The class of monotonic compact initialized rectangular automata admits parameter approximation in polynomial space w.r.t. the automaton size and linear time w.r.t. a given precision n.*

Finally, the optimal parameters of weighted timed automata can be actually computed as they are always integers or arbitrarily close to integers [4], which makes their infima integers. Thus, it is sufficient to approximate the optimal parameters only up to ϵ, such that each ϵ-neighborhood contains at most one vector of integers.

PROPOSITION 14. *Given a monotonic weighted timed automaton $\mathcal{A}$, the value* $\inf\{|\vec{p}| : \vec{p} \in \mathfrak{Par}(\mathcal{A})\}$ *can be computed in polynomial space in $|\mathcal{A}|$.*

Recall that $\inf\{|\vec{p}| : \vec{p} \in \mathfrak{Par}(\mathcal{A})\} = \infty$ if $\mathfrak{Par}(\mathcal{A})$ is empty.

4. MODEL-MEASURING FRAMEWORK

The model-measuring problem [11] asks, given a model M and a specification φ, what is the maximal distance ρ such that all models M' within that distance from M satisfy (or violate) φ. In this section, we adapt the model-measuring problem to the hybrid automata setting. We begin with basic definitions from [11].

Let M be a transition system (model). A *similarity measure* (of M) is a function d_M from timed words into positive real numbers such that for all traces w of M, $d_M(w) = 0$. Such a similarity measure extends to transition systems by $d_M(M') = \sup\{d_M(w) : w \text{ is a trace of } M'\}$. Every similarity measure results from a distance function via fixing the first argument.

DEFINITION 15. *Let M be a transition system and d_M be a similarity measure. For a specification P, the* stability radius *of P in M (w.r.t. d_M), denoted by $sr_{d_M}(P)$, is defined*

as follows:
(1) if $M \models P$, $sr_{d_M}(P) = \sup\{\rho \geq 0 : \forall M'(d_M(M') < \rho \Rightarrow M' \models P)\}$,
(2) if $M \models \neg P$, $sr_{d_M}(P) = sr_{d_M}(\neg P)$,
(3) otherwise, $sr_{d_M}(P) = 0$.

Now, these definitions are specialized to the hybrid automata case. We begin with representing similarity measures by monotonic hybrid automata, a hybrid counterpart of weighted automata.

DEFINITION 16. *Let* $|\cdot|$ *be a norm computable in linear time. A (hybrid) similarity measure* d_M *is* automatic *iff there is a monotonic hybrid automaton* $\mathcal{A}_{dist}$ *such that* $d_M(M') = \inf\{r : \exists \vec{p}. |\vec{p}| \leq r \wedge [M'] \subseteq [\mathcal{A}_{dist}][\vec{p}]\}$.

We assume that a specification is given by a hybrid automaton $\mathcal{A}_P$ that accepts all timed words that violate the specification. We call specifications given in such a way *automatic*. Observe that a transition system M, given by a hybrid automaton $\mathcal{A}_M$, satisfies an automatic property P ($M \models P$) iff the languages recognized by $\mathcal{A}_M$ and $\mathcal{A}_P$ are disjoint. Thus, model checking for hybrid automata reduces to the emptiness problem for hybrid automata.

We define the *model measure* on the basis of the stability radius by scaling the value the stability radius from $[0, \infty]$ to $[\frac{1}{2}, 1]$ if $M \models P$, and $[0, \frac{1}{2}]$ otherwise.

DEFINITION 17. *The* model-measuring problem *is defined as follows: given an automatic similarity measure* d_M *and an automatic specification* P*, compute* $[P]_{d_M}$ *defined by*

(i) if $M \models P$, $[P]_{d_M} = 1 - 2^{-sr_{d_M}(M,P)-1} \quad (\in [\frac{1}{2}, 1])$,

(ii) if $M \models \neg P$, $[P]_{d_M} = 1 - [\neg P]_{d_M} \quad (\in [0, \frac{1}{2}])$,

(iii) otherwise, $[P]_{d_M} = \frac{1}{2}$.

Observe that the minimal norm of parameters $\vec{p}$ such that $[\mathcal{A}_{dist}[\vec{p}]]$ and $[\mathcal{A}_P]$ have nonempty intersection is exactly the stability radius of P in M w.r.t. d_M. Thus, the model-measuring problem for hybrid specifications reduces to the problem of finding the minimal norm of parameters such that $(\mathcal{A}_{dist} \times \mathcal{A}_P)[\vec{p}]$, the product of automata $\mathcal{A}_{dist}$ and $\mathcal{A}_P$, recognizes a nonempty language.

We can restrict instances of the model-measuring problem (a similarity measure and a specification) to be represented by hybrid automata from a given class. We call such a restricted problem *the model-measuring problem over* $\mathfrak{C}$.

As noted in Section 3 the minimal norm of a vector of parameters can be a rational number with arbitrarily long representation. For that reason, we settle for approximation. Corollary 13 and Proposition 14 imply the following:

THEOREM 18. *The model measuring problem over compact initialized rectangular automata can be* ***approximated*** *in polynomial space in the size of automata representing* d_M *and* P.

The model measuring problem over weighted timed automata can be **computed** *in polynomial space in the size of automata representing* d_M *and* P.

5. MODELING HYBRID SIMILARITY MEASURES

In this section we present a systematic approach to the construction of automatic hybrid similarity measures. The main difficulty originates from the following issues. First, the model M is usually complex, therefore modifying its internal structure is a complicated and error-prone task. Ideally, the construction method would yield a similarity measure given only the original hybrid automaton and a description of allowed perturbations. Second, the outcome of the construction should be a parametric hybrid automaton that admits effective approximation of minimal parameters for which its intersection with another hybrid automaton is nonempty. The presented approach addresses both issues.

Hybrid automata combine discrete and continuous control via extending finite state automata by continuous variables. Thus, for modeling automatic hybrid similarity measures, we extend the (discrete) hypervisor approach [11] to the hybrid case. The main idea behind the hypervisor approach is to introduce an external component, called the *hypervisor*, whose task is to govern the execution of the original automaton $\mathcal{A}_M$ by providing alternative switch relations, invariants and flows. A hypervisor runs an external hybrid automaton that using its current location selects the current switch relation, invariants and flows.

Composition of $\mathcal{A}_M$ with a hypervisor produces a monotonic hybrid automaton. In order to guarantee monotonicity of the resulting automaton, we require all constraints to be monotonic in the following sense. An affine constraint $t[\vec{p}]$ parametrized by $\vec{p}$ is monotonic iff for all vectors of real numbers $\vec{c_1}, \vec{c_2}$, if $\vec{c_1} \leq \vec{c_2}$, then $t[\vec{c_1}]$ implies $t[\vec{c_2}]$.

DEFINITION 19. *A* hypervisor *for a hybrid automaton* $\mathcal{A}_M = (\Sigma, L_M, X_M, \langle l_{0,M}, \nu_{0,M}\rangle, Inv_M, Flow_M, \delta_M, F_M)$ *is a quadruple* $H = (\mathcal{A}_H, \tau_H, \mathfrak{Inv}_H, \mathfrak{Flow}_H)$ *satisfying:*

(i) $\mathcal{A}_H = (\Sigma, L_H, \langle l_{0,H}, \nu_{0,H}\rangle, X_H, Inv_H, Flow_H, \delta_H, F_H)$ *is a parametric hybrid automaton.*

(ii) for every $x \in X_M \cap X_H$, $\nu_{0,M}(x) = \nu_{0,H}(x)$

(iii) $\tau_H : L_H \mapsto \mathcal{P}(L_M \times \text{AFF}(X_M \cup X_M^+) \times \Sigma \times L_M)$*, where* $\mathcal{P}(A)$ *denotes the power set of* A,

(iv) $\mathfrak{Inv}_H : L_H \mapsto (L_M \mapsto \text{AFF}(X_M))$,

(v) $\mathfrak{Flow}_H : L_H \mapsto (L_M \mapsto \text{AFF}(\dot{X_M}))$,

(vi) $\mathcal{A}_H$ *has the initial state* $\langle l_I, \nu\rangle$*, an* idle state*, such that* $\tau_H[l_I] = \delta_M$, $\mathfrak{Inv}_H[l_I] = Inv_M$, $\mathfrak{Flow}_H[l_I] = Flow_M$*, and for all* $a \in \Sigma$, $\mathcal{A}_H$ *has a switch* $(l_I, \top, a, l_I)$*, where* $\top$ *is the empty constraint that is always satisfied,*

(vii) all affine constraints in $\tau_H, \mathfrak{Inv}_H, \mathfrak{Flow}_H$ *and* $\mathcal{A}_H$ *are monotonic.*

At each step, the functions $\tau_H, \mathfrak{Inv}_H, \mathfrak{Flow}_H$ determine the transition relation, invariants and flows for $\mathcal{A}_M$. Intuitively, they should encode modifications applied to these components of $\mathcal{A}_M$ rather than their complete descriptions. For example:
(blind a-transitions) Consider $l_a \in L_H$ such that $\tau_H[l_a] = \{(l, s, b, l') : (l, s, a, l') \in \delta_M, b \in \Sigma\}$, i.e., the automaton moves as it would have read an event with a. $\tau_H[l_a]$ can be simply defined uniformly on δ_M, i.e., regardless of the complexity of δ_M.

(bounded deviation of x) Consider $\tau_H[l_x] = \{(l, s, a, l') : (l, s', a, l') \in \delta_M, s' \equiv s[x/(x+y)] \wedge y \leq q \wedge y \geq -q\}$, where $s[x/(x+y)]$ results from substitution x by $x+y$ in s. Intuitively, we allow values of x to deviate from its intended values by at most q.

For a hybrid automaton $\mathcal{A}_M$ and a hypervisor H as in Definition 19, we define the semi-direct product of $\mathcal{A}_M$ and H. The *semi-direct product* $\mathcal{A}_M \ltimes H$ is a parametric hybrid automaton $(\Sigma, L, X, \langle l_0, \nu_0 \rangle, Inv, Flow, \delta, F)$ such that:

- $L = L_M \times L_H$, and $X = X_M \cup X_H$,
- $l_0 = \langle l_{0,M}, l_{0,H} \rangle$, $\nu_0 = \nu_{0,M} \cup \nu_{0,H}$
- $Inv(\langle l_M, l_H \rangle) = \mathfrak{Inv}_H[l_H](l_M) \wedge Inv_H(l_H)$
- $Flow(\langle l_M, l_H \rangle) \equiv \mathfrak{Flow}_H[l_H](l_M) \wedge Flow_H(l_H)$
- $(\langle l_M, l_H \rangle, s, a, \langle l'_M, l'_H \rangle) \in \delta$ iff
  - (i) $(l_H, s_H, a, l'_H) \in \delta_H$, $(l_M, s_M, a, l'_M) \in \tau_H[l'_H]$, and $s = s_M \wedge s_H$, or
  - (ii) $a = \epsilon$, $(l_H, s_H, \epsilon, l'_H) \in \delta_H$ and $l_M = l'_M$
- $F = \{\langle (l_M, l_H), s_M \wedge s_H \rangle : \langle l_H, s_H \rangle \in F_H, \langle l_M, s_M \rangle \in F_M\}$

The semi-direct product defines an automatic hybrid similarity measure. Indeed, due to existence of the idle location, regardless of the values of the parameters, each timed word accepted by $\mathcal{A}_M$ is also accepted by $\mathcal{A}_M \ltimes H$. More precisely, as $\mathcal{A}_M$ can be a parametric automaton itself, for every $\vec{p} \in \mathbb{R}^m$, $[\mathcal{A}_M[\vec{p}]] \subseteq [(\mathcal{A}_M \ltimes H)[\vec{p}]]$. Conversely, any automatic hybrid similarity measure can be obtained by the hypervisor construction. Indeed, for any automatic hybrid similarity measure defined by $\mathcal{A}$ one can define a hypervisor H, which neglects $\mathcal{A}_M$ and simulates $\mathcal{A}$. Therefore, the hypervisor approach is complete, i.e., every automatic hybrid similarity measure can be obtained as a semi-direct product.

All constraints introduced by the hypervisor are monotonic, therefore if $\mathcal{A}_M$ is monotonic, $\mathcal{A}_M \ltimes H$ is monotonic as well. In contrast, there is no natural condition on the hypervisor that would guarantee that the semi-direct product of an automaton from a given class $\mathfrak{C}$ and that hypervisor belongs to $\mathfrak{C}$. The reason for that is that those conditions heavily depend of the class $\mathfrak{C}$.

DEFINITION 20. *Let $\mathfrak{C}$ be a class of hybrid automata. Let $\mathcal{A} \in \mathfrak{C}$ and let H be a hypervisor H for $\mathcal{A}$. The hypervisor H is* admissible *for $\mathfrak{C}$ with $\mathcal{A}$ iff $\mathcal{A} \ltimes H$ belongs to $\mathfrak{C}$.*

The following facts can be easily verified by the reader:

FACT 21. *Every hypervisor $H = (\mathcal{A}_H, \tau_H, \mathfrak{Inv}_H, \mathfrak{Flow}_H)$, that satisfies the following conditions is admissible for the class of weighted timed automata (regardless of $\mathcal{A}_M$): (1) $\mathcal{A}_H$ is a (linearly) weighted timed automaton, (2) $\mathfrak{Inv}_H$ is rectangular, and for every $l_h \in L_H$, for every variable x except for the value variable wt: (3) every switch in $\tau_H[l_h]$ preserves the value of x or resets it to 0, (4) for all $l_m \in L_M$, $\mathfrak{Flow}_H[l_H](l_m)$ implies that all slopes of all variables equal 1.*

FACT 22. *Let $\mathcal{A}_M$ be a compact initialized rectangular automaton. Every hypervisor H such that all components are compact and rectangular, and $\mathcal{A}_M \ltimes H$ is initialized, is admissible for the class of compact initialized rectangular automata with $\mathcal{A}_M$.*

EXAMPLE 23. ***(Pacemaker)*** *Consider a model of a pacemaker, which consists of three components: the sensor, controller and electrodes. The goal of the pacemaker is to ensure that the pulse is in the range 60-70 beats per minute. If there is no heartbeat for a predefined time, the controller sends a signal to the electrodes, which in turn charge their capacitors for some predefined time and fire an impulse.*

The following questions can be expressed (and then approximated) as instances of the model-measuring problem: what are the maximal impulse firing time and latency of the sensor such that the pacemaker model still meets the specification.

The impulse firing time is modeled by a clock x with a predefined time limit T_c. Basically, we need to change this predefined time to a parameter p and ask, what is the maximum value of p, such that the model still meets the specification. This is expressed by a simple hypervisor that has only two locations, an idle location and a parametric location q_p. All the constraints in $\tau_H[q_p], \mathfrak{Inv}_H[q_p], \mathfrak{Flow}_H[q_p]$ remain the same as in $\delta_M, Inv_M, Flow_M$, except that T_c is substituted by $T_c + p$.

The latency of the sensor can be modeled by a hypervisor that captures every heartbeat event and forwards it to the model with a delay. The hypervisor H is defined as $(\mathcal{A}_H, \tau_H, \mathfrak{Inv}_H, \mathfrak{Flow}_H)$, where $\mathcal{A}_H$ is a parametrized timed automaton, which has four locations: an idle location l_I, waiting for a heartbeat l_w, delaying the delivery l_d and delivering a heartbeat to the model l_r. The automaton $\mathcal{A}_H$ can be in the location l_d not longer than p, which is a parameter restricting sensor delays and it can be in the location l_r only for 0 time units. Both $\mathfrak{Inv}_H$ and $\mathfrak{Flow}_H$ in l_w, l_d, l_r are as is the original model. Then, $\tau_H[l_w]$ is equal to δ_M, which corresponds to the usual behavior of the model. The transition relation $\tau_H[l_d]$ specifies that the hypervised automaton ignores a heartbeat event. Finally, $\tau_H[l_r]$ is a blind a transition as defined above; it specifies that the hypervised automaton acts as it would have got a heartbeat event.

Observe that in the above cases the model is a timed automaton and the hypervisors are parametrized timed automata. Therefore, the maximal firing time and the maximal sensor latency can be computed (not only approximated) in polynomial space (Theorem 18).

The impulse firing time and the latency of the sensor from Example 23 represent two types of similarity measures. The similarity measure related to the impulse firing time strongly depends on the model as it essentially asks what is the maximal value of a bound in a specific constraint, whereas the one related to the latency can be described independently of the model. We refer to those two types as *model-dependent* and *model-independent*.

Model-dependent similarity measures are more expressible as any model-independent similarity measure can be considered as model-dependent. On the other hand, tweaking a model may lead to unpredictable results (Example 24). We discuss both approaches in the following sections.

5.1 Model-dependent similarity measures

We begin with an example showing that parameterizing models can effect in non-obvious faults.

EXAMPLE 24. ***(Scheduler)*** *Consider a system consisting of a scheduler S and processes $P_1, \ldots, P_k$. Each process has two private clocks t_I, t_T, clock of individual instructionss and*

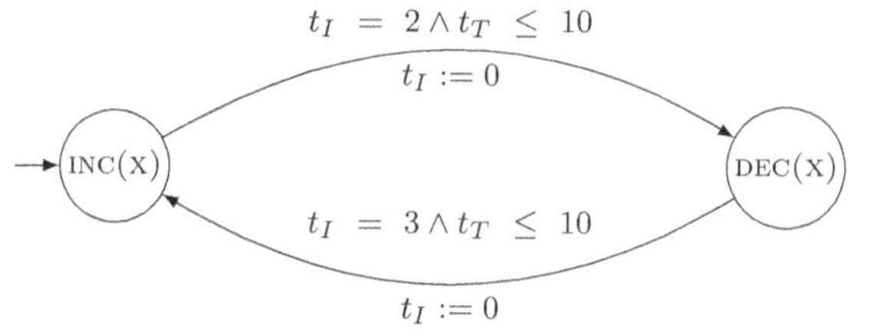

Figure 3: An automaton modeling the process P_1.

a total time clock. The clock t_I is used to model duration of execution of an instruction. Each instruction has its own duration and the clock t_I is reset after each execution of an instruction. The clock t_T is used for preemptive scheduling. A process P can execute instructions only when t_T is below the length of a time slice for P. This clock can be reset by the scheduler; processes are scheduled by resetting their clocks. The scheduler has its own clock that is used to determine times of context switches. An example of a process P_1 with the time slice 10 is depicted in Figure 3. Suppose the length of time slice granted to P_1 is parametrized by p, and the tested value of the parameter would be 7. Then, after instructions INC(X), DEC(X), *the process P_1 is about to execute $dec(x)$ and $t_T = 5$. Then, after 2 time units another process is scheduled, but P_1 executes* DEC(X) *which takes 3 time units before it is suspended. Indeed, when P_1 is resumed it immediately finishes the execution of* DEC(X). *This means that for 1 time unit two processes were running in parallel, which cannot happen in a single-processor model. The problem did not manifest itself in the original model because the length of time slices is equal to the sum of executing times of instructions. That problem can be solved by compelling the scheduler to reset both clocks t_T and T_I, which corresponds to discarding partial computations.*

Another example is a modification of a water-level monitor [1] presented in the introduction.

EXAMPLE 25. ***(Water-level monitor)*** *Both similarity measures discussed in the introduction, the one that parametrizes the latency of the pump and the one modeling the water pipeline failure, can be expressed with the hypervisor approach. The hypervisor that parametrizes the latency of the pump is virtually the same as the hypervisor parameterizing the impulse firing time in Example 23; it substitutes the constant 2 by $2 + p$ in all constraints.*

The hypervisor modeling the water pipeline failure scenario consists of a hybrid automaton $\mathcal{A}_H$ that has 5 locations: an idle location l_I, l_n corresponding to normal water supply, $l_s, l_{s'}$ corresponding to water shortage and l_c corresponding to water absence. It is depicted in Figure 4.

Moreover, $\mathcal{A}_H$ has a clock x and the parameters that bound the periods of the water shortage before and after the water absence (p_1, p_3) and the water absence period (p_3). The constraints on the bottom of each node represent additional constraints on the flow of the original model.

Finally, the norm $2 \cdot (|p_1| + |p_3|) + |p_2|$ applied to the optimal values of parameters corresponds to the maximal overall pipeline failure time tolerated by the water-level monitor.

5.2 Model-independent similarity measures

In this section we show how to define model-independent similarity measures for hybrid automata. A natural way to do that is to define a "distance" between timed words, and on its basis define a similarity measure as a "distance" of timed words from the set of traces of the model L_M. Similarity measures defined in that way are clearly model-independent.

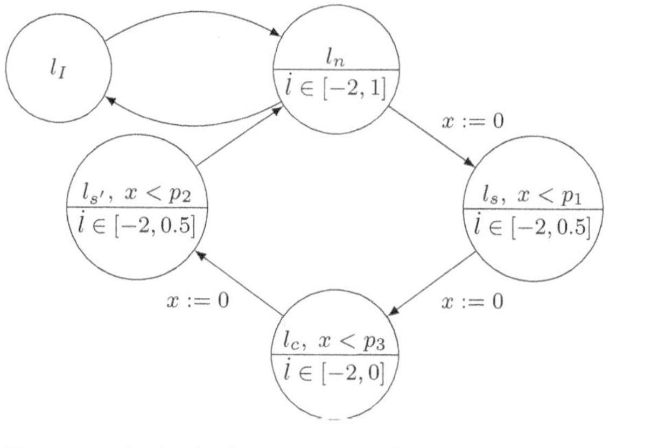

Figure 4: $\mathcal{A}_H$ in the hypervisor modeling the pipeline failure.

In the following, we discuss "distances" between timed words that are computed by monotonic hybrid automata. We call such "distances" *hybrid-automatic weighted relations*, as we do require them to be symmetric and satisfy the triangle inequality. Also, they generalize automatic relations in two ways: their range is the real numbers instead of Boolean values and they are computed by hybrid automata.

We begin with preliminary definitions. Let w_1, w_2 be timed words over Σ and X. For $i \in \{1,2\}$, we define the labeling σ_i on events as $\sigma_i(\langle a, \nu \rangle) = \langle (a, i), \nu_i \rangle$, where $\nu_i : (X \times \{i\}) \cup \{t\} \mapsto \mathbb{R}$ is defined as $\nu_i(\langle x, i \rangle) = \nu(x)$ and $\nu_i(t) = \nu(t)$. The (event) labellings σ_1, σ_2 extend to timed words by applying themselves to each event. We define *the disjoint union* of w_1 and w_2, denoted by $w_1 \oplus w_2$, as the timed word $\Sigma \times \{1,2\}$ consisting of the union of events of timed words $\sigma_1(w_1)$ and $\sigma_2(w_2)$, E.g. $\langle a, 0.4 \rangle \langle b, 2.1 \rangle \oplus \langle b, 0.3 \rangle \langle b, 0.4 \rangle = \langle (b,2), 0.3 \rangle \langle (a,1), 0.4 \rangle \langle (b,2), 0.4 \rangle \langle (b,1), 2.1 \rangle$.

A *weighted relation* is a generalization of the usual relation by allowing its characteristic function to range over $\mathbb{R}^+ \cup \{\infty\}$. We say that a (binary) weighted relation on timed words R is a *hybrid-automatic weighted relation* iff there is a monotonic hybrid automaton $\mathcal{A}_R$ such that for all timed words v, w we have $vRw = \inf\{|\vec{p}| : \mathcal{A}_R[\vec{p}] \text{ accepts } v \oplus w\}$. In particular, vRw may be equal to the value of $v \oplus w$ assigned by a weighted timed automaton $\mathcal{A}_R$. Indeed, it suffices for $\mathcal{A}_R$ to have a single parameter p bounding the value variable val. Then, $\mathcal{A}_R[p]$ accepts $v \oplus w$ iff there is a run of $\mathcal{A}_R$ whose value varible does not exceed p and $\inf\{p : \mathcal{A}_R[p] \text{ accepts } v \oplus w\}$ is the value of $v \oplus w$ assigned by $\mathcal{A}_R$.

Assume that $\mathcal{A}_R$ *contains the timed identity*, i.e., for every timed word v, $\mathcal{A}_R[\vec{0}]$ accepts $v \oplus v$. Observe that d_M defined by $d_M(w) = \inf\{|\vec{p}| : v \in \mathcal{L}(\mathcal{A}_M), \mathcal{A}_R[\vec{p}] \text{ accepts } v \oplus w\}$ is an automatic similarity measure. Clearly, for every M', $d_M(M') \geq 0$ and since $\mathcal{A}_R$ contains the timed identity, $d_M(M) = 0$. The class of timed languages accepted by hybrid automata is closed under projection, hence there is a hybrid automaton computing d_M. Furthermore, it can be defined by a hypervisor in a uniform way:

PROPOSITION 26. *Let R be a hybrid-automatic weighted relation computed by $\mathcal{A}_R$ and let $\mathcal{A}_M$ be a hybrid automaton. The similarity measure defined from $\mathcal{A}_M$ by R can be defined* *by a hypervisor that has a symbolic definition that uses components of $\mathcal{A}_M$ and $\mathcal{A}_R$ as predicates. Moreover, if $\mathcal{A}_R, \mathcal{A}_M$ are weighted timed automata (compact initialized rectangular automata), the automaton $\mathcal{A}_M \ltimes H_R$ is a weighted timed automaton (compact initialized rectangular automaton).*

EXAMPLE 27. *Consider the model from Example 23 and the question of the maximal latency of the sensor tolerated by the model. We decouple a heartbeat event into two consecutive events: an actual heartbeat and an observed heartbeat. Then, we specify that the trace of actual heartbeats and observed heartbeats are in a weighted relation R_d defined as follows. The weighted relation R_d is defined only on pairs of* 1-interleaved *timed-words, i.e., timed words w, v satisfying that between any two events of w, there is at most one event of v and vice versa. For timed words w, v that are 1-interleaved, $untime(w) = untime(v)$ and every event of w is earlier than its counterpart in v, the value of wRv is the maximal delay between any event of w and its counterpart in v. Otherwise, $wRv = \infty$. We show in Section 6, that R_d is a timed-automatic weighted relation.*

6. HYBRID-AUTOMATIC WEIGHTED RELATIONS

We have seen in Section 5.2 that hybrid-automatic weighted relations conveniently express model-independent similarity measures. This motivates the study of their expression power. We show basic construction methods as well as limitations of hybrid-automatic weighted relations. However, the fact that certain weighted relations are not expressible by hybrid automata does not imply that the similarity measures defined by those relations are not hybrid-automatic.

Hybrid-automatic (weighted) relations are substantially different than automatic relations on words (defined in Section 6.2). A key difference between words and timed words is that events in the latter can be arbitrarily dense, i.e., there can be arbitrarily many events in a fixed time interval. In consequence, in the disjoint union $w \oplus v$, there is no bound on the number of events from v between two consecutive events of w and vice versa. As we will see in Theorem 37 this leads to undecidability of simple (in the word case) problems. To avoid that, we define the notion of K-interleaved words, which intuitively means that words are synchronized.

6.1 Compositionality of hybrid-automatic relations

Composition and intersection are two simple constructions that build new hybrid-automatic weighted relations from the ones already defined.

DEFINITION 28. *Let R, S be weighted relations. We define the* composition *$R \circ S$ and* intersection *$R \cap S$, as follows. For all timed words w_1, w_2:*

$$w_1(R \circ S)w_2 = \inf\{w_1Rw_3 + w_3Sw_2 : w_3 \text{ is a timed word}\}$$
$$w_1(R \cap S)w_2 = w_1Rw_2 + w_1Sw_2$$

PROPOSITION 29. *The composition and intersection of hybrid-automatic weighted relations are hybrid-automatic weighted relations.*

Moreover, if the relations R, S are computed by weighted timed automata (compact initialized rectangular automata), then $R \circ S$ and $R \cap S$ are computed by weighted timed automata (compact initialized rectangular automata).

6.2 K-interleaved timed words

In this section, we define K-interleaved property, which intuitively expresses that two words are synchronized. Next, we show that discrete automatic relations can be lifted to the hybrid case assuming that the timed words are K-interleaved. That assumption is essential (Theorem 37).

DEFINITION 30. *Let w_1, w_2 be timed words over disjoint alphabets. We say that w_1, w_2 are K-interleaved iff in any time interval $[t_1, t_2]$ the numbers of events from w_1 and from w_2 differ by at most K.*

We briefly introduce automatic relations on discrete words. The *convolution* of words w_1, w_2, denoted by $w_1 \otimes w_2$, is a word over $(\Sigma \cup \{\#\}) \times (\Sigma \cup \{\#\})$ of length $max(|w_1|, |w_2|)$ such that the i-th letter of $w_1 \otimes w_2$ is a pair of the i-th letters of w_1 and w_2. If $|w_j| < i$, we assume that its i-th letter is $\#$. E.g. $ab \otimes c = (a, c)(b, \#)$. A relation R on $\Sigma^* \times \Sigma^*$ is *automatic* iff there is a finite word automaton $\mathcal{A}_R$ such that for all v, w, vRw holds iff $\mathcal{A}$ accepts $v \otimes w$.

PROPOSITION 31. *Let $K > 0$ and let S be a discrete automatic relation. A weighted (hybrid) relation R defined for all w_1, w_2 as $w_1Rw_2 = 0$, if w_1, w_2 are K-interleaved and $untime(w_1)\, S\, untime(w_2)$, and $w_1Rw_2 = \infty$ otherwise, is a hybrid-automatic weighted relation and it is computed by a monotonic timed automaton.*

A weighted relation R on $\Sigma^* \times \Sigma^*$ is *automatic* iff there is a weighted finite word automaton $\mathcal{A}_R$ such that for all v, w, vRw equals to the value of $v \otimes w$ assigned by $\mathcal{A}$.

PROPOSITION 32. *Let $K > 0$ and let S be an automatic weighted relation. Define a weighted relation R on timed words as follows: for all w_1, w_2, if w_1, w_2 are K-interleaved, $w_1Rw_2 = untime(w_1)\ S\ untime(w_2)$, otherwise $w_1Rw_2 = \infty$. The relation R is a hybrid-automatic weighted relation and it is computed by a monotonic weighted timed automaton.*

Propositions 31 and 32 have virtually the same proofs. The timed automaton computing R neglects time and simulates the automaton computing S. Corresponding events of two timed words may appear at different times, but since w_1, w_2 are K-interleaved, the timed automaton has to remember only last K events to synchronize w_1 and w_2.

DEFINITION 33. *Let $K > 0$ and let z be a continuous variable. We define distances $d_K^{\infty,z}, d_K^{1,z}$ on timed words $w_1 = \langle a_1^1, \nu_1^1\rangle\langle a_2^1, \nu_2^1\rangle \dots \langle a_k^1, \nu_k^1\rangle$, $w_2 = \langle a_1^2, \nu_1^2\rangle\langle a_2^2, \nu_2^2\rangle \dots \langle a_l^2, \nu_l^2\rangle$ as follows: if $k = l$ and w_1, w_2 are K-interleaved:*

$$w_1 dt_K^{\infty,z} w_2 = \max_{i \in \{1,\dots,k\}} |\nu_i^1(z) - \nu_i^2(z)|$$
$$w_1 dt_K^{1,z} w_2 = \sum\nolimits_{i \in \{1,\dots,k\}} |\nu_i^1(z) - \nu_i^2(z)|$$

Otherwise, $w_1 dt_K^{\infty,z} w_2 = w_1 dt_K^{1,z} w_2 = \infty$.

PROPOSITION 34. *For every $K > 0$ and every variable z, the relations $dt_K^{\infty,z}, dt_K^{1,z}$ are hybrid-automatic weighted relations. If z is the time variable, then $dt_K^{\infty,z}, dt_K^{1,z}$ can be computed by, respectively, a monotonic timed automaton and a monotonic weighted timed automaton.*

EXAMPLE 35. *Observe that the relation from Example 27 is computed by a monotonic timed automaton. Indeed, that relation is an intersection of three relations* $dt_1^{\infty,x}$, Id_1 *and* $\geq_1$ *defined as follows.* $dt_1^{\infty,x}$ *is a weighted relation from Definition 33. It is computed by a monotonic timed automaton (Proposition 34). The relation* $w\mathrm{Id}_1 v$ *is defined by* $w\mathrm{Id}_1 v = 0$ *iff* w, v *are* 1*-interleaved and* $untime(w) = untime(v)$*, and* $w\mathrm{Id}_1 v = \infty$ *otherwise. It is computed by a monotonic timed automaton (Proposition 31 applied to the identity relation.) Finally, the relation* $\geq_1$ *is defined by* $w{\geq_1}v = 0$ *iff* w, v *are* 1*-interleaved and every event of* w *is earlier than its counterpart in* v*, and* $w{\geq_1}v = \infty$ *otherwise. It is computed by a monotonic timed automaton that counts the difference of events from* w *and from* v*. Clearly, the difference of events from* w *and from* v *is always* 0 *or* 1 *iff* w, v *are* 1*-interleaved and every event of* w *is earlier than its counterpart in* v*.*

EXAMPLE 36. *(Skorohod distance) The Skorohod distance between functions* $x, y : \mathbb{R}^n \mapsto \mathbb{R}$ *is defined as* $d_S(x, y) = \inf\{\|\mathrm{Id} - \Lambda\|_\infty + \|x - y \circ \Lambda\|_\infty : \Lambda$ *is a bijective continuous function*$\}$*. It has been pointed out in [6], that* d_S *is the right measure to compare hybrid systems. The intuition behind the Skorohod distance is that* Λ *represents distorted time flow, and the distance measures the optimal balance between the distortion of time* ($\|\mathrm{Id} - \Lambda\|_\infty$) *and space* ($\|x - y \circ \Lambda\|_\infty$)*.*

The Skorohod distance can be expressed by an affine hybrid automaton on K*-interleaved timed words. Observe that for all* w, v, $d_S(w, v) = w\, dt_K^{\infty,t} \circ (dt_K^{\infty,z} \cap \mathrm{tId})\, v$*, where* tId *is defined as* $w\, \mathrm{tId}\, v = 0$ *if projections of* w, v *on the time variable are equal, and* $w\, \mathrm{tId}\, v = \infty$ *otherwise. Clearly,* tId *is recognized by a timed automaton.*

Unfortunately, a hybrid-automaton expressing $dt_K^{\infty,z}$ *is neither rectangular nor initialized.*

6.3 Inexpressible hybrid relations

Propositions 31, 32 and 34 refer only to timed words that are K-interleaved. In a way, it is clear that automata with finite memory are not able to process meaningfully piling up events from one of the timed words. However, the question arises, is there a (more general) notion of hybrid automata whose emptiness problem is decidable, but it is strong enough to define nontrivial hybrid-automatic weighted relations without assuming that timed words are K-interleaved? The following theorem proves otherwise.

THEOREM 37. *Let* Id *be a weighted relation defined as follows: for all timed words* w_1, w_2, $w_1 \mathrm{Id} w_2 = 0$ *iff* $untime(w_1) = untime(w_2)$*, and* $w_1\, \mathrm{Id}\, w_2 = \infty$ *otherwise.*

The problem, given a hybrid-automatic weighted relation R*, decide whether there are* w_1, w_2 *such that* $w_1(\mathrm{Id} \cap R)w_2$ *equals* 0*, is undecidable.*

7. CONCLUSIONS

In this paper we presented the model-measuring framework for the hybrid case, where distances are represented by parametrized hybrid automata. The theory developed in this paper applies to any class of hybrid automata, but the model-measuring problem is decidable only on special classes of hybrid automata. We give two examples of such classes, weighted timed automata and compact initialized rectangular automata.

Our future work is to extend the class of hybrid automata for which the model-measuring problem is decidable.

Acknowledgment

This work was supported in part by the Austrian Science Fund NFN RiSE (Rigorous Systems Engineering) and by the ERC Advanced Grant QUAREM (Quantitative Reactive Modeling).

8. REFERENCES

[1] Rajeev Alur, Costas Courcoubetis, Nicolas Halbwachs, Thomas A Henzinger, P-H Ho, Xavier Nicollin, Alfredo Olivero, Joseph Sifakis, and Sergio Yovine. The algorithmic analysis of hybrid systems. *Theoretical computer science*, 138(1):3–34, 1995.

[2] Rajeev Alur and P. Madhusudan. Decision problems for timed automata: A survey. In *SFM*, volume 3185 of *LNCS*, pages 1–24. Springer, 2004.

[3] Tawhid Bin Waez, Juergen Dingel, and Karen Rudie. A survey of timed automata for the development of real-time systems. *Computer Science Review*, 2013.

[4] Patricia Bouyer, Thomas Brihaye, Véronique Bruyère, and Jean-François Raskin. On the optimal reachability problem on weighted timed automata. *FMSD*, 31(2):135–175, October 2007.

[5] Thomas Brihaye, Laurent Doyen, Gilles Geeraerts, Joël Ouaknine, Jean-François Raskin, and James Worrell. On reachability for hybrid automata over bounded time. In *Automata, Languages and Programming*, pages 416–427. Springer, 2011.

[6] Paul Caspi and Albert Benveniste. Toward an approximation theory for computerised control. In *Embedded Software*, pages 294–304. Springer, 2002.

[7] Goran Frehse, Sumit Kumar Jha, and Bruce H Krogh. A counterexample-guided approach to parameter synthesis for linear hybrid automata. In *HSCC*, pages 187–200. Springer, 2008.

[8] Laurent Fribourg and Ulrich Kühne. Parametric verification and test coverage for hybrid automata using the inverse method. *Int. J. Found. Comput. Sci.*, 24(2):233–250, 2013.

[9] Thomas A Henzinger. *The theory of hybrid automata.* Springer, 2000.

[10] Thomas A Henzinger, Peter W Kopke, Anuj Puri, and Pravin Varaiya. What's decidable about hybrid automata? In *STOC*, pages 373–382. ACM, 1995.

[11] Thomas A. Henzinger and Jan Otop. From model checking to model measuring. In *CONCUR*, volume 8052 of *LNCS*, pages 273–287. Springer, 2013.

[12] Thomas Hune, Judi Romijn, Mariëlle Stoelinga, and Frits Vaandrager. Linear parametric model checking of timed automata. *The Journal of Logic and Algebraic Programming*, 52:183–220, 2002.

[13] Joseph S. Miller. Decidability and complexity results for timed automata and semi-linear hybrid automata. In *HSCC*, volume 1790 of *LNCS*, pages 296–309. Springer, 2000.

Abstracting and Refining Robustness for Cyber-Physical Systems*

Matthias Rungger
Department of Electrical Engineering
University of California, Los Angeles
rungger@ucla.edu

Paulo Tabuada
Department of Electrical Engineering
University of California, Los Angeles
tabuada@ee.ucla.edu

ABSTRACT

According to the IEEE standard glossary of software engineering, robustness is the degree to which a system or component can function correctly in the presence of invalid inputs or stressful environment conditions. In this paper we present a design methodology for robust cyber-physical systems (CPS) based on a notion of robustness for CPS termed *input-output dynamical stability*. It captures two intuitive aims of a robust design: bounded disturbances have bounded consequences and the effect of sporadic disturbances disappears as time progresses. Our framework to synthesize robust CPS is based on an *abstraction and refinement* procedure, where the robust CPS is obtain through the refinement of a design for an abstraction of the concrete CPS. The soundness of the approach is ensured through the use of several novel notions of simulation relation introduced in this paper.

Categories and Subject Descriptors

I.2.8 [**Problem Solving, Control Methods and Search**]: Control Theory; I.2.2 [**Automatic Programming**]: Program Synthesis

Keywords

Cyber-Physical Systems; Robustness; Stability; Synthesis

1. INTRODUCTION

Every system design is based on certain assumptions about the environment where the system is supposed to operate. But the run-time environment of a system is not completely known at design-time. It is therefore crucial to provide some guarantees about the system behavior whenever disturbances, i.e., violations of environment assumptions made at design-time, occur. Such guarantees are provided by a robust design.

In this paper, we introduce a methodology for the robust design of cyber-physical systems (CPS). The disturbances are allowed to be of continuous nature, e.g., sensor noise or actuation errors in a feedback control loop, as well as of discrete nature, e.g., hardware errors or software errors in an embedded device.

We introduce a notion of robustness for CPS termed *input-output dynamical stability* which merges existing notions of robustness for continuous systems, such as input-to-state dynamical stability and input-output stability, see e.g. [11, 25], and the recently introduced notion of robustness for discrete systems [27] which was already inspired by continuous notions of robustness. Similarly to the studies [11] and [27], our definition of robustness captures two intuitive goals of a robust design: firstly, bounded disturbances have bounded consequences and secondly, "nominal" system behavior is eventually resumed once disturbances disappear.

We also propose a framework for the design of robust CPS based on an abstraction and refinement process consisting of three main steps: **i)** computation of an *abstraction* or *symbolic model* of a given CPS, i.e., a finite-state system where certain properties of the concrete CPS are omitted; **ii)** robust synthesis for the abstraction; **iii)** refinement of the solution for the abstraction to a solution for the concrete CPS. The abstraction and refinement process is illustrated in Figure 1.

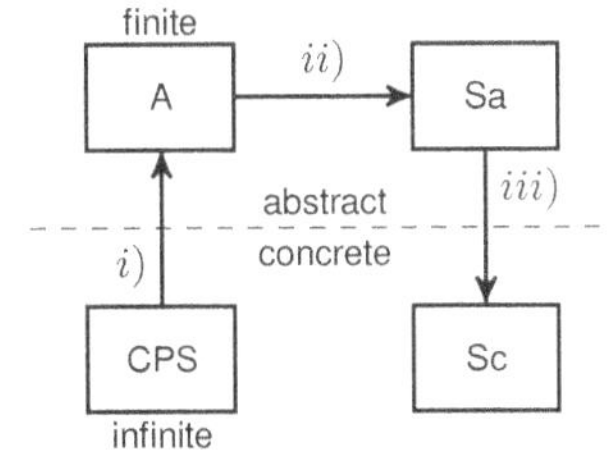

Figure 1: The abstraction and refinement approach: i) compute an abstraction (A) of the CPS; ii) solve the problem in the abstract domain (Sa); iii) refine the abstract solution to a solution (Sc) in concrete domain.

We focus on the first and third steps of the abstraction and refinement procedure, since the robust synthesis problem for finite systems has been solved in [27]. A well-known approach to establish the soundness of the abstraction and refinement procedure is based on simulation relations (SR) [17] and alternating simulation relations (ASR) [1] which are used to relate CPS with their symbolic models. We show in this paper how to modify the existing notions of relations so that they can be utilized to prove the robustness of a system in terms of a related system.

In addition, we introduce *contractive alternating simulation relations* as a tool to refine designs for an abstraction to designs for the concrete system. We introduced recently in [23] contractive SR for the verification of robustness of CPS with the aim to capture certain contraction properties that are often observed for continuous control system in the abstraction process, see e.g. [19, 14, 10]. In this paper we extend this notion to the synthesis of robust CPS. A particular feature of contractive SR allows us neglect continuous

*This work is supported by the NSF awards 1239085, 1136174 and by the NSF Expeditions in Computing project ExCAPE: Expeditions in Computer Augmented Program Engineering.

HSCC'14, 15–17, 2014, Berlin, Germany.
Copyright 2014 ACM 978-1-4503-2732-9/14/04...$15.00
http://dx.doi.org/10.1145/2562059.2562133.

disturbances in the abstract design, but nevertheless establish robustness with respect to continuous and discrete disturbances. As we demonstrate in Section 6, this might lead to a separation of concerns where a continuous design caters to continuous disturbances and the design for the abstract model caters to the discrete disturbances while ensuring that the refined design provides robustness to both continuous and discrete disturbances.

In summary, the main contributions of the proposed abstraction/refinement design methodology are the following: 1) we propose a notion of robustness for CPS; 2) we prove that robust designs for an abstraction can be refined to robust designs for the concrete system whenever the abstraction is related to the concrete system by an ASR; 3) we show how to construct the refined robust design from the abstract one; 4) when using contractive ASR we tailor the abstract design to discrete disturbances, while ensuring the robustness of the refined design with respect to continuous and discrete disturbances.

1.1 Related work

Robustness has been studied in the control systems community for more than fifty years, see [31], and formalized in many different ways including operator finite gains, bounded-input bounded-output stability, input-to-state stability, input-output stability, and several others, see e.g. [25]. Moreover, robustness investigations have been conducted for different system models such as continuous-time systems, sampled-data systems, networked control systems, and general hybrid systems [4]. The notion of robustness described in this paper benefited from all this prior work and was directly inspired by input-to-state stability [25] and its quantitative version input-to-state dynamical stability [11]. Unlike the framework presented in this paper, most of the existing research on robustness of nonlinear control systems does not consider constructive procedures for the verification and synthesis of controllers enforcing robustness. The only exceptions known to the authors are [12, 32, 13]. Unfortunately, the finite-state models that are used in those approaches represent *approximations* of the concrete dynamics, rather than abstractions. Hence, the soundness of those methods is not ensured.

Robustness for discrete systems also has a long standing history. For example, Dijkstra's notion of self-stabilizing algorithms in the context of distributed systems [7] requires the "nominal" behavior of the system to be resumed in finitely many steps after the occurrence of a disturbance. As explained in [27], self-stabilizing systems are a special case of robust systems, as defined in this paper. In addition to self-stabilization, there exist several different notions of robustness for discrete systems. For example, in [24] a systematic literature review is presented, where the authors distill and categorize more than 9000 papers on software robustness. In the following, we focus on the few approaches that provide quantitative measures of robustness for discrete systems and thereby are close to the framework presented in this paper.

Let us first mention two notions of robustness for systems over finite alphabets [28] and reactive systems [3] that we think are the closest to the definition of robustness discussed in this paper. Similarly to our methodology, the deviation of the system behavior from its "nominal" behavior as well as the disturbances are quantified. A system is said to be robust if its deviation from the "nominal" behavior is proportional to the disturbance causing that deviation. Although, this requirement captures the first intuitive goal of robustness, those definitions do not require that the effect of a sporadic disturbance disappears over time. See [27] for a more rigorous comparison of the robustness definitions.

Note that the work in [3] on reactive systems demonstrates how to quantify disturbances and their effects on the system behavior in order to characterize safety specifications in terms of robustness inequalities. However, it is unclear how to quantify disturbances and their effects in order to encode liveness specifications. Some possible notions are given in [2, 8, 29], where the robustness of a system is expressed as the ratio of the number of assumptions and guarantees the system meets. Those notions of robustness are incompatible with our definition of robustness, and further work is needed if we would like to express liveness specifications through the notion of robustness presented in this paper.

There exist different studies that characterize the robustness of discrete systems in terms of a Lyapunov function, as it is done in [6, 18] for discrete event systems, or in [15] for ω-regular automata and in [22] for software programs. Note that Lyapunov functions represent a tool to establish robustness inequalities, but do not provide a direct quantification of the effect of disturbances on the system behavior. Hence, further work is needed to related Lyapunov functions, like those presented in [6, 18, 15, 22], to a robustness inequality that directly quantifies the consequences of disturbances on the system behavior.

Another interesting method to characterize robustness for programs is outlined in [16] and [5]. Programs are interpreted as function that map input data to output data. A program is said to be robust if the associated input-output function is continuous. In comparison to our approach, in [16, 5] a program is assumed to terminate on all inputs and is interpreted as a static function.

2. PRELIMINARIES

We denote by $\mathbb{N} = \{0, 1, 2, \ldots\}$ the set of natural numbers and by $\mathbb{B}_x(r)$ the closed ball centered at $x \in \mathbb{R}^n$ with radius $r \in \mathbb{R}_{\geq 0}$. We identify $\mathbb{B}(r)$ with $\mathbb{B}_0(r)$. We use $|x|$ and $|x|_2$ to denote the ∞-norm and two-norm of $x \in \mathbb{R}^n$, respectively. Given $x \in \mathbb{R}^n$ and $A \subseteq \mathbb{R}^n$, we use $|x|_A := \inf_{x' \in A} |x - x'|_2$ to denote the Euclidean distance between x and A. Given a set $A \subseteq \mathbb{R}^n$ we use $[A]_\eta := \{x \in A \mid \exists k \in \mathbb{Z}^n : x = 2k\eta\}$ to denote a uniform grid in A. For $a, b \in \mathbb{R}$ with $a \leq b$, we denote the closed, open, and half-open intervals in $\mathbb{R}$ by $[a, b]$, $]a, b[$, $[a, b[$ and $]a, b]$, respectively. For $a, b \in \mathbb{Z}$, $a \leq b$ we use $[a; b]$, $]a; b[$, $[a; b[$ and $]a; b]$, to denote the corresponding intervals in $\mathbb{Z}$.

Given a function $f : A \to B$ and $A' \subseteq A$ we use $f(A') := \{f(a) \in B \mid a \in A'\}$ to denote the image of A' under f. A set-valued function or mapping f from X to Y is denoted by $f : X \rightrightarrows Y$. Its domain is defined by $\operatorname{dom} f := \{x \in X \mid f(x) \neq \varnothing\}$. Given a sequence $a : \mathbb{N} \to A$ in some set A, we use a_t to denote its t-th element and $a_{[0;t]}$ to denote its restriction to the interval $[0; t]$. The set of all finite sequences is denoted by A^*. The set of all infinite sequences is denoted by A^ω and we think of elements in $a \in A^\omega$ as sequences $a : \mathbb{N} \to A$. Given a relation $R \subseteq A \times B$ we use $\pi_A(R)$ and $\pi_B(R)$ to denote its projection onto the set A and B, respectively.

We use the following classes of comparison functions:

- $\mathcal{K} := \{\alpha : \mathbb{R}_{\geq 0} \to \mathbb{R}_{\geq 0} \mid \alpha \text{ is cont., str. incr. with } \alpha(0) = 0\}$
- $\mathcal{L} := \{\alpha : \mathbb{N} \to \mathbb{R}_{\geq 0} \mid \alpha \text{ is str. decr. with } \lim_{t \to \infty} \alpha(t) = 0\}$
- $\mathcal{KL} := \{\beta : \mathbb{R}_{\geq 0} \times \mathbb{N} \to \mathbb{R}_{\geq 0} \mid \forall t \in \mathbb{N} : \beta(\cdot, t) \in \mathcal{K}$ and $\forall c \in \mathbb{R}_{\geq 0} : \beta(c, \cdot) \in \mathcal{L}\}$
- $\mathcal{KLD} := \{\beta \in \mathcal{KL} \mid \forall c \in \mathbb{R}_{\geq 0}, \forall s, t \in \mathbb{N} : \mu(c, 0) = c$ and $\mu(c, s + t) = \mu(\mu(c, s), t)\}$

Note that we work only with discrete-time systems and for this reason we have defined the domain of class $\mathcal{L}$ functions as $\mathbb{N}$.

3. ROBUSTNESS FOR CPS

Since CPS exhibit a rich dynamical behavior through the interaction of discrete and continuous components we need an adequate mathematical description that is able to represent its complex dynamics. We use a general notion of transition system as the underlying model of CPS.

DEFINITION 1. *A* system *S is a tuple $S = (X, X_0, U, r)$ consisting of*

- *a set of states X;*
- *a set of initial states $X_0 \subseteq X$;*
- *a set of inputs U containing the distinguished symbol $\bot$;*
- *a transition map $r : X \times U \rightrightarrows X$.*

A behavior *of S is a pair of sequences $(\xi, \nu) \in (X \times U)^\omega$, that satisfies $\xi_0 \in X_0$ and $\xi_{t+1} \in r(\xi_t, \nu_t)$ for all times $t \in \mathbb{N}$.*

A state $x \in X$ is called reachable *if there exists $T \in \mathbb{N}$ and sequences $\xi \in X^T$, $\nu \in U^{T-1}$ with $\xi_{t+1} \in r(\xi_t, \nu_t)$ for all $t \in [0; T[$, $\xi_0 \in X_0$, and $\xi_T = x$.*

A system is called non-blocking *if $r(x, u) \neq \varnothing$ for any reachable state x and any $u \in U$. It is called* finite *if X and U are finite sets and otherwise it is called* infinite.

Behaviors are defined as infinite sequences since we have in mind reactive systems, such as control systems, that are required to interact with its environment for arbitrarily long periods of time. In particular, we are interested in understanding the effect of disturbances on the system behavior. Therefore, the inputs in U are to be interpreted as disturbance inputs. Nevertheless, in order to allow for the possibility of absence of disturbances, we assume that U contains a special symbol $\bot \in U$ that indicates that no disturbance is present.

For simplicity of presentation, we assume throughout this section that the system is non-blocking, i.e., for every state and (disturbance) input there exists at least one successor state to which the system can transition.

In order to be able to talk about robustness properties, we endow our notion of system with cost functions I and O that we use to describe the desired behavior and to quantify disturbances.

DEFINITION 2. *A* system with cost functions *is a triple (S, I, O) where S is a system and $I : X \times U \to \mathbb{R}_{\geq 0}$ and $O : X \times U \to \mathbb{R}_{\geq 0}$ are the* input cost function *and* output cost function, *respectively.*

We now introduce a notion of robustness following well-known notions of robustness for control systems, see e.g. [25]. In particular, we follow the notion of *input-to-state dynamical stability* introduced in [11] and generalize it here to CPS using the cost functions I and O.

DEFINITION 3. *Let (S, I, O) be a system with cost functions, $\gamma \in \mathcal{K}$, $\mu \in \mathcal{KLD}$ and $\rho \in \mathbb{R}_{\geq 0}$. We say that S is (γ, μ, ρ)-*practically input-output dynamically stable ((γ, μ, ρ)-pIODS) with respect to (I, O) *or* (S, I, O) is (γ, μ, ρ)-pIODS *if the following inequality holds for every behavior of S:*

$$O(\xi_t, \nu_t) \leq \max_{t' \in [0;t]} \mu(\gamma(I(\xi_{t'}, \nu_{t'})), t - t') + \rho, \quad \forall t \in \mathbb{N}. \quad (1)$$

We say that (S, I, O) is pIODS *if there exist $\gamma \in \mathcal{K}$, $\mu \in \mathcal{KLD}$ and $\rho \in \mathbb{R}_{\geq 0}$ such that (S, I, O) is (γ, μ, ρ)-pIODS.*

We say that (S, I, O) is (γ, μ)-IODS *if it is $(\gamma, \mu, 0)$-pIODS, and* IODS *if there exist $\gamma \in \mathcal{K}$, $\mu \in \mathcal{KLD}$ such that (S, I, O) is (γ, μ)-IODS.*

If the cost functions are clear from the context or are irrelevant to the discussion, we abuse the terminology and call a system S pIODS/IODS without referring to the cost functions.

In our previous work [27] we used IODS as a notion of robustness for cyber systems. The underlying model were *transducers*, i.e., maps $f : U^* \to Y^*$ that process input streams in U^* into output streams in Y^*. In that framework, the cost functions were defined on *sequences* of input symbols and output symbols, i.e., $I : U^* \to \mathbb{N}$ and $O : Y^* \to \mathbb{N}$. In order formulate such cost functions in the current framework we can compose the transducers computing the input and output costs with the system being modeled so that input and output costs are readily available as functions on the states and inputs of the composed system.

Let us describe how the IODS inequality (1) realizes the intuitive notion of robustness described in the introduction. For the following discussion, suppose we are given a system with cost functions (S, I, O) that is (γ, μ)-IODS. We use the output cost to specify preferences on the system behaviors: less preferred behaviors have higher costs. In particular, the cost should be zero for the nominal behavior. Similarly, we use the input costs to quantify the disturbances. Hence, the input costs should be zero if no disturbances are present, i.e., $I(\xi_t, \nu_t) = 0$ when $\nu = \bot^\omega$. Since, $\gamma(0) = 0$ and $\mu(0, s) = 0$ for all $s \in \mathbb{N}$, zero input cost implies zero output cost which, in turn, implies that the system follows the desired behavior. Moreover, inequality (1) implies that bounded disturbances lead to bounded deviations from the nominal behavior. Suppose $I(\xi_t, \nu_t) \leq c$ holds for some $c \in \mathbb{R}_{\geq 0}$ for all $t \in \mathbb{N}$. Note that γ is monotonically increasing and $\mu(c, t) \leq \mu(c, 0) = c$ holds for all $t \in \mathbb{N}$. Therefore, (1) becomes

$$O(\xi_t, \nu_t) \leq \gamma(c) \quad \forall t \in \mathbb{N}.$$

In addition, inequality (1) ensures that the effect of a sporadic disturbance vanishes over time. Suppose there exists $t' \in \mathbb{N}$ after which the input cost is zero, i.e., $I(\xi_t, \nu_t) = 0$ for all $t \geq t'$. Then it follows from the definition of $\mu \in \mathcal{KLD}$ that

$$\mu(\gamma(I(\xi_{t'}, \nu_{t'})), t - t') \to 0, \quad t \to \infty.$$

Hence, the output cost is forced to decrease to zero as time progresses.

We refer the reader to our previous work [27] for a further demonstration of the usefulness of inequality (1) to express robustness of cyber systems. We showed in [27] that verifying if a cyber system is robust can be algorithmically solved in polynomial time. Similarly, the problem of synthesizing a controller to enforce robustness of a cyber system is solved in polynomial time. Moreover, we provide some examples of robust cyber systems in the sense of inequality (1).

4. PRESERVATION OF IODS BY SIMULATION RELATIONS

In this section we introduce simulation relations between two systems and answer the following question:

Under what conditions is pIODS preserved by simulation relations?

We consider three different types of relations: exact simulation relations (SR), approximate simulation relations (aSR) and approximate contractive simulation relations (acSR).

Bisimilarity and (bi)simulation relations were introduced in computer science by Milner and Park in the early 1980s, see e.g. [17], and have proven to be a valuable tool in verifying the correctness of programs. Approximate SR [9, 20, 26] have been introduced in the control community as a generalization of SR in order to enlarge the class of systems which admit finite abstractions (or symbolic models). We refine the notion of aSR to acSR, with the aim of capturing a contraction property that is often observed in concrete systems, see e.g. [14, 19, 20]. Intuitively, the existence of a SR from system S to system $\hat{S}$ implies that for every behavior of S there exists a behavior of $\hat{S}$ satisfying certain properties. In the classical setting, one would ask that the output of the two related behaviors coincides, from which behavioral inclusion follows, i.e., for every behavior of S there exists a behavior of $\hat{S}$ such that both behaviors generate the same output sequence. For our purposes, as we want to preserve the IODS inequality, we require that the input costs and output costs satisfy $\hat{I} \leq I$ and $O \leq \hat{O}$ along those related behaviors. The satisfaction of these inequalities allows us to conclude that $(\hat{S}, \hat{I}, \hat{O})$ being pIODS implies that (S, I, O) is pIODS.

For notational convenience we use $R_X := \pi_{X \times \hat{X}}(R)$ to denote the projection of a relation $R \subseteq X \times \hat{X} \times U \times \hat{U}$ on $X \times \hat{X}$. Moreover, we use $U(x) := \{u \in U \mid r(x, u) \neq \varnothing\}$ to denote the set of inputs for which the right-hand-side is non-empty.

4.1 Exact simulation relations

Let us introduce the definition of simulation relation which allows us to preserve robustness properties.

DEFINITION 4. *Let S and $\hat{S}$ be two systems. A relation $R \subseteq X \times \hat{X} \times U \times \hat{U}$ is said to be a* simulation relation (SR) from S to $\hat{S}$ *if:*

1. *for all $x_0 \in X_0$ exists $\hat{x}_0 \in \hat{X}_0$ such that $(x_0, \hat{x}_0) \in R_X$;*
2. *for all $(x, \hat{x}) \in R_X$ and $u \in U(x)$ there exists $\hat{u} \in \hat{U}(\hat{x})$ such that*
   - *(a) $(x, \hat{x}, u, \hat{u}) \in R$;*
   - *(b) for all $x' \in r(x, u)$ there exists $\hat{x}' \in \hat{r}(\hat{x}, \hat{u})$ such that $(x', \hat{x}') \in R_X$.*

Let (S, I, O) and $(\hat{S}, \hat{I}, \hat{O})$ be two systems with cost functions. We call a SR R form S to $\hat{S}$ an input-output SR (IOSR) from (S, I, O) to $(\hat{S}, \hat{I}, \hat{O})$ *if*

$$\hat{I}(\hat{x}, \hat{u}) \leq I(x, u) \quad \textit{and} \quad O(x, u) \leq \hat{O}(\hat{x}, \hat{u}) \tag{2}$$

holds for all $(x, \hat{x}, u, \hat{u}) \in R$.

Note that the notion of IOSR for systems with input and output costs is a straightforward extension of the well-known definition of SR for the usual definition of system, see [26].

LEMMA 1. *Let S and $\hat{S}$ be two systems. Suppose there exists an SR R from S to $\hat{S}$, then for every behavior (ξ, ν) of S there exists a behavior $(\hat{\xi}, \hat{\nu})$ of $\hat{S}$ such that*

$$(\xi_t, \hat{\xi}_t, \nu_t, \hat{\nu}_t) \in R, \quad t \in \mathbb{N}. \tag{3}$$

Proof: The proof follows by similar arguments as the proof of [26, Proposition 4.9] and is omitted here. ■

Simulation relations preserve IODS in the following sense.

THEOREM 1. *Let (S, I, O) and $(\hat{S}, \hat{I}, \hat{O})$ be two systems with cost functions and suppose there exists an IOSR R from (S, I, O) to $(\hat{S}, \hat{I}, \hat{O})$. If $(\hat{S}, \hat{I}, \hat{O})$ is (γ, μ, ρ)-pIODS then (S, I, O) is (γ, μ, ρ)-pIODS.*

Note how preservation of pIODS is contra-variant, i.e., while the direction of the simulation relation is from system S to system $\hat{S}$, the propagation of pIODS is from system $\hat{S}$ to system S. Moreover, by taking $\rho = 0$ it follows that $\hat{S}$ being IODS implies S is IODS.

4.2 Approximate simulation relations

Exact simulation relations are often too restrictive when one seeks to relate a physical system to a finite-state abstraction or symbolic model. In this case, approximate simulation relations were shown to be adequate in the sense that they can be shown to exist for large classes of physical systems [9, 26].

DEFINITION 5. *Let (S, I, O) and $(\hat{S}, \hat{I}, \hat{O})$ be two systems with cost functions. A SR R from S to $\hat{S}$ is called an ε-*approximate input-output SR (ε-aIOSR) from (S, I, O) to $(\hat{S}, \hat{I}, \hat{O})$ *if every $(x, \hat{x}, u, \hat{u}) \in R$ satisfies:*

$$\hat{I}(\hat{x}, \hat{u}) \leq I(x, u) + \varepsilon \quad \textit{and} \quad O(x, u) \leq \hat{O}(\hat{x}, \hat{u}) + \varepsilon. \tag{4}$$

Note that the definition of aIOSR is again a straightforward extension of the well-known notion of approximate SR of systems, see [26]. For $\varepsilon = 0$ the notion of exact IOSR is recovered. However, the notion of aIOSR introduces some flexibility as it allows, for example, the inequality $O(x, u) - \varepsilon \leq \hat{O}(\hat{x}, \hat{u}) \leq O(x, u)$ to hold which is not possible for IOSR. This flexibility is important when we are dealing we infinite state systems where an abstract state in $\hat{X}$ corresponds to a set of states in X.

THEOREM 2. *Let (S, I, O) and $(\hat{S}, \hat{I}, \hat{O})$ be two systems with cost functions and suppose there exists an ε-aIOSR R from (S, I, O) and $(\hat{S}, \hat{I}, \hat{O})$. If $(\hat{S}, \hat{I}, \hat{O})$ is (γ, μ, ρ)-pIODS, then (S, I, O) is (γ', μ, ρ')-pIODS with $\gamma'(c) = 2\gamma(2c)$ and $\rho' = \mu(\gamma'(\varepsilon), 0) + \varepsilon + \rho$.*

4.3 Contractive simulation relations

The construction of abstractions or symbolic models for physical systems described in [20, 21, 26] results in simulation relations that satisfy a certain contraction property. Here we introduce a notion of simulation that captures those contraction properties.

In the following definition of contractive simulation relation from S to $\hat{S}$, we use a function $\mathsf{d} : U \times \hat{U} \to \mathbb{R}_{\geq 0}$ to measure the "mismatch" between two inputs $u \in U$ and $\hat{u} \in \hat{U}$. In various examples, in which we show that two systems are related, the set of inputs $\hat{U}$ of system $\hat{S}$ is actually a subset $\hat{U} \subseteq U$ of the set of inputs of system S and we simply use a norm $|\cdot|$ in U as distance function $\mathsf{d}(u, \hat{u}) = |u - \hat{u}|$, see Example 1, Example 2 and Section 6. However, in the following definition, we simply assume we are given a function $\mathsf{d} : U \times \hat{U} \to \mathbb{R}_{\geq 0}$ without referring to any underlying metric.

DEFINITION 6. *Let S and $\hat{S}$ be two systems, let $\kappa, \lambda \in \mathbb{R}_{\geq 0}$, $\beta \in [0, 1[$ be parameters and consider a map $\mathsf{d} : U \times \hat{U} \to \mathbb{R}_{\geq 0}$. We call a parameterized (by $\varepsilon \in [\kappa, \infty[$) relation $R(\varepsilon) \subseteq X \times \hat{X} \times U \times \hat{U}$ a* κ-approximate (β,λ)-contractive simulation relation ((κ, β, λ)-acSR) from S to $\hat{S}$ with distance function d *if $R(\varepsilon) \subseteq R(\varepsilon')$ holds for all $\varepsilon \leq \varepsilon'$ and for all $\varepsilon \in [\kappa, \infty[$ we have*

1. *$\forall x_0 \in X_0, \exists \hat{x}_0 \in \hat{X}_0 : (x_0, \hat{x}_0) \in R_X(\kappa)$;*
2. *$\forall (x, \hat{x}) \in R_X(\varepsilon), \forall u \in U(x), \exists \hat{u} \in \hat{U}(\hat{x})$:*
   - *(a) $(x, \hat{x}, u, \hat{u}) \in R(\varepsilon)$*
   - *(b) $\forall x' \in r(x, u), \exists \hat{x}' \in \hat{r}(\hat{x}, \hat{u})$:*
     $(x', \hat{x}') \in R_X(\kappa + \beta\varepsilon + \lambda \mathsf{d}(u, \hat{u}))$.

Let (S, I, O) and $(\hat{S}, \hat{I}, \hat{O})$ be two systems with cost functions. We call a (κ, β, λ)-acSR $R(\varepsilon)$ from S to $\hat{S}$ with distance function d *a* κ*-approximate* (β,λ)*-contractive* input-output SR ((κ,β,λ)-acIOSR) from (S, I, O) to $(\hat{S}, \hat{I}, \hat{O})$ with distance function d *if there exist* $\gamma_O, \gamma_I \in \mathcal{K}$ *such that*

$$\begin{aligned}\hat{I}(\hat{x},\hat{u}) &\leq I(x,u) + \gamma_I(\varepsilon') \\ O(x,u) &\leq \hat{O}(\hat{x},\hat{u}) + \gamma_O(\varepsilon')\end{aligned} \tag{5}$$

holds for all $(x, \hat{x}, u, \hat{u}) \in R(\varepsilon)$ *and* $\varepsilon' = \max\{\varepsilon, \mathsf{d}(u, \hat{u})\}$.

Recall that in generalizing IOSR to aIOSR we merely relaxed the inequalities on the costs functions by a constant parameter ε, compare (2) and (4). Here, we go one step further, and relax the inequalities using the generalized gain functions γ_I and γ_O, where ε' in (4) depends on the parameter ε that appears in the definition of the acSR $R(\varepsilon)$ and on the input difference measured in terms of d. This change, in combination with the definition of acSR, allows us to quantify the relaxation in the cost function inequalities as a function of the difference of input histories, see Theorem 3 and the subsequent discussion.

Before we make those statements more precise, let us first introduce an example to illustrate the notion of acSR.

EXAMPLE 1. *We consider a scalar disturbed linear system*

$$x^+ = 0.6x + u. \tag{6}$$

on the bounded set $D := [-1, 1]$. *We start our analysis by casting (6) as a system* S *with* $X := \mathbb{R}$, $X_0 := D$, $U := \mathbb{R}$ *and* $r(x, u) := \{0.6x + u\}$.

Note that D *is forward invariant with respect to (6) in the absence of disturbances, i.e., when* $u = 0$. *Later on, we analyze the invariance property in the presence of disturbances. This motivates our choice of cost functions with* $O(x, u) := |x|_D$ *and* $I(x, u) := |u|$.

We now introduce a symbolic model $\hat{S}$ *of* S *with* $\hat{X} := [D]_{0.2}$, $\hat{X}_0 := \hat{X}$, $\hat{U} := \{0\}$ *and*

$$\hat{x}' \in \hat{r}(\hat{x}, \hat{u}) :\iff |\hat{x}' - 0.6\hat{x}| \leq 0.2.$$

Note that since $O(\hat{x}, \hat{u}) = I(\hat{x}, \hat{u}) = 0$ *for all* $\hat{x} \in \hat{X}$ *and* $\hat{u} \in \hat{U}$, *we define the cost functions for* $\hat{S}$ *to be* $\hat{O} := 0$ *and* $\hat{I} := 0$. *We also introduce the relation* $R(\varepsilon) := R_X(\varepsilon) \times \mathbb{R} \times \{0\}$ *with*

$$R_X(\varepsilon) := \{(x, \hat{x}) \in X \times \hat{X} \mid |x - \hat{x}| \leq \varepsilon\}$$

and show that $R(\varepsilon)$ *is a* $(0.2, 0.6, 1)$*-acSR from* S *to* $\hat{S}$ *with distance function* $\mathsf{d}(u, 0) := |u|$.

Point 1) in Definition 6 is easily verified. Now let $(x, \hat{x}) \in R_X(\varepsilon)$ *and* $u \in U$. *We pick* $0 \in \hat{U}$ *and observe that* $(x, \hat{x}, u, 0) \in R(\varepsilon)$ *holds by definition of* $R(\varepsilon)$. *We proceed with 2.b) of Definition 6. For* $x' \in r(x, u)$ *there exists* $\hat{x}' \in \hat{r}(\hat{x}, 0)$ *with*

$$|x' - \hat{x}'| \leq 0.2 + |0.6x + u - 0.6\hat{x}| \leq 0.2 + 0.6\varepsilon + |u|$$

and it follows that $R(\varepsilon)$ *is a* $(0.2, 0.6, 1)$*-acSR from* S *to* $\hat{S}$. *Moreover, the inequalities (5) are satisfied with* $\gamma_I = 0$ *and* $\gamma_O(c) = c$. *Hence,* $R(\varepsilon)$ *is an acIOSR from* (S, I, O) *to* $(\hat{S}, \hat{I}, \hat{O})$.

Let us now emphasize that there exists no ε*-aIOSR* $\hat{R}$ *from* (S, I, O) *to* $(\hat{S}, \hat{I}, \hat{O})$ *for any finite symbolic model* $\hat{S}$. *For the sake of contradiction, suppose there exists an* ε*-aIOSR* $\hat{R}$ *from* (S, I, O) *to* $(\hat{S}, \hat{I}, \hat{O})$ *and* $\hat{S}$ *is finite. Since* $\hat{S}$ *is finite, there necessarily exists a state* $\hat{x} \in \hat{X}$ *and input* $\hat{u} \in \hat{U}$ *such that the set of related sates and inputs* $\{(x, u) \in X \times U \mid (x, \hat{x}, u, \hat{u}) \in \hat{R}\}$ *is unbounded. As a consequence, we find for any constant* $c \in \mathbb{R}$, *a pair* (x, u) *with* $(x, \hat{x}, u, \hat{u}) \in \hat{R}$ *so that* $O(x, u) = |x|_D > \hat{O}(\hat{x}, \hat{u}) + c$ *and* $\hat{R}$ *cannot be an aIOSR since (4) is violated.*

Conversely, if we bound the set of states and inputs of (6) but consider the modified dynamics $x^+ = x + u$, *then it is easy to compute a relation* $\hat{R}$ *that is an* ε*-aIOSR from* (S, I, O) *to* $(\hat{S}, \hat{I}, \hat{O})$, *but there is no acSR from* $\hat{S}$ *to* S.

We resume the analysis of this example at the end of this section, where we continue the robustness analysis of the invariance property of D *with respect to* S.

The previous example demonstrates that we can use acIOSR to relate an infinite system S with an *unbounded* set of states and/or inputs, with a *finite* system $\hat{S}$, which is not possible using aIOSR.

We point out that any (κ, β, λ)-acIOSR $R(\varepsilon)$ from (S, I, O) to $(\hat{S}, \hat{I}, \hat{O})$ is also an aIOSR, whenever the maximal distance between two related elements in U and $\hat{U}$ is bounded. Let $\alpha \in \mathbb{R}_{\geq 0}$ be given such that $\mathsf{d}(u, \hat{u}) \leq \alpha$ holds for all $(u, \hat{u}) \in \pi_{U \times \hat{U}}(R(\varepsilon))$ and $\varepsilon \in \mathbb{R}_{\geq 0}$. Now we fix ε such that $\kappa + \beta\varepsilon + \lambda\alpha \leq \varepsilon$ holds. Note that we can always find such an ε as we assume $\beta \in [0, 1[$. Then the relation $R' := R(\varepsilon)$ is a SR from S to $\hat{S}$. This observation follows immediately from the definition of $R(\varepsilon)$ since $\kappa + \beta\varepsilon + \lambda\alpha \leq \varepsilon$ implies that $R(\kappa + \beta\varepsilon + \lambda\alpha) \subseteq R'$ which in turn implies that R' is a SR from S to $\hat{S}$. Moreover, if $R(\varepsilon)$ is an acIOSR then R' is an ε'-aIOSR from (S, I, O) to $(\hat{S}, \hat{I}, \hat{O})$ with $\varepsilon' := \max\{\varepsilon, \gamma_O(\max\{\varepsilon, \alpha\}), \gamma_I(\max\{\varepsilon, \alpha\})\}$.

Before we explain how the notions of acSR and acIOSR capture the contraction property of S, we provide a result that mimics Lemma 1.

THEOREM 3. *Let* S *and* $\hat{S}$ *be systems and let* $R(\varepsilon)$ *be a* (κ, β, λ)*-acSR from* S *to* $\hat{S}$ *with distance function* d. *Then there exist* $\mu_\Delta \in \mathcal{KLD}$ *and* $\gamma_\Delta, \kappa_\Delta \in \mathbb{R}_{\geq 0}$ *such that for every behavior* (ξ, ν) *of* S *there exists a behavior* $(\hat{\xi}, \hat{\nu})$ *of* $\hat{S}$ *so that the two behaviors satisfy*

$$(\xi_t, \hat{\xi}_t, \nu_t, \hat{\nu}_t) \in R(\varepsilon_t), \quad t \in \mathbb{N}. \tag{7}$$

with $\varepsilon_{t+1} \leq \max_{t' \in [0;t]} \mu_\Delta(\gamma_\Delta \mathsf{d}(\nu_{t'}, \hat{\nu}_{t'}), t - t') + \kappa_\Delta$.

Theorem 3 exposes one of the key features of an acIOSR. The membership $(\xi_t, \hat{\xi}_t, \nu_t, \hat{\nu}_t) \in R(\varepsilon_t)$ implies $O(\xi_t, \nu_t) \leq \hat{O}(\hat{\xi}_t, \hat{\nu}_t) + \gamma_O(\varepsilon_t)$. Hence, the bound on the output cost O of S in terms of the output cost $\hat{O}$ of $\hat{S}$ depends on the parameter ε_t which is time-varying. In comparison to the definition of aIOSR (see (4)) this parameter varies over time. We established with Theorem 3 a bound on ε_t in terms of the difference (measured by λd) of the input histories $\mathsf{d}(\nu_{t'}, \hat{\nu}_{t'})$ with $t' \in [0; t]$. If we are able to match a disturbance ν_t of S closely (in terms of d) by a disturbance $\hat{\nu}_t$ of $\hat{S}$, we know that the output cost $\hat{O}$ of $\hat{S}$ provides a good estimate for the output cost O of S. Moreover, if after a certain $t' \in \mathbb{N}$ the difference in the input behaviors is zero, i.e., $\mathsf{d}(\nu_t, \hat{\nu}_t) = 0$ for all $t \geq t'$, then the bound on ε_t approaches κ_Δ as $t \to \infty$. Here, we clearly exploit the contraction parameter $\beta \in [0, 1[$ together with the requirement 2.b) in the Definition 6 where the successor states satisfy $(\xi_{t+1}, \hat{\xi}_{t+1}) \in R(\kappa + \beta\varepsilon)$ whenever $(\xi_t, \hat{\xi}_t, \nu_t, \hat{\nu}_t) \in R(\varepsilon)$ and $\mathsf{d}(\nu_t, \hat{\nu}_t) = 0$.

With the following corollary, we provide a bound on ε_t that depends solely on the behavior (ξ, ν) of S and not on the choice of a related behavior $(\hat{\xi}, \hat{\nu})$ of $\hat{S}$.

COROLLARY 1. *Given the premises of Theorem 3, let the function* $\Gamma : X \times U \to \mathbb{R}_{\geq 0} \cup \{\infty\}$ *be given by*

$$\Gamma(x, u) := \sup\{\mathsf{d}(u, \hat{u}) \mid \exists\varepsilon, \exists\hat{x} : (x, \hat{x}, u, \hat{u}) \in R(\varepsilon)\}. \tag{8}$$

For any two behaviors (ξ, ν) *and* $(\hat{\xi}, \hat{\nu})$ *of* S *and* $\hat{S}$, *respectively, that satisfy (7),* ε_t *in (7) is bounded by*

$$\varepsilon_{t+1} \leq \max_{t' \in [0;t]} \mu_\Delta(\gamma_\Delta \Gamma(\xi_t, \nu_t), t - t') + \kappa_\Delta$$

with $\kappa_\Delta = \kappa/(1-\beta)$, $\gamma_\Delta = \lambda/(\beta'-\beta)$ *and* $\mu_\Delta(r,t) = (\beta')^t r$ *for any* $\beta' \in]\beta, 1[$.

We are now ready to state the main result of this section where we show that pIODS is preserved under acIOSR. As in the in case of SR and aSR, the proof strategy is to establish a pIODS inequality for S in terms of the pIODS inequality given for $\hat{S}$. For acIODS, the estimates of the cost functions I and O in terms of the cost functions $\hat{I}$ and $\hat{O}$ depend on the time varying parameter ε_t. That is reflected in the following theorem, by a modification of the input costs I of S to $I' = \max\{I, \Gamma\}$. Here, Γ is the function that we used in Corollary 1 to established a bound on ε_t. It represents the mismatch of the inputs U and $\hat{U}$ measured in terms of d.

THEOREM 4. *Let* (S, I, O) *and* $(\hat{S}, \hat{I}, \hat{O})$ *be systems with costs functions and suppose there exists a* (κ, β, λ)*-acIOSR* $R(\varepsilon)$ *from* (S, I, O) *to* $(\hat{S}, \hat{I}, \hat{O})$ *with distance function* d. *Then,* $(\hat{S}, \hat{I}, \hat{O})$ *being pIODS implies that* (S, I', O) *is pIODS, with* $I'(x,u) = \max\{I(x,u), \Gamma(x,u)\}$ *and* Γ *given by* (8).

If the inequality $\hat{I} \leq I$ holds, we can provide an pIODS type inequality for S that can be easily described in terms of the parameters of the pIODS inequality of $\hat{S}$.

COROLLARY 2. *Given the premises of Theorem 4, suppose* γ_O *satisfies* $\gamma_O(r+r') \leq \gamma_O(r) + \gamma_O(r')$ *and that* $\hat{I}(\hat{x}, \hat{u}) \leq I(x,u)$ *holds for all* $(x, \hat{x}, u, \hat{u}) \in R(\varepsilon)$ *and* $(\hat{S}, \hat{I}, \hat{O})$ *is* $(\hat{\gamma}, \hat{\mu}, \hat{\rho})$*-pIODS, then every behavior* (ξ, ν) *of* S *satisfies*

$$O(\xi_t, \nu_t) \leq \max_{t' \in [0;t]} \hat{\mu}(\hat{\gamma}(I(\xi_{t'}, \nu_{t'})), t-t') + \max_{t' \in [0;t]} \gamma_O\big(\mu_\Delta(\gamma'_\Delta \Gamma(\xi_{t'}, \nu_{t'}), t-t')\big) + \gamma_O(\kappa_\Delta) + \hat{\rho} \tag{9}$$

with $\gamma'_\Delta(r) = \max\{r, \gamma_\Delta(r)\}$, μ_Δ *and* κ_Δ *from Corollary 1.*

Even though in Theorem 4, contrary to the results in Theorem 1 and Theorem 2, we do not characterize the parameters (μ, γ, ρ) of the pIODS inequality for S in dependency of the parameters $(\hat{\mu}, \hat{\gamma}, \hat{\rho})$, inequality (9) provides us with some insights. The first term in the inequality (9) follows from the fact that we were able to successfully verify pIODS for $\hat{S}$. The second term in (9) accounts for the "mismatch" between the inputs U and $\hat{U}$. The last two terms, i.e., the constant offset $\gamma_O(\kappa_\Delta) + \hat{\rho}$, is a result of the lower bound on the parameter $\varepsilon \geq \kappa$ and $\hat{\rho}$ from the pIODS inequality of $\hat{S}$.

We conclude this section with an application of Theorem 4 to Example 1.

EXAMPLE 1 (CONTINUED). *Recall that, every behavior* $(\hat{\xi}, \hat{\nu})$ *of* $\hat{S}$ *satisfies* $\hat{O}(\hat{\xi}_t, \hat{\nu}_t) = 0$ *for all* $t \in \mathbb{N}$. *Therefore* $(\hat{S}, \hat{I}, \hat{O})$ *is* $(\hat{\gamma}, \hat{\mu})$*-IODS with* $\hat{\gamma} = \hat{\mu} = 0$. *We obtain* Γ *for this example by* $\Gamma(x,u) = |u|$ *and the input cost* I' *coincides with* $I = \max\{I, \Gamma\} = I'$. *In addition, the inequality* $\hat{I} \leq I$ *holds and we can apply Corollary 2 to obtain the pIODS inequality for every behavior* (ξ, ν) *of* S *as*

$$|\xi_t|_D \leq \max_{t' \in [0;t]} \mu_\Delta(\gamma_\Delta |\nu_{t'}|, t-t') + \kappa_\Delta \tag{10}$$

with $\kappa_\Delta = 0.2/0.4$, $\gamma_\Delta = 1/(\beta' - 0.6)$ *and* $\mu_\Delta(r,t) = (\beta')^t r$ *for any* $\beta' \in]0.6, 1[$.

Let us shortly describe how this inequality shows the robustness of the invariance of D *with respect to* S *against the disturbances* ν. *First, let us ignore the constant* κ_Δ *on the right-hand-side of* (10). *Then, the distance between the state* ξ_t *and* D *is proportional to the norm of the disturbance* ν_t. *Moreover, the effect of a disturbance at some time* t' *disappears over time since* $\beta^{t-t'}\gamma_\Delta|\nu_{t'}|$ *approaches zeros as* $t \to \infty$. *The constant* κ_Δ *appears in* (10) *because we established the inequality through the use of the symbolic model* $\hat{S}$ *and represents the effect of quantization.*

5. CONTROLLER DESIGN

So far we interpreted the set of inputs U of a system S as disturbance inputs over which we had no control. However, in this section, we assume that the input set U is composed of a set of *control* inputs U^c and a set of *disturbance* inputs U^d, i.e., $U = U^c \times U^d$. Moreover, we introduce a controller that is allowed to modify the system behavior by imposing *restrictions* on the control inputs U^c. In our framework, a *controller for* S consists of a system S_C and a relation R_C. The *controlled system* $S_C \times_{R_C} S$ is given by the composition of S_C with S where R_C is used to restrict the control inputs U^c depending on the current state of S_C and S.

In [27], a synthesis approach has been developed to construct a controller $(\hat{S}_C, \hat{R}_C)$ rendering a *finite* system $\hat{S}$ IODS, i.e., the composed system $\hat{S}_C \times_{\hat{R}_C} \hat{S}$ is IODS[1]. In order to apply those results to a (possibly infinite) CPS S we first compute a finite symbolic model $\hat{S}$ of S and then provide a procedure to *transfer* (or *refine*) a controller $(\hat{S}_C, \hat{R}_C)$ that is designed for $\hat{S}$ to a controller (S_C, R_C) for S. This brings us to the main question answered in this section:

Given (S, I, O), *what are the conditions that a symbolic model* $\hat{S}$ *of* (S, I, O) *needs to satisfy so that the existence of a controller* $(\hat{S}_C, \hat{R}_C)$ *for* $\hat{S}$ *rendering* $\hat{S}_C \times_{\hat{R}_C} \hat{S}$ *pIODS, implies the existence of a controller* (S_C, R_C) *for* S *rendering* $S_C \times_{R_C} S$ *pIODS?*

A well-known approach for controller refinement in connection with symbolic models is based on *alternating simulation relations (ASR)*, see [1] and [26, Chapter 4.3]. In this section, we extend this approach to approximate contractive alternating input-output SR (acAIOSR). An intuitive version of the main result proved in this section is:

Consider two systems (S, I, O) *and* $(\hat{S}, \hat{I}, \hat{O})$, *and let* R *be an acAIOSR from* $(\hat{S}, \hat{I}, \hat{O})$ *to* (S, I, O). *Suppose there exists a controller* $(\hat{S}_C, \hat{R}_C)$ *for* $\hat{S}$ *such that* $(\hat{S}_C \times_{\hat{R}_C} \hat{S}, \hat{I}, \hat{O})$ *is pIODS. Then there exist a controller* (S_C, R_C) *for* S *such that* $(S_C \times_{R_C} S, I, O)$ *is pIODS.*

We provide a precise formulation of this statement in Theorem 5, after we formalize the notions of acAIOSR, controller, and composition of a system with a controller. Moreover, we explain how (S_C, R_C) can be constructed from $(\hat{S}_C, \hat{R}_C)$.

5.1 Alternating simulation relations

In the following definition of an ASR we use a refined notion of input sets associated to states given by:

$$U^c(x) := \{u^c \in U^c \mid \forall u^d \in U^d : r(x, u^c, u^d) \neq \varnothing\}.$$

DEFINITION 7. *Let* S *and* $\hat{S}$ *be two systems, let* $\kappa, \lambda \in \mathbb{R}_{\geq 0}$ *and* $\beta \in [0,1[$ *be parameters and consider a map* $\mathsf{d} : \hat{U} \times U \to \mathbb{R}_{\geq 0}$. *We call a parameterized (by* $\varepsilon \in [\kappa, \infty[$*) relation* $R(\varepsilon) \subseteq \hat{X} \times X \times \hat{U} \times U$ *a* κ-approximate (β,λ)-contractive alternating simulation relation ((κ,β,λ)-acASR) from $\hat{S}$ to S with distance function d *if* $R(\varepsilon) \subseteq R(\varepsilon')$ *holds for all* $\varepsilon \leq \varepsilon'$ *and we have for all* $\varepsilon \in [\kappa, \infty[$

[1]Technically, the controller in [27] is defined in a slightly different manner from $(\hat{S}_C, \hat{R}_C)$. However, it is straightforward to obtain a controller $(\hat{S}_C, \hat{R}_C)$ from the controller given in [27].

1. $\forall \hat{x}_0 \in \hat{X}_0, \exists x_0 \in X_0 : (\hat{x}_0, x_0) \in R_X(\kappa)$;

2. $\forall (x, \hat{x}) \in R_X(\varepsilon), \forall \hat{u}^c \in \hat{U}^c(\hat{x}), \exists u^c \in U^c(x)$,

   (a) $\forall u^d \in U^d, \exists \hat{u}^d \in \hat{U}^d$:
   - $(\hat{x}, x, \hat{u}, u) \in R(\varepsilon)$;
   - $\forall x' \in r(x, u), \exists \hat{x}' \in \hat{r}(\hat{x}, \hat{u})$:
     $(\hat{x}', x') \in R_X(\kappa + \beta\varepsilon + \lambda \mathsf{d}(\hat{u}, u))$;

   with $u := (u^c, u^d)$, $\hat{u} := (\hat{u}^c, \hat{u}^d)$.

Let (S, I, O) and $(\hat{S}, \hat{I}, \hat{O})$ be two systems with cost functions. We call a (κ, β, λ)-acASR $R(\varepsilon)$ from $\hat{S}$ to S with distance function d *a* κ-approximate (β, λ)-contractive alternating input-output SR ((κ, β, λ)-acAIOSR) from $(\hat{S}, \hat{I}, \hat{O})$ to (S, I, O) with distance function d *if there exist $\gamma_O, \gamma_I \in \mathcal{K}$ such that*

$$\begin{aligned} \hat{I}(\hat{x}, \hat{u}) &\le I(x, u) + \gamma_I(\varepsilon') \\ O(x, u) &\le \hat{O}(\hat{x}, \hat{u}) + \gamma_O(\varepsilon') \end{aligned} \tag{11}$$

with $\varepsilon' := \max\{\varepsilon, \mathsf{d}(\hat{u}, u)\}$ holds for all $(\hat{x}, x, \hat{u}, u) \in R(\varepsilon)$.

We call a relation $R(\varepsilon)$ acASR (acAIOSR) *if there exists $\beta \in [0, 1[$, $\kappa, \lambda \in \mathbb{R}_{\ge 0}$ such that $R(\varepsilon)$ is a (κ, β, λ)-acASR (acAIOSR) from $\hat{S}$ to S ($(\hat{S}, \hat{I}, \hat{O})$ to (S, I, O)).*

We illustrate acAIOSR using an example from the literature.

EXAMPLE 2 (DC-DC BOOST CONVERTER). *We consider a popular example from the literature, the boost DC-DC converter, see for example [10]. The dynamics of the boost converter is given by a two-dimensional switched linear system $\dot{\xi}(t) = \bar{A}_u \xi(t) + \bar{B}$ with $\bar{A}_u \in \mathbb{R}^{2\times 2}$, $\bar{B} \in \mathbb{R}^2$ and $u \in \{1, 2\}$. In [10] a symbolic model $\hat{S}$ of the sampled dynamics of the boost converter S is used to compute a controller rendering the set $D = [1.3, 1.7] \times [5.7, 5.8]$ positively invariant. Similarly to the approach in this paper, a symbolic model $\hat{S}$ together with an approximate ASR $\hat{R}$ is first computed. In the second step, a controller $(\hat{S}_C, \hat{R}_C)$ for $\hat{S}$ is computed to render D positively invariant with respect to the symbolic model $\hat{S}_C \times_{\hat{R}_C} \hat{S}$. Afterwards, a controller for S is obtained by refining the controller $(\hat{S}_C, \hat{R}_C)$.*

Note, as the controller refinement in [10] is based on an ε-approximate ASR with constant $\varepsilon \in \mathbb{R}_{\ge 0}$, a disturbance $w \in \mathbb{R}^2$ on the system dynamics $\dot{\xi}(t) = \bar{A}_u \xi(t) + \bar{B} + w$ might lead to a state $\xi(\tau)$ such that the composed system is blocking. Therefore, the resulting controller is prone to fail in the presence of disturbances. Contrary to that, we exploit the contractivity of the matrices $\bar{A}_u$ and construct a robust controller using the introduced notion of acAIOSR.

In this example, we use the same parameters as in [10], and obtain the sampled dynamics of the boost converter as $\xi_{t+1} = A_{\nu_t}\xi_t + B_{\nu_t} + \omega_t$ with the system matrices given by

$$A_1 = \begin{bmatrix} 0.9917 & 0 \\ 0 & 0.9964 \end{bmatrix}, \quad B_1 = \begin{bmatrix} 0.1660 \\ 0 \end{bmatrix},$$
$$A_2 = \begin{bmatrix} 0.9903 & -0.0330 \\ 0.0354 & 0.9959 \end{bmatrix}, B_2 = \begin{bmatrix} 0.1659 \\ 0.0030 \end{bmatrix}.$$

Note that in contrast to [10] we add $\omega_t \in \mathbb{R}^2$ to model various disturbances. We introduce the system $S = (X, X_0, U, r)$ associated with the boost converter by defining $X := \mathbb{R}^2$, $X_0 := D$, $U := U^c \times U^d$ with $U^c := \{1, 2\}$ and $U^d := \mathbb{R}^2$. Note that the inputs $(u^c, u^d) \in U$ of the system S correspond to the control input $u^c = u$ and the disturbance $u^d = w$. The transition function is given by $r(x, (u^c, u^d)) := \{A_{u^c}x + B + u^d\}$. We use the cost functions $I(x, (u^c, u^d)) := |u^d|$ and $O(x, u) := |x|_D$ to quantify the disturbances and to encode the desired behavior.

The symbolic model $\hat{S} = (\hat{X}, \hat{X}_0, \hat{U}, \hat{r})$ that is used in [10] is based on a discretization of D:

$$\hat{X} := \hat{X}_0 := D \cap \{x \in \mathbb{R}^2 \mid x_i = k_i 2/\sqrt{2}\kappa, i \in \{1, 2\}, k_i \in \mathbb{Z}\}$$

with $\kappa = 0.25 \cdot 10^{-3}/\sqrt{2}$. The inputs are given by $\hat{U} := \hat{U}^c \times \hat{U}^d$ with $\hat{U}^c := \{1, 2\}$ and $\hat{U}^d := \{0\}$. The transition function is implicitly given by $\hat{x}' \in \hat{r}(\hat{x}, (\hat{u}, 0)) \iff |\hat{x}' - A_{\hat{u}}\hat{x} - B_{\hat{u}}|_2 \le \kappa$.

We set the cost functions for $\hat{S}$ simply to $\hat{I}(\hat{x}, \hat{u}) := 0$ and $\hat{O}(\hat{x}, \hat{u}) := 0$ since $I(\hat{x}, \hat{u}) = O(\hat{x}, \hat{u}) = 0$ holds for all $\hat{x}$ and $\hat{u}$. Let us introduce the relation $R(\varepsilon) := R_X(\varepsilon) \times R_U$ with

$$\begin{aligned} R_X(\varepsilon) &:= \{(\hat{x}, x) \in \hat{X} \times X \mid |\hat{x} - x|_2 \le \varepsilon\} \\ R_U &:= \{((\hat{u}^c, 0), (u^c, u^d)) \in \hat{U} \times U \mid u^c = \hat{u}^c\}. \end{aligned}$$

We now show that $R(\varepsilon)$ is a (κ, β, λ)-acAIOSR from $\hat{S}$ to S with $\mathsf{d}((u^c, u^d), (\hat{u}^c, 0)) := |u^d|_2$ for $\beta = 0.997 \ge \max\{|A_1|_2, |A_2|_2\}$ and $\lambda = 1$. We first note that $R(\varepsilon) \subseteq R(\varepsilon')$ holds whenever $\varepsilon \le \varepsilon'$. By definition of $\hat{X}_0$ we can see that for every $\hat{x}_0 \in \hat{X}_0$ there exists a $x_0 \in X_0$ such that $(\hat{x}_0, x_0) \in R_X(\kappa)$. We proceed by checking 2) of Definition 7. Let $(\hat{x}, x) \in R_X(\varepsilon)$ and $\hat{u}^c \in \hat{U}^c$. We choose $u^c = \hat{u}^c$ and see that for every $u^d \in U^d$ we have $(\hat{x}, x, (\hat{u}^c, 0), (u^c, u^d)) \in R(\varepsilon)$ and $(\hat{x}', x') \in R_X(\kappa + \beta\varepsilon + \lambda|u^d|_2)$ with $x' \in r(x, (u^c, u^d))$, $\hat{x}' \in \hat{r}(\hat{x}, (\hat{u}^c, 0))$ since

$$|x' - \hat{x}'|_2 \le \kappa + |A_{u^c}x + u^d - A_{u^c}\hat{x}|_2 \le \kappa + \beta\varepsilon + |u^d|_2$$

which shows that $R(\varepsilon)$ is an (κ, β, λ)-acASR from $\hat{S}$ to S. As the inequalities (11) *hold for $\gamma_I = 0$ and $\gamma_O(c) = c$ we conclude that $R_1(\varepsilon)$ is an acAIOSR from $(\hat{S}, \hat{I}, \hat{O})$ to (S, I, O).*

Similarly to previous examples, we exploited the contraction property of the control system to construct an acASR from the symbolic model $\hat{S}$ to S.

We resume the example after we presented the main theorem of this section, where we refine the controller for the symbolic model $\hat{S}$ to a controller for S.

5.2 System composition

In this subsection, we define a general notion of system composition between two systems S_1 and S_2 with respect to a relation $H \subseteq X_1 \times X_2 \times U_1 \times U_2$. Afterwards, we introduce the notion of system composition for the case when H is an acASR $R(\varepsilon)$ from S_1 to S_2. In the next subsection, we use the definition of system composition to define the controlled system.

DEFINITION 8. *The* composition of system S_1 and S_2 with respect to the relation $H \subseteq X_1 \times X_2 \times U_1 \times U_2$, *is denoted by $S_{12} := S_1 \times_H S_2$ and defined by:*

1. $X_{12} := X_1 \times X_2$;
2. $X_{120} := (X_{10} \times X_{20}) \cap H_X$;
3. $U_{12} := U_1 \times U_2$;
4. $(x_1', x_2') \in r_{12}((x_1, x_2), (u_1, u_2)) :\iff$
   (a) $x_2' \in r_1(x_1, u_1)$;
   (b) $x_1' \in r_2(x_2, u_2)$;
   (c) $(x_1, x_2, u_1, u_2) \in H$ and $(x_1', x_2') \in H_X$.

If H is an (κ, β, λ)-acASR $R(\varepsilon)$ from S_1 to S_2 with distance function d, *then we exchange 2) by $X_{120} := (X_{10} \times X_{20}) \cap R_X(\kappa)$ and 4.c) by*

$$(x_1, x_2, u_1, u_2) \in R(e(x_1, x_2)), \quad \text{and} \quad (x_1', x_2') \in R_X(\varepsilon')$$

with $\varepsilon' := \kappa + e(x_1, x_2)\beta + \lambda \mathsf{d}(u_1, u_2)$ *and* $e(x_1, x_2) := \inf\{\varepsilon \in \mathbb{R}_{\geq 0} \mid (x_1, x_2) \in R_X(\varepsilon)\}$.

Intuitively, our definition of system composition corresponds to the well-known definition of parallel composition of the systems S_1 and S_2 with synchronization defined by H, respectively $R(\varepsilon)$. The only transitions allowed on the composed system $S_1 \times_H S_2$ are those for which the corresponding states and inputs belong to H, i.e., $(x_1, x_2, u_1, u_2) \in H$. It is shown in [26] how this notion of composition can describe series, parallel, feedback and several other interconnections. For the case that H is an acASR $R(\varepsilon)$, we require that $(x_1, x_2, u_1, u_2) \in R(\varepsilon)$ where we fix $\varepsilon = e(x_1, x_2)$. With our particular choice of $\varepsilon = e(x_1, x_2)$ we restrict the transitions of the composed system $S_1 \times_{R(\varepsilon)} S_2$ to those states and inputs that are related by the smallest $\varepsilon = e(x_1, x_2)$ possible. In general it is not ensured that the infimal $\varepsilon = e(x_1, x_2)$ is actually attained by the states (x_1, x_2). Therefore, we assume in the following that

$$e(x_1, x_2) < \infty \implies (x_1, x_2) \in R_X(e(x_1, x_2)). \quad (12)$$

Note that this assumption is often satisfied in practice where $R_X(\varepsilon)$ is for example defined by $|x_1 - x_2| \leq \varepsilon$.

5.3 The controlled system and controller refinement

In the following, we use the composition of two systems S_C and S with respect to a parameterized relation $R_C(\varepsilon)$ to define the controlled system $S_C \times_{R_C(\varepsilon)} S$, when the relation $R_C(\varepsilon)$ is an acASR from S_C to S. From a control perspective, the controller $(S_C, R_C(\varepsilon))$ for S can be implemented in a feedback loop as follows. Let us denote the set of initial states $x \in X_0$ for which there exists $x_C \in X_{C0}$ such that $(x_C, x) \in R_{C,X}(\kappa)$ by X_0'. Then initially, **i)** the controller measures the system state $x \in X_0'$ and determines a related controller state $x_C \in X_{C0}$ such that $(x_C, x) \in R_X(\kappa)$; **ii)** the controller picks the control inputs u_C^c and u^c according to 2) in Definition 7 and applies u^c to S; **iii)** the disturbance chooses $u^d \in U^d$ and $x' \in r(x, (u^c, u^d))$; **iv)** the controller measures the new state x' and chooses x_C' and $u_C^d \in U_C^d$ such that $x_C' \in r_C(x_C, (u_C^c, u_C^d))$ and $(x_C', x') \in R_X(\varepsilon')$ for $\varepsilon' = e(x_C', x')$. Now the cycle continues with **ii)**.

Note that in this scenario, the disturbance inputs U_C^d of the controller S_C are not considered as external inputs, but are allowed to be chosen by the controller. This leads us to the following the definition.

DEFINITION 9. *Given a system S, we call the pair $(S_C, R_C(\varepsilon))$ a* controller for S *if S_C is a system, $R_C(\varepsilon)$ is an acASR from S_C to S and the composed system $S_C \times_{R_C(\varepsilon)} S$ is non-blocking, in the sense that for all reachable states (x_C, x) there exists $(u_C^c, u^c) \in U_C^c \times U^c$ such that for all $u^d \in U^d$ there exists $u_C^d \in U_C^d$ for which $r'((x_C, x), ((u_C^c, u_C^d), (u^c, u^d))) \neq \varnothing$, where r' is the transition map of the composed system.*

The interested reader may wish to consult [26, Chapter 6.1] for detailed explanations of why the composition between a controller and a system is only well defined when the relation R_C is alternating. Note that the assumption (13) is consistent with the use of extended alternating simulation relations in the definition of the feedback composition in [26, Definition 6.1].

Let us remark that the controller $(\hat{S}_C, \hat{R}_C)$ rendering the system $\hat{S}$ pIODS that we obtain from the approach in [27] is given in terms of a system $\hat{S}_C$ and an *alternating simulation relation* (ASR) from $\hat{S}_C$ to $\hat{S}$ rather than an acASR. The definition of an ASR is given in [26, Definition 4.22]. Instead of repeating the definition here, we define it in terms of an acASR.

DEFINITION 10. *Let S and $\hat{S}$ be two systems and let $R(\varepsilon)$ be a $(0, 0, 0)$-acASR from $\hat{S}$ to S. The relation $\hat{R} := R(0)$ is called an* alternating simulation relation (ASR) *from $\hat{S}$ to S.*

The composition $S_1 \times_{R_{12}} S_2$ of S_2 and S_1 with respect to an ASR R_{12} follows from Definition 8 with $H = R_{12}$. Similarly, the definition of a controller (S_C, R_C) in terms of an ASR follows in a straightforward manner from Definition 9. No confusion between acASR and ASR should arise, since we always include the parameter ε in the notation when we refer to an acASR (acAIOSR) $R(\varepsilon)$.

In the following, we assume that an ASR R_{12} from S_2 to S_1 satisfies

$$\begin{aligned} &(x_1, x_2, (u_1^c, u_1^d), (u_2^c, u_2^d)) \in R_{12} \implies \\ &\qquad (x_1, x_2, u_1^c, u_2^c) \text{ satisfies 2.a) of Def. 7.} \end{aligned} \quad (13)$$

This implication (13) results in no loss of generality since we can always construct an ASR R_{12}' that satisfies (13) from an ASR R_{12} by simply removing the elements that don't satisfy (13).

Given a system with cost functions (S, I, O) and a controller (S_C, R_C) for S, we abuse the notation and use $(S_C \times_{R_C} S, I, O)$ to refer to the composed system $S_C \times_{R_C} S$ with cost functions $I_C((x_C, x), (u_C, u)) := I(x, u)$ and $O_C((x_C, x), (u_C, u)) := O(x, u)$.

Like in Corollary 1, we define the function

$$\Gamma(x, u) := \sup\{\mathsf{d}(\hat{u}, u) \mid \exists \varepsilon, \exists \hat{x} : (\hat{x}, x, \hat{u}, u) \in R(\varepsilon)\} \quad (14)$$

for an acAIOSR $R(\varepsilon)$ from $\hat{S}$ to S with distance function d and refer to $R(\varepsilon)$ as *acAIOSR from $\hat{S}$ to S with Γ*.

Now we are ready to state the main theorem.

THEOREM 5. *Given two systems with cost functions (S, I, O) and $(\hat{S}, \hat{I}, \hat{O})$, let $R(\varepsilon)$ be an acAIOSR from $(\hat{S}, \hat{I}, \hat{O})$ to (S, I, O) with Γ and let $R(\varepsilon)$ satisfy (12). Suppose there exists a controller $(\hat{S}_C, \hat{R}_C)$ for $\hat{S}$ such that $(\hat{S}_C \times_{\hat{R}_C} \hat{S}, \hat{O}, \hat{I})$ is pIODS and $\hat{R}_C$ satisfies (13). Then there exists a controller $(S_C, R_C(\varepsilon))$ for S such that $(S_C \times_{R_C(\varepsilon)} S, I', O)$ is pIODS with $I' := \max\{I, \Gamma\}$.*

REMARK 1. *Note that we use Theorem 4 to ensure that the controlled system $S_C \times_{R_C(\varepsilon)} S$ is pIODS. If γ_O satisfies the triangle inequality and $\hat{I}(\hat{x}, \hat{u}) \leq I(x, u)$ holds for every $(\hat{x}, x, \hat{u}, u) \in R(\varepsilon)$ and $\varepsilon \in \mathbb{R}_{\geq 0}$, the premises of Corollary 2 are satisfied and it follows that every behavior $((\xi_C, \xi), (\nu_C, \nu))$ of $S_C \times_{R_C(\varepsilon)} S$ satisfies (9).*

REMARK 2. *The controller $(S_C, R_C(\varepsilon))$ for S_C is given by $S_C = \hat{S}_C \times_{\hat{R}_C} \hat{S}$ where $R_C(\varepsilon)$ equals*

$$\{((\hat{x}_C, \hat{x}), x, (\hat{u}_C, \hat{u}), u) \mid (\hat{x}, x, \hat{u}, u) \in R(\varepsilon) \wedge (\hat{x}_C, \hat{x}) \in \hat{R}_{C,X}\}.$$

EXAMPLE 2 (DC-DC BOOST CONVERTER (CONTINUED)). *We use $(\hat{S}_C, \hat{R}_C)$ to denote the controller from [10] that renders D positively invariant with respect to $S_C := \hat{S}_C \times_{\hat{R}_C} \hat{S}$. Therefore, any behavior $((\hat{\xi}_C, \hat{\xi}), (\hat{\nu}_C, \hat{\nu}))$ of $\hat{S}_C \times_{\hat{R}_C} \hat{S}$ satisfies $O(\xi_t, \nu_t) = I(\xi_t, \nu_t) = 0$ and it follows that $\hat{S}_C \times_{\hat{R}_C} \hat{S}$ is $(\hat{\gamma}, \hat{\mu})$-IODS with $\hat{\gamma} = 0$ and $\hat{\mu} = 0$.*

We apply Theorem 5 and conclude that $S_C \times_{R_C(\varepsilon)} S$ is pIODS with input costs $\max\{I, \Gamma\} = |u^d|_2$, since Γ induced by $R(\varepsilon)$ and d is given by $|u^d|_2$. Note that the assumptions of Corollary 2 hold and we can conclude that any behavior $((\xi_C, \xi), (\nu_C, \nu))$ of $S_C \times_{R_C(\varepsilon)} S$ satisfies

$$|\xi_t|_D \leq \max_{t' \in [0;t]} \mu_\Delta(\gamma_\Delta(|\nu_{t'}^d|_2), t - t') + \kappa_\Delta$$

where with $\mu_\Delta(r,t) := (\beta')^t r$, $\gamma_\Delta = 1/(\beta' - \beta)$ and $\kappa_\Delta := \kappa/(1-\beta)$ for some $\beta' \in]\beta, 1[$.

The pIODS inequality implies that the system may leave the set D in the presence of disturbances, however in absence of disturbances the system either stays in $D + \mathbb{B}(\kappa_\Delta)$ or asymptotically approaches $D + \mathbb{B}(\kappa_\Delta)$. Moreover, contrary to the approach in [10] the closed-loop system $S_C \times_{R_C(\varepsilon)} S$ is non-blocking even in the presents of unbounded disturbances.

6. A MOBILE ROBOT EXAMPLE

In Example 2 we used the contraction property of the system matrices to establish an acAIOSR from the symbolic model to the concrete system. As a consequence, we could neglect the continuous disturbances on the symbolic model, but nevertheless establish the pIODS inequality. We demonstrate in this section, how this procedure leads to a *separation of concerns* when designing a robust controller for a mobile robot, where a continuous "low-level" controller and a discrete "high-level" controller provides robustness with respect to continuous and discrete disturbances, respectively. In particular, we use a low-level feedback controller to enforce the contraction property needed to establish an acAIOSR from the symbolic model (without continuous disturbances) to the concrete system. Then we use the synthesis approach in [27] to design a discrete high-level controller that renders the symbolic model robust against discrete disturbances. Afterwards, we refine the discrete controller to the original system according to Remark 2. It follows from Theorem 5 that the controlled robot is robust against the continuous as well as discrete disturbances.

We consider a simple mobile robot that moves in the plane $x \in \mathbb{R}^2$. We assume that we can control (using $u \in \mathbb{R}^2$) the robot independently in the x_1 and x_2 directions. Moreover, the robot drive is equipped with low-level controllers that we use to enforce the sampled-data dynamics

$$x^+ = 0.8x + u + w. \tag{15}$$

We use $w \in \mathbb{R}^2$ to model actuator errors and/or sensor noise. A real-world example of a robot that fits our assumptions is *Robotino*, see [30].

In order to apply the theory from the previous sections, we cast (15) as the system $S_c = (X_c, X_{c0}, U_c, r_c)$ with $X_c = \mathbb{R}^2$, $X_{c0} = \{x_{c0}\}$, $U_c = U_c^c \times U_c^d$, $U_c^c = U_c^d = \mathbb{R}^2$ and r_c is defined in the obvious way.

We assume that the high-level control signal u is sent to the actuator via a wireless connection where package dropouts might occur. However, for simplicity of the presentation, we assume that two packages are never dropped consecutively. We use the system $S_a = (X_a, X_{a0}, U_a, r_a)$ with $X_a = \{a_0, a_1\}$, $X_{a0} = X_a$ and $U_a = U_a^d = D$ and $D = \{\bot, \top\}$ to model that behavior. The dynamics r_a of the model is illustrated in the figure below. Our model of the wireless communication acts like a switch with respect to the control input $\bar{u} \in \mathbb{R}^2$. If a package dropout occurs, i.e., $x_a = a_1$, we apply zero as control input $u = 0$. If no dropout occurs, i.e., $x_a = a_0$, the control input is $u = \bar{u}$ since the robot successfully received a control update.

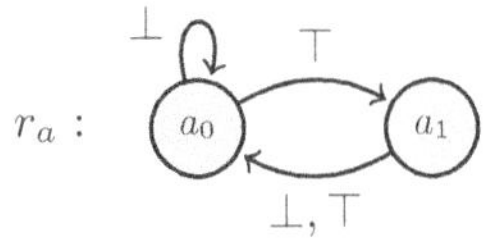

We would like to enforce the periodic behavior which we express as a cycle along the states displayed in Figure 2. In order to express our desired behavior in terms of the output costs, we introduce a system $S_r = (X_r, \{r_0\}, U_r, r_r)$ with $X_r = \{r_i\}$, $i \in \{0, \ldots, 7\}$,

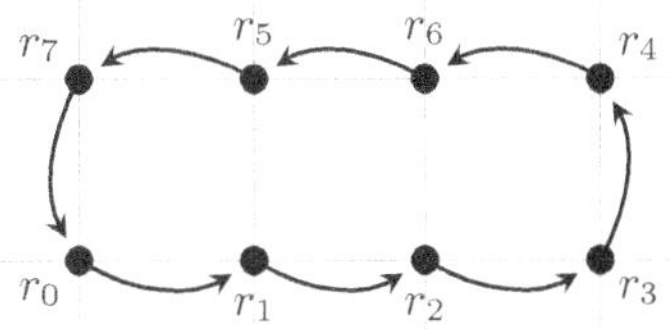

Figure 2: Desired trajectory in the state space.

$X_{r0} = \{r_0\}$, $U_r = \{\epsilon\}$ and $r_r(x_r, u_r)$ given according to Figure 2. The reference states $r_i \in \mathbb{R}^2$ are given by

$$r_0 = [0,0]^\top, r_1 = [1,0]^\top, r_2 = [2,0]^\top, r_3 = [3,0]^\top,$$
$$r_4 = [3,1]^\top, r_5 = [2,1]^\top, r_6 = [1,1]^\top, r_7 = [0,1]^\top$$

The CPS $S = (X, X_0, U, r, I, O)$ is given by the composition of S_c, S_a and S_r, i.e., $X := X_c \times X_a \times X_r$, $X_0 := \{r_0\} \times \{a_0, a_1\} \times \{r_0\}$, $U := U_c \times U_a$. The transition function is defined implicitly by $(x_c', x_a', x_r') \in r((x_c, x_a, x_r), (u_c, u_a))$ iff

$$x_c' \in \begin{cases} r_c(x_c, u_c) & \text{if } x_a = a_0 \\ r_c(x_c, 0) & \text{if } x_a = a_1 \end{cases}$$
$$x_a' \in r_a(x_a, u_a)$$
$$x_r' \in r_r(x_r, \epsilon).$$

We define the output costs $O : X_c \times X_r \to \mathbb{R}_{\geq 0}$ by

$$O(x_c, x_r) := |x_c - x_r|$$

and choose the input costs $I : X_a \times U_c^d \to \mathbb{R}_{\geq 0}$ simply to

$$I(x_a, u^d) := I_d(x_a) + |u^d|,$$

with $I_d(a_0) := 0$ and $I_d(a_1) := 1$, where we omitted the independent variables of O and I. The value of the output costs indicates how well the robot is following the nominal behavior. The costs are zero, if the robot follows the system S_r and non-zero otherwise. The input costs are used to quantify the possible disturbances.

The symbolic model. We continue with the construction of the symbolic model $\hat{S}$ for S. First we introduce the symbolic model $\hat{S}_c$ of S_c based on a discretization of the state space and input space of S_c. We choose $\hat{X}_c = [[-1,4]^2]_\kappa$, $\hat{U}_c^c = [[-3,3]^2]_\kappa$ and $\hat{U}_c^d = \{[0,0]^\top\}$. Note that we neglect the disturbances U_c^d on the symbolic model $\hat{S}_c$. We set the discretization parameter to $\kappa = 0.05$. We obtain the symbolic model $\hat{S}$ again by the composition of $\hat{S}_c$, S_a and S_r. We proceed in the same manner as in the definition of S but use $\hat{S}_c$ in place of S_c. The cost functions $\hat{I}$ and $\hat{O}$ for $\hat{S}$ are defined by $\hat{I}(x_a) := I_d(x_a)$ and

$$\hat{O}(\hat{x}_c, x_a, x_r) := \max\{|\hat{x}_c - x_r| - \kappa, 0\}.$$

We use the synthesis approach in [27] to compute a controller $(\hat{S}_c, \hat{R}_c)$ that renders the system $\hat{S}$ IODS. As a result, we obtain the IODS inequality

$$\hat{O}(\xi_{c,t}) \leq \max_{t' \in [0;t]} \{1.4 I_d(\xi_{c,t'})) - 1.4(t - t')\} \tag{16}$$

for every behavior (ξ_c, ν_c) of the controlled system $S_c := \hat{S} \times_{\hat{R}_c} \hat{S}_c$. Note that with $\gamma = \eta = 1.4$ the effect of the disturbance $x_a = a_1$ at time t disappears after one step. Due to the limited space, we don't provide further details on the controller $(\hat{S}_c, \hat{R}_c)$.

The IODS inequality. Let us introduce the relation $R(\varepsilon) = R_X(\varepsilon) \times R_U \subseteq X \times \hat{X} \times U \times \hat{U}$ defined by

$$R_X(\varepsilon) = \{(x_c, x_{ar}), (\hat{x}_c, \hat{x}_{ar}) \mid |x_c - \hat{x}_c| \leq \varepsilon \wedge x_{ar} = \hat{x}_{ar}\}$$
$$R_U = \{(u_c^c, u_c^d, u_a), (\hat{u}_c^c, \hat{u}_c^d, \hat{u}_a^d) \mid u_c^c = \hat{u}_c^c \wedge u_a^d = \hat{u}_a^d\}.$$

We leave it to the reader to verify that $R(\varepsilon)$ is a (κ, β, λ)-acAIOSR from $\hat{S}$ to S with parameters $\beta = 0.8$, $\lambda = 1$, distance function $\mathsf{d}_{\mathsf{U}}((u_c^c, u_c^d, u_a^d), (\hat{u}_c^c, 0, \hat{u}_a^d)) := |u_c^d|$, $\gamma_I = 0$ and $\gamma_O(c) = c + \min\{c, \kappa\}$.

We apply Theorem 5 and see that the $S \times_{R_c(\varepsilon)} S_c$ is pIODS. Furthermore, from Remark 1 and Corollary 2 the inequality follows

$$
\begin{aligned}
O(\xi_t) \leq & \max_{t' \in [0;t]} \{1.4 I_d(\xi_t) - 1.4(t - t')\} + \\
& \max_{t' \in [0,t]} \tfrac{1}{\beta' - 0.8} (\beta')^{t-t'} |\pi_{U_c^d}(\nu_{t'})| + 0.3
\end{aligned}
$$

for any behavior (ξ, ν) of $S \times_{R_c(\varepsilon)} S_c$ for some $\beta' \in [0.8, 1[$.

This example demonstrates nicely how our results enable us to separate the design procedure to establish robustness with respect to continuous and discrete disturbances. We used the low-level controllers of the robot to enforce the contractive dynamics (15) so that S admits an acAIOSR. We used the discrete design procedure [27] to establish the IODS inequality (16) for the symbolic model with respect to the discrete disturbances. As the previous pIODS inequality shows, the final controlled system is robust with respect to both discrete as well as continuous disturbances.

7. FUTURE WORK

Although the construction of an approximate contractive ASR for a continuous control systems follows by rather simple extensions of the methods presented in [20, 21, 10], a systematic approach to compute approximate contractive ASR for general CPS is still missing. We will address this problem in our future research.

8. REFERENCES

[1] R. Alur, T. Henzinger, O. Kupferman, and M. Y. Vardi. Alternating refinement relations. In *Concurrency Theory*, pages 163–178. Springer, 1998.

[2] R. Bloem, K. Chatterjee, K. Greimel, T. A. Henzinger, and B. Jobstmann. Robustness in the presence of liveness. In *Computer Aided Verification*, pages 410–424, 2010.

[3] R. Bloem, K. Greimel, T. A. Henzinger, and B. Jobstmann. Synthesizing robust systems. In *Proc. of Int. Conf. on Formal Methods in Computer-Aided Design*, pages 85–92, 2009.

[4] C. Cai and A. R. Teel. Characterizations of input-to-state stability for hybrid systems. *Systems & Control Letters*, 58:47–53, 2009.

[5] S. Chaudhuri, S. Gulwani, and R. Lublinerman. Continuity and robustness of programs. *Communications of the ACM*, 55(8):107–115, 2012.

[6] K. H. Cho and J. T. Lim. Stability and robustness of discrete event dynamic systems. *International Journal of Systems Science*, 28:691–703, 1997.

[7] E. W. Dijkstra. Self-stabilizing systems in spite of distributed control. *Communications of the ACM*, 17:643–644, 1974.

[8] R. Ehlers. Generalized Rabin(1) synthesis with applications to robust system synthesis. In *NASA Formal Methods*, pages 101–115. Springer, 2011.

[9] A. Girard and G. J. Pappas. Approximation metrics for discrete and cont. systems. *IEEE TAC*, 52:782–798, 2007.

[10] A. Girard, G. Pola, and P. Tabuada. Approximately bisimilar symbolic models for incrementally stable switched systems. *IEEE TAC*, 55:116–126, 2010.

[11] L. Grüne. Input-to-state dynamical stability and its Lyapunov function characterization. *IEEE TAC*, 47:1499–1504, 2002.

[12] L. Grüne and P. Saint-Pierre. An invariance kernel representation of ISDS Lyapunov functions. *Systems & Control Letters*, 55:736–745, 2006.

[13] S. Huang, M. R. James, D. Nešić, and P.M. Dower. A unified approach to controller design for achieving iss and related properties. *IEEE TAC*, 50:1681–1697, 2005.

[14] W. Lohmiller and J.-J. Slotine. On contraction analysis for non-linear systems. *Automatica*, 34:683–696, 1998.

[15] R. Majumdar, E. Render, and P. Tabuada. Robust discrete synthesis against unspecified disturbances. In *Proc. of the 14th ACM Int. Conf. on HSCC*, pages 211–220, 2011.

[16] R. Majumdar and I. Saha. Symbolic robustness analysis. In *IEEE Real-Time Systems Symposium*, pages 355–363. IEEE Computer Society, 2009.

[17] R. Milner. *Communication and concurrency*. Prentice-Hall, 1989.

[18] K. M. Passino, A. N. Michel, and P. J. Antsaklis. Lyapunov stability of a class of discrete event systems. *IEEE TAC*, 39:269 –279, 1994.

[19] A. Pavlov, N. van de Wouw, and H. Nijmeijer. Convergent systems: analysis and synthesis. In *Control and observer design for nonlinear finite and infinite dimensional systems*, pages 131–146. Springer, 2005.

[20] G. Pola, A. Girard, and P. Tabuada. Approximately bisimilar symbolic models for nonlinear control systems. *Automatica*, 44:2508–2516, 2008.

[21] G. Pola and P. Tabuada. Symbolic models for nonlinear control systems: Alternating approximate bisimulations. *SICON*, 48:719–733, 2009.

[22] M. Roozbehani, A. Megretski, and E. Feron. Optimization of lyapunov invariants in verification of software systems. *IEEE TAC*, 58:696–711, 2013.

[23] M. Rungger and P. Tabuada. A symbolic approach to the design of robust cyber-physical systems. In *Proc. of the 52nd IEEE CDC*, 2013.

[24] A. Shahrokni and R. Feldt. A systematic review of software robustness. *Information and Software Tech.*, 55:1–17, 2013.

[25] E. D. Sontag. Input to State Stability: Basic concepts and results. *Nonlinear and optimal control theory*, 2008.

[26] P. Tabuada. *Verification and Control of Hybrid Systems – A Symbolic Approach*. Springer, 2009.

[27] P. Tabuada, A. Balkan, S. Y. Caliskan, Y. Shoukry, and R. Majumdar. Input-output robustness for discrete systems. In *Proc. of the 10th ACM Int. Conf. on Embedded Software*, pages 217–226, 2012.

[28] D. C. Tarraf, A. Megretski, and M. A. Dahleh. A framework for robust stability of systems over finite alphabets. *IEEE TAC*, 53:1133–1146, 2008.

[29] U. Topcu, N. Ozay, J. Liu, and R. M. Murray. On synthesizing robust discrete controllers under modeling uncertainty. In *Proc. of the 15th ACM Int. Conf. on HSCC*, pages 85–94, 2012.

[30] R. C. Weber and M. Bellenberg. *Robotino Manual, Festo Didactic GmbH & Co*, 2010.

[31] G. Zames. Input-output feedback stability and robustness, 1959–85. *IEEE Control Systems Magazine*, 16:61–66, 1996.

[32] H. Zhang and M. P. Dower. Computation of tight integral input-to-state stability bounds for nonlinear systems. *Systems & Control Letters*, 62:355—365, 2013.

Parameter Synthesis for Polynomial Biological Models[*] [†]

Tommaso Dreossi
University of Udine, Italy
VERIMAG, University Joseph Fourier
2 avenue de Vignate, 38610
GIERES, France
tommaso.dreossi@imag.fr

Thao Dang
CNRS/VERIMAG
2 avenue de Vignate, 38610
GIERES, France
thao.dang@imag.fr

ABSTRACT

Parameter determination is an important task in the development of biological models. In this paper we consider parametric polynomial dynamical systems and address the following parameter synthesis problem: find a set of parameter values so that the resulting system satisfies a desired property. Our synthesis technique exploits the Bernstein polynomial representation to solve the synthesis problem using linear programming. We apply our framework to two case studies involving epidemic models.

Categories and Subject Descriptors

G.1 [**Mathematics of Computing**]: Numerical Analysis

Keywords

Parameter synthesis; system biology; verification

1. INTRODUCTION

Mathematical models have been developed to study mechanisms and principles of biological processes. A particularity of such models is that they usually contain a large number of interdependent parameters, which are necessary to capture the details of components and interactions of the biological systems. To gain insight of a process, its models are often simulated and to this end a numerical value must be specified for every parameter. In order for the model to accurately simulate the actual process, its parameters are estimated by fitting the model outputs with the data obtained from experimental analysis. Nonlinear optimization algorithms can be used to account for a given set of experimental data. However, available experimental data are often incomplete and subject to measurement errors, and therefore they sometimes may not be sufficient to determine precise numerical values of the parameters, especially when the data are qualitative (such as behavioral patterns) rather than quantitative; consequently, uncertainty remains in the resulting parameter values. Even if all the parameters of a model are identifiable, the usefulness of the model also depends on its power to account for new sets of experimental data. Robustness with respect to changes in parameter values is thus an important criterion. To address these issues, it is of great interest to be able to analyze the behaviors of models with uncertain parameters, in order to determine parameter values allowing the model to produce the expected behaviors and to infer generic properties and test hypotheses.

This paper focuses on the following problem: given a dynamical system model with uncertain parameters, constrain the parameter space in order to guarantee that the model satisfies a desired property. For example, in the study of the transmission of communicable disease through individuals, presented in Section 7, one is interested in knowing the infective period durations that make the number of infected individuals exceed a given threshold.

The parametric models we address in this paper are described by polynomial discrete-time dynamical systems. Our motivation for focusing on such systems is that they are largely used to model bio-chemical networks; in addition, algorithms and tools have been developed to build such models from experimental data (see for example [3]). Biological observations are often measurements recorded at pre-determined time intervals, which results in time series of experimental data. To build a model from such observations, discrete-time dynamical systems can be used. Such models are also suited to the processes where the changes in quantitative entities (such as a small population size) at discrete time points can be accurately approximated as a function of their values at some previous time points. A major limitation of these models is that there are many processes where the variables evolve in continuous time, for which a description using differential equations is more appropriate. Differential equations arising in biological systems are generally too complex to be solved analytically, and numerical methods (which essentially operate in discrete time) are often used, but rigorous methods are needed to handle time discretization error. This requires an elaborated study and is not addressed here.

The work described in this paper is built on our results on reachability analysis of polynomial systems [27, 11, 25], inspired by the work on the Bernstein expansion [16]. In

*This work was supported by the Agence Nationale de la Recherche (COMPACS project - ANR Blanc 2013).

†This work was partially supported by Istituto Nazionale di Alta Matematica (INdAM).

HSCC'14, April 15–17, 2014, Berlin, Germany.
Copyright 2014 ACM 978-1-4503-2732-9/14/04 ...$15.00.

this paper, we extend these results to parameter synthesis. Important applications of the Bernstein expansion include global optimization, robust control, reliability analysis, geometric constrain solving, program analysis and compiling optimization [10, 1]. In the studies of hybrid systems, polynomials are used to compute barrier certificates [22], invariants [24] and reachability approximation [21, 8, 9, 2].
Parameter estimation for biological models to match a set of observed data has been considered using various optimization based techniques from model identification (see for example a survey [5] and references therein). Parameter estimation is also formulated as a problem of state estimation from output sequences (by considering the parameters as additional state variables with derivatives equal to 0) [20]. Concerning parameter synthesis for a desired property (rather than to fit experimental data), there have been a number of recent works. The problem of finding a parameter set so that a given set of traces (instead of a model) satisfies a temporal specification is considered in [4]. Our previous work in [14] focused on a variant of the parameter synthesis problem, that is using guided simulation to find parameter values that can falsify a property of the model. The work on parameter synthesis which is the closest to ours is [12, 13] where the parameter set and initial set are represented as a union of boxes and sensitivity analysis is employed to approximate the reachable set. This method can be applied to ordinary differential equations (ODEs). Our work differs from this in the parameter set representation: we use polytopes and refine the parameter set using linear constraints, which allows a more compact representation and discovering the dependence between the parameters. On the other hand, in our method the refinement of the initial set is done dynamically guided by the information on the property violation. In [6] a parameter synthesis algorithm was proposed for Boolean models using model checking; its application to ODEs requires discrete abstractions, which are hard to compute, and a method specialized for multi-affine systems was proposed. Other model-checking based methods for stochastic biochemical model were proposed in [18, 7].
The paper is organized as follows. In Section 2 we introduce basic definitions and state our problem. We then present the main ingredients of our algorithm for parameter synthesis. The algorithm includes an improved version of the method for computing the Bernstein coefficients. Some experimental results on two epidemic models are reported in Section 7.

2. PRELIMINARIES

2.1 Problem statement

Let $\mathbb{R}$ denote the set of reals. Throughout the paper, vectors are often written using bold letters (except for the vector f of dynamics functions). Given a vector $\boldsymbol{x}$, $\boldsymbol{x}_i$ denotes its ith component. We consider a parametric discrete-time dynamical system described by

$$\boldsymbol{x}(k+1) = f(\boldsymbol{x}(k), \boldsymbol{p}) \tag{1}$$

where $\boldsymbol{x} \in \mathbb{R}^n$ is the vector of state variables, $\boldsymbol{p} \in P \subseteq \mathbb{R}^m$ is the vector of uncertain parameters, f is a vector of n multi-variate polynomials of the form $f_i : \mathbb{R}^n \times \mathbb{R}^m \to \mathbb{R}$ for each $i \in \{1, \ldots, n\}$. The set P is called the *parameter set*. We assume that P is a convex polyhedron. The initial state $\boldsymbol{x}(0)$ is inside some set $X^0 \subset \mathbb{R}^n$, called the *initial set*. Given a set $X \subset \mathbb{R}^n$ of states, the image of X by f with all possible parameter values in P, denoted by $f(X, P)$, is defined as follows: $f(X, P) = \{(f_1(\boldsymbol{x}, \boldsymbol{p}), \ldots, f_n(\boldsymbol{x}, \boldsymbol{p})) \mid \boldsymbol{x} \in X, \boldsymbol{p} \in P\}$. The dynamical system (1) generates a set of solutions and at each step the set of all visited states is the image by f of the previous set. The reachable set at step K from an initial set X^0 can be computed as the solution of the following recursion for $j = 0, 1, \ldots, K$:

$$X^{j+1} = \{f(\boldsymbol{x}, \boldsymbol{p}) \mid \boldsymbol{x} \in X^j, \boldsymbol{p} \in P\}.$$

To emphasize that the reachable set is computed for the parameter set P, we denote it by $\mathcal{R}_P^K$.
We focus on the problem of constraining the parameter set P so that the resulting system satisfies a safety property. Let $\mathcal{F}$ be an unsafe set, defined by a constraint g over the state variables: $\mathcal{F} = \{\boldsymbol{x} \mid g(\boldsymbol{x}) \geq 0\}$. Then we want to find a subset $P_s \subseteq P$ such that starting from the initial set X^0, the system does not enter the unsafe set $\mathcal{F}$ up to time K, that is

$$\forall \boldsymbol{p} \in P_s \; \forall j \in \{0, 1, \ldots, K\} \; \forall \boldsymbol{x} \in \mathcal{R}_{P_s}^j : g(\boldsymbol{x}) < 0.$$

The iterative computation of X^j and the test of the safety condition are both based on the Bernstein expansion of polynomials [15], which we recall in the following section.

2.2 The Bernstein expansion

A multi-index is a vector $\mathbf{i} = (\mathbf{i}_1, \mathbf{i}_2, \ldots, \mathbf{i}_n)$ where each $\mathbf{i}_j$ is a non-negative integer. Given two multi-indices $\mathbf{i}$ and $\mathbf{d}$, we write $\mathbf{i} \leq \mathbf{d}$ if for all $i \in \{1, \ldots, n\}$, $\mathbf{i}_i \leq \mathbf{d}_i$. Also, we write $\frac{\mathbf{i}}{\mathbf{d}}$ for $(\mathbf{i}_1/\mathbf{d}_1, \mathbf{i}_2/\mathbf{d}_2, \ldots, \mathbf{i}_n/\mathbf{d}_n)$ and $\binom{\mathbf{i}}{\mathbf{d}}$ for the product of binomial coefficients $\binom{\mathbf{d}_1}{\mathbf{i}_1}\binom{\mathbf{d}_2}{\mathbf{i}_2}\ldots\binom{\mathbf{d}_n}{\mathbf{i}_n}$.
A system of parametric polynomials $\pi : \mathbb{R}^n \times \mathbb{R}^m \to \mathbb{R}^n$ can be represented using the power basis as follows:

$$\pi(\boldsymbol{x}, \boldsymbol{p}) = \sum_{\mathbf{i} \in I^\pi} \mathbf{a}_\mathbf{i}(\boldsymbol{p}) \boldsymbol{x}^\mathbf{i}$$

where $\mathbf{i}$ is a multi-index of size n, $\boldsymbol{x}^\mathbf{i}$ denotes the monomial $\boldsymbol{x}_1^{\mathbf{i}_1} \boldsymbol{x}_2^{\mathbf{i}_2} \cdots \boldsymbol{x}_n^{\mathbf{i}_n}$. The set I^π is called the multi-index set of π. Let $\mathbf{d}$ be the largest multi-index, that is $\forall \mathbf{i} \in I^\pi : \mathbf{i} \leq \mathbf{d}$; we call $\mathbf{d}$ the *degree* of π. The coefficients $\mathbf{a}_\mathbf{i}$ are functions of the parameters $\boldsymbol{p}$ of the form $\mathbb{R}^m \to \mathbb{R}$. The polynomial π can also be represented using the Bernstein expansion. For $\boldsymbol{x} = (\boldsymbol{x}_1, \ldots, \boldsymbol{x}_n) \in \mathbb{R}^n$, the $\mathbf{i}^{th}$ Bernstein polynomial of degree $\mathbf{d}$ is defined as follows: $\mathcal{B}_{\mathbf{d},\mathbf{i}}(\boldsymbol{x}) = \beta_{\mathbf{d}_1,\mathbf{i}_1}(\boldsymbol{x}_1) \ldots \beta_{\mathbf{d}_n,\mathbf{i}_n}(\boldsymbol{x}_n)$ where for a real number y, $\beta_{\mathbf{d}_j,\mathbf{i}_j}(y) = \binom{\mathbf{d}_j}{\mathbf{i}_j} y^{\mathbf{i}_j}(1-y)^{\mathbf{d}_j - \mathbf{i}_j}$. Then, for all $\boldsymbol{x} \in [0,1]^n$, the polynomial π can be written using the Bernstein expansion as follows:

$$\pi(\boldsymbol{x}, \boldsymbol{p}) = \sum_{\mathbf{i} \in I^\pi} \mathbf{b}_\mathbf{i}(\boldsymbol{p}) \mathcal{B}_{\mathbf{d},\mathbf{i}}(\boldsymbol{x})$$

where for each $\mathbf{i} \in I^\pi$ the Bernstein coefficient $\mathbf{b}_\mathbf{i}(\boldsymbol{p})$ is

$$\mathbf{b}_\mathbf{i}(\boldsymbol{p}) = \sum_{\mathbf{j} \leq \mathbf{i}} \frac{\binom{\mathbf{i}}{\mathbf{j}}}{\binom{\mathbf{d}}{\mathbf{j}}} \mathbf{a}_\mathbf{j}(\boldsymbol{p}). \tag{2}$$

Regarding the problem of checking the safety condition, the Bernstein expansion is of particular interest thanks to useful geometric properties of its coefficients. One important property involves the range of π for all $\boldsymbol{x} \in [0,1]^n$:

$$\forall i \in \{1, \ldots, n\} \; \forall \boldsymbol{p} \in P \; \forall \boldsymbol{x} \in [0,1]^n : \; \pi_i(\boldsymbol{x}, \boldsymbol{p}) \in [m_i^\pi, M_i^\pi]$$

where

$$m_i^\pi = min\{\mathbf{b}_{\mathbf{i},i}(\boldsymbol{p}) \mid \mathbf{i} \in I^\pi \wedge \boldsymbol{p} \in P\} \quad (3)$$

$$M_i^\pi = max\{\mathbf{b}_{\mathbf{i},i}(\boldsymbol{p}) \mid \mathbf{i} \in I^\pi \wedge \boldsymbol{p} \in P\} \quad (4)$$

In the above, $\mathbf{b}_{\mathbf{i},i}$ is the ith component of $\mathbf{b}_\mathbf{i}$. We can see here the advantage of the Bernstein expansion in the analysis of parametric systems as it can succinctly capture how the bounds of the reachable set varies as a function of the parameters.
Another property concerns sharpness of the Bernstein coefficients as approximations of the values of the polynomial:

$$\forall \mathbf{i} \in I_v^\pi : \mathbf{b}_\mathbf{i} = \pi(\frac{\mathbf{i}}{\mathbf{d}}) \quad (5)$$

where I_v^π is the set of vertices of the box $[0, \mathbf{d}_1] \times \ldots \times [0, \mathbf{d}_n]$. We call these multi-indices *vertex multi-indices* and their corresponding Bernstein coefficients *vertex coefficients*. Intuively it means that the vertex coefficients match the exact values of the polynomial at some points inside the domain $[0,1]^n$.

3. CONSTRAINING THE PARAMETER SET

In this work we use the following assumptions. First, the safety constraint g is linear in $\boldsymbol{x}$ and all the coefficients $\mathbf{a}_\mathbf{i}$ of the dynamics f are linear in the parameters $\boldsymbol{p}$. This assumption allows us to reduce the synthesis problem to a set of linear programs, as will be shown later. Second, the initial set X^0 is a box in $\mathbb{R}^n$.
To over-approximate the reachable sets at each step up to K, we also use boxes. It is therefore sufficient to explain one iteration. Note that the Bernstein expansion presented in the previous section is valid only for the domains inside the unit box $[0,1]^n$. We therefore define a function v^j that maps the unit box $[0,1]^n$ to X^j, and then we can study the composition $h^j = f \circ v^j$ over the unit box to yield the result for f over X^j. The function h^j is a polynomial and we denote the set of its Bernstein coefficients by $B^{h^j}(\boldsymbol{p}) = \{\mathbf{b}_\mathbf{i}^{h^j}(\boldsymbol{p}) \mid \mathbf{i} \in I^{h^j}\}$. Here we write each Bernstein coefficient as a function of $\boldsymbol{p}$ because they are computed from monomial coefficients which are dependent of the parameters $\boldsymbol{p}$.
Using the property expressed in (3), we can compute a box approximation of the reachable set. For each dimension $i \in \{1, \ldots, n\}$, a lower bound and an upper bound of the reachable set can be determined as follows. For each axis i, $m_i^\pi = min\{\mathbf{b}_{\mathbf{i},i}(\boldsymbol{p}) \mid \mathbf{i} \in I^{h^j} \wedge \boldsymbol{p} \in P\}$ and $M_i^\pi = max\{\mathbf{b}_{\mathbf{i},i}(\boldsymbol{p}) \mid \mathbf{i} \in I^{h^j} \wedge \boldsymbol{p} \in P\}$. From the above analysis we derive Algorithm 1 for bounding the reachable set from a given initial set X^0.

Algorithm 1 Bounding the reachable set at step j

```
1: function ReachStep(X^j, P, f)
2:     v^j ← mapUnitBoxtoDomain(X^j)
3:     h^j ← f ∘ v^j
4:     B^{h^j} ← BernCoeff(h^j)
5:     (m_i^{h^j}, M_i^{h^j}) ← bounds(B^{h^j}) for all i = {1,...,n}
6:     X^j ← [m_1^{h^j}, M_1^{h^j}] × ... × [m_n^{h^j}, M_n^{h^j}]
7: end function
```

To check whether the system does not reach the unsafe set $\mathcal{F}$ we can similarly consider the function $\pi^j = g \circ f \circ v^j$ and let $B^{\pi^j}(\boldsymbol{p})$ be its set of the Bernstein coefficients.

Lemma 1. *The following is a sufficient condition for the system to satisfy the safety property:*

$$\forall \boldsymbol{p} \in P \, \forall j \in \{1, \ldots, K\} \, \forall \mathbf{i} \in I^{\pi^j} : \mathbf{b}_\mathbf{i}^{\pi^j}(\boldsymbol{p}) < 0. \quad (6)$$

Note that g is a linear function, the coefficients in the monomial representation of π^j remain linear in $\boldsymbol{p}$. The above constraints are thus linear inequalities over $\boldsymbol{p}$. An additional remark is that to compute the bounds m_i^π and M_i^π, one can exploit the monotonicity properties of the Bernstein coefficients in order to avoid enumerating all the coefficients. This is discussed in the remainder of this section.
Since each dimension is treated independently, for simplicity of presentation, in what follows we focus on a polynomial $\pi(\boldsymbol{x}, \boldsymbol{p})$ over a set X. We denote by $\mathbf{im}^\pi$ and $\mathbf{iM}^\pi$ the multi-indices corresponding respectively to the minimal and maximal Bernstein coefficients of $\pi(\boldsymbol{x}, \boldsymbol{p})$, called the *min-index* and *max-index*. We first observe the following monotonicity of the Bernstein coefficients of monomials [26]. Given a monomial of n variables $\boldsymbol{x}$ over a domain X, if X lies entirely inside one orthan of $\mathbb{R}^n$, then its Bernstein coefficients are monotone with respect to each variable $\boldsymbol{x}_i \in X$, $i \in \{1, \ldots, n\}$.
The above can be extended to the monomials which are likewise monotone, that is if all the monomials involving $\boldsymbol{x}_i$ in π are either increasingly monotone or decreasingly monotone, then the ith component of $\mathbf{im}^\pi$ and $\mathbf{iM}^\pi$ are either 0 or $\mathbf{d}_i$, that is $\mathbf{im}_i^\pi \in \{0, \mathbf{d}_i\}$, $\mathbf{iM}_i^\pi \in \{0, \mathbf{d}_i\}$. Since before computing the Bernstein coefficients we map the unit box to the domain and compose g with this map, the domains of the functions h^j in Algorithm 1 are the unit box, for which the above monotonicity property of monomials can be applied.

4. EFFICIENT CONTROL POINT COMPUTATION

Despite the advantage of the Bernstein expansion in the set image approximation, the direct computation of the Bernstein control points from the representation using the monomial basis is exponential in the number of variables. The *Matrix* method [23] is a technique using operations on matrices that can reduce the computational complexity by a multiplicative factor. In this section, we propose an improvement that can reduce further the complexity of this technique by performing the multi-dimensional matrix tranposition in a more efficient manner.
The main idea of the Matrix technique is to express the Bernstein control points as a matrix product series. For instance, the univariate polynomial[1] $\pi(x, \boldsymbol{p}) = \sum_{i \in I^\pi} \mathbf{a}_i(\boldsymbol{p}) x^i = \sum_{i \in I^\pi} \boldsymbol{b}_i(\boldsymbol{p}) \mathcal{B}_{d,i}(x)$ can be rewritten as

$$\pi(x, \boldsymbol{p}) = (1 \; x \; x^2 \; \ldots \; x^d) \begin{pmatrix} \mathbf{a}_0(\boldsymbol{p}) \\ \vdots \\ \mathbf{a}_d(\boldsymbol{p}) \end{pmatrix} = \mathcal{X}\mathbf{a}(\boldsymbol{p})$$

or as

$$\pi(x, \boldsymbol{p}) = (\mathcal{B}_{d,0}(x) \; \ldots \; \mathcal{B}_{d,d}(x)) \begin{pmatrix} \mathbf{b}_0(\boldsymbol{p}) \\ \vdots \\ \mathbf{b}_d(\boldsymbol{p}) \end{pmatrix} = \mathcal{B}_\mathcal{X} B(\boldsymbol{p}).$$

[1]In this section we use the notation $\pi(x, \boldsymbol{p})$ instead of $\pi(\boldsymbol{x}, \boldsymbol{p})$ to stress that the vector $\boldsymbol{x}$ has only one element and the multi-index i and degree d are scalars.

Defining the matrix

$$\tilde{U}_x = \begin{pmatrix} 1 & 0 & 0 & \dots & 0 \\ 1 & \binom{1}{0}\binom{d}{1}^{-1} & 0 & \dots & 0 \\ 1 & \binom{2}{1}\binom{d}{1}^{-1} & \binom{2}{0}\binom{d}{2}^{-1} & \dots & 0 \\ \vdots & \vdots & \vdots & \ddots & \vdots \\ 1 & 1 & 1 & 1 & 1 \end{pmatrix}$$

for the unit box interval domain, it holds that $\mathcal{B}_{\mathcal{X}} B(\boldsymbol{p}) = \mathcal{X}\tilde{U}_x^{-1} B(\boldsymbol{p})$ and consequently $B(\boldsymbol{p}) = \tilde{U}_x \mathbf{a}(\boldsymbol{p})$ [23]. Thus, to obtain the Bernstein control points, it is sufficient to multiply the lower triangular matrix $\tilde{U}_x$ by the polynomial coefficients vector $\mathbf{a}(\boldsymbol{p})$.
For multi-variate polynomials, things are slightly more difficult, since the coefficients of the considered polynomial must be collected in a multi-dimensional matrix. Given a multivariate polynomial $\pi(\boldsymbol{x}, \boldsymbol{p})$ of degree $\boldsymbol{d}$, each coefficient $\mathbf{a}_{\boldsymbol{i}}(\boldsymbol{p})$, with $\boldsymbol{i} \in I^{\pi}$, is placed at the position $\boldsymbol{i}$ in the matrix $A(\boldsymbol{p}) \in \mathbb{R}^{\mathbf{d}_1 \times \dots \times \mathbf{d}_n}$. Then, the control points can be computed using the formula

$$B(\boldsymbol{p}) = (\tilde{U}_{\boldsymbol{x}_n}(\dots(\tilde{U}_{\boldsymbol{x}_2}(\tilde{U}_{\boldsymbol{x}_1} A(\boldsymbol{p}))^T)^T \dots)^T)^T$$

where the multi-dimensional transposition consists of a left-shift rotation of the dimensions of the matrix. As an example, if $A(\boldsymbol{p}) \in \mathbb{R}^{\mathbf{d}_1 \times \dots \times \mathbf{d}_n}$ then $A^T(\boldsymbol{p}) \in \mathbb{R}^{\mathbf{d}_2 \times \mathbf{d}_3 \times \dots \times \mathbf{d}_n \times \mathbf{d}_1}$.
To express the operations over multi-dimensional matrices using the operations over standard bi-dimensional matrices, it is to possible to represent a matrix $A(\boldsymbol{p}) \in \mathbb{R}^{\mathbf{d}_1 \times \mathbf{d}_2 \times \dots \times \mathbf{d}_n}$ by a matrix $C(\boldsymbol{p}) \in \mathbb{R}^{\mathbf{d}_1 \times \prod_{i=2}^{n} \mathbf{d}_i}$. In particular, we define the functions $\overrightarrow{\eta} : \mathbb{N}^n \to \mathbb{N}^2$ and $\overleftarrow{\eta} : \mathbb{N}^2 \to \mathbb{N}^n$ to map a n-dimensional index vector $(\mathbf{a}_1, \mathbf{a}_2, \dots, \mathbf{a}_n)$ (specifying a position in a n-dimensional matrix) to a bi-dimensional index vector $(\mathbf{c}_1, \mathbf{c}_2)$ (specifying a position in a bi-dimensional matrix), and vice versa:

$$\overrightarrow{\eta}(\mathbf{a}_1, \mathbf{a}_2, \dots, \mathbf{a}_n) = (\mathbf{a}_1, \sum_{i=2}^{n}(\mathbf{a}_i \prod_{j=2}^{i-1} \mathbf{d}_j))$$

and $\overleftarrow{\eta}(\mathbf{c}_1, \mathbf{c}_2) = (\mathbf{a}_1, \mathbf{a}_2, \dots, \mathbf{a}_n)$ where $\mathbf{a}_n = \lfloor \mathbf{c}_2 / \prod_{i=2}^{n-1} \mathbf{d}_i \rfloor$, $\mathbf{a}_i = \lfloor (\mathbf{c}_2 \bmod \mathbf{a}_{i+1}) / \prod_{j=2}^{i-1} \mathbf{d}_j \rfloor$ for $i = 2, \dots, n-1$, and $\mathbf{a}_1 = \mathbf{c}_1$.
To compute the control points, it remains to define the transposition of the bi-dimensional representation of a multi-dimensional matrix. Starting from an index vector $\mathbf{c}$, a simple way to do so consists of 3 steps: (1) applying $\overleftarrow{\eta}(\mathbf{c}) = (\mathbf{a}_1, \mathbf{a}_2, \dots, \mathbf{a}_n)$, (2) performing the rotation $(\mathbf{a}_2, \mathbf{a}_3, \dots, \mathbf{a}_1)$, and (3) going back to $\overrightarrow{\eta}(\mathbf{a}_2, \mathbf{a}_3, \dots, \mathbf{a}_1) = \mathbf{c}' = \mathbf{c}^T$.
The map $\overrightarrow{\eta}$ requires n sums and $n(n+1)/2$ multiplications, hence $\overrightarrow{\eta} \in \mathcal{O}(n^2)$. And $\overleftarrow{\eta}$ involves $n(n+1)/2$ multiplications, thus $\overleftarrow{\eta} \in \mathcal{O}(n^2)$. The whole procedure requires $\prod_{i=1}^{n} \mathbf{d}_i (\mathcal{O}(n^2) + \mathcal{O}(n^2)) = \mathcal{O}(n^2 \prod_{i=1}^{n} \mathbf{d}_i)$.
To improve the efficiency of this computation, we propose a new method for computing the multi-dimensional matrix transposition operation.
Unfolding $\mathbf{c} = (\mathbf{c}_1, \mathbf{c}_2)$ we observe that

$$\begin{aligned} \mathbf{c} &= (\mathbf{c}_1, \mathbf{c}_2) = \\ &= (\mathbf{a}_1, \mathbf{a}_2 + \mathbf{a}_3\mathbf{d}_2 + \mathbf{a}_4\mathbf{d}_3\mathbf{d}_2 + \dots + \mathbf{a}_n\mathbf{d}_{n-1}\dots\mathbf{d}_2) \end{aligned} \tag{7}$$

and, if $\overleftarrow{\eta}(\mathbf{c}_1, \mathbf{c}_2) = (\mathbf{a}_1, \mathbf{a}_2, \dots, \mathbf{a}_n)$, $(\mathbf{a}_1, \mathbf{a}_2, \dots, \mathbf{a}_n)^T = (\mathbf{a}_2, \mathbf{a}_3, \dots, \mathbf{a}_1)$. Let denote $\mathbf{c}^T = (\mathbf{c}'_1, \mathbf{c}'_2)$, then $(\mathbf{c}'_1, \mathbf{c}'_2) = (\mathbf{a}_2, \mathbf{a}_3 + \mathbf{a}_4\mathbf{d}_3 + \mathbf{a}_5\mathbf{d}_4\mathbf{d}_3 + \dots + \mathbf{a}_n\mathbf{d}_{n-1}\dots\mathbf{d}_3 + \mathbf{a}_1\mathbf{d}_n\mathbf{d}_{n-1}\dots\mathbf{d}_3)$. From (7) it follows that

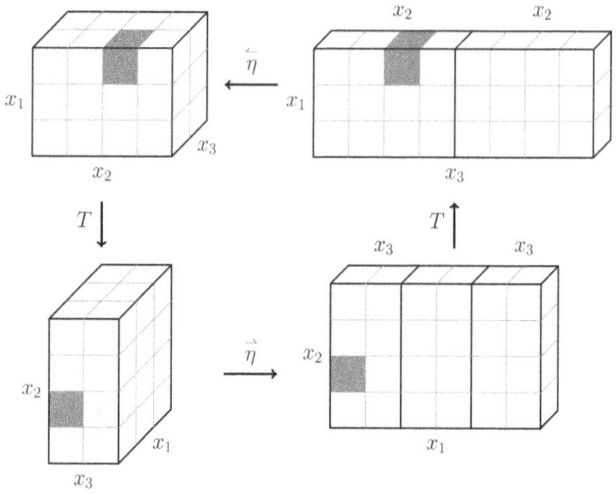

Figure 1: n-dimensional and bi-dimension transposition.

$$\begin{aligned} \mathbf{c}'_1 &= \mathbf{a}_2 \\ \mathbf{c}'_2 &= \frac{(\mathbf{c}_2 - \mathbf{a}_2)}{\mathbf{d}_2} + \mathbf{a}_1 \prod_{i=3}^{n} \mathbf{d}_i. \end{aligned} \tag{8}$$

This means that retrieving efficiently $\mathbf{a}_1$ and $\mathbf{a}_2$ from $\mathbf{c}$, we can quickly compute $(\mathbf{c}'_1, \mathbf{c}'_2) = \mathbf{c}^T$. By the definition in (7), the first element $\mathbf{a}_1$ is $\mathbf{c}_1$, that is $\mathbf{a}_1 = \mathbf{c}_1$. Rearranging (7) we observe that

$$\begin{aligned} \mathbf{c} &= (\mathbf{c}_1, \mathbf{c}_2) = \\ &= (\mathbf{a}_1, \mathbf{a}_2 + \mathbf{a}_3\mathbf{d}_2 + \mathbf{a}_4\mathbf{d}_3\mathbf{d}_2 + \dots + \mathbf{a}_n\mathbf{d}_{n-1}\mathbf{d}_{n-2}\dots\mathbf{d}_2) = \\ &= (\mathbf{a}_1, \mathbf{a}_2 + \mathbf{d}_2(\mathbf{a}_3 + \mathbf{d}_3(\mathbf{a}_4 + \mathbf{d}_4 \dots (\mathbf{a}_n)\dots))) = \\ &= (\mathbf{a}_1, \mathbf{a}_2 + \mathbf{d}_2 q) \end{aligned}$$

from which we deduce that $\mathbf{a}_2 = (\mathbf{c}_2 \bmod \mathbf{d}_2)$. By substitution, from Equation (8), we obtain

$$\begin{aligned} \mathbf{c}'_1 &= (\mathbf{c}_2 \bmod \mathbf{d}_2) \\ \mathbf{c}'_2 &= \frac{(\mathbf{c}_2 - (\mathbf{c}_2 \bmod \mathbf{d}_2))}{\mathbf{d}_2} + \mathbf{c}_1 \prod_{i=3}^{n} \mathbf{d}_i \end{aligned}$$

that allows us to compute directly $\mathbf{c}^T = (\mathbf{c}'_1, \mathbf{c}'_2)$ from $\mathbf{c}$, without passing through the functions $\overrightarrow{\eta}$ and $\overleftarrow{\eta}$. Using the above-described method, the transposition of a single element requires n multiplications, hence, the whole procedure involves $\mathcal{O}(n \prod_{i=1}^{n} \mathbf{d}_i)$, which shows an improvement in efficiency, compared to the standard transposition method. Table 1 reports a comparison between the original method [23] and the improved version using the above new method for computing the transposition of multi-dimensional matrices.

5. SUBDIVISION

Throughout this section we consider the polynomial π over a box domain X and therefore, for simplicity of presentation, we sometimes omit mentioning π and X explicitly in the subsequent discussion (for example when saying the Bernstein expansion, we mean the Bernstein expansion of

n, d	Original method	Improved method
2	0.0018	0.0015
3	0.0091	0.0028
4	0.0285	0.0098
5	0.2328	0.0627
6	3.6336	0.9501
7	77.9803	17.1926

Table 1: Computational times (in seconds). The values n and d correspond to the polynomial dimension and degree, e.g., if $n = d = 4$ then $\mathbf{d} = (4, 4, 4, 4)$.

π over X). Note that the system of constraints (6) over the parameters that guarantee the satisfaction of the property (expressed by the polynomial g) may have no solution due to the image over-approximations inherent to the Bernstein expansion. One way to handle such situations is to subdivide the set X^j to achieve a more precise image approximation. We now explain the subdivision procedure, which can be done efficiently thanks to the properties of the Bernstein expansion [26]. A subdivision in the rth direction ($1 \leq r \leq n$) is a bisection perpendicular to this direction. Let $X = [\underline{\boldsymbol{x}}_1, \overline{\boldsymbol{x}}_1] \times \cdots \times [\underline{\boldsymbol{x}}_r, \overline{\boldsymbol{x}}_r] \times \cdots \times [\underline{\boldsymbol{x}}_n, \overline{\boldsymbol{x}}_n] \subseteq [0,1]^n$. If X is subdivided along the rth component direction at some point $\lambda_r \in [0,1]$, then the resulting two sub-boxes X_A and X_B are $X_A = [\underline{\boldsymbol{x}}_1, \overline{\boldsymbol{x}}_1] \times \cdots \times [\underline{\boldsymbol{x}}_r, \hat{\boldsymbol{x}}_r] \times \cdots \times [\underline{\boldsymbol{x}}_n, \overline{\boldsymbol{x}}_n]$ and $X_B = [\underline{\boldsymbol{x}}_1, \overline{\boldsymbol{x}}_1] \times \cdots \times [\hat{\boldsymbol{x}}_r, \overline{\boldsymbol{x}}_r] \times \cdots \times [\underline{\boldsymbol{x}}_n, \overline{\boldsymbol{x}}_n]$ where $\hat{\boldsymbol{x}}_r = \underline{\boldsymbol{x}}_r + \lambda_r(\overline{\boldsymbol{x}}_r - \underline{\boldsymbol{x}}_r)$.

We use the following notation to express neighboring multi-indices. Let $\mathbf{i} = (\mathbf{i}_1, \ldots, \mathbf{i}_r, \ldots, \mathbf{i}_n)$ be a multi-index, then $\mathbf{i}_{(r,k)} = (\mathbf{i}_1, \ldots, \mathbf{i}_r + k, \ldots, \mathbf{i}_n)$ where $0 \leq \mathbf{i}_r + k \leq \mathbf{d}_r$. We start with $B^{(0)}(X) = B(X) = \{\mathbf{b}^0_{\mathbf{i}} \mid \mathbf{i} \in I^\pi\}$ where $B(X)$ is the set of the Bernstein coefficients for X. We then update $\mathbf{b}^{(k)}_{\mathbf{i}_1,\ldots,\mathbf{i}_r,\ldots,\mathbf{i}_n}$ for $k = 1, \ldots, \mathbf{d}_r$ as follows[2]:

- If $\mathbf{i}_r < k$, $\mathbf{b}^{(k)}_{\mathbf{i}_1,\ldots,\mathbf{i}_r,\ldots,\mathbf{i}_n} = \mathbf{b}^{(k-1)}_{\mathbf{i}_1,\ldots,\mathbf{i}_r,\ldots,\mathbf{i}_n}$.
- If $\mathbf{i}_r \geq k$

$$\mathbf{b}^{(k)}_{\mathbf{i}_1,\ldots,\mathbf{i}_r,\ldots,\mathbf{i}_n} = (1-\lambda_r)\mathbf{b}^{(k-1)}_{\mathbf{i}_1,\ldots,\mathbf{i}_r-1,\ldots,\mathbf{i}_n} + \lambda_r \mathbf{b}^{(k-1)}_{\mathbf{i}_1,\ldots,\mathbf{i}_r,\ldots,\mathbf{i}_n}.$$

To obtain the new coefficients of X_1 after the subdivision of X, we apply the above update rules for $\mathbf{i}_j = 0, \ldots, \mathbf{d}_j$, $j = 1, \ldots, r-1, r+1, \ldots, n$. Then, $B(X_A) = B^{(\mathbf{d}_r)}(X)$. Moreover, we obtain directly the coefficients $B(X_B)$ since for $k = 0, 1, \ldots, \mathbf{d}_r$ the following relation holds:

$$\mathbf{b}_{\mathbf{i}_1,\ldots,\mathbf{d}_r-k,\ldots,\mathbf{i}_n}(X_2) = \mathbf{b}^{(n)}_{\mathbf{i}_1,\ldots,\mathbf{d}_r,\ldots,\mathbf{i}_n}(X_1). \quad (9)$$

The complexity of this procedure is $O(\mathbf{d}_r^{n+1})$.

Let $B_s(X) = B(X_A) \cup B(X_B)$, that is the union of the Bernstein coefficients for the two sub-boxes. It can be proven that the minimal (maximal) coefficient of $B_s(X)$ is not smaller (greater) that the minimal (maximal) one of $B(X)$. This means that subdivision can improve and always preserves the accuracy of range approximation. It is thus of great interest to quickly detect the cases where the set of parameter values satisfying the requirement is truly empty, since in those cases subdivision is not useful, which is stated in the following lemma.

[2]We recall that $\mathbf{d}_r$ is the degree of π in the variable $\boldsymbol{x}_r$.

LEMMA 2. *If there exists a vertex index $\mathbf{i} \in I^\pi_v$ such that $\forall \boldsymbol{p} \in P : \mathbf{b}_{\mathbf{i}}(\boldsymbol{p}) \geq 0$, then there is no $\boldsymbol{p} \in P$ such that*

$$\forall \boldsymbol{x} \in X : \ \pi(\boldsymbol{x}, \boldsymbol{p}) < 0. \quad (10)$$

PROOF. It follows from the sharpness property of the Bernstein expansion (expressed in (5)) that for every value of $\boldsymbol{p}$, there exists a point $\boldsymbol{x} = \frac{\mathbf{i}}{\mathbf{d}}$ inside the domain X such that the vertex coefficient $\mathbf{b}_{\mathbf{i}}(\boldsymbol{p})$ (which is a function of $\boldsymbol{p}$) matches exactly the polynomial for the same value $\boldsymbol{p}$, that is, $\mathbf{b}_{\mathbf{i}}(\boldsymbol{p}) = \pi(\boldsymbol{x}, \boldsymbol{p})$. This implies that for all parameter values $\boldsymbol{p} \in P$ the polynomial always has a non-negative value at some point inside X, which invalidates the statement (10). This proves the lemma. ∎

Hence, before subdividing we can test the condition in (10). If this condition is not satisfied, then we proceed with a subdivision of X. Otherwise, the above lemma indicates that subdividing X is not useful because the set X may contain accumulated over-approximation error which results in the emptiness of the computed parameter set. Therefore, we should move back one more step to subdivide the predecessor set of X. This will be discussed in detail later.

On the other hand, if the polynomial is monotone, this can simplify the update procedure. More concretely, if the polynomial is monotone in a variable $\boldsymbol{x}_i$, to compute the lower and upper bounds m_i and M_i for each sub-box, it suffices to update the coefficients $\mathbf{b}_{\mathbf{i}}$ corresponding to the vertex multi-indices $\mathbf{i}_m \in \{\mathbf{0}, \mathbf{d}_i\}$. From the update procedure we see that the coefficient $\mathbf{b}_{\mathbf{0}}(X_A)$ of the sub-box on the left is the same as $\mathbf{b}_{\mathbf{0}}(X)$ of the original box. It remains to update the other extreme coefficient, which requires updating only $\mathbf{d}_r$ coefficients (for $\mathbf{d}_r$ iterations).

Selection of the subdivision direction

The first task is to find an appropriate component direction for the subdivision to achieve better approximations of the polynomial values by the Bernstein coefficients. We choose as the subdivision direction the one with the largest first partial derivative. The selection is performed by exploiting again the Bernstein form. More concretely, we estimate $\max_{\boldsymbol{x} \in X} |\frac{\partial \pi}{\partial \boldsymbol{x}_r}(\boldsymbol{x})|$ for each variable $\boldsymbol{x}_r$, then we pick r with the largest derivative value over X. The first partial derivative of the polynomial with respect to $\boldsymbol{x}_r$ is given by:

$$\frac{\partial \pi}{\partial \boldsymbol{x}_r}(\boldsymbol{x}) = \mathbf{d}_r \sum_{\mathbf{i} \leq \mathbf{d}_{r,-1}} [\mathbf{b}_{\mathbf{i}_{(r,1)}}(X) - \mathbf{b}_{\mathbf{i}}(X)] \mathcal{B}_{\mathbf{d}_{(r,-1)},\mathbf{i}}(\boldsymbol{x}),$$

where $\mathcal{B}_{\mathbf{d}_{(r,-1)},\mathbf{i}}(\boldsymbol{x})$ is the $\mathbf{i}^{th}$ Bernstein polynomial of degree $\mathbf{d}_{(r,-1)}$ (see Section 2.2).

Finding a subdivision point

Once the subdivision direction r has been chosen, the second task is to find a division point $\lambda_r \in [0,1]$ such that this subdivision can increase as much as possible the feasibility of the resulting correctness conditions on the parameters. Recall the condition (6) for the system to reach the unsafe set at step j: $\forall \mathbf{i} \in I^{\pi^{j-1}}$ $\forall \boldsymbol{p} \in P : \mathbf{b}^{\pi^j}_{\mathbf{i}}(\boldsymbol{p}) \geq 0$. Hence we should subdivide the domain in order to retain as much as possible a subdomain corresponding to non-positive values of π^j. We consider the convex hull C of the projection of all of its control points $v_{\mathbf{i}} = (\frac{\mathbf{i}}{\mathbf{d}}, \mathbf{b}_{\mathbf{i}})$ on the $\boldsymbol{x}_r$-$\mathbf{b}$ plane. An efficient subdivision should separate this intersection from the rest.

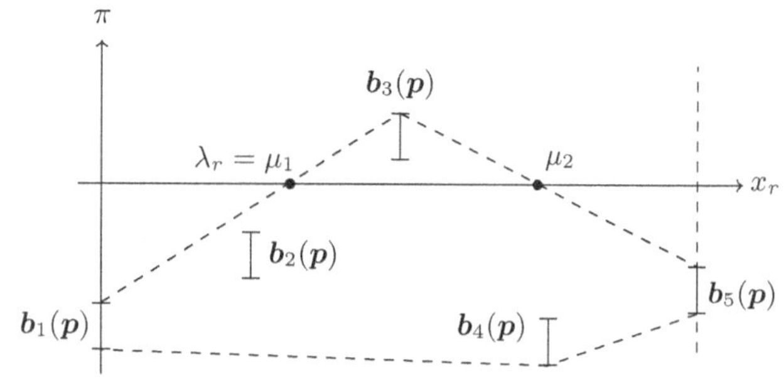

Figure 2: Finding a division point. Since $1-\mu_2 \leq \mu_1$, the chosen subdivision point is $\lambda_r = \mu_1$.

Note that the Bernstein coefficients $\mathbf{b_i}$ are functions of the parameters $\boldsymbol{p}$; to compute this projection, we can determine around each control point a box neighborhood that accounts for the uncertainty in $\boldsymbol{p}$, and then project the vertices of the resulting boxes. The convex-hull operator on 2 dimensions can be efficiently performed using well-known algorithms.
From the 2-dimensional convex hull on the $\boldsymbol{x}_r - \mathbf{b}$ space, we determine the subdivision point as follows. We identify the set E of line segments connecting the control points that intersect with the abscissa $\boldsymbol{x}_r$ (that is their $\mathbf{b}$-coordinates have the opposite signs). Let $[\mu_1, \mu_2]$ be the intersection of C with the abscissa $\boldsymbol{x}_r$. We thus subdivide along this axis at a point which results in the largest interval that does not contain $[\mu_1, \mu_2]$, that is if $1-\mu_2 > \mu_1$, we subdivide at $\lambda_r = \mu_2$, otherwise at $\lambda_r = \mu_1$. In Figure 2 we illustrate this idea with a 2-dimensional example.
The subdivision procedure is repeated until the refined parameter set is not empty, or until the sizes of the subboxes are smaller than some threshold.

6. PARAMETER SYNTHESIS ALGORITHM

We now describe the overall algorithm for parameter synthesis. Most of its procedures involve the theoretical results exposed in the previous sections.
In this algorithm, the precomputed Boolean vector is_{mono} indicates whether the dynamics of a variable is monotone. The main procedure ParaSynth (Algorithm 2) consists of a single loop that iterates until a predefined maximal number K of steps is reached or the parameter set P^j becomes empty. Each iteration computes a map v^j of the unit box to the actual domain, its composition $\pi^j \leftarrow g \circ f \circ v^j$ with the safety constraint g and the dynamics f, and then the control points B^{π^j} (by exploiting the eventual monotonicity of the dynamics (lines 4-6)). Through the function RefParams (line 7), a new refined parameter set P^j is computed and if it is not empty, the algorithm performs a single reachability step computing the new reachable set X^{j+1} (line 9). Figure 3 schematically represents an execution of ParaSynth. The arrows from X^j and P^j to X^{j+1} represent the jth ReachStep call (labeled with $\texttt{RS}^j$); the dashed arrows from X^j to P^j correspond to the jth RefParams execution (labeled with $\texttt{RP}^j$).
RefParams (Algorithm 3) plays a fundamental role, since it refines the parameter set and, on the basis of its emptiness, it determines whether to halt the synthesis algorithm. It takes as input the previous parameter set P^{j-1} and the current control points B^{π^j}, it merges the constraints of P^{j-1} with the new safety constraints (6) to form a new refined parameter set P_{new}. It then checks if P_{new} is not empty (line 3). If so, P_{new} is a good parameter set. Otherwise it verifies whether the sharpness condition is satisfied (line 6) (and the set P_{new} is thus actually empty), or more accurate control points need to be estimated. The emptiness test involves the resolution of a linear program where the number of variables is the dimension of the parameter space, while the number of the new constraints at each step is, in the worst case, the number of the Bernstein control points.
We suppose now that the sharpness condition of Lemma 2 does not hold. In such a case, more precise control points $B_s^{\pi^j}$ are computed by subdividing X^j (line 7) and if the subdivided boxes are large enough, RefParams attempts a refinement of the parameter set with a recursive call on the new control points $B_s^{\pi^j}$ (line 9).
If the sharpness condition of Lemma 2 holds, it means that a subdivision of X^j is useless. Nevertheless, the algorithm does not give up. It might be possible that the computed parameter set is empty because of the approximation error accumulated in the domain X^j during the previous steps. Thus, the last attempt is to recompute the set X^{j-1} in order to reduce the approximation error. To do so, the procedure goes back two steps, splits the set X^{j-2} to two subsets X_A^{j-2} and X_B^{j-2} (line 14) and computes the set X^{j-1} as the union of the applications of ReachStep to X_A^{j-2} and X_B^{j-2}. Finally, it restores the parameter synthesis procedure from the more accurate approximation X^{j-1} (line 17). Figure 4 depicts the backward refiment of the set X^{j-1}.

Algorithm 2 Parameter synthesis w.r.t. g

1: **function** ParaSynth(X^0, P^0, K)
2: $\quad j = 0$
3: $\quad$**repeat**
4: $\quad\quad v^j \leftarrow$ mapUnitBoxtoDomain(X^j)
5: $\quad\quad \pi^j \leftarrow g \circ f \circ v^j$
6: $\quad\quad B^{\pi^j} \leftarrow$ BernCoeff(π^j, is_{Mono})
7: $\quad\quad P^j \leftarrow$ RefParams(B^{π^j}, X^j, P^{j-1})
8: $\quad\quad$**if** $P^j \neq \emptyset$ **then**
9: $\quad\quad\quad X^{j+1} \leftarrow$ ReachStep(X^j, P^j)
10: $\quad\quad$**end if**
11: $\quad\quad j{+}{+}$
12: $\quad$**until** $(j = K) \vee (P^j = \emptyset)$
13: **end function**

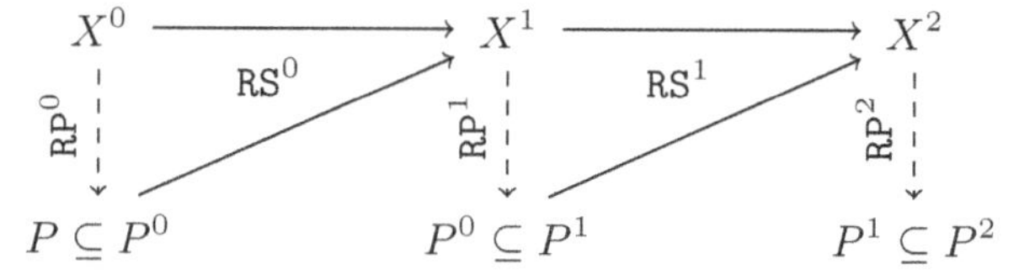

Figure 3: An execution of the parameter synthesis procedure.

7. EXPERIMENTAL RESULTS

We implemented a prototype tool written in MATLAB. We chose this environment because its advanced features in the

Algorithm 3 Parameter refinement

```
function RefParams(B^{π^j}, P^j, X^j)
    P_new ← BuildLS(B_{π^j}, P^j)
    if notEmpty(P_new) then
        return P_new
    end if
    if ¬Sharpness(B^{π^j}, X^j) then
        B_s^{π^j} ← Subdivide(B^{π^j}, X^j)
        if LargeEnough(B_s^{π^j}) then
            return RefParams(B_s^{π^j}, P^j, X^j)
        else
            return ∅
        end if
    end if
    [X_A^{j-2}, X_B^{j-2}] ← Split(X^{j-2})
    X^{j-1} ← ReachStep(X_A^{j-2}, P^{j-2}) ∪
                ReachStep(X_B^{j-2}, P^{j-2})
    ParaSynth(X^{j-1}, P^{j-1}, k - j - 1)
end function
```

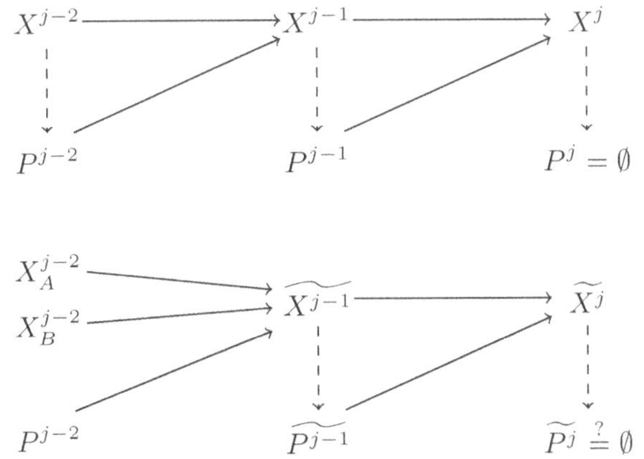

Figure 4: A better approximation $\widetilde{X^{j-1}}$ is achieved by splitting X^{j-2} to X_A^{j-2} and X_B^{j-2}. The letters marked with tilde are labels of the new sets computed after splitting.

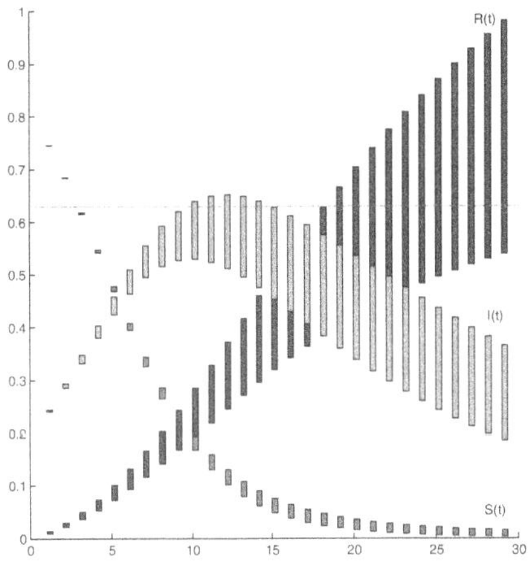

Figure 5: SIR evolution (in percentages) with the initial parameter set $[0.05, 0.0675]$.

manipulation of symbolic formulæ and it additionally can be easily interfaced with and integrated in external tools. All the experiments have been carried out using MATLAB R2012b on an Intel(R) Core(TM)2 Duo (2.40 GHz, 4GB RAM) mounting Ubuntu 12.04.

7.1 SIR model

The first example is a basic epidemic SIR model [19]:

$$\begin{aligned} \dot{S} &= -\beta S I \\ \dot{I} &= \beta S I - \gamma I \\ \dot{R} &= \gamma I \end{aligned}$$

In this model, a fixed population $N = S(t) + I(t) + R(t)$ is grouped in three classes: $S(t)$ is the number of individuals not yet infected and susceptible to the disease, $I(t)$ are the individuals who have been infected and who could infect healthy individuals, and $R(t)$ are those who have been infected and removed from the system, either because become immune or, in the worst case, dead. The parameters β and $1/\gamma$ are respectively the contraction rate of the disease and the mean infective period.

Discretizing the continuous SIR model with the Euler method and a time step h, we obtain the following parametric discrete-time dynamical system: $S_{k+1} = S_k - (\beta S_k I_k)h$, $I_{k+1} = I_k + (\beta S_k I_k - \gamma I_k)h$, $R_{k+1} = R_k + (\gamma I)h$. For this model, the monotonicity property can be exploited (see Section 3), for example the dynamics of S is monotone in I. We consider a population composed by $N = 100$ individuals, of which, at time $t = 0$, $S(t) = 80$ are susceptible, $I(t) = 20$ are infected, and $R(t) = 0$ are removed. Figure 5 depicts the computation result for the contraction rate $\beta = 0.34$, $\gamma \in [0.05, 0.0675]$, time step $h = 1.0$, and $K = 30$. We want to know if there are some values of γ such that the infected individuals are always less than 63, i.e., the safety condition is defined by $g(I) = I - 63$. Our tool found positive answer to the query and synthesized a safe parameter set, which is $[0.0659, 0.0675]$, in 45.83 seconds. Figure 6 depicts the evolution of the population size with the synthesized parameter set. Note that the number of infected individuals does not

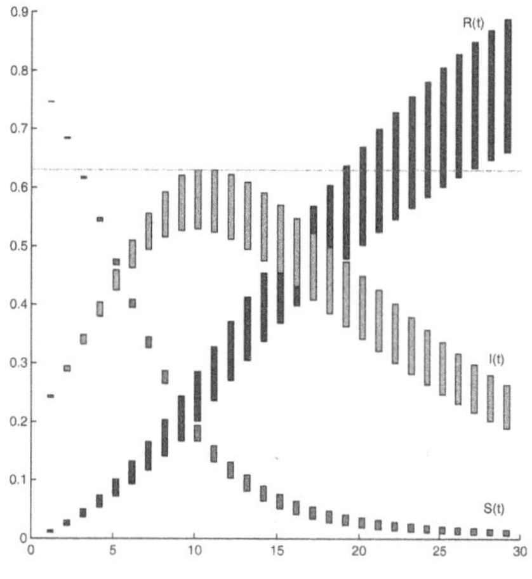

Figure 6: SIR evolution (in percentages) with synthesized parameter.

exceed the threshold 63. The fact that the tool reduces the possible values of γ from $[0.05, 0.0675]$ to $[0.0659, 0.0675]$, can be interpreted as a need to decrease the infection period $1/\gamma$, which allows speeding up the removal of individuals and keeping low the number of the infected ones.
Strengthening the constraint to $g(I) = I - 62.70$, the tool, at the tenth iteration, found an empty safe parameter set. Also, the satisfaction of the sharpness condition is detected, hence at this point subdivision is useless. The tool performed two steps back, splitting the set $X^1 = [32.65, 34.41] \times [49.43, 55.54] \times [11.64, 16.60]$ to

$$X_A^1 = [32.65, 33.53] \times [49.43, 52.49] \times [11.64, 14.12]$$
$$X_B^1 = [33.53, 34.41] \times [52.49, 55.54] \times [14.12, 16.60],$$

and computed

$$\begin{aligned}\widetilde{X^2} &= \widetilde{X_A^2} \cup \widetilde{X_B^2} \\ &= [26.82, 27.89] \times [51.58, 55.85] \times [14.11, 17.66] \cup \\ &\quad [27.20, 28.27] \times [54.93, 59.29] \times [16.74, 20.35].\end{aligned}$$

We can see that

$$\begin{aligned}\widetilde{X^2} = &\ [26.82, 28.27] \times [51.58, 59.29] \times [14.11, 20.35] \subset \\ &\ [26.48, 28.63] \times [51.58, 59.29] \times [14.11, 20.35] = X^2\end{aligned}$$

which means that the subdivision led to a better approximation of the reachable set. Restoring the computation from $j = 2$ with the domain $\widetilde{X^2}$, the tool was able to compute a safe parameter set $\gamma = [0.0668, 0.0675]$ for $g(I) = I - 62.70$. This result shows the benefit of domain splitting in searching for larger safe parameter sets.

7.2 SARS model

We now consider a more complex and realistic epidemic model that describes the *Severe Acute Respiratory Syndrome*, also known as SARS [17]. Differently from the SIR model, in this model the total population size $N = S(t) + E(t) + Q(t) + I(t) + J(t) + R(t)$ is partitioned in six compartments: susceptible individuals $S(t)$ not yet infected by the disease; asymptomatic individuals $E(t)$ that have been exposed to the virus but do not show clinical symptoms of the disease; quarantined individuals $Q(t)$ who were asymptomatic people placed in quarantined because they came in contact with the disease; symptomatic individuals $I(t)$ that show clinical symptoms of SARS and thus considered infected; isolated individuals $J(t)$ that have developed clinical symptoms and have been isolated in order to reduce the contacts with other individuals; recovered individuals $R(t)$ who possess immunity against the disease. The behavior of the susceptible population is governed by

$$\dot{S} = \Pi - \frac{S(\beta I + \epsilon_E \beta E + \epsilon_Q \beta Q + \epsilon_J \beta J)}{N} - \mu S$$

where Π is the rate of inflow individuals into the infected area and $\mu > 0$ is the proportional death rate. The parameters β, $\epsilon_E \beta$, $\epsilon_Q \beta$, and $\epsilon_J \beta$ are the transmission coefficients for symptomatic, asymptomatic, quarantined, and isolated individuals, respectively. From the dynamics of S we can see how these 4 parameters influence the decrease of the susceptible population. The rate of asymptomatic individuals is described by

$$\dot{E} = p + \frac{S(\beta I + \epsilon_E \beta E + \epsilon_Q \beta Q + \epsilon_J \beta J)}{N} - (\gamma_1 + \kappa_1 + \mu)E$$

where p is the rate of undetected entry of infected individuals (such as animal-to-human transmissions), γ_1 is the rate of quarantining, and κ_1 the development of clinical symptoms. The equation

$$\dot{Q} = \gamma_1 E - (\kappa_2 + \mu)Q$$

regulates the rate of change of quarantined individuals, where κ_2 corresponds to the development of clinical symptoms, while

$$\dot{I} = \kappa_1 E - (\gamma_2 + d_1 + \sigma_1 + \mu)I$$

describes the evolution of the symptomatic population, that is decreased at rate γ_2 by isolation, by disease-induced death at rate d_1, and recovery at rate σ_1. The rate of change of isolated individuals is governed by

$$\dot{J} = \gamma_2 I + \kappa_2 Q - (\sigma_2 + d_2 + \mu)J$$

where σ_2 and d_2 are the recovery and disease-induced death rates, respectively. Finally, the rate of recovered individuals is described by

$$\dot{R} = \sigma_1 I + \sigma_2 J - \mu R$$

where symptomatic and isolated individuals recover from the disease at rates σ_1 and σ_2, respectively. Collecting the above-mentioned differential equations and discretizing them with the Euler method with time step h, we obtain a 6-dimensional discrete-time polynomial model. In this case study, we perform computations on data obtained from the SARS outbreak occurred in late 2002 around the area of Hong Kong [17]. The initial values corresponding to the compartments expressed in millions are $S_0 = 6.5$, $E_0 = 124$, $I_0 = 1$, and $Q_0 = R_0 = J_0 = 0$, while the fixed parameter values are $\Pi = 221$, $p = 0$, and $N = 131.5$. The natural death rate is $\mu = 0.05$, the two recovery rates are $\sigma_1 = 0.0337$ and $\sigma_2 = 0.0386$, and disease-induced death rates are $d_1 = 0.015$ and $d_2 = 0.0068$. It is assumed that $d_1 > d_2$ and $\sigma_2 > \sigma_1$, that is the mortality rate of infected individuals is higher than the isolated ones, while the recovery rate of isolated people is faster than the infected ones.

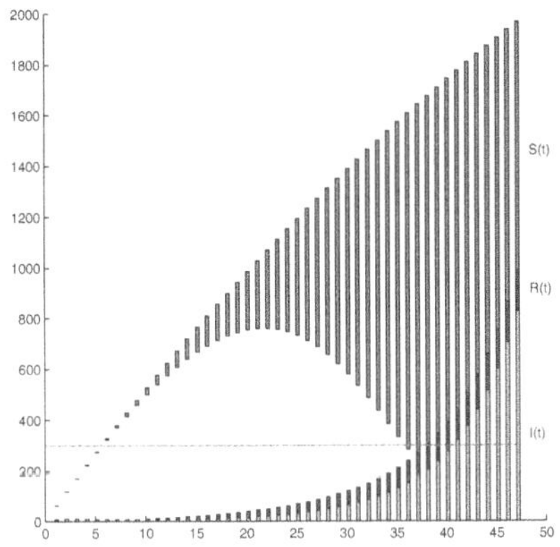

Figure 7: SARS evolution with the unconstrained parameter set.

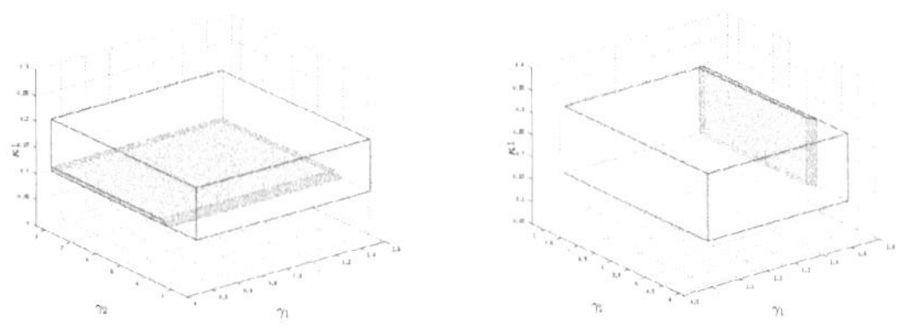

(a) (b)

Figure 8: Projections of the original and synthesized parameter sets.

Regarding the transmission coefficients, the parameter values are $\epsilon_E = \epsilon_Q = 0$, $\epsilon_J = 0.5$, and $\beta = 0.15$.
Finally, the controllable parameters are the quarantining and isolation rates $\gamma_1 \in [0.10, 1.50]$ and $\gamma_2 \in [2.50, 8.25]$, and the clinical symptoms development values $\kappa_1 \in [0.1, 0.2]$ and $\kappa_2 \in [0.1, 0.2]$. Figure 7 depicts the reachability result of the SARS model with the initial unconstrained parameter set. The time step chosen is $h = 0.25$. A unit time corresponds to almost a week, hence the graphs represent the evolution on a time interval of approximatively 14 months. Similarly to the previous case study, we are interested in decreasing the number of infected people $I(t)$ by controlling parameters γ_1, γ_2, κ_1, and κ_2. Analyzing the system without any constraint on the admissible parameter set, we observe (see Figure 7) that there is a peak of almost 800 millions of infected people and approximatively 2000 susceptible individuals. We want to know if it is possible to decrease the maximum number of symptomatic individuals below the threshold of 300. To this end, we formalize the safety condition $g(I) = I - 300 < 0$. Our tool was able to find a positive answer to the query and synthesized safe values for the parameters γ_1, γ_2, κ_1, and κ_2 in 2012.82 seconds. Figure 8(a) shows the projection of the original and the synthesized parameter sets on the variables γ_1,γ_2, and κ_1. The larger box is the original parameter set, while the inner polytope is the result of the synthesis. The evolution of the system with the constrained parameter set is shown in Figure 9. Interpreting the data, we can deduce that the number of infected people can be controlled to exclude low values of the isolation rate. That is, a fast isolation of symptomatic individuals decreases the proliferation of the disease.

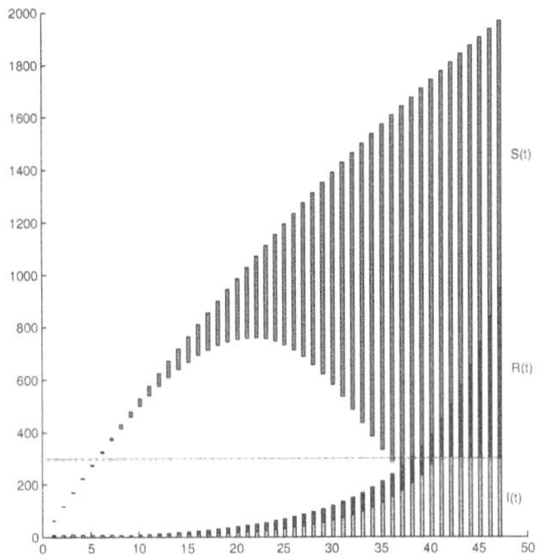

Figure 9: SARS evolution with the synthesized parameter set.

Considering the unsafe set described by the formula $g(E, I) = E + I - 1300$ and the initial parameter set $\gamma_1 \in [0.1, 1.5]$, $\gamma_2 \in [2.5, 8.25]$, and $\kappa_1 \in [0.15, 0.3]$, our tool computed in 2410.32 seconds the synthesized parameter set depicted in Figure 8(b). Note that the result is a polytope, since these parameters are coupled in the dynamics of the state variables in the safety constraint.

8. CONCLUSION

In this paper we described a parameter synthesis algorithm for polynomial dynamical systems and its application to biological models. The algorithm includes a new method for multi-dimensional matrix transposition that allows significantly improving the efficiency of the Bernstein expansion computation. An important advantage of our algorithm is that it can handle a large number of parameters since the computation involving the parameters can be reduced to linear program solving. The experimental results obtained for two biological models are encouraging and we intend to pursue this work in several directions. One is an extension to the problem where the property is described by a set of polynomial constraints, which requires a more sophisticated subdivision technique. To address more complex behavioral specifications in biological systems, we want to extend this work to more expressive constraints described using logical operators and time-dependent queries. Finally, a promising direction to investigate is to develop a more symbolic method to manipulate parametric Bernstein control points.

9. REFERENCES

[1] *Special Issue on the Use of Bernstein Polynomials in Reliable Computing: A Centennial Anniversary*, volume 17. Reliable Computing, December 2012.

[2] M. Althoff. Reachability analysis of nonlinear systems using conservative polynomialization and non-convex sets. In *HSCC'13*, pages 173–182. ACM, 2013.

[3] B. Amos. A computationally efficient algorithm for testing the identifiability of polynomial systems with

applications to biological systems. *Ind. Eng. Chem. Res.*, 49(13):6125–6134, 2010.

[4] E. Asarin, A. Donzé, O. Maler, and D. Nickovic. Parametric identification of temporal properties. In *Proc. of the Second Int. Conf. on Runtime verification*, RV'11, pages 147–160. Springer-Verlag, 2012.

[5] M. Ashyraliyev, Y. Fomekong-Nanfack, J. A. Kaandorp, and J. G. Blom. Systems biology: parameter estimation for biochemical models. *FEBS Journal*, 276(4):886–902, 2009.

[6] J. Barnat, L. Brim, A. Krejci, A. Streck, D. Safranek, M. Vejnar, and T. Vejpustek. On parameter synthesis by parallel model checking. *IEEE/ACM Trans. Comput. Biol. Bioinformatics*, 9(3):693–705, 2012.

[7] E. Bartocci, L. Bortolussi, and L. Nenzi. On the robustness of temporal properties for stochastic models. In *Hybrid Systems and Biology HSB*, volume 125 of *EPTCS*, 2013.

[8] A. Casagrande, T. Dreossi, and C. Piazza. Hybrid automata and epsilon-analysis on a neural oscillator. In *Hybrid Systems and Biology HSB*, volume 92 of *EPTCS*, pages 58–72, 2012.

[9] X. Chen, E. Ábrahám, and S. Sankaranarayanan. Taylor model flowpipe construction for non-linear hybrid systems. In *Proc. RTSSâĂŹ12*. IEEE, 2012.

[10] F. Clauss and I. Chupaeva. Application of symbolic approach to the Bernstein expansion for program analysis and optimization. *Program. Comput. Softw.*, 30(3):164–172, 2004.

[11] T. Dang and R. Testylier. Reachability analysis for polynomial dynamical systems using the Bernstein expansion. *Reliable Computing*, 17(2):128–152, 2012.

[12] A. Donzé. Breach, a toolbox for verification and parameter synthesis of hybrid systems. In *CAV*, pages 167–170, 2010.

[13] A. Donzé, G. Clermont, and C. J. Langmead. Parameter synthesis in nonlinear dynamical systems: Application to systems biology. *Journal of Computational Biology*, 17(3):325–336, 2010.

[14] T. Dreossi and T. Dang. Falsifying oscillation properties of parametric biological models. In *Int. Workshop on Hybrid Systems and Biology HSB*, volume 125 of *EPTCS*, pages 53–67, 2013.

[15] J. Garloff and A. Smith. A comparison of methods for the computation of affine lower bound functions for polynomials. In *Global Optimization and Constraint Satisfaction*, LNCS, pages 71–85. Springer, 2005.

[16] J. Garloff and A. Smith. Rigorous affine lower bound functions for multivariate polynomials and their use in global optimisation. In *Proc. of the 1st Int. Conf. on Applied Operational Research*, volume 1 of *Lecture Notes in Management Science*, pages 199–211, 2008.

[17] A. Gumel, S. Ruan, T. Day, J. Watmough, F. Brauer, V. Driessche, D. Gabrielson, C. Bowman, M. Alexander, S. Ardal, et al. Modelling strategies for controlling sars outbreaks. *Proc. of the Royal Society of London. Series B: Biological Sciences*, 271(1554):2223–2232, 2004.

[18] S. K. Jha and C. J. Langmead. Synthesis and infeasibility analysis for stochastic models of biochemical systems using statistical model checking and abstraction refinement. *Theor. Comput. Sci.*, 412(21):2162–2187, May 2011.

[19] W. Kermack and A. McKendrick. A contribution to the mathematical theory of epidemics. *Proceedings of the Royal Society Of London: Series A, Physical and Mathematical Sciences*, 115:700–721, 1927.

[20] G. Lillacci and M. Khammash. Parameter estimation and model selection in computational biology. *PLoS Computational Biology*, 6(3), 2010.

[21] A. Platzer and E. Clarke. The image computation problem in hybrid systems model checking. In *HSCC'07*, volume 4416 of *LNCS*, pages 473–486. Springer, 2007.

[22] S. Prajna and A. Jadbabaie. Safety verification of hybrid systems using barrier certificates. In *HSCC'04*, volume 2993 of *LNCS*, pages 477–492. Springer, 2004.

[23] S. Ray and P. Nataraj. A matrix method for efficient computation of bernstein coefficients. *Reliable Computing*, 17(1):40–71, 2012.

[24] E. Rodríguez-Carbonell and A. Tiwari. Generating polynomial invariants for hybrid systems. In *HSCC'05*, volume 3414 of *LNCS*, pages 590–605. Springer, 2005.

[25] M. Sassi, R. Testylier, T. Dang, and A. Girard. Reachability analysis of polynomial systems using linear programming relaxations. In *ATVA 2012*, volume 7561 of *LNCS*, pages 137–151. Springer, 2012.

[26] A. P. Smith. *Enclosure Methods for Systems of Polynomial. Equations and Inequalities.* PhD thesis, Universität Konstanz, Germany, 2012.

[27] R. Testylier and T. Dang. Analysis of parametric biological models with non-linear dynamics. In *Int. Workshop on Hybrid Systems and Biology HSB*, volume 92 of *EPTCS*, pages 16–29, 2012.

Compositionality Results for Cardiac Cell Dynamics

Md. Ariful Islam
Stony Brook University
Stony Brook, NY, USA
mdaislam@cs.sunysb.edu

Abhishek Murthy
Stony Brook University
Stony Brook, NY, USA
amurthy@cs.sunysb.edu

Antoine Girard
Université Joseph Fourier
Grenoble, France
antoine.girard@imag.fr

Scott A. Smolka
Stony Brook University
Stony Brook, NY, USA
sas@cs.sunysb.edu

Radu Grosu
Vienna Univ. of Technology
Vienna, Austria
radu.grosu@tuwien.ac.at

ABSTRACT

By appealing to the small-gain theorem of one of the authors (Girard), we show that the 13-variable sodium-channel component of the 67-variable IMW cardiac-cell model (Iyer-Mazhari-Winslow) can be replaced by an approximately bisimilar, 2-variable HH-type (Hodgkin-Huxley) abstraction. We show that this substitution of (approximately) equals for equals is safe in the sense that the approximation error between sodium-channel models is not amplified by the feedback-loop context in which it is placed. To prove this feedback-compositionality result, we exhibit quadratic-polynomial, exponentially decaying bisimulation functions between the IMW and HH-type sodium channels, and also for the IMW-based context in which these sodium-channel models are placed. These functions allow us to quantify the overall error introduced by the sodium-channel abstraction and subsequent substitution in the IMW model. To automate computation of the bisimulation functions, we employ the SOSTOOLS optimization toolbox. Our experimental results validate our analytical findings. To the best of our knowledge, this is the first application of δ-bisimilar, feedback-assisting, compositional reasoning in biological systems.

1. INTRODUCTION

Technological advances in data acquisition and data processing have revolutionized the way we understand biological processes. From the molecular level to the organ level, new mechanisms underlying such processes are uncovered on a regular basis, and then formalized mathematically. If concentrations e.g. of ions, molecules, and proteins play an important role, the models of choice are systems of partial or ordinary differential equations (PDEs/ODEs).

This ever-increasing knowledge about biological processes is reflected in the ever-increasing complexity of the corresponding PDEs. The ionic processes underlying the transmembrane action potentials (APs) exhibited by *excitable* cells (e.g. neurons and cardiac myocytes) are no exception. In the case of myocytes, PDE models have evolved from 4 state variables in the Noble model [17] to 67 state variables in the Iyer-Mazhari-Winslow (IMW) model [12], pushing simulation efforts, not to mention formal analysis, up against the tractability boundary. The original benchmark for neurons was the 4-variable ODE model of Hodgkin and Huxley [10].

Two techniques have proved to be particularly useful in extending the reach of formal analysis: *abstraction* and *decomposition*. Abstraction reduces the size of the system under investigation by neglecting details irrelevant to the properties of interest. Decomposition, as the name suggests, decomposes the system into smaller pieces, which are then analyzed on their own. Together, these two techniques permit *compositional reasoning*: if A_1 abstracts I_1 and A_2 abstracts I_2, then their composition $A_1 \| A_2$ abstracts $I_1 \| I_2$.

Compositional reasoning has proved to be especially useful in the non-numerical setting, with *simulation* and *bisimulation* among the most widely used abstraction techniques. Intuitively, simulation is a game requiring that each move of I from state x_1, with observation o_1, to a state x_2, with observation o_2, can be matched by a move of A from state y_1, with observation o_1, to a state y_2, with observation o_2. Both I and A start in their initial states, and iteratively continue from the successor states. Bisimulation is the symmetric form of this game. Simulation and bisimulation have the very salient property of supporting compositional reasoning in the sense discussed above.

In the numerical setting, the notions of simulation and bisimulation were extended in two ways. First, the moves of the game are assumed to take some (equal) amount of time. Second, identical observations are replaced with the more robust notions of *δ-simulation* and *δ-bisimulation*, where δ is the maximum distance (error) between observations. In a previous paper [16], we used this concept to show that the 13-variable ODE model of the IMW sodium channel, which we denote as Σ_I (see Def. 1 in Section 2), is δ-bisimilar (for a very small δ) to a 2-variable HH-type model, denoted as Σ_H (see Def. 2 in Section 2). Our proof was by construction: we showed that it is possible to identify the parameters of Σ_H such that the observations of the two systems are always less than δ apart.

HSCC'14, April 15–17, 2014, Berlin, Germany.

ACM 978-1-4503-2732-9/14/04 ...$15.00.
http://dx.doi.org/10.1145/2562059.2562138.

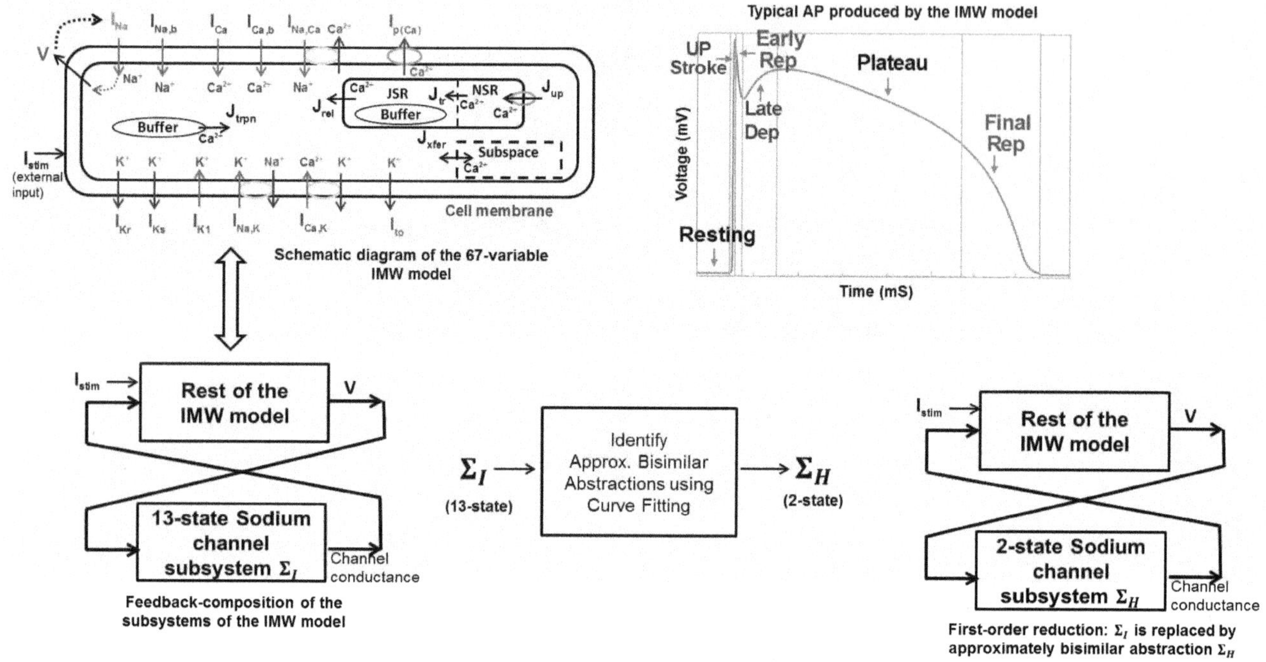

Figure 1: Component-wise model-order reduction of IMW model using abstraction and compositional reasoning.

Unfortunately, δ-bisimulation does not automatically support compositional reasoning. When parallel composition feeds the outputs of subsystem A_1 to the inputs of subsystem A_2 (and vice versa), the error of A_1 with respect to I_1 can get amplified by A_2, which may lead to an even larger error of A_2 with respect to I_2, which is then again amplified by A_1, and so on. For example, in the context of the IMW model, let this model with its sodium channel removed be denoted by Σ_R (the "rest" of the IMW model). Then, replacing Σ_I within $\Sigma_I \| \Sigma_R$ with its δ-bisimilar channel Σ_H may lead to widely divergent behavior by $\Sigma_H \| \Sigma_R$ with respect to $\Sigma_I \| \Sigma_R$ in terms of their APs, even for a very small δ. Careful examination of the problem reveals that this is due to Σ_H not properly closing as the AP reaches the conclusion of its upstroke phase.

To find the proper conditions under which the δ-bisimulation abstraction Σ_H of Σ_I behaves properly with respect to its feedback composition with Σ_R, we enlist the support of *Bisimulation Functions* (BFs) [8]. The value of a BF is required to cover (be greater than) the (observation) distance between all pairs of states of a system (say Σ_R) in isolation, or of the states of one system (say Σ_H) and the states of another system (say Σ_I). See Fig. 8 for a 3D rendering of the BFs relevant to this paper. Once such a cover is found, one can restrict it to the initial states of the system(s) and their successors. Similar to Lyapunov functions, one can search for BFs from among the square polynomials over pairs of states of the system. A popular tool for automating this search is SOSTOOLS, which we use in this paper.

Inspired by the notion of input-to-state stability, the approach of [7] requires that BFs are exponentially decaying, and that the distance between inputs is bounded. The former condition, which corresponds to exponential stability, is stronger than asymptotic stability, but it has a very desirable compositionality property: the BF for the composed systems (for example, the one for $\Sigma_H \| \Sigma_R$ versus $\Sigma_I \| \Sigma_R$) is a linear combination of the BFs for its components (e.g., Σ_H versus Σ_I and Σ_R versus Σ_R). The coefficients of the linear combination quantify the precision of the BF so obtained, and of its associated bisimulation relation.

Applying the compositional reasoning technique described above to the three components Σ_H, Σ_I, and Σ_R proved to be beyond the computational power of SOSTOOLS. Σ_R has $67 - 13 = 54$ variables; consequently, a BF over all pairs of states of Σ_R has 108 variables, one for each pair, and must be computed in a compositional fashion itself. We show how to do this by considering a Σ_R consisting of only its one-variable membrane, which we call Σ_C (see Def. 4). For Σ_C paired with itself, as well as for Σ_I versus Σ_H, SOSTOOLS is able to successfully compute the required BFs.

The other channels, pumps and exchangers of the IMW model can be treated in a similar manner, which is reserved for the full version of the paper. Fig. 1 provides an overview of our approach, which is geared toward incrementally reducing the complexity of cardiac-cell models through the use of δ-bisimilarity-based abstraction and BF-based compositional reasoning. To the best of our knowledge, this is the first application of δ-bisimilar, feedback-assisting, compositional reasoning in biological systems.

The rest of the paper is organized as follows. Section 2 provides relevant background information on the Σ_I and Σ_H models, and on BFs. Section 3 introduces canonical cell models, states our compositionality result, and explains the BF-based approach for establishing the result. Section 4 describes our computation of BFs using SOSTOOLS. Section 5 contains our experimental results. Section 6 considers related work, while Section 7 offers our concluding remarks.

A two-page, poster-style abstract of a preliminary version of this work appeared in [15].

2. BACKGROUND

Cardiac myocytes belong to the class of *excitable cells*, which also includes neurons and skeletal muscle cells. Such cells have the following excitability property: supra-threshold electrical excitation, either external or from neighboring cells, results in a characteristic change in the transmembrane voltage known as the *Action Potential* (AP). See Fig. 1 for a typical AP.

The transmembrane potential of the cell is determined by the differences in the concentrations of sodium (Na), potassium (K), and calcium (Ca) ions present in the extracellular and intracellular mediums. The resulting gradients of concentrations lead to the flow of ions across the membrane that can be measured as an *ionic current* for each type of flow. The ion flow is facilitated by *ion channels* present in the membrane of the cells. Ion channels are proteins that exhibit conformational changes on varying the transmembrane voltage, and are selectively permeable to either Na, K, or Ca ions. Some of the conformations allow ion flow, whereas others inhibit the respective current. The rate of change of voltage resulting from the ion flows is a function of the various ionic currents at any point in time.

Detailed cardiac cell models, such as the 67-variable Iyer-Mazhari-Winslow (IMW) model [12], are dynamical systems that capture the voltage-dependent behavior of the various ion channels responsible for the movement of Na, K, and Ca ions. In these models, each type of channel contributes a subsystem (submodel) that is responsible for the corresponding ionic current. Each such submodel is a mean-field approximation of the channel's collective stochastic behavior. In this paper, we focus on the sodium-channel subsystem of the IMW model.

We define dynamical systems using a 6-tuple $(\mathcal{X}, \mathcal{X}^0, \mathcal{U}, f, \mathcal{O}, g)$, where $\mathcal{X}$ is the *state space*, $\mathcal{X}^0 \subseteq \mathcal{X}$ is the set of *initial conditions*, $\mathcal{U}$ is the *input space*, $f : \mathcal{X} \times \mathcal{U} \to \mathcal{X}$ is the *vector field* defining the dynamics, $\mathcal{O}$ is the set of *outputs*, and $g : \mathcal{X} \to \mathcal{O}$ maps a state to its output. We begin by defining the IMW sodium-channel subsystem.

Definition 1. The *sodium channel model* Σ_I is given by $(X, X^0, \mathcal{V}, f_I, \mathcal{O}, g_I)$. A state $\mathbf{x} \in X \subseteq \mathbb{R}^{13}_{\geq 0}$ is the occupancy probability distribution over the 13 states of the voltage-controlled Continuous Time Markov Chain (CTMC) shown in Fig. 2 in the following order of the state labels: $[C_0, C_1, C_2, C_3, C_4, O_1, O_2, CI_0, CI_1, CI_2, CI_3, CI_4, I]$. The dynamics f_I is given by

$$f_I : \dot{\mathbf{x}} = A_I(V)\ \mathbf{x} \tag{1}$$

where $V \in \mathcal{V} \subseteq \mathbb{R}$, the transmembrane voltage, is the input to the system and $A_I(V)$ is the 13×13 voltage-controlled rate matrix. The off-diagonal entry $A_I(i, j), i \neq j$, is the transition rate from state $\mathbf{x}_j$ to state $\mathbf{x}_i$. For example, $A_I(5, 6) = \delta(V)$, the transition rate from O_1 to C_4. The diagonal entry $A_I(i, i)$ is the sum of all the outgoing rates from state $\mathbf{x}_i$. The transition rates are exponential functions of V, and can be found in Table 1 of [16].

The set of outputs $\mathcal{O} \subseteq \mathbb{R}_{\geq 0}$ contains the conductance values for the states. Given a state $\mathbf{x}$, $g_I(\mathbf{x}) \triangleq \mathbf{x}_6 + \mathbf{x}_7$ maps it to its conductance given by the sum of the occupancy probabilities of the states labeled O_1 and O_2. We use O_I to denote the output when the state can be inferred from the context. The system has a single initial condition $\mathbf{x}_0 \in X^0$, which is defined in Table 4 of [12].

In [16], we presented a two-step curve-fitting procedure for identifying Σ_H, a two-state abstract model that can (approximately) match the output of Σ_I, and is based on the Hodgkin-Huxley (HH) model for neurons [10].

Definition 2. The *HH-type abstraction* Σ_H is given by $(Y, Y^0, \mathcal{V}, f_H, \mathcal{O}, g_H)$. Its state $\mathbf{y} \in Y \subseteq \mathbb{R}^2_{\geq 0}$ measures the degrees of activation, denoted by m, and inactivation of the channel, denoted by h; see Fig. 2. Component $\mathbf{y}_1$ corresponds to m and $\mathbf{y}_2$ corresponds to h. The dynamics f_H is given by

$$f_H : \dot{\mathbf{y}} = A_H(V)\ \mathbf{y} + B_H(V) \tag{2}$$

where $A_H = \begin{bmatrix} -(\alpha_m(V) + \beta_m(V)) & 0 \\ 0 & -(\alpha_h(V) + \beta_h(V)) \end{bmatrix}$ and $B_H = \begin{bmatrix} \alpha_m(V) \\ \alpha_h(V) \end{bmatrix}$ where $V \in \mathcal{V} \subseteq \mathbb{R}$, the transmembrane voltage, is the input. The rates $\alpha_i(V)$ and $\beta_i(V)$, $i \in \{m, h\}$, are given in Eqs. (7)-(10) of Section 3 of [16], and were identified during the two-step curve-fitting process.

The set of outputs $\mathcal{O} \subseteq \mathbb{R}_{\geq 0}$ contains the conductance values for the states. Given a state $\mathbf{y}$, $g_H(\mathbf{y}) \triangleq \mathbf{y}_1^3\mathbf{y}_2$, maps it to its conductance, which corresponds to m^3h. We use O_H to denote the output when the state can be inferred from the context.

The system has a single initial condition $\mathbf{y}_0 = [0.0026, 0.95]^T$, which was obtained after model identification. Details can be found in the discussion of procedure "Parameter Estimation from Finite Traces (PEFT)" in Section 3 of [16].

The *feedback composition* $\Sigma_A || \Sigma_B$ of two dynamical systems Σ_A and Σ_B is obtained by feeding the output of Σ_A as the input to Σ_B and vice versa.

The concept of Input-to-Output Stability (IOS) is key to proving our compositionality results. IOS is formalized using contractive metrics, called bisimulation functions [7], that characterize the joint IOS of two dynamical systems. The following definition is adapted from [7] and uses $\parallel . \parallel$ to denote the squared L2 norm.

Definition 3. Let $\Sigma_i = (\mathcal{X}_i, \mathcal{X}_i^0, \mathcal{U}, f_i, \mathcal{Y}, g_i)$, $i = 1, 2$, be two dynamical systems such that $\mathcal{X}_i \subseteq \mathbb{R}^{n_i}$, $\mathcal{U} \subseteq \mathbb{R}^m$ and $\mathcal{Y} \subseteq \mathbb{R}^p$. A *bisimulation function* (BF) is a smooth function $S : \mathbb{R}^{n_1} \times \mathbb{R}^{n_2} \to \mathbb{R}_{\geq 0}$ such that for every $\mathbf{x}_1 \in \mathcal{X}_1$, $\mathbf{x}_2 \in \mathcal{X}_2$, $\mathbf{u}_1, \mathbf{u}_2 \in \mathcal{U}$:

$$\parallel g_1(\mathbf{x}_1) - g_2(\mathbf{x}_2) \parallel \leq S(\mathbf{x}_1, \mathbf{x}_2), \tag{3}$$

$$\exists \lambda > 0, \gamma \geq 0 : \frac{\partial S}{\partial \mathbf{x}_1} f_1(\mathbf{x}_1, \mathbf{u}_1) + \frac{\partial S}{\partial \mathbf{x}_2} f_2(\mathbf{x}_2, \mathbf{u}_2) \leq -\lambda S(\mathbf{x}_1, \mathbf{x}_2) + \gamma \parallel \mathbf{u}_1 - \mathbf{u}_2 \parallel \tag{4}$$

Next, we present a modified version of Theorem 1 of [7], which captures the joint IOS of two systems.

Theorem 1. Let S be a BF with parameters λ and γ between dynamical systems Σ_i, $i = 1, 2$, and let $\mathbf{x}_1(t)$ and $\mathbf{x}_2(t)$ be two trajectories of the systems. For all $t \geq 0$,

$$\begin{aligned} \parallel g_1(\mathbf{x}_1(t)) - g_2(\mathbf{x}_2(t)) \parallel &\leq S(\mathbf{x}_1(t), \mathbf{x}_2(t)) \\ &\leq e^{-\lambda t} S(\mathbf{x}_1(0), \mathbf{x}_2(0)) + \\ &\frac{\gamma}{\lambda} \parallel \mathbf{u}_1 - \mathbf{u}_2 \parallel_\infty \end{aligned}$$

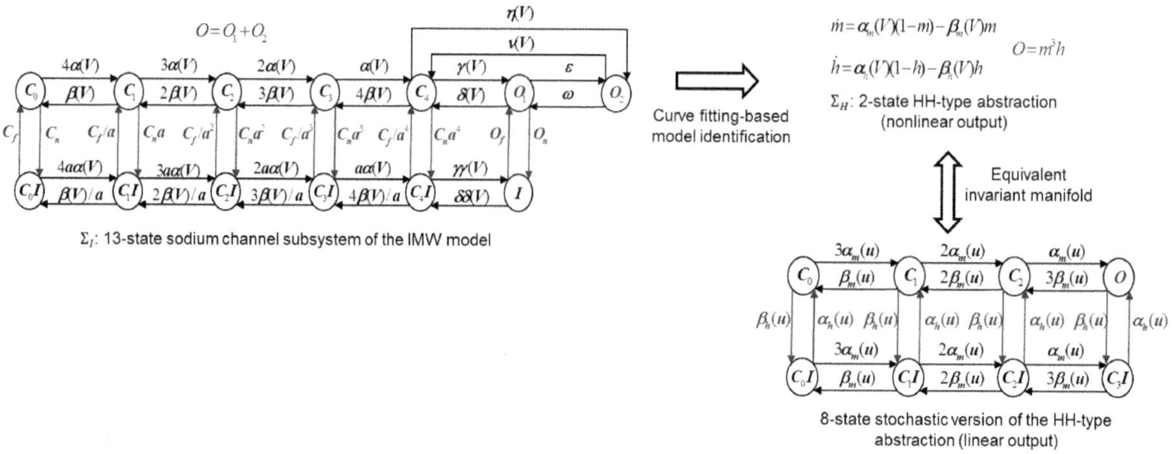

Figure 2: Sodium-channel subsystems used in the CCM: Σ_I is the detailed sodium-channel subsystem used in the IMW model. The 2-state abstraction Σ_H is identified in [16], and has a nonlinear output function m^3h. Σ_H is an exact invariant manifold of an 8-state stochastic model that has linear output. The 8-state version is used for computing BFs in SOSTOOLS.

where $\| \mathbf{u}_1 - \mathbf{u}_2 \|_\infty = sup_{t \geq 0} \| \mathbf{u}_1(t) - \mathbf{u}_2(t) \|$ denotes the maximum difference in the input signals being fed to the two systems.

PROOF. See the supplementary document [11]. □

It follows from Theorem 1 that the existence of a BF between two dynamical systems is a proof of the following IOS property: when *approximately equal* signals are fed as inputs to the two systems, they produce *approximately equal* outputs. When applied to one system, a BF demonstrates the *robustness* of the system to small variations in the input signal. The Lyapunov-like functions-based approach is an extension of *input-to-state* stability of [20].

When subsystems are connected using feedback, their respective BFs can be composed subject to a small-gain condition. We formalize this idea by stating a result based on Theorem 2 of [7].

Theorem 2. Let $\Sigma_i = (\mathcal{X}_i, \mathcal{X}_i^0, \mathcal{U}_i, f_i, \mathcal{O}_i, g_i)$, $i = 1, 2, A, B$, be dynamical systems such that $\mathcal{U}_1 = \mathcal{O}_A$, $\mathcal{U}_A = \mathcal{O}_1$, $\mathcal{U}_2 = \mathcal{O}_B$ and $\mathcal{U}_B = \mathcal{O}_2$. Let S_{12}, parameterized by λ_{12} and γ_{12}, be a BF between Σ_1 and Σ_2. Let S_{AB}, parameterized by λ_{AB} and γ_{AB}, be a BF between Σ_A and Σ_B.

Let $\Sigma_{A1} = \Sigma_A || \Sigma_1$ and $\Sigma_{B2} = \Sigma_B || \Sigma_2$. If the *small-gain condition* (SGC) $\frac{\gamma_{AB}\gamma_{12}}{\lambda_{AB}\lambda_{12}} < 1$ is met, then a BF S can be constructed between Σ_{A1} and Σ_{B2} by composing S_{AB} and S_{12} as follows:

$$S(\mathbf{x}_{A1}, \mathbf{x}_{B2}) = \alpha_1 S_{AB}(\mathbf{x}_A, \mathbf{x}_B) + \alpha_2 S_{12}(\mathbf{x}_1, \mathbf{x}_2) \quad (5)$$

where $\mathbf{x}_{A1} = [\mathbf{x}_A, \mathbf{x}_1]^T$ and $\mathbf{x}_{B2} = [\mathbf{x}_B, \mathbf{x}_2]^T$ and the constants α_1 and α_2 are given by:

$$\begin{cases} \frac{\gamma_{12}}{\lambda_{AB}} < \alpha_1 < \frac{\lambda_{12}}{\gamma_{AB}} \text{ and } \alpha_2 = 1 & \text{if } \lambda_{AB} \leq \gamma_{12} \\ \alpha_1 = 1 \text{ and } \frac{\gamma_{AB}}{\lambda_{12}} < \alpha_2 < \frac{\lambda_{AB}}{\gamma_{12}} & \text{if } \lambda_{12} \leq \gamma_{AB} \\ \alpha_1 = 1 \text{ and } \alpha_2 = 1 & \text{in other cases} \end{cases} \quad (6)$$

PROOF. See the supplementary document [11]. □

3. COMPOSITIONAL APPROACH

In this section, we introduce the voltage subsystem Σ_C representing the cell membrane, which we compose with Σ_I and Σ_H to obtain two *canonical cell models* (CCMs). We then state our compositionality result in terms of the two CCMs, and show how BFs can be used to prove the result.

Definition 4. The *voltage subsystem* Σ_C is a capacitor-like model given by $(\mathcal{V}, \mathcal{V}^0, \mathcal{O}, f_C, \mathcal{V}, g_C)$. State $V \in \mathcal{V} \subseteq \mathbb{R}$ is the voltage. The dynamics of Σ_C is given by

$$f_C : \dot{V} = -G_{Na}(V - V_{Na})\ O \quad (7)$$

where $G_{Na} = 5$ and $V_{Na} = 30\ mV$ are the parameters of the model, and $O \in \mathcal{O} \subseteq \mathbb{R}_{\geq 0}$, the conductance of the sodium channel, is Σ_C's input. The system outputs its state, i.e., for $V \in \mathcal{V}$, $g_C(V) = V$, and the initial condition is $V_0 = -30\ mV$.

As per Eq. (7), V_{Na} represents the equilibrium for a fixed-conductance input. Thus, V takes values in $[-30, 30]$.

In the case of detailed cardiac cell models, such as the IMW model, ion-channel subsystems such as Σ_I and Σ_H take voltage as input from the rest of the model and provide the conductance of the channel as the output. The rest of the model takes the channel conductance as input and outputs the voltage, which is then fed back to the ion-channel subsystems. Next, we define CCMs Σ_{CI} and Σ_{CH} that reflect this feedback-based composition. The models are canonical in the sense that other ion-channel subsystems can be similarly added to obtain a complete IMW model.

Definition 5. Systems Σ_{CI} and Σ_{CH} (see Fig. 3) are obtained by performing feedback-composition on the voltage subsystem Σ_C with ion-channel subsystems Σ_I and Σ_H, respectively; i.e., $\Sigma_{CI} = \Sigma_C || \Sigma_I$ and $\Sigma_{CH} = \Sigma_C || \Sigma_H$. The state spaces, initial conditions, dynamics and outputs are inherited from the subsystems, as explained below. Both Σ_{CI} and Σ_{CH} are autonomous systems and do not receive any external inputs.

A state of Σ_{CI} is given by $[\mathbf{x}, V_I]^T$, where $\mathbf{x}$ is a state of Σ_I and V_I is a state of Σ_C. The subscript I in V_I is used to denote the copy of Σ_C composed with Σ_I. The system dynamics are given by Eqs. (1) and (7). The output is given by $[g_I(\mathbf{x}), V_I]^T$. The initial condition is the pair of the initial conditions of Σ_I and Σ_C.

A state of Σ_{CH} is given by $[\mathbf{y}, V_H]^T$, where $\mathbf{y}$ denotes a state of Σ_H and V_H denotes a state of Σ_C. The subscript H in V_H is used to denote the copy of Σ_C composed with Σ_H. The system dynamics are given by Eqs. (2) and (7). The output is given by $[g_H(\mathbf{y}), V_H]^T$. The initial condition is the pair of the initial conditions of Σ_H and Σ_C.

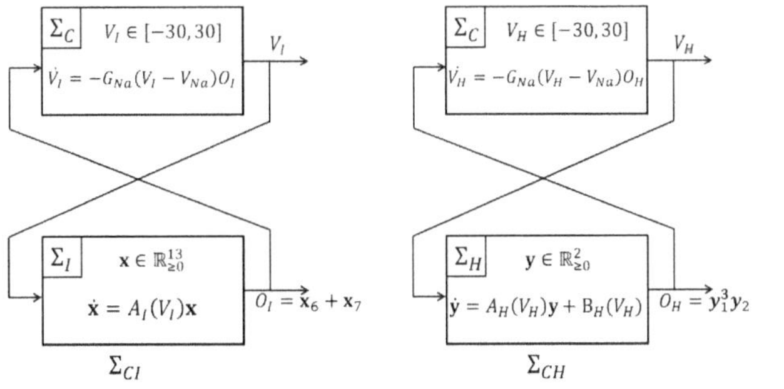

Figure 3: CCMs Σ_{CI} and Σ_{CH}: ion-channel subsystems Σ_I and Σ_H are feedback-composed with Σ_C, which represents the cell membrane. Σ_{CH} is obtained by i) identifying the 2-variable abstraction Σ_H of Σ_I using the curve-fitting procedure given in [16]; and ii) substituting Σ_H for the detailed model Σ_I in the composition Σ_{CI}.

The 2-variable abstraction Σ_H was identified in [16] such that the trajectories of the abstract model approximately match the ones of the detailed model Σ_I. When Σ_I in Σ_{CI} is substituted for by Σ_H to obtain Σ_{CH}, the behaviors of the composite CCMs might diverge. This is due to the feedback composition that tends to amplify deviations in the outputs of either of the subsystems. The goal of the paper is to show that the composite CCMs are indeed approximately equivalent, i.e., the following statement is valid.

Compositionality Result: There exists a BF S between Σ_{CI} and Σ_{CH} that renders the two CCMs to be approximately equivalent in the sense characterized by Theorem 1.

S is computed compositionally as follows. First, the components Σ_I and Σ_H are proved to be approximately equivalent by computing a BF S_{IH} between the two systems. Then, the context Σ_C is proved to be robust to input deviations by computing a BF S_C for it. The computation procedure ensures that the prerequisite SGC condition is satisfied by S_{IH} and S_C, thereby enabling the application of Theorem 2; this results in a BF S between Σ_{CI} and Σ_{CH}. We describe the computation procedure for S_{IH} and S_C in the next section.

4. COMPUTING SUM-of-SQUARES BFs

In this section, we show how to formulate the BFs S_{IH} and S_C as sum-of-squares (SoS) polynomials, thereby enabling us to automate their computation using SOSTOOLS [18], the MATLAB-based SoS optimization toolbox. S_{IH} is a BF between Σ_I and Σ_H, with parameters λ_{IH} and γ_{IH}, while S_C is a BF between Σ_C and itself, with parameters λ_C and γ_C. Values for these parameters must be determined such that the SGC condition of Theorem 2 is satisfied.

I. Rewriting the system definitions

The rate matrix $A_I(V)$ of Σ_I has a zero eigenvalue for all $V \in [-30, 30]$, the values the input can take when Σ_I is composed with Σ_C. The system dynamics are rewritten to make the new rate matrix Hurwitz, which is a necessary and sufficient condition for exponential stability. As the system is a voltage-controlled CTMC, one of the variables is always redundant; i.e., the occupancy probability of one state can be expressed as 1 - (sum of all other occupancy probabilities).

Using this fact, we removed the redundant state occupancy probability corresponding to state I of Fig. 2. The resulting dynamics are affine: $\dot{\mathbf{x}}' = A'_I(V).\mathbf{x}' + B_I(V)$, where the state vector $\mathbf{x}'$ now contains the first 12 probabilities from $\mathbf{x}$. The 12×12 matrix A'_I and the 12×1 affine term B_I can be found in [11]. For a fixed voltage input $V = v$, the equilibrium of the resulting linear system was shifted to the origin by solving $A'_I(v).\mathbf{x}' = -B_I$.

Σ_H has an output function of degree 4, which would require S_{IH} to be an 8th-order polynomial. Higher-order polynomials lead to possibly intractable instances of SoS optimization in SOSTOOLS. To resolve this issue, the 2-state system was converted to an equivalent 8-state stochastic model that has a linear output function. In [14], Σ_H is shown to be the exact invariant manifold of the 8-state voltage-controlled CTMC shown in Fig. 2. S_{IH} is then defined as a quadratic function over 19 (12 + 7) variables, which ensures that the corresponding SoS problem can be solved despite the increase in the number of undetermined coefficients.

The output of Σ_H, m^3h, represents the probability that three *activation (m-type)* gates and one *inactivation (h-type)* gate are open. As they are all independent, we obtain the net probability of the event as m^3h. This event corresponds to the occupancy probability of the state labeled O in voltage-controlled CTMC of Fig. 2, which is the output of this 8-state model. Similarly, the occupancy probability of each of the other 7 states corresponds to a certain number of m-type (maximum 3) and the h-type (maximum 1) gates being open. For example, the state labeled C_1 corresponds to one m-type gate and the h-type gate being open, resulting in a net probability of mh. Similarly, the state labeled C_1I corresponds to one m-type gate being open and the h-type gate being closed, resulting in a net probability of $m(1-h)$.

The 8-state stochastic version has dynamics of the form $\dot{\mathbf{y}} = A_H(V)$, where $y \in \mathbb{R}^8$ is the vector representing the occupancy probability distribution among the eight states in the order $[C_0, C_1, C_2, O, C_0I, C_1I, C_2I, C_3I]$. $A_H(V)$ is an 8×8 matrix similar to $A_I(V)$ in Definition 1. The linear system was converted to its affine form to remove the zero eigenvalue, as was done for Σ_I: $\dot{\mathbf{y}}' = A'_H(V).\mathbf{y}' + B'_H(V)$, by eliminating the state labeled C_3I. The new state vector $\mathbf{y}'$ denotes the occupancy probabilities of the first 7 states from $\mathbf{y}$. The 7×7 rate matrix A'_H and the 7×1 affine term B_H can be found [11]. The output of this system is $\mathbf{y}_4$, corresponding to the occupancy probability of the state labeled O.

For a fixed voltage input $V = v$, the equilibrium of the resulting linear system was shifted to the origin by solving $A'_H(v).\mathbf{y}' = -B'_H$. Similarly, the equilibrium of Σ_C, for a fixed conductance input, was shifted to the origin using an offset of V_{Na}.

II. SoS Optimization

A multivariate polynomial $p(x_1, x_2, \dots, x_n) = p(\mathbf{x})$ is an *SoS polynomial* if there exist polynomials $f_1(\mathbf{x}), \dots, f_m(\mathbf{x})$ such that $p(\mathbf{x}) = \sum_{i=1}^{m} f_i^2(\mathbf{x})$. We denote the set of all SoS polynomials by $\mathbb{S}$. An instance of SoS optimization involves finding an $S \in \mathbb{S}$ such that a linear objective function, whose decision variables are the coefficients of S, is optimized. The constraints of the problem are linear in the decision variables. A formal definition of an SoS optimization instance can be found in the SOSTOOLS user guide (p. 7).

We constructed two instances of SoS optimization: P_{IH} and P_C, to compute $S_{IH}(\mathbf{x}', \mathbf{y}')$ and $S_C(V_I, V_H)$, respectively. The two problems are solved using SOSTOOLS, which internally calls the semidefinite programming solver *sedumi*. We next explain the construction of P_{IH} and P_C.

III. Choosing the form of the SoS BFs

Defining an instance of SoS optimization begins with declaring the form of the desired polynomial. We chose ellipsoidal forms for the BFs using the `sossosvar` function provided by SOSTOOLS: $S_{IH}(\mathbf{x}', \mathbf{y}') = [\mathbf{x}', \mathbf{y}'].Q_{IH}.[\mathbf{x}', \mathbf{y}']^T$ and $S_C(V_I, V_H)$
$= [V_I, V_H].Q_C.[V_I, V_H]^T$. Variables $\mathbf{x}', \mathbf{y}', V_I$, and V_H are declared using the `pvar` polynomial variable toolbox. The coefficients of the BFs, which form the decision variables of the SoS optimization problems, are contained in the positive semidefinite matrices Q_{IH} (19×19) and Q_C (2×2).

Eq. (3), the first constraint defining a BF, was implemented as:

$$P_{IH} : S_{IH} - ((\mathbf{x}'_6 + \mathbf{x}'_7) - (\mathbf{y}'_4))^2 \in \mathbb{S}, \text{ and}$$

$$P_C : S_C - (V_I - V_H)^2 \in \mathbb{S}.$$

IV. Input-space quantization

Eq. (4), the second constraint defining a BF, must be satisfied for all the pairs of states and inputs. The optimizer searches over the state space to optimize Q_{IH} and Q_C, but does not search over the input space. We therefore sampled pairs of inputs to the two subsystems: Σ_I and Σ_H for P_{IH}, and the two copies of Σ_C for P_C. Eq. (4) was thus implemented as follows:

$$P_{IH} : -\left[\frac{\partial S_{IH}}{\partial \mathbf{x}'}\left(A'_I(v_i).\mathbf{x}'\right) + \frac{\partial S_{IH}}{\partial \mathbf{y}'}\left(A'_H(v_j).\mathbf{y}'\right)\right] - \lambda_{IH} S_{IH}(\mathbf{x}', \mathbf{y}') + \gamma_{IH}|v_i - v_j| \in \mathbb{S}, \quad (8)$$

$$P_C : -\left[\frac{\partial S_C}{\partial V_I}\left(-G_{Na}o_i V_I\right) + \frac{\partial S_C}{\partial V_H}\left(-G_{Na}o_j V_H\right)\right] - \lambda_C S_C(V_I, V_H) + \gamma_C|o_i - o_j| \in \mathbb{S}. \quad (9)$$

For P_{IH}, the input pairs are $(v_i, v_j) \in \mathcal{V} \times \mathcal{V}$, where $\mathcal{V} = \{-60, -30, 0, 20, 30\}$. For P_C, the input pairs are $(o_i, o_j) \in \mathcal{O} \times \mathcal{O}$, where $\mathcal{O} = \{0.1, 0.2, 0.3, 0.4, 0.5, 0.6, 0.7, 0.8, 0.9, 1\}$. We use the dynamics of the system, with the origin shifted to the equilibrium corresponding to the input pair (v_i, v_j). Hence, there are no affine terms in the multipliers of $\partial S_{IH}/\partial \mathbf{x}'$, $\partial S_{IH}/\partial \mathbf{y}'$, $\partial S_C/\partial V_I$ and $\partial S_C/\partial V_H$ terms. Note that each input pair contributes one constraint to the corresponding problem. Thus, Eq. (4) was implemented as 25 constraints in P_{IH} and 100 constraints in P_C.

The use of input-space sampling in computing BFs can be justified as follows. As per Theorem 1, BF S_{IH} bounds the difference in the outputs of Σ_I and Σ_H when the maximum difference in the voltage (input) signals is $\| V_I - V_H \|_\infty$. Voltage signals $V_I(t)$ and $V_H(t)$ can be approximated by quantizing them using the set $\mathcal{V}$. At any point in time, the voltage signals would be rounded off to the nearest member of $\mathcal{V}$. The error in the outputs due to the quantization error in the inputs can be bound using sensitivity analysis. Then, the bound on the output difference given by S_{IH} would have to take into account the output error resulting from the quantization.

A similar analysis can be performed for S_C, where the conductance signals would now be quantized using $\mathcal{O}$. Providing revised bounds that reflect input-space quantization is part of our future work.

V. Handling the parameters

Eqs. (8) and (9) were implemented in SOSTOOLS with fixed values for parameters λ_{IH}, γ_{IH} of P_{IH}, and λ_C, γ_C of P_C. The parameter values we used are given in Table 1. We were unable to make λ_{IH} and λ_C decision variables of P_{IH} and P_C, respectively, as Eqs. (8) and (9) would have become nonlinear in the decision variables. Parameters γ_{IH} and γ_C, however, could have been declared as decision variables of P_{IH} and P_C, respectively. We tried this approach and also defined an objective function to minimize the amplification factor γ/λ of Theorem 1. The resulting BF was inferior to our current approach of defining the objective function (see below), and thus the parameters were fixed to the values provided in Table 1.

Problem	BF	λ	γ
P_{IH}	S_{IH}	$\lambda_{IH} = 0.1$	$\gamma_{IH} = 0.001$
P_C	S_C	$\lambda_C = 0.01$	$\gamma_C = 0.0001$

Table 1: Parameter values used for the BFs.

VI. Optimizing the BFs

Theorem 1 implies that $\forall t \geq 0$, the value of the BF bounds the difference in outputs observed from the two systems. Ideally, we want this bound to be as tight as possible. Also, the value of the BF at $t = 0$ is the highest value that it can assume along a pair of the trajectories (as it decays $\forall t > 0$).

To obtain a BF that provides tight bounds on the output difference, we implemented an objective function that minimizes the BF at the initial states of the two subsystems:

$$P_{IH} : \text{Minimize } S_{IH}(\mathbf{x}'(0), \mathbf{y}'(0)) \text{ and}$$
$$P_C : \text{Minimize } S_C(-30, -30),$$

where $\mathbf{x}'(0)$ and $\mathbf{y}'(0)$ represent the initial conditions of Σ_I and Σ_H as per Definitions 1 and 2, respectively.

P_{IH} and P_C were solved in SOSTOOLS. In the process, SOSTOOLS outputs *feasratio*, *pinf*, *dinf* and *numerr*, which reflect the accuracy and reliability of the solutions. Both P_{IH} and P_C were solved by error-free executions with *feasratio* = 1 and *pinf*, *dinf*, *numerr* = 0, resulting in reliable and accurate BFs. SOSTOOLS took 956.17 seconds to solve P_{IH} and 2.43 seconds to solve P_C on an Intel i5 2.5 GHz CPU-based PC with 6 GB of memory.

The computed value of S_{IH}, as defined by the 19×19 matrix Q_{IH}, can be found in the supplementary document [11]. S_C, the BF between Σ_C and itself, was computed as:

$$S_C(V_I, V_H) = 1.27V_I^2 - 1.4599V_I.V_H + 1.27V_H^2.$$

VII. Composing S_{IH} and S_C
The parameters of S_{IH} and S_C, given in Table 1, satisfy the SGC condition of Theorem 2, as $\frac{\gamma_{IH}\gamma_C}{\lambda_{IH}\lambda_C} = 0.0001 < 1$. Applying Theorem 2, we linearly composed S_{IH} and S_C to obtain $S = \alpha_1 S_{IH} + \alpha_2 S_C$, where $\alpha_1, \alpha_2 = 1$. S is a BF between the composite systems Σ_{CI} and Σ_{CH}. As per Theorem 2 of [7], the parameter λ of S can be calculated as

$$\lambda = min\left(\frac{\alpha_1\lambda_{IH} - \alpha_2\gamma_C}{\alpha_1}, \frac{\alpha_2\lambda_C - \alpha_1\gamma_{IH}}{\alpha_2}\right) = 0.009.$$

5. RESULTS

In this section, we experimentally validate BFs S_{IH}, S_C and S, which were obtained as described in Section 4. As per Theorem 1, BFs decay along a pair of trajectories of the two systems under consideration. To this end, we simulated Σ_I and Σ_H (for S_{IH}), Σ_C (for S_C), and Σ_{CI} and Σ_{CH} (for S) using different inputs and initial conditions, and evaluated the BFs along the resulting trajectories.

Empirical validation of the BFs is first provided by plotting them in 2D along the time axis. As the time proceeds in the same manner in both systems, the corresponding BF is plotted for the pair of states occurring at the same time along the trajectories of the systems. The squared difference in outputs observed for the pair of states is also plotted in the same graph. The resulting plots show that the BFs bound the squared Output Difference (OD) and decay in time along the pairs of trajectories, as per Theorem 1.

We also provide 3D plots, where the x- and y-axes measure time, and the BF along with the OD are plotted on the z-axis. This form of plotting allows us to visualize the fact that the BF upper bounds the difference in the outputs for all possible pairs of states. These plots also show that the BF decays along pairs of trajectories, even when there is a delay between the systems (off-diagonal states).

Fig. 4 shows S_{IH} plotted along three pairs of trajectories of Σ_I and Σ_H. Each pair was generated by supplying a pair of constant voltage signals $(V_1(t), V_2(t))$ as inputs to Σ_I and Σ_H, respectively. The two subsystems were initialized as per Defs. 1 and 2, and simulated using MATLAB's *ODE45* solver. S_{IH} was then evaluated along the resulting pair of trajectories after shifting the origin to the equilibrium defined by $(V_1(t), V_2(t))$.

Fig. 4(a) plots, in blue, the OD along two trajectories that receive the same input of -30 mV. S_{IH} is plotted in red and exhibits the decaying behavior predicted by Theorem 1. Fig. 4(b) plots the output difference along two trajectories with the maximum possible difference in inputs: $V_I(t) = -30\ mV$ and $V_H(t) = 30\ mV$. This results in a relatively large OD observed for the two subsystems. S_{IH} is shown to upper bound this difference and decay along the pair of trajectories. Fig. 4(c) inverts the inputs with $V_I(t) = 30\ mV$ and $V_H(t) = -30\ mV$.

S_C characterizes the ability of Σ_C to tolerate small changes in the input conductance signals. In the composite systems Σ_{CI} and Σ_{CH}, these signals are provided by subsystems Σ_I and Σ_H, and thus vary slightly due to the fitting errors incurred by the abstraction process of [16].

As in Fig. 4, S_C is plotted in Fig. 5 along three pairs of trajectories of Σ_C. Each pair of trajectories was generated by supplying constant conductance (input) signals $(O_1(t), O_2(t))$. Σ_C was initialized at $-30\ mV$ and simulated using the Euler method. S_C was evaluated along the resulting trajectories after shifting the origin to the equilibrium, $30\ mV$ (V_{Na}). Fig. 5(a) shows the case when both $O_1(t)$ and $O_2(t)$ were 0.01, resulting in equal voltage traces with an OD of 0. We have not scaled the systems nor the BFs; thus the scale of Fig. 5 is very different from that of Fig. 4. We can see that even when the input conductances vary by a factor of 8, in Fig. 5(c), S_C bounds the OD and decays along the trajectories.

CCMs Σ_{CI} and Σ_{CH} are autonomous dynamical systems and do not receive any external inputs. To visualize the composite BF S, we simulated Σ_{CI} and Σ_{CH} using the Euler method. Fig. 7 plots the trajectories obtained from these simulations. The corresponding conductance traces of Fig. 7(a) and the voltage traces of Fig. 7(b) empirically validate that the composed models are approximately equivalent as predicted by Theorem 2. BF S along this pair of trajectories is plotted in Fig. 6(a). The value of S is dominated by the value of S_C, as it bounds the squared difference of voltages and is much larger than S_{IH}, which bounds differences in probabilities. This is reasonable as voltage is the primary entity of interest when analyzing excitable cells. One could scale subsystem Σ_C such that its output lies in $[0, 1]$ and is thus comparable to the outputs of Σ_I and Σ_H.

To test extreme cases, we simulated Σ_{CI} and Σ_{CH} by initializing Σ_C at different values. Fig. 6(b) shows the OD plotted along pairs of trajectories, where Σ_C in Σ_{CI} starts at $V_I(0) = -30\ mV$ and in Σ_{CH} at $V_H(0) = 30\ mV$. Fig. 6(c) plots the other extreme, where the copy of Σ_C in Σ_{CI} starts at $30\ mV$ and the copy in Σ_{CH} is initialized to $-30\ mV$. S bounds the OD in all these cases and decays along the trajectories.

Fig. 8 provides 3D views of S_{IH}, S_C, and S. Fig. 8(a) was generated as follows. Σ_I an Σ_H were simulated using constant voltage input signals of $V_I(t) = -30$ mV and $V_H(t) = 30$ mV. The two models were simulated using *ODE45*, starting from the nominal initial conditions specified in Defs. 1 and 2 until steady state was reached. Let T denote the time steps $[t_1, t_2, ..., t_n]$ of the two discrete-time simulations, and $O_I(t)$ and $O_H(t)$ denote the resulting conductance (output) time series, with their origins shifted to the respective equilibria. Fig. 8(a) plots in red the squared output difference $(O_I(t_i) - O_H(t_j))^2$ for all $(t_i, t_j) \in T \times T$. S_{IH} is plotted at the pair of states $(\mathbf{x}'(t_i), \mathbf{y}'(t_j))$ obtained in the simulation for all $(t_i, t_j) \in T \times T$, where $\mathbf{x}'$ and $\mathbf{y}'$ denote the origin-shifted versions of $\mathbf{x}$ and $\mathbf{y}$, respectively. The 3D view of S_{IH} shows that the BF provides an upper bound for the OD at all pairs of states of the two systems. It also shows that S_{IH} decays along the trajectories even when the two systems have a delay between them.

Fig. 8(b) was obtained by simulating Σ_C with two constant conductance signals of 0.1 and 0.01. The resulting voltage output signals differ significantly due to a 10-fold difference in the input signals. Fig. 8(c), on the other hand, was obtained by simulating Σ_{CI} and Σ_{CH} using different initial conditions. In both the cases, the respective BFs S_C and S bound the output difference and decay along the trajectories (even when the two systems have a delay between them).

6. RELATED WORK

In response to the increasing complexity of biological models, *model reduction* and *abstraction* have become active areas of research in computational biology. In [4, 6], the au-

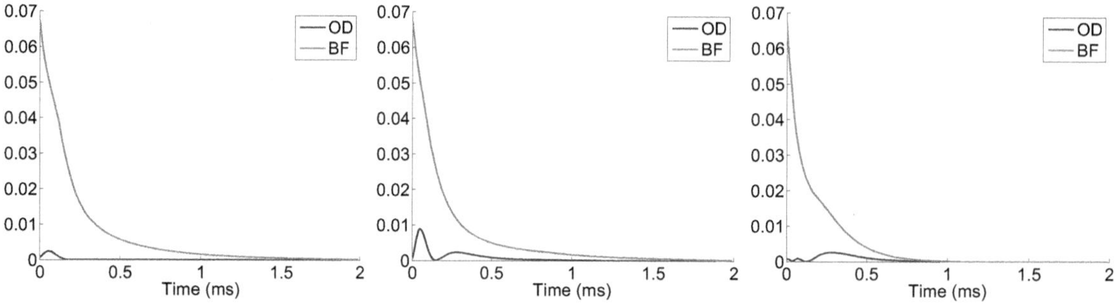

(a) $V_1(t) = V_2(t) = -30\ mV$. (b) $V_1(t) = -30\ mV$, $V_2(t) = 30\ mV$. (c) $V_1(t) = 3\ 0mV$, $V_2(t) = -30\ mV$.

Figure 4: BF S_{IH} and the OD plotted along three pairs of trajectories of Σ_I and Σ_H generated using constant voltage (input) signals. S_{IH} upper bounds the OD and decays along the trajectories.

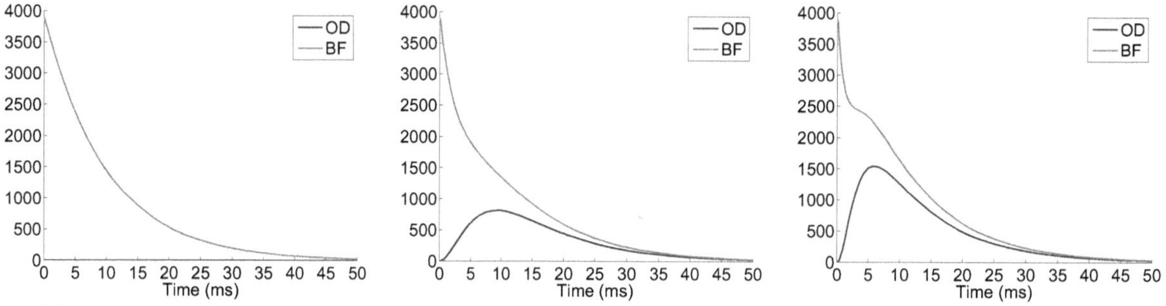

(a) $O_1(t) = 0.01$, $O_2(t) = 0.01$. (b) $O_1(t) = 0.04$, $O_2(t) = 0.01$. (c) $O_1(t) = 0.08\ O_2(t) = 0.01$.

Figure 5: BF S_C and the OD plotted along three pairs of trajectories of Σ_C generated using constant conductance (input) signals. S_C bounds OD even when input signals vary by a factor of 8 (subfig. c).

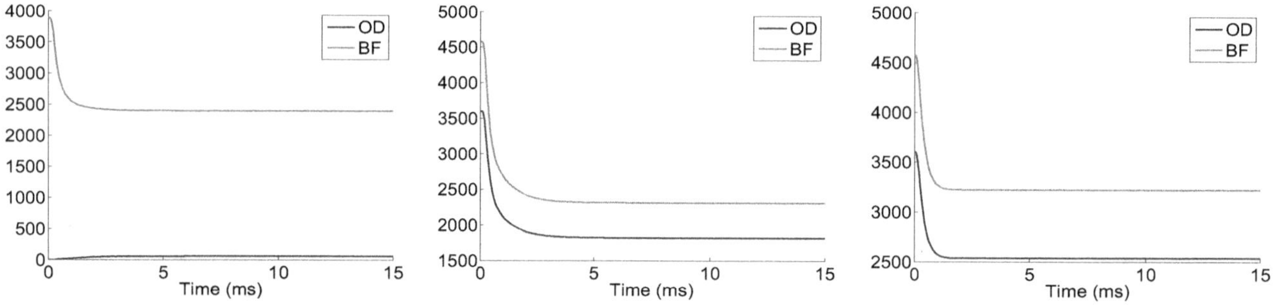

(a) $V_I(0) = -30\ mV$, $V_H(0) = -30\ mV$. (b) $V_I(0) = -30\ mV$, $V_H(0) = 30\ mV$. (c) $V_I(0) = 30\ mV\ V_H(0) = -30\ mV$.

Figure 6: S and OD along pairs of trajectories of Σ_{CI} and Σ_{CH}. Subfig. (a) plots OD and S along trajectories shown in Fig. 7. Subfigs. (b) and (c) plot OD and S along trajectories where Σ_C is initialized at different voltages. Value of OD is dominated by difference of outputs of the two copies of Σ_C, which is in mV. Similarly, value of S is dominated by S_C, which bounds differences in voltages as opposed to S_{IH}, which bounds differences in probabilities.

thors propose the idea of *towers of abstraction*, consisting of a hierarchy of models that capture biological details at varying scales of space and complexity. Compositionality and approximation are vital aspects of constructing such a hierarchy, as pointed out in [5, 9].

Approximate bisimulation equivalence of a detailed model to an abstract model supports such compositional reasoning. In [1], the authors use bisimulation to constrain the *U-projections* of deterministic systems of algebraic differential equations of biochemical networks. The projected automaton is *U-bisimilar* to the original system and thus satisfies the same temporal logic formulae. Compositionality of the models-of-interest is not investigated.

In other related work, a number of efforts, including [3, 19, 2], have been devoted to developing process algebras that are capable of describing biological systems (e.g., interactions among bacteria and bacteriophage viruses) via special biologically motivated operators. Bisimulation in these calculi are typically congruences, thereby allowing compositional reasoning through substitution of equal for equals.

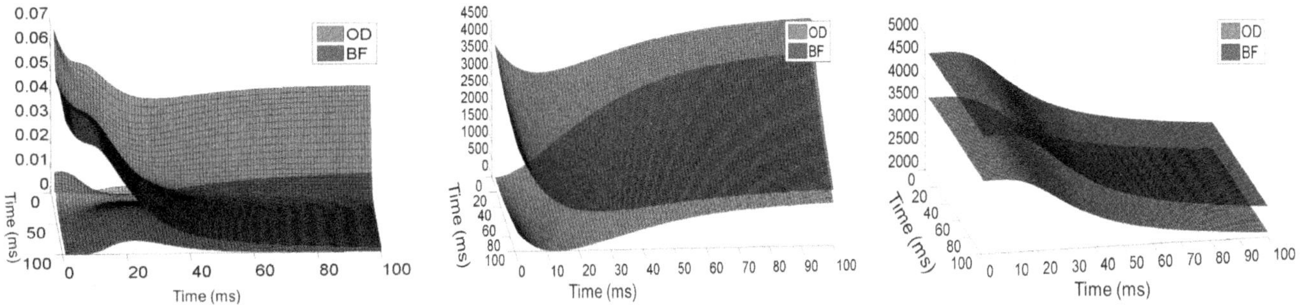

(a) $V_I(t) = -30$ mV, $V_H = 30$ mV. (b) $O_I(t) = 0.1$, $O_H = 0.01$. (c) $V_I(0) = -30$ mV, $V_H(0) = 30$ mV.

Figure 8: 3D visualization of BFs (in blue): S_{IH} in subfig. (a), S_C in subfig. (b) and S in subfig. (c) are plotted for pairs of states obtained at time points $(t_i, t_j) \in T \times T$, where $T = [t_1, t_2, ...]$ are the time steps of discrete-time simulations of the corresponding pairs of systems. The BFs upper bound the OD, plotted in red for all pairs of states, and decay along the trajectories even when there is delay between the two systems. The captions of subfigs. (a)-(b) specify the input signals used for simulation and the caption of subfig. (c) provides the initial conditions used for Σ_C while simulating Σ_{CI} and Σ_{CH}.

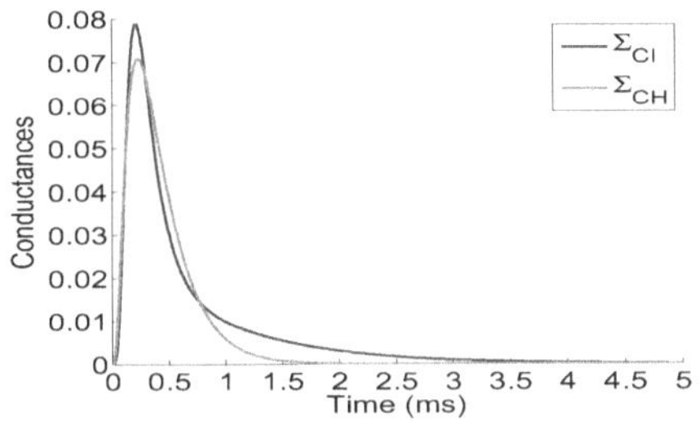

(a) $O_I(t)$ and $O_H(t)$ of Σ_{CI} and Σ_{CH} respectively.

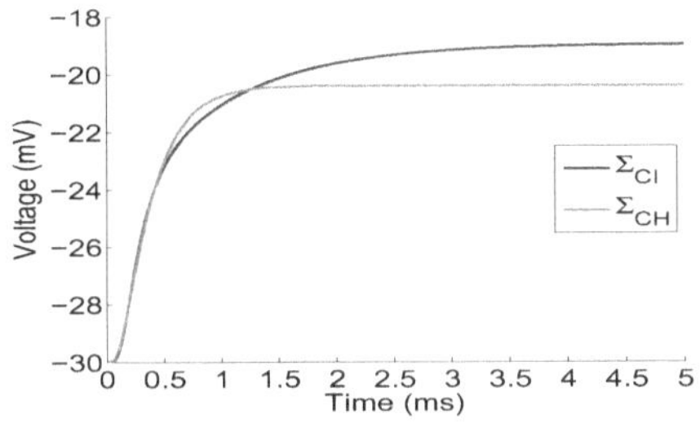

(b) $V_I(t)$ and $V_H(t)$ of Σ_{CI} and Σ_{CH} respectively.

Figure 7: Simulations of Σ_{CI} and Σ_{CH}: when Σ_I is replaced by Σ_H, feedback composition tends to accumulate error incurred due to the abstract component. S proves that these errors remain bounded due to the approximate equivalence of Σ_I and Σ_H, established by BF S_{IH}, and the ability of Σ_C to tolerate deviations in the conductance inputs, established by BF S_C. The mean L1 errors: $O_{Na}: 9 \times 10^{-3}$, V: 1.42 mV.

These approaches typically do not consider continuous system dynamics and feedback through composition.

7. CONCLUSIONS

We used the small-gain theorem of [7] to show that the 13-variable sodium-channel component of the IMW cardiac-cell model can be safely replaced with the δ-bisimilar, 2-variable HH-abstraction we developed in [16]. This substitution of (approximately) equals for equals is "safe" in the sense that, despite the feedback nature of the composition of the sodium-channel component and the rest of the IMW model, the approximation error remains bounded in this context. Our experimental results, which include the SOSTOOLS-based derivation of the appropriate bisimulation functions and their 2-d and 3-d renderings, validate our analytical findings.

When factoring out the sodium-channel component from the IMW model, we are left with a 54-variable subsystem (Σ_R) comprising a multitude of (non-sodium) ionic currents, including potassium and calcium. Applying the compositional reasoning technique discussed above in this context proved to be beyond the computational power of SOSTOOLS. Consequently, we limited our current investigation to a Σ_R consisting of only its one-variable membrane (Σ_C) [12]. The other channels, pumps, and exchangers of IMW can be treated in a similar manner, which is reserved for future work.

Motivated by the challenges we encountered in using SOSTOOLS to find a tightly fitted, exponentially stable cover for the observation distance between *all* pairs of states of a system (or a pair of systems), we plan to investigate how to limit the domain of BFs to *states of interest*: typically those states very close to each other (in terms of their observation distance), and which remain close to each other as time progresses. Such states are δ-bisimilar to each other, for δ sufficiently small. In such cases, we can show that the compositionality result of Theorem 2 still holds, as do the coefficients of the linear combination of the component BFs.

One approach to computing a BF restricted to δ-bisimilar states is to add the constraint $\{(\mathbf{x}_1, \mathbf{x}_2) \mid \| g_1(\mathbf{x}_1) - g_2(\mathbf{x}_2) \| \leq \delta\}$ to the BF optimization problem, where, recall, g_1, g_2 are the respective system output functions. Unfortunately, SOSTOOLS reported that the resulting optimization problem is infeasible. The authors of [13] present an alternative approach to computing BFs restricted to subsets of the state space based on finding two functions g_1', g_2' such that the constraint $\{(\mathbf{x}_1, \mathbf{x}_2) \mid g_1'(\mathbf{x}_1) \geq 0 \wedge g_2'(\mathbf{x}_2) \geq 0\}$ represents the subspace in question. Unfortunately, their approach is not immediately applicable to our problem, as there is no apparent way to decompose the δ-bisimilarity constraint into one based on g_1' and g_2'.

The BFs computed by SOSTOOLS can be scaled by applying an exponential scaling function to them. For a BF S, the scaled version S' would be of the form $S' = S\exp(-CS)$, where $C > 0$. The problem is to find a C such that S' also satisfies both conditions of a BF (Def. 3). Note that scaling can be applied recursively to S. Fig. 9 illustrates the first- and second-order effects of scaling on S_{IH}. For this figure, we used 15 for C in first-level scaling and 42 for C in second-level scaling. Future work will include formalizing this notion of scaled BFs.

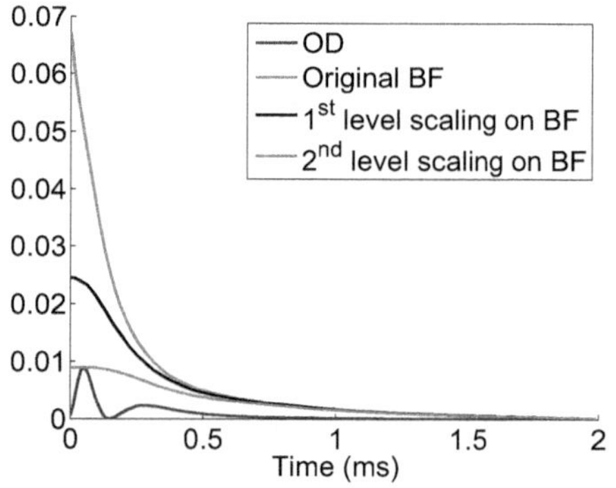

Figure 9: Scaling function applied recursively to S_{IH}. The BF bound on OD is tightened with each level of scaling. All curves use the same pair of trajectories of Σ_I and Σ_H corresponding to input pair (-30,30) mV.

Acknowledgments: We would like to thank the anonymous reviewers for their valuable comments. Research supported in part by NSF grants CCF-0926190 and CCF-1018459, and by AFOSR grant FA0550-09-1-0481.

8. REFERENCES

[1] M. Antoniotti, C. Piazza, A. Policriti, M. Simeoni, and B. Mishra. Taming the complexity of biochemical models through bisimulation and collapsing: Theory and practice. *Theoretical Computer Science*, 325:2004, 2004.

[2] R. Barbuti, A. Maggiolo-Schettini, P. Milazzo, and A. Troina. Bisimulation congruences in the calculus of looping sequences. In *International Colloquium on Theoretical Aspects of Computing (ICTAC'06), LNCS 4281*, pages 93–107. Springer, 2006.

[3] M. Curti, P. Degano, C. Priami, and C. T. Baldari. Modelling biochemical pathways through enhanced pi-calculus. *Theoretical Computer Science*, 325(1):111–140, 2004.

[4] J. Fisher, D. Harel, and T. A. Henzinger. Biology as reactivity. *Communications of the ACM*, 54(10):72–82, October 2011.

[5] J. Fisher and N. Piterman. The executable pathway to biological networks. *Briefings in Functional Genomics*, 9(1):79–92, Jan. 2010.

[6] J. Fisher, N. Piterman, and M. Y. Vardi. The only way is up. In *Proceedings of the 17th International Conference on Formal methods*, FM'11, pages 3–11, Berlin, Heidelberg, 2011. Springer-Verlag.

[7] A. Girard. A composition theorem for bisimulation functions. *Pre-print*, 2007. arXiv:1304.5153.

[8] A. Girard and G. J. Pappas. Approximate bisimulations for nonlinear dynamical systems. In *Proceedings of 44th IEEE Conference on Decision and Control*, Serville, Spain, December 2005.

[9] R. Grosu, G. Batt, F. H. Fenton, J. Glimm, C. L. Guernic, S. A. Smolka, and E. Bartocci. From cardiac cells to genetic regulatory networks. In *Proceedings of the 23rd International Conference on Computer Aided Verification*, pages 396–411. Springer, 2011.

[10] A. L. Hodgkin and A. F. Huxley. A quantitative description of membrane current and its application to conduction and excitation in nerve. *Journal of Physiology*, 117:500–544, 1952.

[11] M. A. Islam. Supplement to compositionality results for cardiac cell dynamics. `www.cs.sunysb.edu/~amurthy/hscc14_supp.htm`, also available on `arxiv.org`, 2013.

[12] V. Iyer, R. Mazhari, and R. L. Winslow. A computational model of the human left-ventricular epicardial myocytes. *Biophysical Journal*, 87(3):1507–1525, 2004.

[13] J. Kapinski, A. Donzé, F. Lerda, H. Maka, S. Wagner, and B. H. Krogh. Control software model checking using bisimulation functions for nonlinear systems. In *47th IEEE Conference on Decision and Control (CDC)*, pages 4024–4029, 2008.

[14] J. P. Keener. Invariant manifold reductions for Markovian ion channel dynamics. *Journal of Mathematical Biology*, 58(3):447–457, July 2009.

[15] Md. A. Islam, A. Murthy, E. Bartocci, S. A. Smolka, and R. Grosu. Compositionality results for cardiac cell dynamics. In *Proceedings of CMSB'13, the 11th Conference on Computational Methods in Systems Biology*, LNCS, Klosterneuburg, Austria, Sept. 2013. Springer.

[16] A. Murthy, Md. A. Islam, E. Bartocci, E. Cherry, F. H. Fenton, J. Glimm, S. A. Smolka, and R. Grosu. Approximate bisimulations for sodium channel dynamics. In *Proceedings of CMSB'12, the 10th Conference on Computational Methods in Systems Biology*, LNCS, London, U.K., October 2012. Springer.

[17] D. Noble. A modification of the Hodgkin-Huxley equations applicable to Purkinje fibre action and pace-maker potentials. *Journal of Physiology*, 160(2):317–352, 1962.

[18] S. Prajna, A. Papachristodoulou, P. Seiler, and P. A. Parrilo. *SOSTOOLS: Sum of squares optimization toolbox for MATLAB*, 2004.

[19] A. Regev, E. M. Panina, W. Silverman, L. Cardelli, and E. Shapiro. Bioambients: An abstraction for biological compartments. *Theoretical Computer Science*, 325(1):141–167, Sept. 2004.

[20] E. D. Sontag. Input to state stability: Basic concepts and results. In *Nonlinear and Optimal Control Theory*, pages 163–220. Springer, 2006.

Powertrain Control Verification Benchmark

Xiaoqing Jin Jyotirmoy V. Deshmukh James Kapinski

Koichi Ueda Ken Butts

Powertrain Control and Model-based Development, Toyota Technical Center, USA.
firstname.lastname@tema.toyota.com

ABSTRACT

Industrial control systems are often hybrid systems that are required to satisfy strict performance requirements. Verifying designs against requirements is a difficult task, and there is a lack of suitable open benchmark models to assess, evaluate, and compare tools and techniques. Benchmark models can be valuable for the hybrid systems research community, as they can communicate the nature and complexity of the problems facing industrial practitioners. We present a collection of benchmark problems from the automotive powertrain control domain that are focused on verification for hybrid systems; the problems are intended to challenge the research community while maintaining a manageable scale. We present three models of a fuel control system, each with a unique level of complexity, along with representative requirements in signal temporal logic (STL). We provide results obtained by applying a state of the art analysis tool to these models, and finally, we discuss challenge problems for the research community.

Categories and Subject Descriptors

I.6.4 [**Simulation and Modeling**]: Model Validation and Analysis; J.7 [**Computers in other Systems**]: Industrial Control; D.2.4 [**Software Engineering**]: Software/Program Verification—*Validation*

Keywords

Hybrid Systems Benchmarks, Automotive Control Systems, Verification, Model Comparison, Model-based Testing

1. INTRODUCTION

Hybrid dynamical systems are prevalent in modern control designs, and many researchers continue to develop new technologies and tools to analyze such systems. Unfortunately, there is a paucity of standard benchmark systems and accompanying requirements that researchers can use to evaluate and compare the efficacy of their analysis techniques. Industrial benchmark problems can be of added value as they exemplify the context, scale, and complexity of real-world hybrid systems challenges. Often, however, industrial models are either proprietary and cannot be shared with the research community or they are too complex to be investigated with academic tools. To address this, we present a suite of benchmark hybrid systems verification problems in the form of a series of models of an automotive powertrain control system along with a collection of formal specifications.

An inherent challenge in the analysis of hybrid systems is that even the simplest of problems run into the problem of undecidability; for example, the problem of reachability analysis for linear hybrid automata was shown to be undecidable [21]. Many researchers have worked on this problem [5, 7], and continue to extend reachability analysis to systems with more interesting nonlinear dynamics [9]. This research area has been served well by efforts such as [15] that have formulated benchmark problems. The benchmarks proposed in [15] are easily extensible, for example a navigation system with a parameterized set of cells on a map-grid. While the original paper evaluated tools such as `d/dt`, CHARON, and a predicate abstraction based verifier on the benchmark problems, these benchmark problems have also successfully influenced more recent research leading to tools such as PHAver [16], SpaceEx [18] and `iSAT` [14].

In this paper, we present three benchmark models, a set of challenge problems and suite of requirements in Signal Temporal Logic (STL) specifying the behavior and performance of the models. The models that we present in Sec. 3 are successive simplifications of the model of an important control problem in the automotive domain, that of air-fuel (A/F) ratio control [10]. In an internal combustion engine, the ratio of air mass to injected fuel has direct implications on the rate of exhaust gas emissions, driveability and fuel efficiency. A three-way catalyst (TWC) system (used in catalytic converters that reduce the amount of undesirable exhaust gases) performs optimally when the A/F ratio is at the stoichiometric value. The control problem for this system is to maintain A/F ratio to this set value.

The first model is the most complex model, implemented using Simulink[1] and contains many features typical of an industrial closed-loop system; i.e., a plant model that captures the physical aspects of the fuel and air subsystems and has elements such as lookup tables (LUTs), variable transport delays, and highly nonlinear dynamics, and a controller model that is a time-triggered system with mode switching behavior that has hysteresis. This model is beyond the capabilities of most existing formal verification tools; with the state of the art, the best one could achieve with this model is simulation-based falsification.

The second model presents hybrid I/O automata (HIOA) models of the plant and the controller and an automaton representing their composition. In this model, we simplify dynamics of some

[1]Simulink™ is a registered trademark of the MathWorks Inc.

HSCC'14, April 15–17, 2014, Berlin, Germany.

ACM 978-1-4503-2732-9/14/04 ...$15.00.
http://dx.doi.org/10.1145/2562059.2562140 .

subsystems, remove time delays, replace lookup tables with continuous functions, and remove certain subsystems. The plant is an HIOA model of a continuous dynamical system, while the controller is an HIOA model of a discrete-time multi-modal dynamical system. The third model is a further simplification in which the controller is modeled with continuous-time differential equations, and all nonpolynomial dynamics are approximated by polynomials. These final two models could, perhaps, be more amenable to formal techniques such as reachable set estimation or stability analysis.

The rest of the paper is organized as follows. We review definitions related to hybrid I/O automata and Signal Temporal Logic in Section 2. In Section 3, we present the three benchmark models and provide a collection of formal requirements for them in Section 4. Section 5 presents samples of analyses of the models using a falsification tool known as S-TaLiRo [6]. Finally, in Section 6, we present verification research challenges.

2. PRELIMINARIES

In this section, we briefly review the terminology that we will use in this paper. We use the formalism of hybrid input/output automata (HIOA) similar to the one presented in [17, 24]. These are essentially hybrid automata extended with ability to process exogenous inputs and produce outputs. We further elaborate on how a hybrid system with a mixture of discrete-time and continuous-time state variables can be modeled by such a hybrid automaton. Finally, we introduce the falsification problem for hybrid systems.

2.1 Hybrid I/O Automata

A hybrid automaton is a useful model of a system that displays continuous-time behavior interleaved with discrete jumps. Hybrid automata with inputs and outputs have additional structure as they allow exogenous time-varying inputs, and observable outputs. Due to this additional structure, HIOA facilitate modular descriptions of subsystems and their compositions to obtain larger systems.

Let $\mathcal{V} = \{v_1, \ldots, v_k\}$ denote a set of variables, such that each of them takes values from possibly different domains. Let $\mathbb{D}(\mathcal{V})$ denote the domain of values for the variables in $\mathcal{V}$. Let $\nu(\mathcal{V})$ denote a valuation for the variables, i.e., a tuple of values from $\mathbb{D}(\mathcal{V})$. In the sequel, we follow the notation that caligraphic symbols (such as $\mathcal{V}$) denote sets of variables $\{v_1, \ldots, v_k\}$ and the corresponding normal capitalized, italic font letters (such as V) to denote $\mathbb{D}(\mathcal{V})$.

Formally, a hybrid input/output automaton (HIOA) $\mathcal{A}$ is defined as a tuple $(\mathcal{L}, \mathcal{X}, \mathcal{U}, \mathcal{M}, \mathcal{G}, \mathcal{R}, \Delta, \mathcal{T}, \mathcal{Y}, \mathcal{I})$, where:

- $\mathcal{L}$ is a finite set of *discrete modes*.
- $\mathcal{X} = \{x_1, \ldots, x_n\}$ is a finite set of n state variables, and following the notation defined before, X denotes the set of all valuations of $\mathcal{X}$. The hybrid state space is thus a subset of the set $\mathcal{L} \times X$. We use $\mathbf{x}$ as an abbreviation for the tuple $(x_1, \ldots, x_n)$.
- $\mathcal{U} = \{u_1, \ldots, u_m\}$ denotes a set of m typed input variables. Note that input variables could be of different types such as $\mathbb{R}$, $\mathbb{Z}$, Booleans, etc. We use $\mathbf{u}$ as an abbreviation for the tuple $(u_1, \ldots, u_m)$.
- $\mathcal{M}$ maps each mode ℓ with a *mode invariant* $\mathcal{M}(\ell) \subseteq X \times U$.
- $\mathcal{G}$ is a set of predicates over $X \times U$.
- $\mathcal{R}$ is a set of functions from $X \times U$ to X.
- $\Delta \subseteq \mathcal{L} \times \mathcal{G} \times \mathcal{R} \times \mathcal{L}$, is a finite set of transitions. For each transition $\delta : (\ell, g, r, \ell') \in \Delta$, $g \in \mathcal{G}$ is its *guard predicate*, and $r \in \mathcal{R}$ its *reset map*.
- Let $\mathbb{T} \subseteq \mathbb{R}^{\geq 0}$ represent the domain of time values. A *trajectory* $\tau_{(\mathcal{X},\mathcal{U})}$ is a function from $\mathbb{T}$ to $(X \times U)$ that describes the valuations of the input variables and state variables over time. $\mathcal{T}$ is a finite or infinite set of trajectories. In an HIOA, a trajectory is often a sequence of alternating *flows* (within modes) and *resets* (consistent with mode transitions). For a given mode ℓ, the flow within the mode is typically the solution trajectory $\mathbf{x}(\cdot)$ of an initial value problem as described by an ordinary differential equation (ODE) of the form $\dot{\mathbf{x}} = f_\ell(\mathbf{x}, \mathbf{u})$ with $\nu(\mathbf{x}) = \mathbf{x}_0$ at time $t = t_0$.
- $\mathcal{Y} \subseteq \mathcal{X}$ denotes a set of typed output variables.
- $\mathcal{I} \subseteq \mathcal{L} \times X$ is the set of possible initial discrete modes and valuations of the state variables.

In what follows, we use $\mathbf{x}(t)$, $\mathbf{u}(t)$ to denote the valuation of the variables $\mathbf{x}$ and $\mathbf{u}$ at time t.

Parallel Composition. Given two HIOA $\mathcal{A}_1$ and $\mathcal{A}_2$, where $\mathcal{A}_i$ is defined as the tuple $(\mathcal{L}_i, \mathcal{X}_i, \mathcal{U}_i, \mathcal{M}_i, \mathcal{G}_i, \mathcal{R}_i, \Delta_i, \mathcal{T}_i\mathcal{Y}_i, \mathcal{I}_i)$, for $i \in \{1, 2\}$, we say that $\mathcal{A}_1$ and $\mathcal{A}_2$ are *compatible* if $\mathcal{X}_1 \cap \mathcal{X}_2 = \emptyset$, $\mathcal{Y}_1 \subseteq \mathcal{U}_2$ and $\mathcal{Y}_2 \subseteq \mathcal{U}_1$.

The parallel composition operation allows compatible HIOA representing two modules to be composed to form a composite module. Note that the input and output variables that are part of the interface between two HIOA disappear as a result of composition. For a given set X, let $X \downarrow Y$ denote projection or the restriction of X to the elements of Y. The composite HIOA $\mathcal{A}_c = \mathcal{A}_1 \parallel \mathcal{A}_2$ representing the parallel composition of $\mathcal{A}_1$ and $\mathcal{A}_2$ as shown above is defined as the tuple $(\mathcal{L}_c, \mathcal{X}_c, \mathcal{U}_c, \mathcal{M}_c, \mathcal{G}_c, \mathcal{R}_c, \Delta_c, \mathcal{Y}_c, \mathcal{T}_c, \mathcal{I}_c)$, where:

- $\mathcal{L}_c = \mathcal{L}_1 \times \mathcal{L}_2$,
- $\mathcal{X}_c = \mathcal{X}_1 \cup \mathcal{X}_2$,
- $\mathcal{U}_c = (\mathcal{U}_1 \cup \mathcal{U}_2) \setminus (\mathcal{Y}_1 \cup \mathcal{Y}_2)$,
- $\nu(\mathcal{X}_c) \in \mathcal{M}_c(\ell_1, \ell_2)$ iff for $i \in \{1, 2\}$, $\nu(\mathcal{X}_c \downarrow \mathcal{X}_i) \in \mathcal{M}_i(\ell_i)$,
- $\mathcal{G}_c$ is a set of predicates over $X_c \times U_c$ and $\mathcal{R}_c$ is a set of functions from $X_c \times U_c$ to X_c.
- A transition δ_c of the form $(\ell_c, g_c, r_c, \ell_c')$ is in the set Δ_c if:
  - There is a transition $\delta_1 \in \Delta_1$ of the form $(\ell_1, g_1, r_1, \ell_1')$, and $\ell_c = (\ell_1, \ell_2)$, $g_c = g_1$, $r_c = r_1$ and $\ell_c' = (\ell_1', \ell_2)$, or,
  - there is a transition $\delta_2 \in \Delta_2$ of the form $(\ell_2, g_2, r_2, \ell_2')$, and $\ell_c = (\ell_1, \ell_2)$, $g_c = g_2$, $r_c = r_2$ and $\ell_c' = (\ell_1, \ell_2')$ or,
  - there are transitions δ_1 and δ_2 as described in the previous cases, and $\ell_c = (\ell_1, \ell_2)$, $\ell_c' = (\ell_1', \ell_2')$, $g_c = g_1 \wedge g_2$, and $r_c = r_1 \cup r_2$.
- $\mathcal{Y}_c = (\mathcal{Y}_1 \cup \mathcal{Y}_2) \setminus (\mathcal{U}_1 \cup \mathcal{U}_2)$,
- A trajectory $\tau_{(\mathcal{X}_c, \mathcal{U}_c)}$ is in $\mathcal{T}_c$ iff for $i = 1, 2$, $\tau_{(\mathcal{X}_i, \mathcal{U}_i)} \in \mathcal{T}_i$.
- $((\ell_1, \ell_2), \nu(\mathcal{X}_c)) \in \mathcal{I}_c$ iff for $i = \{1, 2\}$, $(\ell_i, \nu(\mathcal{X}_c \downarrow \mathcal{X}_i)) \in \mathcal{I}_i$.

Modeling discrete-time updates. In our model, we have a mixture of states that evolve in continuous-time according to dynamics defined by an ODE, as well as states that evolve in discrete-time that stay constant between discrete time-steps. The latter can be modeled by a traditional hybrid automaton using resets.

2.2 Polynomial Hybrid I/O Automata

Let $\mathcal{U}_R$ denote the variables $\mathcal{U}$ restricted to those u_j that take values over $\mathbb{R}$. Let $\mathbb{P}(\mathbf{x}, \mathbf{u}, k)$ denote the set of all polynomial functions from $(\mathcal{X} \times \mathcal{U}_R)$ to $\mathbb{R}$, such that for any polynomial function $f(\mathbf{x}, \mathbf{u}) \in \mathbb{P}(\mathbf{x}, \mathbf{u}, k)$, the maximum degree of any monomial in $f(\mathbf{x}, \mathbf{u})$ is k. Further, let $\mathbb{B}(\mathbf{x}, \mathbf{u}, k)$ denote the infinite set of predicates of the form $g(\mathbf{x}, \mathbf{u}) < c$, where $g \in \mathbb{P}(\mathbf{x}, \mathbf{u}, k)$ and $c \in \mathbb{R}$. A *polynomial hybrid I/O automaton* (PHA) is an HIOA where:

- For each mode ℓ, the flow within the mode is described as a solution trajectory of the initial value problem of an ODE of the form $\dot{\mathbf{x}} = f_\ell(\mathbf{x}, \mathbf{u})$, where $f_\ell \in \mathbb{P}(\mathbf{x}, \mathbf{u}, k)$.
- For each mode ℓ, $\mathcal{M}(\ell)$ is a finite Boolean combination of predicates in $\mathbb{B}(\mathbf{x}, \mathbf{u}, k)$.
- The set $\mathcal{G}$ is a finite subset of the set $\mathbb{B}(\mathbf{x}, \mathbf{u}, k)$.
- The set $\mathcal{R}$ is a finite subset of $\mathbb{P}(\mathbf{x}, \mathbf{u}, k)$.

A well-known subclass of polynomial hybrid I/O automaton is that of *linear hybrid automata* (LHA), where the sets in the above definition are restricted to those with degree $k = 1$. As reachability analysis tools such as SpaceEx [18], and Flow* [9] are applicable for models expressed as LHA and PHA respectively, these are interesting subclasses of the general model.

2.3 Falsification Analysis

In Section 4, we provide some benchmark specifications that characterize desired behavior of the closed-loop system consisting of the plant and the controller. Such *formal* specifications, also known in the automotive world as *verifiable requirements* are typically not expressed in a format amenable to analysis tools. The ultimate goal for automotive control systems is improvement in metrics such as fuel economy, driveability, and lower exhaust gas emissions. With the benchmark specifications, our intent is to map these high-level requirements to checkable requirements on individual subsystems (such as the A/F control subsystem).

To specify requirements, we use the formalism of signal temporal logic (STL) or its close variant metric temporal logic (MTL). These logics are extensions of linear temporal logic (LTL), which is used in software verification to specify correctness of finite or infinite traces of programs. STL and MTL extend the temporal operators provided by LTL with time-intervals, and this allows us to specify real-time requirements. While MTL characterizes time-varying behavior of pre-defined Boolean predicates, STL admits time and frequency-domain properties on signals [12, 13]. Here, we focus on the time-domain specifications using STL. Below we give the formal syntax and semantics of STL, which are similar to those of MTL [23, 4].

Syntax and Semantics of STL. STL is a temporal logical formalism that allows predicates on real-valued *signals*; it is used to specify precise real-time relations between predicates. An n-dimensional signal $\mathbf{x}$ is defined as a function from a time domain (in our case this is some *interval*, i.e., a bounded and closed subset of $\mathbb{R}$) to $\mathbb{R}^n$.

Informally, an atomic unit of an STL formula is some predicate μ on an n-dimensional signal $\mathbf{x}$, and can be converted to an inequality of the form $f(\mathbf{x}) > 0$, where f is any function from $\mathbb{R}^n$ to $\mathbb{R}$. Note that as $\mathbf{x}$ is an n-dimensional signal, this definition allows constraints relating multiple signals. Further, equality constraints can be specified by using Boolean combinations of predicates. Relations between predicate values at different time instants in a signal are specified using *timed temporal operators*. Temporal operators such as $\Box$ ("always"), $\Diamond$ ("eventually") and $\mathbf{U}$ ("until") are commonly used. Each temporal operator ranges over an open time-interval of the form (a, b) where $a, b \in \mathbb{R}$. Other time-intervals such as those with one or both end-points included in the interval are also permitted. We use I to denote any such time-interval. While it is known that the $\Box$ and $\Diamond$ operators can be rewritten using the $\mathbf{U}$ operator, in the following formal syntax we include them for completeness:

$\varphi ::=$	$true$	/* the *true* predicate */
	$\mid \mu$	/* μ: signal predicate $f(\mathbf{x}) > 0$ */
	$\mid \neg\varphi \mid \varphi \wedge \psi$	/* Boolean combinations */
	$\mid \Box\varphi$	/* always */
	$\mid \Diamond\varphi$	/* eventually */
	$\mid \varphi\, \mathbf{U}_I\, \psi$	/* timed until */

The satisfaction of an STL property by a signal is always relative to a specified time instant in the signal. We denote by $(\mathbf{x}, t_0) \models \varphi$ the satisfaction of φ by $\mathbf{x}$ at time t_0. The semantics of STL formulas are inductively defined using first-order logic with quantifiers as follows:

$(\mathbf{x}, t_0) \models$

μ	iff	$\mathbf{x}$ satisfies μ at time t_0
$\neg\varphi$	iff	$(\mathbf{x}, t_0) \not\models \varphi$
$\varphi_1 \wedge \varphi_2$	iff	$(\mathbf{x}, t_0) \models \varphi_1$ and $(\mathbf{x}, t_0) \models \varphi_2$
$\Box_{(a,b)}\varphi$	iff	$\forall t : t \in (t_0+a, t_0+b) \Rightarrow (\mathbf{x}, t) \models \varphi$
$\Diamond_{(a,b)}\varphi$	iff	$\exists t : t \in (t_0+a, t_0+b) \wedge (\mathbf{x}, t) \models \varphi$
$\varphi\, \mathbf{U}_{(a,b)}\, \psi$	iff	$\exists t_1 : t_1 \in (t_0+a, t_0+b) \wedge (\mathbf{x}, t_1) \models \psi \wedge$ $\forall t_2 : t_2 \in (t_0 + a, t_1) \Rightarrow (\mathbf{x}, t_2) \models \varphi$

Falsification Problem. In simple terms, the falsification problem is to determine if given a hybrid system, there is a trajectory of the system that does not satisfy a specific logical requirement. In addition to the Boolean semantics specified above, the logics STL and MTL also allow quantitative semantics. These allow us to define a numeric value known as the *robustness value* or the *satisfaction value* for a property with respect to a given $(\mathbf{x}, t_0)$ (denoted as $\rho(\mathbf{x}, t_0, \varphi)$). Informally, $\rho(\mathbf{x}, t_0, \varphi)$ indicates how strongly $(\mathbf{x}, t_0)$ satisfies φ. A large positive value means $(\mathbf{x}, t_0)$ easily satisfies φ, a small positive value means that $(\mathbf{x}, t_0)$ is very close to violating φ, and a negative value indicates $(\mathbf{x}, t_0) \not\models \varphi$. The quantitative semantics for STL can be found in [12].

When equipped with the quantitative semantics, previous work has framed the falsification problem as the problem of minimizing the robustness value. If the minimum value is negative, a counterexample is obtained. This optimization problem is over a highly nonlinear and hybrid space, and hence traditional optimization techniques may not succeed in finding counterexamples. In [6, 28] the authors have proposed using techniques based on stochastic optimization to find traces with minimum robustness value. In Sec. 5, we present results from experiments using S-TaLiRo to falsify some of our benchmark requirements for each of the benchmark models.

3. MODELS

In this section, we present three different versions of an automotive air-fuel control model. We begin with the most complex version and end with the simplest. All parameter values are listed in the Appendix.

3.1 Abstract Fuel Control System

We present a description of a fuel control model implemented in Simulink. The model contains the air-fuel controller and a mean-value model of the engine dynamics, such as the throttle and intake manifold air dynamics. The controller has provision to operate in either a.) a closed-loop mode using Proportional + Integral (PI) feedback control along with feedforward control based on an observer or b.) an open-loop mode using feedforward control based on the observer.

The plant model consists of the throttle and intake manifold and the air-path dynamics. The throttle and intake manifold models are taken from the Simulink Demo palette [30], which was based on the work by Crossley and Cook [11] (excluding an exhaust gas recirculation system). We assume that the throttle angle θ_{in} (in degrees) and the engine speed ω (in rad/sec) are exogenous inputs to the model.

Throttle Control. An electronic throttle control system takes exogenous throttle commands θ_{in} as input and regulates the throttle plate position θ to the desired setpoint. We model this system with the following first-order ODE:

$$\frac{d\theta}{dt} = 10(\theta_{in} - \theta). \tag{1}$$

Throttle Air Dynamics. The throttle air dynamics subsystem defines the rate at which air flows past the throttle plate, or in other words the rate at which the throttle introduces air into the intake manifold. This rate is denoted by $\dot{m}_{af}$ and often called the *inlet air mass flow rate*. The quantity $\dot{m}_{af}$ is a product of two functions, one is an empirical function of the throttle plate angle given in degrees (denoted by the intermediate variable $\hat{\theta}$), and the other is a function of the atmospheric and manifold pressure. The former is given by the following polynomial equation:

$$\hat{\theta} \;=\; c_6 + c_7\theta + c_8\theta^2 + c_9\theta^3.$$

Let state variable p be the manifold pressure (in units of bar), and let c_{10} represent atmospheric pressure. The inlet air mass flow rate (denoted $\dot{m}_{af}$) in grams per second is given by:

$$\dot{m}_{af} \;=\; 2\hat{\theta}\sqrt{\frac{p}{c_{10}} - \left(\frac{p}{c_{10}}\right)^2}. \qquad (2)$$

Intake Manifold. The following details the manifold dynamics, as found in the Simulink Demo palette [30]. The rate $\dot{m}_c$ at which air flows into the cylinder is a function of the throttle, and is known as the pumping polynomial (the quantity in parentheses in the RHS of (3)). In the controller, we implement an estimator for p, and to model error in estimation, we use the parameter c_{12}.

$$\dot{m}_c \;=\; c_{12}\left(c_2 + c_3\omega p + c_4\omega p^2 + c_5\omega^2 p\right) \qquad (3)$$

According to the ideal gas law, the derivative of the manifold pressure is proportional to the net rate of change of air mass in the intake, which is the difference between the rate at which air enters the manifold ($\dot{m}_{af}$) and the rate at which it is pumped into the cylinder ($\dot{m}_c$). In other words, the ODE for p is given as:

$$\frac{dp}{dt} \;=\; c_1\left(\dot{m}_{af} - \dot{m}_c\right), \qquad (4)$$

Substituting (2) and (3) into (4), we have

$$\frac{dp}{dt} =$$

$$c_1\left(2\hat{\theta}\sqrt{\frac{p}{c_{10}} - \left(\frac{p}{c_{10}}\right)^2} - c_{12}\left(c_2 + c_3\omega p + c_4\omega p^2 + c_5\omega^2 p\right)\right). \qquad (5)$$

Cylinder and Exhaust. The air-fuel path aspects of the model, including the cylinder and exhaust dynamics, are largely based on the development in [20]. Let $\dot{m}_\varphi$ be the rate of flow of fuel into the cylinder, in g/s. The A/F ratio in the cylinder is then given by:

$$\lambda_c(t) = \frac{\dot{m}_c}{\dot{m}_\varphi}. \qquad (6)$$

In reality, there is a variable transport delay incurred when the exhaust gas produced by the engine reaches the oxygen (O_2) sensor for the A/F ratio measurement. This delay is given by a 2D lookup table (LUT 4(b) in the appendix). The LUT values are estimated values, taken from Figure 4.24 in [20]. The table axes are the air mass into the cylinder m_c and the engine speed (n) in rpm (revolutions per minute). The former can be obtained from $\dot{m}_c$ and the engine speed in rad/sec (ω) as $m_c = \frac{\pi \dot{m}_c}{\omega}$. Let the delay value obtained from the table be denoted $\Delta(m_c, n)$. The delayed A/F ratio passes through two first-order transfer functions, representing the exhaust system transport dynamics and the O_2 sensor dynamics. The output of the transfer functions is the measured A/F ratio, denoted $\lambda_m(t)$. Then the ODE governing $\lambda_m(t)$ is given by:

$$\frac{d^2\lambda_m(t)}{dt^2} =$$

$$\frac{1}{0.002}\left(-0.12\frac{d\lambda_m(t)}{dt} - \lambda_m(t) + \lambda_c(t - \Delta(m_c, n))\right). \qquad (7)$$

State	Unit	Description
p	bar	Intake manifold pressure
λ	-	A/F Ratio
p_e	bar	Est. manifold pressure
i	-	Integrator state, PI
$\dot{m}_{af}$	g/s	Inlet air mass flow rate
$\dot{m}_c$	g/s	air flow Rate to cylinder
θ_{in}	degrees	Throttle angle input
θ	degrees	Delay-filtered throttle angle
$\hat{\theta}$	-	O/P of Throttle polynomial
ω	rad/sec	Engine speed
F_c	g/s	Commanded fuel

Table 1: States and Intermediate Variables

Sensor Fault. The oxygen sensor measures the amount of oxygen in the exhaust gas, which is proportional to the air-fuel ratio. The oxygen sensor measurements are fed back to the controller. An external event can trigger a fault in the oxygen sensor. This fault causes the output of the oxygen sensor to raise the `sensor_failed` flag. The controller detects this fault condition and reacts by switching to a mode of operation where only feedforward control is applied, and feedback control is disabled.

Wall Wetting. The wall wetting dynamics are based on the description of the Aquino model described in [20]. The mass of the fuel flowing into the cylinder is given by (8). Parameters $\kappa(\cdot)$ and $\tau(\cdot)$ appear in the Aquino model and depend on several factors including engine speed (in rpm) and the air mass in the cylinder, and are approximated by 2D LUTs (LUT 4(a)). The LUTs presented contain values estimated from those in [20] Figure 2.21.

$$\dot{m}_\varphi = (1 - \kappa(n, m_c))\dot{m}_\psi + \frac{m_f}{\tau(n, m_c)}, \qquad (8)$$

In (8), $\dot{m}_\varphi$ is the fuel mass aspirated into the cylinder, $\dot{m}_\psi$ is the fuel mass injected into the intake manifold. The dynamic equation for the mass of fuel stored in the fuel film, m_f, is given by:

$$\frac{dm_f}{dt} = \kappa(\omega, m_c)\dot{m}_\psi - \frac{m_f}{\tau(\omega, m_c)}. \qquad (9)$$

Equations (8), (9) are taken from (2.60) and (2.61) in [20].

To summarize, a modular view of the plant model is considered with the following interface specifications, and main internal states:

- *Exogenous Inputs*: Throttle Angle (θ_{in}), Engine Speed (ω).
- *Inputs from Controller*: Fuel command (F_c).
- *Outputs to Controller*: Measured inlet air mass flow rate ($\dot{m}_{af}$) and the measured A/F ratio (λ_m).
- *Continuous-valued States*: Intake Manifold pressure (p), two states associated with (7), the state associated with the filter block for the throttle input (θ), fuel stored in the fuel film (m_f), and states associated with the variable delay[2].

Controller. The controller is a sampled-time subsystem with two high-level subsystems: 1.) a Proportional + Integral (PI) feedback controller, 2.) a feedforward controller based on an estimate of the air mass entering the cylinder. The controller is compliant with a standard published by the MathWorks automotive advisory board (MAAB), which is used by the automotive industry. We used Version 3.0 of the MAAB standard [26].

The feedforward controller estimates the rate of air flow into the cylinder based on a measurement of the inlet air mass flow rate

[2] Strictly speaking, a variable system delay requires an infinite number of states to model precisely.

($\dot{m}_{af}$). In a real system, such an observer is a carefully designed system that compensates for delays and noise in the plant model; for example an extended Kalman filter. For simplicity, we choose an "almost perfect" observer, i.e., we assume almost perfect knowledge of the pumping polynomial (modulo some multiplicative error factor) to observe state p (intake manifold pressure), and use the observer state (denoted p_e) to compute the estimated air mass flowing into the cylinder. The feedback PI controller regulates the A/F ratio in closed-loop, and uses the measured A/F ratio to compute the fuel command (F_c). The controller has four modes of operation, that we now detail.

1. *Startup mode*: Standard O_2 sensors produce accurate measurements only when they reach a particular operating temperature; until then the controller operates in an "open-loop" mode, i.e., with only feedforward control. In lieu of modeling the heating dynamics, we model this phenomenon with a timer. The timer limit is assumed to be a range, and once the timer expires, the controller changes mode to a normal mode of operation.
2. *Normal mode*: In this mode, the controller uses both feedback PI control and feedforward control to regulate the A/F ratio.
3. *Power enrichment mode*: This mode represents a situation where the user provides a wide throttle angle (i.e., by depressing the gas pedal more than a certain threshold). In this mode, to satisfy the power and torque demands, the controller uses only feedforward control, and disables feedback correction until the throttle angle is reduced to below a certain threshold. Also, the desired A/F setpoint is adjusted from the standard value of 14.7 down to 12.5.
4. *Fault mode*: This mode represents one or more sensor failures. Again, in this mode the controller switches to open-loop control. Once entered, the system remains in this mode.

Note that in a real system, it is certainly possible for the system to transition to power enrichment mode directly from the startup mode or to encounter a fault in startup mode. We choose not to model these behaviors for simplicity in modeling and analysis. To summarize, the controller can be viewed as a module with the following inputs, outputs and internal states:

- *Inputs from Plant (sensors)*: Inlet air mass flow rate measurement ($\dot{m}_{af}$), Measured A/F ratio (λ_m).
- *Exogenous Inputs*: Throttle angle (θ), Engine speed (ω), Sensor failure event ($fail\_event$).
- *Outputs to Plant*: Fuel command (F_c).
- *States*: Estimate of the rate of air mass pumped into the cylinder (p_e), Integrator state for the PI controller (i), and fuel command state (F_c).

Error Factor Correction. A constant error factor, c_{24}, is included in the oxygen sensor measurement. Also, the inlet air mass flow rate $\dot{m}_{af}$ is measured by the controller; a constant error factor, c_{23}, is included in this measurement. The fuel command produced by the controller and the actual fuel produced by the actuator may be different due to actuator error; a constant fuel injector actuator error c_{25} is included to account for this.

3.2 Hybrid I/O Automaton Model

In this section, we present a simplification of the system dynamics described in Sec. 3.1. Ideally, we would like to perform analysis, including formal verification, on the system introduced in Sec. 3.1, but limitations in existing verification techniques for such systems prevent this. Hence, we present a hybrid automaton version of the system more amenable to extant analysis techniques.

Plant HIOA. Certain aspects of the model described in Sec. 3.1 can present difficulties to some analysis tools, such as the transport delays and LUTs. To address these concerns, this version of the model presents several significant simplifications. We remove the wall wetting subsystem entirely. For the exhaust subsystem, we approximate the variable transport delay (which is accurately described using a delay-differential equation), the sensor dynamics and the transport dynamics by a single first order filter. Thus, we simplify the dynamics of the A/F ratio to the following equation:

$$\frac{d\lambda}{dt} = c_{26}\left(\lambda_c - \lambda\right). \qquad (10)$$

Substituting (3) into (6) and using the fuel command from the controller, F_c, modified by the fuel tolerance factor, c_{25}, we get

$$\frac{d\lambda}{dt} = c_{26}\left(\frac{c_{12}\cdot\left(c_2 + c_3\omega p + c_4\omega p^2 + c_5\omega^2 p\right)}{c_{25}\cdot F_c} - \lambda\right). \qquad (11)$$

We leave the dynamics of the intake manifold pressure (p) unchanged. In effect, the plant dynamics can be modeled by a single mode system, with the continuous states p and λ, where $\mathbf{x}_p = [p\ \lambda]^T$ evolves according the to ODE $\dot{\mathbf{x}}_p = f(\mathbf{x}_p)$, where f is the multi-valued function given by (5) and (11).

We skip the tuple definition of the plant HIOA for brevity. As it has only one discrete mode, the sets Δ_P, $\mathcal{G}_P$, $\mathcal{R}_P$ are empty. The rest of the model (input variables, state variables, output variables, states[3]) are as specified in the modular definition of the plant in Sec. 3.1, except for states that were eliminated. The plant HIOA has a single initial state given by $(\theta \mapsto 8.8°, p \mapsto 0.9833, \lambda \mapsto 14.7)$.

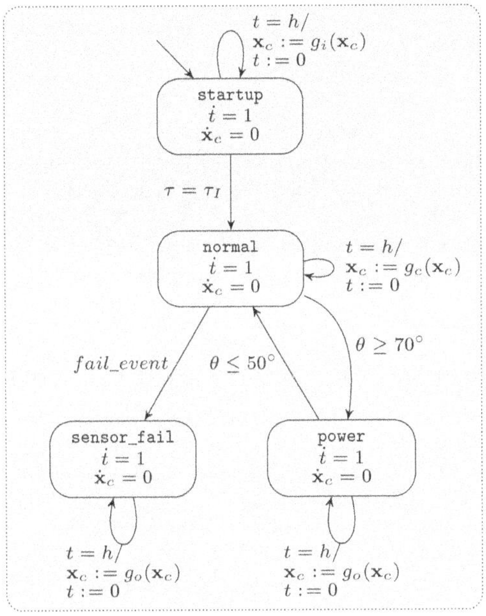

Figure 1: Hybrid I/O Automaton $\mathcal{A}_c$ modeling the controller. The HIOA $\mathcal{A}_p$ for the plant model is a single discrete mode automaton with the ODE $\dot{\mathbf{x}}_p = f(\mathbf{x}_p)$, and we omit its depiction for brevity. Note that the state t in $\mathcal{A}_c$ is not an actual state in the respective models, but is an artifact of modeling a discrete-time system using a HIOA formalsim.

Controller HIOA. The controller HIOA has four discrete modes, and the transition structure is as shown in Fig. 1. The controller HIOA tuple is defined as follows:

[3]Technically, $\dot{m}_{af}$ is not a state in the plant, but is defined as an output variable. To make the plant HIOA well-defined, we can introduce a dummy state in the plant, and allow only those trajectory functions in $\mathcal{T}$ that are consistent with equation 2.

- The set of modes $\mathcal{L}_C$ has four modes (`startup`, `normal`, `power`, `sensor_fail`),
- The set of state variables $\mathcal{X}_C$ is $\{p_e, i, \tau, F_c\}$. We use $\mathbf{x}_c$ as shorthand to represent the tuple of the state variables.
- The set of input variables $\mathcal{U}_C$ is $\{\dot{m}_{af}, fail\_event, \lambda\}$,
- As the controller is a discrete-time system, for any trajectory in $\mathcal{T}$, the flow function for the trajectory in any mode is described by the ODE $\dot{\mathbf{x}}_c = 0$.
- For each mode ℓ, $\mathcal{M}$ maps ℓ to the negation of the conjunction of all the guards on its outgoing transitions.
- The set of guards is $\{fail\_event = true, \tau = \tau_I, \theta \leq 50°, \theta \geq 70°\}$.
- The set of reset functions is a union of two functions $g_c(\cdot)$ and $g_o(\cdot)$. We define the actual functions below.
- The transitions are as depicted in Fig. 1.
- The set of output variables is $\{F_c\}$.
- The set of initial states is the singleton set: $\{(\texttt{startup}, p_e \mapsto 0, i \mapsto 0, \tau \mapsto 0, F_c \mapsto 0.6537)\}$.

We now elaborate on the discrete-time update equations that appear in the reset transitions in Fig. 1. In what follows, h denotes the sample period for the controller, and we use the notation $x[k]$ to mean the value of continuous-time variable x at time $t = kh$, and $k \in \mathbb{Z}_{\geq 0}$ is a sample number.

The quantity p_e denotes the estimated manifold pressure. The dynamics for the estimated manifold pressure are:

$$p_e[k+1] = p_e[k] + hc_1(c_{23} \cdot \dot{m}_{af} - \left(c_2 + c_3\omega p_e[k] + c_4\omega p_e[k]^2 + c_5\omega^2 p_e[k]\right)). \quad (12)$$

Closed-loop discrete dynamics. In the `normal` mode, which is the common operating mode, the controller uses feedback control. The dynamics for the PI controller state and the fuel command are given by

$$i[k+1] = i[k] + hc_{14}(c_{24}\lambda[k] - c_{11}), \quad (13)$$

$$F_c[k+1] = \frac{1}{c_{11}}\left(1 + i[k] + c_{13}(c_{24}\lambda[k] - c_{11})\right) \cdot \left(c_2 + c_3\omega p_e[k] + c_4\omega p_e[k]^2 + c_5\omega^2 p_e[k]\right). \quad (14)$$

Note that the timer is not used in this mode, thus the corresponding update equation is

$$\tau[k+1] = 0.0. \quad (15)$$

The update function g_c is a multi-valued function consisting of the RHSs of equations (12), (13), and (15).

Open-loop discrete dynamics. In the `power` and `sensor_fail` modes, the signal from the O_2 sensor is ignored, and the controller uses only feedforward control, hence the state of the integrator in the PI control does not change. Note that the timer is not used in this mode. Also, in `power` mode, we use $c_{11} = 12.5$, and in `sensor_fail` mode we use $c_{11} = 14.7$. The update equations for the integrator state and the fuel command are given as follows:

$$\begin{aligned} F_c[k+1] &= \frac{1}{c_{11}}\left(c_2 + c_3\omega p_e[k] + c_4\omega p_e[k]^2 + c_5\omega^2 p_e[k]\right), \\ i[k+1] &= 0.0, \\ \tau[k+1] &= 0.0. \end{aligned} \quad (16)$$

Thus, the update function g_o is a multi-valued function consisting of the RHSs of equations (12) and (16).

Startup mode dynamics. In the `startup` mode, in addition to having open-loop control, the controller also uses the timer to count up to τ_I seconds. The update function g_i consists of the the first two update equations from (16), and $\tau[k+1] = \tau[k] + h$.

Controller transitions. As shown in Fig. 1, the controller starts in the `startup` mode using open-loop dynamics, and after τ_I seconds, enters the `normal` mode of operation. If at any time, the effective throttle angle input (θ) is greater than 70°, the controller switches to the open-loop dynamics, and when θ drops below 50°, it switches back to the closed-loop dynamics. In the `normal` mode if there is a sensor failure event detected, the controller switches to the `sensor_fail` mode, and remains there. In `sensor_fail` mode it again uses open-loop dynamics.

Closed-loop HIOA. The closed-loop HIOA is obtained by parallel composition of the plant HIOA and the controller HIOA. As some of the interface variables are eliminated during the composition, the closed-loop HIOA has fewer input and output variables. The closed-loop HIOA has the same basic structure as the HIOA for the controller, except each state also contains the plant dynamics. Further, the update equations and the dynamics do not contain the interface variables, as for each output variable of the plant (resp. controller), the corresponding output variable of the plant (resp. controller) is substituted in the respective input variable of the controller (resp. plant). The final closed-loop HIOA has 6 states (θ, p, λ, p_e, i, F_c), three exogenous inputs (θ_{in}, ω, $fail\_event$), and no outputs.

3.3 PHA model

The model presented in Sec. 3.2 contains features that present unique challenges to hybrid systems verification tools. Specifically, the dynamic equations are not explicitly expressed as polynomial equations. We now present a simplified version of the system, where the continuous-valued dynamics are restricted to the class of polynomials and are converted from mixed continuous/discrete time to ODEs. Such a hybrid system can be analyzed by some tools, including Flow* [9]. We also eliminate the fuel command state in the controller, as the purpose of that state is simply to implement a zero-order hold, which is not required for a model with fully continuous dynamics in each mode (with no resets).

We now present a PHA model of the closed-loop fuel control problem, obtained by applying a host of simplification techniques to the model in Sec. 3.2. We approximate the rational function in (11) with the following second order polynomial function, which is accurate in the range $1.0 \leq \dot{m}_c \leq 20.0$ and $0.5 \leq F_c \leq 1.2$:

$$\frac{d}{dt}\lambda \approx c_{26}(c_{15} + c_{16}c_{25}F_c + c_{17}c_{25}^2F_c^2 + c_{18}\dot{m}_c + c_{19}\dot{m}_c c_{25}F_c - \lambda). \quad (17)$$

Next, we approximate the square root function in (2) with a polynomial, which is accurate in the range $0.5 \leq p \leq 1.0$:

$$\sqrt{\frac{p}{c_{10}} - \left(\frac{p}{c_{10}}\right)^2} \approx c_{20}p^2 + c_{21}p + c_{22}. \quad (18)$$

Applying these substitutions, and using continuous-time versions of the discrete-time update equations, we obtain the following alternative system representation:

$$\begin{aligned} \tfrac{d}{dt}\theta &= 10(\theta_{in} - \theta) \\ \tfrac{d}{dt}p &= c_1(2\hat{\theta}\left(c_{20}p^2 + c_{21}p + c_{22}\right) - c_{12}\left(c_2 + c_3\omega p + c_4\omega p^2 + c_5\omega^2 p\right)) \\ \tfrac{d}{dt}\lambda &= c_{26}(c_{15} + c_{16}c_{25}F_c + c_{17}c_{25}^2F_c^2 + c_{18}\dot{m}_c + c_{19}\dot{m}_c c_{25}F_c - \lambda) \\ \tfrac{d}{dt}p_e &= c_1(2c_{23}\hat{\theta}\left(c_{20}p^2 + c_{21}p + c_{22}\right) - \left(c_2 + c_3\omega p_e + c_4\omega p_e^2 + c_5\omega^2 p_e\right)) \\ \tfrac{d}{dt}i &= c_{14}(c_{24}\lambda - c_{11}), \end{aligned} \quad (19)$$

where F_c is given by:

$$F_c = \tfrac{1}{c_{11}}\left(1 + i + c_{13}(c_{24}\lambda - c_{11})\right) \cdot \left(c_2 + c_3\omega p_e + c_4\omega p_e^2 + c_5\omega^2 p_e\right), \quad (20)$$

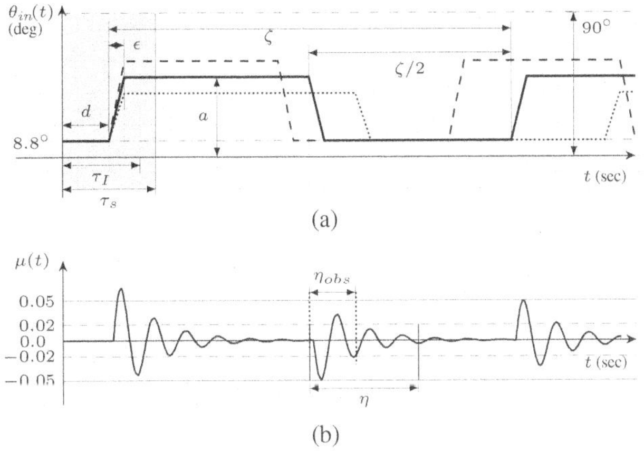

Figure 2: (a) shows a pulse train input (with period ζ, amplitude a, rise time ϵ, and delayed by time d) depicted by a solid line. The dashed and dotted pulse trains lines illustrate other inputs that match the profile. (b) shows the output $\mu(t)$ when the system is excited by the input depicted by the solid line. η_{obs} denotes the observed settling time for the input, while η represents the maximum settling time as specified by requirement (27). The dashed lines denote the settling region, and the solid lines parallel to the dashed lines denote the maximum permitted undershoot/overshoot.

and $\dot{m}_c$ is given by (3).

Again, in any mode with open loop dynamics, the air-fuel ratio signal measurement is not used by the controller, and it only uses feedforward control. The ODEs for states p, λ, and p_e remain as in (19), and the updates for F_c and i are given by the following:

$$F_c = \frac{1}{c_{11}}\left(c_2 + c_3\omega p_e + c_4\omega p_e^2 + c_5\omega^2 p_e\right) \quad (21)$$

$$\frac{d}{dt}p_e = 0.0. \quad (22)$$

4. REQUIREMENTS

In this section, we present typical formal requirements for an A/F ratio control problem. These requirements were formulated by by surveying the A/F ratio control design literature (cf. [10, 29]). We express requirements in STL; please see Sec. 2 for its syntax and semantics. In the sequel, we assume that the simulation time horizon is denoted by the symbol T.

Requirement Format. The expected behavior of most industrial control systems is usually specified with respect to a set of input profiles. Informally, an input profile is a parameterized representation of a possibly infinite set of input signals. For all the requirements described here, we assume the following input profiles: (1) the engine speed (ω) signal profile is the set of constant signals with amplitude in [900, 1100] rpm (approx. [94.25, 115.19] rad/sec), (2) the throttle angle (θ_{in}) signal profile is the set of pulse train signals (with pulse width equal to half the period). We use $\texttt{pulse}(a, \zeta, d)$ as shorthand to symbolically denote a class of pulse train signals, such as those shown in Fig. 2, where a is the pulse amplitude, ζ is the period ($\zeta_{min} < \zeta < \zeta_{max}$) in seconds, and d is some initial delay in seconds before the first pulse (to allow for effects of transients due to initial conditions to dissipate). Here, ζ_{min}, ζ_{max}, and d are fixed constants.

We assume that an input profile can be specified using an STL formula φ_I. For instance, the θ_{in} input profile can be defined using events $\texttt{rise}(a)$ and $\texttt{fall}(a)$ (23 and 24). The $\texttt{rise}$ event specifies that within time ϵ, the throttle angle rises from 8.8° to some value a (where 8.8°< a), and similarly the $\texttt{fall}$ event specifies a falling transition. The time ϵ represents a small unit of time, typically comparable to the the time-step selected by the numerical integration solver.

$$\texttt{rise}(a) \equiv (\theta = 8.8^\circ) \wedge \Diamond_{(0,\epsilon)}(\theta = a) \quad (23)$$

$$\texttt{fall}(a) \equiv (\theta = a) \wedge \Diamond_{(0,\epsilon)}(\theta = 8.8^\circ) \quad (24)$$

Let $\mathbf{u}$ denote the input signals, and $\mathbf{y}$ denote the output signals of the model. A behavioral I/O requirement on the closed-loop model specifies that for a signal u satisfying the input profile φ_I from time 0 onwards, the corresponding output y must satisfy the output requirement φ_O, i.e., $(\mathbf{u}, 0) \models \varphi_I \Rightarrow (\mathbf{y}, 0) \models \varphi_O$. In what follows, we omit the input portion of the requirements, only presenting the requirements on the output signals. For convenience, we define a normalized error signal μ that indicates the error in λ from the reference stoichiometric value λ_{ref}.

$$\mu(t) = \frac{\lambda(t) - \lambda_{ref}}{\lambda_{ref}} \quad (25)$$

Requirements in the $\texttt{normal}$ mode. For all the requirements in $\texttt{normal}$ mode, we use the input profile $\texttt{pulse}(a, \zeta, d)$ and constrain a such that $8.8^\circ < a < 70^\circ$, where 70° is the value of θ_{in} that triggers a transition to the $\texttt{power}$ mode. Also, we do not allow any failure event to occur.

Transient and Steady-state behavior: Measuring both the steady-state and the transient response of the control system with periodic pulse inputs is important. If the control system's response time is not fast enough, then the pulse events can occur before the transients have dissipated, leading to insufficient performance or even instability. Also the rising and falling edges of the pulse signal can trigger overshoots and undershoots in the controlled signal. The first requirement (26) specifies the maximum permitted overshoot or undershoot. Note that the requirement does not include behavior over the initial time interval of $(0, \tau_s)$ (where $\tau_s = \tau_I + \eta_{S\to N}$). This is to exclude behaviors in the startup mode for the first τ_I seconds, and then to allow the controller to settle after transitioning into the $\texttt{normal}$ mode. For our models, we use $\tau_I = 10$ secs, $\eta_{S\to N} = 1$ second. The STL requirement (27) specifies that after each rising or falling edge of the pulse, the signal settles within η seconds, and remains within the settling region (that we define as $\lambda_{ref} \pm 0.02\lambda_{ref}$) until the next rising or falling edge of the pulse can occur. (See Fig. 2(b) for an illustration of these requirements).

$$\Box_{(\tau_s,T)} |\mu| < 0.05 \quad (26)$$

$$\Box_{(\tau_s,T)} \left(\texttt{rise}(a)|\texttt{fall}(a) \Rightarrow \Box_{(\eta,\frac{\zeta}{2})} |\mu| < 0.02\right) \quad (27)$$

Error tolerance: An important quantity for a control system is the error between the desired setpoint and the controlled signal. A standard way of measuring this error is by taking the *root mean square* (RMS) value of the error over the period of time when the controller is in the $\texttt{normal}$ mode. We first define the RMS error accumulated over time t as a signal in (28), where $u(\tau)$ is the Heaviside step function that masks the error in the initial τ_I seconds where the system is not in the $\texttt{normal}$ mode. Here, the calculation starts at τ_I to include the transient error introduced by the transition from the $\texttt{startup}$ mode to the $\texttt{normal}$ mode.

$$\mathbf{x}_{rms}(t) = \sqrt{\frac{1}{t - \tau_I}\int_0^t (\lambda(\tau) - \lambda_{ref})^2 u(\tau - \tau_I) d\tau} \quad (28)$$

Recall that $(\mathbf{x}, 0) \models \Diamond_{[T,T]}\varphi$ means that the property φ holds for $(\mathbf{x}, 0)$ exactly at time T. Thus, requirement (29) states that the RMS error at time T (i.e., the accumulated error over the duration

$(\tau_I, T))$ is less than some value c.

$$\Diamond_{[T,T]} \; \mathbf{x}_{rms} < c \quad (29)$$

Worst-case excursions in the `normal` *mode:* The performance of the controller is sensitive to the accuracy of sensors and actuators. At extremal tolerance values, we require that the worst-case excursions in the A/F ratio remain within a given range around the stoichiometric value. We identified two extreme scenarios corresponding to certain fixed values of the sensor tolerances c_{23} and c_{24} and the actuator error c_{25}.

In the first case, the following set of extremal tolerances: $\{c_{23} = 1.05, c_{24} = 1.01, c_{25} = 1.05\}$, gives rise to a steady-state error in λ, where λ settles to a setpoint that corresponds to the A/F mixture being fuel-rich (i.e., $\mu < 0$). Thus, this set of tolerances leads to the worst case behavior for the undershoot on μ, and requirement (30) specifies the worst-case permitted undershoot $-c_r$.

In the second case, the set of tolerances $\{c_{23} = 0.95, c_{24} = 0.99, c_{25} = 0.95\}$, gives rise to a similar steady-state error in λ; however, here λ settles to a lean A/F mixture (i.e., $\mu > 0$). Thus, this set of tolerances leads to the worst case overshoot on μ, and requirement (31) specifies the worst-case permitted overshoot c_l.

$$\Box_{(\tau_s,T)} \; \mu > -c_r \quad (30)$$

$$\Box_{(\tau_s,T)} \; \mu < c_l \quad (31)$$

Transitioning out of the `power` *mode:* As λ in the `power` mode is regulated in an open-loop fashion and has a different set-point, we want to ensure that the controller is able to settle to a value close to λ_{ref} within a specified time after switching back from the `power` mode. The input profile $\texttt{pulse}(a, \zeta, d)$ for this requirement constrains a differently; the constraint used here is $8.8^\circ \leq a \leq 90^\circ$. This allows the controller to transition to the `power` mode and stay in that mode for approximately $\frac{\zeta}{2}$ seconds. Requirement (32) characterizes this settling-time requirement.

$$\Box_{(\tau_s,T)} \left(\begin{array}{l} \ell{=}\texttt{power} \wedge \Diamond_{(0,\epsilon)} \ell{=}\texttt{normal} \Rightarrow \\ \Box_{(\eta,\frac{\zeta}{2})} \; |\mu| < 0.02 \end{array} \right) \quad (32)$$

Requirements in the `power` **mode.** In the `power` mode, the feed-forward control is expected to provide a fuel-rich air mixture, i.e., the setpoint for the A/F ratio is $\lambda_{ref}^{pwr} = 12.5$. Let $\mu_p(t)$ define the error signal in `power` mode, where λ_{ref} in equation (25) is replaced by λ_{ref}^{pwr}. The input profile for θ_{in} is $\texttt{pulse}(a, \zeta, d)$, where a is constrained such that $70^\circ \leq a \leq 90^\circ$. Such a pulse input maintains the controller in the `power` mode after the initial delay of τ_s seconds. The transient and steady-state requirements for `power` mode are similar in form to the ones for the `normal` mode; however, as there is only open-loop control in this mode, the requirements on λ are typically relaxed. We omit the requirement on settling time for brevity, and in (33) specify that the maximum undershoot/overshoot on λ is within 20% of λ_{ref}^{pwr}.

$$\Box_{(\tau_s,T)} \left(\ell{=}\texttt{power} \Rightarrow |\mu_p| < 0.2\right) \quad (33)$$

Requirement in the `startup` **and** `sensor_fail` **mode.** When the controller is in the `startup` or `sensor_fail` mode, the controller uses open-loop control. The requirements on λ are similar in form to the ones in `normal` mode, but with relaxed bounds on the settling region and transient excursions (we omit the latter for brevity). The input profile $\texttt{pulse}(a, \zeta, d)$ has similar constraints on a as the one for requirements (26),(27). Further, we force a sensor failure event to occur at 15 seconds.

$$\Box_{(0,T)} \left(\left(\begin{array}{l} \ell{=}\,\texttt{startup}|\texttt{sensor\_fail} \\ \wedge\, \texttt{rise}(a)|\texttt{fall}(a) \end{array} \right) \Rightarrow \Box_{(\eta,\frac{\zeta}{2})} \; |\mu| < 0.1 \right) \quad (34)$$

5. ANALYSIS: CASE STUDY

In this section, we provide the results of performing falsification analysis on the three models presented in Sec. 3 with the tool S-TaLiRo. Given the requirements in the previous section[4], S-TaLiRo searches each model for the falsifying counterexample. Table 2 lists the requirement under consideration, the parameter values used, total run-time, number of simulations, and indicates if S-TaLiRo was able to find a counterexample. When testing the requirements, we use the following values for the input profile parameters: $\zeta_{min} = 10$, $\zeta_{max} = 30$, $d = 3$, and $\epsilon = 0.02$.

Conclusions. We present a brief analysis of the experimental results presented in Table 2. The results indicate that each requirement is either falsified by S-TaLiRo, or S-TaLiRo exhausted a given simulation-run budget (1000 simulations) and was unable to falsify the requirement. S-TaLiRo is unable to falsify most of the properties (either transient or steady-state), which may indicate that the quality of the manual abstractions that we performed vis-à-vis high-level requirements is reasonable. However, this can be confirmed only after more rigorous conformance checking.

The tables also indicate that the requirement related to the transition out of the `power` mode (32) is easily falsified for all three models. For all of the simulations explored by S-TaLiRo, once the system transitions from `power` mode back to `normal`, we observe that the normalized error never remains within the designated error bound within the specified settling time η. This is due to the large step in θ_{in} that is applied and also because the λ_{ref} changes instantaneously from 12.5 to 14.7 at the instant of the transition, which causes a significant transient behavior. It is a challenge to design the controller to behavior well in this scenario. Finally, we wish to remark that the requirements expressed in this paper are meant to convey the flavor of how desirable design behavior may be expressed, and should not be interpreted as formal requirements that are valid for actual industrial models. That said, in future work, we aspire to produce a comprehensive suite of requirements that would comprise a benchmark suite to certify desired behavior.

6. ANALYSIS: CHALLENGE PROBLEMS

Abstraction Techniques. We presented three models: the first created by control design experts, and the second and third obtained by successive simplifications. The simplified models represent manual abstractions with no guarantees on fidelity across model versions. Transformations with formal guarantees would be preferable; especially techniques for transforming Simulink models into formal representations such as hybrid automata. This is a stiff challenge as the semantics of the Simulink language are obscure. For continuous-valued aspects of a Simulink model, we can perform numerical linearizations automatically, but the resulting models are only valid near some operating point. Existing works to transform Simulink models to hybrid automata typically focus on small fragments or focus on discrete-time models [1, 25].

Reachable Set Estimation. Bounded-time reachability analysis techniques for hybrid systems try to obtain overapproximations of

[4]Implementing requirements (27), (32), and (34) in S-TaLiRo is difficult, as strictly speaking each is not a single requirement, but specifies a class of requirements for varying values of ζ. For any fixed value of ζ, each requirement is indeed an STL formula. But, we allow S-TaLiRo to choose ζ as an optimization variable, which changes the requirement in each iteration of S-TaLiRo; this is not currently supported. In the actual analysis, we thus use a relaxed form of the requirement, where the term $\frac{\zeta}{2}$ is replaced by $\frac{\zeta_{min}}{2}$.

Table 2: Experimental results of falsification analysis with S-TaLiRo.

		Model 1 (Sec. 3.1)			Model 2 (Sec. 3.2)			Model 3 (Sec. 3.3)		
Req.	Parameters	Time (sec)	Sim.	Falsified?	Time (sec)	Sim.	Falsified?	Time (sec)	Sim.	Falsified?
(26)	$\eta = 1$	5173.27	1000	no	1026.57	1000	no	1569.81	1000	no
(27)	$\eta = 1$	5421.03	1000	no	1097.09	1000	no	1727.83	1000	no
(29)	$c = 0.05$	4188.39	1000	no	1044.54	1000	no	1399.54	1000	no
(30)	$c_r = 0.1$	5296.41	1000	no	1058.50	1000	no	1586.46	1000	no
(31)	$c_l = 0.1$	5589.76	1000	no	1061.15	1000	no	1560.16	1000	no
(32)	$\eta = 1$	5.44	1	yes	1.27	1	yes	1.73	1	yes
(33)	$\lambda_{ref}^{pwr} = 12.5$	4193.46	1000	no	996.58	1000	no	1459.73	1000	no
(34)	$\eta = 1$	3893.06	1000	no	1019.28	1000	no	1521.63	1000	no

the set of reachable states of the system over a fixed time horizon, which are then used to prove system safety. Tools that address this problem continue to mature [2, 3, 9, 16]. The SpaceEx tool [18] provides algorithms currently limited to affine hybrid systems, while Flow* [9] can reason about a larger class of dynamical systems by using higher order approximations. These and other tools in this space face fundamental challenges related to the curse of dimensionality and approximation error with its concomitant false positives.

Certain features of our models, for example the LUTs, exacerbate issues faced by reachability analysis tools. Precise analysis of LUTs requires that each grid element of the LUT be treated as a system mode, typically worsening the conservativeness of the analysis. This is significant, as models of industrial systems often contain LUTs. The variable transport delays indicate that system dynamics are given by a delay differential equation (DDE); DDEs are not handled directly by current reachable set estimation techniques. Finally, a practical limitation is that verification tools require systems to be described in tool-specific formats.

Conformance Checking. As seen in this paper, we often have models representing varying levels of system abstraction. In addition to manual abstractions created for formal analysis, model refinements naturally occur during the development process. Refined models usually include implementation details, e.g., controller output saturation and fixed-point number formats. The general notion of checking behavioral proximity of models is sometimes called *conformance* checking. What it means for two models to be conformant is itself an open problem, as notions of logical equivalence are often inadequate in a hybrid setting. Previous work has focused on notions such as *bisimulation equivalence* [19] using *bisimulation functions*. Existence of a bisimulation function is a property of a model's behaviors over an infinite time horizon, and could be a much stronger notion of conformance than required. On the other hand, bisimulation relations may not be a sufficient comparison; for example, there are examples where a stable system is bisimilar to an unstable system [27]. A possible direction of research is to use hybrid distance metrics [8] to establish conformance.

Stability proofs. Lyapunov techniques have been used for proving system stability [22]. A critical requirement of such analyses is a Lyapunov function. The problem of finding Lyapunov functions for systems with nonpolynomial, hybrid dynamics, such as those described in this paper is open. Furthermore, systems such as those shown in this paper may not have an analytic form of the dynamics for proprietary components, or may have features such as delays and look-up tables. Obtaining Lyapunov functions for both stability proofs and more general verification tasks is a challenge.

7. REFERENCES

[1] A. Agrawal, G. Simon, and G. Karsai. Semantic translation of simulink/stateflow models to hybrid automata using graph transformations. *Electronic Notes in Theoretical Computer Science*, 109:43–56, 2004.

[2] M. Althoff. Reachability analysis of nonlinear systems using conservative polynomialization and non-convex sets. In *Proceedings of Hybrid Systems: Computation and Control*, pages 173–182, 2013.

[3] M. Althoff, O. Stursberg, and M. Buss. Computing reachable sets of hybrid systems using a combination of zonotopes and polytopes. *Nonlinear Analysis: Hybrid Systems*, 4(2):233–249, 2010.

[4] R. Alur, T. Feder, and T. A. Henzinger. The benefits of relaxing punctuality. *Journal of the ACM*, 43(1):116–146, 1996.

[5] R. Alur, T. Henzinger, and P.-H. Ho. Automatic symbolic verifcation of embedded systems. *IEEE Transactions on Software Engineering*, 22(3):181–201, March 1996.

[6] Y. Annapureddy, C. Liu, G. Fainekos, and S. Sankaranarayanan. S-TaLiRo: A tool for temporal logic falsification for hybrid systems. In *Proceedings of Tools and Algorithms for the Construction and Analysis of Systems*, pages 254–257, 2011.

[7] G. Behrmann, R. David, and K. G. Larsen. A tutorial on UPPAAL. In *Formal Methods for the Design of Real-time Systems*, pages 200–236, 2004.

[8] P. Caspi and A. Benveniste. Toward an approximation theory for computerised control. In *Proceedings of 2nd International Conference on Embedded Software*, pages 294–304, 2002.

[9] X. Chen, E. Abraham, and S. Sankaranarayanan. Flow*: An analyzer for non-linear hybrid systems. In *Proceedings of Computer Aided Verification*, pages 258–263, 2013.

[10] J. A. Cook, J. Sun, J. H. Buckland, I. V. Kolmanovsky, H. Peng, and J. W. Grizzle. Automotive powertrain control - a survey. *Asian Journal of Control*, 8:237–260, 2006.

[11] P. R. Crossley and J. A. Cook. A nonlinear engine model for drivetrain system development. In *International Conference on Control*, volume 2, pages 921–925, 1991.

[12] A. Donzé and O. Maler. Robust satisfaction of temporal logic over real-valued signals. In *Proceedings of Formal modeling and analysis of timed systems*, pages 92–106, 2010.

[13] A. Donzé, O. Maler, E. Bartocci, D. Nickovic, R. Grosu, and S. A. Smolka. On temporal logic and signal processing. In

Proceedings of Automated Technology for Verification and Analysis, pages 92–106, 2012.

[14] A. Eggers, N. Ramdani, N. Nedialkov, and M. Fränzle. Improving SAT modulo ODE for hybrid systems analysis by combining different enclosure methods. In *Proceedings of Software Engineering and Formal Methods*, pages 172–187, 2011.

[15] A. Fehnker and F. Ivancic. Benchmarks for hybrid systems verification. In *Proceedings of Hybrid Systems: Computation and Control*, pages 326–341, 2004.

[16] G. Frehse. PHAVer: algorithmic verification of hybrid systems past HyTech. *International journal on Software Tools for Technology Transfer*, 10(3):263–279, 2008.

[17] G. Frehse, Z. Han, and B. Krogh. Assume-guarantee reasoning for hybrid i/o-automata by over-approximation of continuous interaction. In *Proceedings of IEEE Conf. on Decision and Control*, volume 1, pages 479–484, 2004.

[18] G. Frehse, C. Le Guernic, A. Donzé, S. Cotton, R. Ray, O. Lebeltel, R. Ripado, A. Girard, T. Dang, and O. Maler. Spaceex: Scalable verification of hybrid systems. In *Proceedings of Computer Aided Verification*, pages 379–395, 2011.

[19] A. Girard and G. J. Pappas. Approximate bisimulation: A bridge between computer science and control theory. *European Journal of Control*, 17(5-6):568–578, 2011.

[20] L. Guzzella and C. Onder. *Introduction to Modeling and Control of Internal Combustion Engine Systems*. Springer-Verlag, 2nd edition edition, 2010.

[21] T. A. Henzinger, P. W. Kopke, A. Puri, and P. Varaiya. What's Decidable about Hybrid Automata? *Proceedings of the ACM Symposium on Theory of Computing*, 57(1):94 – 124, 1998.

[22] H. Khalil. *Nonlinear Systems*. Prentice Hall PTR, 2002.

[23] R. Koymans. Specifying real-time properties with metric temporal logic. *Real-Time Systems*, 2(4):255–299, 1990.

[24] N. Lynch, R. Segala, and F. Vaandrager. Hybrid I/O automata. *Information and Computation*, 185(1):105 – 157, 2003.

[25] K. Manamcheri, S. Mitra, S. Bak, and M. Caccamo. A step towards verification and synthesis from Simulink/Stateflow models. In *Hybrid Systems: Computation and Control*, pages 317–318, 2011.

[26] Mathworks Automotive Advisory Board. Control Algorithm Modeling Guidelines Using MATLAB, Simulink, and Stateflow, 2012.

[27] P. Prabhakar, G. E. Dullerud, and M. Viswanathan. Pre-orders for reasoning about stability. In *Proceedings of Hybrid Systems: Computation and Control*, pages 197–206, 2012.

[28] S. Sankaranarayanan and G. E. Fainekos. Falsification of temporal properties of hybrid systems using the cross-entropy method. In *Proceedings of Hybrid Systems: Computation and Control*, pages 125–134, 2012.

[29] A. A. Stotsky. *Automotive Engines: Control, Estimation, Statistical Detection*. Springer, 2009.

[30] The MathWorks, Inc. *Simulink User's Guide*. Natick, MA, 2012.

APPENDIX

Symbol	Value	Description
c_1	0.41328	Constant from Ideal Gas Law
c_2	-0.366	Coefficient for Pumping polynomial
c_3	0.08979	Coefficient for Pumping polynomial
c_4	-0.0337	Coefficient for Pumping polynomial
c_5	0.0001	Coefficient for Pumping polynomial
c_6	2.821	Coefficient for $\hat{\theta}$ polynomial
c_7	-0.05231	Coefficient for $\hat{\theta}$ polynomial
c_8	0.10299	Coefficient for $\hat{\theta}$ polynomial
c_9	-0.00063	Coefficient for $\hat{\theta}$ polynomial
c_{10}	1.0	Atmospheric pressure (bar)
c_{11}	14.7/12.5	$\lambda_{ref}/\lambda_{ref}^{pwr}$
c_{13}	0.04	Proportional gain for controller
c_{14}	0.14	Integral gain for controller

Table 3: Model Parameters

n	m_c	$1-\kappa(\cdot)$	$\tau(\cdot)$
1000	0.1	0.80	0.40
1500	0.1	0.70	0.30
2000	0.1	0.70	0.35
2500	0.1	0.80	0.30
3000	0.1	0.90	0.20
1000	0.2	0.70	0.22
1500	0.2	0.66	0.22
2000	0.2	0.65	0.40
2500	0.2	0.73	0.35
3000	0.2	0.85	0.50
1000	0.3	0.66	0.20
1500	0.3	0.66	0.22
2000	0.3	0.63	0.50
2500	0.3	0.66	0.40
3000	0.3	0.80	0.35
1000	0.4	0.60	0.35
1500	0.4	0.60	0.30
2000	0.4	0.60	0.45
2500	0.4	0.60	0.50
3000	0.4	0.70	0.40

(a) LUTs for $1-\kappa(\cdot)$ and $\tau(\cdot)$

n	m_c	Delay
800	0.05	0.25
1000	0.05	0.20
1500	0.05	0.20
2000	0.05	0.20
3000	0.05	0.20
800	0.15	0.30
1000	0.15	0.25
1500	0.15	0.20
2000	0.15	0.20
3000	0.15	0.20
800	0.20	0.40
1000	0.20	0.30
1500	0.20	0.20
2000	0.20	0.20
3000	0.20	0.20
800	0.25	0.80
1000	0.25	0.60
1500	0.25	0.40
2000	0.25	0.30
3000	0.25	0.20

(b) Delay LUT

Table 4: Look-up Tables

Symbol	Value	Description
c_{15}	13.893	Coefficient for A/F polynomial
c_{16}	-35.2518	Coefficient for A/F polynomial
c_{17}	20.7364	Coefficient for A/F polynomial
c_{18}	2.6287	Coefficient for A/F polynomial
c_{19}	-1.592	Coefficient for A/F polynomial
c_{20}	-2.3421	Coefficient for square root polynomial
c_{21}	2.7799	Coefficient for square root polynomial
c_{22}	-0.3273	Coefficient for square root polynomial
c_{12}	0.9	Pressure est. error factor
c_{23}	1.0	MAF sensor error factor
c_{24}	1.0	O_2 sensor error factor
c_{25}	1.0	Fuel inj. actuator error factor
c_{26}	4.0	First-order transfer fun. const.

Table 5: Polynomial Approximation Coefs., Error Tolerances

Dynamic Multi-Domain Bipedal Walking with ATRIAS through SLIP based Human-Inspired Control*

Ayonga Hereid
AMBER Lab
Texas A&M University
College Station, TX 77843
ayonga@tamu.edu

Shishir Kolathaya
AMBER Lab
Texas A&M University
College Station, TX 77843
shishirny@tamu.edu

Mikhail S. Jones
Dynamic Robotics Laboratory
Oregon State University
Corvallis, OR 97331
jonesmik@engr.orst.edu

Johnathan Van Why
Dynamic Robotics Laboratory
Oregon State University
Corvallis, OR 97331
vanwhyj@onid.orst.edu

Jonathan W. Hurst
Dynamic Robotics Laboratory
Oregon State University
Corvallis, OR 97331
jonathan.hurst@oregon-state.edu

Aaron D. Ames
AMBER Lab
Texas A&M University
College Station, TX 77843
aames@tamu.edu

ABSTRACT

This paper presents a methodology for achieving efficient multi-domain underactuated bipedal walking on compliant robots by formally emulating gaits produced by the Spring Loaded Inverted Pendulum (SLIP). With the goal of achieving locomotion that displays phases of double and single support, a hybrid system model is formulated that faithfully represents the full-order dynamics of a compliant walking robot. The SLIP model is used as a basis for constructing human-inspired controllers that yield a dimension reduction through the use of hybrid zero dynamics. This allows for the formulation of an optimization problem that produces hybrid zero dynamics that best represents a SLIP model walking gait, while simultaneously ensuring the proper reduction in dimensionality that can be utilized to produce stable periodic orbits, i.e., walking gaits. The end result is stable robotic walking in simulation and, when implemented on the compliant robot ATRIAS, experimentally realized dynamic multi-domain locomotion.

Categories and Subject Descriptors

J.2 [**Physical Sciences and Engineering**]: [engineering, mathematics and statistics; G.1.6 [**Numerical Analysis**]: Optimization - constrained optimization

Keywords

SLIP model, multi-domain hybrid systems, bipedal walking, hybrid zero dynamics, human-inspired optimization

*This research is supported by CPS grant 1239085 and SRI grant W31P4Q-13-C-009.

HSCC'14, April 15–17, 2014, Berlin, Germany.
Copyright 2014 ACM 978-1-4503-2732-9/14/04 ...$15.00.
http://dx.doi.org/10.1145/2562059.2562143.

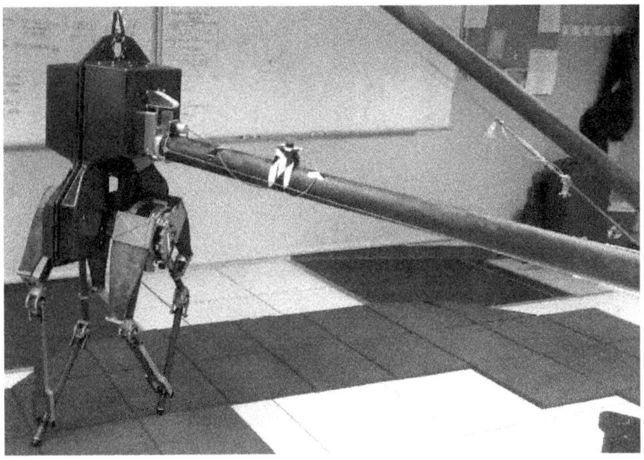

Figure 1: Figure showing front view of ATRIAS. Its motion is constrained to the sagittal plane through a boom connected to its torso.

1. INTRODUCTION

Humans are able to walk with exceptional ease and efficiency. It is postulated that this is due to two major factors: the presence of elasticity in their joints [20], and a mass distribution aimed at conservation of energy [17]. In the case of the former, elasticity allows energy that would otherwise be lost to be stored and used later to replace actuator work. For example, humans handle impacts during a foot strike by storing the kinetic energy rather than dissipating it, then converting the stored energy back to kinetic energy before the end of the step. In fact, [11] shows that the efficiency increases steadily when the positive work is mainly derived from the passive recoil of muscle elastic elements and to a lesser extent from the active shortening of the contractile machinery. In the latter, the mass distribution of humans allows them to be likened to an inverted pendulum model which can swing forward with constant energy; human walking is therefore analogous to the motion of coupled pendula, where the stance leg behaves like an inverted pendulum moving about the stance foot, and the swing leg like a regular pendulum swinging about the hip. This points to reduced models of human locomotion centered around inverted compliant pendula.

Reduced order dynamic models have long been used in biomechanics and robotics to encapsulate the most important dynamic properties of complex systems [12, 18, 21]. The Spring Loaded Inverted Pendulum (SLIP), based upon the concept of coupled compliant pendula, is one such low-dimensional model that has been shown to approximate animal walking and running behaviors in everything from cockroaches, to quail, to kangaroos [9], to humans [8]. ATRIAS, shown in Fig. 1, is a 5-DOF under-actuated robot with series compliance specifically constructed so as to capture the essential elements of the SLIP model and thereby allow for the realization of efficient and natural locomotion on bipedal robots.

The goal of this paper is to provide a formal framework in which to realize SLIP inspired walking gaits on bipedal robots, and realize these formally-generated gaits experimentally to achieve natural locomotion. With this goal in mind, we begin by considering a hybrid system model of ATRIAS. Since it has been shown that humans display multiple discrete phases of walking consisting of double and single support [10, 6], we construct a multi-domain hybrid system model capturing these different phases of walking. In order to achieve the dimensionality reduction enjoyed by the SLIP model, we utilize human-inspired control [4, 3] to construct virtual constraints that project the full-order dynamics of the system to a reduced order model expressed via multi-domain hybrid zero dynamics [19, 22, 23]. A formal result establishes that stable periodic orbits, i.e., walking gaits, for the reduced dynamics imply stable periodic orbits for the full-order dynamics. This observation is utilized in the construction of a SLIP inspired optimization; in particular, walking gaits generated for the SLIP model are used as the cost in an optimization aimed at achieving hybrid invariance of the reduced order dynamics. Novel constructions are utilized to both make this problem computationally tractable and to allow for the inclusion of constraints that will ensure the physical realizability of the resulting walking gaits.

The SLIP-inspired methodology for generating dynamic multi-domain gaits on compliant bipedal robots is applied to ATRIAS both in simulation and experiment. The behavior of the gait is compared against the SLIP walking gait from which it was obtained, and the methods for translating the theoretic constructions to hardware are outlined. The end result is the experimental implementation on ATRIAS and successful demonstration of dynamic multi-domain locomotion. Moreover, the locomotion is remarkably natural looking.

2. MULTI-DOMAIN HYBRID SYSTEM

This section describes the hybrid model of the bipedal robot ATRIAS in detail. ATRIAS (**A**ssume **T**he **R**obot **I**s **A** **S**phere) is a 3D capable, human-scale, bipedal robot conceived and implemented at the Oregon State University Dynamic Robotics Laboratory. Designed to match key characteristics of the SLIP model, ATRIAS uses large springs in series with actuators to drive lightweight four bar mechanisms on each leg which terminate in point feet. This enables ATRIAS to achieve agile, efficient and highly dynamic maneuvers. For the current work, a support boom is used

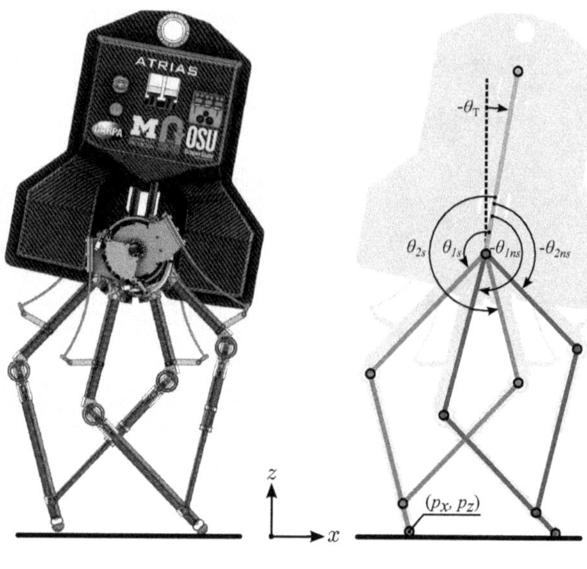

Figure 2: The coordinate configuration of the robot.

to constrain torso rotation and translation to the sagittal plane, effectively planarizing the dynamics. A more detailed description of the robot is presented in [15]. Fig. 1 illustrates the experimental setup.

Robot Configuration. For the 2D model of ATRIAS, we will consider the generalized coordinates of the robot due to the multi-domain structure of the hybrid system. That is, the stance toe position $\{p_x, p_z\}$ and torso pitch angle θ_T of the body fixed frame with respect to world inertia frame will be introduced as the extended coordinates of the robot. By the nature of the parallelogram of four link bars, only two coordinates are needed to characterize each leg, as shown in Fig. 2, where $\{\theta_{1s}, \theta_{2s}\}$ are the angles of the upper two bars of stance leg, $\{\theta_{1ns}, \theta_{2ns}\}$ are the angles of upper two bars of the non-stance leg with respect to the torso, respectively. Since the motors are connected to legs through springs to introduce compliance, additional coordinates are introduced to model the dynamics of the motors, i.e., $\theta_m = \{\theta_{m1s}, \theta_{m2s}, \theta_{m1ns}, \theta_{m2ns}\}$ are the corresponding angles of motor outputs, measured in the same coordinates of the respective joint angles, where θ_i equals θ_{mi} when there is no spring deflection, with $i \in \{1s, 2s, 1ns, 2ns\}$. Therefore the following configuration space $\mathcal{Q}$ is given in the generalized coordinates:

$$\theta_e = \{p_x, p_z, \theta_T, \theta_b, \theta_m\}^T, \tag{1}$$

where $\theta_b = \{\theta_{1s}, \theta_{2s}, \theta_{1ns}, \theta_{2ns}\}$ are the rigid body coordinates. When there is an impact the legs need to be switched accordingly, which is done by using the reset map.

Hybrid System Model. Having described the basics of the hardware setup, the mathematical model of multi-domain walking for this bipedal robot can thus be designed using the framework of hybrid systems [6]. For this paper, we are concerned with a bipedal walking gait consisting of a *single* and a *double* support phase (see Fig. 3). The formal hybrid model for the two-domain locomotion is given by the *tuple*:

$$\mathscr{HC}_A = (\Gamma_A, \mathcal{D}_A, \mathcal{U}_A, S_A, \Delta_A, FG_A), \tag{2}$$

where

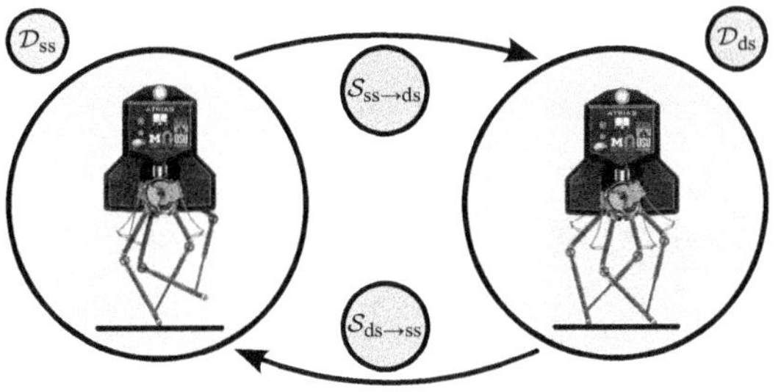

Figure 3: The directed graph of single/double support phase.

- $\Gamma_A = (V_A, E_A)$ is the directed graph specific to this hybrid system, with vertices $V_A = \{\mathbf{ss}, \mathbf{ds}\}$, where **ss** and **ds** represent single and double support phases, respectively, and edges $E_A = \{e_1 = \{\mathbf{ss} \to \mathbf{ds}\}, e_2 = \{\mathbf{ds} \to \mathbf{ss}\}\}$,
- $\mathcal{D}_A = \{\mathcal{D}_{\mathbf{ss}}, \mathcal{D}_{\mathbf{ds}}\}$ is a set of two domains,
- $\mathcal{U}_A = \{\mathcal{U}_{\mathbf{ss}}, \mathcal{U}_{\mathbf{ds}}\}$ is a set of admissible controls,
- $S_A = \{S_{\mathbf{ss}\to\mathbf{ds}}, S_{\mathbf{ds}\to\mathbf{ss}}\}$ is a set of guards,
- $\Delta_A = \{\Delta_{\mathbf{ss}\to\mathbf{ds}}, \Delta_{\mathbf{ds}\to\mathbf{ss}}\}$ is a set of reset maps, and finally
- $FG_A = \{(f_{\mathbf{ss}}, g_{\mathbf{ss}}), (f_{\mathbf{ds}}, g_{\mathbf{ds}})\}$ is a control system on each $\mathcal{D}_v$ for $v \in V_A$.

The two domains $\{\mathcal{D}_{\mathbf{ss}}, \mathcal{D}_{\mathbf{ds}}\}$ are depicted in the Fig. 3. The robot is in the double support phase when both legs are in contact with the ground and transitions to single support phase when one of the legs lifts off the ground. The remainder of this section will be focused on how to construct the individual elements of the two-domain hybrid system considered.

Single Support. In the single support case, the non-stance foot is above the ground. When the non-stance foot strikes the ground, a guard is reached and the transition to the next domain takes place. This implies that the single support domain has the following structure:

$$\mathcal{D}_{\mathbf{ss}} = \{(\theta_e, \dot{\theta}_e, u) : h_{ns}(\theta_e) \geq 0, F^z_{ns}(\theta_e, \dot{\theta}_e, u) = 0\}, \quad (3)$$

where $F^z_{ns}(\theta_e, \dot{\theta}_e, u)$ is the normal force acting on the non-stance foot (as will be formally defined later) and $h_{ns}(\theta_e)$ is the height of the non-stance foot. Similarly, the guard is given by:

$$S_{\mathbf{ss}\to\mathbf{ds}} = \{(\theta_e, \dot{\theta}_e) : h_{ns}(\theta_e) = 0, \dot{h}_{ns}(\theta_e, \dot{\theta}_e) < 0\}. \quad (4)$$

Impacts happens when the non-stance foot hits the ground. The discrete dynamics of the impact of system with compliance can be computed [16, 22] by assuming a perfectly plastic impact of the rigid dynamics and state continuity in the motor positions and velocities [19]; the post-impact states, computed in terms of pre-impact states, is given by:

$$\Delta_{\mathbf{ss}\to\mathbf{ds}}(\theta_e, \dot{\theta}_e) = \begin{bmatrix} \mathcal{R}\Delta_{\theta_e}\theta_e \\ \mathcal{R}\Delta_{\dot{\theta}_e}(\theta_e)\dot{\theta}_e \end{bmatrix}, \quad (5)$$

where $\mathcal{R}$ is the relabeling matrix required to switch the stance and non-stance legs.

The control system $(f_{\mathbf{ss}}, g_{\mathbf{ss}})$ can be obtained from the Lagrangian dynamics of a n-DOF robot. Using the coordinates $\theta = (p_x, p_z, \theta_T, \theta_b)$, we have [19]:

$$D(\theta)\ddot{\theta} + H(\theta, \dot{\theta}) = B_{sp}\tau_{sp}(\theta_b, \theta_m, \dot{\theta}_b, \dot{\theta}_m) + J_s^T(\theta)F_s, \quad (6)$$

$$J_m\ddot{\theta}_m = -\tau_{sp}(\theta_b, \theta_m, \dot{\theta}_b, \dot{\theta}_m) + B_m u, \quad (7)$$

where $D(\theta)$ and $H(\theta, \dot{\theta})$ are obtained from the dynamics of the rigid body system without series compliant actuators, J_m is the motor inertia, $u \in \mathcal{U}$ are the motor control inputs, $B_m \in \mathbb{R}^{4\times4}$ is the motor torques distribution matrix, $J_s(\theta)$ is the Jacobian of the holonomic constraint defined by the height of the stance foot and F_s is the vector of reaction forces acting on the stance foot such that the acceleration of the stance foot is zero and can be computed in terms of state variables and control inputs [14]. Also, $B_{sp} \in \mathbb{R}^{7\times4}$ is the spring force distribution matrix,

$$B_{sp} = \begin{bmatrix} \mathbf{0}_{3\times4} \\ \mathbf{I}_{4\times4} \end{bmatrix}, \quad (8)$$

and $\tau_{sp}(\theta_b, \theta_m, \dot{\theta}_b, \dot{\theta}_m)$ is the vector of spring forces. For series springs, it can be computed by,

$$\tau_{sp}(\theta_b, \theta_m, \dot{\theta}_b, \dot{\theta}_m) = b(\dot{\theta}_m - \dot{\theta}_b) + k(\theta_m - \theta_b), \quad (9)$$

where $k \in \mathbb{R}^{4\times4}$ and $b \in \mathbb{R}^{4\times4}$ are the identified matrices of spring constants and damping coefficients for each spring. Then (6) - (9) can be combined together to give the following control system:

$$\underbrace{\begin{bmatrix} D & \mathbf{0} \\ \mathbf{0} & J_m \end{bmatrix}}_{D_e}\ddot{\theta}_e + \underbrace{\begin{bmatrix} H \\ \mathbf{0} \end{bmatrix}}_{H_e} + \kappa = \underbrace{\begin{bmatrix} \mathbf{0} \\ B_m \end{bmatrix}}_{B_e} u + J_{es}^T F_s, \quad (10)$$

where

$$\kappa = \begin{bmatrix} \mathbf{0}_{3\times4} & \mathbf{0}_{3\times4} \\ k & -k \\ -k & k \end{bmatrix} \begin{bmatrix} \theta_b \\ \theta_m \end{bmatrix} + \begin{bmatrix} \mathbf{0}_{3\times4} & \mathbf{0}_{3\times4} \\ b & -b \\ -b & b \end{bmatrix} \begin{bmatrix} \dot{\theta}_b \\ \dot{\theta}_m \end{bmatrix}, \quad (11)$$

and $J_{es}(\theta_e) = [J_s(\theta) \;\; \mathbf{0}]$.

Having obtained the equations of motion, the control system formed by $(f_{\mathbf{ss}}, g_{\mathbf{ss}})$ is given by:

$$f_{\mathbf{ss}} = \begin{bmatrix} \dot{\theta}_e \\ D_e^{-1}(-\kappa - H_e + J_{es}^T F_s) \end{bmatrix}, g_{\mathbf{ss}} = \begin{bmatrix} \mathbf{0} \\ D_e^{-1}B_e \end{bmatrix}. \quad (12)$$

Double Support. In the double support case, the non-stance foot must remain on the ground. Therefore, the double support domain is given by:

$$\mathcal{D}_{\mathbf{ds}} = \{(\theta_e, \dot{\theta}_e, u) : h_{ns}(\theta_e) = 0, F^z_{ns}(\theta_e, \dot{\theta}_e, u) \geq 0\}, \quad (13)$$

where F^z_{ns} is the normal contact force on the nonstance foot. Since the transition from double support to single support occurs when the normal reaction force on the nonstance foot crosses zero, the guard is given by:

$$S_{\mathbf{ds}\to\mathbf{ss}} = \{(\theta_e, \dot{\theta}_e, u) : h_{ns}(\theta_e) = 0, F^z_{ns}(\theta_e, \dot{\theta}_e, u) = 0\}. \quad (14)$$

For the transition from double support to single support, since there are no impacts involved, the states of the robot remain the same. Therefore the reset map from double support to single support is an identity map: $\Delta_{\mathbf{ds}\to\mathbf{ss}} = \mathbf{I}$.

The control system for the double support will be similar to (10) but with an added constraint on the non-stance foot. This constraint will enforce the non-stance foot to remain on the ground. With this equation, (10) can be modified for the double support case in the following manner:

$$D_e\ddot{\theta}_e + H_e + \kappa = B_e u + J_{es}^T(\theta_e)F_s + J_{ens}^T(\theta_e)F_{ns}, \quad (15)$$

where $J_{ens}(\theta_e) = [J_{ns}(\theta) \quad \mathbf{0}]$ with $J_{ns}(\theta)$ is the Jacobian of the x and y position of the non-stance foot. Accordingly, F_{ns} is the vector of reaction forces acting on the non-stance foot such that the acceleration of the non-stance foot is zero. Moreover $F_{ns} = [F_{ns}^x, F_{ns}^z]^T$, where F_{ns}^x is due to the frictional force in the horizontal direction, and F_{ns}^z is the normal force in the vertical direction which is also used in defining $\mathcal{D}_{\mathbf{ss}}, \mathcal{D}_{\mathbf{ds}}$.

Having obtained the equations of motion, the control system formed by $(f_{\mathbf{ds}}, g_{\mathbf{ds}})$ is given by:

$$f_{\mathbf{ds}} = \begin{bmatrix} \dot{\theta}_e \\ D_e^{-1}(-\kappa - H_e + J_{es}^T F_s + J_{ens}^T F_{ns}) \end{bmatrix}, g_{\mathbf{ds}} = g_{\mathbf{ss}}. \quad (16)$$

3. CONTROLLER DESIGN

This section will describe the methods used to determine the required control input to achieve sustainable and robust multi-domain bipedal walking for the given hybrid system. Previous experimental results have yielded single domain locomotion for robots without series elastic actuators [24, 4] through the successful implementation of human-inspired control. A similar approach will be employed here to achieve two-domain walking on ATRIAS. We begin by selecting a walking gait using the ideal SLIP model. Motivated by this gait, human-inspired control is implemented by picking outputs that elucidate the underlying walking structure through the low-dimensional representation, or "virtual model." It is important to note that emulating a SLIP walking gait through the use of outputs will not necessarily result in a viable walking gait due to the hybrid nature of the system; this will be addressed in detail in the following paragraphs. Nevertheless, combining SLIP walking as a guide for gait generation with formal guarantees on the existence of a stable walking gait will ideally result in more human-like locomotion.

SLIP Model. The spring-mass model consists of a point mass m supported by massless spring legs with fixed rest length l_0 and spring constant k. The springs only act on the mass while in contact with the ground and cannot apply forces during swing. For walking, the hybrid dynamic phases are limited to single support and double support. During double support, the system remains entirely passive with takeoff and transition to single support triggered by zero spring force. During single support, the only control input is the swing leg angle α with touchdown and the switch to double support triggered by the swing leg toe touching the ground. Because the dynamics are almost entirely passive and the only control input is the angle of a massless leg, SLIP model gaits require zero net actuator work.

Walking gaits are generated by selecting a fixed swing leg angle that results in an equilibrium gait, that is, a gait where each step's initial conditions match its final conditions. Given a desired average walking speed and a set of model parameters, a non-linear equation solver is used to find all possible equilibrium gaits. Of these gaits, only one

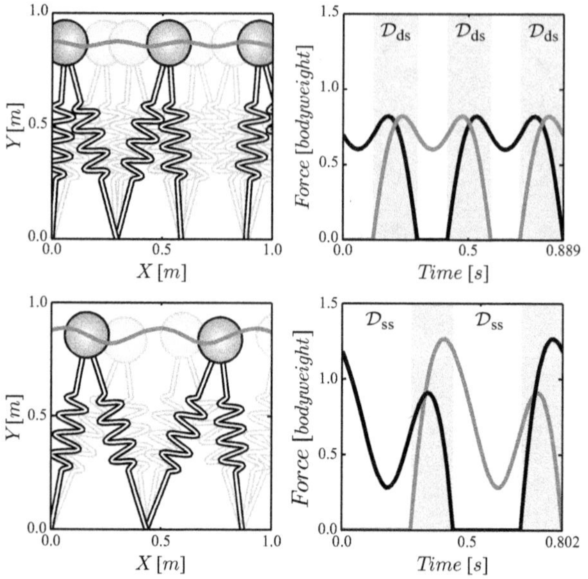

Figure 4: The top plots depict a symmetric SLIP model gait while the bottom plots depict an asymmetric gait. The left plots illustrate the center of mass trajectory and moments of touchdown and takeoff. The plots on the right show the vertical ground reaction force with double support highlighted in grey.

will have a symmetric vertical ground force reaction while the others will be asymmetric. We choose to use this single symmetric gait as it has lower peak forces and a more fluid center of mass trajectory as shown in Fig. 4.

For the purposes of this work we use model parameters that roughly approximate the low-dimensional dynamics of ATRIAS, including the nonlinear spring constant resulting from the four-bar linkage. Doing so enables us to generate relevant center of mass trajectories that take full advantage of the passive dynamics.

Output Definition. As discussed above, the center of mass trajectories are the natural choice to represent the reduced order model [13]. However, for the full-order robotic system, the complex nonlinear expression representing center of mass position will significantly increase the tracking difficulty. Instead, we consider a linear combination of state variables that also capable of approximately characterizing the simple SLIP model dynamics. In particular, the following collection of outputs yields such a representation:

- Virtual stance leg angle: $\theta_{sl} := \left(\frac{\theta_{m2s}+\theta_{m1s}}{2}\right)$,
- Virtual non-stance leg angle: $\theta_{nsl} := \left(\frac{\theta_{m2ns}+\theta_{m1ns}}{2}\right)$,
- Stance knee angle: $\theta_{sk} := (\theta_{m2s} - \theta_{m1s})$,
- Non-stance knee angle: $\theta_{nsk} := (\theta_{m2ns} - \theta_{m1ns})$,

where the virtual leg angles characterize the forward motion of the legs and the knee angles determine the corresponding leg lengths. Note that we use motor angles instead of joint angles due to the following considerations: (1) motor angles are directly controlled, therefore we can track them more precisely, and (2) assuming small spring deflections, motor angles are a good approximation of joint angles which are used to compute center of mass position in the optimization discussed in Sect. 4. The end result is a set of relative degree two outputs for which the corresponding feedback control law is implemented by using input/output linearization.

Canonical Walking Function. The observation that humans and other animals act according to low-dimensional representations during locomotion [2] led to the introduction of the canonical walking function. Defined to be the time solution to a mass-spring-damper system, the canonical walking function is then defined as the linear mass spring damper systems in general mechanical systems:

$$y_H(t,\alpha) = e^{-\alpha_4 t}(\alpha_1 \cos(\alpha_2 t) + \alpha_3 \sin(\alpha_2 t)) + \alpha_5. \quad (17)$$

This becomes apparent by noting that $\alpha_1 = c_0$, $\alpha_2 = \omega_d$, $\alpha_3 = c_1$, $\alpha_4 = \zeta\omega_n$ and $\alpha_5 = g$, where ζ is the damping ratio, ω_n is the natural frequency, $\omega_d = \omega_n\sqrt{1-\zeta^2}$ is the damped natural frequency, c_0 and c_1 are determined by the initial conditions of the system, and g is a gravity related constant.

The canonical walking function is used as the desired trajectories of the previously defined outputs.

Parameterization of Time. *Autonomous* control has several advantages in regard to bipedal robots, the details of which can be found in [7]. Considering this, we introduce a state-based parameterization of time in our system; this is a common practice in [23, 22]. It was observed that the hip position of the SLIP model was monotonously increasing in time. Therefore, the desired outputs's time parameter can be effectively replaced with the robot hip position, yielding the following parameterization of time:

$$\tau(\theta_e) = \frac{\delta p_{\text{hip}}(\theta_e) - \delta p_{\text{hip}}(\theta_e^-)}{\delta p_{\text{hip}}(\theta_e^+) - \delta p_{\text{hip}}(\theta_e^-)}, \quad (18)$$

where $\delta p_{\text{hip}}(\theta_e^-)$ is the forward hip position of the robot at the end of the current step in single support phase, $\delta p_{\text{hip}}(\theta^+)$ is the hip position of the robot at the beginning of the step, with the linearized forward hip position, $\delta p_{\text{hip}}(\theta_e)$, given by:

$$\delta p_{\text{hip}}(\theta_e) = \pi - (L_2 + L_4)\theta_T - L_2\theta_{1s} - L_4\theta_{2s}, \quad (19)$$

where L_2 and L_4 are the lengths of the lower-leg and thigh respectively.

Control Law Construction. Due to the presence of elasticity in ATRIAS, the robot is under-actuated in both *single support* and *double support* phase. Thus we can define the same combination of outputs for both domains. We define the outputs (of relative degree two), as:

$$y(\theta_e) = y^a(\theta_e) - y^d(\tau_i(\theta_e), \alpha), \quad (20)$$

where y^a and y^d are the relative degree two actual outputs and desired outputs, respectively, given by:

$$y^a(\theta_e) = \begin{bmatrix} \theta_{sl}(\theta_e) \\ \theta_{nsl}(\theta_e) \\ \theta_{sk}(\theta_e) \\ \theta_{nsk}(\theta_e) \end{bmatrix}, y^d(\tau,\alpha) = \begin{bmatrix} y_H(\tau,\alpha_{sl}) \\ y_H(\tau,\alpha_{nsl}) \\ y_H(\tau,\alpha_{sk}) \\ y_H(\tau,\alpha_{nsk}) \end{bmatrix}. \quad (21)$$

Importantly, because the parameters for each output are exactly the same on both single support and double support domain, the corresponding controller can easily be implemented on the real robot. In particular, the controllers for the affine control system with relative degree two outputs are defined specifically for each domain:

$$u_v^{(\alpha,\varepsilon)}(\theta_e,\dot\theta_e) = \quad (22)$$
$$-\mathcal{A}_v^{-1}(\theta_e,\dot\theta_e)\left(L_{f_v}^2 y(\theta_e,\dot\theta_e) + 2\varepsilon L_{f_v} y(\theta_e,\dot\theta_e) + \varepsilon^2 y(\theta_e)\right),$$

with $\mathcal{A}_v(\theta_e,\dot\theta_e) = L_{g_v}L_{f_v}y(\theta_e,\dot\theta_e)$ the decoupling matrix for $v \in \{\mathbf{ss},\mathbf{ds}\}$. Again, the choice of outputs implies that this matrix is nonsingular.

Hybrid System. With these feedback controllers introduced for both phases, we obtain a hybrid system:

$$\mathscr{H}_A^{(\alpha,\varepsilon)} = (\Gamma_A, \mathcal{D}_A, S_A, \Delta_A, F_A), \quad (23)$$

where Γ_A, $\mathcal{D}_A$, S_A and Δ_A are as in (2). Also, $F_A = \{f_{\mathbf{ss}}^{(\alpha,\varepsilon)}, f_{\mathbf{ds}}^{(\alpha,\varepsilon)}\}$ is the set of feedback vector fields where:

$$f_{\mathbf{ss}}^{(\alpha,\varepsilon)}(\theta_e,\dot\theta_e) = f_{\mathbf{ss}}(\theta_e,\dot\theta_e) + g_{\mathbf{ss}}(\theta_e,\dot\theta_e)u_{\mathbf{ss}}^{(\alpha,\varepsilon)}(\theta_e,\dot\theta_e), \quad (24)$$

$$f_{\mathbf{ds}}^{(\alpha,\varepsilon)}(\theta_e,\dot\theta_e) = f_{\mathbf{ds}}(\theta_e,\dot\theta_e) + g_{\mathbf{ds}}(\theta_e,\dot\theta_e)u_{\mathbf{ds}}^{(\alpha,\varepsilon)}(\theta_e,\dot\theta_e). \quad (25)$$

Clearly, each individual vector field depends on ε and the parameters for their respective domains, α. The goal of SLIP inspired optimization is to design the parameters α such that the hybrid system $\mathscr{H}_{(\alpha,\varepsilon)}$ has a stable periodic orbit, i.e., a stable walking gait, for sufficiently large ε.

Zero Dynamics. The goal of the feedback control law in (22) is to drive the outputs $y(\theta_e) \to 0$ exponentially. In other words, the controller drives the system dynamics to a parameterized smooth surface, termed as the *zero dynamics surface* [3], with exponential stability. Now we will define them specifically for each domain. First, we consider the *single support* domain; when we consider the generalized coordinates θ_e, the *zero dynamics surface* is defined as:

$$\mathbf{Z}_{\mathbf{ss},\alpha} = \{(\theta_e,\dot\theta_e) \in \mathcal{D}_{\mathbf{ss}} : y(\theta_e) = \mathbf{0}, L_{f_{\mathbf{ss}}}y(\theta_e,\dot\theta_e) = \mathbf{0}\}, \quad (26)$$

where $\mathbf{0}$ is a vector of zeros. Note that we make the dependence of the *zero dynamics surface* on the set of domains explicit. Similarly, for the *double support* domain, we have:

$$\mathbf{Z}_{\mathbf{ds},\alpha} = \{(\theta_e,\dot\theta_e) \in \mathcal{D}_{\mathbf{ds}} : y(\theta_e) = \mathbf{0}, L_{f_{\mathbf{ds}}}y(\theta_e,\dot\theta_e) = \mathbf{0}\}. \quad (27)$$

With the invertible decoupling matrix due to the proper choice of the outputs, the feedback control law in (22) restricts the dynamics to the *zero dynamics surface*. Pick $\theta_z = \{p_x, p_z, \theta_T, \theta_b\}$ with

$$\theta_z = [\mathbf{I}_{7\times 7} \quad \mathbf{0}_{7\times 4}]\,\theta_e := H_z\theta_e. \quad (28)$$

Define $x_z := (\theta_z,\dot\theta_z) \in \mathbf{Z}_{v,\alpha}$, the unactuated states in the Lagrangian model (10), wherein θ_z constitutes a set of local coordinates for $\mathbf{Z}_{v,\alpha}$, where $v \in \{\mathbf{ss},\mathbf{ds}\}$. In particular, we can write the equation of the zero dynamics for a given domain $\mathcal{D}_v$ as

$$\dot x_z = q_v(x_z,\alpha) \quad (29)$$

for a proper selection of outputs and parametrized time defined in Sect. 3, and ground reaction forces computed from the state variables. That being said, the zero dynamics surface only depends on the parameter set of the feedback control law. In fact, we can reconstruct actuated states of the system in the terms of $(\theta_z,\dot\theta_z)$ and parameters α when it is on the *zero dynamics surface*.

With this notation in mind, we can now derive the equation of zero dynamics, independent of the control input.

First, we consider the case of *single support* domain. From the continuous dynamics equation (10), we can write the unactuated component as,

$$D(\theta_z)\ddot{\theta}_z + H(\theta_z,\dot{\theta}_z) + \kappa_z(\theta_e,\dot{\theta}_e) = J_{es}(\theta_z)^T F_s, \qquad (30)$$

where, $\kappa_z(\theta_e,\dot{\theta}_e)$ is the upper 7 rows of the κ in (11). It will be seen from (42) and (43) that, $(\theta_m,\dot{\theta}_m)$ in the expression of κ are a function of parameter α and linearized hip position, which actually only depends on the robots unactuated states. Therefore, we can write that,

$$\kappa_z(\theta_e,\dot{\theta}_e) = \kappa_z(\theta_z,\dot{\theta}_z,\alpha).$$

To fully determine the zero dynamics, the holonomic constraints are differentiated twice and set equal to zero:

$$\frac{\partial J_{es}(\theta_z)\dot{\theta}_z}{\partial t} = J_{es}(\theta_z)\ddot{\theta}_z + \dot{J}_{es}(\theta_z,\dot{\theta}_z)\dot{\theta}_z = 0. \qquad (31)$$

Solving (30) and (31) simultaneously for F_s yields,

$$F_s(\theta_z,\dot{\theta}_z) = (J_{es}(\theta_z)D(\theta_z)^{-1}J_{es}(\theta_z)^T)^{-1}(-\dot{J}_{es}(\theta_z,\dot{\theta}_z)\dot{\theta}_z + J_{es}(\theta_z)D(\theta_z)^{-1}(H(\theta_z,\dot{\theta}_z) + \kappa_z(\theta_z,\dot{\theta}_z.\alpha))) \qquad (32)$$

By substituting (32) into (30), we have the zero dynamics equation of *single support* domain in the form of (29) with,

$$q_{\mathbf{ss}}(x_z,\alpha) = \begin{bmatrix} \dot{\theta}_z \\ D^{-1}(-\kappa - H + J_{es}^T F_s) \end{bmatrix}. \qquad (33)$$

Similarly for the *double support* domain, the following equation holds,

$$q_{\mathbf{ds}}(x_z,\alpha) = \begin{bmatrix} \dot{\theta}_z \\ D^{-1}(-\kappa - H + J_{es}^T F_s + J_{ens}^T F_{ns}) \end{bmatrix}. \qquad (34)$$

where $[F_s \quad F_{ns}]^T$ can be obtained analogously from (32) by replacing J_{es} by $[J_{es} \quad J_{ens}]$.

Main observation. The advantage of zero dynamics is that, instead of full-order dynamics, the low dimensional zero dynamics can be used in the optimization problem introduced in next section *if* the zero dynamics are invariant through the impacts of the system. In particular, the hybrid system $\mathscr{H}_A^{(\alpha,\varepsilon)}$ in (23) obtained by applying human-inspired control to the hybrid control system $\mathscr{HC}_A$ in (2) has *hybrid zero dynamics* if:

$$\Delta_{\mathbf{ss}\to\mathbf{ds}}(S_{\mathbf{ss}\to\mathbf{ds}} \cap \mathbf{Z}_{\mathbf{ss},\alpha}) \subset \mathbf{Z}_{\mathbf{ds},\alpha}, \qquad \text{(HZD1)}$$
$$\Delta_{\mathbf{ds}\to\mathbf{ss}}(S_{\mathbf{ds}\to\mathbf{ss}} \cap \mathbf{Z}_{\mathbf{ds},\alpha}) \subset \mathbf{Z}_{\mathbf{ss},\alpha}. \qquad \text{(HZD2)}$$

The result of hybrid zero dynamics is a stable periodic multi-domain walking gait for the full order system given a stable limit cycle in the (hybrid) zero dynamics. This can be formally summarized as follows:

Theorem 1. *If the hybrid system $\mathscr{H}_A^{(\alpha,\varepsilon)}$ in (23) satisfies* (HZD1) *and if $\mathcal{O}_Z \subset \mathbf{Z}_{\mathbf{ds}} \cup \mathbf{Z}_{\mathbf{ss}}$ is an exponentially stable periodic orbit for the zero dynamics in* (29)*, then there exists $\varepsilon > 0$, such that $\mathcal{O} = \iota_0(\mathcal{O}_Z)$ is an exponentially stable periodic orbit of the full order system, where $\iota_0 : \mathbf{Z}_{\mathbf{ds}} \cup \mathbf{Z}_{\mathbf{ss}} \to \mathcal{D}_{\mathbf{ss}} \cup \mathcal{D}_{\mathbf{ds}}$ is the canonical embedding.*

Space constraints do not allow for a proof of this result, but it essentially follows in a straightforward manner from the results of [5] coupled with the fact that $\Delta_{\mathbf{ds}\to\mathbf{ss}} = \mathbf{I}$. This is why only (HZD1) is required and why, in the future, this condition will be denoted by simply (HZD).

4. OPTIMIZATION

In this section, we will discuss the process of obtaining control parameters and an initial condition on the zero dynamics that result in *hybrid zero dynamics* (HZD) while producing outputs that are as close as possible to those of the SLIP model. More formally, an optimization problem is constructed to solve for parameters of the human-inspired controller α, and a fixed point $(\theta_z^-,\dot{\theta}_z^-)$ that guarantees HZD while simultaneously generating a stable walking gait.

SLIP Inspired Optimization. This section utilizes the fact that the *zero dynamic surfaces* in (26) and (27) are invariant under the flow of closed-loop continuous dynamics, while it is not necessarily invariant for the discrete dynamics. In particular, the invariance of the zero dynamics will be disturbed at the discrete impacts that occur as a result of contact points changing. For the hybrid system of (2), the only impact occurs when the robot transitions from the *single support* domain to the *double support* domain. The goal of this paper is to find a parameter set α^*, which guarantees hybrid invariance of the hybrid system of (2) while tracking the center of mass (CoM) trajectory of the SLIP model as close as possible. In particular, we construct the following constrained optimization problem, called *SLIP Inspired Optimization*:

$$\alpha^* = \underset{\alpha\in\mathbb{R}^{4\times5}}{\text{argmin}} \ \text{Cost}_{\text{SLIP}}(\alpha) \qquad (35)$$
$$\text{s.t} \quad \Delta_{\mathbf{ss}\to\mathbf{ds}}(S_{\mathbf{ss}\to\mathbf{ds}} \cap \mathbf{Z}_{\mathbf{ss},\alpha}) \subset \mathbf{Z}_{\mathbf{ds},\alpha}, \qquad \text{(HZD)}$$

with the SLIP-model-based cost function defined as:

$$\text{Cost}_{\text{SLIP}}(\alpha) = \qquad (36)$$
$$\sum_{k=1}^{K}\sum_{i\in\{x,z\}} \left(p^S_{com,i}[k] - p_{com,i}\left(y^H(t^S[k],\alpha)\right)\right)^2,$$

where discrete times, $t^S[k]$, and discrete values of the CoM position for the SLIP gait, $p^S_{com,i}[k]$, for $i \in \{x,z\}$ obtained from the SLIP walking gait found in Fig. 3, and $p_{com}\left(y^H(t^S[k],\alpha)\right)$ is the approximate center of mass position of the robot computed from the outputs characterized by the canonical walking function. The end result is the least square fit of the CoM trajectory of the robot to that of SLIP model. In other words, we seek to "shape" the dynamics of the robot as close to SLIP model dynamics as possible. The formal goal of this section is to reframe the constraints of (HZD) in a way that it can be practically solvable.

Hybrid Zero Dynamics As discussed in previous section, a hybrid system has *hybrid zero dynamics* (HZD) if the zero dynamics are invariant through the impact. For a rigid body system, the pre-impact states can be explicitly solved for in terms of the parameter α [2]. However, because the system being considered has series elastic actuators, it is not possible to solve explicitly due to high dimensions of zero dynamics surface of the system. The difficulty comes from the fact that the pre-impact states of the zero dynamics coordinates $(\theta_z^-,\dot{\theta}_z^-) \in S_{\mathbf{ss}\to\mathbf{ds}} \cap \mathbf{Z}_{\mathbf{ss},\alpha}$ need to be solved by integrating the dynamics defined in (29).

We assume that a set of points $(\theta_z^-,\dot{\theta}_z^-)$ are the local coordinates of the zero dynamics on the guard. Due to the fact that the guard function $h_{ns}(\theta_e)$ only depends on the rigid body configurations, which is the same as $h_{ns}(\theta_z)$ in this case, the following constraints need to be satisfied:

$$h_{ns}(\theta_z^-, \dot{\theta}_z^-) = 0, \tag{C1}$$

$$dh_{ns}(\theta_z^-)\dot{\theta}_z^- < 0. \tag{C2}$$

Now we expand our parameter set by defining,

$$\beta := \{\alpha, \theta_z^-, \dot{\theta}_z^-\}.$$

The advantage of this definition is that we can solve the pre-impact states explicitly in the terms of β, and simplify the constraints to the same form as in [2]. A point $(\vartheta(\beta), \dot{\vartheta}(\beta)) \in S_{\mathbf{ss}\to\mathbf{ds}} \cap \mathbf{Z}_{\mathbf{ss},\alpha}$ that depends on these parameters can be obtained by solving the equations:

$$\vartheta(\beta) := \theta_e \quad \text{s.t.} \quad y(\mathcal{R}\Delta_{\theta_e}\theta_e) = \mathbf{0}_4 \tag{37}$$

$$\dot{\vartheta}(\beta) = Y^{-1}(\vartheta(\beta)) \begin{bmatrix} \dot{\theta}_z^- \\ \mathbf{0}_4 \end{bmatrix}, \tag{38}$$

where $\mathcal{R}$ is the relabeling matrix and,

$$Y(\vartheta(\beta)) = \begin{bmatrix} H_z \\ dy(\vartheta(\beta)) \end{bmatrix}$$

where H_z is defined in (28) such that $\theta_z = H_z\theta_e$. The equation (37) is easy to solve by the fact that $\theta_e^+ = \mathcal{R}\Delta_{\theta_e}\theta_e$ and $\tau(\mathcal{R}\Delta_{\theta_e}\theta_e) = 0$ implying that: $y(\theta_e^+) = y^a(\theta_e^+) - y^d(0)$. With the proper choice of the outputs, the matrix $Y(\vartheta(\beta))$ is invertible. Thus the (HZD) of the system can be stated as,

$$y(\vartheta(\beta)) = \mathbf{0}, \tag{C3}$$

$$dy\left(\mathcal{R}\Delta_{\theta_e}\vartheta(\beta)\right)\mathcal{R}\Delta_{\dot{\theta}_e}(\vartheta(\beta))\dot{\vartheta}(\beta) = \mathbf{0}, \tag{C4}$$

which guarantee the hybrid invariance of the system through impacts [2].

Physical Constraints. To achieve a physically permissible walking gait, several constraints are imposed on the optimization. The computations of the physical constraints are performed by integrating the zero dynamics of (29) over both *double support* and *single support* domains with the initial condition $\Delta_{\mathbf{ss}\to\mathbf{ds}}(\vartheta(\beta), \dot{\vartheta}(\beta))$. Those constraints are shown as follows:

Ground Reaction Forces: For the *double support* domain, the normal ground reaction forces on non-stance foot should be positive to prevent the reaction force from "pulling" the robot against the ground, i.e.,

$$F_{ns}^z(\theta_z, \dot{\theta}_z, \alpha) > 0, \quad (\theta_z, \dot{\theta}_z) \in \mathcal{D}_{\mathbf{ds}}. \tag{C5}$$

For the *single support* domain, the normal ground reaction forces on stance foot should be positive, otherwise the robot will leave the ground and enter the flight phase, which is not in the scope of this paper. Therefore, we require that:

$$F_s^z(\theta_z, \dot{\theta}_z, \alpha) > 0, \quad (\theta_z, \dot{\theta}_z) \in \mathcal{D}_{\mathbf{ss}}. \tag{C6}$$

The ground reaction forces can be computed by (32).

Friction: To prevent the stance foot from sliding, the following constraint is imposed:

$$F_s^x(\theta_z, \dot{\theta}_z, \alpha) < \mu F_s^z(\theta_z, \dot{\theta}_z, \alpha), \tag{C7}$$

where μ is the coefficient of static friction for the contact between stance foot and the ground.

Foot Clearance: From the definition of the $\mathcal{D}_{\mathbf{ss}}$, the height of the non-stance foot needs to be above the ground during the *single support* domain. The constraint can be expressed as

$$h_{ns}(\theta_z) > 0, \quad (\theta_z, \dot{\theta}_z) \in \mathcal{D}_{\mathbf{ss}}. \tag{C8}$$

Touch Down Angle: To achieve stable walking with the ideal SLIP model discussed in Fig. 3, it requires that the touch down angle, or the angle of attack, denoted as θ_t, needs to be a certain value, $\theta_{\mathcal{TD}}$, determined from the optimal SLIP gait. With the goal of matching the SLIP model dynamics as close as possible, we impose a constraint that the touch down angle of the robot, which is a function of post impact state $\vartheta(\beta)$ in (37), equals the desired value of the stable SLIP walking gait:

$$\theta_t(\vartheta(\beta)) = \theta_{\mathcal{TD}}. \tag{C9}$$

We now have the necessary framework in which to restate the *SLIP Inspired Optimization* problem for multi-domain walking:

$$\beta^* = \underset{\beta \in \mathbb{R}^{4\times 5} \times T\mathcal{Q}_z}{\operatorname{argmin}} \quad \mathrm{Cost}_{\mathrm{SLIP}}(\beta) \tag{39}$$

$$\text{s.t} \quad (\text{C1}) - (\text{C9}). \tag{C}$$

where $\mathcal{Q}_z \subset \mathcal{Q}$ is the configuration space of the zero dynamics coordinates θ_z. The end result is a stable multi-domain walking gait with $\beta = (\alpha, \theta_z^-, \dot{\theta}_z^-)$ consists of the parameters of the human walking function α, and the pre-impact states $(\theta_z^-, \dot{\theta}_z^-)$ of the zero dynamics. The stability of the gait is validated numerically through the use of the *Poincaré* map only for the zero dynamics.

Taking $S_{\mathbf{ss}\to\mathbf{ds}}$ as the *Poincaré* section, define the *Poincaré* map $P^\varepsilon : S_{\mathbf{ss}\to\mathbf{ds}} \to S_{\mathbf{ss}\to\mathbf{ds}}$ which is a partial function:

$$P^\varepsilon(\theta_z, \dot{\theta}_z) = \phi^{\mathbf{ss}}_{T_{\mathbf{ss}}(\theta_z, \dot{\theta}_z)}(\Delta_{\mathbf{ss}\to\mathbf{ss}}(\theta_z^-, \dot{\theta}_z^-)), \tag{40}$$

with $\Delta_{\mathbf{ss}\to\mathbf{ss}}(\theta_z^-, \dot{\theta}_z^-)$ defined as,

$$\Delta_{\mathbf{ss}\to\mathbf{ss}}(\theta_z^-, \dot{\theta}_z^-) = \Delta_{\mathbf{ds}\to\mathbf{ss}}(\phi^{\mathbf{ds}}_{T_{\mathbf{ds}}(\theta_z, \dot{\theta}_z)}(\Delta_{\mathbf{ss}\to\mathbf{ds}}(\theta_z^-, \dot{\theta}_z^-)))$$

where, for $v \in \{\mathbf{ss}, \mathbf{ds}\}$, ϕ^v is the flow generated by the zero dynamics vector field $q_v^{(\alpha,\varepsilon)}$ and $T_v(\theta_z, \dot{\theta}_z)$ is the *time-to-impact* function determined by the first time the flow intersects with the corresponding guard, respectively.

The point $(\theta_z^-, \dot{\theta}_z^-)$ on $S_{\mathbf{ss}\to\mathbf{ds}}$ is a fixed point of P^ε if and only if $(\theta_z^-, \dot{\theta}_z^-) = P^\varepsilon(\theta_z^-, \dot{\theta}_z^-)$. Moreover, if P^ε is exponentially stable with a sufficiently large gain ε, then the fixed point is a stable fixed point and the equivalence of the stability of the fixed point and the corresponding periodic orbit implies that the zero dynamics of the system has a stable periodic orbit [22]. Therefore, by applying the result of Theorem 1 in this paper, we can conclude that parameters obtained from the optimization result in a periodic orbit on the full order system, and thus a stable walking gait is achieved.

5. IMPLEMENTATION AND RESULTS

This section discusses the simulated and experimental results on ATRIAS for the multi-domain walking gait previously obtained. The simulation results show the control system's stability, convergence after perturbations, and SLIP-like behavior. Experimental results show sustainable and dynamic walking on a real robotic platform [1].

Simulation Results. A walking gait was generated through the SLIP-inspired optimization (39), subject to constraints

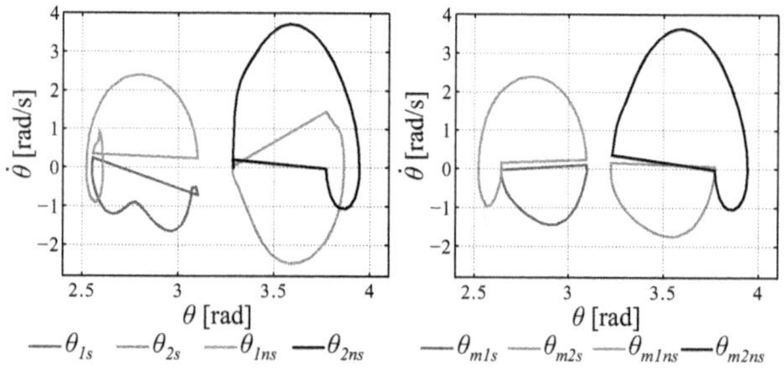

(a) Joint Angles (b) Motor Angles

Figure 5: Stable periodic orbits in the joint angles and motor angles for the walking gait generated through the SLIP-inspired optimization. Note that the difference in shape between (a) and (b) demonstrate the compliance present in the robotic system being considered.

that ensure a physically realizable gait on hardware. The gait was then simulated using the human-inspired controllers introduced in Sect. 3. The resulting periodic orbits can be seen in Fig. 5. The robustness of the gait was also investigated; the system was simulated from a perturbed initial condition to show the output tracking convergence, as depicted in Fig. 6a. Finally, the stability of the gait was numerically verified. For $\varepsilon = 100$, the maximum magnitude of the *Poincaré* eigenvalues, 0.7135, is less than one, establishing the stability of the gait.

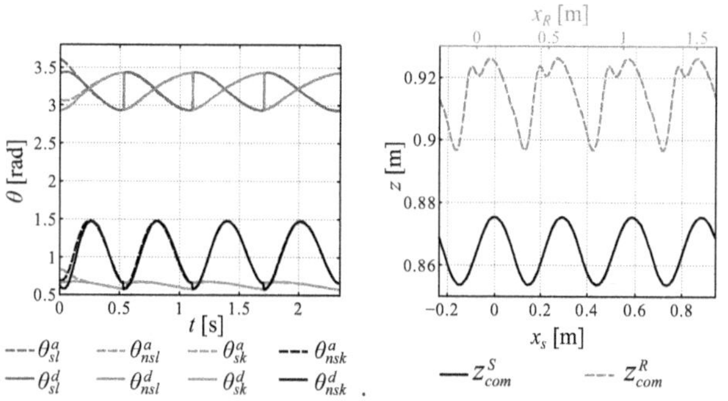

(a) Outputs (b) Center of Mass Position

Figure 6: Simulation results: (a) Desired versus actual outputs starting from a perturbed point. (b) A comparison of the center of mass trajectory between the ideal SLIP gait and the full-order robotic model.

Due to the SLIP-inspired nature of the optimization, the full-order model gait behavior was compared to the ideal SLIP model gait. Although they have different speeds and step lengths, simulation shows that the planar center of mass trajectory of the full-order gait exhibits patterns very similar to that of the SLIP gait, as illustrated in Fig. 6b. Note that the x positions of the two trajectories are on different scales. To show the similarities, x-axis scaling was adjusted between the two gaits so that they are in phase. This difference could be a result of the ideal SLIP model's massless leg assumption. In the SLIP model, the leg is assumed massless, enabling instantaneous swing leg movements during single support phase. Even though the ATRIAS legs are designed to be near massless, the motors have large reflected inertias

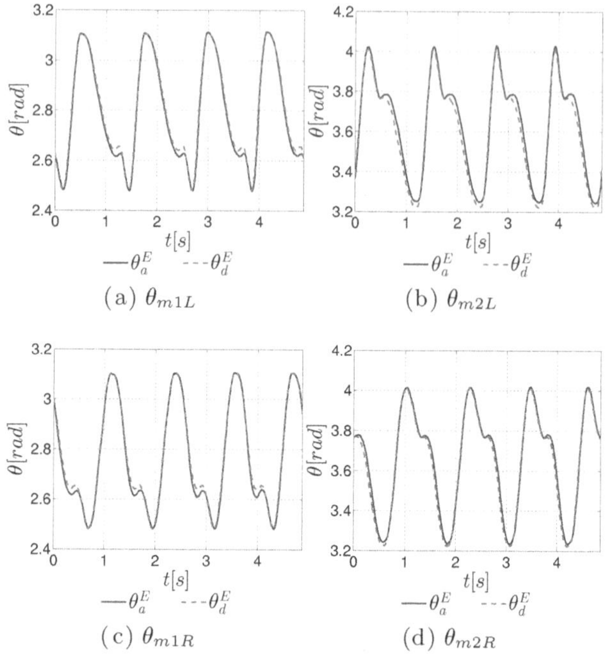

(a) θ_{m1L} (b) θ_{m2L}

(c) θ_{m1R} (d) θ_{m2R}

Figure 7: Comparison of the actual θ^E_a vs. desired θ^E_d motor angle trajectories from the experimentation.

resulting in physical limitations on the leg swing. Therefore, SLIP gaits with very short single support phases may not be physically possible with the full-order model. An additional selection criteria could be used to overcome this, selecting SLIP gaits with an adequate single support duration to allow for leg swing. Moreover, to achieve sustainable walking on a real robot, a proper foot clearance constraint is needed with a maximum non-stance foot height. To satisfy this constraint, the optimization will tend to find gaits with a comparatively high center of mass position. Despite these differences, the full-order system's walking gait is remarkably SLIP-like.

Controller Implementation. For practical realization, we want to find the desired robot joint angles and velocities at each iteration through inverse projection from the HZD surface. Given the HZD surface, we define

$$\xi_1 = \delta p_{\text{hip}}(\theta_e) := c_1\theta_e + c_0, \qquad (41)$$
$$\xi_2 = \delta \dot{p}_{\text{hip}}(\theta_e) := c_1\dot{\theta}_e,$$

where $c_1 \in \mathbb{R}^{11\times1}$, $c_0 \in \mathbb{R}$ are obtained from (19). Since ξ_1 is the linearized position of the hip used to parameterize time (18), we can write $y^d(\tau(\theta_e), \alpha) = y^d(\xi_1, \alpha)$.

Moreover, as a result of selecting outputs that are linear functions of motor angles θ_m, the actual outputs can be written as $y^a(\theta_e) = \mathcal{H}\theta_m$ for $\mathcal{H} \in \mathbb{R}^{4\times4}$ with full row rank. Thus, when the system is constrained to the zero dynamics surface via feedback control, the actual outputs are equal to the desired outputs. Therefore, defining the following functions

$$\Psi(\xi_1, \alpha) := \mathcal{H}^{-1}y^d(\xi_1, \alpha), \qquad (42)$$

$$\Phi(\xi_1, \alpha) := \mathcal{H}^{-1}\frac{\partial y^d(\xi_1, \alpha)}{\partial \xi_1} \qquad (43)$$

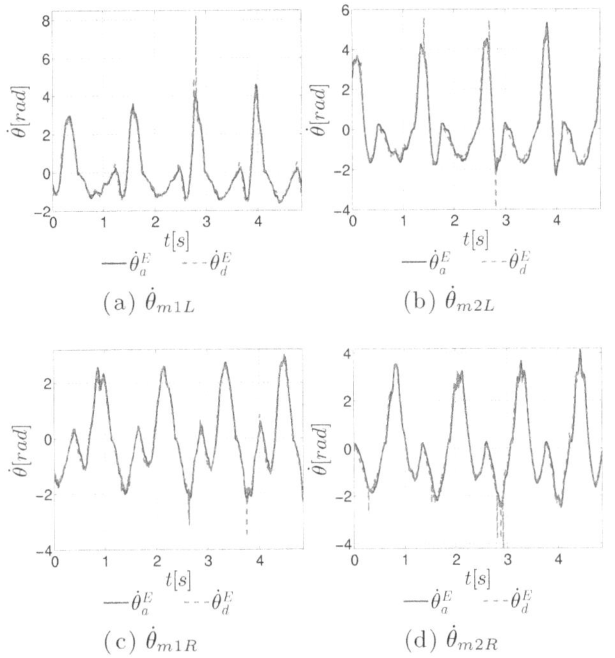

(a) $\dot{\theta}_{m1L}$ (b) $\dot{\theta}_{m2L}$

(c) $\dot{\theta}_{m1R}$ (d) $\dot{\theta}_{m2R}$

Figure 8: Comparison of actual $\dot{\theta}_a^E$ vs. desired $\dot{\theta}_d^E$ motor velocities trajectories from experimentation.

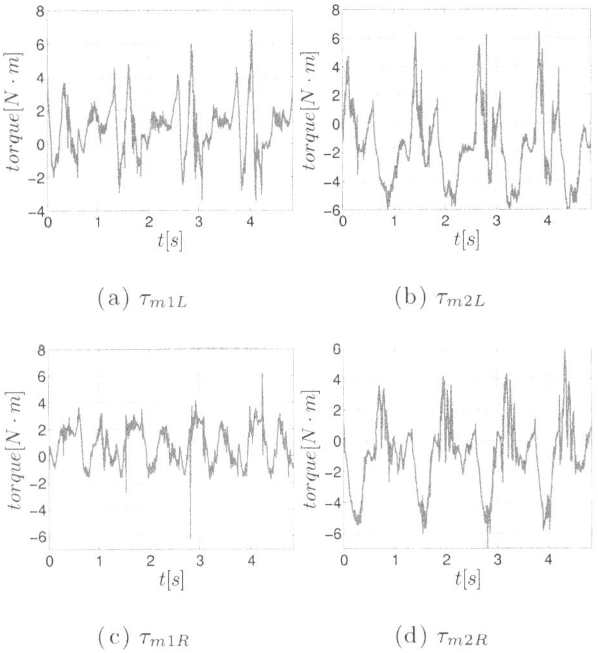

(a) τ_{m1L} (b) τ_{m2L}

(c) τ_{m1R} (d) τ_{m2R}

Figure 10: Corresponding torque input of each motors.

yields the desired motor angles and their corresponding velocities, $\theta_m^d = \Psi(\xi_1, \alpha)$ and $\dot{\theta}_m^d = \Phi(\xi_1, \alpha)\xi_2$. That is, we can reconstruct the desired motor angles and velocities from the system outputs on the HZD surface. Tracking these joint angles and velocities on the robot is equivalent to tracking the outputs of the robot, i.e., the restriction of the dynamics to the partial zero dynamics surface is maintained.

PD controllers are then used to track the desired motor angles and velocities obtained from the HZD reconstruction:

$$\tau_{PD} = -K_p(\theta_m^a - \theta_m^d) - K_d(\dot{\theta}_m^a - \dot{\theta}_m^d), \tag{44}$$

where K_p and K_d are proportional and derivative constant matrices, respectively. Here, the elements of the K_p and K_d matrices depend on their corresponding motors.

Experimental Setup. ATRIAS is supported by a boom that constrains it to the sagittal plane so as to emulate a 2D planar robot. In addition, boom encoders at each degree of freedom provide full feedback on the robot's torso position and rotation relative to the world. During experiments the boom also functions as a safety mechanism to catch the robot in the event of a fall; it does not provide any support in the sagittal plane at any other time.

Each experiment was conducted in a similar manner. The control system was initially enabled while ATRIAS was suspended in the air, allowing the software to drive the robot to an initial pose. ATRIAS was then lowered to the ground and manually given an initial impulse to initiate the walking motion. Fig. 7 and Fig. 8 show the tracking of the motor angles and velocities of the left and right legs during four walking steps with the left leg as the stance leg for the first step. Note that the subscripts 'L' and 'R' in the subtitles represent the left and right leg, respectively. The tracking errors are exceptionally small with motor torque inputs that remain within the robots capabilities (see Fig. 10). This results in a dynamically stable walking gait that visually appears very "SLIP-like". The snapshot in Fig. 9 illustrates the extraordinary similarities between the simulated and experimental gaits. The video of the experiment shows sustainable walking with ATRIAS and is available online [1].

Conclusions. This paper successfully demonstrates underactuated multi-domain walking on the compliant bipedal robot ATRIAS. Our approach starts with a passive walking gait generated by a reduced-order SLIP model that captures the primary dynamics of the robot. From this an optimal walking controller is derived using hybrid zero dynamics. Comparisons of the simulated and experimental results illustrate the effectiveness of the proposed methods and highlight the remarkably natural look of the gait.

6. REFERENCES

[1] Sustained walking of ATRIAS 2.1: `http://youtu.be/yiEbWwC-sR0`.

[2] A. D. Ames. First steps toward automatically generating bipedal robotic walking from human data. In *Robotic Motion and Control 2011*, volume 422 of *LNICS*, pages 89–116. Springer, 2012.

[3] A. D. Ames. First steps toward underactuated human-inspired bipedal robotic walking. In *Robotics and Automation (ICRA), 2012 IEEE International Conference on*, pages 1011–1017. IEEE, 2012.

[4] A. D. Ames, E. A. Cousineau, and M. J. Powell. Dynamically stable bipedal robotic walking with NAO via human-inspired hybrid zero dynamics. In *Hybrid Systems: Computation and Control*, pages 135–44, Beijing, Apr. 2012.

[5] A. D. Ames, K. Galloway, J. Grizzle, and K. Sreenath. Rapidly exponentially stabilizing control lyapunov functions and hybrid zero dynamics. *To appear in IEEE Trans. Automatic Control*, 2013.

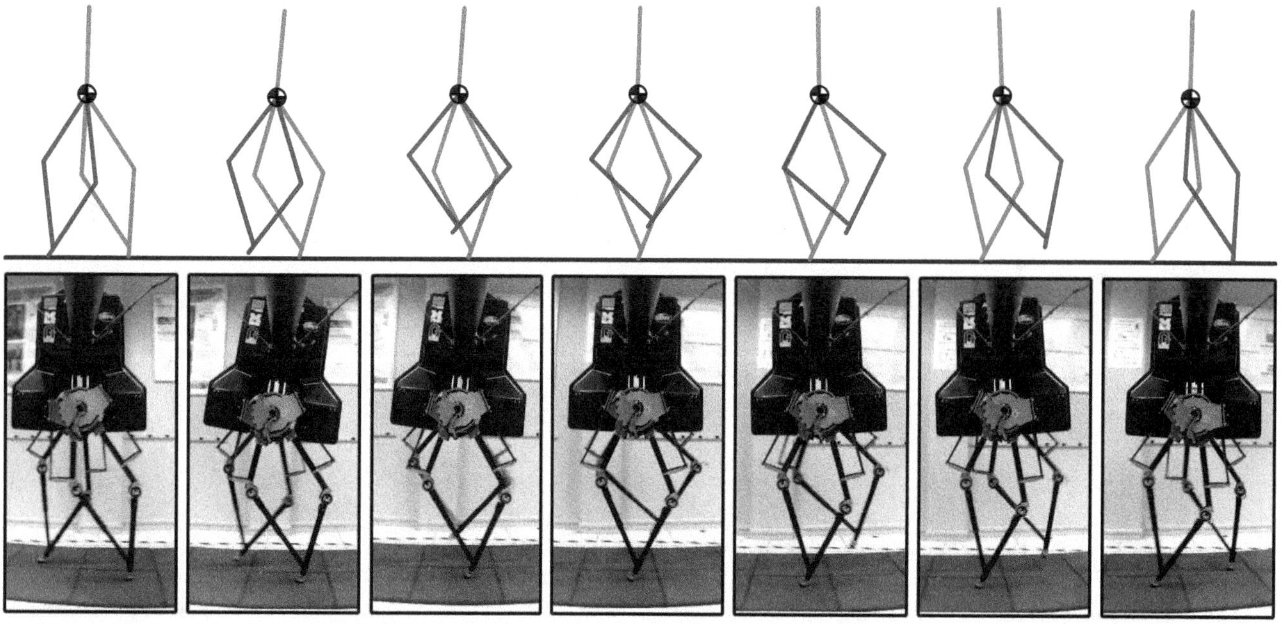

Figure 9: The walking gait snapshot comparison of the simulation and experimental results with ATRIAS over one step.

[6] A. D. Ames, R. Vasudevan, and R. Bajcsy. Human-data based cost of bipedal robotic walking. In *14th Intl. Conf. on Hybrid Systems: Computation and Control*, pages 153–62, Chicago, Apr. 2011.

[7] G. A. Bekey. *Autonomous robots: from biological inspiration to implementation and control.* MIT Press, May 2005.

[8] R. Blickhan. The spring-mass model for running and hopping. *Journal of biomechanics*, 22(11):1217–1227, 1989.

[9] R. Blickhan and R. Full. Similarity in multilegged locomotion: bouncing like a monopode. *Journal of Comparative Physiology A*, 173(5):509–517, 1993.

[10] D. J. Braun and M. Goldfarb. A control approach for actuated dynamic walking in bipedal robots. *IEEE Trans. on Robotics*, 25(6):1292–1303, Dec. 2009.

[11] G. A. Cavagna, N. C. Heglund, and C. R. Taylor. Mechanical work in terrestrial locomotion: two basic mechanisms for minimizing energy expenditure. *American Journal of Physiology-Regulatory, Integrative and Comparative Physiology*, 233(5):R243–R261, 1977.

[12] R. Full and D. Koditschek. Templates and anchors: Neuromechanical hypotheses of legged locomotion on land. *The Journal of Experimental Biology*, 202:3325–3332, 1999.

[13] G. Garofalo, C. Ott, and A. Albu-Schaffer. Walking control of fully actuated robots based on the bipedal slip model. In *IEEE Intl. Conf. on Robotics and Automation*, pages 1456–63, St. Paul, May 2012.

[14] J. W. Grizzle, C. Chevallereau, A. D. Ames, and R. W. Sinnet. 3D bipedal robotic walking: models, feedback control, and open problems. In *IFAC Symposium on Nonlinear Control Systems*, Bologna, Sept. 2010.

[15] C. Hubicki, J. Grimes, M. Jones, D. Renjewski, A. Spröwitz, A. Abate, and J. Hurst. ATRIAS: Enabling agile biped locomotion with a template-driven approach to robot design. *Submitted to International Journal of Robotics Research*, 2014.

[16] Y. Hürmüzlü and D. B. Marghitu. Rigid body collions of planar kinematic chains with multiple contact points. *Intl. J. of Robotics Research*, 13(1):82–92, 1994.

[17] A. D. Kuo, J. M. Donelan, and A. Ruina. Energetic consequences of walking like an inverted pendulum: step-to-step transitions. *Exercise and sport sciences reviews*, 33(2):88–97, 2005.

[18] T. McGeer. Passive dynamic walking. *the international journal of robotics research*, 9(2):62–82, 1990.

[19] B. Morris and J. Grizzle. Hybrid invariance in bipedal robots with series compliant actuators. In *Decision and Control, 2006 45th IEEE Conference on*, pages 4793–4800. IEEE, 2006.

[20] M. Srinivasan. Fifteen observations on the structure of energy-minimizing gaits in many simple biped models. *Journal of The Royal Society Interface*, 8(54):74–98, 2011.

[21] M. Srinivasan and A. Ruina. Computer optimization of a minimal biped model discovers walking and running. *Nature*, 439(7072):72–75, 2005.

[22] E. R. Westervelt, J. W. Grizzle, C. Chevallereau, J. H. Choi, and B. Morris. *Feedback Control of Dynamic Bipedal Robot Locomotion.* CRC Press, Boca Raton, 2007.

[23] E. R. Westervelt, J. W. Grizzle, and D. E. Koditschek. Hybrid zero dynamics of planar biped walkers. *IEEE Trans. on Automatic Control*, 48(1):42–56, 2003.

[24] S. N. Yadukumar, M. Pasupuleti, and A. D. Ames. From formal methods to algorithmic implementation of human inspired control on bipedal robots. In *Algorithmic Foundations of Robotics X*, pages 511–526. Springer, 2013.

Temporal Logic Inference for Classification and Prediction from Data

Zhaodan Kong
Boston University
110 Cummington Street
Boston, MA
zhaodan@bu.edu

Austin Jones
Boston University
15 Saint Mary's Street
Brookline, MA
austinmj@bu.edu

Ana Medina Ayala
Boston University
110 Cummington Street
Boston, MA
duvinci@bu.edu

Ebru Aydin Gol
Boston University
15 Saint Mary's Street
Brookline, MA
ebru@bu.edu

Calin Belta
Boston University
110 Cummington Street
Boston, MA
cbelta@bu.edu

ABSTRACT

This paper presents an inference algorithm that can discover temporal logic properties of a system from data. Our algorithm operates on finite time system trajectories that are labeled according to whether or not they demonstrate some desirable system properties (e.g. "the car successfully stops before hitting an obstruction"). A temporal logic formula that can discriminate between the desirable behaviors and the undesirable ones is constructed. The formulae also indicate possible causes for each set of behaviors (e.g. "If the speed of the car is greater than 15 m/s within 0.5s of brake application, the obstruction will be struck") which can be used to tune designs or to perform on-line monitoring to ensure the desired behavior. We introduce reactive parameter signal temporal logic (rPSTL), a fragment of parameter signal temporal logic (PSTL) that is expressive enough to capture causal, spatial, and temporal relationships in data. We define a partial order over the set of rPSTL formulae that is based on language inclusion. This order enables a directed search over this set, i.e. given a candidate rPSTL formula that does not adequately match the observed data, we can automatically construct a formula that will fit the data at least as well. Two case studies, one involving a cattle herding scenario and one involving a stochastic hybrid gene circuit model, are presented to illustrate our approach.

Categories and Subject Descriptors

I.2.6 [**Learning**]: Knowledge Acquisition; D.2.1 [**Software Engineering**]: Requirements/Specifications; F.4.3 [**Mathematical Logic and Formal Languages**]: Formal Languages; D.4.7 [**Organization and Design**]: Real-Time Systems and Embedded Systems

HSCC'14, April 15–17, 2014, Berlin, Germany.

http://dx.doi.org/10.1145/2562059.2562146.

General Terms

Algorithms, Theory

Keywords

Parametric Signal Temporal Logic; Logic inference; Directed Acyclic Graph; Gene network

1. INTRODUCTION

Reverse engineering has always been a cornerstone of physical and biological science. Given a set of input-output pairs, one can interpret and predict the behavior of the underlying system by inferring properties that are compatible with this data. Reverse engineering can largely be divided into three areas: system identification [16], machine learning [21], and inductive logic programming [15]. In general, properties inferred from reverse engineering can either describe the dynamics of a system or capture some high-level specification that the system satisfies. Inferring dynamics can be a challenging task if very little is known about the system. On the other hand, inferred specifications might be too "coarse-grained" to be useful for problems of interest. Temporal logics [11] bridge these two extremes by incorporating quantitative temporal and spatial constraints when describing dynamic behaviors. For instance, we can use temporal logics to express invariance properties such as "If x is greater than x_r, then within T_1 seconds, it will drop below x_r and remain below x_r for at least T_2 seconds".

In this paper, we address the problem of inferring a temporal logic formula that can be used to distinguish between desirable system behaviors, e.g. an airplane lands in some goal configuration on the tarmac, and undesirable behaviors, e.g. the airplane's descent is deemed unsafe. Moreover, in our approach, the inferred formulae can be used as predictive templates for either set of behaviors. This in turn can be used for on-line system monitoring, e.g. aborting a landing if the descent pattern is consistent with unsafe behavior. Since our procedure is automatic and unsupervised beyond the initial labeling of the signals, it is possible that it can discover properties of the system that were previously unknown to designers, e.g. changing the direction of banking too quickly will drive the airplane to an unsafe configuration.

Most of the recent research on temporal logic inference has focused on the estimation of parameters associated with a given temporal logic structure [1, 22, 12, 2]. In the referred papers, the structure of the formula reflects the domain knowledge of the designer as well as the properties of interest of a given system. However, it is possible that the selected formula may not reflect achievable behaviors or may overlook fundamental features. Furthermore, an important feature of reverse engineering that is absent from the current paradigm is the possibility of deriving new knowledge directly from data, since it requires the user to be very specific about the system properties that are to be inferred. Thus, a natural next step is to infer from data the formula structure in addition to its parameters. As a result, in this work, we guide the search via the robustness degree [8, 6], a signed metric on the signal space which quantifies to what degree a signal satisfies or violates a given formula.

In this paper, we solve the structural inference problem and the parameter estimation problem simultaneously. The structural inference problem is generally hard and even ill-posed [9]. We reduce the difficulty of structural learning by imposing a partial order on the set of *reactive parametric signal temporal logic* (rPSTL) formulae. The defined partial order allows us to search for a formula template in an efficient, orderly fashion while the robustness degree allows us to formulate the inference problem as a well-defined optimization problem.

The paper is outlined as follows. Section 2 reviews signal and parametric signal temporal logic. Section 3 uses a herding example to motivate the inference problem. A new logic called reactive parametric signal temporal logic is defined and the formal problem statement is given in this section. Section 4 presents some properties of rPSTL. The details of our inference algorithm are described in Section 5. Two case studies are presented in Section 6. Finally, Section 7 concludes the paper.

2. SIGNAL AND PARAMETRIC SIGNAL TEMPORAL LOGIC

Given two sets A and B, $\mathcal{F}(A, B)$ denotes the set of all functions from A to B. Given a time domain $\mathbb{R}^+ := [0, \infty)$ (or a finite prefix of it), a *continuous-time, continuous-valued signal* is a function $s \in \mathcal{F}(\mathbb{R}^+, \mathbb{R}^n)$. We use $s(t)$ to denote the value of signal s at time t, and $s[t]$ to denote the suffix of signal s from time t, i.e. $s[t] = \{s(\tau)|\tau \geq t\}$. We use x_s to denote the one-dimensional signal corresponding to the variable x of the signal s.

Signal temporal logic (STL) [17] is a temporal logic defined over signals. The *syntax* of STL is inductively defined as

$$\phi := \mu|\neg\phi|\phi_1 \vee \phi_2|\phi_1 \wedge \phi_2|\phi_1 \mathcal{U}_{[a,b)}\phi_2, \quad (1)$$

where $[a, b)$ is a time interval, μ is a *numerical predicate* in the form of an inequality $g_\mu(s(t)) \sim c_\mu$ such that $g_\mu \in \mathcal{F}(\mathbb{R}^n, \mathbb{R})$, $\sim \in \{<, \geq\}$, and c_μ is a constant.

The *semantics* of STL is defined recursively as

$$\begin{array}{rcl} s[t] \models \mu & \text{iff} & g_\mu(s(t)) \sim c_\mu \\ s[t] \models \neg\phi & \text{iff} & s[t] \not\models \phi \\ s[t] \models \phi_1 \wedge \phi_2 & \text{iff} & s[t] \models \phi_1 \text{ and } s[t] \models \phi_2 \\ s[t] \models \phi_1 \vee \phi_2 & \text{iff} & s[t] \models \phi_1 \text{ or } s[t] \models \phi_2 \\ s[t] \models \phi_1 \mathcal{U}_{[a,b)}\phi_2 & \text{iff} & \exists t' \in [t+a, t+b) \\ & & \text{s. t. } s[t'] \models \phi_2, s[t''] \models \phi_1 \\ & & \forall t'' \in [t+a, t'). \end{array} \quad (2)$$

We also use the constructed temporal operators $\diamondsuit_{[a,b)}\phi = \top\ \mathcal{U}_{[a,b)}\phi$ (read "eventually ϕ"), where $\top$ is the symbol for Boolean constant True, and $\square_{[a,b)}\phi = \neg\diamondsuit_{[a,b)}\neg\phi$ (read "always ϕ"). A signal s satisfies an STL formula ϕ if $s[0] \models \phi$.

The *language* of an STL formula ϕ, $L(\phi)$, is the set of all signals that satisfy ϕ, namely $L(\phi) = \{s \in \mathcal{F}(\mathbb{R}^+, \mathbb{R}^n)|s \models \phi\}$. Given formulae ϕ_1 and ϕ_2, we say that ϕ_1 and ϕ_2 are *semantically equivalent* , i.e., $\phi_1 \equiv \phi_2$, if $L(\phi_1) = L(\phi_2)$.

Parametric signal temporal logic (PSTL) [1] is an extension of STL where c_μ or the endpoints of the time intervals $[a, b)$ are parameters instead of constants. We denote them as *scale* parameters $\pi = [\pi_1, ..., \pi_{n_\pi}]$, and *time* parameters $\tau = [\tau_1, ..., \tau_{n_\tau}]$, respectively. They range over their respective hyper-rectangular domains $\Pi \subset \mathbb{R}^{n_\pi}$ and $\mathrm{T} \subset \mathbb{R}^{n_\tau}$. A full parameterization is denoted by $\theta = [\pi, \tau]$ with $\theta \in \Theta = \Pi \times \mathrm{T}$. The syntax and semantics of PSTL are the same as those for STL. To avoid confusion, we will use ϕ to refer to an STL formula and φ to refer to a PSTL formula. A *valuation* v is a mapping that assigns real values to the parameters appearing in a PSTL formula. Each valuation v of a PSTL formula φ induces an STL formula ϕ_v where each parameter in φ is replaced with its image in v. For example, given $\varphi = (x_s \geq \pi_1)\mathcal{U}_{[0,\tau_1)}(y_s \geq \pi_2)$ and $v([\pi_1, \pi_2, \tau_1]) = [0, 4, 5]$, we have $\phi_v = (x_s \geq 0)\mathcal{U}_{[0,5]}(y_s \geq 4)$.

The robustness degree of a signal s with respect to an STL formula ϕ at time t is given as $r(s, \phi, t)$, where r can be calculated recursively via the *quantitative semantics* [8, 6]

$$\begin{array}{rl} r(s, \mu_{\geq}, t) & = g_\mu(s(t)) - c_\mu \\ r(s, \mu_{<}, t) & = c_\mu - g_\mu(s(t)) \\ r(s, \neg\phi, t) & = -r(s, \phi, t) \\ r(s, \phi_1 \wedge \phi_2, t) & = \min(r(s, \phi_1, t), r(s, \phi_2, t)) \\ r(s, \phi_1 \vee \phi_2, t) & = \max(r(s, \phi_1, t), r(s, \phi_2, t)) \\ r(s, \phi_1 \mathcal{U}_{[a,b)}\phi_2, t) & = \sup\limits_{t' \in [t+a, t+b)} (\min(r(s, \phi_2, t'), \\ & \inf\limits_{t'' \in [t,t')} r(s, \phi_1, t''))) \end{array}$$

where $\mu_{\geq}$ is a predicate of the form $g_\mu(s(t)) \geq c_\mu$ and $\mu_{<}$ is a predicate of the form $g_\mu(s(t)) < c_\mu$.

We use $r(s, \phi)$ to denote $r(s, \phi, 0)$. A *signed distance* from a point $x \in X := \mathcal{F}(\mathbb{R}^+, \mathbb{R}^n)$ to a set $S \subseteq X$ is defined as

$$\mathrm{Dist}_\rho(x, S) := \begin{cases} -\inf\{\rho(x, y)|y \in cl(S)\} & \text{if } x \notin S \\ \inf\{\rho(x, y)|y \in X \setminus S\} & \text{if } x \in S \end{cases} \quad (3)$$

with $cl(S)$ denoting the closure of S, ρ is a metric defined as

$$\rho(s, s') = \sup_{t \in T}\{d(s(t), s'(t))\}, \quad (4)$$

and d corresponds to the metric defined on the domain $\mathbb{R}^n$ of signal s. It has been shown in [8] that $r(s, \phi)$ is an under-approximation of $\mathrm{Dist}_\rho(s, L(\phi))$.

3. PROBLEM STATEMENT

3.1 Motivating Example

We first give a motivating scenario that will serve as a running example throughout the rest of this paper. Consider the example shown in Figure 1. A rancher keeps track of the location of his cattle via GPS devices embedded in ear tags. The rancher herds the cattle to new grazing grounds. While most of the cattle are successfully herded to the rancher's grounds, some wander into someone else's land, indicating that there are likely one or more breaches in the fencing separating the two properties. However, searching for a breach

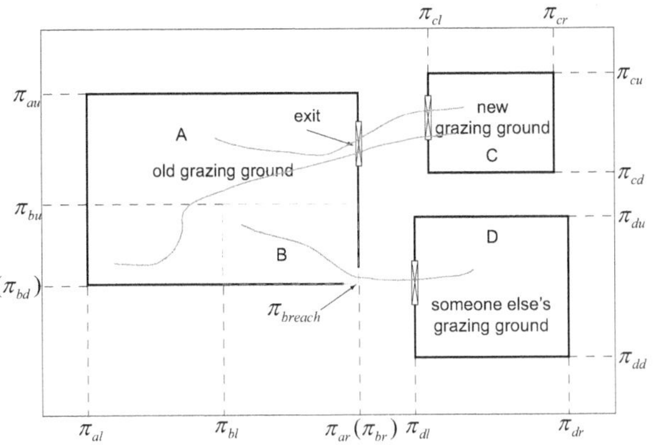

Figure 1: A herding example. The desired behaviors are shown in green, while the undesired ones are shown in red.

in the fencing would be very difficult to do if the property is large.

Consider the following PSTL formula that describes undesirable behaviors

$$\varphi_{und} = \Diamond_{[0,\tau_1)}(\Box_{[0,\tau_2)}(d(s,\pi_{breach}) < d_0) \Rightarrow \Diamond_{[\tau_3,\tau_4)}(\text{Dist}_\rho(s,D) \geq 0)), \tag{5}$$

where π_{breach} is a parameter describing the breach location (the corner of region B), D is someone else's grazing ground, d_0 is a threshold, and d and $\text{Dist}_\rho(.,.)$ are defined in Section 2. The formula reads as "If there is a time t in $[0,\tau_1)$ such that if the cow remains within d_0 of π_{breach} for the next τ_2 seconds, then in at least τ_3 and at most τ_4 seconds, the cow is guaranteed to enter D." The structure of the formula gives quite a bit of insight into the cows' behavior. The sub-formula $\Diamond_{[\tau_3,\tau_4)}(\text{Dist}_\rho(s,D) \geq 0)$ specifies the undesirable behavior (classifies behaviors), and the sub-formula $\Box_{[0,\tau_2)}(d(s,\pi_{breach}) < d_0)$ provides a pre-condition of the undesirable behavior (predicts behaviors). Finding a parameterization of this formula that fits the data has practical value, as searching for the parameter π_{breach} will yield the location of the breach, allowing the farmhands to mend it.

3.2 Reactive Parametric Signal Temporal Logic

We define *reactive parametric signal temporal logic* (rPSTL), a fragment of PSTL that is expressive enough to capture causal relationships that are crucial to a wide range of applications.

The set of predicates used in rPSTL is restricted to the set of linear predicates of the form $(y_s \sim \pi)$ where $\sim \in \{<, \geq\}$, and π is a scale parameter.

The *syntax* of rPSTL is given as

$$\varphi ::= \Diamond_{[\tau_1,\tau_2)}(\varphi_c \Rightarrow \varphi_e) \tag{6a}$$

$$\varphi_c ::= \Diamond_{[\tau_1,\tau_2)}\ell|\Box_{[\tau_1,\tau_2)}\ell|\varphi_c \wedge \varphi_c|\varphi_c \vee \varphi_c \tag{6b}$$

$$\varphi_e ::= \Diamond_{[\tau_1,\tau_2)}m|\Box_{[\tau_1,\tau_2)}m|\varphi_e \wedge \varphi_e, |\varphi_e \vee \varphi_e \tag{6c}$$

where ℓ and m are linear predicates, and τ_1 and τ_2 are time parameters. We refer to φ_c as the *cause formula* and φ_e as the *effect formula.*

The semantics of rPSTL is the same as PSTL. Since rPSTL is a fragment of PSTL, any valuation v of an rPSTL formula induces an STL formula. We call the fragment of all such STL formulae reactive STL (rSTL). Let c_i be real values. The *quantitative semantics* of a signal with respect to an rSTL formula are given by

$$\begin{aligned} r(s,(y_s \geq c_1),t) &= y_s(t) - c_1 \\ r(s,(y_s < c_1),t) &= c_1 - y_s(t) \\ r(s,\Box_{[c_1,c_2)}\phi,t) &= \min_{t' \in [t+c_1,t+c_2)} r(s,\phi,t') \\ r(s,\Diamond_{[c_1,c_2)}\phi,t) &= \max_{t' \in [t+c_1,t+c_2)} r(s,\phi,t') \end{aligned} \tag{7}$$

Formula (6a) can be read as "If there is an instance t in the time interval $[\tau_1,\tau_2)$ such that an event described by formula φ_c occurs, then an event described by formula φ_e will be triggered." For this reason, in an rPSTL (rSTL) formula, we call sub-formula φ_c (ϕ_c) the cause formula and sub-formula φ_e (ϕ_e) the effect formula. We call this fragment reactive PSTL because we say that the system reacts to the cause φ_c by producing an effect φ_e. The causal structure fits the practical needs of automatically identifying causes of certain events, such as unauthorized network intrusion [3]. In this case, the learned cause formula can serve as an on-line monitor for intrusion detection.

rPSTL can be used to express a wide range of important system properties, such as

- Bounded-time invariance, e.g. $\Diamond_{[0,\tau_1)}(\Box_{[0,\tau_2)}(y_s < \pi_1) \Rightarrow \Box_{[\tau_3,\tau_4)}(y_s < \pi_2))$ ("If there exists a time $t \in [0,\tau_1)$ such that if y_s is less than π_1 for the next τ_2 seconds, then it will be less than π_2 everywhere in $[t+\tau_3, t+\tau_4)$.")
- Reachability to multiple regions in the state space, e.g. $\Diamond_{[0,\tau_1)}(\Diamond_{[0,\tau_2)}(y_s \geq \pi_1) \Rightarrow \Diamond_{[\tau_3,\tau_4)}(y_s \geq \pi_2) \vee \Diamond_{[\tau_3,\tau_4)}(y_s < \pi_3))$ ("If there exists a time $t \in [0,\tau_1)$ such that if y_s is greater than π_1 within the next τ_2 seconds, then eventually y_s is either less than π_3 or greater than π_2 from $t+\tau_3$ seconds to $t+\tau_4$ seconds.")

We can approximate (5) with the rPSTL formula

$$\begin{aligned} \varphi^*_{und} =\ & \Diamond_{[0,\tau_1)}(\varphi^*_{und,c} \Rightarrow \varphi^*_{und,e}) \\ \varphi^*_{und,c} =\ & \Box_{[0,\tau_2)}(y_s \geq \pi_{bd}) \wedge \Box_{[0,\tau_2)}(y_s < \pi_{bu}) \wedge \\ & \Box_{[0,\tau_2)}(x_s \geq \pi_{bl}) \wedge \Box_{[0,\tau_2)}(x_s < \pi_{br}) \\ \varphi^*_{und,e} =\ & \Box_{[\tau_3,\tau_4)}(y_s \geq \pi_{dd}) \wedge \Box_{[\tau_3,\tau_4)}(y_s < \pi_{du}) \wedge \\ & \Box_{[\tau_3,\tau_4)}(x_s \geq \pi_{dl}) \wedge \Box_{[\tau_3,\tau_4)}(x_s < \pi_{dr}) \end{aligned} \tag{8}$$

The scale parameters are shown in Figure 1. The formula φ^*_{und} can be interpreted as "If a cow is in B for the next τ_2 seconds ($\varphi^*_{und,c}$), then it is guaranteed to be in D within τ_3 seconds and remain in D for $\tau_4 - \tau_3$ seconds($\varphi^*_{und,e}$)."

Remark 1. (Limitations of rPSTL) There are some temporal properties that cannot be described directly in rPSTL, namely,

- Concurrent eventuality, e.g. $\varphi_{c,e} = \Diamond_{[0,\tau_1)}((y_s < \pi_1) \wedge (x_s \geq \pi_2))$. ("Within τ_1 seconds, y_s is less than π_1 and x_s is greater than π_2 at the same time.")
- Nested "always eventually", e.g. $\varphi_{c,e} = \Box_{[0,\tau_1)}\Diamond_{[\tau_2,\tau_3)}(y_s < \pi_1)$. ("At any time t in the next τ_1 seconds, y_s will be less than π_1 at some point in the interval $[t+\tau_2, t+\tau_3)$.")

The lack of concurrent eventuality means that we cannot directly specify that a trajectory will eventually reach some intersection of half-spaces in the state-space, though we can approximate such properties by specifying $\varphi_{c,e} = \Diamond_{[0,\tau_1)}(y_s < \pi_1) \wedge \Diamond_{[0,\tau_1)}(x_s > \pi_2)$.

The lack of nested "always eventually" limits the periodic properties that may be expressed, but we can approximate such properties by specifying $\varphi_{c,e} = \Diamond_{[\tau_2,\tau_3)}(y_s < \pi_1) \wedge \ldots \wedge \Diamond_{[\tau_2+n\epsilon,\tau_3+n\epsilon)}(y_s < \pi_1)$, that is by selecting n points in the interval $[0,\tau_1)$ ϵ apart and specifying that the property $\Diamond_{[\tau_2,\tau_3)}(y_s < \pi_1)$ is true at all points.

3.3 Problem Description

In this paper, we consider the following problem:

Problem 1. Given a set of labeled signals $\{(s_i, p_i)\}_{i=1}^{N}$, where signal s_i has a finite duration and $p_i = 1$ if s_i demonstrates a desired behavior and $p_i = 0$ if s_i does not, find an rSTL formula ϕ_{des} (or ϕ_{und}) such that

- $s_i \models \phi_{des}$ iff $p_i = 1$ (or $s_i \models \phi_{und}$ iff $p_i = 0$) $\forall i = 1, \ldots, N$ (classification).
- ϕ_{des} (or ϕ_{und}) can be used to determine p_i from a prefix of s_i $\forall i = 1, \ldots, N$ (prediction).

The nature of the problem of interest determines whether ϕ_{des} or ϕ_{und} is needed. For instance, when trying to find possible causes of aircraft crashes, ϕ_{und} is more relevant. In the following, for brevity, we only define the problems involved with ϕ_{des}. Problems involved with ϕ_{und} can be defined similarly.

We approximate the solution to Problem 1 by finding the cause and effect formulae (see (6b)) and (6c)) separately. First, we solve the classification problem by searching for an effect formula $\phi_{des,e}$ that can adequately classify the s_i based on the last $\tilde{t}$ seconds of the observed signals. That is, we assume that the observed desirable or undesirable behaviors occur in the last $\tilde{t}$ seconds of the observed signal s_i. (Please refer to Remark 3 for guidelines for selecting $\tilde{t}$.) Making this assumption yields a significant computational speedup: inferring time bounds for a single formulae over the timescale T requires more computation than inferring time bounds for two formulae over timescales $\tilde{t}$ and $T - \tilde{t}$, respectively.

The classification procedure can be cast as the following optimization problem.

Problem 2. (Classification) Let σ_i be the signal that results from truncating s_i to its final $\tilde{t}$ seconds. Find an effect formula $\phi_{des,e}$ with syntax given by (6c) such that the rPSTL formula $\varphi_{des,e}$ and valuation $v_{des,e}$ minimize

$$J_e(\varphi, v) = \frac{1}{N}\sum_{i=1}^{N} l(p_i, r(s_i, \phi_v)) + \lambda||\phi_v||, \qquad (9)$$

where r is the robustness degree defined in Section 2, ϕ_v is derived from φ with valuation v, l is a loss function, λ is a weighting parameter, and $||\phi_v||$ is the length of ϕ_v (number of linear predicates that appear in ϕ_v).

A natural loss function l is the total number of signals that ϕ_v mis-classifies. Unfortunately, such a discrete measure of success is not helpful for iterative optimization procedures. Instead, we propose to continuize l by using the robustness degree as an intermediary *fitness function,* a measure of how well a given formula fits observed data. We penalize formula length in our approach because if $\phi_{des,e}$ grows arbitrarily long, it becomes as complex to represent as the data itself, which would render the inference process redundant.

After solving Problem 2, we need to find a cause formula $\phi_{des,c}$ that is consistent with the mined rPSTL template $\varphi_{des,e}$ and the full signals s_i. We do this by performing the following optimization.

Problem 3. (Prediction) Find a formula ϕ_{des} that minimizes the cost

$$J_c(\varphi, v) = \frac{1}{N}\sum_{i=1}^{N} l(p_i, r(s_i, \phi_v)) + \lambda||\phi_v||, \qquad (10)$$

where $\varphi = \Diamond_{[0,\tau_1)}(\varphi_c \Rightarrow \varphi_{des,e})$ and $\varphi_{des,e}$ is the solution to Problem 2.

The minimization of l in Problem 2 maximizes the classification quality. Solving Problem 3 after Problem 2 yields a cause formula $\phi_{des,c}$ such that if a system produces a signal prefix that satisfies $\phi_{des,c}$, then p_i is guaranteed to be 1.

4. PROPERTIES OF RPSTL

In this section, we present some properties of rSTL and rPSTL that are essential for the design of our inference algorithm. We define a partial order over $rPSTL$, the set of all rPSTL formulae. The formulae in $rPSTL$ can be organized in a directed acyclic graph (DAG) where a path exists from formula φ_1 to formula φ_2 iff φ_1 has a lower order than φ_2. Finally, for any parameterization, the robustness degree of a signal with respect to a formula $\phi_{1,v}$ is greater than with respect to $\phi_{2,v}$ if φ_1 has a higher order than φ_2. This enables us to find an rSTL formula against which a signal is more robust by searching for a parameterization of an rPSTL formula that is further down the DAG.

4.1 Partial Orders Over rSTL and rPSTL

We define two relations $\preceq_S$ and $\preceq_P$ for rSTL formulae and rPSTL formulae, respectively.

Definition 1.

1. For two rSTL formulae ϕ_1 and ϕ_2, $\phi_1 \preceq_S \phi_2$ iff $\forall s \in \mathcal{F}(\mathbb{R}^+, \mathbb{R}^n), s \models \phi_1 \Rightarrow s \models \phi_2$, i.e. $L(\phi_1) \subseteq L(\phi_2)$.
2. For two rPSTL formulae φ_1 and φ_2, $\varphi_1 \preceq_P \varphi_2$ iff $\forall v$, $\phi_{1,v} \preceq_S \phi_{2,v}$, where the domain of v is $\Theta(\varphi_1) \cup \Theta(\varphi_2)$, the union of parameters appearing in φ_1 and φ_2.

Based on these definitions and the semantics of $rSTL$ and $rPSTL$, we have

PROPOSITION 1. *Both $\preceq_S$ and $\preceq_P$ are partial orders.*

PROOF. (Sketch) A partial order $\preceq$ is a binary relation that is reflexive, transitive and antisymmetric. The equivalence with language inclusion of $\preceq_S$ is used to prove that it is a partial order. The relationship of $\preceq_P$ with $\preceq_S$ is used to show that $\preceq_P$ is a partial order. For example, the antisymmetry of $\preceq_P$ can be proved as follows. If $\varphi_1 \preceq_P \varphi_2$ and $\varphi_2 \preceq_P \varphi_1$, we have

$$\begin{aligned} & \forall v, \phi_{1,v} \preceq_S \phi_{2,v} \text{ and } \phi_{2,v} \preceq_S \phi_{1,v} \\ \Rightarrow\ & \forall v, \phi_{1,v} \equiv \phi_{2,v} \text{ due to antisymmetry of } \preceq_S \\ \Rightarrow\ & \varphi_1 \equiv \varphi_2 \end{aligned}$$

□

Further, we have

PROPOSITION 2. *The partial order $\preceq_P$ satisfies the following properties.*

1. $\varphi_1 \wedge \varphi_2 \preceq_P \varphi_j \preceq_P \varphi_1 \vee \varphi_2$ *for* $j = 1, 2$
2. $\square_{[\tau_1,\tau_2)}\ell \preceq_P \Diamond_{[\tau_1,\tau_2)}\ell$*, where* ℓ *is a linear predicate;*
3. *For two rPSTL formulae,* $\varphi_1 := \Diamond_{[\tau_1,\tau_2)}(\varphi_{c1} \Rightarrow \varphi_{e1})$ *and* $\varphi_2 := \Diamond_{[\tau_1,\tau_2)}(\varphi_{c2} \Rightarrow \varphi_{e2})$*,* $\varphi_1 \preceq_P \varphi_2$ *iff* $\varphi_{c2} \preceq_P \varphi_{c1}$ *and* $\varphi_{e1} \preceq_P \varphi_{e2}$*.*

The first property is an extension of the propositional logic rules $A \wedge B \Rightarrow A \Rightarrow A \vee B$. The second property states "If a property is always true over a time interval, then it is trivially true at some point in that interval". The third property is easy to verify once we consider the semantic equivalence of $\varphi_c \Rightarrow \varphi_e$ and $\neg\varphi_c \vee \varphi_e$. An rPSTL formula can be made more inclusive by either making the effect formula more inclusive or the cause formula more exclusive.

4.2 DAG and Robustness Degree

The structure of rPSTL and the definition of the partial order $\preceq_P$ enable the following theorem.

THEOREM 1. *The formulae in $rPSTL$ have an equivalent representation as nodes in an infinite DAG. A path exists from formula φ_1 to φ_2 iff $\varphi_1 \preceq_P \varphi_2$. The DAG has a unique top element ($\top$) and a unique bottom element ($\perp$).*

PROOF. (Sketch) The proof of this theorem requires the intermediate results that the family of formulae Φ with syntax (6b) and (6c) (e.g. cause and effect subformulae) form a lattice when ordered according to $\preceq_P$. A partially ordered set $< X, \preceq >$ forms a *lattice* if any two elements $x_1, x_2 \in X$ have a join and a meet [4]. In our case, we need to prove that for all $\varphi_1, \varphi_2 \in \Phi$, their join $\varphi_1 \sqcap \varphi_2$ and meet $\varphi_1 \sqcup \varphi_2$ exist and are unique. This can be done by first treating the subformulae $\square_I p$ and $\Diamond_I p$ where p is a linear predicate and I is a time interval $I := [\tau_1, \tau_2)$ as different Boolean predicates. Then the existence and uniqueness of $\varphi_1 \sqcap \varphi_2$ ($\varphi_1 \sqcup \varphi_2$) can be proved by the existence and uniqueness of $\varphi_1 \wedge \varphi_2$ ($\varphi_1 \vee \varphi_2$)[11] by putting formulae in Disjunctive (Conjunctive) Normal Form . Finally, since $< rPSTL, \preceq_P >$ is a lattice, it has an equivalent representation as an infinite DAG [4]. $\square$

An example of such a DAG is shown in Figure 5.

Next, we establish a relationship between the robustness degrees of a signal s with respect to rSTL (rPSTL) formulae ϕ (φ) and the partial order $\preceq_S$ ($\preceq_P$).

THEOREM 2. *The following statements are equivalent:*

1. $\phi_1 \preceq_S \phi_2$*;*
2. $\forall s \in \mathcal{F}(\mathbb{R}^+, \mathbb{R}^n), r(s, \phi_1) \leq r(s, \phi_2)$.

PROOF. $2 \Rightarrow 1$ can be easily proved by using contradiction. As for $1 \Rightarrow 2$, since $L(\phi_1) \subset L(\phi_2)$, for any $s \in \mathcal{F}(\mathbb{R}^+, \mathbb{R}^n)$, we need to first enumerate the following three cases and prove that $1 \Rightarrow 2$ is true for each: (a) $s \in L(\phi_1)$; (b) $s \in L(\phi_1) \cap L(\neg\phi_2)$; and (c) $s \in L(\neg\phi_1) \cap L(\neg\phi_2)$. This can be done by using the relationship between $r(s, \phi)$ and $\text{Dist}_\rho(s, L(\phi))$ as described by (3). $\square$

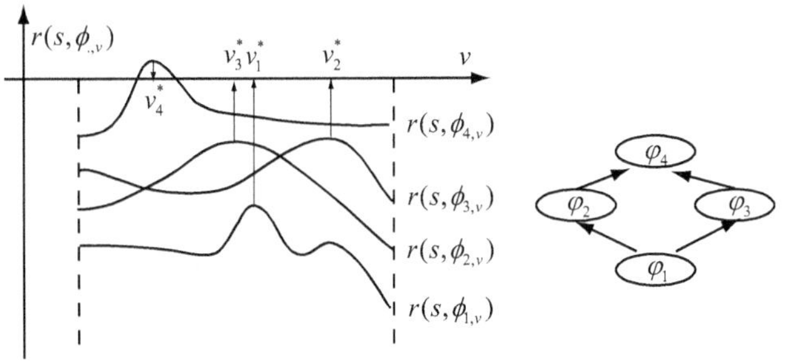

Figure 2: Illustration of the relationship between rPSTL formulae and robustness degree.

COROLLARY 1. *The following statements are equivalent:*

1. $\varphi_1 \preceq_P \varphi_2$*;*
2. $\forall s \in \mathcal{F}(\mathbb{R}^+, \mathbb{R}^n)$ *and* $\forall v, r(s, \phi_{1,v}) \leq r(s, \phi_{2,v})$.

Corollary 1 is illustrated in Figure 2. The formulae are organized according to the relation $\varphi_1 \preceq_P \varphi_2, \varphi_3 \preceq_P \varphi_4$, which means that $r(s, \phi_{1,v}) \leq r(s, \phi_{2,v}), r(s, \phi_{3,v}) \leq r(s, \phi_{4,v})$ for all valuations v.

Theorem 1 and Corollary 1 have important implications for solving Problem 1. The formula inferred by our procedure should be a close representation of the properties that differentiate between desired and undesired behavior. Restricting the inferred formula (shrinking its language) by a small amount should result in a formula that cannot discriminate between the two cases. Thus, the mined formula should in principle be the lowest ordered satisfying formula. The DAG representation of $rPSTL$ can naturally be used to find such a "barely" satisfying formula. The search starts from the most exclusive formula and follows directed edges until a satisfying formula is found. This is shown in Figure 2. The formulae induced from optimal valuations (denoted with $*$ superscripts) of formulae $\varphi_1, \varphi_2, \varphi_3$ are all still violated by s (have negative robustness degrees). Thus, we have to go up the DAG to formula φ_4 to find a formula that s 'barely' satisfies, i.e. a formula with a small yet positive robustness degree.

The interaction between the graph search and parameter estimation is further illustrated in Figure 3. The top left and right plots show the x and y coordinates, respectively, of a single cow's trajectory. The center left (right) figure shows the robustness degree with respect to $\varphi_1 := \Diamond_{[0,\tau)}(x > 100)$ ($\varphi_2 := \Diamond_{[0,40)}(y < \pi)$) for various values of τ (π). Note that by selecting the parameter $\tau(\pi)$ for each φ_i, we can maximize or minimize the robustness degree of the signal with respect to the induced formula $\phi_{i,v}$. The bottom left plot shows the robustness degree for $\varphi_3 := \varphi_1 \wedge \varphi_2$ for various pairs (τ, π) and the bottom right plot shows the robustness degree with respect to $\varphi_4 := \varphi_1 \vee \varphi_2$. Note that $\varphi_3 \preceq_P \varphi_1(\varphi_2) \preceq_P \varphi_4$. By considering φ_3 rather than φ_1 or φ_2 alone, we can find a larger class of rSTL formulae that strongly violate the specification, which is useful for mining formulae with respect to undesirable behavior. Similarly, by considering φ_4, we can find a larger class of formulae that robustly satisfy the behavior. This is useful when we consider large groups of traces, as it is more likely that for two signals s_1, s_2 where $p_1 = 1, p_2 = 0$, we can find a formula $\phi_{j,v}, j \in \{3, 4\}$ such that $r(s_1, \varphi_{j,v}) > 0$ and $r(s_2, \varphi_{j,v}) < 0$ for $i = 1, 2$ than to

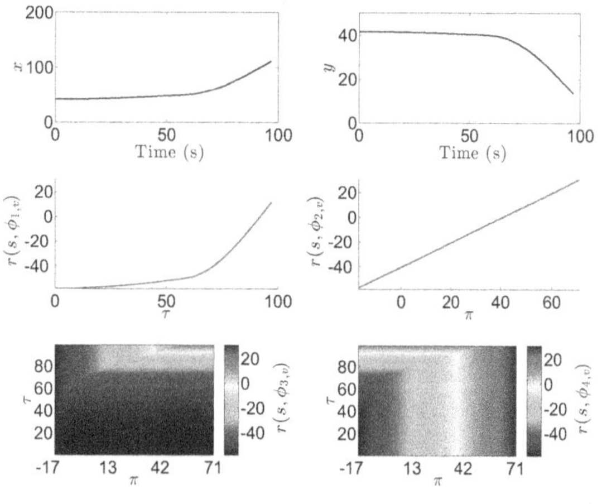

Figure 3: Simple example of formula search using cattle herding data.

be able to find a formula $\phi_{1,v}$ or $\phi_{2,v}$ that achieves the same classification.

5. SOLUTION

In this work, we infer an rPSTL formula by inferring the effect and cause formulae separately. Inferring the formulae separately still constitutes a search on finite subgraphs of the infinite DAG. When searching for the effect formula ϕ_e, we search over only the nodes of form $\Diamond_{[0,\tau_1)}(\top \Rightarrow \varphi_e)$. When searching for the entire formula in the prediction phase, we only search among the nodes of the form $\Diamond_{[0,\tau_1)}(\varphi_c \Rightarrow \varphi_{des,e})$, where $\varphi_{des,e}$ is the effect formula found in the classification phase. The framework for solving Problem 2 is detailed in Alg. 1. The prediction algorithm to solve Problem 3 is similar to Alg. 1.

Initialization.

Our algorithm operates on V, the set of all variables represented in the output signals from the system. The inference process begins in line 4 of Alg. 1, where DAGInitialization(V) generates the basis of the candidate formulae. The basis is a set of linear predicates with temporal operators, called *basis nodes*, of the form $O_{[\tau_1,\tau_2)}(x_s \sim \pi_1)$ where $O \in \{\Box, \Diamond\}$, $\sim \in \{\geq, <\}$ and $x \in V$. Edges are constructed from φ_i to φ_j in the initial graph $\mathcal{G}_1$ iff $\varphi_j \preceq_P \varphi_i$. For example, in the cow herding example if we only consider the (x, y) position of the cow, then the initial graph is shown in Figure 4.

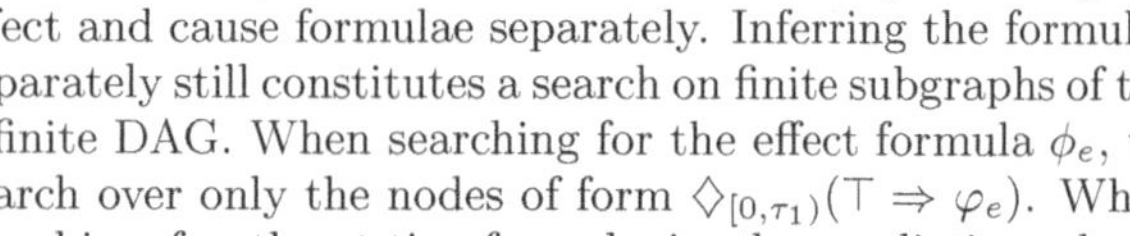

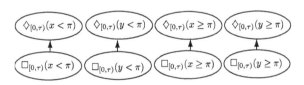

Figure 4: The initial graph $\mathcal{G}_1$ constructed from x, y coordinates.

ListInitialization($\mathcal{G}_1$) (line 5) generates a ranked list of formulae from the basis nodes. Since we do not yet know anything about how well each of the basis nodes classifies

---

Algorithm 1: Classification Algorithm

Input:
A set of labeled signals $\mathcal{S}_e := (s_i, p_i), i = 1, ..., N$;
A variable set V;
A misclassification rate threshold δ;
A formula length bound L_{max}
Output:
A rPSTL formula φ_e along with the corresponding valuation v_e and the misclassification rate q_e.

1 $\mathcal{G}_0 \leftarrow \emptyset$;
2 **for** $i = 1$ *to* L_{max} **do**
3   **if** $i = 1$ **then**
4     $\mathcal{G}_1 \leftarrow$ DAGInitialization(V);
5   *List* $\leftarrow$ ListInitialization($\mathcal{G}_1$);
6   **else**
7     $\mathcal{G}_i \leftarrow$ PruningAndGrowing($\mathcal{G}_{i-1}$);
8   *List* $\leftarrow$ Ranking($\mathcal{G}_i \setminus \mathcal{G}_{i-1}$);
9   **end**
10   **while** *List* $\neq \emptyset$ **do**
11     $\varphi \leftarrow$ PopOutFirstFormula(*List*);
12     $v_{ini} \leftarrow$ ParameterInitialization($\varphi, \mathcal{G}_{i-1}$);
13     $(v, c, q) \leftarrow$ ParameterEstimation($\mathcal{S}_e, \varphi, v_{ini}$);
14   **if** $q \leq \delta$ **then**
15   **return** (φ, v, q).
16   **end**
17     $\mathcal{G}_i \leftarrow$ Maintenance(φ, v, c, q);
18   **end**
19 **end**
20 $k^* \leftarrow$ MinimumCostNode($\mathcal{G}_{L_{max}}$);
21 **return** $(\varphi_{k^*}, v_{k^*}, q_{k^*})$.

---

behaviors, the rank is generated randomly. After the graph is constructed, we find the optimal parameters for each of the nodes.

Parameter Estimation.

PopOutFirstFormula(*List*) (line 11) pops out the lowest ranked formula from *List*. ParameterInitialization($\varphi, \mathcal{G}_{i-1}$) (line 12) randomly generates an initial valuation for φ if $\mathcal{G}_{i-1} = \emptyset$. Otherwise, it initializes the valuations based on those of its parents. ParameterEstimation($\mathcal{S}_e, \varphi, v_{ini}$) (line 13) uses simulated annealing [19] to find an optimal valuation for φ. The robustness degree of a formula generally increases or decreases monotonically in each parameter. However, we use simulated annealing rather than binary searches over the parameters because we are interested in optimizing a loss function of the robustness degree and are not necessarily trying to directly minimize it.

Function Maintenance(φ, v, c, q) (line 17) maintains the DAG by updating the nodes of $\mathcal{G}_i$ with the computed tuple (φ, v, c, q) where φ is the formula, v is the optimal valuation, c is the corresponding cost, and q is the corresponding *misclassification rate*, which is defined as the number of misclassified signals divided by the total number of signals N.

Structural Inference.

After the first set of parameters and costs have been found, the iterative process begins. The definition of the partial order allows for dynamic extension of the formula search space. We cannot explicitly represent the infinite DAG, so we construct a finite subgraph of possible candidate formulae and expand it when the candidate formulae perform insufficiently. PruningAndGrowing($\mathcal{G}_{i-1}$) (line 7) does this by first eliminating a fixed number of nodes with high costs, i.e. those formulae that do not fit the observed data. Pruning the graph to eliminate high cost formulae follows naturally from forward subset selection ideas developed in machine learning [21]. Then, the function grows the pruned $\mathcal{G}_{i-1}$ to include nodes with length i according to graph manipulation rules detailed in Section 4.2. An example of a subset of a graph $\mathcal{G}_2$ grown from the (pruned) basis graph is given in Figure 5.

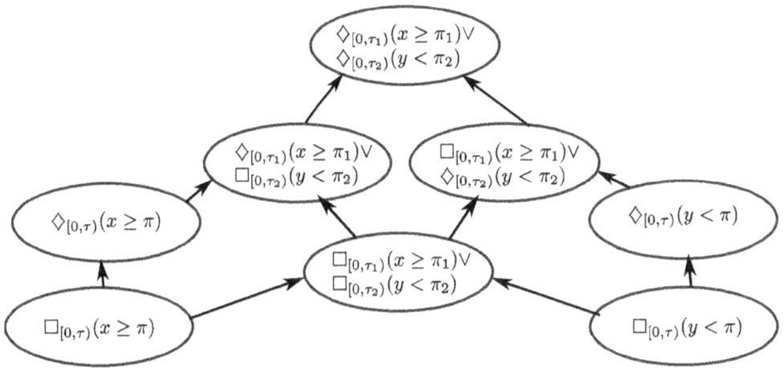

Figure 5: A subset of the DAG $\mathcal{G}_2$ after pruning and expansion

Ranking($\mathcal{G}_i \setminus \mathcal{G}_{i-1}$) (line 8) ranks the newly grown nodes based on a heuristic function

$$\frac{1}{|pa(k_i)|} \sum_{k_{i-1} \in pa(k_i)} J_e(k_{i-1}), \tag{11}$$

where k_i is a node in $\mathcal{G}_{i-1}$, $pa(k_i)$ is the set of k_i's parents, and $|pa(k_i)|$ is the size of $pa(k_i)$. For example, in Figure 5, for $k_i = (\Diamond_{[0,\tau_1)}(x \geq \pi_1) \wedge (\Diamond_{[0,\tau_2)}(y < \pi_2))$, $pa(k_i) = \{\Diamond_{[0,\tau)}(x \geq \pi), (\Diamond_{[0,\tau)}(y < \pi)\}$ and $|pa(k_i)| = 2$.

The iterative graph growing and parameter estimation procedure is performed until a formula with low enough misclassification rate is found or L_{max} iterations are completed. At this point, MinimumCostNode($\mathcal{G}_i$) returns the node with the minimum cost within $\mathcal{G}_i$.

Compared to Alg. 1, the prediction algorithm searches inside the subsection of the DAG of $rPSTL$ corresponding to formulae $\Diamond_{[0,\tau_1)}(\varphi_c \Rightarrow \varphi_{des,e})$, where $\varphi_{des,e}$ is the output of Alg. 1. The prediction algorithm employs the same procedures and continues the search until a formula with a low enough misclassification rate is found.

Complexity.

Without pruning, the discrete layer of the described algorithms runs in time $\mathcal{O}(L_{max} \cdot 2^{|V|})$. Since PruningAndGrowing prunes a constant number of nodes at each iteration, the complexity of the discrete layer is reduced to $\mathcal{O}(L_{max} \cdot |V|^2)$ when pruning is applied. The continuous layer of the algorithm, based on the simulated annealing algorithm, runs in time $\mathcal{O}(L_{max}(n^2 + m) \cdot \log(N))$, with n being the number of samples used in simulated annealing, and m being the number of data points per signal.

Remark 2. It has been shown in [7] that the set of all linear temporal logic (LTL) formulae can also be organized in a DAG using a partial order similar to $\preceq_S$. However, unlike LTL, PSTL can express temporal specifications involving continuous-time intervals and constraints on continuously valued variables. To our own knowledge, our algorithm is the first of its kind which can be used to infer an STL formula by inferring both its PSTL structure and its optimal valuation.

Remark 3. The truncation time $\tilde{t}$ is specified by the user. The truncation time represents a temporal threshold between possible causes of behaviors (described by ϕ_c) and the observed effects of these behaviors (described by ϕ_e). Thus, it should be chosen such that the desirable and undesirable effects can be clearly seen in the truncated signals σ_i. In the absence of any intuition about the value of $\tilde{t}$, its value can be set to half the duration of signals. This is the value we use for both case studies in Section 6.

6. IMPLEMENTATION AND CASE STUDIES

The classification and prediction algorithms were implemented as a software tool called TempLogIn (TEMPoral LOGic INference) in MATLAB. We developed all of the components of our solution in-house, including the graph construction and search algorithms and the simulated annealing algorithm. Our procedure takes as inputs sets of labeled trajectories, desired confidence, a truncation time ($\tilde{t}$) and a maximum formula length, and infers an rSTL formula. The software is available at `http://hyness.bu.edu/Software.html`.

6.1 Herding Example

Table 1: Parameters Defining Relevant Areas (Unit: m)

	$\pi_{.l}$	$\pi_{.r}$	$\pi_{.d}$	$\pi_{.u}$
A	0	50	40	100
B	25	50	40	60
C	100	150	60	100
D	100	150	0	45

The first example we consider is the herding example given in Section 3.1. We generated 600 signals, 120 of which are shown in Figure 6. Table 1 shows the values of the parameters describing the boundaries of the different regions A, B, C, D shown in Figure 1 and Figure 6. The columns correspond to the boundaries: the left boundary $\pi_{.l}$, the right boundary $\pi_{.r}$, the lower boundary $\pi_{.d}$ and the upper boundary $\pi_{.u}$. The starting locations of the signals are chosen randomly within A. The starting velocities are all set to 0. The dynamics of the cow are described by

$$\begin{cases} \dot{x} &= v\cos\alpha \\ \dot{y} &= v\sin\alpha \\ \dot{v} &= a_t \\ \dot{\alpha} &= \omega, \end{cases} \tag{12}$$

where x and y are the cow's coordinates, v is its speed, and α is its heading.[1] The two controls are the tangential

[1]The simple unicycle dynamics (12) is chosen for reader familiarity. The choice of simulated dynamics does not affect the validity of our results, as our algorithm depends on labeled traces and not explicit system models.

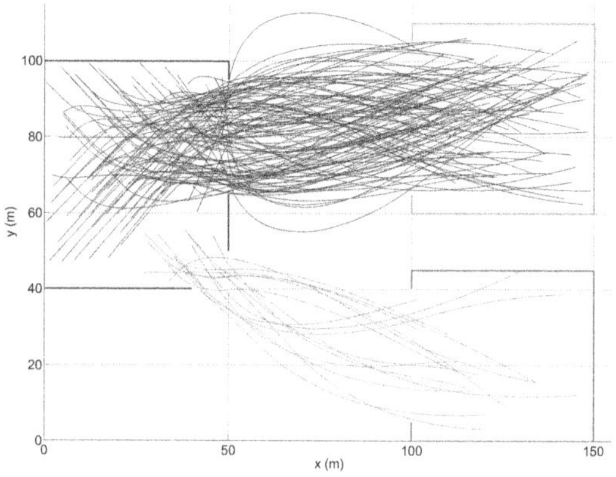

Figure 6: Synthesized trajectories with positive examples shown in black and negative ones shown in purple.

acceleration a_t and the angular velocity ω. These controls are generated based on a hybrid strategy. For a signal with $p_i = 1$ (a positive example), a random point is selected along the exit of A and acts as an attractor. The controls are generated from a potential function, a function of the distance between the selected point and the current location of the cow [14], until the cow reaches the exit. Then, the potential function-based control strategy is used to drive the cow to C. Signals in which $p_i = 0$ (a negative example) are generated similarly. All times are in minutes.

Table 2: Misclassification Rates for $i = 1$ (Classification)

	$\Diamond, <$	$\Box, <$	$\Diamond, \geq$	$\Box, \geq$
x	0.140	0.140	0.213	0.173
y	0	0	0.270	0.233
v	0.325	0.140	0.207	0.140
α	0.140	0.140	0.140	0.140

Classification For this case study, we are interested in inferring $\phi_{und,e}$, the formula describing the signals in which $p_i = 0$ (shown as purple in Figure 6). The variable set V is $\{x, y, v, \alpha\}$. Table 2 shows the misclassification rates of the nodes generated by our algorithm after parameter estimation occurs. The rows correspond to different variable choices. The columns correspond to different temporal operator and inequality combinations. For instance, the first row x and first column $\Diamond, <$ represent $\Diamond_{[\tau_1,\tau_2)}(x < \pi)$. In the following, we use the triple $(x, \Diamond, <)$ to represent it. It can be seen from the table that there are two formulae that have zero misclassification rate (underlined), which means the classification algorithm terminates with $i = 1$. To break the tie between these two formulae, the algorithm chooses the one with a lower cost $J_e(\varphi, v)$. The inferred effect formula is

$$\Box_{[0,3.02)}(y < 47.56), \tag{13}$$

which says that the undesirable cow behavior can be classified as "the y coordinate is always smaller than 47.56 meters for a period of 3.02 minutes". Notice that $y = 47.65$ is located between C and D which means that, for this specific case, we can classify signals by simply looking at their y coordinates.

Table 3: Misclassification Rates for $i = 1$ (Prediction)

	$\Diamond, \geq$	$\Box, \geq$	$\Diamond, <$	$\Box, <$
x	0.168	0.138	0.310	0.245
y	0.243	0.213	0.032	0.008
v	0.140	0.140	0.860	0.140
α	0.140	0.140	0.140	0.140

Prediction We again focus on signals in which $p_i = 0$. Table 3 shows the misclassification rates of the 16 basis nodes. It can be seen that there is no formula ϕ_c of length one that has zero misclassification rate. The three formulae with the lowest misclassification rates are underlined. The algorithm next grows the DAG to include formulae with length 2.

The algorithm then searches the new formulae in order according to the heuristic given in (11). The basis node with lowest cost is $(y, \Box, <)$ and the basis node with second lowest cost is $(y, \Diamond, <)$. The lowest ranked formula is the child of $(y, \Diamond, <)$, i.e. $(y, \Box, <)$, which has already been checked. Thus, the algorithm proceeds to the next lowest ranked candidate,which is the child of $(y, \Box, <)$ and $(x, \Box, \geq)$. This formula is $\Box_{[\tau_1,\tau_2)}(x \geq \pi_1) \wedge \Box_{[\tau_3,\tau_4)}(y < \pi_2)$. The algorithm was able to infer a cause formula with this template that has 0 misclassification rate. The total inferred rSTL formula is

$$\begin{aligned}\phi_{und} = \; & \Diamond_{[0,12.00)}((\Box_{[0,0.65)}(x \geq 25.00) \wedge \\ & \Box_{[0,8.00)}(y < 58.99)) \Rightarrow \Box_{[8.98,12.00)}(y < 47.56)).\end{aligned} \tag{14}$$

The similarity between (14) and (8) shows that our inference algorithm can accurately capture the essence of the undesirable behaviors with the cause formula (LHS of (14)). The two scale parameters inferred by the algorithm are 25.00 and 58.99, which are close to the fencing breach location $(\pi_{bl}, \pi_{bu}) = (25, 60)$ (see Section 3.1 and Table 1). These results are achieved without any expert knowledge.

On a Mac with a 3.06 GHz Intel Core 2 Duo CPU and 6 GB RAM, the classification took 305.5 seconds, and the prediction took 643.1 seconds with n, the number of samples generated in simulated annealing, equal to 100, and m, the maximum number of data point per signal, equal to 200.

6.2 Biological Network

The second example we consider is from synthetic biology. In this field, gene networks are engineered to achieve specific functions [13, 20]. The robustness degree has previously been exploited in gene network design and analysis [18, 2, 5], but to our knowledge, template discovery has never been used to analyze a gene network. We consider the gene network presented in [10]. The network, shown in Figure 7, controls the production of two proteins, namely $tetR$ and RFP. This network is expected to work as an inverter in which the concentrations of $tetR$ and RFP can be treated as the input and the output, respectively. In particular, $tetR$ represses the production of RFP. A high $tetR$ concentration decreases the production rate of RFP, hence the concentration of RFP eventually decreases and stays low. Similarly, if the concentration of $tetR$ is low, then the production of RFP is not repressed, and its concentration eventually increases and stays high.

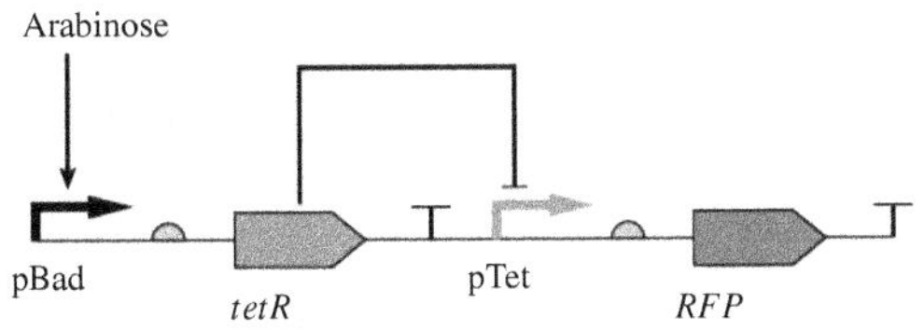

Figure 7: A synthetic gene network. The genes coding for proteins $tetR$ and RFP are shown as colored polygons. The promoters (pBad and pTet) regulating protein production rates are indicated by bent arrows. The regulators ($arabinose$ and $tetR$) are connected to the corresponding promoters.

In [10], a stochastic hybrid system modeling the gene network was constructed from characterization data of the biological network components. Statistical model checking was used to check a temporal logic formula (expressing a property chosen by biology experts) that describes the inverter behavior of the network. In this paper, sample trajectories of this system [2] are used to find a formula that describes the inverter behavior without any prior expert knowledge.

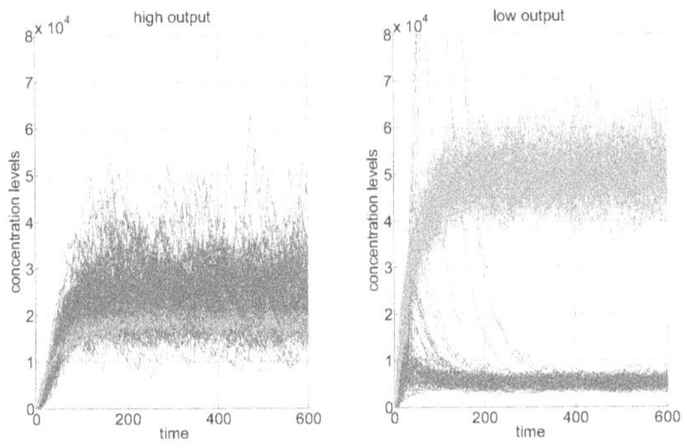

Figure 8: Concentration levels x_{tetR} (green) and x_{RFP} (red) for the high and low output cases. 100 signals are plotted for each protein and each case.

We generated 600 signals, half of which correspond to the low output case (repression) and half of which correspond to the high output case (no repression). Figure 8 shows 200 of these signals. Assume that we are interested in characterizing the low output case ($p_i = 1$ for low output signals). The inferred rSTL formula ϕ_{des} which classifies both cases and describes the pre-conditions for low output is

$$\phi_{des} = \Diamond_{[0,118)}(\Box_{[0,340)}(x_{tetR} \geq 23209) \Rightarrow \Box_{[188,323)}(x_{RFP} < 13479)) \quad (15)$$

This formula captures the repressing effect of $tetR$, and shows that the designed gene network works as expected. In particular, the formula implies that $tetR$ represses the production of RFP when its concentration is higher than 23209 for 340 time units. Moreover, when the production of RFP is repressed, its concentration drops below 13479 within 188 time units. Such quantitative information learned from the formula helps the user to design more complex gene networks.

On the same computer used in the first case study, the classification procedure took 494.0 seconds while the prediction algorithm took 693.7 seconds. For the biological network case study, the number of samples generated by the simulating annealing, n, and the maximum number of data points per signal, m, were 100 and 600, respectively.

[2] $Arabinose$ regulates the production rate of $tetR$. We use trajectories generated at different concentration levels of $arabinose$. As we are interested in cause-effect relationship between $tetR$ and RFP, we omit the concentration of $arabinose$.

7. FINAL REMARKS AND FUTURE WORK

In this paper, we present a temporal logic inference framework, which, given a collection of labeled continuously valued signals, produces temporal logic formulae that can be used to describe and predict desirable and undesirable behaviors. We define reactive parametric signal temporal logic (rPSTL), a fragment of parametric signal temporal logic (PSTL) that can be used to describe causal relationships in systems. We exploit the properties of rPSTL and develop a hybrid temporal logic inference algorithm that searches for a formula template, as well as as its parameterization, that best fits the observed data. Two case studies, one on herding and the other one on biological networks, are used to illustrate our algorithm. The formulae mined from each case study appear to be consistent with the observed behaviors of each system.

While the example considered in Section 6 is relatively simple, the algorithm presented in the paper can be used to infer characteristics of more complex systems. Since our algorithm infers properties without any expert inputs, it is well-suited to tasks such as system reconstruction, e.g. inferring the purpose and capabilities of legacy code, and knowledge discovery, e.g. finding relevant properties of a complex biological network directly from the data. It can also serve as a first step for developing high-fidelity models of a complex system from a massive data set. For instance, from the inferred formula (15), it can be seen that the underlying system acts as an inverter. This conclusion can guide further revisions in experimental design as well as modeling.

Future research in this area includes applying our inference algorithm to more complex data, expanding the class of formulae which may be inferred automatically, and revising our algorithm to fit large data sets and unsupervised learning cases.

8. ACKNOWLEDGMENT

This work was supported in part by ONR MURI N00014-10-1-0952, ONR MURI N00014-09-1051, and NSF CNS-1035588. The authors would like to acknowledge members of CIDAR group at Boston University for providing experimental data for the gene network presented in [10].

9. REFERENCES

[1] E. Asarin, A. Donzé, O. Maler, and D. Nickovic. Parametric identification of temporal properties. In *Runtime Verification*, pages 147–160. Springer, 2012.

[2] E. Bartocci, L. Bortolussi, L. Nenzi, and G. Sanguinetti. On the robustness of temporal properties for stochastic models. In *Proceedings*

Second International Workshop on Hybrid Systems and Biology, volume 125, pages 3–19, 2013.

[3] V. Chandola, A. Banerjee, and V. Kumar. Anomaly detection: A survey. *ACM Computing Surveys (CSUR)*, 41(3):15, 2009.

[4] B. A. Davey and H. A. Priestley. *Introduction to Lattices and Order*. Cambridge University Press, 2002.

[5] A. Donzé, E. Fanchon, L. M. Gattepaille, O. Maler, and P. Tracqui. Robustness analysis and behavior discrimination in enzymatic reaction networks. *PLoS One*, 6(9):e24246, 2011.

[6] A. Donzé and O. Maler. Robust satisfaction of temporal logic over real-valued signals. In *Formal Modeling and Analysis of Timed Systems*, pages 92–106. Springer, 2010.

[7] G. E. Fainekos. Revising temporal logic specifications for motion planning. In *Robotics and Automation (ICRA), 2011 IEEE International Conference on*, pages 40–45. IEEE, 2011.

[8] G. E. Fainekos and G. J. Pappas. Robustness of temporal logic specifications for continuous-time signals. *Theoretical Computer Science*, 410(42):4262–4291, 2009.

[9] L. Getoor and B. Taskar. *Introduction to Statistical Relational Learning*. The MIT Press, 2007.

[10] E. A. Gol, D. Densmore, and C. Belta. Data-driven verification of synthetic gene networks. In *52nd IEEE Conference on Decision and Control (CDC)*, 2013.

[11] M. Huth and M. Ryan. *Logic in Computer Science: Modelling and Reasoning about Systems*. Cambridge University Press, 2004.

[12] X. Jin, A. Donze, J. Deshmukh, and S. Seshia. Mining requirements from closed-loop control models. In *Hybrid Systems: Computation and Control (HSCC)*, 2013.

[13] J. R. Kirby. Synthetic biology: Designer bacteria degrades toxin. *Nature Chemical Biology*, 6(6):398–399, 2010.

[14] S. M. LaValle. *Planning Algorithms*. Cambridge University Press, 2006.

[15] N. Lavrac and S. Dzeroski. *Inductive Logic Programming*. E. Horwood, 1994.

[16] L. Ljung. *System Identification: Theory for the User*. Prentice Hall, 1987.

[17] O. Maler and D. Nickovic. Monitoring temporal properties of continuous signals. *Formal Techniques, Modelling and Analysis of Timed and Fault-Tolerant Systems*, pages 71–76, 2004.

[18] A. Rizk, G. Batt, F. Fages, and S. Soliman. On a continuous degree of satisfaction of temporal logic formulae with applications to systems biology. In *Computational Methods in Systems Biology*, pages 251–268. Springer, 2008.

[19] S. J. Russell and P. Norvig. *Artificial Intelligence: a Modern Approach*. Prentice Hall, 1995.

[20] H. Salis, A. Tamsir, and C. Voigt. Engineering bacterial signals and sensors. *Contrib Microbiol*, 16:194–225, 2009.

[21] H. Trevor, T. Robert, and J. J. H. Friedman. *The elements of Statistical Learning*. Springer, 2001.

[22] H. Yang, B. Hoxha, and G. Fainekos. Querying parametric temporal logic properties on embedded systems. In *Testing Software and Systems*, pages 136–151. Springer, 2012.

Energy and Mean-payoff Timed Games*

Romain Brenguier
Département d'informatique,
Université Libre de Bruxelles
(U.L.B), Belgium
brenguier@ulb.ac.be

Franck Cassez
NICTA,†
Sydney, Australia
franck.cassez@nicta.com.au

Jean-François Raskin
Département d'informatique,
Université Libre de Bruxelles
(U.L.B), Belgium
jraskin@ulb.ac.be

ABSTRACT

In this paper, we study energy and mean-payoff timed games. The decision problems that consist in determining the existence of winning strategies in those games are undecidable, and we thus provide semi-algorithms for solving these strategy synthesis problems. We then identify a large class of timed games for which our semi-algorithms terminate and are thus complete. We also study in detail the relation between mean-payoff and energy timed games. Finally, we provide a symbolic algorithm to solve energy timed games and demonstrate its use on small examples using HyTech.

1. INTRODUCTION

Timed automata [1], respectively timed games [33, 19], are fundamental models to verify, respectively to synthesize controllers for, timed systems which have to enforce hard real-time constraints. Those models were introduced in the nineties and the underlying theory has since then been successfully implemented in efficient analysis tools such as Kronos [15] and UppAal [32] for verification, and UppAal-Tiga [4] for synthesis. The latter has been used to solve industrial case studies, e.g. [28, 20].

Recently, there has been an important research effort to lift verification and synthesis techniques from the Boolean case to the quantitative case, see [26] and references therein. More specifically, lots of progress has been made recently on zero-sum two-player games played on weighted graphs, in which edges are decorated with *costs* or *rewards*, see for example [13, 22, 23, 18], with the objective of setting up a framework for the synthesis of optimal controllers (see also [34] for applications in linear control systems). Important examples of such games are *mean-payoff* and *energy* games [13, 18, 23]. In those games, two players move a token along the edges of a weighted graph whose vertices are partitioned into vertices that belong to player 1, and player 2 respectively. In each round of the game, the player that owns the vertex with the token chooses an outgoing edge and target vertex to move the token to. By playing in such a way, the two players form an infinite path through the graph. Player 1 wins the *mean-payoff objective* if the long-run average of the edge-weights along this path is nonnegative, and he wins the *energy objective*, if there exists a bound $c \in \mathbb{Z}$ such that the running sum of weights of the traversed edges along the infinite path never goes below c (this can model for example that the system never runs out of energy). As the games we consider are zero-sum, player 2 wins when he can enforce the complementary objectives. In the finite state case, the mean-payoff and energy objectives are *inter-reducible*, and this fact was used recently to provide algorithmic improvements to solve mean-payoff games [18].

Extensions of timed automata with costs and rewards have also been studied. In [3, 5], timed automata are extended with continuous variables that are used as *observers*, and allow for modeling accumulation of costs or rewards along executions. The main motivation for studying those extensions is to offer an extra modeling power while avoiding severe intractability of richer models like hybrid automata. Indeed, it has been shown that the reachability problem for weighted/priced timed automata remains decidable [3, 5], and more precisely PSPACE-c [8], while the reachability problem is undecidable already for the class of stopwatch automata [21] (a simple class of hybrid automata). Also the existence of executions in a weighted automaton that ensure a bound on the mean-payoff can also be decided in PSPACE [10]. In this paper, we consider timed extensions of the important classes of mean-payoff and energy games.

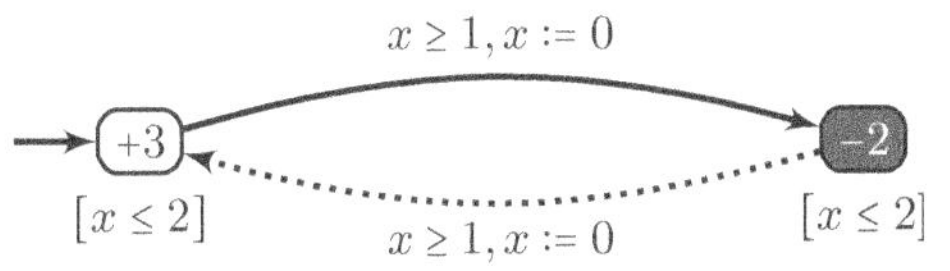

Figure 1: Turn-Based Energy Timed Game $\mathcal{A}$.

Example 1. Fig. 1 gives an example of an energy (turn-based) timed game. `Eve` (player 1) owns the left location and decides when to take the transition from left to right, while `Adam` (player 2) owns the right location and decides when to take the transition from right to left; x is a dense-time clock. Each transition resets the clock x, and when time elapses the energy level grows with derivative 3 in `Eve`'s lo-

†NICTA is funded by the Australian Government through the Department of Communications and the Australian Research Council through the ICT Centre of Excellence Program.
*Work supported by ERC Starting Grant inVEST (279499).

HSCC'14, April 15–17, 2014, Berlin, Germany.
Copyright 2014 ACM 978-1-4503-2732-9/14/04 ...$15.00.
http://dx.doi.org/10.1145/2562059.2562116.

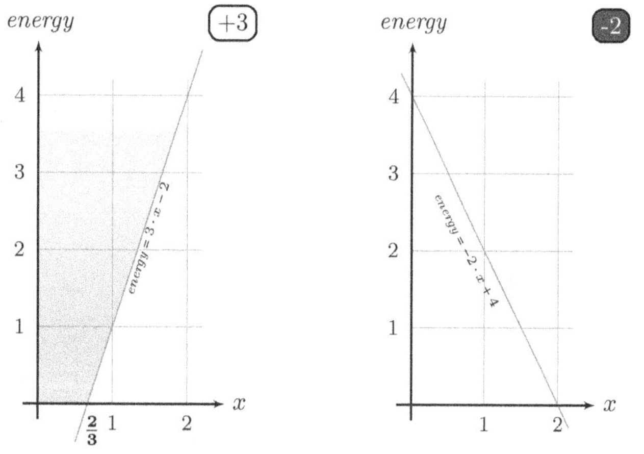

Figure 2: Winning Zones for Timed Game $\mathcal{A}$.

cation and decreases with derivative 2 in Adam's location. In the remaining of this paper, we use the following conventions: plain (resp. dashed) arrows are Eve's (resp. Adam's) transitions; a location *invariant* is enclosed in brackets (e.g. $[x \leq 2]$) and must be satisfied by the valuation of the clocks when the control is in that location; when an edge weight is non zero, we attach it to the edge. Fig. 2, left, depicts the initial energy levels that are sufficient for Eve in order to have a winning strategy against any strategy of Adam, i.e. to ensure an infinite execution in which the energy level never falls below 0. For instance, if the infinite game starts in Eve's location, then if the value of clock x is less than $\frac{2}{3}$, an initial energy level 0 is sufficient; for $x > \frac{2}{3}$, the initial energy level should be larger than or equal to $3 \cdot x - 2$. Similarly, the winning zone in Adam's location is depicted on the right hand side of Fig. 2. The main purpose of this article is to propose algorithmic methods to compute such information.

Unfortunately, for weighted extensions of timed games, even the cost bounded reachability problem is undecidable [17], and we show here that both mean-payoff and energy games are undecidable. This is unfortunate as such cost extensions of timed games are very natural and well-suited to model optimality problems in embedded control [20]. Nevertheless, we believe that the undecidability result should not be an end to the story and we study in this paper *semi-algorithms* (completeness and/or termination is not guaranteed) to solve those two synthesis problems. We also identify a large class of timed games where our semi-algorithms are complete. To the best of our knowledge, there are the first positive results for those objectives on timed automata. There are related works in the literature but they apply to orthogonal classes of games, or to other objectives. Indeed, in [9], it is shown that mean-payoff games are decidable for O-minimal hybrid automata, this class is different from the one identified here as timed automata are not O-minimal hybrid automata. In [30], the authors study the average time per transition problem for turn-based timed games; their results do not apply to mean-payoff, nor to energy objectives.

Contributions. Our contribution is threefold. First, we study the relation between mean-payoff and energy timed games. As we already mentioned, in the finite state case, the mean-payoff and energy objectives are inter-reducible [18]: given a weighted game G, Eve wins the mean-payoff objective if, and only if, she wins the energy objective. We show here that the relationship between the two types of games is more complex in the timed case. We identify conditions under which it is possible to transfer winning strategies for one objective into winning strategies for the other objective, and we show that those conditions are also necessary. Those results are formalized by Thm. 1 and Thm. 2.

Second, Thm. 3 establishes the undecidability of the decision problems associated with energy and mean-payoff timed games. This result is unfortunate but not surprising (it was already conjectured in [7], see page 89). This negative result motivates the main contribution of this paper: we propose two semi-algorithms for synthesizing winning strategies. We first consider a *cycle forming game* (in the spirit of [6]) on the region graph associated with the underlying weighted timed game: the two players move a token on the region graph and the game is stopped as soon as a cycle is formed. In Sect. 3.4, we partition the set of simple cycles of the region graph into those that are *good* for Eve, those that are *good* for Adam, and those that are neither good for Eve nor for Adam. If the formed cycle belongs to the first set then Eve is declared winner of the cycle forming game, if the cycle belongs to the second then Adam is the winner, otherwise it is a draw. Thm. 4 establishes that if Eve wins the cycle forming game then she has also a winning strategy in associated energy games, and Thm. 5 proves a similar result for Adam. Then, we identify a class of weighted timed games, that we call *robust*, for which this reduction to the cycle forming game on the region graph is complete: in this case the good cycles for Eve and the good cycles for Adam partition the set of simple cycles of the region graph. This class covers the class of timed games where costs appear on edges only. Thm. 10 establishes the decidability of the membership problem for the class of robust weighted timed games.

Finally, as the cycle forming game is defined on the region graph, it does not lead to a practical algorithmic solution. This is why we propose in addition a symbolic semi-algorithm to solve energy timed games. In Thm. 13, we show that our symbolic algorithm is also complete on the class of *robust* weighted timed games. In order to show the feasibility of our approach, we have implemented this algorithm as a script for HyTech [27] and ran it on small examples.

Our main theorems and their relation with the different classes of games we consider are depicted in Fig. 3 and 4.

Structure of the paper.

In Sect. 2, we define the mean-payoff and energy timed games. In Sect. 3, we develop semi-algorithms based on reductions to cycle games played on the region graph. In Sect. 4, we identify a class *robust games*, for which the reduction to cycle games is complete. In Sect. 5, we propose a symbolic semi-algorithm which is also complete for robust games.

Due to space constraints, most proofs have been omitted from this paper; they can be found in the full version [16].

2. PRELIMINARIES

In this section, we first recall the definition of concurrent games. Then we review a useful result from [29] that defines a canonical decomposition of infinite paths in a graph into *simple cycles*. Next, we introduce *weighted timed games*, the semantics of which is given in term of infinite concurrent games. Starting from the notion of *weight* (or cost/reward),

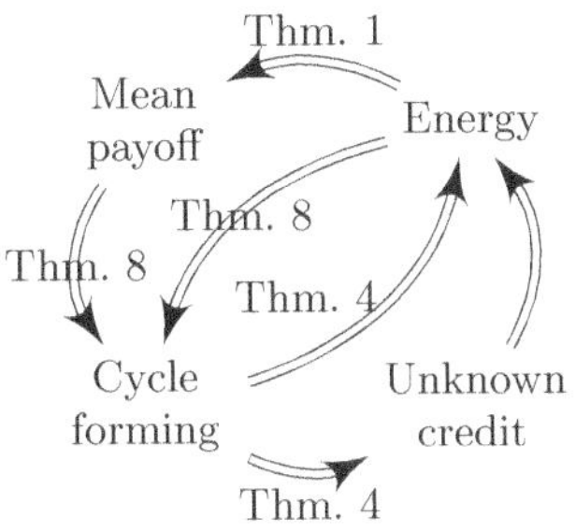

Figure 3: Winning strategies for Eve

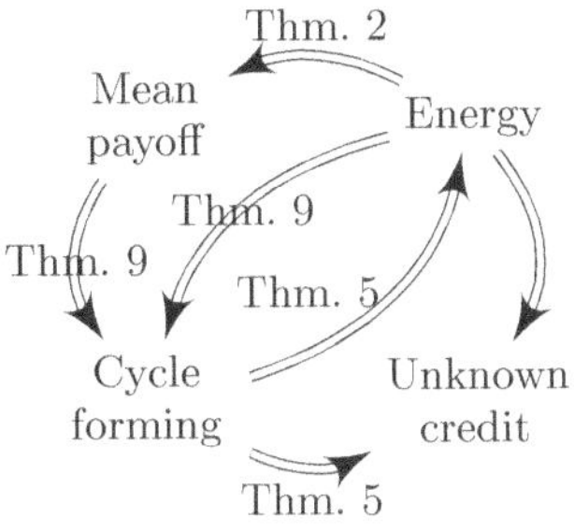

Figure 4: Winning strategies for Adam

we define *mean payoff* and *energy* objectives. We close the section with a study of the relationships that exist between mean-payoff and energy objectives in timed games.

We let $\mathbb{N}$ be the set of natural numbers, $\mathbb{Z}$ the set of integers, $\mathbb{R}$ the set of reals and $\mathbb{R}_+$ the set of non-negative reals.

2.1 Concurrent Games

Definition 1. ([2]) A *concurrent game* between two players Eve and Adam is a tuple $\mathcal{C} = \langle \mathtt{St}, \iota, \mathtt{Act}, \mathtt{Mov}, \mathtt{Tab}, \Omega \rangle$, where:

- $\mathtt{St}$ is the set of *states*;
- $\iota \in \mathtt{St}$ is the *initial* state;
- $\mathtt{Act}$ is the set of *actions*;
- $\mathtt{Mov} : \mathtt{St} \times \{\mathtt{Eve}, \mathtt{Adam}\} \mapsto 2^{\mathtt{Act}} \setminus \{\varnothing\}$ gives for a state and a player the set of *allowed actions*, we let $\mathtt{Mov}(s) = \{(a, b) \mid a \in \mathtt{Mov}(s, \mathtt{Eve}), b \in \mathtt{Mov}(s, \mathtt{Adam})\}$;
- $\mathtt{Tab} : \mathtt{St} \times \mathtt{Act} \times \mathtt{Act} \mapsto \mathtt{St}$ is the *transition function*;
- $\Omega \subseteq (\mathtt{St} \cdot (\mathtt{Act} \times \mathtt{Act}))^\omega$ is the *objective* for Eve.

A concurrent game is *finite* if St and Act are finite. It is *turn-based* if in each state s, one of the players has only one allowed action.

A round of the game consists in Eve and Adam to choose independently and simultaneously some actions, say $a_\exists$ and $a_\forall$ respectively, such that $a_\exists \in \mathtt{Mov}(s, \mathtt{Eve})$ and $a_\forall \in \mathtt{Mov}(s, \mathtt{Adam})$. The pair $m = (a_\exists, a_\forall)$ is an allowed *move* i.e. $m \in \mathtt{Mov}(s)$. By playing finitely (resp. infinitely) many rounds from state $s \in \mathtt{St}$, the players build a finite (resp. infinite) *path*. Formally, a *path* is a finite or infinite sequence $s_0 \cdot m_0 \cdot s_1 \cdot m_1 \cdots s_k \cdot m_k \cdots$ of alternating states and moves, such that $\forall i \geq 0, m_i \in \mathtt{Mov}(s_i)$ and $s_{i+1} = \mathtt{Tab}(s_i, m_i)$. We also write a path as $s_0 \xrightarrow{m_0} s_1 \xrightarrow{m_1} \cdots$. The length, $|\rho|$, of an infinite path ρ is ∞ and the length of a finite path ρ with n moves (ending in s_n) is n and $\mathtt{last}(\rho) = s_n$. We write $\rho_n, n \leq |\rho|$, for s_n, the $n+1$-th state in ρ, and $\mathtt{first}(\rho) = \rho_0 = s_0$. Given a path $\rho = s_0 \xrightarrow{m_0} s_1 \xrightarrow{m_1} \cdots$, we write $\rho_{\leq n}, n \leq |\rho|$ for the prefix of ρ up to s_n that is the finite path $s_0 \xrightarrow{m_0} \cdots \xrightarrow{m_{n-1}} s_n$.

A *play* is an infinite path in $(\mathtt{St} \cdot (\mathtt{Act} \times \mathtt{Act}))^\omega$, and a *history* is a finite path in $(\mathtt{St} \cdot (\mathtt{Act} \times \mathtt{Act}))^* \cdot \mathtt{St}$. The set of plays from s is $\mathtt{Play}(\mathcal{C}, s)$ and $\mathtt{Play}(\mathcal{C}) = \mathtt{Play}(\mathcal{C}, \iota)$. A play is *winning* for Eve if it belongs to the objective Ω.

Definition 2. (Strategies) A *strategy* for Eve (resp. Adam) is a function which associates with a history h an Eve-action in $\mathtt{Mov}(\mathtt{last}(h), \mathtt{Eve})$ (resp. an Adam-action). A pair of strategies $(\sigma_\exists, \sigma_\forall)$ forms a *strategy profile*. Given a strategy profile, its *outcome from state* s, written $\mathtt{Out}_s(\sigma_\exists, \sigma_\forall)$, is the unique play ρ such that: $\rho_0 = s$ and $\forall n \geq 0, \rho_{n+1} = \mathtt{Tab}(\rho_n, \sigma_\exists(\rho_{\leq n}), \sigma_\forall(\rho_{\leq n}))$. Given a strategy $\sigma_\exists$ of Eve, its *outcomes from state* s, written $\mathtt{Out}_s(\sigma_\exists)$, are the set of plays ρ for which there is a strategy $\sigma_\forall$ of Adam, such that $\rho = \mathtt{Out}_s(\sigma_\exists, \sigma_\forall)$. A strategy $\sigma_\exists$ of Eve is *winning*, if for all strategies $\sigma_\forall$ of Adam, $\mathtt{Out}_\iota(\sigma_\exists, \sigma_\forall) \in \Omega$; strategy $\sigma_\forall$ of Adam is *winning*, if for all strategies $\sigma_\exists$ of Eve, $\mathtt{Out}_\iota(\sigma_\exists, \sigma_\forall) \notin \Omega$.

2.2 Decomposition in Simple Cycles

In the sequel we will reduce energy and mean payoff games to games played on the region with *cycles* objectives. In this paragraph we recall the key results [29] related to the decomposition of a play into *simple cycles*. A history $h = s_0 \cdot m_0 \cdot s_1 \cdot m_1 \cdots s_n$ is a *cycle* if $s_0 = s_n, n \geq 1$. A *simple cycle* is a cycle such that for all i and j, $0 \leq i < j < n$, $s_i \neq s_j$. We write $\mathbb{C}(\mathcal{C})$ ($\mathbb{C}$ when $\mathcal{C}$ is clear from the context) for the set of simple cycles in the concurrent game $\mathcal{C}$.

Every history h of a finite game can be uniquely decomposed into a sequence of simple cycles, except for a finite part. The decomposition process maintains a *stack*, $\mathtt{st}(h)$, of distinct states and moves. We write the stack content $s_1 \cdot m_1 \cdot s_2 \cdot \cdots \cdot m_{n-1} \cdot s_n$ where s_1 is at the bottom of the stack and s_n the top. We use the notation $s \in \mathtt{st}(h)$ for $s \in \{s_1, s_2, \cdots, s_n\}$. The *decomposition*, $\mathtt{dec}(h)$, is a set of simple cycles. We define $\mathtt{dec}(h)$ and $\mathtt{st}(h)$ inductively as follows:

- for the single state history s, $\mathtt{dec}(s) = \varnothing$ and $\mathtt{st}(s) = s$.
- let $h' = h \cdot m \cdot s$, m a move, $s \in \mathtt{St}$, be a history.
  - If $s \in \mathtt{st}(h)$, and $\mathtt{st}(h) = \alpha \cdot s \cdot \beta$, then $\mathtt{st}(h') = pop(\mathtt{st}(h), |\beta|)$ and $\mathtt{dec}(h') = \mathtt{dec}(h) \cup \{s \cdot \beta \cdot m \cdot s\}$.
  - else $\mathtt{dec}(h') = \mathtt{dec}(h)$, $\mathtt{st}(h') = push(\mathtt{st}(h), m \cdot s)$.

Note that the stack always contains distinct elements, therefore only simple cycles are added to the decomposition. The elements in the stack from the bottom to the top, form a history $s_0 \cdot m_0 \cdot s_1 \cdot m_1 \cdots s_n$, where $n+1$ is the height of the stack. The decomposition of a play is the union of the decompositions of the finite prefixes of the play.

2.3 Weighted Timed Games

Let X be a finite set of variables called *clocks*. A *clock valuation* is a mapping $v : X \to \mathbb{R}_+$. We let $\mathbb{R}_+^X$ be the set of clock valuations over X. We let $\mathbf{0}_X$ be the *zero* valuation where all the clocks in X are set to 0 (we use $\mathbf{0}$ when X is clear from the context). Given $\delta \in \mathbb{R}_+$, $v+\delta$ denotes the valuation defined by $(v+\delta)(x) = v(x)+\delta$. We let $\mathfrak{C}(X)$ be the set of *convex constraints* on X which is the set of conjunctions of constraints of the form $x \bowtie c$ with $c \in \mathbb{N}$ and $\bowtie \in \{\leq, <, =, >, \geq\}$. Given a constraint $g \in \mathfrak{C}(X)$ and a valuation v, we write $v \models g$ if g is satisfied by v. Given $Y \subseteq X$ and a valuation v, $[Y \leftarrow 0]v$ is the valuation defined by $([Y \leftarrow 0]v)(x) = v(x)$ if $x \notin Y$ and $([Y \leftarrow 0]v)(x) = 0$ otherwise.

Definition 3. A *weighted timed game* [31] (WTG for short) is a tuple $\mathcal{T} = \langle \mathtt{L}, \ell_\iota, X, T_\exists, T_\forall, \mathtt{Inv}, \mathtt{w} \rangle$, where:

- $\mathtt{L}$ is the (finite) set of locations and ℓ_ι is the initial location;

- X is a finite set of clocks;
- $T_\exists, T_\forall \subseteq \mathtt{L} \times \mathfrak{C}(X) \times 2^X \times \mathtt{L}$ are the set of transitions belonging to Eve and Adam respectively, and we let $T = T_\exists \cup T_\forall$; An element of $T_\exists$ (resp. $T_\forall$) is an Eve-transition (resp. Adam-transition).
- $\mathtt{Inv}: \mathtt{L} \to \mathfrak{C}(X)$ defines the invariants of each location;
- $\mathtt{w}: \mathtt{L} \cup T \to \mathbb{Z}$ is a weight function assigning integer weights to locations and discrete transitions.

If, from each location, all the outgoing transitions belong to the same player, $\mathcal{T}$ is said *turn-based*.

Informally, a WTG is played as follows: a state of the game is a pair (ℓ, v) where ℓ is a location and v is a clock valuation such that $v \models \mathtt{Inv}(\ell)$. The game starts from the initial state $(\ell_\iota, \mathbf{0})$. From a state (ℓ, v), each player $p \in \{\mathtt{Eve}, \mathtt{Adam}\}$ chooses (independently) a *timed action* $a_p = (d_p, e_p)$ where $d_p \in \mathbb{R}_+$ and $e_p = (\ell, g, Y, \ell')$ is a p-transition. The intended meaning is that p wants to delay for d_p time units and then fire transition e_p. There are some restrictions on the possible choices of timed actions (d_p, e_p): 1) d_p must be compatible with the current state (ℓ, v) and location invariant, i.e. for all $0 \le d' \le d_p$, $v + d' \models \mathtt{Inv}(\ell)$; 2) e_p must be enabled after d_p time units, i.e. $v + d_p \models g$; 3) the target location's invariant must be satisfied when entering this location, i.e. $[Y \leftarrow 0](v + d_p) \models \mathtt{Inv}(\ell')$.

A timed action satisfying these restrictions is said *legal*. If from a given state, one player has no legal timed action to play (i.e. no discrete action is enabled in the future for this player), it plays a special action $\perp$. At each round of the game, players propose some actions, $a_\exists$ for Eve, and $a_\forall$ for Adam. Either $a_\exists$ is a legal action for Eve; or there are no legal actions for Eve and $a_\exists = \perp$. Similarly for $a_\forall$. We assume that from any reachable state of the game, at least one player has a legal action, hence the pair $(\perp, \perp)$ is never proposed.

To determine the effect of a joint action, we select the player p that chooses the shortest delay d_p. In case both players choose the same delay, the convention is that Adam is selected (this is without loss of generality and other policies can be accommodated for). These informal game rules are formalized in the next section.

2.4 Semantics of Timed Games

Given a timed action $(d, e) \in \mathbb{R}_+ \times T$ with $e = (\ell, g, Y, \ell')$, a state (ℓ, v), the successor state in the WTG is (ℓ', v') if: 1) $\forall 0 \le \delta \le d, v + \delta \models \mathtt{Inv}(\ell)$; 2) and $v + \delta \models g$; 3) and $[Y \leftarrow 0](v + d) \models \mathtt{Inv}(\ell')$. We denote this transition $(\ell, v) \xrightarrow{(d,e)} (\ell', v')$ which accounts for a combined delay transition of d time units followed by the discrete step firing edge e. The *duration* of this transition is $\mathtt{d}((\ell, v) \xrightarrow{(d,e)} (\ell', v')) = d$. Its *reward* (or *weight*) is $\mathtt{w}((\ell, v) \xrightarrow{(d,e)} (\ell', v')) = d \cdot \mathtt{w}(\ell) + \mathtt{w}(e)$.

Given an objective $\Omega \subseteq \left((\mathtt{L} \times \mathbb{R}_+^X) \cdot ((\mathbb{R}_+ \times T_\exists) \times (\mathbb{R}_+ \times T_\forall))\right)^\omega$, the semantics of the WTG $\mathcal{T}$ is the (infinite) concurrent game $\mathcal{C}(\mathcal{T}, \Omega) = (\mathtt{St}, \iota, \mathtt{Act}, \mathtt{Mov}, \mathtt{Tab}, \Omega)$ defined by:

- the set of states is $\mathtt{St} = \mathtt{L} \times \mathbb{R}_+^X$ and the initial state is $\iota = (\ell_\iota, \mathbf{0})$;
- the set of actions is $\mathtt{Act} = \mathtt{Act}_\exists \cup \mathtt{Act}_\forall$, where $\mathtt{Act}_\exists = \mathbb{R}_+ \times T_\exists$ are the actions for Eve and $\mathtt{Act}_\forall = \mathbb{R}_+ \times T_\forall$ are the actions for Adam;
- $\mathtt{Mov}(s, \mathtt{Eve}) \in \left(2^{\mathtt{Act}_\exists} \setminus \{\varnothing\}\right) \cup \{\perp\}$ is the set of legal actions for Eve in s if there is at least one, or $\{\perp\}$ otherwise; and $\mathtt{Mov}(s, \mathtt{Adam})$ is defined similarly.
  Given $(a_\exists, a_\forall) \in \mathtt{Mov}(s, \mathtt{Eve}) \times \mathtt{Mov}(s, \mathtt{Adam})$, we define $\mathtt{Mov}(a_\exists, a_\forall)$ as follows:
  - if $a_\exists = \perp$ (resp. $a_\forall = \perp$) then Adam (resp. Eve) is selected and $\mathtt{Mov}(a_\exists, a_\forall) = a_\forall$ (resp. $\mathtt{Mov}(a_\exists, a_\forall) = a_\exists$);
  - otherwise $a_\exists = (d_\exists, e_\exists)$ and $a_\forall = (d_\forall, e_\forall)$ and: 1. if $d_\exists < d_\forall$, $\mathtt{Mov}(a_\exists, a_\forall) = a_\exists$; 2. if $d_\forall \le d_\exists$ then $\mathtt{Mov}(a_\exists, a_\forall) = a_\forall$;
- Given two actions $a_\exists$ and $a_\forall$, $\mathtt{Tab}((\ell, v), a_\exists, a_\forall) = (\ell', v')$ if $(\ell, v) \xrightarrow{\mathtt{Mov}(a_\exists, a_\forall)} (\ell', v')$.

Let $h = s_0 \xrightarrow{a_1^\exists, a_1^\forall} s_1 \cdots s_{n-1} \xrightarrow{a_{n-1}^\exists, a_{n-1}^\forall} s_n \cdots$ be a finite or infinite path in $\mathcal{C}(\mathcal{T}, \Omega)$. The *duration* and *reward* of h are respectively:

$$\mathtt{d}(h) = \sum_{k=0}^{|h|-1} \mathtt{d}\left(s_k \xrightarrow{\mathtt{Mov}(a_k^\exists, a_k^\forall)} s_{k+1}\right)$$

$$\mathtt{w}(h) = \sum_{k=0}^{|h|-1} \mathtt{w}\left(s_k \xrightarrow{\mathtt{Mov}(a_k^\exists, a_k^\forall)} s_{k+1}\right)$$

A play ρ is said *non-Zeno* if $(d(\rho_{\le n}))_{n \in \mathbb{N}}$ is unbounded. A strategy σ is *immune from Zenoness* if all its outcomes are non-Zeno. A game is said to have *bounded transitions* if there is a bound D, such that for all states (ℓ, v), actions $a_\exists$, $a_\forall$: $\mathtt{d}\left((\ell, v) \xrightarrow{\mathtt{Mov}(a_\exists, a_\forall)} \mathtt{Tab}((\ell, v), a_\exists, a_\forall)\right) \le D$.

2.5 Mean-payoff and Energy Objectives

The *mean payoff* (per time unit) of a play is defined as the long-run average of reward per time unit. Formally, the mean payoff of a play ρ is:

$$\mathtt{MP}(\rho) = \liminf_{n \to \infty} \frac{\mathtt{w}(\rho_{\le n})}{\mathtt{d}(\rho_{\le n})}.$$

Definition 4. We consider the following types of games:

- The *mean payoff game* $\mathcal{T}_{\mathtt{MP}}$ associated with a WTG $\mathcal{T}$, is the game played on $\mathcal{T}$ where the objective (for Eve) is to obtain a non-negative mean payoff: i.e. $\mathcal{T}_{\mathtt{MP}} = \mathcal{C}(\mathcal{T}, \Omega_{\mathtt{MP}})$ where $\Omega_{\mathtt{MP}} = \{\rho \in \mathtt{Play}(\mathcal{C}) \mid \mathtt{MP}(\rho) \ge 0\}$.
- Given an initial credit $c \ge 0$, the *c-energy game* $\mathcal{T}_{E(c)}$ associated to a WTG $\mathcal{T}$, is the game played on $\mathcal{T}$ where the objective $\Omega(c)$ is to maintain the reward of every prefix of every play above $-c$: i.e. $\mathcal{T}_{E(c)} = \mathcal{C}(\mathcal{T}, \Omega(c))$ where $\Omega(c) = \{\rho \in \mathtt{Play}(\mathcal{C}) \mid \forall n \in \mathbb{N}.\ c + \mathtt{w}(\rho_{\le n}) \ge 0\}$.
- The *energy game* associated with a WTG $\mathcal{T}$, is the game $\mathcal{C}(\mathcal{T}, \Omega_E)$ where the objective is $\Omega_E = \cup_{c \ge 0} \Omega(c)$.

Decision problems. For each type of games, we define the associated decision problem:

- *Mean-payoff*: Given a mean payoff game $\mathcal{T}_{\mathtt{MP}}$, is there a winning strategy for Eve in $\mathcal{T}_{\mathtt{MP}}$?
- *c-energy*: Given a c-energy game $\mathcal{T}_{E(c)}$, is there a winning strategy for Eve in $\mathcal{T}_{E(c)}$?

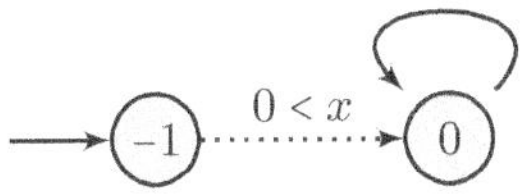

Figure 5: WTG $\mathcal{B}$.

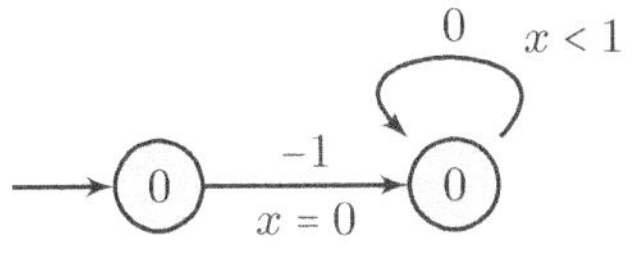

Figure 6: WTG $\mathcal{D}$.

- *Energy*: Given an energy game $\mathcal{T}_E$, is there a winning strategy for Eve in $\mathcal{T}_E$?

We also consider the following related problem:

- *Unknown initial credit*: Given a WTG $\mathcal{T}$, is there a credit c such that Eve has a winning strategy in $\mathcal{T}_{E(c)}$?

We also consider these problems from Adam's point of view.

To conclude this section we study the relations between mean payoff and energy games and state that all decision problems we have defined are undecidable for WTG.

2.6 Relations Between Mean-payoff and Energy Objectives

Obviously, if for some c the c-energy game is won by Eve, then the energy game is also won. In the other direction, if Adam has a winning strategy for the energy game then it is also winning for any c-energy game. In the finite state case the problem of energy and unknown initial credit are equivalent [18]: if Eve has a winning strategy for the energy game she has a memoryless one, and there is a bound on the maximum energy consumed by the outcomes of that strategy. This is not the case in general for WTG as demonstrated by the WTG $\mathcal{B}$ of Fig. 5, for which Eve wins the mean-payoff game and the energy game, but no c-energy game.

While energy and mean-payoff objectives are inter-reducible in the finite state case [18], the relationships between the two classes of objectives, formalized in the next two theorems, is more subtle for weighted timed games.

THEOREM 1. *Let $\mathcal{T}$ be a WTG. If Eve has a winning strategy $\sigma_\exists$ in the energy game $\mathcal{T}_E$ and $\sigma_\exists$ is immune from Zenoness, then $\sigma_\exists$ is a winning strategy in the mean payoff game $\mathcal{T}_{\mathtt{MP}}$.*

Example 2. The following example shows that if we do not have immunity from Zenoness, the property no longer holds. In the game of Fig. 6, any play is winning for Eve in the c-energy game if $c > 1$. However, the total delay of a play is always smaller or equal to 1, hence the mean-payoff is smaller than -1, which means that Eve is losing.

We let $\mathcal{T}^{+\delta}$ be the game $\mathcal{T}$ in which we increase the weights of all locations by $\delta \in \mathbb{R}$. Formally $\mathcal{T}^{+\delta}$ is the WTG $\langle \mathtt{L}, \ell_\iota, X, T_\exists, T_\forall, \mathtt{Inv}, \mathtt{w}_{+\delta} \rangle$, where: 1) $\mathtt{w}_{+\delta}(\ell) = \mathtt{w}(\ell) + \delta$ if $\ell \in \mathtt{L}$; 2) $\mathtt{w}_{+\delta}(t) = \mathtt{w}(t)$ if $t \in T$.

THEOREM 2. *Let $\mathcal{T}$ be a WTG. If there exists $\delta > 0$, such that Adam has a winning strategy $\sigma_\forall$ in the energy game $\mathcal{T}_E^{+\delta}$ which is immune from Zenoness, then $\sigma_\forall$ is a winning strategy in the mean payoff game $\mathcal{T}_{\mathtt{MP}}$.*

Example 3. The following example shows that if we do not add this δ to the weight of locations, the property no longer holds. In the game of Fig. 7, for any initial credit c, Adam wins the c-energy game $\mathcal{T}_{E(c)}$. However Eve has a winning strategy in the mean-payoff game $\mathcal{T}_{\mathtt{MP}}$. She has to choose a delay which increases fast enough so that the weight of the play is small compared to its duration. For instance, if at the n-th step of the game, she chooses to delay for n^2 time units, the average weight of the play will be greater than $-\frac{1}{n}$. Hence it converges towards 0 and the mean-payoff is 0. Notice that if we add a small positive δ to the weight of each location, then following the same strategy, Eve also wins the c-energy game $\mathcal{T}_{E(c)}$ for c greater than $\frac{1}{\delta}$.

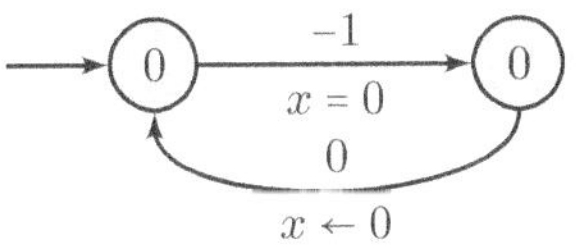

Figure 7: A WTG $\mathcal{T}$.

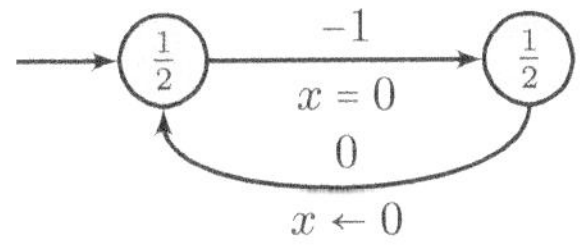

Figure 8: WTG $\mathcal{T}^{+\frac{1}{2}}$.

As already announced in the introduction, all the decisions problems that we have defined on weighted timed games are undecidable. The following theorem can be established (details are given in the full version of this paper) using variants of techniques used in [17, 14]:

THEOREM 3. *The mean-payoff, c-energy, energy and unknown initial credit problems are undecidable for WTG.*

3. A SEMI-PROCEDURE USING REGIONS

In this section, starting from the classical notion of regions [1], we define a finite concurrent game that exploits the relationship between timed paths and their projections in the region graph. We identify simple cycles in the region graph that are *good* for Eve (they roughly correspond to fragments of timed paths with *positive* reward), and others that are *good* for Adam (they roughly correspond to fragments of timed paths with *negative* reward). Thm. 4 tells us that if Eve can force to visit only her good cycles in the region graph then she has a winning strategy in the original energy timed game, and Thm. 5 is a symmetric result for Adam. To formalize those results, we need the notion of *quasi-path*: when we decompose a timed path according to simple cycles of the region graph, we introduce *jumps* inside regions because we remove a fragment of a timed path that starts inside a region and ends up in a possibly different state of the same region. Finally, we show how to solve the cycle forming game. This reduction is not complete: there are games which have winning strategies for Eve (or Adam) that our procedure will not find. However, we identify in Section 4 a class of games for which this reduction is complete.

3.1 Regions

We first recall the classical notion of *regions* [1]. If $k \in \mathbb{N}$, we write $\mathfrak{C}_k(X)$ for the set of constraints in $\mathfrak{C}(X)$ in which constants are integers within the interval $[\![0;k]\!]$. Let $\mathcal{T}$ be a WTG, and let $M = \max\{c \mid x \sim c \text{ is a constraint in } \mathcal{T}\}$. For $\delta \in \mathbb{R}_+$, we write $\lfloor \delta \rfloor$ the integral part of δ and $\mathrm{fr}(\delta)$ its fractional part. The equivalence relation $\equiv_{X,M}$ over $\mathbb{R}_+^X \times \mathbb{R}_+^X$ by $v \equiv_{X,M} v'$ if, and only if: 1) for all clocks $x \in X$, either $\lfloor v(x) \rfloor$ and $\lfloor v'(x) \rfloor$ are the same, or both $v(x)$ and $v(x)$ exceed M; 2) for all clocks $x, y \in X$ with $v(x) \leq M$ and $v(y) \leq M$, $\mathrm{fr}(v(x)) \leq \mathrm{fr}(v(y))$ if, and only if, $\mathrm{fr}(v'(x)) \leq \mathrm{fr}(v'(y))$; 3) for all clocks $x \in X$ with $v(x) \leq M$, $\mathrm{fr}(v(x)) = 0$ if, and only if, $\mathrm{fr}(v'(x)) = 0$;

This equivalence relation naturally induces a partition $\mathcal{R}_{X,M}$ of $\mathbb{R}_+^X$. We write $[v]_{X,M}$ ($[v]$ when X and M are fixed) for the equivalence class of $v \in \mathbb{R}_+^X$. An equivalence class is called a *region*. It is well known that this partition has the following properties: 1) it is compatible with the constraints in $\mathfrak{C}_M(X)$, i.e. for every $r \in \mathcal{R}_{X,M}$, and constraint $g \in \mathfrak{C}_M(X)$ either all valuations in r satisfy the clock constraint g, or no valuation in r satisfies it; 2) it is compatible with time elapsing, i.e. if there is $v \in r$ and $t \in \mathbb{R}_+$ such that $v + t \in r'$, then for all $v' \in r$ there is t' such that $v' + t' \in r'$; 3) it is compatible with resets, i.e. if $Y \subseteq X$ then if $[Y \leftarrow 0]r \cap r' \neq \emptyset$ then $[Y \leftarrow 0]r \subseteq r'$.

A region r is said to be *time-elapsing*, if for any $v \in r$ there is $t > 0$ such that $v + t \in r$. We write $\mathrm{Succ}(r)$ the *successors* of r by time elapsing, it is defined by $r' \in \mathrm{Succ}(r)$ if there is $v \in r$ and $t \geq 0$ such that $v + t \in r'$.

3.2 Region Game

Given an objective $\Omega \subseteq ((\mathtt{L} \times \mathcal{R}_{X,M}) \cdot \mathtt{Act})^\omega$, the *region game* associated with a WTG $\mathcal{T} = \langle \mathtt{L}, \ell_0, X, T_\exists, T_\forall, \mathtt{Inv}, \mathtt{w}\rangle$ is the concurrent game $\mathcal{R}(\mathcal{T},\Omega) = \langle \mathtt{St}, \iota, \mathtt{Act}, \mathtt{Mov}, \mathtt{Tab}, \Omega\rangle$ where:

- $\mathtt{St} = \mathtt{L} \times \mathcal{R}_{X,M}$ and $\iota = (\ell_\iota, \mathbf{0})$ is the initial state;
- $\mathtt{Act}$ is the set of actions. They are either $\bot$ or of the form (r, e, a) where $r \in \mathcal{R}_{X,M}$, $e \in T_\exists \cup T_\forall$ is a transition, and $a \in \{\mathtt{head}; \mathtt{tail}\}$; intuitively, an action is a target region (abstract delay) and a discrete transition. The extra component in $\{\mathtt{head}; \mathtt{tail}\}$ is needed to determine who plays first when the two players choose the same abstract delay (target region).
- Let $s = (\ell, r)$. Action (r', e, a) belongs to $\mathtt{Mov}(s, \mathtt{Eve})$ (resp. $\mathtt{Mov}(s, \mathtt{Adam})$), if: 1) $\exists(\ell, g, Y, \ell') \in T_\exists$ (resp. $T_\forall$); 2) $r' \in \mathrm{Succ}(r)$; 3) $r' \subseteq \mathtt{Inv}(\ell)$; 4) $r' \cap g \neq \emptyset$; 5) and $[Y \leftarrow 0]r' \subseteq \mathtt{Inv}(\ell')$. If there are no such action then only $\bot$ is allowed and this is the only situation in which $\bot$ is allowed.
- Let $s = (\ell, r)$ and $(r_\exists, e_\exists, a_\exists) \in \mathtt{Mov}(s, \mathtt{Eve})$, $(r_\forall, e_\forall, a_\forall) \in \mathtt{Mov}(s, \mathtt{Adam})$. $s' = \mathtt{Tab}(s, (r_\exists, e_\exists, a_\exists), (r_\forall, e_\forall, a_\forall))$ is defined as follows:
  - if $r_\exists \neq r_\forall$, one region is a strict (time abstract) predecessor of the other (as they are both successors of r). If $r_\exists$ is a strict predecessor of $r_\forall$, Eve's action $(r_\exists, e_\exists, a_\exists)$ is selected and otherwise Adam's action $(r_\forall, e_\forall, a_\forall)$ is selected.
  - otherwise $r_\exists = r_\forall$ and two cases arise: 1. either $r_\exists$ is not a time-elapsing region: in this case Adam's move is selected; 2. or $r_\exists$ is a time-elapsing region; which move is selected then depends on the extra components $a_\exists, a_\forall \in \{\mathtt{head}; \mathtt{tail}\}$: if $a_\exists = a_\forall$ then Eve's move is selected and otherwise Adam's move is selected.

  Once an action (r', e, a) with $e = (\ell, g, Y, \ell')$ is selected, the resulting state is $s' = (\ell', r'')$ with $r'' = [Y \leftarrow 0]r'$.

REMARK 1. *In case $\mathcal{T}$ is turn-based, then in each state of $\mathcal{R}(\mathcal{T},\Omega)$ only one player has a choice. The region game can then be seen as a (classical) turn-based finite game.*

Example 4. We want to reduce the problem of finding winning strategies in a WTG to an equivalent problem in the region game. To illustrate the need for the extra component in the actions (i.e. $a \in \{\mathtt{head}; \mathtt{tail}\}$) consider the example of Fig. 9. In the WTG (left), Eve has no winning strategy to win the mean payoff game: Adam can always choose a delay shorter than her from ℓ_0 to enforce location ℓ_2. For the same reason Adam has also no winning strategy. In the region game (right), we abstract away from the actual delays Eve and Adam can propose: they have only one possible choice which is to propose to delay up-to region $0 < x < 1$. To reproduce the possibility that either Eve or Adam are able to propose the smallest delay, we use the choices of both players in $\{\mathtt{head}, \mathtt{tail}\}$.

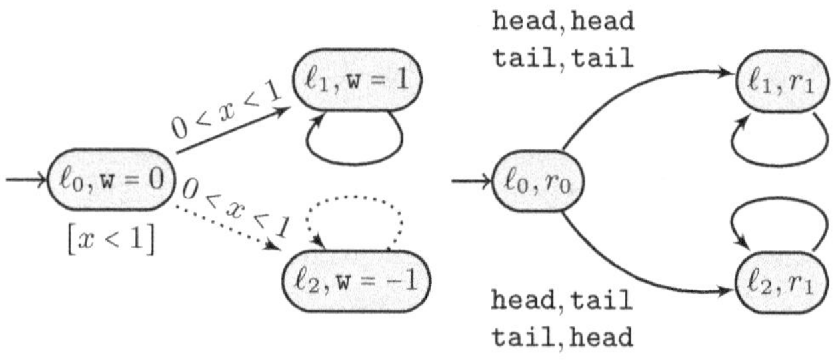

Figure 9: A WTG $\mathcal{T}$ and its associated region game.

3.3 Quasi Paths

A *quasi path* in a WTG is a sequence of states and transitions $\rho = (\ell_0, v_0)\tau_0(\ell_1, v_1)\tau_1 \cdots \tau_{n-1}(\ell_n, v_n)$ such that for all $0 \leq i \leq n-1$ either: 1) τ_i is a move $(a_\exists, a_\forall)$ and $(\ell_i, v_i) \xrightarrow{\mathtt{Mov}(a_\exists, a_\forall)} (\ell_{i+1}, v_{i+1})$; 2) or $\ell_i = \ell_{i+1}$ and $[v_i] = [v_{i+1}]$. In that case τ_i is called a *jump*. We will denote jumps by $\rightsquigarrow$. A *quasi cycle* is a quasi path such that $(\ell_n, [v_n]) = (\ell_0, [v_0])$.

In order to extend the reward to quasi paths, we need a *weight function* $\delta : \mathtt{L} \times \mathcal{R}_{X,M} \mapsto \mathbb{R}$ which attributes a weight to jumps according to the region in which they happen. We define $\mathtt{w}_\delta$ the reward for each transition τ_i, depending on its type: 1) if τ_i is a move $(a_\exists, a_\forall)$ and $(\ell_i, v_i) \xrightarrow{\mathtt{Mov}(a_\exists, a_\forall)} (\ell_{i+1}, v_{i+1})$, then $\mathtt{w}_\delta((\ell_i, v_i)\tau_i(\ell_{i+1}, v_{i+1})) = d \cdot \mathtt{w}(\ell_i) + \mathtt{w}(e)$ where $(d, e) = \mathtt{Mov}(a_\exists, a_\forall)$; 2) otherwise $\tau_i = \rightsquigarrow$, then $\mathtt{w}_\delta((\ell_i, v_i) \rightsquigarrow (\ell_{i+1}, v_{i+1})) = \delta([\ell_i, v_i])$. The reward for the quasi path ρ is then $\mathtt{w}_\delta(\rho) = \sum_{i<|\rho|} \mathtt{w}_\delta((\ell_i, v_i)\tau_i(\ell_{i+1}, v_{i+1}))$.

We define a projection from quasi paths to paths in the region game by forgetting jumps and projecting each state to its associated region. Formally, the projection π is defined inductively: 1. $\pi((\ell, v)) = (\ell, [v])$; 2. $\pi(h \rightsquigarrow (\ell, v)) = \pi(h)$; 3. $\pi\Big(h \cdot (\ell, v) \xrightarrow{a_\exists, a_\forall} (\ell, v')\Big) = \pi(h \cdot (\ell, v)) \xrightarrow{b_\exists, b_\forall} (\ell', [v'])$ where $a_p = (d_p, e_p)$ for $p \in \{\mathtt{Eve}, \mathtt{Adam}\}$, $b_\exists = ([v + d_\exists], e_\exists, \mathtt{head})$, and $b_\forall = ([v + d_\forall], e_\forall, \mathtt{head})$ if $d_\exists < d_\forall$ and $b_\forall = ([v + d_\forall], e_\forall, \mathtt{tail})$ otherwise. It is naturally extended from histories to plays: ρ' is the projection of ρ if for all finite prefixes h of ρ, $\pi(h)$ is a prefix of ρ'. If h is a path in the region game, the path ρ is said *compatible* with h if $\pi(\rho) = h$, and we write $\gamma(h)$ for the set of path compatible with h.

3.4 Reduction to the Region Game

Given a weight function $\delta : \mathtt{L} \times \mathcal{R}_{X,M} \mapsto \mathbb{R}$, we will write $\mathbb{C}_\delta^+$ for the set of simple cycles in the region game that only correspond to quasi cycles rewarding more than δ if δ is positive and more than 0 otherwise. Formally[1]:

$$\mathbb{C}_\delta^+ = \{c \in \mathbb{C} \mid \forall \rho \in \gamma(c).\ \mathtt{w}_\delta(\rho) \ge \max\{\delta(\mathtt{first}(c)), 0\}\}.$$

Given a real number $\varepsilon > 0$, we write $\mathbb{C}_\delta^{-\varepsilon}$ for the simple cycles of the region game that correspond to quasi cycles with weight lower than δ and lower than $-\varepsilon$. Formally[2]:

$$\mathbb{C}_\delta^{-\varepsilon} = \{c \in \mathbb{C} \mid \forall \rho \in \gamma(c).\ \mathtt{w}_\delta(\rho) \le \min\{\delta(\mathtt{first}(c)), -\varepsilon\}\}.$$

The winning condition of the region game will be given by *cycle objectives*. The intuition behind the definition of these objectives, is that if Eve can force the play to see only cycles with positive reward (i.e. in $\mathbb{C}_\delta^+$), the accumulated weight will be positive, except for a finite part. Which means she is winning the c-energy game, if c is big enough to cover the loss of energy in this finite part.

In the region game, we will consider the cases where the objective of Eve is given by $\Omega_\delta^+ = \{\rho \mid \mathtt{dec}(\rho) \subseteq \mathbb{C}_\delta^+\}$. That is, she wins for plays whose decomposition in simple cycles only contains positive cycles.

Given a WTG $\mathcal{T}$, let $W_T = \min_{t\in T}\{\mathtt{w}(t)\} \cup \{0\}$ and $W_L = \min_{\ell\in L}\{\mathtt{w}(\ell)\} \cup \{0\}$.

Theorem 4. *Let $\mathcal{T}$ be a WTG, if Eve has a winning strategy in $\mathcal{R}(\mathcal{T}, \Omega_\delta^+)$ then: 1) she has a winning strategy $\tau_\exists$ in the energy game $\mathcal{T}_E$; 2) if $\mathcal{T}$ has bounded transitions, $\tau_\exists$ is a winning strategy in the energy game $\mathcal{T}_{E(c)}$ for the initial credit $c = |L \times \mathcal{R}_{X,M}| \cdot (W_L \cdot D + W_T)$; 3) if $\tau_\exists$ is immune from Zenoness, then it is winning in the mean payoff game $\mathcal{T}_{\mathtt{MP}}$.*

Remark 2. *We made the hypothesis that there exists a bound on the duration of transitions in order to get the result for the unknown initial credit. Consider the example of Fig. 5. In this game, Eve is winning in the region game for Ω_δ^+, and therefore by Thm. 4 she also wins in the energy game $\mathcal{T}_E$, by Thm. 1 she also wins the mean-payoff game $\mathcal{T}_{\mathtt{MP}}$ if we consider a strategy that is immune from Zenoness. However, the transition going out of ℓ_0 can be taken by Adam at any moment, its duration is not bounded. Indeed, whatever the initial credit is, Adam can force a play which costs more than this credit, by delaying the transition for long enough. Therefore Eve has no winning strategy for any fixed initial credit and the answer to the unknown initial credit problem is negative.*

We now consider the objective for Eve: $\Omega_\delta^{-\varepsilon} = \{\rho \mid \mathtt{dec}(\rho) \notin \mathbb{C}_\delta^{-\varepsilon}\}$. That is, she wins if the decomposition in simple cycle contains at least on simple cycle that is not below $-\varepsilon$.

Theorem 5. *Let $\mathcal{T}$ be a WTG, if Adam has a winning strategy in $\mathcal{R}(\mathcal{T}, \Omega_\delta^{-\varepsilon})$ then 1) he has a winning strategy in the energy game $\mathcal{T}_E$; 2) if $\mathcal{T}$ has bounded transitions, then Adam has a winning strategy in the mean payoff game $\mathcal{T}_{\mathtt{MP}}$.*

3.5 Solving the Region Game

We now show how to solve a finite game with objective of the form $\Omega = \{\rho \mid \forall c \in \mathtt{dec}(\rho).c \in \mathbb{C}^W\}$ or $\Omega = \{\rho \mid \exists c \in \mathtt{dec}(\rho).c \in \mathbb{C}^W\}$. We can then apply this technique to solve the region game. To do so we unravel the game, and stop as soon as a cycle is formed. The play is then winning if the cycle formed belong to $\mathbb{C}^W$. This technique is adapted from [6].

Definition 5. Let $\mathcal{G} = \langle \mathtt{St}, \iota, \mathtt{Act}, \mathtt{Mov}, \mathtt{Tab}, \Omega\rangle$ be a concurrent game with $\Omega = \{\rho \mid \forall c \in \mathtt{dec}(\rho).c \in \mathbb{C}^W\}$ or $\Omega = \{\rho \mid \exists c \in \mathtt{dec}(\rho).c \in \mathbb{C}^W\}$. The unraveling of $\mathcal{G}$, written $\mathcal{U}(\mathcal{G})$, is the tuple $\langle \mathtt{St}', \iota, \mathtt{Act}, \mathtt{Mov}', \mathtt{Tab}', \Omega'\rangle$:

- the set of states is $\mathtt{St}' = \{h \in (\mathtt{St} \cdot (\mathtt{Act} \times \mathtt{Act}))^* \cdot \mathtt{St} \mid \forall i, j \ne i.\ h_i \ne h_j\} \cup \{\uparrow, \downarrow\}$, the set of histories of the original game where all states appear at most once; with the addition of a winning state $\uparrow$ and a loosing state $\downarrow$ for Eve;
- $\mathtt{Mov}'(h, p) = \mathtt{Mov}(\mathtt{last}(h), p)$;
- for an history h and a move $(a_\exists, a_\forall)$, let $s = \mathtt{Tab}(\mathtt{last}(h), a_\exists, a_\forall)$: 1) if s does not appear in h then $\mathtt{Tab}'(h, a_\exists, a_\forall) = h \xrightarrow{a_\exists, a_\forall} s$; 2) otherwise, let i be such that $h_i = s$, and $c = h_{\ge i} \xrightarrow{a_\exists, a_\forall} s$ (notice that such a i is unique): if c belongs to $\mathbb{C}^W$ then $\mathtt{Tab}'(h, a_\exists, a_\forall) = \uparrow$ and otherwise $\mathtt{Tab}'(h, a_\exists, a_\forall) = \downarrow$. Then, from $\uparrow$ and $\downarrow$, there are only self loops, thus $\mathtt{Tab}'(x, a_\exists, a_\forall) = x$ for $x \in \{\uparrow, \downarrow\}$.
- the objective is to reach $\uparrow$, i.e. $\Omega' = (\mathtt{St}' \cdot (\mathtt{Act} \times \mathtt{Act}))^* \cdot (\uparrow \cdot (\mathtt{Act} \times \mathtt{Act}))^\omega$.

Theorem 6. *Let $\mathcal{G}$ be a concurrent game and $\mathcal{U}(\mathcal{G})$ its unraveling. Then Eve has a winning strategy in the unraveled game $\mathcal{U}(\mathcal{G})$ if, and only if, she has a winning strategy in $\mathcal{G}$.*

Theorem 7. *Given a finite concurrent game $\mathcal{G}$ with objective $\Omega = \{\rho \mid \forall c \in \mathtt{dec}(\rho).c \in \mathbb{C}^W\}$ or $\Omega = \{\rho \mid \exists c \in \mathtt{dec}(\rho).c \in \mathbb{C}^W\}$ where $\mathbb{C}^W$ is given by an automaton, deciding if Eve has a winning strategy is* PSPACE*-complete.*

4. ROBUST GAMES

The reduction to the cycle forming game in the region graph is complete when there exists a weight function δ, that partitions the set of simple cycles of the region into good ones for Eve and good ones for Adam.

Definition 6. (Robust game) A WTG is said *δ-robust* if $\mathbb{C} = \mathbb{C}_\delta^+ \cup \mathbb{C}_\delta^{-\varepsilon}$ for some ε. We simply call a WTG *robust* when there exists $\delta : \mathcal{R}_{X,M} \mapsto \mathbb{R}$ such that it is δ-robust.

Remark 3. *Note that a WTG $\mathcal{G}$ where all the costs are discrete (i.e. $\forall \ell \in L.\ w(\ell) = 0$) is robust for $\delta = 0$ and $\varepsilon < 1$. The results of this section implies decidability of the energy problem and mean payoff problem for this class.*

Remark 4. *If $\mathcal{T}$ is robust, then the leafs of $\mathcal{U}(\mathcal{R}(\mathcal{T}))$ are partitioned between winning for Eve and winning for Adam. If, in addition, this game is turn-based, then it is determined. By Thm. 4 and Thm. 9, we can conclude that if $\mathcal{T}$ is robust and turn-based then the energy game $\mathcal{T}_E$ is determined.*

Now, we establish that in a robust WTG, we can decide if Eve can win the energy game. This is a consequence of the following theorem which complements Thm. 4. A symmetric result also holds for Adam.

[1] Note, that this definition is inductive: as a jump in the region (ℓ, r) gives a reward of $\delta(\ell, r)$, we make sure that a (quasi)-cycle on that region always provides a reward larger than or equal to this value.

[2] Note, that the definition for the *good* cycles of Adam is symmetric but slightly stronger as we require that the weight of (quasi)-cycles to be ε-bounded away from zero.

THEOREM 8. *Let $\mathcal{T}$ be a δ-robust WTG: 1) if* **Eve** *has a winning strategy in the energy game $\mathcal{T}_E$ then she has a winning strategy in $\mathcal{U}(\mathcal{R}(\mathcal{T},\Omega_\delta^+))$; 2) if $\mathcal{T}$ has bounded transitions and* **Eve** *has a winning strategy in the mean payoff game $\mathcal{T}_{\text{MP}}$ then she has a winning strategy in $\mathcal{U}(\mathcal{R}(\mathcal{T},\Omega_\delta^+))$.*

THEOREM 9. *Let $\mathcal{T}$ be a δ-robust WTG: 1) if* **Adam** *has a winning strategy in the energy game $\mathcal{T}_E$, then he has a winning strategy in $\mathcal{U}(\mathcal{R}(\mathcal{T},\Omega_\delta^{-\varepsilon}))$; 2) if $\mathcal{T}$ has bounded transitions and* **Adam** *has a winning strategy in the mean payoff game $\mathcal{T}_{\text{MP}}$, then he has a winning strategy in $\mathcal{U}(\mathcal{R}(\mathcal{T},\Omega_\delta^{-\varepsilon}))$.*

Given a weighted timed game, it is decidable whether this game is robust or not. Additionally, we present several complexity results about this problem in the full version of this paper.

THEOREM 10. *The membership problem for the class of robust game is decidable.*

Finally, we can characterize the complexity of deciding the energy problem for robust weighted timed games:

THEOREM 11. *The energy problem for robust games is in* EXPSPACE *and is* EXP*-hard.*

PROOF SKETCH. The algorithm proceeds by constructing the region game and then solving it using the algorithm of Thm. 7. This is correct because of Thm. 4, 6 and 8. □

5. FIXPOINT ALGORITHM

While the reduction to the cycle forming game in the region graph is elegant and allows us to identify a large and natural class of weighted timed games with decidable properties, this reduction does not lead directly to a practical semi-algorithm. In this section, we design a valuation iteration algorithm that can be implemented symbolically using polyhedra, which can be executed on any weighted timed game, and find winning strategies for Eve when it terminates successfully. We also show that termination is guaranteed on robust weighted timed games.

5.1 Value Iteration Algorithm

Our value iteration algorithm is an adaptation of the solution for the finite state case described in [18] to the setting of WTG. It computes successive approximations of the minimal energy level that Eve needs to win the energy game.

Essentially, the semi-algorithm is based on the iteration of an operator that computes successive approximations of the energy level/credit that is necessary for Eve to maintain the energy level positive for k rounds in the energy timed game, where k increases along with the iterations. Most importantly, our algorithm is parameterized by a value $c \in \mathbb{N}$, that represents a maximal energy level that we want to track: if the energy level necessary to stay alive from a given state (l, v) for k rounds is larger than c then (ℓ, v) is considered as loosing. This is a sound approximation when looking for winning strategies. This parameter is important to enforce termination of the analysis. If a fixed point is reached, then it contains enough information to identify winning states (those that are not mapped to $+\infty$ by the operator) and construct winning strategies. If the analysis is negative (no winning strategy found) then this value can be increased. Furthermore, we show that for robust weighted timed games, there is a finite value c which is computable and sufficient to detect winning strategies for Eve.

In this section, we assume the WTG is fixed and transitions, weight functions, etc ... refer to this game. Given $c \in \mathbb{N}$, we write $a \ominus_c b$ for $\max(0, a-b)$ if $a - b \le c$ and $+\infty$ otherwise. In the sequel we consider mappings in $\mathcal{S} = [\texttt{St} \mapsto \mathbb{R}_+ \cup \{+\infty\}]$ that associate with each state an element in $\mathbb{R}_+ \cup \{+\infty\}$.

Given $c \in \mathbb{N}$, the operator $\texttt{lift}_c : \mathcal{S} \mapsto \mathcal{S}$ is defined by:

$$\forall s \in \texttt{St}, \texttt{lift}_c(f)(s) = \inf_{a_\exists} \sup_{a_\forall} \left\{ f(s') \ominus_c \texttt{w}(s \xrightarrow{a_\exists, a_\forall} s') \right\}$$

We let $f_0^c : \texttt{St} \mapsto \mathbb{R}_+ \cup \{+\infty\}$ be the mapping defined by $\forall s \in \texttt{St}, f_0^c(s) = 0$. We then inductively define f_{k+1}^c, for $k \ge 0$ to be $\texttt{lift}_c(f_k^c)$. Thus, $f_n^c(s)$ represents the initial energy level that is needed by Eve to keep the energy level positive for n steps from s. If more than c is needed then $f_n^c(s)$ is set to be $+\infty$ (c being the maximal energy level that we want to track). This is formalized in Lem. 1.

LEMMA 1. *For all state s, index n, credit c, $\varepsilon > 0$:*

$$f_n(s) \ge -\sup_{\sigma_\exists} \inf_{\sigma_\forall} \left\{ w_{/c}(\mathit{Out}_s(\sigma_\exists, \sigma_\forall)_{\le n}) \right\}.$$

where for a history $h = h_0 \xrightarrow{m_0} h_1 \cdots \xrightarrow{m_n} h_n$, $w_{/c}(h) = -\infty$ if $\exists i.\ w(h_i \xrightarrow{m_i} h_{i+1}) < -c - \varepsilon$ and $w(h)$ otherwise.

THEOREM 12 (CORRECTNESS). *If there exists $n \ge 0$ such that $f_{n+1} = f_n$, and $f_n^c(\iota) \ne +\infty$, then for any $\varepsilon > 0$,* **Eve** *has a winning strategy for the c'-energy game $\mathcal{T}_{E(c')}$ with initial credit $c' = f_n^c(\iota) + \varepsilon$.*

In the case of robust game, we show that we can stop the algorithm after a finite number of iterations.

THEOREM 13 (TERMINATION). *Let $\mathcal{T}$ be a WTG and c a fixed credit. If $\mathcal{T}$ is δ, ε-robust and $f_{n_0}^c(\ell_\iota, \mathbf{0}) \ne +\infty$ for $n_0 \ge \left(\frac{c \cdot (|L| \cdot |\mathcal{R}_{X,M}|+1)}{\varepsilon} + 1\right) \cdot |L| \cdot |\mathcal{R}_{X,M}|$ then* **Eve** *has a winning strategy in the energy game.*

If moreover the game has bounded transition, the algorithm is complete.

THEOREM 14 (COMPLETENESS FOR ROBUST GAMES). *Let $\mathcal{T}$ be a robust WTG, which has bounded transitions, and $c = |L \times \mathcal{R}_{X,M}| \cdot (W_L \times D + W_T) + 1$.* **Eve** *has a winning strategy in the energy game $\mathcal{T}_{E(c)}$ if, and only if, $f_{n_0}^c \ne +\infty$.*

5.2 Symbolic Algorithm

We have implemented the previous value iteration algorithm in HYTECH [27]. The implementation is based on the symbolic *controllable timed predecessors* operator defined in [11] and first implemented in HYTECH for cost optimal reachability games [12]. The choice of HYTECH compared to state-of-the-art hybrid systems' analyzers like PHAVer [24] or SpaceEx [25] is motivated by the fact that HYTECH has a built-in script language in which we can define the symbolic *controllable* predecessors operator easily. The symbolic algorithm/program in HYTECH for the example of Fig. 1 is given in the full version of this paper. The result of the computation for the value iteration algorithm with $c = 4$ is depicted on Fig. 2 and show the winning zones for Eve in locations Eve and Adam.

The value iteration algorithm is implemented as the iterative computation of the fixpoint of a safety *hybrid* game. The hybrid game has a special variable E, the energy variable which is the only variable that is not a clock. Each location ℓ of the original WTG has a counterpart location $\ell_{\mathcal{H}}$ in the hybrid game. If $w(\ell) = k \in \mathbb{Z}$ then the derivative of E in $\ell_{\mathcal{H}}$ is given by $\frac{dE}{dt} = k$; each discrete transition (ℓ, g, z, ℓ') of the WTG also has a counterpart transition $(\ell, g, z \wedge E := E + k, \ell')$ if $w(\ell, g, z, \ell') = k$.

A state of the hybrid game is thus defined by $((\ell, v), E)$ where (ℓ, v) is a state of the original WTG. The existence of a winning strategy for the c-energy game $\mathcal{T}$ is reduced to the existence of a winning strategy in the associated hybrid game for the safety objective $E \geq 0$ (in each location.) Let $\mathit{Safe} = \{((\ell, v), E) \mid 0 \leq E \leq c\}$, where the upper bound c is the one used in the `lift` function from subsection 5.1. We define the winning states of the safety hybrid game as the greatest fixpoint of:

$$X = \mathit{Safe} \cap \mathtt{Pred}_t(\mathtt{Up}(\mathtt{cPred}(X)), \mathtt{uPred}(\overline{X}))$$

where `cPred` (controllable predecessor), `uPred` (uncontrollable predecessor), $\mathtt{Pred}_t$ (temporal predecessor) are defined as in [11, 12] and

$$\mathtt{Up}(Y) = \{((\ell, v), e') \mid \exists ((\ell, v), e) \in Y \wedge e' \geq e\}.$$

The `Up` operator captures in our symbolic implementation the role of the bound c in the $\mathtt{lift}_c$ operator: indeed, while the set X_i contains only triples $((\ell, v), e)$ where $e \leq c$, it is clear that we must include in X_{i+1} triples $((\ell', v'), e')$ from which `Eve` can force in one round the upward closure (for the energy level) of safe states in i steps. This is because if `Eve` can win from (ℓ, v) with a given energy level then she can win from that state with any greater energy level.

Example 5. In Fig. 10, plain (resp. dashed) arrows are controllable (resp. uncontrollable) edges. In location ℓ_0, no task is scheduled and the (battery) energy is recharging at rate +3. There is a background task B to be run at least every 2 t.u. if the other task has not arrived (and actually running in location ℓ_1) and a sporadic task S (interrupt) that can happen any time. The task B can be scheduled from location ℓ_0 (this is controllable) and we can stop to run it after at least 1 t.u. (measured by clock x.) The background task B has less priority than S and if S happens it is scheduled and B preempted. If we schedule the background task B, we are rewarded by +2 energy units. In locations ℓ_0, ℓ_1, the sporadic task S can occur (uncontrollable) and in this case it must be scheduled (going to ℓ_2) which consumes energy at rate $-\alpha$. The execution time of S is at most 1 t.u. (measured by clock x) and successive occurrences of S must be separated by at least 2 t.u. (measured by clock y.)

On this example, our symbolic algorithm terminates. If $\alpha = 3$, the HyTech program (in the full version of this paper) gives a minimal initial energy level of 3 to be able to win the game (notice that we start with $y = 2$ and thus the sporadic task can arrive at the initial instant.) The optimal strategy from the point of view of `Adam` is to trigger the sporadic task S as often as possible. While a winning strategy for `Eve` (scheduler) is to wait in location ℓ_0 as long as possible. If the sporadic task arrives again, it is not before 1 t.u. and thus we are rewarded by at least 3 energy credits. If the sporadic does not occur before $x = 2$, we get 6 energy credits, and we can switch to ℓ_1 which increases energy by

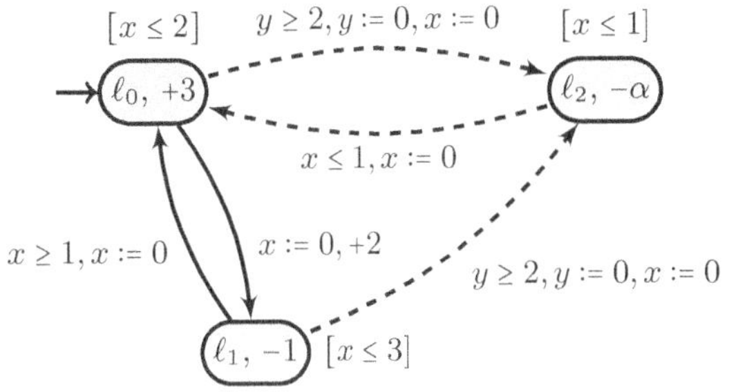

Figure 10: Scheduling Example

2. This ensures winning the energy game, see Fig. 11 for a graphical representation of the winning region. The set of winning state computed by the HyTech program can be used to determine the minimal initial credit for each possible initial state: for example $\mathit{energy} \geq 3$ is necessary for the initial condition $x = 0, y = 2$.)

Now assume $\alpha = 4$. The previous strategy is not winning any more. However, the result of the HyTech program is now: $\mathit{energy} > 4$ (for $x = 0, y = 2$ as initial state.) In this case, while the minimal (infimum) initial credit is 4, there is no strategy realizing this value; the game cannot be won with an initial credit of 4 but rather with any value strictly above 4. Note that this information is collected by our symbolic algorithm but not by the operator $\mathtt{lift}_c$ as this operator is defined using inf, sup operators.

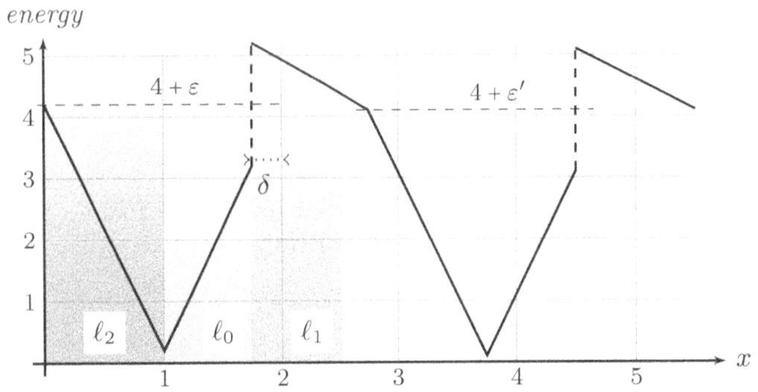

Figure 11: Winning Strategy for `Eve`, $\alpha = 4$.

6. REFERENCES

[1] R. Alur and D. L. Dill. A theory of timed automata. *TCS*, 126(2):183–235, 1994.

[2] R. Alur, T. A. Henzinger, and O. Kupferman. Alternating-time temporal logic. *Journal of the ACM*, 49(5):672–713, Sept. 2002.

[3] R. Alur, S. La Torre, and G. J. Pappas. Optimal paths in weighted timed automata. In *HSCC*, volume 2034 of *LNCS*. Springer, 2001.

[4] G. Behrmann, A. Cougnard, A. David, E. Fleury, K. G. Larsen, and D. Lime. Uppaal-tiga: Time for playing games! In *CAV*, volume 4590 of *LNCS*. Springer, 2007.

[5] G. Behrmann, A. Fehnker, T. Hune, K. G. Larsen, P. Pettersson, J. Romijn, and F. W. Vaandrager.

Minimum-cost reachability for priced timed automata. In *HSCC*, volume 2034 of *LNCS*. Springer, 2001.

[6] H. Björklund, S. Sandberg, and S. G. Vorobyov. Memoryless determinacy of parity and mean payoff games: a simple proof. *Theoretical Computer Science*, 310(1-3):365–378, 2004.

[7] P. Bouyer. From qualitative to quantitative analysis of timed systems – Mémoire d'habilitation à diriger des recherches, 2009.

[8] P. Bouyer, T. Brihaye, V. Bruyère, and J.-F. Raskin. On the optimal reachability problem of weighted timed automata. *Formal Methods in System Design*, 31(2), 2007.

[9] P. Bouyer, T. Brihaye, M. Jurdzinski, R. Lazic, and M. Rutkowski. Average-price and reachability-price games on hybrid automata with strong resets. In *FORMATS*, volume 5215 of *LNCS*. Springer, 2008.

[10] P. Bouyer, E. Brinksma, and K. G. Larsen. Staying alive as cheaply as possible. In *HSCC*, volume 2993 of *LNCS*. Springer, 2004.

[11] P. Bouyer, F. Cassez, E. Fleury, and K. G. Larsen. Optimal Strategies in Priced Timed Game Automata. In *FSTTCS 2004*, pages 148–160, 2004.

[12] P. Bouyer, F. Cassez, E. Fleury, and K. G. Larsen. Synthesis of Optimal Strategies Using HyTech. *Electronic Notes in Theoretical Computer Science*, 119(1):11–31, 2005.

[13] P. Bouyer, U. Fahrenberg, K. G. Larsen, N. Markey, and J. Srba. Infinite runs in weighted timed automata with energy constraints. In *FORMATS*, volume 5215 of *LNCS*. Springer, 2008.

[14] P. Bouyer, K. G. Larsen, and N. Markey. Lower-bound constrained runs in weighted timed automata. In *QEST'12*, pages 128–137, London, UK, Sept. 2012. IEEE Computer Society Press.

[15] M. Bozga, C. Daws, O. Maler, A. Olivero, S. Tripakis, and S. Yovine. Kronos: A model-checking tool for real-time systems. In *CAV*, volume 1427 of *LNCS*. Springer, 1998.

[16] R. Brenguier, F. Cassez, and J.-F. Raskin. Energy and mean-payoff timed games. 2014. http://hal.archives-ouvertes.fr/docs/00/94/30/15/PDF/mainFull.pdf.

[17] T. Brihaye, V. Bruyère, and J.-F. Raskin. On optimal timed strategies. In *FORMATS*, volume 3829 of *LNCS*. Springer, 2005.

[18] L. Brim, J. Chaloupka, L. Doyen, R. Gentilini, and J.-F. Raskin. Faster algorithms for mean-payoff games. *Formal methods in system design*, 38(2):97–118, 2011.

[19] F. Cassez, A. David, E. Fleury, K. G. Larsen, and D. Lime. Efficient on-the-fly algorithms for the analysis of timed games. In *CONCUR*, volume 3653 of *LNCS*. Springer, 2005.

[20] F. Cassez, J. J. Jessen, K. G. Larsen, J.-F. Raskin, and P.-A. Reynier. Automatic synthesis of robust and optimal controllers - an industrial case study. In *HSCC*, volume 5469 of *LNCS*. Springer, 2009.

[21] F. Cassez and K. G. Larsen. The impressive power of stopwatches. In *CONCUR*, volume 1877 of *LNCS*. Springer, 2000.

[22] K. Chatterjee, L. Doyen, and T. A. Henzinger. A survey of stochastic games with limsup and liminf objectives. In *ICALP*, volume 5556 of *LNCS, Part II*. Springer, 2009.

[23] K. Chatterjee, L. Doyen, T. A. Henzinger, and J.-F. Raskin. Generalized mean-payoff and energy games. In *FSTTCS*, volume 8 of *LIPIcs*. Schloss Dagstuhl - Leibniz-Zentrum fuer Informatik, 2010.

[24] G. Frehse. PHAVer: algorithmic verification of hybrid systems past HyTech. *STTT*, 10(3):263–279, 2008.

[25] G. Frehse, C. L. Guernic, A. Donzé, S. Cotton, R. Ray, O. Lebeltel, R. Ripado, A. Girard, T. Dang, and O. Maler. SpaceEx: Scalable Verification of Hybrid Systems. In *CAV*, volume 6806 of *LNCS*, pages 379–395. Springer, 2011.

[26] T. Henzinger. Quantitative reactive modeling and verification. *Computer Science Research and Development*, page 14, 2013.

[27] T. A. Henzinger, P.-H. Ho, and H. Wong-Toi. Hytech: A model checker for hybrid systems. *STTT*, 1(1-2):110–122, 1997.

[28] J. J. Jessen, J. I. Rasmussen, K. G. Larsen, and A. David. Guided controller synthesis for climate controller using Uppaal Tiga. In *FORMATS*, volume 4763 of *LNCS*. Springer, 2007.

[29] M. Jurdziński. Deciding the winner in parity games is in UP and in co-UP. *Information Processing Letters*, 68(3):119–124, 1998.

[30] M. Jurdzinski and A. Trivedi. Average-time games. In *FSTTCS*, volume 2 of *LIPIcs*. Schloss Dagstuhl - Leibniz-Zentrum fuer Informatik, 2008.

[31] S. La Torre, S. Mukhopadhyay, and A. Murano. Optimal-reachability and control for acyclic weighted timed automata. In *IFIP TCS*, volume 2, pages 485–497, 2002.

[32] K. G. Larsen, P. Pettersson, and W. Yi. UPPAAL in a nutshell. *STTT*, 1(1-2):134–152, 1997.

[33] O. Maler, A. Pnueli, and J. Sifakis. On the synthesis of discrete controllers for timed systems (an extended abstract). In *STACS*, pages 229–242, 1995.

[34] P. Tabuada. Controller synthesis for bisimulation equivalence. *Systems & Control Letters*, 57(6):443–452, 2008.

Abstraction, Discretization, and Robustness in Temporal Logic Control of Dynamical Systems*

Jun Liu
University of Sheffield
Mappin Street
Sheffield, S1 3JD, United Kingdom
j.liu@sheffield.ac.uk

Necmiye Ozay
University of Michigan
1301 Beal Avenue
Ann Arbor, MI 48109-2122, USA
necmiye@umich.edu

ABSTRACT

Abstraction-based, hierarchical approaches to control synthesis from temporal logic specifications for dynamical systems have gained increased popularity over the last decade. Yet various issues commonly encountered and extensively dealt with in control systems have not been adequately discussed in the context of temporal logic control of dynamical systems, such as inter-sample behaviors of a sampled-data system, effects of imperfect state measurements and unmodeled dynamics, and the use of time-discretized models to design controllers for continuous-time dynamical systems. We discuss these issues in this paper. The main motivation is to demonstrate the possibility of accounting for the mismatches between a continuous-time control system and its various types of abstract models used for control synthesis. We do this by incorporating additional robustness measures in the abstract models. Such robustness measures are gained at the price of either increased nondeterminism in the abstracted models or relaxed versions of the specification being realized. Under a unified notion of abstraction, we provide concrete means of incorporating these robustness measures and establish results that demonstrate their effectiveness in dealing with the above mentioned issues.

Categories and Subject Descriptors

D.2.4 [**SOFTWARE ENGINEERING**]: Software/Program Verification—*Formal methods*; I.2.8 [**ARTIFICIAL INTELLIGENCE**]: Problem Solving, Control Methods, and Search—*Control theory*; G.4 [**MATHEMATICAL SOFTWARE**]: Reliability and robustness

General Terms

Theory, Verification

*This work is supported in part by a Marie Curie Career Integration Grant PCIG13-GA-2013-617377 (to J.L.) and by University of Michigan startup funds (to N.O.).

HSCC'14, April 15–17, 2014, Berlin, Germany.

ACM 978-1-4503-2732-9/14/04 ...$15.00.
http://dx.doi.org/10.1145/2562059.2562137.

Keywords

hybrid control; temporal logic; abstraction; discretization; robustness

1. INTRODUCTION

Abstraction-based, hierarchical approaches to control synthesis for dynamical systems from high-level specifications naturally lead to hybrid feedback controllers [21]. Such approaches have gained increased popularity over the last few years (see, e.g., [3,8,9,11,12,15,17,21,22,26,28]). The main workflow of these approaches consists of three steps: (i) construct finite abstractions of the dynamical control systems, (ii) solve a discrete synthesis problem based on the specification and abstraction to obtain a discrete control strategy, (iii) refine the discrete control strategy to a hybrid controller that renders the dynamical system satisfy the specification. As the first step in such approaches, how to construct finite abstractions of control systems, in particular, for nonlinear systems, received special attention (see [20, 23] and references therein).

One advantage of abstraction-based methods is that they provide a feedback solution, as opposed to open-loop trajectory generation strategies [7, 25]. Feedback has the potential to reduce the effects of disturbances and deal with sensing and modeling uncertainties. One of the motivations of this paper is to establish these in the context of temporal logic control. We present a unified abstraction framework equipped with certain robustness measures to account for imperfections in measurements and/or models. In particular, we show that, when the abstract system complies with these measures (with respect to a nominal concrete dynamical system), then a discrete control strategy synthesized using the abstract system is valid for (i.e., can be implemented with correctness guarantees on) a family of dynamical systems that can be represented as the nominal dynamical system subject to uncertainty.

We demonstrate the effectiveness of this abstraction framework on various problems commonly considered for control systems, including inter-sample behaviors of a sampled-data system, effects of imperfect state measurements and unmodeled dynamics, and the use of time-discretized models to design controllers for continuous-time dynamical systems. While these issues have been extensively dealt for stability analysis of control systems, they have not been discussed adequately in the context of control for temporal logic objectives. We present these as the main results of the paper.

2. PRELIMINARIES

Notation: $\mathbb{R}^n$ denotes the n-dimensional Euclidean space; $|x|$ denotes a given (but fixed) norm of x for $x \in \mathbb{R}^n$; $\mathbb{R}^+$ denotes the nonnegative real line; given $\delta \geq 0$ and $x \in \mathbb{R}^n$, $B_\delta(x) := \{x' \in \mathbb{R}^n : |x' - x| \leq \delta\}$; given an interval $I \subseteq \mathbb{R}^+$ and $U \subseteq \mathbb{R}^m$, U^I denotes the set of signals from I to U; given a function f, $\text{dom}(f)$ denotes its domain; given $h > 0$, $\mathcal{C}_h$ denotes the space of $\mathbb{R}^n$-valued continuous functions on $[-h, 0]$.

2.1 Linear temporal logics

We use the stutter-invariant fragment of linear temporal logic (denoted by $\text{LTL}_{\setminus\bigcirc}$) to specify system properties. The syntax of $\text{LTL}_{\setminus\bigcirc}$ over a set of atomic propositions Π is defined inductively as:

$$\varphi := \pi \,|\, \neg\varphi \,|\, \varphi \vee \varphi \,|\, \varphi\,\mathcal{U}\varphi,$$

where $\pi \in \Pi$. Atomic propositions are statements on an observation space Y. A labeling function $L : Y \to 2^\Pi$ maps an observation to a set of propositions that hold true. Linear temporal logic formulas are interpreted over observed signals.

Negation Normal Form (NNF): All $\text{LTL}_{\setminus\bigcirc}$ formulas can be transformed into negation normal form, where

- all negations appear only in front of the atomic propositions[1];
- only other logical operators `true`, `false`, $\wedge$, and $\vee$ can appear; and
- only the temporal operators $\mathcal{U}$ and $\mathcal{R}$ can appear, where $\mathcal{R}$ is defined by $\varphi_1\mathcal{R}\varphi_2 \equiv \neg(\neg\varphi_1\mathcal{U}\neg\varphi_2)$, called the *dual until* operator.

For syntactic convenience, we can define additional temporal operators $\Box$ and $\Diamond$ by $\Box\varphi \equiv \texttt{false}\mathcal{R}\varphi$ and $\Diamond\varphi \equiv \texttt{true}\mathcal{U}\varphi$.

Continuous semantics of $\text{LTL}_{\setminus\bigcirc}$: Given a continuous-time signal $\xi \in Y^{\mathbb{R}^+}$, we define $\xi, t \vDash \varphi$ with respect to an $\text{LTL}_{\setminus\bigcirc}$ formula φ at time t inductively as follows:

- $\xi, t \vDash \pi$ if and only if $\pi \in L(\xi(t))$;
- $\xi, t \vDash \neg\pi$ if and only if $\pi \notin L(\xi(t))$;
- $\xi, t \vDash \texttt{true}$ always holds;
- $\xi, t \vDash \texttt{false}$ never holds;
- $\xi, t \vDash \varphi_1 \vee \varphi_2$ if and only if $\xi, t \vDash \varphi_1$ or $\xi, t \vDash \varphi_2$;
- $\xi, t \vDash \varphi_1 \wedge \varphi_2$ if and only if $\xi, t \vDash \varphi_1$ and $\xi, t \vDash \varphi_2$;
- $\xi, t \vDash \varphi_1\mathcal{U}\varphi_2$ if and only if there exists $t' \geq 0$ such that $\xi, t + t' \vDash \varphi_2$ and for all $t'' \in [0, t')$, $\xi, t + t'' \vDash \varphi_1$;
- $\xi, t \vDash \varphi_1\mathcal{R}\varphi_2$ if and only if for all $t' \geq 0$ either $\xi, t+t' \vDash \varphi_2$ or there exists $t'' \in [0, t')$ such that $\xi, t + t'' \vDash \varphi_1$.

We write $\xi \vDash \varphi$ if $\xi, 0 \vDash \varphi$.

Discrete semantics of $\text{LTL}_{\setminus\bigcirc}$: Given a sequence $\rho = \{y_i\}_{i=0}^\infty$ in Y, we define $\rho, i \vDash \varphi$ with respect to an $\text{LTL}_{\setminus\bigcirc}$ formula φ inductively as follows:

- $\rho, i \vDash \pi$ if and only if $\pi \in L(h(y_i))$;
- $\rho, i \vDash \neg\pi$ if and only if $\pi \notin L(h(y_i))$;
- $\rho, i \vDash \texttt{true}$ always holds;
- $\rho, i \vDash \texttt{false}$ never holds;
- $\rho, i \vDash \varphi_1 \vee \varphi_2$ if and only if $\rho, i \vDash \varphi_1$ or $\rho, i \vDash \varphi_2$;
- $\rho, i \vDash \varphi_1 \wedge \varphi_2$ if and only if $\rho, i \vDash \varphi_1$ and $\rho, i \vDash \varphi_2$;
- $\rho, i \vDash \varphi_1\mathcal{U}\varphi_2$ if and only if there exists $j \geq i$ such that $\rho, j \vDash \varphi_2$ and $\rho, k \vDash \varphi_1$ for all $k \in [i, j)$;
- $\rho, i \vDash \varphi_1\mathcal{R}\varphi_2$ if and only if, for all $j \geq i$, either $\rho, j \vDash \varphi_2$ or there exists $k \in [i, j)$ such that $\rho, k \vDash \varphi_1$.

Similarly, we write $\rho \vDash \varphi$ if $\rho, 0 \vDash \varphi$.

[1]Hence all negations can be effectively removed by introducing new atomic propositions corresponding to the negations of current ones. We assume this has been done for all $\text{LTL}_{\setminus\bigcirc}$ formulas involved in this paper.

2.2 Problem Statement

We consider both continuous-time control systems of the form

$$\dot{x} = f(x, u), \tag{1}$$

and discrete-time control systems of the form

$$x^+ = g(x, u), \tag{2}$$

where $x \in \mathbb{R}^n$, $u \in U \subseteq \mathbb{R}^m$, x^+ denotes the next state of x under the difference equation, and both f and g are functions from $\mathbb{R}^n \times \mathbb{R}^m$ to $\mathbb{R}^n$.

Given a control input signal $\mathbf{u} \in U^{[0,T]}$, we assume that there exists a unique solution x defined on $[0, T]$ such that $\dot{x}(s) = f(x(s), \mathbf{u}(s))$ for all $s \in [0, T]$. For the discrete-time system (2), given a sequence of control inputs u_0, u_1, u_2, $\cdots$ in U, a solution to (2) is a sequence x_0, x_1, x_2, $\cdots$ such that $x_{i+1} = g(x_i, u_i)$.

The objective is to design control strategies such that solutions of systems (1) or (2) satisfy a given $\text{LTL}_{\setminus\bigcirc}$ specification. For continuous-time systems, we define a *control strategy* to be a partial function of the form:

$$\sigma(x(\tau_0), \cdots, x(\tau_i)) = \mathbf{u}_i \in U^{[0,\Delta_i]}, \; \forall i = 0, 1, 2, \cdots.$$

The sampling times τ_0, τ_1, τ_2, $\cdots$ satisfy $\tau_{i+1} - \tau_i = \Delta_i$, which is the duration of the control input signal $\mathbf{u}_i$. The control sequence $\mathbf{u}_0$, $\mathbf{u}_1$, $\mathbf{u}_2$, $\cdots$ lead to a solution of (1), which satisfies $\dot{x}(t) = f(x(t), \mathbf{u}(t))$ for all $t \geq 0$, where $\mathbf{u} \in U^{\mathbb{R}^+}$ is the concatenation of the sequence of control input signals $\mathbf{u}_i$'s. For discrete-time systems, a *control strategy* is defined to be a partial function of the form:

$$\sigma(x_0, \cdots, x_i) = u_i \in U, \; \forall i = 0, 1, 2, \cdots.$$

In this paper, we consider systems with full state observations; that is, we let the observation space $Y = \mathbb{R}^n$. Solutions of (1) and (2) are interpreted as signals and sequences in Y, respectively.

Problem Statement (Continuous Synthesis): Given a continuous-time system (1) (or a discrete-time system (2)) and an $\text{LTL}_{\setminus\bigcirc}$ specification φ, find a control strategy for the system such that all of its solutions satisfy φ.

It should be emphasized that φ is interpreted using the continuous semantics for solutions of (1) and discrete semantics for solutions of (2).

2.3 Transition systems

A *transition system* is a tuple $\mathcal{T} = (Q, Q_0, \mathcal{A}, \to_\mathcal{T}, Y, h, \Pi, L)$, where:

- Q is a (finite or infinite) set of states and Q_0 the initial states;
- $\mathcal{A}$ is a (finite or infinite) set of actions;
- $\to_\mathcal{T} \subseteq Q \times \mathcal{A} \times Q$ is a transition relation;
- Y is a (finite or infinite) set of observations;
- $h : Q \to Y$ is an observation map on the states;
- Π is a set of atomic propositions on Y;
- $L : Y \to 2^\Pi$ is a labeling function.

We often write $q \xrightarrow{a} q'$ to indicate $(q, a, q') \in \to$. $\mathcal{T}$ is said to be (i) *finite* if the cardinality of Q and $\mathcal{A}$ are finite, (ii) *infinite* otherwise, and (iii) *metric* if Y is equipped with a metric.

An *execution* of a transition system $\mathcal{T}$ is a sequence of pairs

$$\rho = (q_0, a_0)(q_1, a_1)(q_2, a_2)\cdots,$$

where $q_0 \in Q_0$ and $(q_i, a_i, q_{i+1}) \in \rightarrow_{\mathcal{T}}$ for all $i \geq 0$. A *control strategy* for a transition system $\mathcal{T}$ is a partial function $s : (q_0, a_0, \cdots, q_i) \mapsto a_i$ that maps the execution history to the next action. An *s-controlled execution* of a transition system $\mathcal{T}$ is an execution of $\mathcal{T}$, where for each $i \geq 0$, the action a_i is chosen according to the control strategy s.

2.3.1 Continuous-time control systems as transition systems

Continuous-time control systems can be formulated as transition systems. Given system (1), we define a transition system $\mathcal{T}_c = (Q, Q_0, \mathcal{A}, \rightarrow_{\mathcal{T}_c}, Y, h, \Pi, L)$ by

- $Q = X$ and $Q_0 = X_0$;
- $\mathcal{A} = \bigcup_{\tau\in\mathbb{R}^+} U^{[0,\tau]}$;
- $(q, \mathbf{u}, q') \in \rightarrow_{\mathcal{T}_c}$ if and only if there exists $\xi : [0, \tau] \rightarrow \mathbb{R}^n$ such that $\xi(0) = q$, $\xi(\tau) = q'$, and $\dot{\xi}(s) = f(\xi(s), \mathbf{u}(s))$ for all $s \in [0, \tau]$, where $\mathbf{u} \in U^{[0,\tau]} \subseteq \mathcal{A}$;
- $Y = Q$;
- $h : Q \rightarrow Y$ is defined by $\mathbf{id}_Q$, i.e., the identity map on Q;
- Π is a set of atomic propositions on Y;
- $L : Y \rightarrow 2^{\Pi}$ is a labeling function,

where the state space is restricted to $X \subseteq \mathbb{R}^n$, with initial states in $X_0 \subseteq X$. Each action in $\mathcal{A}$ is a control input signal in $\mathcal{U}^{[0,\tau]}$ for some τ. If we are interested in digital implementations of control systems with a fixed sampling period τ_s, the set of actions can be regarded as $\mathcal{A} = U$ and interpreted as a constant input signal defined on $[0, \tau_s]$ and taking value in U.

2.3.2 Discrete-time control systems as transition systems

Discrete-time control systems can also be formulated as transition systems. Given system (2), we define a transition system $\mathcal{T}_d = (Q, Q_0, \mathcal{A}, \rightarrow_{\mathcal{T}_d}, Y, h, \Pi, L)$ by

- $Q = X$ and $Q_0 = X_0$;
- $\mathcal{A} = U$;
- $(q, u, q') \in \rightarrow_{\mathcal{T}_d}$ if and only if $q' = g(q, u)$;
- $Y = Q$;
- $h : Q \rightarrow Y$ is defined by $\mathbf{id}_Q$, i.e., the identity map on Q;
- Π is a set of atomic propositions on Y;
- $L : Y \rightarrow 2^{\Pi}$ is a labeling function.

Each action in $\mathcal{A}$ is a control input in $\mathcal{U}$.

Having defined (exact) transition system models for (1) and (2), it is possible to rephrase the continuous synthesis problem defined earlier as follows.

Problem Restatement (Continuous Synthesis): Given the transition system $\mathcal{T}_c$ (or $\mathcal{T}_d$) and an $\text{LTL}_{\setminus\bigcirc}$ specification φ, find a control strategy s such that all s-controlled executions of $\mathcal{T}_c$ (or $\mathcal{T}_d$) lead to *solutions of (1)* (or (2)) that satisfy φ.

This is a *continuous* synthesis problem since the state space is still continuous (and hence infinite). Again, it is emphasized that φ, for executions of $\mathcal{T}_c$, is interpreted using the *continuous* semantics that involve solutions of (1). The motivation for doing so will become clear in Section 4.1.

3. ABSTRACTIONS WITH ROBUSTNESS MARGIN

Both the transition system $\mathcal{T}_c$ and $\mathcal{T}_d$ constructed above are infinite, with infinitely many states and actions. Under the assumption that the sets X and U are compact, we can construct finite abstractions of $\mathcal{T}_c$ and $\mathcal{T}_d$ as follows.

These abstractions are induced by an abstraction map. An *abstraction map* $\alpha : Q \rightarrow 2^{\hat{Q}}$ maps the states in Q into a subset of a finite set $\hat{Q}$. Without loss of generality, we assume $\hat{Q}$ is a subset of Q; if not, for each $\hat{q} \in \hat{Q}$, we can pick a point q such that $\hat{q} \in \alpha(q)$ to represent $\hat{q}$. This map α effectively introduces a finite covering of Q given by $\bigcup_{\hat{q}\in\hat{Q}} \alpha^{-1}(\hat{q})$.

DEFINITION 1. Given the continuous-time control system (1), its transition systems representation

$$\mathcal{T}_c = (Q, Q_0, \mathcal{A}, \rightarrow_{\mathcal{T}_c}, Y, h, \Pi, L),$$

and a tuple of positive constants $(\eta, \gamma_1, \gamma_2, \delta)$ satisfying $\gamma_i \geq \eta$ $(i = 1, 2)$, a finite transition system

$$\hat{\mathcal{T}}_c = (\hat{Q}, \hat{Q}_0, \hat{\mathcal{A}}, \rightarrow_{\hat{\mathcal{T}}_c}, \hat{Y}, \hat{h}, \hat{\Pi}, \hat{L})$$

is called an $(\eta, \gamma_1, \gamma_2, \delta)$*-abstraction* of $\mathcal{T}_c$ if there exists an abstraction map $\alpha : Q \rightarrow 2^{\hat{Q}}$ such that

(i) $\hat{Q}$ and $\hat{\mathcal{A}}$ are finite subsets of Q and $\mathcal{A}$ and $\hat{Q}_0 = \bigcup_{q\in Q_0} \alpha(q)$;
(ii) $|q - \hat{q}| \leq \eta$ for all $(q, \hat{q}) \in Q \times \hat{Q}$ such that $\hat{q} \in \alpha(q)$;
(iii) $(\hat{q}, \mathbf{u}, \hat{q}') \in \rightarrow_{\hat{\mathcal{T}}_c}$ if there exists $\xi : [0, \tau] \rightarrow \mathbb{R}^n$ such that $|\xi(0) - \hat{q}| \leq \gamma_1$, $|\xi(\tau) - \hat{q}'| \leq \gamma_2$, and $\dot{\xi}(s) = f(\xi(s), \mathbf{u}(s))$ for all $s \in [0, \tau]$, where $\text{dom}(\mathbf{u}) = [0, \tau]$;
(iv) $\hat{h} = h|_{\hat{Q}}$, i.e., h restricted on $\hat{Q}$, $\hat{Y} = \hat{Q}$, and $\hat{\Pi} = \Pi$;
(v) $\hat{L} : \hat{Y} \rightarrow 2^{\hat{\Pi}}$ is defined by

$$\pi \in \hat{L}(y),\ y \in \hat{Y} \iff \pi \in L(y'),\ \forall y' \in B_\delta(y). \quad (3)$$

We write $\mathcal{T}_c \preceq_{(\eta,\gamma_1,\gamma_2,\delta)} \hat{\mathcal{T}}_c$.

REMARK 1. Since each action in $\hat{\mathcal{A}}$ is a control input signal with some finite duration τ and $\hat{\mathcal{A}}$ is a finite set, there exists a maximum duration for signals in $\hat{\mathcal{A}}$, denoted by $\Delta(\hat{\mathcal{A}})$ or Δ. If we restrict the actions to constant signals of a fixed duration τ_s (e.g., due to periodic sampling and zero-order hold), we have $\Delta = \tau_s$.

Similarly, we can define an $(\eta, \gamma_1, \gamma_2, \delta)$-abstraction of $\mathcal{T}_d$.

DEFINITION 2. Given the discrete-time control system (2), its transition systems representation

$$\mathcal{T}_d = (Q, Q_0, \mathcal{A}, \rightarrow_{\mathcal{T}_c}, Y, h, \Pi, L),$$

and a tuple of positive constants $(\eta, \gamma_1, \gamma_2, \delta)$ satisfying $\gamma_i \geq \eta$ $(i = 1, 2)$, a finite transition system

$$\hat{\mathcal{T}}_d = (\hat{Q}, \hat{Q}_0, \hat{\mathcal{A}}, \rightarrow_{\hat{\mathcal{T}}_d}, \hat{Y}, \hat{h}, \hat{\Pi}, \hat{L})$$

is called an $(\eta, \gamma_1, \gamma_2, \delta)$*-abstraction* of $\mathcal{T}_d$ if there exists an abstraction map $\alpha : Q \rightarrow 2^{\hat{Q}}$ such that

- $(\hat{q}, u, \hat{q}') \in \rightarrow_{\hat{\mathcal{T}}_c}$ if there exists ξ and ξ' such that $|\xi - \hat{q}| \leq \gamma_1$, $|\xi' - \hat{q}'| \leq \gamma_2$, and $\xi' = g(\xi, u)$,

and (i), (iii), (iv) and (v) in Definition 2 hold for $\hat{\mathcal{T}}_d$. We write $\mathcal{T}_d \preceq_{(\eta,\gamma_1,\gamma_2,\delta)} \hat{\mathcal{T}}_d$.

The abstraction relations defined above can be seen as an over-approximation of the system dynamics with discretization granularity η and parameters γ_i $(i = 1, 2)$ to account for mismatches in abstraction. It is, at the same time, an under-approximation on the control actions in the sense that these are restricted to a subset of all available actions. The parameter δ provides a robustness margin which plays an important role in preserving the correctness of executions with respect to a given LTL$_{\setminus\bigcirc}$ specification (closely related to robust interpretations of temporal logic formulas [4]). The above relation essentially defines an alternating simulation from $\mathcal{T}_c$ to $\hat{\mathcal{T}}_c$ ($\mathcal{T}_d$ to $\hat{\mathcal{T}}_d$) [1] that takes into account approximation errors (cf. [19]) and provides robustness margins to accommodate these errors. Here, additional robustness measures are given by γ_i $(i = 1, 2)$, where, as shall be demonstrated by the main results of this paper, γ_1 is useful in accounting for imperfect state measurements, while γ_2 is useful in dealing with uncertainties/mismatches in the models used for controller synthesis.

EXAMPLE 1. We give concrete examples of $\hat{\mathcal{T}}_c$ and $\hat{\mathcal{T}}_d$ by constructing $\hat{Q}$ as a state discretization of Q. Given a positive integer k, let $\mathbb{Z}^n$ denote the n-dimensional integer lattice, which is the lattice in $\mathbb{R}^n$ whose lattice points are k-tuples of integers. For a given parameter $\mu > 0$, define

$$[X]_\mu := \mu\mathbb{Z}^n \cap X, [X_0]_\mu := \mu\mathbb{Z}^n \cap X_0,$$

where $\mu\mathbb{Z}^n := \{\mu z : z \in \mathbb{Z}^n\}$. Clearly, $[X]_\mu$ and $[X_0]_\mu$ are finite sets given that X and X_0 are compacts. As for actions, instead of looking at an infinite set of actions, we consider control input signals of durations within a finite set $\hat{T} := \{k\tau_s : k \in K\}$ and taking values in a finite subset $\hat{U}$ of U, where K is a finite subset of positive integers and τ_s is the minimum sampling period. For example, one can choose $K = \{2^s : s = 0, \cdots N\}$ for some integer $N \geq 0$ (cf. [15]). Finite abstractions for $\mathcal{T}_c$ and $\mathcal{T}_d$ can be defined as in Definitions 1 and 2 with $\hat{Q} = [X]_\mu$, $Q_0 = [X_0]_\mu$, and $\hat{\mathcal{A}} = \bigcup_{\tau\in\hat{T}} \hat{U}^{[0,\tau]}$. Note that this discretization result in conditions (ii) in Definitions 1 and 2 being satisfied with $\eta = \mu/2$. □

3.1 Discrete synthesis

The main reason to construct finite abstractions such as $\hat{\mathcal{T}}_c$ and $\hat{\mathcal{T}}_d$ is to formulate discrete synthesis problems that can be used to solve the continuous synthesis problems previously defined for $\mathcal{T}_c$ and $\mathcal{T}_d$.

Given a set of atomic propositions Π on Y, an LTL$_{\setminus\bigcirc}$ formula over Π can be interpreted over executions of $\hat{\mathcal{T}}_c$ and $\hat{\mathcal{T}}_d$ using the discrete semantics. We can now formulate the discrete problems as follows.

Problem Statement (Discrete Synthesis): Given the transition system $\hat{\mathcal{T}}_c$ (or $\hat{\mathcal{T}}_d$) and an LTL$_{\setminus\bigcirc}$ specification φ, find a control strategy s such that all s-controlled executions of $\hat{\mathcal{T}}_c$ (or $\hat{\mathcal{T}}_d$) satisfy φ.

If there exists a control strategy for $\hat{\mathcal{T}}_c$ (or $\hat{\mathcal{T}}_d$) such that all controlled executions of $\hat{\mathcal{T}}_c$ (or $\hat{\mathcal{T}}_d$) satisfy φ, we say φ is *realizable* on $\hat{\mathcal{T}}_c$ (or $\hat{\mathcal{T}}_d$). We may call control strategies for $\hat{\mathcal{T}}_c$ (or $\hat{\mathcal{T}}_d$) *discrete* (control) strategies and those for $\mathcal{T}_c$ (or $\mathcal{T}_d$) *continuous* (control) strategies.

For the finite abstractions $\hat{\mathcal{T}}_c$ and $\hat{\mathcal{T}}_d$ to be useful, we need to guarantee two things: (i) every discrete control strategy for $\hat{\mathcal{T}}_c$ (or $\hat{\mathcal{T}}_d$) can be implemented to form a control strategy for the continuous system $\mathcal{T}_c$ (or $\mathcal{T}_d$); and (ii) if the discrete strategy solves the discrete synthesis problem for $\hat{\mathcal{T}}_c$ (or $\hat{\mathcal{T}}_d$), then the corresponding continuous strategy solves the discrete synthesis problem for $\mathcal{T}_c$ (or $\mathcal{T}_d$). Establishing these under various scenarios will be the main results of this paper.

3.2 Computation of transitions

A question that remains is how to compute the transitions in $\to_{\hat{\mathcal{T}}_c}$ and $\to_{\hat{\mathcal{T}}_d}$. One way to do this is by simulating a trajectory starting from each of the point in $\hat{Q}$ and estimating the state evolution under the dynamics of (1) and (2).

In the continuous-time case, we rely on the following condition:

$$|x(t;\mathbf{u},\xi) - x(t;\mathbf{u},\zeta)| \leq \beta(|\xi - \zeta|, t), \tag{4}$$

for all $\tau \in \mathbb{R}^+$, $\mathbf{u} \in U^{[0,\tau]}$, and $t \in [0,\tau]$, where $x(t;\mathbf{u},\xi)$ and $x(t;\mathbf{u},\zeta)$ denote solutions of $\dot{x} = f(x,u)$ starting from ξ and ζ and with control input $\mathbf{u}$, respectively, and $\beta : \mathbb{R}^+\times\mathbb{R}^+ \to \mathbb{R}^+$ is a continuous function such that for each fixed t, $\beta(\cdot,t)$ is a class-$\mathcal{K}_\infty$ function[2]. Such a condition is a special case of the notion of incremental forward completeness defined in [28]. Condition (4) essentially defines a continuous dependence condition of (1) on its initial conditions that is uniform for all $\mathbf{u}$ taking values in U. An explicit form of β can usually be obtained using Lyapunov-type techniques. In addition, if (1) is incrementally asymptotically stable [2], β can be chosen as a $\mathcal{KL}$-function[3].

PROPOSITION 1. *Suppose (4) holds. If $(\hat{q},\mathbf{u},\hat{q}') \in\to_{\hat{\mathcal{T}}_c}$ whenever $(\hat{q},\mathbf{u},\hat{q}') \in \hat{Q}\times\hat{\mathcal{A}}\times\hat{Q}$ and $|\hat{q}' - x(\tau;\mathbf{u},\hat{q})| \leq \beta(\gamma_1,\tau) + \gamma_2$, then $\mathcal{T}_c \preceq_{(\eta,\gamma_1,\gamma_2,\delta)} \hat{\mathcal{T}}_c$, where dom$(\mathbf{u}) = [0,\tau]$.*

PROOF. We have to show that $\to_{\hat{\mathcal{T}}_c}$ constructed above contains all transitions $(\hat{q},\mathbf{u},\hat{q}')$ whenever there exists $\xi : [0,\tau] \to \mathbb{R}^n$ such that $|\xi(0) - \hat{q}| \leq \gamma_1$, $|\xi(\tau) - \hat{q}'| \leq \gamma_2$, and $\dot{\xi}(s) = f(\xi(s),\mathbf{u}(s))$ for all $s \in [0,\tau]$.

Consider $x(t;\mathbf{u},\hat{q})$ and $x(t;\mathbf{u},\xi(0))$. We have

$$\begin{aligned}|x(\tau;\mathbf{u},\hat{q}) - \xi(\tau)| &= |x(\tau;\mathbf{u},\hat{q}) - x(\tau;\mathbf{u},\xi(0))| \\ &\leq \beta(|\xi(0) - \hat{q}|,\tau) \leq \beta(\gamma_1,\tau).\end{aligned}$$

It follows that

$$\begin{aligned}|x(\tau;\mathbf{u},\hat{q}) - \hat{q}'| &\leq |x(\tau;\mathbf{u},\hat{q}) - \xi(\tau)| + |\xi(\tau) - \hat{q}'| \\ &\leq \beta(\gamma_1,\tau) + \gamma_2,\end{aligned}$$

which implies that $(\hat{q},\mathbf{u},\hat{q}') \in\to_{\hat{\mathcal{T}}_c}$. □

For discrete-time systems, we replace (4) with the following condition:

$$|g(u,\xi) - g(u,\zeta)| \leq \beta(|\xi - \zeta|), \tag{5}$$

where $u \in U$ and β is class-$\mathcal{K}_\infty$ function.

PROPOSITION 2. *Suppose (5) holds. If $(\hat{q},u,\hat{q}') \in\to_{\hat{\mathcal{T}}_d}$ whenever $(\hat{q},u,\hat{q}') \in \hat{Q}\times\hat{\mathcal{A}}\times\hat{Q}$ and $|\hat{q}' - g(u,\hat{q})| \leq \beta(\gamma_1) + \gamma_2$, then $\mathcal{T}_d \preceq_{(\eta,\gamma_1,\gamma_2,\delta)} \hat{\mathcal{T}}_d$.*

[2]A function $\kappa : \mathbb{R}^+ \to \mathbb{R}^+$ is called a *class-$\mathcal{K}$ function* if it is strictly increasing and $\kappa(0) = 0$; it is called a *class-$\mathcal{K}_\infty$ function* if it is a class-$\mathcal{K}$ function and $\kappa(r) \to \infty$ as $r \to \infty$.
[3]A function $\kappa : \mathbb{R}^+\times\mathbb{R}^+ \to \mathbb{R}^+$ is called a *class-$\mathcal{KL}$* function if, for each fixed t, $\kappa(\cdot,t)$ is a class-$\mathcal{K}_\infty$ function and, for each fixed r, $\kappa(r,t) \to 0$ as $t \to \infty$.

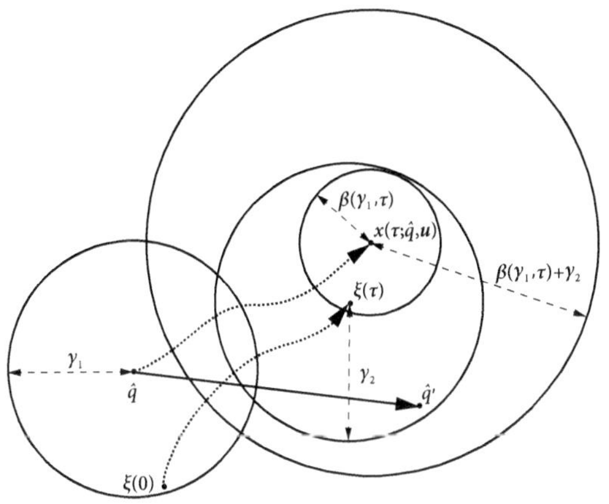

Figure 1: **Proposition 1 provides concrete means to over-approximate $\rightarrow_{\hat{\mathcal{T}}_c}$ by adding $(\hat{q}, \mathbf{u}, \hat{q}')$ to $\rightarrow_{\hat{\mathcal{T}}_c}$ whenever $|\hat{q}' - x(\tau; \mathbf{u}, \hat{q})| \leq \beta(\gamma_1, \tau) + \gamma_2$. In view of condition (4), the ball $B_{\beta(\gamma_1,\tau)}(x(\tau; \hat{q}, \mathbf{u}))$ includes $\xi(\tau)$ for all $\xi : [0, \tau] \rightarrow \mathbb{R}^n$ such that $|\xi(0) - \hat{q}| \leq \gamma_1$ and $\dot{\xi}(s) = f(\xi(s), \mathbf{u}(s))$ for all $s \in [0, \tau]$. Hence, the ball $B_{\beta(\gamma_1,\tau)+\gamma_2}(x(\tau; \hat{q}, \mathbf{u}))$ contains all $\hat{q}' \in \hat{Q}$ that is γ_2-close to $\xi(\tau)$ for some ξ defined above; that is, all $\hat{q}' \in \hat{Q}$ such that $(\hat{q}, \mathbf{u}, \hat{q}') \in \rightarrow_{\hat{\mathcal{T}}_c}$ as required by Definition 1.**

Proposition 1 essentially says that, for each state in $\hat{q} \in \hat{Q}$ and $\mathbf{u} \in \hat{A}$, if we add $(\hat{q}, \mathbf{u}, \hat{q}')$ to $\rightarrow_{\hat{\mathcal{T}}_c}$ for each $\hat{q}' \in \hat{Q} \cap B_\gamma(x(\tau; \mathbf{u}, \hat{q}))$, where $\gamma = \beta(\gamma_1, \tau) + \gamma_2$, then we obtain an $(\eta, \gamma_1, \gamma_2, \delta)$-abstraction of $\mathcal{T}_c$ in the sense of Definition 1. Figure 1 illustrates how transitions in $\rightarrow_{\hat{\mathcal{T}}_c}$ can be computed in Proposition 1. The intuition behind Proposition 2 is similar.

Augmented Progress Properties.

In view of comments above, if τ is sufficiently small compared with γ, then the ball $B_\gamma(x(\tau; \mathbf{u}, \hat{q}))$ will almost always include $\hat{q}$ itself, which introduces a self-transition $(\hat{q}, \mathbf{u}, \hat{q})$ for almost all $\hat{q} \in \hat{Q}$. As we shall treat all non-determinism as adversary when solving the discrete synthesis problem, these self-transitions can render the problem unrealizable if the specification involves making progress. In addition to self-transitions, non-determinism can potentially induce spurious cyclic executions in the abstract system that do not exist in the continuous system (1). To deal with these issues, we can use augmented finite transition systems [17] to enforce additional progress assumptions when solving the discrete synthesis problem. Such progress assumptions can be captured by the following LTL$_{\setminus\bigcirc}$ formula:

$$\varphi_g \doteq \bigwedge_{\mathbf{u} \in \hat{\mathcal{A}}} \bigwedge_{G \in \mathcal{G}(\mathbf{u})} \neg\Diamond\Box((\vee_{\hat{q} \in G} \hat{q}) \wedge \mathbf{u}), \tag{6}$$

where each $G \in \mathcal{G}(\mathbf{u})$ represents a progress group. That is, the set $\bigcup_{\hat{q} \in G} \alpha^{-1}(\hat{q})$ does not contain any invariant sets for system (1) when a fixed $\mathbf{u}$ is repeatedly executed. Such progress groups can be trivially computed for affine or incrementally stable dynamics. It is also possible to approximate them when the dynamics are polynomial [17]. Appropriately encoding these progress properties is essential for achieving certain specifications (e.g., reachability).

Remark 2. Without additional assumption, the estimate $\gamma(\tau) = \beta(\gamma_1, \tau) + \gamma_2$ used by Proposition 1 and illustrated in Figure 1 can be conservative and may lead to too much nondeterminism that renders the discrete synthesis problem unrealizable. One way to overcome this is to assume (1) to be incrementally stable, in which case β can be chosen as a $\mathcal{KL}$ function. We can then choose τ sufficiently large such that

$$\beta(\gamma(\tau), \tau) = \beta(\beta(\gamma_1, \tau) + \gamma_2, \tau) \leq \gamma(\tau),$$

which is always possible since β is a $\mathcal{KL}$ function and $\gamma_2 < \gamma(\tau) \leq \beta(\gamma_1, 0) + \gamma_2$. The above inequality essentially captures how nondeterminism is bounded within two steps of transitions.

4. MAIN RESULTS—IMPLICATIONS OF THE ROBUSTNESS MARGIN

The main objective of this section is to show that, with the notions of abstractions defined in Definitions 1 and 2, we are able to reason about the qualitative properties of solutions of (1) and (2) in a number of different scenarios, including inter-sample behaviors of a sampled-data system, effects of imperfect state measurements and unmodeled dynamics, and the use of time-discretized models to design controllers for continuous-time dynamical systems.

4.1 Continuous correctness by discrete reasoning

When implementing a discrete strategy, perhaps obtained from solving a discrete synthesis problem, we are effectively implementing a hybrid feedback controller such that solutions of (1) (or (2)) satisfy a given specification.

In general, the existence of a discrete control strategy for the discrete synthesis problem for $\hat{\mathcal{T}}_c$ (or $\hat{\mathcal{T}}_d$) with an LTL$_{\setminus\bigcirc}$ formula φ *does not* guarantee the existence of a control strategy that solves the continuous synthesis problem for (1) (or (2)) with the same specification φ. In fact, using discretization-based (or grid point-based), rather than proposition-preserving partition-based, abstractions, we need extra conditions to ensure correctness of continuous executions from discrete reasoning. This motivates (3) in defining abstractions, which essentially captures the idea of contracting and expanding atomic propositions as used in [3, 12]. This extra condition is needed to account for inter-sample behaviors as illustrated in the following simple example.

Example 2. Consider a two dimensional system given in polar coordinates $\dot{r} = -r$ and $\dot{\theta} = \omega$. This is an asymptotically stable linear system, hence incrementally stable. Trajectories of this systems are spiraling towards the origin, such as the trajectory x illustrated in Figure 2. Suppose we are interested in verifying that all trajectories starting from the set A and eventually reach the set B, while not intersecting the set C, which can be captured by the specification $\varphi \equiv (A \rightarrow \Diamond B) \wedge \Box C^c)$, where C^c is the complement of the set C. Suppose that we are using sampled values of x to verify whether $x \vDash \varphi$ and the sampling period is τ_s. For any $\tau_s > 0$, if we choose $\omega = 2\pi/\tau_s$, the trajectory x starting from $(a_0, 0) \in A$ will lead to a sampled sequence of $(a_0, 0)(a_1, 0)(a_2, 0)\cdots$, which clearly satisfies φ. However, $x \nvDash \varphi$ as it intersects with C. This simple example illustrates that extra conditions are needed to account for inter-

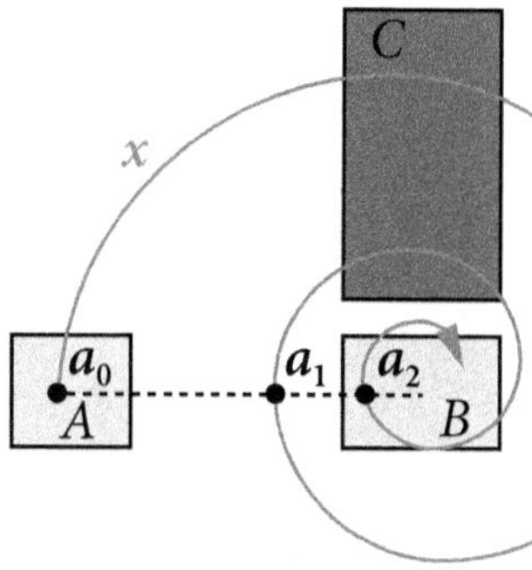

Figure 2: A simple illustration of inter-sample behaviors that violate a given specification, while a sampled sequence satisfies the same specification.

sample behaviors and these conditions will have to depend on system dynamics. □

We let $M = \sup_{x\in X, u\in U} |f(x,u)|$ and Δ be the maximum duration of actions in $\hat{\mathcal{A}}$.

THEOREM 1. *If $\mathcal{T}_c \preceq_{(\eta,\gamma_1,\gamma_2,\delta)} \hat{\mathcal{T}}_c$ with $\gamma_i \geq \eta$ $(i = 1,2)$ and $\delta \geq M\Delta/2 + \eta$, then, given any $LTL_{\backslash\bigcirc}$ formula φ, φ being realizable for $\hat{\mathcal{T}}_c$ implies that φ is realizable for $\mathcal{T}_c$.*

PROOF. By the definition of an $(\eta,\gamma_1,\gamma_2,\delta)$-abstraction, to every control strategy $\hat{f}$ for $\hat{\mathcal{T}}_c$, there corresponds a control strategy f for $\mathcal{T}_c$ such that, to each f-controlled execution of $\mathcal{T}_c$, there corresponds a $\hat{f}$-controlled execution in $\hat{\mathcal{T}}_c$. In fact, this is ensured by the fact that $|q - \hat{q}| \leq \eta$ for all $(q,\hat{q}) \in Q \times \hat{Q}$ such that $\hat{q} \in \alpha(q)$ and the condition $\gamma_i \geq \eta$ $(i = 1,2)$.

We denote this correspondence by ρ to $\hat{\rho}$, where

$$\rho = (q_0, \mathbf{u}_0)(q_1, \mathbf{u}_1)(q_2, \mathbf{u}_2)\cdots$$

and

$$\hat{\rho} = (\hat{q}_0, \mathbf{u}_0)(\hat{q}_1, \mathbf{u}_1)(\hat{q}_2, \mathbf{u}_2)\cdots$$

Each $\hat{q}_i$ is an abstract state corresponding to q_i and hence $|q_i - \hat{q}_i| \leq \eta$ for all $i \geq 0$. Furthermore, corresponding to ρ, there is the solution x with $x(\tau_i) = q_i$ for all $i \geq 0$, where $\tau_0 = 0$ and $\tau_{i+1} = \tau_i + \Delta_i$, where Δ_i is the duration of $\mathbf{u}_i$. We have to show that $\hat{\rho} \vDash \varphi$ implies $x \vDash \varphi$. We prove this by proving a stronger statement: $\hat{\rho}, i \vDash \varphi$ for $i \geq 0$ implies $x, t \vDash \varphi$ for all $t \in J_i = [\tau_i - \Delta/2, \tau_i + \Delta/2] \cap \mathbb{R}^+$.

The proof is by induction on the structure of an $LTL_{\backslash\bigcirc}$ formula.

Case $\varphi = \pi$: To show $x, t \vDash \pi$ for all $t \in J_i$, we have to show that $\pi \in L(x(t))$. This follows from $q_i = x(\tau_i)$, $\pi \in \hat{L}(\hat{q}_i)$, and

$$|x(t) - \hat{q}_i| \leq |x(t) - x(\tau_i)| + |q_i - \hat{q}_i| \leq M\Delta/2 + \eta \leq \delta. \quad (7)$$

Case $\varphi = \varphi_1 \mathcal{U} \varphi_2$: To show $x, t \vDash \varphi$ for all $t \in J_i$, we need to show that, for each fixed $t \in J_i$, there exists $t' \geq 0$ such that $x, t + t' \vDash \varphi_2$ and for all $t'' \in [0, t')$, $x, t + t'' \vDash \varphi_1$. We have $\hat{\rho}, i \vDash \varphi$; that is, there exists $j > i$ such that $\hat{\rho}, j \vDash \varphi_2$ and $\hat{\rho}, k \vDash \hat{\varphi}_1$ for all $k \in [i, j)$. It follows from the inductive assumption that $x, s \vDash \varphi_2$ for all $s \in J_j$ and $x, s \vDash \varphi_1$ for all $s \in J_k$ and all $k \in [i, j)$. Take $t' = \max(\tau_j - \Delta/2, t) - t$. Then $t + t' \in J_j$ and hence $x, t + t' \vDash \varphi_2$. In addition, for all $t'' \in [0, t')$, we have $t + t'' \in J_k$ for some $k \in [i, j)$ and hence $x, t + t'' \vDash \varphi_1$. In fact, $\cup_{i \leq k \leq j-1} J_k = [\tau_i - \Delta/2, \tau_{j-1} + \Delta/2] \cap \mathbb{R}^+ \supseteq [t, \tau_j - \Delta/2) = [t, t + t') \ni t + t''$.

Case $\varphi = \varphi_1 \mathcal{R} \varphi_2$: To show $x(t) \vDash \varphi$ for all $t \in J_i$, we need to show that, for each fixed $t \in J_i$, we have, for all $t' \geq 0$ either $x, t + t' \vDash \varphi_2$ or that there exists $t'' \in [0, t')$ such that $x, t + t'' \vDash \varphi_1$. We have $\hat{\rho}, i \vDash \varphi$; that is, for all $j \geq i$, either $\hat{\rho}, j \vDash \varphi_2$ or there exists $k \in [i, j)$ such that $\hat{\rho}, k \vDash \varphi_1$. Given $t' \geq 0$, let τ_j be such that $t + t' \in J_j$, where $j \geq i$. For this j, we have either $\hat{\rho}, j \vDash \varphi_2$ or that there exists $k \in [i, j)$ such that $\hat{\rho}, k \vDash \varphi_1$. It follows from the inductive assumption that either $x, s \vDash \varphi_2$ for all $s \in J_j$ or there exists $k \in [i, j)$ such that $x, s \vDash \varphi_1$ for all $s \in J_k$. If the former holds, since $t + t' \in J_j$, we get $x, t + t' \vDash \varphi_2$. If the latter holds, since $t + t' \geq \tau_j - \Delta/2 > \tau_k - \Delta/2$ and $\tau_k + \Delta/2 \geq \tau_i + \Delta/2 \geq t$, we know $[t, t + t') \cap J_k \neq \emptyset$. Thus, there exists $t'' \in [0, t')$ such that $x, t + t'' \vDash \varphi_1$.

The other cases are straightforward. □

REMARK 3. The condition $\delta \geq M\Delta/2 + \eta$ can be relaxed by considering a one-step version of it; that is, the relation holds for every single transition $(\hat{q}, \mathbf{u}, \hat{q}') \in \rightarrow_{\hat{\mathcal{T}}_c}$. This can potentially lead to a non-uniform, state-dependent error specification (η becomes a function on $\hat{Q}$) and a state-dependent robustness margin (δ becomes a function on $\hat{Q}$). The bounded M can be taken on the set of concrete states corresponding to $\hat{q}$ and $\hat{q}'$ and the set of inputs u taken by the signal $\mathbf{u}$. Moreover, we can use precise information of the duration of an action $\mathbf{u}$ in each transition (denoted by τ), instead of using a global bound Δ for such τ's.

THEOREM 2. *If $\mathcal{T}_d \preceq_{(\eta,\gamma_1,\gamma_2,\delta)} \hat{\mathcal{T}}_d$ with $\gamma_i \geq \eta$ $(i = 1,2)$ and $\delta \geq \eta$, then, given any $LTL_{\backslash\bigcirc}$ formula φ, φ being realizable for $\hat{\mathcal{T}}_d$ implies that φ is realizable for $\mathcal{T}_d$.*

PROOF. The proof is similar to that for Theorem 1. The only difference is that we do not need to account for inter-sample behaviors. Hence, the condition is weaken to $\delta \geq \eta$, which essentially says that all concrete states corresponding to the same discrete states should satisfy the same propositions. □

4.2 Imperfect state measurement: bounded errors or delays

In practice, state measurements are not perfect, often subject to measurement noise or quantization. Furthermore, delays are ubiquitous in control systems. In this subsection, we consider the robustness of a hybrid controller for (1) that realizes a temporal logic objective with respect to imperfect state measurements. The details of the problem are illustrated in Figure 3.

THEOREM 3. *Suppose that (1) is to be controlled under the situation illustrated in Figure 3. If $\mathcal{T}_c \preceq_{(\eta,\gamma_1,\gamma_2,\delta)} \hat{\mathcal{T}}_c$ with $\gamma_1 \geq hM + \varepsilon + \eta$, $\gamma_2 \geq \varepsilon + \eta$, and $\delta \geq (h + \Delta)M/2 + (\varepsilon + \eta)$, then, given any $LTL_{\backslash\bigcirc}$ formula φ, φ being realizable for $\hat{\mathcal{T}}_c$ implies that φ is realizable for $\mathcal{T}_c$.*

PROOF. Let x_0, x_1, x_2, $\cdots$, be the measurements taken at the plant at times τ_0, τ_1, τ_2, $\cdots$; that is $x_i = x(\tau_i)$ for all $i \geq 0$. As shown in Figure 3, we assume it takes time delay h_1 for the hybrid controller to receive a perhaps noisy measurement given by $\hat{x}_i = x(\tau_i) + e_i$ at time $\tau_i + h_1$. The controller makes a decision and passes on a suggested input

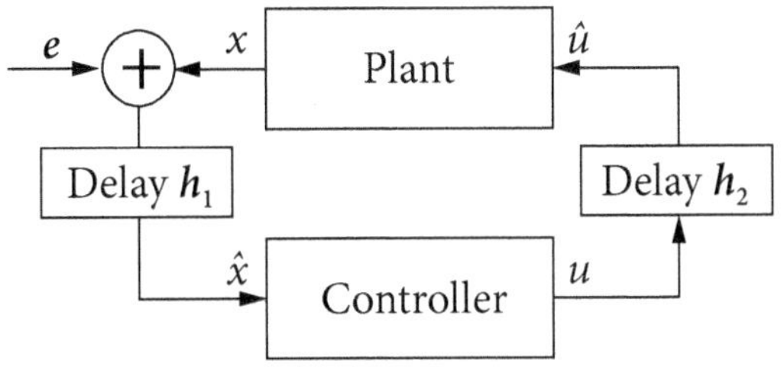

Figure 3: Illustration of a controller that takes delayed (by h_1) and imperfect measurement (subject to measurement errors bounded by ε) from a plant and sends a control input that is received by the plant after another delay h_2 (measured from when the controller receives the measurement and to when the control input has been actuated by the plant). The total round-trip delay $h_1 + h_2$ is not assumed to be constant, but assumed to be bounded by some constant h. While the plant is waiting for the next control input, it keeps on executing the previous one.

$\mathbf{u}_i$ (which includes the duration of $\mathbf{u}_i$ denoted by Δ_i). The plant will receive this input subject to another delay h_2 at time $\tau_i+h_1+h_2$. From this point on, the control input is set to $\mathbf{u}_i$. Between τ_i and $\tau_i + h$, the plant will keep executing the previous input $\mathbf{u}_{i-1}$; initially, between τ_0 and $\tau_0 + h$, assume this input is set to some initial value. We need to be clear how τ_i's are defined: we set $\tau_0 = 0$ and the rest of the sampling times τ_i $(i \geq 1)$ are defined by $\tau_i = \tau_{i-1}+\Delta_{i-1}+h$.

There are two things to prove: (1) every measured states (with delays and noise) are accounted for in the abstraction, so that the discrete control strategy can be implemented. Put more straightforwardly, every measured states should be expected by the controller so that it can make a decision based on the strategy automaton; (2) the plant trajectory $x(t)$, $t \geq 0$, should satisfy the desired specification φ.

The first is ensured by that the transition from $\hat{x}_i$ to $\hat{x}_{i+1}$ is captured by the a transition $\hat{q}_i$ to $\hat{q}_{i+1}$ in the abstraction. We only need to verify that there exists a trajectory ξ of (1) under input signals $\mathbf{u}_i$ such that $|\xi(0) - \hat{q}_i| \leq \gamma_1$ and $|\xi(\Delta_i) - \hat{q}_{i+1}| \leq \gamma_2$ for all $i \geq 0$. We know that $|\hat{x}_i - \hat{q}_i| \leq \eta$ and $|\hat{x}_{i+1} - \hat{q}_{i+1}| \leq \eta$. We also know that $|\hat{x}_i - x(\tau_i)| \leq \varepsilon$, $\tau_{i+1} = \tau_i + \Delta_i + h$ for all $i \geq 0$, and $\mathbf{u}_i$ is activated on $[\tau_i + h, \tau_i + h + \Delta_i]$. Letting $\xi(s) = x(\tau_i + h + s)$ for $s \in [0, \Delta_i]$, then $\xi(0) = x(\tau_i + h)$ and $\xi(\Delta_i) = x(\tau_i+\Delta_i+h)$. It is easy to verify that $|\xi(0) - \hat{q}_i| \leq |x(\tau_i + h) - x(\tau_i)|+|x(\tau_i) - \hat{x}_i|+|\hat{x}_i - \hat{q}_i| \leq hM+\varepsilon+\eta \leq \gamma_1$ and $|\xi(\Delta_i) - \hat{q}_{i+1}| \leq |x(\tau_{i+1}) - \hat{x}_{i+1}| + |\hat{x}_{i+1} - \hat{q}_{i+1}| \leq \varepsilon + \eta \leq \gamma_2$.

Let $x(\tau_i) = q_i$. We have $|q_i - \hat{q}_i| \leq \varepsilon + \eta$ and $\tau_{i+1} - \tau_i = \Delta_i + h$ for all $i \geq 0$. We can prove $x \models \varphi$ following the proof of Theorem 1 with η replaced by $\eta + \varepsilon$ and Δ_i replaced by Δ_i+h. The result follows from $\delta \geq (h+\Delta)M/2+(\eta+\varepsilon)$. □

For discrete-time systems, we do not consider delays in this paper, but the following result gives robustness with respect to measurement errors. The proof is omitted.

THEOREM 4. *Suppose that (2) is to be controlled subject to measurement errors bounded by ε. If $\mathcal{T}_d \preceq_{(\eta,\gamma_1,\gamma_2,\delta)} \hat{\mathcal{T}}_d$ with $\gamma_i \geq \varepsilon + \eta$ $(i = 1, 2)$, and $\delta \geq \varepsilon + \eta$, then, given any $LTL_{\setminus\bigcirc}$ formula φ, φ being realizable for $\hat{\mathcal{T}}_d$ implies that φ is realizable for $\mathcal{T}_d$.*

4.3 Unmodeled dynamics: bounded disturbance or delays

We can also apply the same methodology to prove the effectiveness of the design in the situation where systems (1) and (2) contain unmodeled dynamics that can be treated as bounded disturbance in the right-hand side of (1) and (2).

A general time-delay system can be written as a functional differential equation:

$$\dot{x} = F(x_t, u), \quad t \geq 0, \tag{8}$$

where $F : \mathcal{C}_h \times U \to \mathbb{R}^n$ is a functional with control input $u \in U$, and $x_t(s) = x(t + s)$ for all $s \in [-h, 0]$. We assume that, given any initial condition $x_0 \in \mathcal{C}_h$, (8) has a unique global solution.

We can rewrite F such that it has an *ordinary part* and a *functional part*:

$$F(x_t, u) = f(x, u) + g(x_t, u), \tag{9}$$

where $f : \mathbb{R}^+ \times \mathbb{R}^n \to \mathbb{R}^n$ and $g : \mathcal{C}_h \times U \to \mathbb{R}^n$. This form can be obtained, for example, from (8) by letting $g(x_t, u) := F(x_t, u) - f(x, u)$. The idea is to design controllers for system (8), based on the delay-free model (1). The results rely on the following assumption:

Assumption (Boundedness).
There exists a constant $D_h > 0$ such that $|g(x_t, u)| \leq D_h$ for all $u \in U$ and all solutions x_t of (8) that completely lies in X; that is, $x_t(s) \in X$ for all $s \in [-h, 0]$. □

In most delay models, $D_h \to 0$ as $h \to 0$ for compact sets X and U. We will treat $g(x_t, u)$ as additive disturbances to the right-hand side of (1). Therefore, the results also work for general disturbances satisfying a boundedness condition as in the above assumption. Similar to that for previous results, we let M be such that $|F(x_t, u)| \leq M$ for all $u \in U$ and all solutions x_t of (8) that completely lies in X.

THEOREM 5. *Suppose the boundedness assumption holds and that (8) is to be controlled with a hybrid controller that is designed using the delay-free model (1). If $\mathcal{T}_c \preceq_{(\eta,\gamma_1,\gamma_2,\delta)} \hat{\mathcal{T}}_c$ with $\gamma_1 \geq \eta$, $\gamma_2 \geq (e^{L\Delta} - 1)D_h/L + \eta$, where L is the uniform Lipschitz constant of $f(\cdot, u)$ on X for all $u \in U$, and $\delta \geq \Delta M/2 + \eta$, then, given any $LTL_{\setminus\bigcirc}$ formula φ, φ being realizable for $\hat{\mathcal{T}}_c$ implies that φ is realizable for $\mathcal{T}_c$.*

PROOF. Let x_0, x_1, x_2, $\cdots$, be the measurements taken for the system (8) at times τ_0, τ_1, τ_2, $\cdots$; that is $x_i = x(\tau_i)$ for all $i \geq 0$, where $\tau_0 = 0$ and $\tau_{i+1} = \tau_i + \Delta_i$ for all $i \geq 0$ and $\mathbf{u}_i$ is activated on $[\tau_i, \tau_i + \Delta_i]$ for each $i \geq 0$. The only thing that needs to be proved is that the abstraction based on model 1 actually accounts for all possible behaviors of solutions of (8). That is, each transition from x_i to x_{i+1} is captured by a transition $\hat{q}_i$ to $\hat{q}_{i+1}$ in the abstraction. We only need to verify that there exists a trajectory ξ of (1) under inputs $\mathbf{u}_i$ such that $|\xi(0) - \hat{q}_i| \leq \gamma_1$ and $|\xi(\Delta_i) - \hat{q}_{i+1}| \leq \gamma_2$. Let ξ be a solution of (1) starting from x_i. We have $\xi(0) = \xi(\tau_i)$ and $\dot{\xi}(s) = f(\xi(s), \mathbf{u}_i(s))$ for all $s \in [0, \Delta_i]$. Define $y(s) = x(\tau_i + s)$ for $s \in [-h, \Delta_i]$. Then $y(0) = x(\tau_i)$ and $\dot{y}(s) = F(y_s, \mathbf{u}_i(s)) = f(y(s), \mathbf{u}_i(s)) + g(y_s, \mathbf{u}_i(s))$ for all $s \in [0, \Delta_i]$. Let $z(s) = y(s) - \xi(s)$ for $s \in [-h, \Delta_i]$. It follows that $|\dot{z}| \leq L|z| + D_h$ and $z(0) = 0$, where L is the uniform Lipschitz constant of $f(\cdot, u)$ on X for all $u \in U$ and D_h is the bound on g specified in the assumption. Using a differential inequality on $|z|$, it is easy to establish that

$|z(s)| \leq (e^{Ls}-1)d/L$ for $s \in [0, \Delta_i]$. Therefore, $|\xi(0) - \hat{q}_i| \leq |z(0)| + |x(\tau_i) - \hat{q}_i| \leq \eta \leq \gamma_1$ and $|\xi(\Delta_i) - \hat{q}_{i+1}| \leq |z(\Delta_i)| + |x(\tau_i + \Delta_i) - \hat{q}_{i+1}| \leq (e^{L\Delta} - 1)d/L + \eta \leq \gamma_2$. □

For discrete-time systems, we do not consider delays in this paper, but the following result gives robustness with respect to bounded additive disturbances. The proof is omitted.

THEOREM 6. *Suppose that (2) is subject to additive disturbances bounded by d. If* $\mathcal{T}_d \preceq_{(\eta,\gamma_1,\gamma_2,\delta)} \hat{\mathcal{T}}_d$ *with* $\gamma_1 \geq \eta$, $\gamma_2 \geq d + \eta$, *and* $\delta \geq \eta$, *then, given any* $LTL_{\setminus\bigcirc}$ *formula* φ, φ *being realizable for* $\hat{\mathcal{T}}_d$ *implies that* φ *is realizable for* $\mathcal{T}_d$.

4.4 Justification of time-discretization-based design

There are situations one would like to use a time-discretized model to design controllers for a continuous-time system, for example, when there is already a design methodology proved to be effective for discretized systems. What are the issues that need to be considered to ensure the performance of the resulted controller? This is a standard question in the design of stabilizing controllers (e.g., [5]). Here we consider it in the context of hybrid control for temporal logic objectives.

Let (2) be a time-discretized model for (1), which could be an exact model (e.g., available in the case where f is linear) or an approximate model (such as obtained from applying a numerical scheme). For example, $g(x, u)$ can be defined by $g(x, u) = x + \Delta f(x, u)$ as in a forward Euler scheme with a constant step size Δ. We only consider the case of constant step size and write the time-discretized control system as

$$x^+ = g_\Delta(x, u), \tag{10}$$

where $x \in X \subseteq \mathbb{R}^n$ and $u \in U \subseteq \mathbb{R}^m$ and g_Δ is a suitable one-step numerical scheme with a constant step size Δ.

Assumption (Consistency).
The numerical scheme g_Δ satisfies

$$|x(\Delta; x_0) - g_\Delta(x_0, u)| \leq \Delta C(\Delta),$$

for all $x_0 \in X$ and $u \in U$, where $C(\Delta) \to 0$ as $\Delta \to 0$. □

For example, for the forward Euler scheme with a fixed step size Δ, the above assumption holds with $C(\Delta) = (e^{L\Delta} - 1)/L$, where L is the uniform Lipschitz constant of $f(\cdot, u)$ on X for all $u \in U$.

THEOREM 7. *Suppose the consistency assumption holds and that (1) is to be controlled with a hybrid controller synthesized using the time-discretized model (10). If* $\mathcal{T}_c \preceq_{(\eta,\gamma_1,\gamma_2,\delta)} \hat{\mathcal{T}}_c$ *with* $\gamma_1 \geq \eta$, $\gamma_2 \geq \Delta C(\Delta) + \eta$, *and* $\delta \geq \Delta M/2 + \eta$, *then, given any* $LTL_{\setminus\bigcirc}$ *formula* φ, φ *being realizable for* $\hat{\mathcal{T}}_c$ *implies that* φ *is realizable for* $\mathcal{T}_c$ *and the controlled executions of* $\mathcal{T}_c$ *lead to solutions of (1) that satisfy* φ.

PROOF. Let x_0, x_1, x_2, $\cdots$, be the measurements taken for the system (1) at times τ_0, τ_1, τ_2, $\cdots$; that is $x_i = x(\tau_i)$ for all $i \geq 0$, where $\tau_0 = 0$ and $\tau_{i+1} = \tau_i + \Delta_i$ for all $i \geq 0$, $\mathbf{u}_i \equiv u_i$ on $[\tau_i, \tau_i + \Delta_i]$ for each $i \geq 0$, and u_i is a control input given by the discrete strategy. We need to show that: (1) every measured state is accounted for in the abstraction (computed from the discretized model), so that the discrete control strategy can be implemented; (2) the plant trajectory $x(t)$, $t \geq 0$, should satisfy the desired specification φ. Let $\{\hat{q}_i\}$ denote a sequence of abstract states corresponding to $\{x_i\}$.

To prove (1): for each i, we need to show that there exists ξ and ξ' such that $|\xi - \hat{q}_i| \leq \gamma_1$, $|\xi' - \hat{q}_{i+1}| \leq \gamma_2$, and $\xi' = g_\Delta(\xi, u_i)$. We let $\xi = x_i$ and $\xi' = g_\Delta(x_i, u_i)$. Then $|\xi - \hat{q}_i| \leq \eta \leq \gamma_1$. Moreover, it follows from the one-step consistency assumption that $|x_{i+1} - g_\Delta(x_i, u_i)| \leq \Delta C(\Delta)$ and $|\xi' - \hat{q}_{i+1}| \leq |x_{i+1} - g_\Delta(x_i, u_i)| + |x_{i+1} - \hat{q}_{i+1}| \leq \Delta C(\Delta) + \eta \leq \gamma$.

To prove (2): We can prove $x \vDash \varphi$ following the proof of Theorem 1. □

5. EXAMPLE

We consider a simple cruise control example where the goal is to regulate the vehicle's velocity to a desired range while respecting speed limits. The longitudinal dynamics of the car is given by

$$\dot{v} = u - c_0 - c_1 v^2 \tag{11}$$

where $v \in [v_{\min}, v_{\max}]$ is the velocity of the car, $u \in [-3a, 2a]$ is the scaled input acceleration and c_i for $i = 1, 2$ are proper constants to account for rolling resistance, air drag and head-wind [16], which are chosen as $c_0 = 0.1$, $c_1 = 0.00016$, $a = 0.5$. The unit of velocity is in meters per second (m/s).

We consider a specification of the form

$$\varphi \equiv \square(v \leq 30) \wedge \Diamond\square(v \in [22, 24]),$$

which respects a speed limit of 30 and eventually reaches and stays within the desired range [22, 24]. To demonstrate the results in Section 4, we assume that the measurement of v involves a bounded error in the range $[-\varepsilon, \varepsilon]$ with $\varepsilon = 0.1$ and there is a round-trip delay in sensing, computation, and actuation, as illustrated in Figure 3, that is bounded by a constant $h = 0.01$. For $[v_{\min}, v_{\max}] = [20, 30]$ and $[-3a, 2a] = [-1.5, 1]$, $M = \sup_{v \in [v_{\min}, v_{\max}], u \in [-3a, 2a]} |f(x, u)| = 3a + c_0 + 900c_1 = 1.744$. Therefore, according to Theorem 3, we can choose an $(\eta, \gamma_1, \gamma_2, \delta)$-abstraction with $\eta = 0.05$, $\gamma_1 = 0.1674$, $\gamma_2 = 0.15$, and $\delta = 0.5947$ to formulate a discrete synthesis problem. We compute such an abstraction by discretizing $[v_{\min}, v_{\max}]$ with grid size 0.1. To compute transitions, it is easy to show that the estimate (4) holds with $\beta(r, t) = re^{-40c_1 t}$ on $[v_{\min}, v_{\max}]$ for $u \in [-3a, 2a]$. Proposition 1 is then used to compute transitions. The resulting discrete synthesis problem is solved using TuLiP [27]. Simulation results that illustrate the implementations of the discrete strategies are shown in Figure 4, which demonstrate that it is important to account for measurement errors and delays within the abstractions used for controller synthesis.

6. RELATED WORK

There are two common ways to construct finite abstractions. One is to partition the state space into a finite number of "proposition-preserving" regions (see, e.g., [17, 26]). This approach has the advantage of resulting in a small number of abstract states (given by elements in the partition) and also do not require any stability assumptions on the system dynamics. However, the fact that the computation of transitions in this type of abstraction relies heavily on the geometry of the vector fields with respect to the partition makes it difficult to incorporate robustness measures, especially those to deal with imperfect state information except for some special cases [14].

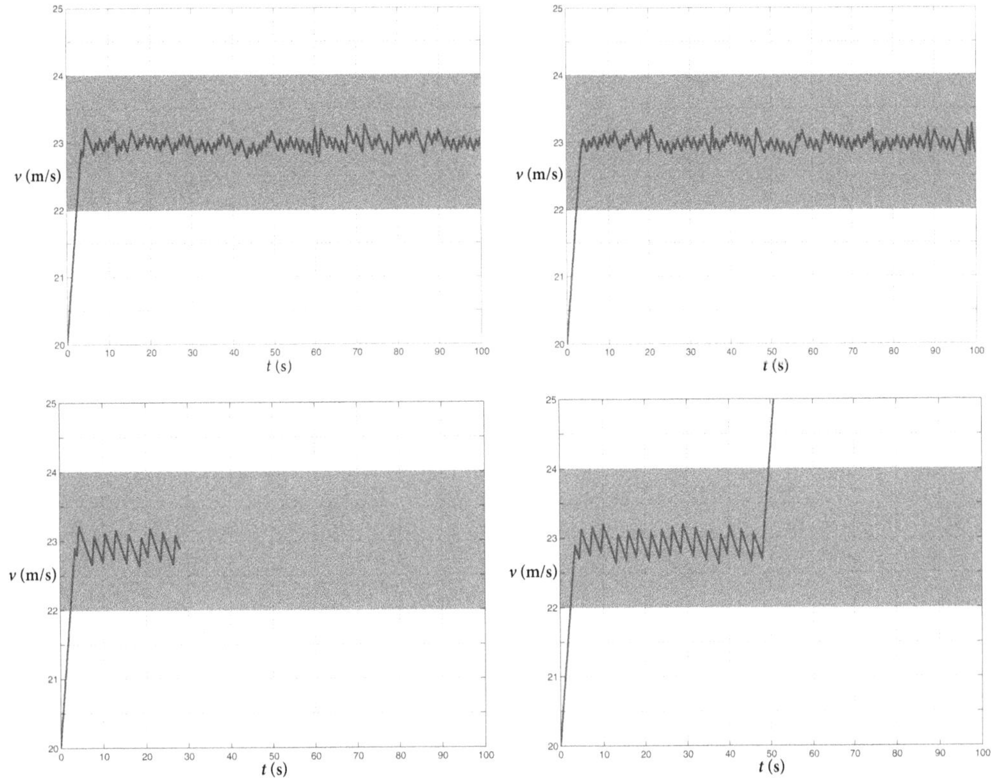

Figure 4: Simulation results for the cruise control example (11), where the system is subject to measurement errors bounded by $\varepsilon = 0.1$ and a delay in sensing, computation, and actuation bounded by $h = 0.01$. We use an $(\eta, \gamma_1, \gamma_2, \delta)$-abstraction (given by Definition 1) of (11) to synthesize a hybrid control strategy. The upper two figures show simulated trajectories generated by a controller synthesized using an $(\eta, \gamma_1, \gamma_2, \delta)$-abstraction with $\eta = 0.05$, $\gamma_1 = 0.1674$, $\gamma_2 = 0.15$, and $\delta = 0.5947$, where γ_i $(i = 1, 2)$ are used to account for measurement errors and delays as shown in Theorem 3. The grey band indicates the desired speed range [22, 24]. The delays and measurements are randomly generated, which clearly led to somewhat random trajectories as opposed to periodic ones. The lower two figures show what could happen if measurement errors and delays are not accounted for within the abstractions, where we have chosen $\gamma_1 = \gamma_2 = \eta = 0.05$, while δ is kept the same. The lower left figure shows a termination of simulation when the measured system state, due to uncertainties in measurements, is mapped to an unexpected discrete state in the controlling automaton. One may keep executing the previous control input if the measurement is unexpected, but this may lead to violation of system specification as shown in the lower right figure.

Another approach is to discretize the state space. This has been extensively used for constructing approximate symbolic models for control systems (see, e.g., [15, 18, 19, 21, 28]) based on the notion of approximate (bi)simulation [6]. In these approaches, a finite transition system model is constructed by discretizing the time, the input space, and the continuous state space. Under certain incremental stability assumptions, the resulting finite system can be shown to be approximately bisimilar to the time-discretized model of a continuous-time control system. The stability assumption can be relaxed [28] if one is interested in constructing simulations instead of bisimulations. The advantage of this approach is that it provides a quantitative measure of the fidelity of abstractions using metric transition systems. However in above mentioned papers, the approximation is between the finite abstraction and the time-discretized model of a continuous-time control system and it is unclear how to handle imperfect state information. In this paper we considered a discretization-based approach and addressed these shortcomings. In particular, we introduced abstractions with robustness margins to rigorously reason about the inter-sample behaviors and to account for imperfections in measurements and models.

The type of robustness considered in this paper is related to but distinct from that of [13, 24]. The focus of [13, 24] is on the design of discrete controllers for finite transition systems (namely, discrete synthesis) against unmodeled disturbances or transitions, whereas the current paper aims to establish robustness of discrete controllers against imperfect measurements and unmodeled dynamics in the continuous plants.

Our work is also related to control of hybrid systems with imperfect state information. In [10], the author considered stability of switched systems with limited information under slow switching. Limited information refers to the situation where the state measurements are taken only at sampling times and quantized using a finite alphabet. This is exactly how the hybrid controller is implemented in this paper: it takes measurements at sampling times, maps it to discrete states in the finite abstractions, and looks for appropriate control actions, based on an automaton that represents a discrete control strategy.

7. CONCLUSIONS

In this paper we presented a notion of abstractions with robustness margins and showed that it is possible to synthesize provably-correct robust feedback controllers based on such abstractions. This allows us to handle various types of imperfections in the models or measurements and to reason about implementation artifacts in a unified fashion. The idea can be naturally generalized to multi-scale abstractions where the abstract states are non-uniformly distributed around the continuous state space. Future work will include investigating such abstractions and combining them with automated refinement procedures to mitigate potential state explosion problem.

8. REFERENCES

[1] R. Alur, T. A. Henzinger, O. Kupferman, and M. Y. Vardi. Alternating refinement relations. In *Proc. International Conference on Concurrency Theory (CONCUR)*, pages 163–178, 1998.

[2] D. Angeli. A Lyapunov approach to incremental stability properties. *IEEE Trans. on Automatic Control*, 47(3):410–421, 2002.

[3] G. E. Fainekos, A. Girard, H. Kress-Gazit, and G. J. Pappas. Temporal logic motion planning for dynamic robots. *Automatica*, 45:343–352, 2009.

[4] G. E. Fainekos and G. J. Pappas. Robustness of temporal logic specifications for continuous-time signals. *Theoretical Computer Science*, 410(42):4262–4291, 2009.

[5] G. F. Franklin, M. L. Workman, and D. Powell. *Digital Control of Dynamic Systems*. Addison-Wesley Longman Publishing Co., Inc., 1997.

[6] A. Girard and G. Pappas. Approximation metrics for discrete and continuous systems. *IEEE Trans. on Automatic Control*, 52:782–798, 2007.

[7] S. Karaman and E. Frazzoli. Sampling-based algorithms for optimal motion planning with deterministic μ-calculus specifications. In *Proc. of American Control Conference (ACC)*, pages 735–742, 2012.

[8] M. Kloetzer and C. Belta. A fully automated framework for control of linear systems from temporal logic specifications. *IEEE Trans. Automatic Control*, 53:287–297, 2008.

[9] H. Kress-Gazit, G. E. Fainekos, and G. J. Pappas. Temporal-logic-based reactive mission and motion planning. *IEEE Trans. Robotics*, 25:1370–1381, 2009.

[10] D. Liberzon. Limited-information control of hybrid systems via reachable set propagation. In *Proc. of the 16th International Conference on Hybrid Systems: Computation and Control (HSCC)*, pages 11–20, 2013.

[11] J. Liu, N. Ozay, U. Topcu, and R. M. Murray. Synthesis of reactive switching protocols from temporal logic specifications. *IEEE Trans. on Automatic Control*, 58(7):1771–1785, 2013.

[12] J. Liu, U. Topcu, N. Ozay, and R. M. Murray. Reactive controllers for differentially flat systems with temporal logic constraints. In *Proc. of the 51st IEEE Conference on Decision and Control (CDC)*, pages 7664–7670, 2012.

[13] R. Majumdar, E. Render, and P. Tabuada. Robust discrete synthesis against unspecified disturbances. In *Proc. of the 14th International Conference on Hybrid Systems: Computation and Control (HSCC)*, pages 211–220, 2011.

[14] O. Mickelin, N. Ozay, and R. M. Murray. Synthesis of correct-by-construction control protocols for hybrid systems using partial state information. In *Proc. of American Control Conference (ACC)*, 2014.

[15] S. Mouelhi, A. Girard, and G. Gössler. Cosyma: a tool for controller synthesis using multi-scale abstractions. In *Proc. of the 16th International Conference on Hybrid Systems: Computation and Control (HSCC)*, pages 83–88, 2013.

[16] G. Orosz and S. P. Shah. A nonlinear modeling framework for autonomous cruise control. In *Proc. of ASME Annual Dynamic Systems and Control Conference joint with JSME Motion & Vibration Conference*, pages 467–471, 2012.

[17] N. Ozay, J. Liu, P. Prabhakar, and R. M. Murray. Computing augmented finite transition systems to synthesize switching protocols for polynomial switched systems. In *Proc. of American Control Conference (ACC)*, 2013.

[18] G. Pola, P. Pepe, M. D. Di Benedetto, and P. Tabuada. Symbolic models for nonlinear time-delay systems using approximate bisimulations. *Systems & Control Letters*, 59(6):365–373, 2010.

[19] G. Pola and P. Tabuada. Symbolic models for nonlinear control systems: Alternating approximate bisimulations. *SIAM J. Control Optim.*, 48:719–733, 2009.

[20] G. Reiszig. Computing abstractions of nonlinear systems. *IEEE Trans. Automatic Control*, 56:2583–2598, 2011.

[21] P. Tabuada. *Verification and Control of Hybrid Systems: A Symbolic Approach*. Springer, 2009.

[22] P. Tabuada and G. J. Pappas. Linear time logic control of discrete-time linear systems. *IEEE Trans. Automatic Control*, 51:1862–1877, 2006.

[23] Y. Tazaki and J. Imura. Discrete abstractions of nonlinear systems based on error propagation analysis. *IEEE Trans. Automatic Control*, 57:550–564, 2012.

[24] U. Topcu, N. Ozay, J. Liu, and R. M. Murray. On synthesizing robust discrete controllers under modeling uncertainty. In *Proc. of the 15th ACM International Conference on Hybrid Systems: Computation and Control (HSCC)*, pages 85–94, 2012.

[25] E. M. Wolff and R. M. Murray. Optimal control of nonlinear systems with temporal logic specifications. In *Proc. of the International Symposium on Robotics Research (ISRR)*, 2013.

[26] T. Wongpiromsarn, U. Topcu, and R. M. Murray. Receding horizon temporal logic planning. *IEEE Trans. Automatic Control*, 57:2817–2830, 2012.

[27] T. Wongpiromsarn, U. Topcu, N. Ozay, H. Xu, and R. M. Murray. TuLiP: a software toolbox for receding horizon temporal logic planning. In *Proc. of the 14th International Conference on Hybrid Systems: Computation and Control (HSCC)*, 2011.

[28] M. Zamani, G. Pola, M. Mazo Jr, and P. Tabuada. Symbolic models for nonlinear control systems without stability assumptions. *IEEE Trans. Automatic Control*, 57:1804–1809, 2012.

Edit Distance for Timed Automata*

Krishnendu Chatterjee
IST Austria

Rasmus Ibsen-Jensen
IST Austria

Rupak Majumdar
MPI-SWS

ABSTRACT

The edit distance between two (untimed) traces is the minimum cost of a sequence of edit operations (insertion, deletion, or substitution) needed to transform one trace to the other. Edit distances have been extensively studied in the untimed setting, and form the basis for approximate matching of sequences in different domains such as coding theory, parsing, and speech recognition.

In this paper, we lift the study of edit distances from untimed languages to the timed setting. We define an edit distance between timed words which incorporates both the edit distance between the untimed words and the absolute difference in time stamps. Our edit distance between two timed words is computable in polynomial time. Further, we show that the edit distance between a timed word and a timed language generated by a timed automaton, defined as the edit distance between the word and the closest word in the language, is PSPACE-complete. While computing the edit distance between two timed automata is undecidable, we show that the approximate version, where we decide if the edit distance between two timed automata is either less than a given parameter or more than δ away from the parameter, for $\delta > 0$, can be solved in exponential space and is EXPSPACE-hard. Our definitions and techniques can be generalized to the setting of hybrid systems, and analogous decidability results hold for rectangular automata.

Categories and Subject Descriptors

F.4.1 [**MATHEMATICAL LOGIC AND FORMAL LANGUAGES**]: Mathematical Logic-Computability Theory

General Terms

Verification, Theory, Algorithms

Keywords

Timed automata; Edit distance; Rectangular hybrid automata

*This research was supported by Austrian Science Fund (FWF) Grant No P23499- N23, FWF NFN Grant No S11407-N23 (RiSE), ERC Start grant (279307: Graph Games), Microsoft Faculty Fellowship Award, and a grant from Toyota Motors North America.

HSCC'14, April 15–17, 2014, Berlin, Germany.

ACM 978-1-4503-2732-9/14/04 ...$15.00.
http://dx.doi.org/10.1145/2562059.2562141.

1. INTRODUCTION

The edit distance [13] between two strings is the minimum cost of a sequence of edit operations (insertion, deletion, or substitution of one letter by another) that transforms one string to another. The edit distance between a string w and a language L is the minimal distance between strings belonging to L and w. The notion of *edit distance* provides a quantitative measure of "how far" one string is from another, or from a given language. It forms the basis for approximately comparing sequences, a problem that arises in many different areas, such as error-correcting codes, natural language processing, and computational biology.

Algorithms for edit distance have been studied extensively for (untimed) words [13, 1, 15, 17, 12, 14]. In this paper, we generalize the definition of edit distance from untimed to timed words. We define the edit distance between two timed words tw and tw$'$ as the lexico-graphic ordering of two components: the first is the (normal) edit distance on their untimed parts, and the second is the maximum difference in time stamps.[1] We study algorithmic aspects of the edit distance between timed words and timed languages. We show that the edit distance between two timed words can be computed in polynomial time. Moreover, we show that the edit distance between a timed word and a timed language generated by a timed automaton can be computed in polynomial space. The corresponding decision problem is PSPACE-complete. A nice by-product of our result is that the edit distance problem for an untimed word and untimed non-deterministic finite-state automaton (NFA) is NL-complete (complete for non-deterministic log-space). The best, previous known upper bound is polynomial time [19].

One can generalize edit distances to capture the distance between two languages: the edit distance between L_1 and L_2 is the supremum over all strings w in L_1 of the edit distance between w and L_2. We show that the edit distance between two timed languages generated by timed automata is not computable. However, we show that the approximate version of the problem, where we ask if the edit distance is either less than α or more than $\alpha+\delta$ for an additive error $\delta > 0$, can be solved in exponential space, and is EXPSPACE-hard.

Our results use the following technical constructions. For the computation of edit distance between a timed word and a timed automaton, we construct two timed automata which are polynomial in the size of the input automaton, and show that the decision problem for edit distance reduces to checking non-emptiness of the constructed automata. The key intuition is to use non-determinism in the timed automata to model edits in the word, and use additional clocks with rectangular constraints to bound the mismatch in time stamps. For the computation of the approximation of edit distance between two timed automata, we generalize the approach for com-

[1] While we focus on this definition, we show that several related definitions have similar algorithmic properties.

putation of edit distance between two untimed automata [3]. The algorithm uses the classical region abstraction, but requires non-trivial generalization of the untimed case [3] to capture the quantitative timing aspects.

Besides intellectual curiosity, our definition and algorithmic computation of edit distances between timed words and timed languages form the foundations of a quantitative approach to timed verification. The calculation of timed edit distance is the basis for *repairing* timed specifications, generalizing the untimed case [3], and for providing robust semantics to timed automata and timed logics [8, 7]. For example, in simulation-based verification of a real-time implementation against a timed automaton model, the simulation trace may differ slightly from the model due to inaccuracies in the implementation and errors in measuring the timing behavior. Thus, a timed trace of the implementation may not be in the model. However, instead of rejecting the implementation, one can quantify the distance between a measured trace and the model. Quantitative semantics for timed and hybrid logics have been the basis for some recent verification tools [9, 6]. Our work can be seen as providing a quantitative semantics for timed automaton models.

Finally, while we focus on timed systems, we sketch how our definitions and algorithmic techniques extend to hybrid automata, with EXPTIME algorithms for the edit distance between a hybrid trace and a rectangular hybrid automaton, and 2EXPTIME algorithm for the approximate distance between two rectangular automata.

2. DEFINITIONS

In this section we first present the basic definition of timed automata, and then the notion of edit distance for them.

2.1 Timed Automata

Timed automata [2] suggest a finite syntax for specifying finite-state automata with real-valued clocks. We first start with the notion of clock constraints.

Clock constraints. For a set X of clock variables, the set $\Phi(X)$ of *clock constraints* ψ is defined inductively by

$$\psi := x \leq d \mid d \leq x \mid \neg\psi \mid \psi_1 \wedge \psi_2,$$

where x is a clock in X and d is a constant in natural numbers.

Timed automata. A *timed automaton* $\mathcal{A}$ over finite words is a tuple $\langle L, \Sigma, C, \rightarrow, \gamma, S_0, F\rangle$, where

- L is a finite set of locations.
- Σ is a finite input alphabet.
- C is a finite set of clocks.
- $\rightarrow \subseteq L \times L \times \Sigma \times 2^C \times \Phi(C)$ gives the set of transitions, where $\Phi(C)$ is the set of clock constraints over C. An edge $(\ell, \ell', \sigma, \lambda, \psi)$ represents a transition from location ℓ to location ℓ' on input letter σ, $\lambda \subseteq C$ represents the set of clocks to be reset with the transition and ψ is a clock constraint over C.
- $\gamma : L \mapsto \Phi(C)$ is a function that assigns to every location an invariant on clock valuations. All clocks increase uniformly at the same rate. When at location ℓ, a valid execution must move out of ℓ before the invariant $\gamma(\ell)$ expires. Thus, the timed automaton can stay at a location only as long as the invariant is satisfied by the clock values.
- $S_0 \subseteq L \times \mathbb{R}_+^{|C|}$ is the set of initial states.
- $F \subseteq L$ is a finite set of accepting locations.

Each clock increases at rate 1 inside a location. A *clock valuation* is a function $\kappa : C \mapsto \mathbb{R}_{\geq 0}$ that maps every clock to a non-negative real. The set of all clock valuations for C is denoted by $K(C)$. Given a clock valuation $\kappa \in K(C)$ and a time delay $\Delta \in \mathbb{R}_{\geq 0}$, we write $\kappa + \Delta$ for the clock valuation in $K(C)$ defined by $(\kappa + \Delta)(x) = \kappa(x) + \Delta$ for all clocks $x \in C$. For a subset $\lambda \subseteq C$ of the clocks, we write $\kappa[\lambda := 0]$ for the clock valuation in $K(C)$ defined by $(\kappa[\lambda := 0])(x) = 0$ if $x \in \lambda$, and $(\kappa[\lambda := 0])(x) = \kappa(x)$ if $x \notin \lambda$. A clock valuation $\kappa \in K(C)$ *satisfies* the clock constraint θ, written $\kappa \models \theta$, if the condition θ holds when all clocks in C take on the values specified by κ. A *state* $s = \langle \ell, \kappa\rangle$ of the timed automaton $\mathcal{A}$ is a location $\ell \in L$ together with a clock valuation $\kappa \in K(C)$ such that the invariant at the location is satisfied, that is, $\kappa \models \gamma(\ell)$. We let S be the set of all states of $\mathcal{A}$. The semantics of timed automata are given as timed transition systems, which is standard [2], and omitted here.

Timed and untimed words. An *untimed word* $w \in \Sigma^*$ is a finite sequence of input letters, and a *timed word* $\mathrm{tw} \in (\Sigma \times \mathbb{R})^*$ is a finite sequence of input letters and time stamps such that the time stamps are non-decreasing. Equivalently a timed word $\mathrm{tw} = (w, \bar{t})$ can be considered as a pair of sequences, where the first sequence $w = (\sigma_1, \sigma_2, \ldots, \sigma_n)$ is the sequence of letters (i.e., the untimed word corresponding to tw), and the second sequence is the corresponding time stamps $\bar{t} = (t_1, t_2, \ldots, t_n)$, and we require that for all $1 \leq i \leq n-1$ we have $t_i \leq t_{i+1}$. The *length* of a timed word tw is the number of letters in it, i.e., the length of the untimed word.

Language of timed automata. A timed word tw induces a set of runs over a timed automaton (see [2] for the standard semantics of runs). A word tw is accepted by an automaton $\mathcal{A}$ if there exists a run that ends in an accepting location. For a timed automaton $\mathcal{A}$ we denote by $\mathcal{L}(\mathcal{A})$ the set of timed words accepted by $\mathcal{A}$.

Clock region equivalence. Clock region equivalence, denoted as $\cong$ is an equivalence relation on states of timed automata. The equivalence classes of the relation are called *regions*, and induce a time abstract bisimulation on the corresponding timed transition system [2]. There are finitely many clock regions; more precisely, the number of clock regions is bounded by $|L| \cdot \prod_{x \in C}(c_x + 1) \cdot |C|! \cdot 4^{|C|}$. For a real $t \geq 0$, let $\mathsf{frac}(t) = t - \lfloor t \rfloor$ denote the fractional part of t. Given a timed automaton $\mathcal{A}$, for each clock $x \in C$, let c_x denote the largest integer constant that appears in any clock constraint involving x in $\mathcal{A}$ (let $c_x = 1$ if there is no clock constraint involving x). Two states $\langle \ell_1, \kappa_1\rangle$ and $\langle \ell_2, \kappa_2\rangle$ are said to be *region equivalent* if all the following conditions are satisfied: (a) $\ell_1 = \ell_2$, (b) for all clocks x, we have $\kappa_1(x) \leq c_x$ iff $\kappa_2(x) \leq c_x$, (c) for all clocks x with $\kappa_1(x) \leq c_x$, we have $\lfloor \kappa_1(x) \rfloor = \lfloor \kappa_2(x) \rfloor$, (d) for all clocks x, y with $\kappa_1(x) \leq c_x$ and $\kappa_1(y) \leq c_y$, we have $\mathsf{frac}(\kappa_1(x)) \leq \mathsf{frac}(\kappa_1(y))$ iff $\mathsf{frac}(\kappa_2(x)) \leq \mathsf{frac}(\kappa_2(y))$, and (e) for all clocks x with $\kappa_1(x) \leq c_x$, we have $\mathsf{frac}(\kappa_1(x)) = 0$ iff $\mathsf{frac}(\kappa_2(x)) = 0$. Given a state $\langle \ell, \kappa\rangle$ of $\mathcal{A}$, we denote the region containing $\langle \ell, \kappa\rangle$ as $\mathsf{Reg}(\langle \ell, \kappa\rangle)$.

Region graph. The region graph $\mathsf{Reg}(\mathcal{A})$ corresponding to a timed automaton $\mathcal{A}$ is the time-abstract bisimulation quotient graph induced by the region equivalence relation. The states of $\mathsf{Reg}(\mathcal{A})$ are the regions of $\mathcal{A}$. In the region graph, for regions R and R', there exists a transition $R \rightarrow R'$ iff there exists $s \in R$ and $s' \in R'$ such that there exists a transition from s to s' in the timed automaton. We denote by $|\mathsf{Reg}(\mathcal{A})|$ the number of states in the region graph, which is bounded by $|C|! \cdot 4^{|C|} \cdot (c_{\max} + 1)^{|C|} \cdot |L|$, where C is the set of clocks, $c_{\max}$ the largest constant in the clock constraints, and $|L|$ is the number of locations.

2.2 Edit distance

In this section we first recall the notion of edit distance for untimed words, and then introduce the definition of edit distance for timed words. Finally we present the definition of edit distance between a timed word and a timed automaton, and between two timed automata.

Edit distance between untimed words. Consider a pair of untimed words w and w'. A *word edit* WE from w to w' is a finite sequence of some deletions, substitutions, and insertions of letters into w such that the sequence of transformations changes w to w'. We denote by $\mathsf{WE}(w,w')$ the set of word edits from w to w', and by $\mathrm{Opt}(w,w')$ the set of optimal word edits between w and w', i.e., $\mathrm{Opt}(w,w')$ is the subset of $\mathsf{WE}(w,w')$ such that every sequence in $\mathrm{Opt}(w,w')$ has the minimal length among the sequences in $\mathsf{WE}(w,w')$. The *edit-distance* $\mathcal{D}(w,w')$ is the minimum number of edits required to transform w to w', i.e., the length of a sequence in $\mathrm{Opt}(w,w')$. A word edit WE is *optimal* if it belongs to $\mathrm{Opt}(w,w')$. Given a word edit WE, we say that the i-th index of w is *retained* if the i-th letter w_i was not deleted by the deletions of WE nor substituted by the substitutions of WE. Also, we say that the i-th index of w *corresponds* to the j-th index of w' if i was retained and there was $j-i$ insertions minus deletions in WE before the i-th index. Note that if index i is retained, there is always some j such that i corresponds to j. Also note that for any index j, there is at most one index i such that index i corresponds to index j.

Informal description. Informally, the edit distance between two timed words is a pair, where the first component is the edit distance between the untimed words, and the second component is the absolute maximal time mismatch. We illustrate with some examples the definition for edit distance between timed words. First consider two timed words where the untimed parts match, i.e., $\mathrm{tw}=(w,\bar{t})$ and $\mathrm{tw}'=(w,\bar{t}')$. Then the first component of the edit distance is 0 and the second component is the absolute maximal mismatch in the timing. Now, consider two timed words $\mathrm{tw}=(w,\bar{t})$, where $w=abcd$ and $\bar{t}=(1,2,3,4)$, and $\mathrm{tw}'=(w',\bar{t}')$ where $w'=abbcd$ and $\bar{t}'=(1,2,2,4,4)$. We first extend the timed word tw to a timed word $\mathrm{tw}''=(w'',\bar{t}'')$ such that $w''=w'$ and the time sequences in $\bar{t}''$ match the ones of $\bar{t}$ for the occurrences that match in w and w''. For example, an extension of tw is $w''=abbcd$ and $\bar{t}''=(1,2,2,3,4)$. Thus the first component of the edit distance is 1, and the second component is also 1.

Extension of timed words. Given a pair of timed words $\mathrm{tw}=(w,\bar{t})$ and $\mathrm{tw}'=(w',\bar{t}')$, we first consider the corresponding untimed words w and w'. Given a word edit WE between w and w', the timed word tw can be *extended* to tw' by WE if for each pair of indices i,j, such that index i of w corresponds to index j of w' under WE, we have that $t_i=t'_j$. In other words, the word edit creates a word whose untimed word matches with w' and the time stamps corresponding to the letters in w match with the time stamps in w. Given a timed word tw, a word w', and a word edit WE between w and w', let $\mathrm{Ext}(\mathrm{tw},w',\mathsf{WE})$ be the set of timed words tw' such that tw can be extended to tw' by WE.

Edit distance between timed words. Let $(a_1,b_1)\in\mathbb{R}^2$ and $(a_2,b_2)\in\mathbb{R}^2$ be two pairs of real numbers, then the *lexico-graphic* ordering $\leq_{\mathsf{lex}}$ and $<_{\mathsf{lex}}$ is defined as follows:

$$(a_1,b_1)\leq_{\mathsf{lex}}(a_2,b_2)\quad\text{iff}\quad(a_1<a_2)\vee(a_1=a_2\wedge b_1\leq b_2);$$

$$(a_1,b_1)<_{\mathsf{lex}}(a_2,b_2)\quad\text{iff}\quad(a_1<a_2)\vee(a_1=a_2\wedge b_1<b_2);$$

and we use similar notations for $\geq_{\mathsf{lex}}$ and $>_{\mathsf{lex}}$. The edit distance for timed words has two components, the first component is the number of edits for the untimed word, and the second component is the maximal mismatch in the time stamps. We consider edit distance between timed words where we consider the lexico-graphic ordering of the two components, i.e., edits to discrete transitions are more costly. Formally, the edit distance $\mathcal{D}(\mathrm{tw},\mathrm{tw}')$ between two timed words is defined as follows, where $\mathcal{D}_1(\mathrm{tw},\mathrm{tw}')$ and $\mathcal{D}_2(\mathrm{tw},\mathrm{tw}')$ are the first and second component, respectively:

1. For a pair of timed words $\mathrm{tw}=(w,\bar{t})$ and $\mathrm{tw}'=(w',\bar{t}')$ of length n, such that $w=w'$, the first component of the edit distance is 0 and the second component $\mathcal{D}_2(\mathrm{tw},\mathrm{tw}')$ is defined as follows:

$$\mathcal{D}_2(\mathrm{tw},\mathrm{tw}')=\max_{1\leq i\leq n}|t_i-t'_i|\ .$$

2. For a pair of timed words $\mathrm{tw}=(w,\bar{t})$ and $\mathrm{tw}'=(w',\bar{t}')$ such that $w\neq w'$ we have $\mathcal{D}_1(\mathrm{tw},\mathrm{tw}')=\mathcal{D}(w,w')$, i.e., the first component is the edit distance of the untimed words. For the second component we first consider the extension of tw and then compute the second component. Formally,

$$\mathcal{D}_2(\mathrm{tw},\mathrm{tw}')=\inf_{\substack{\mathsf{WE}\in\mathrm{Opt}(w,w')\text{ and },\\ \mathrm{tw}''\in\mathrm{Ext}(\mathrm{tw},w',\mathsf{WE})}}\mathcal{D}_2(\mathrm{tw}'',\mathrm{tw}')\ .$$

Note that above we have that the untimed part of tw'' and tw' coincide and hence we apply the definition of the first item above where the untimed parts coincide. Intuitively, we first pick some optimal word edit for the untimed word, and then extend the first word under this word edit, and then compute the second component. Finally, among all the choices we consider the one that minimizes the second component.

PROPOSITION 1 (COMPUTATION OF EDIT DISTANCE). *Given two timed words* tw *and* tw' *the edit distance* $\mathcal{D}(\mathrm{tw},\mathrm{tw}')$ *can be computed in polynomial time.*

PROOF. It is straightforward to find the edit distance between two timed words tw, tw' in polynomial time, and we describe the main ideas below. The first component is computed simply running the classical dynamic programming algorithm of [20] on the untimed words. Given a bound β on the second component, the standard dynamic programming algorithm of [20] is modified to ensure that for all i,j, the i-th character of tw matches the j-th character of tw' iff they use the same letter and the difference between the time stamps is at most β. It is also clear that there are at most $|\mathrm{tw}|\cdot|\mathrm{tw}'|$ different "possible" values for β: the difference between each pair of time stamps (except in the case where no letter match, in which case the value of β is 0). By simply using a binary search algorithm over the possible choices, we get an algorithm with a running time of $O(|\mathrm{tw}|\cdot|\mathrm{tw}'|\cdot\log(|\mathrm{tw}|\cdot|\mathrm{tw}'|))$. □

Edit distance of timed words and timed automata, and between pairs of timed automata. Consider a pair of timed automata $\mathcal{A}$ and $\mathcal{A}'$, and a timed word tw. The edit distance between the pair of automata, and between the timed word and the automaton $\mathcal{A}$ is defined as follows:

1. For the timed word tw and the timed automaton $\mathcal{A}$, the edit distance $\mathcal{D}(\mathrm{tw},\mathcal{A})$ is $\inf_{\mathrm{tw}'\in\mathcal{L}(\mathcal{A})}\mathcal{D}(\mathrm{tw},\mathrm{tw}')$, i.e., the edit distance is the minimal edit distance among all words accepted by the automaton $\mathcal{A}$. Also note that we consider the lexico-graphic ordering to compare the edit distance which consists of a pair of numbers.

2. For the pair of timed automata $\mathcal{A}, \mathcal{A}'$, the edit distance $\mathcal{D}(\mathcal{A}, \mathcal{A}')$ is $\sup_{\mathrm{tw} \in \mathcal{L}(\mathcal{A})} \mathcal{D}(\mathrm{tw}, \mathcal{A}')$, i.e., it is the maximal edit distance between a word in the language of $\mathcal{A}$ to the automaton $\mathcal{A}'$.

3. EDIT DISTANCE BETWEEN A TIMED WORD AND A TIMED AUTOMATON

In this section we consider the edit-distance problem between a timed word and a timed automaton. We show that the problem is PSPACE-complete. We first define the decision problem and start with the lower bound.

Decision problem for edit distance between a timed word and a timed automaton. The *edit-distance decision* problem $\mathsf{EdDec}(\alpha, \beta, \mathrm{tw}, \mathcal{A})$ is as follows: given a non-negative integer α, a number $\beta \in \mathbb{Q} \cup \{\infty\}$, where $\mathbb{Q}$ is the set of rationals, a timed word tw, and a timed automaton $\mathcal{A}$, the decision problem asks whether the edit distance $\mathcal{D}(\mathrm{tw}, \mathcal{A}) \leq_{\mathsf{lex}} (\alpha, \beta)$? In the sequel we always consider $\alpha \in \mathbb{N}$ and $\beta \in \mathbb{Q} \cup \{\infty\}$ such that β is non-negative.

LEMMA 2 (PSPACE LOWER BOUND). *The edit-distance decision problem* $\mathsf{EdDec}(\alpha, \beta, \mathrm{tw}, \mathcal{A})$ *is PSPACE-hard.*

PROOF. Since the reachability problem for timed automata is PSPACE-hard [2], it follows that the non-emptiness question for timed automata (i.e., given a timed automaton $\mathcal{A}$, whether $\mathcal{L}(\mathcal{A})$ is non-empty) is also PSPACE-hard. If the language $\mathcal{L}(\mathcal{A})$ for a timed automaton $\mathcal{A}$ is non-empty, then it accepts a timed word of length say at most d^* (d^* is at most exponential in the size of $\mathcal{A}$ and linear in the size of the region graph). Then the answer to the question $\mathsf{EdDec}(d^* + 1, 0, \epsilon, \mathcal{A})$ is YES iff $\mathcal{L}(\mathcal{A})$ is non-empty, where ϵ is the empty word. The PSPACE lower bound follows. □

PSPACE upper bound. The rest of the section is devoted to presenting a PSPACE upper bound for the edit-distance decision problem $\mathsf{EdDec}(\alpha, \beta, \mathrm{tw}, \mathcal{A})$.

Bound on the components of the edit distance. We start with a bound on the components of the edit distance.

1. *(Bound on the first component).* For a given timed automaton $\mathcal{A}$, if $\mathcal{L}(\mathcal{A})$ is not empty, then as mentioned above $\mathcal{A}$ accepts a word of length at most exponential in the size of the automaton (at most the size of the region graph). Hence the first component of the edit distance between a timed word tw and a timed automaton $\mathcal{A}$ is at most $\max(|\mathrm{tw}|, d)$, where $|\mathrm{tw}|$ is the length of the timed word and d the length of the shortest word in $\mathcal{L}(\mathcal{A})$.

2. *(Bound on the second component).* If the first component is bounded by α, then the second component can be at most $\max\left((|\mathrm{tw}| + \alpha) \cdot c_{\max}, t_{|\mathrm{tw}|}\right)$, where $c_{\max}$ is the greatest number appearing in a clock constraint and $t_{|\mathrm{tw}|}$ is the last time stamp in tw. This is because any run in $\mathcal{A}$ that ensures that the first component is at most α cannot be longer than $(|\mathrm{tw}|+\alpha)$ and we can bound the wait in each move by $c_{\max}$.

PSPACE algorithm. We now give an algorithm which solves the decision problem $\mathsf{EdDec}(\alpha, \beta, \mathrm{tw}, \mathcal{A})$ in polynomial space. We refer to our algorithm as $\textsc{SolEd}(\alpha, \beta, \mathrm{tw}, \mathcal{A})$. Given α, β, tw, and $\mathcal{A}$, we construct two timed automata $\mathcal{A}'$ and $\mathcal{A}''$ and return NO iff $\mathcal{L}(\mathcal{A}')$ and $\mathcal{L}(\mathcal{A}'')$ are both empty, i.e., if either of the automata has a non-empty language, then the answer to the edit-distance decision problem is YES. The construction of $\mathcal{A}''$ given α, β, tw, and $\mathcal{A}$, is the same as the construction of $\mathcal{A}'$ given $\alpha - 1, \infty$, tw and $\mathcal{A}$, and thus we only explicitly give the construction of $\mathcal{A}'$.

Construction of $\mathcal{A}'$ given α, β, tw, and $\mathcal{A}$. The construction of $\mathcal{A}'$ given α, β, tw, and $\mathcal{A}$, is as follows:

1. *(Locations).* The timed automaton $\mathcal{A}'$ contains $(|\mathrm{tw}| + 1) \cdot (\alpha + 1)$ copies of $\mathcal{A}$, each location in each copy is annotated with a pair of integers (j, k), where $0 \leq j \leq |\mathrm{tw}|$ and $0 \leq k \leq \alpha$, where j corresponds to how far the timed word tw has been processed, and k to the number of edits that have been made. The location corresponding to location ℓ in $\mathcal{A}$, annotated with (j, k) is location (ℓ, j, k) in $\mathcal{A}'$. Furthermore there is a location err from which no accepting location can be reached, and corresponds to the fact that more than α edits have been made (i.e., the target on the edit distance has been exceeded).

2. *(Accepting locations).* The only accepting locations in the automaton $\mathcal{A}'$ are the locations in the copies of $\mathcal{A}$, which are annotated with $(|\mathrm{tw}|, k)$ for some k and which correspond to accepting locations of $\mathcal{A}$.

3. *(Clocks).* The set of clocks C' in $\mathcal{A}'$ is C, the set of clocks in $\mathcal{A}$, together with the two additional clocks $\{\mathsf{x}, \mathsf{x}'\}$. The clock x measures the total time used and the clock x' measures the time used in the current location. Hence, x is never reset and x' is reset in every transition.

4. *(Transitions).* The location (ℓ, j, k) has up to $3 \cdot d + 1$ transitions, where d is the number of transitions in location ℓ of $\mathcal{A}$. Each transition from ℓ to ℓ' in $\mathcal{A}$ is copied three times and there is also at most one more transition t. The transition t exists iff $j \neq |\mathrm{tw}|$. If transition t exists, it resets the clock x' (though this is not necessary, but makes it conceptually easier to follow), uses the letter w_{j+1}, and has a clock constraint of $\mathsf{x}' = 0$. That is, it can only be used if no time has passed since arriving in (ℓ, j, k). The transition goes to $(\ell, j + 1, k + 1)$ (the transition t models *insertions* of the next letter). For a fixed transition t' between ℓ and ℓ' in $\mathcal{A}$, the three copies of it from (ℓ, j, k) each resets the same clocks as t', but also the clock x' and otherwise are as follows:

   (a) The first copy has the same clock constraint as t' but goes to location $(\ell', j, k+1)$, if $k < \alpha$ or err otherwise and has the letter ϵ (this copy corresponds to *deletion* of the current letter).

   (b) The second copy only exists if $j < |\mathrm{tw}|$. The second copy (if it exists) also has the same clock constraint as t' but goes to location $(\ell', j + 1, k + 1)$, if $j < \alpha$ or err otherwise and has the letter w_{j+1} (this copy corresponds to *substitution* of the current letter).

   (c) The third copy also only exists if $j < |\mathrm{tw}|$ and that t' is a w_{j+1}-transition. The third copy (if it exists) has the clock constraint $\mathcal{G}(t') \wedge (\mathsf{x} \in [t_{j+1} - \beta; t_{j+1} + \beta])$, where $\mathcal{G}(t')$ is the clock constraint of t' (the clock constraint is the same as for t' if $\beta = \infty$) and goes to location $(\ell, j+1, k)$ and has letter w_{j+1} (this copy corresponds to *no edit* having been made with the current letter).

Intuitively, the transition t' checks for insertions, the first two copies of the transition check for deletions and substitutions, and the final copy of the transition checks for a correct move (i.e., no edits).

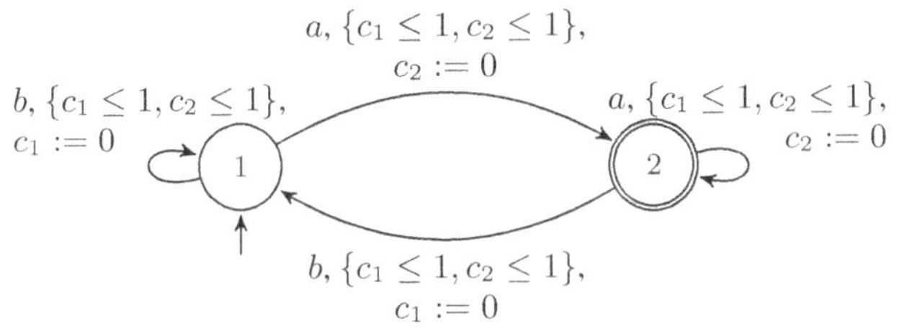

Figure 1: Example automaton $\mathcal{A}$.

5. *(Invariant).* The invariant at location (ℓ, j, k) is the same as in location ℓ.

Before the correctness argument and complexity analysis we first present an example for illustration.

Example. Consider the timed automaton $\mathcal{A}$ for the timed language over a, b which (i) ends in a; and (ii) in which there is a difference in time of at most 1 between each consecutive a's and between each consecutive b's; and (iii) the first move has a delay of at most 1. The automaton consists of two locations, 1 and 2, location 1 is the start location and location 2 is the accepting location. There are two clocks in the automaton c_1 and c_2. The automaton contains four transitions, and each transition has clock constraint $c_1 \leq 1$ and $c_2 \leq 1$. From location j there are two outgoing transitions t_1^j and t_2^j. The transition t_1^j goes to location 1, resets clock c_1, and uses letter b. The transition t_2^j goes to location 2, resets clock c_2, and uses letter a. A pictorial illustration is given in Figure 1.

We then consider the decision problem $\mathsf{EdDec}(1, 1, \mathrm{tw}, \mathcal{A})$, where $\mathrm{tw} = ((a, 2), (b, 3))$. There is an illustration of the timed automaton $\mathcal{A}'$ corresponding to $\mathsf{EdDec}(1, 1, \mathrm{tw}, \mathcal{A})$ in Figure 2. For the sake of readability, we have removed the unreachable locations (which are location $(2, 0, 0)$, location $(1, 1, 0)$ and location $(2, 2, 0)$) in the figure, and instead of annotating the transitions with the letter, clock constraints and resets, we have annotated them only with letters in $\{N, D, I, S\}$, corresponding to a no-edit-transition, a deletion-transition, an insertion-transition, or a substitution-transition, respectively. Note that if there are multiple letters on an edge, then there is a copy of each transition in $\mathcal{A}'$, between the designated locations for each letter.

We see that there are only three paths in the graph of Figure 2 that reaches an accepting location from the start location. The paths correspond to the timed words described below:

1. The sequence N, I which gives the run $(1, 0, 0) \rightarrow (2, 1, 0) \rightarrow (2, 2, 1)$. This sequence corresponds to the timed word $(a, 1)$ in $\mathcal{A}$, which has an edit distance of $(1, 1)$ from $(a, 2), (b, 3)$ (by inserting $(b, 3)$). This timed word is in $\mathcal{A}'$.

2. The sequence N, S which also gives the run $(1, 0, 0) \rightarrow (2, 1, 0) \rightarrow (2, 2, 1)$. This sequence corresponds to the timed word $(a, 1), (a, z)$ in $\mathcal{A}$ for some $z \geq 1$, which has an edit distance of $(1, 1)$ from $(a, 2), (b, 3)$ (by substituting (a, z) with $(b, 3)$). This timed word is in $\mathcal{A}'$.

3. The sequence N, N, D which gives the run $(1, 0, 0) \rightarrow (2, 1, 0) \rightarrow (1, 2, 0) \rightarrow (2, 2, 1)$. This sequence does not correspond to any run in $\mathcal{A}'$: the requirements on the first no-edit-transition is that $c_1 \leq 1, c_2 \leq 1, \mathsf{x} \in [2-1; 2+1]$ (which can only be satisfied by waiting one time unit in the start location), followed by a reset of c_2; and the requirement on the second no-edit-transition is that $c_1 \leq 1, c_2 \leq 1, \mathsf{x} \in [3-1; 3+1]$, but this cannot be satisfied, because $c_1 = \mathsf{x} = 1$ at the start location and any positive amount of waiting will ensure that we violate $c_1 \leq 1$, but we must wait at least one time unit before $\mathsf{x} \in [3-1; 3+1]$. Note that if we considered the decision problem $\mathsf{EdDec}(1, 2, \mathrm{tw}, \mathcal{A})$ instead, then there is such a run, e.g. $(a, 1), (b, 1), (a, 2)$ in $\mathcal{A}'$ and the word $(a, 1), (b, 1), (a, 2)$ has an edit distance of $(1, 2)$ from $(a, 2), (b, 3)$.

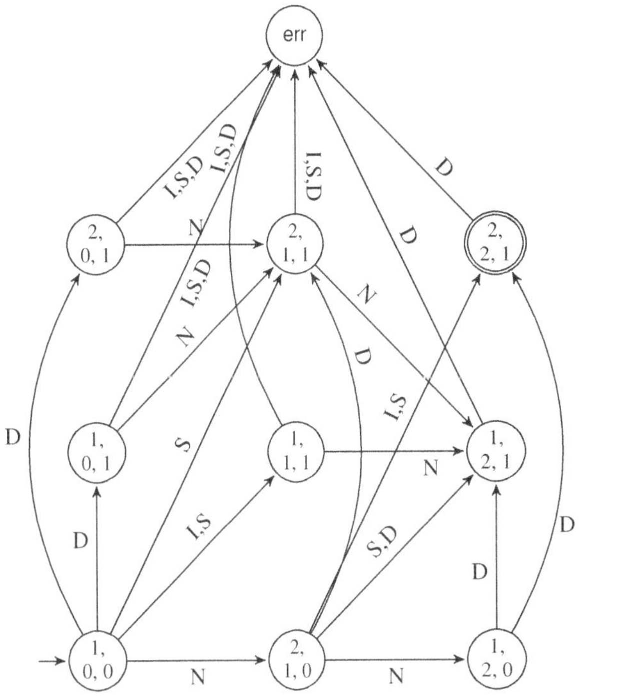

Figure 2: The automaton $\mathcal{A}'$ constructed from the timed automaton $\mathcal{A}$ in Figure 1.

We now establish the correctness of the reduction and then analyse the complexity.

LEMMA 3 (CORRECTNESS ARGUMENT). *The algorithm* $\textsc{SolEd}(\alpha, \beta, \mathrm{tw}, \mathcal{A})$ *correctly solves the decision problem* $\mathsf{EdDec}(\alpha, \beta, \mathrm{tw}, \mathcal{A})$.

PROOF. For a given decision problem $\mathsf{EdDec}(\alpha, \beta, \mathrm{tw}, \mathcal{A})$, we show that $\mathcal{A}'$ or $\mathcal{A}''$ is not empty iff there is a timed word in $\mathcal{A}$, with edit distance at most (α, β) to tw.

1. *(Non-emptiness implies $\mathcal{D}(\mathrm{tw}, \mathcal{A}) \leq_{\mathrm{lex}} (\alpha, \beta)$).* Consider an accepting word tw' of $\mathcal{A}'$ or $\mathcal{A}''$, ending in location $(\ell, |\mathrm{tw}|, k)$ for some k. Let tw'' be the word in $\mathcal{A}$ we get by following the transitions in tw', which are not insertions. Note that such a word exists, since the clock constraints on transitions in $\mathcal{A}'$ and $\mathcal{A}''$ which are not insertions are stronger than in $\mathcal{A}$ and the insertions do not matter (since they go between (ℓ, j, k) and $(\ell, j+1, k+1)$ and no time has passed). Note that tw' and tw spells the same (untimed) word (ignoring ϵ). Therefore, by making the modifications to the untimed word of tw'' as indicated by tw', we obtain tw. Also, note that there are at most k modifications, which is at most α. We now consider two cases: either $k = \alpha$ or $k < \alpha$.

   - If $k = \alpha$ (indicating that $\mathrm{tw}' \in \mathcal{A}'$), then whenever we used a no-edit-transition (or correct-move-transition) from (ℓ, j, k) to $(\ell', j+1, k)$, then the corresponding move in $\mathcal{A}$ was such that the total time T was in $[t_{j+1}-\beta; t_{j+1}+\beta]$ and the letter used was the $(j+1)$-st letter of tw, indicating that no edit has been made and $|t_{j+1} - T| \leq \beta$. Hence the edit distance is at most $(k, \beta) = (\alpha, \beta)$.

- If $k < \alpha$ (indicating that $\mathrm{tw}' \in \mathcal{A}''$, because in such cases the requirements in $\mathcal{A}'$ are stronger than in $\mathcal{A}''$), then using an argument like the preceding and the construction of $\mathcal{A}''$, we get that the edit distance is at most $(k, \infty) <_{\mathsf{lex}} (\alpha, \beta)$.

2. *($\mathcal{D}(\mathrm{tw}, \mathcal{A}) \leq_{\mathsf{lex}} (\alpha, \beta)$ implies non-emptiness).* Consider a timed word $\mathrm{tw}'' \in \mathcal{A}$, such that the edit distance $\mathcal{D}(\mathrm{tw}, \mathrm{tw}'') = \mathcal{D}(\mathrm{tw}'', \mathrm{tw})$ is at most (α, β). We consider the case that $(\alpha - 1, \infty) <_{\mathsf{lex}} \mathcal{D}(\mathrm{tw}'', \mathrm{tw})$ and show that $\mathcal{A}'$ is non-empty (the case $\mathcal{D}(\mathrm{tw}'', \mathrm{tw}) \leq_{\mathsf{lex}} (\alpha - 1, \infty)$ is similar, but in this case we show $\mathcal{A}''$ is non-empty instead of $\mathcal{A}'$). Let WE be a word edit which is used to show that $\mathcal{D}(\mathrm{tw}'', \mathrm{tw})$ is at most (α, β). We now show an accepting run of $\mathcal{A}'$ from tw'' and WE. Define $\ell_1 \in \mathcal{A}$ to be the start location of tw'' and let the corresponding location $(\ell_1, 0, 0)$ be the start location of the run. We can view the sequence of operators that WE makes on tw'' as the following sequence of letter operators: for all $i \geq 1$, the word edit WE first inserts some letters before the i-th letter of tw'', then it either substitutes, deletes, or keeps the i-th letter and then repeats for the $(i+1)$-st letter. Whenever WE inserts a letter into tw'', follow the insertion transition from the current location. In the other cases, there is a corresponding transition t in the word $\mathrm{tw}'' \in \mathcal{A}$. In that case follow the (substitution, deletion, no-edit) transition depending on the choice of WE in the obvious way. Note that if it follows the no-edit case, the time T spent on the sub-word up to transition t must be within β of the time used for the corresponding letter of tw by definition of WE and hence, in each case, we can use the indicated transition. At the end we end up in $(\ell', |\mathrm{tw}|, \alpha)$, where ℓ' is an accepting location of $\mathcal{A}$ the run tw'' ends in. Hence it follows that $\mathcal{A}'$ is non-empty.

The desired result follows. □

LEMMA 4 (SPACE COMPLEXITY ANALYSIS). *The algorithm* SOLED$(\alpha, \beta, \mathrm{tw}, \mathcal{A})$ *can be implemented so that it uses polynomial space.*

PROOF. It is clear from the algorithm that we just need to solve the non-emptiness problem for $\mathcal{A}''$ and $\mathcal{A}'$ in PSPACE. Both automata have at most $n = |L| \cdot (|\mathrm{tw}| + 1) \cdot (\alpha + 1) + 1$ locations and the least common multiple (LCM) of the numbers in the clock constraints is $g \cdot d$, where g is the LCM of the numbers in the clock constraints of $\mathcal{A}$ and d the LCM of the denominators of the time stamps in the timed word tw and β, and the number of clocks is 2 more than the number of clocks $|C|$ of $\mathcal{A}$. This indicates that we get a region abstraction with $(2+|C|)! \cdot 4^{2+|C|} \cdot (g \cdot d+1)^{2+|C|} \cdot n$ regions [2], each region of which can be written in polynomial space and the successors can also be computed in polynomial space. This indicates, similarly to how the non-emptiness problem for $\mathcal{A}$ is solved by Alur and Dill [2], that we can solve the non-emptiness problem for $\mathcal{A}'$ and $\mathcal{A}''$ in polynomial space. The desired upper bound follows. □

THEOREM 5 (COMPLEXITY). *The edit-distance decision problem* $\mathsf{EdDec}(\alpha, \beta, \mathrm{tw}, \mathcal{A})$ *is PSPACE-complete.*

PROOF. The theorem follows from Lemma 2, Lemma 3 and Lemma 4. □

REMARK 6. *We now argue that our construction above for timed automata specialized to untimed automata shows NL-completeness (non-deterministic log-space completeness) for untimed non-deterministic finite automata (NFA). In case of NFA, the second component does not exist. Also given an input untimed word* w*, the edit distance to an NFA* $\mathcal{A}$ *is at most* $\max\{|w|, |L|\}$*, where* L *is the set of locations of* $\mathcal{A}$*. Our construction above applied to NFA reduces the edit distance computation to non-emptiness of NFA. Moreover, since our reduction is local (i.e., it only modifies transitions of every location locally) it can be implemented in log-space. Since emptiness of NFA is NL-complete [11], we obtain the edit-distance computation for an untimed word and an NFA is in NL. The same proof as in Lemma 2 shows that non-emptiness of NFA reduces to the edit-distance computation problem. This gives us the following result.*

COROLLARY 7. *The edit-distance computation problem for an untimed word* w *and an untimed non-deterministic finite automaton (NFA) is NL-complete.*

4. EDIT DISTANCE BETWEEN TIMED AUTOMATA

In this section we consider the computation of edit distance between two timed automata. We first show that the *exact* decision problem is undecidable, and then consider the *approximation* problem. We first formally define the approximation problem as a *promise* problem.

Promise problem. We will consider the following promise problem $\mathsf{PromEd}(\delta, \mathcal{A}, \mathcal{A}', \alpha, \beta)$: Given a rational number $\delta > 0$, a pair of numbers $(\alpha, \beta) \in \mathbb{N} \times (\mathbb{Q} \cup \{\infty\})$, and a pair of timed automata $\mathcal{A}, \mathcal{A}'$, the promise problem asks whether $\mathcal{D}(\mathcal{A}, \mathcal{A}') \leq_{\mathsf{lex}} (\alpha, \beta)$, under the promise that either $\mathcal{D}(\mathcal{A}, \mathcal{A}') \leq_{\mathsf{lex}} (\alpha, \beta)$ or $\mathcal{D}(\mathcal{A}, \mathcal{A}') >_{\mathsf{lex}} (\alpha, \beta + \delta)$. Intuitively the promise problem defines the approximation problem with an *additive* error in the second component.

Significance of the promise problem. We now explain why the promise problem is the appropriate formulation for approximation with additive error. First, given an algorithm for the promise problem with a space (resp. time) bound, we run a modified algorithm which runs as the given algorithm till the space (resp. time) bound has been exceeded; and if the bound has been exceeded, then it terminates and answers UNSURE. Thus even if the promise is not met, the algorithm always terminates in the required resource bound. For our concrete algorithm for the promise problem, the algorithm will always use at most exponential space, and terminate even if the promise is not satisfied, but if the promise is not satisfied, the algorithm may answer incorrectly. An alternative (perhaps more intuitive) approximation formulation is given numbers (α, β), timed automata $\mathcal{A}$ and $\mathcal{A}'$, and $\beta \geq \delta > 0$, if $(\alpha, \beta - \delta) <_{\mathsf{lex}} \mathcal{D}(\mathcal{A}, \mathcal{A}') \leq_{\mathsf{lex}} (\alpha, \beta + \delta)$, the algorithm can answer UNSURE. If it does not, it must (correctly) answer YES if $\mathcal{D}(\mathcal{A}, \mathcal{A}') \leq_{\mathsf{lex}} (\alpha, \beta)$, and NO if $\mathcal{D}(\mathcal{A}, \mathcal{A}') >_{\mathsf{lex}} (\alpha, \beta)$. We argue that solving the promise problem implies a solution to the above formulation, using a similar amount of resources. Given an instance of the problem, first we solve $\mathsf{PromEd}(\delta, \mathcal{A}, \mathcal{A}', \alpha, \beta - \delta)$ and $\mathsf{PromEd}(\delta, \mathcal{A}, \mathcal{A}', \alpha, \beta)$. Note that at least one of the answers is correct. If the results match and is YES, we have $\mathcal{D}(\mathcal{A}, \mathcal{A}') \leq_{\mathsf{lex}} (\alpha, \beta)$ and return YES; if the results match and is NO, we have $\mathcal{D}(\mathcal{A}, \mathcal{A}') >_{\mathsf{lex}} (\alpha, \beta)$ and return NO. If the results do not match, then we have $(\alpha, \beta - \delta) <_{\text{lex}} \mathcal{D}(\mathcal{A}, \mathcal{A}') \leq_{\text{lex}} (\alpha, \beta + \delta)$, and we return UNSURE. Hence we focus on the promise problem and present a solution to it.

4.1 Lower bounds

LEMMA 8 (HARDNESS OF EXACT DECISION PROBLEM). *Given two timed automata $\mathcal{A}$ and $\mathcal{A}'$ and two numbers (α, β), the decision problem whether $\mathcal{D}(\mathcal{A}, \mathcal{A}') \leq_{\text{lex}} (\alpha, \beta)$ is undecidable.*

PROOF. Let $\mathcal{A}$ be a timed automaton accepting all timed words. We will now argue that for a closed timed automaton $\mathcal{A}'$, i.e. where all clock constraints are closed (except towards ∞), we have $\mathcal{D}(\mathcal{A}, \mathcal{A}') \leq_{\text{lex}} (0, 0)$ iff $\mathcal{L}(\mathcal{A}) \subseteq \mathcal{L}(\mathcal{A}')$ (i.e., the language universality problem for closed timed automata). It is clear that if $\mathcal{L}(\mathcal{A}) \subseteq \mathcal{L}(\mathcal{A}')$ then $\mathcal{D}(\mathcal{A}, \mathcal{A}') \leq_{\text{lex}} (0, 0)$ and we will therefore argue that if $\mathcal{D}(\mathcal{A}, \mathcal{A}') \leq_{\text{lex}} (0, 0)$ then $\mathcal{L}(\mathcal{A}) \subseteq \mathcal{L}(\mathcal{A}')$. The argument is as follows. Pick any timed word $\text{tw} = (w, \bar{t})$. We will argue that $\text{tw} \in \mathcal{L}(\mathcal{A}')$. We have that $\mathcal{D}(\text{tw}, \mathcal{A}') \leq_{\text{lex}} (0, 0)$, which by definition, indicates that there is a sequence of timed words $(\text{tw}_i)_{i \in \mathbb{N}}$, such that $\text{tw}_i = (w_i, \bar{t}_i) \in \mathcal{L}(\mathcal{A}')$ and $\mathcal{D}(\text{tw}, \text{tw}_i) \leq_{\text{lex}} (0, \frac{1}{i})$ (that is, for all i we have that $w = w_i$ and the j-th component of $\bar{t}$ and $\bar{t}_i$ differs by at most $\frac{1}{i}$ for all j). Because the clock constraints are closed, we also have that the limit of $(\text{tw}_i)_{i \in \mathbb{N}}$ is in $\mathcal{A}'$. But the limit of $(\text{tw}_i)_{i \in \mathbb{N}}$ is tw. Hence any arbitrary timed word is in $\mathcal{A}'$ and therefore also all timed words. Since the language universality problem for closed timed automata is undecidable, as shown by Ouaknine and Worrell [16], the desired result follows. □

Since Lemma 8 establishes the undecidability of the exact decision problem, we consider the problem of finding the first component exactly, but approximating the second component by an additive error term δ (as defined in the promise problem). Also note that multiplicative approximation is undecidable, since it would still require deciding if the edit distance is precisely $(0, 0)$ or not. We now establish a complexity lower bound for the promise problem.

LEMMA 9 (HARDNESS OF APPROXIMATION). *Given two timed automata $\mathcal{A}$ and $\mathcal{A}'$, two numbers (α, β), and a rational number $\delta > 0$, the promise problem $\text{PromEd}(\delta, \mathcal{A}, \mathcal{A}', \alpha, \beta)$ is EXPSPACE-hard.*

PROOF. As shown in [4], the decision problem for the universality of the untimed language of a timed automaton is EXPSPACE-complete (i.e., given a timed automaton $\mathcal{A}'$, deciding whether for every word w in Σ^* there exists $\text{tw}' = (w', \bar{t}') \in \mathcal{L}(\mathcal{A}')$ such that $w' = w$ is EXPSPACE-complete). We can solve the universality of the untimed language problem using our promise problem. Let $\mathcal{A}$ be a timed automaton accepting all words and then deciding if the first component of the edit distance $\mathcal{D}(\mathcal{A}, \mathcal{A}')$ is 0 coincides with the untimed universality of $\mathcal{A}'$, i.e., $\text{PromEd}(\delta, \mathcal{A}, \mathcal{A}', 0, \infty)$, for any $\delta > 0$, iff the untimed language of $\mathcal{A}'$ is universal. The desired result follows. □

4.2 Upper bound

Simplification. To simplify the remainder, we will assume that $\delta \geq 2$ and all numbers used, i.e. the ones in clock constraints of $\mathcal{A}$ and $\mathcal{A}'$ and the numbers α, β, and δ are integers. If one has an instance of the problem where this is not the case, one can simply scale all clock constraints, β and δ so that they are all integers and $\delta \geq 2$ (by multiplying with two times the LCM of the denominators), and consider $\lfloor \alpha \rfloor$ for the first component of the edit distance. We will furthermore assume that there is a bound of $c_{\max}$ on the time we can wait before moving. This assumption can be removed by including two additional columns corresponding to arbitrary high and arbitrary low difference between time stamps and suitable book-keeping. This will not be done explicitly in the present paper for sake of simplicity in presentation.

Overview of our algorithm. We will now present our algorithm in three stages.

- (Step 1) First we will give an algorithm that finds the first component of the edit distance.
- (Step 2) For a pair of timed automata $\mathcal{A}, \mathcal{A}'$ of edit distance at most (α, β), and two timed words $\text{tw} \in (\mathcal{A})$ and $\text{tw}' \in (\mathcal{A}')$ such that $(\alpha - 1, \infty) <_{\text{lex}} \mathcal{D}(\text{tw}, \text{tw}') \leq_{\text{lex}} (\alpha, \beta)$, we bound the worst case time mismatch, between indices close together in thc words.
- (Step 3) Then finally, we will give an algorithm that tests if $\mathcal{D}(\mathcal{A}, \mathcal{A}') \leq_{\text{lex}} (\alpha, \beta)$, under the promise that either $\mathcal{D}(\mathcal{A}, \mathcal{A}') \leq_{\text{lex}} (\alpha, \beta)$ or $\mathcal{D}(\mathcal{A}, \mathcal{A}') >_{\text{lex}} (\alpha, \beta + \delta)$. For the computation of this step we will define a matrix and the size of the matrix will be determined using Step 2.

The first two steps of the algorithm are relatively straight-forward and we present them below. Finally we present Step 3 in details.

4.2.1 Step 1 and Step 2 of the algorithm

Step 1 of the algorithm. Given two timed automata $\mathcal{A}$ and $\mathcal{A}'$, we want to compute the first component α of the edit distance. First we construct the corresponding region graphs $\text{Reg}(\mathcal{A})$ and $\text{Reg}(\mathcal{A}')$ and annotate on each transition the corresponding letter. By running an algorithm by Benedikt, Puppis and Riveros [3] to compute edit distance between two finite-state (untimed) automata, on the region graphs, we obtain α. The results of [3] also imply that the first component of the edit distance is at most $(|\text{Reg}(\mathcal{A})| + 1) \cdot |\text{Reg}(\mathcal{A}')|$, if it is finite.

Step 2 of the algorithm: Bounding the time difference. We now present the following lemma for Step 2 of the algorithm.

LEMMA 10. *Let a pair (α, β) of numbers, and a pair of timed automata $\mathcal{A}, \mathcal{A}'$ be given, such that $\mathcal{D}(\mathcal{A}, \mathcal{A}') \leq_{\text{lex}} (\alpha, \beta)$. If there exists a timed word $\text{tw} = (w, \bar{t}) \in \mathcal{L}(\mathcal{A})$ such that $\mathcal{D}(\text{tw}, \mathcal{A}') >_{\text{lex}} (\alpha - 1, \infty)$, then for all timed words $\text{tw}' = (w', \bar{t}') \in \mathcal{L}(\mathcal{A}')$, where $\mathcal{D}(\text{tw}, \text{tw}') \leq_{\text{lex}} (\alpha, \beta)$, and for all integers $1 \leq i \leq |\text{tw}|$ and all integers j such that $i - 2 \cdot \alpha \leq j \leq i + 2 \cdot \alpha$ and $1 \leq j \leq |\text{tw}'|$, we have that*

$$|t_i - t'_j| \leq 4 \cdot \alpha \cdot c_{\max} + \beta \ .$$

PROOF. Let a pair of numbers (α, β) and a pair of timed automata $\mathcal{A}, \mathcal{A}'$ be given, such that $\mathcal{D}(\mathcal{A}, \mathcal{A}') \leq_{\text{lex}} (\alpha, \beta)$. Consider a timed word $\text{tw} = (w, \bar{t}) \in \mathcal{L}(\mathcal{A})$, such that $\mathcal{D}(\text{tw}, \mathcal{A}') >_{\text{lex}} (\alpha - 1, \infty)$, and a timed word $\text{tw}' = (w', \bar{t}') \in \mathcal{L}(\mathcal{A}')$, where $\mathcal{D}(\text{tw}, \text{tw}') \leq_{\text{lex}} (\alpha, \beta)$. Let WE be some word edit witnessing $\mathcal{D}(\text{tw}, \text{tw}') \leq_{\text{lex}} (\alpha, \beta)$. Fix some index i in tw. If $i \leq 2 \cdot \alpha$, then note that $0 \leq t_i \leq i \cdot c_{\max} \leq 2 \cdot \alpha \cdot c_{\max}$ and $0 \leq t'_{i+\alpha} \leq (i + 2 \cdot \alpha) \cdot c_{\max} \leq 4 \cdot \alpha \cdot c_{\max}$, because the time can at most increase with $c_{\max}$ in every move, from which the statement follows, for such i. Hence, we only need to consider $i > 2 \cdot \alpha$. Consider some index j in w which correspond to index i of w', then $|i - j| \leq \alpha$, since it is the number of insertions minus deletions before index i. Also note that in any set S of indices in tw' of size $\alpha + 1$, at least one index i' corresponds to some index j' in tw, because otherwise there would be at least $\alpha + 1$ edits. This is especially true for the set of indices $S' = \{j - \alpha, j - \alpha - 1, \dots, j - 2 \cdot \alpha\}$ of size $\alpha + 1$ (note that they are all indices of tw', because $i \geq 2 \cdot \alpha$ and the length of the words cannot differ by more than α). Let

i', j' be some indices such that i' in S' corresponds to j'. We then get that $j' \leq j \leq j' + 3 \cdot \alpha$, by the preceding definition of j'. Because of the correspondence between i' and j' we also get that $|t'_{i'} - t_{j'}| \leq \beta$. Since we can increase the time used by at most $c_{\max}$ in every move and that $\bar{t}$ is monotonically non-decreasing, we also get that $t'_{i'} - \beta \leq t_j \leq t'_{i'} + \beta + 3 \cdot \alpha$. By the same argument we also get that

$$t'_{j-2\cdot\alpha} - \beta \leq t'_{i'} - \beta \leq t_j \leq t'_{i'} + \beta + 3 \cdot \alpha \leq t'_{j-2\cdot\alpha} + \beta + 4 \cdot \alpha$$

and also

$$t'_k - \beta - 4 \cdot \alpha \leq t_j \leq t_k + \beta + 3 \cdot \alpha \ ,$$

where $k = \min(|\,\mathrm{tw}'\,|, j + 2 \cdot \alpha)$. Therefore, by monotonicity of $\bar{t}'$ we get that for all $j - 2 \cdot \alpha \leq i \leq k$, that $|t_j - t'_i| \leq 4 \cdot \alpha + \beta$ and the desired result follows. □

4.2.2 *Step 3 of the algorithm*

We will now give an algorithm that solves the decision problem $\mathsf{PromEd}(\delta, \mathcal{A}, \mathcal{A}', \alpha, \beta)$.

Deducing time passage. Given a timed automaton $\mathcal{A}$, we will consider $\mathsf{Eps}(\mathcal{A})$, which is identical to $\mathcal{A}$, except that (1) it has one more clock x; (2) modifies the clock constraints on the transitions in $\mathcal{A}$; and (3) also adds $|L|$ new transitions, one from each location. For each transition t in $\mathcal{A}$, the corresponding transition in $\mathsf{Eps}(\mathcal{A})$ also includes $\mathsf{x} < 1$ as a part of the clock constraint. For each location ℓ in $\mathcal{A}$, the new transition in $\mathsf{Eps}(\mathcal{A})$ from the corresponding location in $\mathsf{Eps}(\mathcal{A})$ is an ϵ-transition and a self-loop with clock constraint $\{\mathsf{x} = 1 \wedge \bigwedge_{c \in C} c \leq c_{\max}\}$. Note that this ensures that $\epsilon^{-1}(\mathcal{L}(\mathsf{Eps}(\mathcal{A}))) = \mathcal{L}(\mathcal{A})$, where ϵ^{-1} is the function on timed languages that removes all occurrences of the letter ϵ and the corresponding time stamps. The construction ensures that the floor of the total timed used in a prefix of a run is precisely the number of ϵ-transitions used in the prefix. A similar construction was used by Chatterjee and Prabhu [5] for computation of quantitative simulation.

The triple $\mathrm{impact}(\mathrm{tw}, \mathcal{A}, \mathcal{A}', \alpha, \beta) = (A, V, M)$. Given a timed word $\mathrm{tw} = (w, \bar{t})$, a pair of timed automata $\mathcal{A}, \mathcal{A}'$, and some target pair of numbers (α, β), we define the triple $\mathrm{impact}(\mathrm{tw}, \mathcal{A}, \mathcal{A}', \alpha, \beta) = (A, V, M)$. We now describe the components of the triple.

- The first component A is a subset of regions in $\mathsf{Reg}(\mathsf{Eps}(\mathcal{A}))$.
- The second component V is a vector of length α, and each entry in the vector is a subset of regions of $\mathsf{Reg}(\mathcal{A}')$.
- The third component M is a matrix of dimension $(8 \cdot \alpha \cdot c_{\max} + 2 \cdot \beta + 4, \alpha + 1)$. Each entry (a_1, a_2) of M is a subset of regions of $\mathsf{Reg}(\mathsf{Eps}(\mathcal{A}'))$.

To simplify the definition of $\mathrm{impact}(\mathrm{tw}, \mathcal{A}, \mathcal{A}', \alpha, \beta)$, we will now first assign labels to M and V. The rows are labeled $0, \ldots, \alpha$ and the columns are labeled $\{-4 \cdot \alpha \cdot c_{\max} - \beta - 2, \ldots, 4 \cdot \alpha \cdot c_{\max} + \beta + 2\}$. Similarly we assign labels $0, \ldots, \alpha - 1$ to the entries of V. The subset A is the set of regions in $\mathsf{Reg}(\mathsf{Eps}(\mathcal{A}))$ one can get to such that the i-th non-ϵ-transition used is w_i and there are $\lfloor t_i \rfloor$ many ϵ-transitions before that transition. The α-vector V is such that entry a_1 of V contains the regions, which can be reached after a timed word $\mathrm{tw}' = (w', \bar{t}')$, such that $\mathcal{D}(w, w') \leq a_1$ (this is easy to compute on the region graph, using the algorithm by Benedikt, Puppis and Riveros [3], since it only considers the untimed part). Also, a given region $r \in \mathsf{Reg}(\mathsf{Eps}(\mathcal{A}'))$ is in entry (a_1, a_2) of M (where a_1 and a_2 are resp. row and column labels of M) iff there exists a timed word $\mathrm{tw}' = (w', \bar{t}')$, such that (1) one can get to r after having processed tw'; and (2) there exists a word edit WE with at most a_1 edits between tw and tw' such that at every pair of corresponding timed letters i, j, we have that $|\lfloor t_i \rfloor - \lfloor t'_j \rfloor| \leq \beta + 1$; and (3) $\lfloor t_{|\,\mathrm{tw}\,|} \rfloor - \lfloor t'_{|\,\mathrm{tw}'\,|} \rfloor = a_2$.

Feasible and successful impact **triples.** We will call a triple (A, V, M) *feasible* if $\mathrm{impact}(\mathrm{tw}, \mathcal{A}, \mathcal{A}', \alpha, \beta) = (A, V, M)$ for some tw and *successful* if it is feasible and A contains a region with a location of $\mathcal{A}$ which is accepting, but no entry in neither V nor M contains a region with a location of $\mathcal{A}'$ which is accepting. We will now argue that there exists a successful triple iff the answer is NO to the promise problem $\mathsf{PromEd}(\delta, \mathcal{A}, \mathcal{A}', \alpha, \beta)$.

LEMMA 11. *There exists a successful triple (A, V, M) iff the answer is NO to the promise problem* $\mathsf{PromEd}(\delta, \mathcal{A}, \mathcal{A}', \alpha, \beta)$.

PROOF. We will first argue that a successful triple implies that the answer to $\mathsf{PromEd}(\delta, \mathcal{A}, \mathcal{A}', \alpha, \beta)$ is NO. Consider a triple $(A, V, M) = \mathrm{impact}(\mathrm{tw}, \mathcal{A}, \mathcal{A}', \alpha, \beta)$ for some $\mathrm{tw} = (w, \bar{t})$, which is successful. Consider some accepting region r in A and let $\mathrm{tw}' = (w', \bar{t}')$ be some timed word that goes to r from some start location, such that for all i we have that $w_i = w'_i$ and $\lfloor t_i \rfloor = \lfloor t'_i \rfloor$. Such a run exists by definition of impact. We have that $\mathrm{tw}' \in \mathcal{L}(\mathcal{A})$. Assume towards contradiction that there is a $\mathrm{tw}'' \in \mathcal{L}(\mathcal{A}')$ such that $\mathcal{D}(\mathrm{tw}', \mathrm{tw}'') \leq_{\mathsf{lex}} (\alpha, \beta)$. Let r' be the accepting region one reaches in $\mathsf{Reg}(\mathsf{Eps}(\mathcal{A}'))$ after the run $\mathrm{tw}'' = (w'', \bar{t}'')$. First consider the case that $\mathcal{D}(\mathrm{tw}', \mathrm{tw}'') \leq_{\mathsf{lex}} (\alpha - 1, \infty)$. This implies that r' is in entry $(\alpha - 1)$ of V and hence contradicts that (A, V, M) is successful. If, on the other hand $(\alpha - 1, \infty) <_{\mathsf{lex}} \mathcal{D}(\mathrm{tw}', \mathrm{tw}'') \leq_{\mathsf{lex}} (\alpha, \beta)$, then r' is in entry $(\alpha, \lfloor t'_{|\,\mathrm{tw}'\,|} \rfloor - \lfloor t''_{|\,\mathrm{tw}''\,|} \rfloor)$ of M (by Lemma 10, this is an entry of the matrix) and again contradicts that (A, V, M) is successful.

We will now argue that if the answer to $\mathsf{PromEd}(\delta, \mathcal{A}, \mathcal{A}', \alpha, \beta)$ is NO, then there is a successful triple. By definition of $\mathsf{PromEd}(\delta, \mathcal{A}, \mathcal{A}', \alpha, \beta)$ we know that there is a timed word $\mathrm{tw} = (w, \bar{t}) \in \mathcal{L}(\mathcal{A})$ such that for all timed words $\mathrm{tw}' \in \mathcal{L}(\mathcal{A}')$, we have that $\mathcal{D}(\mathrm{tw}, \mathrm{tw}') \geq_{\mathsf{lex}} (\alpha, \beta + 2)$. Fix such a timed word tw. There are two cases. Either for some tw' we have that $\mathcal{D}(\mathrm{tw}, \mathrm{tw}') >_{\mathsf{lex}} (\alpha, \infty)$ or not.

- If we have that $\mathcal{D}(\mathrm{tw}, \mathrm{tw}') >_{\mathsf{lex}} (\alpha, \infty)$, then all entries of V do not contain a region with accepting location. But the requirements to be in entry a_1 of V are satisfied by every region in (a_1, a_2) of M for all a_2. But this implies that the matrix also does not contain a region with accepting location.
- In the other case, there must be a timed word $\mathrm{tw}' = (w', \bar{t}')$ such that $(\alpha, \beta + 2) \leq_{\mathsf{lex}} \mathcal{D}(\mathrm{tw}, \mathrm{tw}') \leq_{\mathsf{lex}} (\alpha, \infty)$. First note that for all $a_1 < \alpha$, no region with an accepting location can be in entry (a_1, a_2) of M nor in entry a_1 for V, because $\mathcal{D}(\mathrm{tw}, \mathcal{A}) >_{\mathsf{lex}} (\alpha - 1, \infty)$. We therefore only need to consider the entries in row α. But then for any word edit with α edits, there must be some index i in w corresponding to index j of w', such that $|t_i - t'_j| \geq \beta + 2$, by definition of edit distance and since we consider that $\delta \geq 2$. But then also $|\lfloor t_i \rfloor - \lfloor t'_j \rfloor| > \beta + 1$, implying that no region with accepting location can be in entry (α, a_2) of M for any a_2.

The desired result follows. □

Computing impact **- the start case.** It is easy to compute $\mathrm{impact}(\epsilon, \mathcal{A}, \mathcal{A}', \alpha, \beta) = (A, V, M)$, because (1) A are simply the regions corresponding to time 0 on all clocks in the start locations; and (2) for each a_1, entry a_1 of V is the set of regions in $\mathsf{Reg}(\mathcal{A})$, reachable in at most a_1 moves; and (3) for each a_1 and

$a_2 \geq 0$, entry $(a_1, -a_2)$ of M (the entries (a_1', a_2'), where $a_2' > 0$ are empty, because the time stamps are always non-negative numbers, and the time for the timed word ϵ is 0) is the set of regions in $\mathsf{Reg}(\mathsf{Eps}(\mathcal{A}))$, reachable in precisely a_1 many non-ϵ-moves and a_2 many ϵ-moves (note that every letter used must be deleted to match ϵ and thus we do not need to consider the requirement on times).

Computing impact **- the move case.** Given $\mathsf{impact}(\mathrm{tw}, \mathcal{A}, \mathcal{A}', \alpha, \beta) = (A, V, M)$, for some A, V, M and for some timed word $\mathrm{tw} = (w, \bar{t})$, we can compute each triple $\mathsf{impact}(\mathrm{tw} \circ (\sigma, t), \mathcal{A}, \mathcal{A}', \alpha, \beta) = (A', V', M')$ for some (σ, t). Let $t' = \lfloor t \rfloor - \lfloor t_{|\mathrm{tw}|} \rfloor$. Then A' is the set of regions one can get to from some region in A, using first t' many ϵ-transitions and then one σ-transition. Each entry a_1 of V' can be computed directly from V, similar to the algorithm by Benedikt, Puppis and Riveros [3] for untimed automata. Also, entry (a_1, a_2) of M' consists of the regions one can get to from some region in (a_1', a_2') of M for $a_2' \in [-4 \cdot \alpha \cdot c_{\max} - \beta - 1, 4 \cdot \alpha \cdot c_{\max} + \beta + 1]$ using (1) no transitions, if $a_1 = a_1' + 1$ and $a_2 = a_2' + t'$ (this corresponds to insertion); or (2) first $(a_2 - a_2' + t')$ many ϵ-transitions and then any non-ϵ-transition if $a_1 = a_1' + 1$ (this corresponds to substitution); or (3) first $\hat{t}_0$ many ϵ-transitions and then some σ-transition, followed by $\hat{t}_1$ many ϵ-transitions and then some non-ϵ-transition, followed by $\hat{t}_2$ many ϵ-transitions and then some non-ϵ-transition and so on until $\hat{t}_n$ many ϵ-transitions and then some non-ϵ-transition, where $n = a_1 - a_1'$ and $a_2 - a_2' + t' = \sum_{i=0}^{n} \hat{t}_i$ (corresponding to one correct move followed by n deletions). It is easy to see that we can always assume that all deletions come directly after a correct move (or appear at the beginning).

Computing impact **- correctness.** We will now argue that our computation of impact satisfy the properties required.

LEMMA 12. *The computation of* impact *is correct.*

PROOF. In both the start case and the move case, it should be clear that the first two components (that is A and V) of the triple are correctly computed.

We now recall the requirements on being in entry (a_1, a_2) of M: A given region $r \in \mathsf{Reg}(\mathsf{Eps}(\mathcal{A}'))$ is in entry (a_1, a_2) of M iff there exists a timed word $\mathrm{tw}' = (w', \bar{t}')$, such that (1) one can get to r after having processed tw'; and (2) there exists a word edit WE with at most a_1 edits between tw and tw' such that at every pair of corresponding indices i, j, we have that $|\lfloor t_i \rfloor - \lfloor t_j' \rfloor| \leq \beta + 1$; and (3) $\lfloor t_{|\mathrm{tw}|} \rfloor - \lfloor t'_{|\mathrm{tw}'|} \rfloor = a_2$.

Start case of M**.** In the start case for M, it is clear that there exists a timed word $\mathrm{tw}' = (w', \bar{t}')$ to each of the regions of entry $(a_1, -a_2)$ of M, because of our use of the region abstraction [2]. Also, it contains a_1 many non-ϵ-moves and a_2 many ϵ-moves, indicating that $\mathcal{D}(\epsilon, \mathrm{tw}') \leq_{\mathsf{lex}} (a_1, \infty)$ (indicating that we satisfy (1)) and that $\lfloor t'_{|\mathrm{tw}'|} \rfloor = a_2$ (indicating that we satisfy (3)). Also, since no word edit can have any corresponding indices between ϵ and tw' we satisfy (2).

Move case of M**.** In the move case, we have $\mathsf{impact}(\mathrm{tw}, \mathcal{A}, \mathcal{A}', \alpha, \beta) = (A, V, M)$ and we must compute each $\mathsf{impact}(\mathrm{tw} \circ (\sigma, t), \mathcal{A}, \mathcal{A}', \alpha, \beta) = (A', V', M')$ for any (σ, t). By Alur and Dill [2] we see that we satisfy (1) (since it indicates that there is a timed word ending in each reachable region). Also, by letting the word edit WE we consider in (2), be any that have the pairs of corresponding indices defined by our correct moves, we see that we satisfy (2). It is clear that we can do the rest of the word edit afterwards in a_1 edits, since we increase the number of edits we need whenever we do not use a correct move. In regards to (3), we have the value of $\lfloor t_{|\mathrm{tw}|} \rfloor - \lfloor t_{|\mathrm{tw}|-1} \rfloor$, from our computation of A'. Wagner and Fischer [20] shows that we can split up a word edit between a word $w \circ \sigma$ and a word w', so that w is edited to w'' and σ is edited to w''' for some $w'' \circ w''' = w$. It is easy to see that this generalises to timed words. Therefore, we must have that tw' can be split up into tw'' and tw''' such that $\mathrm{tw}' = \mathrm{tw}'' \circ \mathrm{tw}'''$ and such that tw'' is in M (because of Lemma 10). From M we get $\lfloor t_{|\mathrm{tw}|-1} \rfloor - \lfloor t'_{|\mathrm{tw}''|} \rfloor$ for all possible tw''. Thus to compute $\lfloor t_{|\mathrm{tw}|} \rfloor - \lfloor t'_{|\mathrm{tw}'|} \rfloor$, we just need $\lfloor t'_{|\mathrm{tw}'''|} \rfloor = \lfloor t'_{|\mathrm{tw}'|} \rfloor - \lfloor t'_{|\mathrm{tw}'''|} \rfloor$, which is easy to find, by counting the number of ϵ-transitions used and is done correctly by the description.

We therefore conclude that also M is computed correctly. □

Space complexity of impact**-triple computation.** Observe that a triple (A, V, M) consists of some exponential number of subsets of exponential sized sets of regions and therefore each triple have at most exponential size. Given the preceding it is also clear that we can compute each successor of the (possibly) exponentially many successors in exponential space. Note that given a feasible triple (A, V, M) it is easy to check in exponential space if the triple is also successful.

The algorithm SolPromEd**.** Our algorithm SolPromEd for solving $\mathsf{PromEd}(\delta, \mathcal{A}, \mathcal{A}', \alpha, \beta)$, is as follows: (1) first compute $\mathsf{impact}(\epsilon, \mathcal{A}, \mathcal{A}', \alpha, \beta)$; and (2) then guess a timed word (with one letter and the floor of the corresponding time stamp at a time) to a successful triple and compute the impact triples using the move case, and check that the triple is successful and then return NO. If there is no successful triple, return YES. The correctness follows from Lemma 11 and Lemma 12. The above algorithm is non-deterministic (since it involves a guess of a timed word) and the space complexity is exponential (since the impact-triple computation and check is exponential space). Since NEXPSPACE=EXPSPACE by Savitch's Theorem [18], we obtain that the algorithm for the promise problem can be implemented in exponential space. Along with Lemma 9 we obtain the following result.

THEOREM 13 (COMPLEXITY OF APPROXIMATION). *The promise problem* $\mathsf{PromEd}(\delta, \mathcal{A}, \mathcal{A}', \alpha, \beta)$ *can be solved in exponential space; and the problem is EXPSPACE-hard.*

Relating our algorithm to the algorithm by Benedikt, Puppis and Riveros [3]. Our algorithm SolPromEd for deciding the decision problem $\mathsf{PromEd}(\delta, \mathcal{A}, \mathcal{A}', \alpha, \beta)$ is similar to the algorithm by Benedikt, Puppis and Riveros [3] for solving the problem of edit distance between untimed languages. There they construct $\mathsf{impact}(w, u\mathcal{A}, u\mathcal{A}', \alpha')$, for some word w, some finite-state (untimed) automata $u\mathcal{A}, u\mathcal{A}'$ and some target α', whereas we construct $\mathsf{impact}(\mathrm{tw}, \mathcal{A}, \mathcal{A}', \alpha, \beta)$, for some timed word tw, some timed automata $\mathcal{A}$ and $\mathcal{A}'$ and some target (α, β). But their construction only have parallels for the first two components of our triple (they do not have the matrix component in their construction). Also, in their construction a given location could only occur once in their vector, in contrast, we can have a given location in each column of M and in V (because, while it is always better to make less errors, it is not clear what the best time mismatch is before the next move).

5. DISCUSSION ON EXTENSIONS AND CONCLUSION

In this work we have considered the edit distance computation for timed automata under the lexico-graphic ordering. We now discuss several extensions that can be obtained from our results.

1. *Point-wise comparison and Pareto curve.* Instead of the lexico-graphic comparison we could also consider point-wise comparison between the components of the edit distance, and then compute the Pareto points where one component cannot be improved without sacrificing the other. The Pareto curve consists of all Pareto points. Consider bounds B_1 and B_2 for the bounds for Pareto curve. Given a solution to the decision problem with point-wise comparison which asks whether the first component is at most α and the second component at most β, the δ-approximation of the Pareto curve bounded by B_1 and B_2, for $\delta > 0$, can be computed as follows: enumerate α from 0 to B_1 as integers, and for a fixed α, choose β iteratively by a binary search in the interval $[0, B_2]$ until the imprecision is smaller than δ, and consider the decision problem for the point-wise comparison with α and β. Our solution for lexico-graphic ordering can also be modified to solve the point-wise comparison. The modifications are as follows: (A) For the solution of Section 3, we remove automaton $\mathcal{A}''$, and in automaton $\mathcal{A}'$ consider a location (ℓ, j, k) to be accepting if ℓ is accepting, and the automaton $\mathcal{A}'$ is non-empty iff $\mathcal{D}_1(\mathrm{tw}, \mathcal{A}) \leq \alpha$ and $\mathcal{D}_2(\mathrm{tw}, \mathcal{A}) \leq \beta$ (i.e., pointwise comparison). Also note that if the language of the input automaton is non-empty, then we have B_1 bounded by $\alpha = \max\{|\,\mathrm{tw}\,|, d\}$ and B_2 bounded by $\max\{(|\,\mathrm{tw}\,| + \alpha) \cdot c_{\max}, t_{|\,\mathrm{tw}\,|}\}$ (refer to the paragraph of Bound on the components of the edit distance in Section 3). (B) For the solution of Section 4, we simply need to remove the vector V from the triple for the solution. Also in this case B_1 is bounded by the product of the size of the region graphs (refer to Step 1 of our algorithm in Section 4).

2. *Delay instead of time mismatch.* In our definition of the second component of the edit distance we considered the more challenging notion of the absolute timing mismatch. Another alternative notion is to consider the delays, where the *delay* Δ_i in index i is the time difference $t_i - t_{i-1}$ between the $(i-1)$-th and i-th move. Then instead of the timing mismatch of t_i and t'_i we could consider the delay mismatch Δ_i and Δ'_i. The problem with the mismatch of delay is technically slightly easier (though has the same computational complexity) and we discuss the details for the solution of Section 4. To find the delay difference between $\mathcal{A}$ and $\mathcal{A}'$, we compute $\mathsf{Reg}(\mathcal{A})$ and $\mathsf{Reg}(\mathcal{A}')$, then label each transition in $\mathsf{Reg}(\mathcal{A})$ with the corresponding letter and some symbol indicating the floor of the delay used. Then each transition t in $\mathsf{Reg}(\mathcal{A})'$ is copied $2 \cdot \beta + 1$ times, one copy for each integer $y \in [-\beta, \beta]$. Let d be the floor of the delay of transition t. We mark the y-th copy of transition t with the corresponding letter of t and a symbol indicating $y + d$. We then run the algorithm of [3] on the resulting graphs. Note that whenever we match a letter, then the difference in delay must be in $[-\beta - 1, \beta + 1]$ as required.

3. *Rectangular hybrid automata.* While we have presented the solution for timed automata, our results also extend to rectangular hybrid automata [10] under discrete-time semantics (where the control state changes at discrete time points). First note that in our solution of Section 3, we either copy transitions, or include additional rectangular constraints, and thus our transformation ensures that if we start with a rectangular hybrid automaton we obtain another rectangular hybrid automaton. Since language emptiness is decidable in EXPTIME for rectangular hybrid automata under discrete-time semantics [10], our solution also extends to rectangular hybrid automata giving decidability in EXPTIME. Finally the solution of Section 4 relied on the region abstraction for timed automata, and since a similar finite-quotient based abstraction exists for rectangular hybrid automata [10], the impact-triple based computation can also be done for rectangular hybrid automata. Intuitively, the computation for timed automata was a PSPACE computation over exponential size structures leading to exponential space bound, and for rectangular automata we have an EXPTIME computation over exponential size structures that gives 2EXPTIME complexity.

Concluding remarks. In this work we extended the notion of edit distance from untimed languages to timed languages defined by timed automata. Our results characterized precisely the decidability and complexity of the computation between timed words and timed automata, and between timed automata. While we established the complexity is PSPACE-complete for timed words and timed automata, the problem is undecidable for a pair of timed automata. For the approximation problem between a pair of timed automata, we establish an exponential space lower and upper bound. We also discussed how our results can be extended to variants with point-wise comparison, delay instead of time mismatch, and the more general model of rectangular automata. We believe our results will provide a theoretical basis for approximate matching between timed words and timed languages.

6. REFERENCES

[1] A. Aho and T. Peterson. A minimum distance error-correcting parser for context-free languages. *SIAM J. of Computing*, 1:305–312, 1972.

[2] R. Alur and D. L. Dill. A theory of timed automata. *Theoretical Computer Science*, 126:183–235, 1994.

[3] M. Benedikt, G. Puppis, and C. Riveros. Regular repair of specifications. In *LICS*, pages 335–344. IEEE Computer Society, 2011.

[4] R. Brenguier, S. Göller, and O. Sankur. A comparison of succinctly represented finite-state systems. In *CONCUR*, pages 147–161, 2012.

[5] K. Chatterjee and V. S. Prabhu. Quantitative timed simulation functions and refinement metrics for real-time systems. In *HSCC*, 2013.

[6] A. Donzé, T. Ferrère, and O. Maler. Efficient robust monitoring of signal temporal logic. In *CAV 2013*, LNCS. Springer, 2013.

[7] A. Donzé and O. Maler. Robust satisfaction of temporal logic over real-valued signals. In *FORMATS*, LNCS, pages 92–106. Springer, 2010.

[8] G. Fainekos and G. Pappas. Robustness of temporal logic specifications for continuous-time signals. *Theoretical Computer Science*, 410(42), 2009.

[9] G. Fainekos, S. Sankaranarayanan, K. Ueda, and H. Yazarel. Verification of automotive control applications using S-TaLiRo. In *Proc. American Control Conference*, 2012.

[10] T. A. Henzinger and P. W. Kopke. Discrete-time control for rectangular hybrid automata. *Theor. Comput. Sci.*, 221(1-2):369–392, June 1999.

[11] J. E. Hopcroft and J. D. Ullman. *Introduction to Automata Theory, Languages, and Computation*. Adison-Wesley Publishing Company, Reading, Massachusets, USA, 1979.

[12] R. Karp. Mapping the genome: some combinatorial problems arising in molecular biology. In *STOC 93*, pages 278–285. ACM, 1993.

[13] V. Levenshtein. Binary codes capable of correcting deletions, insertions and reversals. *Soviet Physics-Doklady*, 10:707–710, 1966.

[14] M. Mohri. Edit-distance of weighted automata: general definitions and algorithms. *Intl. J. of Foundations of Comp. Sci.*, 14:957–982, 2003.

[15] T. Okuda, E. Tanaka, and T. Kasai. A method for the correction of garbled words based on the levenshtein metric. *IEEE Trans. Comput.*, 25:172–178, 1976.

[16] J. Ouaknine and J. Worrell. Universality and language inclusion for open and closed timed automata. In O. Maler and A. Pnueli, editors, *HSCC*, volume 2623 of *Lecture Notes in Computer Science*, pages 375–388. Springer, 2003.

[17] G. Pighizzini. How hard is computing the edit distance? *Information and Computation*, 165:1–13, 2001.

[18] W. J. Savitch. Relationships between nondeterministic and deterministic tape complexities. *J. Comput. Syst. Sci.*, 4(2):177–192, Apr. 1970.

[19] R. A. Wagner. Order-n correction for regular languages. *Commun. ACM*, 17(5):265–268, 1974.

[20] R. A. Wagner and M. J. Fischer. The string-to-string correction problem. *J. ACM*, 21(1):168–173, Jan. 1974.

HSCC'14 Posters

Willem Hagemann *(Carl von Ossietzky University Oldenburg)*: **Reachability Analysis of Hybrid Systems Using Symbolic Orthogonal Projections.**

Austin Jones *(Boston University)*, Mac Schwager *(Boston University)* and Calin Belta *(Boston University)*: **Formal Synthesis of Optimal Information-Gathering Policies.**

Stanley Bak *(Unites States Air Force Research Lab - Rome NY)*: **Reducing the Wrapping Effect when Computing Continuous Successors.**

Goran Frehse *(University of Grenoble)* and Olivier Lebeltel *(CNRS - Verimag)*: **Verification of Control Systems in Space-Time using SpaceEx.**

Kendra Lesser *(University of New Mexico - Albuquerque)* and Meeko Oishi *(University of New Mexico - Albuquerque)*: **Reachability Computation for Partially Observable Discrete Time Stochastic Hybrid Systems.**

Houssam Abbas *(Arizona State University - Tempe)*, Bardh Hoxha *(Arizona State University - Tempe)*, Georgios Fainekos (*Arizona State University - Tempe)* and Koichi Ueda *(Toyota Technical Center - Gardena, CA)*: **Robustness-Guided Temporal Logic Testing for Stochastic Hybrid Systems.**

Jan Kuřátko (*Institute of Computer Science - Academy of Sciences of the Czech Republic)* and Stefan Ratschan *(Institute of Computer Science - Academy of Sciences of the Czech Republic)*: **Combined Global and Local Search for the Falsification of Hybrid Systems.**

Yunus Emre Arslantas *(DLR - German Aerospace Center)*, Thimo Oehlschlägel *(DLR - German Aerospace Center)*, Marco Sagliano *(DLR - German Aerospace Center)* and Stephan Theil *(DLR - German Aerospace Center)*: **Approximation of Attainable Landing Area of a Moon Lander by Reachability Analysis.**

HSCC'14 Demonstrations

Bardh Hoxha *(Arizona State University - Tempe)*, Houssam Abbas *(Arizona State University - Tempe)*, Adel Dokhanchi (*Arizona State University - Tempe)* and Georgios Fainekos (*Arizona State University - Tempe)*: **S-TaLiRo: A Tool for Testing and Verification for Hybrid Systems - Recent Functionality and Additions.**

Goran Frehse *(University of Grenoble)* and Olivier Lebeltel *(CNRS - Verimag)*: **Verification of Control Systems in Space-Time using SpaceEx**

Derek Riley *(University of Wisconsin - Parkside)*, Xiaowei Zhang *(University of Wisconsin - Parkside)* and Xenofon Koutsoukos *(Vanderbilt University)*: **Biodiesel Sim - Crowdsourcing Simulations for Formal Model Analysis.**

Stephan Huck *(ETH Zurich)*: **RCopterX Project.**

Alexander Liniger *(ETH Zurich)*: **ORCA Project.**

Author Index

Abate, Alessandro 41, 193
Allgöwer, Frank 1
Ames, Aaron D. 263
Aréchiga, Nikos 133
Aydin Gol, Ebru 273
Batt, Gregory 143
Belta, Calin 273
Ben, Yue 61
Benveniste, Albert 71
Bogomolov, Sergiy 93
Borgers, Dominicus P. 103
Bourke, Timothy 71
Brenguier, Romain 283
Brunner, Florian D. 1
Butts, Ken 253
Caillaud, Benoit 71
Cassez, Franck 283
Chatterjee, Debasish 11
Chatterjee, Krishnendu 303
Damm, Werner 145
Dang, Thao 233
Deshmukh, Jyotirmoy V. ... 133, 253
Dreossi, Tommaso 233
Ehlers, Rüdiger 203
Feng, Yao 61
Gillula, Jeremy H. 173
Girard, Antoine 243
Goubault, Eric 163
Grosu, Radu 243
Han, Zhi 83
Heemels, Maurice W.P.M.H. 103
Hendrickx, Julien M. 151
Henzinger, Thomas A. 213
Hereid, Ayonga 263
Herrera, Christian 93
Huang, Zhenqi 183
Hurst, Jonathan W. 263
Ibsen-Jensen, Rasmus 303
Islam, Md. Ariful 243
Jackson, Ethan K. 157
Jin, Xiaoqing 253
Jones, Austin 273
Jones, Mikhail S. 263
Jungers, Raphaël M. 151
Kapinski, James 133, 253
Kaynama, Shahab 173
Kieffer, Michel 163
Kolathaya, Shishir 263
Kong, Zhaodan 273
Kundu, Atreyee 11
Lazar, Mircea 1
Lee, Ji-Woong 31
Lesser, Kendra 51
Liu, Jun 293
Majumdar, Rupak 303
Malone, Nick 51
Medina Ayala, Ana 273
Mitra, Sayan 183
Möhlmann, Eike 145
Mosterman, Pieter J. 83
Mullier, Olivier 163
Muñiz, Marco 93
Murthy, Abhishek 243
Oishi, Meeko 51
Otop, Jan 213
Ozay, Necmiye 293
Pagano, Bruno 71
Papadopoulos,
Alessandro Vittorio 113
Podelski, Andreas 93
Pouzet, Marc 71
Prandini, Maria 113
Putot, Sylvie 163
Rakow, Astrid 145
Raskin, Jean-François 283
Riedinger, Pierre 21
Rungger, Matthias 223
Sankaranarayanan, Sriram 133
Simko, Gabor 83, 157
Sistla, A. Prasad 61
Sloth, Christoffer 123
Smolka, Scott A. 243
Tabuada, Paulo 223
Tapia, Lydia 51
Tkachev, Ilya 41, 193
Tomlin, Claire J. 173
Topcu, Ufuk 203
Ueda, Koichi 253
Van Why, Johnathan 263
Vankeerberghen, Guillaume 151
Vivalda, Jean-Claude 21
Westphal, Bernd 93
Wisniewski, Rafael 123
Xiong, Sihan 31
Zamani, Majid 41
Zander, Justyna 83
Žefran, Miloš 61

www.ingramcontent.com/pod-product-compliance
Lightning Source LLC
LaVergne TN
LVHW060136070326
832902LV00018B/2814
* 9 7 8 1 4 5 0 3 2 7 3 2 9 *